### Jon Murray

Jon Murray spent time alternating between travelling and working with various publishing companies in Melbourne (Australia) before joining Lonely Planet as an editor. He was soon travelling again, this time researching Lonely Planet's guidebooks. He has co-authored all editions of this book, written Lonely Planet's *New South Wales & the ACT* and *Cape Town city guide* and updated several other Lonely Planet books, including *Papua New Guinea* and sections of *Australia* and *Africa on a shoestring*. He spends a lot of time battling blackberries on his bush block which is near Daylesford.

### Jeff Williams

Jeff is a Kiwi from Greymouth on New Zealand's wild west coast of the South Island. He now lives in subtropical Brisbane and wonders why the rest of the world doesn't. When not on his laptop computer enthusing over 'that bird', 'this mountain' or 'a great place to stay', he rambles, skis and climbs over whichever country will have him. He is author, co-author or contributor to Lonely Planet's *New Zealand*, *Australia*, *Tramping in New Zealand*, *Outback Australia*, Virginia in the US guide *Washington DC & The Capital Region*, and West African countries for *Africa on a shoestring*. His dream is to write a comprehensive travel guide to the islands of the South Pacific, accompanied by his wife Alison and son Callum.

### Richard Everist

Richard grew up in Geelong, Australia, has travelled a bit and had a wide variety of jobs. He worked full time at Lonely Planet's head office in Melbourne before jumping the fence to become a writer. In late 1994 he was lured back into the home paddock to be Co-General Manager. He has co-written LP's travel survival kits *Nepal* and *Britain*, updated *Papua New Guinea*, and contributed to the shoestring guides for *West Asia*, *Africa*, *Western Europe* and *Mediterranean Europe*.

### From the Authors

**Jon Murray** Thanks to the usual cast of thousands, including the people at Lonely Planet who helped drag this third edition over the line, the many travellers I met while on the road and the many helpful citizens of South Africa, Lesotho and Swaziland. Special mentions to Ilse Witthoft at Spoornet for prompt help with queries, Mick and Di Jones at Malealea Lodge, Lesotho, and to all the bad influences in Cape Town.

**Jeff Williams** A special thanks to Jon Murray ('Mr South Africa') for letting me go to his favourite parts of the country; to my best mate Alison in Brisbane; and to my four-year-old son Callum for his patience (Dad will be home soon!).

Thanks also to Rob, Evan, Muff and Bushie at the Rockey St Backpackers in Jo'burg (as usual my protectors when I wandered along Jo'burg's unsafe paths); Max of Maximum Tours and his staff in Soweto; Darron Raw and his boss the great Ted Reilly (and son Micky) of the Royal Swazi Big Game Parks in Swaziland; the two Welsh rugger buggers who followed me into the wild Kalahari (and gave me one of their Cheltenham club shirts); Randal Arsenault, one of the best musicians in the free world for 'The Peasant Battalions', a great night in Graaff-Reinet and six weeks of little argument; Viz in Pietersburg/Polokwane; Chester in East London; the staff of Pretoria Backpackers; the Drostdy Hotel in Graaff-Reinet; and the staff of the tourist offices in Tzaneen, Louis Trichardt, Khoka Moya Game Reserve, Barberton, Storms River, Jeffreys Bay, Kuruman, Port Elizabeth, Port Alfred, Graaff-Reinet, Kimberley, Upington, Springbok and Mafikeng (remembered in the order they deserve – there are many others that deliberately don't appear).

## This Book
The first edition of this book was researched and written by Richard Everist and Jon Murray. The second and third editions were updated by Jon Murray and Jeff Williams.

## From the Publisher
Richard Plunkett edited this third edition of *South Africa, Lesotho & Swaziland* with assistance from Linda Suttie, Suzi Petkovski, Anne Mulvaney, Kristin Odijk, Peter Cruttenden and Bethune Carmichael. A special thanks to Rupert Haw of Eshowe, KwaZulu-Natal; South Africa's future can't be all that bad.

Mapping and design were coordinated by Geoff Stringer with cartographic assistance from Janet Watson, Trudi Canavan, Anthony Phelan, Lyndell Taylor and Verity Campbell. Illustrations were drawn by Trudi, Greg Herriman, Margie Jung, Sally Gerdan, Reita Wilson, David Andrew and Miriam Cannell. Paul Piaia created the climate charts. David Kemp designed the cover, with cartographic assistance from Adam McCrow.

The Safari Guide was originally written by Geoff Crowther and Deanna Swaney, and illustrated by Matt King; additional material was provided by Jon Murray. Geoff Stringer redesigned it for this edition and David Andrew researched and wrote the Birds section.

## Thanks
Many thanks to the travellers who used the last edition and wrote to us with helpful hints, useful advice and interesting anecdotes. Your names appear at the end of the book.

## Warning & Request
Things change – prices go up, schedules change, good places go bad and bad places go bankrupt – nothing stays the same. So, if you find things better or worse, recently opened or long since closed, please tell us and help make the next edition even more accurate and useful.

We value all of the feedback we receive from travellers. Julie Young coordinates a small team who read and acknowledge every letter, postcard and email, and ensure that every bit of information finds its way to the appropriate authors, editors and publishers.

Everyone who writes to us will find their name in the next edition of this guide; in our newsletter, *Planet Talk*; or in updates on our Web site – so please let us know if you don't want your letter published or your name acknowledged.

# Contents

# EASTERN CAPE PROVINCE

# NORTHERN CAPE PROVINCE

# Map Legend

## ROUTES

Train Route, with Station
Tramway
Walking Tour
Walking Track
Cable Car or Chairlift

### Regional Maps

Freeway
Primary Road
Secondary Road
Unsealed Road
Minor Road

### City Maps

Freeway
Primary Road
Secondary Road
Minor Road
Lane

## AREA FEATURES

City Park, National Park
Building
Pedestrian Mall
Market
Cemetery
Built-Up Area

## BOUNDARIES

International Boundary
Province Boundary

## HYDROGRAPHIC FEATURES

River, Creek
Intermittent River or Creek
Rapids, Waterfalls
Lake, Intermittent Lake
Swamp

## SYMBOLS

CAPITAL ......National Capital
Capital ......Regional Capital
City ......................City
Town ......................Town
Village ....................Village

Place to Stay
Camping Ground
Caravan Park
Youth Hostel
Hut or Chalet
Place to Eat
Pub or Bar
Café

Airport
Archaeological Site
Bank
Battle Site
Border Crossing
Castle, Fort
Cathedral, Church
Embassy
Hindu Temple
Hospital
Mine
Monument
Mosque
Mountain, Hill

Museum
Pass, Tunnel
Petrol Station
Police Station
Post Office
Route Number
Shopping Centre
Swimming Pool
Synagogue
Telephone
Tourist Information
Transport
Winery, Vineyard
Zoo

Note: not all symbols displayed above appear in this book

# Introduction

South Africa, Lesotho and Swaziland make up a beautiful region of Africa that is just beginning to realise its potential.

The national parks are among the greatest in the world and there are few better places to see Africa's wildlife. The thrill of seeing animals like elephants and lions in the wild cannot be overestimated.

The beaches are among the best and least crowded in the world, and the surfing and fishing are as good as you can get. The countryside, particularly the mountains, is spectacular, and the walking and touring possibilities are endless.

The climate is kind, and there is the added advantage that it is summer in Southern Africa while the northern hemisphere is in the depths of winter.

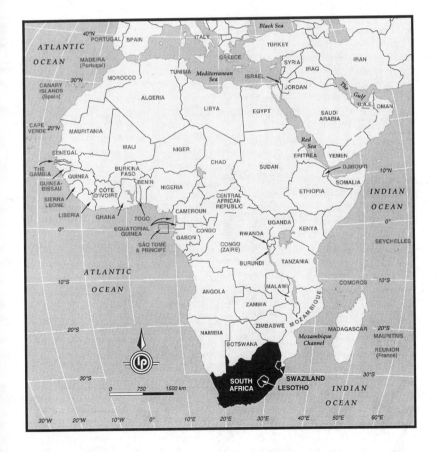

The region's infrastructure, by African standards, is extremely good – the transport and communications systems all work. With the isolation of the past fading, international-standard hotels and restaurants are meeting the demands of foreign visitors. Even away from the more popular areas you can always find somewhere clean and comfortable to stay and somewhere with decent food.

The mixture of cultures is tremendously interesting and all three countries stand to benefit from South Africa's attempt to meld a new society of great energy and significance. It's an exciting time to visit.

Swaziland, in contrast to South Africa's new democracy, retains its beloved monarchy and the tiny country is proof that a pre-industrial culture can thrive in a modern nation. Lesotho, 'the kingdom in the sky', also offers travellers contact with traditional village life, whether pony trekking or hiking through the highland wilderness.

# Facts about the Region

The current national boundaries in Southern Africa are, in large part, creations of the 19th and 20th centuries. The modern nation states owe their form to the competitive ambitions of European imperialist powers, colonists and invaders – not, to a large degree, to intrinsic geographical, cultural or historical logic. South Africa, Lesotho and Swaziland are, therefore, more usefully seen as a whole, at least until the late 19th century in terms of their history, and even today in terms of language, culture, and flora & fauna.

## HISTORY
### Prehistory
Southern Africa's prehistory before the coming of the Iron Age peoples is uncertain. Sites in Mpumalanga and other places have produced evidence of various 'missing links', dating back about three million years, and human bones 100,000 years old have been found in Swaziland.

### San & Khoikhoi
The San (known to Europeans as Bushmen) were nomadic hunters and gatherers, and the Khoikhoi (known as Hottentot) were semi-nomadic hunters and pastoralists. Both groups were closely related, however, so the distinction was by no means hard and fast. Because of this, the term Khoisan is now widely used for both groups.

The San have probably lived in Southern Africa for 40,000 years – the earliest dated painting attributed to them is about 28,000 years old. Culturally and physically, they developed differently from the negroid peoples of Africa.

The San are generally shorter (averaging around 140cm in height) than the Khoikhoi, perhaps because of the richer diet of the Khoikhoi, but there are a number of similarities. Both groups are characterised by fairly light, almost honey-coloured skin; well developed buttocks, which can store reserves of fat; high cheekbones, with an almost

Asiatic cast to their faces; and hair that forms tight curls. There is also a close relationship between the San and Khoikhoi languages, which are the origin of the 'clicks' common in Southern African languages.

It is now believed the Khoikhoi developed from San groups in present-day Botswana. Perhaps they came in contact with pastoralist Bantu tribes, as in addition to hunting and gathering food, they became pastoralists, with cattle and oxen. They migrated south, reaching the Cape of Good Hope about 2000 years ago. For centuries, perhaps even millennia, the San and the Khoikhoi intermarried and coexisted. It was not uncommon for impoverished Khoikhoi to revert to a hunter-gatherer existence, or for San to acquire domestic animals.

The first rivals to the Khoisan were Bantu-speaking tribes. These tribes not only had domestic animals, but farmed crops (particularly maize), were metal workers and potters, and lived in settled villages. They migrated down the east coast, reaching today's KwaZulu-Natal by the 3rd century.

It seems that the first settlements were limited to areas with more than about 600mm of rain, but between the 12th and 15th centuries they expanded onto the highveld of today's Northern Province, Gauteng and Free State. Once again rainfall, or the lack of it, seems to have provided a natural barrier between the Bantu and Khoikhoi. There are no known Bantu settlements west of the Great Fish River or into the territory that receives less than 200mm of rain. The Bantu crops could not survive with less rain.

Although this migration must have made an impact on the eastern Khoisan it seems the two groups either integrated, or found a way to coexist. There was intermarriage and the Xhosa and Zulu languages adopted Khoisan 'clicks'. Khoisan artefacts are commonly found at the sites of Bantu settlements. Curiously, only one Bantu tribe adopted the use of bows and arrows, the most important

## Southern Africa's History

| | |
|---|---|
| c.40,000 BC | San people settle Southern Africa |
| c.300 AD | Bantu people arrive in KwaZulu-Natal area |
| 1487 | Bartholomeu Dias sails around the Cape of Good Hope |
| c.1500 | Sotho people settle in (Basutholand) Lesotho |
| 1652 | Dutch settlement in Table Bay (Cape Town) |
| 1688 | French Huguenots arrive at Cape |
| c.1690 | Boers move into the hinterland |
| c.1750 | Nguni people settle Swaziland |
| 1779 | Dutch fight Xhosa at Great Fish River |
| 1795 | British capture Cape Town |
| 1815 | Shaka Zulu seizes power – the difaqane begins |
| 1820 | British settlers arrive in Eastern Cape |
| 1824 | King Moshoeshoe begins to meld the modern Basutho people |
| 1830s | The Voortrekkers undertake the Great Trek |
| 1838 | Boers defeat the Zulu at Battle of Blood River |
| 1852 | Boer Republic of Transvaal created |
| 1858 | British defeat Xhosa after the disaster of the Great Cattle Killing |
| 1860 | Indians arrive in Natal |
| 1868 | British annexe Basutholand (Lesotho) |
| 1869 | Diamonds found near Kimberley |
| 1871 | Gold discovered in eastern Transvaal |
| 1877 | British annexe the Boer Republic of Transvaal |
| 1881 | Boers defeat British and Transvaal becomes the South African Republic |
| 1886 | Gold discovered on the Witwatersrand |
| 1893 | Mohandas Gandhi arrives in Natal |
| 1897 | Zululand annexed by Britain |
| 1899-1902 | Anglo-Boer War |
| 1905 | Government commission recommends separate development for blacks, with inferior education |
| 1910 | Union of South Africa created, federating the British colonies and the old Boer republics. Blacks denied the vote. Lesotho and Swaziland become British protectorates. |
| 1912 | South African Native National Congress established, the forerunner of the ANC |
| 1913 | Natives Land Act restricts black ownership of land to 7½% of the country |
| 1928 | Communist Party begins agitation for full democracy |
| 1948 | National Party wins government. The party retains control until 1994. Apartheid laws, such as the one making interracial sex illegal, begin to be passed. |
| 1955 | ANC adopts Freedom Charter |
| 1960 | Sharpeville massacre; ANC banned. |
| 1961 | South Africa leaves the Commonwealth and becomes a republic |
| 1963 | Nelson Mandela jailed for life |
| 1966 | Lesotho gains independence from Britain |
| 1968 | Swaziland gains independence from Britain |
| 1975 | South Africa invades Angola |
| 1976 | Soweto uprisings begin |
| 1977 | Steve Biko murdered |
| 1982 | Swazi King Sobhuza II, then the world's longest-reigning monarch, dies |
| 1985 | State of Emergency declared – official murder and torture become rife, black resistance strengthens |
| 1990 | ANC ban lifted; Nelson Mandela freed |
| 1991 | Talks on a new constitution begin; political violence escalates |
| 1992 | Whites-only referendum agrees to reform |
| 1994 | Democratic elections held and Nelson Mandela elected president |

Khoisan weapon. West of the 200mm rain zone, and even in the Drakensberg, the Khoisan were undisturbed until white colonists arrived in the 18th and 19th centuries.

## Bantu

By the 15th century Bantu-speaking peoples had moved inland to settle most of the eastern half of Southern Africa – that is, most of the land suitable for growing staple crops and grazing cattle. These tribes were primarily pastoral, held land in common and undertook some form of agriculture. There were extensive trade links throughout the region. They were Iron Age peoples and the smelting techniques of some tribes were not surpassed in Europe until the Industrial Revolution. Gold, copper and tin were also mined, and shafts 25m deep have been discovered. These were people who, in Zimbabwe, found *every* known gold deposit except one.

Most Southern African Bantu peoples are classified as being either Nguni (Zulu, Swazi, Xhosa) or Sotho-Tswana (Tswana, Pedi, Basotho). This classification is based on 19th-century linguistic theories and is suspect, but there is some evidence for two broad immigration patterns. The Nguni are grouped around the south and east coasts, and the Sotho-Tswana mainly live on the highveld. The origin of the Venda peoples is uncertain, with some historians arguing that they are relatively late arrivals.

Little is known about the history of these tribes and peoples before the twin disasters of European invasion and the *difaqane* (forced migration), when several of the most important modern peoples – the Basotho, the Swazi and the Zulu – became prominent.

## European Exploration

The Muslim expansion across North Africa and the Balkans threw Christian Europe's trade routes into chaos, prompting the Portuguese and Spanish to search for a sea route to India. They sought to guarantee and hopefully monopolise the supply of one of the most precious commodities in medieval times – spices.

At the end of 1487 Bartholomeu Dias and his expedition (two tiny caravels and a store ship) rounded a cape, which Dias named Cabo da Boa Esperança (Cape of Good Hope). Ten years later Vasco da Gama rounded the Cape and finally reached India in 1498.

Portuguese eyes were fixed on the east coast of Africa and on India. It was as if they didn't see Southern Africa, let alone its potential. To them, the region offered little more than fresh water; attempts to trade with the Khoikhoi often ended in violence and the coast and its fierce weather posed a terrible threat to their caravels.

By the end of the 16th century the English and Dutch were beginning to challenge the Portuguese traders, and the Cape became a regular stopover for their scurvy-ridden crews. In 1647 a Dutch East Indiaman was wrecked in Table Bay and the crew built a fort and stayed for a year before they were rescued.

This crystallised the value of a permanent settlement in the minds of the directors of the Dutch East India Company (Vereenigde Oost-Indische Compagnie or VOC). They had no intention of colonising the country, but simply of establishing a secure base where ships could shelter and stock up on fresh supplies of meat, fruit and vegetables. To this end, a small expedition of VOC employees, under the command of Jan van Riebeeck, reached Table Bay on 6 April 1652.

## Company Rule

Although the settlement traded with the neighbouring Khoikhoi there was a deliberate attempt to restrict contact. Partly as a consequence of this, the small number of VOC employees found themselves faced with a labour shortage. Van Riebeeck made two moves to deal with this problem, both with far-reaching consequences. Slaves were imported, mostly from Mozambique, Indonesia and Madagascar, and a handful of burghers were allowed to establish their own farms.

The burghers were still theoretically subject to VOC control, however, and were forced to sell their produce at prices determined by the company. The colony was soon producing fruit, vegetables, wheat and wine so successfully that there was a problem with oversupply. As a result, many farmers turned away from intensive farming to raising livestock.

The number of burghers grew slowly, but steadily. The majority were of Dutch descent, but there were also significant numbers of Germans. Their church was the Calvinist Reformed Church of the Netherlands. In 1688 they were joined by a group of about 150 French Huguenots who were also Calvinists and had fled religious persecution under King Louis XIV. This small group was more significant than might be imagined; in crude numerical terms it increased the white population by over 15%.

Some trace the Afrikaner idea of a chosen people (and racial superiority) to Calvin's doctrine of predestination, which says that an individual's salvation or damnation is preordained. Surrounded by 'primitive heathens', the whites had no doubts which race was superior and who had been chosen.

(the Khoikhoi) yet show so little humanity that truly they more resemble the unreasonable beasts than reasonable man…having no knowledge of God
**Quoted in *The Mind of South Africa*
by Allister Sparks**

### The Boers
The population of whites did not reach 1000 until 1745, but small numbers of free burghers had begun to drift away from the close grip of the company, and into Africa. They had crossed the Oliphants River to the north and were pushing east towards the Great Fish River. These were the first of the *trekboers* (literally 'wandering farmers', ie graziers) – completely independent of all official control, extraordinarily self-sufficient and isolated.

Many pursued a semi-nomadic pastoralist lifestyle, in some ways not far removed from that of the Khoikhoi. In addition to its herds a family might have had a wagon, a tent, a Bible and a couple of guns. As they became more settled a mud-walled cottage would

have been built, but it would – often by choice – be days of hard travel away from the nearest European.

This isolated lifestyle produced courageous individualists, but also a backward people whose only source of knowledge was the Bible. The trekboers (later called just 'Boers') were completely cut off from the great intellectual developments that occurred in Europe in the 18th century – the French Revolution and all the associated ideas of liberalism and democracy.

The Boers' lifestyle and culture, both real and idealised, has been the dominant factor in shaping the Afrikaners view of themselves and their place in Africa.

They possessed guns and a religious faith that established both a physical and an imagined superiority that set them apart absolutely. What evolved was a semiliterate peasantry with the social status of a landed gentry.
**                     *The Mind of South Africa* by Allister Sparks**

### The Impact on the Khoisan
The inevitable confrontations between whites and the Khoisan were disastrous. The Khoisan were driven from their traditional lands, decimated by introduced diseases, and destroyed by superior weapons when they fought back – which they did in a number of major 'wars' and with guerrilla resistance that continued into the 19th century.

Most survivors were left with no option but to work for Europeans in a form of bondage little different from slavery. They were exploited both for labour and for sex and in time also mixed with the slaves who had been imported. The offspring of these unions formed the basis for today's coloured population.

One Khoikhoi group, the Grigriqua, who had originally lived on the west coast between St Helena Bay and the Cederberg, managed to acquire guns and horses. Around 1770, in a pattern to be followed 60 years later by the Boers, they trekked east and north. The Grigriqua were joined by other groups of Khoisan, coloureds and even white adventurers, and proved to be a formidable military force. They reached the highveld

JON MURRAY

DI JONES

MIKE REED

JON MURRAY

JON MURRAY

JON MURRAY

JON MURRAY

Top: Street life, Cape Town; Basotho herd boy in the fields near Malealea, Lesotho.
Middle: Traditional and western dress at the coronation of King Mswati III, Swaziland;
    Waterskiing (easier on a surfboard) is a popular South African pastime, Cape Town.
Bottom: The different faces of South Africa.

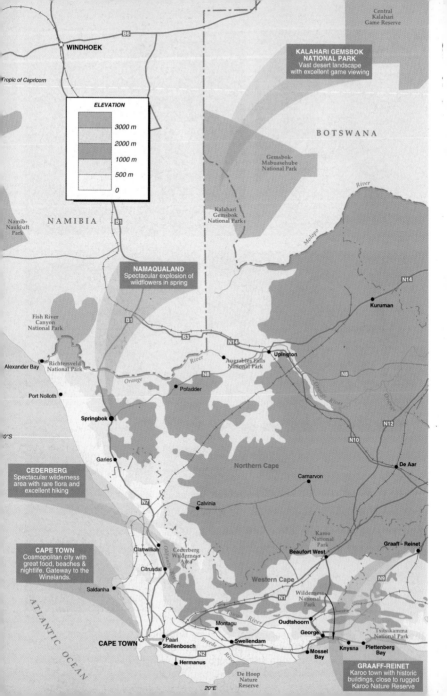

WINDHOEK

B6

Tropic of Capricorn

**KALAHARI GEMSBOK
NATIONAL PARK**
Vast desert landscape
with excellent game viewing

Central
Kalahari
Game Reserve

BOTSWANA

**ELEVATION**

3000 m
2000 m
1000 m
500 m
0

Gemsbok-
Mabuasehube
National Park

Namib-
Naukluft
Park

NAMIBIA

B1

Kalahari
Gemsbok
National Park

River

Molopo

**NAMAQUALAND**
Spectacular explosion of
wildflowers in spring

N14

Kuruman

Fish River
Canyon
National Park

B1

B3

N14

River

Augrabies Falls
National Park

Upington

N8

Alexander Bay

Richtersveld
National Park

Orange

River

N8

Orange

Port Nolloth

Pofadder

N12

Springbok

N10

Garies

Northern Cape

De Aar

**CEDERBERG**
Spectacular wilderness
area with rare flora and
excellent hiking

Carnarvon

Calvinia

Karoo
National
Park

Graaff - Reinet

Clanwilliam

Cederberg
Wilderness
Area

Beaufort West

**CAPE TOWN**
Cosmopolitan city with
great food, beaches &
nightlife. Gateway to the
Winelands.

Citrusdal

N7

Western Cape

N9

Saldanha

N1

Wilderness
National
Park

Montagu

Oudtshoorn

Tsitsikamma
National Park

ATLANTIC OCEAN

CAPE TOWN

Paarl
Stellenbosch

George

Knysna

Plettenberg
Bay

Breede

Swellendam

Mossel
Bay

N2

River

Hermanus

De Hoop
Nature
Reserve

**GRAAFF-REINET**
Karoo town with historic
buildings, close to rugged
Karoo Nature Reserve

20°E

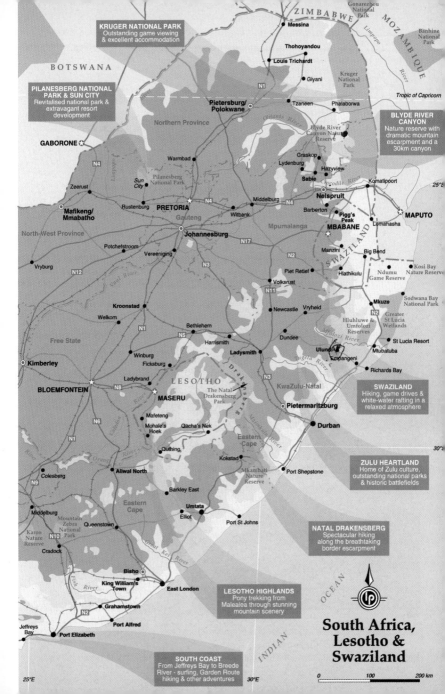

ZIMBABWE

**Gonarezhou National Park**

**Banhine National Park**

**MOZAMBIQUE**

● Messina

● Thohoyandou

● Louis Trichardt

BOTSWANA

**KRUGER NATIONAL PARK**
Outstanding game viewing & excellent accommodation

● Giyani

Kruger National Park

N1

Tropic of Capricorn

**PILANESBERG NATIONAL PARK & SUN CITY**
Revitalised national park & extravagant resort development

Pietersburg/
Polokwane ◉

● Tzaneen

Phalaborwa

Northern Province

*Olifants River*

**BLYDE RIVER CANYON**
Nature reserve with dramatic mountain escarpment and a 30km canyon

GABORONE ☆

● Warmbad

Blyde River Canyon Nature Reserve

● Graskop

Lydenburg ●

● Hazyview

25°S

N4

Zeerust ●

Sun City

Pilanesberg National Park

Sabie ●

*Crocodile River*

Komatipoort ●

● Mafikeng/Mmabatho

Rustenburg ●

**PRETORIA** ☆

N4

Middelburg ●

Nelspruit ◉

**MAPUTO** ◈

Gauteng

Witbank ●

N4

Barberton ●

Pigg's Peak ●

Lomahasha ●

North-West Province

**Johannesburg** ☆

Mpumalanga

**MBABANE** ◉

Potchefstroom ●

N17

Manzini ●

Big Bend ●

SWAZILAND

Vereeniging ●

Vryburg ●

N12

N3

Piet Retief ●

Hlathikulu ●

Ndumu Game Reserve

● Kosi Bay Nature Reserve

*Vaal River*

Volksrust ●

N11

Mkuze ●

Sodwana Bay National Park

**Kroonstad** ●

Newcastle ●

Vryheid ●

Welkom ●

Greater St Lucia Wetlands

Kimberley ◉

Free State

N1

Bethlehem ●

Harrismith ●

Dundee ●

Hluhluwe & Umfolozi Reserves

*Mfolozi River*

St Lucia Resort ●

Winburg ●

Ladysmith ●

Ulundi ●

Mtubatuba ●

**BLOEMFONTEIN** ☆

Ficksburg ●

LESOTHO

The Natal Drakensberg Park

*Tugela River*

Empangeni ●

Richards Bay ●

N8

Ladybrand ●

N6

**MASERU** ☆

KwaZulu-Natal

**SWAZILAND**
Hiking, game drives & white-water rafting in a relaxed atmosphere

Mafeteng ●

N3

**Pietermaritzburg** ◉

N1

Mohale's Hoek ●

Qacha's Nek ●

*Orange River*

Quthing ●

Eastern Cape

**Durban** ●

30°S

**ZULU HEARTLAND**
Home of Zulu culture, outstanding national parks & historic battlefields

Colesberg ●

N9

Kokstad ●

Aliwal North ●

Mkambati Nature Reserve

Port Shepstone ●

Barkley East ●

Middelburg ●

Mountain Zebra National Park

Umtata ●

Elliot ●

Port St Johns ●

**NATAL DRAKENSBERG**
Spectacular hiking along the breathtaking border escarpment

Karoo Nature Reserve

N10

Queenstown ●

Cradock ●

*Great Kei River*

INDIAN OCEAN

Bisho ◉

King William's Town ●

**East London** ●

**LESOTHO HIGHLANDS**
Pony trekking from Malealea through stunning mountain scenery

*Fish River*

N2

Grahamstown ●

Jeffreys Bay ●

Port Alfred ●

● **Port Elizabeth**

LP

**South Africa, Lesotho & Swaziland**

**SOUTH COAST**
From Jeffreys Bay to Breede River - surfing, Garden Route hiking & other adventures

25°E

30°E

0    100    200 km

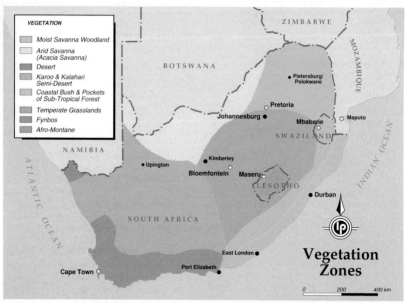

VEGETATION

Moist Savanna Woodland

Arid Savanna
(Acacia Savanna)

Desert

Karoo & Kalahari
Semi-Desert

Coastal Bush & Pockets
of Sub-Tropical Forest

Temperate Grasslands

Fynbos

Afro-Montane

Vegetation
Zones

0    200    400 km

MIKE REED

JON MURRAY

Left: Pincushion proteas of the fynbos floral kingdom bloom alongside a vineyard in the
     Constantia Valley, Western Cape.

Right: The harsh landscape of the Kalahari Gemsbok National Park is home to herds of
     wildebeest, Northern Cape.

around modern-day Kimberley and carved out territory that came to be known as Griqualand. This was forcibly annexed by the British in 1871.

Although small numbers of whites came into tenuous contact with the Sotho-Tswana peoples on the northern frontier in about 1700, the Xhosa to the west of the Great Fish River first encountered the trekboers in the 1770s. The first of nine frontier wars broke out in 1779.

## The British Arrive

Dutch power was fading as the 18th century closed, and in 1795 the British invaded to prevent the Cape falling into French hands. They found a colony with 25,000 slaves, 20,000 white colonists, 15,000 Khoisan and 1000 free blacks (freed slaves).

Power was restricted to a white elite in Cape Town, and differentiation on the basis of colour was deeply entrenched. In large part it was a society that had been hermetically sealed from the rest of the world. With the exception of Cape Town and the immediate hinterland, the country was populated by isolated black and white pastoralists whose lifestyles and beliefs were almost medieval.

The initial British occupation had little impact on society and, in 1803, the colony was handed over to the Batavian Republic (the Netherlands). Not long after, however, in response to the Napoleonic wars, the British once again decided to secure the Cape against French occupation. In 1806, at Bloubergstrand 25km north of Cape Town, the British again defeated the Dutch. The colony was permanently ceded to the British on 13 August 1814.

This time the British did start to meddle in local affairs. The British Empire was reaching its height in power and confidence and was at the vanguard of the new capitalist world. Missionaries were its shock troops and teachers were its foot soldiers. Religion aside, the most important motive was profit, and the empire had a new and seemingly insatiable appetite for labour, raw materials and manufactured goods. Industrialisation

and urbanisation were changing the shape of the world.

## The Settlers

In 1820, 5000 middle class British immigrants arrived to settle near the eastern frontier of the colony. The peaceful land of plenty that had been promoted to them was, in reality, a heavily contested border region. The Boers were on the west side of the Great Fish River, the Xhosa were on the east, and both battled interminably over the coastal plain known as the Suurveld.

The immigrants were intended to create a buffer of market gardeners between the cattle-farming Boers and Xhosa, but the Suurveld ('sour land') was completely unsuitable for intensive cultivation. By 1823 almost half of the settlers had retreated to the towns to pursue the trades and businesses they had followed in Britain.

As a result, Grahamstown developed into a trading and manufacturing centre, quickly becoming the second-largest city in the country. And the relative unity of white South Africa was over – there were now two language groups and two very different cultures. A pattern had also been established – English speakers were highly urbanised and dominated politics, trade, finance, mining and manufacturing, while the Boers were largely uneducated farmers and pastoralists.

Despite their power, however, and despite the fact that they did make some positive changes to institutionalised racism, the settlers' middle class conservatism and sense of racial superiority prevented them from making any radical reforms. Apart from anything else, the system served them too well. Slavery was abolished in 1833, but a Masters and Servants Ordinance perpetuating white control was passed in 1841.

British numbers increased rapidly in Cape Town, the east of the Cape Colony (the Eastern Cape area of today's South Africa), Natal (now KwaZulu-Natal), and, after the discovery of gold and diamonds, parts of the Transvaal (mainly around modern Gauteng). Thanks to the British, the border wars with the Xhosa reached new depths of depravity.

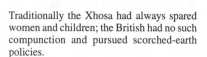

## Highlights & Possible Itinerary

In such a large and diverse region it is very tempting to plan a long trip. Where to go and what to do depends, as anywhere, on your available time and money. It's often the case that the people who have the most money have the least time, and vice versa. You could easily spend a few months meandering around on minibus taxis; you could just as easily spend a week in a luxury private game reserve – and pay not much less.

All of the places mentioned here are accessible by public transport of one sort or another, although in a few areas, such as the Transkei region and Zululand, you won't find many luxury buses and will have to rely on local bus services and minibus taxis. In the national parks you need your own vehicle.

The following list of highlights is by no means exhaustive, but it does give you a roughly circular route. The suggested number of days for each highlight is even more arbitrary – some people stay much longer in each place, others breeze through in an hour or so.

**Cape Town** is one of the world's most beautiful cities, and probably the most relaxed in Africa. It's a manageable size and as well as the best food and nightlife in South Africa, it offers superb natural attractions. There are plenty of beaches (some deserted, some extremely fashionable) and **Table Mountain** is right in the middle of the city. On the city's doorstep is the **Cape of Good Hope**, part of a national park, and the **Winelands** which make an easy day excursion. Cape Town and the Peninsula could easily occupy you for a week.

Although you can easily visit the winelands from Cape Town, it makes sense to *stay* in the Winelands, at least overnight. Many of the vineyards welcome visitors for sampling and cellar door sales, and some offer good food. **Stellenbosch** is a delightful old town and **Franschhoek** is a village set in one of the most beautiful valleys in the country. You'd need at least four days to do justice to the area.

The **Garden Route** is one of South Africa's most well-known attractions (it gets crowded in summer), and with its warm-water beaches, resort towns and forests, it isn't difficult to see why. **Knysna**, set on a beautiful lagoon system and surrounded by forest, is probably the best town to start from, although there is much more to the Garden Route than holiday towns. For example, **Tsitsikamma Coastal National Park** is stunningly beautiful and has famous hiking trails. Just driving through and stopping in a few places could take three days.

**Jeffreys Bay** has perhaps the best surfing in the world, and it's a relaxed little town that welcomes surfies. For the non-surfer, there are great beaches in this area that don't get as crowded as those on the Garden Route. How long to stay? How many waves do you want to catch?

The **Karoo** might not be everybody's cup of tea, but the wide, empty spaces can be fascinating. There are also some very nice old Karoo towns, such as **Calvinia** and **Graaff-Reinet**, which are welcome oases. For a taste of the Karoo and also the rugged mountains that border it, visit **Prince Albert**, not far from Oudtshoorn. Distances are long in the Karoo so allow at least four fairly full days.

The **Transkei region**, once an 'independent Homeland' of the Xhosa people, remains largely undeveloped, and this is its major attraction. A hiking trail runs the length of the region's long subtropical coastline (from five days), and on it is the small, idyllic and backpacker-friendly town of **Port St Johns**. Driving through on the main highway takes a few hours, but you won't really see the area unless you head for the coast and stay at least one night.

**Durban** is the beach resort city for Southern Africa, and in summer it is a lively place. It has a subtropical climate and excellent surf beaches in the heart of the city. With a large population of

Traditionally the Xhosa had always spared women and children; the British had no such compunction and pursued scorched-earth policies.

### The Difaqane

The difaqane ('forced migration' in seSotho) or *mfecane* ('the crushing' in isiZulu) was a time of immense upheaval and suffering among the peoples of Southern Africa.

In the early 19th century the Nguni tribes around the Mkuzi and Tugela rivers (in modern KwaZulu-Natal) underwent a dramatic change from loosely organised collections of chiefdoms into a centralised, militarist state. The process began under Dingiswayo, chief of the Mthethwa, and reached its peak under the chief Shaka, born into a small clan called Zulu.

Dingiswayo (died 1818) was a powerful

Indian-descended people the atmosphere is very different from other South African cities. Two or three days is enough to see the city and the nearby sights, but the coast north and south of Durban might detain you longer.

The spectacular **Drakensberg escarpment** forms the border between South Africa and Lesotho and is a chain of rugged national parks and nature reserves. The area is a magnet for hikers and climbers. You can either travel north parallel to the escarpment or concentrate on the southern Drakensberg, from where there is road entry to Lesotho. It will require a good vehicle or a relaxed timetable to penetrate further into 'the Kingdom in the Sky' from here, however; most people enter from the north side of the country near Maseru. From Durban, travelling north up through the Drakensberg, then west through southern Free State to Maseru could take anywhere from a couple of days to a week, depending on how many stops you make. In **Lesotho** allow at least two or three days to go pony trekking or walking.

The **Zulu heartland** has some outstanding national parks, such as **Hluhluwe/Umfolozi** and the **St Lucia area**, and offers glimpses of Zulu culture. For Anglo-Boer War buffs, this area is littered with important battlefields. You could easily spend a couple of weeks exploring this very diverse region, but travelling fast and allowing only a couple of nights in Natal Parks Board reserves, you might manage to see enough in five days.

**Swaziland** is a very friendly monarchy where the traditional way of life remains strong. There are some good game reserves with hiking and rafting facilities. You can drive the length of the country in a few of hours but a couple of days is best.

**Kruger National Park** is perhaps the best in the world. You would be unlucky not to see any of the 'big five', and the accommodation in the various rest camps is superb and reasonably priced. But avoid Kruger during school holidays! Allow yourself at least three days.

If you exit Kruger in the north, you can wind back south through the **Venda** region and the savanna plains of Northern Province. Allow at least a couple of days.

**Johannesburg** has earned itself a bad reputation for crime, but as the richest and arguably most important city in Africa it's worth a visit. This is where change, good and bad, is happening first in South Africa. You can safely visit **Soweto**, the powerhouse of the new South Africa, on tours run by locals. If Johannesburg sounds too scary, sedate **Pretoria** is just up the road and is a good place to relax. The sights of both places can be seen in three or four days.

Perhaps the world's largest piece of kitsch, **Sun City** is definitely worth visiting, even if you can't afford R10,000 for a suite at The Palace. You can take a day trip from Johannesburg or Pretoria. Nearby is **Pilanesberg National Park**, not as spectacular as some of South Africa's parks, but offering inexpensive accommodation and a good chance to see animals.

**Kimberley**, the diamond city, is a welcome oasis in the harsh Karoo, and also has some worthwhile attractions, such as the excellent Mine Museum and, of course, the Big Hole, from where most of the boom-time diamonds were extracted. An overnight stop is sufficient.

The **Kalahari Basin** verges on desert but it's a remote region with its own magic. **Kalahari Gemsbok National Park**, home to the unique Kalahari lion, is a complete contrast to the crowds at Kruger and other more accessible parks. A couple of very peaceful days can be spent here.

South Africa's astounding **wildflowers** are at their best in the **Namaqualand region**, but the dramatic landscapes and bleakly atmospheric coast are worth visiting at any time. Travelling fairly quickly you could get back to Cape Town from Upington in a couple of days, but this backwater is worth a meander. ∎

leader, who developed disciplined *impis* (regiments) of soldiers. His initial expansion produced local chaos, during which he was succeeded by one of his commanders, Shaka.

Shaka increased the size of the armies and placed them under the control of his officers rather than hereditary chiefs. He began a massive programme of conquest in which his main weapon was terror. Previous inter-tribal conflict had often been settled by

battles between champions, but now there was total war. The best a conquered people could hope for was slavery, but often whole tribes were wiped out and their crops razed. Shaka's soldiers were subject to similar rigours – failure in battle or a wound in the back meant death.

Not surprisingly, tribes in the path of Shaka's increasingly powerful armies fled, and they in turn became aggressors upon their neighbours. This wave of disruption and terror spread throughout Southern Africa, with refugees reaching, and conquering, almost as far as Lake Victoria. Two notable successes among the destruction were the Swazi and Basotho peoples, both of whom used the tide of refugees to their advantage and forged powerful nations (see the Swaziland and Lesotho sections for more information).

The Boers, whose Great Trek coincided with the difaqane, mistakenly believed that what they found – deserted pasture lands, disorganised bands of refugees and tales of brutality – was the normal state of affairs. The Afrikaner myths, now dying hard, that the Great Trek was into unoccupied territory or that the blacks and the Boers both arrived at much the same time, stem from this. The difaqane also added emphasis to their belief that European occupation meant the coming of civilisation to a savage land.

Shaka was killed in 1828 by Dingaan and Umhlanga, his half-brothers. Dingaan became king. He relaxed military discipline and attempted to establish friendly relations with the British traders setting up on the Natal coast, but events were unfolding which were to see the demise of Zulu independence.

### Shaka: Hero or Madman?

Historians have advanced many explanations for the difaqane. Some say that the centralisation of power which enabled the creation of a powerful Zulu state resulted from the ivory trade with the Portuguese at Delagoa Bay (modern Maputo in Mozambique). Inter-tribal cooperation was necessary to keep the trade routes open and standover tactics could win control of the whole lucrative system. It has also been suggested that contact with Europeans taught the tribes the value of large standing armies, impossible to maintain in a loosely organised, decentralised state. Population pressure has also been blamed as it not only produced the likelihood of conflict but in so doing gave the means of relieving it: Shaka's impis were forbidden to marry, and many thousands of people were killed or fled the area during his reign.

Other researchers have concentrated on Shaka's personality, with opinion divided between those who think he was mad and those who maintain that he was a superb tactician. Shaka's disturbed childhood offers scope for Freudians and the scale of his violence is exceptional – on the death of his mother he had thousands of his people killed for displaying insufficient grief – and there have been questions about his asexual nature. His insistence that his soldiers did not marry has often been cited as an example of his perversity, but it is interesting that one of the British demands to Chief Cetshwayo in the 1878 ultimatum was that the Zulu impis be allowed to marry: bachelor soldiers were seen as a greater threat than married ones. ■

Shaka and his armies rode to victory through the judicious use of the shield and stabbing stick devised by Shaka as a means of warfare.

### The Great Trek

From the 1820s groups of Boers dissatisfied with British rule in the Cape Colony had trekked off into the interior in search of freedom. From the mid-1830s increasing numbers of frontier communities were abandoning their farms and crossing the Orange River (Cape Colony's frontier) in a decade of migration known as the Great Trek.

Tensions between the Boers and the government had been building for some time, but the reason given by many trekkers for leaving was the 1833 act banning slavery. Most Boers grudgingly accepted that slavery might be wrong, but the British seemed to go a step further and proclaim the equality of

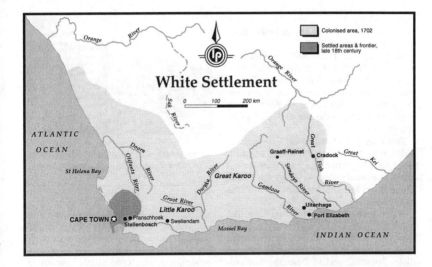

races. This resulted in, for example, servants bringing actions against their masters for non-payment of wages or for assault.

For an illiterate farmer who rarely saw a government official, much less ventured to Cape Town, to be summoned to a distant court which used a language he could not speak, all on the complaint of a coloured servant, was an extreme insult. It seemed to go against nature. If the law would not distinguish between races, how could a race maintain its culture, its purity?

Reports from early treks told of vast, uninhabited – or at least poorly defended – grazing lands, and from 1836 increasing numbers of *Voortrekkers* ('fore-trekkers', pioneers) crossed the Orange River. The trekkers had entered their promised land, with space enough for their cattle to graze and for their culture of anti-urban independence to flourish.

The various trek leaders now occupy high places in the Afrikaner pantheon. Names such as Retief, Potgieter, Trichardt, Van Rensburg, Maritz and Uys are synonymous with daring and enterprise.

The peoples of the plains which were occupied by the trekkers were disorganised by the difaqane; they lacked both horses and firearms so their resistance was easily overcome. The mountains where Moshoeshoe's Basotho nation (later Lesotho) was being melded and the wooded valleys of Zululand were a more difficult proposition, and there began the skirmishes, squabbles and flimsy treaties which were to litter the next 50 years of increasing white domination.

**The Voortrekkers Meet the Zulu** The Great Trek's first halt was at Thaba 'Nchu, near modern Bloemfontein, where a republic was established. After a disagreement, Maritz, Retief and Uys moved on to Natal, and Potgieter headed north to establish the republics of Winburg (in the Free State) and Potchefstroom, then crossed the Vaal River to found Transvaal.

By 1837 Retief's party had crossed the Drakensberg and wanted to establish a republic. Zulu king Dingaan (Shaka's successor) agreed to this and, in February 1838, Retief and some others visited his capital Mgungundlovu (near modern Ulundi) to sign the title deed. It was a trap. The deed assigning all Natal to the Boers was signed but immediately afterwards Dingaan's men massacred the entire party. There was a further massacre at Weenen and other Boer settlements were attacked.

In December 1838 Andries Pretorius arrived in Natal and organised a revenge attack on the Zulus. Sarel Celliers climbed onto a gun carriage to lead the party in a vow that if they won the battle, the Boers would ever after celebrate the day as one of deliverance.

Pretorius' party reached the Ncome River and on 16 December the Zulus attacked. After three hours of carnage the river ran red and was named Blood River by the Boers. Three Boers had slight injuries; 3000 Zulus had been killed.

After such a 'miraculous' victory (the result of good tactics and vastly superior weapons) it seemed that Boer expansion really did have that long-suspected stamp of divine approval, and 16 December was celebrated by whites as the Day of the Vow until 1994, when it was renamed the Day of Reconciliation.

Perhaps more miraculously, when the Boers pushed on to Mgungundlovu they found the remains of Piet Retief and his party and the deed granting them Natal. With both military success and a title deed, it isn't surprising that they considered Natal to be well and truly theirs. That was not to be. The British annexed the republic in 1843 and most of the Boers moved north into the Transvaal, with yet another grievance against the British.

## The Boer Republics

Several short-lived Boer republics sprang up but soon the only serious contenders were the Orange Free State and the Transvaal. The Transvaal Boers were too far away for the British to do much about, but the Orange Free State was more accessible and promised to be a headache because of the Boers' constant encroachment on Basotho land around the Caledon River.

The years between the Battle of Blood River (1838), and the conventions of Sand River (1852) and Bloemfontein (1854), which gave independence to the Transvaal

JON MURRAY

A major feature of the Voortrekker expansion were the massive convoys of wagon trains crossing the land.

and the Orange Free State, are full of confusion and conflict. The Boers knew what they wanted: land and freedom. The aims of the black tribes were similar, but the British government, which commanded the strongest forces in the area, wasn't at all sure of what it wanted.

There were two differing viewpoints in successive British governments. One held that the boundaries of the colony should be expanded to take in the areas settled by the Boers, both to enlarge the colony and to prevent other Europeans having a stake in Southern Africa.

The other view considered that colonies were expensive things. Even India, with its fabulous wealth, was run by a private company rather than the government until after the 1857 Mutiny, and Southern Africa promised much less in the way of trade and taxes. From this viewpoint the Boers shouldn't have been allowed to trek in the first place, and their republics were to be discouraged.

Besides, Britain had non-aggression treaties with many of the peoples with whom the Boers were coming into conflict. When the Boers, as de facto British subjects, broke those treaties, the British were obliged to send in the army to enforce the peace. This was not just out of a desire to see justice prevail. The British knew that any large-scale disturbance had a domino effect and they did not want to upset their precarious relations with tribes bordering the Cape Colony. However, because of changing policies their armies and officials often had no idea of whether they should be restraining Boers, protecting blacks, enforcing British treaties, revenging Boer losses or carving out new British colonies. Nobody knew what orders would arrive on the next mail boat from England.

The Orange Free State was intermittently at war with the powerful Basotho, sometimes with British assistance, sometimes without. At various times the British placed Residents in Bloemfontein and Moshoeshoe's court, annexed the Free State, gave it independence, wrote treaties, tore up the treaties, revised borders, supervised a few ceasefires and finally, in 1871, they annexed Basutholand.

That solved the problem of land for the Orange Free State. The settlement terms of the 1865 Basutho-Orange Free State War had been generous and now there was no chance of Moshoeshoe reclaiming his land from Orange Free State. (After South Africa gained majority rule in 1994, Lesotho raised the issue of the stolen land, but South Africa was not interested in negotiations.)

The Transvaal Republic's problems were mostly internal, with several leaders and breakaway republics threatening civil war until Paul Kruger settled the issue with a short, sharp campaign in 1864.

The financial position of the republics was always precarious. With small populations, no industry and precious little agriculture, they depended entirely on cattle. Most trade was by barter. There were few towns and the infrastructure of a nation was almost entirely lacking. Their contact with the outside world was minimal and that was the way they wanted it.

Just when it seemed that the republics, with their thinly spread population of fiercely independent Boers, were beginning to settle into stable states, diamonds were discovered near Kimberley in 1869. They were discovered on land belonging to the Grigriqua people but to which both the Transvaal and the Orange Free State laid claim. Britain stepped in quickly and annexed the area.

The diamond mines resulted in a rush of European immigrants and a migration of black labour. Towns sprang up in which the 'proper separation' of white and black was ignored. The Boers were disturbed by the foreigners, both black and white, and angry that their impoverished republics were missing out on the economic benefits of the mines.

Meanwhile, Britain became nervous about the existence of independent republics in Southern Africa, especially as gold had been found in the Transvaal. The solution, as usual, was annexation and in 1877 the Transvaal lost its independence.

### Anglo-Boer Wars

After annexation, the Transvaal drifted into rebellion and the First Anglo-Boer War, known by Afrikaners as the War of Independence, broke out. It was over almost as soon as it began, with a crushing Boer victory at the Battle of Majuba Hill in early 1881. The republic regained its independence as the Zuid-Afrikaansche Republiek (ZAR, South African Republic).

Paul Kruger, who had been one of the leaders of the uprising and had earlier led a delegation to London to argue for an end to the annexation, became president of the ZAR in 1883.

Kruger was born in Cape Colony but his family had joined Potgieter's party on the trek into the Transvaal. He received little education and at 16 he left home to run his own farm – an apparently inauspicious background for a man who was to take on the British Empire at its most ravenous.

The British desire to federate the Southern African colonies and republics was growing, but not just because federation would solve local difficulties. Victoria was now Queen Empress and her empire builders had visions of a British Africa stretching from Cairo to the Cape. Almost the only obstacles in the path of that imperial dream were the Boer republics.

With the discovery of a huge reef of gold

Paul Kruger became the first president of the Zuid-Afrikaansche Republiek.

in the Witwatersrand (the area around Johannesburg) in 1886 and the explosive growth of Johannesburg, the ZAR was suddenly host to thousands of *uitlanders* (foreigners), black and white. By 1887 Johannesburg had a stock exchange and a racecourse. Within five years it was a city, complete with wealthy magnates and financiers, none of whom were Afrikaners. The influx of black labour to the area was also disturbing for the Boers, many of whom were going through hard times and bitterly resented the black wage-earners.

With little experience of towns, none of cities, no access to the international finance which poured into the mining companies, and a deep suspicion of foreign ways, Kruger's government did its best to isolate the republic from the gold rush. The foreigners were paying taxes but they were not allowed to vote.

The enormous wealth of the Witwatersrand was an irresistible target for the British imperialists. In 1895 a raiding party lead by Leander Jameson entered the ZAR with the intention of sparking an uprising on the Witwatersrand and installing a British administration. This was a fiasco, but it was obvious to Kruger that the raid had at least the tacit approval of the British government and that his republic was in danger. He formed an alliance with the Orange Free State.

In 1899 the British demanded that voting rights be given to the 60,000 foreign whites on the Witwatersrand. Kruger refused, demanding that British troops massing on the ZAR borders be withdrawn by 11 October or he would consider the republic to be at war.

The British, confident that their vastly superior numbers of experienced troops would win swiftly, took him on. Shocked to find that the Boers were no push-over, the British were for a time in disarray. The Boers first invaded Natal, where they won important battles. They besieged Ladysmith but this, like the siege of Mafeking (now Mafikeng), was a mistake as it gave the British time to bring in more troops and new commanders, Lords Roberts and Kitchener.

The abilities of the Boer *kommandos* (small fighting units, the equivalent of a district militia) were no longer underestimated and an army of 450,000 men was brought to bear on them. The 80,000 Boers from the ZAR, the Orange Free State and the Cape gave way rapidly and by 5 June 1900 Pretoria, the last of the major towns, had surrendered.

It seemed as though the war was over but instead it entered a second, bitter phase. Kommando raiders, freed from the now-broken central command, denied the enemy control of the countryside. There was no possibility that the British could be defeated but maintaining an occupying army would be a very expensive proposition.

The British had no enemy army to face, just kommandos who could instantly become innocuous farmers, and they decided to exact reprisals. If a railway line was blown up, the nearest farmhouse was destroyed; if a shot was fired from a farm, the house was burnt down, the crops destroyed and the animals killed. The women and children from the farms were collected and taken to concentration camps – a British invention. As the guerrilla war dragged on the burnings and detentions became more systematic. By the end of the war 26,000 people, mainly children, had died of disease and neglect in the camps.

The Boer leaders were in a dilemma. Their growing hatred of the British deepened their resolve to fight until the end, but the horror stories from the concentration camps compelled them to finish the war quickly. Public feeling in Britain and Europe was swinging against the British government (largely due to the efforts of Emily Hobhouse, an Englishwoman who worked in the camps), but it was too late to influence the outcome of the war. On 31 May 1902 the Peace of Vereeniging was signed and the Boer republics became British colonies. Paul Kruger fled to Europe, where he died in 1904.

The terms of the peace were generous. The British extracted no payments and in 1906 a new government in Britain granted limited self-government. This was small solace for the Afrikaners, who found themselves again ruled by Britain and in the ignominious position of being poor farmers in a country where big mining ventures and foreign capital made them irrelevant.

### British Rule

The British response after their victory was a curious mixture of appeasement and insensitive imperialism. It was essential for the Boers and British to work together. The nonwhites were scarcely considered, other than as potential labour, despite the fact that they constituted nearly 80% of the country's population. The Peace of Vereeniging did nothing to ensure that blacks or coloureds would be given political rights, despite British propaganda during the war that blacks would be freed from 'Boer slavery' – a failure that was regarded as a betrayal by the tens of thousands who had fought on Britain's side.

After the war, the Cape Colony was the only state where political rights were shared between races, but even there only 15% of the registered voters were nonwhite. Political awareness was growing however. Mohandas (later called Mahatma) Gandhi was working with the Indian populations of Natal and the Transvaal, and men like John Jabavu, Walter Rubusana and Abdullah Abdurahman laid the foundations for new non-tribal black political groups. There was considerable black unrest, which in Natal developed into the Bambatha Rebellion. Bambatha, a Zulu chief, began a guerrilla war of independence, but it was crushed at the cost of 4000 black lives.

The colonial government, under Lord Milner, spent millions of pounds on reconstructing the country after the devastation of the war, although a primary aim was to get the mines functioning again. By 1907 the mines of the Witwatersrand were producing almost one-third of the world's gold.

Resettlement was less successful and poor Boers, ill-equipped for urban life, flooded into the cities. There they found a world dominated by the English and their language, and they were at the mercy of English oppressors. Worst of all, they were forced to

After the Anglo-Boer War, Walter Rubusana began developing non-tribal black political groups.

Abdullah Abdurahman was another key figure in developing black political groups.

compete for jobs with blacks on an equal footing. Partly as a backlash to this, Afrikaans came to be seen as the *volkstaal* (people's language) and a symbol of Afrikaner nationhood, and several nationalistic organisations sprang up.

The former republics were given representative government in 1906/7, and moves towards union began almost immediately. The pressures were largely economic – the smaller provinces were unsustainable in a world that required integrated economies and infrastructures, proper tax bases and centralised bureaucracies.

The most contentious issue was the question of voter franchise, which varied from colony to colony. Despite a major campaign by nonwhites the eventual compromise agreement allowed each colony to retain its existing arrangements, but only whites could be elected to Parliament. English and Dutch were made the official languages.

The Union of South Africa was established on 31 May 1910. Cape Town became the legislative capital, Pretoria (capital of the Transvaal) the administrative capital, Bloemfontein (capital of the Orange Free State) the seat of the Supreme Court, while Pietermaritzburg (capital of Natal) was given financial compensation. The three British High Commission Territories of Basutholand (now Lesotho), Bechuanaland (now Botswana), Swaziland, and Rhodesia (now Zimbabwe) were excluded from the Union.

For information about the history of South Africa from Union to the present day see the South African Facts about the Country chapter.

## FLORA

In some eyes, Southern Africa's most impressive endowment is its flora. There are more than 22,000 species, accounting for 10% of the world's total – that's more than in the USA, which is seven times larger. It is not just impressive numerically, it is both fascinating and spectacularly beautiful.

South Africa is the only country with one of the world's six floral kingdoms within its borders. This is the Cape kingdom, mostly in Western Cape, with its characteristic *fynbos* ('fine bush'), primarily proteas, heaths and ericas. There are over 8500 species, and the Cape Peninsula alone has more native plants than the entire British Isles.

In the drier regions there are weird succulents, dominated by euphorbias and aloes, and annuals, which flower brilliantly after

LUBA VANGELOVA

The protea flower is the national floral emblem of South Africa.

This member of the protea family, the Leucadendron, is endemic to South Africa

**Fynbos – floral kingdom of the Cape**
South American rainforest is, as everyone knows, an immensely important world resource because of its biodiversity. There are over 400 species to be found in every 10,000 sq km. Pretty impressive? Not compared with the world's richest floral kingdom, the Cape floral kingdom, with over 1300 species per 10,000 sq km.

The world's flora is divided into just six 'floral kingdoms' (eg, rainforest, Australia), and as well as being by far the richest, the Cape Floral Kingdom is also by far the smallest. It extends roughly from Cape Town to Grahamstown, on the coast and in the ranges behind the coast. Most of the remaining indigenous vegetation is now found only in protected areas, such as Table Mountain and the Cape Peninsula.

The dominant vegetation is fynbos (literally fine bush), so named because most fynbos species have small, narrow leaves. All told there are nearly 8000 species of plants in the fynbos environment, most of which are found only here.

Some species have an incredibly small range – the world's entire supply occurs within a few hundred square metres. Some members of the dominant fynbos families – proteas, ericas (heaths) and reeds – have been domesticated in other areas and countries, but for many species the clearing of a house site can mean extinction. ■

spring rainfall – see the Namaqualand section in the Northern Cape chapter. An extraordinary number of domesticated flowers grow wild in South Africa – daisies, pelargoniums, gladioli, ixias, arum lilies, strelitzias, irises, freesias, proteas, watsonias, agapanthus and red hot pokers among them.

In contrast to this wealth Southern Africa is very poor in natural forests. Although they were more widespread in the past, they were never particularly extensive. Today only a few remnants remain. Temperate forests occur on the southern coastal strip between George and Humansdorp (Eastern Cape), in the Drakensberg and in Mpumalanga. There is some subtropical forest north-east of Port Elizabeth through the Transkei area and KwaZulu-Natal.

Large areas in the north are covered by savanna-type vegetation, characterised by acacias and thorn trees, such as the umbrella thorn and sweet thorn.

**FAUNA**
The region is rich in wildlife though most of the large game is now concentrated in South Africa's national parks, particularly the huge Kruger National Park.

South Africa has the world's largest land mammal (the African elephant), the second biggest (the white rhinoceros), the third biggest (the hippopotamus), the tallest (the giraffe), the fastest (the cheetah) and the smallest (the pygmy shrew).

Conservation of the native fauna is an active concern and although one can only dimly imagine the extent of the loss since the arrival of Europeans, a significant amount remains. The region is home to the last substantial populations of black and white rhinos – with horns intact – and the problem with elephant numbers is not that they are declining, but that they are increasing too rapidly.

You probably have a better chance of seeing the 'big five' – buffalo, lion, leopard, elephant and black rhino – in South Africa than in any other African country. There is also a lesser known 'little five' – the buffalo weaver, rhinoceros beetle, elephant shrew, leopard tortoise and ant lion – if you are looking for a challenge.

There is a spectacular variety of birds, with 900 species, 113 of which are endemic. They range from the largest in the world (ostrich), the largest flying bird (the Kori bustard), to spectacularly coloured sunbirds, flamingoes, and the extraordinary sociable weaver birds whose huge colonies live in 'cities' of woven grass.

## CULTURE

Superficially, urbanised European culture doesn't seem to differ much from that found in western countries. There are shopping malls, freeways and all the trappings of consumer culture. However, the unique experience of the white people of Africa has given them a self-awareness that has raised culture to an issue of central importance, far beyond the arts pages of a weekend newspaper. Those of Afrikaner and British descent form distinct subgroups.

Despite the strength of traditional black culture in the countryside, the mingling of peoples in South Africa's urban areas means that old cultures are fading and others are emerging. There is nothing new in this: culture is never static and always responds to external events. Even during the short recorded history of the black peoples of Southern Africa there have been several huge cultural changes, caused by the difaqane and white invasion. The idea that a people can have an intrinsic and unchangeable cultural identity was one of the racist myths promulgated by the apartheid regime to justify its Homelands policy.

In Swaziland traditional culture is one of the most powerful forces in society, whereas in Lesotho it persists mainly in rural areas.

Although there are several major and many minor groupings in the traditional black cultures, there are broad similarities. All are based on belief in a masculine deity, ancestral spirits and various supernatural forces. Marriage customs and taboos differ (but are always important) but polygamy (ie, men can have more than one wife but not vice versa) is permitted and a dowry *(lobolo)* is usually paid. First-born males have inheritance rights. Cattle play an important part in many cultures, as symbols of wealth and as sacrificial animals.

Most black peoples belong to the Nguni (Ndebele, Swazi, Xhosa, Zulu) or the Sotho (Tswana, Pedi, Basotho) linguistic and cultural groupings. The Nguni tended to live in scattered, semi-independent settlements, while the Sotho (especially the Tswana) had larger communities. The Nguni feared incest and prohibited marriage to relatives; the Sotho encouraged the marriage of cousins, perhaps because it meant that the dowry remained in the family.

### San

The nomadic San (or Bushman) culture did not survive the impact of white settlement. Introduced diseases and genocide on the part of whites meant that they have virtually disappeared. Many of the survivors interbred with other racial groups and their descendants are now considered to be a part of the coloured population.

There are small numbers of San at Twee Rivieren (Northern Cape Province), Kagga Kamma (Western Cape Province), and Lake Chrissie (Mpumalanga). Larger groups survive in Botswana. Their traditional nomadic hunting lifestyle has completely disappeared, except for the semi-artificial lifestyle of the Kagga Kamma project and a few small bands living in Botswana.

Elaborate rock paintings, found throughout Southern Africa, are the only tangible reminders of the San people.

Although their technology was simple, it was well adapted to the African environment. Their main hunting weapon was the bow and poisoned arrows, and their tracking and hunting abilities were exceptional. The San's principal cultural legacy is their extraordinary art. The rocks and caves of South Africa were their canvas, and the whole country is studded with examples. For natural detail, purity of line and an almost eerie sense of movement, the paintings, some of which date back 26,000 years, cannot be surpassed.

There are quite a number of accessible sites in the KwaZulu-Natal Drakensberg, particularly in Giant's Castle Game Reserve. *The Drakensberg Bushmen & Their Art* by AR Willcox (Drakensberg Publications, R17) has detailed information on a number of the sites.

In the Cape provinces relatively few sites are easily accessible and those that are have often been destroyed by vandalism, or by people who have thoughtlessly sprayed the paintings with water to temporarily brighten the colours. Most are on private land and the owners of the land are rarely forthcoming about their existence, both to protect them from vandals and to prevent any government interference.

## Khoikhoi

Like the San, the Khoikhoi (Hottentot) and their culture have been submerged in the Christianised and westernised coloured population of the Cape provinces. Originally sheep and cattle herders closely related to the San, they have, at least according to official sources, disappeared as a people.

The Khoikhoi were semi-nomadic and, like the San, hunted with bows and arrows. They lived in easily transportable huts, made with saplings covered with woven mats and followed pasturage on a seasonal basis. The Nama, one of the main tribes, still build the characteristic huts (these days using hessian) around Steinkopf in Namaqualand on the north-west coast and are still small-scale pastoralists. Another group, the Griqua, settled around Kokstad.

Dotted around the Cape provinces are small mission stations where the Khoikhoi sought some kind of refuge. Many of these places are still functioning today, including Mamre, Goederwacht, Wittewater, Keimoes, Genadendal, Onseekpans, Elim, Pella and Wuppertal. The people speak a form of Afrikaans, and hymns and choirs are a feature of their communal life.

## Nguni

**Zulu** The Zulu traditionally believe that the creator of the world is Unkulunkulu (the old, old man), but his daughter uNomkubulwana is more important to day-to-day life as she controls the rain. Still more important are ancestors who can make most things go well or badly depending on how assiduously a person has carried out the required sacrifices and observances.

## Zulu Beadwork

Zulu beadwork is worth looking out for. It takes many forms, from the small, square *umgexo*, which is widely available and makes a good gift, to the more elaborate *umbelenja*, a short skirt or tasselled belt worn by women at puberty, but before marriage. Bead anklets *(amadavathi)* are worn by men and women. Today beadwork is still common but, with the exception of traditional ceremonies, it is used mainly for decoration of people or objects, such as a beaded match-box cover.

As in other societies, beads were used for decoration and as symbols of status, but the Zulu people have also traditionally used them as a means of communication, especially as love letters. The colours and arrangement of the beads give the message.

Some of the colours and their meanings are: red, passion or anger; black, difficulties or night; blue, yearning; deep blue, elopement (refers to the flight of the ibis); white or pale blue, pure love; brown, disgust or despondency; and green, peace or bliss. The more subtle meanings of the beads have been largely forgotten and there were always ambiguities. For example, a 'letter' predominantly red and black could be promising a night of passion or it could mean that the sender was annoyed.

Some bead-sculptors make social and political comment in their work, often weaving elaborate tableaux; the most famous exponent was the late Sizakele Mchunu. The Durban Art Gallery has monthly classes in beadwork in an effort to preserve this ancient art. A good place to buy beadwork is at the Dalton Road Hostel market in Durban. One of the best collections on display is in the KwaZulu Cultural Museum, Ulundi. ■

Zulu Beadwork

In common with other peoples, the important stages of life – birth, puberty, marriage, death – are marked by ceremonies. The clothes people wear reflect their status and their age. For example, girls may not wear long skirts until they become engaged. Animal skins are worn to reflect status, with a leopard-skin cloak signifying a chief.

Since Shaka's time, when the Zulu became a large and dominant tribe, the king *(inoksa)* has been the leader of all the people. Before Shaka there was a looser organisation of local chiefs and almost self-sufficient family groups.

The Zulu *kraal* (village) is usually circular, often with a defensive wall of dead saplings and branches. The 'beehive' huts are hemispherical and made of tightly woven grasses. Inside the hut the right-hand side is for the men and the left-hand for the women, with ancestral spirits allocated a space at the rear. The floor is hard-packed dung, so well made

that at Ondini, some floors remain in the kraal that was burnt by British troops in 1879.

Dancing and singing are important and if you see an IFP (Inkatha Freedom Party) demonstration you'll feel something of the power of massed Zulu singing.

**Xhosa** The Xhosa who maintain a traditional lifestyle are known as the red people because of the red-dyed clothing worn by most adults. Different subgroups wear different costumes, colours and arrangements of beads. The Tembu and Bomvana favour red and orange ochres in the dyeing of their clothing while the Pondo and Mpondomise use a very light blue ochre (although chemical dyes are now much in use).

The Xhosa deity is known variously as uDali, Tixo and Qwamata. This deity also figured in the San religion and it's probable that the invading Xhosa adopted it from them. There are numerous minor spirits and a rich folklore which persists in rural areas. A belief in witches (male or female) is strong and witch-burning is not unknown. Most witchcraft is evil, and the main fear is that people will be possessed by depraved spirits. The main source of evil is the *tokoloshe* which lives in water but is also kept by witches. However, water is not always seen as evil. If someone drowns and their body is not recovered, it is assumed, joyously, that they have gone to join the People of the Sea. Often the drowned are reincarnated as people with special knowledge and understanding.

The *igqirha* (spiritual healer) holds an important place in traditional society because they can deal with the forces of nature and the trouble caused by witches. *Amagqirha* wear white. The *ixhwele* (herbalist) performs some magic but is more concerned with health. *Mbongi* are the holders and performers of a group's oral history and are something like a cross between a bard and a court jester.

While there is a hierarchy of chiefs, the structure of Xhosa society is much looser than that of the Zulus.

Many people have the top of their left-hand little finger removed during childhood to prevent misfortune. Puberty rituals also figure heavily. Boys must not be seen by women during the three-month initiation period following circumcision and disguise themselves with white clay or in intricate costumes made of dried palm leaves. In another puberty ritual, a girl is confined in a darkened hut while her friends tour the area singing for gifts.

Marriage customs and rituals are also important. Unmarried girls wear short skirts which are worn longer as marriage approaches. Married women wear long skirts and cover their breasts. They often put white clay on their faces and wear large, turban-like cloth hats. Smoking long-stemmed pipes is also popular among married women.

Beadwork and jewellery are important. The *danga* is a long turquoise necklace which identifies the wearer to their ances-

tors. The *ngxowa yebokwe* is a goatskin bag carried over the left shoulder on important occasions.

**Ndebele** The Ndebele are a Nguni group, surrounded by Sotho groups in Northern Province close to Pretoria, but their strikingly painted houses and the women's elaborate costume and decoration set them apart. Their beadwork is dazzling; women can reach outstanding proportions as they load on 25kg of beads and jewellery. Some of the costume is so elaborate that it cannot be removed without destroying it, and the masses of copper rings on the ankles and neck are there for life.

You can visit Ndebele villages in Botshabelo Nature Reserve, in Mpumalanga near Middelburg, and in the former Homeland of KwaNdebele, near Hammanskraal about 80km north-east of Pretoria.

**Swazi** Mkhulumnchanti is the Swazi deity. Respect for both the aged and ancestors plays a large part in the complex structure of Swazi traditional society. It is a conservative monarchist society and in many ways it is illiberal, but it works and it's popular.

Unlike in many other post-colonial countries, the wearing of traditional clothing is as common among people in the Westernised middle classes as it is among rural labourers. It's not unusual to see a man on his way to work wearing an *amahiya* robe, with a spear in one hand and a briefcase in the other.

The identity of the Swazi nation is maintained by a system of age-related royal regiments which boys join. They graduate to others as they grow older. These regiments provided the military clout to hold off invaders during the difaqane and have helped to minimise the potentially divisive differences between clans while emphasising loyalty to the king and nation. Annual rituals like the important *Incwala* and the *Umhlanga* ceremonies (see the Swaziland section for details) have the same effect.

The rich and vigorous culture of the Swazi people is vested in the monarchy, both the king *(Ngwenyama* – the lion) and his mother *(Ndlovukazi* – the she-elephant). The Swazi people's forebears were a clan living on the coast of modern Mozambique, and even today their most important ritual involves the waters of the Indian Ocean.

Most Swazis rely at least partly on traditional medicine. There are two types of practitioners, the *inyanga* (usually a man) and the *sangoma* (usually a woman). The inyanga analyses problems and predicts the future by studying the patterns of thrown bones. The sangoma is more of a counsellor, although like the inyanga she is also a herbalist. Sangomas in South Africa are pressing to be recognised as part of the health care system.

Singing is important to Swazis and there are many songs to mark occasions or just to pass the time. Some may not be sung except at specified times.

## Sotho

**Northern Sotho** This broad classification covers many unconnected groups. Traditional villages *(kgoros)* were large – the Tswana had towns of 15,000 people – and had a sophisticated political structure.

The various groups each have totem animals, which they must not kill.

The Lobedu (Pedi) people are unique in that they have a Rain Queen, the *Modjadji*, who brings rain to the lush Lebowa area. The *Modjadji* is supposedly immortal, as she does not marry and thus theoretically has no children. In fact, the queen dies by ritual suicide and is succeeded by a daughter. She is regarded with awe by her people and her reputation is widespread: even Shaka avoided attacking the Lobedu. Henry Rider Haggard's novel *She* is based on the story of the original Modjadji, a 16th-century refugee princess.

**Southern Sotho** The Southern Sotho group comprises mainly the Basotho people of Lesotho. See the Lesotho chapter for information on Basotho culture.

## VhaVenda

The VhaVenda people are something of an enigma. No one is certain of their origin, and their traditional economy was based on manufacture and trade rather than agriculture.

Traditional society is matriarchal, with female priests who supervise the worship of female ancestors. The *domba* (python dance) is a puberty rite performed by girls but boys are included in the ceremony. Very few societies allow both sexes to attend puberty rituals.

The VhaVenda, especially the Lemba, mined, smelted and worked iron, copper and gold for centuries. They travelled throughout Southern Africa to trade their metal. Most of these skills were lost when cheaper European metal became available but the quality of Venda iron is astonishingly high. Pottery is an important craft and these skills have survived.

Because of the tsetse fly, cattle have not figured highly in Venda culture.

Before the Venda area acquired 'independent Homeland' status (and a South African-supported dictator) there were about 30 independent chiefdoms, with no overall leader.

## Afrikaner

The Boers' remarkable history, and their geographical isolation combined with often deliberate cultural isolation has created a unique people – often called the white tribe of Africa.

The ethnic composition of the Afrikaners is difficult to quantify, but the former white government estimates 40% Dutch, 40% German, 7.5% French, 7.5% British, and 5% other. Some historians have argued that the '5% other' figure includes a significant proportion of blacks and coloureds – a claim that would still be regarded as highly offensive by many Afrikaners.

The Afrikaners speak Afrikaans, the only Germanic language to have evolved outside Europe. Spoken as a mother tongue by 5.5 million people it is central to the Afrikaner identity, but it has also served to reinforce their isolation from the outside world. The Afrikaners are a religious people and their brand of Christian fundamentalism based on 17th-century Calvinism is still a powerful influence.

Determination and courage were required by the first trekboers who launched themselves into Africa, and again by the Boers in their long and bitter struggle against the British Empire. This history has been heavily mythologised and the concepts of culture and race are tightly fused. Folk songs are sung like hymns at political rallies.

All this has created a proud and resourceful people, quick to violence, with a volatile streak of arrogance and bitterness. In 1948, the new prime minister and Afrikaner patriot DF Malan exclaimed:

The last hundred years have witnessed a miracle behind which must lie a divine plan. Indeed, the history of the Afrikaner reveals a will and a determination which makes one feel that Afrikanerdom is not the work of men but the creation of God.
**Quoted in *The Mind of South Africa* by Allister Sparks**

The South African countryside, with the exception of Eastern Cape, KwaZulu-Natal and the ex-Homelands, is still dominated by Afrikaners, and outsiders are often regarded with a degree of suspicion. Women are still expected to be wives and mothers. Life in the country towns revolves around the Dutch Reformed churches, which include the Nederduitse Gereformeerde Kerk (the NG Kerk), the Gereformeerde Kerk and the Gereformeerde Hervormde Kerk. The NG Kerk, sometimes referred to as the National Party at prayer, is the largest and most influential of the Afrikaner churches; after years of support it explicitly rejected apartheid in 1990.

There are a number of influential Afrikaner cultural organisations, including the secret Afrikaner Broederbond, which has dominated National Party politics, the Federasie van Afrikaanse Kultuuvereniginge (FAK), which coordinates cultural events and movements, and the Voortrekkers, an Afrikaner youth organisation based on the scouting movement.

Significant numbers of Afrikaners still

dream of an independent, racially pure Boer state (Volkstaat) where the only citizens would be descendants of the Voortrekkers or those who fought in the Anglo-Boer wars. Of course, there would be lots of non-citizens with black skins to do the manual work.

The urbanised middle class tends to be considerably more moderate in its chauvinism, but historical events still find echoes in icons like wagon-wheel fences, and people are proud of old Boer names. Regular *braais* (barbecues) are compulsory. Afrikaner rednecks tend to belong to the 'one-two-three' crowd – one litre of brandy, two litres of Coke and a three-litre Cortina.

## Other Europeans

Aside from the Afrikaners, the majority (around 1.9 million) of European South Africans are of British extraction. There is also a large and influential Jewish population (130,000); significant minorities of Portuguese (36,000), many of whom are refugees from Angola and Mozambique; Germans (34,000); Dutch (28,000); Italians (16,000) and Greeks (10,000).

The British have always had a slightly equivocal position in South African society, exemplified by a not so friendly Afrikaans term: *soutpiel*, literally meaning salt dick and referring to a man with one foot in South Africa and one in Britain. The Afrikaners have often felt (rightly in many cases) that the English-speakers' commitment to Africa was less than their own. Apart from anything else, many of the British who arrived in the 20th century can return 'home' if things get really tough.

The British are much more highly urbanised than the Afrikaners and, particularly up until the 1960s, completely dominated the mining, manufacturing, financial and retail sectors, much to the resentment of the Afrikaners. Although they have traditionally been regarded as a more liberal force politically, a significant number supported the National Party governments.

Their numerical inferiority meant that the English-speakers were doomed to political impotence, but with some noble exceptions their opposition to apartheid was at best muted. It is hard not to come to the cynical conclusion that they were happy to let the Afrikaners do the dirty work, while they, in their dominant economic position, reaped many of the benefits. They even had the luxury of tut-tutting from the corner.

Most lead a suburban existence that, except for the ubiquitous servants, could be transplanted unchanged from Australia or North America.

The English-speaking community does not burn with a sense of grievance or mission. It has no positive, purposeful creed. It lacks cohesion: it is an amorphous community with little sense of any collective identity. They do not even have a proper name: 'English-speaking South Africans' is an appellation so vague as to make them almost anonymous.
*The Mind of South Africa* by Allister Sparks

## RELIGION
### South Africa

Most of the country is Christian, but among the Christians there is enormous diversity, from the 4000 African Indigenous churches to the racist sects which have split from the Dutch Reformed churches. The Indigenous churches are run by and for blacks, independent of the mainstream white churches. They broadly follow either the Ethiopian line, which broke away from the early Methodist missions, or the later Zionist line, which developed as a result of the activities of American Pentecostal missions early this century. The largest church in the country is the Zion Christian Church, whose members wear a silver star on a green background. At Easter each year millions of people congregate at the church's headquarters at Moria near Tzaneen in Northern Province.

The Dutch Reformed churches cover at least three major groups of Afrikaner churches, all conservative. The Church of England is also represented; it gained a high profile because of the anti-apartheid battles of Archbishop Desmond Tutu, who has now retired.

Hindus make up about 70% of the Indian population and about 20% are Muslims.

A minority of blacks follow traditional

religions. Among different peoples, beliefs and practices vary, although there is usually a belief in a supreme deity, but with more emphasis on ancestor worship. Magic plays a large part in beliefs and ceremonies. The distinction between religion and what would be considered folklore in western societies is blurred on a day-to-day level. So much so that many more blacks have no problem in combining Christianity with traditional beliefs, in much the same way that Christianity adopted 'pagan' rituals in its spread through Europe.

### Seven Million Silver Stars

If you're travelling between Tzaneen and Pietersburg/Polokwane (Northern Province), you might notice a giant Star of David painted on the side of a mountain. This marks the site of Moria, Zion City, home of the Zion Christian Church (ZCC). You have probably seen many members of the church. They are the people who wear a metal Star of David, often on a green ribbon. There are seven million of them, and they belong to the largest independent church in Africa.

Each Easter since its founding by Edward Lekganyane in 1910, the church has held a huge gathering at Moria. These days the attendance is around three million people! Part of the reason for the ZCC's popularity is that it allows its members to hold traditional beliefs, most importantly ancestor worship.

The Easter gathering is notable for its lack of trouble. This is perhaps helped by the fact that participants aren't supposed to eat during the four days, while constantly engaged in prayer and dancing. ∎

### Lesotho

Lesotho is a largely Catholic country, thanks to the French missionaries who helped King Moshoeshoe. Traditional beliefs still play their part in daily life.

### Swaziland

Nearly half the population belong to the Zion Apostolic Church. While traditional religion is not widely practised, Swazi traditional culture continues strongly and many ceremonies have religious significance.

# Language

In all three countries English is one of the official languages and in most places you'll find English speakers, although outside the main towns in Lesotho and Swaziland you might have to search for one.

In Lesotho the other official language is seSotho and in Swaziland it's siSwati.

South Africa's official languages were once English and Afrikaans but nine others have been added: isiNdebele, seSotho sa Lebowa, seSotho, siSwati, Xitsonga, Setswana, Tshivenda, isiXhosa and isiZulu. The most widely spoken are Afrikaans, English, seSotho, isiXhosa and isiZulu. The relegation of Afrikaans from one of two official languages to one of 11 has caused some anguish among Afrikaners, who fear for the language's survival. Still, the proportion of TV and radio programmes, road signs and forms, etc, in Afrikaans is still way above the 9.1% allowed.

In South Africa, forms, brochures and timetables are usually printed in both English and Afrikaans; road signs alternate between the two languages. Most Afrikaans speakers also speak good English, but this is not always the case in small rural towns and among the older generations. However, it's not uncommon for blacks in cities to speak at least six languages – whites can usually speak two.

With so many languages, compromises are inevitable, and in the black townships where all the languages come into contact with each other, pure forms are disappearing. The common tongue used in most townships is either a hybrid form of isiZulu and isiXhosa or some variation on seSotho. Although language purists find this development unfortunate these hybrids are fast becoming the most important communication links. It is quite possible that one will be

officially developed and recognised as a lingua franca.

Fanakalo, a pidgin language based on Afrikaans, English and Zulu, was developed for use by black workers. This was once hailed as a future lingua franca, but for many blacks it represents oppression and it is rarely used outside the workplace.

The TALK (Transfer of African Language Knowledge) project aims to teach African languages by teaming up each student with a mother-tongue speaker. This method of learning has proved highly successful, and of course it's also a good way to get to know another culture. TALK courses run for at least six weeks and cost from R250 (most of which goes to the mother-tongue speaker). For information contact TALK (☎ (011) 487 1798), 155 Hunter St, Bellevue East, Johannesburg, 2198; in Cape Town phone ☎ (021) 487 1798.

If you're completely lost for words, remember that the thumbs-up gesture is a universal gesture of goodwill, and can have an amazingly positive effect.

## SOUTH AFRICAN ENGLISH

English has undergone some changes during its time in Africa. Quite a few words have changed meaning, new words have been appropriated, and a distinctive accent, thanks to the influence of Afrikaans, has developed. British rather than US practice is followed in grammar and spelling. In some cases British words are preferred to their US equivalent (eg, lift not elevator, petrol not gas). See the glossary at the back of this book for some examples.

## AFRIKAANS

Although Afrikaans has been closely associated with the tribal identity of the Boers, it is also spoken as a first language by many coloureds. Ironically, it was probably first used as a common language by the polyglot coloured community of the Cape, and passed back to whites by nannies and servants. Around 5.5 million people speak the language, roughly half of whom are Afrikaners and half of whom are coloured.

Afrikaans developed from the High Dutch of the 17th century. It has abandoned the complicated grammar and incorporated vocabulary from French, English, indigenous African languages and even Asian languages (thanks to East Asian slaves). It's inventive, powerful and expressive, but it was not recognised as one of the country's official languages until 1925; before then it was officially regarded as a dialect of Dutch.

Afrikaans is a phonetic language and words are generally pronounced as they are spelled, with the characteristic guttural emphasis and rolled 'r' of Germanic languages. The following pronunciation guide is not exhaustive, but it includes the more difficult sounds that differ from English.

| | |
|---|---|
| **a** | like 'u' in pup |
| **e** | like 'e' in hen |
| **i** | like 'e' in angel |
| **o** | like 'o' in fort, or 'oy' in boy |
| **u** | like 'e' in angel but with lips pouted |
| **r** | should be rolled |
| **aai** | like 'y' in why |
| **ae** | like 'ah' |
| **ee** | like 'ee' in deer |
| **ei** | like 'ay' in play |
| **oe** | like 'oo' in loot |
| **oë** | like 'oe' in doer |
| **ooi** | like 'oi' in oil, preceded by w |
| **oei** | like 'ooey' in phooey, preceded by w |
| **tj** | like 'ch' in chunk |

## Greetings & Civilities

| | |
|---|---|
| Hello. | *Hallo.* |
| Good morning, sir. | *Goeiemore, meneer.* |
| Good afternoon, madam. | *Goeiemiddag, mevrou.* |
| Good evening, miss. | *Goeienaand, juffrou.* |
| Good night. | *Goeienag.* |
| please | *asseblief* |
| Thankyou. | *Dankie.* |
| How are you? | *Hoegaand?* |
| Good thank you. | *Goed dankie.* |
| pardon | *ekskuus* |

## Profanity & Abuse

Although these words are not attractive they are in reasonably common use in South Africa. It's not a wise idea to use them yourself but, in certain situations, it may be necessary to know what they mean.

| | |
|---|---|
| black person | *kaffir* (derogatory, dangerous to use!) |
| nigger lover | *kaffirboetie* |
| Afrikaner | *Dutchman* |
| English South African | *soutpiel* |
| redneck | *rooinek* |
| dero/bum | *bergie* |
| redneck conservative | *gom* |
| narrow-minded | *verkrampt* |
| black threat | *swart gevaar* |
| homosexual man | *moffie* |

## Useful Words & Phrases

| | |
|---|---|
| yes | *ja* |
| no | *nee* |
| What? | *Wat?* |
| How? | *Hoe?* |
| How many/ how much? | *Hoeveel?* |
| When? | *Wanneer?* |
| Where? | *Waar?* |
| emergency | *nood* |
| Do you speak English/Afrikaans? | *Praat u Engels/u Afrikaans?* |
| I only understand a little Afrikaans | *Ek verstaan net 'n bietjie Afrikaans* |
| Where do you live? | *Waar woon u?* |
| What is your occupation? | *Wat is jou beroep?* |
| Where are you from? | *Waarvandaan kom u?* |
| from ... | *van ...* |
| overseas | *oorsese* |
| yes/no/maybe/sure | *ja-nee* |
| soon | *nou-nou* |
| Isn't that so? | *Né?* |
| sons | *seuns* |
| daughters | *dogters* |
| wife | *vrou* |

| | |
|---|---|
| husband | *eggenoot* |
| mother | *ma* |
| father | *pa* |
| sister | *suster* |
| brother | *broer* |
| nice/good/pleasant | *lekker* |
| bad | *sleg* |
| cheap | *goedkoop* |
| expensive | *duur* |
| party | *jol* |

**Numbers**

| 1 | *een* |
|---|---|
| 2 | *twee* |
| 3 | *drie* |
| 4 | *vier* |
| 5 | *vyf* |
| 6 | *ses* |
| 7 | *sewe* |
| 8 | *agt* |
| 9 | *nege* |
| 10 | *tien* |
| 11 | *elf* |
| 12 | *twaalf* |
| 13 | *dertien* |
| 14 | *veertien* |
| 15 | *vyftien* |
| 16 | *sestien* |
| 17 | *sewentien* |
| 18 | *agtien* |
| 19 | *negentien* |
| 20 | *twintig* |
| 21 | *een en twintig* |
| 30 | *dertig* |
| 40 | *veertig* |
| 50 | *vyftig* |
| 60 | *sestig* |
| 70 | *sewentig* |
| 80 | *tagtig* |
| 90 | *negentig* |
| 100 | *honderd* |
| 1000 | *duisend* |

**Days of the Week**

| Monday | *Maandag* (abbreviated to *Ma*) |
|---|---|
| Tuesday | *Dinsdag (Di)* |
| Wednesday | *Woensdag (Wo)* |
| Thursday | *Donderdag (Do)* |
| Friday | *Vrydag (Vr)* |
| Saturday | *Saterdag (Sa)* |
| Sunday | *Sondag (So)* |

**Travel Terms**

| am | *vm* |
|---|---|
| pm | *nm* |
| arrival | *aankoms* |
| daily | *daagliks* |
| departure | *vertrek* |
| from | *van* |
| public holiday | *openbare vakansiedag* |
| return | *retoer* |
| single | *enkel* |
| ticket | *kaartjie* |
| to | *na* |
| today | *vandag* |
| tomorrow | *môre* |
| travel | *reis* |
| weekly | *weekblad* |
| yesterday | *gister* |

**Getting Around – town**

| art gallery | *kunsgalery* |
|---|---|
| at the corner | *op die hoek* |
| avenue | *laan* |
| bank | *bank* |
| building | *gebou* |
| church | *kerk* |
| city | *stad* |
| city centre | *middestad* |
| enquiries | *navrae* |
| exit | *uitgang* |
| information | *inligting* |
| left | *links* |
| office | *kantoor* |
| pharmacy/chemist | *apteek* |
| police | *polisie* |
| police station | *polisiestasie* |
| post office | *poskantoor* |
| right | *regs* |
| road | *pad, weg* |
| rooms | *kamers* |
| station | *stasie* |
| street | *straat* |
| tourist bureau | *toeristeburo* |
| town | *dorp* |
| traffic light | *robot* |

## Getting Around – country

| | |
|---|---|
| bay | *baai* |
| beach | *strand* |
| car | *kar* |
| caravan park | *woonwapark* |
| field/plain | *veld* |
| ford | *drift* |
| freeway | *vrymaak* |
| game reserve | *wildtuin* |
| hiking trail | *wandelpad* |
| highway | *snelweg* |
| lake | *meer* |
| marsh | *vlei* |
| mountain | *berg* |
| point | *punt* |
| river | *rivier* |
| road | *pad* |
| track | *spoor* |
| utility/pick-up | *bakkie* |

## Food & Drinks

| | |
|---|---|
| barbecue | *braaivleis/braai* |
| beer | *bier* |
| bread | *brood* |
| cheese | *kaas* |
| chicken | *hoender* |
| cup of coffee | *koppie koffie* |
| dried and salted meat | *biltong* |
| farm sausage | *boerewors* |
| fish | *vis* |
| fruit | *vrugte* |
| glass of milk | *glas melk* |
| hotel bar | *kroeg* |
| meat | *vleis* |
| pork | *varkvlies* |
| steak | *biefstuk* |
| tea | *tee* |
| vegetables | *groente* |
| water | *water* |
| wine | *wyn* |

## SISWATI

SiSwati is the language of the Swazi people. It is very similar to Zulu, and the two speakers can understand one another. Tonality (rising and falling 'notes' in the words) plays a part in siSwati, and there are some clicks to contend with.

## Useful Words & Phrases

| | |
|---|---|
| Hello (to one person) | *sawubona* ('I see you' – friendly or respectful greeting) |
| Hello (to more than one person) | *sanibona.* |
| How are you? | *kunjani?* |
| I'm fine. | *kulungile.* |
| Goodbye (if you are leaving) | *sala kahle* (stay well) |
| Goodbye. (if you are staying) | *hamba kahle* (go well) |
| please | *tsine* |
| I thank you. | *ngiyabonga* |
| We thank you. | *siyabonga* |
| yes | *yebo* (an all purpose greeting) |
| no | (click) *ha* |
| sorry | *lucolo* |
| Do you have? | *une yini?* |
| How much? | *malini?* |
| today | *lamuhla* |
| tomorrow | *kusasa* |
| yesterday | *itolo* |
| Is there a bus to? | *kukhona ibhasi yini leya?* |
| When does it leave? | *isuka nini?* |
| morning | *ekuseni* |
| afternoon | *entsambaba* |
| evening | *kusihlwa* |
| night | *ebusuku* |

## SESOTHO

There are two forms of seSotho, the language of the Sotho peoples. Southern Sotho is spoken in Lesotho and by Basotho people in South Africa. It's useful to know some words and phrases if you're planning to visit Lesotho, especially if you want to trek in remote areas.

## Greetings

| | |
|---|---|
| Greetings father. | *lumela ntate* |
| Peace father. | *khotso ntate* |
| Greetings mother. | *lumela 'me* |
| Peace mother. | *khotso 'me* |
| Greetings brother. | *lumela abuti* |
| Peace brother. | *khotso abuti* |

| | |
|---|---|
| Greetings sister. | *lumela ausi* |
| Peace sister. | *khotso ausi* |

There are three ways to say 'How are you?':

| | |
|---|---|
| How are you? | *o kae? (singular)* |
| | *le kae? (plural)* |
| How do you live? | *o phela joang? (s)* |
| | *le phela joang? (p)* |
| How did you get up? | *o tsohele joang? (s)* |
| | *le tsohele joang? (p)* |

The answers to these questions are:

| | |
|---|---|
| I am here | *ke teng (s) re teng (p)* |
| I live well | *ke phela hantle (s)* |
| | *re phela hantle (p)* |
| I got up well | *ke tsohile hantle (s)* |
| | *re tsohile hantle (p)* |

These questions and answers are quite inter-changeable. Someone could ask you *o phela joang?* and you could answer *ke teng*.

When trekking, people always ask *lea kae?* (Where are you going?) and *o tsoa kae?* or the plural *le tsoa kae?* (Where have you come from?). When parting, use the following expressions:

| | |
|---|---|
| Stay well. | *sala hantle* (s) |
| | *salang hantle (p)* |
| Go well. | *tsamaea hantle (s)* |
| | *tsamaeang hantle (p)* |

Add *ntate* or *'me* (or *bo*) for the plural.

'Thank you' is *kea leboha* (pronounced 'keya lebowah'). The herd boys often ask for money *(chelete)* or sweets *(lipompong)* (pronounced dee-pom-pong). If you want to say 'I don't have any', the answer is *ha dio* (pronounced 'ha dee-oh').

## ISIXHOSA
The language of the Xhosa people is isiXhosa, the dominant indigenous language in Eastern Cape Province, although you'll meet isiXhosa speakers everywhere.

| | |
|---|---|
| Good morning. | *molo* |
| Goodnight. | *rhonanai* |
| Do you speak English? | *uyakwazi ukuthetha siNgesi?* |
| father (term of respect for older man) | *bawo* |
| Are you well? | *uphilile na namhlanje?* |
| Yes, I am well. | *ewe, ndiphilile kanye* |
| Where do you come from? | *uvela phi na okanye ngaphi na?* |
| I come from ... | *ndivela ...* |
| When do we arrive? | *siya kufika nini na?* |
| The road is good. | *indlela ilungile* |
| The road is bad. | *indlela imbi* |
| I am lost | *ndilahlekile* |
| Is this the road to ...? | *yindlela eya ... yini le?* |
| Would you show me the way to ...? | *Ungandibonisa na indlela eye ...?* |
| Is it possible to cross the river? | *kunokwenzeka ukuwela umlambo?* |
| How much does it cost? | *idla ntoni na?* |
| day | *usuku* |
| week | *iveki* |
| month (moon) | *inyanga* |
| east | *empumalanga* |
| west | *entshonalanga* |

## ISIZULU
Zulu people speak isiZulu. As with several other Nguni languages, isiZulu uses a variety of 'clicks', very hard to reproduce without practice. Many people don't try (the 'Kwa' in KwaZulu is a click, but you rarely hear it from whites) although it's worth the effort, if just to provide amusement for your listeners. To ask a question, add *na?* to the end of a sentence.

| | |
|---|---|
| Please | *jabulisa* |
| Thank you. | *ngiyabonga* |
| Where does this road go? | *iqondaphi lendlela na?* |

| | | | |
|---|---|---|---|
| Which is the road to ...? | *Iphi indlela yokuya ku...?* | east | *impumalanga* |
| Is it far? | *Kukude yini?* | west | *intshonalanga* |
| yes | *yebo* | water | *amanzi* |
| no | *cha* | food | *ukudla* |
| north | *inyakatho* | lion | *ibhubesi* |
| south | *iningizumi* | rhino (black) | *ubhejane* |
| | | rhino (white) | *umkhombe* |

# Regional Facts for the Visitor

## PLANNING

### When to Go

**South Africa** In many places, especially the lowveld, summer can be uncomfortably hot. In KwaZulu-Natal and Mpumalanga, humidity can also be annoying. The warm waters of the east coast make swimming a year-round proposition. Spring is the best time for wildflowers in the Northern and Western Cape provinces and they are at their peak in Namaqualand (Northern Cape) from mid-August to mid-September. Winters are mild everywhere except in the highest country, where there are frosts and occasional snowfalls. There is skiing in Lesotho and in Eastern Cape Province. Summer brings warmer weather but also rain and mist to the mountains.

Many South Africans take their annual holidays in summer, with several overlapping waves of holiday-makers streaming out of the cities from mid-December to late January. Then, as well as during the other school holidays, resorts and national parks are heavily booked and prices on the coast can more than double. The KwaZulu-Natal coast, especially south of Durban, is packed. The South African provinces have slightly different dates for school holidays and they all change annually. Roughly, there are two-week holidays in April, a month around July, a month around September, and about two months from early December to late January. The peak time is mid-December to early January. Contact Satour for the exact dates.

**Lesotho** Lesotho is worth visiting year-round, but the weather can determine what

---

### On the Net

For travel information, travellers' letters and a travellers' bulletin board check out the Lonely Planet web site: http://www.lonelyplanet.com

For more general tourist information and some links, the South African embassy in the USA has a useful site: http://www.safrica.net

South Africans are very quick to pick up on new technology, and there many useful websites emanating from the country. The internet country code for South Africa is za. Check out SAA (South African Airways) routes on the web at: http://vwv.is.co.za/saa/pak/

Spoornet (the company that runs passenger trains) has routes and timetables and a good email contact address at: www.spoornet.co.za/

As well as the Spoornet site, there's a good site run by a dedicated railways enthusiast, with useful information and news, plus some very esoteric items and details of steam train options: www.ru.ac.za/departments/iwr/staff/daf/sartrain.html

For backpacker-oriented tours and services, check out the Africa Travel Centre's site: www.kingsley.co.za/millennia/bp&atc.htm

You can book accommodation in national parks over the net, from the Travel South Africa home page: http://africa.com/docs/satravel.htm

This page also has links to Satour and the Western Cape Tourism Board.

A great way to keep up with news and entertainment listings is to visit the *Weekly Mail & Guardian* home page: http://www.mg.co.za/mg/

Arthur Goldstuck is a collector of South African urban legends (his books include *The Leopard in the Luggage*) and is a connoisseur of the net, with a web page at: www.legends.org.za/arthur/

For an interesting list of South African organisations (including detailed news from the ANC), go to: http://minotaur.marques.co.za/saorg.htm

South Africa's largest gay web page is at www.gaysa.co.za/, with information on entertainment, travel services and restaurants, plus some more adult-oriented stuff.

There's a sparse Lesotho page at: http://www.sas.upenn.edu//Africa_Studies/Country_Specific/Lesotho.html ■

you do. In winter be prepared for cold conditions and snow. In summer, it's rain and mist which have to be taken into account. In remote areas (which make up a large proportion of the country) roads are often cut by flooding rivers in summer.

**Swaziland** Swaziland's climate is much the same as that of Mpumalanga, with hot summers alleviated by rain on the high country, and mild winters with little rain. The two most important Swazi cultural ceremonies, the Umhlanga (Reed) Dance and the Incwala ceremony are held in August or September and late December or early January, respectively.

## Maps

**South Africa** Good maps are widely available. Lonely Planet's *South Africa, Lesotho & Swaziland travel atlas* is a handy companion to this book. The Map Studio series is recommended and, as always, Michelin maps are excellent.

The Map Office (☎ (011) 339 4951), 3rd Floor, Standard Bank Building, De Korte St, Braamfontein, Johannesburg, sells government topographic maps for R9 a sheet. You probably have a better chance of quick service if you deal with this shop rather than battle with the bureaucracy. The Map Office's postal address is Box 207, Wits 2050, Gauteng.

The 1:50,000 scale maps of the KwaZulu-Natal Drakensberg drawn by Peter Slingsby are a must for hikers. Trails are shown with detailed information such as dangerous river crossings, distances and difficult sections. They are usually available at the various trailheads.

**Lesotho** The Department of Land Surveys & Physical Planning in Maseru sells some excellent maps of Lesotho. Best for driving is the 1:250,000 map (1994) which covers the whole country (yes, it's that small) and costs M30. For trekking or driving in very rugged areas you might want the 1:50,000 series, at about M10 each. The problem with

these maps is that Lesotho's rapid programme of road building and upgrading has left them behind. Ask the friendly staff at the department for the latest information.

The maps are produced in conjunction with the British government and you can buy them in the UK from the Ordnance Survey, Romsey Rd, Southampton, SO9 4DH, UK. To order maps from Lesotho write to the Department of Land Surveys & Physical Planning, Ministry of the Interior, PO Box 876, Maseru 100, Lesotho.

**Swaziland** The free maps available in various brochures and at the tourist office in Mbabane are good enough to get around this tiny country, although if you're driving you might have to ask directions if you get off the main roads. There's a good 1:250,000 scale map available from the Surveyor-General's office at the Ministry of Works in Mbabane (PO Box 58), and if you're serious about hiking there are also 1:50,000 maps.

## What to Bring

With such a variety of things to do in the region, it's hard to generalise about what to bring. With so much dramatic scenery and so many good nature reserves, binoculars will come in handy.

A sleeping bag is vital for budget travellers, useful in backpackers' hostels and in rondavels (circular huts) and cabins in the caravan parks. Camping is definitely a viable option.

You can buy just about anything you need in the major cities in South Africa, and clothes are often cheaper than in western countries. Lightweight camping equipment and other specialised items are of good quality but there isn't much choice and prices tend to be high. A very limited range of consumer goods is available in Swaziland and Lesotho.

## VISAS

For many visitors, Lesotho is the only country that requires a visa before arrival (and you can arrange this in South Africa).

See the Facts for the Visitor chapters for each of the three countries for detailed information.

## BOOKS

Most books are published in different editions by different publishers in different countries. As a result, a book might be a hardcover rarity in one country and readily available in paperback in another. Fortunately, bookshops and libraries search by title or author.

A number of excellent writers can help unlock something of the region's soul, not least Nadine Gordimer, the 1991 Nobel Prize winner. The South African publishing industry churns out high-quality coffee table books (such as *The Ndebele* by Margaret Courtney Clarke, R253) and there is an increasing number of guidebooks for most activities.

### Lonely Planet

Lonely Planet also publishes the *Cape Town city guide* (US$9.95), with more detail on that great city than can fit in this book; the *South Africa, Lesotho & Swaziland travel atlas* (US$14.95) to help you get around; *Africa – the South* (US$25.95), with information on the whole of Southern Africa; and the classic *Africa* (US$29.95) for budget travellers setting out to explore the continent.

### Guidebooks

Satour, the national tourism organisation, publishes glossy guides to hotels and guesthouses (paperback, about R30) and to B&Bs (paperback, about R30). Each establishment is graded, which is useful up to a point.

The Automobile Association (AA) publishes some handy paperback guides to caravan parks and hotels. They have reasonably descriptive entries but don't venture into giving opinions. The *Guide to Caravan Parks in Southern Africa* and *Guide to Hotels in Southern Africa* cost around R30 each.

The paperback *Swaziland Jumbo Tourist Guide* by Hazel Hussey has some useful information hidden among the glossy ads. It's geared towards South Africans going away for weekends.

The owner of Sani Lodge, a backpacker hostel on Sani Pass, produces a handy little guide to Lesotho (about R15).

### History & Politics

There are no longer any 'standard' histories of South Africa; most of the old ones have been discredited and the new ones have yet to be written. For a brief introduction, Kevin Shillington's *History of Southern Africa* (paperback, about R60) is good, although it is intended as a school text. For a more partisan, but nonetheless accurate view, *Foundations of the New South Africa* by John Pampallis (paperback, R35) was originally written as a history textbook for exiled South African students in Tanzania and gives South African history from the ANC's point of view.

*A History of the African People of South Africa* by Paul Maylam (paperback, about R40) is a detailed and fascinating book.

The best introduction to white South African history is *The Mind of South Africa* by Allister Sparks, (paperback, R40). It's opinionated, and some will find it controversial, but it's readable and insightful – highly recommended. Also good is *The Afrikaners – Their Last Great Trek* by Graham Leach (paperback, R40). It gives a detailed analysis of the Afrikaner people and their political development. Allister Sparks' latest book, *Tomorrow is Another Country* (paperback, R61), is the fascinating inside story of the Convention for a Democratic South Africa (CODESA) negotiations.

For a history of the ANC, read *South Africa Belongs to Us* by Francis Meli (paperback, R68).

The 'They Fought for Freedom' series of paperbacks, published by Maskew Miller Longman, cost around R21 each and feature important figures from recent South African history, including Steve Biko, Yusef Dadoo, Ruth First, Chris Hani and Oliver Tambo. For the story (so far) of a turbulent life, read

*The Lady – the Life & Times of Winnie Mandela* by Emma Gilbey (paperback R51).

If you're at all interested in the political process, buy *Election '94 South Africa*, edited by Andrew Reynolds (paperback, R40), which gives a fascinating and detailed account of the parties and the election. *Political Organisations in South Africa A-Z* by Hennie Kotze and Anneke Greyling (paperback, about R70) covers every significant political group, which can be handy if you become baffled by acronyms. It's updated annually.

For detailed insights into the Boer side of the Anglo-Boer wars, read *Jan Smuts: Memoirs of the Boer War*, edited by Spies & Nattras (hardback, R90).

## Culture

*Indaba My Children* (paperback, R68) is an interesting book of folk tales, history, legends, customs and beliefs, collected and told by Vusamazulu Credo Mutwa.

*Religion in Africa* (paperback R122), published by the David M Kennedy Centre at Princeton University, is thick and scholarly but is one of the few books that gives an overview of this subject.

In Lesotho you occasionally see booklets on various aspects of Basotho culture, often produced under the auspices of the various missions. These are worth reading because they tend to be straight descriptions or oral history, without the ideological and intellectual baggage of scholarly texts. Two titles which are available in Maseru with a bit of searching are *Customs & Superstitions in Basutholand* by Justinus Sechefo (M10.60) and *Basutho Music & Dancing* by AG Mokhali (M5.70).

## Personal Accounts

Some books seem to have such a powerful sense of place they become compulsory reading for foreign visitors to a country. There can be no more obvious or important example than Nelson Mandela's autobiography, *Long Road to Freedom* (hardback, R100; R500 for an autographed copy) –

despite the fact that the man was behind bars for nearly three decades.

If you want to read more of Mandela's words, look for the collections of his writings and speeches in *The Struggle is My Life* and *Nelson Mandela Speaks* (paperback, about R50 each). They can be pretty dry but do offer an insight into the steadfastness of this amazing man – and also how his message was refocussed depending on the audience he addressed. He might be a hero of the people but he is also a consummate politician.

For a white perspective on the apartheid years read the excellent *My Traitor's Heart* by Rian Malan (paperback, R46). It is an outstanding autobiography of an Afrikaner attempting to come to grips with his heritage and his future. Breyten Breytenbach, a political prisoner and exile under the apartheid regime, writes of his return to South Africa in *Return to Paradise* (paperback, R45). It's a very personal and rather poetic account.

Gillian Slovo, novelist and daughter of Joe Slovo, has written about life with a famous father in *Every Secret Thing*. Joe Slovo, who lived just long enough to take his place in the new democratic government, was one of the few white heroes of the liberation struggle.

*The Lost World of the Kalahari* and *The Heart of the Hunter* by Laurens van der Post (paperbacks, about R45) both chronicle the author's exploration of the Kalahari and give a sympathetic interpretation of San culture. The analysis is poetic and thought-provoking, giving an insight into the mystical relationship between nomadic hunters and their world.

*Jock of the Bushveld* by Sir James Percy Fitzpatrick was written in 1907. As well as being a story about the relationship between a man and his dog, it is a vivid portrayal of the time when the country was still dependent on ox-wagons for its transport. It's a classic. In the same class is John Buchan's *Prester John*. It's a typical Buchan 'ripping yarn', with some interesting descriptions of people and landscape among the racist jingoism.

## Literature

Nadine Gordimer was awarded the Nobel Prize for Literature in 1991. Her first novel, *The Lying Days*, was published in 1953. In her subsequent novels she has explored with a merciless eye South Africa, its people and their interaction. *The Conservationist* was the joint winner of the 1974 Booker Prize. Her more recent work explores the inter-racial dynamics of the country. Look for *July's People* and *A Sport of Nature*.

JM Coetzee is another contemporary writer who has received international acclaim; *The Life & Times of Michael K* won the 1983 Booker Prize.

*Being There*, edited by Robin Malan (paperback, R35), is a good introductory collection of short stories from Southern African authors, including Doris Lessing and Nadine Gordimer.

The most famous exponent of the short story in South Africa is Herman Charles Bosman. He wrote mainly in the 1930s and '40s and is reminiscent of Australia's Henry Lawson. Bosman is an accessible writer and is widely popular for stories that blend humour and pathos, and capture the essence of rural South Africa. The most popular collection is *Mafeking Road*, but there are a number of compilations available.

My favourite Bosman is the novella *Wilemsdorp*. It is set in a narrow-minded Transvaal town, but one which is seething with sex (seduction, adultery and illegal 'miscegenation'), murder and suicide. And *dagga* – it contains 'stoned and on the run' scenes unmatched until Hunter S Thompson. The ostensible theme is that a white man is brought dreadfully low by associating with a nonwhite woman and by smoking dagga (the drug of choice of the 'natives'), but you get the feeling that Bosman was much more ambivalent. On the other hand, most of Bosman's humorous short stories set in Jurie Steyn's post office in Drogevlei (a fictitious hamlet in the Zeerust area of North-West Province) contain gratuitous and extremely offensive jokes about the 'natives'.

**Jon Murray**

Alan Paton was responsible for one of the most famous South African novels, *Cry the Beloved Country* (paperback, R38), an epic that follows a black man's suffering in a white and urban society. It was written in 1948. Paton returned to the theme of apartheid in *Ah, but Your Land is Beautiful*. André Brink, author of *A Dry White Season,* which was made into an unusually accurate Hollywood film, is another noted South African author worth reading.

*Circles in a Forest* by Dalene Mathee, translated from Afrikaans, is a historical novel about the area around Knysna, written from the Afrikaner point of view. It's melodramatic, moving and entertaining – the story of the woodcutters and elephants who lived in the forests – a must if you spend time on the Garden Route.

As you travel around the Karoo you'll notice several old houses with plaques proclaiming them an 'Olive Schreiner house'. Olive Schreiner (1855-1920) wrote *The Story of an African Farm* (published 1883) which was immediately popular and established her enduring reputation as one of South Africa's seminal novelists. Despite the novel being adopted as part of the folk heritage of white South Africa, Schreiner was a feminist, an anti-racist (to an extent) and held left-wing political views.

Published literature by nonwhite authors is in short supply but that situation will change.

## Special Interest Books

**Animals** *Mammals of Southern Africa* by Chris & Tilde Stuart (paperback, R70) includes a great deal of information and many excellent photos. *Whale Watching in South Africa* by Peter Best (paperback, R17) contains handy information about the leviathans you have a good chance of seeing.

**Birds** *Newman's Birds of Southern Africa* by Kenneth Newman (paperback, R81) is an excellent, comprehensive field guide with full-colour paintings.

Ian Sinclair's pocket-sized *Southern African Birds* (paperback, R46) is an excellent guide with colour photos, particularly suitable for a short-term visitor as it does not cover obscure birds. Sinclair's larger *Field*

*Guide to Southern African Birds* (paperback, R76) is more comprehensive.

**Flora** *Southern African Trees* by Piet van Wyk (paperback, R43) is a handy little guide full of information and photos.

*Namaqualand in Flower* by Sima Eliovson (paperback, R60) is a detailed book on the flora of Namaqualand. It has excellent colour plates.

**Reserves** *Guide to Southern African Game & Nature Reserves* by Chris & Tilde Stuart (paperback, R70) gives comprehensive coverage of every game and nature reserve, with lots of maps, photos and basic information.

**Surfing** *Surfing in South Africa* by Mark Jury (paperback, R30) is one of the best surfing guides around, with good tips and maps. This book is out of print but you might find a secondhand copy.

**Astronomy** If you're from the northern hemisphere, you might want a guide to all those unfamiliar stars. There's the *Struik Pocket Guide to the Night Skies of South Africa* (paperback, R28).

**Walking** *Exploring Southern Africa on Foot; Guide to Hiking Trails* by Willie & Sandra Olivier (hardback, R80) doesn't cover all the trails (there are so many!) but otherwise this book is simply outstanding. Highly recommended.

*The Complete Guide to Walks & Trails in Southern Africa* by Jaynee Levy (hardback, R110) *does* cover all trails and contains an extraordinary amount of information. It's not a trail guide but gives you a good idea of what a walk entails in advance. It's far too big and heavy to carry.

Lots of small books detail walks in various areas of the country. Look for *Western Cape Walks* by David Bristow (paperback, R50) which covers 70 walks of varying length and standard.

**Wine** *John Platter's South African Wine Guide* (paperback, about R45) is updated annually and is incredibly detailed, covering all available wines. More down-to-earth is *The South African Plonk Buyer's Guide* by David Briggs (paperback, about R25).

## FILM & PHOTOGRAPHY

Film, cameras and accessories are readily available in larger towns. Processing is generally of a high standard. The approximate price for 24-exposure negative film is R50, plus R45 for processing and printing.

In Swaziland and Lesotho be careful about taking photos of soldiers, police, airports and government buildings. This also applies to police and defence installations in South Africa.

## TIME

All three countries use South African Standard Time (SAST), which is two hours ahead of GMT/UTC, seven hours ahead of US Eastern Standard Time, and eight hours behind Australian Eastern Standard Time. There is no daylight saving.

## ELECTRICITY

Most power systems are 220/230V AC at 50 cycles per second. The Pretoria system is 250V and the Port Elizabeth system is 220/250V. This means that appliances rated between 220 and 250V AC will work anywhere.

JON MURRAY

The bizarre three-pin South African powerpoint.

Plugs have three large round pins. Adaptors aren't easy to find, but you can buy leads suitable for plugging into laptop computer chargers, etc, for about R6 at electronics shops in the big cities. If your appliance doesn't have a removable lead, you can always buy a South African plug and have it wired on (assuming that the appliance takes AC and is rated at the correct voltage!).

## WEIGHTS & MEASURES

All three countries use the metric system. See the inside back cover of this book for conversion from other units.

## HEALTH

Apart from malaria and bilharzia in some areas, and the possibility of hikers drinking contaminated water, there are few health problems in these countries. Good medical care is never too far away except in the remote areas, where air evacuation of emergency cases is routine. Make sure you have enough insurance.

Travel health depends on your pre-departure preparations, your day-to-day health care while travelling and how you handle any medical problem or emergency that does develop. If you're planning to venture into less developed areas of Africa you might want to read *Staying Healthy in Asia, Africa & Latin America*, Moon Publications. This is probably the best all-round guide to carry as it's compact but very detailed and well organised. There's also *Travellers' Health* by Dr Richard Dawood (Oxford University Press). It's comprehensive, easy to read, authoritative and also highly recommended, although rather large to lug around.

*Travel with Children* by Maureen Wheeler (US$11.95) is a Lonely Planet guide which includes basic advice on travel health for young children.

### Problem Areas

Malaria is mainly confined to the eastern half of the region (northern KwaZulu-Natal, Mpumalanga, Northern Province and Swaziland), especially on the lowveld. Kalahari

---

### Everyday Health

Normal body temperature is up to 37°C or 98.6°F; more than 2°C (4°F) higher indicates a high fever. The normal adult pulse rate is 60 to 100 per minute (children 80 to 100, babies 100 to 140). As a general rule the pulse increases about 20 beats per minute for each °C (2°F) rise in fever.

Respiration (breathing) rate is also an indicator of illness. Count the number of breaths per minute: between 12 and 20 is normal for adults and older children (up to 30 for younger children, 40 for babies). People with a high fever or serious respiratory illness breathe more quickly than normal. More than 40 shallow breaths a minute may be an indicator of pneumonia. ■

---

Gemsbok National Park (Northern Cape) and some areas of North-West Province might also be malarial.

Bilharzia is also found mainly in the east but outbreaks do occur in other places so you should always check with knowledgeable local people before drinking water or swimming in it.

While hiking in the ex-Homelands, Lesotho or Swaziland, or wherever you find yourself drinking from streams, make sure that there isn't an upstream village, even if there is no bilharzia. Typhoid is rare but it does occur, as does Hepatitis A. Industrial pollution is common in more settled areas.

### Medical Problems & Treatment

The number one rule in a medical emergency or serious illness is to get qualified help as soon as possible.

**Sunburn** Both on the lowveld and in the mountains you can get sunburnt surprisingly quickly, even through cloud. The hole in the ozone layer affects Southern Africa and you risk skin cancer later in life if you are exposed to too much UV radiation. Use a sunscreen and take extra care to cover areas which don't normally see sun – eg, your feet. A hat provides added protection, and you

## Predeparture Preparations

If you wear glasses take a spare pair and your prescription. Losing your glasses is a major hassle but there are plenty of optometrists in South Africa where you can get new spectacles.

If you use a particular medication regularly, take the prescription or, better still, part of the packaging showing the generic rather than the brand name (which may not be locally available), as it will make getting replacements easier. South Africa tends to sell drugs over-the-counter which would require a prescription in some other countries, but it's still a wise idea to have a legible prescription with you to show that you legally use the medication.

**Vaccinations** Assuming that you are up to date with your boosters for the standard childhood vaccinations such as TB, polio and tetanus, no additional vaccinations are essential. Off the beaten track typhoid is a possibility (as it is almost everywhere in the world) so make sure your vaccination is current. If you're planning to spend time in remote villages a hepatitis shot might not be a bad idea.

People who have travelled through the yellow-fever zone in Africa (or South America) must have an International Certificate of Vaccination against yellow fever before entering South Africa.

**Health Insurance** A travel-insurance policy to cover theft, loss and medical problems is a wise idea. Although there are excellent private hospitals in South Africa, the public health system is underfunded and overcrowded and is not free. Services such as ambulances are often run by private enterprise and are expensive. If you suffer a major illness or injury in the ex-Homelands, Swaziland or Lesotho you might want to use your air-evacuation cover. There is a wide variety of policies and your travel agent will have recommendations. The international student travel policies handled by STA or other student travel organisations are usually good value. Check the small print:

- Some policies specifically exclude 'dangerous activities' which can include scuba diving, motorcycling, even trekking. If such activities are on your agenda you don't want that sort of policy.

- You may prefer a policy which pays doctors or hospitals directly rather than you having to pay on the spot and claim later. If you have to claim later make sure you keep all documentation. Some policies ask you to call back (reversing the charges) to a centre in your home country where an immediate assessment of your problem is made.

- Check if the policy covers ambulances or an emergency flight home. If you have to stretch out you will need two seats and somebody has to pay for them! ■

should also use zinc cream or some other barrier cream for your nose, lips and ears. Calamine lotion is good for easing mild sunburn.

**Heat Exhaustion** Dehydration or salt deficiency can cause heat exhaustion. Take time to acclimatise to high temperatures and make sure you get sufficient liquids – don't rely on feeling thirsty to indicate when you should drink. Not needing to urinate or very dark yellow urine is a danger sign. Remember to always carry a water bottle with you on long trips.

Salt deficiency (eg through excessive sweating) is characterised by fatigue, lethargy, headaches, giddiness and muscle cramps. Salt tablets may help but much better (and safer) are rehydration mixes which are available from chemists. Sports drinks are fine for mild cases. Vomiting or diarrhoea can also deplete your liquid and salt levels. Anhydrotic heat exhaustion, caused by an inability to sweat, is quite rare. Unlike other forms of heat exhaustion it is likely to strike people who've been in a hot climate for some time.

**Heat Stroke** This serious, potentially fatal, condition can occur if the body's heat-regulating mechanism breaks down and the body temperature rises to dangerous levels. Long, continuous periods of exposure to high temperatures can leave you vulnerable to heat stroke.

Avoid excessive alcohol or strenuous activity when you first arrive in a hot climate.

The symptoms are feeling unwell, not sweating very much or at all and a high body temperature (39°C to 41°C). Where sweating has ceased the skin becomes flushed and red. Severe, throbbing headaches and lack of coordination will also occur, and the sufferer may be confused or aggressive. Eventually the victim will become delirious or convulse. Hospitalisation is essential, but meanwhile get victims out of the sun, remove their clothing, cover them with a wet sheet or towel and then fan them continually.

**Cold** Too much cold is just as dangerous as too much heat, particularly if it leads to hypothermia.

Hypothermia occurs when the body loses heat faster than it can produce it and the core temperature of the body falls. It is surprisingly easy to progress from very cold to dangerously cold due to a combination of wind, wet clothing, fatigue and hunger, even if the air temperature is above freezing. It is best to dress in layers; silk, wool and some of the new artificial fibres are all good insulating materials. A hat is important, as a lot of heat is lost through the head. A strong, waterproof outer layer is essential, as keeping dry is vital. Carry basic supplies, including food containing simple sugars to generate heat quickly, and lots of fluid to drink.

Symptoms of hypothermia are exhaustion, numb skin (particularly toes and fingers), shivering, slurred speech, irrational or violent behaviour, lethargy, stumbling, dizzy spells, muscle cramps and violent bursts of energy. Irrationality may take the form of sufferers claiming they are warm and trying to take off their clothes.

To treat hypothermia, first get the patient out of the wind and/or rain, remove any wet clothing and replace it with dry, warm clothing. Give them hot liquids – *never* alcohol – and some high-kilojoule, easily digestible food. This should be enough for the early stages of hypothermia, but if it has gone further it may be necessary to place the

## Medical Kit Check List

Consider taking a basic medical kit including:

- [ ] **Aspirin** or paracetamol (acetaminophen in the US) – for pain or fever.
- [ ] **Antihistamine** (such as Benadryl) – useful as a decongestant for colds and allergies, to ease the itch from insect bites or stings, and to help prevent motion sickness. Antihistamines may cause sedation and interact with alcohol so care should be taken when using them; take one you know and have used before, if possible.
- [ ] **Antibiotics** – useful if you're travelling well off the beaten track, but they must be prescribed; carry the prescription with you.
- [ ] **Loperamide** (eg Imodium) or Lomotil for diarrhoea; prochlorperazine (eg Stemetil) or metaclopramide (eg Maxalon) for nausea and vomiting.
- [ ] **Rehydration** mixture – for treatment of severe diarrhoea; particularly important for travelling with children.
- [ ] **Antiseptic** such as povidone-iodine (eg Betadine) – for cuts and grazes.
- [ ] **Multivitamins** – especially for long trips when dietary vitamin intake may be inadequate.
- [ ] **Calamine lotion** or **aluminium sulphate spray** (eg Stingose) – to ease irritation from bites or stings.
- [ ] **Bandages** and Band-aids
- [ ] **Scissors, tweezers** and a **thermometer** (note that mercury thermometers are prohibited by airlines).
- [ ] **Cold and flu tablets** and throat lozenges. Pseudoephedrine hydrochloride (Sudafed) may be useful if flying with a cold to avoid ear damage.
- [ ] **Insect repellent, sunscreen, chap stick** and **water purification tablets**.
- [ ] **A couple of syringes**, in case you need injections in a country with medical hygiene problems. Ask your doctor for a note explaining why they have been prescribed.

victim in a warm sleeping bag and get in with them. Do not rub patients or place them near a fire or remove their wet clothes in the wind. If possible, place a sufferer in a warm (not hot) bath.

**Malaria** This serious disease is spread by mosquito bites. If you are planning to travel in endemic areas it is extremely important to take malarial prophylactics. Symptoms include headaches, fever, chills and sweating which may subside and recur. Without treatment malaria can develop more serious, potentially fatal effects. Antimalarial drugs do not actually prevent the disease but suppress its symptoms. Consult your doctor for advice on the prophylactic most suitable for Southern Africa.

A considerable part of the South African population live in malarial areas and many more people travel to them, so South African doctors and chemists have good information and advice.

When travelling in malarial areas the main recommendations are:

1. Avoid being bitten! Mosquitoes that transmit malaria bite from dusk to dawn and during this period travellers are advised to:
   • wear light-coloured clothing
   • wear long pants and long-sleeved shirts
   • use mosquito repellents containing the compound DEET on exposed areas
   • avoid highly scented perfumes or aftershave
   • use a mosquito net

2. While no antimalarial is 100% effective, taking the most appropriate drug significantly reduces the risk of contracting the disease.

3. No one should ever die from malaria. It can be diagnosed by a simple blood test. Symptoms range from fever, chills and sweating, headache and abdominal pains to a vague feeling of ill-health, so seek examination immediately if there is any suggestion of malaria.

Contrary to popular belief, once a traveller contracts malaria they do not have it for life. One of the parasites may lie dormant in the liver but this can be eradicated using a specific medication. Malaria is curable, as long as the traveller seeks medical help when symptoms occur.

**Bilharzia** Bilharzia is carried in water by minute worms. The larvae infect certain varieties of freshwater snails found in rivers, streams, lakes and, particularly, dams. The worms multiply and are eventually discharged into the water surrounding the snails.

The worm enters through the skin, and the first symptom may be a tingling and sometimes a light rash around the area where it entered. The worm eventually attaches itself to your intestines or bladder, where it produces large numbers of eggs. Weeks later, when the worm is busy producing eggs, a high fever may develop. A general feeling of being unwell may be the first symptom; once the disease is established, abdominal pain and blood in the urine are other signs.

Avoiding swimming or bathing in fresh water where bilharzia is present is the main method of preventing the disease. If you do

---

**Water Purification**
Practically everywhere in this region high-quality water is available and you need not fear drinking from taps. Hikers drinking from streams might be at risk of water-borne diseases (eg, gastroenteritis or, rarely, typhoid) especially if they take water downstream of unsewered villages.

The simplest way of purifying water is to boil it thoroughly for 10 minutes. At high altitude water boils at a lower temperature, so germs are less likely to be killed.

Simple filtering doesn't remove all dangerous organisms, so if you cannot boil water it should be treated chemically. Chlorine tablets (Puritabs, Steritabs or other brand names) will kill many but not all nasties, including giardia and amoebic cysts. Iodine is very effective in purifying water and is available in tablet form (such as Potable Aqua), but follow the directions carefully and remember that too much iodine can be harmful.

If you can't find tablets, use tincture of iodine (2%). Four drops of tincture of iodine per litre or quart of clear water is the recommended dosage; the treated water should be left to stand for 20 to 30 minutes before drinking. Iodine crystals (dangerous things to have around) can also be used to purify water but this is a more complicated process, as you have to first prepare a saturated iodine solution. ■

get wet dry off quickly and dry your clothes as well. Seek medical attention if you have been exposed to the disease and tell the doctor your suspicions, as bilharzia in the early stages can be confused with malaria or typhoid.

**Diarrhoea** Simple things like a change of water, food or climate call all cause a mild bout of diarrhoea, but a few rushed toilet trips with no other symptoms is not indicative of a major problem.

Dehydration is the main danger with any diarrhoea, particularly in children or the elderly as dehydration can occur quite quickly. Under all circumstances fluid replacement (at least equal to the volume being lost) is the most important thing to remember. Urine is the best guide to the adequacy of replacement – if you have small amounts of concentrated urine, you need to drink more. Weak black tea with a little sugar, soda water, or soft drinks allowed to go flat and diluted with 50% clean water are all good. With severe diarrhoea a rehydrating solution is preferable to replace minerals and salts lost. Commercially available oral rehydration salts (ORS) are very useful; add them to boiled or bottled water. In an emergency you can make up a solution of six teaspoons of sugar and half a teaspoon of salt to a litre of boiled or bottled water.

Lomotil or Imodium can be used to bring relief from the symptoms, although they do not actually cure the problem. Only use these drugs if you do not have access to toilets, eg if you *must* travel. For children under 12 Lomotil and Imodium are not recommended. Do not use these drugs if the person has a high fever or is severely dehydrated.

In certain situations antibiotics may be required: diarrhoea with blood or mucous (dysentery), any fever, watery diarrhoea with fever and lethargy, persistent diarrhoea not improving after 48 hours and severe diarrhoea. In these situations gut-paralysing drugs like Imodium or Lomotil should be avoided.

A stool test is necessary to diagnose which kind of dysentery you have, so you should

**Nutrition**
If your food is poor or limited in availability, if you're travelling hard and fast and therefore missing meals, or if you simply lose your appetite, you can soon start to lose weight and place your health at risk.

Make sure your diet is well balanced. Cooked eggs, tofu, beans, lentils (dhal in India) and nuts are all safe ways to get protein. Fruit you can peel (bananas, oranges or mandarins for example) is usually safe (melons can harbour bacteria in their flesh and are best avoided) and a good source of vitamins. Try to eat plenty of grains (including rice) and bread. Remember that although food is generally safer if it is cooked well, overcooked food loses much of its nutritional value. If your diet isn't well balanced or if your food intake is insufficient, it's a good idea to take vitamin and iron pills.

In hot climates make sure you drink enough – don't rely on feeling thirsty to indicate when you should drink. Not needing to urinate or small amounts of very dark yellow urine is a danger sign. Always carry a water bottle with you on long trips. Excessive sweating can lead to loss of salt and therefore muscle cramping. Salt tablets are not a good idea as a preventative, but in places where salt is not used much adding salt to food can help. ∎

seek medical help urgently. Where this is not possible the recommended drugs for dysentery are norfloxacin 400mg twice daily for three days or ciprofloxacin 500mg twice daily for five days. These are not recommended for children or pregnant women. The drug of choice for children would be co-trimoxazole (Bactrim, Septrin, Resprim) with dosage dependent on weight. A five-day course is given. Ampicillin or amoxycillin may be given in pregnancy, but medical care is necessary.

**Amoebic dysentery** is more gradual in the onset of symptoms, with cramping abdominal pain and vomiting less likely; fever may not be present. It will persist until treated and can recur and cause other health problems.

**Giardiasis** is another type of diarrhoea. The parasite causing this intestinal disorder is present in contaminated water. The symptoms are stomach cramps, nausea, a bloated stomach, watery, foul-smelling diarrhoea and frequent gas. Giardiasis can appear several weeks after you have been exposed to the parasite. The symptoms may disappear for a few days and then return; this can go on for several weeks. Tinidazole, known as Fasigyn, or metronidazole (Flagyl) are the recommended drugs. Treatment is a 2g single dose of Fasigyn or 250mg of Flagyl three times daily for five to 10 days.

**Hepatitis** Hepatitis is a general term for inflammation of the liver. It is a common disease worldwide. The symptoms are fever, chills, headache, fatigue, feelings of weakness and aches and pains, followed by loss of appetite, nausea, vomiting, abdominal pain, dark urine, light-coloured faeces, jaundiced (yellow) skin and the whites of the eyes may turn yellow.

**Hepatitis A** is transmitted by contaminated food and drinking water. The disease poses a real threat to the western traveller. You should seek medical advice, but there is not much you can do apart from resting, drinking lots of fluids, eating lightly and avoiding fatty foods. People who have had hepatitis should avoid alcohol for some time after the illness, as the liver needs time to recover.

**Hepatitis E** is transmitted in the same way. It can be very serious in pregnant women.

There are almost 300 million chronic carriers of **Hepatitis B** in the world. It is spread through contact with infected blood, blood products or body fluids, for example through sexual contact, unsterilised needles and blood transfusions, or contact with blood via small breaks in the skin. Other risk situations include having a shave, tattoo, or having your body pierced with contaminated equipment. The symptoms of type B may be more severe and may lead to long term problems.

**Hepatitis D** is spread in the same way, but the risk is mainly in shared needles.

**Hepatitis C** can lead to chronic liver disease. The virus is spread by contact with blood usually via contaminated transfusions or shared needles. Avoiding these is the only means of prevention.

**Sexually Transmitted Diseases** Sexual contact with an infected partner spreads these diseases. While abstinence is the only 100% preventive, using condoms is also effective. Gonorrhoea and syphilis are the most common of these diseases; sores, blisters or rashes around the genitals, discharges or pain when urinating are common symptoms. Symptoms may be less marked or not observed at all in women. Syphilis symptoms eventually disappear completely but the disease continues and can cause severe problems in later years. The treatment of gonorrhoea and syphilis is by antibiotics.

There are numerous other sexually transmitted diseases, for most of which effective treatment is available. However, there is no cure for herpes or AIDS.

**HIV/AIDS** HIV (Human Immunodeficiency Virus) may develop into AIDS (Acquired Immune Deficiency Syndrome). Any exposure to blood, blood products or bodily fluids may put a person at risk. In many developing countries transmission is predominantly through heterosexual sexual activity. Apart from abstinence, the most effective preventive is always to practise safe sex using condoms. It is impossible to detect the HIV-positive status of an otherwise healthy-looking person without a blood test.

South Africa, Lesotho and Swaziland are probably not as badly affected by AIDS as some areas of Africa and a belated public awareness campaign has begun. However, AIDS is certainly present and widespread in the heterosexual community.

### Women's Health
**Gynaecological Problems** Poor diet, lowered resistance due to the use of antibiotics for stomach upsets and even contraceptive pills can lead to vaginal infections when travelling in hot climates. Keeping the genital area clean, and wearing skirts or loose-fitting trousers and cotton underwear will help to prevent infections.

Yeast infections, characterised by a rash, itch and discharge, can be treated with a vinegar or even lemon juice douche or with natural yoghurt. Nystatin suppositories are the usual medical prescription. Trichomoniasis is a more serious infection; symptoms are a discharge and a burning sensation when urinating, and if a vinegar water douche is not effective, medical attention should be sought. Flagyl is the prescribed drug. Male sexual partners must also be treated.

**Pregnancy** Most miscarriages occur during the first three months of pregnancy, so this is the most risky time to travel. The last three months should also be spent within reasonable distance of good medical care, as quite serious problems can develop at this time. Pregnant women should avoid all unnecessary medication, but vaccinations and malarial prophylactics should still be taken where possible – ask a doctor. Additional care should be taken to prevent illness and particular attention should be paid to diet and nutrition.

## WOMEN TRAVELLERS

Most South African men, whatever their colour, have sexism in common. People who do anything technical or physical (including sport) are inevitably referred to as 'guys', serious newspapers have 'pretty miss' photos and you'll be expected to take a serious interest in beauty contests, of which there are many. Until recently, modelling was one of the few prestigious careers open to most South African women. If you want to find out what life for women was like in western countries in the '50s, talk to well-off white women in South Africa.

Newfangled ideas such as the equality of the sexes haven't filtered through to many people, especially away from the cities. Although urban attitudes are more liberal, the statistics for sexual assault are horrendous, particularly in the black townships. Common sense and caution, particularly at night, are essential.

A non-black woman travelling alone is a rarity (not being married sets you apart, for a start). This gives single women a curiosity value that makes them conspicuous, but will also bring forth numerous generous offers of assistance and hospitality. It is always difficult to quantify the risk of assault – and there is one – but plenty of women do travel alone safely in Southern Africa.

Obviously the risk varies depending on where you go and what you do. Hitching alone is extremely foolhardy, for instance. The best advice on what can and can't be undertaken safely will come from local women. Unfortunately, many white women are likely to be appalled at the idea of lone travel and will do their best to discourage you with horrendous stories, often of dubious accuracy.

What risks there are, however, are significantly reduced if two women travel together or, even better, if a woman travels as part of a mixed-sex couple or group. However you travel, especially inland and in the more traditional black communities, it's best to behave conservatively. On the coast, casual dress (and undress) is the norm, but elsewhere dress modestly (full-length clothes that aren't too tight) if you do not wish to draw attention to yourself.

In traditional black cultures, women often have a very tough time, but this is changing to some extent because a surprising number of girls have the opportunity to stay at school while the boys are sent away to work.

Many of the staff in tourist offices, government departments and so on are well-educated black women. It's worth talking to them to get their perspective on the region's problems. Their outlook on life is often much closer to the average visitor's than that of the manicured white staff.

## GAY & LESBIAN TRAVELLERS

South Africa's new constitution guarantees freedom of sexual choice and there are small but active gay and lesbian scenes in Cape Town, Johannesburg and Durban. However, the new constitution is a radical departure from the old laws and it will be a while before the more conservative sections of society fully accept it. Outside the cities, in both black and white communities, homosexuality remains taboo. Luckily, a Cape Town travel agency, Gay esCape, has extensive listings of gay-friendly accommodation, restaurants, activities and more around the country. See the Cape Town section of the Western Cape chapter for details.

## DANGERS & ANNOYANCES
### Natural Dangers

Throughout the region keep in mind the natural dangers, from freezing storms in the Drakensberg to crippling heat on the lowveld. Bilharzia isn't the only danger in the water – crocodiles and hippos can be deadly. Be careful near any lowveld stream.

### Animals

Crocodiles are now rare but they do occur in lowveld rivers and streams. Hippos can also be very dangerous. If you meet one (most likely on or near the KwaZulu-Natal north coast) do not approach it and be prepared to get away or up a tree very fast. Lions, rhinos and elephants are very unlikely to be encountered when you are walking, but take seriously the warning not to get out of your vehicle in wildlife reserves.

**Snakes**  Out of the water, venomous snakes are a potential problem. To minimise your chances of being bitten, always wear boots, socks and long trousers when walking through undergrowth where snakes may be present. Don't put your hands into holes and crevices, and be careful when collecting firewood.

Snake bites do not cause instantaneous death and antivenenes are usually available. Keep the victim calm and still, wrap the bitten limb very tightly, as you would for a sprained ankle, and attach a splint to immobilise it. Then seek medical help, if possible with the dead snake for identification. Don't attempt to catch the snake if there is even a remote possibility of being bitten; in any case the victim must not blunder around trying to catch the snake. Tourniquets and sucking out the poison are now comprehensively discredited.

LUBA VANGELOVA

Baboons exhibit fairly scant regard for the property of others whan encountered in national parks throughout the region.

Although reaching medical assistance is of paramount importance, weigh up the dangers of moving the victim. The tightly wrapped bandage means that the poison enters their system slowly and, hopefully, at a rate their body can cope with. If the victim is moved their blood circulation will speed up, delivering large doses of poison.

**Ticks**  Ticks are present in many areas and it's easy for them to jump onto you as you brush past bushes. An insect repellent may keep them away. Vaseline, alcohol or oil will persuade a tick to let go. You should always check your body and clothes if you have been walking through a tick-infested area (practically any scrubland, even in city limits – such as Table Mountain in Cape Town), as they can spread typhus or 'tick-bite fever'. Apparently ticks like to congregate under camel thorn trees.

### South Africa

Crime rates in the cities are soaring and some crime is pretty nasty. Be very careful at night

## Survival Tactics

None of these countries is particularly danger-ous, especially compared to other African countries – or even North America. However, in the cities you should be cautious. Johannes-burg is earning a reputation as the mugging capital of Southern Africa and some of the crime is violent. There are some simple rules that should help keep you out of trouble in big cities.

- Never carry anything you can't afford to lose
- Never look like you might be carrying valu-ables (wearing an extravagant T-shirt makes you look just as rich as wearing jewellery or a suit does)
- Avoid groups of young men; trust older mixed-sex groups
- Always have some money to give if you are mugged
- Don't resist muggers
- Listen to local advice on unsafe areas
- Avoid deserted areas (such as downtown on weekends) even in daylight

Unfortunately, the most effective tactics are the most difficult for newcomers to use:

- Don't look apprehensive or lost
- Don't assume that everyone is out to get you
- Make friends!

happens to be 'white', it usually doesn't hurt to make it clear that you are not South African.

Many non-whites can tell that white visitors aren't South African by their attitude. However, when I was researching the first edition of this book in 1992, before the tourist boom, many non-white people were puzzled by my attitude to them, and some came to the conclusion that I was an Anglican minister. Flattering, but desperately sad.

**Jon Murray**

### Lesotho

The last Friday of the month is when many people are paid, and by mid-afternoon some towns become like street parties. These can be fun but as the day wears on some of the drunks become depressingly familiar to an Australian – over-friendly, boisterous and ultimately aggressive. In Maseru this phe-nomenon usually expresses itself as a big night in the discos, but be careful.

Outside a few large towns crime is negli-gible and aggressive racism almost unheard of.

If you're hiking without a guide you might be hassled for money or 'gifts' by shepherds in remote areas. There's a very slight risk of robbery. However, the best way to ensure problems is to greet people with suspicion and show a lack of generosity.

### Swaziland

Street crime in Mbabane and Manzini is rising so take common-sense precautions such as being careful at night and not walking home drunk. Elsewhere, courtesy and respect for local customs are all that is required.

The permitted blood-alcohol level for drivers is 0.15%, triple that of many other countries, so watch out for drunk drivers.

### DRUGS

Marijuana was an important commodity in the Xhosa's trade with the San. Today *dagga* or *zol* is illegal but widely available. There are heavy penalties for use and possession but it's estimated that the majority of black men smoke the drug. The legal system

and bear in mind that daylight muggings are not uncommon in parts of Johannesburg.

The large-scale political violence that gave South Africa such a bad reputation in the months and years leading up to the 1994 election has all but vanished. However, it's a moot point whether being attacked in a town-ship is a result of political, antisocial or criminal motives. It's unwise for an outsider of any race to venture into a township without knowing the current situation and, usually, without a guide.

Incidents such as taxi wars (between rival minibus taxi companies) have lead to massa-cres. Once again, it's a matter of knowing the current situation and avoiding being in the wrong place at the wrong time. There are very, very few wrong places and times.

Most blacks aren't racist, but if your skin

doesn't distinguish between soft and hard drugs.

South Africa is reputed to be the world's major market for Mandrax, which is now banned in many countries (including South Africa). Its use has devastating effects. Now that the country has rejoined the world economy, drugs such as cocaine and heroin are becoming widely available, and their use accounts for much property crime.

## ACTIVITIES

The obvious activities in the region are wild-life viewing, wine tasting, hiking and watersports. However, there's much more on offer, especially since international visitors began to arrive in large numbers. South Africa offers the most, because of its size and variety, not to mention the infrastructure and capital necessary to arrange many activities,

JON MURRAY
A visit to the Belcher Winery in Paarl is a very indulgent way to pass the time.

but Lesotho and Swaziland shouldn't be overlooked.

See the Facts for the Visitor chapters of the three countries for details.

# Regional Getting There & Away

This chapter gives general information on the various methods of travelling to Southern Africa, and how to go about finding the ticket(s) that will suit you. For specific information on travel to and from South Africa, Lesotho or Swaziland, see those countries' Getting There & Away sections. These also cover travel between the three countries.

However you're travelling, it's worth taking out travel insurance. Work out what you need. You may not want to insure that grotty old army surplus backpack, but everyone should be covered for the worst possible case: an accident, for example, that will require hospital treatment and a flight home. It's a good idea to make a copy of your policy, in case the original is lost.

If you are planning to travel for a long time, the insurance may seem very expensive, but if you can't afford it, you certainly won't be able to afford a medical emergency overseas.

## AIR

About 50 airlines fly to South Africa, a great increase on the handful that operated during the apartheid days. However, Southern Africa still isn't exactly a hub of international travel. Airfares to or from Europe, North America and Australia certainly reflect that. About the only relief you'll get are fares for the low season which fortunately coincides with the nicest weather. The region's main international airport is in Johannesburg but there are an increasing number of flights to Cape Town and a few to Durban.

Low-season fares to Southern Africa from Europe and North America are typically applicable in April and May while the high season is between July and September. The rest of the year, with the exception of several weeks around Christmas, which is considered high season, falls into the shoulder season category.

### Buying a Plane Ticket

The plane ticket will probably be the single most expensive item in your budget, and buying it can be an intimidating business. There is likely to be a multitude of airlines and travel agents hoping to separate you from your money. It is always worth putting aside a few hours to research the current state of the market.

Start early; some of the cheapest tickets have to be bought months in advance, and some popular flights sell out early. Talk to other recent travellers – they may be able to stop you making some of the same old mistakes. Look at the ads in newspapers and magazines (not forgetting the expatriate press, such as *SA Times* in the UK), consult reference books and watch for special offers. Then phone around travel agents for bargains. (Airlines can supply information on routes and timetables; however, except during inter-airline wars, they do not supply the cheapest tickets.) Find out the fare, the route, the duration of the journey and any restrictions on the ticket. (See Restrictions in the Air Travel Glossary boxed text in this chapter.) Then sit back and decide which is best for you.

You may discover that those impossibly cheap flights are 'fully booked, but we have another one that costs a bit more ...' Or the flight is on an airline notorious for its poor safety standards and leaves you in the world's least favourite airport in mid-journey for 14 hours. Or they claim only to have the last two seats available on that flight for the whole of July, which they will hold for you for a maximum of two hours. Don't panic – keep ringing around.

Use the fares quoted in this book as a guide only. They are approximate and based on the rates advertised by travel agents at the time of going to press. Also, quoted airfares do not necessarily constitute a recommendation for the carrier.

If you're travelling from the UK or the

USA, you'll probably find that the cheapest flights are being advertised by obscure bucket shops whose names haven't yet reached the telephone directory. Many such firms are honest and solvent, but there are a few rogues who will take your money and disappear, to reopen elsewhere a month or two later under a new name. If you feel suspicious about a firm, don't give them all the money at once – leave a deposit of 20% or so and pay the balance when you get the ticket. If they insist on cash in advance, go somewhere else. And once you have the ticket, ring the airline to confirm that you are actually booked onto the flight.

You may decide to pay more than the rock-bottom fare by opting for the safety of a better known travel agent. Firms such as STA Travel, which has offices worldwide, Council Travel in the USA or Travel CUTS in Canada are not going to disappear overnight (touch wood), and they do offer good prices to most destinations.

Once you have your ticket, write the number down, together with the flight number and other details, and keep this infor-

## Air Travel Glossary

**Apex** Apex, or 'advance purchase excursion', is a discounted ticket which must be paid for in advance. There are penalties if you wish to change it.

**Baggage Allowance** This will be written on your ticket: usually one 20kg item to go in the hold, plus one item of hand luggage.

**Bucket Shop** An unbonded travel agency specialising in discounted airline tickets.

**Bumped** Just because you have a confirmed seat doesn't mean you're going to get on the plane – see Overbooking.

**Cancellation Penalties** If you have to cancel or change an Apex ticket there are often heavy penalties involved; insurance can sometimes be taken out against these penalties. Some airlines impose penalties on regular tickets as well, particularly against 'no show' passengers.

**Check In** Airlines ask you to check in a certain time ahead of the flight departure (usually 1½ hours on international flights). If you fail to check in on time and the flight is overbooked the airline can cancel your booking and give your seat to somebody else.

**Confirmation** Having a ticket written out with the flight and date you want doesn't mean you have a seat until the agent has checked with the airline that your status is 'OK' or confirmed. Meanwhile you could just be 'on request'.

**Discounted Tickets** There are two types of discounted fares – officially discounted (see Promotional Fares) and unofficially discounted. The lowest prices often impose drawbacks like flying with unpopular airlines, inconvenient schedules, or unpleasant routes and connections. A discounted ticket can save you other things than money – you may be able to pay Apex prices without the associated Apex advance booking and other requirements. Discounted tickets only exist where there is fierce competition.

**Full Fares** Airlines traditionally offer first class (coded F), business class (coded J) and economy class (coded Y) tickets. These days there are so many promotional and discounted fares available from the regular economy class that few passengers pay full economy fare.

**Lost Tickets** If you lose your airline ticket an airline will usually treat it like a travellers' cheque and, after inquiries, issue you with another one. Legally, however, an airline is entitled to treat it like cash and if you lose it then it's gone forever. Take good care of your tickets.

**No Shows** No shows are passengers who fail to show up for their flight, sometimes due to unexpected delays or disasters, sometimes due to simply forgetting, sometimes because they made more than one booking and didn't bother to cancel the one they didn't want. Full fare passengers who fail to turn up are sometimes entitled to travel on a later flight. The rest of us are penalised (see Cancellation Penalties).

**On Request** An unconfirmed booking for a flight, see Confirmation.

mation somewhere separate. If the ticket is lost or stolen, this information will help you get a replacement.

It's sensible to buy travel insurance as early as possible. If you buy it the week before you fly, you may find, for example, that you're not covered for delays to your flight caused by industrial action.

### Air Travellers with Special Needs

If you have special needs of any sort – you've broken a leg, you're vegetarian, travelling in a wheelchair, taking the baby, terrified of flying – you should let the airline know as soon as possible so that they can make arrangements accordingly. You should remind them when you reconfirm your booking (at least 72 hours before departure) and again when you check in at the airport. It may also be worth ringing round the airlines before you make your booking to find out how they can handle your particular needs.

Airports and airlines can be surprisingly helpful, but they do need advance warning. Most international airports will provide

**Open Jaws** A return ticket where you fly out to one place but return from another. If available this can save you backtracking to your arrival point.

**Overbooking** Airlines hate to fly empty seats and since every flight has some passengers who fail to show up (see No Shows) airlines often book more passengers than they have seats. Usually the excess passengers balance those who fail to show up but occasionally somebody gets bumped. If this happens guess who it is most likely to be? The passengers who check in late.

**Promotional Fares** Officially discounted fares like Apex fares which are available from travel agents or direct from the airline.

**Reconfirmation** At least 72 hours prior to departure time of an onward or return flight you must contact the airline and 'reconfirm' that you intend to be on the flight. If you don't do this the airline can delete your name from the passenger list and you could lose your seat. You don't have to reconfirm the first flight on your itinerary or if your stopover is less than 72 hours. It doesn't hurt to reconfirm more than once.

**Restrictions** Discounted tickets often have various restrictions on them – advance purchase is the most usual one (see Apex). Others are restrictions on the minimum and maximum period you must be away, such as a minimum of 14 days or a maximum of one year. See Cancellation Penalties.

**Standby** A discounted ticket where you only fly if there is a seat free at the last moment. Standby fares are usually only available on domestic routes.

**Tickets Out** An entry requirement for many countries is that you have an onward or return ticket, in other words, a ticket out of the country. If you're not sure what you intend to do next, the easiest solution is to buy the cheapest onward ticket to a neighbouring country or a ticket from a reliable airline which can later be refunded if you do not use it.

**Transferred Tickets** Airline tickets cannot be transferred from one person to another. Travellers sometimes try to sell the return half of their ticket, but officials can ask you to prove that you are the person named on the ticket. This is unlikely to happen on domestic flights, but on an international flight tickets may be compared with passports.

**Travel Agencies** Travel agencies vary widely and you should ensure you use one that suits your needs. Some simply handle tours while full-service agencies handle everything from tours and tickets to car rental and hotel bookings. A good one will do all these things and can save you a lot of money but if all you want is a ticket at the lowest possible price, then you really need an agency specialising in discounted tickets. A discount ticket agency, however, may not be useful for other things, like hotel bookings.

**Travel Periods** Some officially discounted fares, Apex fares in particular, vary with the time of year. There is often a low (off-peak) season and a high (peak) season. Sometimes there's an intermediate or shoulder season as well. At peak times, when everyone wants to fly, not only will the officially discounted fares be higher but so will unofficially discounted fares or there may simply be no discounted tickets available. Usually the fare depends on your outward flight – if you depart in the high season and return in the low season, you pay the high-season fare. ∎

escorts from the check-in desk to the plane where needed, and there should be ramps, lifts, accessible toilets and reachable phones. Aircraft toilets, on the other hand, are likely to present a problem; travellers should discuss this with the airline at an early stage and, if necessary, with their doctor.

Guide dogs for the blind often have to travel in a specially pressurised baggage compartment with other animals, away from their owner, though smaller guide dogs may be admitted to the cabin. All guide dogs will be subject to the same quarantine laws (six months in isolation etc) as any other animal when entering or returning to countries currently free of rabies, such as Britain or Australia.

Deaf travellers can ask for airport and in-flight announcements to be written down for them.

Children under two travel for 10% of the standard fare (or free, on some airlines), as long as they don't occupy a seat. They don't get a baggage allowance either. 'Skycots' should be provided by the airline if requested in advance; these will take a child weighing up to about 10kg. Children aged between two and 12 years can usually occupy a seat for half to two-thirds of the full fare, and do get a baggage allowance. Prams can often be taken as hand luggage.

### The USA

The *New York Times*, the *LA Times*, the *Chicago Tribune* and the *San Francisco Examiner* all produce weekly travel sections in which you'll find any number of travel agents' ads. *Travel Unlimited* (PO Box 1058, Allston, MA 02134) publishes details of the cheapest airfares and courier possibilities for destinations all over the world from the USA.

Council Travel and STA Travel have offices in major cities nationwide. You may have to produce proof of student status and in some cases be under 26 years of age to qualify for their discounted fares.

North America is a relative newcomer to the bucket-shop traditions of Europe and Asia so ticket availability and the restrictions attached to them need to be weighed against what is offered on the standard APEX or full economy tickets.

It may well be cheaper in the long run to fly first to London on Virgin or another inexpensive airline, then buy a bucket-shop ticket from there to Africa. Do some homework before setting off. Magazines specialising in bucket-shop advertisements in London (see The UK below) will post copies so you can study current prices before you decide on a course of action.

From the US west coast it should be possible to get some good deals via Asia. Malaysian Airline System (MAS) flies from Los Angeles to Kuala Lumpur (Malaysia) and from there to Johannesburg and Cape Town. There are no direct flights, but MAS usually has good stopover deals. From Cape Town, MAS flies to Buenos Aires, so you could put together a very interesting trip.

There are direct flights between New York and Johannesburg and there was talk of a direct flight starting up between Washington DC and Johannesburg, but this is yet to be confirmed.

### Canada

Travel CUTS has offices in all major cities. The *Toronto Globe & Mail* and the *Vancouver Sun* carry travel agents' ads. *Great Expeditions* (PO Box 8000-411, Abbotsford, BC V2S 6H1) is useful.

### The UK

The majority of travel agents in Britain are registered with the ABTA (Association of British Travel Agents). If you have bought your ticket from an ABTA-registered agency which then goes out of business, the ABTA will guarantee a refund or arrange an alternative flight. Buying your ticket from unregistered bucket shops is riskier but sometimes cheaper. London is the national centre for bucket shops, although all major cities have unregistered agencies as well.

The following companies are reliable:

Africa Travel Centre
   4 Medway Crt, Leigh St, London WC1H 9QX,

(☎ (0171) 387 1211) – specialising in Africa, with a video lounge and free newspaper

Campus Travel
52 Grosvenor Gardens, London SW1W OAG (☎ (0171) 730 8111) – offices in large YHA Adventure Shops

CTS
44 Goodge St, London W1 (☎ (0171) 637 5601)

STA Travel
86 Old Brompton Rd, SW7 (☎ (0171) 937 9962), tube: South Kensington – the largest, worldwide student/budget agency

Trailfinders
194 Kensington High St, W8 (☎ (0171) 938 3939) – a complete travel service, including a bookshop, information centre, visa service and immunisation centre

It's worth checking the Sunday newspapers for ads. In London, there are also several magazines with lots of info and ads:

*Trailfinder* A magazine put out quarterly by Trailfinders (see previous list of agencies). It's free if you pick it up in London but if you want it mailed, it costs UK£8 for four issues in the UK or Ireland and UK£12 or the equivalent for four issues in Europe or elsewhere (airmail).

*Time Out* This is London's weekly entertainment guide, containing travel information and advertising. It's available everywhere. Subscription enquiries should be addressed to Time Out Subs, Unit 8, Grove Ash, Bletchley, Milton Keynes MK1 1BZ, UK.

*TNT Magazine* This is a free magazine which can be picked up at most London Underground stations and on street corners around Earls Court and Kensington. It caters to Australians and New Zealanders working in the UK and is full of travel advertising. They're at 14-15 Child's Place, Earls Court, London SW5 9RX, UK (☎ (0171) 373 3377).

In these magazines, you'll find discounted fares to Johannesburg as well as other parts of Africa. Many of them use Aeroflot or Eastern European and Middle Eastern Airlines.

### Europe

There are bucket shops by the dozen in Paris, Amsterdam, Brussels, Frankfurt and a few other places. In Amsterdam, NBBS is a popular travel agent.

### Australia & New Zealand

STA Travel and Flight Centres International are major dealers in cheap airfares. The Africa Travel Centre (☎ (02) 9267 3048) specialises in African travel and has lots of free information. The best publications for finding good deals are the Saturday editions of the *Sydney Morning Herald* and the Melbourne *Age*. Discuss your options with several travel agents before buying because many have very little experience with inexpensive routings to Africa.

There are flights from Sydney and Perth to Johannesburg and Cape Town – New Zealanders will have to get to Sydney. Fares are steep so it makes sense for Australasians to think in terms of a RTW ticket or a return ticket to Europe with a stopover in Southern Africa.

### Asia

Hong Kong is the discount plane ticket capital of the region. Its bucket shops are at least as unreliable as those of other cities. Bangkok is another possibility. Ask the advice of other travellers before buying a ticket. STA, which is reliable, has branches in Hong Kong, Tokyo, Singapore, Bangkok and Kuala Lumpur.

Air India flies from Bombay to Johannesburg and Durban. There are marginal bucket shops in New Delhi, Bombay and Calcutta. In New Delhi, Tripsout Travel, 72/7 Tolstoy Lane, behind the Government of India Tourist Office, Janpath, is recommended. It's very popular with travellers and has been in business for many years.

### Africa

Most regional African airlines fly to/from South Africa. For example, Air Afrique flies to various West African countries; Air Gabon flies to Libreville (Gabon), with connections to West Africa and Europe; Uganda Airlines flies to Harare (Zimbabwe) and Uganda; Air Namibia flies between Cape Town and Windhoek (and on to Europe); and Air Botswana flies to various Southern African cities. There are plenty of other regional airlines and South African Airways (SAA) also has inter-Africa flights. Some European airlines stop in African countries en route to South Africa.

## LAND

If you're planning an overland trip through Africa you really need a copy of Lonely Planet's *Africa on a shoestring*.

With the exception of the Israel-Egypt connection, all overland travel to Africa has to be done through Europe and involves a ferry crossing.

In the past, you had a choice of two routes south through Africa: through the Sahara from Morocco to West Africa, or up the Nile from Egypt to Uganda or Kenya. The latter is now impossible due to the civil war in southern Sudan. If your starting point in Africa must be Egypt, this will entail a flight from Cairo – or at best from Khartoum – to Kampala or Nairobi. Alternatively, fly to Eritrea or Ethiopia and travel south to Kenya from there.

It's impossible to travel overland between the two north-south routes due to the road-block imposed by Libya; those wishing to travel between Morocco, Tunisia and Egypt will have to fly. As this book went to press, overland travel from West Africa to East or Southern Africa was also not possible due to civil wars in Congo (Zaïre) and Congo-Brazzaville. Some overland tour companies were flying from Gabon to Kenya and continuing overland from there.

From Nairobi, there are several ways to reach Zimbabwe, Botswana and Namibia. The most popular route seems to be the TAZARA railway between Dar es Salaam in Tanzania (accessible by bus or plane from Nairobi) and Kapiri Mposhi in Zambia, from where it's possible to pick up another train on to Lusaka and Livingstone (both also in Zambia). It's extremely inexpensive for the distance travelled but be prepared for a slow pace and uncomfortable conditions.

Another option takes you across Tanzania to Kigoma on Lake Tanganyika, then by steamer to Mpulungu (Zambia) and overland to Chitipa (Malawi) or Lusaka (Zambia). It's also possible to enter Zambia at Nakonde or Malawi between Mbeya and Karonga. There's no public transport along the latter route so it will require hitching.

Once you're in Zambia, it's fairly straight-forward getting to Lusaka or Livingstone and entering Zimbabwe at Chirundu, Kariba or Victoria Falls, or Botswana at Kazungula. There are good straightforward connections from Botswana and Zimbabwe to Johannesburg. See the South Africa Getting There & Away chapter for details of these routes.

### Overland Tours

Although the days of travelling from Cairo to the Cape are over for the time being, quite a few overland operators have taken up the trans-Sahara route through Morocco and West Africa, across to Central Africa, then flying over Congo (Zaïre) to East Africa and on to Zimbabwe, Botswana and South Africa. These trips are very popular, but aren't for everyone. They are designed primarily for first-time travellers who feel uncomfortable striking out on their own or for those who prefer guaranteed social interaction to the uncertainties of the road.

If you have the slightest inclination towards independence or would feel confined travelling with the same group of 25 or so people for most of the trip (quite a few normally drop out along the way), think twice before booking something like this. One reader who found her truck hell, had read this warning but says that she was distracted by the colour brochures. So – think twice and close your eyes!

If you'd like more information or a list of agents selling overland packages in your home country, contact one of the following Africa overland operators, all of which are based in the UK (Exodus and Encounter also have offices in Australia, New Zealand, USA and Canada):

Dragoman
   Camp Green, Kenton Rd, Debenham, Suffolk IP14 6LA (☎ (01728) 86 1133; fax 86 1127)
Encounter Overland
   267 Old Brompton Rd, London SW5 9JA (☎ (0171) 370 6845)

Exodus Expeditions
9 Weir Rd, London SW12 0LT (☎ (0181) 673 7966)
Guerba Expeditions
101 Eden Vale Rd, Westbury, Wiltshire BA13 3QX (☎ (01373) 82 6689)
Top Deck
The Adventure Centre, 131-135 Earls Court Rd, London SW5 9RH (☎ (0171) 330 4555; fax 373 6201)

There's a modest boom in overland truck journeys from South Africa to other African countries. Most of these are round trips. Once again, these are mainly for people who haven't the confidence to travel on their own and many of the customers are white South Africans who are just beginning to realise that the rest of the continent isn't full of bloodthirsty savages, but can't quite conceive of actually mixing too much with locals. On the other hand, many backpackers go along and have a good time. Companies include African Routes, Epic, Wayfarers and Which Way Adventures. Many hostels will book you on a truck trip.

### Private Vehicles

Drivers of cars and riders of motorbikes will need the vehicle's registration papers, liability insurance and an International Driving Permit in addition to their domestic licence. Beware: there are two kinds of international permit, one of which is needed mostly for former British colonies. In Africa you will also need a *Carnet de passage en douane*, which is effectively a passport for the vehicle, and acts as a temporary waiver of import duty. The carnet may also need to list any expensive spares that you're planning to carry with you, such as a gearbox. This is designed to prevent car-import rackets. Contact your local automobile association for details about all documentation.

Liability insurance is not available in advance for many out-of-the-way countries, but has to be bought when crossing the border. The cost and quality of such local insurance varies wildly, and you will find in some countries that you are effectively travelling uninsured.

Anyone planning to take their own vehicle with them needs to check in advance what spares and petrol are likely to be available. Lead-free petrol is not on sale worldwide, and neither is every little part for your car.

### Bicycle

Cycling is a cheap, convenient, healthy, environmentally sound and above all a fun way of travelling. One note of caution: before you leave home, go over your bike with a fine-toothed comb and fill your repair kit with every imaginable spare. As with cars and motorbikes, you won't necessarily be able to buy that crucial gizmo for your machine when it breaks down somewhere in the back of beyond as the sun sets.

Bicycles can travel by air. You *can* take them to pieces and put them in a bike bag or box, but it's much easier simply to wheel your bike to the check-in desk, where it should be treated as a piece of baggage. You may have to remove the pedals and turn the handlebars sideways so that it takes up less space in the aircraft's hold; check all this with the airline well in advance, preferably before you pay for your ticket.

### SEA

Swaziland and Lesotho are both landlocked, but South Africa is an important stop on world shipping routes. It *is* possible (if not easy or cheap) to get here by cargo ship (see the Getting There & Away chapter in the South Africa section), and plenty of cruise ships call in at Cape Town and Durban.

### WARNING

The information in this chapter is particularly vulnerable to change: prices for international travel are volatile, routes are introduced and cancelled, schedules change, special deals come and go, and rules and visa requirements are amended. Airlines and governments seem to take a perverse pleasure in making price structures and regulations as complicated as possible. You should check directly with the airline or a travel agent to make sure you understand how a fare (and ticket you may buy) works. In addition, the travel industry is highly competitive and there are many lurks and perks.

The upshot of this is that you should get opinions, quotes and advice from as many airlines and travel agents as possible before you part with your hard-earned cash. The information given in this chapter should be regarded only as a pointer and is not a substitute for your own careful, up-to-date research.

Safari Guide

# PRIMATES

### Baboons
*Papio ursinus* (Chacma Baboon)

The Chacma baboon, just one of at least five species of baboon, is the one most commonly sighted in Southern Africa. The dog-like snouts of baboons give them a more aggressive appearance than most other primates, which have much more human-like facial features. Having said that, when you watch them playing or merely sitting around contemplating their surroundings, it's difficult not to make anthropomorphic comparisons.

Baboons live in large troops of up to 150 animals, each of which has its own two to 30 sq km area and is headed by one dominant male. Individuals spend much of their time searching for insects, spiders and birds' eggs.

They've also discovered that lodges, camp sites and picnic areas provide easy pickings, especially those occupied by idiotic tourists who throw food and leave their tents unzipped. Often baboons become such a nuisance that they have to be dealt with harshly by park officials, so please resist the temptation to feed them!

Farmers hunt baboons (which are not protected in South Africa), so you'll see them most often in parks and reserves, or on steep mountain passes. Other than people, baboons' greatest enemies are leopards, for whom they're a favourite meal. Young baboons are also taken by lions and hunting dogs.

DAVID WALL

Chacma Baboon

### Bushbabies
*Otolemur crassicaudatus* (Greater or Giant Bushbaby)
*Galago senegalensis* (Lesser Bushbaby)

The greater bushbaby, which resembles an Australian possum, is in fact a small pro-simian (lemur-like) creature about the size of a rabbit. It inhabits forest areas in the east of South Africa and in southern Swaziland, but it's nocturnal and is therefore rarely observed. The bushbaby has a small head, large rounded ears, dark brown fur, a thick bushy tail and the enormous eyes that are typical of nocturnal primates. On average, adults weigh under 2kg and measure 80cm in length, but 45cm of this is tail.

The lesser bushbaby is about half the size of the greater bushbaby. It is a very light grey and has yellowish colouring on the legs. It is present in Kruger National Park and Northern Province.

Greater or Giant Bushbaby

## Samango Monkey (White-Throated Guenon)
*Cercopithecus mitis*

Also known as the white-throated guenon or diademed monkey, the Samango monkey inhabits much of eastern Africa. In South Africa you're most likely to see it in KwaZulu-Natal, especially in the north-east.

The face is grey to black, but most of the back and the flanks and upper limbs have a greenish cast. The rump is yellow and the lower limbs are black. Mature males make coughing sounds; females and young of both sexes make chirping and chattering sounds.

The Samango monkey feeds in the early morning and late afternoon in the higher treetops, descending into shady areas during the day. They normally live in social groups of four to 12 and eat mainly shoots, leaves, young birds, insects, moss, fungi, fruit, berries and eggs. They occasionally even raid plantations, taking chickens. Enemies include leopards, pythons and eagles.

Samango Monkey (White-Throated Guenon)

## Vervet Monkey (Savanna Monkey)
*Cercopithecus aethiops*

The playful vervet monkey is Southern Africa's most common monkey. It occurs in much of the east of the country and along the Orange River, as well as the Eastern Cape coast. It's easily recognisable by its black face fringed with white hair. The hair is yellowish-grey hair elsewhere, except on the underparts, which are whitish. The male has an extraordinary bright blue scrotum.

Vervet monkeys usually live in woodland and savanna, running in groups of up to 30. They're extremely cheeky and inquisitive, as you may well find when camping in the game reserves. Many have become habituated to humans and will stop at nothing to steal food or secure handouts, including making themselves welcome at dining tables or inside tents or cars.

DAVID WALL
Vervet Monkey (Savanna Monkey)

# CARNIVORES

In East African parks, carnivores are the animals most seriously affected by tourism, and often find themselves trailing dozens of white minibuses while trying to hunt. In South African parks, however, tourism is better regulated, so natural patterns are little altered by human onlookers.

Just remember to keep as low a profile as possible; if an animal is obviously hunting, try to control your excitement and avoid the temptation to move in too close, lest you distract the predator or spook the intended prey.

## Mongooses

*Mungos mungo* (Banded Mongoose)
*Galerella pulverulenta* (Small Grey Mongoose)

Southern Africa has at least eight species of mongoose, but the most common is the banded (or Zebra) mongoose, which is present in Kruger National Park and Northern Province, and the small grey mongoose which occurs in the Cape provinces.

The banded mongoose is brown or grey, measures about 40cm in length, weighs 1.3 to 2.3kg, and is easily identified by the dark bands which stretch from the shoulder to the tail. The small grey is about the same size but has no bands.

Banded mongooses are very sociable animals, living in packs of 30 to 50 individuals. They emit a range of sounds which they use for communication within the pack. When threatened they make growling and spitting noises, much like a domestic cat. Small greys are usually solitary.

Being diurnal animals they enjoy sunning themselves by day, but at night, they retire to warrens in rock crevices, hollow trees and abandoned anthills.

A mongoose's favourite foods are insects, grubs and larvae, but they'll also eat amphibians, reptiles, birds, eggs, fruit and berries. Its main predators are birds of prey, though they are also taken by lions, leopards and wild dogs.

Banded Mongoose

## Bat-Eared Fox
*Otocyon megalotis*

True to its name, the bat-eared fox is basically a long-legged fox with enormous ears. As you'd expect, its sense of hearing is exceptional. Its tail is very bushy and the body is brown with white markings and black-tipped ears. The bat-eared fox eats mainly insects, small animals, fruits and berries, and while foraging for subterranean insects it can hear even faint sounds coming from below ground. By lowering its head towards the soil, ears parallel, it can use a sort of triangulation to get an exact fix on potential food. This is followed by a burst of frantic digging to capture the prey.

The bat-eared fox normally inhabits multi-roomed burrows with several entrances, which it either digs or takes over. It's active at night, especially just after sunset. Its only enemies are large birds of prey and hyenas. They live in much of the western half of South Africa and there's a good chance of seeing some in Kalahari Gemsbok National Park.

The bat-eared fox is often mistaken for the **Cape Fox** *Vulpes chama*, which occurs in much the same area. The cape fox has smaller ears and is lighter in colour – it looks more like a European fox.

Bat-Eared Fox

## Black-Backed Jackal
*Canis mesomelas*

Black-backed jackals occur widely in all three countries, although they are disliked by farmers so they tend to be restricted to parks and reserves.

Their backs, which are actually more grizzled than black, are wide at the neck and taper to the tail. Although jackals are dogs, their bushy tails and large ears cause them to more closely resemble foxes.

Jackals are mostly scavengers, and commonly hang around kills awaiting morsels. If nothing is forthcoming they'll often hunt insects, birds, rodents and even the occasional small antelope. They also hang about outside human settlements and often go for sheep, poultry and young calves or foals.

Each jackal pair looks after a home territory of around 250 hectares. Pups are born in litters of five to seven. Although they don't reach maturity until they're almost a year old, most jackal pups are on their own at the age of just two months, and are especially vulnerable to enemies, such as leopards, cheetahs and eagles.

In Kruger National Park you might also see the **Side-striped Jackal** *Canis adustus*, which is slight-ly larger and has a more uniform grey appearance.

DAVID WALL

Black-Backed Jackal

### Cape Clawless Otter
*Aonyx capensis*

The Cape clawless otter, a river otter, is found in wet areas of the eastern half of South Africa and in Lesotho and Swaziland. In South Africa's Eastern Cape Province it occurs in the intertidal zone, especially in Tsitsikamma Coastal National Park. It has a light greyish brown back; the snout, face and throat are white or cream-coloured and each cheek has a large rectangular spot. Unlike most otters, Cape clawless otters don't have webbed feet, and although some are truly clawless, others have short pointed claws on the third and fourth toes.

The otters are normally active by day, and with a bit of luck may be seen playing, swimming and diving throughout the afternoon. In areas where they're hunted by humans, however, otters have adopted a nocturnal schedule.

Their main foods include fish, crabs, frogs, and both bird and crocodile eggs. Their only known natural enemy is the crocodile.

Cape Clawless Otter

### Caracal (African Lynx)
*Felis caracal*

Once considered to be a true lynx, the caracal is now placed in the small-cat genus *Felis*. The caracal is certainly very cat-like, and despite its sometimes sleepy appearance is the fastest cat of its size.

The caracal is distinguished by its height (about 50cm at the shoulder), relatively small head, long, narrow ears densely tufted with long hairs at the tips, lack of whiskers on the face, and long, stout legs. The colour of the coat ranges from reddish-brown to yellow-grey, with a white underside and a black line joining the nose and eye.

Caracals are 80 to 120cm long (including a tail of 20 to 30cm), and weigh between 13 and 23kg. They live in porcupine burrows, rocky crevices or dense vegetation. They inhabit many areas, but prefer dry country (woodland, savanna and scrub) and avoid sandy deserts.

Their favourite prey are birds, rodents and other small mammals, including young deer. They stalk their prey until a quick dash or leap can capture it. They are usually active at twilight, but they may hunt by night in hot weather and by day in cold weather. They are generally solitary animals, but might sometimes be seen in pairs with their young. They are believed to be territorial, marking the territory with urine sprays. The calls are typical of cats – miaows, growls, hisses and coughing noises.

Litters of one to four kittens (usually three) can be born at any time of the year. The kittens open their eyes after 10 days, are weaned at 10 to 25 weeks, and can breed from as young as six months.

Caracal (African Lynx)

## Cheetah
*Acinonyx jubatus*

The cheetah is one of nature's most magnificent accomplishments; this sleek, streamlined and graceful creature exists in limited numbers in Kruger and Kalahari Gemsbok national parks, and has been reintroduced to some parks in KwaZulu-Natal.

Although it superficially resembles a leopard, the cheetah is longer and lighter, and has a slightly bowed back and a much smaller and rounder face. It stands around 80cm at the shoulder, measures around 210cm in length, including the tail, and weighs from 40 to 60kg.

Normally cheetahs hunt in early morning or late evening. While hunting, a cheetah stalks its prey as closely as possible. When the time is ripe, it launches into an incredible 100m sprint in which it can reach a speed of up to 110km/h. However, this phenomenal speed can only be sustained for a short distance. If it fails to bring down its intended victim, it gives up and tries elsewhere. The prey, often a small antelope, may be brought to the ground with a flick of the paw to trip it up. Other favourite meals include hares, jackals and young warthogs.

The main breeding period is between March and December, when mature females produce litters of two to four cubs. The cubs reach maturity at around one year, but stay with the mother much longer to learn hunting and survival skills. Cheetahs rarely fight, but do suffer from predation by lions, leopards and hyenas; most victims are cubs.

HUGH FINLAY

Cheetah

## Civet (African Civet)
*Viverra (Civetticus) civetta*

The civet is a medium-sized omnivore around 40cm high at the shoulder and 90cm long, excluding the tail, with some canine features and short, partially retractile claws. Its long, coarse and mainly grey coat is specked with a varying pattern of black spots, with one set of black bands stretching from the ears to the lower neck and another around the upper hind legs. The head is mostly greyish white and the small, rounded ears are tipped with white hairs. Another conspicuous feature is a set of musk glands in the anal region which produce a foul-smelling oily substance used to mark territory. This musk is used in manufacturing perfumes, though in western countries it's collected from captive animals.

They occur in Northern Province and Mpumalanga, although they are solitary, nocturnal animals and hard to spot; by day they nestle in thickets, tall grass or abandoned burrows.

Civets have a varied diet consisting of amphibians, birds, rodents, eggs, reptiles, snails, insects (especially ants and termites), berries, young shoots and fruit. Litters consist of up to four cubs, which have a similar but slightly darker colour to the adults.

Civet (African Civet)

## Genet
*Genetta genetta (felina)* (Small-Spotted Genet)
*Genetta tigrina* (Large-Spotted Genet)

More than the civet, the genet resembles the domestic cat, although the body is considerably longer, the long, coarse coat has a prominent crest along the spine and the tail is longer and bushier. The basic colour varies from grey to fawn, patterned from the neck to the tail with dark brown to black spots. The tail, which has a white tip, is banded with nine or 10 similarly coloured rings.

The small-spotted genet occurs throughout South Africa, except in KwaZulu-Natal, while the large-spotted genet lives mainly in Swaziland, Northern Province, KwaZulu-Natal and along the south coast.

Genets live singly or in pairs in riverine forests and dry scrub, savanna and open country. They're agile climbers, but are seldom sighted because they're only active nocturnally. By day they sleep in abandoned burrows, rock crevices or hollow trees, or up on high branches, apparently returning to the same spot each day.

Genets may climb trees to seek out nesting birds and their eggs, but normally hunt on the ground. Like the domestic cat, they stalk prey by crouching flat on the ground. Their diet consists of small rodents, birds, reptiles, insects and fruits. They're well known for being wasteful killers, often eating only small bits of the animals they catch. Like domestic cats, genets spit and growl when angered. Litters typically consist of two or three kittens.

Small-Spotted Genet

## Honey Badger (Ratel)
*Mellivora ratel*

The honey badger is of a similar size and shape to the European badger and is every bit as ferocious. They've even been known to attack creatures as large as Cape buffalo! They're present throughout the region except in the Free State and Lesotho. They are normally active between dusk and dawn.

Honey badgers subsist on fish, frogs, scorpions, spiders, and reptiles, including poisonous snakes; at times they'll even take young antelopes. They also eat a variety of roots, honey, berries and eggs, and are adept at raiding rubbish bins.

Honey Badger (Ratel)

## Hunting Dog
*Lycaon pictus*

The scruffy looking hunting dog (or wild dog) is now rare, and in this region occurs only in Kruger National Park. It's the size of a large domestic dog, but has big, round ears and a blotchy black, brown and white coat, with a white tail.

Hunting dogs rarely scavenge, preferring to kill their own prey. They move in packs of four to 40 and work well together. Once the prey has been selected and the chase is on, two lead dogs will chase hard while the rest pace themselves; once the first two tire another pair steps in, and so on until the quarry is exhausted. Favoured prey include springbok, impala and other mid-sized antelope, but they can kill animals as large as buffalo.

Litters of seven to 15 pups are born in grass-lined burrows; by six months of age they're competent hunters and have abandoned the burrow. The hunting dog has no common predators, although unguarded pups may fall prey to hyenas and eagles.

Hunting Dog

## Hyena
*Crocuta crocuta* (Spotted Hyena)
*Hyena brunnea* (Brown or African Laughing Hyena)

Hyenas appear distinctly canine, but are generally larger and more powerfully built than your average dog, and have a broad head, large eyes, weak hindquarters and a sloping back that gives them a characteristic loping gait when running. The short coat is dull grey to buff-coloured and patterned with black spots except on the throat. Its powerful jaws and teeth enable it to crush and swallow bones, which give its scat a characteristic calcium whitewash.

Both the spotted and the African laughing hyenas live in Kruger National Park, and may still be found in parts of Northern Province.

Hyenas have highly developed senses of smell, sight and hearing, which are all important in locating carrion or live prey and for mutual recognition among pack members and mating pairs. Carrion does form an important part of their diet, but hyenas are also true predators. Running hyenas can reach speeds of up to 60km/h and a pack of them will often bring down small antelope, wildebeest and zebras. They also stalk pregnant antelope to snatch and kill the newly born calf – and occasionally the mother as well. They also prey on domestic stock.

During the mating season – especially on moonlit nights – hyenas assemble in large numbers for a bit of night-time chorus, which sounds like hell has broken loose. In their den, females produce a litter of up to four pups after a gestation period of about 110 days. The pups are weaned at around six weeks old and are on their own shortly. Humans are the hyena's main enemies, but wild dogs will occasionally kill or mutilate a hyena that approaches a kill.

MIKE SCOTT

Hyena

### Leopard (Panther)
*Panthera pardus*

Leopards are among the most widespread of African carnivores but in this region farming and hunting has restricted them to Northern Province, parts of Mpumalanga and Swaziland, the Drakensberg escarpment in KwaZulu-Natal and Lesotho, and in the mountain ranges of Eastern and Western Cape provinces.

They're mainly nocturnal and are therefore rarely observed. Leopards are agile and climb as well as domestic cats, and normally spend their days resting in trees up to 5m above the ground. They also protect their kills by dragging them up trees.

The leopard's short orange coat is densely covered with mostly hollow black spots, although some individuals – often called panthers – are black all over. The underparts are white with fewer spots. Leopards are heard more often than seen; their cry sounds very much like a hacksaw cutting through metal.

This powerfully built animal uses cunning to catch its prey, which consists mainly of birds, reptiles and mammals including large rodents, dassies, warthogs, small antelope, monkeys and baboons (a particular favourite). Occasionally, they also take domestic animals.

Leopards are solitary animals, except during the mating season when the male and female cohabit. A litter of up to three cubs is produced after a gestation period of three months.

DAVID WALL

Leopard (Panther)

### Lion
*Panthera leo*

Lions are big attractions in Kruger and Kalahari Gemsbok national parks, where indigenous populations still exist. They are also being reintroduced to other parks. Lions are most active in the late afternoon, but spend much of the day lying under bushes or in other attractive places.

Lions are hardly the human-eaters their reputation would have you believe, but older or irritable individuals do occasionally attack people, so take seriously the warnings not to get out of your vehicle in national parks.

Lions are territorial beasts. A pride of up to three males and 15 accompanying females and young will defend an area of anything from 20 to 400 sq km, depending on the type of terrain and the amount of game food available. Lions generally hunt in prides. Although they cooperate well together, lions aren't the most efficient hunters and as many as four out of five attempts are unsuccessful.

Cubs are born in litters of two or three and become sexually mature by 1½ years. Males are driven from the family group shortly after, but don't reach full maturity until around six years of age. Unguarded cubs are preyed on by hyenas, leopards, pythons and hunting dogs.

ALEX DISSANAYAKE

Lion

## Serval
*Felis (Lepitailurus) serval*

The serval, a type of wild cat, is about the size of a domestic cat but has much longer legs. It inhabits thick bush and tall grass around streams in Northern Province and parts of Swaziland, KwaZulu-Natal and eastern Free State.

Servals stand about 50cm high and measure 130cm long, including the tail. Their dirty yellow coat is dotted with large black spots which form lines along the length of the body. Other prominent features include large upright ears, a long neck and a relatively short tail.

It's an adept hunter, favouring birds, hares and rodents, and can catch birds in mid-flight by leaping into the air. Owing to its nocturnal nature, the serval is usually observed only in the early morning or late evening.

Kittens are born in litters of up to four. Although they leave their mother after one year, they don't reach sexual maturity until two years of age.

Serval

# UNGULATES

## Antelope
### Bushbuck
*Tragelaphus scriptus*

Bushbuck

Although the bushbuck exists in Northern Province and Mpumalanga and down through KwaZulu-Natal to the south coast, it's a shy and solitary animal and is rarely sighted.

Standing about 80cm at the shoulder, the bushbuck is chestnut to dark brown in colour. It has a variable number of white vertical stripes on the body between the neck and rump, and usually two horizontal white stripes lower down which give the animal a harnessed appearance, as well as a number of white spots on the upper thigh and a white splash on the neck. Normally only the males grow horns, but females have been known to grow them on rare occasions. The horns are straight with gentle spirals and average about 30cm long.

Bushbuck are rarely found in groups of more than two, and prefer to stick to areas with heavy brush cover. When startled they bolt and crash loudly through the undergrowth. They're nocturnal browsers, yet rarely move far from their home turf. Though shy and elusive they can be aggressive and dangerous when cornered. Their main predators are leopards and pythons.

### Common or Grey Duiker
*Silvicapra grimmia*

As the name would suggest, the common duiker is the most common of the 16 duiker species in Africa and it lives throughout this region. Even so, it's largely nocturnal and is sighted only infrequently. Duikers usually live in pairs, and prefer areas with good scrub cover. Only 60cm high at the shoulder, the common duiker is greyish light-brown in colour, with a white belly and a dark brown vertical stripe on the face. Only the males have horns, which are straight and pointed, and grow to only 20cm in length.

Common duikers are almost exclusively browsers and only rarely eat grasses, though they appear to supplement their diet with insects and guinea fowl chicks. They're capable of going without water for long periods but will drink whenever water is available.

The rare **blue duiker** *(Cephalophus monticola)* is sometimes spotted on the south-east coast. It's significantly smaller than the common duiker and its coat is grey or dark brown with a characteristic blue sheen.

Common or Grey Duiker

## Eland
*Taurotragus oryx*

The eland is the largest antelope species, standing about 170cm at the shoulder; a mature bull can weigh up to 1 tonne. Oddly enough, eland resemble some varieties of cattle native to the Indian subcontinent. Those remaining in this region live in Kruger National Park, with a few to be found in the KwaZulu-Natal Drakensberg.

Eland have light brown coats with up to 15 vertical white stripes on the body, although they're often almost indistinguishable. Both sexes have horns about 65cm long, which spiral at the base and sweep straight back. The male of the species has a much hairier head than the female, and its horns are stouter and shorter.

Eland prefer savanna scrub to open spaces, but they avoid thick forest. They feed on grass and tree foliage in the early morning and late afternoon, and are also active on moonlit nights. They normally drink daily, but can go for a month or more without water.

Eland usually live in groups of around six to 12, but herds can contain as many as 50 individuals. A small herd normally consists of several females and one male, but in larger herds there may be several males, which is made possible by a strict hierarchy. Females reach sexual maturity at around two years and can bear up to 12 calves in a lifetime. The young are born in October or November.

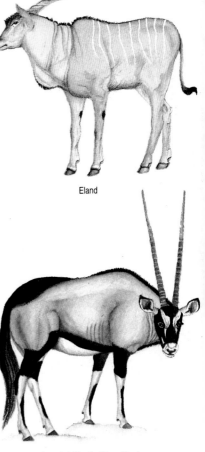

Eland

## Gemsbok (South African Oryx)
*Oryx gazella*

The gemsbok, a large grey antelope standing around 120cm at the shoulder, is common in the Kalahari Gemsbok National Park. It is a solid but stately animal, with impressively long, straight horns, an attractive grey-fawn body with black on the flanks and white on the underside, and a black and white pattern on the face. The tail is hairy, like a horse's.

Gemsbok are principally grazers, but will also browse on thorny shrubs. They can survive for long periods without water.

Herds vary from five to 40 individuals, but the bulls normally prefer a solitary existence.

Gemsbok (South African Oryx)

Greater Kudu

## Greater Kudu
*Tragelaphus strepsiceros*

The beautiful greater kudu, one of the largest ante-lope, is found in Northern Province, Kruger National Park, parts of Mpumalanga and Swaziland, and in some of the wilder areas inland from the south coast. Kudu prefers hilly country with fairly dense bush cover.

Kudu stand around 1.5m at the shoulder, with a long neck and broad ears, and weigh up to 250kg, yet they're very regal in appearance. Their bodies are light grey in colour with six to 10 vertical white stripes along the sides and a white chevron between the eyes. The horns, carried only by males, form large spirals; an old buck can have up to three complete twists.

Kudu live in small herds of up to five females and their young, but during rainy periods, the herds often split. The normally solitary males occasionally band into small herds.

Kudu are mainly browsers and can eat a variety of leaves which would be poisonous to other animals. On occasion, they also eat grasses.

Although they're somewhat clumsy, when on the move kudu can easily clear obstacles of over 2m and are known for their unhealthy habit of leaping in front of oncoming vehicles.

## Grysboks
*Raphiceros sharpei* (Sharpe's Grysbok)
*Raphicerus melanotis* (Cape Grysbok)

Sharpe's grysbok is a small, stocky antelope which is reddish-brown with a pale red underside. The back and sides are speckled with individual white hairs from the nape of the neck to the rump, hence the Afrikaans name grysbok, or 'grey buck'. Sharpe's grysbok stand only about 50cm high and weigh no more than 9kg. Only the males have horns, which are small, sharp and straight. It is found in the north-east of South Africa, in both bushy and woodland savanna country and rocky koppies, feeding primarily on shoots and leaves. They also like to munch the reeds which grow in wetlands.

The Cape grysbok looks similar to Sharpe's, but it is found only in the extreme south-west of South Africa, where it inhabits the unique *fynbos* vegetation – and sometimes feeds on vines in the Cape Winelands area, making it unpopular.

Grysbok are solitary, and you'll rarely see more than two together. They're most active from morning to late afternoon, spending the night resting in bushy thickets and stony outcrops.

Sharpe's Grysbok

## Hartebeest
*Alcelaphus buselaphus (Red Hartebeest)*
*Sigmoceros lichtensteinii (Lichtenstein's Hartebeest)*

The hartebeest is a medium-size antelope. Once found in this region, it has been reintroduced to many parks including Kruger, Kalahari Gemsbok and Addo Elephant national parks.

Hartebeest are easily recognised by their long, narrow face and short horns, which are distinctively angular and heavily ridged. In both sexes, the horns form a heart shape, hence their name (which means 'heart beast' in Afrikaans). The back slopes away from the humped shoulders and is light brown, becoming lighter towards the rear and underside.

Hartebeest prefer grassy plains for grazing but are also found in sparsely forested savanna or hills. They feed exclusively on grass and usually drink twice daily, although they can go for months without water if necessary.

They're social beasts and often mingle with animals such as zebra and wildebeest. Sexual maturity is reached at around two years, and hartebeest can calve at any time of year, although activity peaks in February and August. Predators are mainly the large cats, hyenas and hunting dogs.

Hartebeest

## Impala
*Aepyceros melampus*

The graceful impala is found in large numbers in Kruger National Park, as well as in Northern Province, parts of Swaziland and north-eastern KwaZulu-Natal.

Individuals weigh from 50 to 60kg and stand about 80cm at the shoulder. The coat is a glossy rufous colour, though more pale on the flanks, and the under-parts, rump, throat and chin are white. A narrow black band runs from the middle of the rump to about halfway down the tail and there's also a vertical black stripe on the back of the thighs. Males have long, lyre-shaped horns averaging 75cm in length.

Impala are gregarious animals, and males have harems of up to 100 females, although 15 to 20 are more common. Single males form bachelor groups, and there is fierce competition and fighting between them during the rutting season. The normal gestation period is six to seven months, but that can be prolonged if low rainfall has produced insufficient grass to nourish the young. Males usually leave the herd before they reach breeding age.

Impala are known for their speed and ability to leap; they can spring as much as 10m in a single bound or 3m off the ground – and frequently do – even when there's nothing to jump over! And it's lucky they can; impala are the rabbits of Africa, and make a tasty meal for all large predators, including lions, leopards, cheetahs, wild dogs and even hyenas.

HUGH FINLAY

Impala

Klipspringer

### Klipspringer
*Oreotragus oreotragus*

The delicate little klipspringer, which stands about 50cm at the shoulder, is shy and easily disturbed. It's easily recognised by its curious tip-toe stance – the hooves are adapted for balance and grip on rocky surfaces – and the greenish tinge of its coarse speckled hair. The widely-spaced 10-cm-long horns are present only on the male.

Klipspringers normally inhabit rocky outcrops and are found in many places in this region, from Northern Province to the KwaZulu-Natal Drakensberg, to the coastal ranges in the three Cape provinces. They also venture into adjacent grasslands, but when alarmed they retreat into the rocks for safety. These amazingly agile and sure-footed creatures are capable of bounding up impossibly rough rock faces. They get all the water they need from their diet of greenery and go for long periods without drinking.

Each male has a clearly defined territory and lives with one or two females. They reach sexual maturity at around one year, and females bear one calf twice annually. Calves may stay with their parents for up to a year, but young males normally establish their own territory even sooner.

Main predators are leopards, crowned eagles, jackals and baboons.

Nyala

### Nyala
*Tragelaphus angasii* (Common Nyala)
*Tragelaphus buxtoni* (Mountain Nyala)

The medium-size nyala is one of Africa's rarest and most beautiful antelope. Males are grey with a mane and long hair under the throat and hind legs. They also have vertical stripes down the back and long, lyre-shaped horns with white tips. Females are a ruddy colour with vertical white stripes, but have no horns.

Nyalas are found in Kruger National Park and a few remaining habitats in north-eastern KwaZulu-Natal. Their main foods are shoots, buds, bark, fruit and leaves of trees and bushes. During the dry season they're active only in the morning and evening, while during the rains, they more often feed at night.

Female nyala and their young live in small groups, with one older dominant male to guard and defend them from young males, which organise their own social groups. Nyala defend themselves bravely against humans and enemies – mainly leopards and lions. The young may even be taken by baboons and birds of prey.

## Oribi
*Ourebia ourebi*

Similar to the duiker in appearance, the small oribi is relatively difficult to see; your best chance of spotting one is in one of the parks in the KwaZulu-Natal Drakensberg.

Oribi are a uniform golden brown with white on the belly and the insides of the legs. The males have short straight horns about 10cm long. The oribi's most distinguishing mark – although you'll need binoculars to spot it – is a circular patch of naked black skin below the ear, which is actually a scent gland. Another identifying characteristic is the tuft of black hair on the tip of the short tail.

Being quite small, the oribi has many predators, including the larger cats. They usually graze on high grass savanna plains, where they're well sheltered from predators. They can go without water for long periods, but if it's available, they'll drink. When alarmed they bolt, making erratic bounces with all four legs held rigid. It's thought this helps them with orientation in high grasses. After 100m or so, they stop to assess the danger.

Oribi are territorial and usually live in pairs. They reach sexual maturity at around one year, and the females bear one calf twice annually.

Oribi

## Reedbuck
*Redunca arundinum* (Common Reedbuck)
*Redunca fulvorufula* (Mountain Reedbuck)

The dusky brown reedbuck is found on wetlands or riverine areas in parts of Northern Province, Swaziland and KwaZulu-Natal. It never strays more than a few kilometres from a permanent water source. The rarer mountain reedbuck inhabits a wider area, in hill country from Northern Province down through Swaziland, Lesotho, KwaZulu-Natal, Free State and Eastern Cape Province.

These medium-size antelope stand around 80cm at the shoulder and males have distinctive forward-curving horns. The underbelly, inside of the thighs, throat and underside of the bushy tail are white.

Reedbuck are territorial and live in small groups of up to 10 animals. Groups usually consist of an older male and accompanying females and young. Their diet consists almost exclusively of grass and some foliage.

At mating time, competing males fight with spirit. After sexual maturity at 1½ years, females bear one calf at a time. Predators include big cats, hyenas and hunting dogs.

Reedbuck

Ringed (Common) Waterbuck

### Ringed (Common) Waterbuck
*Kobus ellipsiprymnus*

The ringed waterbuck, so called because of the bulls-eye ring around its rump, has white markings on the face and throat. It's a solid animal with a thick, shaggy, dark brown coat, white inner thighs and proportionally long neck and short legs. It's commonly seen in Kruger National Park and sometimes in the north-east corner of KwaZulu-Natal.

Only the males have horns, which curve gradually outward before shooting straight up to a length of about 75cm. Waterbuck are good swimmers and readily enter the water to escape predators. They never stray far from water, and a male's territory will always include a water source. Herds are small and consist of cows, calves and one mature bull, while younger bulls live in small groups apart from the herd.

The bulk of the waterbuck's diet consists mainly of grass, but it also eats some foliage. Sexual maturity is reached at just over one year, although a male will not become dominant in the herd until around five years of age. Females and younger males are permitted to wander at will through territories of breeding males.

Predators such as lions, leopards and hunting dogs go for the young calves and females, but mature waterbucks are not a favoured prey species because of their tough flesh and the distinct odour of the meat.

### Roan Antelope
*Hippotragus equinus*

The roan is one of Southern Africa's rarest antelope species, but still exists in Kruger National Park. As a grazer, it prefers tall grasses and sites with ample shade and fresh water.

The roan is the third largest antelope species, after eland and kudu, reaching up to 150cm at the shoulder. It bears a striking resemblance to a horse. Bulls can weigh up to 270kg.

The coat varies from reddish fawn to dark rufous, with white underparts and a conspicuous mane of stiff, black-tipped hairs stretching from the nape to the shoulders. There's another mane of sorts on the underside of the neck, consisting of long dark hairs. The ears are long, narrow and pointed, with a brown tassel at the tip. The face has a distinctive black and white pattern. Both sexes have curving, back-swept horns up to 70cm long.

It has an extremely aggressive nature and fight from an early age, thus deterring predators. For most of the year roans are arranged in small herds of normally less than 20 individuals, led by a master bull. However, in the mating season, bulls become solitary and take a female from the herd. The pair remain together until the calf is born, after which the females and calves form a separate herd; when the dry season comes, the females and calves rejoin the original herd.

Roan Antelope

## Sable Antelope
*Hippotragus niger*

The sable is present in Kruger National Park and nearby areas of Northern Province. Sable are slightly smaller than roan, but are more solidly built. The colouring is dark brown to black, with a white belly and face markings. Both sexes carry 80-cm sweeping horns, but those of the male are longer and more curved. Sable feed mainly on grass, but foliage accounts for around 10% of their diet.

Sable live in territorial herds of up to 25 – sometimes more in the dry season – and are active mainly in the early morning and late afternoon. Each herd occupies its own area, within which each individual male has his own territory of up to 30 hectares.

Females start bearing calves at around three years of age; most are borne in January and September. Like the roan, the sable is a fierce fighter and has been known to kill lions when attacked. Other predators include leopards, hyenas and hunting dogs.

Sable Antelope

## Springbok
*Antidorcas marsupialis*

The springbok, the only gazelle in Southern Africa, is found in the north-western corner of South Africa, including Kalahari Gemsbok National Park.

Springbok are easily recognised by their white head, with a black stripe connecting the nose and eye. The fawn-coloured back and white belly are separated by a ruddy brown stripe along the animal's side. Both male and female springbok have ribbed, lyre-shaped horns of medium length. It's one of several species of antelope known for its pronking (leaping vertically in the air).

They generally move in herds of 20 to 100 animals; sometimes herds of several hundred can be seen. Male springbok are only territorial during the rutting season, when they collect harems of females and defend them against other potential suitors. At other times, herds consist of mixed groups of males and females, although groups made up entirely of bachelors are often observed.

Springbok are active early in the morning and from late afternoon to dusk. They also emerge on nights with strong moonlight. They eat grass and the leaves of low bushes, and occasionally dig out roots and tubers. Females calve from December to January.

They drink often, but can survive for long periods without water. Occasionally, in conditions of severe drought, huge herds migrate in search of water; in the great migration of 1896, the surface area covered by millions of springbok was 220km long and 25km wide. In Namibia, great herds, driven mad by thirst or hunger, have in the past flocked to the coast, drank seawater and died, leaving the shoreline littered with carcasses.

DEANNA SWANEY

Springbok

### Steenbok
*Raphiceros campestris*

The steenbok, sometimes spelt 'steinbock', bears a resemblance to both the duiker and the grysbok, with a short tail and proportionally long and slender legs. The back and hindquarters range from light reddish brown to dark brown, and on the upper edge of the nose is a black, wedge-shaped spot. Males have small, straight and widely separated horns.

Steenbok live mainly on open plains, but can be found almost anywhere in this region. They're solitary animals, and only have contact with others during the mating season.

Normally, steenbok are active in the morning and evening, but may stay out late when there's a bright moon. At other times, they seek out high grass or bear holes which offer some protection from enemies, which include leopards, eagles, pythons, monitor lizards, jackals and hyenas.

DEANNA SWANEY

Steenbok

### Tsessebi (Topi)
*Damaliscus lunatus*

The tsessebi is like the hartebeest in appearance but is darker – in some cases appearing almost violet – with black patches on the rear thighs, front legs and face. Its horns, carried by both sexes, curve gently up, out and back. The tsessebi is found in Kruger National Park.

A highly gregarious antelope, it lives in herds of at least 15 and frequently mingles with wildebeest, hartebeest and zebras. During the mating season, bulls select a well-defined patch which they defend against all rivals, while females wander from one patch to another. After mating, herds divide into separate male and female groups.

Tsessebi are exclusively grazers. Although they can live on dry grasses spurned by other antelope, they prefer floodplains and moist areas which support lush pasture. When water is available they drink frequently, but they are also capable of surviving long periods without water as long as sufficient grass is available. Lions are their main predators.

Tsessebi (Topi)

### Wildebeest (Gnu)

*Connochaetes taurinus* (Blue Wildebeest or Brindled Gnu)
*Connochaetes gnou* (Black Wildebeest or White-tailed Gnu)

The wildebeest, also called the gnu after its low and languid grunt, is to the African savanna what the bison once was to the American prairies. Wildebeest are gregarious, to say the least, and sometimes move about in herds up to tens of thousands strong, normally in association with zebras and other herbivores, accompanied by a cacophony of amusing snorts and low grunts. In South Africa, numbers are today much smaller, but you'll see wildebeest in many of the drier national parks, from Kalahari Gemsbok to Kruger.

The wildebeest's ungainly appearance makes it unmistakable; it's heavily built and has a massive head and wild, frayed mane. It has been described as having the forequarters of an ox, the hind parts of an antelope and the tail of a horse.

During the mating season, groups of up to 150 females and their young are gathered by up to three bulls, which defend a defined territory against rivals, even when on the move. At the end of the mating season, breeding herds are reabsorbed into the main herds.

Wildebeest are almost exclusively grazers, and move constantly in search of good pasture and water. Because they prefer to drink daily and can survive only five days without water, wildebeest will migrate up to 50km to find it. During the rainy season they graze haphazardly, without any apparent social organisation, but in the dry season they coalesce around waterholes.

Major predators include lions, cheetahs and wild dogs, and hyenas are also partial to young wildebeest calves.

# Other Ungulates
### Cape Buffalo
*Syncerus caffer*

Cape (or African) buffalo occur in Kruger National Park, with some smaller populations in north-eastern KwaZulu-Natal and elsewhere. Both sexes have the distinctive curving horns which broaden and almost meet over the forehead, but those of the female are usually smaller. Their coloration varies from ruddy brown to black.

Buffalo have a penetrating gaze, and one safari operator has noted that 'buffalo always look at you as if you owe them a lot of money'. Although for the most part they're docile and stay out of humans' way, these 800kg creatures can be very dangerous and should be treated with caution. Solitary rogue bulls and females protecting young are the most aggressive.

Cape buffalo are territorial, but when food and water are plentiful the herds, which normally consist of 100 or more individuals, may disperse over an area 100km in diameter. However, they never stray far from water, especially in dry periods.

TONY WHEELER

Wildebeest (Gnu)

TONY WHEELER

Cape Buffalo

DAVID WALL

Giraffe

GEOFF CROWTHER

GEOFF CROWTHER

Hippopotamus

## Giraffe
*Giraffa camelopardalis*

As well as odd specimens in game reserves and parks around the country, you'll find giraffe in Kruger National Park and nearby.

The name giraffe is derived from the Arabic *zarafah* ('the one who walks quickly').

The average male is around 5.5m tall. Females are 4.5m and are normally lighter in colour and have less well-defined markings. Both sexes have 'horns', actually just short projections of skin-covered bone and probably a remnant of what might once have been antlers. Despite the giraffe's incredibly long neck, it still has only seven cervical vertebrae – the same number as all mammals, including humans.

Giraffes are out and about in the early morning and afternoon, browsing on acacia. You may be surprised to see them chewing bones, a practice known as *pica*, which indicates a shortage of minerals in their diet. When the sun is high and hot, they relax in a cool, shady spot. At night they also rest for several hours.

Giraffes most often drink in the late afternoon or early evening, but they must go through all sorts of contortions to reach water level. They're at their most vulnerable at waterholes and always appear hesitant and visibly nervous when drinking. In fact, if they feel the slightest uncertainty about the safety of the situation, they'll often forgo their drink altogether.

## Hippopotamus
*Hippopotamus amphibius*

The hippo is found in many watercourses in northeastern South Africa, and in Swaziland. The best places to see them are in Kruger National Park and the St Lucia Wetlands reserves in KwaZulu-Natal.

Hippos, as you probably already know, are huge, fat animals with enormous heads and short legs. When fully grown they weigh in at 1350 to 2600kg. Their ears, eyes and nostrils are so placed that they can remain inconspicuously above water even when the animal is submerged.

Hippos spend most of the day submerged, feeding on bottom vegetation and surfacing only occasionally to grab a breath of air before plunging again. Only at night do they emerge from the water, often wandering up to several kilometres from their aquatic haunts to graze. They're voracious feeders and can consume up to 60kg of vegetable matter, mostly a variety of grasses, each night. They urinate and defecate in well-defined areas – often in the water – dispersing the excreta with their tails.

They're very gregarious animals and live in schools of 15 to 30 or more. Each school generally contains an equal number of bulls and cows (with their calves) and hippo society operates under an established hierarchy. They may appear placid, but the males do frequently fight among themselves for dominance and some of the resulting wounds can be quite horrific.

Virtually every male hippo bears the scars of such conflicts.

To humans, hippos are statistically Africa's most dangerous animal. Most accidents occur when hippos surface beneath boats and canoes or when someone sets up camp on a riverside hippo run or blocks a hippo's retreat route to the water.

Hippos breed year-round. Cows give birth to a single calf after a gestation period of 230 days and suckle it both in the water and on land for four to six months. At this time it begins to graze on its own. Hippos live for about 30 years and sexual maturity is reached at about four years.

The hippo's only natural predators are lions and crocodiles, which prey on the young. Though they occasionally tangle fishing nets, they're considered beneficial because their wallowing stirs up the bottom mud and their excreta is a valuable fertiliser which encourages the growth of aquatic organisms.

GEOFF CROWTHER

Hippopotamus

### Rhinoceros

*Ceratotherium simum* (White or Square-lipped Rhinoceros)
*Diceros bicornis* (Black or Hook-lipped Rhinoceros)

White rhinos are in fact lighter in colour (and much bulkier) than black rhinos, but their name is a corruption of *wide*-lipped rhino, as opposed to the hook-lipped black rhino.

Rhinos are Africa's most endangered large animals, thanks mainly to the Asian belief that rhino horn has medicinal and aphrodisiac properties, and the Yemeni notion that all real men need a dagger made of rhino horn. Poaching has caused dramatic declines in rhino numbers in recent years, and in many countries they've been completely exterminated.

Luckily for visitors to South Africa and Swaziland, poaching is not out of control, and you have a very good chance of getting close to rhino in Kruger National Park, and in several parks in KwaZulu-Natal and in Swaziland.

Black rhinos are browsers, living in scrubby country and eating mainly leaves, shoots and buds, while white rhinos are grazers and prefer open plains.

While white rhinos are generally docile, black rhinos are prone to charging when alarmed, but their eyesight is extremely poor and chances are they'll miss their target anyway. They've even been known to charge trains or elephant carcasses!

Rhinos reach sexual maturity by five years but females first breed at around seven years of age. Calves average 40kg at birth and grow to 140kg at three months of age. Adult black rhinos weigh from 800kg to 1.1 tonnes but the much larger white rhinos tip the scales at 1.2 to 1.6 tonnes. Both species are solitary, only socialising during the mating season. Calves stay with the mother for up to three years, although they're weaned after one year.

DAVID WALL

White or Square-Lipped Rhinoceros

DAVID WALL

Black or Hook-Lipped Rhinoceros

TONY WHEELER

Warthog

## Warthog
*Phacochoerus aethiopicus*

Warthogs are found in parts of Northern Province, Kruger National Park, north-eastern KwaZulu-Natal and elsewhere. They take their name from the rather unusual wart-like growths on the face. They usually live in family groups, known as 'sounders', which include a boar, a sow and three or four young. Their most endearing habit is the way they trot away with their thin tufted tail stuck straight up in the air like antennae.

Males are usually larger than females, measuring up to a metre long and weighing around 100kg. They grow two sets of tusks; the upper ones curve outwards and upwards and grow as long as 60cm; the lower ones are usually less than 15cm long.

Warthogs feed mainly on grass, but also eat fruit and bark. In hard times they'll burrow with their snout for roots and bulbs. They also rest and give birth in abandoned burrows, or sometimes excavate cavities in abandoned termite mounds. Piglets are born in litters of two to eight.

DAVID WALL

Zebra

## Zebra
*Equus burchelli* (Common or Burchell's Zebra)
*Equus zebra zebra* (Cape Mountain Zebra)

Zebras were once widely distributed, but today you'll only see them in parks and reserves such as Kruger National Park (Burchell's zebra) and Mountain Zebra National Park (Cape mountain zebra). Burchell's zebras have shadow lines between the black stripes; mountain zebras don't have shadows but do have a gridiron pattern of black stripes just above the tail.

Zebras are grazers but occasionally browse on leaves and scrub. They need water daily and rarely wander far from a water hole. They often mingle with other animals, such as wildebeest, elephants and impala.

During the breeding season, stallions engage in fierce battles for control over a herd of mares. A single foal is born after a gestation period of 12 months. Lions are the zebra's worst enemy, but they're also taken by hyenas and wild dogs.

# OTHER MAMMALS

### Aardvark (Antbear)
*Orycteropus afer*

The porcine-looking aardvark has thick and wrinkled pink-grey skin with very sparse and stiff greyish hair. Its has an elongated tubular snout and a round, sticky, pink tongue, which are used to lap up ants and termites dug from nests and rotting wood with the long claws of its front feet.

Aardvarks dig metre-long holes which are also used as burrows by many other species, including hares, hyenas, jackals, warthogs, owls and rodents. They normally emerge only at night, but in the morning after a cold night they may bask in the sun awhile before retiring underground. When aardvark holes are occupied, the entrances are sealed except for small ventilation holes. When confronted by an enemy, aardvarks somersault and bleat loudly or if there's time, quickly excavate a refuge. When cornered, they resist attack with the foreclaws, shoulders and tail.

Aardvarks are normally solitary animals; only mother and offspring live together. They are found all over this region and can co-exist with cattle farms.

Aardvark (Antbear)

### African Elephant
*Loxodonta africana*

African elephants are much larger than their Asian counterparts and their ears are wider and flatter. A fully grown bull can weigh more than 6½ tonnes.

Elephants are present in Kruger National Park, some parks in KwaZulu-Natal, and a few others, including the Addo Elephant Park, where you'd be unlucky not to see elephants. There are also a very few in the forests around Knysna.

Both males and females grow tusks, although the female's are usually smaller. The tusks on an old bull can weigh as much as 50kg each but 15 to 25kg is more usual.

Elephants are gregarious animals, and usually live in herds of 10 to 20. These herds will consist of one mature bull and a couple of younger bulls, cows and calves, but herds may incorporate up to 50 individuals. Old bulls appear to lose the herding instinct and eventually leave to pursue a solitary existence, rejoining the herd only for mating. Because elephants communicate using a range of sounds, herds often make a great deal of noise: snorting, bellowing, rumbling and belching produced by the trunk or mouth. The best-known elephant call, however, is the high-pitched trumpeting which they produce when they're frightened or want to appear threatening.

Herds are on the move night and day in pursuit of water and fodder, both of which they consume in vast quantities. An adult's average daily food intake is about 250kg. Elephants are grazers and browsers and feed on a wide variety of vegetable matter, including grasses, leaves, twigs, bark, roots and fruits, and they

DAVID WALL

African Elephant

DAVID WALL

African Elephant

frequently knock down quite large trees to get at the leaves. Especially in drought years, they're capable of turning dense woodland into open grassland in a relatively short time. Because of this destructive capacity they're often perceived as a serious threat to a fragile environment, but some schools of thought maintain that elephant damage is necessary in the natural cycle of the bushveld.

Mineral salts obtained from 'salt licks' are also essential in an elephant's diet. Salt is dug out of the earth with the tusks and devoured in large quantities.

Elephants breed year-round and have a gestation period of 22 to 24 months. Expectant mothers leave the herd along with one or two other females and select a secluded spot to give birth, then rejoin the herd a few days later. Calves weigh around 130kg at birth and stand just under a metre high. They're very playful and are guarded carefully and fondly by their mothers until weaned at two years of age. They continue to grow for the next 20 years, reaching puberty at around 10 to 12 years. On average, an elephant's life span is 60 to 70 years, though some individuals reach the ripe old age of 100 or more.

### Cape Pangolin
*Manis temminckii*

The Cape pangolin (also called Temminck's Ground Pangolin) is one of four species of African pangolins, but it is the only species in Southern Africa. Pangolins are sometimes known as scaly anteaters because they're covered with large rounded scales over the back and tail, with hair only around the eyes, ears, cheeks and belly. Their primary foods include ants and termites dug from termite mounds, rotting wood and dung heaps. They walk on the outside edges of their hands, with claws pointed inward. They rarely excavate their own holes, however, and prefer to live in abandoned aardvark holes.

Despite the name, Cape pangolins are present mainly in Swaziland and the north and north-east of South Africa, including Kruger National Park. They normally keep to dry scrubby country, especially areas with light sandy soil. They're mainly nocturnal but are most active between midnight and dawn and are therefore rarely seen.

Cape Pangolin

## Hyrax
*Procavia capensis* (Rock Dassie or Rock Hyrax)

Southern Africa's most common hyrax species is the rock dassie, or rock hyrax. This small but robust animal is about the size of a rabbit, with a short and pointed snout, large ears and thick fur. The tail is either absent or reduced to a stump.

Rock dassies occur practically everywhere there are mountains or rocky outcrops.

Hyraxes are sociable animals and live in colonies of up to 60 individuals, usually in rocky, scrub-covered locales, such as rock koppies. They feed in the morning and evening on grass, bulbs, roots, grasshoppers and locusts. During the rest of the day hyraxes sun themselves on rocks or chase each other in play. Where they're habituated to humans (such as on top of Table Mountain in Cape Town) they're often quite tame, but otherwise they dash into rock crevices when alarmed, uttering shrill screams. They have excellent hearing and eyesight.

Hyraxes breed all year and have a gestation of around seven months, which is a remarkably long period for an animal of this size. Up to six young are born at a time, and are cared for by the entire colony. Predators include leopards, wild dogs, eagles, mongooses and pythons.

Despite its small size, the hyrax is thought to be more closely related to the elephant than any other living creature, but the exact relationship is unclear.

Rock Hyraxes

## Short-Tailed Porcupine
*Hystrix africaeaustralis*

The prickly porcupine, the largest rodent native to Southern Africa, can weigh as much as 24kg and measure up to a metre in length. It occurs all over this region but is nocturnal and quite difficult to observe. On cooler days, it may emerge during daylight hours.

Porcupines are covered with a spread of long black and white banded quills from the shoulders to the tail. Along the ridge from the head to the shoulders runs a crest of long coarse hair, which stands on end when the animal is alarmed.

For shelter, they either occupy rock caves or excavate their own burrows. Their diet consists mainly of bark, tubers, seeds and a variety of plants and ground-level foliage. The young are born during the hot summer months, normally in litters of one or two.

DEANNA SWANEY

Short-Tailed Porcupine

PETER ROBINSON

Fish Eagle

Jackass Penguin

# BIRDS

Birds rate highly among the many attractions of South Africa. For sheer abundance and variety, few parts of the world offer as much for the bird-watcher, whether expert or beginner. South Africa is host to nearly 10% of the world's bird species – over 900 species have been recorded in the region. More than 130 are endemic to Southern Africa and most of these are found in South Africa.

With the exception of nocturnal, cryptic (camouflaged) or rare species, birds can be easily seen – not just in national parks and game reserves, but at popular tourist destinations and even in the middle of large cities.

Bird-watching is a popular pastime for residents and visitors alike; birds and birdlore are not only intrinsic to ancient African customs, they have been assimilated into the lives of white settlers, and there is an English and an Afrikaans name for nearly every type. Visitors will find ample books and other publications on birds.

The astonishing variety of the country's birdlife can be attributed to the number of habitats. The climate ranges from cool temperate with winter rainfall in the south-west, to a hot tropical zone with summer rains in the north-east, and the main habitats can be separated into seven categories: forest; savanna; fynbos; grassland; Karoo; fresh water areas (rivers, marshes, lakes, pans, and their adjoining shores); and seashore areas (including areas of brackish water where fresh water meets salt in lagoons and estuaries).

Many species of birds are wide-ranging, but the vast majority have feeding, breeding or other biological requirements which restrict them to a habitat or group of habitats. Therefore, to see a wide variety a visitor should try to take in as many different habitats as possible.

All the national parks and game reserves feature a great range of birdlife. (For a complete rundown on national parks and game reserves, refer to the national parks sections in the individual country chapters.) Those particularly known for their rich birdlife include the Kruger and Pilanesberg national parks in northern South Africa; Ndumu and Mkuzi game reserves, Lake St Lucia and Oribi Gorge in KwaZulu-Natal; and Karoo, West Coast and Bontebok national parks in Western Cape. Also worth noting are the nature reserves of Eastern Cape's Wild Coast, and Golden Gate National Park in Free State.

Following is a group-by-group description of some of the birds you'll see in South Africa. This is not a comprehensive list; the focus is on common, unusual and spectacular species. Using the colour photos in this section, you should be able to identify most bird families and a few common species. For more detailed descriptions refer to one of the readily available field guides.

**Ostrich** The largest and heaviest of all birds, the ostrich is a wide-ranging inhabitant of grassland and savanna and the only member of this flightless group found on the continent.

**Seabirds** Into this broad category can be lumped a number of bird families which hunt over the open sea. They include Africa's one resident penguin, the jackass penguin; the various petrels, shearwaters and albatrosses, which usually live far out to sea and only return to land to breed; the beautiful gannets and their tropical relatives the boobies, that feed by plunging from a great height after fish; frigatebirds, who by their marauding habits have also been known as man o'war birds; and the fish-eating cormorants (shags), which also make use of brackish and freshwater habitats.

**Waterfowl** This large group includes the familiar ducks and geese. As their collective name suggests, they are found almost exclusively around waterways. Some species are specialists of inland swamps, while others have a broader habitat preference and can be seen on coastal lagoons or even in city parks and gardens. Only the South African shelduck and Cape shoveler are endemic to the region; other members of this highly mobile group roam across the continent looking for suitable places to feed and breed.

**Birds of Prey** South Africa's hawks, eagles, vultures, falcons and the unique secretary bird fall under this broad heading and together number nearly 70 species. Their presence is almost ubiquitous and you'll soon notice a few different species, from soaring flocks of scavenging vultures to the stately bateleur perched atop a koppie, from where it surveys the surrounding plain for prey. Many have specialised prey or habitat requirements: the osprey and the striking fish eagle of large waterways feed almost exclusively on fish; and the pygmy falcon is so small it nests in the colonies of sociable weavers.

**Cranes** These graceful, long-legged birds superficially resemble storks and herons, but are typically grassland-dwelling birds. The crowned crane is eccentrically adorned with a colourful crest. The blue or Stanley crane is South Africa's national bird.

**Long-legged Wading Birds** Virtually any waterway will have its complement of herons, egrets, storks, spoonbills and/or ibis. All species have long legs and necks, and bills adapted to specific feeding strategies: herons and egrets have dagger-like bills for spearing fish and frogs; spoonbills have peculiar, flattened bills which they swish from side to side to gather small water creatures; ibis have long, down-curved bills to probe in soft earth or seize insects; and storks have large powerful beaks to snap up small animals and fish. Members of this group range in size from the tiny, secretive bitterns to the enormous Goliath heron

ROB DRUMMOND

Cape Gannet Colony

MIKE REED

Crowned Crane

PETER ROBINSON

Blacksmith Plover

ROB DRUMMOND

Crested Barbet

ROB DRUMMOND

Speckled Mousebird

(standing 1.4m tall) and the hideous Marabou stork, which often gather around a kill and feed on carrion. Some storks are migratory and may be nearly absent from a region until they arrive in autumn, often in vast numbers; Abdim's stork is particularly noteworthy because large flocks arrive suddenly when on migration. An unusual member of this group is the hamerkop, a small heron-like bird that makes an enormous nest of twigs and grass.

**Migratory Waders** Every year millions of shorebirds arrive in Southern Africa after completing a journey of many thousands of kilometres from their breeding grounds in the northern hemisphere. Generally nondescript in their winter plumage, these migratory 'waders' present an identification challenge to the keen birdwatcher. A number of species are resident – plovers, dikkops and their close relatives the gulls and terns. With few exceptions these birds are found near fresh and saline waterways, feeding along the shores on small creatures or probing the intertidal mud for worms. The migrants include the long-distance champions, the sandpipers and plovers. Residents include the boldly marked blacksmith plover, lapwings and the odd dikkops – lanky, cryptic, nocturnal species with weird wailing cries.

**Pigeons & Doves** Familiar to city and country dwellers alike, members of this worldwide family make up for their lack of colour by their ubiquity. The various species of the region have adapted to virtually every habitat: the rock pigeon to crags and peaks; the cinnamon dove to forest floors; and the African green pigeon to a nomadic life following the fruiting of trees. The rock pigeon is easily seen on Table Mountain.

**Louries** In South Africa, three beautifully coloured species of these medium-sized birds inhabit forests. They can be difficult to see because they hide in the canopy; often you will only catch a tantalising view as one flies across a clearing, showing its broad, rich crimson wing patches. A fourth species, the grey lourie, is often seen in noisy parties in thornveld; its raucous call has earned it the alternative name 'Go-away Bird'.

**Barbets & Woodpeckers** There are a few species of woodpeckers in the region, but perhaps more conspicuous are their colourful, tropical cousins the barbets. Rather than drilling into bark after grubs like woodpeckers, barbets have strong, broad bills adapted to eating fruit and a variety of insect prey.

**Mousebirds** This uniquely African group comprises a small group of common but rather plain birds. They are so named because they forage by crawling up tree trunks and along branches, dragging their long tails behind them and appearing, as their name suggests, like tree-dwelling rodents.

**Honeyguides** Honeyguides display one of the most remarkable behaviours of any bird. They seek out mammals such as the ratel (honey badger) or even humans, then 'guide' them to a beehive. Once it has attracted the attention of a 'helper', the honeyguide flies a short way ahead then waits to see if it is being followed. In this way it leads its 'helper' to the hive and while the obliging creature, which could also be a genet, mongoose or baboon, breaks open and robs the hive, the honeyguide feeds on wax and bees' larvae and eggs.

**Kingfishers** Colourful and active, the 10 species found in South Africa can be divided into two groups: those which typically dive into water after fish and tadpoles (and as a consequence are found along waterways); and those that usually live away from water for much of their lives, preying on lizards and large insects. Of the former, the giant kingfisher reaches 46cm in height and the jewel-like malachite and pygmy kingfishers a mere 14cm. The less brightly coloured 'forest' kingfishers are inhabitants of woodland and forest.

**Bee-Eaters, Rollers & Hoopoe** The various species of bee-eaters and rollers are colourful relatives of the kingfishers; they are commonly seen perched on fences and branches – sometimes in mixed flocks – from where they pursue flying insects, particularly, as their name suggests, bees and wasps. The most stunning of all is the carmine bee-eater. Mention should also be made of the bizarre hoopoe, a salmon pink migrant from Europe and Asia that sports a dashing black and white crest.

**Owls** Many African tribes have deep superstitions about these nocturnal birds of prey. Owls have soft feathers (which make their flight inaudible to prey), exceptional hearing and can turn their heads in a 180° arc to locate their prey. The prey varies according to the species: from insects, mice and lizards among the smaller species, to the roosting birds and small mammals favoured by others. South Africa has some splendid examples, such as the Cape eagle owl.

**Nightjars** Another nocturnal group, these small birds are not related to owls, although their plumage is soft and their flight silent. Nightjars roost on the ground by day, their subtle coloration making a perfect camouflage among the leaves and twigs. At dusk, they take to the wing and catch insect prey. Although these birds are not uncommon, you may be oblivious to their presence until one flies up near your feet. The identification of several species is difficult and often relies on call, but when flushed during the day nightjars typically fly to a nearby horizontal branch and perch there, allowing you a closer look.

ROB DRUMMOND
Giant Kingfisher

ROB DRUMMOND
Pied Kingfisher

DOUG LAING
Carmine Bee-Eaters

ROB DRUMMOND
Hoopoe

Sociable Weaver's communal nest

Masked Weaver          Red Bishop

ALL PHOTOGRAPHS ABOVE BY ROB DRUMMOND

Pin-Tailed Whydah

DOUG LAING

Malachite Sunbird

**Swifts & Swallows** Although unrelated, these two groups are superficially similar and can be seen chasing flying insects just about anywhere. Both groups have long wings and streamlined bodies adapted to lives in the air, both fly with grace and agility after insect prey, and both are usually dark in coloration. However, swallows differ in one major aspect: they can perch on twigs, fences or even the ground while swifts have weak legs and rarely land except at the nest. In fact, swifts are so adapted to life in the air that some are even known to roost (sleep) on the wing!

**Finches, Weavers & Widows** This large group includes many small but colourful species, readily seen in flocks at camping grounds, along roads and wherever there is long grass. All are seed eaters and while some, such as the various sparrows, are not spectacular, others develop showy courtship plumage and tail plumes of extraordinary size. The sociable weaver makes enormous communal nests of grass and straw that can literally cover the crown of a tree and resemble a thatched cottage (other species will perch on the 'thatch' and even build a nest on top). The sparrows come typically in shades of brown and grey; widows are similar while not breeding, but males moult into black plumage with red or yellow highlights when courting. Whydahs are predominantly black with a lighter breast coloration and develop striking tail plumes during courtship. The bishops moult from drab coloration to brilliant reds and yellows – during courtship, a field can have a black and red dot every few metres as males perch on top of stems trying to attract a mate.

**Starlings** At any of the game parks you'll sooner or later see fast-flying flocks of iridescent starlings. Intelligent, opportunistic and adaptable, starlings in Africa have reached the pinnacle of their evolution. Colourful, noisy and gregarious, there are many species, including the glossy starling, the bizarre wattled starling, the red-billed oxpecker (often seen clinging to game, from which they prise parasitic ticks and insects), and the red-winged starlings that hang around the peak of Table Mountain.

**Larks & Pipits** Larks and pipits may not be the most spectacular group of birds, but in Southern Africa they are diverse and, biologically, are significant to the grasslands they inhabit. Many are endemic to the region and for the keen birdwatcher, their identification can pose some real challenges.

**Sunbirds & Sugarbirds** Sunbirds are small, delicate nectar feeders with sharp down-curved bills. The males of most species are brilliantly iridescent while the females are more drab. Sunbirds are commonly seen feeding on the flowers of proteas, etc. The two species of sugarbirds are endemic to the Cape and, while less colourful than their relatives the sunbirds, the males sport long, showy tail feathers.

South Africa

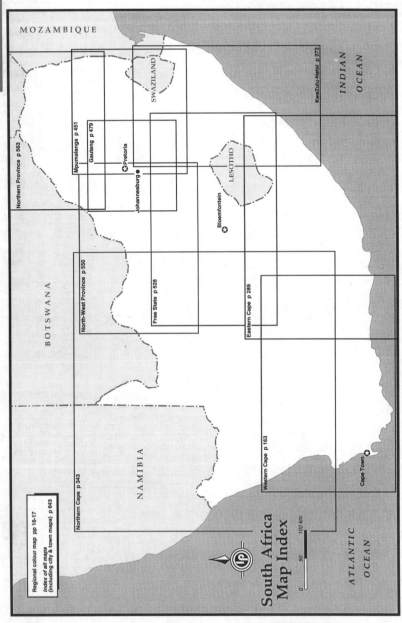

MOZAMBIQUE

INDIAN OCEAN

KwaZulu-Natal p 373

SWAZILAND

Northern Province p 563

Mpumalanga p 451

Gauteng p 479

✪ Pretoria

● Johannesburg

LESOTHO

✪ Bloemfontein

BOTSWANA

North-West Province p 550

Free State p 528

Eastern Cape p 289

NAMIBIA

Northern Cape p 343

Western Cape p 163

✪ Cape Town

Regional colour map pp 16–17
Index of all maps
(including city & town maps) p 643

South Africa
Map Index

ATLANTIC OCEAN

0    50    100 km

# Facts about the Country

## HISTORY
### Aftermath of War

The second Anglo-Boer War ended in May 1902 with the defeat of the Boer republics (the Zuid-Afrikaansche Republiek, or Transvaal, and the Orange Free State). The British had pursued a scorched earth policy to deny the Boer guerrillas supplies, while Boer women and children had been confined to concentration camps. The country was devastated and there was a legacy of enormous bitterness, particularly on the Boer side; 22,000 British, 34,000 Boer and 15,000 black lives had been lost.

The colonial government, under Lord Milner, spent millions of pounds reconstructing the country. Attempts were made to rebuild the Boers' agricultural base, but tens of thousands of Boers, ill-equipped for urban life, flooded into the cities. There they found a world dominated by the English and their language. Worst of all, they were forced to compete for jobs with blacks on an equal footing. Partly as a backlash to this Afrikaans came to be seen as the *volkstaal* (people's language), a symbol of Afrikaner nationhood, and several nationalistic organisations sprang up.

The British realised that reconstruction could only occur in some sort of partnership with the Boers. In 1906/7, the former republics were given representative government, and moves toward union began almost immediately. The pressures were largely economic – the smaller provinces were unsustainable in a world that required integrated economies and infrastructures, proper tax bases and centralised bureaucracies.

The most contentious issue was the question of voter franchise, which varied from colony to colony. Despite a major nationwide campaign by nonwhites, the eventual compromise agreement allowed each colony to retain its existing arrangements, but only whites could be elected to parliament. The only province where nonwhites did have

## SOUTH AFRICA AT A GLANCE

**Area:** 1,220,000 sq km
**Population:** 37.8 million
**Population Growth Rate:** 1.7%
**Capitals:** Pretoria (administrative), Cape Town (legislative), Bloemfontein (judicial)
**Head of State:** President Nelson Mandela
**Official Languages:** Afrikaans, English, isiZulu, isiXhosa, seSotho, seSotho saLebowa, Setswana, Tshivenda, Xitsonga, siSwati, isiNdebele
**Currency:** Rand (R)
**Exchange Rate:** R4.56 = US$1
**Per Capita GNP:** US$2930 (Purchasing power parity: US$4065)
**Literacy:** 82%
**Infant Mortality:** around 5%

## Highlights

- **Cape Town** – best food and nightlife in South Africa; close to Table Mountain, the Cape of Good Hope and the Winelands (page 164)
- **Kruger National Park** – perhaps South Africa's main attraction; a must-see! (page 458)
- **The Drakensberg** – spectacular escarpment on the South Africa-Lesotho border; a magnet for hikers and climbers (page 421)
- **Zulu heartland** – outstanding national parks, glimpses of Zulu culture, and important battlefields (page 401)
- **Transkei** – largely undeveloped region with superb warm-water surf beaches and excellent hiking trails (page 330)

political rights to any meaningful degree was the Cape Province – the franchise was based on a wealth qualification – but even there only 15% of the registered voters were non-white.

## Union of South Africa

The Union of South Africa was established on 31 May 1910. Cape Town was the legislative capital, Pretoria the administrative capital, Bloemfontein the seat of the Supreme Court, and Pietermaritzburg was given financial compensation. The British High Commission Territories of Basutoland (now Lesotho), Bechuanaland (now Botswana) and Swaziland, and Rhodesia (now Zimbabwe) were excluded from the Union.

English and Dutch were made the official languages – Afrikaans was not recognised as the official language until 1925.

The first election was held in September 1910. The South African National Party (soon known as the South African Party, or SAP), a diverse coalition of conciliatory Boer groups under General Louis Botha and the brilliant General Jan Smuts, won the

Louis Botha, member of the South African Party, became the first prime minister in 1910.

election and Botha became the first prime minister.

The most divisive issues were raised by General Barry Hertzog who championed Afrikaner interests, advocated separate development for the two white groups and independence from Britain. He and his supporters formed the National Party (NP).

Soon after the union was established, a barrage of repressive legislation was passed. It became illegal for black workers to strike; skilled jobs were reserved for whites; blacks were barred from military service; and pass laws, restricting black freedom of movement, were tightened.

In 1912, Pixley ka Isaka Seme formed a national democratic organisation to represent blacks. It was initially called the South African Native National Congress, but from 1923, it was known as the African National Congress (ANC).

In 1913 the Natives Land Act set aside 7.5% of South Africa's land for black occupancy. No black African (and they made up more than 70% of the population) was allowed to buy, rent or be a sharecropper outside this area. Thousands of squatters were evicted from farms and forced into increasingly overcrowded and impoverished reserves, or into the cities. Those who remained were reduced to the status of landless labourers.

The main players were on the scene and the foundations for modern apartheid were laid. From the first day of union, race relations would be the major problem facing the country.

## WWI

In 1914 South Africa, as a part of the British Empire, found itself automatically at war with Germany and saddled with the responsibility of dealing with German South West Africa (now Namibia). South Africa's involvement on the British side prompted the last major Afrikaner rebellion – over 300 men were killed. After the war, South West Africa became a part of South Africa under 'mandate' from the League of Nations.

During the war, General Smuts rose to

international prominence, becoming a member of the British War Cabinet (along with his old enemy, Lord Milner) without ever facing a British election. Smuts made an important contribution to the establishment of the League of Nations and perhaps because he, too, had once been defeated in war, he was one of the few who saw the Treaty of Versailles as 'an impossible and wrong peace'. He became South Africa's second prime minister in 1919.

## Fusion
In 1924 the National Party under Hertzog came to power, with an agenda that included promoting Afrikaner interests, independence and racial segregation. In the 1929 election the *swart gevaar* (black threat) was made the dominant issue for the first time, with Hertzog successfully portraying himself and the NP as the champion of the whites and Smuts and the SAP as advocates of racial equality.

In reality, their respective positions were not so far apart and, in 1933, the two parties formed a coalition, with Hertzog as prime minister and Smuts as his deputy. The 'Fusion' or 'Pact' government did not collapse until 1939, and then over the question of South Africa's participation in WWII. Hertzog – who argued for neutrality – was forced to resign in favour of Smuts by the Governor-General.

Fusion had been rejected by Dr DF Malan and his followers. They formed the Purified National Party, which quickly became the dominant force in Afrikaner political life. The Afrikaner Broederbond, a secret Afrikaner brotherhood, became an extraordinarily influential force behind the party and a range of political, cultural and economic organisations designed to promote the *volk* (Afrikaners).

Parity with the English, Hertzog's goal, was no longer enough for the resurgent Afrikaners. At the far right, the Ossewa-Brandwag (Sentinels of the Ox-wagon, or OB) grew into a popular militaristic organisation with strong German sympathies, and an obvious affinity with Hitler's doctrine of

a master race. Elements within the organisation pursued an active policy of sabotaging the South African war effort. Nonetheless, many thousands of South Africans volunteered for military service, and troops fought for the Allies with distinction in North Africa and Italy.

The economy boomed during the war and the black urban population nearly doubled. Enormous squatter camps grew up on the outskirts of Johannesburg and, to a lesser extent, outside the other major cities. Black labour became increasingly important to the burgeoning mining and manufacturing industries. Conditions in the townships were appalling, but poverty was by no means only the province of blacks; wartime surveys found that 40% of white school children were malnourished.

## Apartheid
The National Party fought the 1948 election on the basis of its policy of *apartheid* (literally, the state of being apart). They gained around 40% of the vote and won 70 of the 150 seats. In coalition with the Afrikaner Party, which had won nine seats, they took control. With the help of creative electoral boundaries The National Party held power right up to the first democratic election in 1994.

Malan lost no time in instituting the necessary legal apparatus. Mixed marriages were prohibited. Interracial sex was made illegal. Every individual was classified by race and a classification board was established to rule in questionable cases. The Group Areas Act enforcing the physical separation of residential areas was promulgated. The Separate Amenities Act created separate public facilities – separate beaches, separate buses, separate toilets, separate hospitals, separate schools and separate park benches. The pass laws were further strengthened: blacks were compelled to carry identity documents at all times and were prohibited from remaining in towns, or even visiting them, without specific permission.

Thanks to the Dutch Reformed churches, apartheid was given a religious justification:

SOUTH AFRICA

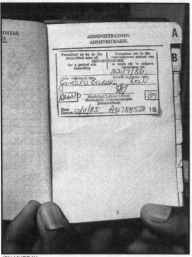

JON MURRAY

The Group Areas Act required blacks to carry a pass book at all times.

the separateness of the races was divinely ordained and the volk had a holy mission to preserve the purity of the white race in its promised land.

Until WWII there was nothing even vaguely unusual about racist attitudes or whites dominating nonwhite people. White South Africans had been, to a large degree, in step with the attitudes of the time. The English, French, Belgian, Dutch and Portuguese all saw the possession of colonies and domination of their indigenous people as their natural right.

Allister Sparks, in *The Mind of South Africa,* argues that the Nazis' excesses created a revulsion towards racism that sparked a revolution in attitudes among whites. The days of guiltless racial domination ended with WWII. However, at the very time the rest of the white world was attempting to abandon old prejudices, and to pack up the old colonial empires and go home, white South Africa moved decisively in the opposite direction. Of course, there was no 'home' to which a 10th-generation Afrikaner could return.

## Black Action

In 1949 the ANC developed a programme of action that for the first time advocated open resistance in the form of strikes, acts of public disobedience and protest marches. These continued intermittently throughout the 1950s, with occasional violent clashes.

In June 1955, at a congress held at Kliptown near Johannesburg, a number of organisations, including the Indian Congress and the ANC, adopted a Freedom Charter. This articulated a vision of a non-racial democratic state and is still central to the ANC's vision of a new South Africa.

### The Broederbond

Conspiracy theorists will love the secretive Broederbond, the Afrikaner organisation behind the National Party governments of the apartheid era. Founded in 1918, the 'band of brothers' was pivotal in the development of apartheid – its members formulated the plan and implemented it from the highest office. Every National Party prime minister and president was a member of the organisation.

At its height in the 1970s it was believed to have 12,000 members in every public institution from the churches to the armed forces, and had founded two universities and helped build many of the country's biggest businesses, as well as controlling Afrikaner cultural groups.

Open by invitation only to male Protestant Afrikaners, it comprised the intellectual elite of teachers, lawyers, journalists, businessmen and senior civil servants. At initiation members are sworn to secrecy and to serve Afrikanerdom.

In the 1980s the Broederbond and the unity of Afrikaner politics began to fracture. One former chairman, Dr Andries Treurnicht, quit the National Party and founded the Conservative Party. Another, Carel Boshoff, founded the conservative Afrikaner Volkswag, and retired to the town of Orania in Northern Cape to live in a whites-only community (where visitors aren't welcome). The Broederbond finally abandoned apartheid in the early 1990s, causing its membership to plummet.

**Richard Plunkett**

## Hendrik Verwoerd – apartheid's main architect

Among the creators of the apartheid system, Hendrik Verwoerd was the National Party leader who implemented it in its most extreme form. When he came to power in 1958, apartheid shifted from being a policy of racial separation and discrimination to one of stripping black South Africans of all the rights of citizenship.

It was Verwoerd who established the Homelands and began the forcible removal of millions to these invariably uneconomic pieces of territory. As Minister of Native Affairs in the National Party governments of DF Malan and JG Strijdom, he had honed his ideas of setting up black puppet states and emptying the other 87% of South Africa of non-whites. Much of the apartheid legislation was his. By 1978, he said, South Africa would be a whites-only country, but for black guestworkers. Among his other policies was bringing black education totally under government control, attempting to nip in the bud any black intelligentsia. He also laid down the laws that black townships would have no civic centres, no businesses bigger than grocery stores, and no public institutions, to encourage blacks to live in tribal Homelands.

An austere, intellectual man, Verwoerd studied psychology in Germany in the 1930s, under the unavoidable influence of the Nazis and their doctrines of racial purity and superiority. He became a leading ideologue in the Broederbond. It's no coincidence that this most extreme of the Afrikaner leaders was not, in fact, an Afrikaner by birth. Born in the Netherlands in 1901, he emigrated with his family to South Africa when he was two years old. It was not until he was in his teens that the family moved to Free State and Verwoerd lived in a solidly Afrikaner environment. Like Hitler, Stalin and Napoleon, the partial outsider became the ultra-nationalist. It was Verwoerd who took South Africa out of the Commonwealth and made it a republic in 1961, fulfilling an Afrikaner dream.

Although Verwoerd was killed on the floor of the Cape Town parliament by a deranged parliamentary messenger in 1966, his apartheid system will take years to be fully unravelled. His son-in-law and widow live in the all-white town of Orania in Northern Cape, which they hope will be the foundations of a new, purely white Afrikaner state. Perhaps the quote that best sums up Verwoerd's dreams for his country was this: 'If South Africa must choose between being poor and white or rich and multiracial, then it must rather choose to be white.'

**Richard Plunkett**

On 21 March 1960 the Pan African Congress (PAC) called for nationwide demonstrations against the hated pass laws. When demonstrators surrounded a police station in Sharpeville (near Vereeniging) police opened fire, killing 69 people and wounding 160. In many domestic and international eyes the struggle had crossed a crucial line – there could no longer be any doubts about the nature of the white regime.

Soon after, the PAC and ANC were banned and the security forces were given the right to detain people indefinitely without trial. Prime Minister Hendrik Verwoerd announced a referendum on whether the country should become a republic, and a slim majority of white voters gave their approval to the change. Verwoerd withdrew from the (British) Commonwealth, and in May 1961 the Republic of South Africa came into existence.

Nelson Mandela became the leader of the underground ANC and Oliver Tambo went abroad to establish the organisation in exile. As increasing numbers of black activists were arrested, the ANC and PAC began a campaign of sabotage through the armed wings of their organisations, respectively Umkhonto we Sizwe (Spear of the Nation; usually known as MK) and Poqo (Pure). In July 1963 Nelson Mandela, along with a number of other ANC and communist leaders, was arrested, charged with fomenting violent revolution and sentenced to life imprisonment.

The time comes in the life of any nation when there remain only two choices: submit or fight. That time has now come to South Africa. We shall not submit and we have no choice but to hit back by all means within our power in defence of our people, our future and our freedom ... Refusal to resort to force has been interpreted by the government as an invitation to use armed force against the people without any fear of reprisals.

**Umkhonto we Sizwe manifesto, 1961**

## The Homelands

Verwoerd was assassinated in parliament in 1966 (there was apparently no political motive) and was succeeded by BJ Vorster,

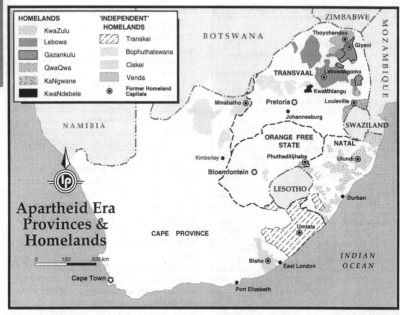

who was followed in 1978 by PW Botha. Both men continued to pursue the insane dream of separate black Homelands and a white South Africa.

The plan was to restrict blacks to Homelands that were, in terms of the propaganda, to become self-sufficient, self-governing states on the traditional lands of particular tribal groups. In reality, these traditional lands had virtually no infrastructure, no industry and were therefore incapable of producing sufficient food for the burgeoning black population. They were based on the land that had been set aside for blacks in the 1913 Natives Lands Act. Under the plan, 13% of the country's total land area was to be the home to 75% of the population.

Irrespective of where they had been born, blacks were divided into one of 10 tribal groups and were made citizens of the Homeland that had been established for their group. Blacks had no rights in South Africa and could not even be present outside their particular Homeland without a pass and explicit permission.

The Homelands policy ignored the fact that in the 19th century, the tribes had been in a complete state of chaos because of the difaqane, and that the ethnological grounds for distinguishing 10 tribal groups were extremely shaky. In the meantime, there had been extremely rapid urbanisation and economic integration – blacks had lived and worked on 'white' land and in 'white' cities for several generations.

Millions of people were forcibly dispossessed and resettled – in particular, the elderly, the unfit, the unemployed, women and children were targeted. Their houses were flattened and they were dumped in Homelands they had often never seen. They were given rations for a limited period, but were expected to be self-sufficient on over-populated countryside that was rapidly exhausted. There was intense, widespread suffering. In particular, families were fractured as the men were forced to return alone to the cities as guest workers without rights.

The crusading government banned the employment of blacks as shop assistants, receptionists, typists and clerks. The construction of housing in the black locations (dormitory suburbs for black workers) was halted, and enormous single-sex hostels were built instead. Despite this, many families returned to the cities as soon as they could. Life was tough in the squatter camps where they were forced to live, but the Homelands were worse.

The Homelands were first given internal self-government, and were then expected to accept a nominal independence. Chief Mangosuthu Buthelezi, who controlled the KwaZulu legislature with the help of his Inkatha movement, attempted to unite the Homeland leaders in resistance to South Africa's ploy.

However, power proved irresistible to the leaders of Transkei, Bophuthatswana, Venda and Ciskei. Between 1976 and 1981 the collaborators accepted 'independence', and then proceeded to crush all resistance to themselves and to the South African government.

### The Frontline States
In 1966 the United Nations began a series of unsuccessful attempts to take over the administration of South West Africa. South Africa's mandate (dating from the end of WWI) was withdrawn and its presence in the country was declared unlawful. South Africa's response was to deploy a large military force against SWAPO (South West Africa People's Organisation), the liberation movement that began a guerrilla war of independence.

After a coup in 1974, Portugal began to withdraw from its African colonies. By 1975 both Angola and Mozambique had become independent and South Africa was confronted by two Marxist-oriented black states sympathetic to the ANC and PAC. In addition, Botswana and Lesotho were also outspoken in their criticism of apartheid and supported black movements.

In 1975 and '76 the South African Defence Force (SADF) made full-scale invasions of Angola both to attack SWAPO bases and to aid UNITA and the FNLA, organisations fighting the Cuba-backed MPLA regime which had seized power. In Mozambique, South Africa supported the rebel Renamo guerrillas against the socialist Frelimo government.

In 1980, after a bitter guerrilla war, Robert Mugabe was elected prime minister of an independent Zimbabwe (formerly Rhodesia) and South Africa found itself the last white-controlled state in Africa. Increasing numbers of western countries imposed sanctions of various kinds and the ANC and PAC received direct support from the governments of black Africa (with the exception of Malawi and Swaziland), many of whom were, in turn, receiving support from communist countries.

South Africa increasingly saw itself as a bastion besieged by communism, atheism and black anarchy. From 1978 to 1988 the SADF made a number of major attacks inside Angola, Mozambique, Zimbabwe, Botswana and Lesotho. These ranged from full-scale deployment in Angola and Namibia to more limited attacks on ANC targets in Lesotho.

In 1988 the formidable SADF suffered its first major reverse at the town of Cuito Cuanavale in Angola, largely due to the intervention of the Cubans and particularly their airforce. The war suddenly began to look very expensive in terms of both lives and material gain and serious negotiations commenced.

Thanks in no small part to Mikhail Gorbachev's new spirit of détente a peace was finally brokered. This opened the way for independence in Namibia. In early 1989 South African troops withdrew from Namibia and Cuban troops withdrew from Angola. An election was held in Namibia under UN auspices and SWAPO won a huge majority. Namibia became independent in 1990.

The SADF was (and still is) the largest and best equipped army in Africa, although it's now called the South African National Defence Force (SANDF). All white males were liable for national service. As a result of arms embargoes, and thanks to Armscor (the government armaments producer), the army became remarkably self-sufficient in supplies and equipment. Thousands of young white South Africans were forced into exile to avoid conscription. Thousands more were scarred mentally and physically by the vicious struggles in Namibia and Angola, or in the townships of South Africa.

## Soweto Uprising

Within South Africa, large-scale violence finally broke out on 16 June 1976 when the Soweto Students' Representative Council organised protests against the use of Afrikaans (regarded as the language of the oppressor) in black schools. Police opened fire on a student march, beginning a round of nationwide demonstrations, strikes, mass arrests and riots that, over the next 12 months, took over 1000 lives.

Steve Biko, the charismatic leader of the Black Consciousness movement, which stressed the need for psychological liberation and black pride, was killed in September 1977. Unidentified security police bashed him until he lapsed into a fatal coma – he went without medical treatment for three days and finally died in Pretoria. At the subsequent inquest, the magistrate found that no one was to blame.

South Africa was never to be the same again – a generation of young blacks committed themselves to a revolutionary struggle against apartheid and the black communities were politicised. World opinion turned decisively against the white regime. The white South Africans, however, were by no means ready to face reality.

PW Botha rewrote the constitution in 1983 and two-thirds of the white population supported the changes. The powers of the state president were increased and three legislative chambers of parliament were created: a House of Assembly for whites, a House of Representatives for coloureds, and a House of Delegates for Indians. Needless to say, the white chamber was larger than the other two put together.

Apart from completely alienating three-quarters of the population (the blacks, who were given no role at all), it was an insanely complicated system. What chamber should control what? Each chamber administered its own education department, the whites controlled black education, and there were education departments within each of the Homelands.

Violent protest built up steadily over the next two years until, in 1985, the government declared a state of emergency which was to stay in force for five years. The media was strictly censored and, by 1988, 30,000 people had been detained without trial. Thousands were tortured. The violence was not only between the United Democratic Front (UDF), which had adopted the ANC's Freedom Charter, and the government, but increasingly between Inkatha and the UDF.

Botha repealed the pass laws, but this failed to mollify the black protesters and also created a white backlash. Dr Andries Treurnicht – Dr No – and his Conservative Party developed into a serious force and a number of neo-Nazi paramilitary groups emerged, notably the frightening Afrikaner-Weerstandsbeweging (AWB). The AWB was

### Soweto Uprisings

Try to see the film *A Dry White Season* (1989), a powerful depiction of the 1976 Soweto uprisings and the vicious reaction by the police state, tacitly condoned by the majority of whites. The role of the *Rand Daily Mail* newspaper as a liberal voice is emphasised – but what the film doesn't show in its 'happy' ending is that the paper was soon to be banned by the government. The film is based on a novel by André Brink. This is, for a Hollywood movie, a remarkably straight telling of an horrific story. The only problem is that for the sake of the story the scale of the events is reduced to a few goodies and baddies. In reality, the detentions, torture and murders involved thousands and thousands of innocent people, mainly blacks but including a few whites. ■

distinctive, both for its swastika lookalike emblem and the demagoguery of its now jailed leader Eugène Terre'Blanche – Eugène White Earth.

Botha's reforms also failed to impress the rest of the world, and economic sanctions began to bite. In particular, foreign banks refused to roll over government loans and the value of the rand collapsed. In late 1989, Botha was replaced by FW De Klerk.

### Reform

At his opening address to the parliament on 2 February 1990, De Klerk announced that he would repeal discriminatory laws and the ANC, PAC and the Communist Party were legalised. Media restrictions were lifted, and De Klerk undertook to release political prisoners not guilty of common-law crimes. On 11 February he released Nelson Mandela, 27 years after he had first been incarcerated. In March, at an occasion that would have been totally unimaginable three years earlier, both men attended the independence celebrations of Namibia.

During 1990 and '91, virtually all the old apartheid regulations were repealed. The Separate Amenities Act, the Group Areas Act (which reserved racially-based residential areas) and the Population Registration Act (classifying people by race) were all swept away.

On 21 December 1991, the Convention for a Democratic South Africa (CODESA) began negotiations on the formation of a multiracial transitional government and a new constitution extending political rights to all groups. The convention was attended by delegates from every major organisation in the country, with the exception of the Conservative Party and other far-right groups like the AWB.

After losing a by-election to the Conservatives, De Klerk showed his shrewdness and political nerve by calling a referendum seeking a mandate for his policies of change. In a result that exceeded the most optimistic predictions, 68.7% of the white electorate gave that mandate and clearly rejected the Conservative Party and its right-wing allies.

As South Africa's last white president, FW De Klerk paved the way for the end of apartheid.

In the cities the vote in favour of reform exceeded 80%; it was much closer in the conservative countryside, especially in the Transvaal and northern Cape, but only one of the 12 electoral districts, Pietersburg in the northern Transvaal, recorded a negative vote.

After nearly 350 years of domination, the great majority of whites had accepted that they could no longer deny equal political and human rights to the nonwhite population. Remarkably, most of the nonwhite population and its leaders seemed to harbour very little bitterness and the ANC consistently emphasised that whites were not in any way 'the enemy'.

The right-wing response to this crushing loss was muted, but with 30% of the white population behind them, fanatical and heavily armed right-wing groups were still a potential threat to reform.

### Township Violence

From the mid-1980s the majority of deaths attributed to political violence were the result of black-on-black violence. The Human Rights Commission estimated that more than 4300 people died in 1993 alone. There were clashes between political rivals, tribal enemies, opportunistic gangsters, and between those who lived in huge migrant-workers' hostels and their township neighbours.

The violence was often characterised as straightforward tribal war between members of the right-wing Zulu-based Inkatha party and left-wing Xhosa-based ANC. Inkatha's leader, Chief Mangosuthu Buthelezi, is a skilful politician who played an ambiguous role fighting for black (particularly Zulu) rights on one hand, but receiving direct financial and military support from the white regime on the other. Buthelezi's fear that his people would be dominated in a new, unitary state controlled by the ANC came close to precipitating civil war several times on the way to the 1994 election. Nevertheless, this view of the township violence is too simple.

The roots of the violence were clearly buried in the years of apartheid. Firstly, there was (and still is) massive economic and social deprivation in the black communities. In some areas over 90% of the population is unemployed, and living conditions for most people are appalling. The government's migrant-worker policies broke up millions of families, and black education and health policies were completely inadequate. Whole generations were brutalised by political and criminal violence.

The enormous single-sex hostels (sometimes housing more than 10,000 men) were often at the centre of the violence. There is a cultural gulf between the educated, urbanised blacks in the township suburbs and those in the hostels, many of whom are recent arrivals from traditional communities in the countryside (where the cult of the warrior survives). During the years of township violence the hostels became virtually ungovernable armed camps inhabited by men who were unemployed, uneducated, and unused to city life in the centre of township suburbs. Violent clashes were hardly surprising, even without the addition of political, cultural and linguistic differences.

There is also clear evidence that sections of the white-controlled security forces were covertly involved in the killing. In addition to sins of commission, including assassinations, there were sins of omission – the forces often appeared unwilling to intervene, especially in cases where Inkatha supporters had been on a rampage.

### Towards Democracy

The CODESA negotiations did not proceed smoothly or easily but it was apparent that both the National Party and the ANC were determined that free elections of some sort would take place. However, thrashing out the details was a complex process and the ANC suspected that the government was committed to drawing it out as long as possible. The political violence that was wracking the country could only hurt the ANC's vote at the election.

In June 1992, 42 men, women and children were massacred in Boipatong, a township south of Johannesburg, allegedly by members of the nearby KwaMadala hostel, controlled by the Inkatha movement. Witnesses in the township and a black police constable consistently alleged that security forces were involved. For the ANC, Boipa-

Chief Buthelezi, leader of the Inkatha Freedom Party.

tong was the final straw, and they withdrew from CODESA.

No longer involved in negotiations, the ANC played its trump card – mass action. Months of strikes and a rekindling of fervour for the struggle among grassroots ANC supporters convinced the government to agree to some of the ANC's demands and the talks resumed. The violence continued to build and non-military white targets were attacked. Chris Hani, the popular secretary general of the Communist Party, was assassinated by right-wingers.

By now the CODESA talks had become a straight negotiation between the National Party and the ANC, excluding the smaller parties. The Zulu-based Inkatha movement (now called the Inkatha Freedom Party – IFP) and some of the Homelands governments left CODESA, demanding a federal structure for the new constitution. Right-wing whites, who wanted a *Volkstaat* (literally, people's state – a Boer homeland), joined them in an unlikely alliance.

With white support drifting to the right-wing parties, the National Party needed to hurry negotiations. Also, it needed to demonstrate that it was not simply handing the country over to the ANC. The Nationals demanded an interim government with power-sharing arrangements and a hand in writing the final version of the constitution. The ANC didn't want the old government to retain any real control after the election, but at the same time it could not afford to frighten the whites. The radical right-wing was as much a threat to the ANC as it was to the Nationals, and it was essential for the economy that as few whites as possible fled the country.

A compromise was reached and both sides accepted an interim government of national unity to rule after the election for no more than five years. They also agreed that the final version of the constitution be written within two years by members of the new parliament to be elected on 26 and 27 April 1994.

The right-wing threat was lessened when the right's most respected leader, General

## The Old South Africa

It's useful to have an idea of how the old South Africa operated, if only to understand some of the quirks you'll find in the new South Africa.

South Africa had a Westminster-style system of government, modified several times, from union in 1910 until 1984, when the constitution was rewritten. The constitution promised to 'uphold Christian values and civilised norms ...'

There were three chambers to the parliament, for coloureds, Indians and whites. Blacks could not vote (most blacks were not considered to be citizens of South Africa). The State President had enormous power, including the power to decide whether an issue was an 'own affair' or a 'general affair'. Own affairs were deliberated by the individual houses and general affairs by all three. That was the theory, anyway. Since the white chamber was larger than the others combined, whites retained control when it counted. In addition, there was the President's Council which had the power to resolve deadlocks, and nearly half the members were nominated by the president.

As a result of the compromises made at the time of union there were three capitals: Pretoria, the administrative capital and capital of the Transvaal; Cape Town, the legislative capital and capital of the Cape Province; Bloemfontein, the judicial capital and capital of the Orange Free State. The only provincial capital to miss out on the action was Pietermaritzburg, the capital of Natal.

There were four provinces: Transvaal (most of Gauteng, Northern Province and Mpumalanga, and part of North-West Province), Natal (now KwaZulu-Natal), the Orange Free State and Cape Province (most of Northern, Eastern and Western Cape provinces). There were once elected provincial assemblies, but after 1986 the provinces were run by authorities appointed by the president.

In addition there were the Homelands, the cornerstones of apartheid. The six 'self-governing Homelands' – Gazankulu, KwaNdebele, KaNgwane, KwaZulu, Lebowa and QwaQwa – had internal self-government. Transkei, Ciskei, Venda and Bophuthatswana were considered by South Africa (but not by the United Nations) to be independent countries. They had their own puppet presidents, armies, border controls and ludicrous trappings such as 'international airports'.

One of the many fringe benefits for white South Africans was that these 'independent countries' weren't bound by South Africa's puritanical laws. A visit to a Homeland casino, to gamble or see a porn movie, became a popular outing. ∎

Constand Viljoen, hastily formed the Freedom Front party and agreed to participate in the election. Viljoen had learned that the right-wing militants were not the inheritors of Boer ideals but a rabble of thugs. Just days before the election, Chief Buthelezi's IFP also agreed to participate.

Two last-minute amendments to the interim constitution help to explain why these holdouts joined in: one enabled the setting-up of a committee to consider the establishment of a Volkstaat and the other allowed future provincial governments to recognise traditional monarchs – by far the most powerful of whom is the Zulu king.

### Free Elections

Across the country at midnight on 26-27 April 1994, *Die Stem* (the old national anthem) was sung and the old flag was lowered. Then the new rainbow flag was raised and the new anthem, *Nkosi Sikelele Afrika* (God Bless Africa) was sung – once, people were jailed for singing this beautiful hymn.

Voting for 'special' voters (mainly the old and disabled) had been held on the 26th, under the eyes of thousands of foreign observers and an equally large foreign press corps. Although there had been a couple of serious bombings by far-right militants, it was clear that the biggest problems when general voting began the next day would be poor organisation and a lack of ballot papers.

This proved to be the case, and the 27th was a day of queues several kilometres long, closed polling stations, and allegations of irregularities. Surprisingly, though, this didn't result in chaos and people generally took the delays in good spirit. That night the army was called in to help print and airlift nine million additional ballot papers and on the 28th voting proceeded more smoothly. The polls were kept open until everyone who wanted to vote had done so, and there was a further day of voting in remote areas in some of the ex-Homelands. Observers agreed that there had been some problems and probably some cheating, but on the whole the election was free and fair. More importantly, the vast majority of South Africans perceived it to be so.

The biggest problems were in KwaZulu-Natal and during the counting process there was considerable behind-the-scenes work (including the juggling of figures) to compensate for logistical and political hitches.

The ANC won 62.7% of the vote, less than the 66.7% which would have enabled it to overrule the interim constitution. However, as the interim constitution is largely the work of the ANC, that isn't a problem, and the public perception that it cannot ride roughshod over the constitution is good for stability. As well as deciding the national government, the election decided the provincial governments, and the ANC won in all but two of the provinces.

The National Party won 20.4% of the vote, enough to guarantee it representation in cabinet. Given that white voters are only 15% of the electorate this is a good result for the party. De Klerk became one of the deputy presidents, beside Thabo Mbeki of the ANC. The Nationals also won the provincial election in Western Cape, thanks to a scare-mongering campaign aimed at the coloured population.

The IFP won 10.5% of the national vote and Chief Buthelezi became Minister for Home Affairs. However, in a dispute over concessions granted before the election, he and the IFP have considered boycotting the National Assembly. The IFP had a decisive victory in the KwaZulu-Natal provincial election, but Buthelezi has had a falling-out with the Zulu royal family, so the domestic politics of the province will remain interesting for some time to come. A return to serious violence is not impossible.

The only other parties to win seats in the National Assembly were the white conservative Freedom Front (2.2%), the mainly white liberal Democratic Party (1.7%), the black hard-line PAC (1.3%) and the African Christian Democratic Party (0.5%).

For the full story of the election, read the excellent book *Election '94 South Africa* edited by Andrew Reynolds (paperback, R40).

## Nelson Rolihlahla Mandela

Nelson Mandela, the son of the third wife of a Xhosa chief, was born on 18 July 1918 in the small village of Mveso on the Mbashe River. When he was very young his family moved to Qunu, south of Umtata. He attended school in the Transkei before going to Johannesburg where, after a few false starts, he undertook legal studies and set up a law practice with Oliver Tambo. He shunned the opportunities offered to educated blacks and adopted a more militant stance, aspiring to help in the liberation of his people.

In 1944 he helped form the youth league of the African National Congress (ANC) with Walter Sisulu and Oliver Tambo. Its aim was to end the racist policies of the white South African government. Mandela took up boxing to keep fit. He met Nomzamo Winnifred Madikizela ('Winnie') who he married after receiving a divorce from his first wife, Evelyn.

In 1964, after establishing the ANC's military wing Umkhonto we Sizwe, he was captured and sentenced to life imprisonment at the infamous Robben Island prison near Cape Town. In the early 1970s rules were sufficiently relaxed to allow Mandela to write his now-famous prison notebooks and teach politics.

Mandela was released from prison in 1990 after the ANC was declared a legal organisation. In 1991 he was elected president of the ANC and began the long negotiations which were to end minority rule. He shared the 1993 Nobel Peace Prize with FW De Klerk and, in the first free elections the following year, was elected president of South Africa.

On 2 May 1994, in front of Coretta Scott King, wife of the late Martin Luther King Jr, he said to his people: 'You have shown such a calm, patient determination to reclaim this country as your own and now the joy that we can loudly proclaim from the rooftops: Free at last! Free at last! I stand before you humbled by your courage, with a heart full of love for all of you. I regard it as the highest honour to lead the ANC at this moment in our history. I am your servant ... this is the time to heal the old wounds and build a new South Africa.'

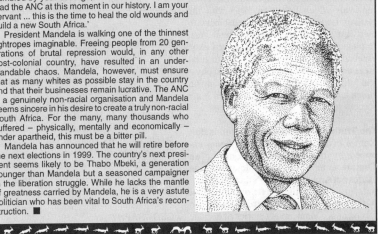

President Mandela is walking one of the thinnest tightropes imaginable. Freeing people from 20 generations of brutal repression would, in any other post-colonial country, have resulted in an understandable chaos. Mandela, however, must ensure that as many whites as possible stay in the country and that their businesses remain lucrative. The ANC is a genuinely non-racial organisation and Mandela seems sincere in his desire to create a truly non-racial South Africa. For the many, many thousands who suffered – physically, mentally and economically – under apartheid, this must be a bitter pill.

Mandela has announced that he will retire before the next elections in 1999. The country's next president seems likely to be Thabo Mbeki, a generation younger than Mandela but a seasoned campaigner in the liberation struggle. While he lacks the mantle of greatness carried by Mandela, he is a very astute politician who has been vital to South Africa's reconstruction. ∎

## The New South Africa

Despite the scars of the past and the enormous problems ahead, South Africa today is an immeasurably more optimistic and relaxed country than it was a few years ago. (For the majority, that is. Many in the white minority seem to have forgotten how terrified they were of godless 'miscegenation' or being overrun by Communist savages, and consider that the high crime rate is the worst fate that could befall a nation.) New and old arts and cultures, long denigrated, are flowering. There is a lot of catching up to do and the next few years will be very exciting.

The people of South Africa seem to have invented a political structure strong enough to hold together the diverse cultures of the country, although whether it is flexible enough to allow each group to fulfil its legitimate aspirations remains to be seen.

Economic inequality remains a thorny problem. Although the apartheid system is dead, economic apartheid lives on, despite affirmative-action programmes. With an economy geared to low wages and a legacy of very poor education for blacks, it will be a generation at least before the majority gain much economic benefit from their freedom. As a traveller you'll notice just how little black involvement there is in the economy. Chances are that the only black-owned business you will deal with is a minibus taxi company.

**Land Reform** The most important piece of legislation passed in the first session of the new parliament was the Land Rights Bill. It sets out to reverse (or compensate) the forced removals which began in 1913 with the Natives Lands Act that allowed blacks to own just 13% of the country's total area. Implementing the bill has not proved easy, especially as many landless blacks in rural areas are still subject to economic and physical intimidation by white farmers living on stolen land. However, there have been some success stories.

**The Truth & Reconciliation Commission** Crimes of the apartheid era are being exposed by the Truth & Reconciliation Commission. This admirable institution carries out Archbishop Tutu's dictum, 'Without forgiveness there is no future, but without confession there can be no forgiveness'. Many, many stories of horrific brutality and injustice have been heard by the commission over the past few years, offering some cathartic relief to people and communities still shattered by their past.

The commission operates by allowing victims to tell their stories and perpetrators to confess their guilt – and thus escape punishment for their crimes. Those who choose not to appear before the commission will face criminal prosecution if their guilt can be proven, and that's the problem. Although some soldiers, police and 'ordinary' citizens

Archbishop Desmond Tutu was a major force behind raising international opposition to the South African government.

have confessed their crimes, it seems unlikely that the human rights criminals who gave the orders and dictated the policies will appear, and it has proven difficult gathering evidence against them.

Some reject even the idea of the Truth Commission. In June 1997, the leader of the neo-Nazi AWB, Eugène Terre'Blanche, was sentenced to six years in jail for trying to murder one black man and assaulting another. Several dozen rightwingers turned up at the Johannesburg court wearing khaki to show support for their leader.

**GEOGRAPHY**
South Africa is divided into nine provinces: Gauteng, Northern, Mpumalanga, Free State, KwaZulu-Natal, North-West, Northern Cape, Eastern Cape and Western Cape.

Most of these provinces were formed during the run-up to the 1994 election and were carved from the old provinces of Cape, Transvaal, Orange Free State and Natal. Some of the new provinces changed their names after 1994 (eg, Eastern Transvaal became Mpumalanga) and it's possible that others will do so.

The Homelands no longer exist as political entities, but because of their very different histories and economies it will be some time before you don't notice a marked change when you cross one of the old borders. In this guide we sometimes refer to the old Homelands by name. Transkei and Ciskei have been absorbed into Eastern Cape (a small chunk of Transkei has been claimed by KwaZulu-Natal), Venda into Northern Province, and Bophuthatswana into the North-West (Thaba 'Nchu, an isolated chunk of Bop, is in Free State). The smaller Homelands (Gazankulu, Lebowa, KaNgwane, KwaNdebele, KwaZulu and QwaQwa), which were regarded as self-governing rather than independent countries by the apartheid regime, have been more easily reabsorbed into the surrounding provinces.

Pretoria and Cape Town are locked in a struggle for the status of legislative capital. Pretoria points out that it is ridiculous to have the parliament so far from the public servants, and that within 200km of the city is 27% of the country's population, most of the country's 11 official languages are spoken, there are 14 airports and so on. However, Cape Town could well retain the parliament. The country's real, unofficial capital has always been Johannesburg. It lies at the centre of an enormous urban conurbation known as the PWV (Pretoria, Witwatersrand, Vereeniging – now Gauteng Province). It is the largest, richest and most important city in the country.

The provincial capitals are: Johannesburg (Gauteng), Pietersburg/Polokwane (Northern Province), Nelspruit (Mpumalanga), Mafikeng (North-West Province), Bloemfontein (Free State), Kimberley (Northern Cape), Cape Town (Western Cape), Bisho (Eastern Cape) and Pietermaritzburg (KwaZulu-Natal).

South Africa is a big country, nearly 2000km from the Limpopo River in the north to Cape Agulhas in the south, and nearly 1500km from Port Nolloth in the west to Durban in the east. It's mostly dry and sunny, lying just to the south of the Tropic of Capricorn – Sydney, Australia, is almost the same latitude as Cape Town, and Brisbane, Australia, is about the same as Johannesburg. The major influence on the climate, however, is not latitude, but topography and the surrounding oceans.

The country can be divided into three major parts: the vast interior plateau (the highveld), the narrow coastal plain, (the lowveld) and the Kalahari Basin. In the east of the country the divide between the highveld and lowveld is marked by dramatic escarpments, notable the Drakensberg. Although Johannesburg is not far south of the tropics, its altitude, around 1700m above sea level, and its distance from the sea moderates its climate. It is 1500km further north than Cape Town, but its average temperatures are only 1°C higher.

The cold, nutrient-rich Benguela current from the Antarctic runs north up the west coast, lowering temperatures and severely limiting rainfall. The warm Agulhas current from the tropical Indian Ocean runs south down the east coast. Durban is an average 6°C warmer than Port Nolloth and receives 16 times more rain (1000mm), although they are on much the same latitude.

## CLIMATE

The eastern plateau region (including Johannesburg) has a dry, sunny climate in winter with maximum temperatures around 20°C and crisp nights, with temperatures dropping to around 5°C. Between October and April there are late-afternoon showers often accompanied by spectacular thunder and lightning, but it rarely gets unpleasantly hot. Heavy hailstorms cause quite a lot of damage each year. It can, however, get very hot in the Karoo (the semi-desert heart of all three Cape provinces) and the far north (the Kalahari).

The Western Cape has dry sunny summers with maximum temperatures around 26°C. It is often windy, however, and the southeasterly 'Cape Doctor' can reach gale force. Winters can get cold, with average minimum temperatures of around 5°C, and maximum temperatures of around 17°C, with occasional snow on the higher peaks.

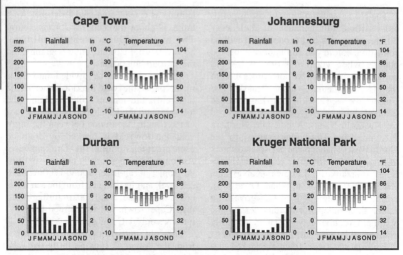

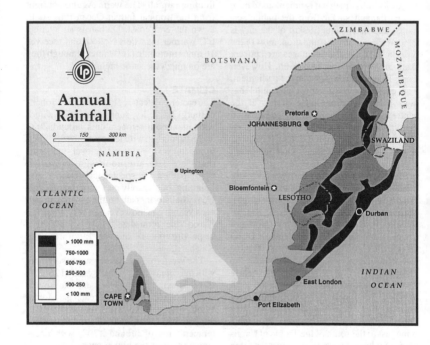

The coast north from the Cape becomes progressively drier and hotter. Along the south coast the weather is temperate, but the east coast becomes increasingly tropical the further north you go. The Transkei region of Eastern Cape and KwaZulu-Natal can be hot and unpleasantly humid in summer, although the highlands are still pleasant; this is a summer rainfall area. The Mpumalanga and Northern Province lowveld gets very hot in summer, when there are spectacular storms. In winter the days are sunny and warm.

## GOVERNMENT

The new constitution, which was passed into law in 1996 (from 1994 until then an interim constitution was in place), is one of the most enlightened in the world – not surprising when you consider the long struggle for freedom. Among the many Fundamental Rights proclaimed is the right not to be discriminated against on any grounds and 'in particular: race, gender, sex, ethnic or social origin, colour, sexual orientation, age, disability, religion, conscience, belief, culture or language'. That must cover just about everything except shoe size. There has been some whining that the constitution gives too much protection to 'criminals' – once again, this isn't surprising considering the massive abuse of the legal system by the apartheid regime, and the fact that many members of the government endured this abuse, notably one Nelson Mandela.

The constitution gives an amnesty for political crimes committed between 8 October 1990 and 6 December 1993.

There are two houses of parliament: a National Assembly of 400 members and a Senate of 90 members. Members of the National Assembly are elected directly (using the proportional representation method – there are no constituencies) but members of the Senate are appointed by the provincial legislatures. Each province, regardless of its size, appoints 10 senators.

The head of state is the president, currently Nelson Mandela. The president is elected by the National Assembly (and thus will always be the leader of the majority party) rather than directly by the people. A South African president has more in common with a Westminster system prime minister than a US president, although as head of state he/she does have some executive powers denied most prime ministers.

The government which was formed after the 1994 elections was a government of national unity, with some power-sharing arrangements. Each party winning more than 5% of the vote for the National Assembly (the IFP, NP and ANC) was entitled to proportional representation in Cabinet, and Cabinet decisions are supposed to be reached by consensus. However, the NP has withdrawn from the government to concentrate on learning to be an opposition party (something which doesn't come naturally to it, and it shows) and the IFP can't make up its mind whether it wants to be in or out.

There are also provincial legislatures, with memberships varying according to population: Northern Cape is the smallest with 30 members, Gauteng the largest with 86. Each province has a premier. Provincial governments have strictly limited powers and are bound by the national constitution.

In addition to the western-style democratic system there is a system of traditional leaders: a Council of Traditional Leaders, to which all legislation pertaining to indigenous law, traditions or customs must be referred. Although the Council cannot veto or amend legislation it can delay its passage. In each province where there have been recognised traditional authorities (every province except Gauteng, Western Cape and Northern Cape), a House of Traditional Leaders will be established, with similar powers to the Council. These houses will be controversial, as 'recognised traditional authorities' could include those which were created by the various white governments, and which usually encouraged blacks to reject the ANC and other liberation organisations.

An amendment to the constitution passed just two days before the 1994 election allows provincial legislatures to 'provide for the institution, role, authority and status of a traditional monarch'. This applies mainly to the powerful Zulu king and might be a can of worms waiting to be opened.

Meanwhile, democracy is alive and very well. Members of the new parliament who also served in the old parliament are amazed that ANC members ask ministers tricky questions, and that ANC members of parliamentary committees query legislation and actually refer it back to the people for their input. You might be told that the government has suffered many scandals since coming to power, but take this with a grain of salt. Remember that South Africans are not used to a free press, an accountable government, and dissent which doesn't court jail or a bullet.

South Africa has rejoined the Commonwealth.

## ECONOMY

South Africa's economy is a mixture of First and Third World with a marked disparity in incomes, standards of living, lifestyles, education and work opportunities. On one hand there is a modern industrialised and urban economy; on the other there is a subsistence agricultural economy little changed from the 19th century.

While there is tremendous poverty, on an African scale the economy is not only reasonably successful, but it dwarfs all the other economies on the continent. The success is based, to a large degree, on tremendous natural wealth and an abundance of low-paid black labour.

South Africa accounts for 50% of electricity produced in Africa, 40% of the continent's industrial output, 45% of mining production, and is also the largest agricultural exporter by a wide margin.

Within South Africa, wealth is further concentrated in Gauteng, which, it is claimed, accounts for about 65% of the country's gross domestic product (GDP) and no less than 25% of the entire continent's gross product.

South Africa has a well-developed infrastructure with a good road and rail system linking the interior of the country, and the wider region, with a number of modern ports. There is tremendous potential for the

### Legal System

South Africa's legal system is a blend of the Roman-Dutch and British systems. The British influence is seen most strongly in criminal justice procedures. Cases are tried by magistrates or judges without juries, at the instigation of police 'dockets' or private actions. Clients are represented by solicitors (prokureurs in Afrikaans) and advocates (advokates – the equivalent of barristers).

Magistrates (landdrost) in Afrikaans) were first appointed while the colony was under VOC rule, and they were essentially governors of their areas. Drostdys, the homes and offices of the landdrost, are today some of the earliest and most impressive buildings in the country. The Drostdy Museum at Swellendam (Western Cape) and the various Drostdy buildings in Graaff Reinet (Eastern Cape) are among the best examples.

Unlike a British magistrate, whose decisions are partially influenced by the values of the local community, the landdrost was a company and later government official responsible for enforcing policy rather than dispensing an abstract justice. This notion persisted, and until the new constitution came into force in 1994 the judicial system was subservient to the government, in particular the State President, resulting in some politicised decisions.

Now, the highest power in the land is the constitution, which is interpreted and enforced by the new Constitutional Court. Choosing the members of the court was one of the most crucial post-election tasks for the new South Africa. Although women are under-represented (so what's new?), the court is generally accepted as an eminent and impartial body.

The Constitutional Court's independence was demonstrated in 1995 when it decided that capital punishment was unconstitutional and banned it. This was despite a large majority of South Africans being in favour of capital punishment (more than 100 people were hanged each year throughout the 1980s). With one of the world's most enlightened constitutions and a court willing and able to defend it, the legal system will be a major factor in ensuring the success of the new South Africa. ∎

### Executive Outcomes

Since the end of sanctions, South Africa's most notorious export has been Executive Outcomes, the mercenary company which specialises in securing valuable mining areas for governments plagued by rebels.

Based in Pretoria, Executive Outcomes is headed by South African Defence Force veteran Eeben Barlow. Most of the company's employees are veterans of the wars in Namibia and Angola, including members of the feared Koevoet units. With thousands of soldiers with experience in bush warfare being laid off from the armed forces, South Africa has become a recruitment ground for mercenaries.

Executive Outcomes has been most active in Sierra Leone and Angola. In Sierra Leone they took control of territory around the Kono diamond field in the country's east for the government of Captain Valentine Strasser, allegedly being paid with a share of profits from the mine. Some reports note that the locals were grateful to Executive Outcomes for bringing peace to the area, protecting them both from the rebels and the army.

In Angola, the company fought for the former enemies of the SADF, the MPLA government of Jose Eduardo Dos Santos, against the former South African client Jonas Savimbi and his UNITA forces. That's business. The company secured the vital diamond mines in the north of country, although there are allegations of massacres of villagers found to be inconveniently in the way.

The company also inadvertently sparked a political upheaval in distant Papua New Guinea in 1997. They were hired by the government of Prime Minister Sir Julius Chan to go to work against the rebels of the Bougainville Revolutionary Army, who have kept the valuable Panguna copper mine closed for more than 10 years. The PNG Defence Force resented the government's US$24m contract and forced the prime minister to resign. Executive Outcomes departed in a hurry and left tonnes of military hardware, which turned out to be second-rate at best and barely useable.

But Executive Outcomes is only one small facet of South Africa's businesses going international with the end of sanctions. From modern supermarkets in Zambia, to Tanzanian breweries, to Afrikaner farmers taking up huge tracts of land in Mozambique's Niassa province, Africa's biggest economy is making its influence felt in neighbouring countries especially. Executive Outcomes itself is part of a group of companies which invests in mining, water supplies and other more peaceful ventures across Africa.

**Richard Plunkett**

economy to facilitate development in the rest of Southern Africa. Wars and trade sanctions have seriously hampered the whole region, and both by virtue of its wealth and its infrastructure, South Africa holds the key to its recovery.

Until the discovery of diamonds at Kimberley (1869) and the gold reef on the Witwatersrand (1886) the economy was exclusively agricultural. Since then, mineral wealth has been the key to development. Mining remains central to the economy, and South Africa is the world's leading supplier of gold, chromium, manganese, vanadium and platinum. Mining accounts for over 70% of exports and 13% of GDP. The manufacturing industry grew rapidly during and after WWII, mostly to meet local demand. Oddly, it was the aggressively anti-socialist apartheid governments which instituted massive state ownership of industry, and it is the quasi-socialist ANC government which is privatising industry.

Previous governments successfully sought, through involvement in the economy, to redirect wealth into Afrikaner hands. The private sector is highly centralised and is dominated by the enormous, interrelated De Beers and Anglo-American corporations. Their combined stockmarket capitalisation is over four times greater than their nearest competition.

Towards the end of white minority rule, international sanctions bit deeper, and black mass action also destabilised the economy. Add to that a general world economic downturn and a serious drought, and the economy was in serious trouble. The country faced an annual inflation rate running at around 15% and unemployment was rising.

Both inflation and massive unemployment remain problems. Moreover, even if the economy recovers to its boom-time peak, almost the only people to immediately benefit will be whites. Blacks in South Africa have never shared in the fruits of their labour and it will be very difficult for the government to ensure that they do so in future. The economy is still geared to a limitless pool of black labour paid Third World rates, and restructuring will be a long and slow process.

Some of the proposed changes seem to miss the point. For example, most domestic workers (ie, maids) are paid just R400 a month. It has been suggested that a domestic workers' training course be established, with the graduates commanding wages of R800 to R1000 a month. Sure, the wages might more than double but they would still be pathetic and a system of gross inequality amounting to servitude would still be in place.

It's still disturbingly common for whites to justify low black wages by saying, 'the black man doesn't have the same expenses as the white man'. True, a house in Soweto doesn't cost as much as a house in Sandton, but so what? In many counties similar arguments were once used to justify lower wages for women performing the same jobs as men. On the other hand, some white liberals see themselves as performing a social service by employing maids. Buying a pension plan for a maid is seen as an enlightened thing to do – the idea that the maid might earn a living wage so that she can make her own decisions is still an alien one. There is a long way to go.

The challenges the whites face are not dissimilar to those facing the rest of the First World. Is it ever possible to justify gross economic inequality that is based on race or nationality? Can, for instance, a Californian defend their wealth to a Mexican (who by a stroke of fate was born a mile south of an arbitrary border), or for that matter, an Australian justify their wealth to an Indonesian?

The difference for South Africa is that these questions must be dealt with and solved within the country itself. The government must find a way to both create and redistribute wealth without alienating the white community, foreign investors or the majority of poverty-stricken people.

Apart from travelling in minibus taxis and maybe taking a township tour, there is practically no situation (except for donating to beggars) where your money goes directly to the poorest people. Even your R30 for a hostel bunk contributes only a few cents to the wages of the black staff.

## POPULATION & PEOPLE

Of the population of 37.9 million, some 27.9 million are black, 5.6 million white, 3.4 million coloured (ie, mixed race) and 1 million of Indian descent. Some 60% of the whites are of Afrikaner descent and most of the rest are of British descent. There are reported to be several million illegal African immigrants as well, mostly in Gauteng.

Most of the 'coloured' population lives in Northern and Western Cape provinces. Most South Africans of Indian descent live in KwaZulu-Natal.

The former Transvaal (now divided into

---

### Enforcing Law & Order

The police force has been reorganised and for most people a police car is no longer a sign of very bad trouble approaching. In Soweto, I saw a police car pull up outside a guy's house, and the white officer got out, not bothering to put on his cap or remove his cigarette, but making sure his pistol-grip shotgun was handy. The householder walked down his drive, arms spread in greeting, beaming and saying, 'Welcome the South African police'. A wise precaution? Taking the piss? Maybe a little each way.

In the first months of the new South Africa the police had trouble winning prosecutions in the courts. It seems that they were not used to ideas such as the rules of evidence, and 'confessions' were much harder to come by.

Newspapers carried the all-too-familiar pictures of mainly white police firing into a crowd of mainly black protesters the day after a demonstration in Cape Town turned nasty. Someone pointed out that this wasn't compatible with the new South Africa, and that in other countries police used shields and batons to disperse crowds – perhaps the police should look into acquiring some. It was then discovered that the police had owned riot control gear for years but had never bothered to use it, preferring shotguns.

Public attitudes to violence are also a little warped. The morning after striking security guards held a demonstration in the centre of Johannesburg, firing their guns in the air and (maybe) at police, smashing up shops and looting, the newspapers carried the story on the front page. But it wasn't the main story. The big headlines read 'Bus Chaos in City', because there had also been a (peaceful) bus drivers' strike. ■

## Dealing With Racism

In its 1986 confession of the sin of apartheid, the General Synod of the Dutch Reformed Church defined racism:

*'Whoever in theory or by attitude and deed implies that one race, people, or group of people is inherently superior, or one group of people is inherently inferior, is guilty of racism. Racism is a sin which tends to take on collective and structural forms. As a moral aberration it deprives a human being of his dignity, his obligations and his rights. It must be rejected and opposed in all its manifestations because it leads to oppression and exploitation.'*

Not a bad definition (if sexist). In this book we make use of the old apartheid terms: white, black, coloured and Asian. We thought hard before including them, because this does in some ways perpetuate the offensive notion that skin colour is a useful or accurate distinguishing characteristic. By using these terms are we not implicitly validating a racist philosophy? Perhaps this is true to an extent, but it is impossible to pretend that these distinctions have disappeared from South Africa. It is also true that many non-racists proudly identify themselves with one or other of these groups.

The bottom line is that we have no problem with someone arguing there are cultural differences (based on language, shared beliefs, ancestry, place of birth, tribe, political belief, or religion) which sometimes correlate to some degree with skin colour. We do have a problem if these generalisations do not allow for the existence of numerous individual exceptions, or if they are used to justify inequality, intolerance or pre-judgement.

Visitors to South Africa will find that although the apartheid regime has been dismantled, cultural apartheid still exists. To an extent, discrimination based on wealth is replacing that based on race (so most visitors will automatically gain high status) but there are plenty of people (mainly whites) who sincerely believe that a different skin colour means a different mindset. A few believe it means inferiority.

If you aren't white, many white South Africans will register it, even if they don't do anything about it. This constant awareness of race as an issue, even if it doesn't result in problems, is one constantly annoying feature of travel in South Africa, whatever your skin colour.

Racial discrimination is illegal in South Africa but it's unlikely that the over-worked and under-resourced police force will be interested in most complaints. Tourism authorities are likely to be more sensitive. One or two travellers have complained about not being admitted to caravan parks or B&Bs in rural areas. This is definitely not common but it can happen. If you think that racism has been displayed by any of the places mentioned in this book, please let us know.

**White** If your skin colour is white, it will be assumed by most white South Africans that you are essentially the same as them, although perhaps brainwashed by anti-apartheid propaganda. In many ways people from developed countries (whatever their skin colour) lead similar lives to white South Africans but there are some very important differences. For a start, if you've saved for your trip by, say, cleaning offices or working in a petrol station, you will get some startled reactions from whites. And don't offer to help wash the dishes. Non-white South Africans might view you with suspicion but usually this vanishes when they find out that you aren't South African.

**African** If you are of African descent, you will probably find some white resentment at your obvious economic status. Also, black South Africans were lowest on racism's ladder and the lies taught about them will take some time to wear off. On the other hand, do not assume a special bond with black South Africans. The various indigenous peoples of South Africa form distinct and sometimes antagonistic cultural groups. Pan-Africanism is a force in politics here, but not the dominant force. There's no special reason (other than an interest in strangers) why someone from France or the USA will receive a warmer welcome than a trader from Ghana or an illegal immigrant from Mozambique.

**East Asian** East Asians were a problem for apartheid – Japanese were granted 'honorary white' status, and people from other East Asian countries are probably indistinguishable from Japanese to insular South Africans. Grossly inaccurate stereotyping and cultural ignorance will probably be the main annoyances you will face.

**Indian** Indians in South Africa were discriminated against by the whites and were seen as collaborators by the blacks. If you are of Indian descent this could mean some low-level antagonism.

**Anyone Else?** People who didn't fit easily into one of the above categories were lumped together as 'coloured'. In some ways the coloureds were treated better than the blacks but they were perhaps despised more – the macho apartheid culture gave some respect to African warrior cultures. ■

Gauteng, Northern Province, Mpumalanga and much of North-West Province) and Free State are the Afrikaner heartlands. People of British origin are concentrated in KwaZulu-Natal and Western and Eastern Cape.

The Homelands system was based on the white wishful thinking that the various black groups had areas to which they belonged and where most of them lived – and if they didn't live there they would be 'assisted' to do so. There are places of historical and traditional importance to the different peoples, but you will find blacks from all groups and tribes throughout South Africa.

Although the Homelands no longer have any political meaning and were never realistic indicators of the area's cultural diversity, it's useful to have some idea of where the Homelands were and who lived (and still live) in them. The Homelands and their peoples were:

Bophuthatswana – Tswana
Ciskei – Xhosa
Gazankulu – Tsonga
KwaNdebele – Ndebele
KwaNgwane – Swazi
KwaZulu – Zulu
Lebowa – Lobedu (Pedi)
QwaQwa – southern Sotho
Transkei – Xhosa
Venda – VhaVenda

Zulus are the largest group in the region (seven million), followed by the Xhosa (six million) and the various northern Sotho peoples, most of whom are Tswana. The smallest group are the VhaVenda (500,000).

## ARTS & CULTURE

For information on traditional cultures, black and white, see the Facts about the Region chapter. The Books section in the regional Facts for the Visitor chapter suggests some South African literature.

Although South Africa is home to a great diversity of cultures, most were suppressed during the apartheid years. To an extent, the Homelands kept alive some of the traditional cultures but in a static form. The day-to-day

realities of traditional and contemporary cultures were ignored, trivialised or destroyed. The most striking example of this was the bulldozing of both District Six, a vibrant multicultural area in Cape Town, and Johannesburg's Sophiatown, where internationally famous musicians learned their craft in an area once described as 'a skeleton with a permanent grin'.

Many artists, black and white, were involved in the anti-apartheid campaign and some were banned. In a society where you could be jailed for owning a painting deemed politically incorrect, serious art was forced underground and blandness ruled in the galleries and theatres. Many people asked themselves whether it was ethically possible to produce art in such circumstances. For an overview of South African art during these bad times, see *Resistance Art in South Africa* by Sue Williamson (paperback, R97).

It will take time for the damage to be undone, but there are hopeful signs. Many galleries are holding retrospectives of black artists, contemporary and traditional, and musicians from around Africa perform in major festivals.

Jazz was about the only medium in which blacks and whites could interact on equal terms, and it remains tremendously important. Theatre was also important for blacks, as an art form and also as a means of getting the political message across to illiterate comrades. Johannesburg's Market Theatre was and is the most important venue in the country.

One of the most exciting aspects of the new South Africa is that the country is in the process of reinventing itself and, with such a large proportion of the population marginalised from the economic mainstream, this is occurring without much input from professional image makers. The new South Africa is being created on the streets of the townships and the cities.

## NATIONAL PARKS & RESERVES

National parks and reserves are probably South Africa's premier attraction, generally much more interesting than the towns and

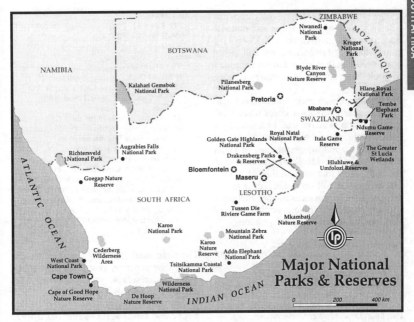

Major National
Parks & Reserves

cities. The scenery is spectacular, the fauna
and flora are abundant and the prices are
extremely reasonable.

In addition to the South African National
Parks Board, the various provinces also have
conservation bodies. In fact, the provinces
control wilderness areas that are sometimes
larger and more spectacular than the better
known national parks. Unless otherwise
indicated, however, the following parks all
fall under the control of the National Parks
Board. Please note that only a small selection
of South Africa's national parks is listed
here.

A useful book is Chris & Tilde Stuart's
*Guide to Southern African Game & Nature
Reserves* published by Struik in South Africa.

Many of the Homelands once had their
equivalents of the National Parks Board and
with several of the old provinces now split
into smaller provinces, the jurisdiction of the
various bodies is in a state of flux. The
National Parks Board wants to take over

control of some of the provincial parks but
the provinces are resisting. It's probable that
some of the contact addresses for parks listed
here will change.

In many national parks (mainly those with
dangerous animals), visitors are confined to
vehicles. If you don't have a car the best way
both to get to and around the parks is to rent
a vehicle (4WD is not necessary). If the cost
is shared among a group it need not be high,
and probably lower than the cost of taking a
bus tour. The quality of the infrastructure and
information is high so you don't need a
guide.

If you do want to do overnight walks in
any of the other parks or reserves, it is necessary to get permits from the appropriate
authorities in advance, and you are nearly
always restricted to official camp sites or
huts. There's no wandering off with a pack
on your back whenever you feel like it. Book
well in advance – preferably before you
leave home.

The national parks all have rest camps that offer a variety of good-value accommodation, from cottages to camp sites. Most of the camps have restaurants, shops and petrol pumps. Although it is not usually necessary to book camp sites, it is necessary to book cottages.

The entrances to parks and reserves generally close around sunset; check if you think you are going to arrive late. Listed here are some of the main booking addresses; for others see the following summary of major parks and the individual park entries later in the book. Note that some of the old provincial offices are still operating, some aren't. Expect the new provinces to open their own offices; check with Satour or the National Parks Board for the latest information.

South African National Parks Board
PO Box 787, Pretoria 0001 (☎ (012) 343 1991; fax 343 0905); Foreign Desk & Group Bookings (☎ (012) 343 2007; fax 343 2006)
PO Box 7400, Rogge Bay, Cape Town 8012 (☎ (021) 22 2810; fax 24 6211)
www.africa.com/venture/saparks/index.htm
Free State, Dept of Nature Conservation
PO Box 517, Bloemfontein 9300 (☎ (051) 70511)

**Too Many Elephants**

Unlike most other African countries, South Africa's problem is that it has too many elephants, and they are increasing in number every year. Elephants in the national parks are culled, despite protests from environmentalists who feel that there should be better ways of controlling the population than killing 'surplus' animals. The culled elephants present another problem: what is to be done with their tusks?

South Africa doesn't sell ivory, but there is pressure to do so. Selling the stockpiles would raise much-needed cash to help conservation projects. However, it can be argued that even legal and responsible ivory sales would encourage poachers who are destroying elephant herds elsewhere in Africa.

How could you be sure that the ivory you bought really came from a culled South African elephant? If your country relaxed its complete ban on importing ivory to allow sales of South African ivory, would its ability to stop the importation of illegal ivory be compromised? ■

Natal Parks Board
PO Box 662, Pietermaritzburg (☎ (0331) 47 1981; fax 47 1980)
www.npb.co.za
Cape Nature Conservation
This organisation controlled all nature reserves in the old Cape Province. It will probably retain control of the Western Cape reserves. PO Box X9086, Cape Town (☎ (021) 483 4085)
Eastern Cape
The provincial parks in the three regions which comprise Eastern Cape are officially controlled by Eastern Cape Tourism, but in reality there are, for the moment at least, several semi-autonomous bodies. For parks in the old Ciskei area contact Eastern Cape Tourism, PO Box 186, Bisho, Eastern Cape Province (☎ (0401) 95 2115; fax 92 765); for parks in the old Transkei area contact the Department of Agriculture & Forestry (☎ (0471) 31 2712) in Umtata; for the rest of the province contact (☎ (041) 55 7761) in Port Elizabeth.

There are many private game reserves and while they generally cost more than public parks and reserves, you can usually get closer to the animals. Before deciding which private reserve to visit, it's worth contacting a specialist travel agent to find out if there are any special deals going. Pathfinders Travel (☎ (011) 453 1113/4; fax 453 1483), Senderwood Square, 17 Chaucer Ave, Bedfordview, Johannesburg, is very helpful. After hours contact Annemarie Berger (☎ /fax (011) 706 6629).

We still haven't got the reserve system figured out. Actual national parks are few and no camping is permitted at most nature reserves, which may be private, municipal or other; private landholders have trails and accommodation available at a price. Many hikes, and all or any length, have to be booked and paid in advance (a risk as the climate is not the best down south). For the most part camping will be in municipal and private parks. Municipalities do quite a lot, having wildflower reserves, bird observations, and hiking trails as well as information centres, but this seems likely to be curtailed (no money), just when the country is being swamped with tourists.

**Noel Gross**

### Western Cape Province

**Bontebok National Park** Proclaimed to protect the last herds of bontebok, a beautiful antelope unique to the Cape provinces, the park is only small. It is just south of Swellendam.

**Cape of Good Hope Nature Reserve** The reserve protects a dramatic coastline and some of the best examples of fynbos, the unique Cape floral kingdom. There are numerous walks, a number of beaches (there's 40km of coast within the reserve), hard-to-spot eland, bontebok, rhebok, grysbok and abundant bird life.

**Cederberg Wilderness** The Cederberg Wilderness, administered by Cape Nature Conservation, is 71,000 hectares of rugged valleys and peaks (up to 2000m), characterised by extraordinary sandstone formations. The vegetation is predominantly mountain fynbos, and includes the rare Clanwilliam cedar. Mammals include the baboon, rhebok, klipspringer and predators like the honey badger and caracal. There are extensive walks, and the nearest major town is Clanwilliam.

**De Hoop Nature Reserve** De Hoop includes a scenic coastline with lonely stretches of beach, rocky cliffs, large coastal sand dunes, a freshwater lake and the Potberg mountain range. This is one of the best places to see both mountain and lowland fynbos. Fauna includes the Cape mountain zebra, bontebok and a wealth of bird life. The coast is an important breeding area for the southern right whale. The reserve covers 41,000 hectares to the east of Bredasdorp and is administered by Western Cape Province. Hikers can tackle beach walks and trails of various lengths on Potberg mountain.

**Karoo National Park** The park, near Beaufort West, encloses 32,000 hectares of classic Karoo landscape and a representative selection of its flora and fauna. There's a three-day hiking trail and excellent accommodation.

Both parks (Karoo and Kalahari Gemsbok national parks) get about eight out of 10. They fail on presentation, not much information, no adequate maps and lamentable walking trails. Both feature three-day hikes of about 30km. Initially we thought we must come back in cooler weather and do them, so spectacular is the country, but both routes are ridiculous and the parks could be better enjoyed with properly constructed shorter trails – the construction is a bare minimum and not user-friendly at all.

**Noel Gross**

## Eastern Cape Province
**Tsitsikamma Coastal National Park** This park encompasses a narrow band of spectacular coast between Plettenberg Bay and Jeffreys Bay. It is traversed by one of the most famous walks in the country – the Otter Trail, which is an easy five-day, 41km trail along the coast. Unfortunately, it is booked months in advance and there is virtually no chance of getting a place. It's still worth visiting for some of the shorter day-walks – which can include a very good section of the Otter Trail.

**Addo Elephant National Park** The park protects the last remnant of the great herds that once roamed the province. It is only small, but the unusual bush (spekboom, sneezewood and guarri) supports a high density of elephants. You would be unlucky not to see one of the 130 elephants living in the park, which is north of Port Elizabeth.

**Karoo Nature Reserve** The reserve, just outside Graaff-Reinet, has extraordinary flora, with the weird Karoo succulents well represented. There's also wildlife, interesting bird life and spectacular rock formations. There are a number of day walks and one overnight hike. The reserve is within walking distance of the town.

**Mountain Zebra National Park** Covering only 6500 hectares, this park was proclaimed to ensure the survival of the Cape mountain zebra – there are now more than 200 in the park and many more around the province. The park covers the rugged northern slopes of the Bankberg range and there are magnificent views across the mountains and the Karoo plains.

**Transkei Area** The Transkei area's coastline is largely untouched, and there are several conservation areas set aside. **Mkambati Nature Reserve** is a coastal reserve with some great scenery, including the Misikaba River Gorge. Other reserves include **Dwesa** and **Cwebe**, between Coffee Bay and Kei Mouth; **Hluleka**, on the Coffee Bay Trail; and **Silaka**, just south of Port St Johns.

## Northern Cape Province
**Kalahari Gemsbok National Park** The Kalahari Gemsbok National Park is not as well known or famous as many other African parks, but it is, nonetheless, one of the greatest. Including the Botswana section (there are no fences) the park exceeds 36,000 sq km. This allows the unhindered migration of animals who, because of the unpredictable rainfall, are forced to travel great distances to reach water and food.

Although the countryside is described as semi-desert (with around 200mm of rain a year) it is richer than it appears and supports large populations of birds, reptiles, small mammals, springbok, blue wildebeest, red hartebeest,

## Where to See the Big Five

The short answer is: go to Kruger National Park. If you want to see the largest variety of wildlife in the one reserve, then Kruger (or one of the private reserves bordering Kruger) is the place for you.

However, it's possible to see the Big Five (and, of course, many other equally interesting animals) in other parks and reserves, many of which have a special attraction of their own. Those listed here are the best-known or the most interesting.

The place *not* to see the Big Five is anywhere near Cape Town (although elusive leopards might still live in the mountains). This was the first area to be settled by people with guns and the large, dangerous animals were killed off a long time ago. Nearly all of the reserves with Big Five animals are in the east and the north of the country.

**Lion** Lions are being reintroduced to several parks but the best place to see them (other than Kruger) is Kalahari Gemsbok National Park (Northern Cape).

**Elephant** Addo Elephant Park (Eastern Cape) is relatively small and is home to quite a large herd. Itala and Hluhluwe-Umfolozi game reserves (KwaZulu-Natal) also have elephants. Off the beaten track and requiring some planning to reach, Tembe Elephant Park (KwaZulu-Natal) protects South Africa's last free-ranging herds.

**Leopard** Leopards live just about everywhere in South Africa, including in most parks and reserves. However seeing one isn't easy.

**Rhino** You have a good chance of seeing white rhino at close range in Hluhluwe-Umfolozi (KwaZulu-Natal) but white rhinos aren't a member of the Big Five. The black rhino, which qualifies for the Big Five because of its bad-temper and unpredictability (remember that the five animals were the most popular animals for hunters) can also be seen in Hluhluwe-Umfolozi but there are fewer of them.

**Cape Buffalo** Itala (KwaZulu-Natal) has Cape buffalo. ■

---

gemsbok and eland. These in turn support a large population of predators – there is arguably no better place to see lions, leopards, cheetahs, hyena, jackals and foxes.

**Augrabies Falls National Park** This park, 120km west of Upington, features the dramatic Augrabies Falls, where the Orange River drops into a solid granite ravine. Particularly when the river is in flood, the sight is spectacular, but for many the area is most interesting for the rich variety of plant life that survives in almost desert conditions.

**Goegap Nature Reserve** This reserve, 10km from Springbok, is famous for its extraordinary display of spring flowers and its nursery of over 200 amazing Karoo and Namaqualand succulents. In addition to the flora, there are springbok, zebras and birds. It is administered by Northern Cape Province, but there is no accommodation.

**Richtersveld National Park** The Richtersveld was proclaimed a park in 1991, and as yet there is little infrastructure. It protects 162,000 hect-

ares of mountainous desert, bordering the Orange River in the north-west corner of the province. The countryside and the flora are spectacular. The park is very rugged and it will be a while before it is easily accessible.

## Mpumalanga

**Blyde River Canyon Nature Reserve** A spectacular 60km canyon follows the Blyde River down from the Drakensberg escarpment to the lowveld, and has a huge range of flora and fauna.

## Northern Province

**Lapalala Wilderness** This private reserve north in the Waterberg mountains has white rhinos, zebras, blue wildebeests and several antelope species, plus crocodiles in the bilharzia-free rivers. You can canoe or hike. Book on ☎ (011) 453 7645.

**Lesheba Wilderness** In the Soutpansberg range, this private reserve has dramatic and varied country and there are plenty of animals, including rhinos. Book on ☎ (015) 593 0076.

**Wolkberg Wilderness** There is good hiking in this wilderness area in the northern tail of the Drakensberg, as well as some strands of indigenous forest. The fair number of animals include a few shy leopards and hyena. Book hiking trails through SAFCOL (☎ (013) 764 1058), in Sabie.

**Nwanedi National Park** In the underdeveloped Venda area, this park is on the northern side of the Soutpansberg mountains and the country is lowveld rather than rainforest. Book through the Ditike Craft Centre (☎ (0159) 41577; fax 41048), which is the information centre in Thohoyandou.

**Kruger National Park** Kruger is one of the best parks in Africa, if not the world. With all of the 'big five' animals (lion, elephant, buffalo, leopard, black rhino), inexpensive accommodation and walking trails (book early), it's not to be missed.

**Private Reserves near Kruger Park** The area just west of Kruger Park contains a large number of private reserves, usually sharing a border with Kruger and thus you may be able to see most of the 'big five' animals. Most of the reserves offer bush camps, walking and open-vehicle game drives. They are often extremely expensive.

**Timbavati** is jointly owned by a large number of people dedicated to conservation. Within it are a number of operations, some reasonably priced. See the Northern Province chapter for more details.

## KwaZulu-Natal

Most major parks and reserves in KwaZulu-Natal are administered by the Natal Parks Board. The Board's HQ in Pietermaritzburg is where you book all accommodation (with the exception of camp sites, which are booked through the individual parks and reserves). You can make phone bookings with a credit card (☎ (0331) 47 1981). The office is open on weekdays from 8.30 am to 12.45 pm and 2 to 3.30 pm. There's also a desk where you can make bookings in Durban's Tourist Junction centre.

In addition to camp sites there are 16 categories of accommodation, ranging from self-contained bungalows to caves, although not all are found in all the parks.

**Drakensberg Reserves** Along with Golden Gate Highlands National Park in the Free State, there are two main reserves in the dramatic KwaZulu-Natal Drakensberg; **Giant's Castle Game Reserve** and **Royal Natal National Park**. Both have spectacular scenery, walking trails and good accommodation. In addition there are the **Mkhomazi, Mzimkulu** and **Mzimkulwana** wilderness areas, with excellent hiking.

**Hluhluwe & Umfolozi Reserves** These large, adjoining game reserves have rhinos, lions and elephants. Umfolozi's wilderness trails offer guided hiking.

**Itala Game Reserve** With facilities rivalling much more expensive private reserves, the Natal Parks Board's flagship reserve is worth visiting.

**Lake St Lucia Area** This complex of Natal Parks Board reserves centres on Lake St Lucia on the north coast. There are crocodiles and hippos as well as good fishing and hiking trails.

**Ntendeka Wilderness** In the Zulu heartland, this is a beautiful area of grassland and indigenous forest, with some dramatic cliffs. There are hiking trails. For more information phone ☎ (0386) 71883.

**Ndumu Game Reserve** On the Mozambique border, about 100km north of Mkuze, this remote reserve has black and white rhinos, hippos, crocodiles, antelope and a wide range of bird life. Book through the KwaZulu Department of Nature Conservation (☎ (0331) 94 6696) in Pietermaritzburg.

**Tembe Elephant Park** This park on the Mozambique border was established in 1991 to protect South Africa's last free-ranging elephants. There are now about 100 in the area. Currently you can only visit the park on a tour. Book through the KwaZulu Department of Nature Conservation (☎ (0331) 94 6696) in Pietermaritzburg.

## Free State

**Golden Gate Highlands Park** One of the spectacular Drakensberg reserves, this national park is close to the northern border of Lesotho in the Free State. The main attraction is the scenery, through which you can walk or ride horses. Book accommodation through the National Parks Board.

**Tussen Die Riviere Game Farm** This game farm near Aliwal North has more animals than any other in the Free State, mostly various antelope species but also white rhinos and hippos.

**QwaQwa Conservation Area** This reserve is in the foothills of both the Maluti mountains and the Drakensberg. It was once administered by the QwaQwa Tourism & Nature Conservation Corporation (☎ (058) 713 4444; fax 713 4342) in Phuthaditjhaba; the old office is still functioning and is now run by Free State, but no official name change yet. Trails must be booked at least two weeks in advance.

**Stokstert Hiking Trail** This overnight trail is in the Caledon River Conservancy Area, around Smithfield in southern Free State. This huge area (300,000 hectares) is on the land of 65 farmers who have adopted conservation-minded techniques.

## North-West Province

**Pilanesberg National Park** The park surrounds Sun City and covers 500 sq km of mountainous extinct volcanic craters. It is well worth visiting. There are black and white rhinos, giraffes, and all sorts of bucks.

# Facts for the Visitor

## TOURIST OFFICES

The South African Tourist Corporation (Satour) is the main government tourism organisation. It produces useful brochures and maps, mostly geared to short-stay, relatively wealthy visitors. Satour brochures are generally free if you get them outside South Africa but there's a charge for many of the brochures in the country. Satour's web site, which has an accommodation-booking function (which didn't work when we tried it), is at www.africa.com/satour/index.htm

The head office is in Pretoria at 442 Rigel Ave South, Erasmusrand 0181 (☎ (012) 347 0600; fax 45 4889). Satour offices abroad include:

Australia
Level 6, 285 Clarence St, Sydney NSW 2000 (☎ (02) 9261 3424; fax 9261 3414)
France
61 rue La Boëtie, 75008, Paris (☎ (01) 45 61 01 97; fax 45 61 01 96)
Germany
Alemannia Haus, An der Hauptwache 11, D-60313 Frankfurt/Main 1, Postfach 101940, 60019 Frankfurt (☎ (69) 929 1290; fax 28 0950)
Japan
Akasaka Lions Building, 2nd Floor, 1-1-2 Moto Akasaka, Minato-ku, Tokyo 107 (☎ (3) 3 478 7601; fax 3 478 7605)
UK
5-6 Alt Grove, Wimbledon, London SW19 4DZ (☎ (0181) 944 8080; fax 944 6705)
USA
500 Fifth Ave, 20th Floor, New York, NY 10110 (☎ (212) 730 2929, ☎ (800) 822 5368; fax (212) 764 1980)
Suite 1524, 9841 Airport Blvd, Los Angeles, CA 90045 (☎ (310) 641 8444, ☎ (1-800) 782 9772; fax (310) 641 5812)
Zimbabwe
Offices 9 & 10, Mon Repos Building, Newlands Shopping Centre, Harare (☎ (04) 70 7766; fax 78 6489)

Satour used to have a network of offices around South Africa, but these are closing as it concentrates on international promotion.

The gap is supposedly being filled by provincial tourism bodies, but while some are working well (eg, the Eastern Cape Tourism Board), others aren't yet producing much beyond glossy brochures and platitudes. At a local level, most towns have tourist offices; if not, you can usually get information at the library or the town hall.

## VISAS & DOCUMENTS
### Visas

The visa situation has changed several times since 1994, and could change again, so check before you arrive.

Entry permits are issued on arrival to holiday visitors from many Commonwealth countries and other countries including Japan, Ireland, Switzerland and Germany. You are entitled to 90 days, but they usually write the date of your flight home as the date of expiry.

If you aren't entitled to an entry permit you'll need to get a visa (free) before you arrive. They aren't issued at the border. It's worth getting a visa before you depart for Africa, but allow a couple of weeks for the process. There are embassies in Australia, Brazil, Canada, France, Germany, Italy, the Netherlands, Spain, the UK and the USA, among other countries. South Africa has at least consular representation in most countries.

If you do need a visa (rather than an entry permit) it must be multiple-entry if you plan to go to a neighbouring country (such as Lesotho) then return to South Africa.

On arrival you might have to satisfy an immigration officer that you have sufficient funds for your stay in South Africa. Obviously, 'sufficient' is open to interpretation, so it pays to be neat, clean and polite.

If you arrive by air you must have an onward ticket of some sort. An air ticket is best but overland seems to be OK. If you arrive in South Africa overland things are usually more relaxed.

**Visa Extensions** Apply for visa or entry-permit extensions, or a re-entry visa, at the Department of Home Affairs in Cape Town, Pretoria, Durban or Johannesburg. Extensions cost a massive R360.

**African Visas** South Africa is a gold-mine for travellers hunting visas to other African countries. These can be very difficult to collect as you travel around, so if you're starting in South Africa it makes sense to get as many as you can here. See the following Embassies section for African representation in South Africa.

### Documents
All people who have travelled through the yellow-fever zone in Africa or South America (including Brazil) must have an International Certificate of Vaccination against yellow fever. Vaccination against smallpox and cholera is not required.

### EMBASSIES
### South African Embassies & Missions
South Africa now has embassies in quite a few African countries, unlike the situation in the apartheid years when the only embassies were in Lilongwe (Malawi) and St Denis (Réunion). It's likely that more South African embassies will open throughout Africa in the near future.

Australia
    Rhodes Place, Yarralumla, Canberra ACT 2600 (☎ (02) 6273 2424; fax 6273 2669)
Brazil
    Rua Lauro Muller 116/1107 (Torre Rio Sul), Botafogo 22299, Rio de Janeiro (☎ (021) 542 6191; fax 542 6043)
Canada
    15 Sussex Drive, Ottawa K1M 1M8 (☎ (613) 744 0330; fax 744 8287)
    Suite 2515, Exchange Tower, Toronto M5X 1E3 (☎ (416) 364 0314; fax 363 8974)
Denmark
    1st Floor, Montergade 1, Copenhagen DK-1011 (☎ (01) 18 0155)

France
    59 Quai d'Orsay, Paris 75007 (☎ (01) 45 55 92 37; fax 45 51 88 12)
Germany
    Auf der Hostert 3, Bonn 53173 (☎ (0228) 82010; fax 35 2579)
Israel
    Yakhin House, 2 Kaplan St, Tel Aviv 64734 (☎ (03) 525 2566)
Kenya
    Lonrho House, Standard St, Nairobi (☎ (02) 228469; fax 223687)
Malawi
    Impco Building, City Centre, Lilongwe 3 (☎ (09265) 73 3722)
Mozambique
    745 Avenida Julius Nyerere, Maputo (☎ (01) 490059)
Namibia
    RSA House, cnr Jan Jonker St and Nelson Mandela Dr, Klein Windhoek, Windhoek, PO Box 23100 (☎ (061) 229765; fax 224140)
Netherlands
    Wassenaarseweg 40, The Hague (☎ (70) 392 4501; fax 45 8226)
Réunion
    Immeuble Cie des Indes, 20 Rue de la Compagnie BP 1117, 97482 Saint Denis Cedex (☎ (09262) 21 5005; fax 41718)
Spain
    Edificio Lista, Calle de Claudio Coello 91-6, Madrid (☎ (01) 435 6688; fax 593 1384)
Sweden
    Linnégatan 76, 11523 Stockholm (☎ (0946) 24 3950; fax 660 7136)
Tanzania
    c/o Oysterbay Hotel, Touré Drv, Oyster Bay (6km north of Dar es Salaam) (☎ (051) 68062)
Uganda
    Plot 9, Malcolm X Ave, Kololo, Kampala (☎ /fax (041) 259156)
UK
    South Africa House, Trafalgar Sq, London WC2N 5DP (☎ (0171) 930 4488; fax 839 1419)
USA
    3051 Massachusetts Ave NW, Washington DC 20008 (☎ (202) 232 4400; fax 265 1607)
    Suite 300, 50 North La Cienega Blvd, Beverly Hills, CA 90211 (☎ (213) 657 9200; fax 657 9215)
Zimbabwe
    Temple Bar House, Baker Ave, Harare (☎ (04) 75 3147)

### Foreign Embassies & Missions in South Africa
Most countries have their main embassy in Pretoria, with an office or consulate in Cape

Town, which becomes the official embassy during Cape Town's parliamentary sessions. However, some countries also maintain consulates (which can arrange visas and passports) in Johannesburg. Some only have representation in Johannesburg.

Angola
CPK Building, 153 Oliver St, Brooklyn, Pretoria (☎ (012) 46 6104)
Australia
292 Orient St, Arcadia, Pretoria (☎ (012) 342 3740; fax 342 4222)
Botswana
2nd Floor, Futura Bank House, 122 De Korte St, Braamfontein, Johannesburg (☎ (011) 403 3748). There is also an office in Cape Town.
Canada
1103 Arcadia St, Hatfield, Pretoria (☎ (012 342 6923; fax 342 3837)
Congo-Brazzaville
960 Arcadia St, Arcadia, Pretoria (☎ (012) 342 5507)
Congo (Zaïre)
423 Kirkness St, Sunnyside, Pretoria (☎ (012) 344 1510)
Egypt
270 Bourke St, Muckelneuk, Pretoria (☎ (012) 343 1590)
Eritrea
1281 Cobham Rd, Queenswood, Pretoria (☎ (012) 333 1302)
Ethiopia
2nd Floor, Southern Life Plaza, 1150 Schoeman St, Hatfield, Pretoria (☎ (012) 342 6321)
France
807 George Ave, Arcadia, Pretoria (☎ (012) 43 5564; fax 43 3481)
Gabon
1st Floor, Southern Life Plaza, 1150 Schoeman St, Hatfield, Pretoria (☎ (012) 342 4376)
Germany
180 Blackwood St, Arcadia, Pretoria (☎ (012) 344 3854; fax 343 9401)
Ghana
1038 Arcadia St, Hatfield, Pretoria (☎ (012) 342 5847)
Ivory Coast
795 Government Ave, Arcadia, Pretoria (☎ (012) 342 6913)
Kenya
302 Brooks St, Menlo Park, Pretoria (☎ (012) 342 5066)
Lesotho
6th Floor, West Tower, Momentum Centre, 343 Pretorius St, Pretoria (☎ (012) 322 6090)

Malawi
770 Government Ave, Arcadia, Pretoria (☎ (012) 342 0146)
Morocco
Cnr Schoeman and Fahrenden Sts, Arcadia, Pretoria (☎ (012) 343 0230)
Mozambique
7th Floor, Cape York House, 252 Jeppe St, Johannesburg (☎ (011) 336 1819)
7th Floor, 45 Castle St, Cape Town (☎ (021) 26 2944)
Namibia
209 Redroute, Carlton Centre, Johannesburg (☎ (011) 331 7055)
Main Tower, Standard Bank Centre, Cape Town (☎ (021) 419 3190)
Nigeria
Cnr Bolton & Newport Sts, Parkwood, Johannesburg (☎ (011) 442 3620)
138 Beckett St, Arcadia, Pretoria (☎ (012) 343 2021)

## Your Own Embassy

As a tourist, it's important to realise what your country's embassy can and can't do. Generally speaking, they won't help much in emergencies if the trouble you're in is remotely your own fault. Remember that you are bound by the laws of the country you're in. Embassies will not be sympathetic if you end up in jail after committing a crime locally, even if such actions are legal in your own country. In genuine emergencies you might get some assistance, but only if other channels have been exhausted. For example, if you need to get home urgently, a free ticket home is exceedingly unlikely – the embassy would expect you to have insurance. If you have all your money and documents stolen they might assist you with getting a new passport, but a loan for onward travel is out of the question. Embassies used to keep letters for travellers or have a small reading room with home newspapers, but these days the mail holding service has been stopped, and even their newspapers tend to be out of date.

On the more positive side, if you are heading into very remote or politically volatile areas you might consider registering with your embassy, so they know where you are, but make sure you tell them when you come back too. Some embassies post useful warning notices about local dangers or potential problems. The US embassies are particularly good for providing this information and it's worth scanning their noticeboards for 'travellers advisories' about security, local epidemics, dangers to lone travellers, etc. ■

Rwanda
> Suite 113, Infotech Building, 1090 Arcadia St, Arcadia, Pretoria (☎ (012) 342 1740)

Sao Tomé & Principe
> 33 Long St, Cape Town (☎ (021) 23 3979)

Swaziland
> Suite 105, Infotech Building, 1090 Arcadia St, Arcadia, Pretoria (☎ (012) 342 5782/4; fax 342 5682)

Sweden
> 9th Floor, Old Mutual Building, 167 Andries St, Pretoria (☎ (012) 21 1050; fax 323 2278)

Tanzania
> 845 Government Ave, Arcadia, Pretoria (☎ (012) 342 4393)

The Netherlands
> 825 Arcadia St, Arcadia, Pretoria (☎ (012) 344 3910; fax 343 9950)

Tunisia
> 850 Church St, Arcadia, Pretoria (☎ (012) 342 6282)

Uganda
> Suite 402, Infotech Building, 1090 Arcadia St, Arcadia, Pretoria (☎ (012) 342 6031)

UK
> Greystoke, 225 Hill St, Arcadia, Pretoria (☎ (012) 43 3121)

USA
> 7877 Pretorius St, Arcadia, Pretoria (☎ (012) 342 1048; fax 342 2244)

Zambia
> Sanlam Building, cnr Festival & Arcadia Sts, Hatfield, Pretoria (☎ (012) 342 1541)

Zimbabwe
> 17th Floor, 20 Anderson St, Johannesburg (☎ (011) 838 5620)

## CUSTOMS

South Africa, Botswana, Namibia, Swaziland and Lesotho are all part of the South African Customs Union, which means the internal borders are effectively open from a customs point of view. When you enter the union, however, you're restricted in the normal way to personal effects: one litre of spirits, two litres of wine and 400 cigarettes. Motor vehicles must be covered by a triptyque or carnet. For information contact the Department of Customs & Excise in Pretoria (☎ (012) 28 4308).

## MONEY

The unit of currency is the rand (R), which is divided into 100 cents. The import and export of local currency is limited to R500. There is no black market.

South Africa has introduced new coins and notes. The only old note you might see is the R5 (which has been replaced by a coin) but old coins are common, making it difficult to establish familiarity. The coins are: 1, 2, 5, 10, 20 and 50 cents; 1, 2 and 5 rand. The notes are: 5 (being withdrawn), 10, 20, 50, 100 and 200 rand. The R200 note looks a lot like the R20 note, so take care.

The Thomas Cook agent is Rennies Travel, a large chain of travel agencies. They also change other brands of travellers' cheques and their rates are good. There are American Express offices in the big cities, although 16 branches have closed because of security problems. Nedbank is associated with American Express. Most banks change travellers' cheques in major currencies, with various commissions. First National Bank is the Visa agent and is supposed to change Visa travellers' cheques without commission, but many branches don't know this.

Keep at least some of the receipts when changing money as you'll need to show them to reconvert your rands when you leave.

Thomas Cook has travellers' cheques in rand, useful for the countries covered in this book but less so outside Southern Africa.

Credit cards, especially MasterCard and Visa, are widely accepted. Many ATMs give cash advances. The nationwide Standard Bank is part of the worldwide Cirrus network and you can get money from its ATM machines if your card bears the Cirrus logo. Opening a bank account in South Africa is not really possible, as no bank will accept a foreign address from an account holder.

### Exchange Rates

| Australia | A$1 = | R3.63 |
|---|---|---|
| Canada | C$1 = | R3.38 |
| France | 1FF = | R0.88 |
| Germany | DM1 = | R2.99 |
| Italy | L100 = | R0.30 |
| Japan | ¥100 = | R4.08 |
| Sweden | Skr1 = | R0.69 |
| United Kingdom | UK£1 = | R7.22 |
| USA | US$1 = | R4.56 |

The exchange rates quoted were those in effect when this book was being researched. The rand is a shaky currency, and it's likely that you will get more rands for your dollar (or whatever) when you arrive. However, it's also likely that many costs will rise as the rand falls – see Costs, below.

## Costs

Although South Africa is certainly not as cheap to travel in as many poorer African countries, it is very good value by European, US and Australian standards. This is due, in large part, to the collapse in the value of the rand, which gives those converting from a hard currency a major advantage. Don't expect imported or manufactured goods (including books) to be cheap, though.

On the negative side, inflation is high so the prices in this book can be expected to rise at a corresponding rate. However, the rand is also likely to continue to devalue (meaning you'll get more rands when you convert from another currency). Inflation and devaluation may well cancel each other. For example, hostel beds have stayed at around US$7 for years now, even though the price in rands has risen from R20 to R30.

Shoestring travellers will find that camping or staying in hostels, on-site caravans or bungalows where they can self-cater are the cheapest options, often working out to around R30 per person. Sit-down meals in restaurants (without getting into haute cuisine) consistently work out to between R30 and R40 per person, less in pubs. Steak dishes, in particular, are incredibly cheap. Fresh produce is good value.

The distances in South Africa are large, so transport can be sparse and expensive; hiring or buying a car can be worthwhile both for convenience and economy.

It's not all good news on costs. Top-end hotels, as well as mid-range places in some popular destinations, have taken advantage of increased international visitor numbers by hiking prices significantly. Cape Town can be one of the more expensive cities in the world unless you are prepared to consider other accommodation options (which can be

### Value Added Tax
There is a Value Added Tax (VAT) of 14%, but foreign visitors can reclaim some of their VAT expenses on departure. This applies only to goods that you are taking out of the country; you can't claim back the VAT you've paid on food or car rental, for example. Also, the goods have to be bought at a shop participating in the VAT Foreign Tourist Sales scheme.

To make a claim you need the tax invoices (usually the receipt, but make sure that the shop knows that you want a full receipt). They must be originals – no photocopies. You also have to fill in a form or two and show the goods to a customs inspector  The total value of the goods must exceed R250. After you've gone through immigration you pick up your refund cheque – at some airports you can then cash it immediately at the bank, in any major currency. If your claim comes to more than R3000 your cheque is mailed to your home address.

You can claim only at the international airports in Johannesburg, Cape Town and Durban, at the Beit Bridge and Komatipoort land borders and at some harbours. At airports, make sure you have the goods checked by the inspector *before* you check-in your luggage. You make the actual claim after you have gone through immigration. ■

as good as or better than hotels). Remember that Cape Town has a very long history of enticing travellers, showing them a good time and emptying their wallets.

### Tipping
Tipping is pretty well mandatory because of the very low wages. Around 10 to 15% is usual.

## POST & COMMUNICATIONS
South Africa has reasonably good post and telephone systems, although neither work quite as efficiently as in many other developed countries.

### Post
Most post offices are open from 8.30 am to 4.30 pm on weekdays and from 8 am to noon on Saturday. Aerograms (handy, prepaid letter forms) and standard size postcards cost R1. Airmail letters cost R1.40 per 10g (R1 to

## How Much Is...?

Hostel dorm bed – R25
Hostel double room – about R75
Cottage, sleeping two – from R60
Two-star hotel room – from R90/150 a single/
    double
Five-star hotel room – around R400/500 a single/
    double
36-exposure transparency (slide) film – R26
36-exposure print film – R20
36-exposure processing & prints – R50
Hamburger & chips – R10
Steak – from R20
1 litre milk – R2
1 loaf bread – R2
1 stubby beer – R2.50
A one-way economy air ticket from Johannes-
    burg to Cape Town – R670
Deluxe bus from Johannesburg to Cape Town
    – R290
Minibus taxi from Johannesburg to Cape Town
    – R150

Southern African countries). Internal letters cost R0.60. Internal delivery can be very slow and international delivery isn't exactly lightning fast. If you ask someone in South Africa to mail you something, even a letter, emphasise that you need it sent by airmail, otherwise it will probably be sent by sea mail and could take months to reach you.

### Telephone

Local telephone calls are timed and although you get a decent amount of time for each R0.30 unit, if you're calling a government department you might go through a few units.

Except in remote country areas, telephones are fully automatic with direct dialling facilities to most parts of the world.

When using a public phone you might find that you have credit left after you've finished a call. If you want to make another call don't hang up or you'll lose the credit. Press the black button under the receiver hook.

All telephone books give full details of service numbers and codes. They also carry long lists of numbers that are due to change. The phone system seems to be in a perpetual

state of upgrading and there's a good chance that many of the numbers (including some area codes) in this guidebook will have changed by the time you get to South Africa.

Long-distance and international telephone calls are expensive. You'll use up a large chunk of an R10 phonecard with a 'Hello, how are you, please ring me back on...' call to Australia. There are many privately-run 'phone centres' where you can make calls without coins. These are more convenient than using a public phone, but also more expensive. The most expensive place to make calls is your hotel room. Charges are simply outrageous, never less than double what you would pay for a public phone and often a lot more. Even using your home country's 'Direct' service incurs a fee of at least R5 in many hotels.

### Useful Numbers

| | |
|---|---|
| Enquiries (national & international) | 1025 |
| Enquiries (local) | 1023 |
| Collect calls (national) | 0020 |
| Collect calls (international) | 0090 |

To make an international call, dial ☎ 09 then your county's access code. Some are given below:

| | |
|---|---|
| Australia | 61 |
| Botswana | 267 |
| Canada | 1 |
| Denmark | 45 |
| France | 33 |
| Germany | 49 |
| Japan | 81 |
| Netherlands | 31 |
| New Zealand | 64 |
| Spain | 34 |
| Sweden | 46 |
| UK | 44 |
| USA | 1 |

To avoid high charges when calling home, dial your 'Direct' number, which puts you through to an operator in your country. You can then either place a call on your 'phone home' account, if you have one, or place a reverse-charge call. The Australian operators (and maybe the others) are used to dealing with stressed-out travellers and can be very helpful.

| | |
|---|---|
| Australia Direct | 0800 990061 |
| Belgium Direct | 0800 990032 |
| Canada Direct | 0800 990014 |
| Denmark Direct | 0800 990045 |
| Ireland Direct | 0800 990353 |
| Japan Direct | 0800 990081 |
| Netherlands Direct | 0800 990031 |
| New Zealand Direct | 0800 990064 |
| UK Direct – BT | 0800 990044 |
| UK Direct – Call UK | 0800 990544 |
| USA Direct – AT&T | 0800 990123 |
| USA Direct – MCI Call USA | 0800 990011 |
| USA Direct – Sprint Express | 0800 990001 |

**Fax & Email**
South Africans are very quick to adopt new technology; you can fax most organisations and businesses. Phone books list fax numbers. The private phone centres (see Telephone section, above) also send faxes.

Email is becoming common, and there are an increasing number of Internet cafés where you can send and receive email.

**NEWSPAPERS & MAGAZINES**
Major English-language newspapers are published in the cities and sold across the country, although in Afrikaans-speaking areas and the ex-Homelands they may not be available in every little town.

During the years of the emergency (1985 to 1990) all media were heavily censored, and although the papers are now free to print pretty much what they like, the art of political journalism is in its infancy. You see very few pieces analysing government policy.

The Johannesburg *Star* is a good middle-of-the-road daily, although there can't be many other serious broadsheets in the world with a 'back-page girl' (always clothed but often poolside – her reported aspirations usually involve a career in modelling).

*The Sowetan* is the biggest selling paper in the country and its background of support for the Struggle makes it interesting reading.

Despite catering to a largely poorly educated audience, it has a much more sophisticated political and social outlook than the major white papers. Some of its education supplements are outstanding. *The Nation* and *South* are other black papers which upheld journalistic standards during the apartheid years. *IMVO* (roughly, 'my view') is published weekly in both English and Xhosa editions and is sold mainly in Eastern Cape Province. The paper was founded in 1884 and is essential reading if you want to understand the situation in this volatile area of the country.

The best newspaper/magazine for investigative journalism, sensible overviews and high-quality columnists, not to mention a week's worth of Doonesbury and an excellent entertainment section, is *The Weekly Mail & Guardian*. It also includes a shortened version of the British *Guardian*'s international edition, which itself includes features from *Le Monde* and the *Washington Post*.

For an insight into conservative white thinking, buy *The Citizen*.

**RADIO & TV**
The mainstream SABC stations (AM and FM) play dreary music and offer drearier chat about recipes and the like, but stations geared to black audiences often play good music. Radio Lotus caters to South Africans of Indian descent and plays a lot of weird and wonderful Indian film music. Cigarette ads are still played on radio and there are some gems that sound like they were made in the '50s.

The BBC World Service is available on short-wave, medium-wave and, if you're near Lesotho (where the transmitter is), FM. If you're about to travel through Africa the Beeb's nightly *Focus On Africa* programme is essential listening.

The monolithic and conservative South African Broadcasting Corporation (SABC) was the mouthpiece of the government, and although times have changed decisively you'll still find most of its fare rather timid. There are a few exceptions, though, such as the flamboyant Dali Tambo's innovative talk show *People of the South*. Soap opera fans are in for a treat, as US daytime soaps are shown in prime time, and Brits and Aussies hooked on *Home & Away* can catch up on some very early episodes. *Melrose Place* dubbed into Afrikaans is a must.

Most programmes are in Afrikaans or English, but with 11 official languages to accommodate, that will change. Unfortunately, subtitling is rare.

As well as the SABC there is the pay channel M-Net, which shows some good movies. Some of the Homelands had their own TV stations and some of these are still in operation.

## TIME
South African Standard Time is two hours ahead of GMT/UTC (at noon in London it's 2 pm in Johannesburg); seven hours ahead of USA Eastern Standard Time (at noon in New York it's 7 pm in Johannesburg); and eight hours behind Australian Eastern Standard Time (at noon in Sydney it's 4 am in Johannesburg). There is no daylight saving.

## BUSINESS HOURS
Banking hours vary, but are usually between 9 am and 3.30 pm on weekdays. Many branches also open from 8.30 to 11 am on Saturday. Post offices usually open from 8.30 am to 4.30 pm on weekdays and 8 am to noon on Saturday. Both banks and post offices close for lunch in smaller towns.

Most shops are open between 8.30 am and 5 pm on weekdays and Saturday morning. Bars usually close around 11 pm except in the major cities. Outside the cities it's difficult to get a drink without a meal on Sunday.

## PUBLIC HOLIDAYS
Public holidays underwent a dramatic shake-up after the 1994 elections. For example, the Day of the Vow, which celebrated the massacre of Zulus, has become the Day of Reconciliation. The officially ignored but widely observed Soweto Day, marking the student uprisings which eventually led to liberation, is now celebrated as Youth Day. Public holidays and approximate dates are:

| | |
|---|---|
| *New Year's Day* | 1 January |
| *Human Rights Day* | 21 March |
| *Good Friday* | (varies) |
| *Family Day* | 17 April |
| *Constitution Day* | 27 April |
| *Workers' Day* | 1 May |
| *Youth Day* | 16 June |
| *Women's Day* | 9 August |
| *Heritage Day* | 24 September |
| *Day of Reconciliation* | 16 December |
| *Christmas Day* | 25 December |
| *Day of Goodwill* | 26 December |

## School Holidays
It's useful to know the dates of school holidays, as accommodation at reserves and resorts is at a premium during these times. The dates for 1997 are given below; dates for following years will be slightly different. Contact Satour for the exact dates.

Gauteng, Mpumalanga, North-West & Northern Province
   27 March–14 April, 28 June–21 July, 27 September–6 October, 10 December–mid-January
Free State, Northern Cape & Western Cape
   21 March–7 April, 21 June–15 July, 20 September–30 September, 10 December–mid-January
KwaZulu-Natal & Eastern Cape
   27 March–7 April, 28 June–20 July, 20 September–28 September, 5 December–mid-January

## ACTIVITIES
### Organised Activities & Tours
With increasing numbers of foreign visitors, many outfits aimed at the 'adventure' or 'eco' market are appearing. They offer a range of activities, such as hiking, canoeing and rafting, and some have trips into other African countries. There are plenty of options, so shop around. We've had many good and a few bad reports from travellers who have tried some of these outfits. The bad reports mainly concern the operators' inexperience, so hopefully they will have either learnt or gone out of business by the time you arrive.

The best way to find out who is currently reliable is to ask other travellers. Hostels often take bookings for adventure activities and travel, but remember that a particular hostel might have an agreement with a particular company. See what the others are offering. Also, it might be possible to book larger companies through a travel agent in your home country.

Two of the larger 'alternative' companies are African Routes (☎ (031) 304 6358; fax 304 6340) and Drifters (☎ (011) 888 1160; fax 888 1020).

For something a little different, see what you can arrange with Max Maximum Tours (☎ (011) 933 4177). Max runs Soweto tours (he lives there) but has proved useful to budget travellers wanting to negotiate longer trips.

In addition to longer trips, many smaller outfits offer day trips and these can be excellent. Cape Town in particular has interesting activities, but keep your eyes open everywhere.

### Hiking

South Africa has an excellent system of hiking trails, usually with accommodation. They are popular and most must be booked well in advance. Satour's brochure on hiking is useful but if you plan to do a lot of hiking pick up a copy of Jaynee Levy's *Complete Guide to Walks & Trails in Southern Africa* (hardback, R110). A new edition is overdue, so some of the contact details are out of date, but it's still highly recommended.

There are many hiking clubs; contact the Hiking Federation of South Africa (☎ (011) 886 6524; fax 886 6013; email sahiker@cis. co.za). The federation tries to keep up with the constantly changing information about trails, permits and contact addresses, so they are good people to talk to. They publish a booklet (R10) with lots of useful information.

Several of the adventure-travel outfits offer organised hikes.

Most trails are administered by the National Parks Board or the various Forest Regions, although the Natal Parks Board controls most trails in KwaZulu-Natal. Some of the best known trails (and their relevant authorities) are:

KwaZulu-Natal
  Giant's Cup – up to five days in the southern Drakensberg.

Also 'wilderness trails' and guided walks in Umfolozi, Mkuzi and St Lucia national parks. Natal Parks Board.

Mpumalanga
  Blyderivierspoort – up to five days in the Blyde River Canyon area. Blyde River Canyon Nature Reserve (☎ (013) 759 4000), PO Box 1990, Nelspruit 1200.
  Kruger National Park – 'wilderness trails' and guided walks. National Parks Board.

Northern Province
  Soutpansberg – up to four days in the Soutpansberg range. SAFCOL (☎ (013) 764 1058)
  Mabudashango – four days in ex-Venda. Department of Agriculture & Forestry, Private Bag X2247, Sibasa 0970 (☎ (015581) 31211).

Free State
  Rhebok – two days in Golden Gate Highlands National Park. National Parks Board.

Western Cape
  Outeniqua – up to eight days in indigenous forest near Knysna. Regional Director, Southern Cape Forest Region, Private Bag X12, Knysna 6570 (☎ (0445) 23037).
  Otter Trail – five days on the coast in Garden Route. National Parks Board.

Eastern Cape
  Wild Coast – three five-day sections along the Transkei coast. Nature Conservation Division, Agriculture & Forestry Department, Private Bag X5002, Umtata, Eastern Cape (☎ (0471) 31 2711).
  Amatola – up to six days in ex-Ciskei. Eastern Cape Tourism Board, PO Box 186, Bisho, Eastern Cape (☎ (0401) 95 2115).

There are many, many other trails. Wilderness areas offer superb hiking in remote areas with few facilities. Some of them include:

Cederberg Wilderness Area, Western Cape. Contact Chief Nature Conservator, Cederberg State Forest, Private Bag X1, Citrusdal 7340 (☎ (022) 921 2289).
Mkhomazi, Mdedlelo & Mzimkulu Wilderness Areas, KwaZulu-Natal Drakensberg. Natal Parks Board.
Ntendeka Wilderness Area, KwaZulu-Natal. State Forester, Ngome State Forest, Private Bag X21306, Vryheid 3100 (☎ (0386) 71883).

### Air Sports

Flying, hang-gliding, ballooning and parachuting are popular activities. Cape Town's Table Mountain must be one of the most beautiful hang-gliding sites, but there are numerous possibilities along the escarpment and particularly in the Drakensberg. Flying lessons are cheap on an international scale, and flying conditions are superb. Learner pilots are attracted to South Africa from around the world.

### Bird-Watching

With 900 species of birds, 113 of which are endemic, South Africa is a paradise for bird-watchers. The regional variation is huge so keen bird-watchers should aim to cover a range of habitats – Kruger National Park is particularly renowned. Even those with a passing interest will find that binoculars and a field guide are worthwhile investments.

There are bird-watching clubs in the major cities.

### Canoeing & Rafting

South Africa is a dry country with few major rivers by international standards. This limits the canoeing and rafting potential, but there are, nonetheless, some interesting possibilities. The Orange River is the giant among South African rivers, running west across the country for 2340km. Other major rivers include the Tugela (KwaZulu-Natal), the Komati (Mpumalanga and Swaziland) and the Olifants, Berg and Breede (Western Cape).

Rafting and canoeing trips on the Orange River in the far north-west, where it forms the border with Namibia, have become very popular. The main attraction is that you float through a beautiful desert wilderness; the rapids are not demanding.

The Tugela offers more challenging rafting, although it is highly variable depending on the rainfall. It is at its best from late December to mid-March.

One of the biggest operators is Felix Unite, with offices in Johannesburg (☎ (011) 803 9775; fax 803 9603) and at Cape Town's Tourist Rendezvous Centre (☎ (021) 762 6935; fax 761 9259).

### Diving

The KwaZulu-Natal north coast, particularly around Sodwana Bay, offers excellent warm-water diving and there are some good reefs. In addition, most resort towns along Western Cape's Garden Route have diving schools.

### Fishing & Hunting

Sea fishing is a popular pastime and there is a wide range of species in the warm and cold currents which flow past the east and west coasts respectively. River fishing, especially for introduced trout, is popular in parks and reserves, with some good highland streams in Lesotho. You usually need a licence, generally available for a few rand at the park office. In some places equipment is available for hire.

Hunting is a bit of a misnomer. It is generally conducted as part of the annual cull in private game reserves and the animals don't stand much of a chance. Still, hunting is tremendously popular and many more people apply to take part in the culls than there are places available.

The other version of hunting involves rich tourists paying enormous fees to shoot just about anything they want in private reserves. There's something very sick about someone spending US$50,000 on shooting a rhino to death.

### Horse-Riding

Many places, including some national parks, offer horse-riding. There are overnight and longer trails.

### Rock Climbing

There are some challenging climbs, especially in the KwaZulu-Natal Drakensberg and over the escarpment in Lesotho. Contact the Mountain Club of South Africa, 97 Hatfield St, Cape Town 8001 for addresses of regional clubs. In Johannesburg there's the South African Climbers Club, 71 12th St, Parkhurst 2153.

### Surfing

South Africa has some of the best, least crowded surfing in the world. Most surfers will have heard of Jeffreys Bay, but there are myriad alternatives, particularly along the east and south coasts. The best time of the year for surfing in KwaZulu-Natal and the south coast is early winter – April to July.

Boards and surfing gear can be bought in most of the big coastal cities. New boards sell for R850 to R1100; secondhand boards for R250 to R600. A Rip Curl steamer sells for about R500. If you plan to surf Jeffreys Bay you'll need a decent-sized board – it's a big, very fast wave.

It's now out of print but you might find a secondhand copy of *Surfing in Southern Africa* by Mark Jury, which has excellent practical information on when and where to go. A reader tells us that there's a copy in the Jeffreys Bay library.

### Winery Tours

The valleys to the east of Cape Town have some of the best and most beautiful vineyards in the world. First planted at the end of the 17th century, they have thrived in an ideal climate. The buildings are typical of Cape Dutch architecture and the surrounding mountains are superb. The classic tourist promotional material, showing rows of immaculately tended vines, and a whitewashed, thatched homestead overshadowed by blue mountains, is the reality.

The wine itself is cheap and of a high standard. Most vineyards and wineries are open to the public and have free tastings. Good quality wine can be bought for less than R10, but an average figure would be from R15 to R25. If you have a vague interest, the wineries can absorb a couple of days. If you are really interested you'll need at least a week. Numerous tours are available from Cape Town.

### Wildlife Safaris

South Africa can boast very well organised national parks and reserves. Rest camps in game reserves are built within protected enclosures, the roads are of a high standard, and it is easy to tour them in a private car. There are a large number of privately owned game reserves where tours are conducted in open vehicles.

For visitors without their own transport, many companies arrange coach tours.

Springbok Atlas (☎ (011) 493 3780) and Connex Travel (☎ (011) 884 8110) are two of the larger operators. However, these tours are expensive. It would be cheaper (and probably more fun) to hire a car.

Several adventure-travel outfits aimed at the backpacker market offer safaris, including the Bundu Bus (☎ (011) 693 1621; fax 693 1808), with three-night/four-day tours of Mpumalanga and Kruger for about R700.

### Mountain Biking

South Africans have discovered mountain biking and have taken to it in a big way. Some reserves and parks are putting in mountain-bike trails.

Quite a few outfits organise trips. Contact Casual Adventures (☎ (011) 650 7090, ☎ (012) 998 5963; fax (012) 98 2591; email rowan@ilink.nis.za), PO Box 99856 Garsfontein, Pretoria 0042.

### WORK

South Africa is experiencing massive unemployment. As a result, the authorities are making it more difficult for foreigners to obtain work permits or residence permits. There are stiff penalties for people caught employing illegal foreign workers, although we haven't heard of any waiters or barpeople being busted. The bottom line is that work cannot be guaranteed.

The best time to look for casual work in restaurants and bars on the coast is in October and November, before the holiday season starts and before university students finish term. Don't expect decent pay – something like R3.50 to R5 per hour, plus tips (which can be good), is usual. However, you can usually make enough to live on.

### ACCOMMODATION

Many places, including caravan parks, have seasonal rates. The high season is usually the summer school holidays, especially around Christmas and the New Year, and Easter. Prices can double or triple and there might be a minimum stay of a week. The other school holidays are often high season as well, but some places classify them as mid-season and charge a little less.

There's one annoying thing to watch out for in accommodation advertising. You might see an advertisement for a three-star hotel boasting that rooms cost 'from R120'. It means R120 *per person* in a twin or double room. A single room might cost R200.

Satour has a star-rating system and a book which lists rated accommodation (all types except hostels and caravan parks) across the country. This is handy to carry around with you, although as with all rating systems based solely on features, it isn't totally reliable. For example, a crummy hotel and a good hotel can have the same rating because both offer TV, phone and ensuite bathroom. Also, places pay to be in the guide, so the selection is nowhere near comprehensive nor necessarily representative.

### Bottom End

Other than backpacker hostels and self-catering cottages (usually on farms), both of which have become a boom industry, there's a scarcity of budget accommodation. Rock-bottom hotels are few – poor whites are usually too poor to travel – and almost none cater to the country's poorest people, the blacks. There were once cheap boarding houses for whites but many have closed because of the recession. However, if you're prepared to camp or pay a little more for a B&B, accommodation is plentiful and generally good.

### Middle

This price range is where you'll find the really good-value accommodation, with the best bargains in B&Bs and guesthouses, plus accommodation in parks and reserves.

### Top End

There are some simply outstanding places to stay if you're prepared to pay for them: private game reserves, quality guesthouses and lodges, and the odd superb hotel. Unfortunately, many not-so-superb hotels are cashing in on the tourist boom, and there can be some expensive disappointments if you aren't selective.

### Camping

Camping and caravans are very popular with whites and most towns have a cheap municipal caravan park or resort close to the centre of town. These can be very basic, but are often both pleasant and good value. The National Parks Board and the provincial authorities operate quality camping grounds. Depending on the level of facilities, camp sites (without power) range from about R30 to R45 (cheaper in parks and reserves). In summer at beach resorts you might have to pay R80 or more for a site, as they are geared to large tents and family holidays. You might be able to negotiate a lower rate for a two-person tent, but don't count on it. There's a good chance that a popular resort town will have a backpacker hostel where you could pitch your tent for R20 or less.

Many places, especially the privately owned caravan parks and resorts, don't permit you to use non-porous groundsheets (ie, the floor of most small tents). This is to stop the grass being killed by tents pitched for weeks at a time, so if you're only staying a night or two you might convince the manager that your tent won't do any harm. It's probably best just to avoid the subject. Some caravan parks don't allow tents at all. Often, this is due to bad experiences with drunken locals. If you make it clear that you're a clean-living foreigner you might get a site.

Chains such as Aventura have elaborate resorts, with guards on the gate, swimming pools, restaurants and sometimes on-site supermarkets. A lot of the accommodation is in chalets and cottages (see below). Club Caravelle is another reliable chain; their resorts tend to be less elaborate and have a wider variety of standards and prices.

In some rural areas of the ex-Homelands (where there are few official camp sites) you can still camp for free. *Always* ask permission from the nearest village or home before setting up. This is not just good manners; you risk robbery or worse if you ignore local sensibilities. Permission to camp given by children doesn't count. Find the most important person you can but don't go stomping into a village demanding to see the chief.

## Self-Catering Cottages

The cheapest self-catering accommodation is usually in farm cottages, which can be excellent value. You might find something for about R50 for two people, although most start around R70. They are usually comfortable but in some you'll have to do without electricity and you might even have to pump water. Small town information centres are the best places to find out about inexpensive farm cottages, and in a small community there's a chance that you can get a ride to the cottage if you don't have transport.

Self-catering cottages are often available in caravan parks and resorts, both municipal and private. The National Parks Board has excellent-value, fully equipped cottages. Most of these cottages are aimed at family groups, so they can be a little expensive for one or two people, starting around R100. Of course, this is great value if there are a few of you.

To confuse things, self-catering cottages are also called chalets, cabins and rondavels (which refer to circular, often thatched, huts). At the top end, a comfortable cottage will be equipped with air-conditioning, bedding and a fully equipped kitchen. At the bottom end, a rondavel might simply have a couple of bunks, with mattresses but no bedding, a table and chairs, and a basin – rudimentary but adequate if you are travelling with a sleeping bag and basic cooking equipment.

## House-Sitting

This is one way to beat the cost of accommodation and to get a glimpse of what life is like for white South Africans. As long as you don't look like a liability, about the only qualifications required are that you don't have children and that you like animals (you'll probably be looking after a large dog or two). House & Home Sitting used to be a national agency but now operates only in Johannesburg (☎ (011) 701 1905). It charges about R20 per night for two people, usually

with a minimum stay of around two weeks. It's worth asking tourist offices in other places as there might be local agencies.

## Hostels

The past few years have seen an explosion in the number of backpacker hostels. South Africa has gone from being one of the least to one of the most backpacker-friendly countries in the world. However, the hostels are clustered in the popular areas, such as Cape Town and along the Garden Route, so there are still large areas of the country where camping is the only option for shoestringers. Nearly all hostels are of a high standard and a dorm bed costs in the region of R30 a night. Many hostels also offer private rooms which cost about R80 to R100 a double. Some will let doubles as singles for a little less.

It seems likely that more hostels will open; for the latest list, look out for the little *BUG* (Backpackers' Up-To-Date Guide), available in some hostels.

The international YHA organisation is represented (it's called Hostelling International here) and has a number of hostels. You can contact their head office in Cape Town at 101 Boston House, 46 Strand St (☎ (021) 419 1853; fax 21 6937). There are also fledgling local organisations which are still in a state of flux. Nearly all hostels carry information on other hostels regardless of their affiliation.

## 'Overnight Rooms'

Many small towns on major routes have at least one place offering *kamers* (rooms) primarily to locals travelling on a budget. Try asking at the café (milk bar) or at the petrol station. The standard of accommodation varies but is usually pretty basic. If there's a caravan park in town you'd probably be better off there. Expect to pay around R60 a double.

## B&Bs & Guesthouses

The distinction between a B&B and a guesthouse is usually pretty vague. Even places offering a number of guest rooms are usually just private houses (admittedly fairly large

## Guesthouse & B&B Organisations

Many regions have B&B organisations (ask at local tourist offices). For a nationwide chain, contact Bed 'n Breakfast Pty Ltd (☎ (011) 482 2206; fax 726 6915), PO Box 91309, Auckland Park, 2006 Johannesburg. This company handles bookings for many places, with rates from R110/180 to R180/200 for singles/doubles. There's a booking fee of R20, although that covers more than one place if you want to book several. For the addresses of their many regional offices contact the central office in Johannesburg.

For consistently excellent places to stay covering a wide range of budgets, travel with the booklets produced by the Portfolio Collection: The Bed & Breakfast Collection (with singles/doubles from about R100/120 to R450/600), The Retreats Collection (guesthouses and lodges), averaging around R200/300 and up) and The Country Places Collection (guesthouses, hotels and game lodges, from R300/500 and way up). Contact them in Johannesburg at Shop 5E, Mutual Square, Oxford Rd, Rosebank, 2196, by mail at PO Box 52350, Saxonwold 2123, by phone on ☎ (011) 880 3414 or by fax on ☎ (011) 788 4802. Highly recommended.

There's also the South African Farm Holiday Association (☎ (021) 96 8621), 'Farm & Country Holiday', Head Office, PO Box 247, Durbanville, Cape Town 7550. ■

houses) and the service provided is always very personal.

There is an enormous number of B&Bs, and it's a rare town that doesn't have at least one. Some of the cheapest places aren't much better than basic Overnight Rooms but on the whole the standard is extremely high.

If you're travelling on the sort of budget which would allow you to stay in B&Bs in the UK or cheap motels in Australia or the USA, you will be pleasantly surprised by the standards and prices of B&B places here. Unlike a British B&B, many South African establishments offer much more than someone's spare room, and unlike a motel they are individual and often luxurious. Antique furniture, a private verandah, big gardens and a pool are common. Many have separate guest entrances and en-suite bathrooms.

Breakfasts are enormous and usually ex-

cellent. Many hosts offer regional specialities and traditional dishes which give you an insight into South African food which you don't get in restaurants.

In big towns the houses are usually out in suburbia or in the countryside, which might be an attraction but can make them difficult to get to if you don't have transport.

### Hotels

Before the boom in B&B accommodation, almost every town in the country had at least one hotel offering reasonable accommodation and meals. Now, many of the cheaper places have found that they can't compete and have either lifted standards and prices or have stopped offering accommodation altogether. This is a pity, as some old country town pubs were basic but pleasant places with real atmosphere.

The average country town hotel rated two stars charges from around R150/200 a single/double, often including breakfast. There might be cheaper rooms with shared bathrooms (maybe R80 per person) but this isn't usual. In areas of tourist interest, prices are usually higher. It's rare to find a hotel which is less than clean and comfortable, and the bar is always a good place to meet locals. Most rooms have TV and direct-dial phones. Larger towns have more expensive hotels as well.

In the ex-Homelands the hotel situation is a bit different. There is almost always a top-end Sun hotel with an attached casino, but with a few exceptions the smaller pubs are usually just drinking places.

### FOOD

Despite the fact that South Africa produces some of the best meat, fresh produce and seafood in the world, the food is often disappointing. The British can take most of the blame. Large steaks (admittedly, usually excellent), overboiled vegetables and fried chips seem to be the staple diet for whites. Vegetarians will have difficulty away from the main cities.

In the cities and in tourist areas such as the Western Cape Winelands and along the

## Hotel Chains

The rapidly expanding **Formule 1** chain (☎ (011) 440 1001; fax 440 2800) offers basic but modern, clean and secure accommodation at around R120 for up to three people. They are sterile but reasonable places. There are Formule 1 hotels in Beaufort West, Cape Town, Jo'burg (three locations), Nelspruit and Port Elizabeth.

The **Holiday Inn** chain (☎ 0800 117711 toll-free) has several levels of hotels. Holiday Inn Garden Court hotels are reliably comfortable, usually modern hotels with low service levels – there's no room service, for example. Singles/doubles cost around R270/320. There are a few Holiday Inns and Holiday Inn Crowne Plazas which offer higher levels of service and charge from around R500/600, with very large weekend discounts. Holiday Inn Express is a new level which is soon to be introduced. It is the budget end of the chain and offers 'no frills' rooms (ie, no service – although it's hard to see how there could be less service than in Garden Courts) for under R200.

The **Southern Sun** group is associated with Holiday Inn and has some more expensive hotels.

**Protea** (☎ 0800 11 9000 toll-free for central booking; fax (011) 484 2752) is another large chain of mid-to-high range hotels. Room rates vary quite a lot, but the average price is around R250 to R300. Most Protea places are existing hotels which have decided to join the chain, so standards can be a bit inconsistent. The Karos chain (☎ (011) 484 1641 or (021) 434 3344) charges a little more.

**Sun International** (☎ (011) 780 7800; fax 780 7443) is a chain of tourist hotels, almost all of which are in the ex-Homelands – because gambling was legal in the Homelands and Sun hotels invariably have casinos attached. Standards and prices vary a little but are never less than high. An average Sun hotel costs about R350/500 a single/double (more on weekends); you can pay over R10,000 a night for a suite at the Palace in Sun City.

See the earlier Guesthouse & B&B Organisations boxed text for information on the Portfolio Collection, which has some outstanding places to stay. ■

Garden Route, a few places serve more interesting (and healthy) food, showing what can be done with some imagination. Unfortunately, you're more likely to find restaurants offering international dishes that have been South Africanised. Minestrone is not supposed to be 'a hearty broth'; Thai chicken shouldn't have 'a rich honey sauce'. Basically, if a dish can have spices removed and sugar or animal fat added in large amounts, it will. It is worth sampling some of the traditional Cape cuisine, which is an intriguing mix of Malay and Dutch.

Prices are remarkably consistent. In pubs and steakhouses, steak or fish will cost between R25 and R35. Pizzas, also popular, cost around R20.

Most restaurants are licensed, but some allow you to bring your own wine, especially in the Cape. This works out cheaply, especially if you've done the rounds of a few vineyards. Ring ahead to check the restaurant's policy.

Most hotels allow nonguests to use their dining rooms and, even if you're travelling

on a tight budget, it's worth trying the breakfast buffet in an expensive hotel. You'll pay around R25 but you will definitely have enough food to last you all day – and enough cholesterol to fill your quota for at least a week. Many whites also eat two other meals of this size each day, so it's easy to see why many white men use belts not so much to hold up their trousers but to restrain an avalanche of fat. God knows how white women stay thin.

*Boerewors* (farmers' sausage) is the traditional sausage and is sold everywhere. Even committed carnivores can find it unappetising but that's partly because what you're being sold sometimes isn't boerewors but *braaiwors* (BBQ sausage), an inferior grade. Real boerewors must be 90% meat, of which 30% can be fat. You can imagine what goes into unregulated braaiwors!

There is a small but increasing number of restaurants serving African dishes, most of which don't originate in South Africa. The staple for most blacks is rice or *mielie* (maize) meal, often served with a fatty stew.

## Glossary of Food Terms

*biltong*
dried meat made from virtually anything
*braaisvleis* or *braai*
a barbecue in any other country, but a religious ritual in South Africa
*bredie*
traditional dish; vegetables and lamb braised and stewed
*bobotie*
traditional dish; delicately flavoured Malay curry served with stewed fruits and chutney
*boerewors*
spicy sausages (often sold like hot dogs by street vendors), essential at any *braai*
*bunny chow*
quarter of a loaf of bread hollowed out and filled with curry; a black takeaway speciality
*groente*
vegetables
*kingklip*
an excellent firm-fleshed fish, usually served fried
*kroeg*
hotel bar
*line fish*
school fish, usually fresh
*mielies*
maize
*mieliemeal*
maize porridge; the staple diet for rural blacks, served with stew
*monkey gland sauce*
sweet and spicy sauce served with steak
*mopane worms*
caterpillars found on mopane trees, dried and served in spicy sauce – a crunchy snack
*peri-peri*
a spicy pepper sauce
*potjiekos*
traditional stew cooked at *braais* in three-legged pots
*samosa*
spicy Indian pastry
*snoek*
a firm-fleshed migratory fish that appears off the Cape in June and July, sometimes served smoked, salted or as a curry
*steak*
usually plate-sized and served with sauce; see *monkey gland sauce*
*Steers/Spur*
ubiquitous steakhouse chain
*vleis*
meat
*waterblommetjie bredie*
traditional dish; mutton stew with water-hyacinth flowers (faintly peppery) and white wine

Although it isn't especially appetising it's cheap. Servings of rice and stew are sold for about R7 around minibus taxi parks.

### DRINKS
#### Pubs

Surprisingly, there are few 'traditional' bars and pubs in South Africa. Johannesburg, Durban and especially Cape Town have a wide range of drinking places, but in smaller towns the situation is dire. Most towns have at least one hotel. Franchised bars, such as O'Hagans, are appearing in larger towns, and while they are reasonable places, they aren't exactly steeped in atmosphere. Think of fast-food 'restaurants'.

In the bad old days most pubs had a bar (or *kroeg*) where the white men would drink, a Ladies Lounge/Bar where white couples would drink, and a hole in the wall where bottles would be sold to the blacks or coloureds. Since the collapse of apartheid, hotels are obliged to serve everyone everywhere, but unofficial segregation is the norm.

In most places, blacks have taken over the bar and white males have taken over the Ladies Bar. As far as we could discover, women are not served through the wall. You will find the occasional white couple in the Ladies, but unaccompanied females (white or black) are rarely seen in any part of any hotel.

The men in the Ladies are very often embittered travelling salesmen, travel writers and drunks, who study the bottom of their glasses as if they were looking into a crystal ball. In general the bar, with its cheerful and gregarious black clientele, will be far more congenial for travellers, once they have established their bona fides. Be warned that in the bar, beer is usually served in a 750ml bottle.

Draught beers are unusual, and served in large (500ml) or small (250ml) glasses. Usually you will be sold lager-style beer in cans or stubbies (small bottles) for around R4. There are a number of lager brands: Castle and Black Label are probably the most popular, but Amstel and Carlsberg are also good. In the Cape provinces, look out for Mitchell's Beers which come from a couple of small breweries. Windhoek beer, brewed in Namibia, is popular with aficionados because it is made with strictly natural ingredients. Brandy & coke is a popular poison – brandy's popularity dates back to the early days of white settlement.

The alcohol content of beer is around 5%, about the same as Australian beer but much stronger than UK or US beer. Even Castle Lite is 4% alcohol.

## Wine

Wine was first made in South Africa in 1659. It is now an enormous industry, employing around 30,000 people in Western Cape Province. The wine is of a high standard, and very reasonably priced. If you buy direct from a vineyard you can get bottles for as little as R6.50, but in a bottle store R12 and up is a more realistic price. Of course, you can pay a lot more and, as always, there is a pretty close correlation between quality and price. Most restaurants have long wine lists and stock a few varieties in 250ml bottles, which is very handy if you want to try a few wines or are eating alone.

There are over 2500 South African wines on the market. No wine may use any estate, variety, vintage or origin declaration on its label without being certified and carrying a certification sticker to that effect. No South African sparkling wine may be called champagne, although a number of producers use Chardonnay and Pinot Noir blends and the méthode champenoise.

There is a range of excellent dry whites made from Sauvignon Blanc, Riesling, Colombar and Chenin Blanc. The most widely available blends are called Blanc de Blanc (mainly Chenin Blanc), and Premier Grand Crû (usually Colombar, Chenin Blanc and Riesling; this is not a quality classification as in France).

The most popular red varieties are Cabernet Sauvignon, Pinotage (an interesting local variety crossed from Pinot and Cinsaut, which was known as Hermitage), Shiraz, Cinsaut and Pinot Noir. There are some excellent fortified wines (sherry, port, hanepoot, jerepigo and muscadel) and very high quality brandies.

A few low-alcohol wines are available, and they aren't bad.

## ENTERTAINMENT

The low-class 'jazz halls' of the Coloured people's quarters in Durban, with their night-long orgies of drinking, gambling, indecent dancing and immorality, illustrate the depths of degradation to which the Natives, and in this case Asiatics of both sexes, fall when left to their own devices.

*South Africa, A Planned Tour,* AW Wells, 1939

The writer would have been pleased that the apartheid governments stamped out this sort of behaviour. Unfortunately for those of us who think that it sounds pretty good, the stifling effects of the apartheid years have not yet worn off and nightlife remains a scarce commodity.

In Cape Town, Durban and Johannesburg you can find most forms of entertainment associated with big, westernised cities. The quality is often high but the range is limited. There are good entertainment listings (which include the small but healthy 'alternative' scene) in the *Weekly Mail*.

Visiting a township *shebeen* (a previously illegal bar) is probably the most interesting entertainment, and some have good music and dancing. However, it's potentially very dangerous. You'd be crazy to enter a township at night (or even during the day) without a trustworthy guide. Some hostels and backpacker-oriented activities outfits run tours which visit shebeens.

Outside the three big cities nightlife comes down to bars and cinemas.

## SPECTATOR SPORT

Sport is a very important part of life here, and if your country happens to be playing against South Africa you'll have an easy topic of conversation.

A few years ago I was in South Africa when the Springboks played the Wallabies (the Australian rugby team). Like most Australians, I live in a state that doesn't play rugby, so I wouldn't know a scrum from a sideline, but I was still expected to know intimate details about the Aussie team, and to care deeply about the result. The Wallabies lost, and the manager of the hotel sent a bottle of champagne to my room as consolation. On another occasion I was queuing at a very slow Spoornet ticket window. When I finally reached the front of the queue the ticket clerk realised that I was Australian, closed his window (much to the annoyance of the people behind me) and took me into a back room to show me that most of the clerks were watching an Australia/South Africa Test (cricket) match.

**Jon Murray**

It was agreed that South African international sporting teams would no longer be named Springboks because of the all-white connotations of the name. It had been boasted that no black would ever wear a Springbok jumper. However, there is almost

no chance that the new name, the Proteas, will catch on, and even Desmond Tutu now argues that the Springbok name should be retained.

South Africa returned to the Olympic Games in 1992, its first appearance since the 1960 Games. At the 1996 Atlanta Games, South Africans won three gold medals, swimmer Penny Heyns bagging two and Josia Thugwane scoring an inspirational win in the men's marathon – the first black South African to wear an Olympic medal. Cape Town made a bid to be the first African city to host the Olympic Games, but lost the 2004 games to Athens.

## Cricket

Cricket fans tend to be English-speakers but for a while after South Africa's return to international sport in the 1992 World Cup, cricket occupied centre stage. The euphoria following South Africa's surprising runner-up success in the competition probably helped the Yes vote in the referendum on constitutional reform.

Cricket was the first of the 'whites-only' sports to wholeheartedly adopt a non-racial attitude, and development programmes in the townships are beginning to pay dividends.

## Golf

Naturally a white sport in South Africa (as elsewhere), the international profile of South African golf has been kept up by champions such as Gary Player and Ernie Els, the world No.1 golfer in mid-1997. Although barred from hosting official tour tournaments in the apartheid days, South Africa staged big-money events, notably Sun City.

## Rugby

Rugby (Union, not League) was traditionally the Afrikaners' sport until the 1995 World Cup, which was hosted and won by South Africa. The entire white and coloured population went rugby mad – the black population was officially part of the celebrations but the response was a little muted. Rugby had been seen (and continues to be seen by many whites) as epitomising the Afrikaners' he-man social values. And those values were closely linked to apartheid values.

Still, there are now rugby development programmes in the townships, and Ellis Park echoed to 65,000 mainly white fans chanting 'Nelson' when the president, wearing a Springbok jumper, met the teams at the World Cup final.

### Soccer

Soccer is the most popular sport among blacks (and thus is by far the most popular sport in the country – a fact you wouldn't guess by reading the sports pages). The national team (known as 'bafana bafana' – the boys) won the prestigious Africa Cup in 1996 (helped, perhaps, by Nigeria's boycott of the event), thus making three big come-backs in the three major sports since the country was readmitted to world sport. Major teams in the local competition include the Kaiser Chiefs and the Orlando Pirates (known as Bucs, as in Buccaneers), both from the Johannesburg area.

### Tennis

Tennis has strong traditions in South Africa:
the national South African championship is one of the longest continuously run tourna-ments in the world. For a time it was an open event, attracting the world's top players (including former winners Arthur Ashe and Evonne Goolagong) but reverted to a nation-al field when South Africa was banned from hosting official tournaments.

Like golfers, tennis players were free to compete on the world stage because they were in an individual sport and therefore deemed to be representing themselves rather than their country. They were barred from team events like the Davis Cup in the mid-1970s. Despite several countries refusing to grant visas to South Africans, Johan Kriek and Kevin Curren managed to stake out places in the world top 10 in the 1980s, with Wayne Ferreira and Amanda Coetzer follow-ing suit in the '90s.

### Jukskei

The most popular of the traditional Afrikaner games is *jukskei*. This game is something like horseshoe-tossing but uses items associ-ated with trek-wagons. Kroonstad (in Free State) is the centre for national competition.

# Getting There & Away

This chapter deals with travel to/from South Africa only. For information on alternative routes that involve other African destinations and overland routes north of Zimbabwe, Botswana and Namibia see the introductory Getting There & Away chapter.

Johannesburg is the most important gateway to the region for both land and air transport, although an increasing number of flights use Cape Town and some go to Durban.

See the Johannesburg section in the Gauteng chapter for a list of airline addresses and phone numbers. There aren't many discount travel outlets in South Africa, but as always it is worth shopping around. The following companies will give you a good start:

South African Students' Travel Service (SASTS)
This is a national student travel organisation (you don't have to be a student to use its services). Once, this organisation was mainly concerned with getting South African students to Europe and back, but now it offers good deals on one-way tickets as well – definitely worth checking out. You'll find them in the Student Union Building, University of Witwatersrand (☎ (011) 716 3045), in Johannesburg. There are also offices at universities in Cape Town, Durban, Grahamstown, Pietermaritzburg and Port Elizabeth.
Rennies Travel
This is a comprehensive network of agencies throughout South Africa and is the agent for Thomas Cook.
Pathfinders Travel
This small agency specialises in ecotourism and personalised itineraries. It's at Senderwood Square, 17 Chaucer Ave, Bedfordview, Johannesburg (☎ (011) 453 1113/4, or 706 6629 after hours; fax 453 1483).

**Departure Tax**
There's an airport departure tax of R18 for domestic flights, R39 to regional African countries and R60 for other international flights. The tax is usually included in the ticket price. ∎

## WITHIN AFRICA
Most Southern African airlines fly to South Africa, plus some of the larger airlines from across the continent.

### Botswana
**Air** Between them Air Botswana and Comair have daily flights between Gaborone and Johannesburg (R550), and Cape Town (R1050).

**Bus** Greyhound buses run between Johannesburg and Gaborone three times a week for R95. Minibus taxis run from Mafikeng (North-West province) to Gaborone for about R25. Mafikeng is accessible from Johannesburg on City to City/Transtate buses (R50).

**Border Crossings** Most land border crossings between Botswana and South Africa are open between 7 or 8 am and 4 pm. The main border crossings are Ramatlhabama, north of Mafikeng, which is open from 7 am to 4 pm; Pioneer Gate, north-west of Zeerust, which is open from 7 am to 8 pm; and Tlokweng Gate, north of Zeerust, which is open from 7 am to 10 pm.

### Lesotho
See the Lesotho Getting & Away chapter for information on land routes, including hiking and horse trails through the Drakensberg, and border crossings.

**Air** SAA flies frequently between Moshoeshoe international airport, 18km from Maseru, and Johannesburg in South Africa. A one-way fare from Johannesburg costs R370 and from Cape Town it's R570. There are some deals on return fares – ask a travel agent.

**Bus** City to City/Transtate buses run from Johannesburg to Maseru for R60.

## Mozambique
**Air** SAA flies between Johannesburg and Maputo for about R450.

**Bus** Panthera Azul (☎ (011) 337 7409 or 887 0383) runs buses from Johannesburg to Maputo three times a week for about R190.

**Train** The *Komati* runs between Johannesburg and Maputo. See the Train section in the Getting Around chapter for details.

## Namibia
**Air** Air Namibia connects Windhoek with Johannesburg (R880) and Cape Town (R930).

**Bus** Intercape Mainliner buses run between Cape Town and Windhoek four times a week for R295. See the Cape Town section of the Western Cape chapter for details. You can travel between Windhoek and Johannesburg with Intercape (a total fare of R375), but you might have to stay overnight in Upington.

**Border Crossings** You can't cross the Namibia-South Africa border to/from the Kalahari Gemsbok National Park. The nearest alternative is to cross at Rietfontein. The main crossing west of Upington is at Nakop and on the west coast it's at Vioolsdrif. All three crossings mentioned are open 24 hours.

## Swaziland
See the Swaziland Getting There & Away chapter for details on land routes and border crossings.

**Air** Royal Swazi Airlines flies to Johannesburg daily (R410).

**Bus** A City to City/Transtate bus runs between Johannesburg and Manzini via Mbabane (the capital) on weekdays for R65. Alternatively, take the Baz bus, which runs through Swaziland en route between Johannesburg and Durban. See the South Africa Getting Around chapter for more details on both options.

## Zimbabwe
**Air** Air Zimbabwe (☎ (011) 331 1541; fax 331 6970 in Johannesburg) flies from Johannesburg to Harare daily (R860). There are also flights to Bulawayo and Victoria Falls. Some flights leave from Durban.

**Bus** Translux runs four services a week between Johannesburg and Harare (some services run via Bulawayo) for R200. See the Translux section in the Getting Around chapter for details. There are several other operators, such as the cheaper Zimbus (☎ (011) 883 7802). Ask around at the Rotunda bus station in Johannesburg for current deals. Translux also runs daily between Johannesburg and Victoria Falls (R210), via Bulawayo (R160 from Johannesburg).

See Johannesburg (Gauteng chapter) and Messina (Northern Province chapter) for information on minibus taxis.

**Train** The *Limpopo* runs weekly between Johannesburg and Harare for R321/220 in 1st/2nd class. The *Bulawayo* runs weekly between Johannesburg and Bulawayo for R235/168. There is no 3rd class on these trains.

**Border Crossings** The only border post between Zimbabwe and South Africa is at Beitbridge on the Limpopo River, which is open from 6 am to 8 pm. Lengthy waits used to be common but apparently things have improved lately. There's a lot of smuggling, so searches can be thorough. Messina is the closest South African town to the border (15km) and this is where you can change money.

## AUSTRALIA
The return flight between Australia and Johannesburg is expensive, at around A$2278 for a standard mid-season economy fare. You should be able to find a discounted fare for around A$1800. Air Mauritius has a few direct flights from Perth to Mauritius with a stopover, then a direct flight to Johannesburg. It has other flights to South Africa

via Mauritius originating in Singapore, Hong Kong and Bombay (Mumbai).

Malaysia Airlines often has the cheapest flights from Sydney or Melbourne to Johannesburg and Cape Town. The hassle is that you fly via Kuala Lumpur, a long way out of the way. There are more-or-less-direct connections but you might want to take advantage of Malaysia Airlines' stopover deals in Malaysia.

The other alternative is to check out round-the-world deals or a return ticket to Europe via Southern Africa.

From South Africa, South African Students' Travel Service (SASTS) has one-way cheapies to Sydney from as low as R4230. The cheapest flight of all is from Johannesburg to Perth, from R3660.

### UK

Flight prices from the UK are quite competitive, and there are some charter flights. It's worth shopping around, but you should be able to get a return flight to Johannesburg for under £450. Some airlines will allow you to fly into Cape Town and leave from Johannesburg or vice versa.

Although it is a long-haul flight, it's pretty easy to handle (nothing like flying to Asia or Australia). The flight takes about 13½ hours, but it is overnight and South Africa is only two hours ahead of GMT/UTC, so the body clock doesn't get too badly out of whack.

There are also interesting tickets available that include other ports in Africa, such as Cairo, Nairobi and Harare. If you have plenty of time up your sleeve, you may find some good value round-the-world tickets that can build in Johannesburg. Return tickets to Australia via Johannesburg are also worth looking at.

About the cheapest consistently available fare directly to Southern Africa from London is the laborious flight on Balkan Bulgarian Airlines, stopping in Sofia (Bulgaria). Given the bare bones service, combined with typically severe overbooking and an obstinate reluctance to change reservations or tickets, it may be worthwhile to pay for something more reliable.

For a cheap one-way fare from South Africa to the UK, talk to SASTS. It will probably put you on a flight to New York, from where you catch another cheapie to Heathrow. Could be an interesting option and you might find a ticket for about R2900.

### EUROPE

Most of the major European airlines fly to Johannesburg, with many flights continuing on to Cape Town. An increasing number, including British Airways, fly direct to Cape Town.

### ASIA

Air India, Cathay Pacific, Malaysia Airlines, Singapore Airlines, Thai Airways and other Asian airlines now fly to South Africa – most to Johannesburg. A cheap fare from Johannesburg to Kuala Lumpur (Malaysia) costs about R4670.

From South Africa, a cheap one-way fare to India costs from R2900 (Johannesburg to Bombay). Air India has a twice-weekly service between Bombay (Mumbai) and Johannesburg and Durban.

### NORTH AMERICA

SAA flies to/from New York and Miami, and by now there should be direct flights to/from Washington, DC. You should be able to purchase singles/returns from New York for US$1335/1750, and from Los Angeles for US$1926/2149. Particularly if you are coming from the west coast of the USA, it is worth looking into fares via Asia. It is also worth exploring the possibility of flying to London and buying a bucket shop ticket there.

### SOUTH AMERICA

SAA and Varig-Brazilian Airlines link Johannesburg and Cape Town with Rio de Janeiro and Sao Paulo. Currently, Malaysia Airlines offers good deals on flights to Buenos Aires. SASTS might find you a one-way ticket from Johannesburg or Cape Town to Buenos Aires for about R4860.

## SEA
### Cruises
Cape Town is a major port of call for cruise ships, and many stop at Durban as well.

### Freighter
Jumping a tramp freighter and enjoying a cheap and grungy experience is largely a thing of the past, thanks to the containerisation of most cargo services. There might be local services where a quite chat with an officer can get you on board, but for long-distance travel you are limited to container vessels.

Many container lines do take a limited number of passengers, and while the voyage will be considerably more expensive than flying, the per-day cost can be reasonable. Accommodation can be anything from the owners' suite to a bunk in a self-contained cabin. Passengers generally eat with the officers, and the food is usually good.

The best source of information about routes and the shipping lines plying them is the *OAG Cruise & Ferry Guide* (it used to be called the *ABC*), published quarterly by the Reed Travel Group in the UK. Your travel agent might have a copy.

A few companies take bookings for freighters. Given the complex nature of freight routes (delays and diversions are common) it might be best to deal with one of them. They include:

Strand Cruise & Travel Centre
  Charing Cross Shopping Centre Concourse, London WC2N 4HZ, UK (☎ (0171) 836 6363; fax 497 0078)
Freighter World Cruises Inc
  180 South Lake Ave, Suite 335, Pasadena CA 91101, USA (☎ (818) 449 3106; fax 449 9573)
Sydney International Travel Centre
  Level 8, 75 King St, Sydney 2000, Australia (☎ (02) 9299 8000; fax 9299 1337)

# Getting Around

South Africa is geared towards travel by private car, with some very good highways but limited and expensive mainstream public transport. If you want to cover a lot of country in a limited time, hiring or buying a car might be necessary. If you don't have much money but have time to spare, you can hitch to most places, and if you don't mind a modicum of discomfort there's the extensive network of minibus taxis, cheap buses and 3rd-class train seats.

## AIR

The domestic service of South African Airways (SAA) is sometime called SA Express. To most destinations there are plenty of daily flights. Fares aren't cheap, but if you plan to do a lot of flying in South Africa check with a travel agent before you leave home for special deals on advance purchase tickets. Once you're in South Africa there are a few discount options.

Most SAA flights have a limited number of 15% discount seats, sold on a first-come, first-served basis. If you book and pay 10 days in advance there's a 30% discount and one month in advance earns you 50% off (Apex fare). There are also big discounts on late-night flights (ask for 'slumber fares').

The free baggage allowance is 40/30/20kg in 1st/business/economy class. Excess baggage is charged at R11 per kilogram.

SAA flights can be booked at travel agents or by phoning local booking offices:

| | |
|---|---|
| Bloemfontein | (051) 47 3811 |
| Cape Town | (021) 403 1111 |
| Durban | (031) 361 1111 |
| East London | (0431) 44 5202 |
| George | (0441) 73 8448 |
| Johannesburg | (011) 356 1111 |
| Kimberley | (0531) 22 431 |
| Port Elizabeth | (041) 507 3158 |
| Pretoria | (012) 328 3215 |
| Upington | (054) 23161 |

**What's *this* place?**
You might still encounter apartheid-era problems of navigation. Most maps didn't (and many still don't) show black townships or 'locations'. That isn't so much of a problem when these areas are on the outskirts of a town, but in many cases, especially in the minor apartheid-era Homelands such as Lebowa or KaNgwane (which themselves didn't make it onto many maps), you can be driving along and come to a large town which just isn't on the map. People naturally give directions involving these major but invisible towns, and if you're using the local transport system you might have a hard time working out just where the bus or minibus taxi is going. ■

SA Airlink competes with SAA on a few major domestic routes and also has flights to smaller places not served by SAA. Make bookings at travel agents or phone toll-free on ☎ 0800 114 799. Another smaller airline flying the main routes is SA Express (☎ (011) 978 5569).

Comair is known for arranging fly-in packages to Kruger and private game reserves but is now developing into a general domestic airline, operating in conjunction with British Airways. Book at travel agents or on ☎ (011) 921 022 in Johannesburg, toll-free ☎ 080 961 1196 in Eastern and Western Cape and ☎ 080 131 4155 in Durban.

There are also several regional airlines, such as National Airlines (☎ (021) 934 0350/1) which flies between Cape Town, Springbok, tiny Kleinsee and Alexander Bay, and Sun Air (☎ (011) 397 2244) which flies between Pilanesberg (Sun City) and Cape Town, Durban and Johannesburg.

## BUS

Translux, part of the semi-privatised government transport service called Autonet, runs most long-distance buses. The other main national operator is Greyhound, which covers quite a lot of the country at similar fares to Translux. In the western half of the country Intercape Mainliner has useful services at fares a little lower than Translux.

With the exception of City to City/Transtate (poor relations of Translux) and local services geared towards blacks, bus travel isn't cheap. Return fares are double the one-way fares.

Greyhound offers Houndabout, a bus pass deal, but it isn't very good value, especially if you plan to sometimes use alternate transport, such as minibus taxis. A much better deal is offered by the innovative Baz Bus.

### The Baz Bus

The Baz Bus is an excellent alternative to the major bus lines. It is aimed at backpackers, but its routes, organisation and service levels make it very useful to travellers on any budget. Its bus fleet is described as 'semi-luxury', but that's being a little modest.

The Baz Bus offers hop-on hop-off fares between Johannesburg and Cape Town via the Drakensberg, Durban and the Garden Route, plus a very useful loop from Durban up through Zululand and Swaziland and back to Johannesburg, passing close to Kruger National Park. This loop runs through what is arguably the most interesting part of the region and no other transport options cover it.

The major fares are Johannesburg to Cape Town (via Durban), R595; and Cape Town to Johannesburg (via Durban and Swaziland) R670. You can also buy sector tickets. It's hoped that in the near future the routes and frequencies will be expanded, and that the Durban-Swaziland-Johannesburg loop will run in both directions.

The Baz Bus drops off and picks up at many hostels along the way, and has transfer arrangements with some hostels in less accessible places, such as Coffee Bay and Port St Johns in the Transkei. Most hostels take bookings, or you can phone ☎ (021) 439 2323 or fax (021) 439 2343. The email address is bazbus@icon.co.za and for the latest information check out their web site (http://www.icon.co.za/bazbus/).

### Translux

Translux runs express services on the main routes. Tickets must be booked 24 hours in advance. You can get on without a booking if there's a spare seat, but you won't know that until the bus arrives and if there isn't a seat you could have a couple of days' wait for the next bus. You usually can't book a seat to a nearby town, but prices for short sectors are exorbitant anyway – you're better-off looking for a local bus or a minibus taxi.

Computicket takes bookings, as do many travel agents and some railway stations. There are also reservations offices around the country, including:

| | |
|---|---|
| Bloemfontein | (051) 408 3242 |
| Cape Town | (021) 405 3333 |
| Durban | (031) 361 8333 |
| East London | (0431) 44 2333 |
| Johannesburg | (011) 774 3333 |
| Port Elizabeth | (041) 507 3333 |
| Pretoria | (012) 315 2333 |

Translux offices have details of the few remaining City to City services (which are cheaper than Translux) but they won't tell you about them unless you ask.

### Major Translux Routes

The fares quoted below are for peak season. There are small discounts from late January to mid-March, from mid-April to mid-June, from late July to mid-September and from early October to the end of November. The frequency of services can change seasonally.

Unfortunately, nearly all services run through the night, so you miss out on the scenery.

Note that services running south from Johannesburg originate in Pretoria, and those running north from Johannesburg run through Pretoria. The trip time between the cities is about 45 minutes and long-distance fares to/from Johannesburg and Pretoria are usually the same.

**Johannesburg – Cape Town via Bloemfontein**
Daily service, 19 hours (overnight). Stops (with fares from Jo'burg/Cape Town) include Bloemfontein (R160/285), Beaufort West (R240/170), Worcester (R300/110), Cape Town (R330/-).

**Johannesburg – Cape Town via Kimberley**
Five services a week, 18 hours (overnight). Stops (with fares from Jo'burg/Cape Town) include Kimberley (R165/285), Beaufort West (R240/170), Worcester (R300/110), Cape Town (R330/-).

**Johannesburg – Durban** Daily service, 8½ hours (daylight). There's also at least one express service daily that takes an hour less. Stops (with fares from Johannesburg/Durban) include Harrismith (R110/115), Pietermaritzburg (R120/30), Durban (R145/-).

**Johannesburg – East London** Daily service, 12½ hours (overnight). Stops (with fares from Jo'burg/East London) include Bloemfontein (R160/200), Queenstown (R180/65), King William's Town (R200/65), East London (R240/-).

**Johannesburg – Harare (Zimbabwe)** Four services a week, 17 hours (overnight). Stops (fares from Johannesburg/Harare) include Pietersburg/Polokwane (R90/180), Louis Trichardt (R100/165), Messina (R115/145), Harare (R230/-).

**Johannesburg – Knysna** Daily service, 17½ hours (overnight). On Sunday and Thursday the southbound buses run via Kimberley and on Wednesday and Friday the northbound buses do. On the other days buses run via Bloemfontein. Stops (with fares from Jo'burg/Knysna) include Bloemfontein (R160/230), Kimberley (R165/195), Beaufort West (R240/120), Oudtshoorn (R250/50), Mossel Bay (R250/50), George (R250/40), Knysna (R250/-).

**Johannesburg – Lusaka (Zambia) via Harare (Zimbabwe)** Two services a week, 25 hours. Stops (with fares from Jo'burg/Lusaka) include Pietersburg/Polokwane (R90/260), Louis Trichardt (R100/235), Messina (R115/220), Harare (R230/95), Lusaka (R310/-).

**Johannesburg – Port Elizabeth** Daily service, 15 hours (overnight). On Tuesday and Sunday, southbound buses run via Cradock, on Monday and Saturday northbound buses do. On the other days buses run via Graaff-Reinet. Stops (with fares from Jo'burg/Port Elizabeth) include Bloemfontein (R160/195), Cradock (R220/185), Graaff-Reinet (R220/135), Port Elizabeth (R260/-).

**Johannesburg – Umtata** Four services a week, 13½ hours (overnight). Stops (with fares from Jo'burg/Umtata) include Pietermaritzburg (R110/130), Kokstad (R140/80), Umtata (R160/-).

**Johannesburg – Victoria Falls (Zimbabwe)** Two services a week, 21 hours. Stops (with fares from Jo'burg/Victoria Falls) include Pietersburg/Polokwane (R90/170), Louis Trichardt (R100/160), Messina (R115/150), Bulawayo (R180/70), Victoria Falls (R220/-). There are also five services a week which go only as far as Bulawayo.

**Cape Town – Durban** Daily service, 20 hours (overnight). Stops (with fares from Cape Town/Durban) include Paarl (R110/330), Beaufort West (R170/2650, Bloemfontein (R285/160), Bethlehem (R310/120), Pietermaritzburg (R330/30), Durban (R340/-).

**Cape Town – East London** Five services a week, 16 hours (overnight). Stops (with fares from Cape Town/East London) include Paarl (R110/210), Beaufort West (R170/180), Graaff-Reinet (R190/180), Cradock (R195/165), Queenstown (R200/65), King William's Town (R210/65), East London (R210/-).

**Cape Town – Port Elizabeth via Coastal Route** Daily service, 10 hours (daylight and good scenery), also an overnight service running a slightly different route four times a week. Stops (with fares from Cape Town/Port Elizabeth) include Swellendam (R75/130, daylight service only), Mossel Bay (R95/115), Oudtshoorn (R115/100), George (R115/100), Knysna (R120/80), Plettenberg Bay (R125/50), Storms River (R140/40 daylight service only), Port Elizabeth (R140/-).

**Cape Town – Port Elizabeth via Mountain Route** Three services a week, 12 hours (overnight). Stops (with fares from Cape Town/Port Elizabeth) include Paarl (R110/140), Robertson (R115/125), Montagu (R115/125), Oudtshoorn (R115/100), Port Elizabeth (R140/-).

**Durban – Port Elizabeth** Daily service, 10½ hours (overnight). Stops (with fares from Durban/Port Elizabeth) include Port Shepstone (R80/205), Kokstad (R95/185), Umtata (R135/145), East London (R165/90), Grahamstown (R200/65), Port Elizabeth (R210/-).

## Transtate & City to City

Transtate originally carried people from the Homelands, Lesotho and Swaziland to and from the big cities where they were guest workers under the apartheid regime. So it was cheap, ran very interesting routes and stopped just about everywhere. In a sense it was Third World transport, but compared with buses in most Third World countries, it was luxurious.

Unfortunately, Transtate services are being wound back. Private bus lines are filling the gap but they are usually far less reliable and comfortable.

Transtate stops and the few offices can be difficult to find. Buses often stop at train stations (ask about the 'railways bus'), so you can try asking there. A black employee is more likely to be of help than a white one. Most remaining services originate in Johannesburg – see the Johannesburg Getting There & Away section of the Gauteng chapter for more information.

City to City, another semi-government Autonet line, used to run similar routes to Translux but at cheaper fares. It was used by poorer whites. Most City to City routes have closed and the line has been merged with Transtate. This fiddling about with the cheaper bus lines has been a favourite occupation of Autonet for some time and it's entirely possible that the City to City and Transtate union will unravel, or that the whole loss-making enterprise will be sold off to private operators.

The bottom line is that it's worth using City to City/Transtate but difficult to find current and reliable information about them.

## Other Long-Distance Lines

Greyhound offers services on much the same routes as Translux at much the same prices. The exception is the daily express run between Johannesburg and Kimberley (R90). There are a couple of Greyhound routes where you don't have the option of taking Translux. There's a daily service between Johannesburg and Nelspruit (R120), and a daily service between Johannesburg and Gaborone (Botswana) (R105). Greyhound's Johannesburg to Durban service runs through parts of Zululand to Richards Bay, then down the coast to Durban, which is handy. There's also an express service which follows the same route as Translux but takes only six hours.

Greyhound has booking offices in the major cities, or see a travel agent.

Intercape Mainliner is a major line in the western half of the country and generally charges appreciably less than Translux. Routes include Johannesburg to Upington (R175), Cape Town to Upington (R150), Upington to Windhoek (Namibia) (R200), Cape Town to Windhoek (R325), Cape Town to Port Elizabeth (R140), and Port Elizabeth to East London (R80). In summer there are also services between Johannesburg and Cape Town (R320), and between Johannesburg and Port Elizabeth (R140) and the Garden Route. See the relevant towns for more information.

## TRAIN

Spoornet, the company which runs South Africa's railway system, has been partially privatised and the result was the closing of passenger services on all but the main lines. The only regular passenger services are on 'name trains'. They are a good way to get between major cities and 3rd class is very cheap, if uncomfortable. Another advantage is that, unlike the long-distance buses, fares on short sectors are not inflated.

On overnight trains the fare includes a sleeping berth (except in 3rd class) but there's an R18 charge for bedding hire. You can also hire a private compartment (sleeping four in 1st class and six in 2nd class) or a coupe (sleeping two in 1st class and three in 2nd). Breakfast costs R13 and other meals are available.

First and 2nd class must be booked at least 24 hours in advance (you can book up to three months in advance); you can't book 3rd class. Most stations accept bookings, or phone one of the major reservation centres:

| | |
|---|---|
| Bloemfontein | (051) 408 2941 |
| Cape Town | (021) 405 3871 |

| Durban | (031) 361 7621 |
| East London | (0431) 44 2719 |
| Johannesburg | (011) 773 2944 |
| Kimberley | (0531) 88 2631 |
| Nelspruit | (013) 288 2203 |
| Port Elizabeth | (041) 507 2400 |
| Pretoria | (012) 315 2401 |

## Name Train Routes & Fares

Return fares are double one-way fares (given here in 1st/2nd/3rd class). Fares have not risen for many years, and while a rise has been rumoured for some time, all that has happened so far is that the 25% discount which used to apply to every fare is disappearing.

For detailed routes and timetables, Spoornet has a web site; http://www.spoornet.co.za/1pass00.htm.

Gricers (train fanatics) will be interested in David Forsyth's site – he's a 'ferroequinologist' with strong views – but even the less fanatical should take a look, as he provides some information that the Spoornet site doesn't; http://www.ru.ac.za/departments/iwr/staff/daf/satrain.html.

**Algoa** Johannesburg – Port Elizabeth, daily, 19 hours. Departs from Johannesburg at 2.30 pm, departs from Port Elizabeth at 2.30 pm. Stops include Kroonstad, R54/38/22 from Johannesburg, R196/133/82 from Port Elizabeth; Bloemfontein, R95/65/39, R156/106/65; Cradock R183/124/77, R68/47/28; and Port Elizabeth, R240/162/101.

A 1st/2nd class compartment for the whole trip costs R720/730, and a coupe is R360/365.

**Amatola** Johannesburg – East London, daily, 20 hours. Departs from Johannesburg 12.45 pm, departs from East London at midday. Stops include Kroonstad, R53/38/23 from Johannesburg, R173/120/77 from East London; Bloemfontein, R92/65/41, R134/93/60; Queenstown, R172/119/77, R53/38/23; and East London, R215/149/96.

A 1st/2nd class compartment for the whole trip costs R646/670, and a coupe is R323/335.

**Bosvelder** Johannesburg – Messina, daily, 15 hours. Departs from Johannesburg at 6.50 pm, departs from Messina at 2.45 pm. Stops include Pretoria, R25/19/10 from Johannesburg, R124/86/51 from

Messina; Pietersburg/Polokwane, R83/58/33, R66/47/27; Louis Trichardt, R112/78/46, R37/27/14; and Messina, R139/95/56.

A 1st/2nd class compartment for the whole trip costs R418/428, and a coupe is R209/214.

**Bulawayo** Johannesburg – Bulawayo (Zimbabwe), 24 hours. Departs from Johannesburg at 3.25 pm on Tuesday, departs from Bulawayo at 9 am on Thursday. The fare is R253/168 in 1st/2nd class – no 3rd class.

A 1st/2nd class compartment for the whole trip costs R706/756, and a coupe is R353/378.

**Diamond Express** Pretoria – Bloemfontein via Kimberley, daily except Saturday, 15 hours (10 hours between Johannesburg and Kimberley). Departs from Johannesburg at 8.40 pm, departs from Bloemfontein at 5 pm. The fare between Johannesburg and Kimberley is R113/77/45, with the luxury Diamondpax class costing R164.

A 1st/2nd class compartment for the whole trip costs R382/393, and a coupe is R191/196.

**Komati** Johannesburg – Komatipoort, daily, 12 hours. Departs from Johannesburg at 5.45 pm, departs from Komatipoort at 6.07 pm. Stops include Pretoria, R25/19/10 from Johannesburg, R106/75/42 from Komatipoort; Middelburg, R56/40/22, R76/54/30; Nelspruit, R99/69/39, R33/25/13; Komatipoort, R121/85/48.

A 1st/2nd class compartment between Johannesburg and Komatipoort costs R364/382, and a coupe is R182/191.

Three times a week the train runs on to Maputo (Mozambique). Fares from Johannesburg to Maputo are R151/108/50. A 1st/2nd class compartment between Johannesburg and Maputo costs R454/486, and a coupe is R227/243.

**Limpopo** Johannesburg – Harare (Zimbabwe), 26 hours. Departs Johannesburg on Friday at 8.30 am and Harare on Sunday at 7 am. Stops at Pretoria, R27/21 from Johannesburg, R305/209 from Harare; Pietersburg/Polokwane, R92/65, R241/165; Louis Trichardt, R125/87, R208/143; Messina R154/107, R179/123; Beitbridge, R159/110, R174/120; and Harare, R321/220. No 3rd class on this train.

A 1st/2nd class compartment for the whole trip costs R964/990, and a coupe is R482/495.

**Southern Cross** Cape Town – Port Elizabeth, 24 hours. Departs from Cape Town on Friday at 6.15 pm, departs from Port Elizabeth on Sunday at 8.45 am. Stops and fares from Cape Town include Swellendam, R52/38/21; George, R86/62/35;

Oudtshoorn, R96/69/39; and Port Elizabeth, R159/114/65.

A 1st/2nd class compartment for the whole trip costs R636/684, and a coupe is R318/342.

**Trans Karoo** Johannesburg – Cape Town, daily, 27 hours. Departs from Cape Town at 9.20 am, departs from Johannesburg at 10.10 am. Stops include Kimberley, R113/77/41 from Johannesburg, R224/152/94 from Cape Town; De Aar, R161/110/67, R176/119/74; Beaufort West R214/145/90, R122/84/51; and Cape Town, R340/230/140.

A 1st/2nd class compartment for the whole trip costs R1020/1036, and a coupe is R510/518.

**Trans Natal** Johannesburg – Durban, daily, 13½ hours. Departs from both Johannesburg and Durban at 6.30 am. Stops include Newcastle R78/52/31 from Johannesburg, R97/65/39 from Durban; Ladysmith, R104/69/42, R71/48/29; Estcourt, R118/78/48, R57/39/23; Pietermaritzburg, R142/93/58, R33/23/13; and Durban R164/108/67.

A 1st/2nd class compartment for the whole trip costs R492/486, and a coupe is R246/243.

**Trans Oranje** Cape Town/Durban, 30½ hours. Departs from Cape Town on Monday at 6.50 pm, departs from Durban on Wednesday at 5.30 pm. Stops include Wellington, R26/19/10 from Cape Town, R410/276/173 from Durban; Beaufort West R122/84/51, R313/211/132/; R260/176/109; Kimberley R224/152/94, R213/145/90; Bloemfontein R258/174/108, R178/121/75; Kroonstad R298/201/125, R139/95/58; Bethlehem R325/219/137, R111/76/46; Ladysmith, R366/247/154, R69/48/29; Pietermaritzburg R403/272/170, R32/24/13, and Durban R425/286/179.

A 1st/2nd class compartment for the whole trip costs R1276/1288, and a coupe is R638/644.

## The Blue Train

Some people come to South Africa just to ride on the famous *Blue Train*, running between Pretoria/Johannesburg and Cape Town. This 25-hour journey is one of the world's most luxurious train trips – dressing for dinner is customary. If you can't afford to take the whole trip, consider a section. For example, from Cape Town to Worcester, near the Winelands, the cheapest seats are about R300, including lunch.

*Blue Train* bookings can be made in Johannesburg (☎ (011) 774 4469), Cape Town (☎ (021) 218 2672), Pretoria (☎ (012) 315 2436) and Durban (☎ (031) 361 8425). For group bookings (for 10 or more people) phone (011) 773 7631. Some travel agents, both in South Africa and in other countries, take bookings. Departures are on Monday, Wednesday and Friday. The train leaves Jo'burg at 10.10 am, and arrives in Cape Town at noon the next day. Northbound, it leaves Cape Town at 11 am. The train is popular and you should book well in advance.

As well as the Cape Town run, a lowveld route has been added, between Johannesburg and Nelspruit, and there are occasional trips to Victoria Falls in Zimbabwe.

## Steam Trains

There are a few steam train trips to be made, (and longer steam train tours; see the Tours section later in this chapter). They include the *Apple Express* from Port Elizabeth, the *Outeniqua Choo-Tjoe* between Knysna and George, and the *Banana Express* along the KwaZulu-Natal South Coast from Port Shepstone. See the Western Cape, Eastern Cape and KwaZulu-Natal chapters.

## Local Trains

There are Metro services in and around several cities. Trains in the Johannesburg area no longer suffer the political violence which turned them into death-traps before 1994, but you should still get advice before taking one, especially in 3rd class. Robbery is a possibility in 3rd class anywhere.

## MINIBUS TAXI

If you don't have a car the only way to get between many – most – places is to hitch or take a minibus taxi.

If you've come overland through Africa you're in for a pleasant surprise. Minibus taxis here are less crowded and in better condition than in other countries, although most don't carry luggage on the roof so stowing packs can be a hassle. From Johannesburg to Cape Town you'll pay R150, slightly more than 3rd class on the train.

As well as the usual 'leave when full'

taxis, there is a small but increasing number of door-to-door services, which you can book. These tend to run on the longer routes and, while they cost a little more, they are convenient.

Minibus taxis tend to run on relatively short routes, generally only to neighbouring towns, although you'll nearly always find a few running to a distant big city. Because many of the taxi services shuttle blacks between the location or township where they live and the town where they work (often a long way apart), and because townships and locations are rarely named on maps, finding out where a taxi is going can be a problem, and there's always a chance that you'll end up stuck on the 'wrong' side of a big town. Which brings us to the question of safety.

Away from the big cities robbery on taxis is not much of a problem, and since the 1994 elections, politically motivated attacks on taxis have ceased. But these have been replaced by commercially motivated attacks in isolated outbreaks of 'taxi wars' between rival companies. Crowded taxis have been machine-gunned. However, given the number of taxis the incidence of attacks is very low if you avoid problem areas. Cape Town's taxi war flares regularly and a few other areas have had trouble. Read the newspapers and ask around.

The biggest risk is bad driving and poor

maintenance. This is more of a concern on long trips, when the driver will become very tired (and maybe drunk); you should be safe enough on short trips.

Whites have a very poor opinion of the driving skills of minibus taxi drivers. I suspect that this is largely because overloaded taxis travel slowly on highways and interrupt all those BMWs travelling at 180km/h. In the many thousands of kilometres I've driven in South Africa I've seen a lot of taxis that looked to be on the point of falling apart, but never any bad driving. Taxis I've travelled in have been relatively comfortable and, compared to similar transport in, say, Nigeria or Pakistan, not frightening.

Jon Murray

## CAR & MOTORCYCLE

South Africa is a good country to drive in. Most major roads are excellent and carry relatively little traffic, and off the big roads are some interesting backroads to explore.

The country is crossed by National Routes (N1, etc), and on some sections a toll is payable. This is based on distance and varies considerably, from about R3 to nearly R20. There's always plenty of warning that you're about to enter a toll section, and there's always an alternative route.

Toll roads are indicated by a black 'T' in a yellow circle. The turn-off for the alternative route is indicated by a black 'A' in a yellow circle. Be prepared for inadequate signposting on alternative routes. Most signs will direct you to small towns or just give route numbers, not the direction of the big city you're heading for.

Most roads are numbered (R123, for example). Signposts show these numbers and when you ask directions most people refer to these numbers rather than destinations, so it pays to have a good road map. The AA's free city and regional guides are very useful, especially their route maps which help you through the maze of freeways which surround even small towns.

Petrol stations are often open 24 hours – because of cheap labour. Fuel costs around R1.50 per litre, depending on the octane level you choose. Unleaded petrol is now becoming widely available. Many petrol sta-

---

**Minibus Taxi Etiquette**
- People with lots of luggage (usually women) sit in the first row behind the driver.
- Pay the fare with coins, not notes. Pass money forward (your fare and those of people around you) when the taxi is full. Give it to one of the front seat passengers, not the driver. If you're sitting in the front seat you might have to collect the fares and make change.
- If you sit on the folding seat by the door it's your job to open and close the door when other people get out. You'll have to get out of the taxi each time.
- Say 'Thank you!' when you want to get out, not 'Stop!'

tions accept credit cards, but a significant number aren't yet connected to the electronic banking system.

## Road Rules

You can use your driving licence if it carries your photo, otherwise you'll need an International Driving Permit, obtainable from a motoring organisation in your country.

South Africans drive on the left-hand side of the road just like in the UK, Japan and Australia.

There are a few local variations on road rules. The main one is the 'four-way stop', which can occur even on major roads. If you're used to a system where drivers on major roads always have priority over drivers on smaller roads you'll definitely need to stay alert. When you arrive at a four-way stop, you must stop. If there are other vehicles at the intersection, those which arrived before you get to cross before you. Before you proceed, make sure that it *is* a four-way stop – if so, you can safely cross ahead of approaching cars; if you've mistaken an ordinary stop sign for a four-way stop, the approaching cars won't be slowing down ...

**Speed Limits** The speed limit is 100km/h (roughly 60 miles per hour), and 120km/h on most major highways. Some dangerous sections of rural roads have a limit of less than 100km/h, while the usual limit in towns is 60km/h.

If you stick to the highway speed limit you'll feel lonely – most white traffic travels much faster, most black traffic travels much slower.

## Hazards

South Africa has a horrific road fatality rate. In 1997, the toll for the four-day Easter holiday was 306 dead, and the annual rate is pushing 10,000. With a population of about 38 million – the vast majority of whom don't own cars – that's appalling. Most of the carnage is caused by dangerous driving.

**Other Drivers** On highways, fast cars com-

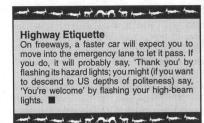

**Highway Etiquette**
On freeways, a faster car will expect you to move into the emergency lane to let it pass. If you do, it will probably say, 'Thank you' by flashing its hazard lights; you might (if you want to descend to US depths of politeness) say, 'You're welcome' by flashing your high-beam lights. ■

ing up behind you will expect you to move over into the emergency lane to let them pass. The problem is that there might be animals, pedestrians or a slow-moving vehicle already in the emergency lane. Don't move over unless it's safe.

It is becoming common for an overtaking car to rely on *oncoming* traffic to move into the emergency lane! This is sheer lunacy and you must remain constantly alert. When two cars travelling in opposite directions decide that they will overtake despite oncoming traffic, things get really hairy, especially if the protagonists are travelling at the usual 160km/h!

Head-on collisions between fast white-driven cars must account for an awful lot of road deaths, but who do whites blame for the high accident rate? Blacks, of course. They say that if it wasn't for those slow-moving black vehicles, they wouldn't have to drive so dangerously. Sure.

Drivers on little-used rural roads often speed and they often assume that there is no other traffic. Be careful of oncoming cars at blind corners on country roads.

Drink-driving has not been treated as a problem until recently. It is a major hazard – be careful.

**Roads** In the ex-Homelands beware of dangerous potholes, washouts, unannounced hairpins and the like.

Anywhere in the country you don't have to get very far off the beaten track to find yourself on dirt roads. Most are regularly graded and reasonably smooth and it's often possible to travel at high speed. Don't! If you're cruising along a dirt road at 100km/h and you come to a corner, you won't go around that corner, you'll sail off into the veld. If you put on the brakes to slow down you'll probably spin or roll. If you swerve sharply to avoid a pothole you'll go into an exciting four-wheel drift then find out what happens when your car meets a telegraph pole. Worst of all, if another car approaches and you have to move to the edge of the road, you'll lose control and collide head-on.

On dirt roads that are dry, flat, straight, traffic-free and wide enough to allow for unexpected slewing as you hit potholes and drifted sand, you could, with practise, drive at about 80km/h. Otherwise, treat dirt as you would driving on ice.

**Animals & Pedestrians** In rural areas slow down and also watch out for people and animals on the roads. Standard white advice is that if you hit an animal in a black area, don't stop – drive to the nearest police station and report it there. This might be paranoia or arrogance, but then again it might not be. If the animal you hit is a cow or a horse, leaving the scene might not be an option.

**Weather** Thick fog can slow you to a crawl during the rainy season. This is particularly a problem in KwaZulu-Natal, where it can be a clear day on the coast while up in the hills visibility is down to a few metres. Hailstorms on the lowveld can damage your car.

**Crime** Car-jacking is a problem in Johannesburg and to a lesser extent in the other big cities. People have been killed for their cars. Stay alert and keep windows wound up at night.

### Rental

The major international companies, such as Avis (☎ 08000 21 111 toll-free) and Budget (☎ 0800 016 622 toll-free), are represented. They have offices or agents across the country. Their rates are high, but if you book through your local agent at home before you arrive they will be significantly lower – but

---

### Giving Lifts

In rural areas you'll see many black hitchhikers. While I was driving in South Africa I made a point of picking up hitchhikers (partly because I knew that I'd be soon hitching myself and needed all the good karma I could get). I met a great many nice people and had conversations I wouldn't have had in most other situations, where the black/white role-playing of South African society stultifies relationships.

Whites warn you not to pick up hitchhikers (no surprise), but so do an increasing number of blacks. That advice might be good near big towns or if the hikers are a group of young men, but if you failed to give a lift to an old man in the middle of nowhere, or a woman with a baby in the rain, I'd say that the apartheid mentality had corrupted your thinking. On the other hand, the only hitchhikers I regretted picking up were a group of poor whites who stubbed out cigarettes on the seats. ■

**Jon Murray**

---

still higher than the cheaper companies in South Africa.

Other than the big companies there are local companies. These come and go, but currently the larger companies include Imperial (☎ 0800 131 000 toll-free) and Tempest (☎ 0800 031 666 toll-free). They have agents in the cities and a few other places.

A step down from these are smaller and cheaper outfits. There seems to be a constant supply of new companies which burst onto the scene with dramatically reduced rates, then either fold or hike their prices. This is good news for visitors. Alisa (☎ 0800 021 515 toll-free) has been around for a while and still offers a good deal. Still further down the scale are outfits in the big cities renting older cars. These can be good value for getting around a local area but usually not for longer trips.

**Rates** If you hire a category B car (usually a smallish Japanese car such as a Corolla with a 1.6 litre motor, manual transmission and air-con) for five days with at least 200 free kilometres per day, with full collision and theft waivers, you'll pay in the region of

R230 per day with the larger companies and from about R190 with the smaller companies. Many hostels can arrange better deals, from around R120 per day. Zebra Crossing in Cape Town seems to have a way with rental companies.

**Choosing a Deal** South Africa is a big country, but unless you are a travel writer on a tight schedule, you probably don't need unlimited kilometre rates. For meandering around, 400km a day should be more than enough, and if you plan to stop for a day here and there, 200km a day might be sufficient. However, if you're renting with an international company and you book through the branch in your home country, you'll probably get unlimited kilometres at no extra cost.

One-way rentals aren't usually a problem with the larger companies, between major cities, anyway. They might be with the smaller companies.

Read the contract carefully before you sign. Some insurance policies don't cover you or the car for 'political unrest', so avoid stone-throwers. Hail damage is a distinct and costly possibility so see if it's covered. Many contracts used to stipulate that you couldn't enter townships – maybe that has changed, but check.

When you're getting quotes make sure that they include VAT, as that 14% slug makes a big difference.

Choose a car powerful enough to do the job. The smallest cars are OK for one person but with any more they'll be straining on the hills, which even on major highways are steep. Steep hills can also make automatics unpleasant to drive.

**Insurance Excess** One problem with nearly all car rental companies is the excess – the amount that you are liable for before the insurance takes over. Even on a small car you will pay at least R2500 and as much as over R4000 for a single-vehicle accident. Visitors with little experience of driving on dirt roads have a high accident rate on South Africa's dirt roads, so this could be an important consideration.

**Camper Vans** A way around South Africa's high accommodation and transport costs is to hire a camper van. Note that one-way rentals might not be possible or attract big fees with these vehicles.

One company with a range of deals is Leisure Mobiles (☎ (011) 477 2374; fax 477 2321) in Johannesburg at 22 Amatola Villas, Montpark Dr (corner of John Adamson Dr), Montgomery Park 2195. Toyota Landcruiser campers sleeping four cost from around R3700 a week with unlimited kilometres. There are also basic two-person 'bakkie' campers – Toyota Hi-Lux pick-ups with a canopy, mattress, sleeping bags, gas stove and cooking utensils. Weekly rates with unlimited kilometres are about R2900.

### Purchase
Buying your own car is one way around the high cost of transport – if you can sell it again for a good price. See Getting There & Away in the Johannesburg and Cape Town sections for details.

### Motorbike Rental
Renting a bike isn't cheap but the idea of riding around South Africa is attractive. See the Cape Town Getting There & Away section for more information.

### BICYCLE
South Africa is a good country to cycle in, with a wide variety of terrain and climate, plenty of camping places and many good roads, most of which don't carry a lot of traffic. Most of the National Routes are too busy for comfort, although there are quieter sections, in northern KwaZulu-Natal and the Cape provinces.

Keep in mind that parts of South Africa are very hilly and even on main roads gradients are steep.

Much of the country (except for Western Cape and the west coast) gets most of its rain in summer, in the form of violent thunderstorms. When it isn't raining it can be hot, especially on the lowveld where extreme heat and humidity make things pretty unpleasant in summer. See the Climate

SOUTH AFRICA

section in the Facts about the Region chapter for more details.

Distances between major towns can be long but except in isolated areas like the Karoo or Northern Province you're rarely very far from a village or a farmhouse (in Australian terms, that is – you'll sometimes feel very alone if you've come from Europe).

Away from the big cities you might have trouble finding specialised parts, although there are basic bike shops in many towns.

If you decide to give up and take public transport you might have to arrange expensive transport for your bike with a carrier, as train lines are few and far between and buses aren't keen on bikes in their luggage holds. The exception to this is City to City/Transtate. Minibus taxis don't carry luggage on the roof.

Theft is a problem – bring a good lock and chain.

Where you go depends on how long you have, how fit you are and what you want to do. There are a few places where meandering between small towns is possible (although these tend to be hilly areas) such as the southern Free State. Cycling through the Transkei area of Eastern Cape (a mountain bike would be best here) would be a good adventure and the northern lowveld offers endless empty plains.

There is a boom in mountain biking (usually with support vehicles, braais and beer – see the Activities section of the

---

**Transporting Your Bicycle Overseas**
It's possible to bring your own bike by plane. Some airlines just want you to cover the chain, remove the pedals and turn the handlebars sideways; others require it to be completely dismantled and in a box. Cardboard bike boxes are available for a small charge or free from bike shops. Your bike is probably safer if it's not in a box, as it will probably be stowed upright or on top of the other luggage. My bike has flown 11 times, suffering a few scratches (in India) and one badly buckled wheel (at Heathrow).

**Jon Murray**

---

regional Facts for the Visitor chapter) so mountain bikes are sold everywhere. The bottom end of the top-quality range cost about R2500. Touring bikes are harder to come by except in the major cities.

## HITCHING

Hitching is never entirely safe in any country, and it's not a form of travel we can recommend. People who decide to hitch should understand that they are taking a small but potentially serious risk. They will be safer if they travel in pairs and let someone know where they are going.

That said, hitching is sometimes the only way to get to smaller towns, and even if you're travelling between larger ones the choice is sometimes to wait a day or two for a bus or hitch. Make it obvious that you're a clean-cut foreign visitor. You might have to wait a while for a lift, especially on major roads, but when you get one there's a good chance that you'll be offered other hospitality, such as a bed for the night.

It helps to carry a sign stating your destination. Rather than writing out the whole word, use the number-plate prefix for the town or area you want. For example, CA is Cape Town, ND is Durban.

If you've waited long enough for a lift and want to flag down a minibus taxi you'll have to exert yourself (maybe wave money) because whites so rarely use them that the driver won't think of stopping for you.

Hitching always involves a degree of risk, but this is particularly so in and around major cities. You are best to catch public transport well beyond the city limits before you start to hitch.

We've only heard of one traveller having police problems while hitching, and they weren't the usual problems:

If you're hitching the Calvinia-Keimoes route and get stuck in Kenhardt, one of the policemen's wives has rooms to rent. The policeman was so keen for us to stay that he knocked the price down and then (we're sure) diverted the traffic to prevent us getting a lift. He underestimated our stickability and we got a lift in a truck three hours later.

**Kate Wall**

## LOCAL TRANSPORT

Getting around in towns isn't easy, and many of them sprawl a long way. This is a major pain if you're hitching, especially if the town is bypassed by the freeway. The big cities and some of the larger towns have bus systems. Services often stop running early in the evening. Many towns, even some quite large ones, don't have taxis. If there is a taxi, chances are you'll have to telephone for it. You can sometimes make use of minibus taxis but they tend not to run through the areas where there are hotels. Often, you'll end up walking.

In Durban and a few other places you'll find that mainstay of South-east Asian public transport, the tuk-tuk. Tuk-tuks run mainly in downtown or tourist areas.

In Cape Town you can hire scooters, and this will probably catch on in other places.

## TOURS

### Air

Comair (☎ (011) 921 0333) has several 'Wings to the Wild' packages, flying to Kruger National Park and the adjacent private reserves. For example, the Skukuza Costcutter is a three-night package for about R3600 per person for two people, flying from Johannesburg.

### Bus

The main coach tour operators are Springbok-Atlas (☎ (021) 25 1271; fax 25 1267) and Connex (☎ (011) 884 8110; fax 884

3090). They have a wide range of fairly expensive tours covering popular routes, as well as day tours. Their clientele tends to be older tourists.

There is a multitude of other companies, with backpackers (and less formal visitors in general) increasingly well catered for. For information on safari-style tours and adventure holidays see the Activities section in the regional Facts for the Visitor chapter.

### Train

Union Ltd Steam Rail Tours (☎ (021) 405 4391; fax 405 4395), a division of Spoornet, runs restored steam trains. The *Union Limited* was the pre-*Blue Train* king of the line in South Africa, running to Cape Town with passengers meeting liners to Europe.

The six-day Golden Thread tour, on the *Union Limited*, runs from Cape Town along the coast to Oudtshoorn and back, a leisurely trip on some very scenic lines. It costs R2500 per person including meals and bedding – not bad value. There are also various 15-day steam safaris, from R6000 per person. The train was in its time luxurious and it has been meticulously restored. Passengers have more room than they once did, though, as two people share four-berth compartments and singles get two-berth compartments.

Another company doing similar things is Rovos Rail (☎ (012) 323 6052; fax 323 0843) which runs superbly restored old trains within South Africa and elsewhere.

# Western Cape Province

Western Cape Province takes in the south-western corner (and many of the attractions) of the old Cape Province, including Cape Town, the Winelands and the Garden Route. One of the highlights of a visit to South Africa is discovering the extraordinary flora, and this is most spectacularly represented in Western Cape, which is home to the prolific Cape floral kingdom.

Most of the province was populated by Khoisan tribes when the whites first arrived. Tragically, very few Khoisan survived, and their traditional cultures and languages have been almost completely lost.

The province is also home to the so-called 'coloureds', people who have diverse origins and didn't fit neatly into the apartheid system's pigeonholes. Most people who were classified as coloured are descended from the Khoisan, slaves (from Asia and Africa), Xhosa and Europeans. Most lead westernised lifestyles; they're overwhelmingly Christian, and most speak Afrikaans.

Until apartheid really got going in the 1950s they were quite closely integrated with the Europeans; they even had voting rights. Distinctive sub-groups include the Nama and Griqua and the Cape Muslims of the Cape Peninsula, who were imported from east Asia as slaves and have maintained their Islamic traditions.

Before Europeans arrived there were few or no Bantu peoples in the area, but many Bantu, particularly Xhosa, have gravitated to the Cape and the larger towns and cities in search of work.

## HISTORY

Khoikhoi tribes with a pastoralist semi-nomadic lifestyle inhabited the Cape Peninsula and most of the best grazing land along the south and west coasts. They coexisted with their close relatives the San, who were nomadic hunter-gatherers capable of surviving in the driest corners of Africa.

Portuguese explorers charted the coast

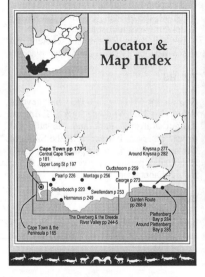

## HIGHLIGHTS

- Cape Town – one of the world's most beautiful cities: Table Mountain, great beaches, historic buildings and the Cape of Good Hope
- Cape Winelands around historic Paarl and Stellenbosch
- Whale-watching at Hermanus
- Ostrich farms at Oudtshoorn
- Knysna's lagoon and steam train
- Warm-water surf beaches, resort towns and forests of the Garden Route

from the 15th century, and the first permanent white settlement was established in Cape Town by the Dutch in 1652. Explorers, hunters and cattle-farming trekboers quickly fanned out into the surrounding countryside. By the second half of the 18th century, the Khoisan were decimated and the whites were battling with the Xhosa tribes in the east, a struggle that would continue for the next 100 years.

In 1806 the British seized the Cape from

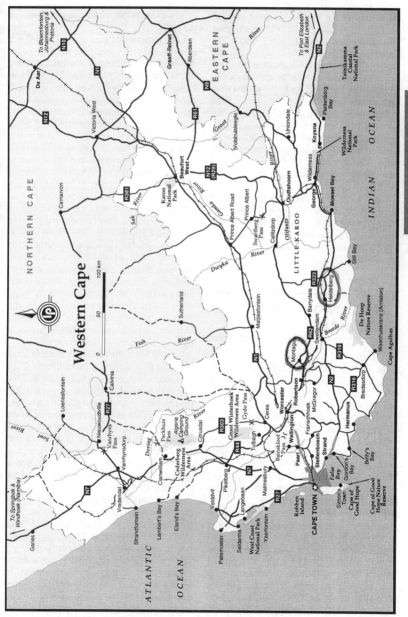

the Dutch for the second and final time, to prevent the strategically important port falling into the hands of the French. The Cape remained a British colony until the Union of South Africa was instituted in 1910.

Between 1834 and 1840, approximately 15,000 Afrikaners left the Cape on the Great Trek to the north where they established independent republics. Their relationship with the British colony was uneasy at best. One of the primary reasons they left was to escape the British administration, but they were still dependent on British ports and were clearly overshadowed by the power of the British Empire.

During the 1899-1902 Anglo-Boer War there was little direct impact on the Western Cape area but not surprisingly, many people were deeply ambivalent about the war, and many Afrikaners joined the Boer republics' forces.

# Cape Town & the Peninsula

Cape Town, or Kaapstad, is one of the most beautiful cities in the world. No matter how long you stay, the image of the mountains and the sea will be seared into your mind.

About 40km from the Cape of Good Hope, near the southern tip of the vast African continent, Cape Town is one of the most geographically isolated of the world's great cities. Dominated by a 1000m-high, flat-topped mountain with virtually sheer cliffs, it's surrounded by superb mountain walks, vineyards and beaches.

Pointless debates attempt to compare Cape Town with great coastal cities like Rio de Janeiro, Sydney, San Francisco and Vancouver. None can surpass the drama of Cape Town's site or its 350 years of recorded history. Long before travel writers' hyperbole devalued the language, Francis Drake's chronicler described the Cape of Good Hope as 'The most stately thing, and the fairest cape we saw in the whole circumference of the earth'.

Like all South African cities, Cape Town is two-faced – European but not European, African but not African – a volatile mixture of the third and first worlds. The cafés in Long St and the bars around the Victoria & Alfred Waterfront could be in any cosmopolitan capital, but the townships on the bleak, windswept plains to the east of the city could only be in Africa. There are few places where there is a more stark difference between rich and poor. Apartheid allowed the whites to reserve some of the world's most spectacular real estate, and the contrast between Crossroads and Clifton is complete – black and white.

Cape Town has the reputation for being the most open-minded and relaxed city in South Africa, but the scars of apartheid run deep. Outside of the black townships, however, there is nothing like the sense of tension that pervades Jo'burg. Perhaps it is partly because the coloureds are in many ways culturally integrated, but in the western-style city centre you could easily imagine the problems of South Africa are a figment of journalistic imagination.

Cape Town is the capital of Western Cape Province (it was the capital of the old Cape Province which covered more than half the country) and is the parliamentary capital of the republic. Pretoria can mount a good case for being made parliamentary capital in the new South Africa, but it's unlikely to succeed.

Cape Town works as a city in a way that few on the African continent do. There is a sense of history, and even in the centre, historical buildings have been saved. There are restaurants, cafés and bars, parks and gardens, markets and shops – all the things that make living in a city worthwhile. And then there are a few things that most cities don't have: mountains, magnificent surf beaches and outstanding vineyards.

Cape Town is a highlight of any visit to South Africa. If you can, give yourself at least a week, but you may well find – like many before you – that a week is far too short.

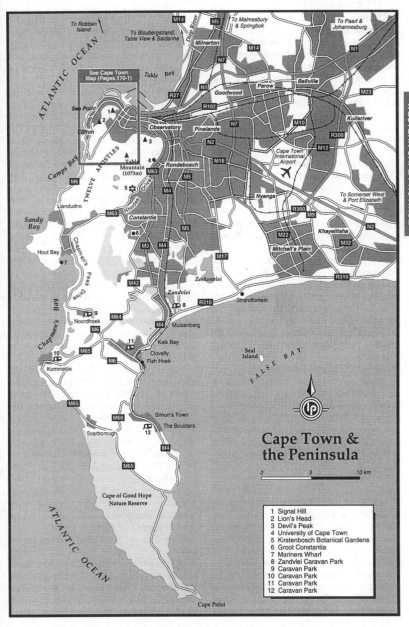

## Cape Town & the Peninsula

0       5       10 km

1  Signal Hill
2  Lion's Head
3  Devil's Peak
4  University of Cape Town
5  Kirstenbosch Botanical Gardens
6  Groot Constantia
7  Mariners Wharf
8  Zandvlei Caravan Park
9  Caravan Park
10 Caravan Park
11 Caravan Park
12 Caravan Park

## HISTORY
### The Earliest Peoples

The human history of the Cape began tens of thousands of years ago with Stone-Age tribes. They were followed by the San, hunter-gatherers who left no sign of their occupation beyond superb cave paintings. By the time the first Portuguese mariners arrived, however, the Cape was occupied by Khoikhoi, close relatives of the San, who were semi-nomadic sheep and cattle pastoralists.

### The European Navigators

The Portuguese came in search of a sea route to India and that most precious of medieval commodities – spice. Bartholomeu Dias rounded the Cape in 1487 naming it Cabo da Boa Esperança (Cape of Good Hope), but his eyes were fixed on the trade riches of the east coast of Africa and the Indies.

In 1503 Antonio de Saldanha became the first European to climb Table Mountain. The Portuguese, however, were not interested in settling on the Cape. It offered little more than fresh water; attempts to trade with the Khoikhoi often ended in violence and the coast and its fierce weather posed a terrible threat to their tiny caravels.

### The First European Settlers

By the end of the 16th century the English and Dutch were beginning to challenge the Portuguese traders, and the Cape of Good Hope became a regular stopover for their scurvy-ridden crews. In 1647, a Dutch East Indiaman was wrecked in Table Bay and its crew built a fort and stayed for a year before they were rescued.

This crystallised the value of a permanent settlement in the minds of the directors of the Dutch East India Company (Vereenigde Oost-Indische Compagnie, or VOC). They had no intention of colonising the country, but simply of establishing a secure base where ships could shelter and stock up on fresh supplies of meat, fruit and vegetables.

Jan van Riebeeck was the man they chose to lead a small expedition in his flagship *Drommedaris*. His specific charge was to build a fort, barter with the Khoikhoi for meat products and to plant a garden. He reached Table Bay on 6 April 1652, built a mud-walled fort not far from the site of the surviving stone castle, and planted gardens that have now become the Botanical or Company's Gardens.

In 1660, in a gesture that takes on an awful symbolism, van Riebeeck planted a bitter-almond hedge to separate the Khoikhoi and the Europeans. It extended around the western foot of Table Mountain down to Table Bay – sections can still be seen in Kirstenbosch Botanical Gardens. The hedge may have protected the 120 Europeans but, having excluded the Khoikhoi, there was a chronic labour shortage. In another wonderfully perverse move, van Riebeeck then proceeded to import slaves (many of whom were Muslim) from Madagascar, India, Ceylon, Malaya and Indonesia.

The European men of the community were overwhelmingly employees of the VOC and overwhelmingly Dutch – a tiny official elite and a majority of ill-educated soldiers and sailors, many of whom had been pressed into service. In 1685 they were joined by around 200 French Huguenots, Calvinists who had fled from persecution by King Louis XIV.

The population of whites did not reach 1000 until 1745, but small numbers of free (meaning non-VOC) burghers had begun to drift away from the close grip of the company, and into other areas of Africa. These were the first of the trekboers and their inevitable confrontations with the Khoisan were disastrous. The indigenous people were driven from their traditional lands, decimated by introduced diseases, and destroyed by superior weapons when they fought back. The survivors were left with no option but to work for Europeans in a form of bondage little different from slavery.

There was a shortage of women in the colony so the female slaves and Khoisan survivors were exploited both for labour and sex. In time, the slaves also intermixed with the Khoisan. The offspring of these unions formed the basis for sections of today's coloured population.

The VOC maintained almost complete control, but the town was thriving – providing a comfortable European lifestyle to a growing number of artisans and entrepreneurs who serviced the ships and crews. Cape Town was known as the Tavern of the Seas, a riotous port used by every navigator, privateer and merchant travelling between Europe and the East (including Australia).

In the early days of European settlement, animals common in the area included lion, elephant, hippo, black rhino, buffalo, hyena and leopard. They were very soon killed off and the great slaughter of Southern Africa's wildlife began.

## Cape Muslims

Cape Muslims (generally called Cape Malays by whites) are South Africans of long standing. Although many were brought to the early Cape Colony as slaves, others were political prisoners and exiles from the Dutch East Indies. Some of the first prisoners on Robben Island were Muslims. People were brought from countries as far apart as India and modern Indonesia, but their lingua franca was Malay (at the time an important trading language), which is why they came to be called Cape Malays.

A common language and religion, plus the presence of important political and religious figures, helped a cohesive community to develop. It has survived intact over the centuries, and even resisted some of the worst abuses of the apartheid decades.

Around Cape Town is the Circle of Karamats made up of the tombs of about 25 saints from the community. One of the first was Sheikh Yusef, a Batavian exiled to the Cape in the late 17th century. On the voyage out, his ship ran low on water, and the Sheikh obligingly turned sea water to fresh water. Another important exile was Tuan Guru from Tidor, who arrived in 1780. During his 13 years on Robben Island he copied the Koran from memory (his version is apparently quite accurate) and later helped establish the first mosque.

A visit to Bo-Kaap, the 'Malay' Quarter, is a must, and while wandering around by yourself is rewarding, it's worth taking one of the tours run by local residents. Tana-Baru Tours (☎ (021) 24 0719; fax 23 5579) is very good and has a two-hour walking or driving tour for about R45. See the Tours section for more information. ■

## The British Invade & Colonise

Dutch power was fading by the end of the 18th century and in response to the Napoleonic Wars, the British decided to secure the Cape. In 1806, at Bloubergstrand 25km north of Cape Town, the British defeated the Dutch and the colony was permanently ceded to the Crown on 13 August 1814.

The slave trade was abolished in 1808, and the remaining Khoisan, who were virtually treated as slaves, were finally given the explicit protection of the law (including the right to own land) in 1828, moves that contributed to Afrikaners' dissatisfaction and the Great Trek (1834-40).

At the same time that these apparently liberal reforms were introduced, however, the British introduced new laws that laid the basis for an exploitative labour system little different from slavery. Thousands of dispossessed blacks sought work in the colony, but it was made a crime to be in the colony without a pass, and without work. It was also a crime to leave your job. In 1854, a representative parliament was formed in Cape Town, but much to the dismay of the Dutch and English farmers to the north and east, the British government and Cape liberals insisted on a multiracial constituency (albeit with financial qualifications that excluded the vast majority of blacks and coloureds).

The discovery and exploitation of diamonds and gold in the centre of South Africa in the 1870s and 80s led to rapid changes. Cape Town was soon no longer the single dominant metropolis in the country, but as a major port it too was a beneficiary of mineral wealth that laid the foundations for an industrial society. The same wealth led to imperialist dreams of grandeur on the part of Cecil John Rhodes (who became the premier of the Cape Colony in 1890) who had made his millions at the head of De Beers Consolidated Mines.

In 1860, construction of the Alfred Basin in the docks commenced, finally making the port storm-proof. In 1869, however, the Suez Canal was opened, and Cape Town's role as the Tavern of the Seas began to wane. Today, the massive supertankers that are too big to use the Suez are also too big to enter Table Bay, so they are serviced by helicopter.

In 1895, Rhodes sponsored the unsuccessful Jameson Raid, which attempted to overthrow the South African Republic (Transvaal), under President Kruger, and bring it into a federation under British control. Rhodes was forced to resign, but the fiasco made the 1899-1902 Anglo-Boer War almost inevitable. Cape Town avoided any direct bloodshed in the terrible conflict, but it did play a key role in landing and supplying the half a million imperial and colonial troops who fought on the British side.

After the war, the British made some efforts towards reconciliation and moves towards the union of the separate South African provinces were instituted. The question of who would be allowed to vote was solved by allowing the provinces to retain their existing systems: blacks and coloureds retained a limited franchise in the Cape (although only whites could become members of the national parliament and eligible blacks and coloureds only constituted around 7% of the electorate) but did not have the vote in other provinces.

The issue of which city should become the capital was solved by the unwieldy compromise of making Cape Town the seat of the legislature, Pretoria the administrative capital, and Bloemfontein the seat of Appellate Division of the Supreme Court. The Union of South Africa came into being in 1910.

## Apartheid & the Townships
In 1948 in the first election after WWII, the National Party stood on its policy of apartheid and narrowly won. In a series of bitter court and constitutional battles, the right of the coloureds to vote in the Cape was removed and the insane apparatus of apartheid was erected.

Since the coloureds had no Homeland, the western half of the Cape Province was declared a 'coloured preference area', which meant no black could be employed unless it could be proved there was no suitable coloured person for the job. No new black

housing was built. As a result, illegal squatter camps mushroomed on the sandy plains to the east of Cape Town. In response, government bulldozers flattened the shanties, and their occupants were dragged away and dumped in their Homelands. Within weeks the shanties would rise again.

In 1960 the African National Congress (ANC) and the Pan African Congress (PAC) organised marches against the hated pass laws, which required blacks and coloureds to carry passbooks which authorised them to be in a particular area. At Langa and Nyanga on the Cape Flats, police killed five protesters. In response to the crisis a warrant for the arrest of Nelson Mandela and other ANC leaders was issued. In mid-1963 Mandela was captured and sentenced to life imprisonment. Like many black leaders before him, Robben Island, in the middle of Table Bay, was his prison.

District Six, just to the east of the city centre, was the suburb that, more than any other, gave Cape Town its cosmopolitan atmosphere and life. It was primarily a coloured ghetto, but people of every race lived there. It was a poor, overcrowded but vibrant community. The streets were alive with people, from children to traders, buskers to petty criminals. Jazz was its life blood and the district was home to many musicians, including the internationally known Dollar Brand. Being so close, it infected the whole city with its vitality.

This state of affairs naturally did not appeal to the National Party Government so, in 1966, District Six was classified as a white area. The 50,000 people, some of whose families had been there for five generations, were evicted and dumped in bleak and soulless townships like Athlone, Mitchell's Plain and Atlantis. Bulldozers moved in and the coloured heart was ripped out of the city. Today District Six is an open wasteland, a depressing monument to the cruelty and stupidity of the government.

The government tried for decades to eradicate squatter towns, such as Crossroads, which were focal points for black resistance to the apartheid regime. In its last attempt

## Pagad versus Gangsters

Rashaad Staggie's horrific (and televised) death made international news in 1996 and brought the activities of People Against Gangsterism And Drugs (Pagad) to the forefront of Western Cape politics. After a lynch mob burned then repeatedly shot the dying gangster, Pagad was labelled as a group of violent vigilantes by both white and black politicians. However the group retains strong support in the coloured community. Bizarrely, reactions to Pagad included a march by gangsters demanding protection of their human rights.

Pagad members are mainly coloured Muslims living in the bleak townships of Mitchell's Plain, where coloureds were dumped by the apartheid regime after being forcibly removed from their homes near central Cape Town. The group sees itself as defending the coloured community from the crooked cops and drug lords who allow gangs to control the coloured townships.

But this is South Africa and nothing is as simple as it seems. The gangs in the coloured townships grew out of a desperate need for the coloured community to organise itself against criminals from the neighbouring black townships. Gang members saw themselves as upright citizens defending their community. Many blacks bitterly resented the coloureds because they received 'favoured' treatment from the apartheid government and because blacks perceived the coloureds as not being active in the fight against apartheid.

This squabbling between apartheid's victims must have been immensely satisfying to the apartheid regime, and given its record of dirty tricks, it's reasonable to suppose that the government helped keep the quarrels bubbling. Even the ANC had to accommodate the gangsters to ensure the safety of their electioneering teams in the coloured townships during the 1994 elections.

To further complicate the issue, Pagad is in danger of being hijacked by an Islamic fundamentalist group. The battles between Pagad and the gangsters continue, with shootings and bombings. Although Pagad is mainly a Western Cape phenomenon, Pagad-style vigilante action has flared around Jo'burg, resulting in serious riots.

Rashied, Staggie's surviving brother and leader of the Hard Livings gang, has formed a political party of 'reformed gangsters' which will stand against Pagad candidates in the 1999 elections. ∎

between May and June 1986 an estimated 70,000 people were driven from their homes and hundreds were killed. Even this brutal attack was unsuccessful and the government accepted the inevitable and began to upgrade conditions. Vast new townships are now rapidly growing at Khayelitsha and Mitchell's Plain.

## ORIENTATION

On first impression, Cape Town is surprisingly small. The city centre lies to the north of Table Mountain and east of Signal Hill, and the old inner city suburbs of Tamboerskloof, Gardens and Oranjezicht are all within walking distance of it. This area is referred to as the City Bowl. When you look down on the city from the cableway stations you'll see why – the whole area is contained in a bowl formed by the steep sides of the mountain.

On the other side of Signal Hill, Sea Point is another older suburb densely populated with high-rise flats, apartments, hotels, restaurants and bars.

In some ways the peninsula seems remarkably undeveloped, an impression exaggerated by the untameable fynbos-cloaked mountains that form its spine. In the 1985 South African census, the entire Cape Peninsula's white population numbered 540,000, and this gives the City Bowl its scale.

The main white dormitory suburbs spread quite a distance to the north-east of the city (either side of the N1 to Paarl, from Goodwood, Parow and Bellville through to Kraaifontein) and to the south, skirting the eastern flank of the mountains and running down to False Bay (from Observatory to Rosebank, Rondebosch, Constantia and through to Muizenberg).

There are some small towns and suburbs that cling to the coast. On the Atlantic side, exclusive Clifton and Camps Bay are accessible by coastal road from Sea Point or

WESTERN CAPE PROVINCE

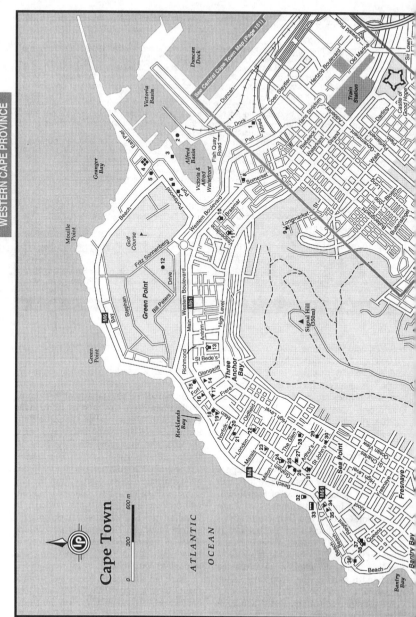

Cape Town

0    300    600 m

ATLANTIC
OCEAN

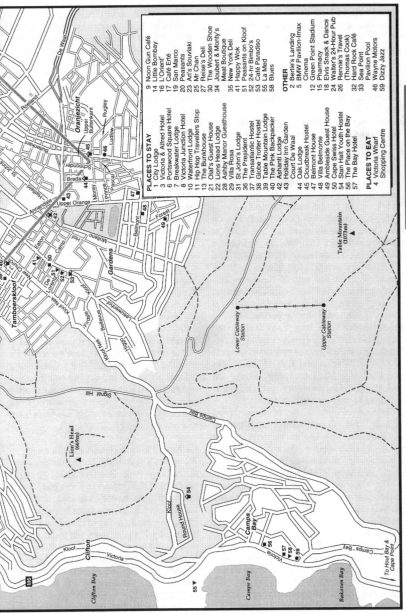

WESTERN CAPE PROVINCE

**PLACES TO STAY**

1 City Lodge
3 Victoria & Alfred Hotel
6 Portswood Square Hotel
7 Breakwater Lodge
8 Victoria Junction Hotel
10 Waterfront Lodge
11 Hip Hop Travelers Stop
13 The Bunkhouse
21 Olaf's Guest House
22 Lions Head Lodge
29 Ashby Manor Guesthouse
30 Villa Rosa
31 St John's Lodge
36 The President
37 Transatlantic Hostel
38 Globe Trotter Hostel
39 Table Mountain Lodge
40 The Pink Backpacker
42 Ashanti Lodge
43 Holiday Inn Garden
   Court De Waal
44 Oak Lodge
45 Cloudbreak Hostel
47 Belmont House
48 Villa Belmonte
49 Ambleside Guest House
50 Cape Swiss Hotel
56 Stan Halt Youth Hostel
56 The Place on the Bay
57 The Bay Hotel

**PLACES TO EAT**

4 Victoria Wharf
  Shopping Centre
9 Noon Gun Café
14 Little Bombay
16 L'Orient'
17 Café Erté
19 San Marco
20 Peasants
23 Ari's Souvlaki
25 Mr Chan
27 Reise's Deli
30 The Wooden Shoe
34 Joubert & Monty's
   Meat Boutique
35 New York Deli
41 Happy Wok
51 Peasants on Kloof
52 24-hr Bimbo's
53 Café Paradiso
55 La Med
58 Blues

**OTHER**

2 Bertie's Landing
5 BMW Pavilion-Imax
   Cinema
12 Green Point Stadium
15 Pharmacy
18 Elvis Snack & Dance
24 Walter's 24-Hour Pub
26 Rennie's Travel
   (Thomas Cook)
32 Hard Rock Café
33 Sea Point
   Pavilion Pool
46 Wayne Motors
59 Dizzy Jazz

through Kloof Nek, the pass between Table Mountain and Lion's Head. Camps Bay is a 10 minute drive (car or bus only) from the city centre, but as you go further south, the towns (Llandudno, Hout Bay and Kommetjie) become more inaccessible by public transport. The False Bay towns from Muizenberg to Simon's Town can all be reached by rail.

Of course, if you include blacks, coloureds and Asians the peninsula's population figures jump dramatically. The 1985 census counted 280,000 blacks, one million coloureds and 18,000 Asians. These numbers were almost certainly inaccurate at the time, particularly in the case of the blacks, and they are now virtually meaningless.

No-one knows how many blacks live on the Cape, although some put the figure at about one million. Thousands arrive from the old Xhosa Homelands of Transkei and Ciskei every month. Most live on the bleak sandy plain to the east of the mountains known as the Cape Flats. South-east from the cooling towers of the power station at Athlone, the townships lie between the N2 freeway and False Bay. They include the venerable squatter camps around Crossroads, and the enormous new developments at Mitchell's Plain and Khayelitsha. There are also large black townships around the industrial developments at Atlantis and Philadelphia to the north of Table Bay.

The spectacular Cape of Good Hope (which is not Africa's southernmost point – see the later Cape Agulhas section) is 70km by road to the south of the city centre. The extraordinary indigenous flora is protected within the Cape of Good Hope Nature Reserve.

The Cape is the meeting point for two great ocean currents that have a major impact on the climate of South Africa, and the Cape itself. The cold Benguela current (from around 8°C) runs up the west side of the Cape from Antarctica. The warm Agulhas current (around 20°C) swings around Madagascar and the east coast from the equatorial waters of the Indian Ocean and, if you're lucky, into False Bay. If you're not, the spring/summer south-easterly will blow in cold water.

The obvious impact for visitors is that you have to be pretty hardy to enjoy swimming on the Atlantic side of the Cape, but there are much more far-reaching climatic consequences. In brief, the Benguela current is rich in sea life, but it is too cold to evaporate easily so the west coast of South Africa is extremely dry.

## INFORMATION

As well as the tourist offices and other services listed here, the best sources of information are the backpacker hostels – a good hostel knows *everything*.

At the Tourist Rendezvous, at the main train station, you'll find the Captour desk (☎ (021) 418 5214/5) and many other desks of interest to visitors, including car hire, accommodation booking and adventure activities. Captour is the body which oversees tourism in and around Cape Town, but it's a private organisation and lists only those businesses which pay their membership fees. This includes pretty much all the major places, but for more obscure information (such as minibus taxi routes), Captour cannot help. Also, the accommodation booking service is inclined to suggest more expensive places (especially B&Bs), so it's worthwhile pressing them if you find that you are being offered places that are beyond your budget.

The Tourist Rendezvous complex is open from 8.30 am to 6 pm on weekdays, from 8.30 am to 3 pm on Saturday and from 9 am to 1 pm on Sunday.

### National Parks & Reserves Offices

As well as a desk at the Tourist Rendezvous, the National Parks Board (☎ (021) 22 2810; fax 24 6211) has offices in a restored Victorian building on the corner of Long and Hout Sts. It's open weekdays from 9 am to 4 pm. If you're heading to any of the national parks (especially Kruger) and want to be sure of accommodation, bookings are essential. Outside of school holidays it's not necessary to book camping sites. Phone for bookings and inquiries or write to PO Box 7400, Roggebaai 8012.

For information on the extensive and

excellent provincial parks contact Cape Nature Conservation (☎ (021) 483 4051), 1 Dorp St (not far from the corner of Long St).

### Visa Extensions

The Department of Home Affairs (☎ (021) 462 4970) is at 56 Barrack St.

### Money

Money can be changed at any commercial bank; they're open from 9 am to 3.30 pm on weekdays and many open on Saturday morning.

American Express is on Thibault Square (at the end of St George's Mall) (☎ (021) 21 5586) and at the Victoria & Alfred Waterfront (☎ (021) 21 6021). The Waterfront office is open from 10 am to 5 pm daily.

Rennies Travel is the agent for Thomas Cook and has branches on the corner of St George's and Hout Sts (☎ (021) 26 1789) open Monday to Friday from 8.30 am to 4.30 pm, and Saturday morning; 182 Main Rd, Sea Point (☎ (021) 439 7529); and at the Waterfront (☎ (021) 418 3744).

You can change money at the airport although the rates aren't as good as you'll get in town.

You can use the machines at BOB (First National) banks for Visa cash advances – there's a branch in St George's Mall on the corner of Shortmarket St and a machine at the train station.

### Post & Communications

The GPO is on the corner of Darling and Parliament Sts and is open weekdays from 8 am to 4.30 pm and Saturday from 8 am to noon. It has a poste restante counter in the Main Hall (identification is theoretically required).

The public phones in the post office are open 24 hours, but they're often very busy. There are also plenty of privately run public phone businesses, where you can make calls (and usually send faxes) without coins. Check their rates first; they are much more expensive than a normal public phone. A handy office is Postnet, on Hout St between Adderley St and St George's Mall. You can use the phone and fax, and send Federal Express parcels.

If you're looking for a quiet public phone in the city centre, there's one in the foyer of the Cultural History Museum.

Connection Internet Café (☎ (021) 419 6180; fax 419 6208; email mandy@ postman.co.za), on Heerengracht between Hans Strijdom and Coen Steytler (across from the US embassy), opens at 9 am on weekdays, 10 am on Saturday and 2 pm on Sunday. Closing time is around 9 pm. There's another Internet café, iCafé, on Long St near the Long St Baths. As well as Internet access (from R10 for half an hour) you can make international phone calls at standard Telkom rates, which are *much* lower than the rates charged in hotels or at other private phone services. Standard rates are charged from 8 am to 8 pm on weekdays, all other times are charged at an economy rate. Some rates per minute are:

| To | Standard | Economy |
| --- | --- | --- |
| Australia | R4.69 | R3.99 |
| France | R7.84 | R4.88 |
| Germany | R8.59 | R7.07 |
| UK | R6.39 | R4.88 |
| USA/Canada | R5.33 | R4.43 |

### Foreign Consulates & Trade Missions

Most countries have their main embassy in Pretoria, with an office or consulate in Cape Town, which becomes the official embassy during Cape Town's parliamentary sessions. A surprising number of countries also maintain consulates (which can arrange visas and passports) in Jo'burg. Some countries, like Mozambique and Zimbabwe, only have representation in Jo'burg.

The following is not a comprehensive list. If your consulate is not listed, consult the Yellow Pages telephone directory under consulates and embassies. Many are open in the morning only.

Australia
    14th Floor, BP Centre, Thibault Square (☎ (021) 419 5425)

WESTERN CAPE PROVINCE

Belgium
 Vogue House, Thibault Square (☎ (021) 419 4960)
Canada
 Reserve Bank Building, 30 Hout St (☎ (021) 23 5240)
Denmark
 Southern Life Centre, 8 Riebeeck St (☎ (021) 419 6936)
France
 2 Dean St, Gardens (☎ (021) 23 1575)
Germany
 825 St Martini Gardens, Queen Victoria St (☎ (021) 24 2410)
Israel
 Church Square House, Plein St (☎ (021) 45 7205)
Italy
 2 Grey Pass Gardens (☎ (021) 241 1256)
Japan
 Standard Bank Centre, Heerengracht (☎ (021) 25 1695)
Namibia
 Main Tower, Standard Bank Building, cnr Adderley St & Hertzog Blvd (☎ (021) 419 3190)
Netherlands
 100 Strand St (☎ (021) 21 5660)
Sweden
 17th Floor, Southern Life Centre, 8 Riebeeck St (☎ (021) 25 1687)
UK
 Southern Life Centre, 8 Riebeeck St (☎ (021) 25 3670)
USA
 4th Floor, Broadway Centre, Heerengracht (☎ (021) 21 4280)
Zimbabwe
 Strand Tower, 66 Strand St (☎ (021) 461 4710)

## Travel Agencies

Most hotels and hostels offer tour booking (although not always a full range of options) and many have good deals on car hire. Some hostels (such as The Backpack) offer services which rival those of a travel agency, and they are usually better informed about budget options than mainstream travel agencies.

The South African Students' Travel Service (SASTS) is a national organisation with offices at universities around the country. You don't have to be a student to use their services. They offer all the regular services plus student and youth cards, youth hostel membership, and special fares and flights during vacations. They also know about cheap tours through Africa. They are at the University of Cape Town (Upper Campus), Leslie Building Concourse (☎ (021) 685 1808).

Rennies Travel has a comprehensive network of agencies, with a distinctive red livery, throughout South Africa, and Cape Town is no exception. It's the agent for Thomas Cook travellers' cheques and handles international and domestic bookings. It will also arrange visas for a moderate charge. See the previous Money section for locations and phone numbers.

A reader has recommended Worldwide Travel (☎ (021) 419 3840), 12th floor, 2 Long St, as a good place to buy international air tickets. A handy travel agency for straight business is Intercape Travel & Tours (☎ (021) 419 8888), in the train station. Visa Services (☎ (021) 21 7826), 4th floor, Strand Towers, 66 Strand St, arranges visas.

You should at least check out what's on offer at The Africa Travel Centre (☎ (021) 23 5555; fax 23 0065) at The Backpack hostel, 74 New Church St. It books all sorts of travel and activities including day trips, kloofing, hire cars and extended truck tours of Africa. The rates are good. As the centre has been in business for some time, it has vetted many of the operators – and there are some cowboys out there. Other hostels also make bookings, but usually not with as wide a range of options or such professional service.

See the Gay Scene section later in this chapter for Gay esCape, an excellent gay travel agency.

## Bookshops & Maps

Exclusive Books, at the Waterfront (☎ (021) 419 0905), has an excellent range; it's open until 9.30 pm on Saturday and from 11 am to 5 pm on Sunday. The main mass-market bookshop/newsagent is CNA, with numerous shops around the city.

If you're staying for more than a week or so, and have a car, consider buying Map Studio's excellent Cape Town street directory (R76, or R51 for the smaller A-Z version). As well as directories and country maps (which you can buy at CNA and many other outlets) the Map Studio (☎ (021) 462 4360), Struik House, 80 McKenzie Rd, Gardens, sells other series including Michelin and government topographic maps, excellent for hiking.

Ulrich Naumann's (☎ (021) 23 7832), 17 Burg St, has a good range of German-language books.

### Medical Services

Medical services are of a high standard. Doctors are listed under Medical in the phone book, and they generally arrange for hospitalisation, although in an emergency you can go directly to the casualty department of Groote Schuur Hospital (☎ (021) 404 9111) – where in 1967 Dr Christiaan Barnard made the first successful heart transplant – which is at the intersection of De Waal (M3) and the Eastern Boulevard (N2) to the east of the city. Ring the police (☎ 10111) to get directions to the nearest hospital.

Many doctors make house calls; hotels and most other places to stay can arrange a visit.

The Glengariff Pharmacy, Main Rd (corner of Glengariff), Sea Point, is open until 11 pm daily. There's another pharmacy open until 11 pm daily, in the city centre on Darling St between Plein and Parliament Sts.

For vaccinations, the British Airways Travel Clinic (☎ (021) 419 3172; fax 419 3389) is at Room 1027 in the Medical Centre, Adderley St.

### Emergency

The contact numbers for emergency services are:

| | |
|---|---|
| ambulance | ☎ 10177 |
| fire brigade | ☎ 461 4141 |
| police | ☎ 10111 |
| tourist police | ☎ 418 2852 |
| AA | ☎ 21 1550 |
| Lifeline | ☎ (021) 461 111 |
| Rape Crisis Centre | ☎ (021) 47 9762 |

### Dangers & Annoyances

Cape Town is probably one of the most relaxed cities in Africa, which can instil a false sense of security. People who have travelled overland from Cairo without a single mishap or theft have been known to be cleaned out in Cape Town – generally doing something stupid like leaving their gear on a beach while they go swimming.

Paranoia is not required but common sense is. There is tremendous poverty on the peninsula and informal redistribution of wealth is reasonably common. The townships on the Cape Flats have an appalling crime rate and unless you have a trustworthy guide they are off-limits (the triangular segment south of Athlone and the N2). If violence on the flats gets out of control even the N2 can become unsafe – you probably shouldn't drive it late at night when traffic is sparse.

The rest of Cape Town is reasonably safe. Care should be taken in Sea Point late at night. Walking to/from the Victoria & Alfred Waterfront is not recommended once it starts to get dark. As always, listen to local advice. There is safety in numbers.

Swimming at all the Cape beaches is potentially hazardous, especially for those inexperienced in surf. Check for signs warning of rips and rocks, and unless you really know what you're doing only swim in patrolled areas.

The mountains in the middle of the city are no less dangerous just because they are in the city. Weather conditions can change rapidly, so warm clothing and a good map and compass are always necessary.

Another hazard of the mountains is ticks, which can get onto you when you brush past vegetation – see the Health section in the Facts for the Visitor chapter.

### Climate & When to Go

Cape Town has what is described as a Mediterranean climate. Weather is not really a critical factor in deciding when to visit. There are no terrible extremes of temperature, although it can be relatively cold and wet for a few months over winter. It can get very crowded during the school holidays, particularly around Christmas (mid-December to the end of January) and Easter, when prices jump markedly and it can be difficult to find a place to stay. Late summer/early autumn, from February to April, is the best time to visit.

One of the Cape's most characteristic phenomena is the famous Cape Doctor, the south-easterly wind that buffets the Cape and lays Table Mountain's famous tablecloth. It can be a welcome breeze in summer, but it can also be a wild gale, particularly in spring. When it really blows you know you're clinging to a peninsula at the southern end of Africa, and there's nothing between you and the Antarctic.

In winter, between June and August, temperatures range from 7°C to 18°C but there are pleasant, sunny days between the gloomy ones. The prevailing winds are north-westerly.

From September to November the weather is unpredictable with anything from bright warm days to howling south-easterly storms, with winds reaching 120km/h. Wildflowers are at their best during the months of August and September.

December to March can get pretty hot, although average maximum temperatures are only 26°C. The Doctor generally keeps things bearable and it is usually relatively calm in the mornings. From March to April, and to a lesser extent May, the weather

remains good, and the wind is at its most gentle.

It can be very smoggy after a few still days – luckily, consecutive still days aren't all that common. Much of the smog comes from cooking fires in the huge squatter camps, and the smoke drifts around Table Mountain into the City Bowl.

### Laundry
There are laundrettes scattered throughout the suburbs, although if you're staying in any sort of budget accommodation you'll probably have a laundry on the premises. It's simpler to do a bag wash (they wash, dry and fold your clothes), around R15. Same-day laundry is available at Nannucci Dry Cleaners which has branches everywhere, including Shop 35, ground floor, Golden Acre Centre; Unity House, Long St; 57 Main Rd, Green Point; 152A Main Rd, Sea Point; and 67 Station Rd, Observatory.

### Work
The best time to look for work is October to November, before the high season starts and before university students begin holidays. Because of high unemployment and fears about illegal immigration from the rest of Africa, there are very tough penalties for employers taking on foreigners without work permits. So far this doesn't seem to have stopped foreigners getting jobs in restaurants or bars but this might change. Don't expect decent pay – something like R5 per hour plus tips (which can be good) is usual.

Hostels might know of fruit-picking work, especially in the Citrusdal, Ceres and Piketberg areas. The pay is negligible but you'll get free accommodation.

If you have recognised childcare and first-aid qualifications, Supersitters (☎ (021) 439 4985) might be able to find you baby-sitting work. In this conservative society there might not be much demand for male sitters.

### Left Luggage
There's a left luggage facility next to Platform 24 in the main train station, open

**Weather Lore**
The weather in Cape Town can change rapidly and often. Many people use Table Mountain as a weather forecaster, and it's apparently quite accurate. Some things to watch for:

- If there is heavy cloud on Lion's Head, rain is coming.
- If the tablecloth (cloud) shrouds the mountain, the Cape Doctor (a south-easterly change) is coming.
- If there is no cloud around the upper cable station (visible from all over town) there is no wind on Clifton Beach.

weekdays from 6 am to 5.45 pm, and weekends from 6 am to 2.30 pm.

## Library Membership
Visitors can take out temporary library memberships for a small fee at the City Library, in the Town Hall on Darling St.

## Camera Repairs
For camera repairs go to Camera Care, on Castle (Kasteel) St between Burg St and St George's Mall. Prolab, 177 Bree St (on the corner of Pepper St), will do slide processing and mounting in two hours for less than R35 for 36 – and they do a good job. They also sell professional film which has been kept in the right conditions.

## CITY BOWL MUSEUMS
### Bo-Kaap Museum
The small but interesting Bo-Kaap Museum (☎ (021) 24 3846), 71 Wale St, gives an insight into the lifestyle of a prosperous, 19th century Muslim family. The house itself was built in 1763. It's open between 9.30 am and 4.30 pm from Tuesday to Saturday; entry is R1. This whole area is well worth a stroll.

The Waterkant area of Bo-Kaap (around Waterkant St on the north-eastern edge of Signal Hill) forms a distinct area. It is now occupied by yuppies and it's the centre of the gay scene. The prime real estate was quickly snapped up by whites after the apartheid regime began its forced removals of Muslims, dumping them on the Cape Flats. But after this first assault the residents of Bo-Kaap organised and fought back, winning the battle to stay in homes that their families had occupied for centuries.

The Waterkant area wasn't always socially desirable. Most Muslims came here as slaves or political prisoners, but there was a small proportion of common criminals who were given the choice between the guillotine (which was situated in the Waterkant) and serving time on Robben Island. Most chose the island and those who survived came back to live in the Waterkant. The stigma remained until quite recently.

### District Six Museum
On the corner of Buitenkant and Albertus Sts, this simple museum (☎ (021) 461 8745) is as much *for* the people of the now-vanished District Six as it is about them. The floor is covered with a large-scale map of District Six, and ex-residents are encouraged to label their old homes and features of their neighbourhood. After District Six was bulldozed, the government changed the street grid and the names of the few remaining roads. The formerly vibrant community now exists only in the memories of those who lived there. There are a few other interesting displays, but the best reason to visit is to talk with the staff.

The museum is open daily except Sunday from 10 am to 4 pm. Admission is by donation.

See the earlier Apartheid & the Townships section for more information on District Six.

### Cultural History Museum
This interesting museum at the mountain end of Adderley St is the former slave lodge of the VOC, but it has gone through several incarnations since then – including the Supreme Court and the Legislative Assembly – and major physical alterations. The museum is open from 9.30 am to 4.30 pm Monday to Friday; entry is R5.

### Bertram House Museum
Bertram House (☎ (021) 24 9381) on the corner of Orange St and Government Ave (the walkway through the Company's Gardens) is a Georgian house filled with antiques which once belonged to wealthy English-descended South Africans. It's interesting to compare the architecture and furnishing of this house to that of old Cape Dutch houses, such as Koopmans de Wet – the Georgian comes off second-best.

The museum is open Tuesday to Saturday from 9.30 am to 4.30 pm; admission is R2.

### Jewish Museum
The Jewish Museum (☎ (021) 45 1546), 84 Hatfield St (next to the Art Gallery in the Company's Gardens), is in the oldest synagogue in South Africa. It contains items of Jewish historical and ceremonial significance. It's open Tuesday and Thursday from 2 to 5 pm and Sunday from 10.30 am to noon. Entry is free.

## Rust-en-Vreugd

This 18th century house (☎ (021) 45 3628), at 78 Buitenkant, was once the home of the state prosecutor. It now houses part of the William Fehr collection of paintings and furniture, featuring some important watercolours and engravings by renowned early South African artists like Baines. There's also a pleasant garden.

The museum is open from 9 am to 4 pm on weekdays and on weekends over summer and occasionally at other times. Admission is free.

## South African Museum

The South African Museum (☎ (021) 24 3330), at the mountain end of the Company's Gardens, is the oldest and arguably the most interesting museum in South Africa. It has some startlingly lifelike displays of San

---

### City Sights & Walking Tour

The following walk around the City Bowl could take the best part of a day, depending on the stops you make, although it is only about 6km long.

The **Castle**, as the oldest surviving building in Cape Town, seems the most appropriate place to start a walking tour. Van Riebeeck's original mud-walled fort was a little to the west of the stone castle that replaced it (built between 1666 and 1679) and survives today. See the separate Castle of Good Hope section.

Walk to the west across the **Grand Parade**, once a military parade ground, and now a bleak and windy car park. On Wednesday and Saturday mornings a section is kept clear for a flea market. The impressive old Town Hall on the southern side (1905) has been superseded by a much less attractive Civic Centre on the other side of the station.

Buses leave from the station side of the Parade, and minibus taxis compete for customers amid the friendly chaos on the Strand. At the Plein St end, an interesting bunch of permanent stalls form a colourful bazaar. Spices and takeaway food are sold – the samosas are cheap and excellent.

Circle around the post office and enter the **Golden Acre Centre** (1978) which was built on the site of the old railway station, and dubbed 'the golden acre' by locals because of its valuable real estate. It has several levels of shops and is linked to more shops in the Strand Concourse (including Captour) that runs under the intersection of Adderley and Strand Sts. Black tiles on the floor indicate the waterline before land reclamation in the 1930s.

Exit onto Adderley St, named after a British parliamentarian and historically regarded as Cape Town's main street. Until 1849 it was named the Heerengracht, or Gentlemen's Canal, after a canal of the same name in Amsterdam.

Turn left along Adderley towards Table Mountain and continue until you reach the **Groote Kerk**, the mother church for the Dutch Reformed Church (Nederduitse Gereformeerde Kerk, or NG Kerk). The first church on the site was built in 1704, but the current building dates from 1841 (open 10.30 am to noon and 2 to 3 pm). A number of early notables have tombs inside.

The next building is the **Cultural History Museum**, originally the VOC's slave lodge and brothel. The impressive façade was designed in 1811 and the building was later used as a debating chamber for the Cape Colony Legislative Council. (See the City Bowl Museums section.)

Follow the road as it turns right at the gardens (becoming Wale) past **St Georges Cathedral**, designed by Herbert Baker in 1897. This was Archbishop Desmond Tutu's cathedral. Turn right into St Georges St, which is now almost completely a pedestrian mall. The **Rhodes Building** (1900) was the Cape Town office for De Beers Consolidated Mines.

Turn left at Longmarket and you come out on **Greenmarket Square**, one of the most interesting spots in the city. It was created as a farmers' market in 1710 and is now home to a flea market (open daily). The **Townhouse Museum** (1761) on the corner of Burg St and Longmarket was the original city watch house, and now houses the Michaelis Collection of 16th & 17th-century Dutch and Flemish oil paintings (open 10 am to 5 pm every day, admission free). The building itself might be more interesting than the generally dour artworks, and there's a balcony overlooking bustling Greenmarket Square. Also note the magnificent Art Deco architecture of the building opposite, on the Shortmarket side of the square.

Walk back towards Table Mountain along Burg St and turn right into Church St, which is lined with art and antique shops. The pedestrianised section is a flea market specialising in antiques and bric-a-brac. Turn right down **Long St** which, along with Church St, retains a strong historical atmosphere, with elegant cast-iron decorated balconies and numerous old buildings. One of the oldest

communities (made with casts taken from living people in 1911) and interesting exhibits of other indigenous cultures. As an indirect testimony to Cape Town's importance as a stopping-place for ships, the museum holds some Pacific island artefacts left here by Captain Cook on his way home from his great voyages of discovery.

Despite some updating, it's still a good, old-fashioned museum with cases and cases of stuffed animals (some overstuffed, like the rotund platypus) and bloodthirsty dioramas of dinosaurs which must have inspired generations of young imaginations. The most interesting of the new displays is the whale room, where you can hear whale noises while looking at models suspended high in the air.

There is also a planetarium (☎ (021) 24 3330) in the complex, which could help

is the atmospheric **Sendinnestig Museum** (1802) at No 40, originally a missionary church (open Monday to Friday, 9.15 am to 4.15 pm). On the first Friday of the month the old gas lights are lit between 1 and 2 pm.

Continue until you reach Strand St. Turn right and a short distance on your right is **Koopmans de Wet House** (1701), a classic example of a Cape townhouse and furnished with antiques. It's a quiet, self-satisfied house holding its own in the centre of a big city. The house is open from Tuesday to Saturday between 9.30 am and 4.30 pm; entrance is R2, free on Friday.

Backtrack along Strand St passing, on the right-hand side in the block before Buitengracht, the old **Lutheran Church**, which was converted from a warehouse in 1780, and the next-door parsonage **Martin Melck House**.

Cross Buitengracht, and you enter the old **Cape Muslim Quarter** (sometimes erroneously referred to as the Malay Quarter), the historical residential suburb for the descendants of the Asian slaves and political prisoners imported by the Dutch. The steep streets, some of which are still cobbled, and 18th-century flat-roofed houses and mosques are still home to a strong Muslim community. This group miraculously survived apartheid, but it is less certain it will survive unfettered capitalism. The cottages on the Waterkant edge of the Quarter have been bought by yuppies and while those streets might be neat and freshly painted, they are also lifeless.

Turn left down Rose St, which after a couple of hundred metres forms a T-intersection with Wale St. Here you will find a restored house, the **Bo-Kaap Museum**, which gives an insight into the lifestyle of a Cape Muslim family. It's open between 9.30 am and 4.30 pm from Tuesday to Saturday; admission is R2.

Walk down the hill, cross Buitengracht and keep going until you reach Long St. Turn right into Long St and follow it until it becomes Orange St. The **Long St Baths** on the corner are still in operation. Turn left into Orange St, and left again into Grey's Pass which takes you past the excellent **South African Museum**, which is open daily from 10 am to 5 pm. Entry costs R3 (free on Wednesday). It has some fascinating displays on indigenous black culture (see Museums).

From here, you enter the top end of the **Botanical Gardens**, also known as The Company's Gardens. This is the surviving six hectares of Van Riebeeck's original 18 hectare vegetable garden which was planted to provide fresh produce for the VOC's ships. As sources of supply were diversified, the garden was gradually changed to a superb pleasure garden with a magnificent collection of botanical species from South Africa and the world. The gardens are open from 9.30 am to 4 pm. The **Gardens Restaurant**, at the Adderley St end of the Gardens, to the north of the oak-lined Government Ave, serves drinks and reasonably priced food and has inside and outside seating.

On the south side of Government Ave (Wale St end), are the **Houses of Parliament**. Opened in 1885, they have been enlarged several times. Continue towards the mountain, and past **De Tuynhuys**, the president's office, which has been restored to its 1795 appearance.

Next on the left, on the south-eastern side of the gardens, is the **South African National Gallery** which has a permanent collection of important South African paintings and also holds temporary exhibitions. It's open daily from 10 am to 5 pm; from 1 pm on Monday.

Leave the gardens by Gallery Lane and turn left into St Johns (towards the bay), take the next left and then next right into Parliament. This takes you through to **Church Square** where the burghers would unhitch their wagons while they attended the Groote Kerk. Slaves were also auctioned under a tree in the square (the spot is now marked with a plaque).

Continue down Parliament, keeping your eyes open for some of the Art Deco details on the buildings. Turn right on Darling St and you're back at the Grand Parade where you started. Phew! ∎

**WESTERN CAPE PROVINCE**

## PLACES TO STAY
1 Formule 1 Hotel
8 Diplomat Holiday Flats
9 Tulbagh Protea Hotel
12 The Lodge
21 Holiday Inn Garden Court St George's Mall
34 Cape Town Inn
37 Cape Sun Hotel
49 Metropole Hotel
64 Holiday Inn Garden Court Greenmarket Square
67 Tudor Hotel
82 Townhouse Hotel
83 Pleinpark Travel Lodge
94 Carlton Heights Hotel
103 Holiday Inn Garden Court De Waal
104 Mount Nelson Hotel
113 Albergo Backpackers
120 The Backpack & Africa Travel Centre
121 Zebra Crossing
122 Mijloff Manor Hotel
123 Leeuwenvoet House
124 Underberg Guesthouse

## PLACES TO EAT
29 Spur Steakhouse
52 Nino's
53 Le Petit Paris
56 World of Coffee
59 Wellington Dried Fruit
66 Karima's Café
70 Off Moroka Café Africaine
74 Mark's Coffee Shop
93 Kaapse Tafel Restaurant
99 Bistrot la Boheme
100 Roxy's Coffee Bar
101 Maria's Greek Restaurant
107 Blue Plate
109 Rustica
111 Rozenhof
114 Sukothai
115 Mario's Coffee Shop
118 KD's Bar & Bistro
119 Café Bar Deli

## ENTERTAINMENT
2 Nico Malan Complex
10 The Fireman's Arms
11 The Bronx
13 Café Manhattan
14 Brunswick Hotel
25 Long Street Theatre
26 Browne's Café du Vin
27 Crew Bar
28 Café Comic Strip
31 Shebeen on Bree
32 Hemingways
57 District Six Café
63 The Purple Turtle
65 Magnet
73 Manenberg's Jazz Café
86 The Fringe
87 The Shed
88 Kimberley Hotel
89 Perseverance Tavern
98 Stag's Head Hotel
106 Little Theatre
112 Firkin Brew Pub Company
117 Labia Cinema

## MUSEUMS
36 Koopmans de Wet House
69 Townhouse Museum
77 Bo-Kaap Museum
81 Cultural History Museum
85 District Six Museum
90 Rust-en-Vreugd
95 South African Museum
96 National Gallery
97 Jewish Museum
105 Bertram House

## OTHER
3 Broadway Centre
4 Connection Internet Café
5 Civic Centre
6 Jan & Maria van Riebeeck Statues
7 Tulbagh Square
15 BP Centre
16 Thibault Square
17 American Express
18 British Airways Travel Clinic
19 Trustbank Centre
20 Southern Life Centre
22 Tourist Rendezvous
23 Train Station
24 Namibia Trade & Tourism
30 Imperial Car Rental
33 Avis Car Rental
35 Budget Car Rental
38 Golden Acre Centre
39 City Bus Terminal
40 Castle of Good Hope
41 Grand Parade
42 Bus Information Kiosk
43 GPO
44 OK Bazaars
45 Postnet
46 Rennies Travel
47 Camera Care
48 Ulrich Naumann Bookshop
50 National Parks Board Office
51 Surf Centre
54 Pezulu (Crafts)
55 Stuttaford's Town Square
58 Town Hall
60 Pharmacy
61 BOB (First National Bank)
62 Greenmarket Square
68 African Image (Crafts)
71 Groote Kerk
72 Church Square
75 Mike Hopkins Cycles
76 Tempest Car Rental
78 Cape Wine Cellar
79 St George's Cathedral
80 Houses of Parliament
84 Department of Home Affairs
91 Botanical (Company's) Gardens
92 Alisa Car Rental
102 Gardens Centre
108 Afrogem
110 Le Cap Motorcycle Hire
116 Spar Supermarket

northerners unravel the mysteries of the southern hemisphere's night sky.

The museum is open daily from 10 am to 5 pm; entry is R3 (free on Wednesday). Planetarium shows are given at 1 pm on Tuesday and Thursday, at 2 and 3.30 pm on Saturday

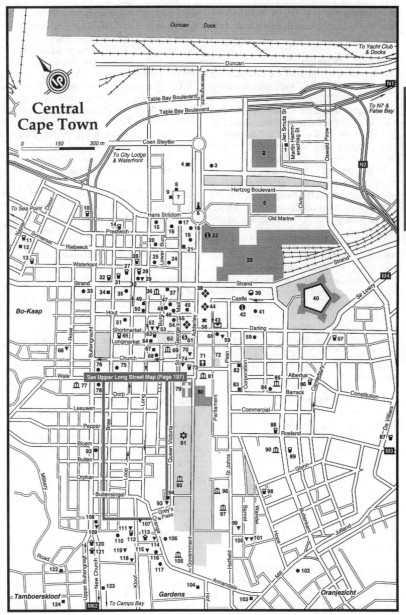

and Sunday, and at 8 pm on Tuesday and Wednesday. Admission is R6 (R7 for evening shows).

### Townhouse Museum

The Townhouse Museum on Greenmarket Square is another old Cape Dutch building. It dates from 1761, although there has been considerable alteration to suit its changing roles as a watch-house, the first city hall and, in 1916, Cape Town's first public gallery. Today it houses the Michaelis Collection of Dutch and Flemish paintings and etchings from the 16th and 17th centuries. As well as the art, it's worth visiting for the architecture and the views from the balcony overlooking bustling Greenmarket Square. The museum is open from 10 am to 5 pm daily and admission is free.

### NATIONAL GALLERY

This small but exquisite gallery (☎ (021) 45 1628) in the Company's Gardens was always worth visiting for its architecture, but now it also has some very interesting exhibitions which begin to redress the imbalance from the apartheid days. There's a good shop with some interesting books and a pleasant café with snacks and light meals. The gallery is open from 10 am to 5 pm every day (from 1 pm on Monday). Admission is free.

### HOUSES OF PARLIAMENT

On the south side of Government Ave (Wale St end) are the Houses of Parliament (☎ (021) 403 2911), which were opened in 1885 and enlarged several times since. During the parliamentary session (usually late January to June) gallery tickets are available; overseas tourists must present their passports. During the recess (usually July to January) there are free guided tours (☎ (021) 403 2198) on weekdays at 11 am and 2 pm. Go to the Old Parliament Building entrance on Parliament St.

### LONG ST BATHS & SWIMMING POOL

The Turkish baths and heated pool (☎ (021) 210 3302) at the mountain end of Long St are something of an anachronism, but they

have been restored and are very popular. The pool is open from 7 am to 9 pm on weekdays, until 8 pm on Saturday and from 8 am to 7 pm on Sunday. You have to get there at least an hour before closing time. Admission costs R6 (less if you just want a hot bath).

The Turkish baths are segregated. For men they are open from 9 am to 8.30 pm on Tuesday, Wednesday and Friday, and from 8 am to noon on Sunday. For women the hours are from 8.30 am to 8.30 pm on Monday and Thursday and from 9 am to 6 pm on Saturday. A Turkish bath costs R35, a massage costs R25, and a bath and massage is R50.

### CASTLE OF GOOD HOPE

Built near the site of Van Riebeeck's original mud-walled fort, the Castle was constructed between 1666 and 1679 and is one of the oldest European structures in Southern Africa. The impressive 10m-high walls have never had to repel an attack, but the Castle is nonetheless a striking symbol of the might of the VOC.

The Castle is still the headquarters for the Western Cape Military command but its tourist potential has been recognised and visitors are welcome. A small shop sells drinks and cheap snacks.

Within the Castle are a couple of museums with collections of furniture and paintings. The paintings, mainly of Cape Town in the past, are fascinating.

There are guided tours hourly between 10 am and 3 pm, and taking one of these is the only way to see many of the sights. However, if you're visiting one of the excellent temporary exhibitions (lately they have focused on anti-apartheid themes) held in a hall in the Castle, you can do a little solo wandering. The Castle closes at 4 pm. Admission (from the Grand Parade side) costs R5.

### SIGNAL HILL

Signal Hill separates Sea Point from the City Bowl. There are magnificent views from the 350m-high summit of Signal Hill, especially at night. Head up Kloof Nek Rd from the city and take the turn-off to the right at the top of the hill. At this intersection you also turn off for Clifton (also to the right) and the lower cableway station (left).

## NOON GUN

At noon, every day except Sunday, a cannon is fired from the lower slopes of Signal Hill. You can hear it all over town. Traditionally this allowed the burghers in the town below to check their watches. You can walk up to the cannon through Bo-Kaap – take Longmarket St and keep going up until it ends. The Noon Gun Café is a good place to gather your senses after they've been frazzled by that big bang.

## TABLE MOUNTAIN & CABLEWAY

The cableway is such an obvious and popular attraction you might have difficulty convincing yourself that it is worth the trouble and expense. It is. The views from the top of Table Mountain are phenomenal, and there are some excellent walks on the summit. The mountain is home to over 1400 species of flowering plants, which are particularly spectacular in spring. It's also home to rock dassies (hyraxes), those curious rodent-like creatures whose closest living relative is the elephant. They like to be fed.

If you do plan to walk, make sure you're properly equipped with warm and waterproof clothing. Table Mountain is over 1000m high and conditions can become treacherous quickly. There's a small restaurant and shop at the top, where you can also post letters and faxes.

The cable cars don't operate when it's dangerously windy, and there's obviously not much point going up if you are simply going to be wrapped in the tablecloth. Ring in advance (☎ (021) 24 5148 or 24 8409) to see if they're operating. Weather conditions permitting, they operate from 8 am to 9.30 pm in November, 7 am to 10.30 pm from December to mid-January, 8 am to 9.30 pm from mid-January to the end of April and from 8.30 am to 5.30 pm the rest of the year. The best visibility and conditions are likely to be first thing in the morning or in the evening.

The cableway carried its 10-millionth passenger in 1994. It has never had a fatality. New cable cars were introduced in 1997, increasing capacity and cutting down on the three or four-hour queues.

To get to the lower cable station, catch the Kloof Nek bus from outside OK Bazaars in Adderley St to the Kloof Nek terminus and connect with the cableway bus. By car, take Kloof Nek Rd and turn off to the left (signposted). An adult return is R50 and you can also buy a single ticket – it's possible to walk up or down the mountain to/from both the City Bowl side or the Kirstenbosch Botanical Gardens side. See the Activities section for more information.

## VICTORIA & ALFRED WATERFRONT

The Victoria & Alfred Waterfront is pitched at tourists, but it's atmospheric, interesting and packed with restaurants, bars, music venues and shops.

The development seems to have given the whole city a boost, and is tremendously popular, day and night. There is an information centre (☎ (021) 418 2369), in the middle of the complex, where you can get free maps of the Waterfront. It's open daily but not in

### The Tablecloth

As if Table Mountain is not spectacular enough in itself, for much of the summer it is capped by a seemingly motionless cloud that drapes itself neatly across the summit. An Afrikaner legend explained the phenomena by telling of an old burgher, who was fond of his pipe, attempting to outsmoke the devil in a competition.

Meteorologists have come up with an equally intriguing explanation. The south-easterly wind picks up moisture as it crosses the Agulhas current and False Bay. When it hits Table Mountain it rises and as it reaches cooler air temperatures around 900m above sea level it condenses into thick white clouds. As the clouds pour over the plateau and down into the City Bowl they once more dissolve in the warmer air at around 900m.

Table Mountain just happens to be at the perfect height and place, and the tablecloth is a dynamic and hypnotic sight. ∎

the evenings. There's also an information kiosk in the Victoria Wharf mall that stays open until 9 pm in summer.

Despite all the development, it remains a working harbour and that is the source of most of the Waterfront's charm. Most of the redevelopment has been undertaken around the historical Alfred and Victoria Basins (constructed from 1860). Although these wharves are too small for modern container vessels and tankers the Victoria Basin is still used by tugs, harbour vessels of various kinds, and fishing boats. There is still a smell of diesel and salt and the bustle of real boats and people doing real work.

Large modern shipping uses the adjacent Duncan and Ben Schoeman docks. These were constructed from the mid-30s and the sand excavated was used to reclaim the foreshore area north-east of the Strand. The Castle used to be virtually on the shorefront, and the old high water line actually passes through the Golden Acre Centre. The Waterfront is *the* place to go for nightlife. There is strict security and although it is safe to walk around, there are plenty of merry men so lone women should be a little cautious. The restaurateurs along Main Rd in Sea Point are reeling – a big proportion of their trade has been stolen. See the Places to Eat and Entertainment sections for information on the numerous restaurants and bars, although if you just go for a wander you'll find something that appeals.

There is a downside to the Waterfront, and many visitors quickly tire of it. The big shopping malls and the residential developments around the newly re-flooded Alfred Basin mean that it's becoming a self-contained suburb. And it's an antiseptic, security-conscious and decidedly white suburb. Transport logistics and economics can present almost as many barriers to nonwhites as the old laws.

### Cruises
A trip into Table Bay should not be missed. Few people nowadays have the privilege of reaching the Tavern of the Seas by passenger ship, but something of the feeling can be captured by taking a harbour cruise. The view of Table Mountain hasn't changed.

See Waterfront Charters (☎ (021) 25 3804), Port Captain's Building, Pier Head (across from Bertie's Landing) for a variety of cruises, including a half-hour cruise for just R8.

### Aquarium
The aquarium is well worth a visit. It features denizens of the deep from both the cold and warm oceans which border the Cape Peninsula, including great white sharks, which gather in False Bay. There are touch-tanks for the kids and the astounding kelp forest, which is alone worth the R22 admission.

### Getting There & Away
Shuttle buses run from Adderley St in front of the Tourist Rendezvous, then up Strand St, with a stop near the Cape Sun Hotel, to the centre of the Waterfront. They also leave from near the Hard Rock Cafe in Sea Point. They depart half hourly from early to late and cost R1.20.

If you're driving, there are free parking spaces, which are often full, but there's usually space in the car park beneath the Victoria Wharf complex.

### KIRSTENBOSCH BOTANICAL GARDENS
The Kirstenbosch Botanical Gardens (☎ (021) 762 1166) on Rhodes Drive, Constantia, are one of the most beautiful gardens in the world, and are a must for any visitor to Cape Town. They have an incomparable site on the eastern side of Table Mountain, right at the foot of the final steep escarpment, overlooking False Bay and the Cape Flats. The 36 hectare landscaped section seems to merge almost imperceptibly with the 492 hectares of fynbos (see the boxed text) that cloak the mountain slopes.

In 1895, Cecil Rhodes (of De Beers and Jameson Raid fame) purchased the eastern slopes of Table Mountain as part of a plan to preserve a relatively untouched section, and bequeathed the property to the nation on his death in 1902. The impressive granite

**Rhodes Memorial** was constructed further around the mountain towards the city (off Rhodes Drive). There is also a café here. The memorial is a popular place from which to see the sun rise on New Year's Day.

Portions of the hedge that Jan van Riebeeck planted in 1660 to isolate his settlement from the Khoikhoi can still be seen. Although there are some magnificent oaks, Moreton Bay fig trees and camphor trees, the gardens are devoted almost exclusively to indigenous plants. About 9000 of Southern Africa's 22,000 plant species are grown in the gardens. They are predominantly from the winter rainfall region, but there are also large numbers of hardy species from other parts of the country. There is always something flowering, but the gardens are at their best between mid-August and mid-October. A new conservatory is atmosphere-controlled and displays plant communities from a variety of terrains, the most interesting of which is the Namaqualand/Kalahari section, with baobabs, 'quiver' trees and others.

The gardens have been thoughtfully laid out and include a fragrance garden that has been raised so you can more easily sample the scents of the plants, a Braille Trail, a *koppie* (rock outcrop) that has been planted with pelargoniums, and sections featuring cycads, aloes, euphorbias, ericas and, of course, proteas. There are also three signposted circular walks that explore the natural forest and fynbos that surround the cultivated section.

As a nod to the new South Africa, the gardens are growing muti plants, used by sangomas in traditional medicine, to help conserve the supply in the wild.

The information office (open daily from 8 am to 4.45 pm) gives maps and advice on various walks. The very casual restaurant, serving snacks and inexpensive meals, is open daily.

The gardens are open year-round from 8 am, closing at 7 pm from September to March, and 6 pm from April to August; entry is R5. There are guided walks on Tuesday and Saturday from 11 am for approximately 1½ hours.

## Getting There & Away
It is possible to catch buses from Mowbray station on the Simon's Town line, but there aren't many. Phone Golden Arrow (☎ 080 121 2111) for an up-to-date timetable. A minibus taxi running from the main train station to Wynberg might take you within walking distance of the gardens, but check the route carefully.

You can walk uphill to the upper station of the Table Mountain cableway. This could be done in three hours by someone of moderate fitness. Make sure you have a map (from the Kirstenbosch information centre or the Table Mountain shop) and are prepared for a sudden change in weather. The trails are all well marked, and steep in places, but the cableway station is not signposted from the gardens or vice versa.

## GROOT CONSTANTIA
Groot Constantia is the oldest and grandest vineyard and homestead in the Cape – a superb example of Cape Dutch architecture. It embodies the gracious and refined lifestyle the wealthy Dutch created in their adopted country. Groot Constantia was built by one of the early governors, Simon van der Stel, in 1692. Not surprisingly, van der Stel could not bear to be parted from his creation; after his retirement he refused to return to Europe and stayed until he died in 1712.

In the 18th century, Constantia wines were exported around the world and were highly acclaimed. Today, the estate is owned by a syndicate, and fine wines are still produced. Unfortunately, it's a bit of a tourist trap, but it's worth visiting, especially if you don't have time to explore the Winelands around Stellenbosch – but if you've been to Boschendal you don't need to come here. Try to avoid visiting on a weekend; it can get very crowded.

The beautiful homestead has been carefully restored and appropriately furnished. The nearby wine museum traces the history of wine from the 6th century BC. Entry is R2 and the building is open from 10 am to 5 pm daily.

You can take a guided tour of the modern

## Cape Dutch Architecture

During the last years of the 17th century a distinctive Cape Dutch architectural style began to emerge. Thanks to Britain's wars with France, the British turned to the Cape for wine, so the burghers prospered and, during the 18th and 19th centuries, were able to build many of the impressive estates that can be seen today.

Although there is no direct link between the Cape Dutch style and the Dutch style, they are recognisably related.

The building materials were brick and plenty of plaster, wood (often teak) and reeds to thatch the roof.

The main features of a Cape Dutch manor are the *stoep* (a raised platform, the equivalent of a verandah) with seats at each end, a large central hall running the length of the house, and the main rooms symmetrically arranged on either side of the hall. Above the front entrance is the gable, the most obvious feature, and there are usually less elaborate gables at each end. The house is covered by a steep, thatched roof and is invariably painted white (a traveller with an eye to commerce reckoned that if you wanted to make your fortune in South Africa you would get a monopoly on white paint).

The front gable, which extends up above the roof line and almost always contains an attic window, most closely resembles 18th century Dutch styles. The large ground-floor windows have solid shutters. The graceful plaster scrolls of the gable are sometimes reflected in the curve on the top of the front door (above which is a fanlight, sometime with elaborate woodwork) but sometimes the door has neo-classical features such as flat pillars or a simple triangle above it. This combination of styles works surprisingly well.

Inside, the rooms are large and simply decorated. The main hall is often divided by a louvred wooden screen, which probably derives from similar screens the Dutch would have seen in the East Indies. Above the ceilings many houses had a *brandsolder*, a layer of clay or brick to protect the house if the thatching caught fire. The roof space was used for storage, if at all.

Perhaps the loveliest of all the manors is **Boschendal**, near Franschhoek and Stellenbosch, although **Groot Constantia** in Cape Town is also very fine. To see the slightly different style of the Cape Dutch townhouse, visit **Koopmans de Wet House**, now a museum in downtown Cape Town. And to get an idea of how pervasive this indigenous style is, just travel around the country and see the many, many imitation Cape Dutch houses, walls, gates, etc.

One of the best books on Cape Dutch architecture is the modern facsimile edition of the 1900 book *Old Colonial Houses of the Cape of Good Hope* by Alys Fane Trotter, (hardback, about R200). It includes an interesting introduction by Herbert Baker, the British architect whose work includes the Union Buildings in Pretoria and Connaught Place in New Delhi (India). Only 1500 copies of the facsimile edition were printed, but you have a reasonable chance of finding one in the antiquarian bookshops in Cape Town. ■

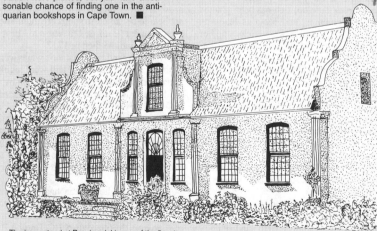

The homestead at Boschendal is one of the finest examples of Cape Dutch architecture.

wine-making operation for R7; hourly in season, and at 11 am and 3 pm out of season. Wines are on sale, including on Sunday. Prices range from R7 to R26 per bottle; the '89 Governor's reserve red bordeaux is their top wine. For R8 you can taste five wines – and you get to keep the glass. Tastings are free if you do the cellar tour, and are available between 10 am and 4.30 pm; sales stay open until 5 pm.

There are a number of places to eat (see Places to Eat later) and for provisions, there's the excellent Old Cape Farm Stall on the corner of Constantia and Groot Constantia Rds.

### Getting There & Away
A visit to Groot Constantia could easily be combined with a visit to the Kirstenbosch Botanical Gardens. Unfortunately there is no direct public transport to either.

## ATLANTIC COAST
The Atlantic coast of the Cape Peninsula has some of the most spectacular coastal scenery in the world. The combination of beaches and mountains is irresistible. The beaches include the trendiest on the Cape, and the emphasis is on sunbaking rather than swimming. Although it is possible to find shelter from the summer south-easterlies, the water comes straight from the Antarctic (courtesy of the Benguela current) and swimming is nothing if not exhilarating.

Buses and taxis run through Victoria Rd from the city to Hout Bay, but after that, you're on your own. Hitching is reasonably good.

On the more popular beaches in the city area you might see the work of sand artists, who create huge and complex naive artworks in return for donations. They will make to measure if you want. Unfortunately, the council regards them as a nuisance and wants to make them pay a licence fee.

### Bloubergstrand & Table View
Bloubergstrand, 25km to the north of the city on Table Bay, was the site for the 1806 battle between British and Dutch forces that resulted in the second British occupation of the Cape. This is also the spot with the most dramatic (and photographed) view of Table Mountain – you know, the one with wildflowers and sand dunes in the foreground, surf and, across the bay, the cloud-capped mountain ramparts looming over the city.

This is a boom area for antiseptic new suburbs but the village of Bloubergstrand itself is still quite small. There are a couple of small resorts where you can have a braai, buy snacks and find some long, uncrowded, windy stretches of sand. This is windsurfer territory, but there's also some surfing, best with a moderate north-easterly wind, a small swell and incoming tide. The Beach Club (keep going through Bloubergstrand) is a pleasant spot with takeaways available. Blue Peter has been recommended as a good spot for sundowners (drinks at sunset).

**Getting There & Away** Unfortunately, you'll need a car. Take the R27 north from the N1.

### Robben Island
Robben Island, offshore from the city centre, was a prison from the early days of the VOC right up until the first years of majority rule. Even at the beginning it was home to some famous political prisoners, exiled from the Dutch East Indies, but the most famous of them all was one of the last – Madiba, also known as Nelson Mandela. If you read his book, *Long Walk to Freedom* (and you really should), you will learn something of life on the island but not the harshest side. Mandela's account is very mild, partly because recrimination is not on his agenda but also because the great man's presence was such that he was spared some of the brutalisation suffered by other prisoners.

The island served as a 'university' for the ANC as many of the organisation's leaders were imprisoned there at one time or another, and they taught the junior comrades who served time there, and learned of developments in the outside world from them.

Tours of Robben Island (☎ (021) 419 1300) run from Jetty 1 at the Victoria &

Alfred Waterfront at 9 am, 11 am and 1.15 pm (returning at 12.30, 2.30 and 4.45 pm). The charge is R80.

### Sea Point
Separated from the City Bowl by Signal Hill, Sea Point is a bustling residential suburb with numerous multistorey apartment buildings and hotels fringing the coast. It's one of the most densely populated suburbs in Africa. Main and Regent Rds are lined with restaurants, cafés and shops. The coast itself is rocky and swimming is dangerous. However, there are four tidal swimming pools and plenty of bronzed bodies take advantage of the sun. The Sea Point Pavilion pool (at the end of Clarens St) is open from 8.30 am to dusk; entry is R4. The pool is huge but a sunny day will heat it up. If it's 12°C in the ocean the pool will be about 20°C.

A number of reefs produce good waves. Solly's and Boat Bay, near the Sea Point Pavilion, have lefts and rights that work on a south-east wind. Further along the beach towards Mouille Point there are a number of left reefs.

**Getting There & Away** To get there, catch any Clifton, Bakoven or Camps Bay bus from the main bus station (R2.60) – or walk. There's a pedestrian promenade above the beach.

### Clifton
There are four linked beaches at Clifton accessible by steps from Victoria Rd. They're the trendiest, busiest beaches on the Cape, and although they have the advantage of being sheltered from the wind, the water is cold. Consequently, the favoured activities are sunbaking, people-watching, tennis and frisbee. It's *very* hard to remember you're in Africa, although when you do, the obsessive pursuit of brown skin in a country where skin colour is such an issue, seems particularly bizarre.

There's a friendly and relaxed mood, although the occupants and atmosphere tend to vary with each beach. Fourth Beach, at the Camps Bay end, is the most accessible and popular with families, and there's a shop at the Fourth Beach car park (on the Ridge, off Victoria Rd). First Beach is definitely the place to be seen.

**Getting There & Away** There are frequent buses from OK Bazaars, Adderley St, and minibus taxis from the train station. Buses cost R2.60, minibus taxis a bit less. It's a pleasant 3km walk from Sea Point (Hard Rock Cafe) and another 1km or so to Camps Bay. In summer there's no point driving to Clifton as you won't be able to park.

### Camps Bay
Camps Bay is one of the most beautiful beaches in the world. The fact that it is within 15 minutes of the city centre makes it even more extraordinary. It is often windy and it is certainly not as trendy as the beaches at Clifton, but it is more spectacular. The Twelve Apostles running south from Table Mountain tumble into the sea above the broad stretch of white sand.

It is amazing how relatively unspoilt and uncrowded it is. The only drawbacks are the wind and the temperature of the water. There are no lifesavers and strong surf, so take care. There's a small batch of shops and restaurants, including the trendy Blues, and St Elmo's. Accommodation possibilities range from the five star Bay Hotel to the Stan Halt Youth Hostel, a stiff 20 minute walk up the hill towards Kloof Nek.

**Getting There & Away** There are frequent buses from OK Bazaars, Adderley St, and minibus taxis from the Strand. Buses cost R2.60, minibus taxis about the same. It's a 1km or so walk to the more sheltered coves at Clifton.

### Llandudno
Although it's only 18km away, Llandudno seems completely removed from Cape Town, let alone Africa. It's a small, exclusive seaside village clinging to steep slopes above a sheltered beach. There are no shops. The remains of the tanker *Romelia*, wrecked in 1977, lie off Sunset Rocks. There's surfing

on the beach breaks (mostly rights), best at high tide with a small swell and a south-easterly wind.

## Sandy Bay

Sandy Bay is Cape Town's unofficial nudist beach. Like many such beaches, there are no direct access roads. From the M6 turn towards Llandudno, keep to the left-hand side of this road and head towards the sea until you reach the Sunset Rocks parking area. It's a 20 minute walk to the south. There can be waves; best at low tide with south-easterly wind.

## Hout Bay

Hout Bay opens up behind the almost vertical Sentinel, and the steep slopes of Chapman's Peak. Inland from the 1km stretch of white sand, there is quite a large and fast-growing satellite town that still manages to retain something of its village atmosphere. The southern arm of the bay is still an important fishing port and processing centre for snoek and crayfish.

Perched on a rock in the bay near the end of Chapman's Peak Drive is a bronze leopard. It has been sitting there since 1963 and is a reminder of the wildlife which once roamed the area's forests – which have also vanished.

The information centre (☎ (021) 790 4053) is in the Trading Post store on the main road and is open daily (reduced hours in the off-season).

The Hout Bay Museum (☎ (021) 790 3270), 4 St Andrew's Rd, tells the story of Hout Bay. The World of Birds, Valley Rd, is an aviary with 450 species of bird. Although caging birds is not an attractive idea, a real effort has been made to make the aviaries large and natural.

There are daily launch trips from Hout Bay, with Circe Launches (☎ (021) 790 1040). The one-hour trips (about R25) run out to Duiker Island, with its colony of Cape fur seals. There's at least one trip daily all year, at 10.30 am, and many more in summer, for which you can't book.

You can hire a Hobie cat on the beach.

There are a number of restaurants, including a wharfside complex, Mariner's Wharf. See the Places to Eat section for details, and the Places to Stay section for accommodation in Hout Bay.

**Getting There & Away** Buses to Hout Bay (R5.30) leave from outside OK Bazaars on Adderley St. There are several early in the morning before 9 am, a few in the middle of the day and several between 2.15 and 5.30 pm, but there aren't many on weekends. Minibus taxis do the route for about the same price.

## Chapman's Peak Drive

This 10km drive is cut into the side of sheer mountain walls, between layers of brilliantly coloured sedimentary rock. There are great views over Chapman's Bay and back to the Sentinel and Hout Bay. It is one of the great scenic drives in the world and should not be missed.

## Noordhoek

About 30km south of Cape Town in the shadow of Chapman's Peak, Noordhoek has a 5km stretch of magnificent beach. Favoured by surfers and walkers, it tends to be windy and dangerous for swimmers. The Hoek, as it is known to surfers, is an excellent right beach break at the northern end that can hold large waves (only at low tide) and is best with a south-easterly wind. There's a caravan park here.

## Long Beach

At the Kommetjie end of Chapman's Bay, Long Beach is another popular surf beach, with an attractive caravan park. There are lefts and rights, best with a south-easterly or south-westerly wind. Take the turn-off to Kommetjie and turn right before the village. The nearest shop is in Kommetjie.

## Kommetjie

Kommetjie is a smallish crayfishing village with a quiet country atmosphere. There's a pub with bar lunches, a restaurant, a couple of caravan parks, a few shops, and not much more. It is, however, the focal point for surfing on the Cape, offering an assortment of reefs that hold a very big swell. Outer Kom is a left point out from the lighthouse. Inner Kom is a more protected, smaller left with lots of kelp (only at high tide). They both work best with a south-easterly or south-westerly wind.

## FALSE BAY

False Bay lies to the south-east of the city. Although the beaches on the east side of the peninsula are not quite as scenically spectacular as those on the Atlantic side, the water is often 5°C warmer, or more, and can reach 20°C in summer. This makes swimming far more pleasant. Suburban development along the coast is considerably more intense, presumably because of the railway which runs all the way through to Simon's Town.

On the east side of False Bay, Strand and Gordon's Bay are a cross between satellite suburbs and beach resorts. They have great views back to the Cape and are themselves in the shadow of the spectacular Hottentots-Holland Mountains. There's a superb stretch of coastal road that rivals Chapman's Peak Drive, with a great caravan park and a couple of spots where you can get access to the beach – the surf can be very dangerous for swimmers.

During October and November, False Bay is a favoured haunt for whales and their calves – southern right, humpback and bryde (pronounced 'breedah') whales are the most commonly sighted. They often come quite close to the shore.

See the Places to Stay and Places to Eat sections for more on the False Bay towns.

### Getting There & Away

On weekdays trains run between Cape Town and Fish Hoek every half hour to 9 pm; every second one runs through to Simon's Town (hourly). On weekends nearly all trains run through to Simon's Town, and they're more or less hourly. Cape Town to Muizenberg is R5/2.20 in 1st/3rd class, Simon's Town is R6.80/2.90. The journey takes a bit over an hour.

## Muizenberg

Unless the sun is shining, Muizenberg can be pretty bleak, but when it is sunny, you can escape the fairly tacky shorefront for a broad white beach that shelves gently and is generally safer than most of the peninsula beaches. Surf at the peninsula end of the beach, in front of the 19th century bathing boxes (which are let by the season – you can't hire one for the day).

## Kalk Bay

Kalk Bay (or Kalkbaai) was named after the lime kilns that in the 17th century produced lime from seashells for painting buildings. In 1806 it became a whaling station, and it is still a busy fishing harbour, particularly during the snoek season, which peaks during June and July, but can begin earlier. To the north of the harbour, there's an excellent left reef break (best with a west to north-westerly wind).

The Brass Bell, on the bay side of the train station, with a terrace right beside the sea, is a favourite spot for seafood braais and live music.

## Clovelly & Fish Hoek

Both these resorts/suburbs have wide safe beaches. Clovelly is flanked by sand dunes. Peers Cave, which can be reached by climbing the dunes behind 19th Avenue, is named after the man who discovered the fossilised skeleton of a man who lived 15,000 years ago. South from Kalk Bay there are numerous grottoes and caves that have been occupied by humans.

## Simon's Town (Simonstad)

Named after Simon van der Stel, an early governor, the town was the VOC's official winter anchorage from 1741 – it's sheltered from the winter north-easterlies that created havoc for ships in Table Bay. The British turned the harbour into a naval base in 1814 and it has remained one ever since.

There is an information bureau (☎ (021) 786 3046) at the Simon's Town Museum (off the main road about 600m south of the train station), which traces the history of the town and port. It's in the old Governor's Residency, built in 1777. Both are open from 9 am to 4 pm on weekdays and from 11 am to 4 pm on weekends; admission to the museum is R2. Next door is the South African Navy Museum, open daily from 10 am to 4 pm. Cameras are not allowed.

**Seaforth Beach** This beach is the nearest to Simon's Town and is a safe and sheltered family swimming spot. Head south from Simon's Town along St George's and after the navy block turn off into Seaforth Rd. Take the second right into Kleintuin Rd. Day visitors are charged R4 entry.

**The Boulders** A bit further on, but still within walking distance of Simon's Town are The Boulders. As the name suggests, this is an area with a number of attractive coves among large boulders that offer shade and shelter. The sea is calm and shallow in the coves so The Boulders is popular with families. Take the coast road south and turn left into Miller Rd. Day visitors are charged R4 entry. The Boulders are also home to a growing colony of jackass penguins.

### Strand
Strand is quite a large satellite town, built along a nice stretch of gently shelving beach. It's very much a city by the surf, but some people like this combination.

### Gordon's Bay
Pretty much a southerly continuation of Strand's sprawl, Gordon's Bay is smaller and has camping accommodation close to the beach.

### CAPE OF GOOD HOPE NATURE RESERVE
This is a beautiful peninsula. If the weather is good – or even if it isn't – you can easily spend at least a day here. In some ways, the coastline here is not as dramatic as that between Clifton and Kommetjie, but there is drama nonetheless. There are numerous walks, a number of beaches (there's 40km of coast within the reserve), a great cross

section of the Cape's unique flora (fynbos) as well as baboon, hard-to-spot eland, bontebok, rhebok, grysbok, and abundant bird life. It's particularly beautiful in spring when the wildflowers are in bloom.

There are a number of picnic places where you can braai; the Homestead Restaurant on the main road, which is moderately expensive; and a kiosk near Cape Point. A tramway takes you right up to the point from the kiosk, although there's no reason not to walk.

The reserve is open daily from 7 am to 6 pm. Maps and firewood are available at the gate. The entrance fee is R5 per person and R5 per surfboard.

### Getting There & Away
The only public transport to the Cape is with Rikki's (who run those Asian-style mini-mini buses), which run from Simon's Town (accessible by train) and cost about R70 per hour. Numerous tours include Cape Point on

**Do Not Feed the Baboons!**
There are signs all over Cape Point warning you not to feed the baboons. This isn't just some mean-spirited official stricture designed to keep baboons from developing a taste for crisps and chocolate. One group told me about how they stopped and opened the car windows to take photos of baboons. 'The next thing we knew, the baboons were in the car and we were out of the car. It took about half an hour before they were satisfied that they'd thoroughly trashed the interior, and we drove back to the rental agency in a car full of baboon shit.'

JON MURRAY

their itineraries. Day Trippers (☎ (021) 461 4599 or 531 3274) and perhaps other backpacker-oriented companies take along mountain bikes, so you can ride in the nature reserve and along Chapman's Peak Drive on the way to/from the Cape. They say they haven't yet lost anyone over the edge ...

Consider getting a group together and hiring a car for the day. If you plan to loop around the peninsula, start at Kirstenbosch Botanical Gardens and Groot Constantia, stock up on supplies at the Old Cape Farm Stall and head down through Muizenberg. If you tackle the drive clockwise you'll be on the right side of the road to stop and take in the unforgettable views. The section along Chapman's Peak Drive and on to Llandudno and Clifton is one of the most spectacular marine drives in the world.

## CAPE FLATS

For the majority of Cape Town's inhabitants, home is in one of the townships out on the desolate Cape Flats: Guguletu, Nyanga,

Philippi, Mitchell's Plain, Crossroads or Khayelitsha. The first impression as one approaches is of an endless, grim, undifferentiated sprawl, punctuated by light towers that would seem more appropriate in a concentration camp. In fact, some parts are acceptable, not all that far removed from suburbs anywhere, while others are as bad as any Third World slum.

Cape Town's townships have played a major role in the struggle against apartheid. See Apartheid & the Townships in the History section for more details. Given its history, the courtesy and friendliness that is generally shown to visitors is almost shocking.

You should try to get objective advice on the current situation. This isn't easy, however, since most whites would never dream of visiting. Visiting without a companion who has local knowledge is likely to be foolish. If a trustworthy resident is happy to escort you, however, you should have no problems, and tours have operated safely for years.

### The Townships

Most residents of Cape Town live in one of the Cape Flats townships. Although all the townships are depressing and inconveniently situated, not all present scenes of squalor and misery, partly because the coloured population received favoured treatment under the apartheid regime, and there was also a programme of building a little decent housing in some of the black townships. It has been suggested that this was a way of dividing the black community and thus defusing its opposition to apartheid.

Most blacks live either in hostels or in shacks in the vast squatter camps. However, unlike the hostels in Jo'burg, which were cut off from the life of the surrounding township and became armed camps, hostels in Cape Town are integrated with the community. Some are owned by the city council, others by large companies such as Coca Cola.

Until the pass laws were abolished, hostels were for men only. They lived in basic units, each accommodating 16 men who shared one shower, one toilet and one small kitchen. Tiny bedrooms each housed three men. After the pass laws were abolished, most men brought their families to live with them (previously, if you didn't have a job outside the Homelands you were not allowed to leave). So now each unit is home to 16 *families*; each room sleeps three families. Some people have moved out of the hostels and built shacks, but the hostels remain the source of electricity, water and sanitation. Rent is R7.50 per month, but over the years many bed spaces (called 'squares' – your own square, the size of a single bed, was your sole private area) have been sublet, and the most recent arrivals can pay up to R50 per month.

All the black townships except Khayelitsha have hostels. Khayelitsha, with a population of one million, consequently has a huge proportion of squatters.

There are a few day hospitals in the townships, but for an illness requiring an overnight stay, residents have to travel into the city. A hospital is now being built at Khayelitsha.

If you're going to really understand Cape Town, it's essential that you visit the Cape Flats. They are still off-limits to lone visitors but there are some tours. Paula Gumede's One City Tours (☎ (021) 387 5351 or 387 5165) is excellent and charges R75. Other companies such as Day Trippers (see Activities) also visit the townships. ■

Nowadays, it's not so much political violence as crime that is the problem.

## ACTIVITIES

The boom in backpacker accommodation has led to a boom in backpacker-oriented activities. There are some excellent choices. Day Trippers (☎ (021) 461 4599 or 531 3274) gets excellent feedback from travellers, and Steve really knows his stuff. On most of their trips they take along mountain bikes, so you can do some riding if you want. Most tours cost around R120 and include Cape Point, the Winelands (including a visit to a township on the way) and whale-watching.

The Hip Hop Travellers Stop hostel runs its own Bizzy Buzzy Bus Tours (☎ (021) 439 1842), with similar itineraries and prices.

## Kloofing

The Table Mountain area is full of kloofs (cliffs or gorges) and kloofing is a way of exploring them that involves climbing, walking, swimming and jumping. It's a lot of fun. Kloofing requires local knowledge, equipment and experienced guides, so it's best to go along with one of the adventure activities outfits. Several offer kloofing; Day Trippers claims to have been the first. It offers kloofing between November and April and charges about R120.

## Diving

Cape Town has a wide variety of diving – the Agulhas and Benguela currents create a unique cross section of marine conditions. Diving can be undertaken at any time of the year, but is best from June to November. The water on the False Bay side is warmer then and the visibility is greater. There are a number of excellent shore dives. Hard and soft corals, kelp beds, wrecks, caves and drop-offs, seals and a wide variety of fish are some of the attractions. There are several dive operators, such as Ocean Divers International (☎ /fax (021) 439 1803), Ritz Plaza, Main Rd, Sea Point. A certificate course costs around R750.

## Surfing

The Cape Peninsula has fantastic surfing possibilities – from gentle shorebreaks ideal for beginners to 3m-plus monsters for experts only. There are breaks that work on virtually any combination of wind, tide and swell direction.

In general, the best surf is along the Atlantic side, and there is a string of breaks from Bloubergstrand through to the Cape of Good Hope. Most of these breaks work best in south-easterly conditions. The water can be freezing (as low as 8°C) so a steamer wetsuit, plus booties, is required.

With the exception of the excellent left reef at Kalk Bay, the False Bay beaches tend to be less demanding in terms of size and temperature (up to 20°C), and work best in north-westerlies. There's a daily surf report on Radio Good Hope at 7.15 am.

Surprisingly there aren't many surf shops on the peninsula, but the Surf Centre (☎ (021) 23 7853) at 70 Loop St (corner of Hout St) in the city centre has a good stock of wetsuits and second-hand boards. It also rents boards and wetsuits.

---

### The Flying Dutchman

According to the most popular version of the Flying Dutchman Legend, a ghost ship haunts the Cape because its captain once bet his soul he could round the Cape in a storm – and failed. In the spooky equinoxial sea-mists it doesn't seem too unlikely that the ancient square-rigger with its doomed crew might appear. In fact, the Flying Dutchman is 'sighted' near the Cape Peninsula more often than anywhere else in the world.

The Cape has a fearsome reputation for wrecking ships. Part of the reason is the fast-flowing current a few kilometres offshore. Ships that avoid the current by sailing between it and the coast are at risk if one of the area's violent storms sweeps in. And there's a good chance one will – the Cape of Good Hope was originally called the Cape of Storms. If the wind is blowing in the opposite direction to the current, freak waves can also develop. If you add to this a panicky crew claiming to see a ghost ship flying before the wind, then avoiding the shoals might be almost impossible. ■

## Walking

There are some fantastic walks around the peninsula, including to Lion's Head, on Table Mountain and in the Cape of Good Hope Nature Reserve.

It is important to be properly equipped with warm clothing, a map and compass. There are numerous books, brochures and maps that give details. Shirley Brossy's *Walking Guide to Table Mountain* (paperback, R30) details 34 walks. Mike Lundy's *Best Walks in the Cape Peninsula* (paperback, R40) is also useful. Serious climbers could contact the Mountain Club of South Africa (☎ (021) 45 3412), 97 Hatfield St. Guided walks are available and Captour has details.

Walking up (or down) Table Mountain is definitely possible – more than 300 routes have been identified. However, it is a high mountain and claims lives from time to time. It's safe enough if you are properly prepared with warm clothing and emergency food and water, and if you stick to the path. The trouble is, thick mists can make the paths invisible, and you'll just have to wait until they lift. You should always tell someone where you are going and you should never walk alone. Captour can put you in touch with a guide, and adventure activity outfits such as Day Trippers can give advice. Climbing the mountain is such a popular pastime that there's a good chance you'll meet someone who will invite you along.

None of the routes is easy, but the Platteklip Gorge walk on the City Bowl side is at least straightforward. Unless you're fit, try walking down before you attempt the walk up. It took me about 2½ hours from the upper cable station to the lower, taking it fairly easy. One of the scariest walks is to go to the lower cableway station and head straight up. The hikers you see from the cable car, perched like mountain goats on apparently sheer cliffs, are taking this route. I'm told that it isn't as difficult as it looks.

## Other Activities

Several canoeing operators run short trips from Cape Town (as well as their regular longer trips). Felix Unite (☎ (021) 762 6935; fax 761 9259) is the major operator.

Abseiling off Table Mountain (or Chapman's Peak, depending on the weather) with Abseil Africa (☎ (021) 25 4332) costs R90 (plus the cableway fare, if applicable). Head along to their desk at the Tourist Rendezvous at 11 am, daily. On Thursday and Saturday they also have day tours to 'Kamikazi Kanyon' (R190), which include hiking, kloofing and abseiling through a waterfall.

The Argus Tour from Cape Town to the peninsula is held in the second week of March and is the largest bicycle race in the world, with over 20,000 entries. Some entrants are deadly serious but many people go along for some fairly strenuous fun. See the Getting Around section for information on hiring bikes.

If you want to try water-skiing, or just want to have a fun day of falling over in the water, try Sunfish (☎ 083 261 7542). Monika, a German water-ski champion, has a good boat and equipment and takes groups to Rietvlei Lake (near Bloubergstrand) for a braai on an island and as much high-speed action as you could want. Recommended. It costs R160 (including transport and lunch) and you can book at most hostels. Monika also does ocean crayfishing trips for R160.

## SPECIAL EVENTS

The Cape Festival used to be held annually early in March, with music from classical to jazz and everything in between. Whether or not it continues has yet to be decided. The university suburb of Observatory has a weekend festival sometime in spring.

## ORGANISED TOURS

For a quick orientation on a fine day you can't beat Topless Tours (☎ (021) 448 2888), which runs a roofless double-decker bus. The two hour city tour (R30) between Dock Rd in the Waterfront and the Tourist Rendezvous departs about six times a day, less often (if at all) in winter. Longer tours are also available.

See the earlier Activities section for the

### The Coon Carnival

The Coon Carnival is a long-standing festival involving the coloured community. *Coon* Carnival? Yes, but the name derives from a side alley of racism, not the apartheid highway. It seems that the coloured community was impressed by a touring black-&-white minstrel show and decided to emulate it. Traditionally, the Coon Carnival allowed some licence, and revellers would grab passers-by and black their faces with boot polish. During the apartheid era, the carnival was moved to a stadium, away from the streets, so that sort of thing couldn't happen. Problems caused by rival promoters mean that the carnival may not continue. ■

various outfits running outings aimed at backpackers.

Major tour companies include Springbok Atlas Tours (☎ (021) 417 6545) and Hylton Ross (☎ (021) 438 1500). Hylton Ross also has an office on Quay Five at the Waterfront and as well as its tours it can book quite a few other things around the country.

Several companies offer eco-oriented tours of the Cape and longer trips further afield. They include Greencape Tours (☎ (082) 891 5266 or (021) 797 0166). The maximum group size is seven people and a consensus of customers can alter the itinerary.

One City Tours (☎ (021) 387 5351 or 387 5165) has an excellent, three hour township tour for R75. This tour is a must.

Tana-Baru Tours (☎ (021) 24 0719; fax 23 5579) offers a two hour walk or drive through Bo-Kaap (the 'Malay' quarter). Shereen Habib lives in Bo-Kaap and is an excellent guide, as much for her knowledge of day-to-day life in this vibrant community as for her historical insights. Tours cost R45 and Shereen will take as few as one person; highly recommended. If you're going to take any tour of this area, make it this one, rather than a white-run bus tour that treats the area like a zoo.

Shereen's husband runs a Cape Flats tour, concentrating more on the coloured residen-

tial areas. We haven't tried it, but it should be good.

Court Helicopters (☎ (021) 25 2966/7) has 20-minute flights from near the Waterfront to Hout Bay then back to Table Mountain and down over the City Bowl. It's spectacular and well worth R990 for four people. There's also a sunset flight (covering the same route) for R210 per person (minimum two people).

See the earlier Victoria & Alfred Waterfront section for information on boat cruises.

At least once a month there are steam train excursions to Simon's Town or Franschhoek, for about R50. Contact Union Ltd Steam Rail Tours (☎ (021) 405 4391) at the Tourist Rendezvous.

## PLACES TO STAY

There is a huge number of options and most people will find something that suits their pocket, but note that top-end hotel prices have soared way out of line with other costs in the country. If you have any difficulties, contact the Captour accommodation service.

In the high season – basically December through to Easter – prices can jump by up to 100% and many places will be fully booked. School holidays are always busy, but if you plan to visit during the summer school holidays in particular, booking is essential. Now that Cape Town is gaining a reputation as one of the world's better cities to visit, it would be wise to book at any time of year.

The rates at many places fluctuate according to demand, and it's always worthwhile asking about special deals. For longer stays, rates are definitely negotiable.

## PLACES TO STAY – BOTTOM END
### Caravan Parks

There are no particularly central caravan parks, so if you do intend to camp, a car is virtually a prerequisite. The exception is *Zandvlei Caravan Park* (☎ (021) 788 5215), The Row, Muizenberg, which is within walking distance (about 2km) of the Muizenberg station (on the Simon's Town line) and the beach (about 1km). Walk east around the civic centre and pavilion, turn right onto

**WESTERN CAPE PROVINCE**

Atlantic Beach Rd, which doglegs and crosses the mouth of the Zandvlei lagoon, and take the first left after the bridge down Axminster Rd, which becomes The Row. For two people the tariff ranges from R25 to R50 in December and early January.

*Fish Hoek Beach Caravan Park* (☎ (021) 782 5503), Victoria Rd, Fish Hoek, is also accessible by train but doesn't allow tents. Van sites cost from R30, rising to R66. The caravan parks at Kommetjie and Noordhoek do take tents but you need a car to get to them. A bit closer to town, but still handy for Atlantic surf beaches, *Chapman's Peak Caravan Park* (☎ (021) 789 1225), Dassenheuwel Ave, Noordhoek, is in a beautiful setting. Rates are about R30 for two people, rising to R50 from mid-December to mid-January. *Millers Point Caravan Park* (☎ (021) 786 1142), about 5km from Simon's Town, on the Cape Point side, is on a small private beach and has just 12 sites. It doesn't always accept tents.

### Hostels

You sometimes get the impression that every second person in South Africa is turning their house into a B&B. In Cape Town it seems that the people who didn't open a B&B opened a hostel instead.

Competition between hostels is fierce and you can expect most places to offer free pickups, discounts at local businesses and a good range of excursions. Some hostels tout at the airport, which means that eventually all of them will have to. Being greeted by a scrum of hostel touts isn't the best way to arrive after a long flight, so consider patronising the hostels that don't tout.

**Costs** Prices fluctuate with demand and most hostels are keenly aware of what the competition is charging. You'll pay about R35 for a dorm and between R90 and R110 for a double. Rates seem to rise by about 15% a year but that is offset by the fall in the value of the rand. When converted to a harder currency, such as US dollars, rates haven't risen in years. Many hostels make up in beer sales what they lose in low bed prices.

**Which Hostel?** Just about any hostel is a good hostel if you like the people staying there. If you have the suspicion that you've landed in some sort of tacky, backpackers' version of the Costa del Sol, full of boozy xenophobes, just try another hostel – there are some distinct personalities.

We haven't included every hostel here – there are just too many. Listed below is a selection of good hostels (old favourites, new favourites and the inexplicably popular), but just because a hostel isn't listed doesn't mean that it isn't good.

Unless otherwise indicated, you can assume that the hostels mentioned here have private rooms as well as dorms but you can't assume that any will be vacant when you arrive, so book ahead.

**City Bowl** *The Backpack* (☎ (021) 23 4530; fax 23 0065; email backpack@gem.co.za), 74 New Church St (the top of Buitengracht), was the first non-IYH hostel in Cape Town and one of the first in South Africa (yes, five years ago you could count the number of hostels in the country on one hand). It is arguably still the best hostel in town, as Lee and Tony are constantly making improvements and innovations. There's a good bar/café and a pool. It's about a 15 minute walk from the train station, or you can catch the Kloof Nek bus from Adderley St, outside OK Bazaars. Check out their web site for information on the hostel, and on tours and activities available from the Africa Travel Centre at the hostel: www.kingsley.co.za/millennia/bp@atc.htm.

A few doors up at 82 New Church St is the friendly *Zebra Crossing* (☎ /fax (021) 22 1265), which is smaller, quieter and more personal – and slightly cheaper. There's a good piano and a good atmosphere. It's one of our favourites.

Down in Long St hostels have been mushrooming lately. The first was *Long St Backpackers* (☎ (021) 23 0615), at No 209. It is in a block of 14 small flats, with four beds and a bathroom in each – this is one hostel where you don't have to queue for a shower. Standards have risen lately and it's

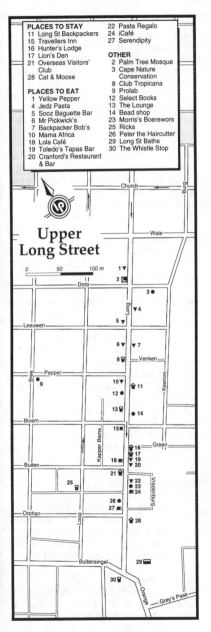

PLACES TO STAY
11 Long St Backpackers
15 Travellers Inn
16 Hunter's Lodge
17 Lion's Den
21 Overseas Visitors'
   Club
28 Cat & Moose

PLACES TO EAT
1 Yellow Pepper
4 Jedz Pasta
5 Sooz Baguette Bar
6 Mr Pickwick's
7 Backpacker Bob's
10 Mama Africa
18 Lola Café
19 Toledo's Tapas Bar
20 Cranford's Restaurant
   & Bar

22 Pasta Regalo
24 iCafé
27 Serendipity

OTHER
2 Palm Tree Mosque
3 Cape Nature
   Conservation
8 Club Tropicana
9 Prolab
12 Select Books
13 The Lounge
14 Bead shop
23 Morris's Boerewors
25 Ricks
26 Peter the Haircutter
29 Long St Baths
30 The Whistle Stop

Upper Long Street

WESTERN CAPE PROVINCE

a pleasant place. The *Overseas Visitors' Club* (☎ (021) 24 6800; fax 23 4870; email hross@ovc.co.za), 236 Long St (near the corner of Buiten), has dorm beds only. It's a nice old building, with high-quality facilities and a pub-like bar, but it doesn't really have a backpacking atmosphere – although some might consider this a bonus. It sometimes closes in winter. *Cat & Moose* (☎ (021) 23 5456; fax 23 8210) is a new place near the Long St Baths, and it's a comfortable warren of rooms in an historic building. Russian is spoken here.

*Oak Lodge* (☎ (021) 45 6182; fax 45 6308; email oaklodge@lantic.co.za) is at 21 Breda St, Gardens. What can I say? You'll love it or hate it. The hostel was once a commune until the astute communards saw that they'd have more fun (and make some money) if they turned it into a backpacker hostel. They have done a good job, and it's one of the most interesting hostels in town. I haven't actually stayed there but every time I visit I end up spending the night on a couch. There's a big bar (with murals), a good kitchen and smoking and nonsmoking dorms. They have a web site: www.lantic.co.za/oaklodge.

*Ashanti Lodge* (☎ (021) 23 8721; fax 23 8790; email ashanti@iafrica.com), 11 Hof St, Gardens (a block from Orange St), is in a big old house which was once a guesthouse, so the facilities are good (including a decent pool and a big bar) and the rooms are comfortable. This place has definite potential. *Cloudbreak* (☎/fax (021) 461 6892; email cloudbrk@gem.co.za) is a friendly little place at 219 Buitenkant St.

**Sea Point & Nearby** *Waterfront Lodge* (☎ (021) 439 1404; fax 439 4875), 6 Braemar Rd, Green Point, is close to the Waterfront and not too far from the city. It's a large, relaxed and friendly place with very good facilities, including a large garden and two pools. Jeff is one of the better hosts in town.

*Hip Hop Travellers Stop* (☎ (021) 439 2104), 11 Vesperdene Rd, Green Point, describes itself as being on the Waterfront. It isn't, but it is one of the closest hostels to the Waterfront. The hostel also describes itself as lively and it is that. The free beer on check-in gets you started. Hip Hop is in a pleasant old house and has a pool and a garden where you can camp.

*The Bunkhouse* (☎ (021) 434 5695), 23 Antrim Rd, Three Anchor Bay, is pretty well equidistant from the Waterfront, Sea Point and the city – although it's a bit of a walk to any of them. At the far end of Sea Point is *The Globe Trotter* (☎ (021) 434 1539), 17 Queens Rd.

The people who have the Stumble Inn hostel in Stellenbosch and the hostel and fine guesthouse at Boulders Beach (Simon's Town) have opened a new place, *One on Main*, (☎ (021) 439 9471/2/5; email stumble@ iafrica.com). It's at 1 Main Rd (corner of Boundary St) in Green Point. We haven't seen it yet, but they know what they are doing and it should be good.

**Camps Bay**  The *Stan Halt Youth Hostel* (☎ (021) 438 9037), The Glen, Camps Bay, is near the Round House Restaurant, which is better signposted than the hostel. In fact, the hostel buildings were once the stables for the Round House, which was built as a hunting lodge. The hostel, a very pleasant national monument, has a beautiful position, surrounded by trees, with a great view. You pay for this, however, with a steep, 15 minute walk to the nearest shops and restaurants in Camps Bay. Dorm beds (only) cost less here than in most other hostels and even less if you are an IYH member (that's YHA to Australians). This would be a good place to spend a few days recuperating from an overdose of nightlife. Take the Kloof Nek bus from outside OK Bazaars in Adderley St to the top of Kloof Nek, then take the road to the right. It's a longish but pretty walk. Like all other IYH hostels in South Africa, this one has 24-hour access and there are no chores – it's the same deal as any backpacker place, in fact.

**Observatory**  This suburb, a favourite with students, is a long way from the city centre

and the Waterfront – by Cape Town standards, anyway. It's only a few minutes to the city by car or train, and it is a nice neighbourhood with some good music venues and places to eat – a good place to hang out for a while. A minibus taxi from town costs R1.50 (get off at Chippies for the hostel), and a train costs R2.20/1.50 in 1st/3rd class (don't take luggage in 3rd class and don't travel at rush hour).

The *Green Elephant* (☎/fax (021) 448 6359), 57 Milton Rd (on the corner of Lytton), is a two storey house in a walled garden. It's run by experienced travellers and it seems to be one of the more maniacally happy hostels in town. And how many other hostels can boast a tree-climbing dog?

**False Bay**  The *Abe Bailey Youth Hostel* (☎ (021) 788 2301), on the corner of Maynard and Westbury Rds, Muizenberg, is a quiet IYH hostel with dorms and doubles. It's a short walk to the beach and it's near Valsbai station on the Simon's Town railway line. Also accessible by train is *Harbourside Backpackers* (☎ (021) 788 2943; fax 788 6452), 136 Main Rd, Kalk Bay, in a pub across from the beach and close to Kalk Bay train station. It's a little rough and ready but the rooms are nice, with mezzanine beds and sea views. It's also a little cheaper than many places.

Further around at Boulders Beach, Simon's Town, *Boulders Beach Backpackers* (☎ (021) 786 1758) is right on the beach and is a pleasant enough place in a great location. If you want a bit of a splurge, stay at the excellent guesthouse next door, where there's a good restaurant (see Places to Stay – Middle). Both the hostel and the guesthouse are run by the people who have the very popular Stumble Inn in Stellenbosch. The hostel is about 2km south of Simon's Town train station. A Rikki between the station and the hostel costs about R1.50.

**Guesthouses**
*Travellers Inn* (☎ (021) 24 9272; fax 74 9278), 208 Long St, is in one of the old wrought-iron decorated buildings and was

once the British Guesthouse; that name is still on the door. It has been taken over by enthusiastic new management and is undergoing a much-needed refurbishment. Singles (they really are singles) cost R90/120 in the low/high seasons and doubles are R120/160, including a make-it-yourself breakfast.

*The Lodge* (☎ (021) 21 1106), 49 Napier St, used to be one of the nicer little hostels but the owners have wisely decided to get out of that cutthroat game and concentrate on running The Lodge as a very pleasant, inexpensive guesthouse. It's well located, in the newly yuppified edge of the old Cape Muslim quarter, and not far from the city and the Waterfront. B&B costs from around R100 per room, up to as high as R200 in season.

*St John's Lodge* (☎ (021) 439 9028), 9 St John's Rd, on the corner of Main Rd, is both a hostel and a guesthouse, with the usual hostel facilities such as kitchens and good information. It's an attractive old building with wide verandahs and you're sure to meet other travellers here. The rooms are fairly small and fairly basic but it's friendly and good value at R45/90. You'll pay nearly twice that in the high season. The lodge has its own security patrol covering the surrounding streets, so it's pretty secure.

## PLACES TO STAY – MIDDLE
### B&Bs & Guesthouses

The Bed 'n Breakfast organisation (☎ (021) 683 3505; fax 683 5159) has a number of members around the Cape Peninsula. The accommodation is exceptionally good value. Most rooms are in large, luxurious suburban houses (often with swimming pools) and all have private bathrooms; there are also self-contained flats and cottages available. The only problem is that Bed 'n Breakfast prefers advance bookings (at least a day or so) and most houses are difficult to get to without private transport. Prices start at around R70/100 per person in the low/high seasons. You can pay a lot more than this.

The Captour accommodation booking service at the Tourist Rendezvous can also help. The Portfolio people also list some

excellent places to stay. See the Facts for the Visitor chapter for their address, or pick up their booklets at the Tourist Rendezvous.

There are a great many B&Bs and guesthouses – the following is just a small sample.

**City Bowl** *Belmont House* (☎ (021) 461 5417), 10 Belmont Ave, Oranjezicht, is a small but comfortable guesthouse overlooking the City Bowl, charging from R100/170 a single/double to R120/190 in the high season. There are kitchen facilities and they say that they'll give you a discount if you're carrying this book. *Ambleside Guesthouse* (☎ (021) 45 2503), 11 Forest Rd, Oranjezicht, has comfortable singles/doubles and family rooms, and a fully equipped guest kitchen. Doubles start at R85 per person, more with private bathroom.

**Sea Point** *Ashby Manor Guesthouse* (☎ (021) 434 1879; fax 439 3572), 242 High Level Rd, Fresnaye, is a rambling old Victorian house, on the slopes of Signal Hill above Sea Point. All rooms have a fridge and hand basin and there is a kitchen. Singles/doubles go for about R90 per person, higher in season. There's also a two bedroom flat, from R280. *Villa Rosa* (☎ (021) 434 2768), 277 High Level Rd (on the corner of Arthur's Rd), Sea Point, is a nice old house, restored into a quality guesthouse. Well-equipped rooms start at R180/290 a single/double, rising to R220/380 in peak season. *Olaf's Guest House* (☎ /fax (021) 439 8943), 24 Wisbeach Rd, also has high-quality accommodation, starting at R320 a double. German is spoken here.

**Simon's Town** Right across from pretty Boulders Beach, with its penguin colony, *Boulders Beach Guesthouse* (☎ (021) 786 1758; fax 786 1825; email stumble@iafrica.com), is a good new place with an excellent café and restaurant. Single/double rooms with ensuite cost R210/300 (R245/340 with sea view) and there are two self-catering units, each with two bedrooms, at R450.

WESTERN CAPE PROVINCE

### Self-Catering

There are a number of agencies that specialise in arranging fully furnished houses and flats, including Cape Holiday Homes (☎ (021) 419 0430), 31 Heerengracht, PO Box 2044, Cape Town 8000; and Private Places (☎ (021) 52 1200; fax 551 1487), 102 South Point Centre, Loxton Rd, Milnerton 7441.

**City Bowl** *Diplomat Holiday Flats* (☎ (021) 25 2037, 2341), right in the city on Tulbagh Square, is one of those rare places where the quality of the accommodation is higher than the quality of the foyer would suggest. It's old-fashioned but clean and in good condition. The rooms are large and the two-room flats have an enormous lounge. There is a huge array of rates and seasons, but basically the rate for two people in a single bedroom flat is R170; for three/four people in a two bedroom flat it's R290/360. Add about 30% from December to mid-January.

*Gardens Centre Holiday Flats* (☎ (021) 461 5827) is the distinctive multistorey building on Mill St, Gardens. The single-bedroom flats are above an excellent small shopping mall and although the flats only go up to the 5th floor, the views are still good. Rates vary widely according to the season, starting at around R240 for two people and rising by about 15% at peak times.

**Atlantic Coast** *Lions Head Lodge* (☎ (021) 434 4163), 319 Main Rd (on the corner of Conifer), Sea Point, has rooms and self-catering apartments. The nightly rate is from R230/350 a single/double. If you stay longer than a day or so, the rates fall.

The Hout Bay information centre can tell you about self-catering cottages and apartments in that area. Something reasonable will cost from about R150 for two people.

A great spot if you have a car, *Flora Bay Bungalows* (☎ (021) 790 1650), Chapman's Peak Drive, Hout Bay, has magnificent ocean views. One room 'oceanettes' are from R140 to R220 per night depending on the season; two-bedroom units cost between R240 and R360.

**False Bay** *Oatlands* (☎ (021) 786 1410), Seaforth Beach Front, Simon's Town, is a member of the Club Caravelle chain and has self-catering rondavels for R190 a double in mid-season. Next door, the *Blue Lantern* (☎ (021) 786 2113) has serviced chalets for a little less.

### Hotels

**City Bowl** There's a member of the *Formule 1* hotel chain (☎ (021) 418 4664) downtown between Jan Smuts and Martin Hammerschlag, offering basic but comfortable rooms for R114 for up to three people.

The *Tudor Hotel* (☎ (021) 24 1335), Greenmarket Square, is a homely little hotel (30 rooms) with a great position right in the middle of town, but away from main roads. It could do with renovation but it's OK. Parking is available nearby (at a price). Singles/doubles start at R150/200 including breakfast.

The *Metropole Hotel* (☎ (021) 23 6363), 38 Long St, is an attractive old-style hotel, with a dark, wood panel interior. Their prices are very reasonable considering the degree of comfort offered. In the low season, smallish standard rooms are R170/205, luxury rooms are R230/270 and there are more-expensive suites. *Carlton Heights Hotel* (☎ (021) 23 1260), on Queen Victoria St, opposite the South African Museum, is well located and fair value although the rooms are small. Standard rooms start at R210/280, rising to R265/350 around Christmas.

The two star *Pleinpark Travel Lodge* (☎ (021) 45 7563), on the corner of Corporation and Barrack Sts, is a conveniently located hotel with reasonable prices. It's OK, but only OK. Rates start at around R240 a double including breakfast. In the same league is the high-rise *Cape Town Inn* (☎ (021) 23 5116), on the corner of Strand and Bree Sts. Further out of town, but still within walking distance, the *Cape Swiss Hotel* (☎ (021) 23 8190), on the corner of Kloof and Camp Sts, is another characterless but decent hotel. Rates start at around R220 a double, higher in peak season.

**Waterfront Area** The *Breakwater Lodge* (☎ (021) 406 1911; fax 406 1070), Portswood Rd, should be one of the best places to stay, as it's in a restored jail hard by the Waterfront and the prices aren't bad. However, as well as being a restored jail it's also a restored tertiary institution and the rooms are very small. Some people like it, although the rates seem high for what you get – R239 per room.

**Atlantic Coast** In Hout Bay, *Chapman's Peak Hotel* (☎ (021) 790 1036) has rooms from R270 in mid-season. The rooms aren't flash but it's a pleasantly relaxed place. *The Beach House Hotel* (☎ (021) 790 4228), Royal Ave, charges R220 a double, including breakfast. No children under 14.

**False Bay** The *Lord Nelson Inn* (☎ (021) 786 1386), 58 St George's St, Simon's Town, is a small, old-style pub. In the main street of Simon's Town overlooking the harbour, it's accessible by train. Singles/doubles start at R240/290, 15% more in the high season. Although this is a pleasant, refurbished place, it isn't great value, and the more expensive rooms overlooking the sea (which is largely obscured by a shed in the naval dockyards) get traffic noise.

### PLACES TO STAY – TOP END

Prices at top-end places are out of kilter with other prices in the country. Cape Town's tourist boom combined with a shortage of top-end beds (and some sharp opportunism) means that room rates are equivalent to those in countries with average incomes many times higher than South Africa's. New hotels are being built, so hopefully some sanity will return.

### City Bowl

Staying at the *Mount Nelson Hotel* (☎ (021) 23 1000), 76 Orange St, is like stepping back in time to the great days of the British Empire. Dating from 1899, the hotel is set in seven acres of parkland, a short walk through the Company's Gardens to the city. Part of the Venice Simplon Orient Express group,

the rooms are full of character. Mid-season rates start at around R800/1100. Unfortunately, the exterior is painted in a pink and grey colour scheme that makes it look like an underfunded institution of some kind.

In complete contrast, the five star *Cape Sun* (☎ (021) 23 8844), Strand St, is a large, modern, multistorey hotel in the middle of the city. It has a swimming pool, fitness centre and several restaurants. Rates are similar to those at the Mount Nelson.

Less expensive but still very good is the four star *Townhouse Hotel* (☎ (021) 45 7050; fax 45 3891), 60 Corporation St (on the corner of Mostert St), which charges from R260/360 with only a slight rise in summer. Rooms with numbers ending in six have good views of the mountain.

*Mijloff Manor Hotel* (☎ (021) 26 1476), 5 Military Rd, Tamboerskloof, was once an attractive small hotel in a converted mansion – now it has grown into a reasonable, but quite large hotel, with a lot of new rooms. Rates start at R250 and rise steeply.

There are a few members of the Holiday Inn Garden Court chain, including:

Greenmarket Square
  On Greenmarket Square (☎ (021) 23 2040; fax 23 3664), R270/290
St George's Mall
  On the corner of Riebeeck St and St George's Mall (☎ (021) 419 0808; fax 419 7010), R290/340
De Waal
  Mill St, Gardens (☎ (021) 45 1311; fax 461 6648), R280/310

As well as the hotels, there are some outstanding top-end guesthouses, such as *Villa Belmonte* (☎ 462 1576; fax 462 1579), 33 Belmont Ave, Oranjezicht. It's an ornate Italianate villa with excellent facilities, charging from around R380/560 a single/double. The *Underberg Guesthouse* (☎ (021) 26 2262) on the corner of Carstens St and Tamboerskloof Rd is a very nice place, restored Victorian but not too fussy. Rooms start at R230/350, including breakfast. Nearby at 10A Tamboerskloof Rd, *Table Mountain Lodge* (☎ (021) 23 0042; fax 23 4983) is

WESTERN CAPE PROVINCE

another restored house with B&B from R284/308. Not far away at 93 New Church St, *Leeuwenvoet House* (☎ (021) 24 1133; fax 24 0495) is another quality guesthouse with rooms from R285/330, including a huge breakfast.

## Atlantic Coast

Close to both the city and the Waterfront, *City Lodge* (☎ (021) 419 9450; fax 419 0460), on the corner of Dock Rd and Alfred St, is a big place, something like an upmarket motel. Room rates start at R260/310 a single/double. The *Victoria Junction Hotel* (☎ (021) 418 1234; fax 418 5678), at the corner of Somerset/Main and Ebenezer Rds, is a big new member of the Protea chain in a stylishly recycled building. It hadn't opened at the time of writing but it looks as though it will be the flagship of this sometimes inconsistent chain.

The *Victoria & Alfred Hotel* (☎ (021) 419 6677; fax 419 8955), right in the middle of the Waterfront, has everything a five star hotel should have. Its position is brilliant, the rooms are lovely, and it's heavily booked. Definitely first choice if you have the money and if swimming is not a priority – singles/doubles start at R590/900. On the Green Point side of the Waterfront, the *Portswood Square Hotel* (☎ (021) 418 3281; fax 419 7570), Portswood Rd, is a new four star hotel. Rates start at R420/545. The rooms aren't especially large but it's a pleasant place.

*The Place on the Bay* (☎ (021) 438 7069; fax 438 2692), on the corner of Victoria Rd and The Fairways in Camps Bay, is a large complex of modern, very comfortable self-catering apartments. The two-bedroom apartments have a double bed and two singles, plus a couch in the downstairs lounge that sleeps an adult or two children. Low-season rates start at R200 per person for a studio apartment and R650 for a two bedroom suite. In the high season you'll pay from R1000 for a studio and from R2000 for a suite. The penthouse comes with a chef and a butler and costs much, much more.

If you want to be close to a beautiful

beach, consider the five star *The Bay Hotel* (☎ (021) 438 4444), a luxurious hotel across the road from the Camps Bay beach. Singles/doubles start at R465/600 in the low season and R800 a double (only) in the high season. For a sea view you'll pay at least R620/900 or R1360 in the high season.

Further to the south at Kommetjie, the *Kommetjie Inn* (☎ (021) 783 4230) is a refurbished seaside hotel with rooms starting at around R250/330, more in summer.

## PLACES TO EAT

Cape Town could easily claim to be the gastronomic capital of Africa. Unlike the rest of South Africa there's a cosmopolitan café/restaurant culture. Whites go out to eat. Why they do here, and not elsewhere, is a mystery – perhaps it's harder to find live-in cooks, or perhaps the city's history as the Tavern of the Seas has simply created a more dynamic urban culture.

There is a tremendous variety of cuisines and you can spend a lot of money, or a little. Although you have to go looking for it, the traditional Cape cuisine – a curious cross between Dutch/European and Indonesian/Malay – is worth searching for. And there are restaurants specialising in Italian, Greek, Portuguese, American, Indian, Chinese and French. The quality of the ingredients is high. Fruit and vegetables are excellent, most coming from nearby. The seafood is top quality, and the local wines are sensational.

Most of the inner neighbourhoods in the City Bowl have some good places to eat but the greatest concentration is at the Victoria & Alfred Waterfront. The biggest range of budget places is in Sea Point – a stroll down Main Rd will turn up something that will appeal to most palettes and pockets.

The popular *St Elmo's Restaurant & Pizzeria* is a chain worth looking out for. It has wood-fired pizza ovens with pizzas from under R20 and a range of reasonably priced pastas, seafood and steaks. Among others, it has branches at 118 Main Rd, Sea Point; The Broadway, Beach Rd, Camps Bay; and Village Square, Hout Bay. Those catering for themselves should check the Woolworth's supermarkets (there's one on Main Rd, Sea Point and another in the city centre). They're a bit pricey, but they have a wide range of high-quality foods, including fresh fruit and vegetables and some excellent frozen and semi-prepared meals. For more exotic deli items try *Amigos* at the top end of Kloof St.

The cheapest meal in town is at the *Hare Krishna Centre* on the corner of St Andrews and Teddington Rds, not far from Rondebosch train station. Free vegetarian meals (and a Hare Krishna 'festival') are available on Wednesday at 6 pm and Sunday at 3 pm.

### City Centre

**Cafés & Snacks** There is quite a range of cheap takeaway-type places in the city centre – you'll come across plenty as you wander around. One good place to start if you're getting peckish is the so-called Fruit and Vegetable Market at the Adderley St end of the Grand Parade. There's a cheap bakery and a number of stalls that sell various Indian takeaways, including excellent samosas. There are also a couple of places inside the Golden Acre Centre.

*World of Coffee*, on Adderley St near Darling St, offers a chair and caffeine when you need to recuperate. Another possibility is *Mark's Coffee Shop* (☎ (021) 24 8516), 105 St George's Mall (on the corner of Church St), the oldest coffee shop in Cape Town, with good coffee and reasonably priced light meals.

If it isn't too busy, *Cycles* is a pleasant terrace outside the Holiday Inn, overlooking Greenmarket Square. There's a large menu and prices aren't too bad. Just across from Cycles, in the art-deco Namaqua Building on the corner of Burg St, *Le Petit Paris* is a pleasant, trendy café, good for a coffee and a snack during the day.

*Mr Pickwicks Deli*, 158 Long St, is a licensed, deli-style café that stays open very late for good snacks and meals. Try the footlong rolls. It's just the place to recuperate in a civilised atmosphere after a night out at the clubs.

*Off Moroka Café Africaine*, 120 Adderley St, near Church St, is a very pleasant place to sample some fairly genuine African food and listen to tapes of African music. It's open daily, except Sunday, for breakfast and lunch. Breakfast starts at R12, soup is R9 and salads cost between R10 and R15. There are also sandwiches and pancakes.

*Sooz Baguette Bar*, 150 Long St, has inexpensive snacks and meals, and is about the only place in the city (other than hotel dining rooms) to get breakfast on a Sunday morning. Not far away is *Backpacker Bob's*, a bar and café serving fuel such as bangers and mash (R12.50) and lamb chops (R15).

*The Tea Garden* in the Company's Gardens is licensed and has quite a large menu. There are snacks as well as standards such as omelettes (R15), salads (from R12), chicken dishes from R20 and steaks from R25. It's open for breakfast.

*Wellington Dried Fruit* is a Cape Town institution. It's a long, narrow store on Darling St near Plein St, selling a huge range of dried and glacé fruit, deli items, tinned foods and *lots* of lollies (sweets, candy) – well worth a visit even if you don't want to buy anything. For processed meat, *Morris's Boerewurst* on Long St near the corner of Buiten is legendary.

Just up from the City Bowl in the Cape Muslim quarter, *Karima's Café*, on the corner of Rose and Longmarket, is a takeaway selling a few Cape Muslim snacks. Karima herself is friendly and very knowledgeable about the area.

**Meals** If you're looking for a pleasant and stylish place to have lunch in the city centre, try *Squares*, a bright, good-value restaurant in Stuttaford's Town Square, overlooking St George's Mall. A good meal will set you back about R40, but there are plenty of snacks for less. At the *Tudor Hotel* on Greenmarket Square, pub meals are well under R30, with daily specials around R15. The *Ploughman's Pub* on Church Square isn't anything special but it's OK for a beer and a lunchtime meal such as bangers and mash.

The *Spur* family steakhouse on Strand St near the corner of Loop serves standard dishes at standard prices – around R30 for a steak. It would come in handy for refuelling after a night at the nearby clubs, but unfortunately it closes around the time the action is getting under way – at 1 am on Friday and Saturday, midnight Monday to Thursday and 11 pm on Sunday. It's open for breakfast, though, so you could still end your night there if you've had a particularly good time.

*Nino's* (☎ (021) 24 7466), on Greenmarket Square, looks as though it's a tourist trap attracting patrons from the Holiday Inn across the street, but it's actually a good, Italian-run restaurant and pizzeria. As in most South African Italian restaurants, Nino's dishes are not quite the same as the originals; but unlike most, Nino's have added spices and adventurous ingredients. Try the veal pizzaiola (R30) or for something lighter but still good, a chicken salad (R18). It's open from 8 am to 6 pm on Monday and Tuesday, until 10.30 pm from Wednesday to Friday and to 5 pm on Saturday.

The *Kaapse Tafel Restaurant* (☎ (021) 23 1651), 90 Queen Victoria St, is a pleasant little restaurant that serves a variety of traditional Cape dishes. There are entrées such as Cape pickled fish (R12.50) and seafood bobotie (R15). Main courses (most R25 or R30) include Malay chicken biryani, bobotie, waterblommetjie bredie and springbok goulash.

The Metropole Hotel, 38 Long St, has the *Commonwealth Restaurant*, serving pub-style meals at reasonable prices. On Sunday it has a roast lunch for less than R30.

*Yellow Pepper*, 138 Long St, has a casual atmosphere and fairly inexpensive, fairly interesting food, with main courses under R15. It's worth trying. It's open during the day (not Sunday) and also from 7.30 pm on Friday and Saturday.

A little further up Long St, on the corner of Pepper St, *Mama Africa* is a stylish bar and restaurant with interesting decor and a slightly African menu. You'll be offered a choice of rice or pap with your meal. Main courses cost around R25 to R35. There's live African music playing on Friday and Saturday nights.

On the rim of the City Bowl, relaxed *Café Manhattan* is on the corner of Dixon St and Waterkant. It's a neighbourhood bar and restaurant which has been renovated without losing its casual appeal. The food is inexpensive and good, and vegetarians are catered for. It's open from midday until late on weekdays and from late afternoon on weekends.

## Gardens & Tamboerskloof

This area is becoming populated with places to eat. A night out could involve a beer in the Stag's Head Hotel on Hope St (rowdy) or the Perseverance Tavern on Buitenkant (civilised), dinner at Maria's Greek Restaurant or Rozenhof, and finishing with Irish coffees at Roxy's Coffee Bar.

**Cafés & Snacks** *Mario's Coffee Shop*, on Rheede St, not far from several hostels, is a bit shabby but it has excellent and very cheap meals. It's open from 8 am to 4 pm. A big breakfast is R12 – a ridiculously big breakfast is R18 and a mixed grill is R20. There are also burgers and inexpensive pasta dishes. Not far away, on the corner of Kloof and Park, *KD's Bar & Bistro* is popular with impoverished students and backpackers.

*Roxy's Coffee Bar* (☎ (021) 461 4092), on Dunkley Square, is self-consciously bohemian and serves good coffee (including a long list of alcoholic coffees, from R8) and light meals from under R20. It's open from noon to 2 am on weekdays, from 7 pm on Saturday. *Café Paradiso*, on Kloof St on the corner of Malan St, is a fashionable, but informal, upmarket café. It's a bit pricey and I'm not as much of a fan as many locals are, but the outdoor tables are a nice place to sip a drink and watch Kloof St go by.

**Meals** *The Perseverance Tavern* (☎ (021) 461 2440), 83 Buitenkant (across from Rust-en-Vreugd), is an old pub, built in 1808 and licensed since 1836. It's a bit of a rabbit warren inside, with bar areas and plain wooden tables. In addition to beer (some draught) and an excellent range of wines, they serve decent pub food from a blackboard menu. There's a relaxed atmosphere, and you'll find generous meals for R20 to R30. On Friday nights it can be too crowded to move.

Dunkley Square (between Dunkley, Wandel, Barnet and Vrede Sts) has a number of places, most with outdoor tables. On a warm night this is a nice place to linger over a meal. Roxy's Coffee Bar has already been mentioned. *Maria's Greek Restaurant* (☎ (021) 45 2096) is a small taverna, with plastic tablecloths, naive-style murals and good-value food (although some dishes still subscribe to the 'more is better' school of South African cuisine). There are starters such as taramasalata (R10.50), Greek salad (R12.50) and mezze platter (R41). Mains include roast lamb (R35) and spanakopita (R21). Maria's is open from 7 to 11.30 pm daily. Next door is *Dunkley Inn* and across from the square is *Bistrot la Boheme*, a trendy place with a fairly standard menu.

New and currently very popular, *Rustica* (☎ (021) 23 5474, booking advised), 70 New Church St, is an excellent modern Italian restaurant. Most main courses cost between R20 and R30. Not far away, in a recycled building off Kloof St near the corner of Rheede St, is one of the trendiest places in town, the big *Café Bar Deli*. It's open from breakfast until 1 pm (midnight for meals) daily except Sunday and it's usually packed. Surprisingly, given the hip crowd and industrial decor, the food is not only excellent, with an emphasis on fresh and healthy dishes, but it's also very good value. Tapas are around R6.50, pasta R20 and salads R16. The enormous Bar Deli platter is just R24.50.

Just down the street, but a world away in atmosphere, *Rozenhof* (☎ (021) 24 1968), 18 Kloof St, is one of the best restaurants in town. Its small but interesting seasonal menus are big on quality but not too bad on prices. Starters and salads are around R20 and most main courses cost around R40. Across the road, *The Blue Plate* is another good upmarket restaurant.

*Sukothai* (☎ (021) 23 4725), 50 Orange St on the corner of Dorman St, is a good Thai restaurant. It's open for lunch on weekdays and for dinner most nights. The menu includes the less complicated Thai standards. On Kloof St, on the corner of Union St, *The Happy Wok* is an offshoot of Sukothai and sells similarly good meals and takeaways at much lower prices, around R22 for most main courses. The emphasis here is more on Chinese.

The *Mount Nelson Hotel* offers High Tea on the terrace, with lots of cakes, lots of waiters and a grand piano. Expect to pay about R40.

## Victoria & Alfred Waterfront

New restaurants and nightspots are mushrooming here, and the Waterfront information centre has a sizeable booklet listing them all. As well as the franchised places such as *St Elmo's* and *Spur*, there are some interesting places to eat, although most are aimed squarely at tourists. An exception is the group of smaller places in the King's Warehouse, next to the Red Shed Craft Workshop. You can buy from various stalls and eat at common tables. *Ari's*, the Sea Point institution for Middle Eastern dishes, has a branch here.

The *Musselcracker Restaurant*, upstairs in the Victoria Wharf shopping centre, has a seafood buffet for R66. There's also the relaxed *Musselcracker Oyster Bar*, a good place for a drink and some seafood. Oysters are R35 a dozen.

The *Green Dolphin* (☎ (021) 21 7471), beneath the Victoria & Alfred Hotel, is a popular restaurant with excellent live jazz, nightly from 8 pm. If there's an international act in town it will probably play here. There's a cover charge of R10 (R6 if you don't have a view of the stage). The jazz is probably more important than the food, but it isn't bad, with starters around R20 and mains around R40.

One of the cheap and cheerful options is *Ferryman's Tavern*, adjoining Mitchell's Waterfront Brewery. The emphasis is on an interesting variety of freshly brewed beers and good-value pub meals. To give you an idea, calamari starter is R15, fish and chips costs R17 and steaks are under R30.

For fish and chips overlooking the water, head for *Fisherman's Choice*, where you can takeaway or eat in. Fish and chips costs R24 and seafood boxes are R28.

*Caffe San Marco* (☎ (021) 418 5434) is the offspring of the San Marco restaurant in Sea Point, and here you can sample some of the famed Italian cooking at lower prices. Pizzas and pastas start at around R18.

There are many other restaurants – it's a matter of walking around and seeing what appeals. There are a couple of places on Bertie's Landing, across a 20m channel from the main Victoria & Alfred complex – take the ferry (R2) from near the Old Customs House, otherwise it's quite a long walk around the basin.

## Sea Point

There are dozens of places to eat along Main and Regent Rds, between the suburbs of Three Anchor Bay and Queens, although since the advent of the Waterfront this is no longer Cape Town's premier restaurant strip. The following suggestions start at the Three Anchor Bay end.

There are surprisingly few Indian restaurants in Cape Town. One worth considering is *Little Bombay* (☎ (021) 439 9041), 245 Main Rd. It's a Hindu-run 'pure-veg' restaurant and the meals are good value, eg full thalis with entrées cost R32, mini thalis are R22. The spices have been toned down for South African palates but they will cook you the real thing if you ask. It's open daily for lunch and dinner. *L'Orient* (☎ (021) 439 6572), 50 Main Rd (near the corner of Marine Rd), is a good restaurant with fairly genuine Malaysian and Indonesian dishes. Most main courses start at around R30. It's open for dinner daily except Monday.

*Café Erté*, on Main Rd near the corner of Frere, is a relaxed (despite the stark black-and-deco paint job), gay-friendly bar and café open from 11 am to 5 am. You can have snacks such as burgers for R15 and for larger meals of modern cuisine with lots of fresh ingredients, two people can probably eat and drink for under R70.

*San Marco* (☎ (021) 49 2758), 92 Main Rd (on the corner of St James), is a long-established and excellent formal Italian restaurant, with some of the few professional waiters in town. They let it go to their heads, sometimes. Prices match the quality. You might find an entrée under R25, a pasta under R35 and a main course under R45, but why not forget about the bill and enjoy some great food. It's open daily except Tuesday for dinner, plus lunch on Sunday. The gelateria in front of the restaurant has delicious takeaway gelati and other ice cream.

*Peasants*, just off Main Rd on Wisbeach St, is a pizza and pasta place offering food a little better than the franchise places, with dishes starting at around R30.

*Ari's Souvlaki* (☎ (021) 439 6683), 150 Main Rd (on the corner of Oliver Rd), is a very popular Sea Point institution famous for felafels and souvlaki. Shawarma is R15. The food is good although, as is usual in this country, a little blander than the original.

For kerbside tables and good snacks go to *Reise's Deli* on Main Rd near Arthur's Rd. It's open from 8.30 am to 7 pm daily. Nearby on St John's Rd, beneath St John's Lodge, *The Wooden Shoe* (☎ (021) 439 4435) is the oldest surviving steakhouse in Cape Town, if not South Africa. It's tiny but it's very good and specialises in Austrian dishes. Prices are reasonable.

Right on the beachfront, a short walk down Clarens St from Main Rd, the *Hard Rock Café* (☎ (021) 434 1573), 118 Beach Rd, is in a large warehouse-like structure; there's also a pleasant outdoor deck. There's live music on Wednesday, Friday and Saturday. Salads are around R18, fish or steak are R35 and there are cheaper snacks.

For biltong, which can be vacuum-packed for export (but no matter how it's packed you can't take it home to Australia or the USA), try *Joubert & Monty's Meat Boutique*, 53 Regent Rd, near the corner of Clarens St. Next door is *New York Deli*, where bagels are the speciality.

## Camps Bay

Camps Bay is a pleasant destination for an evening drink and meal, especially if the south-easterly isn't howling. A stroll on the beach, followed by a beer at one of the pavement tables, and dinner in Blues is a genuine pleasure. For those on a budget there's a *St Elmo's*.

*Blues* (☎ (021) 438 2040), upstairs in The Promenade centre, Victoria Rd, is in a large, airy room overlooking the beach. The crowd tends to be relatively young and informal, but smart – this is a place to be seen. The menu is interesting and the prices are surprisingly reasonable – from around R35. Booking is recommended in the evening and during the day on summer weekends.

*La Med* (☎ (021) 438 5600) is another casual but upmarket place in Camps Bay. It's at the Glen Country Club and often has live music.

**Observatory**

Observatory is an inner-city suburb to the east of the city and Devil's Peak. It's convenient to the University of Cape Town and is favoured by student types, although yuppies are starting to realise the suburb's advantages.

The main batch of restaurants is only a short walk from the Observatory train station (on the Simon's Town line), 10 minutes and R2.20/1.50 in 1st/3rd class from the main train station. There are frequent trains until 10 pm Monday to Saturday, until 8 pm on Sunday. From the station, walk west (towards the mountain) along Trill Rd until it intersects with Lower Main Rd. Turn right and walk through to the intersection with Station Rd – most places are around here. Turn left on Station for the Heidelberg Hotel, a popular student bar.

All the following places are on Lower Main Rd. Just south of Trill Rd is *Stews R Us*, with good-value and filling meals. On the other side of Lower Main Rd on the corner of Trill is *Elaine's* (☎ (021) 47 2616), a good Indian/Asian restaurant with curries for around R30. On the opposite corner is the *Zulu Warrior Café* and a few doors up from here is *Die Blou Okapi*, a studenty café with good, cheap food. Breakfast (served all day) is just R10 and there are pittas from R4.50.

It's open until 2 am daily. Just next door is its antithesis, the trendy *Observatory Café*, which is also a bar. A little along from here is *Pancho's Mexican Restaurant* with good-value food (most dishes under R25) and a cheerful atmosphere. Across the road from Pancho's is *Seasons*, a vegetarian restaurant – the meal I had there was too bland, if healthy.

*Fiddlewoods Restaurant* (☎ (021) 448 6687), 40 Trill Rd (near the corner of Lower Main Rd), serves modern, delicious and healthy food. Many dishes are vegetarian and they start at less than R20. Next door, set back from Trill Rd, is *Café Ganesh*, which is trendy but cool. *The Planet* on Station Rd opposite the Heidelberg Hotel is a bar and restaurant with budget specials.

*Africa Café* (☎ (021) 47 9553), 213 Lower Main Rd (on the corner of Bishop), serves African dishes from across the continent. There's an all-you-can-eat communal feast for R59 per person. It's open for dinner nightly except Sunday.

Not in Observatory but on the way there, at 297 Albert Rd in Woodstock, *The Palace* (☎ (021) 47 9540) *is* palatial and its clients are mainly wealthier members of the Muslim community. It's run by Boete Achmad, who has been a big name in Cape Town catering for nearly 50 years. Curries start at around R30, rising to about R70 for prawn curry, and steaks are around R40. There are also set menus. It's pricey but a nice change from standard restaurants.

**Hout Bay**

At the northern end of Chapman's Peak Drive this place was a fishing village, and there are still a number of fish factories. It's a popular destination, especially on weekends. *Snoekies* at the far end of Hout Bay harbour has a fresh-fish shop, or try *The Laughing Lobster* for fried fish and piping hot chips. Both places are open seven days a week from 8.30 am to 5.30 pm. *Fish on the Rocks* in the same area is basically a takeaway for workers at the fish factories, but they do very good fish and chips at reasonable prices.

Mariner's Wharf (☎ (021) 790 1100) is a harbour-front complex with a restaurant and open-air bistro, both specialising in fish. It is a tourist trap but a lot of work has gone into it and it's quite pleasant. The nautical antiques *are* antiques, not plastic reproductions. *Mariners' Wharf Grill* has some less expensive dishes such as fish pie and salad (R25), but most fish dishes are pricey. There's a fish market in the complex, so you could buy and cook your own.

### False Bay

**Kalk Bay** The *Brass Bell* (☎ (021) 788 5455), Kalk Bay station, is right between the railway line and the sea, with magnificent views over False Bay. Besides the restaurant, the Bell has two bars and an open-air patio. It isn't cheap, but it is worth it.

There's live music every Saturday afternoon which drifts on into the night, and on some evenings (check the papers). The Brass Bell was a legendary rock venue, but the music is now considerably less rowdy. If you want to see music at the Brass Bell but can't afford the meal prices, there are a number of good places across the road, such as *Cafe Matisse* with snacks and pizzas.

**Boulders Beach** The *Penguin Point Café* is a pleasant café with sea views from the deck, but it's also a good restaurant. There are snacks such as spicy kedgeree (R19), starters such as calamari (R16 and prepared much more imaginatively than in most restaurants) and dishes such as pasta (R28).

### Groot Constantia

Groot Constantia is the oldest and grandest of the Cape's wine estates. The buildings date from 1685 and have been beautifully restored. It's a bit of a tourist trap, but it's worth visiting, especially if you don't have time to explore the Winelands around Stellenbosch. See the earlier Groot Constantia section for things to see and do at the estate. Another good-value restaurant, nearby, is in the Kirstenbosch Botanical Gardens.

The *Tavern*, beside the modern cellars

near the main homestead, has a pleasant outdoor eating area, although it is expensive. You'll pay about four times more for a bottle of wine here than it costs in the nearby cellar. The *Jonkerhuis* looks as if it will be expensive, but it's actually good value. It's in an old, restored estate house, a short walk from the main homestead. Teas and light lunches are served daily from 10 am to 5 pm. There are some great cakes and pastries, and at lunch there are some traditional dishes such as bobotie and rice (R35) and chicken pie (R35) as well as standard and lighter dishes.

### Kirstenbosch Botanical Gardens

The *restaurant* at Kirstenbosch Botanical Gardens (☎ (021) 797 7614) is good value. It is open daily for breakfasts, teas and lunches; there are indoor and outdoor eating areas. It's not formal or flash but you can get something cheap and filling like bangers and mash (R15), a vegetable platter (R17) or a steak (from R20). On Sunday there's a roast lunch for about R25. It's open from 9 am to 5 pm Monday to Friday, and from 8.30 am to 5 pm on Saturday and Sunday.

### ENTERTAINMENT

Cape Town is returning to its roots – the old Tavern of the Seas has dusted itself down and is back in the business of beguiling doubloons from visiting foreigners. If you're staying at a top-end place your doubloons will already be flowing fairly rapidly, but even if you're paying a pittance for a hostel bunk there are still plenty of wallet-emptying temptations. Although there aren't many stand-out entertainment venues, the city has such a good atmosphere (especially in summer) that many people put in some very long nights drifting from bar to club to bar to club...

You can't do without the entertainment guide in the *Weekly Mail & Guardian*. *The Cape Times* newspaper has an entertainment section on Friday. *Going Out in the Cape* is a monthly booklet listing most mainstream events; it's sold at various information offices for R3.

For any entertainment bookings, contact

Computicket (☎ (021) 21 4715), a computerised booking agency that has *every* seat for *every* theatre, cinema and sports venue on its system. You can be shown the available seats and get your ticket on the spot. It has outlets in the Golden Acre Centre, at the Waterfront and many other places. In addition to the entertainment sphere, it also accepts classified advertisements for major newspapers and bookings for various bus lines.

To see how the majority of Cape Towners enjoy themselves, take a tour of clubs in the townships. These are a little hard to come by, unfortunately, as operators go in and out of business quickly. Ask at Captour for those currently running.

### Bars & Clubs

Several pubs and bars are covered in the Places to Eat section. In particular, don't forget the *Brass Bell* on Kalk Bay station overlooking the sea and the *Perseverance Tavern* in Gardens.

Wednesday, Friday and Saturday are the big nights in the clubs. In the city centre, the blocks around Bree, Loop and Long Sts and say, Waterkant, are incredibly lively all night long on summer weekends. The actual entertainment rarely matches this level of activity (most clubs play techno to expensively dressed young suburbanites and visiting Vaalies) but it's a good buzz. Cover charges are around R10.

Bars and clubs in this area come and go quite rapidly, but some seem to survive, such as *Café Comic Strip*, Loop St, which is pretty standard, with lots of bouncers and lots of young whites from the outer suburbs. On the next corner is *Browne's Café du Vin*, currently the home of acid jazz. Around here you'll find plenty of other places, such as the *Havana Bar*, the *Crew Bar* and *Carlos O'Brien's*. A reader recommends *The Rockin' Shamrock* (Loop St), 'but only if you like dancing on the tables and the bar'.

For less clean-cut entertainment, try Riebeeck St around Loop and Bree Sts, where there are strip shows and the like.

The strip clubs might not be very savoury but they are culturally interesting. This is where you're likely to meet up-country Afrikaner men who are in the big city for a spree. Amid the smashing of all sorts of racial and sexual taboos you can almost see their Calvinist upbringing beginning to crumble. It's like something out of William Faulkner.

**Jon Murray**

Currently the place to be seen is *Hemingways*, an upmarket nightclub in the impressive old Martin Melck House on Strand St, between Bree and Buitengracht. Admission is a hefty R20 but a foreign accent (especially a US one) combined with model looks might get you in free. It's that sort of place.

The *Shebeen* on Bree serves beer in 750ml bottles and drinks in tin cups – and the bar is lined with young whites sitting around waiting for something to happen. Apparently that something includes good township jazz, but there wasn't much happening when I dropped by. If you want to see a real shebeen, take a township tour or get yourself an invitation from someone who knows what they are doing. The *Fireman's Arms*, on the corner of Buitengracht and Mechau (near Somerset), is one of the few old pubs left in town and it dates from 1906. There's a cheerful bar and a lounge where you can buy cheap meals.

At the Waterfront, *Cantina Tequila* is currently very popular with visitors, and the *Quay 4 Bar* is still crowded. There are plenty of other places. *Blue Rock*, Main Rd, Sea Point, is a smallish, coolish bar specialising in cocktails (complete with juggling barpeople) and hoping to attract an 'unpretentious yuppie' crowd. It plays good music, sometimes live, and stays open very late.

*The Purple Turtle*, on Shortmarket St around the corner from Greenmarket Square, has a relaxed and student pub-like atmosphere. There are meals and bands, although it seems to be a place where people meet before going on to the clubs. The crowd at *The Lounge*, upstairs at 194 Long St, tends to the alternative, and it's a small, relaxed place. It's in the narrow section of Long St with all the iron-lace balconies and its own balcony is a great place for a drink on a hot night. *District Six Café*, on the corner of Sir Lowry Rd and Darling St, is similar but more down-to-earth – it's a dim but friendly place that describes itself as a 1990s pub. It's open from 8 pm to 4 am from Monday to Thursday and until 6 am on Friday and Saturday.

A grungy neighbourhood bar with a reputation among fastidious Cape Towners as catering to 'bergies' (bums, tramps, deros), *The Whistle Stop* is actually not bad. It's about the only bar in the city area where you'll drink with ordinary people of all colours in anything like an ordinary bar atmosphere. The Whistle Stop is at the top end of Long St, near the Long St Baths and is open until 4 am daily.

Away from the centre but not too far to go by Rikki or taxi, *The Shed*, De Villiers St, Gardens, is a bar and a pool hall. It attracts an interesting crowd and the decor is good. *The Fringe*, 46 Canterbury St, Gardens, is a relaxed and unpretentious place where people actually dance to enjoy themselves. The night I called by it was full of happy young lesbians. Thursday is reggae night.

The *Stag's Head Hotel* (☎ (021) 45 4918), 71 Hope St, Gardens, is a very popular pub. It's one of the few English/Australian-style downmarket pubs in South Africa. The ground floor bar has a motley assortment of locals staring morosely into their beers, the ground floor lounge (rear) has a younger crowd, but the real action happens upstairs with plenty of pool tables, pinball machines and loud music (sometimes live).

The *Heidelberg Hotel*, Station St (near the corner of Lower Main Rd), Observatory, is another classic – the clientele is dominated by students and the name of the game is drinking beer. What else are hotels for? Nearby on Lower Main Rd is *Rolling Stones*, a large, upstairs pool hall with a long balcony that's a nice place to have a drink. As with everywhere else in Cape Town, the tables are not full-size (we'd be pleased to hear if you have found a full-size table) but it's a good spot. Opening hours are noon to 3 am, daily.

For a bar/cafeteria which has zero design qualities but a friendly atmosphere, go upstairs from the train station's Strand St entrance. The clientele is exclusively non-white. For something completely different try *Forries* (The Forester's Arms) in the leafy suburb of Newlands, on the corner of Newlands Ave and Manson Close. There are good pub meals starting at about R20 for bangers and mash. Another pleasant middle-class watering hole to try out is *Barristers*, nearby on the corner of Kildare and Main Sts (not Main Rd).

### Live Music

Several music venues are covered in the Places to Eat section. The *Green Dolphin* is a top-class jazz venue at the Waterfront, and the *Brass Bell* at the Kalk Bay station has live bands on Wednesday and Saturday night, and Saturday and Sunday afternoon.

Occasionally there is live music at *Quay 4* on the Waterfront. There is nearly always something on at *The Pumphouse* (☎ (021) 25 4437), also at the Waterfront. It's a great venue – it's in the old pumphouse for the adjacent dry docks – but it's fairly small and can be ridiculously crowded.

One of the best places for a drink, a snack and live jazz is *Manenberg's Jazz Cafe*, upstairs on Adderley St on the corner of Church St. It's a pleasant place with tables on the balcony and a relaxed and racially mixed clientele. There's a cover charge of R10 at night (more if there's a big act).

One of the best venues is unfortunately a long way from the city. The *River Club* (☎ (021) 448 6117), near the corner of Station Rd and Liesbeek Parkway, Observatory, often hosts big-name bands with a cover charge of around R10. There's another club on the premises, *The Water Room*.

*Dizzy Jazz* (☎ (021) 438 2686) is on the corner of The Drive and Camps Bay Drive, just off Victoria Rd in Camps Bay. It's open daily until very late and has live jazz from Thursday to Sunday.

For classical music, see what's on at the *town hall* (☎ (021) 462 1250), where the Cape Town Symphony has regular concerts. The *Nico Malan* complex also has classical music (see Theatre).

## Cinema

See the local press for a rundown of cinemas and the films they are showing.

The best cinema for 'mainstream alternative' films is the *Labia* (☎ (021) 24 5927), named after Count Labia, 68 Orange St, Gardens. Most shows cost a very reasonable R12. Similar fare is offered at the *Baxter Theatre* (☎ (021) 689 1069), Main Rd, Rondebosch, on the corner of Woolsack. There are Nu-Metro cinemas at the Waterfront and on Adderley St for commercial fare.

At the Victoria & Alfred Waterfront, in the flashy BMW Pavilion, the *Imax cinema* offers Imax-format films (shown on a giant square screen). There are hourly shows from 11 am to 11 pm.

## Theatre

The *Baxter Studio*, Woolsack Rd, Rosebank, and the *Little Theatre*, Orange St, are venues for non-mainstream productions.

The various theatres in the large *Nico Malan* complex (gradually becoming known as the Nico to avoid the apartheid-era connotations of the Malan name) on the foreshore have ballet, opera and more mainstream theatre – at prices way below what you would pay in Europe. After an evening performance you'll have to phone for a taxi as there is no rank and walking isn't very safe in this area after dark.

## Gay Scene

Although there's quite a healthy gay scene there aren't many exclusively gay venues. Most are close together in the Waterkant area. *The Bronx* is a small bar and cabaret venue on the corner of Main Rd/Strand St and Napier St between the city and Green Point. When there's entertainment (usually on Saturday night) it starts at around 10 pm. *Angels* on Main Rd in Green Point is a mixed dance venue. *Café Manhattan*, a bar and restaurant, is nearby, up on the corner of Waterkant and Dixon Sts. *Café Ertè* (see Places to Eat) on Main Rd in Sea Point is a gay-friendly place that stays open late for after-club recuperation.

The Cape Town Queer Project is a massive party held at the River Club every year in mid-December.

Gay esCape (☎ (021) 23 9001; fax 23 5907; email gayesc@cis.co.za), 2nd floor, 7 Castle St, is a gay-oriented travel agency which books tours and accommodation across the country. It's also a good source of information on other things, such as good restaurants and venues in and around Cape Town. Check out their web site at www.icafe.co.za/gayes.

## Elvis Snack & Dance

This place wouldn't warrant a heading all to itself or even an entry in this book, except that it's about the only example of genuine eccentricity you'll come across in this country. It's a tiny (and probably unlicensed) bar adjoining a tiny barber shop (just R13 for a haircut), run by Michael, a devoted fan of Elvis. He'll sing you a song if you ask nicely and buy a beer at an inflated price. Elvis Snack & Dance is on Main Rd in Sea Point, to the city side of the San Marco restaurant, and sometimes stays open very late.

## THINGS TO BUY

You'll find most things you need at shops in the city centre, but if you hunger for a suburban mall, try Cavendish Mall, off Protea Rd in Claremont, the most stylish shopping centre in Cape Town.

## Markets

In addition to the specialised markets (see the following sections) there are markets in Greenmarket Square (daily) and at Green Point (between the Waterfront and Sea Point) on Sunday. The market at Grand Parade (Wednesday and Saturday) doesn't sell much of interest to visitors but it is much livelier than the others, with people scrambling for bargains, mainly clothing.

## Crafts

There are craft shops all over town, but don't forget that few items come from the Cape Town area. For traditional crafts you're better off looking in the part of the country where they originate. There are, however, some township-produced items such as recycled tin boxes and toys, which are local and make great gifts.

The Siyakatala stall in the craft market at the Waterfront sells items made by self-help groups in the townships, and the quality is as good as anywhere. In St George's Cathedral is a small shop worth looking at. It has some guidebooks and craft – and you know that the profits are going to people who need them.

African Image, on the corner of Church and Burg Sts, has an interesting range of new and old craftworks and artefacts. Prices are reasonable, eg flowers made from aluminium cans cost R6 – you can pay R20 elsewhere. Nearby on Church St, Out of Africa, on the Church St mall, is a very expensive but very good craft/antique shop. Pezulu, 70 St George's Mall (near Hout St), is upstairs and can be difficult to spot, but it's worth making the effort.

A craft market is held on Sunday on Dock Rd, just outside the Waterfront, with a more tourist-oriented art and craft market held in the Waterfront near the Maritime Museum on weekends. Mnandi Textiles, 90 Station St (near the corner of Lower Main Rd), Observatory, sells interesting printed cloth and some clothing made from it. You'll find cloth printed with everything from ANC election posters to animal patterns. A few blocks away at 190 Lower Main Rd, Evelyn Kubukeli's sangoma shop has been recommended as the place to pick up your traditional medicines.

### Antiques, Collectables & Old Books

South Africa's long isolation from the outside world means that there are troves of old goods for sale at very reasonable prices.

The Junk Shop, on the corner of Long and Bloem Sts, has some intriguing junk from many eras. In the same area there are several good second-hand and antiquarian bookshops, although the legendary Cranfords has closed. Not far away, Church St between Long and Burg Sts is a pedestrian mall where a flea market is held on Thursday, Friday and

Saturday (daily in summer) and there are several antique shops.

### Camping Gear

There's a branch of the excellent Camp & Climb chain (☎ (021) 23 2175) at 6 Pepper St, near the corner of Long St. Cape Union Mart chain has branches at the Victoria & Alfred Waterfront (☎ (021) 419 0019) and others in the Cape Sun Gallery (an underground shopping arcade) and on the corner of Spin and Corporation Sts. For quite a bit of gear, the big department stores (like OK Bazaars in Adderley St) will be cheaper, however.

### Wine

The wines produced in the Cape are of an extremely high standard and they are very cheap by international standards. It is worth considering having a few cases shipped home, although you will almost certainly have to pay duty. Even so, when you can buy excellent wines for R30 and under, you might still consider it worthwhile. Several companies will freight wine for you, including Vaughan Johnson's Wine Shop (☎ (021) 419 2121; fax 419 0040) at the Waterfront.

### Other Things to Buy

Afrogem (☎ (021) 24 8048), 64 New Church St, produces jewellery and other items from semi-precious stones, gold and silver, and you can call in and see how it's done on a free guided tour. Its large showroom has some rather tempting gift ideas. Tours are available from 8.30 am to 4.30 pm on weekdays (to 3.30 pm on Friday) and the showroom is open daily except Sunday from 8.30 am to 5 pm.

### GETTING THERE & AWAY
### Air

Cape Town has an increasingly busy international airport. If you have the choice, arriving here is much nicer than arriving in Jo'burg.

Distances in South Africa are large, so if you're in a hurry some domestic flights are definitely worth considering. Fares quoted here are full economy, but big discounts are available – see the Getting Around chapter. SAA flies between Cape Town and major centres including Durban (R787), East London (R684), Jo'burg (R787), Kimberley (R661), Port Elizabeth (R513) and Upington (R627).

National Airlines (☎ (021) 934 0350; fax 934 3373) has flights every weekday going to Springbok (R764) and Alexander Bay (R807).

International airlines with offices in Cape Town include:

Air France
    Golden Acre Centre (☎ (021) 21 4760; fax 21 7061)
Air India
    20th Floor, Trustbank Centre (☎ (021) 418 3558)
Air Mauritius
    11th Floor, Strand Towers, 66 Strand St (☎ (021) 21 6294; fax 21 7321)
British Airways
    12th Floor, BP Centre, Thibault Square (☎ (021) 25 2970)
KLM
    Main Tower, Standard Bank Centre (☎ (021) 21 1870)
Lufthansa
    Southern Life Centre, 8 Riebeeck St (☎ (021) 25 1490)
Malaysia
    Safmarine House, 22 Riebeeck St (☎ (021) 419 8010)
Namib Air
    Standard Bank Centre (☎ (021) 21 6685)
Qantas
    BP Centre (☎ (021) 25 2978)
SAA
    Southern Life Centre, 8 Riebeeck St (☎ (021) 403 1111)
Singapore Airlines
    14 Long St (☎ (021) 419 0495)
Swissair
    Southern Life Centre, 8 Riebeeck St (☎ (021) 21 4938)
Varig
    (☎ (021) 21 1850)

## Bus

All long-distance buses leave from the main train station. The main buslines operating out of Cape Town are:

Translux
    The national busline running many major routes at major prices. The Translux office (☎ (021) 405 3333; fax 405 2545) is on the Adderley St side of the station block and is open from 7.30 am to 6 pm Monday to Saturday and from 11.30 am to 5 pm on Sunday. Phone bookings are taken from 8 am to 5 pm on weekdays and from 8 am to noon on Saturday.
Greyhound
    The other national line runs fewer routes from Cape Town, at prices a little higher than Translux (☎ (021) 418 4312; fax 418 4315).
Intercape Mainliner
    Some extremely useful services, including along the west and south coasts. A little cheaper than the majors (☎ (021) 386 4400, 24 hours). The office is not far from the Translux office and is open from 6 am to 8 pm daily.

**Jo'burg** Translux, Greyhound and Intercape run to Jo'burg at least daily for about R320, via either Bloemfontein or Kimberley (about 17 hours). Intercape also runs to Jo'burg via Upington, for a total of R280. You might have to change buses in Upington but it is usually a direct connection; if so Cape Town to Jo'burg takes about 19 hours.

**Garden Route** Translux runs at least daily to Port Elizabeth (R125 and 11 hours from Cape Town) via Swellendam (R65), Mossel Bay (R85), Oudtshoorn (R100 – not all services stop here), George (R100), Knysna (R105), Plettenberg Bay (R110) and Storms River (R125).

Intercape runs the Garden Route twice daily at slightly lower fares. Even cheaper is the weekly Chilwans Intercity (☎ (021) 934 4786) bus to Port Elizabeth (R100). It departs from the upper deck of the train station on Friday and returns on Sunday.

If you plan to visit several Garden Route towns check out the options on the Garden Route Hopper (☎ (041) 55 4000) and the Baz Bus (☎ (021) 439 2323) – most hostels take bookings.

**Mountain Route** Like the Garden Route, the mountain route takes you east from Cape Town, but inland for the first half of the trip. If you can find a daylight service this route is more scenic than the Garden Route. Translux runs to Port Elizabeth (R125) three times a week via Robertson (R100), Montagu (R100) and Oudtshoorn (R100).

Munnik Coaches (☎ (021) 637 1850) departs from the upper deck at the train station and runs to Montagu thrice weekly for R35.

**Eastern Cape** City to City (a Translux subsidiary) runs daily from Cape Town to Umtata (R115, 19 hours) via Worcester, Beaufort West and Graaff-Reinet. It's a useful route (although slow), but unfortunately much of the journey is at night. Transtate (a poor cousin of City to City once designated for black travellers) runs to Umtata once a week, along much the same route as City to City. It's a slower but cheaper trip.

Translux services to Port Elizabeth (R140, 12 hours) connect with a daily bus to Durban via East London and Umtata.

**Durban** Translux services to Port Elizabeth connect with a service to Durban. The total trip takes about 24 hours and costs over R300 – consider finding a discount air ticket. A slightly faster Translux service runs to Durban via Bloemfontein.

**West Coast & Namibia** Intercape runs to Upington (R130) via Citrusdal (R70 from Cape Town) and Clanwilliam (R85). From Upington you can get an Intercape bus to Windhoek (Namibia) for R200. Intercape also has a direct service between Cape Town and Windhoek (R295), running via Springbok (R165).

City to City (book through Translux) runs to Upington for R240.

## Train

Several long-distance trains run to/from Cape Town, although the local area Metro service is the best way to get to the Winelands area, especially to Stellenbosch (see the following Getting Around section). All trains leave from the main Cape Town train station, where the booking office (☎ (021) 405 3871) is open from 7.30 am to 4 pm on weekdays and from 7.30 to 11 am on Saturday.

There's a luggage storage facility next to Platform 24, open from 7 am to noon and 12.30 to 6.50 pm Monday to Thursday, 6 am to noon and 12.30 to 6 pm on Friday, 7 to 11 am on Saturday and 7 am to 1 pm on Sunday. The charge is R5 per item per 24 hours.

**Trans Karoo to Jo'burg** The daily *Trans Karoo* is competitive in price, but much slower than the bus (about 25 hours instead of 17). Still, this is an interesting train journey. First/2nd/3rd-class fares are R326/220/137 (more for a sleeper).

**Trans Oranje to Durban** It's also possible to travel between Cape Town and Durban on the weekly *Trans Oranje*. However, this would be rather an eccentric decision, because although the price is competitive at R425/286/179, it takes an awful long time – over 36 hours. The train runs via Bloemfontein, about 20 hours and R258/174/108 from Cape Town.

**Southern Cross to Port Elizabeth** Although the weekly trip takes about 24 hours it's an interesting route, with stops including Huguenot (Paarl), Robertson, Ashton (near Montagu), Swellendam, George and Oudtshoorn. Fares from Cape Town include Swellendam, R52/38/21; George, R86/62/35; Oudtshoorn, R96/69/39; and Port Elizabeth, R159/114/65.

**Blue Train** See the introductory Getting Around chapter for information on the *Blue Train*. If you can't afford to take the train all the way to Jo'burg, consider a shorter journey. For example, the cheapest ticket to Matjiesfontein, where you can stay in the wonderful Lord Milner Hotel, is R600. For information on the *Blue Train* phone ☎ (021) 405 2672.

## Minibus Taxi

Long-distance minibus taxis cover most of the country with an informal network of routes. Although they have traditionally been used by blacks only, an increasing number of whites (mainly foreign backpackers) are now using them – for very good reasons. Minibus taxis are a cheap and efficient way of getting around. The driving can occasionally be hair-raising, but it is mostly OK, especially compared with similar transport in other African countries. As their clientele is largely black, they'll often travel via townships and will usually depart very early in the morning or in the early evening to cater to the needs of commuting workers and shoppers.

In Cape Town, most taxis start picking up passengers in a distant township, especially Langa and Nyanga, and perhaps make a trip into the train station if they need more people, so your choices can be limited. Currently some of the townships aren't totally off-limits to outsiders, but nor are they great places to be wandering around in the early hours of the morning carrying a pack. *Do not* go into a township without accurate local knowledge, and preferably with a reliable local guide! Langa is currently relatively safe (however these things can change) and long-distance taxis leave from the Langa shopping centre early in the morning. A local area minibus taxi from the train station to Langa costs about R2.50. A taxi to Jo'burg costs about R150 but the trip is long, uncomfortable and potentially dangerous because of driver fatigue. Between a few people, hiring a car would be cheaper.

**Door-to-Door Minibus Taxi** Atkins Transport (☎ (021) 951 2045, best between 8 am and 9 pm) runs a daily door-to-door taxi to Springbok for R90.

Abader's Long Distance Minibus (☎ (021) 418 1346) departs from Platform 24 at Cape Town train station at 8 pm on a nightly run along the Garden Route to Plettenberg Bay. Stops and fares from Cape Town/Plettenberg Bay include: Swellendam (R45/55), Mossel Bay (R60/25), George (R65/15), Knysna (R70/10) and Plettenberg Bay (R80). The trip takes eight hours or so and lands you in towns in the early hours of the morning, so it's inconvenient and unscenic. The return trip departs Plettenberg Bay at 8.30 am so you do get to see some of the country.

**Car & Motorcycle**
**Rental** Major international companies such as Avis (☎ 0800 021 111 toll-free), 123 Strand St; and Budget (☎ 0800 016 622 toll-free), 63A Strand St, are represented.

The larger local companies, such as Imperial (☎ 0800 118 898 toll-free), on the corner of Loop and Strand Sts; and Tempest (☎ 0800 031 666 toll-free), on the corner of Buitengracht and Wale Sts, offer comparable service to the major companies at slightly lower rates.

The smaller, cheaper local companies come and go – at the time of writing two of the more prominent were Alisa (☎ 0800 21515 toll-free), 139 Buitengracht, and Panther (☎ (021) 511 6196; fax 511 7802). You'll find plenty of brochures for other cheaper outfits at the Tourist Rendezvous and at hostels – read the small print! Their businesses are booming because of the increasing numbers of budget travellers to hit Cape Town, and there can be some good

deals. There are so many companies and factors involved in deciding what's best for you (Do you really need 400 free kilometres a day if you're just tootling around Cape Town and the Winelands? Can you drop the car in Jo'burg?) that you really need to gather as many brochures as you can, sit down with a beer and do some sums. At the time of writing, some smaller companies were offering deals of around R800 per week with unlimited kilometres.

Le Cap Motorcycle Hire (☎ (021) 23 0823; fax 23 5566), 3 Carisbrook St, hires bikes and also runs longer tours. If you're looking for cheap transport you'd be better off hiring a car, but it's very tempting to explore South Africa by bike – warm weather, good roads and spectacular scenery. You need to be over 23 and have held a motorbike licence for two years to rent one of the Kawasaki KLR650s. The daily rate is R150 plus R15 helmet hire plus R0.60 per kilometre. There are deals for longer rentals which include free kilometres.

Le Cap also rents 100cc scooters for R100 per day, including a helmet and 100 free kilometres. You need to be 18 and have a motorbike licence. Another outfit plans to rent 50cc mopeds, but they might have trouble on the steep hills.

**Purchase** There are many used car dealers on Voortrekker Rd between Maitland and Bellville. Voortrekker is the R102 and runs west from Salt River, south of and pretty much parallel to, the N1.

Some dealers might agree to a buy-back deal. John Wayne at Wayne Motors (☎ (021) 45 2222; fax 45 2617), 13 Roeland St, reckons that, for example, he might be able to sell you a car for R6500 and guarantee to buy it back for R3500. He says that you have a fair chance of selling it privately for more than that.

Whether you're buying the car from a dealer or privately, make sure that the details correspond accurately with the ownership (registration) papers and that there is a *current* licence disk attached to the windscreen. Check the owner's name against their

## Buying A Car

Johannesburg is the best place to buy cheap cars in South Africa, but Cape Town is the nicest. The process is inevitably time consuming and Cape Town is a much more enjoyable place to waste a week or two. Prices do tend to be a bit higher so it's not a bad place to sell, but as the market is smaller you might wait longer. Cars that have spent their lives around Cape Town are more likely to be rusty than those kept inland, but as one dealer told me, 'What's wrong with rust? It just means that the car is cheaper'.

The main congregation (or is 'pack' a better word?) of used car dealers is on Voortrekker Rd between Maitland and Bellville. Voortrekker is the R102 and runs west from Salt River, south of, and pretty much parallel to, the N1.

Some dealers might agree to a buy-back deal, such as John Wayne at Wayne Motors (☎ (021) 45 2222; fax 45 2617), 13 Roeland St. He'll guarantee a buy-back price but he reckons that that you have a fair chance of selling the car privately for more than that. He doesn't deal in rock-bottom cars, though.

Dealers have to make a profit, however, so you'll pay less if you buy privately. The *Cape Times* has ads every day, but the big day is Thursday. The *Weekend Argus* also has a good selection. Whoever you're buying from, make sure that the details correspond accurately with the ownership (registration) papers and that there is a *current* license disk on the windscreen. Check the owner's name against their identity document and the engine and chassis numbers. Consider getting the car tested by the AA (Automobile Association).

Cheap cars will often be sold without a roadworthy certificate. A certificate is required when you register the change of ownership, and pay tax for a license disk. Roadworthys used to be difficult to get but now some private garages are allowed to issue them, and some will overlook minor faults. A roadworthiness certificate costs R120.

Present yourself along with the roadworthy, a current license disk, an accurate registration certificate, a completed change of ownership card (signed by the seller), a clear photocopy of your ID (passport) along with the original, and your wallet to the City Treasurer's Department, Motor Vehicle Registration Division (☎ (021) 210 2385/6/7/8/9) in the Civic Centre, Cash Hall, on the foreshore. It's open from 8 am to 2 pm and distributes blank change-of-ownership forms. Ring ahead to check how much cash you'll need, but it will be under R200. It is hard to find decent-quality used cars at low prices, although a glut of cheap new models on the market might see used prices fall. You will be lucky to find a reliable vehicle for under R8000. Of course, if nothing serious goes wrong, you will hopefully get most of your money back when you sell.

In the meantime, however, you'll have a lot of money tied up. Insurance for third-party damages and theft is a very good idea. Unfortunately, it is surprisingly difficult to find an insurance company to take your money if you don't have a permanent address and/or a local bank account. If this concerns you, start shopping around early so you can figure out a way to meet their conditions – before you get the car. You'll need to budget around R250 a month. We would be interested to hear of any companies that are helpful to travellers.

Insurance companies will take cash if you buy a year's worth of insurance, but if you just want a month or so you must have a bank account. You might be able to negotiate paying a year's worth with a pro-rata refund the left-over when you sell the car, but get an agreement in writing, not just a vague promise. ∎

---

identity document and the engine and chassis numbers. Consider getting the car tested by the AA. Cheap cars are often sold without a roadworthy certificate. A certificate is required when you register the change of ownership and pay tax for a licence disk.

### Hitching & Arranged Lifts

Hitching around Cape Town is generally easy. Those planning to hitch longer distances should either start in the city centre, or catch public transport to one of the outlying towns, eg Paarl for Johannesburg, Somerset West for the Garden Route and Durban, and Malmsbury or Citrusdal for points north. The idea is to miss the surrounding suburbs and especially the Cape Flats where safety can be a real issue.

In the city centre, make a sign and start at the foreshore near the entry to the Victoria & Alfred Waterfront where the N1 (to Jo'burg), the N7 (to Windhoek), and the N2 (to the Garden Route) all converge.

Lift Net (☎ (021) 785 3802, 088 128 3727

AH) connects drivers with passengers. It's a lot more expensive than hitching but cheaper than most other forms of transport. From Cape Town you'll pay R160 to Jo'burg, R60 to George, R120 to Bloemfontein, R190 to Durban and R190 to Windhoek (Namibia). You need to give at least 24 hours notice. Office hours are 9 am to 5 pm on weekdays and 9 am to 1 pm on weekends.

Hostel notice boards often have offers of lifts.

## GETTING AROUND
### The Airport
Intercape's Airport Shuttle (☎ (021) 934 5455/6) links the main train station (outside Platform 24) and the airport. The shuttle has a counter in the domestic terminal. The scheduled service costs R30; coming from the airport, the shuttle can usually drop you off where you want if it's reasonably close to the city centre, for another R5. If you want to be picked up for a trip outside the regular schedule it will cost about R60 or R120 for the whole vehicle.

Taxis are expensive; expect to pay nearly R150.

A traveller who couldn't find a taxi after he arrived downtown from the airport reports finding someone to carry his bag to the hotel. He recommends negotiating the fee – I'd recommend having pretty good insurance!

### Bus
Cape Town has a pretty effective bus network centred on the Table Bay, Castle St side of the Grand Parade – the Golden Acre terminal. You can get almost anywhere in the city for under R3. Buses are the only means of getting along the Atlantic coast; trains service the suburbs to the east of Table Mountain.

There's a helpful information kiosk at the Parade terminal. It's open from 7.45 am to 5.45 pm Monday to Friday and from 8 am to 1 pm on Sunday. There are a couple of inquiry numbers (☎ (021) 934 0540 and 0801 21 2111).

A bus to Sea Point costs R1.40, to Camps Bay R2.60 and to Hout Bay R5.30. If you are using a particular bus regularly, it's worth buying clipcards, which give you 10 trips at a discount price. Travelling short distances, most people wait at the bus stop and take either a bus or a minibus taxi, whichever arrives first.

### Train
Metro commuter trains are a good way to get around. The Metro information office (☎ (021) 405 2991) is in the main train station near the old locomotive opposite Platform 23. It's open from 6 am to 6.45 pm Monday to Saturday and 7 am to 5 pm on Sunday.

Local trains have 1st and 3rd-class carriages. It's reasonably safe to travel in 3rd class (but check the current situation) but don't do it during peak hours (crowds offer scope for pickpockets), on weekends (lack of crowds offer scope for muggers) or when carrying a lot of gear. We've had the odd report of people having problems in both 1st and 3rd class.

Probably the most important line for travellers is the Simonstad/Simon's Town line that runs through Observatory and then around the back of the mountain through upper-income white suburbs such as Rosebank, down to Muizenberg and along the False Bay coast. Biggsy's (☎ (021) 405 3870) is a privately run bar and dining car attached to some services running between Cape Town and Simon's Town. You need a 1st class ticket and about R4 to enter.

Local trains run some way out of Cape Town, to Strand (on the east side of False Bay) and into the Winelands to Stellenbosch and Paarl. Some 1st/3rd-class fares are: Muizenberg, R5/2.20; Paarl, R10/4.40; Simon's Town, R6.80/2.90; Stellenbosch, R8.70/3.80; and Observatory, R2.20/1.50.

### Taxi
As always, taxis are expensive, but worth considering late at night or if you are in a group. There is a taxi rank at the Adderley St end of the Grand Parade in the city, or phone Star Taxis (☎ (021) 419 7777), Marine Taxi (☎ (021) 434 0434) or Sea Point Taxis

(☎ (021) 434 4444). There are often taxis in Greenmarket Square, near the Holiday Inn, and outside the Cape Sun on Strand St. A taxi from the station to Sea Point could cost R30; to Tamboerskloof it will be around R15. For a cheaper alternative see the Rikki's section following.

## Minibus Taxi

Minibus taxis cover most of the city with an informal network of routes. They are a cheap and efficient way of getting around the city. They go virtually everywhere and can have flexible routes. Minibus taxis cost a little less than the municipal buses.

The main terminus is on the upper deck of the train station, accessible from a walkway in the Golden Acre Centre or from stairways on Strand St. It's well organised and finding the right rank is easy. In the suburbs, you just hail them from the side of the road – point your index finger into the air. Coming into the city from Sea Point, taxis run via either Strand or Riebeeck Sts. There's no way of telling which route the taxi will take except by asking the driver.

There has been a sporadically violent 'war' between rival taxi firms, so check the current situation.

## Rikki's

Rikki's tiny, open vans provide Asian-style transport in the City Bowl and nearby areas for low prices. Telephone Rikki's (☎ (021) 23 4888) or just hail one on the street – you can pay a shared rate of a few rand or more if you phone for the whole van. They run between 7 am and 6 pm daily except Sunday and go as far afield as Sea Point and Camps Bay. From the train station to Camps Bay a single-person trip will cost about R12; to Tamboerskloof it will be about R5. Rikki's also operates out of Simon's Town (☎ (021) 786 2136).

Although it's cheap and fun, Rikki's might not be the quickest, as there is usually a certain amount of meandering as other passengers are dropped off.

## Bicycle

The Cape Peninsula is a great place to explore by bike, but there are hills and distances can be deceptively large – it's nearly 70km from the centre to Cape Point. Unfortunately you aren't supposed to take bikes on suburban trains.

Many hostels hire bikes and some of them are in reasonable condition. For a trouble-free bike contact Mike Hopkins (☎ (021) 23 2527), 133A Bree St (near the corner of Wale St), or Day Trippers (☎ (021) 461 4599 or 531 3274).

Apparently a bike-route map of Western Cape Province is in production.

# Winelands

The wine-producing region around Stellenbosch, sometimes known as the Boland, is only one of the important wine-growing regions in South Africa, but it is the oldest and most beautiful.

The small community at Cape Town established by the Dutch East India Company soon began to expand into the surrounding regions that had been inhabited by the Khoikhoi. The fertile and beautiful valleys around Paarl and Stellenbosch were settled from the 1670s onwards.

Although Jan van Riebeeck had planted vines and made wine himself, it was not until the arrival of Simon van der Stel in 1679 that wine-making seriously began. Van der Stel created Groot Constantia, the superb estate on the flanks of Table Mountain, but he also passed on his wine-making skills to the burghers settling around Stellenbosch. From 1688 to 1690, 200 French Huguenots arrived in the country. They were granted land in the region, particularly around Franschhoek (French Corner) and, although only a few had direct wine-making experience, they gave the infant industry fresh impetus.

The vineyards form a patchwork in the fertile valleys and seem to be overshadowed by dramatic mountains. The Franschhoek, Wemmershoek, Dutoits and Slanghoek ranges are all over 1500m high, and they start pretty close to sea level: the Franschhoek and Bainskloof passes that cross them are among the most spectacular in the country.

There are some pine plantations on the lower flanks, but the mountains are mostly cloaked in dense and shrubby mountain fynbos, a part of the prolific Cape floral kingdom. This includes the ericoid (heath-like plants) and protea families.

Stellenbosch is the most interesting and lively town, Franschhoek has the most spectacular location and Paarl is a busy commercial centre with plenty to see. All three are historically important and attractive, and all three promote wine routes around the surrounding wineries. This region is the oldest European-settled region in the Cape, and at times there is an almost European atmosphere – in South African terms this means it is extremely well endowed with restaurants and interesting accommodation. It is worth considering a splurge on either a nice restaurant, guest-house or both!

It is possible to see Stellenbosch and Paarl on day trips from Cape Town. Both are accessible by train, but Stellenbosch is the easiest to get around if you don't have a car. If you really want to do justice to the region and spend time exploring the many wine routes, you'll need wheels. Bicycle wheels will do.

While you're tasting the very fine wines, spare a thought for the coloured labourers who do most of the actual work in producing them. The infamous 'tot' system, whereby labourers' wages were partly paid in wine, still survives in some areas. Apart from the sheer economic injustice of this, the social and physical results were and are disastrous. For calculated cruelty there can't be many worse systems.

## STELLENBOSCH

Stellenbosch was established as a frontier town on the banks of the Eerste River by Governor Van der Stel in 1679. It's the second oldest town (after Cape Town) in South Africa, and one of the best preserved. The town is full of architectural and historical

gems (Cape Dutch, Georgian and Victorian), and is shaded by enormous oak trees. There are several interesting museums, not least the Village Museum, which consists of four buildings dating from 1709 to 1850.

The Afrikaans-language University of Stellenbosch, established in 1918, plays an important role in Afrikaner politics and culture. There are over 12,000 students, which means there is actually quite a thriving nightlife in the town (something of a rarity in South Africa). Don't expect liberal attitudes, though.

### Orientation

The train station is on the western side of town, a short walk from the centre. The railway line effectively forms the western boundary of the town and the Eerste River, the southern. Dorp St, which runs roughly parallel to the river, is the old town's main street and is lined with numerous fine old buildings. The commercial centre now lies between Dorp St and the university to the east of the Braak. The Braak is the old town square.

### Information

The Stellenbosch Publicity Association (☎ (021) 883 3584), 36 Market St, is open Monday to Friday from 8 am to 5 pm, Saturday from 9.30 am to 5 pm and Sunday from 9.30 am to 4.30 pm. This must be one of the busiest tourist offices in the country but the staff are extremely helpful, especially when it comes to recommending B&Bs and providing information on nearby wineries. Pick up the excellent free brochure *Discover Stellenbosch on Foot*, with a walking-tour map and information on many of the historic buildings (also available in German), and *Stellenbosch & Its Wine Route*, which gives opening times and tasting information about the three dozen or so nearby wineries.

Guided walks leave from the publicity association three times a day. They cost R45 per person (minimum three people).

There's a Thomas Cook/Rennies foreign exchange office on Bird St a block from Dorp St.

WESTERN CAPE PROVINCE

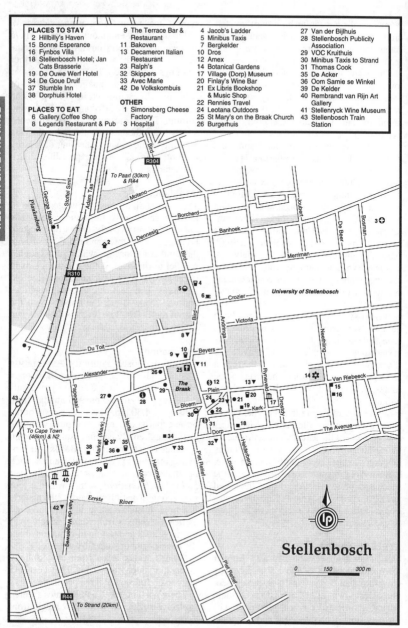

**PLACES TO STAY**
2 Hillbilly's Haven
15 Bonne Esperance
16 Fynbos Villa
18 Stellenbosch Hotel; Jan
   Cats Brasserie
19 De Ouwe Werf Hotel
34 De Goue Druif
37 Stumble Inn
38 Dorphuis Hotel

**PLACES TO EAT**
6 Gallery Coffee Shop
8 Legends Restaurant & Pub

9 The Terrace Bar &
   Restaurant
11 Bakoven
13 Decameron Italian
   Restaurant
23 Ralph's
32 Skippers
33 Avec Marie
42 De Volkskombuis

**OTHER**
1 Simonsberg Cheese
  Factory
3 Hospital

4 Jacob's Ladder
5 Minibus Taxis
7 Bergkelder
10 Dros
12 Amex
14 Botanical Gardens
17 Village (Dorp) Museum
20 Finlay's Wine Bar
21 Ex Libris Bookshop
   & Music Shop
22 Rennies Travel
24 Leotana Outdoors
25 St Mary's on the Braak Church
26 Burgerhuis

27 Van der Bijlhuis
28 Stellenbosch Publicity
   Association
29 VOC Kruithuis
30 Minibus Taxis to Strand
31 Thomas Cook
35 De Acker
36 Oom Samie se Winkel
39 De Kelder
40 Rembrandt van Rijn Art
   Gallery
41 Stellenryck Wine Museum
43 Stellenbosch Train
   Station

**Stellenbosch**

0   150   300 m

Ex Libris, on Andringa St, is a good book-shop with all the glossy coffee-table books but also novels and a few Lonely Planet guides. There's also an interesting selection of old books on South Africa. A couple of doors south is a music shop with a good range of CDs and some inexpensive cassettes.

## Village Museum
The Village (Dorp) Museum is a group of carefully restored and period-furnished houses dating from 1709 to 1850 – eventually a house from the 1920s will be included. The main entrance, on Ryneveld St, leads into the oldest of the buildings, the Schreuderhuis. The whole block bounded by Ryneveld, Plein, Drostdy and Kerk Sts is occupied by the museum and includes most of the buildings and some charming gardens. Grosvenor House is on the other side of Drostdy St. The museum is open from Monday to Saturday between 9.30 am and 5 pm, and on Sunday from 2 to 5 pm. Admission is R5.

## Van der Bijlhuis
This building dates back to 1693, when it formed part of one of the area's original farms, and has in the past been a tannery. It is now the administrative centre for the Village Museum and three rooms are open to the public during office hours.

## Braak
The Braak (Town Square) is an open stretch of grass surrounded by important buildings. In the middle, the **VOC Kruithuis** (Powder House) was built in 1777 to store the town's weapons and gunpowder and now houses a small military museum. On the north-west corner, the **Burgerhuis** was built in 1797 and is a fine example of the Cape Dutch style; most of it is now occupied by Historical Homes of South Africa, a company established to preserve important architecture. **St Mary's on the Braak Church** was completed in 1852.

## Bergkelder
This should be your first stop if you are

interested in the area's wines. For R8 you get a slide show, a cellar tour and tastings of up to 12 wines. You get to pour your own, so take it easy or it might be your last stop for the day! The Bergkelder is a short walk from the train station; tours are held at 10 am, 10.30 am (in German) and 3 pm.

## Simonsberg Cheese Factory
Very popular with hungry backpackers, the cheese factory (☎ (021) 883 8640) has tastings and sells inexpensive cheese between 8.30 am and 4.30 pm. It's west of the railway line at 9 Stoffel Smit St.

## Rembrandt van Rijn Art Gallery
This small gallery houses 20th century South African works; even if these don't interest you, it's worth visiting to see the house, which was built in 1783. It's open Monday to Friday from 9 am to 12.45 pm and 2 to 5 pm, Saturday from 10 am to 1 pm and 2 to 5 pm, and Sunday from 2.30 to 5.30 pm.

## Stellenryck Wine Museum
The small wine museum has some old furniture and wine-making paraphernalia – the most impressive item is the massive wine press, which you can see on the corner of Blersch and Dorp Sts. It's open daily (afternoon only on Sunday).

## Brandy Museum
The international history of brandy and the role it has played in the Cape are traced through a collection of pictures and displays. The museum (☎ (021) 881 3875), in the Van Ryn Brandy Cellar, is open daily.

## Oom Samie se Winkel
Uncle Sammy's Shop at 84 Dorp St is a tourist trap, but it's still worth visiting for the amazing range of goods – from high kitsch to genuine antiques and everything else in between.

## Activities
There are 90 walks in the Stellenbosch area – the tourist office has details. Jonkershoek is a small nature reserve within a timber

## Stellenbosch Wineries

The Stellenbosch Wine Route was the first to be established in South Africa and it's still the most popular. With nearly three dozen wineries offering sales and tastings there's a lot to see. The information centre has maps of the wine route or, for more specialised information, contact the wine route office (☎ (021) 886 4310; fax 886 4330). The office has a web site (www.active.co.za/stellenbosch/wine_route).

The wineries listed here are just a small sample:

**Blaauwklippen** This beautiful 300-year-old estate (☎ (021) 880 0133) is 4km south of Stellenbosch on the R44 to Somerset West. It has several fine Cape Dutch homesteads. Apart from recent vintages of white, red, sparkling and port there's a farm shop selling chutneys, jams, salamis and pickles. Cellar tours are held on weekdays at 11 am and 3 pm, and on Saturday at 11 am (more often in December and January). Tastings and wine sales are available Monday to Friday from 9 am to 5 pm, and Saturday from 9.15 am to 1 pm. In December and January there are cellar tours on weekdays at 11 am and 3 pm and at 11 am on Saturday. From 1 October to Easter, noon to 2 pm, a so-called coachman's lunch is sold.

**Hartenberg Estate** Founded in 1692, Hartenberg (☎ (021) 882 2541) is about 10km north-west of Stellenbosch, off the road running from Koelenhof to Kuilsrivier. Thanks to a micro-climate it produces 16 varieties and blended wines. It's open for tastings and sales (including some house wines available only at the cellar) on weekdays from 9 am to 5 pm, on Saturday from 9 am to 3 pm and on from December to March on Sunday from 10.30 am to 3 pm. Lunch is available daily except Sunday from noon to 2 pm.

**Morgenhof** This winery (☎ (021) 889 5510) is 4km north of Stellenbosch on the R44 to Paarl. It, too, is an old estate with fine architecture. Whites and reds are available for tasting and for sale on weekdays from 9 am to 4.30 pm, Saturday from 10 am to 3 pm and also on Sunday from November to April. Picnic basket lunches are available in the old stables or the surrounding lawns from October to April from noon to 2 pm. In winter you can eat inside.

**Neil Ellis Wines** In the Jonkershoek Valley, this smaller winery (☎ (021) 887 0649) produces a small range of excellent red and white wines. From November to March it's open for sales and tastings on weekdays from 9 am to 4.30 pm and on Saturday from 9 am to 1 pm and 2 to 4.30 pm; the rest of the year it's open on weekdays from 9 am to 1 pm and 2 to 4.30 pm. ∎

plantation which offers walking and biking trails. Admission is R5 per car. Ask the publicity association about permits and maps of the Vineyard Hiking Trails.

Amoi Horse Trails (☎ (082) 650 5794) offers tailor-made rides. For example, a three hour ride with a visit to a winery and a tasting costs R115 per person. There are no minimum numbers and they'll match you with a horse to suit your skill level.

Aqua Energy on Reyneveld St sells surf gear, including second-hand boards. The nearest surf is at Strand, just 20km away.

The parachute club (☎ (021) 58 8514) offers tandem jumps.

A food and wine festival is held in late October.

### Places to Stay

*Stumble Inn* (☎ /fax (021) 887 4049; email stumble@iafrica.com), 14 Mark St, is a hostel in a nice old house with wooden floors and a good atmosphere. A pool is planned (it has been 'planned' for a few years now). The owners are travellers and a good source of information. They arrange budget outings in the area, including to the beach at Strand and to a *shebeen* (drinking establishment) in Khayamandi, an enormous township between Stellenbosch and Cape Town. Dorm beds are R25 and doubles are R70. They rent bikes (R40) and also offer a good, cheap winery tour (R45). Stumble Inn is popular, so it would pay to book ahead.

The other hostel is a more recent arrival

but it also gets positive feedback. *Hillbilly's Haven* (☎ (021) 887 8475), 24 Dennesig St, has dorm beds for R30 and doubles for R80. You can also camp.

The publicity association produces a booklet listing many B&B possibilities, from around R60 per person (you'll have to press them to tell you about the very cheapest). If you have transport, ask them about self-catering cottages out of town, which can be great bargains.

*De Goue Druif* (☎ (021) 883 3555), on historic Dorp St (No 110), a rambling old house built in 1811, has very comfortable suites. Singles/doubles are from R260/390 with an excellent breakfast. They also have a simpler self-catering cottage and a very pleasant apartment in the block behind the house – it's recommended.

The *Stellenbosch Hotel* (☎ (021) 887 3644), on the corner of Dorp and Andringa Sts, is a rather idiosyncratic country hotel, but it is also very comfortable. A section dating from 1743 houses the excellent Jan Cats Brasserie, a bar and a dining room. The accommodation is in a modern section. Singles/doubles cost from R330/480.

Outside Stellenbosch, *Nassau Guest Farm* (☎ (021) 881 3818) has well-equipped cottages for about R180 per person, and a collection of vintage cars. *Sanddrif Guest Farm* (☎ (021) 881 3075), also out of town on Stellenbosch Kloof Rd, is a Cape Dutch-style house among vineyards and B&B costs from R240/350. Dutch, German and French are spoken here.

### Places to Eat

There are 70 places to eat and drink in Stellenbosch and several of the nearby vineyards have restaurants attached.

**Snacks & Cafés** The *Rustic Café* off Bird St near Legends stays open until 4 am. Another late-night student hangout is the *Gallery Coffee Shop* on Crozier St. It has a reputation for being super-cool, but it's a relaxed and friendly place. The coffee is good, it's licensed and there are cheap snacks. You can

buy some amusing (if a little obscure) postcards by a local outfit called Bitterkomix.

There are various places to eat in the *Studentesentrum* at the university, although most of these are franchise outlets and not especially cheap. Walk up Crozier St until it ends at the car park, and continue straight on. Look for the signs to the Langenhoven – Studentesentrum.

*Bakoven*, at the entrance to the Bank-centrum, has pies and burgers. For takeaway seafood, *Skippers* is a high-quality fish and chippery, on Dorp St near the corner of Louw St, with a few tables.

**Restaurants** *Legends Restaurant & Pub* on the corner of Du Toit and Bird Sts is good value and very popular with students. Lunches cost under R20. For good food at reasonable prices try *Avec Mari*, 105 Dorp St. It seems to be a fairly formal restaurant but it is in fact friendly and relaxed, with a contemporary attitude to food and customers. It's open from Tuesday to Sunday for lunch and dinner (no dinner on Sunday). The menu is sort of Mediterranean with a nouvelle cuisine influence, which is a relief after the gargantuan servings you usually have to plough through. Main courses are around R30 – it's recommended. If it's gargantuan portions you're after, try *Ralph's*, Andringa St. Main courses start at around R30 and go much higher.

*De Volkskombuis* (☎ (021) 887 2121), Aan de Wagenweg on the outskirts of town, is one of the best places in the Cape to sample traditional cuisine, and it is favoured by locals, not just tourists. The service is both friendly and competent, a rare combination. Try the Cape country sampler (four traditional specialities) for R42. Booking is advisable. The restaurant is in an attractive Cape Dutch homestead designed by Sir Herbert Baker and the terrace looks across fields to Stellenbosch Mountain. Booking is advisable.

*Jan Cats Brasserie* (☎ (021) 887 3644) is in the Stellenbosch Hotel at the corner of Dorp and Andringa Sts. This colourful restaurant features straightforward dishes like pastas for R20, or Cape bobotie with sambal and yellow rice for R25. If the restaurant was named Jan's Cat rather than Jan Cats, then presumably the statue of the Stellenbosch Hotel's cat, in front of the City Hall on Plein St, would be the animal in question. The *Decameron Italian Restaurant*, on Plein St, is classy and has authentic Italian food. A good meal will set you back about R60, but it's worth it.

### Entertainment

The students give Stellenbosch quite a lively nightlife. It's relatively safe to walk around at night, so it's worth checking a few of the options before you settle. Stumble Inn produces a handy pub crawl map for its guests.

On Alexander, facing the Braak, is *Dros* – dark, panelled, pub-ish and a good place for a drink. There's sometimes live music. Next door, *The Terrace* has pub food from R15.

Not far away, *Legends Restaurant & Pub* on the corner of Du Toit and Bird Sts usually has a DJ and sometimes live music. When it's crowded it might be interesting but when it isn't the bar is pretty unappealing. Further along Bird St, *Jacob's Ladder* is a sizeable and relaxed upstairs bar with local 'alternative' bands some nights.

*De Kelder*, 63 Dorp St, has a pleasant atmosphere and is popular with German backpackers. *De Acker* on the corner of Dorp and Herte Sts is a pub – a classic student drinking hole with cheap grub from R18. *Finlay's Wine Bar* on Plein St is another rowdy, cheerful place.

### Getting There & Away

**Train** Metro trains run the 46km between Cape Town and Stellenbosch; 1st/3rd class is R8.70/3.80 (no 2nd class) and the trip takes about one hour. For inquiries phone Stellenbosch station (☎ (021) 808 1111).

**Bus** Buses to Cape Town are expensive and you can't book this short sector. Translux stops here on the run between Cape Town and Port Elizabeth, charging R20 or R40, depending whether you take a Mountain Route or a Coastal Route bus. See the Cape Town Getting There & Away section for

more information. Fares are about the same as those from Cape Town.

**Minibus Taxi** A taxi to Strand (and thus the beach) can cost as little as R3.50. A taxi to Paarl is about R6 but you'll probably have to change taxis en route.

### Getting Around

Budget Rent-a-Car (☎ (021) 883 9103) at 98 Dorp St rents bicycles as well as cars. With largely flat countryside (unless you try to cross Franschhoek Pass), this is good cycling territory. Rikki's (☎ (021) 887 2203) runs its tiny vans here, and R3 (sharing) will get you just about anywhere in town. Stellenbosch Motorcycles (☎ (021) 883 9805), Latsky St, rents motorbikes.

## FRANSCHHOEK

Franschhoek is really nothing more than a village, but it's tucked into arguably the most beautiful valley in the Cape. There is an interesting museum commemorating the French Huguenots who settled in the region, and there are a number of good wineries and restaurants nearby.

### Orientation & Information

The town straggles along the main road from Stellenbosch and Paarl. At the eastern end it reaches a T-junction, with the Huguenot Memorial Museum directly in front. Turn left for the spectacular Franschhoek Pass.

The very helpful information centre (☎ (021) 876 3603) is in a small building on the main street, next to Dominic's Pub. Pick up a map of the area's scenic walks. In season the centre is open from 9 am to 5 pm on weekdays, 10 am to 2 pm on Saturday and 10 am to 1 pm on Sunday.

### Huguenot Memorial Museum

The Huguenots were French Protestants who fled France as a result of persecution in the 17th century. Some went to Holland, and 200 found their way to South Africa. Some of the names of the original settlers are among the most famous Afrikaner dynasties in the country: Malan, de Villiers, Malherbe, Roux,

Barre, Thibault and Marais. The museum was opened in 1976 to celebrate their history and to house the genealogical records of their descendants. It's quite a fascinating place, but it's not clearly laid out and it is pretty hard work to find your way around. There's an excellent collection of 17th and 18th century Cape Dutch furniture. The museum is open Monday to Friday from 9 am to 5 pm, Saturday from 9 am to 1 pm and 2 to 5 pm, and Sunday from 2 to 5 pm. Admission is R4.

### Places to Stay

The information centre will tell you about B&Bs and other accommodation in town and the district. In town the cheapest B&Bs cost around R120 a double but prices drop if you stay out of town. *Chamoix Guest Cottages* (☎ (021) 876 3531), self-catering cottages on a vineyard, charges about R50 per person. Other places also have whole cottages for about R120.

*Hotel Huguenot* (☎ (021) 876 2092), on Huguenot Rd, is in the centre of town. It's a rather garish old-style country hotel but is reasonably comfortable. Each room has a private bathroom and the rate is around R120/200 a single/double. *La Cotte Inn* (☎ (021) 876 2081), also on Huguenot Rd, is on the western outskirts of town. It has a certain idiosyncratic charm and charges a little less than Hotel Huguenot. Travellers report that the rates might be open to negotiation.

*Auberge Bligny* (☎ (021) 876 3767), 28 Van Wijk St, is one of the town's oldest houses and is now a guesthouse with six pleasant guest rooms. Singles/doubles cost from R145/165 with breakfast. No children. This place used to be called The Anchor. Readers recommend *Reeder Lodge*, a self-catering cottage near the information centre which charges R80 per person.

*Le Quartier Francais* (☎ (021) 876 2248), 16 Huguenot Rd, is the top place to stay in Franschhoek. It has very large guest rooms with fireplaces, huge beds and stylish decor set around a grassy courtyard. Dinner, bed and breakfast costs from R595/790.

### Places to Eat

There are quite a few places to eat, and the village is so small that it's easy to stroll around and see what appeals. *Dominic's Country Pub & Restaurant* is on the main street but has a pleasant, shady lawn where you can have coffee, pastries or meals. As well as the usual steaks (R27) there are light meals such as Cape Malay pickled fish (R15) or trout and salad (R20).

Further along, *Le Quartier Francais* (☎ (021) 876 2248) is a highly acclaimed restaurant, but it is not pompous or ridiculously expensive. For anyone who really likes their food it is highly recommended. It's on the main street of Franschhoek, but it opens out onto a cottage garden with views of the surrounding mountains. Entrées are around R20, main meals like roast rabbit or trout sausages range from R35 to R45 or you can spend more on dishes such as braised shank of springbok with waterblommetjie, couscous and spiced oranges. There are interesting desserts from R12. If the restaurant is beyond your budget there are also the bistro and deli, both open from noon to 5 pm for takeaways and lighter meals.

### Getting There & Away

It's possible, if you're fit, to bicycle between Stellenbosch and Franschhoek. Otherwise, Borland Passenger Transport (☎ (021) 872 2114) has infrequent buses between Paarl and Franschhoek.

### BOSCHENDAL

Boschendal lies between Franschhoek and Stellenbosch on the Pniel Rd (the R310) and is probably the most beautiful of all the Cape wineries: you *must* visit. Tucked in below some startling mountains, the Cape Dutch homestead (open daily from 11 am to 5 pm), the winery buildings and the vineyard are almost too beautiful to be real.

The estate is open daily but sales and tastings are not available on Saturday afternoon or Sunday.

There is an expensive but excellent restaurant with table d'hôte for R85. It's open daily for lunch; booking is essential (☎ (021) 874

1031). For something lighter, but still excellent, go to *Le Café*, in one of the old buildings on the oak avenue. You can just have a coffee (or try the home-made lemonade) or something more substantial.

An even better alternative, if the weather is halfway decent, is *Le Pique Nique*, where simple meals are served outside under umbrellas on the lawn from 1 November to 30 April. A basket including paté, french bread and smoked-trout roulade is made up for you. Again, you must book ahead. It is not cheap at R42.50, but it is worth it.

## PAARL

Paarl is a large commercial centre on the banks of the Berg River, surrounded by mountains and vineyards. There are actually vineyards and wineries within the sprawling town limits, including the huge Kooperatieve Wijnbouwers Vereniging (better known as the KWV), a co-operative that both regulates and dominates the South African wine industry.

The town is less touristy than Stellenbosch, in part because it is not as compact and historically coherent and it is more difficult to get around on foot. However, there is still quite a lot to see, and the surrounding countryside and vineyards are beautiful. There are some great walks in the Paarl Mountain Nature Reserve.

There's some excellent Cape Dutch architecture, and some significant monuments to Afrikaner culture. The surrounding valley was settled by Europeans in the 1680s and Paarl was established in 1720. It became a centre for wagon building, but it's most famous for its important role in the development and recognition of Afrikaans as a separate language.

In 1953 Paarl gained the dubious distinction of being the first town in the country to use a new style of bus – with separate doors for white and nonwhite passengers.

### Orientation & Information

Main St is 15km long and runs the entire length of the town, paralleling the Berg River and the railway line. Main St is shaded by

| PLACES TO STAY | | 5 | First National Bank |
| 2 | Manyano Centre | 6 | Keg & Owl |
| 18 | Grande Roche Hotel | 8 | Afrikaans Language Museum |
| **PLACES TO EAT** | | 9 | Mosque |
| 4 | Jefferson's Family Restaurant | 10 | Oude Pastorie |
| 7 | Nando's | 13 | Paarl Valley Publicity Association |
| 11 | Panarotti's Pizza | 14 | Jailhouse Bar |
| 12 | Kontrehuise; Coffee Place; Lady Jayne's Pub & Restaurant | 15 | Huguenot Church |
| | | 17 | Klein Vredenburg Mansion |
| 16 | Pipers Tavern | 19 | Schoongezicht Homestead |
| 23 | Labourie Restaurant | 20 | La Corncorde, Head Office of KWV |
| **OTHER** | | 21 | KWV Cellars |
| 1 | Dal Josefal Train Station | 22 | Paarl Train Station |
| 3 | Huguenot Train Station | | |

**Paarl**

oaks and jacarandas and is lined with many historic buildings. The busy commercial centre is around Lady Grey St.

The Paarl Valley Publicity Association (☎ (021) 872 3829), 251 Main St, on the corner of Auret St, has an excellent supply of information on the whole region. The staff are particularly helpful for arranging accommodation in some of the many guesthouses that have sprung up around Paarl and will make free bookings. The office is open from 9 am to 5 pm Monday to Friday, 9 am to 1 pm on Saturday and 10 am to 1 pm on Sunday.

### Paarl Mountain Nature Reserve

This popular reserve is dominated by three giant granite domes which loom over the town on its west side. The domes apparently glisten like pearls if they are caught by the sun after a fall of rain – hence 'Paarl'. The reserve has mountain fynbos and a particularly large number of proteas. There's a cultivated wildflower garden in the middle that would make a nice spot for a picnic, and there are numerous walks with excellent views over the valley.

Access is from the 11km-long Jan Phillips Drive, which skirts the eastern edge of the reserve; both the Afrikaans Language Monument and the reserve are signposted from Main St. The picnic ground is about 4km from Main St. A map showing walking trails is available from the publicity association.

### Oude Pastorie

The old parsonage (1714) on Main St houses a collection of Cape Dutch antiques and relics of Huguenot and early Afrikaner culture. It's open weekdays from 9 am to 1 pm and 2 to 4 pm. Admission is free.

### Afrikaans Language Museum

The birth of Afrikaans is chronicled in the home of Gideon Malherbe, the meeting place for the Association of True Afrikaners and the birthplace of the first Afrikaans newspaper. The house has been painstakingly restored. It's open weekdays from 9 am to 1 pm and 2 to 5 pm. Admission is free.

### Afrikaans

Afrikaans is based on Dutch, but in Africa, exposed to the diverse cultures of the Cape, it has been transformed into an independent language. Grammatical forms have been simplified and the vocabulary influenced by German, French, Portuguese, Malaysian, indigenous African languages and English. Dutch remained the official language, however, and Afrikaans was given little formal recognition, especially after the takeover of the Cape by the English in 1806 when a deliberate policy of anglicisation was pursued.

The Afrikaners, however, deeply resented the colonial approach of the British and began to see their language as a central foundation of their own culture. In 1875 a teacher at Paarl Gymnasium High School, Arnoldus Pannevis, inspired a number of Paarl citizens to form the Genootskap van Regte Afrikaners (the Association of True Afrikaners) who developed and formalised the grammar and vocabulary. Strangely, virtually all the founding members were descended from the French Huguenots.

A small press was set up in the house of Gideon Malherbe and the first issue of an Afrikaans newspaper, *Die Afrikaanse Patriot*, was published, followed by many books. Malherbe's house is now a museum, and a large monument has been erected to the east of the town. ■

### Places to Stay

The *Berg River Resort* (☎ (021) 863 1650) is about 5km from Paarl on the Franschhoek road (the R45), alongside the Berg River. It's an attractive municipal park with a swimming pool, canoes, trampolines and a café. There are five pricing seasons. Sites for two people cost R30, rising to R60; chalets cost from R130 for two people, and from R240 in the peak season. The management is surprisingly friendly for a caravan park, and they can collect you from the station.

*Borschen Meer Leisure Resort* (☎ (021) 863 1250) is a manicured and high-security resort, although prices aren't too high, with chalets from R70 per person. There are also sites.

Backpackers could consider the *Manyano Centre* (☎ (021) 862 2537, or 862 5074 after hours) on Sanddrift St. It's an enormous

## Paarl Wineries

The information centre has a Wine Route brochure with a good map, showcasing a dozen or so of the area's wineries. Here is a small sample.

**Kooperatieve Wijnbouwers Vereniging (KWV)** Paarl is home to a unique phenomenon – the huge KWV wine co-operative (☎ (021) 807 3007). The KWV was formed in 1918 when farmers were struggling to deal with problems of oversupply. Today, the KWV has statutory authority to completely regulate South Africa's grape production and prices.

It also purchases grapes and makes high quality wines, sherries and ports, which are mostly sold overseas (they attempt to avoid direct competition with their members within the country). Some KWV port and sherry is available inside South Africa because there is little direct competition; the wines, with the exception of those from Laborie, are only sold overseas. The fortified wines, in particular, are amongst the world's best. The huge Cathedral Cellar is definitely worth seeing.

On weekdays there are tours and tastings (R10) in German at 10.15 am and in English at 11 am and 2.15 pm. On Wednesdays there are also tours in French at 3 pm. On Saturdays there are German tours at 10.15 am and English tours at 11 am. The knowledgeable tour leaders can give you suggestions for touring the winelands. The tours start in the KWV cellars on Kohler, not at La Concorde, the impressive head office on Main St. As well as the formal tours you can have a tasting R6, but only in December.

**Laborie** (☎ (021) 807 3390), Taillefer St, is the KWV's showcase vineyard, right in the centre of Paarl, just off the main road. In addition to selling wines, there is a restaurant in an old Cape Dutch homestead. The food is good but it's fairly pricey and they get a lot of tour groups – you should book. There is a long wine list but few are sold by the glass and fewer in small bottles. It's open daily for lunch and from Tuesday to Saturday for dinner. Tours of the winery are held during school holidays only, at 9.30 and 11.15 am and 2.15 and 3.30 pm.

**Landskroon Estate** (☎ (021) 863 1039) is an old, pleasant estate with a nice terrace overlooking the vines where you can sit and contemplate the view. It's about 6km from town on the R44. It's open from 8 am to 5 pm on weekdays and from 8.30 am to 12.30 pm on Saturday. From November to the end of April they serve a 'vintner's platter' on weekdays, and there are some good cheeses for sale.

**Nederburg Winery** (☎ (021) 862 3104) is one of the biggest, best known and most acclaimed Cape wineries. In the past, the sheer size and professionalism of the operation meant it was not an especially friendly place to visit, but that has changed somewhat and several readers report receiving hospitality here. Tastings and wine sales are available Monday to Friday from 8.30 am to 5 pm and on Saturday from 9 am to 1 pm. Tours in English, German, French and Spanish are available but you have to book in advance. The estate is about 7km from Paarl, off the road to Wellington. ■

accommodation complex used mainly by groups, although there's a fair chance that you'll be the only guest. Beds are R25 and it's wise to bring a sleeping bag. If you're coming on a weekend, ring in advance. Huguenot train station is closer than the main Paarl station.

*Queenslin Guest House* (☎ (021) 863 1160), 2 Queen St, has a couple of rooms in a modern house overlooking the valley. You're guaranteed a hospitable welcome from the friendly family. Rates are around R110/170 a single/double. As usual, the publicity association is the place to get detailed information on the other B&Bs and farm cottages.

*The Berghof* (☎ (021) 871 1099) describes itself as not quite a guesthouse, not quite a hotel, but it is like a quality hotel with the service that is lacking in some mid-range places. You'll definitely need a vehicle to get there, as it's a long way up the side of the valley, with correspondingly excellent views down over the town. Rooms cost from R120/200 (more between December and April).

Cecil John Rhodes definitely had an eye for quality, so the fact that he once lived in the building that has become *Mooikelder Manor House* (☎ (021) 863 8491) points to its class. It's a beautifully restored Cape Dutch homestead, with a pool and terrace with great views, about 5km north of Paarl. Singles/doubles cost R235/390.

*Mountain Shadows* (☎ 021) 862 3192) is another magnificent place to stay outside Paarl; it too is in a restored Cape Dutch mansion (built in 1823 and now a national monument). There are only a small number of guests, a swimming pool and excellent food. The owners also arrange hunting, fishing and sightseeing tours. B&B rates start from around R200 per person, rising in season. On the slopes of Paarl Mountain is the five star *Grande Roche Hotel* (☎ (021) 863 2727), where rooms cost from R1200, with breakfast.

### Places to Eat

Several of the vineyards around Paarl have restaurants and they are probably the best places to eat if you're sightseeing. See the boxed text on Paarl Wineries for details.

*Kontrehuis* (☎ (02211) 22808), 193 Main St, is behind the Zomerlust guesthouse. It has very good-value steak meals from R25. Next door is *Lady Jayne's Pub & Restaurant*, in a Cape Dutch building. Off the courtyard behind Lady Jayne's, the *Coffee Place* is a pleasant spot to escape the world.

*Panarotti's Pizza*, 263 Main St (on the north-east corner of Faure St), looks like the usual bland franchise and the food isn't bad, although genuine Italian it ain't. It's open from 10 am to midnight. *Jefferson's Family Restaurant* is a steakhouse in the same mould as Spur, Mike's Kitchen etc: predictable but reliable, with over-friendly service.

*Pipers Tavern* on the corner of Main and Zeederberg Sts has toasted sandwiches, fish and chips and other light dishes.

### Getting There & Away

Several interesting bus services come through Paarl so it is easy to build it into your itinerary. However, the bus segment between Paarl and Cape Town is much more expen-sive than the train, so take a train to Paarl and then link up with the buses.

**Bus** Travelling on from Paarl you have a number of options. Paarl is a stop on the Translux services between Cape Town and Johannesburg (R310 from Paarl), Durban (R330), Port Elizabeth (Mountain Route, R140) and East London (R210, running via Graaff-Reinet, R165). Greyhound also runs to these places at similar fares. Intercape runs between Cape Town and Jo'burg at slightly cheaper fares than the others.

City to City/Transtate (a subsidiary of the government-owned Translux) runs daily to Umtata (R135, 16 hours), via some interesting Karoo towns. Transtate runs a cheaper bus to Umtata, along much the same route. Chilwans Bus Services (☎ (021) 54 2506, 905 3910) runs a basic bus on a similar route as far as Oudtshoorn, at much lower fares but not daily.

**Train** There are a reasonable number of Metro trains between Cape Town and Paarl, at least a couple in the morning and a couple in the afternoon from Monday to Friday. The services are less common on weekends. A 1st/3rd class ticket from Cape Town to Paarl is R10/4.40 and the trip takes about 1¼ hours.

You can travel by train from Paarl to Stellenbosch, but you will have to take a Cape Town-bound train and then change at Muldersvlei.

### AROUND PAARL
#### Wellington

Just a few kilometres from Paarl is Wellington, a sedate and quite pretty little town. Between the two towns is the large **Mbekweni** township. Mbekweni was created in 1945 but there is little infrastructure to match its half-century history. Because of a stipulation by the landowner whose property was used by the railway, all trains must stop in Wellington. This includes the *Blue Train* and it also included King George VI's train in 1947.

The information centre (☎ (021) 873

4604) is on Hoof St, not far from the train station and near the corner of Kerk St, the main street.

Out of town, *Bloublommetjieskloof Farm* (☎ (021) 873 3696), Olyvenbosch Rd, is an organic farm with a dorm (R35) and a double (R100). They will collect you from the station.

### Bainskloof Pass

Bainskloof is one of the great mountain passes of South Africa and there just happens to be a superb caravan park halfway along. Andrew Bain developed the road through the pass between 1848 and 1852. Other than having its surface tarred, the road has not been altered since then, and it is now a national monument. It's a magical drive which would be even better to experience on bicycle.

The R303 runs from Wellington, across Bainskloof to meet another road running south to Worcester and north to Ceres.

The Western Cape authorities run the *Tweede Tol Caravan Park*, open only between October and May. It is a magical spot. There are swimming holes on the Witrivier and the camp site is surrounded by magnificent fynbos. Camping costs R30 for up to three people plus R5 per vehicle. The gates are open from 7.30 am to 4.15 pm (out of hours, try the left-hand gate; it may appear to be chained, but probably just has the chain looped through it).

There are several nearby walks, including the five hour **Bobbejaans River Walk** to a waterfall. This walk actually starts back at Eerste Tol and you need to buy a permit for a few rand from Hawequas Conservation Area office (☎ (021) 887 0111), 269 Main St, Paarl. This is also where you make bookings for the Tweede Tol Caravan Park, although they'll probably only be necessary in school holidays.

The **Pataskloof Trail** is a long, day walk that begins and ends at the Bakkies Farmstall & Tea Room on the road leading up to the pass from Wellington. You can make it an overnight walk by arranging to stay in a cave on the trail.

# West Coast & Swartland

The region immediately to the north of Cape Town that straddles the N7 highway is often further divided into two contiguous regions – the West Coast and Swartland.

Around 60 million years ago the coastal zone west of the N7 was a sandy unproductive area of unstable dunes that were left behind when the sea retreated. The Swartland, both sides of the N7 and east to the foot of the mountains, is a rich agricultural area of rolling plains.

The barren western coastal strip has been transformed into productive country, thanks to the stabilisation of the dunes by the Australian Port Jackson wattle, with its very distinctive golden flowers. But the wattle now poses a major threat to the indigenous flora, which in this region belongs to the Cape floral kingdom often described as fynbos. The fynbos is one of the region's major attractions, especially in late winter and early spring when wildflowers carpet the remaining coastal dunes (especially in the West Coast National Park).

The coast, because of its relative barrenness and cold water, has only recently been discovered by Capetonian holiday-makers. These people were attracted by the distinctive, though somewhat bleak, landscape and the fact that it was relatively undeveloped. There are now several popular resorts, including Yzerfontein and Langebaan. There are also important fishing towns (Saldanha, St Helena Bay and Lambert's Bay) whose fleets exploit the rich fishing in the cold, nutrient-rich Benguela current. For reasons that are not understood, however, the fishing has recently declined seriously.

The Swartland (Black Land) was, it is now believed, named after the dark foliage of the distinctive *renosterbus* scrub that covered the plains. The soil is not black, but it is fertile. Combined with the winter rainfall, the soil enables farmers to produce over 20% of South Africa's wheat, as well as high-quality wine.

Before white settlement the plains were occupied by the Khoikhoi Grigriqua people, while the mountains were the province of the San. Piketberg is named after the guards (pickets) who were stationed here in the 1670s to protect the Cape Town settlers from Khoisan attacks.

Except for the Cederberg Wilderness Area, this region need not have a high priority for short-term visitors, although many will travel through on their way to the north. The west coast does not compare to the south and east coasts. However, the West Coast National Park is worth visiting, especially in August and September (for wildflowers), and Eland's Bay has a beautiful location and fantastic surf.

### Getting There & Away

Most public transport through this area travels from Cape Town north along the N7, either going all the way to Springbok and Namibia or leaving the N7 and heading through Calvinia to Upington. Getting to the coastal towns west of the N7 isn't easy if you don't have a car.

Intercape Mainliner's services between Cape Town and Upington and between Cape Town and Windhoek (Namibia) run past Citrusdal and Clanwilliam. Upington buses leave Cape Town at 7 pm on Sunday, Monday, Wednesday and Friday, arriving in Citrusdal (R80 from Cape Town) at 9.30 pm, Clanwilliam (R90) at 10.15 pm and Upington (R150) at 5.30 am. The return bus leaves Upington at 7.45 pm on Tuesday, Thursday, Friday and Sunday, arriving in Clanwilliam (R130 from Upington) at 3 am and Citrusdal (R135) at 3.45 am. Windhoek buses leave Cape Town at 2 pm on Sunday, Tuesday, Thursday and Friday, arriving in Citrusdal at 4.15 pm and Clanwilliam at 4.45 pm. The return bus comes through Clanwilliam at 8.30 am on Tuesday, Thursday, Saturday and Monday (45 minutes later at Citrusdal).

City to City runs between Cape Town and Upington about three times a week, charging a little less than Intercape.

### YZERFONTEIN

Yzerfontein is a large holiday village on an interesting stretch of coast. It's not green and beautiful, but it definitely has some dramatic views over rugged, rocky coastline. There are many enormous holiday homes, but nothing more than a garage/café in the way of shops and a *caravan park* (behind the dunes along the seafront).

There is a left point for surfers that works on south-east winds and moderate south-westerly swells.

### WEST COAST NATIONAL PARK

The West Coast National Park is one of the few large reserves along South Africa's coastline. It covers around 18,000 hectares and runs north from Yzerfontein to just short of Langebaan, surrounding the clear, blue waters of the Langebaan Lagoon. Unfortunately, these waters might not be so clear in the future, as a steel mill is being built in Saldanha, on the north shore of the lagoon.

The park protects wetlands of international significance and important seabird breeding colonies. In summer it plays host to enormous numbers of migratory wading birds. The most numerically dominant species is the delicate-looking curlew sandpiper (which migrates north from the sub-Antarctic in huge flocks), but flamingoes, Cape gannets, crowned cormorants, numerous gull species and African black oystercatchers are among the hordes. The offshore islands are home to colonies of jackass penguins.

The park's vegetation is predominantly sandveld, which means it is made up of stunted bushes, sedges and many flowering annuals and succulents. There are some coastal fynbos in the east. The park is famous for its wildflower display, usually between August and October. Several game species can be seen in the part of the park known as the Postberg section, including a variety of small antelope, wildebeest, bontebok and eland.

The rainy season is from May to August. The summer is dry with hot days, sometimes with morning mists. The park is only about

120km from Cape Town, so it could easily be visited on a day trip if you have transport.

### Orientation & Information
The park is made up of a peculiar mix of semi-independent zones, some of which are only leased by the national park authorities. The roads in the park are dirt and can be quite heavily corrugated. The park begins 7km south of Langebaan (it's clearly signposted) and it's over 80km from Langebaan to the northern end of the Postberg section and return; allow yourself plenty of time.

### LANGEBAAN
Langebaan has been discovered by developers, so although it does have an unusual and rather beautiful location it is rapidly being spoilt. Unfortunately, the negative aspects of development have not been matched by any real vibe or nightlife, or even things to do. The best arguments in its favour are that it overlooks the Langebaan Lagoon – which has excellent sailing and windsurfing – and is the base for the West Coast National Park. The abundance of spring flowers here can reach Namaqualand proportions.

### Places to Stay & Eat
There are three caravan parks owned and run by the local municipality, but none allow tents. This is to avoid rowdy parties of young Cape Towners, so if you don't look like trouble you might be able to persuade the manager to let you camp. The *Old Caravan Park* (☎ (02287) 22115) has shady (but sandy) sites right next to the lagoon in the centre of town. The *New Caravan Park*, on Suffren St, is very ordinary – a sort of large suburban block, surrounded by houses. *Seabreeze Caravan Park*, off the road into town and some way from the centre, has bungalows.

A traveller recommends the *Oliphantscop Farm Inn* (☎ (02287) 22326), across the road from the large Mykonos time-share complex, for both mid-range accommodation and excellent food.

*Die Strandloper* (☎ (02287) 21278) is an open-air restaurant on the beach, specialising

in seafood. It gets good reviews. You must book, and bring your own alcohol.

### Getting There & Away
No public transport, not even a minibus taxi, runs to Langebaan. Saldanha is the nearest town with public transport to/from Cape Town.

### SALDANHA
Saldanha shares the lagoon with Langebaan. It's a large working town dominated by an enormous iron-ore pier, navy yards and fish-processing factories. Not a pretty place, but if you're missing the sights and sounds of gritty urban life, wandering around Saldanha's harbour area is a balm.

### Orientation & Information
The main road into town is Saldanha Rd, but Main (Hoof) Rd is the road that runs from the shopping centre up to the headland, along the back bay. The information centre (☎ (02281) 42088) is off Saldanha Rd, just before you get into town.

Despite the town's industrial aura the bays are pleasant and, because they are sheltered, much warmer than the ocean. Hoedjies Bay, near the town centre, is the most popular for swimming. You can rent a canoe or a boat at The Slipway restaurant (see Places to Eat), which also runs boat trips on the harbour, at 11.30 am and 3 pm (R25, minimum eight people).

### Places to Stay
*Saldanha Holiday Resort* (☎ (02281) 42247) is not special but it is right on the Hoedjies Bay beach. Small four-bed cottages without bedding cost from around R60, more on weekends and much more in summer. Tent sites start at around R30.

On Main St, overlooking the back bay, the *Saldanha Bay Protea Hotel* (☎ (02281) 41264) is anonymous but has a good location. Rooms cost R289. The nearby *Hoedjiesbaai Hotel* (☎ (02281) 41271) has recently been renovated but still charges a little less.

## Places to Eat

*The Laughing Mussel* is a seafood takeaway (with a few tables) at the top end of Main Rd, overlooking the bay. On a sunny day it's a nice place for a snack, from under R10. If you want fish and chips, buy them here. Even the seagulls wouldn't eat the ones we bought at one of the more basic takeaway places. Across the road from The Laughing Mussel is *Mermaid's Restaurant*, which has dishes such as cold crayfish and Greek salad for R40. There are also cheaper choices.

Down in the docks, right on the waterfront, *The Slipway* is a nice place for a lazy meal. You'll pay from around R30 for main courses. It's open daily from breakfast to late afternoon, with dinner on Friday and Saturday (perhaps nightly in season).

## Getting There & Away

City to City runs daily between Cape Town and Saldanha, departing from Cape Town at 5 pm on weekdays and Sunday, at 9 am and 1 pm on Saturday and also at 9.45 am on Friday. The return trip departs from Saldanha at 6 am daily, except on Sunday, when it departs at 12.30 pm. There's an extra bus at 1 pm on Friday and 12.30 pm on Saturday. The fare is around R45.

There's at least one taxi a day to Cape Town (about R25), from the Shell service station on Main Rd, near the Hoedjiesbaai Hotel. Local taxis (ask around the Spar supermarket) run north to Vredenburg (R3), where you can pick up taxis to Paternoster. It's difficult to make connections with taxis heading further up the coast because most run direct from Cape Town along the N7.

No taxis run all the way to Langebaan, but some do go past the turn-off on the R27.

## PATERNOSTER

Paternoster is a sleepy fishing village. There's a clutch of simple whitewashed homes where the coloured fishing families live – and which are suddenly becoming highly desirable as weekenders for rich Cape Towners. Paternoster might not be very sleepy much longer and the fishing families probably won't be living in houses with sea views.

The surrounding countryside is attractive, with an almost English feel. The rolling hills are scattered with strange granitic outcrops that could almost be human-made henges. The **Columbine Nature Reserve** is 3km past the town and protects 263 hectares of coastal fynbos around Cape Columbine. There's a small camping and caravan park which is open all year from sunrise to sunset. The wildflowers are spectacular in spring.

## Places to Stay

The *Paternoster Hotel* (☎ (022) 817 52703) is an old-style country hotel, virtually on the beachfront, with B&B for R85 per person. Bookings are advised for weekends; it's a popular venue for people interested in fishing, and the fish and crayfish braais are famous. There's a dinner-dance on Saturday.

The rather windy Columbine Nature Reserve (☎ (022) 752 1718), administered by the Cape Province, has basic *camping* facilities for about R15.

## ELAND'S BAY

Depending on which direction you're travelling, Eland's Bay is the first or last really attractive spot on the West Coast. Mountains run down into the sea and there's a large lagoon which is favoured by all sorts of interesting waterbirds (including flamingo, although they are nomadic and don't hang around). There's very high-quality surf.

Despite the spectacular location, the town is unattractive, with the inevitable fish factory and a poverty-stricken coloured population. Still, you don't go to Eland's Bay for the town, you go for the beaches and to explore beautiful **Baboon Point**. The town has basic facilities: a run-down hotel, a petrol station and a Standard Bank.

## Surfing

This is a goofy-footer's paradise with extremely fast left-point waves working at a range of swell sizes. The bay can hold a very big wave. The main left-point break is virtually in front of the hotel, a bit around towards the crayfish factory – it breaks along a rocky shelf in thick kelp, after south-west winds on a low and incoming tide. There's a right beach break and more lefts on Baboon Point, along the gravel road past the crayfish factory.

### Places to Stay

The *municipal caravan park* (☎ (0265) 745) is a basic park right by the beach. It's pretty exposed to the wind. Sites are R25. *Hotel Eland* (☎ (0265) 640) also overlooks the beach and charges R90/180 a single/double for B&B. The 'Europeans Only' sign above the entrance to the bar has been painted out, but only just.

### Getting There & Away

On Friday a taxi runs to Cape Town for about R50. Ask at the shop in the 'location' on the road into town.

If you're driving south it's worth taking the dirt road that runs along the north bank of the wide and reedy estuary. You can cross over at the hamlet of Rodelinghuys and head south through nice country to the village of Aurora or keep going to join the N7 at Piketberg.

Coming down the dusty dirt road from Lambert's Bay, the turn-off to Eland's Bay takes you onto another dirt road, but this has a toll of R6.50. If you don't want to pay this, head down the toll road a short way and there's a map showing the longer but free route.

### LAMBERT'S BAY

Lambert's Bay is an unattractive fishing town on a bleak stretch of the west coast. It's dominated by fish-processing factories – visions of Cannery Row – and the major attraction is the rookery of Cape gannets. A crayfish festival on the first weekend of November is apparently quite lively.

If you are a bird-lover, you may be tempted to visit because you can walk out onto a breakwater to the gannet rookery. Thousands of aggressive birds mill around making a racket and snapping at each other. Their 'nests' are mere scrapes in the clay. The

mystery is how the birds manage to find their own particular nest and put up with the appalling smell, although there does seem to be a lot of noisy brawling. There are likely to be only small numbers of birds from May to July. They lay between September and November, and the chicks hatch 40 days later.

Claiming Lambert's Bay as a tourist destination takes considerable vision and optimism. The town's development has been particularly unsympathetic to the environment. Eland's Bay, 27km to the south, is a completely different story, however, and if you do stay at Eland's you might come in to Lambert's Bay for supplies.

If you're heading north to Doring Bay consider taking the inland route on minor dirt roads which run through some interesting rolling country. Drive slowly and watch for tortoises crossing the road. Local lore has it that if you squash a tortoise you will get a flat tyre.

### Places to Stay

The *municipal caravan park* (☎ (027) 432 2238) to the north of town beside the beach (off Korporasie St) is OK, with sites from R35 for two people or R45 with a private bathroom. There is a long list of rules, including: '3.12, Female servants are allowed on own responsibility but no male or local servants may be brought into the camping area'.

Aside from the caravan park, the only cheapish option is *Laberine Flats* (☎ (027) 432 2232), behind the Laberine supermarket, which is on the beachfront road. They're self-contained and modern, and the higher storeys have good views – of the gannet colony. Prices start at R100 a double, rising by increments to reach R170 in December.

The *Marine Protea Hotel* (☎ (027) 432 1126) is a typical example of the genre – a bit tacky, but plenty of comfort. Rooms cost R219.

### Places to Eat

*Muisbosskerm* (☎ (027) 432 1017), 5km south of town, is an open-air seafood restaurant, the original of a growing number on the West Coast. A meal costs around R50, more if you have crayfish. *Bosduifklip* (☎ (027) 432 2735) is another open-air place, 4km out of town. Bookings are essential at both places.

## PIKETBERG & AROUND

Piketberg is quite an attractive small town overlooking the beautiful rolling pastoral land at the foot of the Elandskloof range. It's nestled in the lee of a hill, part of the last small range before the coastal plain.

The drive to/from Piketberg is not nearly as bleak and dry as the coastal plain further north, but it is still sandy and flat. **Velddrif** is an unprepossessing town on the edge of a large estuary (there are a couple of hotels). **St Helena Bay** is a lovely sheltered stretch of water, but there is no real beach. There are half a dozen large fish-processing factories and their associated depressing workers' 'locations' at **Stompneusbaai**.

## OLIFANTS RIVER VALLEY

The scenery changes dramatically at the Piekenaarskloof Pass; coming north on the N7 you suddenly overlook the densely populated and intensively cultivated Olifants River valley. The elephant herds that the explorer Jan Danckaert found in 1660 have long gone.

Today the river provides irrigation for acres of grape vines and orange trees, which are beautifully maintained by a huge coloured labour force. The comfortable bungalows of the white farmers are surrounded by green and leafy gardens, masking them from the shanties where the coloureds live. There doesn't even appear to be a token paternalistic effort on behalf of the cheap labour.

On the valley floor are some acclaimed wineries and co-ops (specialising in white wine) and you can get details of a wine route at tourist information centres. The eastern side is largely bounded by the spectacular Cederberg range, which is protected by the extensive Cederberg Wilderness Area. The wilderness area has several great camping grounds and several walks; it's famous for its bizarre rock formations, its fynbos and its San paintings. The whole area is famous for spring wildflowers.

Citrusdal and Clanwilliam, to the south and north of the wilderness area, are the two main towns in the area.

As an alternative to the N7, there's a spectacular road (the R303) between Citrusdal and Ceres (to the south), a great drive through the Cederberg Wilderness Area from Citrusdal to Clanwilliam, and another spectacular route (the R364) running between Clanwilliam and Calvinia (in Northern Cape to the north-east).

## CEDERBERG WILDERNESS AREA

The Cederberg is a rugged mountainous area of valleys and peaks extending roughly north-south for 100km, pretty well between Citrusdal and Vanrhynsdorp. A good proportion is protected by the 71,000 hectare Cederberg Wilderness Area, which is administered by Cape Nature Conservation. The highest peaks are Sneeuberg (2028m) and Tafelberg (1932m), and the area is famous for its weathered sandstone formations, which sometimes take bizarre shapes. San paintings can be seen in some of the caves that have been formed.

The area is also famous for its plant life, which is predominantly mountain fynbos. Once again, spring is the best time to see the wildflowers, although there's plenty of interest at other times of the year. The vegetation varies with altitude, but includes the Clanwilliam cedar (which gives the region its name) and the rare snowball protea. The Clanwilliam cedar survives only in relatively small numbers, growing between 1000m and 1500m, and the snowball protea (now found only in isolated pockets) only grows above the snow line.

There are small populations of baboon, rhebok, klipspringer, grysbok and predators like caracal, Cape fox, honey badger and rarely seen leopard.

### Orientation

The Cederberg offers excellent hiking and is divided into three hiking areas of around

WESTERN CAPE PROVINCE

24,000 hectares. Each area has a network of trails. However, this is a genuine wilderness area with a genuine wilderness ethos. You are *encouraged* to leave the trails and little information is available on suggested routes. It's up to you to survive on your own. Similarly, you probably won't be given directions to the area's rock art. Work out for yourself where the Khoisan were likely to have lived. The book *Some Views on Rock Paintings in the Cederberg* by Janette Deacon might help.

There is a buffer zone of conserved land between the wilderness area and the farmland, and here more intrusive activities such as mountain biking are allowed. Pick up a copy of the mountain-biking trail map from the Citrusdal information centre.

## Information

The rainfall (around 900mm) falls mainly in winter, and snow is possible from May to the end of September. There's no real season for walking; winter is tough but exhilarating, summer can mean problems with water.

The main office for the area is at Citrusdal, where the Chief Nature Conservator (a very knowledgeable and approachable chap) has his office. There's also an office at the Algeria Camping Ground.

A permit is required if you want to walk, and the number of visitors per hiking area is limited to 150 people. The maximum group size is 12 and the minimum is two; three would be safer. Maps (R7) are available at Algeria and the Chief Nature Conservator's office.

If you want to be certain you will get a permit you are advised to apply well in advance. Outside school holidays and weekends, however, there is a chance you will be able to get one on the spot, but you should definitely at least phone before arriving to make sure. Permits must be booked through the Chief Nature Conservator, Cederberg, Private Bag XI, Citrusdal 7340 (☎ (022) 921 2289 during office hours). Bookings open on 1 February for the March to June period, 1 June for July to October and 1 October for November to February. The cost is R6 per person per day, plus the R3 park admission charge.

The entrance to the Algeria Camping Ground closes at 4.30 pm (9 pm on Friday). You won't be allowed in if you arrive late. Permits have to be collected during office hours, so if you're arriving on Friday evening you'll need to make arrangements.

We spent five days hiking in the Cederberg from Algeria. Great hiking, especially for the budget conscious. After you've paid for your permit the huts are free. The huts are *basic* (by New Zealand standards) but for zero rand, that's OK. Plenty of places to camp if the huts are full. We only saw two hikers in five days.

**Kate Wall**

## Places to Stay

*Algeria Camping Ground* is in a beautiful spot alongside the Rondegat River, the headwaters of the Olifants River. The grounds are manicured, and shaded by huge blue gums and pines. It's a bit of a shame that they didn't use indigenous trees, but it's still an exceptional camp site. There are swimming holes and lovely spots to picnic beside the river. Camping costs about R30, more in peak periods. Day visitors (not allowed during peak periods) are charged about R3.

There's another excellent camping ground in the *Kliphuis State Forest* near the Pakhuis Pass on the R364, about 15km north-east of Clanwilliam. There's a small camping ground surrounded by rock walls and cut by a fresh mountain stream. Facilities are fairly spartan, but there's water, toilets and showers. A camp site is about R40.

You'll need to book either of these camp sites in the same way that you book hiking. There are basic huts for hikers in the wilderness area.

See the following Citrusdal and Clanwilliam entries for places to stay outside the Cederberg Wilderness Area. On the southeastern side of the wilderness area, the *Kromrivier Tourist Park* (☎ (027) 482 2807) has tent sites for about R25 for two and doubles for R90; there's also *Sanddrif Cederberg Camping* (☎ (027) 482 2825).

### Getting There & Away

The Cederberg range is about 200km from Cape Town, accessible from Citrusdal, Clanwilliam and the N7.

There are several roads in to Algeria, and they are all spectacular. It takes about 45 minutes to get from Clanwilliam by car, much longer if you give in to normal human emotion and stop every now and again. Algeria is not signposted from Clanwilliam, but you just follow the road above the dam to the south. Algeria *is* signposted from the N7 and it's only 20 minutes from the main road; there's an amazing collection of plants along the side of the road, including proteas.

There are some dusty but interesting backroads which run south-east through Sederberg and on to Ceres. Sederberg is not much more than a big old farm, where you can buy fuel and stay in huts (about R80). There's a good walk from the farm up to the Wolfsberg Crack (a well-known rock formation), about two hours.

Public transport into Algeria is nonexistent, so you might want to go to Citrusdal and start walking from there. It should take about two days to walk from Citrusdal to Algeria, entering the wilderness area at Boskloof. The Chief Nature Conservator's office in Citrusdal has information on this route. Cederberg Lodge in Citrusdal will drive guests.

### CITRUSDAL

Citrusdal is a small town which makes a good base for exploring the Cederberg – both the wilderness area and the surrounding mountains, which can be equally interesting. There are good sources of information and good farmstay accommodation. The area is embracing the idea of ecotourism and mountain biking, and hiking trails are being developed. And, of course, there's the prime attraction of hiking in the Cederberg Wilderness Area.

August and September is wildflower season, and the displays can be spectacular.

The Sandveldhuisie Country Shop & Tea Room (☎ (022) 921 3210) on Kerk St is also the information centre – and it gets our vote for the friendliest and most helpful in South Africa. It's open from 9 am to 4.30 pm on weekdays and until noon on Saturday. In flower season it's open daily. The shop sells cakes, herbs and local art and craft. Not far away is the office of the Chief Nature Conservator for the Cederberg Wilderness Area.

If you're planning to hike in the Cederberg and don't have transport you can start walking from Citrusdal rather than go through the hassle (and it is a hassle) of finding transport to Algeria, the usual starting point. There was talk of a new outfit starting up, offering guided walks in the Cederberg. If this has happened, it will be worth considering, as the guide has an outstanding knowledge of the area. The information centre will know the current situation.

A few kilometres out of town, **Craig Royston** is a large old farm building housing a café, shop and small museum. There's nothing very unusual about this but two things make Craig Royston unique: it hasn't been renovated to within an inch of its life, and the old shop is where the farmworkers still buy their supplies. It's a welcome relief after all those squeaky-clean tourist ventures where the only nonwhites you meet are pushing brooms. There are excellent light meals and you can sample (and buy) local wines. The proprietor is a local artist and she is a refreshing person to meet in rural South Africa. Craig Royston is open daily and the turn-off is near The Baths turn-off from the road in from the highway; it's signposted but the signs are small. If you arrive in Citrusdal when the information centre is closed, this is a good place to come for information.

### Places to Stay

Much of the accommodation is out of town. The exception is *Cederberg Lodge* (☎ (022) 921 2221), a reasonable small-town hotel. Rooms cost from R113/174 a single/double, more in summer and in August and September (flower season).

There are plenty of farmstays in the area, either B&Bs or self-contained cottages, and some places will collect you from the information centre. These are probably the best options, whatever your budget. You can get dinner, bed and breakfast for as little as R100 per person, or a self-catering cottage from about R120. These rates might be slightly negotiable, especially for backpackers.

*The Baths* (☎ (022) 921 3609) is a health spa about 16km from Citrusdal. It's a fairly simple place in a pretty wooded gorge and could be a good place to relax for a few days. Expect to pay around R25 for a camp site, from R20 per person for a room (minimum R80) and from R135 a double for a flat. Prices rise on weekends. They will pick you up from the bus stop on the highway.

*Van Meerhoff Lodge* (☎ (022) 921 2231) is a fancy new hotel near the top of the Piekenierskloof Pass (on the R44), overlooking Citrusdal. There are luxury chalets (from R160/R280), two restaurants and a swimming pool.

### Getting There & Away
See Getting There & Away at the beginning of the West Coast & Swartland section for details of buses. Intercape stops at a petrol station on the highway outside town; Translux comes into town and stops at the hotel. Minibus taxis to Cape Town and Clanwilliam stop at the Caltex service station.

There's an excellent scenic road (the R303) over Middelburg Pass into the Koue (Cold) Bokkeveld and a beautiful valley on the other side, which is only topped by the Gydo Pass and the view over the Ceres valley (see the Ceres Getting There & Away entry later in this chapter). The backroad into the wilderness area is also excellent.

### CLANWILLIAM
Clanwilliam is a popular weekend resort. The attraction is the town itself (which has some nice examples of Cape Dutch architecture and a pleasant main street), the proximity to the Cederberg and, most importantly for domestic tourists, the Clanwilliam Dam, which attracts hordes of noisy water-skiers. If you're in this part of the world, by all means use the Clanwilliam shops, then head to the mountains. There are some beautiful roads into the Cederberg and a great drive over the Pakhuis Pass to Calvinia (see the

Calvinia entry in the Northern Cape Province chapter).

The information centre (☎ (027) 482 2024) is in the old jail at the top end of the main street. It's open on weekdays and Saturday morning, and every day in flower season.

### Places to Stay & Eat
If you have a tent or van, the best spot to stay near Clanwilliam is *Kliphuis State Forest*, about 30 minutes away just before the Pakhuis Pass on the R364 – see the earlier Cederberg Wilderness Area entry.

The *Clanwilliam Dam Municipal Caravan Park & Chalets* (☎ (027) 482 1933) overlooks the water-skiing action; it's on the other side of the dam from the N7. Travellers arriving here after weeks in Namibia are pleased to be able to pitch their tents on lush, grassy sites (R20). The chalets are very nice, but you would have to book ahead for the busy periods – school holidays and weekends. Rates start at around R120 for two people.

The information centre can put you in touch with B&Bs charging from R55 per person and there are farmstays in the area.

The comfortable and popular *Strassberger's Hotel Clanwilliam* (☎ (027) 482 1101) is a country pub which has been renovated to a high standard. It is good value at R120/210 (R170/310 in flower season), including breakfast. There's a pool. They also have an annexe in a delicensed pub nearby where rooms cost R85 per person, with breakfast. This isn't as nice as the hotel. *Faint du Barrys* (☎ (027) 482 1537), 13 Ougsburg Drive, is a pleasant guesthouse charging the same rates as the hotel. There is disabled access.

The Hotel Clanwilliam has an à la carte restaurant, *Reinhold's*, in a building across the road, but the hotel dining room is cheaper and quite flash enough. A good set-menu dinner costs R45.

### Getting There & Away
**Bus** See Getting There & Away at the beginning of the West Coast & Swartland section

region showing interesting drives and walks around the plateau of the Matzikamaberg, and they can advise about the wonderful local wildflowers.

### Places to Stay & Eat

The fairly basic *Vanrhynsdorp Caravan Park* (☎ (002327) 91287) has plenty of lawn. Rooms are around R50, and a camp site is R30.

*Van Rhyn Guest House* (☎ (02727) 91429) is in a nice old house. It would be good for groups and for those who are self-sufficient – it's a bit sparse and lonely. It is preferable to book in advance, as there is no-one living at the property itself. On the other side of the town centre, not far from the town hall, there's another B&B, *Lombard Guesthouse* (☎ (02727) 91424). The Vanrhynsdorp Hotel has changed its name to *Namaqualand Country Lodge* (☎ (02727) 91633), but it's still an old country pub with plain but acceptable mid-priced rooms.

The enormous Shell service station has a *Motorstop Restaurant* and takeaway food.

### Getting There & Away

See Getting There & Away at the beginning of the West Coast & Swartland section for details of buses. All the buses that go through Citrusdal also come through Vanrhynsdorp (which is the turn-off for Calvinia and Upington). It's about 1½ hours between Vanrhynsdorp and Clanwilliam.

### AROUND VANRHYNSDORP

The area around Unionskraal, about 10km to the south-east, is particularly renowned for flowers, and there are some interesting drives and walks around the plateau of the Matzikamaberg and Gifberg ranges.

There is a stunning road trip between Vanrhynsdorp and Calvinia. Starting at Vanrhynsdorp in the Knersvlakte, which is usually about as inhospitable as you can imagine, you climb the Vanrhyns Pass into a totally different world.

You will discover numerous references to the road-building Bains. Andrew Bains built a number of famous passes and roads in the

---

## Rooibos Tea

Rooibos 'tea' is made from the leaves of the *Aspalathus linearis* plant, grown in the Cederberg region of Western Cape Province. 'Malay' slaves first discovered that the plant could be used to make a beverage, although it was not until this century that a Russian immigrant, Benjamin Ginsberg, introduced it to the wider community, and it didn't become a cash crop until the 1930s. Despite this, some brands feature trek wagons and other icons of old Afrikanerdom, and the packets make good souvenirs.

Rooibos, literally 'red bush', is a red-coloured tea with a distinctive aroma. It contains no caffeine and much less tannin than normal tea. This is probably its major health benefit, although it's claimed to have others, including minute amounts of minerals such as iron, copper and magnesium. It's also a great thirst quencher, drunk straight or with lemon or milk.

You can visit the Rooibos Tea Natural Products works (☎ (027) 482 2155), near Clanwilliam, by arrangement. ∎

---

for details of buses. All the buses that go through Citrusdal also come through Clanwilliam. It's about 45 minutes between the two towns.

**Minibus Taxi** Taxis running between Springbok and Cape Town come through Clanwilliam. From Clanwilliam the fare to Cape Town or Springbok is about R40.

### VANRHYNSDORP

Vanrhynsdorp lies in the shadow of the distinctive Matzikamaberg Mountain in the desolate Knersvlakte, the valley of the Sout (Salt) River. It's an archetypal country town – pretty dull, really. The surrounding country is very dry, but framed by dramatic mountains. However, like much of the West Coast, it can explode into colour after decent rains.

The town itself, with the exception of a couple of old buildings, is nothing special. There are the basic necessities of life – a bank, a post office and a pub. The information counter (☎ (02727) 91552) in the old town hall has a good map of the immediate

1850s, although he had no formal training as an engineer. In the latter half of the 19th century he was succeeded by his son Thomas, who built a further 25 passes in the southern and western Cape. Vanrhyns Pass is one of Thomas' engineering masterpieces.

In spring you can go from virtual desert to pleasant green wheat fields in 1km or so as the crow flies. There are great views from the top of the pass. It soon starts to dry off again as you head to Calvinia, but there can be superb flowers and the countryside is majestic, with mountains ringing the plateau. See the Around Calvinia entry in the Northern Cape Province chapter for more information.

## VREDENDAL

Vredendal is quite a large and modern town with a good range of shops servicing the farmers from the surrounding irrigation country. The 'Nie-Blankes' ('Nonwhites') sign above one of the bar doors has been lightly painted over.

## STRANDFONTEIN & DORING BAY

Strandfontein is a holiday town, but it's hard to understand its appeal. Like the rest of the West Coast, it's dry, bleak and treeless. Maybe you have to be a sheep farmer from the Karoo to see the magic. The beach is ordinary but there are plenty of rock pools and some surf. There are few facilities – a pub, a caravan park (☎ (02723) 51169) and some holiday houses.

Doring Bay is linked to Strandfontein by about 10km of dusty road that follows the coastline. If you combined the facilities of these towns you might have one decent hamlet, but as it is facilities are thin. Doring Bay is a working town, with fish processing and crayfish and diamond boats (the diamonds are literally vacuumed from the sea floor). *Louis Roodt Beach Resort* (☎ (02723) 51169) has shaded camp sites and a few cottages.

Particularly in October and November, keep your eyes open for whales, which come within 50m or 100m of the beach. There are also great flower displays during spring.

# Breede River Valley

This region lies to the north-east of the Winelands on the western fringes of the Little Karoo. It's dominated by the Breede River Valley, but it's mountainous country and includes some smaller valleys. The valley floors are intensively cultivated with orchards, vineyards and wheat.

European settlers displaced the Khoisan and had settled most of the valleys by the beginning of the 18th century. The area did not really take off, however, until passes were pushed through the mountains in the 19th century. The headwaters of the Breede River (sometimes called the Breë), in the beautiful mountain-locked Ceres basin, escape via Mitchell's Pass and flow southeast for 310km before meeting the Indian Ocean at Whitesands. Many tributaries join the Breede, and by the time it reaches Robertson it has been transformed from a rushing mountain stream to a substantial river.

Tulbagh and Ceres have generous winter rainfalls, but west of Worcester the countryside becomes increasingly dry; even around Worcester it's semi-desert. The climate is excellent if you like clear skies, but the farms are heavily dependent on irrigation, mainly from the Breede.

Many travellers are likely to come through the region because it is bisected by the N2 between Cape Town and the north-east. Since the opening of the 4km Huguenot Toll Tunnel east of Paarl, towns like Robertson and Montagu are more quickly accessible from Cape Town (around a two hour drive), although if you do use the tunnel you'll miss the wonderful views from the old Du Toitskloof Pass.

Look out for the *Cape Fruit Routes* map in information centres. It covers places in the Breede River Valley and also around the Winelands and east to the Montagu area.

## TULBAGH

Tulbagh is one of the most complete examples of an 18th and 19th century village in

South Africa. It can feel a little like Disneyland, particularly when you discover that many of the buildings were substantially rebuilt after earthquakes in 1969 and 1970, but it is a beautiful spot, and the best buildings were restored with painstaking care. There is a whole street of Cape Dutch architecture and the town is overshadowed by the Witsenberg range.

Although most of Tulbagh's surviving buildings date from the first half of the 19th century, the Tulbagh Valley was first settled in 1699. The village began to take shape after the construction of a church in 1743. It was to here, on the outer rim of the settled European areas, that early trekboer families would bring their children out of the wilderness to be baptised.

### Orientation & Information

The town's main street, Van der Stel St, is parallel to Church St, the famous street in which every building has been declared a national monument. A visitor's first port of call should be 4 Church St (☎ (0236) 30 1348), part of the Old Church Folk Museum, which includes a photographic history of Church St and a general information counter.

### Oude Kerk Volksmuseum

The Old Church Folk Museum is a museum complex actually made up of four buildings. Start at No 4; then visit the beautiful Oude Kerk itself (1743); follow this with No 14, which houses the museum's collection of Victorian furniture and costumes, and then No 22, which is a reconstructed town dwelling from the 18th century.

The complex is open weekdays from 9 am to 5 pm, and weekends from 10 am to 4 pm. Admission is R4.

### Places to Stay

*Kliprivier Park Resort* (☎ (0236) 30 0506) on the edge of town is quite pleasant, with reasonable modern chalets from R150 for two people on weekends, slightly less during the week. Caravan sites are available.

*Hotel Tulbagh* (☎ (0236) 30 0071) and *Hotel Witzenberger* are rather ordinary old country hotels, neither with any particularly appealing features.

There are plenty of guesthouses and farmstays. *De Oude Herberg* (☎ (0236) 30 0260), 6 Church St, is a guesthouse in the old Tulbagh main street, surrounded by old buildings, and is built in traditional Cape architecture. It has been a guesthouse since 1885 (although not continuously) and B&B is available from R150 per person. It's a very friendly and very pleasant place (no smoking and no children under 12).

*Die Oliene* (☎ (0236) 30 1160) is a farm 6km out of town with good self-catering cottages for R150 or less. Ask at the information centre for details of other B&Bs and guesthouses (averaging around R80/170 a single/double) and farmstays (from R50 per person self-catering).

### Places to Eat

The *Paddagang Restaurant* (☎ (0236) 30 0242) is in a beautiful old homestead with a vine-shaded courtyard and serves snacks and light meals, as well as some traditional Cape dishes such as waterblommetjie (R27) and local wines. The restaurant is open from 9 am to 5 pm for breakfast (R20 and very good), lunch and tea.

*Die Oude Herberg* restaurant is open during the day, with breakfast (R18), light lunches (R19 for smoked trout) and snacks. Dinner is also available but you must book by 4 pm – on a weekend it would pay to book well in advance. An excellent three course meal costs R38. Readers have recommended the restaurant at the *Hotel Tulbagh*, which is run separately from the hotel by a German chef.

### Getting There & Away

**Minibus Taxi** Most taxis leave from the 'location' (black residential area), on the hill just outside town, but you might find one at Tulbagh Toyota (the Shell service station) on the main street. The fare to Cape Town's Belville train station is R15 and to Ceres it's R10.

**Car & Motorcycle** If you keep going along Tulbagh's main street you'll get to the

WESTERN CAPE PROVINCE

Drostdy and the wine co-op. This road takes you quickly up to the head of the valley (overlooked by the rugged mountains of the Groot Winterhoek Wilderness Area) but it doesn't lead anywhere. To get back to the R44 (running between Ceres and Piketberg, which is on the N7), head back up Tulbagh's main street. Halfway up the hill leading away from the town centre, turn right. There's a small, faded, black-and-white AA sign pointing to Kaapstad (Cape Town) and Gouda. If you follow the R44 north, you leave the valley and suddenly find yourself in very flat, very dry sheep country reminiscent of Australia.

### Getting Around
You can hire bikes at 30 Church St (☎ (0236) 30 1448).

## CERES
Ceres is sometimes referred to as the Switzerland of South Africa. The town has a superb location on the western side of a green and fertile bowl that is ringed by the rugged Skurweberg range. The passes into the valley are particularly spectacular.

Ceres is the most important deciduous fruit and juice-producing district in South Africa, and seems remarkably prosperous in comparison with many regional towns. The surrounding countryside is densely populated and intensively farmed, and the town itself is an attractive, shady place. The Ceres fruit juice that's been saving you from a diet of sugary drinks all over South Africa is packed here.

The valley has a very high rainfall, with 1100mm of rain falling mostly between June and September. The valley has four well-defined seasons. It can get very cold in winter with temperatures dropping well below zero (snow on the mountains), and hot in summer (36°C). It is beautiful in spring and autumn, but particularly in autumn, when the fruit trees change colour.

The vicious winds that make life uncomfortable on the coast in winter don't reach here.

### Information
There's an information office (☎ (0233) 61287) in the municipal offices on the corner of Owen and Voortrekker Sts (coming from the south, turn left at the first robots). It has information on tours and activities in the surrounding area and is open from 9.30 am to 5 pm on weekdays and from 9 am to 1 pm on Saturday.

### Togryers' Museum
Ceres was once a famous centre for making horse-drawn vehicles. Consequently, the Transport Riders' Museum, 8 Oranje St (one street north of and parallel to Voortrekker St), has an interesting collection of buggies, wagons and carriages. It's open from 9 am to 1 pm and 2 to 5 pm on weekdays (closed on Monday afternoon) and on Saturday morning. Admission is R2.50.

### Ceres Nature Reserve
The nature reserve at the foot of Mitchell's Pass, to the north of the main road, has some pleasant signposted footpaths through the fynbos. The pride of the reserve was some San paintings, but they have been seriously damaged by vandals. There are plans to restore them, but you can see why San paintings are rarely promoted. There's an information office with some interesting displays, unfortunately in Afrikaans only. Contact the Ceres information centre for opening times.

### Places to Stay
There are two caravan parks dating from the days when one was for the coloureds and one was for the whites. Although the days of apartheid are over, coloureds are rare visitors at the Pine Forest Resort and whites are even rarer visitors at the Island Holiday Resort. You can perhaps guess which one has the best facilities.

*Pine Forest Resort* (☎ (0233) 21170) is about 1km from the centre of town and is signposted from the main road (left down Krige or Plantasie Sts as you enter town). It's one of the most luxurious camping grounds ever created – there's a variety of different-standard lodges, a recreation hall, rowing boats, mini golf, trampolines, Olympic swimming pool, playgrounds, fishing etc. Rates for three people in chalets start at R70 (R85 in the high season) and camp sites are R38 (R55 in season). The staff have organised a half day walk in the nearby mountains, and a two day walk (overnight with tent). Maps and details are available from the office.

*Island Holiday Resort* (☎ (0233) 21400), on Bloekom St, has a range of comfortable bungalows with three price tiers (depending on the season). Rondavels sleeping four cost just R65, rising marginally in the high season and on weekends. There are also various categories of more expensive bungalows. A tent site is R30 (R35 in the high season). To get there you pass through the nonwhite area of town, where small shacks and houses straggle over surprisingly sandy soil. This might make the Island a more interesting place to stay.

*Die Herberg Guesthouse* (☎ (0233) 22325) is really quite attractive, in spite (or because) of being completely kitsch. It's also very good value. Singles/doubles start at R90/150. There's also the more expensive *Belmont Hotel* (☎ (0233) 21150) at the end of Porter St. The big Sunday lunch buffet is very popular.

The information centre will help you find B&Bs, from R50 per person.

### Getting There & Away
**Bus** Kruger bus service (☎ (0233) 65901) runs basic buses to Cape Town at 4 am and 9 am from Monday to Saturday, and at 3 pm on Sunday.

**Minibus Taxi** Long-distance taxis leave from opposite the John Steyne library. Peres & Sons (☎ (0233) 65901) has a taxi to Cape Town (about R25), departing from Ceres at 9 am Tuesday to Friday and 4 am on Saturday and Monday. Their taxis leave Cape Town's main taxi rank at 3 pm. If Peres can't help, try phoning C Fontein (☎ (0233) 22863).

## AROUND CERES
### Middelburg & Gydo Passes
The Middelburg and Gydo passes should not be missed if you're in the vicinity of Ceres. Coming from Citrusdal you almost immediately hit a very bumpy dirt road that takes you up into the Cederberg. Middelburg is an impressive pass, but the really good views are on the Ceres side when you come out into a narrow valley completely walled by raw, rock hills with rich mineral colouring.

In stark contrast to the hills, the floor of the valley is irrigated so it is usually emerald green, and there is a patchwork of orchards. The reds, ochres and purples of the rocky mountains, the blue of the sky, the blossom of the orchards, fresh green pastures, wildflowers, dams and wading birds are more like a dream than anything else.

About 20km from Ceres you hit a sealed road. Coming south you feel as if you've lost altitude, so when you come out on the 1000m Gydo Pass overlooking the Ceres Valley, the world seems to drop away at your feet. The valley is a beautiful bowl of green surrounded by mountains.

### Mitchell's Pass
The Breede River, forcing its way between the mountains surrounding Ceres, provided the key to the development of the valley. Originally, the settlers dismantled their wagons and carried them over the mountain, but in 1765 a local farmer built a track along the river.

In 1846 the remarkable Andrew Bain began construction of a proper road. It was completed in 1848 and became the main route onto the South African plateau to the north, remaining so until the Hex River Pass was opened in 1875. Mitchell's Pass cut the travel time to Beaufort West from three weeks to one week. The pass has recently been rebuilt to highway standards, but you can still enjoy the views and appreciate what a remarkable engineer Bain was.

## WORCESTER
Worcester is a service centre for the rich farmland of the Breede River Valley. It's a

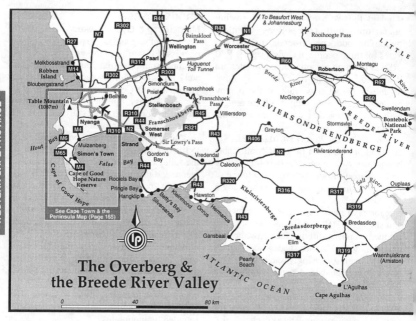

**The Overberg &
the Breede River Valley**

large and fairly nondescript town, particularly in comparison with the surrounding countryside and nearby Robertson, Montagu, Ceres and so on. However, the farm museum and botanic garden are definitely worth visiting.

### Orientation & Information

Most of the town lies to the south of the N1. There are some impressive old buildings near and around the edge of Church Square (off High St), including the one housing the publicity association (☎ (0231) 71408), 75 Church St. It's open from 8 am to 4.30 pm on weekdays and from 8.30 am to 12.30 pm on Saturday.

### Beck House

Just off the town square, Beck House is a charming 1841 house furnished in late-Victorian style. The outbuildings, including a stable, bath house and herb garden, are

particularly interesting. It's open weekdays from 9 am to 1 pm and 2 to 5 pm, Saturday from 8.30 am to 5 pm and Sunday from 2 to 5 pm.

### Kleinplasie Farm Museum

This farm museum (☎ (0231) 22225) is excellent, one of the best in South Africa. It takes you from a Khoikhoi camp, to a trekboers hut, to a complete functioning 18th century farm complex. It's a 'live' museum, meaning there are people wandering around in period clothes and rolling tobacco, making soap, operating a smithy, milling wheat, spinning wool and so on. The place is fascinating and can easily absorb a couple of hours. A miniature train runs around the complex, leaving hourly.

At the museum shop you can buy single bottles of wine that are a whisker more expensive than direct from the winery next door, where you will often have to buy a case

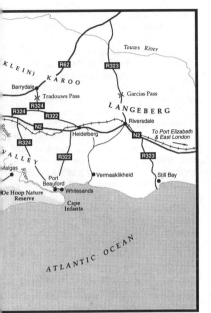

WESTERN CAPE PROVINCE

2.5km from the centre of town. It includes 140 hectares of natural semi-desert vegetation (with both Karoo and fynbos elements) and 10 hectares of landscaped garden where many of the plants have been labelled. If your interest has been piqued, this is an ideal opportunity to identify some of the extraordinary indigenous plants.

There is something to see at any time of the year; bulb plants flower in autumn, the aloes flower in winter and the annuals flower in spring. There's also a collection of weird stone plants and other succulents. The garden is open daily from 8 am to 4 pm and admission costs R2.

### KWV Cellar
This modern cellar and brandy distillery (☎ (0231) 70785) isn't as famous as the one in Paarl but it is the largest in the world under one roof. Tours (R7) are held at 9.30 and 11 am and 1.30 and 3.30 pm during the week, and also on Saturday morning from December to April.

### Places to Stay & Eat
*Burger Caravan Park* (☎ (0231) 23461), De la Bat Rd close to the N1, is pretty ordinary, but it would do at a pinch and it is next to the town's swimming pool. Tent sites cost R22. *Nekkies* (☎ (0231) 70945) is a better alternative. It's on the Breede River en route to Rawsonville, about 5km from the centre of town.

The *Cumberland Hotel* (☎ (0231) 72641), 2 Stockenstroom St, is expensive and tacky but comfortable enough. Rooms cost about R300. There are cheaper rooms but they are small and dark.

There are a number of small restaurants in the streets around the main shopping area. *St Gerans*, on Church/Kerk St, is recommended – steaks start at around R30.

### Getting There & Away
**Bus** Most buses stop at the train station. Translux buses running the Mountain Route from Cape Town to Oudtshoorn and Port Elizabeth, and to East London, stop in Worcester, as do Transtate and City to City

(holding a dozen). Prices are very, very reasonable, ranging from about R6 to R25. For a significantly more potent alcoholic experience, pick up a flask of *witblitz* (white lightning), a traditional Boer distilled spirit. It's strong stuff but not bad. Our favourite is the rooibos-flavoured variety. We've forgotten how much a flask costs – not much – it's all a bit of a blur.

The museum is open from 9 am to 4.30 pm daily (from 10.30 am on Sunday). Admission is R8. It's best to visit in the morning when you can see activities like bread-baking.

The museum is badly signposted, which is a bit strange considering how slick the rest of the operation is. Look for signs to the Kleinplasie Winery, which is next door to the museum.

### Karoo National Botanic Garden
This is an outstanding garden (☎ (0231) 70785), about 1km north of the N1 and

buses to Umtata. Munnik and Chilwans buses also run here. See the Cape Town Getting There & Away section for more information.

Translux and Greyhound services between Cape Town and Jo'burg/Pretoria stop in Worcester. The fare to Cape Town with Translux is a steep R110.

**Train** For bookings phone ☎ (00231) 29 2202/3. The daily *Trans Karoo* between Cape Town and Jo'burg stops in Worcester. From Worcester to Cape Town 1st/2nd/3rd class tickets are R47/33/19; from Worcester to Jo'burg it's R290/196/122. The *Southern Cross* between Cape Town and Port Elizabeth also stops here on Friday evening heading east, early Monday morning heading west. The extremely circuitous *Trans Oranje* to Durban also stops here.

**Minibus Taxi** There are several rival long-distance taxi companies in town and they use different stops. One company, WUTA Taxis, stops near the corner of Tulbagh and Barry Sts, near the entrance to the train station. A daily taxi to Cape Town (R20) leaves sometime after 6 am and there are less regular but probably daily taxis to Robertson (R13) and to Ashton (R15), the town at the bottom of the pass that runs up to Montagu. Other places to find taxis are near the corner of Grey and Durban Sts and around the OK Bazaar on High St. A useful service to Ceres (about R22) via Tulbagh leaves from the Shoprite supermarket.

## ROBERTSON

Robertson is an attractive, prosperous, rather complacent little town – 6000 rose bushes, jacarandas and oaks line the streets, and the problems of South Africa seem a very long way away. It's now the centre for one of the largest wine-growing areas in the country and is also famous for horse studs. As one traveller said:

There is very little to see or do in Robertson, but I spent one of my more relaxing nights in South Africa here. While walking around the neat streets I couldn't

shake the idea that I'd somehow wandered into a wholesome US sitcom from the early 1960s.

The information centre (☎ 02351) 4437) on Church St is open Monday to Friday from 9 am to 5.30 pm, and on Saturday morning.

At 62 Church St, two doors along from the information centre, is a laundromat open until 9 pm (earlier closing for service wash).

The **museum**, at 50 Paul Kruger St (on the corner of Le Roux St, a few blocks northeast of the central church), has a notable collection of lace. It is open from 9 am to noon daily except Sunday and tea is served in the garden on the second and fourth Friday of the month.

There are a couple of overnight **hiking trails** which take you into the mountains above Robertson, offering great views. The information centre has details.

### Places to Stay & Eat

*Silverstrand Resort* (☎ (02351) 3321) is a large complex on the banks of the Breede River, off the R60 to Worcester. It gets pretty hectic during the high season and it's too far from town (3km) to be convenient for backpackers. Apart from that, it has a very attractive spot on the river. There are tent sites and chalets at average prices.

The *Grand Hotel* (☎ (02351) 3272), 68 Barry St, on the corner of White St, is a rare example of a hotel where the quality of the rooms is better than the quality of the foyer would suggest. It has been tastefully renovated and has a friendly and welcoming atmosphere. Some rooms have balconies. There are a couple of cheerful English-style pub bars downstairs. Single/double rooms go for R140/220 with breakfast, and there might still be a few cheaper rooms with shared bathrooms. The proprietors also arrange tours of the surrounding countryside. *Simone's Grill Room & Restaurant* has standard prices – kingklip and steaks around R35 – but the food is of an unusually high standard. They have a very good-value set-menu lunch for R25 and a popular Sunday carvery where you can eat as much as you like for R35.

The information centre can tell you about other options, including self-catering farm cottages which start at around R50 per person.

## Getting There & Away

**Bus** Translux Mountain Route buses to Port Elizabeth (via Oudtshoorn and Knysna) stop at the train station. See the Cape Town Getting There & Away section for more details. Fares from Robertson include: Cape Town, R115; Oudtshoorn, R40; Knysna, R95; and Port Elizabeth, R125.

The cheaper Chilwans (☎ (021) 54 2506, 905 3910) runs to Cape Town and Oudtshoorn, and Munnik Coaches (☎ (021) 637 1850) runs to Cape Town and Montagu on weekends.

Robertson Travel (☎ (02351) 61329), in the small Plaza shopping centre, is the agent for Budget hire cars. It closes for lunch between 12.30 and 2 pm (it's that sort of town).

**Train** The weekly *Southern Cross* between Cape Town and Port Elizabeth stops here on Friday night heading east and early on Monday morning heading west.

**Minibus Taxi** Taxis running between Cape Town (R25) and Oudtshoorn (R75) stop at the Shell service station on the corner of Voortrekker and Barry Sts. These taxis also run through Montagu (R25). There are no daily services.

## MCGREGOR

McGregor feels as if it has been forgotten. It's one of the best-preserved mid-19th century villages in the country, with numerous thatched cottages surrounded by orchards, vegetable gardens and vineyards. It has no through roads, and the only reason you'll go there is if someone tells you that it is a quiet and beautiful spot – ideal if you want to get away from it all. If you want to get back to it all, there are about 30 wineries within half an hour's drive.

You can rent bikes in the village – your guesthouse will help you organise it.

Between Robertson and McGregor lies **Vrolijkheid Nature Reserve** with bird hides and about 150 species to see. There's an 18km circular walking trail in the reserve.

The **Boesmanskloof Hiking Trail** begins at Die Galg, about 15km south of McGregor, and winds 14km through the fynbos-covered Riviersonderend Mountains to the small town of Greyton. For permits contact Vrolijkheid Nature Reserve (☎ (02353) 621). Most people walk the trail in both directions, with an overnight stop in either McGregor or Greyton. You can't camp on the trail. Places to stay in Greyton include the good *Posthaus* guesthouse, *Greyton Lodge* and *Greyton Hotel*. The start of the trail marks the end of a long-abandoned project to construct a pass across the Langeberg Range.

## Places to Stay & Eat

Guesthouses are the major industry in this village and more are opening all the time. As well as the sample of places listed here there are self-catering cottages on nearby farms. The information centre in Robertson has a complete list.

*Old Mill Lodge* (☎ (02353) 841) is a beautiful old building surrounded by a clutch of modern cottages that have been tastefully and comfortably decorated. It's a beautiful spot, and if you feel active there's a swimming pool and nearby fishing. The cottages have two bedrooms and en suite bathrooms. Dinner, bed and breakfast costs R205/370 a single/double. The food is excellent and you eat in the old mill house looking out across a vineyard – highly recommended. It also has cold lunches for R15, although you'll need to give at least an hour's notice.

The lovely *McGregor Country Cottages* (☎ (02353) 816) is a complex of seven cottages surrounding an apricot orchard. Several of the cottages are national monuments. The cottages are fully equipped and the charges are around R160 a double and up – great value.

*Green Gables* (☎ (021) 761 5846 for bookings) is less spectacular but still pleasant and charges R155/250 a single/double with breakfast.

# The Overberg

The Overberg, which literally means 'over the mountains', is the region south and west of the Franschhoek range, and south of the Wemmershoek and Riviersonderend ranges, which form a natural barrier with the Breede River Valley. Although the Franschhoek and Sir Lowry's passes make the region easily accessible today, in the past it was sufficiently isolated for distinctive communities to develop. The N2, the main coastal highway to Port Elizabeth and Durban, crosses Sir Lowry's Pass; those approaching Cape Town from Port Elizabeth will be greeted with fantastic views across Strand, the Cape Flats and False Bay to the mountains of the Cape Peninsula.

Alternatively, the R44 around Cape Hangklip from Strand is one of the most spectacular coastal roads in the world. It's in the same sort of class as Chapman's Peak Drive on the Cape Peninsula, and it's much less busy. There are a couple of caravan parks on the R44, but the first hotel is in Kleinmond. In summer, Hermanus is a popular seaside resort; in spring, it's famous for the whales that frequent its shores.

This region's wealth of coastal and mountain fynbos is unmatched; most species flower somewhere in the period between autumn and spring. The climate basically follows the same pattern as Cape Town. It's described as a temperate Mediterranean climate with relatively mild winters and warm summers. Rain falls throughout the year, but peaks in August. It can be very windy any time.

## KOGEL BAY

From Gordon's Bay, the R44 skirts a magnificent stretch of coast facing out onto False Bay and dominated by 1000m fynbos-cloaked mountains. Kogel Bay has good beach breaks (dangerous for swimmers) and an excellent caravan park, right on the beach.

*Kogel Bay Pleasure Resort* (☎ (024) 56 1286) is a large, basic caravan park (with

cheaper than average sites) but its position is hard to beat, although it is exposed to south-westerly winds.

## ROOIELS BAY

There isn't much to this hamlet, but it is on an excellent little beach with a lagoon for sedate swimming.

*The Drummond Arms* (☎ (02823) 28458) is a small, new building with friendly hosts, good-value pub lunches and some simple, inexpensive accommodation.

## BETTY'S BAY

Betty's Bay is a small holiday village just east of Cape Hangklip. There are some interesting roads around the Cape itself and the surrounding area is renowned for the variety of fynbos it supports. The nearby Harold Porter National Botanical Gardens (☎ (028 23) 9711) protect some of this fynbos, and are definitely worth visiting. There are paths exploring the area and, at the entrance, tearooms and a formal garden where you can picnic. The gardens are open from 8 am to 6 pm daily; entry is R4. There's a colony of jackass penguins at Stony Point.

## KLEINMOND

Kleinmond is not a particularly attractive town, but it is close to a wild and beautiful beach. Most people will stop only briefly on their way through to Hermanus, but there are a couple of places to stay. If the weather is good, you could be tempted to stop here. There are a couple of municipal caravan parks: *Palmiet Caravan Park* (☎ (02823) 4050) on the west side of town is right on the beach and is the more attractive. Sites cost from around R35.

## HERMANUS

Hermanus is a popular seaside resort within easy day-tripping distance of Cape Town (122km). It was originally a fishing village, and still retains vestiges of its heritage, including an interesting museum at the old harbour. It's increasing fame is as a place to view whales swimming close to shore.

There are some great nearby beaches,

**PLACES TO STAY**
1 Zoete Inval
3 Kenjockity Guesthouse
8 Windsor Hotel
20 Marine Hotel
24 Hermanus Esplanade

**PLACES TO EAT**
6 St Tropez; San Remo Spur
9 Mallards
10 Something Special
11 Rossi's Pizzeria &
   Italian Restaurant
12 Ouzari Greek Trattoria
14 Burgundy Restaurant
18 Hoy Ming
21 Bientang's Cave

**OTHER**
2 Hospital
4 Hermanus
   Accommodation Centre
5 Hermanus Publicity
   Office
7 Post Office
13 Surf Shop
15 Village Square
   Shopping Centre
16 First National Bank
17 O'Hagan's
19 Cycle Scene
22 Museum
23 Book Cottage

Hermanus

most west of the town centre. Rocky hills, reminiscent of the Scottish highlands, surround the town, and there are some good walks and a nature reserve, protecting some of the prolific fynbos. The pleasant town centre is well endowed with restaurants. Bear in mind that Hermanus gets very busy in December and January during the school holidays.

### Orientation & Information

Hermanus is a large town with extensive suburbs of holiday and retirement homes, but the town centre, around the old harbour, is easy to get about on foot. The new working harbour is at the eastern end of town.

The Hermanus Publicity Office (☎ (0283) 22629), 105 Main (Hoof) Rd, is helpful and has a worthwhile supply of information about the town and district, including walks and drives in the surrounding hills. It's open from 9 am to 4.30 pm on weekdays, and on weekends during the whale season and in December.

A craft market is held on Friday and Saturday at Lemms Corner, the north-east corner of Main Rd and Harrow St.

The Surf Shop on Main Rd is open daily

in summer and rents boards (surf and body) for R25 a day. They also rent diving gear. Cycle Scene, also on Main Rd, rents mountain bikes for R25 a day and tandems for R50. Lagoon Boat Hire (☎ (0283) 77 0925) at Prawn Flats, a lagoon 7km west of the town centre, off the road to Stanford and past the suburbs of big holiday houses, rents canoes for about R15 per hour and a variety of other small craft.

## Whales

Between June and November, southern right whales *(Eubalaena australis)* come to Walker Bay to calve. There can be 70 whales in the bay at once. This species was hunted to the verge of extinction (South Africa was a whaling nation until 1976), but its numbers are now recovering. Humpback whales *(Megaptera novaeangliae)* are also sometimes seen.

Whales often come very close to shore and there are some excellent vantage points from the cliff paths that run from one end of Hermanus to the other. The best places are Castle Rock, Kraal Rock and Sievers Point. There's a telescope on the clifftop above the old harbour.

It's only recently that the people of Hermanus bothered to tell the outside world that the whales were regular visitors. They took them for granted. Now, however, the tourism potential has been recognised and just about every business in town has adopted a whale logo. There's also a whale crier, who walks around town blowing on a kelp horn and carrying a blackboard which shows where whales have been recently sighted. A Whale Festival is held in the first week of October.

Despite all this commercialism, boat-viewing of whales is still banned (you can be jailed for up to six years if you approach or remain within 300m), so the mighty creatures have the bay to themselves.

Although Hermanus is the best-known whale-watching site, whales can be seen all the way from False Bay (Cape Town) to Plettenberg Bay and beyond.

## Old Harbour

The old harbour clings to the cliffs in front of the town centre; there's a small museum and a display of old fishing boats. There's an annexe to the museum in the old schoolhouse on the market square. The museum is open daily except Sunday from 9 am to 1 pm and 2 to 5 pm; entry is R3.

## Places to Stay

**Hostels** The *Hermanus Travellers' Lodge* (☎ (0283) 22829) is on a farm out of town (they'll collect you) and charges R20 for camping, R25 for dorms and R60 for a double. Two of the guesthouses in town cater to backpackers. *Kenjockity Guesthouse* (☎ (0283) 21772), 15 Church St, has a fairly small backpackers' room where a bunk costs R30, more if you need bedding. A bit further away from the sea, the *Zoete Inval* guesthouse (☎ (0283) 21242), 23 Main Rd, has dorm beds for R30. Rates in the guesthouse start at R80/120. Several travellers have written to recommend this place.

**Caravan Parks** Unfortunately, the closest caravan parks to town (and they aren't very close) do not allow tents or bakkies. *Schulphoek Resort* does but it's quite a way from town. The turn-off is on the main road just west of Hermanus but then it's a long way to the resort down a lonely road to the end of a point. 'Resort' is very optimistic – it's a basic camping area with few facilities and no on-site management. Contact the municipal offices for details.

**B&Bs, Guesthouses & Self-Catering** Out of season, self-catering cottages can be great value shared between a few people, and even in season you can find places for less than R250. The publicity office has listings or you can book through the Hermanus Accommodation Centre (☎ (0283) 70 0004), not far from the publicity office, on Church St. Self-catering flats and houses on their books start at around R150 in the low season and from R300 in the high season. B&Bs range from between R70 and R150 per person.

Of the several guesthouses, *Kenjockity*

*Guesthouse* (☎ (0283) 21772), 15 Church St, has fair-sized rooms. While they are nothing special the guesthouse has a nice atmosphere and is a good size. Rooms start at about R95 per person, R125 with attached bathroom. You'll pay more in December.

*Hermanus Esplanade* (☎ (0283) 23610), on Marine Drive, has apartments overlooking the sea. Smaller apartments cost from R150 to R190 for two people. You probably won't find a vacancy in December.

**Hotels** The *Windsor Hotel* (☎ (0283) 23727) is a large old place on Marine Drive which seems to make its living from coach tours. As well as the old section there's a new wing that has good (if small) rooms with full-length windows overlooking the sea, just across the road. At the right time of the year there's a good chance of seeing a whale without getting out of bed! Low-season rates (May to the end of October) are R167/244 for singles/doubles, with breakfast (R147/ 210 without sea views); high season doubles (only) cost R268 (R248 without sea views). From mid-December to early January the rates are even higher.

The *Marine Hotel* (☎ (0283) 21112; fax 21533) is a grand, old-style hotel which has been superbly renovated. It's comfortable and it's in a good spot. Singles/doubles cost from R213/302 (R346/370 sea-facing) up to R504/528, which is very good value.

**Places to Eat**

Hermanus seems set to have a boom in eating places, so it's likely that there will be more choice by the time you arrive.

There are a couple of interesting possibilities on High St, which runs parallel to Main Rd. *Rossi's Pizzeria & Italian Restaurant* (☎ (0283) 22848), 10 High St, has a pleasant and relaxed atmosphere. It has a range of pasta dishes (from R15 to R23), pizzas (from R15) and steak or line fish (from R35). It's open nightly from 6.30 pm. *Something Special*, across the road from Rossi's, is a pleasant café serving snacks and reasonably priced meals.

*St Tropez* (☎ (0283) 23221), 28 Main Rd,

has good-value pub lunches for under R15, although it is more expensive at night (closer to R20).

The *Burgundy Restaurant* (☎ (0283) 22800), Marine Drive, is one of the most acclaimed and popular restaurants in the province. Prices are surprisingly reasonable, and booking is recommended. There's a garden area with sea views. Main courses are around R35 to R40 at lunch, more at dinner. At lunch there are also cheaper snacks such as the whale watchers' platter of cold meats, cheeses, salad and paté for R19.50.

Right down on the water, between the museum and the Marine Hotel, *Bientang's Cave* (☎ (0283) 23454) really *is* a seaside cave, containing a good restaurant where you can eat a steak meal for under R20. Someone told us about a memorable meal here with a whale nuzzling the rocks a metre or so from their table.

**Getting There & Away**

The only bus service (apart from tours) between Cape Town and Hermanus is Chilwans (☎ (021) 905 3910 in Cape Town), which has an evening service from Cape Town to Gansbaai via Hermanus on Friday and Saturday for about R20.

There aren't many minibus taxis. You might find one running to Bellville (Cape Town) for R20, but not daily. The taxi park, such as it is, is behind the publicity office.

**AROUND HERMANUS**

There are several walks and drives in the hills behind the town – the publicity office has maps. The 1400 hectare **Fernkloof Nature Reserve** is particularly worth visiting if you are interested in fynbos.

The road south from Hermanus passes through some pretty country with quite a bit of fynbos. The next town south is **Stanford**, a largish, quiet town a little way inland. Next along is **Gansbaai**, also quiet but on the coast, then **Pearly Beach**. On one of the inland routes between Gansbaai and Cape Agulhas is **Elim**, a picturesque mission village. Unfortunately, a good part of the picturesqueness is due to poverty.

**WESTERN CAPE PROVINCE**

## CAPE AGULHAS

Cape Agulhas is the southernmost point of the African continent – latitude 34° 49' 58.74". On a stormy day it really looks like the next stop is the South Pole, with green seas, squall clouds and sheets of low, shattered rock. Otherwise it isn't especially impressive, but it does have that air of anticlimax which attends the end of any great journey. Congratulations, all you Africa-overlanders. Where are you going next?

The **lighthouse**, built in 1848 and the second oldest in South Africa, has been restored and is open to the public from Tuesday to Saturday from 9.30 am to 4.45 pm, Sunday from 10 am to 1.30 pm. There's a tearoom in the building.

There isn't much in the hamlet of Cape Agulhas, but **Struisbaai**, about 6km east, is a little larger and has a caravan park. There's also a 14km-long beach there.

The country around Bredasdorp, Struisbaai and Cape Agulhas is very low-key by South African standards – it's rolling wheat and sheep country. For information on this part of the Overberg, go to the friendly Bredasdorp Publicity Association (☎ (02481) 42584) on Dirkie Uys St.

## WAENHUISKRANS (ARNISTON)

Waenhuiskrans, which means wagon-house cliff (after the enormous cavern eroded into the cliffs 1km from the village) is the official name of this isolated fishing/holiday village. It is also often referred to as Arniston, however, after a ship that was wrecked near there in 1815 with the loss of 372 lives.

The coast is certainly wild, and it is not surprising it has claimed many ships. The town has charm, however, and is notable for its restored thatch cottages. There are also some long stretches of sandy beach.

### Places to Stay

*Arniston Hotel* (☎ (02847) 59000) is a very classy getaway overlooking the wild waves of the south coast and surrounded by windswept dunes and whitewashed fisherfolk's cottages. Singles/doubles are R360/520 including breakfast. *Arniston Lodge* (☎ 2847)

59175), 23 Hoofweg, is a very comfortable B&B charging from R180/250.

At the other end of the scale, the *Caravan Park* (☎ (02847) 59620) has basic four-bed bungalows, with shared facilities and no bedding or crockery, for about R95. Sites are available at the caravan park, but they are a pricey R48.

## DE HOOP NATURE RESERVE

De Hoop (pronounced 'huu-op') is one of the best of the reserves administered by Cape Nature Conservation. It includes a scenic coastline with lonely stretches of beach, rocky cliffs, large coastal sand dunes, a freshwater lake and the Potberg range.

This is one of the best places to see both mountain and lowland fynbos and a diverse cross section of coastal ecosystems. Fauna includes the Cape mountain zebra, bontebok and a wealth of bird life. The coast is an important breeding area for the southern right whale.

Hikers can tackle beach walks, an 8km trail along the cliffs of the De Hoop Vlei (Lake), and day trails of various lengths on Potberg. An overnight mountain-bike trail has also been laid out, and it would be nice riding. You have to book in advance.

There is good snorkelling along the coast, and since it is to the east of Cape Agulhas the water is reasonably warm. There are cottages (from R80 for four people – great value) and camp sites (R40), but these must be booked in advance (☎ (028) 542 1126).

The reserve covers 36,000 hectares, plus 5km out to sea. It's about 260km from Cape Town, and the final 50km from either Bredasdorp or Swellendam is along gravel roads. The only access to the reserve is via Wydgeleë on the Bredasdorp to Malgas road. At Malgas a manually operated *pont* (pontoon ferry) on the Breede River still operates. The village of Ouplas, 15km away, is the nearest place to buy fuel and supplies. Gates are open daily from 7 am to 6 pm; entry costs R3 per person. The office is open from 8 am to 4 pm on weekdays and only from 8 to 11 am on weekends.

The brochure warns that 'litterbugs will be

fed to the vultures' – it's probably a joke, but how many jokes have you seen on official brochures in South Africa?

## SWELLENDAM

As well as being a very pretty town with a real sense of history, Swellendam offers those with transport a good base for exploring quite a range of country. The Breede River Valley and the coast are within easy reach, as is the Little Karoo. Swellendam is about midway between Cape Town and George, the first town on the Garden Route. Even if you don't have wheels there's the chance to walk in indigenous forest quite close to town.

Swellendam is dotted with old oaks and on its south side is surrounded by beautiful rolling wheat country, but it backs up against a spectacular ridge, part of the 1600m Langeberg range (author Breyten Breytenbach describes the town as 'lying in the crook

of well-dressed, elderly mountains'.) The distinctive square-topped outcrop is known locally as 12-O'Clock Rock because the sun at noon is very close to the rock, making it impossible for anyone in town to see what is going on up there. We were told that this was a favourite place for diamond smugglers to carry out their business, but it seems a long way to go. You can walk up and back in a day.

### History

Swellendam dates from 1746 and is the third oldest European town in South Africa. The swift expansion by independent farmers and traders beyond the Cape Peninsula meant that by the 1740s they had drifted too far beyond the Dutch East India Company's authorities at Stellenbosch to be controlled.

As a result, Swellendam was established as the seat of a *landdrost*, an official representative of the colony's governor whose

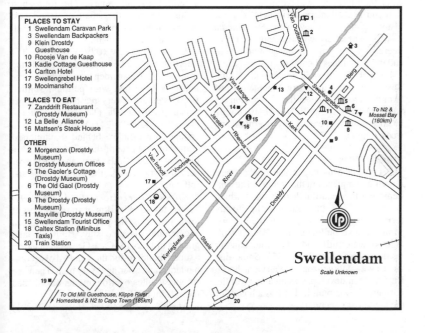

PLACES TO STAY
1 Swellendam Caravan Park
3 Swellendam Backpackers
9 Klein Drostdy
   Guesthouse
10 Roosje Van de Kaap
13 Kadie Cottage Guesthouse
14 Carlton Hotel
17 Swellengrebel Hotel
19 Moolmanshof

PLACES TO EAT
7 Zanddrift Restaurant
   (Drostdy Museum)
12 La Belle Alliance
16 Mattsen's Steak House

OTHER
2 Morgenzon (Drostdy
   Museum)
4 Drostdy Museum Offices
5 The Gaoler's Cottage
   (Drostdy Museum)
6 The Old Gaol (Drostdy
   Museum)
8 The Drostdy (Drostdy
   Museum)
11 Mayville (Drostdy Museum)
15 Swellendam Tourist Office
18 Caltex Station (Minibus
   Taxis)
20 Train Station

To N2 &
Mossal Bay
(160km)

To Old Mill Guesthouse, Klippe River
Homestead & N2 to Cape Town (185km)

**Swellendam**

Scale Unknown

duties combined those of local administrator, tax collector and magistrate. The residency of a landdrost was known as a *drostdy* and included his office and courtroom as well as his family's living quarters. The Swellendam Drostdy is the only 18th century drostdy to survive, and it is now the centrepiece for one of the best museum complexes in South Africa. Official vandalism has ensured that Swellendam, pretty as it is, has not remained a perfect jewel. In 1974 the main road was widened, unfortunately resulting in the loss of many old oaks and older buildings.

## Information

Swellendam Tourist Office (☎ (0291) 42770) in the old mission, or Oefeninghuis, on Voortrek St (the main street) is open Monday to Friday from 9 am to 5 pm, and Saturday from 9 am to 12.30 pm. Note the twin clocks, one of which is permanently set at 12.15 pm. This was the time for the daily service; the illiterate townspeople only had to match the working clock with the painted one to know when their presence was required.

If you're at all interested in architecture or history, pick up a copy of the *Swellendam Treasures* brochure which details scores of interesting buildings in and around Swellendam. It includes a good map.

For permits to walk in Marloth Nature Reserve in the Langeberg Mountains, just 3km from town, contact the Nature Conservation Department (☎ (0291) 41410) during business hours. There are day, overnight and week-long hikes.

## Drostdy Museum

The Drostdy Museum is one of the finest museum complexes in the country. The centrepiece is the beautiful drostdy itself, which dates from 1746. In addition to the drostdy there is the Old Gaol, part of the original administrative buildings, the Gaoler's Cottage, a watermill and Mayville, another residence dating back to 1853. Some distance away, Morgenzon, 16 Van Oudtshoorn Rd, has been developed as an annexe of the museum. It was built in 1751 as a house for the landdrost's secretary.

The complex is open weekdays from 9 am to 4.15 pm, and weekends from 10 am to 3.45 pm; entry is R5.

## Places to Stay

*Swellendam Caravan Park* (☎ (0291) 42705) is in a lovely spot near the Morgenzon museum, a 10 minute walk from town, tucked under the mountains and surrounded by leafy farms. Sites cost around R35 and there are chalets. It's a nice place but if you have transport consider staying at Bontebok National Park, 6km from town.

*Swellendam Backpackers* (☎ (0291) 42648) is at 5 Lichtenstein St. It's a pleasant enough place, charging about R30 for a dorm bed and R25 for camping. A traveller warns that the phone rates here are extremely high.

There are many excellent B&Bs and guesthouses in and around Swellendam, and they are the best accommodation options. The tourist office has a full list.

*Roosje Van de Kaap* (☎ (0291) 43001), 5 Drostdy St, is a friendly little guesthouse in a refurbished old house. The four guest rooms overlook the small pool and cost around R90 per person with breakfast. There's a restaurant here.

*Moolmanshof* (☎ (0291) 43258), 217 Voortrek St, is a beautiful old home dating from 1798. The garden is superb and the house is furnished with period furniture. B&B rates are a very reasonable R90 per person per night. The *Old Mill Guesthouse* (☎ (0291) 42790), 241 Voortrek St, is a cottage in a meadow behind the antiques/craft shop and café of the same name. It's a pleasant place. B&B costs about R90 per person or you can take the whole cottage and self-cater.

*Klippe Rivier Homestead* (☎ (0291) 43341; fax 43337), 1km or so south-west of town, just across the Keurbooms River, is an exceptional place to stay. Built on land granted in 1725, the Cape Georgian manor is a superb building and the standard of accommodation and catering is very high. There are six guest suites overlooking an oak-shaded lawn, from R260 per person.

At the *Swellengrebel Hotel* (☎ (0291)

41144), Voortrek St, the older rooms are fairly cramped (from R149/189) but newer double rooms (R220) are OK. The *Carlton Hotel* (☎ (0291) 41120) is looking pretty tired and charges from R70/120 or R60/100 with shared bathroom.

### Places to Eat
*Mattsen's Steak House* on Voortrek St near the tourist office is popular. A big dinner costs about R50 and there are light meals and snacks.

*Zanddrift Restaurant* adjoins the museum and is in a building that dates from 1757. It's open only from 9 am to 5 pm, unfortunately. Breakfast is a must, with a huge platter of omelette, ham, cheese, paté, fruit and so on, all for R25. It's available all day. Other dishes depend on what's available that day.

The café at the *Old Mill Guesthouse*, 241 Voortrek St, is open for lunch (and dinner for guests staying in the cottage). Light meals cost around R15. More substantial dishes include springbok steaks, guinea-fowl pies and other interesting specialities.

For an excellent night out, phone *Klippe Rivier Homestead* (☎ (0291) 43341) to see if they have room at dinner for nonguests. A three course set menu costs R65.

### Getting There & Away
**Bus** Intercape runs to Cape Town and Port Elizabeth. Fares include Cape Town, R65; Mossel Bay, R65; Knysna, R90; and Port Elizabeth, R120. The Swellengrebel Hotel is the Intercape agent.

Greyhound (☎ (0291) 42374) and Translux have similar services at higher prices. Some Translux buses also run to Oudtshoorn (R80). Milestone Tours (☎ (0291) 42137), 8 Cooper St, is the Translux agent.

**Train** The weekly *Southern Cross* between Cape Town and Port Elizabeth stops here.

**Minibus Taxi** Taxis stop at the Caltex service station on Voortrek St, opposite the Swellengrebel Hotel. There's a daily service to Cape Town for R38, and to Mossel Bay for a little more.

### BONTEBOK NATIONAL PARK
Bontebok National Park (☎ (0291) 42735), 6km south of Swellendam, is a small chunk of land set aside to ensure the preservation of the bontebok, an unusually marked antelope that once roamed the region in large numbers. Unfortunately, it has been reduced to the verge of extinction.

As a national park, Bontebok doesn't offer much competition to Kruger et al, but as a nice place to relax it's hard to beat.

The park falls within the coastal fynbos area and is on the banks of the Breede River (swimming is possible). It boasts nearly 500 grasses and other plant species; in the late winter and early spring, the veld is covered with flowers. In addition to the bontebok there is the rhebok, grysbok, duiker, red hartebeest and mountain zebra. Bird life is abundant.

Admission is R11 per vehicle. There are six-berth 'chalavans' for R77 plus R12 per person (book through the National Parks Board) and pleasant camp sites for R35 for two people.

# The Little Karoo

The Little (or Klein) Karoo is a region bordered in the south by the Outeniqua and Langeberg ranges, and in the north by the Swartberg range about 60km away. It runs east from Montagu for about 300km to Uniondale, and is more fertile and better watered than the harsher Great Karoo to the north. The region is renowned for ostriches, which thrive in the dry and sunny climate; for magnificent wildflower displays; and for the spectacular kloofs and passes that cut through the mountains.

Most people travelling between Cape Town and the Garden Route stick to the coast the whole way but there's a very interesting alternative: the Mountain Route running via Worcester, Robertson, Montagu, Barrydale, Ladismith and Calitzdorp, Oudtshoorn and George. It's much easier to get between Cape Town and the Garden Route by a direct minibus taxi on this route than along the coast (although it's a gruelling trip), and plenty of bus services run it.

## MONTAGU

Montagu, founded in 1851, is the first town up the pass from the Breede River Valley (described earlier in this chapter) – once you pop through the Kogmanskloof Pass near Robertson you are suddenly in a very different world. It's a good place to go if you want to escape the 20th century and get a brief taste of the Little Karoo.

The town is populated by artists and other refugees, and there's a peaceful old-world atmosphere. There are some restored old buildings (23 national monuments), some nice places to stay and some good opportunities to explore the spectacular surrounding mountains.

Originally, access to the town required numerous crossings of the river until 1877 when master engineer Thomas Bain (son of

Andrew) completed the small tunnel that is still in use today. The British added a fort on top in 1899.

### Orientation & Information

The town is small, so it's easy to get around on foot. There's a particularly good tourist information office (☎ (0234) 42471) that can provide information on accommodation (including a good range of B&Bs and self-catering cottages), walks and hikes. It's open on weekdays (sometimes closing for lunch) and on Saturday morning.

### Montagu Museum & Joubert House

The Montagu Museum is in the old mission church on Long St, and includes interesting displays and some good examples of antique furniture. Joubert House, a short walk away but also on Long St, is also attached to the museum. It's the oldest house in Montagu (built in 1853) and is restored to its Victorian finery.

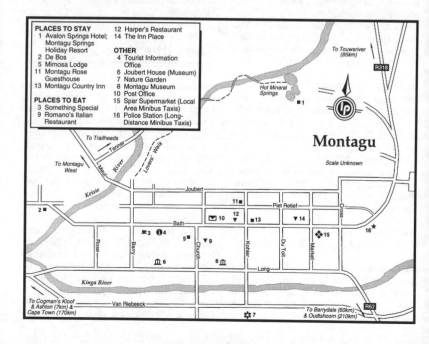

PLACES TO STAY
1 Avalon Springs Hotel;
   Montagu Springs
   Holiday Resort
2 De Bos
5 Mimosa Lodge
11 Montagu Rose
   Guesthouse
13 Montagu Country Inn

PLACES TO EAT
3 Something Special
9 Romano's Italian
   Restaurant

12 Harper's Restaurant
14 The Inn Place

OTHER
4 Tourist Information
   Office
6 Joubert House (Museum)
7 Nature Garden
8 Montagu Museum
10 Post Office
15 Spar Supermarket (Local
   Area Minibus Taxis)
16 Police Station (Long-
   Distance Minibus Taxis)

Montagu

Scale Unknown

To Touwsriver
(85km)

R318

Hot Mineral
Springs

To Trailheads
To Montagu
West

Keisie

Kinga River

To Cogman's Kloof
& Ashton (7km) &
Cape Town (170km)

Van Riebeeck

To Barrydale (60km)
& Oudtshoorn (210km)

R62

LUBA VANGELOVA

JON MURRAY

JON MURRAY

JON MURRAY

LUBA VANGELOVA

Left: Ivy covered facade of the University of Cape Town.
Top: Cape Town's grand Houses of Parliament, built in 1885.
Middle: Cape Town – Victoria & Alfred Waterfront; Ndebele artwork, National Gallery.
Bottom: Table Mountain viewed from Bloubergstrand, a classic image of South Africa.

JON MURRAY

JON MURRAY

RICHARD EVERIST

RICHARD EVERIST

Top: Beach huts at Muizenberg on False Bay, south of Cape Town.
Middle Left: The town hall clocktower, Cape Town.
Middle Right: The dramatic Swartberg Pass, home to many fynbos plant species.
Bottom: Surfin' RSA, Elands Bay, Western Cape.

## Places to Stay

On the edge of town, *De Bos* (☎ (0234) 42532) is a guest farm with camping (R15 per person), a backpackers' barn (R20), a bungalow (R25 per person) and an en suite double room for R80. There's a pool.

*Mimosa Lodge* (☎ (0234) 42351; fax 42418), on Church St, is a very good guesthouse in a beautifully restored old building. It charges from R250/450 for dinner, bed and breakfast. *Montagu Country Inn* (☎ (0234) 41115), Bath St, is a refurbished old hotel charging R155/260 for B&B.

The information office has details of several B&Bs from around R70 per person. There are also inexpensive self-catering farmhouses and cottages available. For example, the Venters (☎ (0234) 42203) have a *farmhouse* 7km from town that sleeps six people and costs R120 a night. They also have a cottage without electricity sleeping five for just R55.

The luxurious *Avalon Springs Hotel* (☎ (0234) 41150) has mineral springs, warm pools, massages and gyms. Rates start at R215/360.

Right on top of the Langeberg Mountains, Neil Burger (☎ (0234) 42471) has several accommodation options including a *stone chalet* for R70 a double. Neil runs the tractor trips up the mountain.

## Places to Eat

*Something Special* is a craft/coffee shop in a beautiful old Cape Dutch building. There are footpath tables, but if you sit inside you're more likely to strike up a conversation with the friendly and knowledgeable owners. It's open during the day, every day. *Harper's Restaurant*, on Bath St near the post office, is very pleasant and reasonably priced.

*Romano's Italian Restaurant* (☎ (0234) 42398) has soup for R5, pasta for R18, pizza for around R20 and fillet steak for R30. Locals say that the best pizzas are to be found at *Da Vinci's Pizzeria*, out at the Avalon Springs Hotel complex. *Montagu Country Inn* has inexpensive pub meals and also a dining room.

## Getting There & Away

**Bus** Translux stops here on the run between Cape Town (R100) and Port Elizabeth (R110). Munnik Coaches (☎ (021) 637 1850) runs thrice weekly between Cape Town and Montagu for just R35.

**Minibus Taxi** Taxis running between Cape Town and Oudtshoorn stop near the police station.

## AROUND MONTAGU
### Montagu Hot Mineral Springs
The hot springs are on an attractive site about 3km from town; they are hot (45°C), radioactive and are renowned for their healing properties.

The spa is a very weird phenomenon to find in the Karoo – you just don't expect so many people for a start. The luxurious *Avalon Springs Hotel* (☎ (0234) 41150) has mineral springs, warm pools, massages and gyms. Rates start at R165/260. Near the hotel is a large time-share resort, *Montagu Springs Holiday Resort* (☎ (00234) 42235), which has four-person chalets for R120 during the week, rising on weekends and holidays and in December.

### Bloupunt & Cogman's Kloof Trails
The information office handles bookings for overnight cabins near the start of the Bloupunt and Cogman's Kloof walks. The huts are fairly basic (wood stoves, showers and toilet facilities) but they are cheap. There are also several camp sites.

The Bloupunt Trail is 15km long and can be walked in six to eight hours; it traverses ravines and mountain streams, and climbs to 1000m. The flora includes proteas, ericas, aloes, gladioli and watsonias. The Cogman's Kloof Trail is 12km and can be completed in four to six hours; it's not as steep as the Bloupunt Trail. Both trails start within walking distance of the town.

### Niel's Farm
Niel Burger takes spectacular tractor-trailer rides to the top of the Langeberg range, from where you can look way down into the

Breede River Valley. Even locals enjoy the trip, so it must be something special. The three hour trip costs about R15 and usually operates on Wednesday at 10 am and Saturday at 9.30 am and 2 pm. You can have a delicious lunch of *potjiekos* (traditional pot stew) with home-made bread for R25. Niel also has an overnight cabin with 20 beds. For information and bookings, contact the Montagu information office; you'll need transport to get to the farm.

## MONTAGU TO OUDTSHOORN

From Montagu, the R62 runs through the upper end of the Little Karoo, through some interesting scenery.

**Barrydale** is a compact town in a small green valley. *Tradouw Guesthouse & Hostel* (☎ (028) 572 1434), 46 Van Riebeeck St, is an informal place in an old trading store. Dorms go for R30 and you can camp for R10 per person. There are also singles and doubles.

From Barrydale you can continue east on the R62 to Calitzdorp and Oudtshoorn, or head south on the R324, which runs down through **Tradouw Pass** (where you might see baboons) and then branches to run east to Heidelberg and west down a very pretty valley to Swellendam, passing on the way small villages such as **Zoar**. The setting is picturesque but there is little work in the area and many people travel to Cape Town, returning to their families on weekends.

**Calitzdorp** is a little old town where the wineries are famous for their ports. *Calitzdorp Guesthouse & Coffee Shop* (☎ (04437) 33453) on Van Riebeeck St has accommodation and has been recommended. You pay around R130 per person for dinner, bed and breakfast. There's also *Calitzdorp Spa* (☎ (04437) 33371) with mineral springs and singles/doubles for R80/ 100. You can also camp.

If you're heading for Oudtshoorn and have a little time to spare, consider leaving the main road (which mainly follows the drier valley floor) at Calitzdorp and taking the small road running along the north side of the range, through some very pretty country. You can join this road either just

west of Calitzdorp (look for signs pointing to Kraaldorings, Kruisrivier or Matjiesrivier) or some way east of Calitzdorp.

## OUDTSHOORN

Oudtshoorn is the tourist capital of the Little Karoo. It's a large, sedate place with some nice old buildings. Its claim to fame is the ostrich industry, and the farmlands around Oudtshoorn are thick with the birds. You can watch ostrich races, ride ostriches and buy ostrich biltong, ostrich feathers and ostrich eggs. This sort of entertainment palls fairly quickly, but luckily Oudtshoorn is also well situated as a base for exploring the very different environments of the Little Karoo, the Garden Route and the Great Karoo. The nearby Swartberg Pass and Seweweekspoort are geological, floral and engineering masterpieces – two of South Africa's scenic highlights.

### Orientation & Information

While it's reasonably easy to get around the town centre on foot, nearly all the main 'attractions' are beyond walking distance from town – this means that a car, or a willingness to take a tour or hitchhike, is virtually essential. The main commercial street is Hogg (High) St, to the east of Baron van Rheede St. Oudtshoorn is 506km from Cape Town and 60km from George.

Oudtshoorn Tourist Bureau (☎ (044) 279 2532) is on Baron van Rheede St next to Queen's Hotel. It's open weekdays from 8 am to 5 pm and on Saturday morning. Ask here about the numerous B&Bs in town and about tours of the local sights.

Kuriopik, on the corner of Langenhoven Rd and Hogg St, sells ostrich products and curios. Die Oude Pastorie, 43 Baron van Rheede St, sells crafts and souvenirs.

Oudtshoorn's phone numbers were due to change while this book was in production. We have given the new numbers here but in case there are delays and you have trouble getting through, try the old number – change the area code to 0443 and delete the first 7.

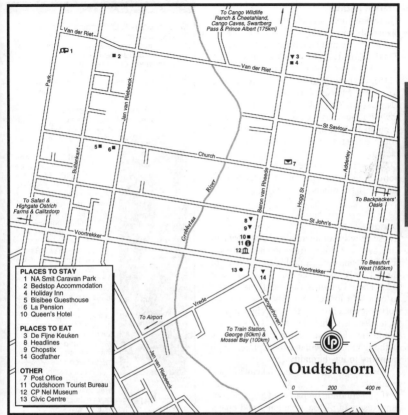

WESTERN CAPE PROVINCE

PLACES TO STAY
1  NA Smit Caravan Park
2  Bedstop Accommodation
4  Holiday Inn
5  Bisibee Guesthouse
6  La Pension
10  Queen's Hotel

PLACES TO EAT
3  De Fijne Keuken
8  Headlines
9  Chopstix
14  Godfather

OTHER
7  Post Office
11  Outdshoorn Tourist Bureau
12  CP Nel Museum
13  Civic Centre

Oudtshoorn

## CP Nel Museum

The museum, on Baron van Rheede St, is a striking sandstone building, completed in 1907 at the height of the ostrich feather boom. There are extensive displays tracing the history of the ostrich and the boom, as well as on the history of the Karoo. The museum also features a reconstructed grocery shop of the boom years and a synagogue. The museum is open Monday to Saturday from 9 am to 1 pm and 2 to 5 pm, and on Sunday from 2.30 to 5 pm. Entry is free.

## Cango Wildlife Ranch & Cheetahland

Roughly 3km from the town centre, this is one of the few attractions it is feasible to visit on foot. Crocodiles, cheetahs, lions and leopards are on display (you can pat a cheetah). The complex is open daily from 8 am to 5 pm, with 45-minute tours starting every 20 minutes. Entry is R18.

The floods which raged through Oudtshoorn in late 1996 extensively damaged the ranch, and at the time of writing it had not yet reopened, although it was expected to eventually.

WESTERN CAPE PROVINCE

## Ostrich Farms

There are three ostrich show farms, each open daily and offering a guided tour of about two hours: Safari Ostrich Farm (☎ (044) 272 7311), 6km from town on the Mossel Bay road; Highgate Ostrich Farm (☎ (044) 272 7115), 10km from town, signposted turn-off from the Mossel Bay road; and Cango Ostrich Farm (☎ (044) 272 4623), 14km from town on the Cango Caves road. Admission is about R18. Ring for details, especially if you are interested in activities like ostrich racing.

Some people find the Cango farm the least commercial (and it now has a butterfly farm attached), but others say that Highgate is the best.

## Cango Caves

These heavily commercialised but spectacular caves are 30km from town. There's a restaurant and curio complex and a choice of three hourly tours, costing R10, R18 and R25. The R10 tour is very brief – it's better to choose a longer tour. The R25 tour involves some crawling through tight places. A reader says that this isn't so good for asthmatics because of the high humidity (although our particular asthma prefers high humidity to low humidity).

There's a restaurant, and takeaways are available.

If you continue on past the Cango Mountain Resort (a pleasant camping and chalet complex) up the dirt road for 8km, you'll come to the pretty **Rust en Vrede Waterfall**, which runs year-round. The falls are in a reserve which closes at 4.30 pm.

## Klein Karoo Nasionale Kunstefees

The new Little Karoo National Arts Festival (with the unfortunate acronym of KKK) is held in Oudtshoorn in early autumn. It was established as an Afrikaans festival to support arts and culture in that language, which is the first language of a majority of whites and nearly all coloureds, and the second language of many blacks. The festival has great potential for bridging the huge gulfs separating many Afrikaans speakers,

### Oudtshoorn & Ostriches

The Oudtshoorn region was settled in the early 19th century, and the town itself was proclaimed in 1863. Its development is intertwined with the growth of the ostrich-feather industry, which began around 1870. By the turn of the 20th century, feathers were a highly fashionable trimming for ladies' hats and clothing in Europe.

The growers around Oudtshoorn came to be known as feather barons. An average ostrich

DAVID WALL

cock would yield around 10 kg of feathers a year, the feathers were easily transportable and they commanded incredible prices. The industry boomed in the years before WWI, and at its height there were 750,000 ostriches in the region. The feather barons built ostentatious palaces with their profits.

During the war, feathers fell from grace as a fashion item. They have never recovered their former position, yet the industry continues. Feathers are still used by the fashion industry, and in dusters. Skins are used for handbags, shoes and wallets, and the ostrich meat is dried and cured to make biltong.

It is still possible to see signs of the boom years around Oudtshoorn, but many of the palaces have either fallen into ruin or remain in private hands. ■

but for the moment at least it is discovering the pitfalls of trying to do so.

The 1997 festival was marred by drunken Afrikaner racists hurling abuse (and beer cans) at non-white acts, but it also showcased that rare part of Afrikanerdom, the radical fringe of Afrikaner youth culture. It takes a lot of guts to go against the conservative norms of Afrikanerdom and as a result many of these acts weren't wishy-washy liberal but very confrontational, exploring sexual and racial taboos.

Between this 'depravity' and being expected to applaud non-whites, it's no wonder that many ordinary Afrikaners found the festival a rather bewildering experience. Long may it run.

### Places to Stay – bottom end

*NA Smit Caravan Park* (☎ (044) 272 4152), on Park Rd, has sites for R35/40 in the low/high season, rondavels from R75/100 for two and chalets. On the other side of town, *Kleinplaas Resort* (☎ (044) 272 5811) has sites from R45 (no tent sites in December and early January) and four-bed chalets for R180/200 in the low/high seasons.

*Backpackers' Oasis* (☎ (044) 279 1163), 3 Church St, is in a large and relaxed house with a good-sized yard and a decent pool. It's friendly and well run. They arrange budget tours to the ostrich farms and further afield, and they hire mountain bikes. They'll take you and your bike to the top of Swartberg Pass and you can ride back – that would be an amazing buzz. Dorm beds are R30, doubles are R75 and camping is R18 per person.

*Bedstop Accommodation* (☎ (044) 272 4746), 69 Van der Riet St, isn't in the same league as the guesthouses mentioned below but it's perfectly OK and charges from just R60. *Feather Inn* (☎ (044) 279 1727), on the corner of Hope and Hogg Sts, is a pub charging about R75 per person.

### Places to Stay – middle & top end

*La Pension* (☎ (044) 279 2445), 169 Church St, is a good place to stay. There's a good-sized pool, a sauna and a large garden. There's a range of accommodation types, from standard B&B to a two bedroom unit. Prices start at around R80/114 for singles/doubles.

Next door at 171 Church St, *Bisibee Guesthouse* (☎ (044) 272 4784) is a little more expensive, from R80/160, but it's excellent. It's a really pleasant old home in immaculate gardens, under the care of Isabé Fourie – highly recommended. Mrs Fourie's guesthouse was one of the first in Oudtshoorn and it remains one of the best.

Other B&Bs and guesthouses include *The Old Parsonage* (☎ (044) 272 4784), 141 Hogg St, and *Adley House* (☎ (044) 272 4533), 209 Jan van Riebeeck Rd. There are plenty of others – see the information centre for more details.

*Queen's Hotel* (☎ (044) 272 2101), on Baron van Rheede St, is an attractive old-style country hotel charging from R200/290, with breakfast. The *Holiday Inn* (☎ (044) 272 2201), on the corner of Baron van Rheede and Van der Riet Sts, has singles/doubles R270/520.

Out of town, the *Cango Mountain Resort* (☎ (044) 272 4506) is quite a way from the caves of the same name but is in similarly attractive country, with hills and trees and a reservoir/dam. Coming from Oudtshoorn take the signposted turn-off about 7km before the caves; the resort is another 3km along. Tent sites for two people cost R40/45 in the low/high season. Chalets start at R115 in the low season and go up to R205 for up to six people.

### Places to Eat

Most places serve ostrich in one form or another. *Godfather*, 61 Voortrekker St, is a bar and restaurant open daily for dinner only. As well as standards such as pasta (from R18), pizza (R15 to R40) and steaks (from R32), you can try springbok steaks (from R26) or exotic dishes such as ostrich antipasto (R32).

*De Fijne Keuken* (☎ (044) 272 6403), on Baron van Rheede St, comes highly recommended for its varied menu and good food. It serves everything from breakfast (R16.50) to main courses such as ostrich (from R36) and Karoo lamb (R28.5). Light meals such as pasta cost under R20. If you're staying at the hostel you get a discount.

*Headlines*, Baron van Rheede St, is pleasant enough in a kitsch sort of way. Soups are R8, chicken is from R25 and steaks start at R27. There are also snackier dishes. Next to Cheetahland is a member of the *Cranzgot's* pizza chain.

The *coffee shop* between the information centre and Queen's Hotel has crepes available for less than R10 and the coffee is good. Across the road from the information centre is *Bernard's Taphuis*, which serves Karoo country cuisine, with main courses for around R35.

### Getting There & Away

**Bus** Translux runs the Mountain Route three times a week. Fares from Oudtshoorn include: Cape Town, R100; Montagu, R40 (standby only); Knysna, R50 (standby only); and Port Elizabeth, R90.

Intercape, Greyhound and Translux stop in Oudtshoorn on the route between Knysna (Intercape runs to Plettenberg Bay) and Jo'burg/Pretoria. Translux fares from Oudtshoorn include Bloemfontein, R180; Kimberley, R180; and Jo'burg, R230.

There are more transport options down in George than in Oudtshoorn, and a Garden Line Transport workers' bus runs between George and Oudtshoorn for R9.50. Unfortunately it departs Oudtshoorn at 5.30 am.

**Train** The weekly *Southern Cross* between Cape Town and Port Elizabeth stops here.

**Minibus Taxi** Taxis aren't easy to find – try Union St near the Spar supermarket.

### UNIONDALE

An old fort overlooks Uniondale, and there is a great landscape of flat-topped Karoo koppies to the north. The town is surrounded by rocky hills and wheat fields, pointing to the increased rainfall. Further south of the spectacular Uniondale Port, the narrow Kouga and Kammanassie valleys, known as the Long Kloof, are quite different again. They are only one range from the sea and are green and fertile, with fruit trees and ostrich farms.

The information office (☎ (044) 752 1024) can tell you about B&Bs. A reader recommends *The Cottages Guesthouse* (☎ (044) 752 1354) on Voortrekker St, which charges about R65 per person.

# The Karoo

Although some of the Karoo is in Western Cape, it doesn't respect provincial boundaries and sprawls into Eastern and Northern Cape as well. The section of the Karoo around the lovely town of Graaff-Reinet is possibly the most interesting – see the Karoo section in the Eastern Cape Province chapter.

The term Karoo is used to describe most of the old Cape Province interior, and covers almost one-third of South Africa's total area. It lies on the great South African plateau and is demarcated in the south and west by the coastal mountain ranges, and to the east and north by the mighty Orange River.

The population is sparse; off the main highways you can drive for hours without seeing another car. It is certainly not an untouched wilderness – the San and Khoikhoi who roamed the region and hunted vast herds of antelope have gone, replaced by farmers and sheep. Despite this, the Karoo feels untouched. There are very few obvious signs of human occupation, apart from the roads snaking over the plains.

Although the main Karoo towns are all linked by public transport, it is best to have a vehicle. There's nothing like stopping in the middle of nowhere, listening to the silence and wandering off the road into the veld. The road network is excellent; even the unsealed roads are of a high standard.

### PRINCE ALBERT

Prince Albert is a beautiful, peaceful little town, dozing on the edge of the Karoo at the foot of the Swartberg Pass. You can easily visit on a day trip from Oudtshoorn or the coast. I'd prefer to stay in Prince Albert and make a day trip to Oudtshoorn, although we have had reports of overt racism from one of the places to stay and the people we met at the information centre were somewhat old-fashioned in this respect.

The town was founded in 1762 and there are some interesting examples of Cape

## Flat, Hot & Boring?

For some people the Karoo means nothing more than flat hot roads and a long and boring trip between Johannesburg and Cape Town. For others, however, the Karoo is one of the most exhilarating regions in South Africa.

As for being flat, some parts are. But others are mountainous, and you are rarely out of sight of a spectacular range hovering on the horizon. The Swartruggens, the Komsberg, the Hantamsberg, the Nuweveldberg, the Groot Swartberg, the Sneeuberg, the Bankberg, and the Baviaanskloofberg, and the Grootwinterhoekberg are just some of the Karoo ranges over 1500m (a number top 2000m).

The Karoo mountains and hills change colour depending on your proximity, the time of the day, or the weather. They are blue or black in the distance, but close up they reveal reds, yellows and oranges. They form fantastic shapes, although many take the classic Karoo form – dolerite-capped koppies, which are flat-topped, and sheer sided. There are a number of spectacular mountain passes, particularly around Oudtshoorn.

There are some interesting old towns, richly endowed with distinctive architecture (especially Graaff-Reinet). Many towns, however, are isolated backwaters, service centres for the surrounding countryside, but this gives them a quiet charm. They seem far removed from the problems of the 20th century.

The seemingly inhospitable environment also produces a fascinating flora of two main sorts: succulents and woody shrubs. The drier the country (the further west you go) the more succulents there are – and they're weird. There are mesembryanthemums, euphorbias and aloes, among others. The woody shrubs need somewhat easier conditions and include pentzias, daisies and saltbushes.

As for being hot, summer temperatures average 33°C but can go a lot higher. The moment the sun sets, however, the temperature plummets. In winter, frosts are common, although day-time temperatures average a pleasant 18°C. Rain is distributed fairly evenly over the year, the main fall occurring in March and April. The best time to visit is spring or autumn when the weather is fine and temperatures during the day are in the mid-20°Cs. Since the main rainfall is likely to be in autumn, this is also when the wild flowers are at their best, although in some areas (notably around Prince Albert), September is the best month to view them. ■

Dutch, Victorian and Karoo styles. The real world seems to have passed it by.

Despite being surrounded by very harsh country, the town is green and fertile, thanks to the run-off from the mountains. A system of original water channels runs through town and most houses have a sluice gate, which they are entitled to open for a certain number of hours each week. Arriving here after a long, hot drive through the Karoo is wonderful – just seeing trees again is refreshing. Peaches, apricots and grapes are grown.

Ostriches, which are surprisingly fragile creatures in their infancy, are reared here from hatching to three months old because of the kind climate.

The **Fransie Pienaar Museum** is open from 2 to 5 pm on weekdays.

### Places to Stay & Eat

*The Prince Albert of Saxe-Coburg Lodge* (☎ (04436) 267) is on the main street, across from the hotel, and charges from R60 per person, with breakfast. The owners are very experienced hikers and a great source of information. They also offer guided hikes.

On the south (Swartberg Pass) edge of town, Elaine Hurford's *Dennehof Karoo Guesthouse* (☎ (04436) 227) is in the town's oldest house (dating to 1835). As well as the usual accommodation, there's also the self-contained Olyfhuis (Olive House) in its own little vineyard. Backpackers can stay here for R50. Elaine can also arrange package tours that include accommodation, meals and activities.

There are several other guesthouses in town (see the list on the museum's verandah) and it seems likely that more will open.

The *Swartberg Hotel* (☎ (04436) 332), 77 Church St (the main street), is a nice old pub which is being renovated. Rates include breakfast and start at R160/250 a single/double. The dining room provides excellent dinners, as well as next door in the café where good meals and snacks are also served during the day.

*Sampie se Plaasstal* on the main street is a farm-produce stall but much, much better than most. They sell dried fruit (including *meëbos*, parchment-like sheets), nuts, game meat, biltong and some delicious home-made pastries.

### Getting There & Away

Most people visit by driving over one of the area's passes from Oudtshoorn, or from the N1 between Cape Town and Jo'burg. However, if you've come for hiking there's no reason not to take a train, which is cheaper than the buses.

**Bus** The nearest Intercape, Translux and Greyhound stop (on the run between Cape Town and Jo'burg/Pretoria) is at Laingsburg, 120km or so away, but you can arrange to be dropped at Prince Albert Rd, the railway halt. Some places to stay in Prince Albert will collect you from here.

**Train** The nearest train station is Prince Albert Rd, 45km north-west of Prince Albert. The daily *Trans Karoo* between Cape Town and Jo'burg stops here, and some places to stay in Prince Albert will collect you. First/2nd/3rd class fares from Prince Albert Rd to Cape Town are R98/68/41; to Jo'burg they are R238/161/100.

**Minibus Taxi** There must be some sort of public transport between Prince Albert and the rest of the world but we couldn't find any. White citizens grudgingly admitted that there might be some taxis 'for the coloured people' running to Oudtshoorn, but the guys pumping petrol at the garage (usually the best place to ask about taxis) said that there weren't any. Let us know if you have better luck.

**Car & Motorcycle** Coming from Beaufort West, it's worth leaving the N12 at Seekoegar and then cutting across some bleak Karoo on a dirt road. Otherwise, leave the N1

at Kruidfontein or Prince Albert Rd. Coming from Oudtshoorn, you have the choice between taking the Swartberg Pass or the marginally less spectacular and longer route via Meiringspoort.

### AROUND PRINCE ALBERT

Prince Albert is a good base for both seeing the Karoo and hiking on the more than 100km of trails in the Swartberg. Overnight walks have to be booked through Cape Nature Conservation (☎ (0443) 29 1739) and cost about R15 per night. **Tierberg Trails** offer a rare opportunity for long walks through the Karoo.

There's a good drive east to **Klaarstroom** (another interesting old town) along the foot of the mountains. The road runs along a nice valley, overwhelmed by the Groot Swartberg range, which is cut by more dramatic gullies, clefts and waterfalls. On the R329 between Prince Albert (40km) and Klaarstroom (10km), **Remhoogte Hiking Trail** can be walked in about five hours but there is a camping place on the trail.

**Meiringspoort**, south of Klaarstroom and on the N12 route between Beaufort West and Oudtshoorn, is extraordinary, following a river that cuts right through the Swartberg range. It's not quite in the same class as Swartberg Pass, partly because it's a main road and partly because it's not as deep or as narrow.

### Hell

In a narrow valley in the Swartberg range is Hell, or **Gamkaskloof**. The first citizens of Hell were early trekboers, who developed their own dialect. There was no road into Hell until the 1960s and the few goods that the self-sufficient community needed were carried by donkey from Prince Albert. Maybe it's a coincidence, but within 30 years of the roads being built all the farmers had left. Now the area is part of a nature reserve and there is a camp site.

The road to Hell (paved with dirt) turns off the Swartberg Pass road about 20km from Prince Albert and extends for another 47km, passing through **Seweweekspoort Pass**.

## Swartberg Pass

Swartberg Pass, a route between the Little Karoo and the Karoo, is arguably the most spectacular in the country. It's 24km long and reaches nearly 1600m in height; it's another Thomas Bain pass, built between 1881 and 1888.

Proteas, watsonias and other fynbos are prolific. After the summit (*Die Top*), where there are incredible views over the bleak Karoo and, on the other side, the greenery of the Little Karoo, the road meanders down into a fantastic geology of twisted sedimentary layers. The best picnic sites are on the north side; the gorge narrows and in spring is full of pelargoniums. There are quiet spots where you can sunbathe or swim.

Don't be put off by the warning signs at each end of the pass. It's a fairly easy drive as long as you take it very slowly. The road is narrow, there are very long drops and many of the corners are blind. The pass is sometimes closed after bad storms – some very bad storms in 1996 caused extensive damage and there might still be problems on this road. Ask at Prince Albert or Oudtshoorn about the current situation. ■

This is an incredibly narrow gorge with raw, multicoloured rocks and mountains towering above. The road follows a stream and there are several good spots to picnic. You have to return the same way, but this is not a hardship. If possible, allow yourself the best part of a day to explore (or try hiking from Prince Albert).

## BEAUFORT WEST

Beaufort West is the archetypal stopover town, although it also serves as an important centre for the Karoo. There must be more service stations here per head than in any other town in South Africa. It is not completely lacking in appeal, but most people will be happy to snatch a cold drink, a few litres of petrol and perhaps a sleep.

In summer Beaufort West is a sluice gate in the torrent of South Africans heading for the coast. Accommodation is booked out and prices rise. Maybe because this is such a travel crossroads, there are a lot of kids begging aggressively.

Dr Christiaan Barnard (who performed the first heart transplant) was born here and there's a small museum. The Karoo National Park, 12km out of the town, is definitely worth visiting and also has excellent accommodation.

### Places to Stay & Eat

*Beaufort West Caravan Park* (☎ (0201) 2800), at the south end of Donkin St, the main street, is an ex-municipal park, now privatised. It would do. They have on-site caravans for hire at R32.50 per person and tent sites at R32.50 for two. If you do have camping equipment and transport, however, go to the Karoo National Park.

There are many places offering 'overnight rooms'. The best deal is at *Donkin House* (☎ (0201) 4287), 14 Donkin St (north end). It's fairly basic but friendly and rooms cost just R50 per person. There might also be dorms. Across the road and up a notch or two is *Christie's Overnight* (☎ (0201) 51682), with rates starting a little higher than those at Donkin House. If you demand sterile environs, try the *Formule 1* (☎ (0201) 52421), 144 Donkin St, at R114 for up to three people.

*Karoo Lodge* (☎ (0201) 3877) on the corner of Donkin and Kerk Sts offers simple overnight accommodation in a big old pub for R75/150 with breakfast. It's reasonable but pretty spartan.

The town's older hotels are suffering from this competition and are fading fast. The *Oasis Hotel* (☎ (0201) 3221) is large and uninspiring, with fair single/double rooms from R95/160. The *Royal Hotel* (☎ (0201) 3241) is a little more expensive and a little better, although the rooms don't have direct-dial phones.

*Ye Olde Thatch* (☎ (0201) 2209), 155 Donkin St, has four guest suites from R95 to R170 a double. The *restaurant* here is the best place to eat in town, and it charges less than the franchised *Saddles* steakhouse next to the Formule 1.

## Getting There & Away

**Bus** Beaufort West is a junction for many bus services. Most buses stop on Donkin St outside the Oasis Hotel. The hotel is the Translux agent.

**Jo'burg/Cape Town** Intercape, Translux and Greyhound stop here on their daily service between Jo'burg/Pretoria and Cape Town. Both run via Bloemfontein and Translux has another service running via Kimberley five times a week. Intercape also alternates between Bloemfontein and Kimberley. Fares from Beaufort West with Translux include: Cape Town, R170; Paarl, R155; Bloemfontein, R135; Kimberley, R145; and Jo'burg, R240.

**Jo'burg/Garden Route** Greyhound and Translux run between Jo'burg and Knysna. Greyhound runs via Bloemfontein and Translux alternates between Bloemfontein and Kimberley. From Beaufort West the Translux fare to Oudtshoorn is R50 and to Mossel Bay, George or Knysna it's R120. Intercape runs twice a week between Plettenberg Bay and Jo'burg via Bloemfontein at slightly cheaper fares.

**Cape Town/Eastern Cape/Durban** Translux runs between Cape Town and East London five times a week. Stops and fares from Beaufort West include: Graaff-Reinet, R125; Cradock, R125; Queenstown, R155; King William's Town, R180; and East London, R180. Most days there's also a Translux service between Cape Town and Durban (R265 from Beaufort West) that runs a roundabout route through Bloemfontein (R135) and the Free State highlands.

City to City runs daily between Cape Town to Umtata (about R120 from Beaufort West). Transtate's cheaper service between Cape Town and Umtata also stops here.

**Train** The train station is on Kerk St. The *Trans Karoo* stops here on the daily journey between Cape Town and Jo'burg. The southbound train arrives in Beaufort West at 4.23 am and the northbound at 6.05 pm. From Beaufort West to Cape Town 1st/2nd/3rd class tickets are R122/84/51; from Beaufort West to Jo'burg they are R214/145/90.

**Minibus Taxi** Most taxis stop at the BP station at the south end of Donkin St, not far from the caravan park. Destinations include Cape Town (R80), Oudtshoorn (R40) and King William's Town (R70).

## KAROO NATIONAL PARK

Although the Karoo dominates the South African plateau, it was for many years neglected by conservationists. People are now beginning to appreciate the landscapes and the fragile ecosystems and extraordinary flora that have evolved to survive the region's climatic extremes.

The Karoo National Park was proclaimed in 1979 and covers 33,000 hectares of impressive Karoo landscapes and representative flora. The plains carry a variety of short shrubs, with well-wooded dry watercourses and mountain grasslands at higher elevations.

The park has 61 species of mammal, the most common of which are dassies and bat-eared foxes. The antelope population is small, but some species have been reintroduced and their numbers are growing. These include springbok, kudu, gemsbok, reedbuck, red hartebeest and rhebok. Mountain zebra have also been reintroduced as has the odd rhino.

## Information

The entrance gates are open from 5 am to 10 pm and the main reception desk is open from 7.30 am to 8 pm. Day visitors are charged R13 per vehicle. There's a shop and an à la carte restaurant. There are two short nature trails and an 11km day walk, in addition to the Springbok Hiking Trail. There are also day or overnight 4WD guided trails.

## Springbok Hiking Trail

The Springbok trail goes through a variety of habitats and altitudes and provides magnificent views. A maximum of 12 people are permitted on the trail, which is now open all year, on the premise that if people are crazy enough to hike in a Karoo summer it's probably best to let them. It's a three day, two night trail. Hikers stay overnight in huts, and the cost is R60 per person.

## Places to Stay

Bookings should be made through the

National Parks Board. The cottages and chalets are all new and of a high standard – they are fully equipped and air-conditioned. Rates start at R220 for two people in a chalet. There's also a very pleasant and inexpensive caravan park.

## MATJIESFONTEIN

Matjiesfontein (pronounced 'mikeys...') is a small railway siding that has remained virtually unchanged for 100 years, its impressive buildings incongruous in the bleak Karoo landscape. People stop here on their way to/from Jo'burg – if not for a night, at least for a cup of coffee.

A night in the hotel would be worth a stopover on the train trip between Jo'burg and Cape Town, although 24 hours in Matjiesfontein might be a bit long unless you have a good book. You could take the train here from Cape Town (arriving at 2.46 pm), stay the night and catch the 8.25 am train back again next day. It's a 5½ hour trip.

The developer of the hotel and the other establishments was one Jimmy Logan, who once ran every railway refreshment room between the Cape and Bulawayo. Matjiesfontein was his home base, and the hotel and other accommodation, together with the dry climate, attracted wealthy people as a health resort.

As well as the attractive old buildings there's a museum (R2) in the train station that's worth a look.

### Places to Stay

The very grand *Lord Milner Hotel* (☎ (023) 551 3011) is a period piece with rooms from R155/240 with breakfast (no children under 12). One of the grander rooms has twin baths! The same people also run a nearby (everything in this village is 'nearby') renovated *boarding house* with rooms at R125/190 with breakfast.

### Getting There & Away

The daily *Trans Karoo* between Cape Town and Jo'burg stops here. Fares to Jo'burg in 1st/2nd/3rd class are R261/177/110; to Cape Town they're just R75/52/31.

# Garden Route

The heavily promoted Garden Route encompasses a beautiful bit of coastline from Still Bay in the west to just beyond Plettenberg Bay in the east.

The narrow coastal plain is often forested, and is mostly bordered by extensive lagoons which run behind a barrier of sand dunes and superb white beaches. Inland, its boundary is the Outeniqua and Tsitsikamma ranges, which are between 1000m and 1700m high. The semi-desert Karoo lies on the other side of the mountains and can be reached via several of the most spectacular passes in the country. The Garden Route has some of the most significant tracts of indigenous forest in the country – giant yellowwood trees and wildflowers like ericas, proteas, gladioli, arum lilies, strelitzia, watsonias and agapanthus. The forests are still harvested commercially and there are also large eucalypt and pine plantations.

The climate is kind. Average minimum temperatures are around 13°C in winter and average maximums only reach the mid-20s in summer (although it can be as high as 40°C). There's plenty of sun throughout the year, but the best weather is likely to be in February and March, and the highest chance of rainfall and grey days is from August to October.

The area is a favourite for all water sports: swimming, surfing, fishing and sailing. Most people come just to laze in the sun and, if the weather becomes cloudy, to tackle some of the numerous short walks along the coast or in the hills.

Although the Garden Route is unquestionably beautiful, it is also quite heavily (and tackily) developed – reminiscent in some ways of Australia's east coast. Prices jump by at least 30% in mid-season (late January to May) and more than double over the high season (December, January and Easter). Unless you're staying in hostels you might find the prices and the crowds ridiculous in the high season.

There are a couple of national parks and some other reserves along this bit of coast, but they are small and the walking trails in the national parks are very poor indeed, being ill-constructed and poorly maintained – so few people use them. (The Elephant Trails near Knysna were much better.) The long-distance trails, for which you have to book well in advance, are the thing to do, but as short trails they are terrible, and the bits we've seen of the long ones are just as bad ... particularly as no flexibility is allowed and one must stay in huts with dozens of other people.

**Noel Gross**

### Travelling the Route

Transport connections are good. Both the Baz Bus (see the introductory Getting Around chapter) and the Garden Route Hopper (☎ (041) 55 4000; fax 55 8402 or book at hostels) offer hop-on, hop-off services between Cape Town and the Garden Route. They run door-to-door between hostels and other places to stay. The Hopper offers a daily service (the Baz Bus probably will soon) and runs as far east as Cintsa near East London. Cape Town to Cintsa with unlimited stopovers costs R300, and you can buy shorter sectors. Tickets are valid for 27 years!

Travelling between neighbouring Garden Route towns with the major bus lines is very expensive and you can't book short sectors, so unless you have a pass with Baz or the Hopper you should take minibus taxis or hitch.

Translux (☎ (021) 405 3333), Greyhound (☎ (021) 418 4310) and Intercape Mainliner (☎ (021) 386 4400) run at least daily from Cape Town to Port Elizabeth via the main Garden Route towns and there are also some

cheaper options, both buses and minibus taxis. The weekly *Southern Cross* train between Cape Town and Port Elizabeth stops in some Garden Route towns. See Getting There & Away in the Cape Town section earlier in this chapter for details of transport from that city.

The three companies also run between Jo'burg/Pretoria and the Garden Route.

> ### Just a lot of Hype?
> Feedback from readers is evenly divided between those who think our coverage of the Garden Route is too negative and those who think we give it too much attention.
>
> The sort of time you have on the Garden Route depends on what you want to do and how you're travelling. The main attractions are the beaches and the forests, although the latter are probably more of an attraction to South Africans, for whom forests are a rarity. There are some excellent walks, and it's worthwhile buying a copy of *On Foot in the Garden Route* by Judith Hopley, paperback and hardback, R32. It's sold in some of the information centres along the Garden Route.
>
> Backpackers are well catered for, with plenty of hostels in hot competition to make sure you have a good time and stay as long as possible. The hostels also make it feasible for those on a budget to stay during the peak summer season, when prices at other places soar. Still, you'd be advised to book ahead whether you're staying in a hostel or an up-market hotel.
>
> Remember, if you depart from South Africa without having seen the Garden Route it isn't a disaster; if you depart having seen *only* the Garden Route, it might be. ∎

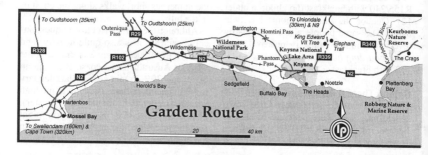

Greyhound and Translux run to Knysna and Intercape goes further, to Plettenberg Bay. Heading south, Greyhound has services on Thursday and Sunday, Translux on Monday, Tuesday, Wednesday, Friday and Saturday, and Intercape on Tuesday and Friday. Northbound, there are Greyhound services on Monday and Friday, Translux on Monday, Tuesday, Thursday, Friday and Sunday, and Intercape on Sunday and Thursday.

From the Garden Route, fares to Pretoria are the same as fares to Jo'burg; add an hour of travelling time.

### Between Jo'burg and the Garden Route with Translux

| Knysna to | Fare | Hours |
|---|---|---|
| George | R40 | 1 |
| Mossel Bay | R50 | 1¾ |
| Oudtshoorn | R50 | 3 |
| Beaufort West | R120 | 5½ |
| Kimberley | R195 | 11 |
| Bloemfontein | R230 | 10¼ |
| Jo'burg | R250 | 17 |

| Jo'burg to | Fare | Hours |
|---|---|---|
| Bloemfontein | R160 | 6 |
| Kimberley | R165 | 6½ |
| Beaufort West | R240 | 12 |
| Oudtshoorn | R250 | 14½ |
| Mossel Bay | R250 | 15¾ |
| George | R250 | 16½ |
| Knysna | R250 | 17 |

From Port Elizabeth (see the Eastern Cape Province chapter) you can connect with buses to East London, Umtata and Durban.

There are many, many tours of the Garden Route, with the more mainstream operators charging around R2500/4400 a single/ double on a three night, four day tour. Backpackers (and anyone else) can pay considerably less and probably have a better time on Lisa's tour (☎ (082) 414 4294), which costs around R800 for three nights/ four days. Just don't drink too much of her *mampoes* (a sort of very strong schnapps) or you'll sleep through it all!

### STILL BAY

Still Bay (Stilbaai) is a large, middle-class holiday village. It's on a lovely part of the coast with a large river inlet, but the town itself is rather ugly. The time-share cowboys are starting to move in. For surfers, there's a very good-quality right-point break with long rides. It's best in winter, like most south-coast breaks; south-westerlies are offshore.

There's a *caravan park* and *holiday cottages*.

### MOSSEL BAY

Mossel Bay (Mosselbaai) was once one of the jewels of the Garden Route, although there's quite a lot of sprawl now, mainly due to the Mossgas gas/petrol conversion refinery on the outskirts. Despite this it's still a fairly sleepy country town, with some pretty sandstone buildings, and it claims to have the mildest climate in the world (whatever that means). It also has the only north-facing beach in the country.

The first European to visit the bay was the

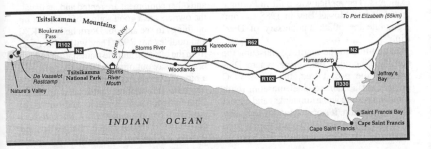

Portuguese explorer Bartholomeu Dias in 1488, and he was followed by Vasco da Gama in 1497. From then on, many ships stopped to take on fresh water, and to barter for provisions with the Gouriqua Khoikhoi who lived in the region. A large milkwood tree beside the spring was used as a postal collection point – expeditions heading east would leave mail to be picked up by ships returning home.

The spring and the tree still exist, and you can post letters (they receive a special post mark) from a mail box on the site.

European farmers established themselves in the area in the second half of the 18th century. In 1786 the Dutch East India Company constructed a granary (not far from the post office tree and now part of the museum complex) and Mossel Bay developed as a port. It has been a holiday centre for some time too – at The Point are some ramshackle beach shacks which have attained 'historic' status.

### Orientation & Information

The town lies on the northern slopes of Cape St Blaize. The museum complex, which overlooks the bay, is the best place to start your exploration. The information centre (☎ (0444) 91 2202) is nearby on Market St.

### Bartholomeu Dias Museum Complex

The highlight of the complex is the replica of the vessel that Dias used on his 1488 voyage of discovery. This caravel is incredibly small. Seeing it brings home the extraordinary skill and courage of the early explorers. The replica was built in Portugal and sailed to Mossel Bay in 1988 to commemorate the 500th anniversary of Dias' trip.

In addition to the maritime museum, the complex includes the spring where Dias watered the postal tree, the 1786 VOC granary, an acclaimed shell museum (with some interesting aquarium tanks) and a local history museum. It's open Monday to Friday from 9 am to 1 pm and 2 to 5 pm, Saturday from 10 am to 1 pm and Sunday from 2 to 5 pm.

### Boat Trips

Two boats, the *Infante* and the *Romonza*, offer daily (hourly, sometimes) boat trips to Seal Island for about R30, from the harbour behind the train station. In late winter and spring it's not unusual to see whales on the trip.

### Diving

Diaz Pro-Dive (☎ (0444) 7293), by the harbour, offers NAUI, and Mossel Bay Divers (☎ (0444) 91 1441), in the Protea Santos Hotel, offers PADI courses.

**Shark Diving** Although there are several shark diving outfits operating out of Cape Town, several readers have written to recommend Infante Shark Diving in Mossel Bay, both for the price (about R400) and the experience. The information centre has details.

### Jumping

Both bridge jumping and bungie jumping are offered near Mossel Bay – the hostels and the information centre have details.

### Places to Stay

There are two adjacent municipal caravan parks (*Bakke* and *Santos*) on the pretty Dias Strand, the bay beach, and also *Punt* on The Point, a little further from the town centre but close to the surf. Contact both these places on ☎ (0444) 91 2915. All have chalets and tent sites from R30 to R65 in peak season.

*Mossel Bay Backpackers* (☎ (0444) 91 3182) is on the corner of Mint and Marsh Sts, not far from The Point. It is run by the owners of the guesthouse around the corner. Bikes and other equipment are rented and, as usual, the owners are a good source of information on things to see and do. Dorm beds are R30 and doubles are R90. They will collect you from the bus stop and the train station (which is some way out of town). Another place in a nice old house has opened at 121 High St (from the information centre head up Kerk/ Church St for several blocks and turn right into High St). It's called *Park Backpackers* (☎ (0444) 91 1800) and it charges around R25 for a dorm bed.

Right on Santos Beach you can stay in an old (well, disused) train called the *Santos Express* (☎ (0444) 91 1995). Out of season you can stay for R30 (R55 with breakfast) but in season you have to pay for a whole coupe (R75, sleeps two) or compartment (R125, sleeps four). You need your own bedding. Things are a bit cramped but you can't beat the position.

There are quite a few guesthouses and B&Bs in town; the information centre has a list. Not far from the museum, the *Old Post Office Tree Guesthouse* (☎ (0444) 91 3738) is a very comfortable setup, more like a hotel than a guesthouse in size. It has a great view overlooking the bay. Singles/doubles start at around R215/350.

There's nothing terribly wrong with the *Ocean View Hotel* (☎ (0444) 3711), but it's too big and too depressingly 60s to be attractive. Rooms cost from R85/130, rising steeply in summer. *Protea Santos* (☎ (0444) 7103) has a good position overlooking the bay. A hassle is that the staff can't actually tell you how much the rooms cost more than a day or so in advance. You'll probably pay around R250, but who knows?

In Danabaai, a small coastal village just west of Mossel Bay, *Friends B&B* (☎ (0444) 98 1269), 35 Erica St, has been recommended by several readers and locals. It costs about R95 per person but it is apparently well worth the money. You can arrange horse-riding and surfing lessons. On the R328 midway between Mossel Bay and Oudtshoorn, *Eight Bells Mountain Inn* (☎ (0444) 95 1544) is a mid-range place that gets good feedback.

### Places to Eat

The *Gannet Restaurant* (part of the Old Post Office Tree Guesthouse near the museum) has a bright and informal atmosphere. At lunch you'll spend between R40 and R60, a little more at dinner.

The *Pavilion* is right on Santos Beach, in a 19th century bathing pavilion. There are snacks for about R20; line fish start at R35, and steaks at R45.

*Nello's Pizzeria & Coffee Bar* is in the courtyard of Vintcent Place, a Georgian building on the corner of Marsh and Bland Sts in the centre of town. Nello is Italian and his food is authentic. Pizzas start at around R15. Further along Marsh St at the corner of Kloof St is the *Bay Tavern*, a local pub in a renovated sandstone building. It has reasonable pub food such as fish and chips (R18), bangers and mash (R20) and huge steaks (R25 to R40).

*At The Point* is a franchised steakhouse.

### Getting There & Away

**Bus** Mossel Bay is off the highway and long-distance buses don't come into town but drop you at the Voorbaai Shell station, 7km from town. The hostels can usually collect you if you give notice.

Greyhound, Intercape and Translux stop here on their Cape Town to Port Elizabeth services. Translux fares include: Cape Town, R95; Knysna, R55 (you can't book this sector); Plettenberg Bay, R90; and Port Elizabeth, R115.

Translux stops in Mossel Bay on its route between Knysna and Jo'burg, via either Bloemfontein or Kimberley. Fares from Mossel Bay include: Knysna, R50 (you can't book this sector); Bloemfontein, R230; Kimberley, R195; and Jo'burg, R250. A similar service is offered by Greyhound at similar prices and Intercape runs between Plettenberg Bay and Jo'burg via the Garden Route at slightly lower prices.

Most backpackers use either the Baz Bus or the Garden Route Hopper.

**Minibus Taxi** See Getting There & Away in the Cape Town section earlier in this chapter for information on a door-to-door service for the Garden Route.

### GEORGE

George is a large, prosperous town that bills itself as the capital of the Garden Route. It was founded in 1811 and lies on a coastal plateau at the foot of the Outeniqua range, 432km east of Cape Town, 320km west of Port Elizabeth and 8km from the coast. It's one of the fastest-growing towns in South

Africa and has a population of over 75,000 people.

The town is pleasant enough, with lots of trees and a good selection of restaurants (both unusual in South Africa). It's not a bad place to spend a night but unless you have a car it's too far from the coast. However, there are some good hikes and one or two outfits running interesting adventure activities.

### Orientation & Information

George is a large place and quite spread out. The N2 enters town from the south on York St, which is a long, four lane avenue, terminating at a T-junction with Courtenay St – west for Oudtshoorn, east for Wilderness. The main commercial area is on the east side of York St around Hibernia and Market Sts.

The tourist office (☎ (0441) 863 9295/6), 124 York St, has a lot of information and some handy maps.

The Market Lane shopping centre has a few craft shops and places to stop for a coffee. On Tuesday and Friday a *boeremark* (farmers' market) is held here from 7 am to mid-morning. There's a laundromat at 57 York St.

### George Museum

The town's old drostdy (1813) houses the museum and has general exhibits on the surrounding area, particularly on the timber industry. There is also a large collection of antique instruments. It's open weekdays from 9 am to 4.30 pm, and Saturday from 9 am to 12.30 pm. PW Botha, last of the hardline apartheid presidents, hails from this area and there are (or were) displays on his career.

### Outeniqua Choo-Tjoe

One of the prime reasons to visit George is the famous *Outeniqua Choo-Tjoe*, a steam train running along a spectacular line to Knysna. Two trains run daily except Sunday and some public holidays, departing George at 9.30 am and 1 pm, and departing Knysna at 9.45 am and 2.15 pm. The fare to Knysna is R25, R35 return (valid for six months). Reservations are recommended. For more details contact Spoornet (☎ (0441) 73 8202).

The trip is fairly long (nearly three hours), so if you have to return to your starting point to collect your car, consider using the services of a company which will drive you back in a van. The tourist office has details.

### Activities

Seal Adventures (☎ (0441) 878 0325 or 083 654 8755) offers a good range of activities: abseiling (including a descent through a big waterfall), hiking, canoeing, horse-riding and mountain biking. As a guide to prices, an abseiling trip which also involves hiking and canoeing costs R155, including lunch. A full day's canoeing costs R100. They can pick you up from other Garden Route towns for a small fee.

### Places to Stay

*George Tourist Resort* (☎ (0441) 74 5205), York St, is a large caravan park about a 20 minute walk from the city centre. Rondavels cost from R140 for four people and there are more expensive chalets. Sites start at R40.

*George Backpackers' Hostel* (☎ (0441) 74 7807), 29 York St (the main road from the N2), is also quite a long walk south of the centre of town. The hostel is in a rather typical suburban house. There's a big garden with a pool, good facilities and a helpful manager. Dorm beds are R30, doubles are a low R80 and you can camp for R20. You can rent a bike, there are various outings, such as canoe trips, and guests get a discount on the *Outeniqua Choo-Tjoe* train fare.

The tourist office has lists of B&B places in and around town, starting at around R60 per person.

*George Lodge International* (☎ (0441) 74 6549), 86 Davidson Rd (left at the north end of York St), is very much an overnight stop, but it's not bad. Singles/doubles are about R110/150.

The old Outeniqua Hotel at 123 York St has been reincarnated as the *Protea Foresters Hotel* (☎ (0441) 74 4488) and charges from R250 a room. There are several top-end options such as the *King George III* (☎ (0441) 74 7659), from R310/365, and the

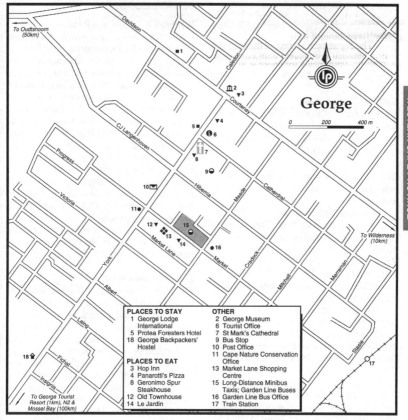

To Oudtshoorn (50km)

Davidson

Caledon

Courtenay

George

0    200    400 m

CJ Langenhoven

Progress

Hibernia

Meade

Cathedral

Victoria

Market Lane

York

Market

Cradock

Mitchell

Merriman

Albert

To Wilderness (10km)

Laing

Fichat

Staple

18

Insignia

To George Tourist Resort (1km); N2 & Mossel Bay (100km)

17

**PLACES TO STAY**
1 George Lodge International
5 Protea Foresters Hotel
18 George Backpackers' Hostel

**PLACES TO EAT**
3 Hop Inn
4 Panarotti's Pizza
8 Geronimo Spur Steakhouse
12 Old Townhouse
14 Le Jardin

**OTHER**
2 George Museum
6 Tourist Office
7 St Mark's Cathedral
9 Bus Stop
10 Post Office
11 Cape Nature Conservation Office
13 Market Lane Shopping Centre
15 Long-Distance Minibus Taxis; Garden Line Buses
16 Garden Line Bus Office
17 Train Station

*Fancourt Hotel* (☎ (0441) 70 8282), from R650.

**Places to Eat**

The *Copper Pot* (☎ (0441) 70 7378) is a very good restaurant serving interesting food at relatively high prices. If these are beyond you, just go next door to the *Wine Barrel* (☎ (0441) 70 7378), which shares a kitchen with the Copper Pot but is markedly cheaper. A good meal and drinks might cost R60. The Copper Pot is open from Tuesday to Friday for lunch and from 7 pm nightly except Sunday. The Wine Barrel is open on week-

days for lunch and from 6 pm nightly. Both restaurants have recently moved from the town centre to 12 Montague St in the suburb of Blanco (on the way to the Fancourt Hotel).

Another quality restaurant is the *Old Townhouse* (☎ (0441) 74 3663), 20 Market St. It's in an 1847 building (now a national monument) made from brick, mud and yellowwood.

*Hop Inn*, 70 Courtenay St, is a friendly bar and restaurant with a young crowd. The gimmick is a couple of old trains, but they have been used well – opening onto a decent-sized room – so they are not claustrophobic.

The menu is meat, meat and meat, with the odd seafood dish such as seafood T-bone. You'll pay around R30.

The *Signalman's Arms*, at the train station, is a pleasant pub loaded with railway memorabilia, with meals for about R20.

### Getting There & Away

**Air** SAA flies to George's PW Botha airport about 15km south of town. The full economy one-way fare from Cape Town is R445; from Jo'burg it's a pricey R787.

**Bus** Most buses stop in St Mark's Square, behind the Geronimo Spur steakhouse on the main street.

Greyhound, Intercape and Translux stop here on their services from Cape Town to Port Elizabeth. Translux fares include: Cape Town, R115; Mossel Bay, R40; Knysna, R55; Plettenberg Bay, R50; and Port Elizabeth, R100. See the Cape Town Getting There & Away section earlier in this chapter for more information.

Intercape, Greyhound and Translux also stop in George on the run between Knysna (runs from Plettenberg Bay) and Jo'burg via either Bloemfontein or Kimberley. Translux fares from George include: Knysna, R55; Bloemfontein, R230; Kimberley, R195; and Jo'burg, R250.

Chilwans Bus Services (☎ (021) 54 2506, 905 3910) has a useful (if slow and not luxurious) service from Cape Town to Port Elizabeth. Buses leave Cape Town on Friday and return on Sunday.

**Train** The weekly *Southern Cross* between Cape Town and Port Elizabeth stops here early Saturday morning heading east and on Sunday evening heading west. First/2nd/3rd class fares to Cape Town are R114/62/35; to Port Elizabeth they're R108/59/33.

**Minibus Taxi** The taxi park is on St Mark's Square. See Getting There & Away in the Cape Town entry earlier in this chapter for information on a door-to-door service running the Garden Route.

## AROUND GEORGE
### Montagu & Outeniqua Passes

It is hard to believe that a mere 20km from the green and fertile country around George, on the other side of the Outeniqua range, there is the dry semi-desert country of the Little Karoo. One interesting loop is out on the Montagu Pass and back on the Outeniqua Pass (from Oudtshoorn). The Montagu is a quiet dirt road that winds its way through the mountains; it was opened in 1843 and is now a national monument. Take a picnic, because there are some great picnic sites and beautiful fynbos to admire along the way. The views from the Outeniqua Pass are actually more spectacular than from the Montagu, but that is a main road so it's a lot more difficult to stop when you want to.

Note that Montagu Pass was severely damaged by storms in late 1996 and it wasn't immediately repaired due to a lack of funds.

### Seven Passes Road

The Seven Passes road to Knysna used to be the main road link, and it is easy to imagine how difficult and dangerous it must have been for the pioneers and their ox-wagons. The views are nice enough, but most of the countryside is now dominated by pine, gum trees and Port Jackson wattle, leaving only small patches of fynbos. The road is still unsurfaced for quite a way and parts are rough thanks to the timber trucks, so the trip will take two hours. The scenery is nice and comfortable rather than wild and dramatic. The views from the coastal road are more spectacular.

### Herold's Bay

There's nothing much in town except one small shop, but there is a pleasant though small beach and a beautiful bit of coast, just south of George. The town gets very crowded in the high season and on summer weekends, but it is a quiet and sleepy place at any other time.

*Herold's Bay Caravan Park* (☎ (0441) 872 9400) is a terrific spot close to the beach and has sites from about R35, more in season. *Dutton's Cove Resort* (☎ (0441) 872

9205) is an attractive village of comfortable rondavels and chalets (some sleeping up to six people) with great views overlooking Herold's Bay (it's about 1km up a very steep hill from the beach). It is recommended. There is a bewildering array of standards, seasons and sizes. Basically, two people pay from R90 in the lowest season. Prices rise in five steps to the highest season, when they start at R200.

### Victoria Bay
Victoria is a tiny, picturesque bay at the foot of steep cliffs, also south of George. There's a small beach and a cluster of holiday houses. It's a popular surf spot (perhaps the best surf on the Garden Route) with a right-point break, best with north-west winds. There's a *caravan park* (☎ (0441) 74 4040) and *Sea Breeze Holiday Cottages* (☎ (0441) 71 1583).

### WILDERNESS
Wilderness is no longer an apt description for this small holiday town, as holiday houses, resorts and hotels now sprinkle the hills. Still, it is a beautiful stretch of coast to the east and west with the blue sea, rolling breakers, miles of white sand, sheltered lagoons and the lush mountain hinterland that have made Wilderness a very popular destination. The N2 and the George-to-Knysna railway line parallel the coast, but everything is quite widely scattered, making life difficult if you don't have a vehicle.

The Wilderness Eco-Tourism Association (☎ (0441) 877 0045) runs the information centre and can help with accommodation bookings. It's open on weekdays from 8.30 am to 6 pm and from 8.30 am to 2 pm on Saturday.

### Places to Stay
*Lakes Holiday Resort* (☎ (0441) 877 1101) on the Touw River, off the N2 past Wilderness but before the Wilderness National Park, has excellent caravan facilities and free sailboarding and canoeing. Four-person cabins start at R145 for two people in the off-season and climb to R530 in the high

season; Likewise, camp sites jump from R40 to R100!

*Hikers' Inn* (☎ (0441) 877 0105), 362 Waterside Rd, gets good feedback. Dorms cost R30, doubles R80 and camping costs R40 for two. Also getting good feedback is *Fairy Knowe Backpackers* (☎ 0441) 847 1285), in a beautiful area just out of town, by the Touw River. You can get here on the *Outeniqua Choo-Tjoe* train (you need to tell them that you want to stop at Fairy Knowe station) or by driving into Wilderness, then following Waterside Rd (the continuation of the main street) to the Fairy Knowe turn-off, from where it's a couple of hundred metres.

*Wilderness Holiday Inn Garden Court* (☎ (0441) 91134) is right between the N2 and the beach, about 2km from Wilderness. Singles/doubles start at R274/348. The old *Fairy Knowe Hotel* (☎ (0441) 877 11004), on Dumbleton Rd, is on the banks of the Touw River; take Waterside Rd from Wilderness. There are riverside rooms and thatched rondavels. Rooms cost from R300. We've had the odd report that standards are slipping, but the good location means that you should at least check it out.

### Getting There & Away
Intercape's twice-daily service between Cape Town (R105, 5½ hours from Wilderness) and Port Elizabeth (R80, 4½ hours) stops here. Buses actually stop on the highway at Flat Rock. Greyhound also stops here and although Translux doesn't advertise a stop in Wilderness, you might be able to arrange it.

The most pleasant way to get here is on the *Outeniqua Choo-Tjoe* steam train from George or Knysna.

### WILDERNESS NATIONAL PARK
Wilderness National Park encompasses the area from Wilderness and the Touw River in the west to Sedgefield and the Goukamma Nature Reserve in the east. The southern boundary is the ocean and the northern boundary is the Outeniqua range. It covers a unique system of lakes, rivers, wetlands and

estuaries that are vital for the survival of many species.

There are three types of lakes in the park: drowned river valleys (like Swartvlei); drowned low-lying areas among the dune system (like Langvlei); and drowned basins that have been formed by wind action (like Rondevlei). The rich bird life includes the beautiful Knysna loerie and many species of kingfisher.

There are several nature trails taking in the lakes, the beach and the indigenous forest. The **Kingfisher Trail** is a day walk that traverses the region and includes a boardwalk across the intertidal zone of the Touw River. The lakes offer anglers, canoeists, windsurfers and sailors an ideal venue. Pedal boats and canoes can be hired at Wilderness Camp, and there is also a small shop.

Day visitors are charged R12 per vehicle. The reception office is open from 8 am to 1 pm and 2 to 5 pm.

### Places to Stay

Those who stay in the park are well placed to take advantage of the best that the Garden Route can offer – great beaches and walks. There are two camps: *Wilderness Camp* (4km east of Wilderness itself and a short walk from the beach) and *Ebb & Flow Camp*. Both offer camping for R45 for two people, plus R12 for additional people. Wilderness Camp has a range of accommodation, starting with six-berth caravans at R110 plus R15 per adult. Ebb & Flow has two-bed huts starting at R90 for two people. There are substantial discounts on camping and accommodation outside major school holidays.

Book accommodation through the National Parks Board, and camp sites direct with the park (☎ (0441) 877 1197).

### Getting There & Away

Wilderness Camp is signposted from the N2. Those without vehicles could catch any of the Garden Route buses or the *Outeniqua Choo-Tjoe* to Wilderness, and walk from there.

### BUFFALO BAY

Buffalo Bay (Buffelsbaai) is a small holiday village built on a point 10km west of Knysna – a sandy beach runs all the way to Brenton-on-Sea. It's 10km from the N2 along the Goukamma Valley, and the Goukamma Nature Reserve is close by. There aren't many facilities, but there is a shop and a great caravan park right beside an excellent right reef break (southerly swell, south-westerly winds). There's also B&B accommodation.

### GOUKAMMA NATURE RESERVE

This reserve is accessible from the Buffels Bay road. It protects 14km of rocky coastline, some weathered sandstone cliffs, dunes covered with coastal fynbos and forest, and Groenvlei, a large freshwater lake. There are some small antelopes and much bird life – 150 species, including the Knysna loerie, have been recorded.

Most of the reserve is only accessible by foot. There are two easy trails: an 8km circular trail and a 14km trail. A suspension bridge over the Goukamma River takes hikers to the start of the trail.

There are picnic, braai and toilet facilities on the banks of the Goukamma River. The gates are open from 8 am to 6 pm.

### KNYSNA

Knysna (the 'k' is silent) is a large and bustling place with a holiday atmosphere. It was developed as a timber port and shipbuilding centre, thanks to the enormous protected lagoon, which opens up behind high sandstone cliffs, and the rich indigenous forests of the area. The continuing legacy of the timber industry is a number of excellent woodwork and furniture shops and a thriving artistic community.

A new waterfront development and at least four upmarket hotels will add to the increasing pace of life in Knysna (and might remove any reason to visit). This may finally force the building of a bypass road – currently the narrow main street is also the N2. However, a bypass would involve killing off some of the indigenous forest around Knysna, and there's precious little left.

WESTERN CAPE PROVINCE

WESTERN CAPE PROVINCE

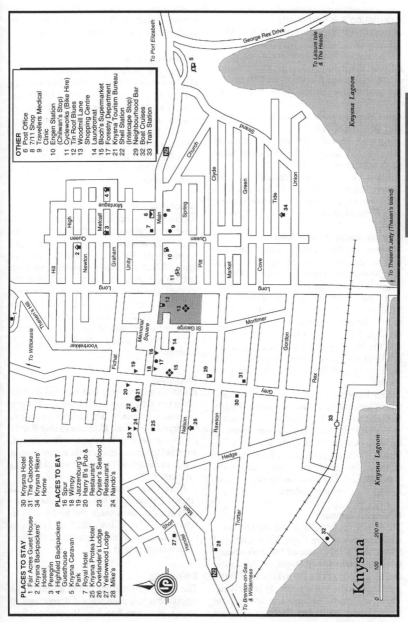

# Knysna

0      100      200 m

**PLACES TO STAY**
1  Fair Acres Guest House
2  Knysna Backpackers' Hostel
3  Peregrin
4  Highfield Backpackers Guesthouse
5  Knysna Caravan Park
7  Royal Hotel
25 Knysna Protea Hotel
26 Overlander's Lodge
27 Yellowwood Lodge
28 Mike's
30 Knysna Hotel
31 The Caboose
34 Knysna Hikers' Home

**PLACES TO EAT**
16 Spur
18 Wimpy
19 Jazzenburg's
20 Harry B's Pub & Restaurant
23 Oyster's Seafood Restaurant
24 Nando's

**OTHER**
6  Post Office
8  7/11 Shop
9  Travellers Medical Clinic
10 Engen Station (Chilwan's Stop)
11 Cycleworks (Bike Hire)
12 Tin Roof Blues
13 Woodmill Lane Shopping Centre
14 Laundromat
15 Bloch's Supermarket
17 Forestry Department
21 Knysna Tourism Bureau
22 Shell Station (Intercape Stop)
29 Neighbourhood Bar
32 Boat Cruises
33 Train Station

## Orientation & Information

Almost everything of importance is on Main Rd.

The tourism bureau (☎ (0445) 82 5510), 40 Main Rd, has a good range of information on the region and is open from 8.30 am to 5 pm on weekdays and on Saturday morning. You can't miss the office; there's an enormous elephant skeleton out the front. Next door is Rennies Travel.

Knysna Travel, opposite the Standard Bank at the entry to the Woodmill Lane shopping centre, sells bus tickets.

There is a travellers medical clinic on Queen St near the corner of Main Rd. It's a good spot to get vaccinations if you're planning further travels.

## Knysna National Lake Area

The National Parks Board regulates and controls the development of the Knysna Lagoon and the catchment area of the Knysna River, which flows into the lagoon.

It's not a national park wilderness area. Much is still privately owned, and the lagoon is used by industry and for recreation. The National Parks Board's brief is to make sure that the ongoing development balances the needs of the environment and the human community and doesn't lead to ecological disaster.

The lagoon covers 13 sq km. The protected area starts just to the east of Buffalo Bay and follows the coastline to the mouth of the Noetzie River. The lagoon opens up between two sandstone cliffs, known as The Heads. There are good views from a lookout on the eastern head, and a nature trail on the western head. The National Parks Board has an office on Thesen's Island.

## Mitchell's Brewery

Those who have been in the country for a while, particularly in Cape Town, may well have come across some of Mitchell's beers, which include a draught lager, a bitter, a stout and an ale. Mitchell's (☎ (0445) 24685) is a small operation, but it seems to be thriving. There are tours through the brewery on weekdays at 10.30 am. Tastings (R6) are available during the brewery's weekday opening hours and on Saturday morning.

## Knysna Oysters

Oysters are grown in the lagoon, and are highly acclaimed by gourmets. The Knysna Oyster Company (☎ (0445) 22168), on Thesen's Island, sells direct to the public. A tasting of eight oysters, with trimmings, costs R15.50. If you just want to take oysters away, they're R1.40 each. The shop is open from 8 am to 5 pm Monday to Thursday, 8 am to 3.30 pm on Friday and 9 am to 3 pm on weekends.

## Witlokasia

Follow Grey St uphill and eventually you'll leave town and emerge on the wooded slopes of the hills behind. On top is the sprawling township of Witlokasia (not the official name). There is at least one shebeen up here, next to the municipal clinic, and even the tourism bureau says that it's safe to visit (which is astonishing), but it would pay to check the current situation. It's too far to walk, but a continual stream of minibus taxis run up there, leaving from behind Bloch's supermarket.

## Elephants

It's extremely unlikely that you will see one of the few remaining wild elephants, but you can visit a couple of hefty babies on a farm between Knysna and Plettenberg Bay. For an admission price of R15 you walk with two young elephants as they eat their way around a flowery field of fynbos. It's a delightful experience.

A wild female has been seen in the area since the youngsters arrived and she apparently tries to show them the best places to find food. This is important, as fynbos is nutritionally poor (the elephants on the farm are fed supplements).

## Swimming

The town is built along the east side of the lagoon, but you need wheels if you want to get to an ocean beach – Brenton-on-Sea,

## The Knysna Elephants

In the forests around Knysna live the last wild elephants in the southern Cape (with the exception of those in the Addo Elephant National Park). The elephants live deep in the forest and are so rarely seen that their dung is labelled and recorded! You can, however meet a couple of young elephants on a farm near Knysna.

The forest is still commercially logged for prized yellowwood and stinkwood, so the elephants are basically in a zoo maintained for tourists, not a wilderness area.

It was recently discovered that the elephant population had shrunk to just one. Some more elephants were introduced from Kruger, however, the lone Knysna elephant was so freaked-out by these newcomers that he fled. The Kruger elephants (accustomed to herds and savanna) were so freaked-out at finding themselves alone in a forest that they pursued him. The chase went on for days and one of the new elephants died of exhaustion. ■

16km to the west, and Noetzie, 11km to the east, are both superb.

### Lagoon Cruises

The MV *John Benn* (☎ (0445) 21693) has cruises on the lagoon for R27.50. You must book. The same people also have the Featherbed cruise, which departs at 10 am and runs across to the other side of the lagoon to the **Featherbed Nature Reserve** and includes a walk and a drive. It costs R35.

### Boat Hire

Tait Marine (☎ (0445) 24460), 6 Long St, rents motor boats, canoes, hobie cats and dinghies.

### Diving

Diving in the lagoon is interesting and there's a wreck to explore. Beneath Tapas Jetty you might meet the unique Knysna seahorses. Waterfront Divers (☎ (0445) 22938) is at East Head and charges about R800 for an open-water certificate course. It also rents gear.

### Hiking & Mountain Biking

The Forestry Department (☎ (0445) 82 5466; fax 82 5461) has an office upstairs in the same shopping centre as the Wimpy bar, on Main Rd. This is where you book walking trails and collect maps and information. Overnight hikes cost R15 per day, including the use of trail huts.

The **Outeniqua Trail** is popular and takes a week to walk, although you can also do two or three-day sections. Other trails through the forest include the three **Elephant Trails** and the superb but tough **Harkerville Trail**.

Bicycles aren't allowed on the walking trails but two bike trails have been developed. Out of season you can use the hiking huts.

### Places to Stay – bottom end

**Caravan Parks** There are plenty to choose from. At one end of the scale is the small, simple, cheap and friendly *Knysna Caravan Park* (☎ (0445) 22011), which is the closest to town and has sites (only) from R15 to R30. At the other end of the scale is *Woodbourne Resort* (☎ (0445) 23223), an attractive caravan park not far from The Heads on George Rex Drive. Tent sites are R35 plus R6 per person, rising to an astronomical R100 for two people plus R40 for each extra person from December to mid-January. There are also two or three-bedroom chalets. For two people they cost from R150 for two people in the lowest season (add R25 for each additional person) to R500 for four people (add R40 for each extra person) in the highest season.

**Hostels** There are currently five hostels, and with so much competition and such seasonal business the rates are fairly flexible. Expect to pay a little less than you would in Cape Town.

*Highfield Backpackers Guesthouse* (☎ (0445) 82 6266), 2 Graham St, is just that – a very pleasant little guesthouse for backpackers. Their rates are a little lower than the other places, too. *Peregrin* (☎ (0445) 23747), 37 Queen St, is also a pleasant place to stay and is well equipped and kept very clean.

WESTERN CAPE PROVINCE

*Overlander's Lodge* (☎ (0445) 62 5920), 11 Nelson St, is behind the Spar supermarket. The owner runs the Knysna Adventure Centre, with good hiking and canoeing trips. *Knysna Backpackers' Hostel* (☎ (0445) 22554), 12 Newton St, is a large Victorian house on the hill a few blocks up from the main street. *Knysna Hikers' Home* (☎ (0445) 24362), 17 Tide St, is a few blocks on the lagoon side of the main street, in a more ordinary house.

**The Caboose** *The Caboose* (☎ (0445) 82 5850) is an interesting concept – quality budget accommodation with a train theme. It's attractive and has been well designed. Unfortunately, the theme has been taken a little too seriously, as the rooms (with attached bathroom) really are about the same size as sleeping compartments: *tiny*. Still, there are plenty of spacious public areas so it might be OK if you don't plan on doing anything except sleeping in your room. It's a nice place but not for the claustrophobic. Rooms cost R69/104, with breakfast.

### Places to Stay – middle & top end

*Under Milk Wood* (☎ (0445) 22385), George Rex Drive, is a group of high-quality chalets with a great location near East Head, with a small but pretty lagoon beach. There are canoes and small boats. The well-equipped chalets sleep four and cost from R270 for two people, plus R50 for each additional person. In the high season they cost from R600 for four people.

On George Rex Drive, *Ashmead Resort* (☎ (0445) 23172) has a variety of chalets and units on the waterfront, surrounded by the last pocket of indigenous forest on the lagoon. There are extensive gardens and a swimming pool. Rates start at around R130/170/200 for two people in a small self-catering flat in the low/middle/high seasons. B&B costs from R110/170 a single/double in the low season, R120/190 in the middle season and R135/220 in the high season.

*Lightley's Holiday Cruisers* (☎ (0445) 87 1026; fax 87 1067), on the west side of the White National Road Bridge over the Knysna

River, has two to eight-berth cruisers for hire. The cruisers are fully equipped, except for bedding, and you can navigate up to 16km upriver from The Heads. Rates vary radically depending on the boat and the season, but can be as little as R175 (not including fuel).

**B&Bs/Guesthouses** Several of the smaller guesthouses, especially those on the main road in from George, have occasional price wars and offer doubles for about R110. This is unlikely to happen in summer. Try *Mike's* (☎ (0445) 21728), at 67 Main Rd.

*Fair Acres Guest House* (☎ (0445) 22442) in Thesen's Hall has great views and large grounds, with B&B from R130/180. *Yellowwood Lodge* (☎ (0445) 82 5906), 18 Handel St, is a beautiful old Victorian-period house with very comfortable rooms from R120 per person, rising to R200, with breakfast. Smoking is not allowed inside and children under 15 aren't allowed anywhere.

There's a home accommodation booking agency (☎ (0445) 82 6200).

**Hotels** The *Royal Hotel* on Main Rd gets as low as R75 per person in the off-season. The *Knysna Hotel* (☎ (0445) 21151) on Grey St has B&B for around R100 per person, rising to R200 in the high season (which is a lot to pay for this place). The *Knysna Protea Hotel* (☎ (0445) 22127), 51 Main Rd, charges from about R250 – also a little high.

### Places to Eat

There are plenty of snack and coffee places in town. For some cheap, fresh oysters, head to the *Knysna Oyster Company* on Thesen's Island.

Originally an old boiler room, the *Pelican Restaurant* in Woodmill Lane shopping centre is now a trendy restaurant. Cajun and Southern (USA) dishes are the speciality, plus seafood and even a few choices for vegetarians. Prices are reasonable and there's a good atmosphere.

The popular *Tapas Restaurant* (☎ (0445) 21927), at Thesen's Jetty, is right on the lagoon. You can fill up on tapas for around R25 and a steak from R28.

Out at The Heads and in a beautiful setting, *Cranzgot's* has a coffee shop with breakfast from R10 and inexpensive snacks and lunches. Cranzgot's is also a restaurant with pasta from R25 and steaks from about R35. There's a bar as well.

A reader recommends *The Roast House* on the corner of Grey and Rawson Sts. They paid R35 'for as much as we could eat and everything was delicious'. Another reader recommends *Makintoshes Country Store* as an excellent place to stock up on supplies for picnics. You can also buy organic produce. It's on Long St in the Thesen building.

### Entertainment
In the *bar* behind the Pelican Restaurant, bands play some nights after 10 pm. *Tin Roof Blues* on the main street has a good balcony and sometimes live music with an R10 cover charge. *Tapas Restaurant* sometimes has live music.

### Getting There & Away
**Bus** The tourism bureau sells Translux and Intercape tickets. Greyhound and Translux stop on Main Rd at the Toyota dealer, Intercape stops on Main Rd at the Shell service station and Chilwans stops on Main Rd at the Engen service station. As usual, for travel between nearby towns on the Garden Route you're better off looking for a minibus taxi than travelling with the major bus lines, which are very expensive on short sectors.

Greyhound, Intercape and Translux stop here on their Cape Town to Port Elizabeth services. Translux fares include: Cape Town, R120; Mossel Bay, R55; George, R40; and Port Elizabeth, R80. See the Cape Town Getting There & Away section earlier in this chapter for more information.

Chilwans Bus Services (☎ (021) 54 2506, 905 3910) has a useful (if slow and not luxurious) service between Cape Town and Port Elizabeth, departing from Cape Town on Friday and returning on Sunday.

Intercape, Greyhound and Translux run from Knysna to Jo'burg/Pretoria. See the

Travelling the Route section under Garden Route earlier in this chapter for some fares and journey times.

**Train** The historic *Outeniqua Choo-Tjoe* steam train runs between Knysna and George every day except Sunday and public holidays. See the George Getting There & Away section earlier in this chapter for details.

**Minibus Taxi** Most taxis stop in the car parks behind Bloch's supermarket. A taxi to Plettenberg Bay costs R8. Taxis depart for Cape Town in the morning from about 7.30 am and cost about R70. See the Cape Town Getting There & Away section earlier in this chapter for information on a door-to-door service on the Garden Route.

**Car & Motorcycle** If you're heading to Oudtshoorn, consider going via Prince Alfred's Pass and Uniondale. The road is dirt and quite steep in places but if you take it easy it's OK.

### Getting Around
Even if you have a car, the traffic jams that develop on the main street (much worse than anything you'll find in Cape Town) will make you look for alternative transport. Rikki's (☎ (0445) 6540) small vans zip around town. There are some set fares, including: Tapas Jetty, R4 per person (R3 for more than three people); the oyster farm R4 (R3); The Heads, R10 (R6); and Leisure Isle Beach, R12 (R10).

Knysna Cycleworks (☎ (0445) 82 5153), 18A Spring St, is one of several places renting good bikes.

### AROUND KNYSNA
#### Prince Alfred's Pass
The Knysna to Avontour road climbs through the Outeniqua range via the beautiful Prince Alfred's Pass. Prince Alfred's is regarded by some as being even better than the superb Swartberg. Needless to say it was built by a Bain, in this case Thomas, in the 1860s. Be

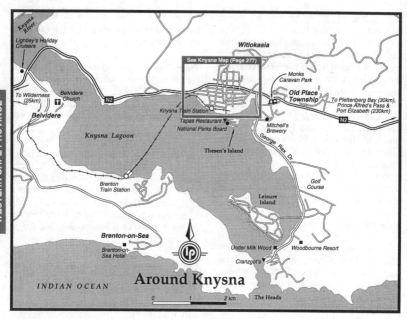

Around Knysna

warned that the road is a bit rough and it's slow going.

Outside Knysna, the road passes through pine and eucalypt plantations and indigenous forest (the home of Knysna's elephants). There are few really steep sections, but the pass does reach a height of over 1000m, and there are magnificent views to the north before the road winds into the Langkloof Valley.

### Belvidere

Belvidere, on the road to Brenton-on-Sea, is notable for a Norman-style church built in the 1850s for a homesick Englishman. It sounds weird, but it is a beautiful sight. Captain Duthie, who built the church, also built a Georgian house nearby. *Belvidere House* (☎ (0445) 87 1055), as it is known, has been turned into the main building for a group of surrounding guest cottages. The rest of the large village is also very pretty (and

rich), but there are so many signs telling you not to do things that visiting isn't much fun.

### Brenton-on-Sea

Brenton-on-Sea overlooks a magnificent 8km-long beach, stretching all the way from the west head of Knysna Lagoon to Buffalo Bay. Fynbos-covered hills drop to white sand and blue sea.

The *Brenton-on-Sea Hotel* (☎ (0445) 81 0081) has a fantastic location right on the beach. Rooms overlook the sea and cost from R195/320 a single/double with breakfast, rising to R275/430 from December to April. There are also some excellent chalets with two bedrooms (sleeping six) and a lounge, kitchenette and bathroom from R360 to R800.

### Noetzie

Not to be outdone by Captain Duthie at Belvidere, another romantic English family built holiday homes in a mock-castle style. The homes are still privately owned, and are not as bad as you might imagine. Their location is certainly fine. Noetzie has a lovely surf beach (spacious but dangerous) and a sheltered lagoon running through a forested gorge. It's a steep trail between the car park and the beach.

## PLETTENBERG BAY

Plettenberg Bay is a beautiful resort, with that rare combination of mountains, white sand and crystal-blue water. It's a trendy and popular destination, so things tend to be upmarket. However, there is a hostel and the full-time locals are very friendly. It's not a bad place to spend time. Better, perhaps, than Knysna – especially if you want to be on the beach. The winter population of 10,000 jumps to 50,000 during the summer holiday season.

Plett, as it is often known, is 520km east of Cape Town and 240km west of Port Elizabeth.

Especially between February and April, if your budget allows and the weather is kind, it's hard to imagine a better place to spend a couple of days. The main idea at Plett is to spend the day on the beach and the night in the pub. The road west to Knysna is not particularly interesting, but the scenery to the east is superb, with some of the best coast and indigenous forest in South Africa.

### Orientation & Information

Plett is a big place and quite spread out. The town centre is on a high promontory overlooking the Keurbooms River lagoon and Beacon Island. The hostel is up here, but camping accommodation is some way from the centre.

The publicity association (☎ (04457) 34065), on Kloof St, has a great deal of useful information, ranging from accommodation to a craft trail and walks in the surrounding hills and reserves. It's open from 9 am to 5 pm Monday to Friday and until 12.30 pm on Saturday. Make sure you pick up the *Plettenberg Bay to Tsitsikamma* booklet.

### Activities

There's a lot to do in Plett. Backpackers will find that the hostel can organise most things, often at a discount.

For information on the surrounding **nature reserves** and walks through the reserves contact the Chief Directorate, Nature & Environmental Conservation (☎ (04457) 32125), 7 Zenon St. Ask them about **canoeing** on the Keurbooms River. There's an overnight canoe trail and they rent canoes. **Mountain-bike trails** are being developed in the area and Outeniqua Biking Trails (☎ (04457) 7644) offers two-day rides. A couple of places offer **diving**: Plett Dive Centre (☎ (04457) 30303) and Ocean Divers (☎ (04457) 31158). Equitrailing (☎ (0445) 9718) offers **horse-riding**.

### Places to Stay

There is a great deal of holiday accommodation in town and nearby, and out of season there can be some bargains. The publicity association has a full list. If you want to rent a house or a flat, contact an agent such as The Accommodation Bureau (☎ (04457) 32101), Main St. Out of season you might get an apartment for R150 or less.

**Caravan Parks** There is a lot of this type of accommodation in the area. The following is a selection. *Robberg Resort & Caravan Park* (☎ (04457) 32571) is 7km to the west of Plett (5km if you walk on the beach) but it's in an excellent location. Bring supplies. Sites cost R17 per person in the low season and R25 (minimum R75) in the high season. There are also chalets.

*Keurbooms Aventura Resort* (☎ (04457) 9309) is on the river east of town, just upstream from the highway. Sites for two people range from R28 plus R15 per person in the lowest season, way up to R84 plus R15 per person in the highest season. The cheapest four-person chalets start at R125, and nearly triple that at the busiest times.

**Hostels** *Albergo* (☎ (04457) 34434), 8 Church St, is the more attractive sibling of the Albergo in Cape Town and is a well-run,

WESTERN CAPE PROVINCE

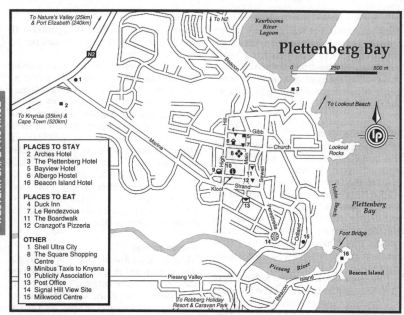

PLACES TO STAY
2  Arches Hotel
3  The Plettenberg Hotel
5  Bayview Hotel
6  Albergo Hostel
16  Beacon Island Hotel

PLACES TO EAT
4  Duck Inn
7  Le Rendezvous
11  The Boardwalk
12  Cranzgot's Pizzeria

OTHER
1  Shell Ultra City
8  The Square Shopping
   Centre
9  Minibus Taxis to Knysna
10  Publicity Association
13  Post Office
14  Signal Hill View Site
15  Milkwood Centre

friendly place that encourages activities in town and in the area. They say that they can organise anything. There are dorms for R30 and doubles for R90 or you can camp. A few B&B-style places have jumped on the backpacking bandwagon – ask the publicity association.

**Hotels** The *Bayview Hotel* (☎ (04457) 31961), right in town on the corner of Main and Gibb Sts, is modern, small and pleasant, and charges from R150 per person. *Arches Hotel* (☎ (04457) 32118), near the N2, is an ugly place to look at, but is good value at about R80 per person in the low season. It's a long walk to the beach from this hotel and an even longer one up the hill to get back again.

*Beacon Island Hotel* (☎ (04457) 31120) is a multistorey hotel on Beacon Island (linked to the rest of Plett by a causeway). The position is spectacular. Expect to pay around R700 a double.

**Out of Town** East of Plett, near Tsitsikamma Coastal National Park, are many more places to stay, including *Woodgate Farm* (☎ (04457) 48690), a small working farm with simple backpacker accommodation (from R25) and friendly hosts who'll drive you to trailheads. If you're driving, turn north (left if you're coming from Plett) off the N2 at The Crags, a village about 16km east of Plett, and left again after 2.1km. Woodgate is 1.3km further along. If you don't have transport they can pick you up from The Crags.

*Hog Hollow* (☎ (04457) 48769; email hog.hollow@pixie.co.za) is an old farmhouse in the forest offering accommodation from R225/350 in the lowest season and from R365/472 in the highest, with breakfast. The chef here has an extraordinary CV, so the dinners (Monday to Saturday) are memorable. A 2½ hour walk down a forested gorge takes you to the ocean. You'll need to phone for directions.

*Forest Hall* (☎ (04457) 48869) is an historic country house set in 220 hectares of forest adjoining a beach. It's now a wonderful guesthouse with rates starting at about R350 per person. The turn-off on the N2 is just east of The Crags.

**Places to Eat**

A popular place to hang out, with locals, surfies and visitors, is *The Boardwalk*. It's an excellent café with soup (eg spinach) for R9.50 and calamari for R12. Other main courses start at around R25 and there are plenty of snacks.

There are more places in the main shopping area, along Main St. *Le Rendezvous* (☎ (04457) 31390) is a long-running survivor serving seafood at reasonable prices, and *Kelly's Restaurant & Pub* (☎ (04457) 33077) is a little cheaper. *Cranzgot's Pizzeria* has excellent pizzas for around R24 and steaks for around R35. It's popular, so you might have to wait for a table in the evenings – there's a bar. The *Continental Café* in Sun Plaza is good.

**Getting There & Away**

**Bus** Buses heading east stop on the highway across from the Shell Ultra City, those heading west stop at the Shell Ultra City.

Greyhound, Intercape and Translux stop here on their services from Cape Town to Port Elizabeth. Translux fares include: Cape Town, R125; Mossel Bay, R90; George, R50; Knysna, R40 (it's less than a fifth that much by minibus taxi); and Port Elizabeth, R50. See the Cape Town Getting There & Away section earlier in this chapter for more information.

Intercape also runs to Jo'burg via the Garden Route and Oudtshoorn twice a week in season for about R250.

Chilwans Bus Services (☎ (021) 54 2506, 905 3910) runs a slow bus from Cape Town to Port Elizabeth via the Garden Route. It leaves Cape Town on Friday and returns on Sunday.

**Minibus Taxi** Most long-distance taxis stop at the Shell Ultra City on the highway. See the Cape Town Getting There & Away section earlier in this chapter for information on a door-to-door service running the Garden Route. However, it's a long way to Plett from Cape Town, and by minibus taxi the journey can take hours longer than the bus.

Taxis to Knysna (R8) leave from the corner of Kloof and High Sts.

**AROUND PLETTENBERG BAY**

The best-known reserve near Plett is the Tsitsikamma Coastal National Park. It is in Eastern Cape Province – see that chapter.

**Robberg Nature & Marine Reserve**

The reserve (☎ (04457) 32125) is 9km south-east of Plett. From Piesang Valley follow the airport road until you see signs to the reserve. The reserve protects a 4km-long peninsula with a rugged coastline of cliffs and rocks. There's a circular walk approximately 11km in length, with rich intertidal marine life and coastal-dune fynbos. The

WESTERN CAPE PROVINCE

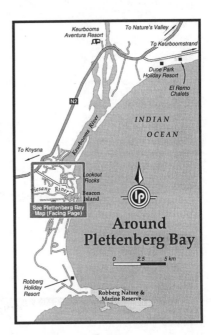

Around Plettenberg Bay

peninsula acts as a sort of marine speed bump to larger sea life, with mammals and fish spending time here before moving on.

## Keurbooms Nature Reserve

The reserve is 7km north-east of Plett. It covers a hilly plateau with steep cliffs and banks above the Keurbooms River. Fynbos covers the plateaux, and there's forest on the steeper slopes. There is a short one hour hiking trail along the river banks. A canoe trail goes further up the river to an overnight hut that sleeps 12 people. The reserve is open from 6 am to 6 pm, but visitors must get a permit from the directorate office in Plett.

## Bloukrans Pass

The road from Plett to Knysna cuts across a fairly uninteresting plateau that is dominated by pine and eucalypt plantations. The road to the east of Plett, however, is brilliant. Don't take the toll road, but turn off to Nature's Valley and the Bloukrans Pass. It's a beautiful drive across a plain with plenty of surviving fynbos, but the road plunges in and out of deep gorges that have been cut by rivers running out to sea.

Nature's Valley and Bloukrans Pass are surrounded by beautiful indigenous forests that make you realise what terrible devastation there has been in the region. The forests are dominated by the Outeniqua yellow-wood, a large, classically proportioned tree with a scaly trunk. There's a great view of the N2 bridge and numerous attractive picnic spots.

# Eastern Cape Province

Eastern Cape Province is a diverse and, compared with Western Cape Province, largely undeveloped area. It includes the former homelands of Ciskei and Transkei, so most of its population is Xhosa-speaking. The former Transkei region has a separate section in this chapter because it remains a fairly homogeneous area of the country.

The province's long coastline extends from Tsitsikamma Coastal National Park and Cape St Francis and Jeffreys Bay (famous for their surf) in the west, through Port Elizabeth and the Sunshine Coast to the Shipwreck Coast of the old Ciskei area, past East London and into the spectacular subtropical Wild Coast of the old Transkei.

Inland, the rolling hills around Grahamstown are known as Settler Country, after the British migrants who settled in the area in the early 19th century. This was the 'border' between expansionist Boer farmers and the Rharhabe or Ciskei Xhosa. Both groups, heavily dependent on cattle, claimed the Suurveld grazing land (the strip from Algoa Bay to the Great Kei River). The Settler Country also includes the highlands which lead up into the foothills of the main South African plateau and Lesotho.

Further north and on the plateau is the semi-desert Karoo and the lazy old towns of Cradock and Graaff-Reinet, all worth visiting.

The rainfall and climate reflect the geographic variation, with around 700mm of rain (mostly in summer) and a moderate climate on the coast; heavy rainfall of over 1000mm (including snow in winter) in the mountains; and low rainfall of around 450mm on the fringes of the Karoo. The Eastern Cape is the meeting point for four types of flora: the subtropical forest (found in sheltered valleys) of the summer rainfall area; the *fynbos* of the Western Cape winter rainfall area (on the coastal plains); the eastern grasslands at higher altitudes; and succulent thorny scrub in the river valleys.

## HIGHLIGHTS

- Uncrowded beaches and great coastal walking trails
- Strong Xhosa culture
- Addo Elephant National Park, with near-guaranteed sightings
- Beautiful old towns like Graaff-Reinet and Cradock – oases in the hot, empty Karoo

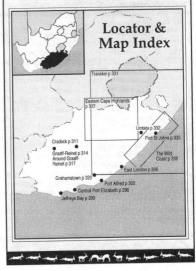

## INFORMATION

The Eastern Cape Tourism Board (Ectour, ☎ (0401) 95 2215; fax (0401) 92756) is based in Tourism House, Phalo Ave, in the former Ciskei capital of Bisho (now Eastern Cape's capital). Use these numbers to book accommodation in the former homeland's reserves and along the popular Amatola, Zingcuka Loop, Katberg and Shipwreck walking trails.

The main regional offices are: Wild Coast (☎ (0471) 31 2885) in Umtata; Central (☎ (0431) 47 4730) in East London; and Western (☎ (041) 55 7761) in Port Elizabeth.

## The Xhosa

Most of Eastern Cape is populated by groups of Nguni peoples who occupied the coastal savanna of South Africa, but those living west of the Great Fish River are relatively recent arrivals. Being graziers and agriculturists, the Nguni could venture no further west than a line roughly following the Great Fish River – most of the land to the west receives less than the 200mm of summer rainfall required for cropping. There is no satisfactory explanation for the differences between the coastal Nguni and the Sotho of the highveld, or when the distinctions between the two main Bantu groups began. It is believed, however, that Iron Age Bantus had reached the Great Kei River by 1000 AD.

The history of the original Xhosa clans can be dated back to the early 17th century, when small communities of Nguni pastoralists were loosely united in kingdoms. They first came into contact with Boers in the 1760s. Both groups were heavily dependent on cattle, and both coveted the grazing land in the area known as Suurveld (the coastal strip from Algoa Bay to the Great Kei River).

In 1771, Governor Van Plettenberg convinced some chiefs to consider the Great Fish River as the boundary between VOC and Xhosa territory. Conflict was inevitable, however, and the first of nine major frontier wars broke out in 1779 – skirmishing and brigandage (by blacks and whites) was virtually continuous for the next century.

By the beginning of the 19th century, the Xhosa were under pressure in the west from white expansion, in the east and north from peoples fleeing from the difaqane. After the Sixth Frontier War (1834-35) the British declared the land between the Great Kei and Keiskamma rivers the Province of Queen Adelaide, and allowed the Xhosa a limited degree of independence. In 1846, however, white colonialists invaded (the theft of an axe at Fort Beaufort was the flimsy pretext), beginning the Seventh Frontier War. In its aftermath, British Kaffraria was established, with its capital in King William's Town.

Increasing numbers of Xhosa were influenced by missionaries and drawn into the European cash economy as peasant labourers, but the great leader Sandile provided a focal point for traditionalists and continued resistance. In 1840, Sandile became the paramount chief of the Rharhabe or Ciskei Xhosa; he was to mobilise the Xhosa in a last, increasingly desperate attempt to retain their land and resist white influence. He was a key figure in the Seventh, Eighth (1850-53) and Ninth (1877-78) Frontier Wars.

Sandile was also involved in the 'Great Cattle Killing', the Xhosa suicide of 1857. A young girl, Nongqawuse, saw visions that the Xhosa believed revealed how they could reconcile themselves with a spirit world that allowed the theft of their land and destruction of their culture. The spirits required the sacrifice of cattle and crops – in return the whites would be swept into the sea. As a result of this enormous and desperate sacrifice it is estimated that of a Xhosa population of 90,000 in British Kaffraria, 30,000 died of starvation and 30,000 were forced to emigrate as destitute refugees.

In 1866, British Kaffraria became part of the Cape Province. The Xhosa had been devastated by years of struggle, but in 1877-78 they once again fought for their independence in the Ninth Frontier War. ■

## WARNING

Although many of the roads within the old Ciskei and Transkei are of a reasonable standard, there is a real likelihood of children and livestock frequently straying onto them. Care is required.

# Nature's Valley to the Kei River

Eastern Cape Province has a long and diverse coastline. Apart from the beautiful forests of Tsitsikamma Coastal National Park, the coast between Cape St Francis and East London is best known for its surf, but even if you aren't a surfie this section of coast might come as a relief after the intense tourist development of the Garden Route. In particular, the stretch of coast between the Great Fish River almost to East London is relatively undeveloped, except for the Sun hotels and casinos that featured in most homelands.

## NATURE'S VALLEY

Nature's Valley is a small settlement at the mouth of the Groot River, at the western end of the Tsitsikamma Coastal National Park. The neighbouring ranges have yellowwood

### South African Architecture

Top: Squatter's shacks in Kliptown, one small part of sprawling Soweto, Gauteng.
Middle: Thatching a Cape Dutch cottage; Batswana hut decoration, North-West Province.
Bottom: Solid old house in the Karoo town of Calvinia, Northern Cape.

Left: Hiking through the mangroves along the Umtafufu River, Eastern Cape.
Right: A taste of the weird and wonderful creatures at the Owl House, Nieu-Bethesda, Eastern Cape.
Bottom: The impoverished Transkei region is dotted with Xhosa huts, Eastern Cape.

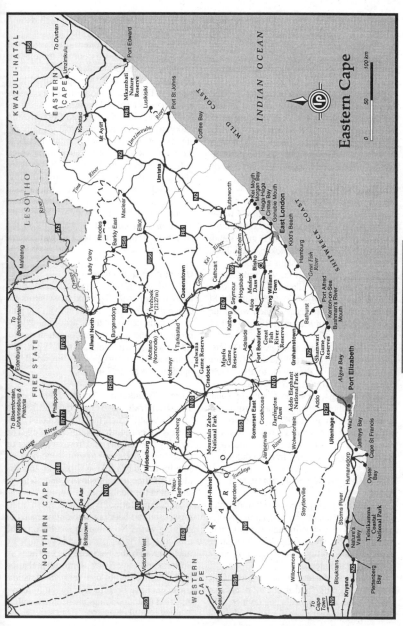

forest, and the 5km stretch of beach is magnificent. The acclaimed Otter Trail ends here, the Tsitsikamma Trail begins here (see the Tsitsikamma Coastal National Park section), and there are many day walks. It's a beautiful spot.

There's only one shop in the area, easily recognised with its gaudy pink and mauve paintwork. It doesn't have a great range of hiking supplies but a good meal of fish at its restaurant is R35. There are over 300 houses in Nature's Valley, but only a small percentage are permanently occupied.

### Places to Stay

*Hikers' Haven* (☎ (04457) 6805), 411 St Patrick's Rd, also known as *Nature's Valley Guesthouse*, is a large and very comfortable home in town, catering to B&B guests and, in the attic dorm, to backpackers and hikers. B&B costs R95 per person and a bed (not a bunk) in the dorm is R35; you must book. They hire mountain bikes for R25 per day. *Tourist Lodge* (☎ (04457) 6681) at 218 St Georges Ave is a pleasant chalet, worth the R95 per person in season (R10 less out of season).

A National Park camping ground, *De Vasselot*, is on the river east of the town (take the main road) and a 2km walk to the beach. Camp sites are from R50 for two people and good forest huts are R65. A 40% seasonal discount applies to camping rates from May to the end of August; a 20% discount applies at any other time except school holidays. If you stay in the huts you'll have your own canoe which you can use free of charge.

### TSITSIKAMMA COASTAL NATIONAL PARK

This national park protects 100km of coast between Plettenberg Bay and Humansdorp. It includes a narrow strip starting 5km out to sea and encompassing the shoreline, steep cliffs and coastal hills, finishing at the edge of the coastal plateau.

The coastal plateau lies at the foot of the Tsitsikamma range and is cut by rivers that have carved deep and abrupt ravines. The flora includes evergreen forest (stinkwood

and yellowwood), ferns, lilies, orchids and coastal fynbos, including proteas.

The Cape clawless otter, after which the Otter Trail is named, is one of the elusive animals, but there are also baboons, monkeys and some small antelope. Bird life is plentiful. Diving and snorkelling are rewarding – there is a special snorkel route.

The area has a high rainfall (around 1200mm a year), but the climate is temperate. The main centre for the national park is the Storms River Mouth Rest Camp, which is 68km from Plettenberg Bay, 99km from Humansdorp and nearly 10km from the N2.

Several short day walks give you a taste of the coastline, so it is worth visiting even if you can't tackle the five day Otter Trail. The four hour circuit to a waterfall on the first part of the Otter Trail is particularly rewarding.

### Orientation & Information

The park gate is 6km from the N2. It's open from 5.30 am to 9.30 pm and day visitors are charged R8 for entry. It's 2km from the gate to the main camp, with its accommodation, restaurant and information/reception centre. Reception is open from 7 am to 7.45 pm. The shop has drinks, supplies and firewood; it's open from 8 am to 7.45 pm.

### Otter & Tsitsikamma Trails

The **Otter Trail** is one of the most acclaimed hikes in South Africa, hugging the coast from Storms River Mouth to Nature's Valley. The five day (four night) walk fords a number of rivers and gives access to some superb coast. The longest day's hike is 14km, so there is plenty of time to walk slowly, and swim or snorkel in the tidal pools.

Accommodation is in huts with mattresses, but no bedding, cooking utensils or running water. No camping is allowed. The trail costs R220 per person and bookings are made through the National Park offices in Pretoria and Cape Town. Unfortunately, the trail is booked up to one year ahead. Some travellers have been lucky enough to arrive and find that a booking has been cancelled, but this is unlikely.

We did a few kilometres of the start of the famous Otter Trail, which included a lot of strenuous rock-hopping along the coast – no fun with a heavy pack – and at the end there is a cliff to scramble down. Perhaps the worst feature of the walk is that it involves going to a place called Storms River Mouth, where a dramatic bit of coastline has been totally wrecked for tourists. The narrow bit of land at the base of the coastal cliffs has been terraced, grassed and covered with 'chalets' and 'oceanettes', apart for a vast area where locals can park their huge caravans and annexes.

**Noel Gross**

The **Tsitsikamma Trail** parallels the Otter Trail, but takes you inland through the coastal forests. It's also five days/four nights long and as it begins at Nature's Valley and ends at Storms River Mouth (the opposite direction to the Otter Trail) you could combine the two. Unlike the Otter Trail there is little difficulty getting a booking; midweek you might have it to yourself, except in school holidays. Accommodation is in huts. Book through the Forestry Department (Knysna is convenient) or contact De Vasselot Nature Reserve near Nature's Valley for more information.

### Places to Stay & Eat
There are different types of cottages; all except the forest huts are equipped with kitchens (including utensils), bedding and bathrooms. Forest huts use communal facilities and cost R80 a double. Log cabins cost R255 a double, with larger models costing R490 for up to four people. 'Oceanettes' also sleep four and cost R490. All accommodation except forest huts has a 20% discount from the start of May to the end of August.

There are also camp sites for R55 a double plus R18 for each additional person, with a 40% discount from May to August and a 20% discount the rest of the year, excluding school holidays. Bookings must be made through the National Parks offices in Pretoria and Cape Town.

*Storms River Restaurant* at the reception complex has great views over the coast and surprisingly reasonable prices. Lunches are cheap – soup is R7, a pie R5 and a salad plate R7.

### Getting There & Away
There is no public transport to the Storms River Mouth Rest Camp, which is an 8km walk from the N2. Buses run along the N2 – see the Cape Town and Port Elizabeth sections for details. Hopper and Baz buses both stop at Nature's Valley.

## STORMS RIVER
There can be some confusion between Storms River and the Tsitsikamma Coastal National Park. From the N2, the Storms River signpost points to the village that lies outside the national park. Despite what some maps show, the turn-off is east of the national park's turn-off. The turn-off to the park headquarters is signed as Storms River Mouth.

Storms River is a tiny and scattered hamlet with tree-shaded lanes, a couple of places to stay and an outdoor centre, Storms River Adventures. Not far east on the N2 is the **Big Tree**, a humungous 36m Outeniqua yellow-wood, and a forest with many other fine examples of candlewood, stinkwood and assegai. An interpretative trail describes the trees in this, one of the best preserved forests in South Africa; entry to the trail is R2 per person.

Rumour has it that the world's highest **bungy jump** is being set up at the Bloukrans River bridge, to the west of Storms River.

Hopper and Baz buses both stop at Storms River.

### Activities
The adventure outfit Storms River Adventures (☎ (042) 541 1609) is based in the centre of the village; the office is open from 8.30 am to 6 pm. It operates **blackwater tubing** trips of four to five hours duration down the scenic Storms River. The guides are very professional and the cost of R150 includes lunch and permits; wetsuit hire is R25.

**Walking trails** include the Plaatbos Forest Trail (four options) and the 4.2km Ratel Trail which starts at the Big Tree. You can hire mountain bikes at the Storms River Adventures centre (R40 for a day) and then attempt the 22km **Storms River Cycle Route**, a

EASTERN CAPE PROVINCE

round trip which should take three to four hours. The new **Robbehoek Biking Trail** (☎ (042) 750 3952) has chalets for both hikers and bikers.

### Places to Stay

*Stormsriver Village Backpackers* (☎ (042) 541 1711) charges R35 for a dorm, R90 for a double; pluses here are the gardens and views. *The Armagh* (☎ (042) 541 1512) has a dorm in the loft; dorm beds are R35. The pleasant guest rooms are R180 for up to three people.

*Tzitzikamma Forest Inn* (☎ (042) 541 1711) is a hotel which, while not especially fancy, has a certain old-world charm after the tour buses depart. There are manicured lawns and a pool. Whether it's worth R195 per person B&B, is another matter.

*Storms River Guesthouse* (☎ (042) 541 1711) is a clean, comfortable place with a huge lounge area; it costs R65 for B&B. The friendly *Ploughmans Rest* (☎ (042) 541 1726), just off the east side of the road before you enter Storms River, has B&B for R125 per person.

Eight kilometres east of Storms River is the *Tsitsikamma Lodge* (☎ (042) 750 3802), a collection of log cabins with all mod cons; it costs R195 per person B&B in deluxe suites, R175 in garden cabins and R150 in standard cabins. A home-cooked buffet dinner is R55.

### CAPE ST FRANCIS

While the beach is good, the treeless cape is covered in unattractive fibro-cement houses and is basically bleak and ugly. To add insult to injury, the reef seldom produces rideable surf. If it does, it will certainly be considerably better at Jeffreys Bay. Nearby Oyster Bay often has a wave when everything else is flat.

Still bleak but not as ugly (unless you think upper middle-class ghettos are ugly) is the nearby village of **St Francis Bay**, off the road to the Cape. Just about every building is a whitewashed, thatched-roofed Cape Dutch imitation. For information, contact the publicity association (☎ (0423) 94 0076).

*Cape St Francis Backpackers'* (☎ (0423) 94 0420) on Da Gama Rd, 200m from Seal Point and its historic lighthouse, has camping for R30 for two (R6 for an extra person), dorm beds for R20 and comfy doubles for R140.

As someone who saw the surf film *Endless Summer* at an impressionable age, Cape St Francis was burnt into my mind as the most perfect wave in the world. In my fevered imagination it became a sort of Shangri-La. The reality is massively disappointing.
**Richard Everist**

### JEFFREYS BAY

Surfing is *the* reason to come to J Bay. Once a sleepy surfie hollow, it is now a flashy town with rampant development but it's also very friendly and might be just the place to spend a few surf-soaked, sun-drenched days.

The surf is sensational; few would disagree that J Bay has the best waves in Southern Africa and among the best in the world. Shaun Tomson ('champ') has claimed Supertubes as the most perfect wave in the world. It can be better than a three minute ride from Boneyards to the end. Kitchen Windows, Magnatubes, Supertubes, Tubes, The Point, Phantoms and Albatross – if you have ever waxed a board, you know! And there are always shells on the beach for older, less committed, beachcombers to discover.

### Information

The friendly, helpful Jeffreys Bay Tourism (☎ (0423) 93 2588), on the corner of Beverland and Da Gama, is open on weekdays from 8 am to 5.30 pm and Saturday morning from 8.30 am to noon. Aloe Afrika Tours & Trails (☎ (0423) 93 2313) has tours to Addo, Shamwari and surfing spots, as well as horse trails and bike trips.

### Surfing

Country Feeling runs most of the surf shops in town and has a factory making their clothing. J Bay Surf Co, on the corner of Da Gama and Goedehoop, sells new boards for R850 to R1100. There's a fairly limited stock of second-hand boards for R200 to R600; a Rip Curl steamer sells for R500. You can hire

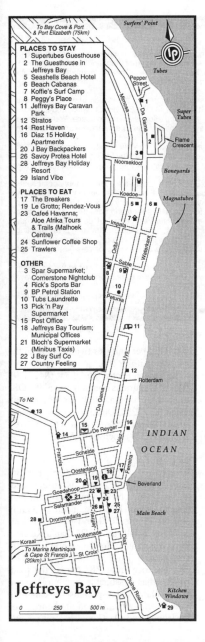

**PLACES TO STAY**
1 Supertubes Guesthouse
2 The Guesthouse in
  Jeffreys Bay
5 Seashells Beach Hotel
6 Beach Cabanas
7 Koffie's Surf Camp
8 Peggy's Place
11 Jeffreys Bay Caravan
   Park
12 Stratos
14 Rest Haven
16 Diaz 15 Holiday
   Apartments
20 J Bay Backpackers
26 Savoy Protea Hotel
28 Jeffreys Bay Holiday
   Resort
29 Island Vibe

**PLACES TO EAT**
17 The Breakers
19 Le Grotto; Rendez-Vous
23 Cafeé Havanna;
   Aloe Afrika Tours
   & Trails (Malhoek
   Centre)
24 Sunflower Coffee Shop
25 Trawlers

**OTHER**
3 Spar Supermarket;
  Cornerstone Nightclub
4 Rick's Sports Bar
9 BP Petrol Station
10 Tubs Laundrette
13 Pick 'n Pay
   Supermarket
15 Post Office
18 Jeffreys Bay Tourism;
   Municipal Offices
21 Bloch's Supermarket
   (Minibus Taxis)
22 J Bay Surf Co
27 Country Feeling

**Jeffreys Bay**

boards for R10 per hour (R50 per day) and
wetsuits for the same rate – rent from
Koffie's Surf Camp or Country Feeling. You
can get surfing lessons for R12.50 per hour
including wetsuit and surfboard. Also, bicycles are R35, and scooters R55 for the day
from Aloe Afrika Tours & Trails.

### Places to Stay

**Budget** There are heaps of crash pads now!
*Jeffreys Bay Caravan Park* (☎ (0423) 93
1111) is exposed, but it has an ideal situation
beside the sea, midway between the town
centre and the surf. For two people a site
costs R40 (R50 in summer). There are three
other caravan parks nearby.

Budget hostels have sprung up like junior
grommets at a 'new wave' rave. *Island Vibe*
(☎ (0423) 93 1625), 10 Dageraad St, is definitely the 'pick' of these places. Sitting
above Kitchen Windows it may get a bit of
wind, but it epitomises J Bay, and the atten-
dant 'raft' of surfies attests to its prime
location. Dorm beds are an absolute steal at
R20. The owners love the beach, where they
walk their dog, and they love to share J Bay's
secrets.

*J Bay Backpackers* (☎ (0423) 93 1379),
12 Jeffrey St, is an adequate little place
where dorm beds go for just R25, and
doubles in confined cottages go for R60.
Another hostel, *Rest Haven* (☎ (0423) 93
1248), 20 De Reyger St (up from the post
office), has singles/doubles for R30/50 (a
minimum stay of two nights). The rambling
*Koffie's Surf Camp* (☎ (0423) 93 1530)
hosted the Springbok Nude Girls recently;
the 'girls' (all male, actually) apparently left
their underwear behind. If you are a surfie,
you will find paradise here; a dorm bed is
R25.

A fair way north of the centre is *Bay Cove*
(☎ (0423) 96 2291), an excellent purpose-
built B&B which is R60 per person; the full
breakfast and the very tidy twin rooms make
this place great value. *Peggy's Place* (☎ (0423)
93 2160) at 8A Oribi St can be hard to find
as it's secluded; it has clean dorms/rondavels
for R25/60.

EASTERN CAPE PROVINCE

## Surfing in Eastern Cape Province

If you can overcome your fear of sharks – and who of us can? – this is one of the greatest surfing venues in the known world. For excellent uncrowded surf with some of the friendliest locals around, head the Kombi anywhere between J Bay and Kei Mouth. These people manage to extricate themselves from the fleshpots and go on to world stardom. Wendy Botha (world women's champion), Dave Malherbe, Brad Bricknell and Daryl Fox are all local.

**Jeffreys Bay** is world-famous; those with the slightest interest in the motion of waves will have heard of Supertubes. Also consider nearby Cape St Francis, seen in *Endless Summer*, and Claptons Coils. J Bay is a surfie town and the locals respect you if you afford them some space. You will find a handy collection of grots at The Grotto. Keep your eye on the low pressure systems – anything above 1000 millibars and you will be in heaven.

Heading north skip PE, stopping only for a burger and a perv at Hobie Beach, and rock on to **Port Alfred**. There are excellent right-handers from the east pier of this sleepy fishing town. In December it hosts the end of the SA series of the Samsung Surf competition with partying, bands and a few hangovers.

Travelling through the old **Ciskei** on the way to East London there are some remote secret spots – don't expect the locals to reveal them, explore yourself. Then **East London**, home to the legendary Nahoon Reef, known to be the most consistent wave in RSA. A thick juicy wave that rises from deep water and thumps down on a boulder reef. If you find yourself stuck in the bowl this wave will rattle your bones. Nahoon Beach and The Corner are the nursery for EL grommets. Due to the abundance of swell this is the place to hang out, while the Buccaneer's, next to the Sugarshack, is the meeting place for those in the know. Buy these guys a beer and they will let you in on Graveyards and Yellow Sands. Nahoon is not as sharky as it is made out to be – but we make no promises (keep your legs up)!

Up **north** check out Whacky Point on a big swell – this is serious – an horrendous barrelling right-hander. Watch out for Doughnut Rock at the end. Cross the Kei by pont and search for *the wave* which locals reckon is on a par with Supertubes – it does exist!

**Chester Mackley, The Sugarshack**

**Middle** J Bay Tourism can put you in touch with some very reasonable B&Bs and guest-houses. You can find something for R70 or less per person but be prepared to pay up to R110. Recommended are *Supertubes Guest-house* (☎ (0423) 793 2957), 8 Pepper St, near the famous surf break of the same name; *Stratos* (☎ (0423) 93 1116), 11 Uys St, near Main Beach; and *The Guesthouse in Jeffreys Bay* (☎ (0423) 93 1878) at 17 Flame Crescent.

*Beach Cabanas* (☎ (0432) 93 2323), near the Seashells Beach Hotel, is modern and close to the surf. Low-season rates are R180 for a six bed room. The very impressive *Diaz 15 Holiday Apartments* (☎ (0423) 93 1779) cost R250 for two-bed units in the low season.

*Jeffreys Bay Holiday Resort* (☎ (0423) 93 1330) on Drommedaris St is within easy walking distance of the main beach and has a variety of self-catering units. There's a pool and tennis courts. Low-season rates start from R110 per unit (for two people); in the high season it is R160.

The *Savoy Protea Hotel* (☎ (0423) 93 1106) is a luxurious option in town. It's OK, but nothing exceptional. Expect to pay around R200/290. Directly in front of Magnatubes, *Seashells Beach Hotel* (☎ (0423) 93 1104) has less--expensive rooms.

### Places to Eat

*The Breakers* (☎ (0423) 93 1975), Ferreira St, overlooking the water, is an excellent place to go for a bit of a splurge. Other than pasta for about R25, the menu is mainly seafood in the R40-and-over bracket. *Chokker's Takeaway* on Da Gama Rd near the Savoy Protea Hotel has good food at cheap prices. There are pastas from R15, curry and rice from R8. Across the road, *Trawlers* has reasonable hamburgers and fish and chips, and it specialises in calamari.

*Le Grotto*, upstairs on the corner of Goedehoop and Da Gama, has pizzas and

1kg steak (R30) but the service is slow. Nearby are the much better *Rendez-Vous* for breakfasts and light meals; *Café Havanna*, in the Malhoek Centre, for continental fare; and the excellent *Sunflower Coffee Shop* for vegetarian meals.

The *Belafonte Floating Restaurant* at the Marina Martinique, a few kilometres south of town, looks like a big Mississippi steamboat. You eat as you ride through the channels; there is something to suit every taste and budget from R28 up. *Dock of the Bay* (☎ (0423) 96 1565) is right on the edge of the ocean at Clapton's Beach, also south of town. An absolute seafood feast is R65. It is not open every day, so phone in advance.

### Entertainment

*Rick's Sports Bar* in the Magnatubes Building in Da Gama Rd is the preferred drinking spot of the local surfies. It's a noisy sort of place.

*Cornerstone*, near the Spar supermarket in Da Gama Rd, is an alternative club with live music. Popular with locals and visitors, it hosts big South African bands. *O'Hagan's*, opposite the Savoy Protea Hotel in Da Gama Rd, has a nice bar with an international beer selection.

### Getting There & Away

**Bus** Intercape stops at the Savoy Protea Hotel on its daily run between Cape Town (R130, 15 hours) and Port Elizabeth (R45), via the Garden Route and Swellendam. Translux buses on the Garden and Mountain routes between Cape Town and Port Elizabeth stop at Humansdorp on the N2, but at the time of writing they no longer ran to J Bay.

The Hopper Bus (☎ (041) 55 4000) which runs from Port Elizabeth to Cape Town (R215 for a 10 sector pass) stops at J Bay daily (at 8.30 am westwards, 3.45 pm eastwards). The Baz Bus (☎ (021) 439 2323) stops at hostels on Monday and Thursday (eastwards), Tuesday and Friday (westwards); J Bay to Cape Town is R175, and to Port Elizabeth R25.

**Minibus Taxi** Taxis depart from Bloch's supermarket. You'll have to take a taxi to Humansdorp (R4.50) and pick up another there. Humansdorp to Port Elizabeth is R15.

## PORT ELIZABETH

Port Elizabeth's city centre is on steep hills overlooking Algoa Bay and there are some pleasant beaches and parks, virtually in the centre of town. Although this seems an excellent start, and the city also has some interesting historical architecture, the 20th century has been unkind. What must once have been a fine example of a Victorian/Edwardian port city has, unfortunately, been the victim of neglect.

To compensate, Port Elizabeth (almost universally known as 'PE') bills itself as the Friendly City. Of course, it's personality not appearance that counts in life. Remarkably, given the hype, PE *is* a genuinely friendly place. Quite a few travellers who have washed up here have had a good time; there's a thriving nightlife.

In theory, there are over one million people in the city, although as always the number of blacks and coloureds is probably underestimated. The theory says there are roughly 200,000 whites, 200,000 coloureds and 600,000 blacks. There are some enormous townships around PE and its sister city Uitenhage, where all the problems of poverty and violence are well represented.

Blacks have not always found PE friendly. It was in PE's Sanlam Centre that Steve Biko, the inspirational Black Consciousness leader, was interrogated and beaten into a coma. After three days lying chained, naked and unconscious in his cell, he was loaded into the back of a jeep that took him 1200km over back-roads to a prison hospital in Pretoria, where he died on 12 September 1976. At the subsequent inquest, the magistrate found that no-one was to blame. In June 1997, the Truth and Reconciliation Commission heard an apology on behalf of the South African medical profession for its failure to treat Biko. Mr Peter Folb, head of pharmacology at the University of Cape Town, apologised directly to Biko's widow Ntsiki and his brother Khaya, saying two doctors had falsified Biko's medical records on the request of the police.

EASTERN CAPE PROVINCE

## Orientation

Port Elizabeth is 1115km from Jo'burg, 785km from Cape Town and 310km from East London. It's a major transport hub.

The train station (for buses and trains) is just to the north of the Campanile, an unmistakable bell tower (which you can climb for a donation), now isolated from the city by a ghastly freeway. The left-luggage office in the train station is open from 8 am to 5 pm, Monday to Friday.

Donkin Reserve, immediately behind the town centre, has good views over the bay. It's a handy point to get your bearings. The pyramid in the reserve is a memorial; the lighthouse beside the pyramid houses the information centre. The reserve is flanked by some fine Victorian architecture: on the north side by a row of terraces, on the west by the Edward Protea Hotel.

The city centre has been more heavily policed (and there has been a noticeable reduction in crimes such as bag-snatching).

Still, many businesses have moved out to the wealthy white western suburbs, difficult to access if you don't have a car. The industrial areas and the city centre should be avoided at night. The city's main beachfront is considered one of the safest in the country.

## Information

**Tourist Offices** The well-organised Tourism Port Elizabeth (☎ (041) 52 1315), with 24 hour voice mail (☎ (041) 56 0773), has an excellent supply of information and maps, including *Donkin Heritage Trail* (R5) which details a walk around the city's historic buildings. The office is in the light-house building in Donkin Reserve; it is open 8 am to 4.30 pm Monday to Friday, on weekends from 9.30 am to 3.30 pm.

A satellite information office (☎ (041) 55 5427), on the beachfront in the old Children's Museum, Humewood, operates daily and is open from 9 am to 5 pm; it offers a variety of budget tours (eg Addo R100/50 for

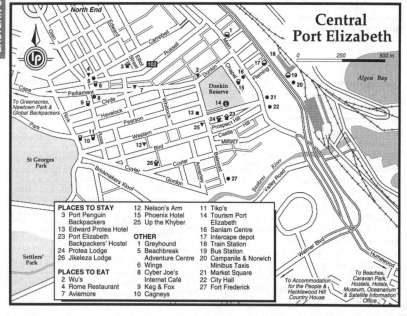

Central Port Elizabeth

| PLACES TO STAY | | |
| --- | --- | --- |
| 3 Port Penguin Backpackers | 12 Nelson's Arm | 11 Tiko's |
| 13 Edward Protea Hotel | 15 Phoenix Hotel | 14 Tourism Port Elizabeth |
| 23 Port Elizabeth Backpackers' Hostel | 25 Up the Khyber | 16 Sanlam Centre |
| 24 Protea Lodge | **OTHER** | 17 Intercape depot |
| 26 Jikeleza Lodge | 1 Greyhound | 18 Train Station |
| | 5 Beachbreak Adventure Centre | 19 Bus Station |
| **PLACES TO EAT** | 6 Wings | 20 Campanile & Norwich Minibus Taxis |
| 2 Wu's | 8 Cyber Joe's Internet Café | 21 Market Square |
| 4 Rome Restaurant | 9 Keg & Fox | 22 City Hall |
| 7 Aviemore | 10 Cagneys | 27 Fort Frederick |

EASTERN CAPE PROVINCE

adults/children, townships R60). Ectour (☎ (041) 55 7761) at 25 Donkin St has regional information.

**Money** Amex (☎ (041) 35 1225) has an office on Pamela Arcade, 2nd Ave, Newton Park, north-west of the city centre. Rennies Travel (☎ (041) 34 3536) is in the Murray & Roberts Building, 48-52 Ring St, Green-acres – a long way from the town centre.

### Settlers' Park & Fort Frederick
Although Settlers' Park is virtually in the centre of the city, it includes 54 hectares of cultivated and natural gardens in the valley of the Baakens River. With the main emphasis on native plants and flowers, it's also a good place for bird life. The main entrance is on How St (off Park Drive, which circles St Georges Park and its sporting fields) – there's a great view from the car park.

Fort Frederick, on Belmont Terrace, over-looking the Baakens River, was built in 1799 to defend the original harbour at the river mouth. It has never fired a shot in anger.

### Port Elizabeth Museum & Oceanarium
This is one of the best and largest museums in the country. There are some interesting anthropological and archaeological exhibitions, a tropical house and snake park, and an oceanarium, complete with dolphin demonstrations. The complex is open daily from 9 am to 1 pm and 2 to 5 pm; the dolphins perform at 11 am and 3 pm. Entry to the museum is R2/1 for adults/children, to the snake park and tropical house it is R7/4, and to the oceanarium R12/7.

### Beaches
Port Elizabeth is a major water sports venue – it hosted the 1995 world windsurfing championships. The beaches are south of the centre. Take Humewood Rd from the city; this becomes Beach Rd, then Marine Drive. Kings Beach stretches from the harbour breakwater to Humewood Beach; both of these are sheltered. Hobie Cats and surfers make for Hobie Beach, about 5km from the city centre.

There's a public pool in St Georges Park and a tidal swimming pool at MacArthur Baths on Kings Beach Promenade.

### Activities
Ndlovini Tours (☎ (041) 51 2572) operates tours to Walmer (Gqebera) to see **township life**, squatter camps, *shebeens* (for a traditional meal) and Resource Development Programme projects – the cost is R60 per person, meal included.

The tourist **steam train** *Apple Express* runs on a day trip to Thornhill and back, with a two hour stop for a *braai*. Along the way it crosses over the highest narrow-gauge bridge in the world. The trip costs R50/25 for adults/children.

There are seven or more **walks** for which you can get guides. Paradise Expeditions (☎ (041) 55 1977) provides refreshments and transport to/from the trails for R110.

Good **diving** sites around PE include some wrecks and the St Croix Islands, a marine reserve. Several outfits offer diving and courses, including Ocean Divers (☎ (041) 55 6536), African Coastal Adventures (☎ (041) 66 2259) and Prodive (☎ (083) 659 2324).

**Sports Equipment** Sporting gear (mountain bikes, boogie boards, windsurfers) is sold and hired out by Beachbreak Adventure Centre (☎ (041) 55 4384), 109 Russell Rd.

### Places to Stay
**Budget** *Sea Acres* (☎ (041) 53 2407), Beach Rd, Humewood, opposite the pedestrian pier, is the closest caravan park to town. It's not great but there are plenty of trees. Sites cost R45 plus R10 per person, with a big discount if you don't have a car. Basic four-bed huts cost R110 and there is a variety of fully equipped (including TV) rondavels and chalets/cottages from R220 to R460 for up to six people.

The pick of the inner-city hostels is the small, clean and well-presented *Jikeleza Lodge* (☎ (041) 56 3721) at 44 Cuyler St; camping is R15, dorms are R30, doubles and twins are R40 per person. It is run by keen travellers who happily transport you to the beach, and pick you up from anywhere in PE.

The friendly, well-managed *PE Backpackers' Hostel* (☎ (041) 56 0697), 7 Prospect Hill Rd, is in a 100 year old building (it shows) in a good location, within walking distance of the city and the places to eat and drink up on the headland. Dorms are R30, doubles are R40 per person.

Also central is the double storey *Port Penguin Backpackers* (☎ (041) 55 4499), 67B Russell Rd; dorms are from R25 per night. It is difficult to find – enter the limited parking area from Elliott St. The ragged *Protea Lodge* (☎ (041) 55 1721), 17 Prospect Hill Rd, may wish to entice the traveller dollar – it is nothing like a backpackers' and should only be a last resort.

*Kings Beach Backpackers* (☎ (041) 55 8113), 41 Windermere Rd, Humewood, is the best beach option. This place epitomises what we mean by 'backpackers' – adequate 'digs' in friendly surroundings. The dorms for R30, and doubles for R40 per person, are worth it. *Brookes Hill Bunkhouse* (☎ (041) 56 0088), Brookes Hill Drive, Humewood, is an alternative if Kings Beach is full.

Out of town are *'Accommodation for the People'* (☎ (041) 51 1781) at 106 Heugh Rd in Walmer; the new but not necessarily 'flash' *Global Backpackers* (☎ (041) 34 3768) at 75 Cape Rd (R30 for a dorm) – it needs lots of work; and *Spring Valley Farm* (☎ (041) 72 1882/2313), a holiday farm with ranch-style bunk rooms. The farm is at 17 Destades Rd, Colleen Glen – 20 minutes drive north of the city centre.

**B&Bs & Guesthouses** Tourism Port Elizabeth assists with B&B bookings; there's also a B&B association (☎ (041) 33 3716). Most places charge between R80 and R130 per person. *Hacklewood Hill Country House* (☎ (041) 51 1300), at 158 Prospect Rd, Walmer, is one of the top guesthouses in the region; singles/doubles are R540/R720.

**Hotels** *Hotel Formule 1* (☎ (041) 55 6380) is on the corner of La Roche Drive and Beach Rd; a room for one to three is R119 (a simple

breakfast is R7 extra). *The Caboose* (☎ 56 0088), Brookes Hill Drive, Humewood, is a good-value place modelled on a 'sleeper train'. Its only drawback (but the reason for its economy) are the claustrophobic little rooms with plastic shower/toilet cubicles; the rates for singles/doubles/triples are R79/118/137.

The *Edward Protea Hotel* (☎ (041) 56 2056), on Belmont Terrace in the heart of the city, is a gracious, old-style Edwardian hotel with comfortable rooms. It's a superior member of the Protea chain. Standard single/double rooms are R195/230, single/double sea-facing rooms are R220/260. Breakfast is R25 extra, but it's worth it.

The *Humewood* (☎ (041) 55 1558), 33 Beach Rd, is another older hotel, on the seafront south of the city centre; standard rooms are R160/190 and sea-facing rooms are R175/220, including breakfast.

*City Lodge* (☎ (041) 56 3322), on the corner of Beach and Lodge Rds in Summerstrand, south of the city, is a fairly flash place with singles/doubles for R180/ 210. *Holiday Inn Garden Court – Kings Beach* (☎ (041) 52 3720), corner of Beach and La Roche, has singles/doubles for R279/ 318.

Port Elizabeth's best hotel, the *Marine Protea* (☎ (041) 53 2101), Marine Drive, Summerstrand, has single/double rooms for R410/R460.

### Places to Eat

*Cyber Joe's Internet Café*, 123 Parliament St, is open noon to midnight every day for cyberspace travel over a coffee. *Wu's* at 11 Belmont Terrace in the centre is open 24 hours for vegetarian meals, a good selection of coffee and decent music. There are cheap places at The Bridge, Greenacres, including the ever-reliable *Mike's* and *Steers*.

If you haven't yet experienced the full splendour of a South African breakfast, head along to the dining room at the dignified *Edward Protea Hotel*. A stupendous breakfast in a nice room costs R25 – a bargain. Non-guests are welcome.

One of the better restaurants in the country, *Aviemore* (☎ (041) 55 1125) specialises in fresh local produce and game, superbly prepared. If your palate is hanging out for cuisine (South African provincial) rather than just food, this is the place to come. Most mains are under R40 and there are some very interesting entrées from R25.

The *Rome Restaurant*, on Campbell St near the corner of Russell St, is a pizza and pasta place with an all-you-can-eat deal on Tuesday. If you're paying by the dish, prices aren't bad, with pasta at R17. It's popular, so you might have to wait for a table.

*Up the Khyber*, an Indian restaurant on the corner of Western and Belmont, sometimes has an all-you-can-eat deal for R13. It is vegan-friendly, unlike most South African places.

The *Phoenix Hotel* (☎ (041) 56 3553), 5 Chapel St, is an entertainment institution, with live music. The food is good value, with T-bone and chips for R15.

*Blackbeard's Lookout & Seafood Tavern* is in the Brookes Pavilion on the main beachfront; it has sumptuous platters for R50-plus. *Nelson's Arm* at 3 Trinder Square in the centre specialises in line fish, crayfish and oysters; meals are from R30 to R40. *Tides*, at 8th Ave, Summerstrand Village, open daily for lunch and dinner, is another quality seafood place.

### Entertainment

For some reason Wednesday seems to be the biggest night in the pubs and clubs, although Friday and Saturday are pretty popular as well. Few places have cover charges. The free *In Town Tonight* details the venues.

The *Phoenix Hotel*, 5 Chapel St, is a small, dark and very friendly pub with live music on some nights. Other night venues include *Club 2night* on Main St (techno/dance); *Cagneys* off Rink St; and *Wings* on Russell St near the corner of Rose St. *Tiko's*, on Rose St in the centre, attracts backpackers (mostly on the say-so of nearby hostels) and those who like their music a little folksy.

The Brookes Pavilion has a number of restaurants/nightspots such as *Tequila Sunrise*, the 'in' place at the moment; and *Tapas Al Sol* – as the name suggests, a tapas bar. A

little further down on Hobie Beach is the Boardwalk, with *Cadillac Jack's*, *Barney's* and *Einsteins* (funk/disco).

### Getting There & Away

**Air** SA Airlink (☎ (041) 51 2310) flies from PE to Jo'burg (R650) daily, and PE to Cape Town (R513) daily except Saturday.

**Bus** Greyhound buses (☎ (041) 56 4879) depart from the rear car park, 107 Main St; reservations can also be made at the Computicket office, Greenacres Centre (☎ (041) 34 4550). The Translux office (☎ (041) 507 3333) is in the Ernest & Young Building in Ring Rd, Greenacres. Intercape (☎ (041) 56 0055) only accepts telephone bookings; it departs from the corner of Fleming and North Union Sts (behind the old post office) or the Edgar's entrance at Greenacres shopping mall.

**Heading West** Translux has a daily bus to Cape Town (R130) via the Garden Route. Stops include Plettenberg Bay (R55), Knysna (R75), George (R80), Oudtshoorn (R80), Mossel Bay (R95) and Swellendam (R120) – there is also a daily service in the other direction. Both depart at 8 am in the morning. There is an additional service on Monday, Wednesday, Friday and Saturday in both directions. Translux also runs to Cape Town via what it calls the Mountain Route. On Tuesday, Thursday and Sunday a bus leaves Port Elizabeth at 8.30 pm and follows the Garden Route to Oudtshoorn, then runs via Montagu (R115), Paarl (R130) and Stellenbosch, arriving in Cape Town at 8.30 am. The return bus leaves Cape Town at 6 pm on Monday, Wednesday and Friday, arriving in PE at 5.50 am.

Intercape also has two daily Garden Route services linking Cape Town and Port Elizabeth (they do not go via Oudtshoorn). Buses leave Cape Town station at 7 am and 8 pm and PE at 7 am and 8 pm; the fare is R140 (10 hours).

Greyhound's daily Durban-Cape Town service stops in PE; to Durban it is R220, and to Cape Town R145.

EASTERN CAPE PROVINCE

The Baz Bus (☎ (021) 439 2323) runs from Cape Town to PE (R120) on Monday, Tuesday, Thursday and Friday. It runs in the other direction on Wednesday, Thursday, Saturday and Sunday. The Hopper Bus (☎ (041) 55 4000) runs daily from PE to Mossel Bay, where it links with a shuttle to Cape Town (R170).

**Heading North** Greyhound has nightly buses from PE to Jo'burg (R275, 17 hours). Translux has a Tuesday, Wednesday, Thursday, Friday and Sunday service from PE to Jo'burg (R245) via Graaff-Reinet and Bloemfontein. There is also a Monday and Saturday service via Cradock. Intercape has a Sunday and Thursday service from PE to Jo'burg (R240).

**Heading East** Translux runs to Durban (R195) daily, via Grahamstown (R70), East London (R85), Umtata (R135) and Port Shepstone (R190). Buses depart from PE at 7 am, arriving in Durban at 8.30 pm. They depart Durban at 6.30 am, arriving in PE at 7.45 pm. Greyhound also runs to Durban (R220) daily. Intercape runs between PE and East London (R80) on Sunday, Monday, Wednesday, Friday and Saturday, via Port Alfred. Buses depart from PE at 7 am, from East London at 1.30 pm.

The Baz Bus (☎ (021) 439 2323) runs from PE to Durban (R185) on Tuesday and Friday. It runs in the other direction on Thursday and Sunday.

**Train** The *Algoa* operates between PE and Jo'burg, via Bloemfontein. Trains depart from PE at 2.30 pm daily and arrive in Jo'burg at 9 pm the next day. Trains depart from Jo'burg at 2.30 pm daily and arrive at PE at 9.25 am the next day. First/2nd class fares are R240/162.

The *Southern Cross* runs between PE and Cape Town, departing from PE at 8.45 am on Sunday and arriving in Cape Town at 8.40 am the next day. Trains depart from Cape Town at 6.15 pm on Friday and arrive in PE at 5.50 pm the following day. For enquiries

contact Spoornet (☎ (041) 507 2400). First/2nd class fares are R212/152.

**Minibus Taxi** Norwich long-distance taxis (☎ (041) 55 7253) depart from under the freeway near the bell tower; there's an office in a small 'wendy house' (shed). Norwich taxis run daily to Cape Town (R100, nine hours) and on Monday, Wednesday and Friday to Jo'burg (R170, 12 hours).

Most taxis leave from the large townships surrounding PE and can be difficult to find. The taxi park on Strand St, a few blocks north of the bell tower, is for the local area.

There is a luxury minibus, J-Bay Sunshine Express (☎ (041) 51 3790), between Jeffreys Bay, PE and other coastal areas.

**Car** All the big car-rental operators have offices in Port Elizabeth, or at the airport: Avis (☎ (041) 51 1306), Budget (☎ (041) 51 4242) and Imperial (☎ (041) 51 4214). Try also Economic Car Hire (☎ (041) 51 5826), 104 Heugh Rd, Walmer.

### Getting Around
There's no public transport to the airport. A taxi costs around R25. Taxis and hire cars are available at the airport. For taxis, contact City Taxis (☎ (041) 34 2212) or Hurter's Radio Cabs (☎ (041) 55 7344).

Algoa Bus Company (☎ (041) 41 4241) runs a scheduled central-city service to the beachfront, the centre, St Georges Park, Greenacres and the Bridge shopping complex. It departs from a number of places in the city centre, especially Main St.

### ADDO ELEPHANT NATIONAL PARK
Addo is 72km north of Port Elizabeth near the Zuurberg range in the Sundays River valley. It's a small park (14,550 hectares) protecting the small remnant of the huge elephant herd that once roamed across the Eastern Cape. It's a beautiful park with curious flora, and you are almost guaranteed of seeing elephant.

Unfortunately, elephants and farmers don't happily coexist. The idea of the gentle harmless elephant doesn't wash when you see the amount of damage they can do – they're like bulldozers that eat and drink. When farmers started to develop the area at the beginning of the 20th century, they found themselves in conflict with the herds.

A Major Pretorius was commissioned to deal with the 'menace', and until he was stopped by a public outcry he seemed likely to succeed. It was thanks to two local landowners, the Harveys, who allowed the elephants to stay on their land, that any survived. Addo was proclaimed a national park in 1931 when there were only 11 elephants left.

Today some 200 elephant roam the park. They can survive at this unusually high density thanks to the weird Addo bush, which is close to elephant gourmet. The dominant plant (and elephant meal) is the pink-flowered spekboom *(Portulacaria afra)* which grows to a height of about 3m and has a small succulent leaf. There are also aloes, vygies and pelargoniums – there's a great display of flowers after spring rains. And where elephants do their business you'll find the busy dung beetle.

### Information

The entrance gate is open from 7 am to 7 pm. The roads around the park are dirt and can become impassable in the wet, so the park is closed if there has been heavy rain. If in doubt, phone ahead (☎ (0426) 40 0556). Day visitors are charged R20 per vehicle. A well-stocked shop is open from 8 am to 7 pm daily.

It's best to arrive at the park by mid-morning and to stake out one of the water holes where the elephants tend to gather during the heat of the day – there are about 45km of roads so it pays to take advice from a ranger on where to go.

### Places to Stay & Eat

Make accommodation bookings at the National Parks office in Pretoria or Cape Town. Six-bed cottages cost R500 for up to four people, breakfast included; two-bed chalets are R220; chalets with two single beds and a double sleeper couch cost R270 for two; and two-bed rondavels with a bathroom but no

kitchen are R200 for two. Extra adults/children are R60/30 each. Bedding is supplied in all huts. There's also a small but pleasant *camping area*, with sites for R36 for two people plus R10 per additional person. There's also a communal kitchen and a restaurant (open from 8 am to 10 pm daily).

### Getting There & Away

It's an interesting drive from Port Elizabeth to Addo, although there are some very depressing townships and industrial developments in the immediate vicinity of PE. The park is signposted from the N2. Alternatively, you can travel via Uitenhage; there are attractive citrus farms along the banks of the Sundays River from Kirkwood to Uitenhage.

Those without transport can take tours from Port Elizabeth – contact Tourism Port Elizabeth for suggested operators.

### SHAMWARI GAME RESERVES

These luxurious private reserves, 30km east of Addo Elephant National Park (75km from PE), are dedicated to restocking large tracts of land with animals which were once common in the region – elephant, white and black rhino, leopard and giraffe.

Accommodation starts at R950/1250 in the low season, R1100/1600 in the high season, including all meals and activities. For B&B only, prices start at around R800 a double. Book on ☎ (042) 851 1196.

### BUSHMAN'S RIVER MOUTH

This river mouth (Boesmanriviermond) is an expensive holiday resort on a beautiful bit of coast – for those wanting a quiet holiday in unspoilt surroundings. A 4km hiking trail runs from the river mouth to Kwaaihoek, where Bartholomeu Dias erected a cross in 1488. The eponymous *camping ground* (☎ (0464) 81227) is an attractive sheltered spot, and foreigners are given a warm welcome. The rate is R30 plus R5 per person in the low season.

The Kenton/Bushman's Publicity Association (☎ (0464) 82418) will provide more information on activities and accommodation. If you are driving, turn off the N2 to the

R72 as soon as you can. There are attractive rolling hills and a 'dunefield' (also known as a dune sea) around Alexandria, and scenic forest which runs for 10km along the coast.

## PORT ALFRED

Port Alfred is an interesting town in transition between being a genuine fishing village (with a large black population) and an up-market holiday resort with a huge artificial island development. Some people would argue that it has already been spoilt, but some visitors will find it a bustling, enjoyable place to stay for a night or longer. It's often called The Kowie, after the river.

The climate is excellent – gentle and subtropical. Surfers will find good right-hand breaks at the river mouth; for golfers there's a famous, extremely beautiful golf course, one of the four 'Royals' in South Africa; and for the adventurous there's 'dune skiing' (sandski board hire is R5).

### Information

The visitors' bureau (☎ (0464) 41235; fax 24 4139), on the east bank of the river in the Market Buildings, is open from 8.30 am to 1 pm and 2 to 4 pm weekdays, 8.30 am to noon Saturday. It has brochures for R0.25 listing places to stay, walks and canoe trails.

### Activities

Three Sisters Horse Trails (☎ (0464) 71 1269) has daily **rides**, either on the beach (one hour, R60) or in the bush (two hours, R75).

The two day Kowie Canoe Trail is a fairly easy 18km **canoe trip** upriver from Port Alfred, with an overnight stay in a hut at Horseshoe Bend. For bookings (well in advance) and canoe hire, contact Kowie Canoe Trail, Box 217, Port Alfred 6170 (☎ (0464) 42230). The cost is R20 per person per day for a double canoe and R20 per night for a permit. There's a pleasant 8km

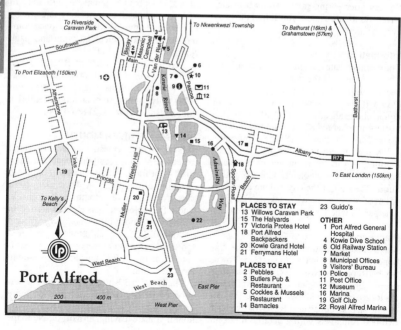

Port Alfred

**PLACES TO STAY**
13 Willows Caravan Park
15 The Halyards
17 Victoria Protea Hotel
18 Port Alfred Backpackers
20 Kowie Grand Hotel
21 Ferrymans Hotel

**PLACES TO EAT**
2 Pebbles
3 Butlers Pub & Restaurant
5 Cockles & Mussels Restaurant
14 Barnacles
23 Guido's

**OTHER**
1 Port Alfred General Hospital
4 Kowie Dive School
6 Old Railway Station
7 Market
8 Municipal Offices
9 Visitors' Bureau
10 Police
11 Post Office
12 Museum
16 Marina
19 Golf Club
22 Royal Alfred Marina

**hiking trail** through the Kowie Nature Reserve; the cost is R2.50 per person.

Kowie Dive School (☎ (0464) 42213) at 43 Van der Riet St has **diving** courses for R850, a resort course for R250 and an introductory pool dive for R60. The best diving is in May and August. The winter water temperature (18°C to 24°C) is actually higher than in summer (12°C to 18°C). Visibility is not outstanding, but there are plenty of big fish, sponges and soft corals. Locals claim that the reef here is South Africa's most colourful.

**Places to Stay**

*Port Alfred Backpackers* (☎ (0464) 43020), 29 Sports Rd, crams its clientele into overcrowded dorms (R30 for such little space in a sterile atmosphere) – hopefully they will amend this. To experience claustrophobia, take the first left turn as you directly approach the marina (off the R72) and follow the resort security fence; the hostel is on your left.

The *Willows Caravan Park* (☎ (0464) 24 5201) is reasonably close to town, near the bridge over the Kowie River. A camp site is R30, rising to R40 over Christmas. *Riverside Caravan Park* (☎ (0464) 42230), on Mentone Rd, is also on the west side of the river, but it's some way north of the town centre and more than an easy walk from the beach. It's a pleasant spot (although it probably gets crowded in season). Caravan sites are R35 for two people, rising to R70 in season (there are no tent sites). Chalets are R140 for two in the low season, R260 for four (minimum) in the high season.

The visitors' bureau lists numerous B&Bs. Estate agents, including Kevin Heny (☎ (0464) 41110), let apartments/cottages on a longer-term basis.

*Ferrymans Hotel* (☎ (0464) 41122), on the river bank and the closest hotel to the beach, has rooms for R75/85 per person in the low/high season, with breakfast. In an old building, the hotel has a bar and very cheap meals, including a Sunday braai.

Up on the corner of Grand St and Princes Ave, *Kowie Grand Hotel* (☎ (0464) 41150) is beginning to look a little tired but still has comfortable rooms with TVs and great views of the river and ocean. Singles/doubles are R110/170 plus R20 for breakfast. *Victoria Protea Hotel* (☎ (0464) 41133), East Bank, is a comfortable pub. You pay as low as R280 a double when it's slow, otherwise R225/345 for B&B.

By far the best place to stay is *The Halyards* (☎ (0464) 42410), Royal Alfred Marina, Albany Rd. It's a very comfortable waterfront hotel with attractive Cape Cod architecture. The rooms are large, well equipped, and look over the harbour; they are a bargain at R200/300 in mid-season.

**Places to Eat**

*Butlers Pub* is a very pleasant place for a beer, a snack or a meal. It's on the west bank of the river and has a nice verandah. Most dishes on the pub-meals menu cost well under R20 and are available from 11 am to 11 pm. Restaurant meals are available from noon to 2.30 pm and from 6.30 to 9.30 pm. The menu includes entrées such as grilled mussels (R11) and mains such as vegetarian platter (R21) and calamari (R25).

The popular and informal *Barnacles* (☎ (0464) 42410) overlooks the marina and commands great views. It's the spot to have a cold beer and a hot pizza. A seafood pizza costs R28; other varieties cost less. The dining room at the *Kowie Grand Hotel* (☎ (0464) 41150) has good-value traditional meals and the Sunday lunches are famous.

New places include *Guido's* on the beach for pizza (R25), good ambience and late-night boozing; and *Pebbles* on Main Rd for delectable steak and kebab meals (from R25).

**Getting There & Away**

Intercape buses stop here on the run between Port Elizabeth (R60) and East London (R55) on Sunday, Monday, Wednesday, Friday and Saturday. The Baz Bus also does drop-offs on Tuesday and Friday (eastwards), Thursday and Sunday (westwards); the cost to East London is R50, to Port Elizabeth R50 and to Durban R220.

## SHIPWRECK COAST

This stretch of coast, the graveyard for many ships, is still largely unspoilt because it was once part of the Ciskei Homeland. There are a couple of resort towns and the inevitable casino/hotel, but it is still easy to get away from it all here.

### Shipwreck Hiking Trail

Although the potential length of the trail, from the Great Fish River to the Ncera River, is 64km, it is possible to do any section as there are several easy entry and exit points. This is one of the few walking areas in South Africa where hikers can set their own pace, camp more or less where they choose and light fires. They are rewarded with wild, unspoilt sections of surf beach, rich coastal vegetation and beautiful estuaries.

The climate is generally mild and excellent, although it can rain at any time of the year. The walking is relatively easy – light shoes are all you will need. There are no facilities – hikers must carry water, tents and cooking equipment. Water is only available at the resorts and holiday townships. Hikers can camp on the beach, but not on private property at the Fish River and Mpekweni Sun hotels. Fires made from driftwood are permitted providing they are on sand away from vegetation.

It's 11.5km from the Great Fish River (easily accessible from Port Alfred, because of the Fish River Sun) to Mpekweni (where there is another Sun); 11km from Mpekweni to Bira River (where the coastal road bends inland); 20km from Bira River to Hamburg (a small village with a great hostel); 6km from Hamburg to Kiwane Resort; 15.5km from Kiwane to the Ncera River; and another 29km to East London. The trail must be booked with Ectour, Bisho (☎ (0401) 95 2115) and costs R20 per person per night.

There are backpackers' buses and minibus taxis on the coastal road between Port Alfred and East London, and between Grahamstown and East London. See those entries for more details.

In *Complete Guide to Walks & Trails in Southern Africa*, Jaynee Levy recommends the sections from the Great Fish River to Bira River and from Hamburg to Kiwane Resort. The area is covered by the official 1:50,000 topographic maps *Prudhoe, Hamburg* and *Kidd's Beach*.

### The Shipwreck Coast 'Suns'

The *Fish River Sun* (☎ (0405) 66 1101) at the estuary of the Great Fish River is one of the best of Sun's hotel/casinos. The attractive buildings are only a stone's throw from the sea. The complex includes restaurants and bars, a pool, an 18 hole Gary Player golf course, and squash and tennis courts. Horse-riding is also offered. Needless to say, it isn't cheap. Singles/doubles start at R340/440, depending on the time of the week and year.

The *Mpekweni Sun Marine Resort* is also run by the ubiquitous Sun group. It's about 11.5km east of the Great Fish River and is more of a family resort than the Fish River Sun. The hotel is beside the sea; there's a restaurant, several bars and a pool. In addition to a surf beach, there's a protected lagoon. This makes almost every water sport possible. Singles/doubles start at R375/535 during the week, R395/550 on weekends.

Intercape bus services between Port Elizabeth and East London stop here.

### Hamburg

The small village of Hamburg, at the wide river flats at the mouth of the Keiskamma River, is near some of the best coast in South Africa. The river flats are home to many birds, especially migrating waders in summer. They also offer good fishing. The name Hamburg is derived from a village established by soldiers of the British German Legion in 1857.

*Hamburg Oyster Lodge* (☎ (0405) 88 1020), one of SA's original backpackers', offers slightly rough-and-ready self-catering accommodation and a good backpackers' section where dorm beds are R25 (doubles are R35 per person). They offer ultra-cheap cruises and fishing trips on the lagoon (R10 for a few hours). A new place, *Clive's*, is operated by the Clive of Oyster Lodge. On Tuesday, both places pick up from East

London. The highlight here is the R50 seafood buffet – eat to believe!

The *Hamburg Hotel* (☎ (0405) 88 1061) is a comfy family hotel with dinner, bed and breakfast for R99 per person (more in summer).

There's a daily minibus taxi to/from East London, about 100km east. Fortunately, the reliable Baz Bus picks up and drops off here (R60 from Port Elizabeth, R25 from East London).

## EAST LONDON

This bustling port with 750,000 residents (surrounding townships included) has a good surf beach and a spectacular bay which curves around to huge sand hills. The port, on the Buffalo River, is the country's largest river harbour. After being hit hard by the recession, EL (as it is universally known) is regaining its family-holiday atmosphere. Still, the surfside suburbs of Quigney and Beach are rather drab on cool, windy days.

If it is the quintessential beach/surfie lifestyle you are after, you have gravitated to the right place – a perfect place for making contacts before heading to Jeffreys Bay.

### Orientation

The main downtown street is Oxford St, with the city centre extending from about Argyle St south to Fleet St. Fleet St runs east, passing Currie St (which runs down to Orient Beach) and eventually, after a few corners and name changes, meets The Esplanade.

East of the river mouth, Orient Beach is popular with families and has a tidal pool. Eastern Beach is the long main beach fronting The Esplanade, but Nahoon Beach on the northern headland is better, with great surf. The best surfing is towards Nahoon Point.

Mdantsane, west of the town on the M3, was founded in 1962 to house EL's black workers, and is now the largest town in the area with a population estimated to be in excess of 330,000. It is the second largest township in South Africa, after Soweto. There should be township tours by now.

### Information

The Municipal Tourist Authority (☎ (0431) 26015) is on Argyle St behind the city hall. It's open from 8.30 am to 4.30 pm on weekdays, and from 8.30 to 11 am on Saturday (when it is most needed). Rennies Travel (☎ (0431) 23611) is at 33A Terminus St.

At the Telkom office, Gladstone St, you can make international calls between 8 am and 4 pm Monday to Thursday, until 3.30 pm on Friday, and from 8 to 11.30 am Saturday. The auto association (☎ (0431) 21271) is at 27 Fleet St.

Outdoor Living in Central Square on Gladstone St has hiking equipment. Screaming Blue Surfboards at 6 The Esplanade hires boards for about R20 per day, and they occasionally have wetsuits for hire; it's the best place to get surf equipment. For board repairs, go to Wet Addiction Surf Co in the SBDC Building, off Commercial Rd.

Get info about diving clubs in the area at Pollock's Sport & Surf (☎ (0431) 24921) in Bell St, Vincent Park. Anglers can get information from East Cape Angling Tours (☎ (0431) 47 2930) – they provide guides and equipment. For fishing charters, contact one Mr MacArthur (☎ (0431) 35 2604).

### Things to See & Do

The small **aquarium** on the beachfront is worth a look; entry is R5 (children R2.50).

The **East London museum** is at the north end of Oxford St, on the corner of Lukin Rd. Exhibits include the world's only dodo egg, a coelacanth model and Xhosa displays. It is open from 9.30 am to 5 pm on weekdays, 9.30 am to noon on Saturday and 11 am to 4 pm on Sunday; entry is R2.50 for adults.

The **Ann Bryant Art Gallery** is on St Marks Rd north of the museum, in an old mansion which is a mixture of Cape Dutch and Victorian styles. It is open from 9.30 am to 5 pm on weekdays, 9.30 am to noon on Saturday and on every third Sunday of the month. The gallery has a representative collection of South African artworks.

Queen's Park has a small **zoo**, open daily; admission is R5 (children R2.50). **Gately House**, near the entrance to Queen's Park, is

EASTERN CAPE PROVINCE

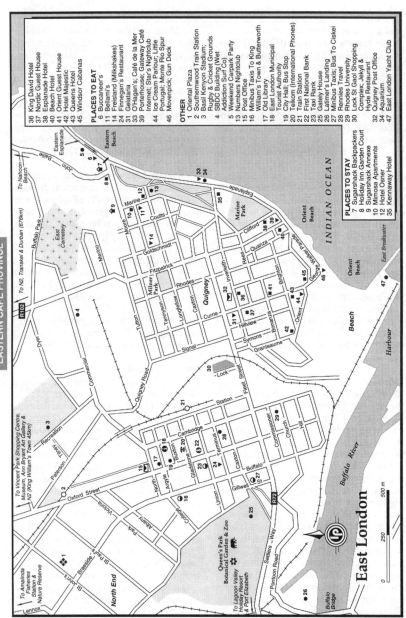

East London

INDIAN OCEAN

**PLACES TO EAT**
6 Buccaneer's
11 Bellami's
14 Freisland (Milkshakes)
24 Finnegan's Restaurant
31 Gelataria
33 O'Hagan's; Café de la Mer
39 Porterhouse; Gateway Café
Internet; Star's Nightclub
44 Ice Cream Parlour; Little
Portugal; Monte Rio Spur
46 Movenpick; Gun Deck

36 King David Hotel
37 Nordic Guest House
38 Esplanade Hotel
40 Beach Hotel
41 Orient Guest House
42 Hotel Majestic
43 Queens Hotel
45 Windsor Cabanas

**OTHER**
1 Oriental Plaza
2 Southernwood Train Station
3 Basil Kenyon Stadium;
Rugby & Cricket Grounds
4 SBDC Building (Wet
Addiction Surf Co)
13 Weekend Carpark Party
15 Numbers Nightclub
16 Post Office
16 Minibus Taxis To King
William's Town & Butterworth
17 East London Municipal
Tourist Authority
18 Old Library
19 City Hall; Bus Stop
20 Telkom (International Phones)
21 Train Station
22 First National Bank
23 Taxi Rank
25 Gately House
26 Latimer's Landing
27 Minibus Taxis; Bus To Ciskei
28 Rennies Travel
29 Rhodes University
30 Lock St Gaol Shopping
Complex; Jekyll &
Hyde Restaurant
32 Quigney Post Office
34 Aquarium
47 East London Yacht Club

**PLACES TO STAY**
7 Sugarshack Backpackers
8 Holiday Inn Garden Court
9 Sugarshack Annexe
10 Mimosa Apartments
12 Hotel Osner
35 Kennaway Hotel

furnished in period style. It was closed at the time of writing for renovations.

The **Guild Theatre** in the Civic Centre at the north end of Oxford St, near the corner of Lukin Rd, is a busy place in season, with everything from ballet to beauty contests. The **Arts Theatre Club**, Paterson St, has musicals (even enjoyed by surfies); the R30 entry includes a meal.

**Latimer's Landing** is a harbourside development near the Buffalo River, with restaurants and shops. If there are enough people you can hire the yacht *Miscky* (☎ (0431) 35 2232) for sailing cruises. The *Albatross* (odd name for a boat) has one to two-hour trips; it leaves every two hours from the wharf (R25). The double-decker *Tug & Ferry* (☎ (0431) 43 1188) cruises the Buffalo (R15).

Not far up the Nahoon River, in Dorchester Heights, is a great swimming place – Windmill Hole; park in Snowy Waters Rd, then walk upstream along the riverbank for about 20 minutes.

Aficionados of good music will enjoy East London's **April Reggae Festival**.

### Places to Stay

**Bottom End** About 12km south of town, just off Marine Drive in Cove Rock, is the picturesque *Lagoon Valley Holiday Resort* (☎ /fax (0431) 46 1080). It is a great place for bird-watchers as over 15 species have been spotted in the park. In the high season it is expensive – caravan sites (up to four people) are R65 per night, with a R275 deposit. Out of season, sites are R20 plus R10 per person. In the high season, cottages are R180 plus R15 per person.

*Sugarshack Backpackers* (☎ (0431) 28240), run by the inimitable Chester (a keen surfer), is in a great position near the beach on Eastern Esplanade; dorm beds cost R30. To get there from town, take the Beach bus from Oxford St which ends up in Moore St, walk down to the beach and enter the one-way road; it is immediately on your left. The 'shack' has free surfboards, hires mountain bikes (R20), and organises booze cruises up the Nahoon River in a rubber duckie (R35).

The Sugarshack has an annexe in Moore St; quieter clients should request a bed there. (The Baz Bus drops off at both places.)

*Selborne B&B* (☎ (0431) 726 9666), 9 Salisbury Rd, Vincent (it gets Chester's nod), has beds if the Sugarshack is full. Luxury B&B singles/doubles cost R120/150.

Not great, but an alternative, is the *Beach Hotel* (☎ (0431) 43 9156), on Fitzpatrick Rd near The Esplanade; it has rooms from R75/115. There's sometimes a live band, and there's dancing every night in the African Nite Club. *Hotel Majestic* (☎ (0431) 43 7477) in Orient Rd has a few rooms for R60/95, but it is rough!

**Middle & Top End** Towards the south end of Currie St near Orient Beach is *Queens Hotel* with singles/doubles for R95/120 including breakfast. It is a great place to stay if you want to meet locals in the disco.

The Hotel Osner's *Mimosa Apartments* (☎ (0431) 43 3433) on Marine Terrace are self-contained units costing R185/215; they're good value but often booked out. *Windsor Cabanas* (☎ (0431) 43 2225), on Currie St, is more upmarket and costs R295/340, breakfast included. Their *Courtyard* is slightly cheaper (because it's cramped); the rooms are from R240/295. A reader recommends Hotel Osner's *Embassy Apartments* (☎ (0431) 43 0182), Fitzpatrick St, with good doubles for R170.

The *Esplanade Hotel* (☎ (0431) 22518), on Clifford St near the beachfront, is a good mid-range hotel with rooms from R130. The B&B weekend rates are even better – about R95/115 for a single/double; most rooms have a sea view. The *King David* (☎ (0431) 23174), 25 Inverleith Terrace in Quigney, has singles/doubles from R165/200.

*Hotel Osner* (☎ (0431) 43 3433), on the beach north of the aquarium, has rooms from R250. North of here is *Holiday Inn Garden Court* (☎ (0431) 27260), on the corner of John Bailie Rd and Moore St. Rooms cost from R264/288 (breakfast is R27). Another member of the Osner group, the *Kennaway* (☎ (0431) 25531), has rooms for R250 for either one or two people.

## Places to Eat

Most of the beachfront hotels have restaurants. For a value breakfast (R20) try the coffee shop at the front of the Mimosa Apartments. There are a number of coffee shops on The Esplanade near O'Hagans, including an ice cream shop and a *Café de la Mer*. On the corner of Goldschmidt and Tennyson Sts is *Friesland*, with reputedly the best milkshakes in the country.

There's a bar and cafeteria at the train station with very good food for R15 to R20. *Finnegan's Restaurant*, on Terminus St west of Oxford St, is a good option, with cheap pub lunches for R15.

On Orient Beach, near the car park at the end of Currie St, is *Movenpick*, an upmarket Swiss place with meals from R35 to R40. Next to Movenpick is *Gun Deck*, with good old-fashioned pub meals.

*Jekyll & Hyde* in the Lock St Gaol shopping complex has pub meals for R20. In the Orient Mall, Currie St, at *Little Portugal* you can get mouthwatering prawns, paella and bacalhau (and sangria to wash it down); main courses start at R28. On The Esplanade is the popular *O'Hagan's* where you can get burgers, steaks, chicken and salads – a full meal is R35-plus, burgers are from R16.

Steakhouses abound – check the takeaway publication *Mr Delivery*. *Monte Rio Spur* is on Orient St near the beach; *Porterhouse* is in the Papagallo Building on The Esplanade; and there are two *Steers*, on Oxford St, Central, and on Devereaux Ave, Vincent Park. All of these places charge about R30 for mains.

*Bellami's*, at the bottom of Tennyson St, has modern cuisine – a three course meal is available from R55 to R60; try the tuna steak or any of the chef's choices and you can't go wrong. At *Buccaneer's*, you can get a hearty T-bone with vegies and chips for less than R20.

Latimer's Landing has the *Sportsmans Bar* which serves pub lunches (R15) and dinners; *Hunter's Jetty*, where they serve meat parrillada-style (on skewers); and the *Tug & Ferry*, a double-decker cruiser, which has a pub menu.

## Entertainment

EL'ers know how to enjoy themselves; there is no shortage of party venues. Many restaurants have live entertainment on Friday or Saturday nights. There is often live music at *Jekyll & Hyde*; a more sedate band plays at *Movenpick* on the weekend; and *Jacqueline's*, in Nahoon, rocks on Saturday night. The top place, however, is *Buccaneer's*, with happy hour from 7 to 9 pm Wednesday, and live bands on Wednesday, Friday and Saturday. Next door, on weekend nights, in a car park, is the best party in town – buy drinks from one of the ambulatory vendors (or 'bakkie top' bars) and mix with the grooving black population.

There are a few nightclubs; perhaps the most popular one with the local crowd is *Numbers* near the Hotel Osner. Latimer's Landing has a good feel to it at night and *O'Hagan's*, upstairs, is good on Friday night. *Star's* in the Papagallo Building also has a good reputation for late-night fun.

For Internerds, there is an Internet café, *Gateway*, on The Esplanade. The Gay Social Society can be contacted at PO Box 709, East London.

If you have children, try the Water Park in West Bank (near the race track); for R15 kids can ride endlessly on the supertube and speed slides.

The shops along Oxford St in the city's commercial centre are sometimes found wanting – you can get all the essentials at the Vincent Park shopping centre, which also has a cinema complex; follow Fitzpatrick St to the Northeast Expressway, take the Pearce/Gleneagles Sts exit west, then go right at Chamberlain Rd and left into Devereaux Ave.

## Getting There & Away

**Bus** Translux (☎ (0431) 44 2333) has buses to Jo'burg/Pretoria (R225), Cape Town (R195), Umtata (R75) and Port Elizabeth (R85); they depart from the train station.

Greyhound stops at Shell Auto Care, Amalinda, several kilometres from the city centre (a taxi to town is R25) en route between Durban (R165) and Port Elizabeth (R100).

Intercape (☎ (0431) 53 3184) has five buses weekly from EL to Port Elizabeth (R80). Minilux (☎ (0431) 41 3107) also runs to Port Elizabeth (R75); buses depart from EL at 7 am Tuesday to Friday, and at 4 pm Sunday. It stops at the train station and the Orient Theatre.

The Baz Bus (☎ (021) 439 2323) runs from Port Elizabeth to Durban via EL on Tuesday and Friday; the cost is R85 to PE, R150 to Durban. It runs in the other direction to Cape Town on Thursday and Sunday.

**Train** The *Amatola* (☎ (0431) 44 2719) from EL to Jo'burg departs daily at noon, arriving in Jo'burg at 8.15 am the following day. The fare to Jo'burg in 1st/2nd class is R215/ 149. It goes via Bloemfontein, where it connects with a Cape Town service.

**Minibus Taxi** There are two main areas to find minibus taxis, both in the black area of town west of Oxford St. On the corner of Buffalo and Argyle Sts are long-distance minibus taxis to the north of East London; further south, on the corner of Caxton and Gillwell Sts, are taxis for King William's Town, Bisho and the local area. East London to KWT is R7, to Jo'burg from KWT is R105.

**Getting Around**
Most city buses stop at the city hall on Oxford St. For information on bus times and routes phone Amatola Regional Services (☎ (0431) 21251). One of the most useful is the Beach route, which runs down Oxford St, east along Fleet, Longfellow and Moore Sts then back along The Esplanade to Currie St and back to Fleet St and the city.

There's a taxi rank on Union St (☎ (0431) 27901) on the corner of Oxford St.

**Tours** Various half-day tours of the city and the nearby area cost R25 per person; contact the tourist office or Amatola Tours (☎ (0431) 43 0472), in the Lock St Gaol complex.

## AROUND EAST LONDON
### Strandloper Hiking Trail
This five day trail runs between Kei Mouth and Gonubie. It is administered by Ectour, in conjunction with Cape Nature Conservation (☎ (043) 841 1888; 8 am to noon). To walk the trail is R27/35 per day unguided/ guided. If you're thinking of walking the trail you'll need a copy of the tide tables, as there are several estuaries to cross and it's dangerous to do so when the tide is flowing out. The *Daily Despatch* has the monthly tide tables. The trained guides have been briefed on walking the trail, flora and fauna, shells, the Strandloper middens and shipwrecks along the coast. The Strandlopers'('beach walkers') were a Khoisan tribe who lived on the southern coast gathering food from the sea, but disappeared as a distinct people after white settlement. A useful booklet is available for R5.

There are four overnight *huts*, the cost of which is included in the booking fee. One of them is a converted pumphouse with a tidal swimming pool in front – it is underneath the Kei Mouth lighthouse. Camping on the beach is prohibited but the coast is littered with resorts, most of which have tent sites. The trail is usually walked from Kei Mouth, where there is a *caravan park* and a couple of *hotels*. Gonubie has many places to stay.

## EAST LONDON TO THE KEI RIVER
There are many resorts on the coast north of East London. The East Coast Resorts turn-off from the N2 will get you to most of them.

The first series of beaches to the north are centred around **Gonubie**, with a small nature reserve where 130 species of birds, mostly waterfowl, have been recorded. The reserve is reached from the N2; follow the signs to Gonubie, turn off before the municipal offices and follow 7th St to its end.

The next concentration of beaches is around **Haga-Haga**, a small village about 72km north of East London (30km of this is on gravel road after you turn off the N2). There are a couple of nature reserves in the region. The northern tip of **Cape Henderson Nature Reserve** adjoins Haga-Haga.

This scenic reserve has sandy beaches, rugged coastline and coastal forest.

To the north of Haga-Haga, and reached by turning off the N2 onto the R349, are Morgan Bay and the Kei Mouth. **Kei Mouth** is the last resort before the Wild Coast. Fishing and beachcombing attract most of the visitors to this region.

### Places to Stay & Eat

There are two caravan parks in Gonubie, *Gonubie* (☎ (0431) 40 2021) and *Yellow Sands* (☎ (0431) 38 3043). The *Gonubie Hotel* (☎ (0431) 40 4010) is good value at R75/110 for singles/doubles, B&B.

Some 38km north-east of East London is *Buccaneer's Retreat* (☎ (0431) 38 3012) in Cintsa West, reached by a rough 2km dirt road which runs off the well-signposted East Coast Resort Rd. It has dorm beds for R30 and doubles/cottages for R40 per person. A big plus here is the free use of canoes, surfboards and paddle skis for play on the Cintsa River. There is also a pool, floodlit volleyball court, poolside café, a variety of day hikes and a booze cruise (R5).

The retreat's interesting 4WD Transkei Tour departs daily at 7.30 am, via a bumpy series of roads (and vehicle ferry), for the Kei Mouth. The trip includes swimming and 'dare' jumping in rock pools, visits to a traditional rural Xhosa village and to the wreck of the *Jacaranda* (1974), canoeing on the Kabonqaba River, and sundowner drinks at Morgan Bay cliffs; the cost is R120.

*Cintsa East Caravan Park* (☎ (0431) 38 5064), across the estuary from Buccaneer's (and reached by a much better road) has tent sites for R30 for two, and log cabins for R110; it is recommended.

*Haga Haga Hotel* (☎ (043) 372 6302) costs from R130 per person including dinner and breakfast; all rooms face the sea.

At Morgan Bay there is a caravan park at the *Morgan Bay Hotel* (☎ (043) 841 1062). The hotel is quite expensive but meals in its restaurant are good value: hamburgers are R7, fish and chips R15 and steak R20.

The Kei Mouth *municipal caravan park* (☎ (043272), ask for 4) is on the main road

into town. One of the cheapest places along the coast is *Kei Sands Hotel* (☎ (043272), ask for 11 or 47); it is R40 per person in the off-season, B&B.

# The Karoo

The Karoo, a vast semi-desert, lies on the great South African plateau. It is demarcated in the south and west by the coastal mountain ranges and to the east and north by the mighty Orange River. It's a dry, hot and inhospitable region, but intriguing for its sense of space. See the Karoo section in the Western Cape Province chapter for more information.

### BURGERSDORP

Burgersdorp is quite a big country town nestled in a dry Karoo valley, but with trees, a beautiful old church and a laid-back, old-fashioned atmosphere. *Hotel Jubilee* (☎ (051) 653 1840) is a graceful country pub with singles/doubles for R85/120.

There's a nice drive to/from Queenstown over the **Penhoek Pass**, although the northern side is not so spectacular, and **Molteno** is a flyspeck. Forget it.

### MIDDELBURG

Middelburg is a nondescript town, nestled on a plain just north of the Sneeuberg range – the nearby **Lootsberg Pass** is spectacular.

There's a rather ordinary *caravan park* (☎ (04924) 21337), next to the municipal pool; sites are R20. *Country Protea Inn* (☎ (04924) 21126) overlooks the pleasant town square and has B&B singles/doubles for R189/239. *Hotel Middelburg* (☎ (04924) 21100), on Meintjies St, is not as nice, but is cheaper (R95/135 B&B).

### CRADOCK

Cradock is a busy agricultural centre on the banks of the Great Fish River, 240km from Port Elizabeth. It was established as a military outpost in 1813 and is now a busy commercial centre for the rich farming dis-

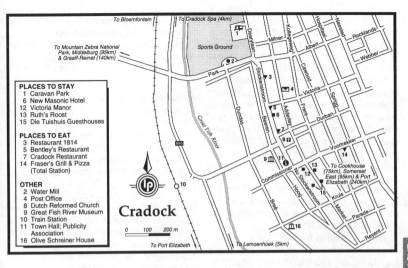

**PLACES TO STAY**
1 Caravan Park
6 New Masonic Hotel
12 Victoria Manor
13 Ruth's Roost
15 Die Tuishuis Guesthouses

**PLACES TO EAT**
3 Restaurant 1814
5 Bentley's Restaurant
7 Cradock Restaurant
14 Fraser's Grill & Pizza
  (Total Station)

**OTHER**
2 Water Mill
4 Post Office
8 Dutch Reformed Church
9 Great Fish River Museum
10 Train Station
11 Town Hall; Publicity
   Association
16 Olive Schreiner House

**Cradock**

trict along the river banks. A warm climate and plentiful water supply ensure a variety of crops.

The town has retained some interesting old buildings and there's a distinct Karoo atmosphere, created largely by shady trees, the river and a superb church (built in 1867 and modelled on St Martin's in the Fields, London).

Numerous vendors on the roads leading in and out of the town sell wire windmills – the Karoo 'symbol'. These are working models (well, the blades spin) and can be beautifully crafted. The price depends on the size and the amount of work that has gone into the piece, but you should be able to buy a good one from R10 to R30.

Get information (opinionated and, occasionally, racist in tone) at the Cradock Publicity Association (☎ (0481) 2383) in the Town Hall Building.

**Things to See & Do**
The **Olive Schreiner House** is a good example of a typical Karoo house. Novelist Schreiner *(Story of an African Farm)* lived here as a girl, and Cradock is the centre of

the country where she taught, wrote and spent part of her married life. The house is open weekdays from 8 am to 12.45 pm and 2 to 4.30 pm. Schreiner is buried on a farm at Buffelshoek, 24km south of Cradock on the Mortimer Rd.

The **Great Fish River Museum** was originally the parsonage of the Dutch Reformed Church. The house was built in 1825 and the displays depict pioneer life in the 19th century. The museum is open on weekdays from 8 am to 1 pm and 2 to 4 pm, and Saturday from 8 am to noon.

**Places to Stay**
The municipal *caravan park* (☎ (0481) 3443) has powered sites for R17 plus R7 per person. It's a pleasant spot by the sports ground on unguarded banks of the river.

It is almost worth making a special trip to Cradock just so you can stay in *Die Tuishuis* (☎ (0481) 71 1322). This is a unique concept in accommodation – in one of Cradock's old streets, cottages have been beautifully restored and are rented on a nightly basis. You have your own cottage, with a lounge and fireplace, kitchen and garden. Staying in

EASTERN CAPE PROVINCE

one of the cottages is like stepping back in time. Home furnishings can include wind-up gramophones complete with 78rpm records. It costs R130 per person including breakfast, with dinner available for R30.

*Cradock Spa* (☎ (0481) 2709), 4km north of town on the Marlow Rd, has natural sulphur spring water (its plus) but, otherwise, it's a sterile Afrikaner kraal surrounded by a huge barbed-wire fence (one of its many negatives). There is camping (R19 without power), prison-like brick cells ('chalets') for R90 to R100 out of season (R20 more in season), and a bar which is less than welcoming to those with the slightest of liberal ideals. A better budget alternative is *Ruth's Roost* (☎ (0481) 3530) at 56 Market St; singles/doubles are R55/95.

The competition for Die Tuishuis is *Victoria Manor* (☎ (0481) 71 1650), a pleasant, big old country pub with rooms from R90 to R110 per person (breakfast is R20). The *New Masonic Hotel* (☎ (0481) 3115), Stockenstroom St, is pretty plain compared with the competition. Singles/doubles/triples are R110/180/230.

### Places to Eat

In the Total service station on Voortrekker St is *Fraser's Grill & Pizza*; dishes are the standard steak and seafood (around R25 to R30) with occasional all-you-can-eat pizza deals. Recommended for breakfast and lunch is *Restaurant 1814* on Stockenstroom St; the nearby *Bentley's* for a range of family meals; and the *Cradock* for steaks. *Lemoenhoek* (☎ (0481) 2514), 5km south of town, has great lashings of 'Karoo' food for R35 per person.

### Getting There & Away

Translux stops at the Total station (Struwig Café) on the run between Cape Town (R180) and East London (R160) via Beaufort West (R120), Graaff-Reinet (R105), Queenstown (R120) and King William's Town (R145). Buses to Cape Town depart from Cradock (Struwig Motors) at 7.35 pm; and to East London at 4.35 am.

The *Algoa* train between Port Elizabeth

and Jo'burg stops here at 7.01 pm heading north, and at 4.43 am southbound.

Most minibus taxis leave from the nearby township, but if you ask at the service stations in town you might get lucky.

## MOUNTAIN ZEBRA NATIONAL PARK

This magnificent national park is on the northern slopes of the 2000m Bankberg range and has superb views over the Karoo. It's a small park (around 7000 hectares) devoted to the protection of one of the rarest animals in the world – the mountain zebra *(Equus zebra, 'bergkwagga')*.

The mountain zebra is distinguished from other zebra species by its small stature, reddish-brown nose and dewlap (a loose fold of skin hanging beneath the throat). It has no shadow stripes, a white stomach and a distinctive gridiron pattern on the rump, with stripes continuing down the legs.

Mountain zebra were probably never numerous, but by the 1960s there were less than 50 of them. It is believed that 500 is the minimum necessary to guarantee their survival. At present there are over 200 in this national park and another 200-plus in other parks and reserves around the Cape provinces.

The park has superb mountain scenery and unique vegetation. Thick patches of sweet thorn and wild olive are interspersed with grasslands and succulents. In addition to the zebra, the park supports black wildebeest, eland, red hartebeest, kudu, blesbok, duiker, steenbok, reedbuck and springbok. The largest predator is the caracal, and there are several species of small cats, genet, bat-eared fox and black-backed jackal. Some 200 bird species have been recorded.

There's a limited network of gravel roads in the park, plus the three day Mountain Zebra Trail and two short day walks.

### Information

The entrance gate is open between 1 October and 30 April from 7 am to 7 pm, and between 1 May and 30 September from 7.30 am to 6 pm. Day visitors are charged R10 each. It's quite feasible to get a taste of the park in a half-day excursion from Cradock. There's a shop and restaurant in the main camp.

## Mountain Zebra Trail
The trail takes three days and totals 25.6km. The first day covers about 9km and includes a steep climb. The second day also covers about 9km, climbing the slopes of the Bankberg range. The third day is a short 7km, returning you to the main office.

Despite the up-and-down hiking, there is plenty of time to pace yourself and watch the game – summer heat is the only real problem. There are two overnight huts; camping is not allowed. Hikers must carry their own sleeping bags, food supplies and eating utensils. If possible, book in advance (☎ (0481) 2427 or 2486; fax (0481) 3943); the price per person is R65.

## Places to Stay & Eat
The most interesting place to stay is the restored historic farmhouse *Doornhoek*, built in 1836 and hidden in a secluded valley within the park. The six bed Doornhoek costs R430 for up to four people and R60/30 per extra adult/child.

Alternatively there are comfortable, fully equipped four-bed *cottages*. These cost R245 for one or two people, and R60/30 per extra adult/child. There's also a pleasant *camping area* with sites for R36 for two people, plus R10 for each additional person. There is a 20% discount on accommodation from the beginning of June to the end of September, excluding school holidays.

The *restaurant* is open for breakfast and dinner; main meals are around R35. The shop has all necessities and is open all day. Bookings should be made with the National Parks office in Cape Town or Pretoria.

## SOMERSET EAST
This attractive old town at the very foot of the 1600m Bosberg range is sometimes referred to as the oasis of the Karoo, since it receives a soaking 600mm of rainfall (thanks to the mountains). After the dry country to the north and south, the rich forest on the mountain slopes is a surprise. The area was

first settled in the 1770s and a village was established in 1835.

The museum and information bureau (☎ (0424) 31448) are in a classic Georgian building at the top end of Beaufort St. They have some useful leaflets, including *A Stroll through Old Somerset East*. The complex is open on weekdays from 9 am to 5 pm and Saturday from 10 am to noon.

## Bosberg Nature Reserve & Trail
The reserve covers 2000 hectares of diverse habitats – mountain fynbos on rocky parts of the plateau, thickly wooded ravines with stinkwood and yellowwood, a dense grassland on the highest parts, and Karoo shrubs and grasses on the lower areas.

There are several possible walks, including the 15km circular **Bosberg Hiking Trail**, with an overnight hut which sleeps 10 people (R20 per person) and has toilet facilities. Hikers must register, and those planning to stay overnight must book in advance. For inquiries and bookings contact the municipality (☎ (0424) 31448).

## Places to Stay
The *caravan park* (☎ (0424) 31376) is 3km from the town centre past the golf course, tucked into a valley surrounded by the Bosberg Nature Reserve; sites are R25. The *Somerset Hotel* (☎ (0424) 32047), 83 Charles St, charges R95/145 for B&B, and R85 for singles with shared bath.

## GRAAFF-REINET
Graaff-Reinet is perhaps the quintessential Karoo town – it is often referred to, with justification, as the 'gem of the Karoo'. If you visit only one inland town in the Eastern Cape, make it this one.

Graaff-Reinet is situated in a cleft in the magnificent Sneeuberg range on a defensible bend of the Sundays River. The fourth oldest European town in South Africa, it has a superb architectural heritage that, fortunately, has been recognised and restored.

Over 220 buildings (mostly private houses) have been declared national monuments – they range from Cape Dutch houses with

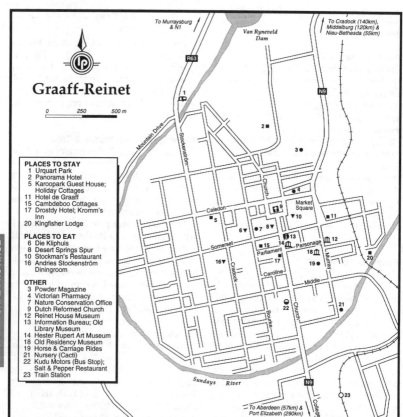

**Graaff-Reinet**

0    250    500 m

**PLACES TO STAY**
1  Urquart Park
2  Panorama Hotel
5  Karoopark Guest House;
   Holiday Cottages
11  Hotel de Graaff
15  Cambdeboo Cottages
17  Drostdy Hotel; Kromm's
   Inn
20  Kingfisher Lodge

**PLACES TO EAT**
6  Die Kliphuis
8  Desert Springs Spur
10  Stockman's Restaurant
16  Andries Stockenström
   Diningroom

**OTHER**
3  Powder Magazine
4  Victorian Pharmacy
7  Nature Conservation Office
9  Dutch Reformed Church
12  Reinet House Museum
13  Information Bureau; Old
   Library Museum
14  Hester Rupert Art Museum
18  Old Residency Museum
19  Horse & Carriage Rides
21  Nursery (Cacti)
22  Kudu Motors (Bus Stop);
   Salt & Pepper Restaurant
23  Train Station

their distinctive gables to classic flat-roofed Karoo cottages and ornate Victorian villas. The excellent Karoo Nature Reserve is within walking distance of town. For those who just wish to see the interesting architecture, a horse and carriage ride (R10) is a great way to get around town.

### History
In 1786 a *landdrost* (an official whose duties combined those of local administrator, tax collector and magistrate) was despatched to establish order in the lawless Cape interior. When not fighting among themselves,

trekboers were in constant conflict with the Khoisan in the Sneeuberg and the Xhosa to the east around the Great Fish River. On one occasion, in 1775, they invited the Khoisan to a feast then surrounded and slaughtered them.

The landdrost of Graaff-Reinet didn't have much luck – in 1795 the citizens drove him out and established a short-lived independent republic. The British re-established limited control during their first occupation at the end of the 18th century but the expansionist Boers continued to provoke trouble. On two occasions around the turn of the century the Khoisan and Xhosa joined forces to fight the Europeans.

Between 1824 and 1840, the Boers' continued dissatisfaction with Cape Town's control led to the Great Trek, and Graaff-Reinet became an important stepping stone for Voortrekkers heading north. It continues to be an important commercial and trading centre, linking the Karoo with the south.

### Orientation & Information

This compact town lies within a bend of the Sundays River, overshadowed by the rocky Sneeuberg. It is 672km from Cape Town, 837km from Jo'burg and 290km from Port Elizabeth; thus it is only an extra 96km from Jo'burg to Cape Town via Colesberg, Graaff-Reinet and Beaufort West, compared with the more direct route. Graaff-Reinet has an excellent Karoo climate with a summer rainfall (340mm) mostly falling around March.

The information bureau (☎ (0491) 24248) in the Old Library building on the corner of Church and Somerset Sts is open weekdays from 8 am to 12.30 pm and 2 to 5 pm, Saturday from 9 am to noon and Sunday from 10 am to noon. It's one of the friendlier info centres and has lots of maps and information about the town and surrounding nature reserve, including farms that offer B&B. If you have an interest in architecture, *Graaff-Reinet: National Monuments & Places of Interest* is a must.

Chalanie Tours (☎ (0491) 22893) and Valley Tours (☎ (0491) 23978) operate tours to the Valley of Desolation (at sunset with sundowner drinks, R60), to Nieu-Bethesda (R100) and to the Karoo Nature Reserve (R50).

### Museums

**Reinet House** This museum on Murray St, built between 1806 and 1812, is a beautiful example of Cape Dutch architecture. It is now furnished with a collection of 18th and 19th century furniture. The cobblestone rear courtyard and garden has one of the largest grapevines in the world. It's open on weekdays from 9 am to 12.30 pm and 2 to 5 pm, Saturday from 9 am to noon and Sunday from 10 am to noon. Admission is R3.

**Old Residency** The Old Residency in Parsonage St is another well-preserved 19th century house, now displaying a large collection of firearms. It has the same opening times as Reinet House; entry is R2.

**Old Library** On the corner of Church and Somerset Sts, the Old Library houses the information bureau as well as collections of photos and clothing from the 19th century, fossils (including some nasty reptile skulls) from the Karoo, and paintings. It has the same opening times as the information bureau; entry is R3.

**Hester Rupert Art Museum** This museum, on Church St, was originally a Dutch Reformed Mission church that was consecrated in 1821. It now displays an exhibition of contemporary South African art. It is open on weekdays from 10 am to noon and from 3 to 5 pm, and weekends from 10 am to noon.

**Drostdy & Stretch's Court** The residence of a landdrost was known as a *drostdy* and included his office and courtroom as well as his family's living quarters. The Graaff-Reinet drostdy on Church St was built in 1806. It has been beautifully restored and is now the focus of a unique hotel complex. The reception and the hotel restaurant are in the drostdy, while guests stay in restored mid-19th century cottages, originally built for freed slaves, along Stretch's Court behind. There's the restored old slave bell which was unveiled, in a piece of awful irony, by Prime Minister John Vorster, one of the arch-criminals of apartheid.

### Microflights

A local daredevil offers microflights over the Valley of Desolation – sensational and very scary. A 20 to 35 minute flight enables you to see the town, the valley and the game reserve and costs R7 a minute. The safest weather conditions are usually early morning or late afternoon, also the best times for spotting game in the reserve. Phone (☎ (0491) 91 0027) for info.

**EASTERN CAPE PROVINCE**

## Places to Stay

*Urquart Park* (☎ (0491) 22136), to the north of town just across the Sundays River bridge and near the Van Ryneveld Dam, isn't a particularly attractive caravan and camping ground. There are, however, some excellent new chalets. A tent site is R25 (R35 in season) plus R2 per person. Basic rondavels start at R46/60 a single/double (R70 in season); and bungalows are R50/75 (R85 in season). The fully equipped chalets cost R100 for two plus R10 for each extra person (R130 minimum in the high season).

*Cambdeboo Cottages* (☎ (0491) 23180), 16 Parliament St, are restored old Karoo cottages, with *reitdak* (reed ceilings) and lovely yellowwood floors. All are national monuments. They're very comfortable, pleasant and fully equipped, with linen supplied. A coffee shop serves breakfast and light meals, and there's a pool and a braai area. It costs R150 for two, with extra adults charged R40. In December and January the minimum charge is R190.

*Karoopark Holiday Cottages* (☎ (0491) 22557), 81 Caledon St, has pleasant self-contained cottages from R150 to R170 a double, plus R15 for each extra person (more in season). In the guesthouse section singles/doubles (with over-the-top fussy decor) cost from R100/220.

The *Drostdy Hotel* (☎ (0491) 22161), on Church St, is simply outstanding, whatever your criteria. The main part of the hotel, including the dining room, is in a beautifully restored drostdy. A whole 'street' has been taken over by the hotel – and the old Karoo workers' cottages (originally slaves' quarters) have been restored, adapted and comfortably furnished. If you were ever going to splurge, this would be the time. Single rooms are R190, doubles range from R225 to R325. Suites, some of them whole cottages, start at R425. Breakfast is R28. Booking ahead is recommended.

*Hotel de Graaff* (☎ (0491) 24191) on Market Square charges R80/160.

There are plenty of B&Bs, starting at around R50 to R60 per person. One place that has been recommended by a traveller is

*Mrs Stegman's* (☎ (0491) 25359), 95 Bourke St. She charges R50/100 for singles/doubles. The information bureau has a complete listing (also of self-catering farm cottages). *Kingfisher Lodge* (☎ (0491) 22657), 33 Cypress Grove, is a really upmarket B&B – it's a historical home in a quiet setting with its own wine cellar. It starts from R125 per person rising to about R175.

## Places to Eat

One of the best spots is the excellent *Kromm's Inn* behind the Drostdy Hotel, in an old building that has been carefully redeveloped. There's a pleasant outdoor area under an old vine. At the moment, it only serves light snacks but the pub is open daily.

With its superb atmosphere, the dining room at the *Drostdy Hotel* (☎ (0491) 22161) is an unmissable experience. When was the last time you dined in an 18th century room illuminated by candelabra? Table d'hôte (buffet) lunches are R30, and dinners are R47. You can also order à la carte. An after-dinner drink in the pleasant bar, or in the garden on a hot night, is a delight. You don't have to be a guest to dine here.

*Andries Stockenström Diningroom* (☎ (0491) 24575), 100 Cradock St, is recommended. There's a set-menu dinner for R60, nightly except Sunday; you must book.

For light meals there is *Stockman's* opposite the church; *Desert Springs Spur* at 22B Church St (with a good salad bar and great vegetarian platter for R23); and *Die Kliphuis*, 46 Bourke St, for light lunches and coffee. *Salt & Pepper*, 90 Church St, is so characterless that it has character. Burgers start at R14, chicken and chips is R16, and steak meals start at R25.

## Getting There & Away

**Bus** The information bureau is the Translux agent, but it's closed on Sunday. Translux stops here on its run from Cape Town (R175) to East London (R165), via Paarl (R155), Beaufort West (R115), Cradock (R115), Queenstown (R135) and King William's Town (R155). Buses to Cape Town depart from Kudu Motors (on Church St) at 9.45

pm, and buses to East London depart at 2.55 am.

City to City/Transtate also stops in Graaff-Reinet on its daily run from Cape Town to Umtata, via Beaufort West, Cradock and Queenstown; the fare is much less than Translux. Buses to Cape Town depart from Kudu Motors at 9 pm, to Umtata at 2.45 am.

**Minibus Taxi** Taxis leave from the northernmost Engen station on Church St or from Market Square. Major destinations are Port Elizabeth, Cape Town and Jo'burg. For more information try phoning Jaftha Taxi Service (☎ (0491) 93 0039).

## AROUND GRAAFF-REINET
The R57 south-west from Graaff-Reinet is not as spectacular as other roads in the triangle formed by Middelburg, Somerset East and Graaff-Reinet, but it's not boring. Until Aberdeen the road follows to the south of the Sneeuberg. It flattens out after Aberdeen, but

mountains are still visible at the edge of the plain. The passes around Willowmore and Uniondale are superb, cutting through high, dry mountains.

### Karoo Nature Reserve
This reserve, which virtually surrounds Graaff-Reinet, protects 16,000 hectares of mountainous veld, typical of the Karoo. The flora is extraordinary, with the weird Karoo succulents well represented. There's also game, interesting bird life, spectacular rock formations, and great views overlooking the town and the plains. It's a lot more interesting for the average visitor than some other desiccated bits of the Karoo.

The reserve can be divided into three main sections: the game-viewing area to the north of the dam; the east section, with the overnight Drie Koppe Hiking Trail; and the west section, with the Valley of Desolation.

The **game-viewing area** is open from about 7 am to dusk. There are buffalo, eland,

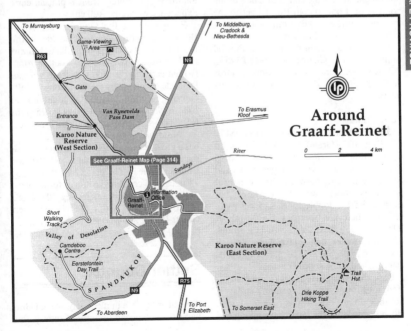

kudu, hartebeest, wildebeest, springbok and many smaller mammals. Visitors must stay in their vehicle.

The **Valley of Desolation** can be reached by car on a steep but sealed road. There are simply outstanding views over the town and the rugged valley. It's the sort of place that makes you wish you were an eagle. There's a 1.5km circuit walk. It is open 24 hours and there is no entrance fee.

The **Eerstefontein Day Trail**, also in the western section, can be reached from Mountain Drive. There are three trail options: 5km, 11km and 14km long. Wildebeest, kudu, springbok and smaller antelope species can be seen in this section. Permits are available from a self-help permit box at the Spandaukop gate.

The **Drie Koppe Hiking Trail** is in the mountains of the reserve's eastern sector. Plenty of game, including mountain zebra, can be seen. An overnight hut can accommodate 10 people in bunks; it costs R15 per person plus R2 for the entry fee. The starting point is on Lootsfontein Rd. To get to the trail, you must get a key from the conservation office in Graaff-Reinet.

Bookings and inquiries should be directed to the Officer in Charge (☎ (0491) 23453), PO Box 349, Karoo Nature Reserve, Petrus de Klerk Building, Bourke St, Graaff-Reinet 6280.

### Farm Trails

Trails of the Cambdeboo (☎ (0491) 91 0546), PO Box 107, Graaff-Reinet 6280, is an organisation of farmers who have restored old farm cottages and developed walks and activities on and between their beautiful properties. Rates vary between farms but average R80 a double, plus R15 per extra person. There are backpacker rates (about R15), although these are intended for groups of hikers rather than individuals. Still, it doesn't hurt to ask. Some places are self-catering and some supply meals.

Sneeuberg Farm Holidays is another collection of farms with self-catering cottages, but they do not offer walks between farms. However, most of the farms have hiking and other activities. The Graaff-Reinet information bureau has a brochure listing these and other farmstays in the area.

### NIEU-BETHESDA

In the tiny and isolated village of Nieu-Bethesda is the extraordinary **Owl House** – home, studio and life's work of artist Helen Martins (1898-1976). Whether it's a monument to madness or a testament to the human spirit is difficult to say (there is no shortage of art critics offering fashionable theories). Whichever is the case, the idea of a lone woman creating such *weird* things in this tiny village in the middle of the Karoo is mind-boggling. It even shakes the standard view of apartheid-era South Africa being a drab and conformist society.

Describing the Owl House and its sculptures isn't easy, and anyway it's the impact of the whole and its context which is most affecting – go and see for yourself. The Owl House is lit by candlelight every Friday, Saturday and Sunday from 8 pm; an eerie experience worth the R20 entry.

Even without the Owl House, Nieu-Bethesda is worth a look to get an idea of life in rural hamlets. The pretty village has dirt roads, a store or two and a pleasant tearoom (which certainly wouldn't be there without the trade generated by the Owl House). Self-catering accommodation is available at *Nieu-Bethesda Cottage* (☎ (04923) 758) for R50/90 a single/double without breakfast. *Stokkiesdraai Guesthouse* (☎ (04923) 711) has a great restaurant (R30 for a three course meal) and comfortable rooms (R50/80 for singles/doubles). *On the Edge* (☎ (04923) 740) has self-contained cottages for R40/80.

The drive here is interesting (there are several turn-offs from the N9 between Graaff-Reinet and Middelburg) but remember that there's no petrol in Nieu-Bethesda.

# Settler Country

As well as the area immediately around Grahamstown, the heart of Settler Country, this

## The Settlers

In 1820, English settlers, duped by their government into believing they were arriving in a peaceful land of plenty, arrived at Algoa Bay. In reality they were arriving at a heavily contested border region with Boers on one side of the Great Fish River and Xhosa on the other, both battling interminably over the country known as the Suurveld.

The Suurveld was suitable for cattle grazing, and Boers and Xhosa rustled each others' herds mercilessly. Grahamstown was at the centre of the maelstrom. In 1819 in the Fifth Frontier War, 9000 Xhosa under the leader Makanda attacked Grahamstown and very nearly defeated the garrison. The story goes that Makanda would have succeeded had he not observed the Xhosa war code and given free passage to a woman who carried a hidden keg of gunpowder to the defenders.

The only government-sponsored migration in South Africa's history was intended to create a buffer of market gardeners between the cattle-farming Boers and Xhosa, but the Suurveld was completely unsuitable for intensive cultivation. It was not long before the 1000 immigrant families found farming untenable. The odds were stacked against them: inexperience, hostile neighbours, labour shortages, floods, droughts and crop diseases all played a role. By 1823 almost half of the settlers had retreated to the townships to pursue trades and businesses they had followed in England.

As a result, Grahamstown developed into a trading and manufacturing centre. Most of the trade was between whites and blacks. Axes, knives and blankets were exchanged for ivory and skins. Travelling merchants, using Grahamstown as their base, ventured further and further afield. Tradespeople among the settlers produced ironmongery, wagons and clothes.

Port Elizabeth and Port Alfred developed to service what had quickly become the second largest city in the Cape Colony. The Sixth Frontier War (1834-35) sent even more refugees into Grahamstown, and the surrounding countryside was almost totally abandoned. ∎

section covers most of the old Ciskei homeland (the Ciskei coast, known as the Shipwreck Coast, is covered in the earlier Nature's Valley to the Kei River section).

## GRAHAMSTOWN

Grahamstown is the capital of Settler Country. When the British settlers first arrived this was a hotly disputed border area. The Xhosa were on one side of the Great Fish River, the Boers on the other. It still feels like a strange English transplant, emphasised by the lack of neon signs and billboards. There are some fine churches and 19th century buildings.

A large student population (4000) attending Rhodes University adds some (perhaps not much) life to the church-going Grahamstown merchants. There are 40 churches, all of which draw healthy congregations.

### Information

The efficient and friendly Tourism Grahamstown (☎ (0461) 23241), on Church Square, is open weekdays from 8.30 am to 5 pm (to 4 pm on Friday), and Saturday from 9 to 11 am. They can put you in touch with B&Bs (with rates from R75 to R150) and they also have a useful *What's On* magazine and *Where to Stay in and around Grahamstown*. Tourism Grahamstown can be difficult to spot – it's in a small building next to the large white Standard Bank on Church Square. They are also the Budget car rental agency.

GBS Travel (☎ (0461) 22235), 84 High St, handles bookings for all local travel as well as being the agent for Avis.

The Standard Bank is on Church Square. The Grahamstown Building Society (the Thomas Cook agent), 18 Hill St, does not charge commission.

### Albany Museum

The Albany Museum (☎ (0461) 22312) has four components. The most interesting is the wonderfully eccentric **Observatory Museum**, on Bathurst St, which is highly recommended. Originally a private house, it includes the only camera obscura in the southern hemisphere – a complicated series of lenses, a bit like a periscope. The camera obscura only functions in clear weather.

The **Natural Sciences Museum**, on Somerset St, depicts the history of early humanity, but also has some interesting African and Xhosa artefacts, including a Xhosa hut.

The **National History Museum**, also on Somerset St, houses a collection of family

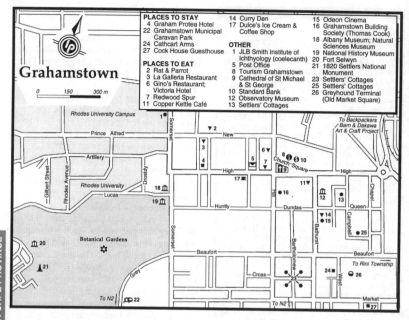

**Grahamstown**

PLACES TO STAY
4 Graham Protea Hotel
22 Grahamstown Municipal Caravan Park
24 Cathcart Arms
27 Cock House Guesthouse

PLACES TO EAT
2 Rat & Parrot
3 La Galleria Restaurant
6 Gino's Restaurant; Victoria Hotel
7 Redwood Spur
11 Copper Kettle Café

14 Curry Den
17 Dulce's Ice Cream & Coffee Shop

OTHER
1 JLB Smith Institute of Ichthyology (coelacanth)
5 Post Office
8 Tourism Grahamstown
9 Cathedral of St Michael & St George
10 Standard Bank
12 Observatory Museum
13 Settlers' Cottages

15 Odeon Cinema
16 Grahamstown Building Society (Thomas Cook)
18 Albany Museum; Natural Sciences Museum
19 National History Museum
20 Fort Selwyn
21 1820 Settlers National Monument
23 Settlers' Cottages
25 Settlers' Cottages
26 Greyhound Terminal (Old Market Square)

treasures, furniture, military memorabilia, paintings and historical photos.

Admission is R3 (R1.50 for children) for the Observatory, and R3 combined for the Natural Sciences and National History museums. All three places are open on weekdays from 9.30 am to 1 pm and 2 to 5 pm. On weekends, the Natural Science Museum is open Saturday from 9.30 am to 1 pm and 2 to 5 pm, Sunday from 2 to 5 pm; the History Museum is open Saturday and Sunday from 2 to 5 pm; and the Observatory, Saturday from 9 am to 1 pm. **Fort Selwyn**, a military museum on Gunfire Hill, and the fourth component, is open by appointment only (☎ (0461) 22397).

The first **coelacanth** ever discovered is exhibited in the JLB Smith Institute of Ichthyology, part of Rhodes University.

### Dakawa Art & Craft Project
Begun in the African National Congress' (ANC) Dakawa refugee camp in Tanzania,

the project (☎ (0461) 29393) moved to Grahamstown in 1991 when the ban on the ANC was lifted. It aims to teach people skills and to provide an outlet for their work, mainly weaving, graphic art and textile printing; it is at 4-11 Froude St.

### Special Events
The town hosts the very successful National Festival of Arts (based at the 1820 Settlers National Monument) and an associated Fringe Festival. The Fringe alone has more than 200 events. The festival runs for 11 days, beginning in early July; accommodation can be booked out a year in advance. For more information contact the 1820 Foundation (☎ (0461) 27115). The Scifest (☎ (0461) 23402), held in mid-April, is a feast of interactive science for the layperson.

### Places to Stay
The cheapest place is *Backpackers Barn* (☎ /fax (0461) 29720) at 4 Trollope St;

dorms are R30 and doubles R40 per person. Phone for a free lift from town. It was closed when we visited so we can't tell you what it is like inside – you can tell us.

*Grahamstown Municipal Caravan Park* (☎ (0461) 30 6072) is in a pleasant spot, although it's a bit of a walk from the centre of town. A camp site is R25, basic rondavels with no bedding are R60 for four, and five-person chalets are R125.

B&Bs, of which there are 40 or so, and farmstays (about 20), are booked with Tourism Grahamstown; expect to pay R75/150 for singles/doubles at both B&Bs and farm-stays.

To taste the flavour of 19th-century Grahamstown, stay at *Cathcart Arms* (☎ (0461) 27111), 5 West St, the oldest operating hotel in South Africa. It dates from 1825 and has pleasant rooms, a nice garden and a pool. There's also an à la carte restaurant. Singles/doubles are R175/250 including breakfast – a little expensive for what is an interesting but not flash country pub. The public bar with its mainly black drinkers is a lot more interesting than the ladies' bar.

*Graham Protea Hotel* (☎ (0461) 22324), 123 High St, is in a characterless building, but is comfortable and well located. Singles/doubles cost R249/289, B&B. *Settlers' Inn* (☎ (0461) 27313) is reached from the N2 and is signposted. It has a pub and restaurant; singles/doubles cost R195/290 (kids under 18 pay for breakfast only).

The *Cock House* (☎ /fax (0461) 31 1287), an 1820s National Monument at 10 Market St, is by far the best place to stay in town if you can afford it. The guest rooms are impeccably presented and merit that 'special occasion' visit; the cost is R210/380 for singles/doubles. The meals are exceptional; breakfast is cooked on an original 'Welcome Dover' stove.

### Places to Eat

There are plenty of cafés and takeaway places. *Gino's*, in Hill St, is popular for pizza, pasta, steak and burgers. *Redwood Spur*, 97 High St, is a decent example of the genre; expect to pay from R25 to R30 for most main

meals. *Curry Den* sells takeaways and *The Copper Kettle Café*, a standard country town café, is open till late on Friday and Saturday. *Dulce's Ice Cream & Coffee Shop*, 98 High St, is a favourite breakfast and lunchtime haunt of locals.

*The Rat & Parrot*, at 59 New St, serves traditional pub fare; popular with students, it is open from lunchtime till late, Tuesday to Saturday. *La Galleria*, an Italian place at 28 New St, is open Tuesday to Saturday until late; bookings (☎ (0461) 23455) are essential. The restaurant at the Cock House (see Places to Stay) comes highly recommended.

### Getting There & Away

**Bus** Leopard Express (☎ (0461) 24589) runs from Grahamstown to Port Elizabeth daily for R40. There is also the Bee Bus (☎ (082) 651 6646) which runs to Port Elizabeth, Port Alfred and Kenton-on-Sea; inquire at Tourism Grahamstown.

Translux stops here (Cathcart Arms Hotel) on its daily run between Port Elizabeth (R85) and Durban (R185, 11 hours), via King William's Town (R85), East London (R85) and Umtata (R130). Buses leave Grahamstown for Durban at 8.30 am, and for Port Elizabeth at 6 pm.

Greyhound stops here at Old Market Square (West St) daily on the Durban to Port Elizabeth run; it is R65 to Port Elizabeth, R90 to East London and R190 to Durban.

**Minibus Taxi** You'll find taxis on Raglan St (the continuation of Beaufort St), but most leave from Rini, the location on the hill at the far eastern end of Raglan St. Fares and destinations include: Fort Beaufort R17, King William's Town R27, Port Elizabeth R27 and East London R29.

### BATHURST

On the road between Port Alfred and Grahamstown, this scattered village of trees, lanes and hedges is a pleasant place to break your (short) journey. Founded in 1820, it is the site of South Africa's oldest unaltered Anglican church. There are a number of minor attractions in the area; pick up information

EASTERN CAPE PROVINCE

and a map from the Bathurst Arms, opposite the Pig & Whistle.

On the road from Port Albert to Grahamstown, near the turn-off to Bathurst, **Summerhill Farm** (☎ (0464) 25 0833) has a big pineapple and a reconstructed Xhosa village where you can buy handicrafts. There are farm tours (R8) and meals. Admission to see the video only is R2.50; the farm is closed on Monday.

There's a basic *caravan park* (☎ (0464) 25 0639) in town. *Talking Drum Backpackers'* (☎ (0461) 41 3107), 100m from the Bathurst Arms, has dorms for R20 and doubles for R30 per person. It also conducts drum-making workshops.

The *Pig & Whistle Pub* (☎ (0464) 25 0673), Kowie Rd, could be in England – not all that surprising considering it is in the centre of the Settler Country, and was built in 1831. It's a popular stop on the road from Port Alfred to Grahamstown for good-value pub lunches (salads R12.50, calamari R21, steaks from R23 to R30 and a good selection of wines). Bookings are essential for Sunday lunch – and remember there's 'no thirst like Bathurst'. B&B here is R110 per person.

The *Bathurst Arms*, across the road next to the Curiosity Shop, has a restaurant and rooms (for the same price as the Pig & Whistle).

## KING WILLIAM'S TOWN

Originally established by the London Missionary Society in 1826, King William's Town (usually known as KWT) became an important military base in the interminable struggle with the Xhosa. After the Seventh Frontier War (1846-47), British Kaffraria was established with KWT as its capital.

Although the former homeland of Ciskei's nominal capital was Bisho (now the Eastern Cape provincial capital), KWT remains the real commercial and shopping centre for the region. Ciskei's boundaries were carefully drawn to exclude KWT's valuable real estate. Bisho does have some grandiose government buildings and a Sun hotel/casino, but KWT has the shops, banks and bustling streets. There are several interesting build-ings dating from the mid-19th century, and a good museum, but no pressing reason to stay.

The library (☎ (0433) 23450), Ayliff St, has tourist information, including Eastern Cape Tourism brochures, which might save a trip to Bisho.

### Kaffrarian Museum
The Kaffrarian Museum's collection was begun by the local naturalists' society in 1884, and consequently has a large natural history section. Pride of place is given to the stuffed corpse of Huberta, the hippo that became famous between 1928 and 1931 when she wandered along the coast from St Lucia in Natal to the vicinity of King William's Town (where she was shot).

The most interesting displays, however, are in the Xhosa Gallery in the old post office building. The gallery has some excellent material on the cultural history of the Xhosa. One highlight is the fantastic wire cars made by local craftspeople.

### Places to Stay & Eat
The *caravan park* (☎ (0433) 23160) at the Grahamstown entry to town is pleasant enough, but a bit noisy; sites are R22. There are a few hotels, but the best options are the *Amatola Sun* in Bisho, and places in East London.

The East Cape Accommodation Network (☎ (0433) 23369), Upper Mount St, is a booking agency and travel service for the whole region.

Places to eat include *St Louis Spur*, corner of Alexandra Rd and Cathcart St; *El Greco Steakhouse*, Alexandra Rd; and *Squirrel's Coffee Shop*, 74 Cathcart St.

### Getting There & Away
Translux buses run between Cape Town (R185 from KWT) and East London (R70) via Beaufort West (R165), Graaff-Reinet (R155), Cradock (R145), Queenstown (R70) and Cathcart (R70). Westbound buses depart from KWT (at the El Greco) at 3.20 pm on Sunday, Monday, Wednesday, Friday and Saturday; eastbound buses depart at 8.40 am daily except Tuesday and Thursday.

## Ciskei

In 1981, Ciskei was given pseudo-independence by the prophets of apartheid. Ciskei's total area was a tiny 8500 sq km; about 180km long and 60km wide. The million people who were forced to live in Ciskei did not have enough land for agriculture on any economic scale, nor for subsistence. There was no industry or natural resources.

In March 1990, the dictatorial inaugural president, Lennox Sebe, was removed from power by a coup that had the support of the South African government. Sebe, who fled to Pretoria, was not lamented by many. In the words of the *Eastern Province Herald*, 'Ciskei's neighbours have witnessed corruption, poor administration, fraternal feuds and assassinations'.

Brigadier Ouba Joshua Gqozo took Sebe's place, and the South African government assumed control of key posts in the Ciskei government and defence forces. Gqozo attempted to consolidate his power by reintroducing a system of local government based on compliant 'traditional' headmen, replacing democratic residential associations affiliated with the ANC.

In late 1991, conflict over this issue, the question of continuing 'independence', and the role of the ANC led to the declaration of a state of emergency. On 7 September 1992, the Ciskei army opened fire on a peaceful ANC demonstration, killing over 30 marchers.

Ciskei has been reabsorbed into South Africa but the effects of the period of neglect are all too evident. Shanty villages still dot the overgrazed hills. The huts within the villages and the villages themselves are scattered, so it is impossible to deliver services efficiently. The inhabitants are dependent on expensive minibus taxis to get to shops, schools and medical services. Huge numbers of men still travel to the big cities to find work, leaving behind their wives and children who fend for themselves as best they can. Sometimes the man will be willing and able to send back money. Sometimes he won't.

Today, Ciskei's former capital Bisho, with its wealth of administrative buildings, has been designated the capital of Eastern Cape Province. In reality, most business is conducted in East London and Port Elizabeth, and Bisho's inhabitants commute to nearby King William's Town to get essential supplies. ∎

KWT is a stop on the Translux run between Jo'burg (R225) and East London, via Aliwal North (R110 from KWT) and Bloemfontein (R170 from KWT).

## BISHO

Bisho, once the capital of Ciskei, is now the capital of Eastern Cape Province. It was originally the black location for nearby King William's Town. The centre of Bisho does have some shops, but it was built to house Ciskei's bureaucrats and politicians, so there is a compact bunch of suitably grandiose and ugly public buildings – now in the service of the new provincial bureaucracy. Curiosity might inspire a visit, but the only practical reason would be to visit the Eastern Cape Tourism Board (Ectour).

### Information

Ectour, the Eastern Cape Tourism Board (☎ (0401) 95 2115; fax 92756), is opposite the post office; they have brochures and also handle bookings for hiking trails in the former Ciskei region. Rennies Travel (☎ (0401) 93095) is in the North Block of the Phalo Building, not far from Ectour.

Regular buses run from King William's Town's bus ranks to nearby Bisho.

### Places to Stay

The *Amatola Sun* (☎ (0401) 91111) is part of the Sun International chain, which specialises in high-quality casino/hotels. The Amatola is no exception; besides slot machines and roulette tables there's golf, tennis, swimming and several restaurants. Singles/doubles start at R320/410.

## AMATOLA & KATBERG MOUNTAINS

The area north and west of King William's Town is partly degraded grazing land and partly rugged mountains with remnant indigenous forest. There are some good walks.

### Getting There & Around

The easiest way into this area is via King William's Town or Queenstown. City to

City/Transtate buses stop in Katberg, Fort
Beaufort and Alice on the Queenstown to
King William's Town run (daily except
Sunday). There are a few minibus taxis.

### Amatola Trail
This six day (105km) trail begins at the
Maden Dam, 23km north of King William's
Town, and ends at the Tyumie River near
Hogsback. Accommodation is in huts.

The Amatola ranks as one of South
Africa's top mountain walks, but it is pretty
tough and should only be attempted if you
are reasonably experienced and fit. Walkers
are rewarded with great views, although
about a third of the walk goes through dense
forest, and numerous streams with waterfalls
and swimming holes.

The trail must be booked with Ectour; it
costs R20 per person per night.

The two day **Pirie-Evelyn** and **Zingcuka
Loop** trails both incorporate parts of the
Amatola Trail; book with Ectour.

### ALICE & FORT HARE
Alice was established as a missionary and
military centre in 1847 (strange how the two
things seem to go together). It's now a busy
little town, close to the University of Fort
Hare. The university was established in 1916
as the South African Native College, and has
played an important role in the development
of Southern Africa. Previous students include Nelson Mandela, Oliver Tambo,
Robert Mugabe (prime minister of Zimbabwe) and Kenneth Kaunda (former
president of Zambia).

Within the university, the **FS Malan Museum** has displays of traditional costumes,
charms and medicines; it's open Monday to
Friday from 8 am to 4.30 pm. Parts of the
original **Fort Hare** are also preserved in the
grounds.

### Getting There & Away
Frequent minibus taxis run from King
William's Town to the main gates of the
university and to Alice; they cost around R8.
From Alice to Fort Beaufort is R4.50 and to

Hogsback it's R10, but you'll probably have
to change taxis en route.

### FORT BEAUFORT
In 1846 a relative of Sandile, the leader of
the Rharhabe or Ciskei Xhosa, stole an axe
from a shop in Fort Beaufort. In a rather
disproportionate retaliation, a mixed force of
regular soldiers and volunteers invaded the
semi-independent Xhosa province of Queen
Adelaide, beginning the Seventh Frontier
War or the War of the Axe (1846-47). Today,
Fort Beaufort is a small, attractive backwater
with interesting historical relics.

### Historical Museum
This museum, on Durban St in the old
officers' mess, contains a large collection of
firearms, curios and paintings (including one
by Thomas Baines). There is a small craft
shop behind the museum and an enthusiastic
group is creating an interesting complex. It's
open from 8.30 am to 5 pm on weekdays and
8.30 am to 1 pm on Saturday.

### Places to Stay
Since Deane's burned down, the *Savoy
Hotel*, at 53 Durban St opposite the museum,
is the best hotel in town, although it is not
inspiring and charges R150/210 (breakfast is
R20); there are some cheaper older rooms.
Next door, at No 47, *Pete's Accommodation*
(☎ (0435) 32101) has pleasant singles/dou-
bles for R80/110.

### HOGSBACK
Hogsback is a small resort area high in the
beautiful Amatola Mountains, about 100km
north-west of Bisho. The village has a sprinkling of holiday homes and old-style
mountain guesthouses. The atmosphere is a
little like a fading hill station in India.

The steepest slopes around Katberg and
Hogsback are still covered in beautiful indigenous rainforest; yellowwood, assegai and
tree fuchsia are all present. There are also,
sadly, large pine plantations on land which
was once forest. The peaks are high and bare,
similar to the Scottish highlands.

There are some great walks and drives in

the area. You can buy booklets detailing walks for a few rand at the Hogsback store. Some of the best roads are unsealed, so check locally before tackling anything ambitious, and definitely think twice if it has been snowing (which happens a couple of times each winter). This is a summer rainfall area, and thunderstorms and mists are common.

## Places to Stay
The SAFCOL *Hogsback Caravan Park* (☎ (045) 962 1055), near the forestry station above town, has attractive unserviced sites for R20 plus R5 per person. The office is a long walk from the camping area – you have to keep going along the main road past the camping area, then down a side road. Maybe it's better to let them find you – they usually wander through at dusk and collect fees.

*Hogsback Arminel Mountain Lodge* (☎ (045) 962 1005) has pleasant rondavels, a beautiful garden and a pool. Dinner, bed and breakfast is extremely reasonable at R150 per person; prices rise in season. Out of season, the weekend special – Friday dinner to Sunday lunch – is R250.

*Hogsback Inn* (☎ (045) 962 1006) is not quite as appealing or as cheap as the Lodge, but it is still rather pleasant. It has a huge garden, log fires and a pool. Dinner, bed and breakfast costs from R160/260 for singles/doubles in the low season. From mid-December to early January there's a minimum stay of five days at R200/330 per day.

*King's Lodge Hotel* (☎ (045) 962 1024) isn't in the same league but it's OK, with rooms from R175 a double and self-catering units from R155 plus R25 per person.

## KATBERG AREA
Katberg, 110km north-west of Bisho, is a small town at the foot of a wooded range. The surrounding countryside is still much as it was when it was in Ciskei – overworked, underfunded and almost medieval.

It's an interesting drive to Hogsback, 27km to the east. There are some great views around the Katberg Pass. The road over the pass is unsealed; although it is in reasonable condition check locally before tackling it

after a lot of rain, and definitely think twice if it has been snowing (which happens a couple of times each winter). This is a summer-rainfall area, and thunderstorms and mists are common.

## Places to Stay
*Katberg Protea Hotel* (☎ (04094) 31151), 8km uphill from the village, is nothing short of luxurious. There are lots of pleasant walks in the vicinity and the hotel offers horse-riding, swimming, squash and tennis. The food is famous and it's a great place for a long weekend if you don't mind kicking back in front of a log fire if the weather sets in. Singles/doubles start at around R285/420 fully inclusive, but ask about specials.

## Katberg Trail
A 42km two day walk begins and ends at the Katberg Forest Station, just below the Katberg Pass. Accommodation is provided in a timber cabin at Diepkloof. It's a fairly easy hike, but you do cover a reasonable distance: 20km on the first day, 22km on the second. You can extend the hike into the Mpofu Game Reserve, where there's a hut. The trail is R30 per person per night; book with Ectour, Bisho (☎ (0401) 95 2115).

## EASTERN CAPE GAME RESERVES
There are three main game reserves administered by Ectour (☎ (0401) 95 2115; fax 92756) in Bisho; entry to all reserves is R10/2.50 for adults/children.

The **Tsolwana Game Reserve** (☎ (0408) 22026) is an 8500 hectare reserve, 57km south-west of Queenstown. It protects some rugged Karoo landscape south of the spectacular Tafelberg (1965m) and adjoining the Swart-Kei River. The reserve has rolling plains interspersed with valleys, cliffs, waterfalls, caves and gullies. There are three vegetation systems: Karoo scrub, fynbos and grassland, and savanna.

There is a similarly diverse range of animals, including large herds of antelope, rhino, giraffe and mountain zebra. The largest four-legged predator is the Cape lynx.

There is the two day Tsolwana Nature

EASTERN CAPE PROVINCE

Trail and gravel roads for game viewing. The guided two night walk is about R220 per person (minimum four people). The park is managed in conjunction with the local Tsolwana people, who benefit directly from the jobs and revenue produced.

The 23,000 hectare **Double Drift Game Reserve** (☎ (04049), ask for 403), between Fort Beaufort and Alice, has been combined with the Sam Knott Nature and Andries Vosloo Kudu reserves to form the **Great Fish River Reserve**. Much large game can be seen in this area of thick bushveld which is sandwiched between the Great Fish and Keiskamma rivers. The 36km Double Drift Foot Safari follows the Great Fish River.

North of Fort Beaufort is the compact but interesting 7500 hectare **Mpofu Game Reserve** (☎ (040452), ask for 11). Mpofu means 'eland' and you are likely to see this, the largest of antelopes. The grassland and valley bushveld make the region ideal for game viewing.

### Places to Stay
Tsolwana has three comfortable lodges – *Lily Fountain, Otterford* and *Indwe* – in old farmhouses, each with a lounge, dining room, three bedrooms (each with two beds) and two bathrooms. The tariff is R280 for up to four people and R50 for each additional person.

Double Drift also has three comfortable lodges – *Double Drift* (R160 for four), *Mbabala* (R280) and *Mvubu* (R180 for two in double-bed lodge). Mpofu has two lodges – *Ntloni* and *Mpofu* (R280 for up to four, R50 extra persons). There are two trail huts, *Phumlani* and *Fundani*, in Tsolwana; all bookings (trails included) with Ectour.

# Eastern Cape Highlands

This area is surrounded on three sides by the former Transkei and also has a short border (but no crossing point) with Lesotho. It's high country, in the southern tail of the main Drakensberg, sparsely settled with sheep-farming communities and trading towns doing business with Transkei. Winter brings snowfalls and even in summer Barkly and Naudersnek passes can be very cold – watch out for ice if you're driving. It's a bleak but atmospheric area.

While the Drakensberg here isn't as spectacular as in KwaZulu-Natal, there are no crowds or resorts and there's good walking. There are trails near Rhodes, Lady Grey, Elliot, Barkly East and Maclear.

### Getting There & Away
Some City to City/Transtate buses running from the East Rand (near Jo'burg) or Welkom to Transkei pass through the area, stopping variously at Sterkspruit, Elliot, Lady Grey and Maclear. A City to City/Transtate bus from Cape Town to Matatiele (KwaZulu-Natal) goes via Dordrecht, Indwe, Elliot and Maclear.

There isn't much public transport, not even minibus taxis, but a tourist train runs from Barkly East to Aliwal North (see the Zigzag Railway boxed text further on).

### BARKLY EAST
This town on the R58, with its scenic and mountainous location, bills itself as the 'Switzerland of South Africa'. It is also the terminus of the 157km **Zigzag Railway**.

The municipal *caravan park* (☎ (04542), ask for 123) is in Victoria Park. *Drakensberg Hotel* (☎ (04542), ask for 277), on the corner of Cole and Greyvenstein Sts, has singles/doubles from R95/140.

The **trout fishing** near Barkly East is reputedly among the best in the country. Anglers are well looked after at the *Gateshead Lodges* (☎ (04542), ask for 7211 or 7502). These include *Gateshead*, a farmhouse on the Bokspruit trout-fishing stream; *Tipperary, Glen Nisbett* and *Bothwell* at the north end of the Bokspruit; *Hollywood* on the Sterkspruit; and *Carabas*, giving access to the Upper Kraai River.

### ELLIOT
Nestled in a scenic region south-east of Barkly East, Elliot is the centre of a very

EASTERN CAPE PROVINCE

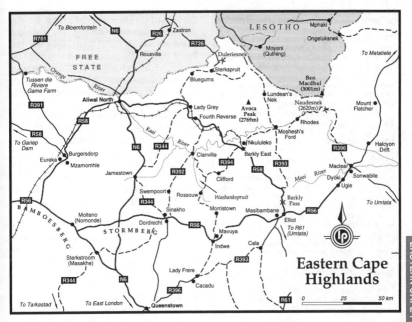

Eastern Cape
Highlands

interesting area. The Xhosa name for the town is Ecowa, referring to the mushrooms which grow here in summer.

Local attractions are the **Gatberg**, a peak that seems to have a hole bored through its centre; the lofty **Kransies**, from where you can sometimes see the sea 80km away; and the **Baster Footpath**, a historic stock route. On Denorbin farm, near Barkly East between Barkly East and Elliot, are some well-preserved examples of **San paintings** in a 32m-long 'gallery'.

Near Elliot is the start of the 39km, three day **Ecowa Hiking Trail**. Numbers on the trail are restricted to 10 and you have to provide your own supplies; for information, contact the Elliot municipality (☎ (045) 313 1011).

The *caravan park* is 2km from town at the Thompson Dam. The inexpensive *Merino Hotel* (☎ (045) 313 1137), on the corner of Maclear and Mark Sts, is R80 per person, with breakfast. *Mountain Shadows* (☎ (045)

313 2233), 20km north of town on the R58, is more expensive.

## LADY GREY

The countryside around Lady Grey, some 50km east of Aliwal North, is quite beautiful, with the Witteberge as an impressive backdrop. Founded in 1861, the town was named after the wife of a Cape governor, Sir George Grey. The Zigzag Railway passes through town.

*Mountain View Country Inn* (☎ (05552), ask for 112), on Botha St, is a small place with a dinner, bed and breakfast rate of R130 per person.

## MACLEAR

This is a trading town on the junction of the R396 and R56. North-west of town, just before **Naudesnek Pass** (the highest pass in South Africa at 2620m), are exposed fossilised **dinosaur footprints**, believed to

## The Zigzag Railway

The 157km zigzag railway line from Aliwal North to Barkly East is a magnet for railway buffs. The line, which winds tortuously through the mountainous Witteberge, took over 30 years to construct. A steam locomotive has been allocated to the line and it is hoped that it will operate three times weekly.

The line incorporates eight reverses through the mountains. It was originally intended that the Karringmelkspruit valley be bridged at a height of 90m and a tunnel constructed on the far side of the bridge. The tunnel was completed in 1911 but never used; some say that the ship carrying the bridge girders from England was sunk by a German U-boat during WWI. Six zigzags, or line reverses, were constructed instead (the other two reverses are where the line crosses the Kraai River).

The grades on the line are steep, with 1:35 quite common. Between the fourth and fifth reverses the grade is 1:30. This is understandable given the fact the train must climb from 1355m at Aliwal North to 1991m at Drizzly Siding, the highest point on the line and the highest siding in South Africa.

The train leaves Aliwal North at 6.15 am, Lady Grey at 8.30 am and arrives at Barkly East at 12.30 pm. For a current schedule and fares (these change), call ☎ (0551) 34224. ■

be 200 million years old; the earliest evidence of dinosaurs in South Africa.

The *Central* (☎ (045) 323 1005) and the *Royal* (☎ (045) 323 1176) hotels offer B&B for about R90 per person; in both places, not all rooms have bathrooms.

## RHODES

It can get cold up here! The town is about halfway between Maclear and Barkly East on the R396. Rhodes is a picturesque village with some quaint old buildings.

South African skiers once headed to Oxbow in Lesotho but have now turned their attention to the 'safer' skifields near Rhodes.

The centre for skiing is nearby **Tiffindell**, and with snow-making facilities they guarantee a ski season of at least 100 days. Tiffindell (2800m) is in an area of breathtaking mountain scenery. Nearby is **Ben Macdhui** (3001m), where the slopes provide

the vertical to 'shred the rad'; there are ski-lifts to get you up to the top. The Tiffindell *mountain hut* (☎ (011) 640 7416) has full board from R200 per person in summer (in winter, it is from R300 to R550 and includes ski-lift and equipment hire). Summer activities include mountain biking, horse-riding, grass-skiing and rock climbing.

The charming *Rhodes Hotel* (☎ (04542), ask for Rhodes 21) looks very much as it would have when it operated as the Horseshoe Hotel a century ago. Rooms with fireplaces and furnished with antiques are about R150 per person for B&B. Their 4WD trips to Ben Macdhui are R30 per person and horse-riding trips are R25 per person.

## ALONG THE N6

The N6 highway runs along the western side of the highlands. It crosses the magnificent Stormberg range, an area of rugged natural beauty.

## ALIWAL NORTH

On the Orange River, the border between Eastern Cape and the Free State, Aliwal North is a largish town popular for its mineral baths and hot springs. There's a big **spa complex** a few kilometres from the old town centre; ask at the library (☎ (0551) 2362) for a copy of *Aliwal North Information*.

### Places to Stay & Eat

There are plenty of places to stay near the spa, but if you're just passing through, the *Balmoral Hotel* (☎ (0551) 2543), in Somerset St, is R90 per person; breakfast is R22 extra.

The spa *caravan park* charges R15 for a site plus R10 per person. Further along the road, *Thatcher's Spa* (☎ (0551) 2772) has rooms from R90 per person, and R110 with breakfast. *Umtali Motel* (☎ (0551) 2400) has singles/doubles with breakfast for R120/190 and, at the *Aliwal Health Springs Hotel* (☎ (0551) 3311), B&B is R85/160.

For takeaways and sit-down meals there is the *Koffehuis* on Grey St. Out at the spa there is *Green Trees*; formerly a Wimpy and the fare reflects that name. If you crave African-style food, *Ezibeleni*, corner of Grey and

Murray Sts, has samp, pap and fish balls for about R7.50.

### Getting There & Away

A daily City to City/ Transtate bus stops here at 4.15 am on the Jo'burg-Queenstown run (at 10 pm northwards).

Translux stops here on its Jo'burg-East London run and Greyhound on its Jo'burg-Port Elizabeth run; both services stop at Nobby's Restaurant.

The nearest passenger train station is at Burgersdorp, 60km south-west, on the Jo'burg-East London *(Amatola)* line. For tourists, there's the North-East Cape Zigzag Railway, a service between Aliwal North and Barkly East (see the boxed text earlier).

The minibus taxi and black bus stop is on Grey St, near the corner of Somerset St.

### QUEENSTOWN

This town was established in 1847 and laid out in the shape of a hexagon for defence purposes. This pattern enabled defenders to shoot down the streets from a central point, but fortunately no shots were fired in anger.

The Stormberg Tourism Association office (☎ (0451) 2265) is in Shop 17 in the Old Market business centre. There are some fine buildings in town, including the 1882 **town hall** with its impressive clocktower, and the **Old Market building** in the Hexagon. **Queens College**, over 100 years old and one of many fine schools in town, has a reputation for producing great cricketers – including Tony Greig and Darryll Cullinan .

There is good fishing in nearby dams. Aficionados of all colours talk bait, lures and line strength (in the pub) then head for **Bongolo Dam**, about 5km from town on the Lady Frere road, to catch black bass and blue gill. Others head to **Xonxa Dam** in Transkei in pursuit of eels, carp (which is dried and used for fishballs) and other fish.

### Places to Stay & Eat

*Longview Lodge* (☎ (0451) 4939), 9 Longview Crescent, has singles/doubles for R90/120.

The *Hexagon* (☎ /fax (0451) 3015) and *Jeantel* (☎ /fax (0451) 81428) hotels are adjoining but the entrance to the latter is on Shepstone St. Discount rooms are R110/150 (breakfast is R25) and the best rooms are R125/165. The *Grand Hotel* (☎ /fax (0451) 3017), 41 Cathcart St, is slightly cheaper.

There isn't a great choice of places to eat. Steak-eaters will appreciate *Buffalo Springs Spur* at 125 Cathcart St and *Buccaneers Sports Pub & Grill* (similar to the Spur) in the Pick 'n' Pay supermarket, also Cathcart St; a steak meal at either is R30.

### Getting There & Away

Queenstown is well served by City to City/Transtate buses, with daily services to Jo'burg. There's a service to King William's Town daily except Sunday. Translux buses pass through on the East London- Jo'burg and East London-Cape Town runs; they stop at the Shell Ultra City (Queenstown to East London is R70, to Jo'burg R170 and to Cape Town R190).

Greyhound passes through Queenstown on the Jo'burg-Port Elizabeth run; the bus stops at Shell Ultra City. The fare from Queenstown to Port Elizabeth is R160; to Jo'burg it's R205.

### CATHCART & STUTTERHEIM

At the base of the Windvogelberg about 60km south of Queenstown, **Cathcart** was established as a frontier post after the Eighth Cape-Xhosa War of 1856. The library (☎ (045) 633 1022), with its imposing neo-classical façade, is worth a look.

The small *Royal Hotel* (☎ (045) 633 1145) on Carnarvon St charges about R70/110 for B&B. There are several holiday farms in the vicinity; ask at the library.

**Stutterheim** (referred to as 's-s-Stutt'), a small town 160km inland from East London, is close to the Kologha and the Amatola trails. The Stutterheim Tourism Bureau (☎ (0436) 31443) is at 34 Maclean St.

*Eagle's Ridge Country Hotel* (☎ /fax (0436) 31200), 6km from Stutterheim on the R352, via the Keiskammahoek and Kologha Forest roads, costs about R125 per person, B&B.

# Transkei

Transkei can still be considered a distinct entity, even though in the new South Africa the homeland has been absorbed into Eastern Cape Province. Formerly it comprised three areas – a pocket of land which bordered Lesotho to the east of Aliwal North; the main section which runs north of the Kei River all the way up to the Umtamvuna River with the Drakensberg as its western boundary; and another pocket along the Umzimkulu River. The latter is now part of Eastern Cape but it is surrounded by KwaZulu-Natal – a great deal of grass-roots politicking will decide which province eventually claims it.

Transkei's major attraction is its coastline, where you'll find superb warm-water surf beaches and lush subtropical vegetation. There is a good range of accommodation and some excellent hiking trails. Away from the coast the hills are dotted with villages. If you plan to hike inland remember that traditional life continues in the rural areas. Always ask permission before camping, but never approach a chief's house without an invitation.

Summers on the coast are hot and humid. Inland, summers can be hot, but many areas have winter frosts. Most rain falls in March, and spring also sees heavy rains. Unsealed roads can be impassable after rain, especially on the coast's clay soil.

## UMTATA

Umtata, the main town in the Transkei, was founded in 1871 when Europeans settled on the Umtata River at the request of the Tembu tribe, to act as a buffer against Pondo raiders. Today Umtata is a cracked, crowded (considered by some dangerous) town: a capital city of 100,000 people with a village atmosphere. With its litter, power cuts and phones that don't always work, Umtata bears little resemblance to the rural town it was before the creation of Transkei, but unless you prefer

### Transkei History

Although the people of this area are collectively known as Xhosa there are several distinct groups – the Bomvana, Pondo, Thembu, Mfengu, Mpondomise and the Xhosa themselves (eg Gcaleka, Ndalambe and Ngqika).

The Xhosa peoples living east of the Kei River (that is, they lived trans-Kei from the Cape Colony) came under the domination of the Cape Colony government from about 1873, but it was not until 1894, with the defeat of Pondoland, that the whole of modern Transkei came under European rule.

The Cape government became concerned that the newly annexed areas in the Transkei region were altering the racial balance of the colony's electoral roles. At this time any man in the colony could vote providing he owned a certain amount of property. With large numbers of Africans now citizens of the colony it was feared that their votes might actually change things, so the rules were altered. Property held communally could no longer be used to claim voting rights, effectively disenfranchising most of the Transkei's indigenous population.

There were, however, some people in the Transkei who were qualified to vote and politicians could not entirely ignore the democratic process. A political culture developed in the Transkei and it was hoped that reforms could be made constitutionally, despite the stacked deck.

These reforms never really happened. The Transkei was initially governed by local councils under the authority of European magistrates, and after the Union of South Africa in 1910 it was granted an almost powerless 'national' council. In the 1950s the South African apartheid regime chose Transkei as the first area to be given limited self-government in its Homelands scheme. This was a farce, as the impoverished Homeland depended on South Africa, both for funding and for the wages of migrant labourers. Revolts in the 60s protested against South African-backed chiefs who led the Transkei deeper into apartheid, but they were put down decisively.

In 1976, the Transkei became an 'independent Homeland'. If its independence had been internationally recognised it would have been classified as one of the world's poorest countries and one of Africa's most densely populated. Now it has been reabsorbed into the Eastern Cape Province of South Africa (not without difficulty), and hopefully its problems will be addressed. ■

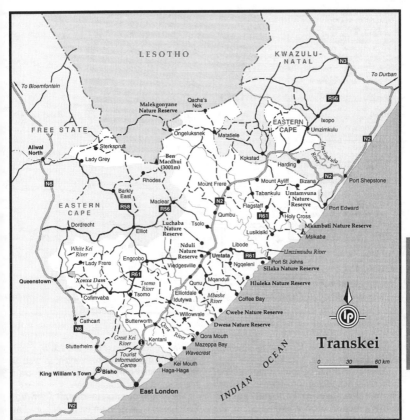

Transkei

0    30    60 km

neat kerbing to vitality the change was for the better. It's a bustling place, wonderfully free of racism.

**Orientation & Information**

Most of the hotels and services are in the grid of the small original town. The tourist office (☎ (0471) 31 2885) is upstairs on the corner of Victoria and York Sts; it also has an information caravan at the Shell Ultra City. Wild Coast Central Reservations (☎ (0471) 23766; ask for Gladys Ramncwana) takes bookings for the various hotels and resorts on the coast.

Book the Wild Coast Trail, other hiking trails and accommodation at nature reserves at the Nature Conservation Division of the Agriculture & Forestry Department (☎ (0471) 31 2711) on the 3rd floor of the Botha Sigcau Building, the office tower on Leeds St. The postal address is Private Bag X5002, Umtata. With prompting, and after innumerable questions, the staff may deign to help you. Excellent maps of coastal trails are R2 and other publications are available – seek Duncan Butchart's *A Guide to the Coast & Nature Reserves of Transkei* (R10).

There are Standard banks and a First

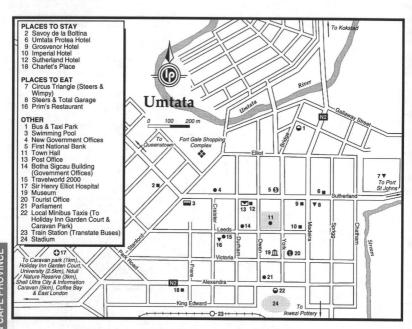

PLACES TO STAY
2 Savoy de la Boltina
6 Umtata Protea Hotel
9 Grosvenor Hotel
10 Imperial Hotel
12 Sutherland Hotel
18 Charlet's Place

PLACES TO EAT
7 Circus Triangle (Steers & Wimpy)
8 Steers & Total Garage
16 Prim's Restaurant

OTHER
1 Bus & Taxi Park
3 Swimming Pool
4 New Government Offices
5 First National Bank
11 Town Hall
13 Post Office
14 Botha Sigcau Building (Government Offices)
15 Travelworld 2000
17 Sir Henry Elliot Hospital
19 Museum
20 Tourist Office
21 Parliament
22 Local Minibus Taxis (To Holiday Inn Garden Court & Caravan Park)
23 Train Station (Transtate Buses)
24 Stadium

EASTERN CAPE PROVINCE

National bank in town. Do your banking here before heading to the Wild Coast.

There's a swimming pool on the corner of Sutherland St and Stanford Terrace; it's open daily but closes between 12.30 and 2 pm. The town's cinema, on Sutherland St, is the imaginatively named 'Umtatarama'.

### Things to See & Do

The **museum**, opposite the tourist office, displays traditional costumes and beadwork. It's open weekdays from 8 am to 4.30 pm (3.30 pm on Friday); entry is by donation.

**Nduli Nature Reserve**, in a valley on the southern outskirts of the city, covers only 200 hectares but has several species of antelope (impala, steenbok and blesbok), many birds, and a garden of indigenous plants (aloe, euphorbia, cycad and small succulents). The entrance is off the N2, 3km south of Umtata.

**Luchaba Nature Reserve**, on the Umtata Dam, just north of the city, combines grass-land and open water. There are zebra, wilde-beest and some antelope species, as well as many wetland birds. The reserve adjoins a water sport recreational area.

The **Wonk'umntu Handicraft Centre** is about 5km west of town on the N2 heading towards Butterworth, near the new Shell Ultra City. About 3km from the town centre (take the road heading towards Queenstown) is the **Izandla Pottery**, which produces stoneware.

**Ikwezi Pottery** (☎ (0471) 35 0701), to the south at the Ikwezi location, is reached via Mnukwana St, an extension of Sprigg St in Umtata. This is a self-help programme for the disabled.

A new addition to the national icons is the childhood home of Nelson Mandela. The first president of free South Africa was born in the village of Mvezo on the Mbashe River. He spent most of his childhood, however, at **Qunu**, 31km south-west of Umtata. On the opposite side of the road to the Xhosa village in which Mandela played as a child is a heavily guarded 'presidential country residence' – do not attempt to photograph it. No-one will stop you if you wish to wander into Qunu – you can ask to be directed to the Mandela family home.

## Places to Stay

*Umtata Caravan Park* is opposite the hospital on the main road west of the centre. Sites cost R15 per person, with a minimum charge of R25. People have illegally erected dwellings on available flat land near the park – perhaps it is not the place to stay at the moment.

The crummy *Sutherland Hotel* (☎ (0471) 31 2281), on Sutherland St (if you can find it amidst a ramshackle of shops and empty beer bottles), has doubles without bath for R70. On Leeds St, the *Imperial Hotel* (☎ (0471) 31 1675) charges (we think) from R70/90, including breakfast. Try for an upstairs room, as some of the downstairs rooms don't have bathrooms and are noisy. For colonial-era atmosphere the *Grosvenor Hotel* (☎ (0471) 31 2118), on the corner of Sutherland and Madeira Sts, is better and costs R140 per person for dinner, bed and breakfast.

*Savoy de la Boltina* (☎ (0471) 31 0791/2), out on the Queenstown bypass, has been upgraded and includes a restaurant and bar; about R100 per person. The Protea chain's upmarket *Umtata Protea Hotel* (☎ (0471) 31 0721), once the Windsor, is at 36 Sutherland St, near the corner of Madeira St; a room here costs R269/295 for singles/doubles. *Holiday Inn Garden Court* (☎ (0471) 37 0181), south of town on the N2, has quality rooms from R239/278.

The new *Charlet's Place* (☎ (0471) 31 1751) at 55 Alexander Rd is a breath of fresh air; singles/doubles are R180/300 without bathroom, R220/360 with bathroom (includes dinner, breakfast and five items of laundry daily). There is a bar and restaurant.

## Places to Eat

Numerous places call themselves tearooms, but they are all just takeaways and there's almost nowhere to sit down and have a coffee. Three noisy, crowded *Wimpy* bars can be found in the Munitata Building, corner of Sutherland and Owen Sts; at the new Circus Triangle on Port St Johns road; and by the Holiday Inn.

There are also two *Steers*, one next to the Total Garage opposite the Grosvenor Hotel and the other in the Circus Triangle. In Owen St there's a *Chinese* takeaway.

A good bar and restaurant, popular with locals and expats, is *Prim's* in Metropolitan Place on the corner of Leeds and Craister Sts. It's upmarket; entrées are expensive but superb – calamari for R16, mussels for R18 and prawn cocktail for R24. Their chef's special, fillet medallions, is R36, and crayfish is R50. You should book for dinner.

Out of town, in the Fort Gale shopping complex, is a good Italian place, *La Piazza*, where a small pizza costs from R20.

The Holiday Inn has a great bar, *Carmen's*, named after the energetic personality who has kept it for several years.

## Getting There & Away

Still no-one in Umtata seems to have any idea about the state of local transport into, out of, or around Transkei (we made this comment in the last edition). Perhaps these two Umtata travel agents will have a better idea: Travelworld 2000 (☎ (0471) 31 2011) and East-West Travel (☎ (0471) 22587).

**Air** Eastern Air (☎ (0471) 36 0021), formerly Transkei Airways, flies to Jo'burg daily (except Saturday), to Durban on weekdays. SA Airlink (☎ (0471) 36002) has services to Port Elizabeth (and on to Cape Town) on Monday, Wednesday, Thursday and Friday (economy/Apex one way for R456/228), and to Jo'burg daily except Saturday (R593/296).

**Bus** City to City/Transtate stops at the train station; it runs to Jo'burg daily (R95). Translux stops at the Shell Ultra City, quite a way from the town centre. From here the buses go through the town centre, so get your luggage from the hold here and ask to be dropped in town. Translux has a daily service from Port Elizabeth to Durban which stops in Umtata. A bus leaves Durban at 6.30 am and departs from Umtata at 12.45 pm, and another leaves Port Elizabeth at 7 am and arrives in Umtata at 2.30 pm. The fare to Durban is R120, and R130 to Port Elizabeth.

Greyhound has a daily Durban-Port Elizabeth-Cape Town service which departs Durban at 8.35 am and reaches Umtata about 2.45 pm; the bus goes in the other direction also daily, departing from Cape Town at 9 pm and reaching Umtata around 3 pm the following day. Durban to Umtata is R120, Umtata to Port Elizabeth is R130, and Umtata to Cape Town is R275. The bus stops at Shell Ultra City.

**Minibus Taxi** Minibus taxi services depart from the main bus and taxi park near Bridge St. Services from Umtata include: Port St Johns and Coffee Bay, both R15, Butterworth R20, Kokstad R40 and East London R40.

## WESTERN & SOUTHERN TRANSKEI

The best-known part of the Transkei is the Wild Coast. There are, however, many interesting places to the west of the N2 and south along it. To the south-west is a fascinating region of rolling hills and picturesque Xhosa villages.

The R359 runs between Queenstown and Elliot. You once had to negotiate a couple of notorious border posts to cross this part of the Transkei, so few people did; the border posts have gone. The numerous **dams** on the Great Kei, White Kei and Tsomo rivers attract anglers in search of eels and other fish. The villages in this region consist of scattered, brightly coloured houses set against dramatic mountain backdrops. It's a magical place where the pace of life has changed little in centuries.

On the N2, just north of the Great Kei, **Butterworth** is the oldest town in the region, having been established around a Wesleyan mission in 1827. There's not much to see in this sprawling place but two **waterfalls** near

town, the cascades of the Gcuwa and the falls of the Qolora, are worth a visit.

There's a country club, the *Butterworth Hotel* (☎ (0474) 3531) and the upmarket *Wayside Protea* (☎ (0474) 3531). B&B at the latter is R200/240.

**Idutywa** gets its name from a tributary of the Mbashe River. North-east of the town are the **Colleywobbles**, a place of great beauty with unusual rock formations studding the cliffs overlooking the Mbashe. The *hotel* (☎ (0474) 27 1040) on Richardson Rd is a typical country hotel, OK for a stopover; a single with breakfast is R120.

## PORT ST JOHNS

This idyllic little town on the coast at the mouth of the Umzimvubu River has tropical vegetation, dramatic cliffs, great beaches, a relaxed atmosphere and no robots. It is about as close as you'll come to the new rural South Africa, with a dominant black population in town. It's name comes from the *Sao Joao*, wrecked here in 1552.

Port St Johns (PSJ) is deliciously backward. There is no information office as yet; the information in this section comes mostly from Kirk of PSJ Backpackers'. Queues at the bank are tediously long so bring adequate cash with you. The phones outside the post office take old (pre-'Mandela money') coins; usually one of the phones is working. Don't post letters here – they will be lucky to get to Umtata.

### Silaka Nature Reserve

Silaka is a small coastal reserve just south of PSJ, running from Second Beach to Sugarloaf Rock. Bird-watchers will be delighted by the species in the forest next to the Gxwaleni River.

By the shoreline there are many interesting tidal rock pools. Near the estuary, where the Gxwaleni flows into the sea, aloes grow down almost to the water. Clawless otters are often seen on the beach and white-breasted cormorants *(Phalacrocorax carbo)* clamber up onto Bird Island. Magic!

## Places to Stay

Backpackers will enjoy this town's ambience. The convivial *PSJ Backpackers'* (no telephone; fax (0475) 44 1057) is near the heart of town, in an old colonial-style house at the top of a hill, where you get glimpses of the beach and town, and all the noise and atmosphere of Africa you desire. From the taxi and bus stop in town walk along the main road parallel to the river, take the fourth road on the right after the post office and then go up the third driveway on the right. You can camp for R15, sleep in the dorm for R22 or take a double for R30 per person.

A permaculture farm, *Sunsplash Farm/Pete's Place*, is up in the hills behind PSJ on Lusikisiki Rd. There are views from the farm down to the 360m headlands forming the Gates of Port St Johns (Mts Thesiger and Sullivan). It costs R20 to camp here among the exotic forest of flowers and fruit trees or it is R25 per person in the dorm, R30 for singles and doubles. You can buy organically grown vegetables in season.

Back in town, the *Coastal Needles Hotel* charges from R70/100, with breakfast. It's central but there are better options away from the town centre. Heading down the coast, *Cape Hermes Hotel* on First Beach charges from R95 per person in the low season, B&B.

Five kilometres further along is Second Beach, and the *2nd Beach Backpackers* (no telephone), with dorm beds for R25; ask at PSJ Backpackers' and you will probably get a lift here. There is snorkelling gear and surfboards for hire. Nearby is *Bulolo Holiday Resort* (☎ (0475) 44 1245), with four and five-bed rooms for R100/125/150; and the *Municipality Holiday Resort* (☎ (0475) 44 1045), with two/three/four-bed rondavels for R50/60/120.

*The Lodge* (☎ (0475) 44 1171), also at Second Beach, is superbly situated on the lagoon and has views across to a dramatic surf beach. There can't be many places in the world with a better location. It's a simple place, with tidy rooms for about R100 per person, B&B.

Four kilometres north of PSJ near the Pon-

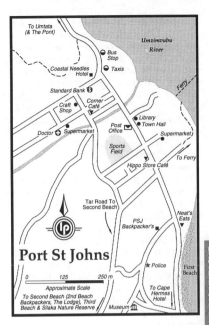

doland Bridge is *The Pont* (☎ (0475) 44 1324) with camping for R15 and dorm beds for R35; meals are cooked on request. In Mtumbane township is *Mama Constance's Place* (no telephone). A traditional breakfast and dinner are included in the price of R32 per person. You are invited to join the locals at their favourite shebeen or, at the opposite end of the morality scale, in church. Get a map and directions from PSJ Backpackers'.

## Places to Eat

You came to PSJ for the solitude, not the food. *Corner Café* in the main street serves breakfast (R7); *Hippo Store Café*, on the same street as the town hall, is good for a simple African dinner (R7 to R9); and *Neat's Eats* by the beach has takeaways. Or do what the locals do – buy cheap mussels, crayfish and line fish and cook your own meal.

## Getting There & Away

If you're coming to PSJ from Durban or Port

Elizabeth catch the Baz Bus (☎ (021) 439 2323) to Umtata. It collects passengers from all Durban hostels between 8 and 9 am on Wednesday and Saturday, from Port Elizabeth hostels between 7 and 7.30 am on Tuesday and Friday. From Steers in Umtata, where you will be dropped, take a minibus taxi to PSJ (R15). The Baz Bus costs R115 from Durban to Umtata, and R130 from Port Elizabeth.

Other possibilities from Durban are Translux (R120) and Greyhound (R130) to Umtata from where you catch a minibus taxi to PSJ. The buses stop at the Shell Ultra City, 4km from the minibus rank in Umtata. You have to get a minibus taxi back to town (R1.50) and then catch another to PSJ.

If you're driving from Durban take the N2 to Port Shepstone, continue along the coast to Port Edward and then take the R61 to PSJ. There is a good sealed road to Lusikisiki and then 20km of dirt road; watch out for maniacal drivers on blind corners. The very scenic road (part of the R61) from Umtata to PSJ is sealed, and police speed traps enforce the low speed limit.

The ferry (R1) is the fastest way to get across the river to Agate Terrace (even though there is a bridge 4km upstream).

## COFFEE BAY

Coffee Bay, finally 'discovered' by backpackers, now boasts three budget hostels. It is about the only town of size, apart from Port St Johns, near the sea. No-one is sure how it got its name, but there is a theory that a ship wrecked here in 1863 deposited its cargo of coffee beans on the beach. The Xhosa name *Tshontini* refers to a dense wood nearby.

Three rivers flow into the sea near here – the Henga ('place of the whale'), Mapuzi ('place of pumpkins') and the Bomvu ('red'). The scenery is dramatic, with cliffs behind and a 1km-long beach. The rustic **golf course** has great views. With the cliffs close by, your 'slice' can be costly.

### Places to Stay & Eat

Competition is fierce for backpacker bucks in Coffee Bay. *Coffee Bay Backpackers*

(☎ (0471) 37 0335) is the first you come to when you cross the river. Externally, the building looks like a concrete box but inside it is comfortable. There is a good common room, kitchen and bar (and a well-used braai area outside). Camping is R15, dorms R25, and doubles in cottages are R35 per person; all have access to hot showers.

Directly across the road is *Woodhouse* (☎ (083) 300 1711), an attractive building with a large garden area in front. When we checked it out (with the intention of staying) we decided not to stay because of the unclean state of the rooms shown to us (some unsavoury foam-rubber mattresses tossed on to a very dirty wooden floor). The rest of the place seemed fine, with a fully equipped kitchen and delightful verandah. Costs match the 'opposition' across the road.

The pick of the places is the isolated *White Clay* (☎ (0475) 44 2004), over the hill behind Coffee Bay; the owners will transport you and your gear from Coffee Bay Backpackers (otherwise it's a 10 minute walk). There are great views of the ocean crashing below from this cosy place; its only drawback is the occasional lack of good drinking water. Costs are the same as at Coffee Bay Backpackers.

The bungalow-style accommodation at the *Ocean View Hotel* (☎ (0475) 44 2005) is just metres from the beach. There is a restaurant in the hotel and delicious seafood snacks are served in the bar. It is R145 per person for dinner, bed and breakfast (high season R160).

You can buy mussels, crayfish and other seafood from locals and there is a well-stocked *grocery store* in the village. Coffee Bay Backpackers organises visits to a local *restaurant* where kids sing Xhosa songs while you enjoy a hearty traditional three course meal; it is good value at R25.

### Getting There & Away

To get to Coffee Bay take the sealed road that leaves the N2 at Viedgesville. When you reach Coffee Bay, continue past the derelict Lagoon Hotel, cross the river and you come to the backpackers' enclave. A minibus taxi from Umtata to Coffee Bay costs R15 and takes an hour. Coffee Bay Backpackers meets the Baz Bus at Steers in Umtata.

## WILD COAST
The Transkei coast is notoriously dangerous for ships. Shipwrecked sailors were the first Europeans to visit this part of the world, and few were rescued or made the harrowing journey to Cape Town or Lourenço Marques (now Maputo, Mozambique). One party struggled through to Cape Town to organise a rescue ship, but when it arrived most of the women had disappeared or were living with the Xhosa and didn't want to be rescued.

About 40,000 hectares of indigenous forest survives along the coast. While there is plenty of bird life (and butterflies galore), the numbers of animals are dwindling.

### Places to Stay & Eat
Port St Johns and Coffee Bay are the only real towns on the coast, but there are a number of hotels and resorts. These are undergoing a shake-up, so check first with Wild Coast Reservations in Umtata. Most are family-oriented places charging from R100 per person, rising dramatically (from R175) around Christmas; prices include meals.

There are fairly frequent minibuses from Umtata to Port St Johns and Coffee Bay, and with patience you can get to most places on public transport or by hitching.

Near the mouth of the Great Kei there are a few places. If you're travelling north from East London turn off the N2 onto the R349; on the south side of the Kei there are self-catering *Suncoast Cabanas* for R120 per person, R200 in the high season. (If you're travelling south on the N2 from Umtata take the Kentani road in Butterworth.) Cross the Kei on a punt (R20 for a car) and soon you reach *Seagulls Hotel* (☎ (0474) 3287), which costs R115/195 per person on weekdays/weekends (starting at R175 in the high season). There is a restaurant and a beach bar.

About a 20 minute drive north of Seagulls is *Trennerys* (☎ (0474) 4102), which has thatched bungalows for R135/220 per person on weekdays/weekends (R195 in the

---

### Wild Coast Shipwrecks
Famous Wild Coast shipwrecks include the *Sao Joao* (St John) which was wrecked in a storm in June 1552. After a harrowing journey, only eight of the original 440 survivors (over 100 drowned) made it to Ilha de Moçambique, 1600km away. Two years later the *Sao Bento* was wrecked near the mouth of the Umtata River; one of the survivors had been on the *Sao Joao* and, faced with the prospect of another epic attempt to survive, died in despair. The *Santo Alberto* sank near the Hole in the Wall in 1593 while heading for Portugal, supposedly with a huge cargo of New World gold.

The British East Indiaman *Grosvenor*, which sank in August 1782 on the way home from India, is another reputed treasure ship. There's even a legend that Persia's Peacock Throne was on board. Only 18 survivors made it to the Dutch settlement at the Cape.

One of the latest sinkings was the cruise liner *Oceanos*, which went down in 1991. ∎

---

high season). On Saturday night the restaurant features a seafood extravaganza.

The next hotel further north is *Wavecrest* (☎ (0474) 3273), near the mouth of the Nxaxo River. It is reached from Butterworth via Kentani; turn left at Kentani. It is R130/220 per person on weekdays/weekends.

The next collection of places, at the mouth of the Qora River, is reached from the N2 by turning off at Idutywa and taking the road via Willowvale. On the south side of the river is *Mazeppa Bay* (☎ (0431) 42 0382); full board is R120 per person (R155 in the high season). *Kob Inn* (☎ (0474) 4421), one of the more famous places on the Wild Coast, is an hour's walk north of Mazeppa Bay. It too is reached by car from Idutywa via Willowvale. Cottages cost R130 (from R185 in the high season). It is not unusual for this hotel to provide fresh oysters and mussels as bar snacks.

*The Haven* (☎ (0474) 62 0247) is further north near the Cwebe Nature Reserve, close to the mouth of the Mbashe River. Singles/doubles in thatched bungalows cost R135/280 (from R150 in high season). Coming from the south you can reach The Haven via

| | | | |
|---|---|---|---|
| 1 | Wild Coast Sun Hotel | 18 | Hole in the Wall (Ocean View Hotel) |
| 2 | Mnyameni | 19 | Mhlahlane |
| 3 | Umtentu | 20 | Amanzimyama |
| 4 | Msikaba | 21 | Xora |
| 5 | Lambazi | 22 | The Haven |
| 6 | Lupatana | 23 | Mbashe |
| 7 | Drew's Camp | 24 | Nqabara |
| 8 | Umzimpunzi | 25 | Shixini |
| 9 | Manteku | 26 | Kob Inn |
| 10 | Agate Terrace | 27 | Mazeppa Bay Hotel |
| 11 | Silaka | 28 | Mazeppa Point |
| 12 | Umngazi River Bungalows | 29 | Cebe |
| 13 | Mngazana Mouth | 30 | Wavecrest |
| 14 | Mpande | 31 | Kobonqaba |
| 15 | Hluleka | 32 | Trennerys |
| 16 | Ngcibe | 33 | Seagulls Hotel |
| 17 | Anchorage Hotel | 34 | Gxara |

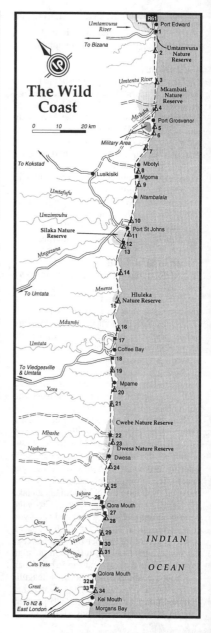

Xhora (Elliotdale); turn off at the village of Qunu (Nelson Mandela's birthplace), 31km south of Umtata. It is about 70km from Qunu to the hotel and the road is unsealed from Xhora. If you're coming from the north, turn off at Viedgesville, 20km south of Umtata.

South of Coffee Bay is the *Hole in the Wall* (☎ (0475) 44 2002) with rooms and self-catering chalets; B&B in the hotel is R85 (R105 in the high season). The landmark after which the hotel is named is a 2km walk away. The signposted turn-off to the Hole in the Wall is about 22km before Coffee Bay.

North of Coffee Bay, near the mouth of the Umtata River, is the *Anchorage* (☎ (0471) 34 0061). Anglers flock here in droves. Rooms cost R135 per person. Either head east from Umtata and take the road south-east from Ngqeleni or take the Coffee Bay road. If you take the latter, keep an eye out for the signposted road to Umtata Mouth, well before you get to Coffee Bay.

*Umngazi River Bungalows* (☎ (0471) 22370) is the next accommodation to the north. Bungalows cost R160; R25 more with a sea view and R15 more again in the high season. To get there take the sealed road to Port St Johns. About 10km before PSJ take the signed turn-off south to Umngazi Mouth.

Top of the price tree (and the northernmost of the hotels) is the *Wild Coast Sun* (☎ (0471)

## Bird-Watching on the Wild Coast

The Wild Coast is a great place to take *Roberts Birds of South Africa*, *Newman's Birds of Southern Africa* and a pair of high-powered binoculars.

In Mkambati the strelitzias in the grasslands are a fertile 'watching ground' for Gurney's sugarbird *(Promerops gurneyi)* and the lesser doublecollared sunbird *(Nectarinia chalybea)*. The forests are alive with birds: the trumpeter hornbill *(Bycanistes bucinator)*, rameron pigeon *(Columba arquatrix)*, forest weaver *(Ploceus bicolor)* and noisy Cape parrots *(Poicephalus robustus)* can all be spotted.

The lagoon at Hluleka is a great spot to see the African jacana *(Actophilornis africanus)* tiptoeing across the waterlilies. Near the rivers of the reserve there is an absolute feast of kingfishers: the pied *(Ceryle rudis)*, pygmy *(Ispidina picta)*, brownhooded *(Halcyon albiventris)*, halfcollared *(Alcedo semitorquata)* and giant *(Ceryle maxima)* kingfishers all frequent these areas. The forests are full of robins such as the Cape *(Cossypha caffra)*, starred *(Pogonocichla stellata)*, chorister *(Cossypha dichroa)* and brown *(Erythropygia signata)*.

In the forest clearings of Cwebe look for the blackheaded oriole *(Oriolus larvatus)*, the black saw-wing swallow *(Psalidoprocne holomelas)* and the crowned hornbill *(Tockus abboterminatus)*. In the reeds by the lagoon, spectacled *(Ploceus ocularis)*, thickbilled *(Amblyospiza albifrons)* and yellow *(Ploceus subaureus)* weavers build nests. Water dikkop *(Burhinus vermiculatus)* inhabit the white mangroves.

The many estuaries of Dwesa are good places to look for the shy, furtive African finfoot *(Podica senegalensis)* and the rare white-backed night heron *(Gorsachius leuconotus)*. By the sea there are African black oyster-catchers *(Haematopus ostralegus)*, at their northern limit, and the curious turnstone *(Arenaria interpres)*. Occasionally jackal buzzards *(Buteo rufofuscus)* can be seen soaring in the thermals above Kolobe Point. The forests are particularly rich with species such as Narina trogons *(Apaloderma narina)*, green twinspots *(Mandingoa nitidula)* and Knysna woodpeckers *(Campethera notata)*. ∎

ROB DRUMMOND

The Yellow-billed hornbill is one of the most striking birds to be found in the area.

59111), near the KwaZulu-Natal border and south of Port Edward. It's a glitzy place geared to holiday-makers and casino enthusiasts. Singles/doubles are R355/465, or R425/555 on weekends. The Sun is reached from the Kokstad region via Bizana on the R61. If coming from Durban, turn off the N2 at Port Shepstone and follow the R61 (and numerous signs).

There are also camp sites and huts on the Wild Coast Trail and in the various nature reserves (see the following sections).

## WILD COAST NATURE RESERVES

There are five coastal reserves (from north to south: Mkambati, Silaka, Hluleka, Cwebe and Dwesa) and the Wild Coast Trail tra-verses them all. Silaka, which fringes Port St Johns, was covered earlier.

### Mkambati

Mkambati is an 8000 hectare coastal reserve with some great scenery, including the Msikaba and Mtentu river gorges. The reserve takes its name from the mkambati, or Pondo coconut palm *(Jubaeopsis caffra)*, as this is the only place in the world where it is found. In the grassland you can see patches of the banana-like *Strelitzia nicolai*. Orchids abound in the rocky recesses of gorges; and proteas, tree ferns and date palms are found on the river banks.

You can take canoes (R7.50 an hour) up the Msikaba, navigable upstream for 2km;

there are also walking trails. A shop sells basic food, and entry to the reserve is R5.

You get here from Flagstaff, 65km south of the N2 – take the turn-off to Holy Cross Mission just north of Flagstaff. There are also buses running from Port St Johns to Msikaba on the southern edge of the reserve.

### Hluleka

Hluleka, a scenic reserve which combines sea, lagoons and forest, is midway between Port St Johns and Coffee Bay. The coast is rocky, although there is a quiet lagoon which is flanked by a large saltmarsh. As in Mkambati, there is a diverse range of flora.

To get here take the road from Umtata to Port St Johns and turn off to the right at Libode, about 30km from Umtata. The reserve is about 90km further on. The road isn't good but cars can usually handle it.

### Cwebe & Dwesa

These adjoining reserves about midway between Coffee Bay and Kei Mouth take in about 6000 hectares of coastal land. Both have tracts of forest as well as good beaches, and there are hiking trails. The reserves are separated by the Mbashe River.

In Cwebe you can walk to the Mbanyana Falls or to the lagoon where, if you are lucky, you may see the Cape clawless otter in the late afternoon. On the southern edge of the reserve near the Mbashe is a small cluster of white mangroves where sesarmid crabs and mudskippers are found near the stems. To get to Cwebe take the Xhora (Elliotdale) turn-off from the N2 (about 40km south-east of Umtata). The reserve is 65km further on; the road to The Haven Hotel is signposted.

Dwesa, one of the most beautiful reserves in South Africa, is bounded by the Mbashe River in the north and the Nqabara River in the south. In the estuaries of both rivers are mangrove communities. Crocodiles have been reintroduced to the Kobole River, although they are rarely sighted. You may see the herd of eland come down to the beach near the Kobole estuary in the late afternoon.

For Dwesa, turn off the N2 at Idutywa (40km north of Butterworth) on the road to Gatyana (Willowvale). Continue until you come to a fork with another sign to Gatyana – take the other, unmarked direction. After heavy rain this is no place for ordinary cars.

### Places to Stay

There is self-catering accommodation at Mkambati, Silaka, Hluleka and Dwesa reserves, and camp sites at Cwebe and Dwesa. Sites cost about R15 and chalets around R50 per person, although during peak holiday times you might have to take the whole chalet for about R120. All the coastal reserves are on the Wild Coast hiking trail and some trail huts are in the reserves.

Accommodation and sites must be booked at the Department of Agriculture & Forestry in Umtata. Ask for current information on roads into the reserves, as some wash out during spring and summer rains.

### WILD COAST HIKING TRAIL

The five day Coffee Bay Trail, running from Port St Johns to Coffee Bay, has been extended to cover the length of the Transkei coast. A walk along this trail is an unforgettable experience – bottlenose dolphins are seen frolicking out at sea, the locals you meet as you wait for ferries welcome you into their villages, and the starry nights are hauntingly quiet. To walk the whole trail takes about two weeks; most people only do a section.

Three major sections of the trail are described in *Exploring Southern Africa on Foot: the Guide to Hiking Trails* – Coffee Bay to the Mbashe River (44km, four days); Port St Johns to Coffee Bay (60km, five days); and the Umtamvuna River to Port St Johns (100km; six to 11 days).

The walking isn't especially difficult, but some planning is required as you have to take along all your own supplies. Water is available at trail huts (about 12km apart) and from the streams and rivers, but it must be purified.

The trails must be booked at the Department of Agriculture & Forestry in Umtata, and must be walked from north to south. Good maps of the trail sections are available at the department for R1.50 each. There is comprehensive interpretative information on the reverse side of the maps.

The sections and walking fees are: Umtamvuna to Msikaba River (R20), Msikaba River to Port St Johns (R40), PSJ to Coffee Bay (R35), Coffee Bay to Mbashe River (R30) and Dwesa to Kei River (R35).

As well as trail huts there are 15 camping areas along the coast (Mbotyi camping area has closed) where you can camp for up to 31 days. There are from eight to 40 sites available at these places. Most are near the huts and share their basic facilities; most sites are from R5 to R10. Book sites at the Nature Conservation Division of the Agriculture & Forestry Department (☎ (0471) 31 2711), 3rd floor, Botha Sigcau Building, Leeds St, Umtata. Although the sites are on the hiking trail, most can also be reached by car, although you'll need a 4WD to get to some. The trail also passes near the hotels and resorts scattered along the coast.

### Warning

Many rivers cut across the trail and crossing them presents the main difficulty for hikers. There are ferries at a few of the larger rivers, but some require wading or swimming. It's important that you know what the tide is doing before you cross – about 30 minutes after low tide is the safest time. You'll need a plastic bag to protect your pack. *Never* try to cross a river while wearing your pack, and wear shoes in case of stone fish or stingrays. It's usually easier to cross a little upstream from the mouth, where you're less likely to encounter the sharks which sometimes enter the estuaries.

### NORTHERN TRANSKEI

On the N2 between Umtata and Kokstad in KwaZulu-Natal are some sizeable towns such as Qumbu, Mt Frere and Mt Ayliff. Other large towns in the north are Bizana and Lusikisiki, both in the north-east and not far from the coast. North of the Kokstad corridor is the isolated tract of Eastern Cape, with Umzimkulu as its main centre.

In Mt Frere, the *hotel* (☎ (04772) 171) has singles/doubles for R40/60.

**Umtamvuna Nature Reserve** is being developed as a twin to the reserve across the Umtamvuna Gorge in KwaZulu-Natal. It's an area rich in flora – the prehistoric-looking Eastern Cape cycad *(Encephalartos altensteinii)* grows on the cliffs.

EASTERN CAPE PROVINCE

# Northern Cape Province

Northern Cape is the largest and most sparsely populated of South Africa's provinces. The mighty Orange River is a lifeline that runs through a country that becomes desert-like on the fringes of the Kalahari and in the Karoo. The Orange and its tributary, the Vaal, combine to create the longest and largest river in South Africa, but its flow can vary significantly depending on the rainfall on the highveld.

Along the river there are intensely cultivated, irrigated farms. To the north of the river, bordering Botswana, there's sparsely wooded acacia savanna and grasslands – cattle-ranching country. To the south, there's the Karoo, with woody shrubs and succulents – sheep-farming country.

The Orange flows west to form the border between South Africa and Namibia, and this area of Northern Cape is spectacularly harsh country, including the isolated and magnificent Richtersveld National Park. South of here is Namaqualand (sometimes spelt as 'Namakwaland'), justly world-famous for its extraordinary spring flowers. Northern Cape's coast is singularly bleak, with cold seas breaking onto a near-desert coast. To the south the coast improves somewhat and there is good surfing.

The indigenous human population is varied, although the San people once occupied most of the drier regions, including the Kalahari. Small numbers of San continue to lead semi-traditional lifestyles in isolated parts of Botswana. The Batswana people settled as far west as Kuruman and one of the Khoikhoi groups, the Grigriqua, who were displaced from the south-west, settled Griqualand in the area west of Kimberley. The first white explorers entered the region in the 1760s, but relatively large numbers of whites only began to move into the region in the second half of the 19th century. After diamonds were discovered near Kimberley in 1869, the British annexed Griqualand West (including Kimberley).

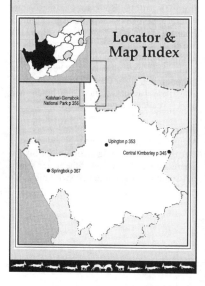

## HIGHLIGHTS

- Huge distances, vast horizons and stunning landscapes
- Springtime in Namaqualand – the world's best flower show
- Remote Kalahari Gemsbok National Park – catch a glimpse of the unique Kalahari lion
- Kimberley – interesting old town, synonymous with diamonds

Kimberley is still synonymous with diamonds, which were discovered on a farm owned by the De Beer family. The De Beers sold their farm to a syndicate for the princely sum of £6300 (compared with the £100 million or so worth of diamonds that were found). Their name survives with the enormous De Beers company, now one of the world's most powerful mining companies.

Two possible routes between Jo'burg and Cape Town run through this region. The most direct is the N12, which skirts the Free

State and runs through Kimberley (worth an overnight stop). The N12 route is 1434km all up, marginally more than the N1 through Bloemfontein.

It is also possible to head west to the extraordinary Kalahari Gemsbok National Park and down the west coast via Namaqualand. This is closer to 2000km, not counting travel within the park, or any side trips.

Most of the area has warm temperatures year-round. It can get very hot in summer and cold at night in winter. Summer maximums average 33°C; winter maximums average 19°C and minimums of 2°C.

## KIMBERLEY

Kimberley, the capital of Northern Cape, would never have existed had it not been for a human fascination for things that glitter. It is still synonymous with diamonds, and mining continues, although for most visitors its interest lies in its historical role: this was where De Beers Consolidated Mines began and Cecil John Rhodes (of Rhodesia) and Ernest Oppenheimer made their fortunes.

The town is not particularly prepossessing – it is a mining town, after all. Still, after a long trip across the Karoo, the relatively bright lights of Kimberley are a welcome

## Cecil Rhodes

Cecil John Rhodes (1853-1902), the sickly son of an English vicar, was sent to South Africa in 1870 to improve his health. After working on his brother's farm in Natal, Rhodes left for the new diamond fields near Kimberley in 1871. By 1887 he had founded the De Beers Company and could afford to buy Barney Barnato's Kimberley Mine for £5,000,000. By 1891 De Beers owned 90% of the world's diamonds and Rhodes also had a stake in the fabulous reef of gold discovered on the Witwatersrand (near Johannesburg).

Rhodes was not satisfied with merely acquiring personal wealth and power. He personified the idea of Empire and dreamed of 'painting the map red', building a railway from the Cape to Cairo (running through British territory all the way) and even had far-fetched ideas of bringing the USA back under British rule. The times were right for such dreams, and Rhodes was a favourite of Queen Victoria as well as the voters (both Boer and British) in the Cape. In 1890 he was elected Prime Minister of the Cape Colony.

To paint Africa red, Rhodes pushed north to establish mines and develop trade. Although he despised missionaries for being too soft on the natives, he used them as stalking horses in his wrangling and chicanery to open up new areas. He was successful in establishing British control in Bechuanaland (later Botswana) and the area that was to become Rhodesia (later Zimbabwe), but the gold mines there proved to be less productive than those on the Witwatersrand. The Transvaal Republic in general and Paul Kruger in particular had been causing Rhodes difficulty for some time.

Both men were fiercely independent idealists with very different ideals, and there was no love lost between them.

It irked Rhodes that Kruger's republic of pastoralists should be sitting on the richest reef of gold in the world, and the republic was also directly in the path of British expansion.

The miners on the Witwatersrand were mainly non-Boers, who were denied any say in the politics of the republic. This caused increasing resentment, and in late 1895 Rhodes' crony Leander Starr Jameson led an expedition into the Witwatersrand with the intention of sparking an uprising among the foreigners.

The Jameson raid was a fiasco. All the participants were either killed or captured, and Jameson was jailed. The British government was extremely embarrassed when it became apparent that Rhodes had prior knowledge of the raid and probably encouraged it. He was forced to resign as Prime Minister and the British government took control of Rhodesia and Bechuanaland, his personal fiefdoms.

Rhodes's health deteriorated after these disasters. His empire-building days were over, but one more stock episode from the Victorian omnibus awaited: an honourable chap becomes entangled in the schemes of a glamorous and ruthless woman, in this case the Princess Randziwill. She was later jailed for her swindles.

After his death in 1906, Rhodes' reputation was largely rehabilitated by his will, which devoted most of his fortune to the Rhodes Scholarship, which still sends winners from around the Commonwealth (and other nations such as Germany and the USA) to study at Oxford University. ■

sight. The Mine Museum is one of the best in the country; the Big Hole is pretty amazing; Galeshewe township oozes history of the struggle against apartheid; and the silence of the Karoo will be forgotten amid the din of Kimberley's many fine pubs.

## History

Diamonds were discovered in the Kimberley region in 1869, and by 1872 there were an estimated 50,000 miners in the vicinity. Most lived in tents, although some built small houses with galvanised iron and tarpaulins.

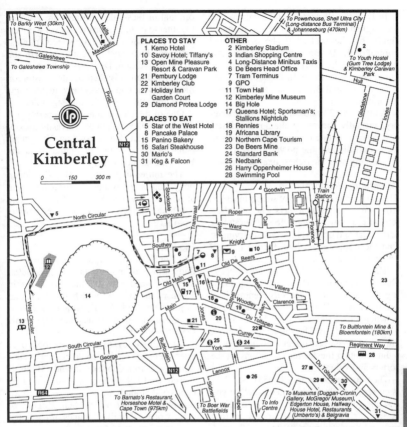

**Central Kimberley**

PLACES TO STAY
1 Kemo Hotel
10 Savoy Hotel; Tiffany's
13 Open Mine Pleasure Resort & Caravan Park
21 Pembury Lodge
22 Kimberley Club
27 Holiday Inn Garden Court
29 Diamond Protea Lodge

PLACES TO EAT
5 Star of the West Hotel
8 Pancake Palace
15 Panino Bakery
16 Safari Steakhouse
30 Mario's
31 Keg & Falcon

OTHER
2 Kimberley Stadium
3 Indian Shopping Centre
4 Long-Distance Minibus Taxis
6 De Beers Head Office
7 Tram Terminus
9 GPO
11 Town Hall
12 Kimberley Mine Museum
14 Big Hole
17 Queens Hotel; Sportsman's; Stallions Nightclub
18 Rennies
19 Africana Library
20 Northern Cape Tourism
23 De Beers Mine
24 Standard Bank
25 Nedbank
26 Harry Oppenheimer House
28 Swimming Pool

Water was scarce and sanitary conditions were appalling. Most supplies were transported by ox-wagons from Port Elizabeth, so most necessities were extremely expensive. It was thought that the diamonds lay at a depth of 15 to 18m, which allowed virtually anyone with a shovel to get at them.

In 1871 diamonds were discovered at a small hill, which came to be known as Colesberg Koppie (later Kimberley), and the excavation of the Big Hole commenced. A number of problems faced the diggers, not least of which how to allow each miner access to their claims (which measured about nine by 7m). These claims were even further subdivided; eventually there were 1600 claims and over 30,000 men toiling in an area, roughly 300 by 200m.

The miners soon found that diamonds continued to be found as they dug further and further down. As they did so, the difficulties of managing the insane anthill increased. The ever-growing crater was soon crisscrossed by an elaborate spider web of ropes and pulleys, which were used to haul out the gravel. The chaos couldn't continue indefinitely; to make things worse, diamond prices dropped because of overproduction.

In 1871 the 19-year-old, tubercular son of an English parson arrived at the diamond fields; by the mid-1870s he had gained control of the De Beers mine, and from this base he bought every claim and mine he could lay his hands on. In 1889, after a long battle, he bought Barney Barnato's Kimberley mines.

A little over 20 years after the first discovery, virtually the entire diamond industry was owned by one company, which was in turn controlled by the powerful Cecil John Rhodes, by now the richest man in Africa.

## Orientation & Information

The city centre is a tangle of streets inherited from the not-so-distant days when Kimberley was a rowdy shantytown, sprawling across flat and open veld. If you're trying to find the train station, look for the red and white communications tower.

The city's most noticeable skyscraper is Harry Oppenheimer House, a striking building to the south of the city centre. It is occupied by De Beers Diamond Trading and is where all South Africa's diamonds are graded and valued. The south side windows are slanted to prevent direct sunlight entering – thus creating the desired conditions for the sorters and valuers.

The information centre (☎ (0531) 82 7298) is currently in the library on Chapel St; you can get good maps and brochures on Kimberley. It's open weekdays from 8 am to 5 pm, and Saturday from 8.30 to 11.30 am. A tourist centre is due to open in the new municipality building on the corner of Dalham and Eureka Sts. The antique tourist tram to the Big Hole starts at the town hall on the corner of Old Main St and Transvaal Rd (see Getting Around later in this section for details).

Northern Cape Tourism (☎ (0531) 31434) in Flaxley House, Du Toitspan Rd, has some information. Rennies Travel (☎ (0531) 81 1825/6) is at 43 Du Toitspan Rd.

## Kimberley Mine Museum

This excellent open-air museum is on the western side of the Big Hole. Forty-eight original or facsimile buildings are grouped together to form a reconstruction of Kimberley in the 1880s. There are streets, miners' cottages, shops, auction rooms, a tavern and so on. In addition, De Beers Hall has a collection of diamonds; there are demonstration models of diamond-recovery technology, and a dramatic view over the Big Hole.

One of the old businesses in operation is the skittle alley, which offers vastly trickier amusement than tenpin bowling. You get six balls for R3. To dig for diamonds at the English Claim costs R4 for one bucket.

The museum (☎ (0531) 31557) is open daily from 8 am to 6 pm; entry is a bargain at R10/6 for adults/children. There's also a café here, with breakfast for R15 and burgers from R10.

## Big Hole

The Big Hole is the largest hole in the world dug entirely by manual labour. It is 800m deep and water now fills the hole to within 150m of the surface, which still leaves an impressive void. Don't forget, however, there is over four times as much hole below the water's surface.

The Kimberley Mine, which took over after open-cast mining could no longer continue, went to a depth of around 1100m. It closed in 1914. Altogether 14½ million carats of diamonds are believed to have been removed from under Colesberg Koppie. In other words, 28 million tonnes of earth and rock were removed for three tonnes of diamonds. To best see the Big Hole you must enter via the museum and pay the entry fee.

## Anglo-Boer War Battlefields

At the beginning of the 1899-1902 war against the British, the Boers, after swift early victories, got bogged down in lengthy sieges at Ladysmith in Natal, and at Mafeking (now Mafikeng in North-West Province) and Kimberley in Northern Cape. The siege of Kimberley lasted for 124 days before the relief of the town was effected on 15 February 1900.

Several major battles were fought in the vicinity of the town, both during the siege and after. The most important was Magersfontein on 11 December 1899, when the famous Highland Brigade was decimated by entrenched Boers. Other important battles include Graspan, Modder River, Paardeberg and Sunnyside. For tours, contact ☎ (0531) 81 4006. The entry fee is R8 per car.

On Atlas St, Kimberley, the **McGregor Museum** (☎ (0531) 32645) has information on the Anglo-Boer war; it is open Monday to Saturday from 7 am to 5 pm, Sunday 2 to 5 pm. (Rhodes sat out the siege in two downstairs rooms of this building.)

At some battlefields, interpretive centres are being built, and a connecting driving route between sites is being planned.

### Galeshewe

The satellite township of Galeshewe rates with Soweto as an important source of 'ideas' people for the struggle against apartheid. It includes the house and grave of Sol Plaatje, a founding member of the African National Congress (ANC), noted journalist and the first black South African to write a novel in English; the home of Robert Sobukwe, founder and first president of the then 'Pan Africanist Congress' (PAC); and the Self Help Scheme implemented by Helen Joseph, former secretary of the Federation of South African Women and an organiser of the 1956 mass demonstration in Pretoria against the extension of passes.

To get there take a minibus taxi from the town hall in Kimberley.

### Duggan-Cronin Gallery & Africana Library

The Duggan-Cronin Gallery (☎ (0531) 32 645/6), on Edgerton Rd in the suburb of Belgravia, features a unique collection of photographs of black tribes taken in the 1920s and 1930s – before many aspects of traditional tribal life were lost. The gallery is open weekdays from 9 am to 5 pm, Saturday from until 1 pm and Sunday from 2 to 5 pm. Entry is R3, or R2 for students.

The **Africana Library** in Du Toitspan Rd covers the period of first contact between the Tswana and missionaries. Included in the collection is Robert Moffat's copy of his translation of the Old Testament into Tswana. For more details, see the Moffat Mission in the Around Kuruman section.

### De Beers Tours

De Beers Tours take groups to the treatment and recovery plants at Bultfontein Mine, departing from the Visitors' Centre at the mine gate. Tours start at 9 and 11 am, Monday to Friday, and cost R7.

Underground Tours (☎ (0531) 82 9651, 80 7270, after hours 32259) are run on weekdays at 8 am (9.30 am on Tuesday), and cost R45. You can't wear contact lenses (because of the pressure at the depths you'll descend to) and you must be at least 16 years of age. The tours are 3½ hours long.

### Places to Stay

The *Big Hole Open Mine Pleasure Resort and Caravan Park* (☎ (0531) 80 6322) is an attractive park with a pool, but very little shade. The mine museum and Big Hole are a short walk away. Tent sites are R10 and R5 per person. The shadier *Kimberley Caravan Park* (☎ (0531) 33582), 2.5km out of town on Hull St, is not recommended.

*Kimberley Youth Hostel* (☎ (0531) 28577), also known as Gum Tree Lodge, is about 5km from town at the intersection of Hull St and the Bloemfontein road. It's a large and pleasant place, in an old jail with shady lawns and a pool. Accommodation is in fairly basic flats, which act as either dorms or private rooms. Dorms cost R25 and singles/doubles (in flats with a stove and fridge) are R40/50.

The information centre has details of B&B places, which charge from about R75 per person. The pick of the bunch is the sumptuous *Edgerton House* (☎ (0531) 81 1150) at 5 Edgerton Rd in fashionable Belgravia, where rooms start at R285/350. Also recommended is *Pembury Lodge* (☎ (0531) 81 6965) at 11 Currey St, for R110/150.

The fact that *Halfway House Hotel* (☎ (0531) 25151), on the corner of Egerton and Du Toitspan Rds, has a drive-in bar might not seem a particularly big selling point if you're staying here. It's a pleasant old-style pub, however, with a friendly atmosphere. Rooms are good value at R95/140, including breakfast. This place gets its name from the time when Cecil John Rhodes, afraid to dismount his horse and reveal his true height, invented the concept of the ride-in bar. Now horse gives way to car at South Africa's first drive-in pub.

The cheapest hotel alternative is the modern *Kemo Hotel* (☎ (0531) 71 1023), Aster Rd, which has rooms for R60/120 – it doesn't get many tourists. The *Horseshoe Motel* (☎ (0531) 82 5267), Memorial Rd, is a comfortable place with a pool. Rooms with TV, air-con and telephone start at R116/180.

*Holiday Inn Garden Court* (☎ (0531) 31751), Du Toitspan Rd, is a large hotel delivering high standards at a reasonable price; rooms start at R243, breakfast is R26.

Also on Du Toitspan Rd, *Diamond Protea Lodge* (☎ (0531) 81 1281) has rooms from R207. Protea also owns the three star *Savoy Hotel* (☎ (0531) 82 6211) on De Beers Rd, where rooms cost R199/219.

### Places to Eat

If you're looking for something cheap and delicious, *Panino Bakery* on the corner of Jones St and Old Main Rd has a mouthwatering selection of cakes, biscuits, pies and bread at good-value prices.

On Market Square, near the tram terminus, *Pancake Palace* is a trendy-looking café that does crêpes only; however, they are good and inexpensive, with most dishes under R10. Also overlooking Market Square, *Safari Steakhouse*, upstairs on the corner of Old Main Rd and Jones St, is highly regarded by locals. The service is good and the steaks are the best in town. It is a bit expensive though, at around R30 for a 200g steak or R40 for a 320g steak.

One of the most relaxed and popular places is *Umberto's* on Du Toitspan Rd near the Halfway House Hotel. It serves snacks, pasta and more substantial meals at average prices – a large pizza with avocado and pineapple is about R25, and it's open from early until late. Occasionally, Umberto gets up and

gives an impromptu opera solo. *Mario's*, also on Du Toitspan Rd, is another Italian family place with a large menu; prices are similar to Umberto's.

At the old-style and atmospheric *Star of the West Hotel*, North Circular Rd, there are meals for under R14 and steaks from R19, including chips, rolls and salad. You can reach it on the tourist tram.

The drive-in bar at the *Halfway House Hotel* on Du Toitspan Rd is a bit of a disappointment – it's nothing more than a car park; however, inexpensive pub lunches are served inside.

*Tiffany's* in the Savoy Hotel, De Beers Rd, also receives a hearty 'lekker' from locals – the food is continental and there's a full wine list. *Barnato's*, Dalham Rd, is one of the poshest places in this rough-and-tumble town; the food is excellent.

A good place for Sunday lunch is *Goloi's* at the Phoenix Hotel. It serves an inexpensive four course meal in winter (with soup) and a three course meal (no soup) in summer. Take Synagogue Rd (which turns into Central Rd) towards the Bultfontein mine; just before you pass under the train bridge you'll see the Phoenix on the corner.

### Entertainment

There's live music on Friday and Saturday nights at the *Halfway House*'s (known locally as 'The Half') pleasant rooftop beer garden. *Powerhouse*, on the Transvaal road, is a nightclub that sometimes has live music; it has a mainly black clientele.

*Queens Hotel*, on Stockdale St in the centre of town, has gambling upstairs, *Stallions* (a techno place) at ground level and the *Sportsman's* pub next door – this precinct really hots up. The *Star of the West* often has live bands playing in its big beer garden. There are pool tables and a cocktail bar upstairs. The *Keg & Falcon*, Du Toitspan Rd, is for the older crowd – you have to be over 23 to get in.

### Getting There & Away

**Bus** Many services run to/from Jo'burg,

## Cruising & Boozing

Kimberley is the ideal destination for the avid pub crawler and its proliferation of 'frontier' bars imparts a distinctive flavour befitting a mining town. So stack away your diamonds, write down the taxi number, have a quick bite to eat and then go for it. (Realise that the local harriers ('fun runners') can brave all the town's major bars in a two hour-plus dash).

Start off at the iron and wood *Star of the West*, one of South Africa's oldest pubs (1873) – you can get here on the Kimberley tram. Not far away is the next stop, the *Kimberlite*, with a drive-in bar (remember, you are in a taxi). Next, taxi it to the *Halfway House Hotel*, the first of South Africa's ride- (horse) and drive-in pubs and mix with the kids. They will stand in awe of your enterprise.

Not far away is the *Keg & Falcon* – for the taste of a more mature crowd – who will also sympathise with your enterprise. Damn it – back to town to the *Queens Hotel* (directions at this stage only known to the sober taxi driver) for a brace of gambling, techno-pop and non-stop argument in the *Sportsman's Bar* next door. ■

about six hours from Kimberley. The cheapest is Greyhound's daily service for R88.

Translux stops in Kimberley on the Monday, Wednesday, Friday, Saturday and Sunday run between Jo'burg/Pretoria (R160 from Kimberley) and Cape Town (R270). Translux has a similar but more expensive service, terminating in Knysna (11 hours). Heading to Knysna, buses depart from Kimberley at 8.35 pm on Sunday and 10.35 pm on Thursday; going the other way, buses run to Jo'burg/Pretoria at 2.45 am on Wednesday and Friday. The fare to Knysna is R185.

Intercape stops in Kimberley on the twice-weekly run (Sunday and Tuesday) between Cape Town (R250, 10 hours) and Pretoria (R150, seven hours). Services in the other direction are on Monday and Saturday.

Northern Cape Bus Service (☎ (0531) 81 1062), 5 Elliot St, is the Greyhound agent in Kimberley. Greyhound, Intercape and Translux stop at Shell Ultra City on the N12.

**Train** For information on trains contact Spoornet (☎ (0531) 88 2100). The *Trans Karoo* runs daily between Cape Town and Jo'burg/Pretoria via Kimberley. The southbound train leaves Jo'burg at 12.30 pm, arrives in Kimberley at 8.50 pm and Cape Town 17½ hours later at 2.15 pm. The northbound train leaves Cape Town at 9.20 am and arrives in Kimberley at 1.53 am the next day and in Jo'burg at 10.15 am. From Kimberley to Cape Town, 1st/2nd/3rd-class tickets are R225/152/95; from Kimberley to Jo'burg they're R115/80/50.

The *Diamond Express* runs overnight between Jo'burg/Pretoria and Bloemfontein via Kimberley daily, except Saturday. Fares are as for the *Trans Karoo*.

The *Trans Oranje* between Cape Town and Durban takes a slow and roundabout route via Kimberley; contact Spoornet for details.

**Minibus Taxi** The taxi area is around the Indian shopping centre off Bultfontein St (where there's a produce market and takeaways). You'll also find long-distance taxis here, a short distance from the rest, near Crossley St.

Destinations include Bloemfontein (R35), Cape Town (R110), Jo'burg (R70), Kuruman (R63) and Upington (R70). If you're heading for Mafikeng you can take a taxi to Hartswater for R23, then a taxi to Taung (R5) and pick up another there.

### Getting Around

Kimberley has one surviving antique tram that runs between the town hall and the mine museum. On weekdays it departs from the town hall at 15 minutes past the hour, every hour daily. A one way trip is R3, a return R6. A minibus taxi around town costs about R1.30. For a regular taxi from the pubs, telephone AA Taxi ☎ (0531) 861 4015.

### VAALBOS NATIONAL PARK

This relatively new national park (1986) of 23,000 hectares is divided into two by a belt of private land. It takes its name from the camphor bush, or 'vaalbos' in Afrikaans. It is now a sanctuary for the black rhino, and some 26 species of large mammal exist here.

Bird life is also prolific, with the martial eagle, bateleur and vulture being regularly seen. It is the only park in the country where three distinct ecosystems are present – Karoo, grasveld and Kalahari.

The park, 61km north-west of Kimberley on the R31, is still being developed. It is open to day visitors, but there are also self-catering chalets nearby (built close to water holes) for overnight stays; for more information contact ☎ (053) 561 0088. Entry to the park for two persons and their car is R17.

### BRITSTOWN

Britstown is at the crossroads of the N10, between the south coast and Namibia, and the N12, between Kimberley and Cape Town. It's in the centre of a prosperous sheep-grazing area and is a pleasant enough little town.

There are a few places of the 'overnight rooms' ilk, the best being the *Transkaroo Hotel* (☎ (053) 672 0027). Rooms with shared bath start at R60 per person, and standard rooms are R150/170 for a single/double or R185/195 for a triple/quad. *Mirage Toeriste-kamers* (☎ (053) 672 0310) has clean rooms from R50/70.

### DE AAR

De Aar is a major service centre for the Karoo, but its claim to fame is as a railway junction – one of the busiest in South Africa. 'De aar' means 'the artery' and refers to the arterial rivers in this area, but could equally refer to the importance of the railway lines.

De Aar is too big to be called a one horse town – maybe it's a two horse town. There is so little to see or do here that an overnight stay can be unnerving.

#### Places to Stay & Eat

The minuscule *Van Der Merwe Municipal Caravan Park* (☎ (05363) 2131) on Cilliers St has sites for R25.

*De Aar Hotel* (☎ (05363) 2181), Fried-lander St, has air-conditioned rooms, but a depressing atmosphere. It's way overpriced at R145/245, including breakfast.

As well as the reasonable dining room at

De Aar Hotel, there's a restaurant in historic *Olive Schreiner House* on the corner of Grundlingh and Van Zyl Sts. The author Olive Schreiner lived here from 1907 to 1913. You get good lunches here Monday to Friday, and dinners on Wednesday, Friday and Saturday.

#### Getting There & Away

**Train** The *Trans Karoo* and *Blue Train* (Jo'burg/Pretoria-Cape Town), and *Trans Oranje* (Durban-Bloemfontein-Kimberley-Cape Town) pass through here.

### COLESBERG

For a major stopover on the N1 between Cape Town and Bloemfontein, Colesberg is an attractive place. It's a classic Karoo town, founded in 1829, and many old buildings have survived. There's a beautiful Dutch Reformed church (NG Kerk) built in 1866. Shops with verandahs still front onto the main street, and there are attractive houses and cottages on the side streets.

The friendly information centre is in the museum (☎ (051) 753 0678) on Murray St; it's open weekdays. The museum houses important archives of the Anglo-Boer War.

#### Places to Stay

During the high season, from mid-December to mid-January, and the school holidays accommodation in Colesberg can book up.

On the outskirts of town on Kerk St, the dusty *Colesberg Caravan Park* (☎ (051) 753 0040) has sites for R30.

The best place in town is *The Lighthouse* (☎ (051) 753 0043), 40A Church St, a comfortable and homey guesthouse. It's sparkling clean and is furnished with old farm furniture. The rate is a reasonable R80/120 for a single/double.

The information centre (☎ (051) 753 0582) lists many other 'overnight accommodation' places, which range from ordinary B&Bs to restored Karoo Tuishuis – town cottages of wealthy Karoo farmers.

The *Central Hotel* (☎ (051) 753 0734) is considerably bigger than it looks from the street. It's a bit faded, but in general it's comfortable and efficiently run. It has rooms for R80/145, or from R165/175 with bath. *Merino Inn* (☎ (051) 753 0782) on the town outskirts (Cape Town side) is a comfortable yet characterless motel inside; outside it's strikingly ugly. It has rooms from about R140/210.

Six km north of Colesberg on the Philippolis road (R717), *Van Zylsvlei Motel* (☎ (051) 753 0589) is a quiet, older-style place, with singles/doubles from R80/150. It has a pleasant restaurant.

### Places to Eat

The tea room at the *Avon Nursery* on the main street has a shady courtyard (in which hidden speakers softly pipe songs from *The Sound of Music*), although the menu is limited to snacks. Close by, the medium to rare *Pop In* looks pretty ordinary, but is, say locals, the place for steaks.

Colesberg also has plenty of chains, such as *Wimpy* and *Golden Egg*.

### AROUND COLESBERG

The R57 between Colesberg and Middelburg crosses a classic Karoo landscape. The **Lootsberg Pass**, south of Middelburg, is spectacular and the countryside is dramatic.

At **Doornkloof Nature Reserve**, northwest of Colesberg and just off the R369 (and on the shores of PK Le Roux Dam), you may see mountain reedbuck, grey duiker, kudu and steenbok (and if you're very lucky, aardvark, aardwolf and bat-eared fox).

### KURUMAN

Just when you were starting to get very depressed about Northern Cape country towns, you get to Kuruman. This town feels as if it sits at the edge of rather wild and interesting country – and it does. Kuruman derives from a San word, but the area was also settled by the Batlhaping, a Batswana tribe, when the first whites appeared in the area around 1800. West of Kuruman there's a long, empty stretch of road to Upington, and a landscape of low, sandy ranges.

There is a **Raptor Rehabilitation Centre** (☎ (05373) 30464) on Tsening Rd; it has a

map of the best routes to follow in search of the birds of prey. The centre is open weekdays from 8 am to 5 pm, Saturday until noon and Sunday from 11 am to noon.

The skies now have to be shared with a recent influx of human soarers. Kuruman has become world renowned as a paragliding centre, with several height and distance records being achieved here. For more information contact Fly Africa (☎ (011) 43 4918) and Fly Cross Country (☎ (011) 883 5017).

### Orientation & Information

The main through road is Hoof St (Main St), and most businesses are concentrated around the intersection of Hoof and Voortrekker Sts. There's a useful tourist office (☎ (05373) 21095) on Hoof St adjacent to The Eye. It's open from 8 am to 5 pm weekdays and until noon on Saturday.

### Eye of Kuruman

The Eye is an amazing natural spring that produces 18 to 20 million litres of water a day, every day. It has never faltered. The surrounding area has been developed into a pleasant enough picnic spot, and a good place to break your journey – note the masked weaver birds and their nests over the pond. Entry is R1/0.50 for adults/children.

### Places to Stay

*Kuruman Caravan Park* (☎ (05373) 21479), Voortrekker St, is a pleasant spot to break your journey. There are some extremely good-value chalets and some shady camp sites. All are short walks from the centre of town and the Eye. The chalets are well equipped and pleasant, and go for R46 a double, R115 for three beds and R145 for four beds. Booking is recommended, especially during the school holidays.

The *Savoy Hotel* (☎ (05373) 21121) has recently undergone a revamp. Singles/doubles with breakfast are R110/150. By comparison the *Grand Hotel* (☎ (05373) 21148) is pretty slick in a small-town way – with air-conditioning, coffee machines and TV, but you pay for what you get. Rooms with breakfast are R110/190. You don't want

NORTHERN CAPE PROVINCE

a room near the disco, which is a 'private club, members only' – it's a fair bet that white skin will ensure instant entry.

The most expensive and luxurious accommodation in town can be found at the large, somewhat incongruous *Eldorado Motel* (☎ (05373) 22191) on the outskirts of town (the N14). B&B costs from R180/290 (negotiable on weekends).

Last, but not least, *Riverfield Guesthouse* (☎ (05373) 30003) on Seodin Rd is a B&B with an ebullient host, Alfie. The bar here is a great meeting place, the rooms are good value (especially the cosy rondavel) at R145/195 and the breakfast is mighty.

### Places to Eat
The hotel dining rooms are good for a sit-down meal, particularly *Eldorado*; a full three course meal is about R40. For a snack, such as asparagus tart (R5) and coffee, *De Oude Drostdy* next to The Eye is a good choice. The town's best place is *Over-devoor*, Hoof St, with 'Kalahari cuisine' – I understand this is meat plus meat.

The apotheosis of Afrikaner bars is the fiercely conservative bastion, the *Tavern Bar* in the Grand Hotel. The ennui here can be cut with a knife – yet it does have a centrepiece spicy sausage *(wors)* collection!

### Getting There & Away
**Bus** Kuruman is a stop on Intercape's Windhoek (Namibia) to Jo'burg via Upington service; see the Upington section further on for more details. Fares from Kuruman include Jo'burg (R130), Upington (R85) and Windhoek (R285).

**Minibus Taxi** The taxi park is next to the Shop Rite supermarket on Voortrekker St (if coming from Jo'burg turn right at the robots). Very few taxis run west from Kuruman. Examples of destinations and fares include Jo'burg (R100), Kimberley (R40), Mafikeng (R70) and Vryburg (R25).

### AROUND KURUMAN
Moffat Mission

The mission was the first white settlement in the area and was established by the London Missionary Society in 1816 to work with the local Batlhaping people. The mission site, 4km from the Eye on the road to Hotazel, was chosen at a cultivable part of the valley. The clay-lined furrow, used to carry water from the Eye, still exists.

The mission was named after Robert and Mary Moffat, two courageous Scots who worked at the mission from 1817 to 1870. They converted the Batswana to Christianity, started a school and translated the bible into Tswana. The mission became a famous staging point for explorers and missionaries heading further into Africa. The Moffat daughter, Mary, married David Livingstone in the mission church.

The mission is a quiet and atmospheric spot, with stone and thatch buildings shaded by large trees. The entry of R5/2 for adults/children also gets you to a copy of the Lord's Prayer, printed on the mission's old press.

### Hotazel & Van Zylsrus
Definitely the most interesting thing about Hotazel is its name. Say it quickly: 'hot as hell'. The sealed road from Kuruman runs parallel to a low range of hills looking out over the vast, hot flatness to the north-east.

Van Zylsrus is a dusty little frontier town, one of the most isolated in South Africa. There's a stop sign, a petrol station, post office and pub – all the necessities of life. I guess they must be saving up for the robot. The pub is the *Gemsbok* (☎ (05378) 238), which has rooms for R80 per person or R70 with shared bath, including breakfast.

### UPINGTON
Upington is on the banks of the Orange River and is the principal commercial town in the far north. It's an orderly, prosperous place, full of supermarkets and chain stores, and generally very friendly.

The surrounding area is intensively cultivated thanks to the limitless sunlight and irrigation water. Cotton, wheat, grapes and fruit are all produced. It's a good place to stock up on supplies for Kalahari Gemsbok. The small **Spitskop Nature Reserve**, 15km

north of Upington, has gemsbok, zebra and other antelope. There are short hiking trails.

### Information
The helpful tourist office (☎ (054) 27064) is in the foyer of the town library. A staff member is there from 8 am to 5.30 pm on weekdays, but there's a desk with plenty of brochures accessible during the longer library hours, which include Saturday morning from 8 am to noon.

A branch of the First National Bank is on the north-west corner of Schroder and Hill Sts, and the Standard Bank is on the corner of Hill and Scott Sts.

There's a laundromat on Scott St, near the Oranje Hotel. In summer, you'll probably be in desperate need of the swimming pool in the park off Le Roux St.

### Activities
Theuns Botha (☎ (054) 22336) operates Spitskop Safaris, which runs informal, flex-

ible tours to the Kalahari Gemsbok and Augrabies Falls national parks, and can also organise hunting trips. Kalahari Safaris (☎ (082) 493 5041, (054) 902, ask for 919722) have also been recommended by readers.

River Runners (☎ (021) 762 2350) and Felix Unite (011) 803 9775) offer canoe trips down the Orange River. Bushmanland Horse Trails (☎ (054) 451 0077) have rides around the Augrabies islands on the Orange River.

### Places to Stay – bottom end
*Die Eiland Resort* (☎ (054) 31 1553) is a fair walk from town, on the south bank of the Orange River; cross the bridge at the north end of town signposted for Prieska. There are pleasant tent sites for R28 for two, and a range of huts and bungalows which vary in price depending on their age and facilities.

There are rondavels at R72/106 for a single/double; four-bed huts from R130; and three-person units from R130.

On Morant St, just north of the stadium, *Yebo Guesthouse & Backpackers* (☎ (054) 24226) is a fantastic stopover, with a pool, excellent CD and book collection and impeccable rooms; great value at R50 for B&B.

Right in the town centre, but more expensive, *Oranjerivier Overnight Rooms* (☎ (054) 24195) offers spartan, clean and fairly large rooms. Despite the ducted air-conditioning, I'd guess that it gets pretty hot in summer. A single with breakfast is R149 (bed only R139) and a four-bed room is R218 (R208 without breakfast). It's on Mark St, near Checkers supermarket.

### Places to Stay – middle

There is a number of guesthouses, such as *Three Gables* (☎ (054) 23041), 34 Bull St, which charge around R80 per person. The tourist office has a list of the others, including *Lemon Tree Cottage* (☎ (054) 22255) at 14 Butler St, which costs R200 per person.

There are two Protea hotels, opposite each other on the corner of Lutz and Schroder Sts. *Oasis Protea Lodge* (☎ (054) 31 1125) is a pleasant if characterless place, with rooms for around R250 – ask about specials. The older *Upington Protea Hotel* (☎ (054) 25414) charges from R245 a double (R285 for a river view), with weekend specials.

The new *River City Lodge* (☎ (054) 31 1971) on Park St has splendid rooms for R165. The *Oranje Hotel* (☎ (054) 24177) on Scott St is more plain, but it's surprisingly large with air-conditioning and TV. Rooms with breakfast are R180/220, or a family room for R320 sleeps six.

### Places to Eat

Under the Upington Protea Hotel is *Spur Steakhouse* with all the usual grills from about R25; there's a good salad bar. *Saddles* on Market St is another of this ilk only larger – perhaps the steaks are bigger? *Le Must*, meaning that you 'must' go there, is on Schroder St; the R32 Veal Neil comes with

pecan, pieces of biltong, port wine and strongly reasserts the restaurant's title.

For entertainment there is *Rumours* 3km from town on Toekons St, parallel to Swartmoder Rd (the Namibia road). To get a chance to mix with the town's coloured and black populations, go to *Club Fantasy* on Van Wyk St, the *Bundu Bar* on Lutz St and *Cool Down* in the market area.

Definitely avoid the racist, parochial Afrikaners in the *Upstairs Bar* on Basson St.

### Getting There & Away

**Air** SA Express flies to/from Jo'burg daily (R660) and to/from Cape Town (R630) daily, except Saturday. There are also flights to Kimberley (R410).

**Bus** The Intercape office (☎ (054) 27091) is on Lutz St. Two Intercape services run through Upington, giving good links to the rest of the country. On Monday, Tuesday, Thursday, Friday and Saturday a bus leaves Upington at 5.30 am, heading for Jo'burg/Pretoria via Kuruman and Potchefstroom. The trip to Jo'burg takes nine hours and costs R175. Coming in the other direction, buses for Upington depart from Jo'burg/Pretoria on Tuesday, Wednesday, Thursday, Friday and Sunday. These services connect with buses to/from Windhoek (Namibia). The overnight journey between Upington and Windhoek takes 10 hours and costs R200.

Intercape also has buses running to/from Cape Town (R150, 10½ hours), via Calvinia (R110 from Upington, R120 from Cape Town) and Clanwilliam (R130, R90). Heading south, buses depart from Upington at 7.45 pm on Tuesday, Thursday, Friday and Sunday; buses heading north depart from Cape Town at 7 pm on Sunday, Monday, Wednesday and Friday. This service connects with the Jo'burg/Pretoria service.

There is no longer a passenger train.

**Minibus Taxi** You'll find taxis near the Checkers supermarket on the corner of Mark and Basson Sts. Not all long-distance taxis leave from here, but it's a good place to start asking. Protea Taxis has an office on the corner of Le Roux and Grobler Sts and you might be able to book a seat on its services. (The refreshment rooms at the train station are a mine of transport information.)

Upington taxis can take a long time to fill, but there is generally at least one per day to major destinations, such as Cape Town (R90), Jo'burg (R100), Kimberley (R70) and Windhoek (R150).

VIP Taxis (☎ (0251) 22006) operates a weekday taxi from Port Nolloth to Upington. It picks up at the Masonic Hotel in Springbok at 3 pm, returning from Upington the following morning at 7 am. It costs from R60 to R70.

**Car** If you want to see Kalahari Gemsbok and are short of time, it makes sense to fly to Upington and hire a car. There's an Avis agent (☎ (054) 25746) at the airport. The Oasis Protea rents 4WD vehicles from R475 per day with unlimited kilometres.

## KALAHARI GEMSBOK NATIONAL PARK

The Kalahari Gemsbok National Park is not as famous as many other African parks, but it is, nonetheless, one of the greatest.

The accessible section of the park lies in the triangular segment of South Africa between Namibia and Botswana. This region covers 9510 sq km; however, the protected area continues on the Botswana side of the border (there are no fences), where there are another 28,500 sq km. The South African park was proclaimed in 1931 and the Botswana park in 1938.

Together, the two sections make up one of the largest protected wilderness areas in Africa, allowing the unhindered migration of antelopes forced to travel great distances, in times of drought, to reach water and food.

Although the countryside is described as semi-desert (with around 200mm of rain a year), it is richer than it appears and supports large populations of birds, reptiles, small mammals and antelopes. These in turn support a large population of predators.

All the animals are remarkably tolerant of cars. This allows you to get extraordinarily close to animals which are otherwise wild – it's as if you were invisible.

The landscape is beautiful – reminiscent in some ways of central Australia. The Nossob and Aoub rivers (usually dry) run through the park and meet each other a few kilometres north of the entrance at Twee Rivieren. Much of the wildlife is concentrated in these river beds, where there are windmills and water holes (the only significant human interference in the ecology of the park). This makes wildlife viewing remarkably successful.

In the south, the Nossob River is between 100 and 500m wide, with grey camel thorn trees between the limestone banks. In the north, the river bed opens up to more than a kilometres wide and becomes sandy. The bed of the Aoub is narrower and deeper. Between the two rivers there is an area with the characteristically red Kalahari dunes (red thanks to iron oxide). In other areas the sand varies from pink and yellowish to grey.

Various grasses and woody shrubs survive on the dunes, and there are occasional shepherd's trees and grey camel thorns. There's a greater variety of vegetation in the river beds, including the camel thorns, black thorn, raisin bush and driedoring.

### Flora

Only hardy plants survive the periodic droughts that afflict the Kalahari. Many have adapted so that they produce seed within four weeks of a shower of rain.

The river beds have the widest variety of flora. The Nossob River is dominated by camel thorn trees *(Acacia erioloba)* in the north and grey camel thorn trees *(Acacia haematoxylon)* in the south. The grey camel thorn is a shrub on the dunes, but grows into a tree in the river beds. Its grey foliage is sparser than that of the camel thorn.

Most of the dead trees in the Nossob River are camel thorns that were killed in fires in 1968 and 1974; fortunately young trees survive fires. Sociable weaver birds favour the camel thorns for their huge nests, and all sorts of creatures feed off the foliage and seeds.

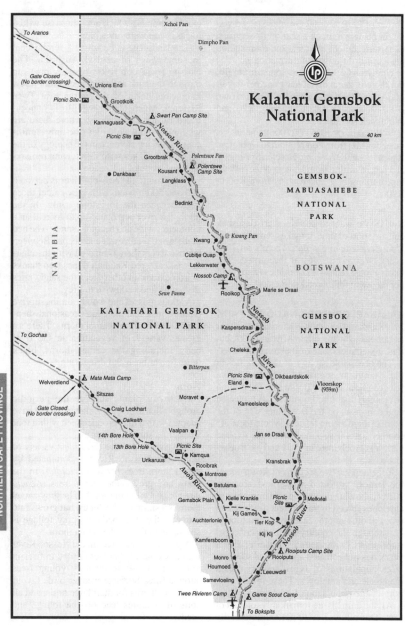

# Kalahari Gemsbok National Park

0        20        40 km

Xchoi Pan

Dimpho Pan

To Aranos

Gate Closed
(No border crossing)          Unions End

Picnic Site

Grootkolk

Swart Pan Camp Site

Kannaguass

Picnic Site

Nossob River

Grootbrak          Polentswe Pan

Dankbaar          Kousant          Polentswe
Camp Site

Langklass

Bedinkt

GEMSBOK-
MABUASAHEBE
NATIONAL
PARK

NAMIBIA

Kwang          Kwang Pan

Cubitje Quap

Lekkerwater

Nossob Camp

Sewe Panne          Rooikop          Marie se Draai

BOTSWANA

KALAHARI GEMSBOK
NATIONAL PARK

Nossob

Kaspersdraai

GEMSBOK
NATIONAL
PARK

To Gochas

Cheleka          River

Bitterpan

Picnic Site          Dikbaardskolk

Welverdiend          Mata Mata Camp          Eland

Vloorskop
(959m)

Sitszas          Moravet

Kameelsleep

Gate Closed
(No border crossing)          Craig Lockhart

Dalkeith

14th Bore Hole          Vaalpan          Jan se Draai

13th Bore Hole

Picnic Site

Urikaruus          Kamqua          Kransbrak

Auob River          Rooibrak

Montrose          Gunong

Batulama

Gemsbok Plain          Kielie Krankie          Picnic
Site          Melkvlei

Kij Games

Auchterlonie          Tier Kop          Nossob River

Kij Kij

Kamfersboom

Monro          Rooiputs Camp Site

Houmoed          Rooiputs

Samevloeiing          Leeuwdril

Twee Rivieren Camp          Game Scout Camp

To Bokspits

Various grasses and woody shrubs survive on the dunes, and there are occasional shepherd's trees *(Boscia albitrunca)*, with white bark and a dense thicket of short low branches where many animals take refuge in the heat of the day. The driedoring shrub *(Rhigozum trichotomum)*, with fine leaves and forked branches, is the most common shrub in the park.

Many of the animals depend on plants as their source of water. In particular, the tsamma *(Citrillus lanatus)* is an important source of water – it's a creeper with melon-like fruit. There are several types of prickly cucumber that are important for the survival of animals, especially the gemsbok.

## Fauna

Finding fauna requires luck, patience and a little intelligence. No one can be guaranteed of seeing one of the big predators, but you are more likely to in the Kalahari than in many other places. Most expected species of wildlife, with the exception of elephant, giraffe and zebra, are found in the park.

Spend an hour or so in the morning and the afternoon by a water hole. Watch for signs of agitation among herds of buck – they don't automatically flee at the sight of a predator, but wait until the predator commits itself to a charge before they run. The lions like to walk along the roadsides because the soft dust is kind to their paws. Look for recent prints, as the lion may have moved off the road at the sound of your vehicle. Binoculars are essential (see the Wildlife Viewing boxed text in the Kruger National Park section of the Mpumalanga chapter for more tips).

**Birds** Some 215 species of birds have been recorded. Perhaps the most dramatic are the raptors, including impressive species like the bateleur, martial eagle, red-necked falcon and tawny eagle.

The secretary bird is a common sight, strutting self-importantly over the clay pans, and the kori bustard, the largest flying bird in Africa, is also common.

Perhaps the most distinctive sight, how-ever, are the huge thatched nests of the socia-ble weaver bird. The bird itself is not particularly interesting, looking a bit like a common sparrow; however, they live in many-chambered nests that can last for more than a century and are inhabited by as many as 200 birds. The birds weave twigs and straw together in the crowns of acacias, on quiver trees and atop telephone poles.

**Mammals** There are 19 species of predator, including the dark-maned Kalahari lion, cheetah, leopard, wild dog, spotted and brown hyena, black-backed jackal, bat-eared fox, Cape fox, honey badger and suricate.

Most numerous is the springbok, but there are also large numbers of gemsbok, eland, red hartebeest and blue wildebeest.

## Orientation

Visitors are restricted to four roads; one running up the bed of the Nossob River, one running up the bed of the Aoub River, and two linking these two. Visitors must also remain in their cars, with the exception of a small number of designated picnic spots.

The only negative point about the park is that although the river beds are the best places to view wildlife, it can become almost claustrophobic being stuck in a car and enclosed by the river banks. The opportunities to really get a feel for the empty expanses of the Kalahari are limited – the exceptions are the roads linking the rivers, and they should not be missed. Still more loops are needed to take you into the veld, and walks need to be organised. A few dead-end roads with viewpoints have been added recently.

There are rest camps at Twee Rivieren, Nossob and Mata Mata. The speed limit is 50km/h. The minimum travelling time from the entrance gate at Twee Rivieren to Nossob is 3½ hours and to Mata Mata it's 2½ hours. No travelling is allowed after dark. Allow plenty of time to get to the camps.

## Information

The best time to visit is in June and July, when the weather is coolest (below freezing at night) and the animals have drawn in to

NORTHERN CAPE PROVINCE

the bores along the river beds. August is windy and, for some reason, is a favourite time for tour buses. From September to October is the wet season, and if it does rain, many of the animals scatter out across the plain to take advantage of the fresh pastures. November is quiet, and daily temperatures start to increase. Despite the fact that temperatures frequently reach 45°C in December and January, the chalets in the park are fully booked by school holiday-makers.

Entry is R23 for vehicles plus R14/7 per adult/child. All the rest camps have shops where basic groceries, soft drinks and alcohol can be purchased (fresh vegetables are hard to come by); the shops are open from 7 am until 30 minutes after the gates close. It's definitely worth stocking up outside the park, and having sufficient utensils to make breakfast and lunch. Petrol and diesel are available at each camp. There are public card and coin phones at Twee Rivieren, and a pool.

The gate opening hours are:

| | |
|---|---|
| January-February | 6 am to 7.30 pm |
| March | 6.30 am to 7 pm |
| April | 7 am to 6.30 pm |
| May | 7 am to 6 pm |
| June-July | 7.30 am to 6 pm |
| August | 7 am to 6.30 pm |
| September | 6.30 am to 6.30 pm |
| October | 6 am to 7 pm |
| November-December | 5.30 am to 7.30 pm |

### Organised Tours

Several operators run expensive tours to Kalahari Gemsbok. Kalahari Safaris (☎ (082) 493 5041, (054) 902 ask for 91 9722) has been recommended by an LP reader as being thoroughly professional.

### Places to Stay & Eat

There is accommodation both inside and outside Kalahari Gemsbok. Twee Rivieren has the only restaurant.

**Inside the Park** There are rest camps at Twee Rivieren, Mata Mata and Nossob; all have a range of huts and chalets (equipped with bedding, towels, cooking and eating utensils), plus camping facilities. Accommodation at Twee Rivieren is air-conditioned. All camps have tent sites, without electricity, with communal ablution facilities for R36 for up to six people (R10 for extra people).

Tent sites are usually available, but booking is advised for huts/chalets from June to September and during holiday periods. Book with the National Parks Board in Pretoria (☎ (012) 343 1991; fax 343 0905) or Cape Town (☎ (021) 222 810l; fax 24 6211).

At *Mata Mata*, three-bed huts with shared facilities cost R95 and six-bed cottages with kitchen cost R220 for one to four people (plus R60/30 for extra adults/children).

*Nossob* has three-bed huts with shared facilities for R95, three-bed huts with attached bath for R220 and cottages for up to four people for R230.

*Twee Rivieren*, the largest camp, has three-bed chalets with kitchen and bathroom for R245, and four-bed chalets for R285.

The pleasant *Lapa Restaurant* at Twee Rivieren overlooks the camp and offers surprisingly reasonable value. Hors d'oeuvres are R12, a mixed grill is R35 and chicken is R25. It's open from 7 am to 9 pm, but you should let staff know you're coming (by 6 pm for dinner). There's also a *snack bar* selling burgers and other takeaways.

**Outside the Park** In the nominal hamlet of Andriesvale, *Motel Molopo* (☎ (054902) ask for Askham 91 6213) is about 60km south of the Twee Rivieren gate. It's a comfortable, attractive spot with a pool and thatched chalets, and there's an à la carte restaurant. It's about 45 minutes to Twee Rivieren, so you're within striking distance of the national park. The chalets are R120 per person, including breakfast, or you can camp for R30. If you're aiming for the park, but arrive late, this motel could save your bacon. It has been recommended by travellers.

There are a number of other places, mainly farms, offering accommodation en route between Upington and the park.

### Getting There & Away

It's a solid five or six hour drive from Twee

Rivieren to Kuruman (385km), and at present you have to cover a significant distance on dirt. It's 280km from Upington to the Twee Rivieren entrance gate, made up of about 220km on tar, 60km on dirt roads. The bitumen is being gradually extended.

Be very careful driving on the dirt, as we've had several letters from travellers who wrecked their cars on this trip. If you stop, don't pull too far off the road or you might become bogged in the sand. Beware of loose gravel which make corners treacherous, and particularly around Bokspits, there are patches of deep sand which give you a bit of a shock if you hit them at speed. No petrol is available between Twee Rivieren and Upington, so start out with a full tank.

It's important to carry water, as you might have to wait a while if you break down. When the temperature is over 40°C you can dangerously dehydrate quickly.

## UPINGTON TO SPRINGBOK

West of Upington the road initially follows the course of the Orange River, and passes through oases of vineyards and the pleasant little towns of **Keimoes** and **Kakamas**. The turn-off to Augrabies Falls National Park, 40km north, is at Kakamas.

Several members of the Orange River **Wine Cellars** are open for sales on weekdays and Saturday mornings; however, they don't necessarily offer tastings. Groblershoop (☎ (05472) 47) and Grootdrink (☎ (0020) ask for Grootdrink 3002) – good name for a wine cellar – are south-east of Upington on the N10. It's a much different tasting experience here than in the Western Cape.

In Keimoes, there's a *caravan park* or two and the *Keimoes Hotel* (☎ (054) 461 1084), which has singles/doubles for R65/110; breakfast is R20 and dinner is R26. Kakamas has *Die Mas Camping* (☎ (054) 431 1150) and *Waterweil Protea Hotel* (☎ (054) 431 0838), with rooms from R205.

From Kakamas to Pofadder things are considerably duller, but then you enter a wide, bleak valley and, as you near Springbok, dramatic piles of boulders litter the landscape – you have entered Namaqualand.

## AUGRABIES FALLS NATIONAL PARK

The Augrabies Falls National Park (☎ (054) 451 0050) is more than just an impressive waterfall. Certainly the falls can be spectacular (particularly if they are carrying a lot of water), but the most interesting facet of the park is the fascinating desert/riverine environment on either side of the river.

The name of the falls derives from the Nama word for 'place of great noise'. The Orange River meanders across the plain from the east, but following an uplift in the land around 500 million years ago it began to wear a deep ravine into the underlying granite. The ravine is 18km long and has several impressive cataracts. The main falls drop 56m – the Bridal Veil Fall on the north side drops 75m.

The park has a harsh climate, with an average rainfall of only 107mm, and daytime summer temperatures that often reach 40°C. It covers an area of 82,000 hectares, and the flora includes kokerbooms, the Namaqua fig, several varieties of thorn trees and succulents. The park has 47 species of mammal, most of which are small. These include klipspringer and other antelope species, rock dassie (hyrax) and ground squirrel. Black rhino, eland, springbok and kudu have been introduced on the north bank (which is not yet open to the public).

**Information** The park authorities have developed quite a village around the falls, with an excellent complex, including a restaurant, open-air café, cottages and a caravan park. Maps and information are available from the main reception desk; there is also a well-stocked shop here (but it has few hiking supplies). Both are open from 7 am to 9 pm daily. The entry fee per vehicle is R20, and the entrance gate is open from 6.30 am to 10 pm April to September, otherwise from 6 am.

**Activities** There are three hour-long nature walks and some interesting drives. At a minimum, allow an hour to look at the falls, a couple of hours at least to explore the park and an hour or so in the pleasant open-air café that overlooks the ravine.

NORTHERN CAPE PROVINCE

The popular three-day **Klipspringer Hiking Trail** runs along the southern bank of the river. Two nights are spent in huts built from local stone, which can sleep 12 people. Camping is not allowed. Hikers must supply their own sleeping bags and food. Booking in advance is advised; the per-person charge is R65. The walk is closed from mid-October to the end of March, because of the heat.

The Black Rhino day tour, by 4WD and boat, costs R240/120 per adult/child (with a minimum of two people and a maximum of seven); day visitors also have to pay park admission. It is necessary to book night game drives in advance.

**Places to Stay & Eat** There's a *camping ground* with a camp kitchen; sites are R36 for two, plus R10 for each extra person. Self-contained accommodation includes four-person cottages for R385 and chalets from R245 for two people (plus R60/30 for an extra adult/child). Many of the cottages and chalets have outstanding views and are within earshot of the falls. Book with the National Parks Board in Pretoria (☎ (012) 343 1991; fax 343 0905) or Cape Town (☎ (021) 22 2810; fax 24 6211).

Just outside the park is the *Augrabies Falls Hotel* (☎ (054) 451 0044), an austere looking place with rooms from R95/90 with/without bathroom.

There's a *cafeteria* selling sandwiches and cold drinks and an à la carte *restaurant*, with meals like fillet steak or chicken for R30. The cold water dispenser is free – if you are here in summer, it's likely you'll drink it dry.

**Getting There & Away** Private transport is essential. The park is 30km north-west of Kakamas and 120km from Upington.

### POFADDER

Aside from its evocative name (which is not only the name of a snake, but also a short, fat sausage – and a local chief, after whom the town is named), there's really not much to Pofadder. The town is something of a byword as an archetypal little place in the middle of nowhere. Namaqualand begins to

the west, and the countryside is dry, expansive and beautiful.

There are a couple of banks, a 24 hour petrol station, a *municipal caravan park* (☎ (02532) ask for 46) and other accommodation, such as *Pofadder Overnight Flats* (☎ (02532) ask for 19), which charges R65 per person. The *Pofadder Hotel* (☎ (02532) ask for 43) is a kitsch and comfortable country hotel with a pool. B&B is R145/240 with air-conditioning; singles with fan only are R110.

### PELLA

Pella is a small mission surrounded by extensive groves of date palms. It was started in 1812 by the London Missionary Society, abandoned after the murder of the missionary, and refounded by French Catholics in 1882. The extraordinary church was built by an untrained French missionary, armed only with an encyclopaedia.

You can hike from Pella to Pofadder in at least four days. The trail is open from early May to late September and runs via Onseepkans, another small Catholic mission station. For information contact the Pofadder municipality (☎ (02532) 46).

# Namaqualand

Namaqualand is an ill-defined region in the north-west corner of the Northern Cape Province, north of Vanrhynsdorp and west of Pofadder. It is a rugged, mountainous plateau that overlooks a narrow, sandy coastal plain and the bleak beaches of the west coast. In the east it runs into the dry central plains that are known as Bushmanland.

The cold Benguela current runs up the west coast and creates a barren desert-like environment. However, this apparently inhospitable environment produces one of the world's natural wonders. Given decent winter rains there is an extraordinary explosion of spring flowers that covers the boulder-strewn mountains and plains with a multicoloured carpet. Namaqualand's flora

## Namaqualand Flora

Although the wildflowers of the Western Cape are spectacular, they are overshadowed by the brilliance of the Namaqualand displays. Generally, the Namaqualand flowers bloom a couple of weeks earlier than those further south, so it makes sense to begin your flower viewing in the north.

The optimum time to visit varies from year to year, but the best chance to catch the flowers at their peak is between mid-August and mid-September, although the season can begin early in August and extend to mid-October. Unfortunately for overseas visitors with fixed itineraries, there can be no guarantee you will be in the right place at the right time. A visit is worth the gamble, however, because even without the flowers, the countryside, though beau, is beautiful.

The flowers depend on rainfall, which is variable, and the blooms can shrivel quickly in hot winds. Many of the flowers are light-sensitive and only open during bright sunshine. Overcast conditions, which generally only last a day or two, will significantly reduce the display, and even on sunny days the flowers only open properly from around 10 am to 4 pm. They also face the sun (basically northwards), so it is best to travel with the sun behind you.

DAVID ELSE

The Kokerboom is a peculiar tree adapted to the conditions of the region.

Although there is no strict dividing line between the Cape floral kingdom (which runs roughly from Clanwilliam to Port Elizabeth), the Namaqualand flora, which is part of the Palaeotropical kingdom, begins north of Vanrhynsdorp. There can be flowers on the plains between Nuwerus and Garies, but the major spectacle begins around Garies and extends to Steinkopf in the north. Springbok is considered the flower capital.

Namaqualand is itself broken into different regions. The dry, sandy coastal belt (the sandveld) gets only around 50mm of rain a year, although the frequent fogs that roll in off the cold Benguela current provide enough moisture for succulents, including euphorbias, aloes and mesembryanthemums.

Inland are the rocky mountains of the escarpment (on the western side of the N7), with a number of spectacular passes overlooking the coastal plain. The mountains are still mostly dry, but the rainfall increases to around 100mm, which is sufficient for wheat farming. The fallow fields are prime habitats for the flowering annuals (daisies, oxalis and gazanias). The hills around Springbok and Nababeep have more rain (around 150mm) and a particularly rich variety of flowers.

Another zone can be found in the Kamiesberg range, which is to the east of Kamieskroon. This area is well watered, and consequently has a bushier scrub. The plain to the east of Springbok and north to Vioolsdrif produces more brilliant annuals.

Trees are scarce, although visitors will certainly see the characteristic kokerboom, or quiver tree *(Aloe dichotoma)*, an aloe that can grow to a height of 4m, on the hills. The tree stores water in its trunk and is known as the quiver tree, because the Khoisan used its branches as quivers. The branches fork until they form a rounded crown with large spiky leaves. The quiver tree has large yellow blooms in June or July.

In the north you'll see 'halfmens', or Elephant trunk *(Pachypodium namaquanum)*, weird tree-like succulents with a long, inelegant trunk topped by a small 'face' of foliage. They always look to the north, and there's a legend that they are the transformed bodies of Khoikhoi people who were driven south during a war. Those who turned to look towards their lost lands were transformed into trees.

The best flower areas vary from year to year, so it is essential to get local advice on where to go. Most locals will happily tell you, or you can contact the local tourist authorities (Jopie Kotze at the Springbok Restaurant is particularly helpful).

There are generally good flowers east of the N7 between Garies and Springbok. Even if there are no flowers, there are spectacular roads between Kamieskroon and Hondeklip Bay, Springbok and Hondeklip Bay, Garies and Hondeklip Bay, Springbok and Port Nolloth, and through the Kamiesberg south-east of Kamieskroon to Garies. The Goegap Nature Reserve (the entrance is south-west of Springbok) and the hills around Nababeep are other reliable venues. Wandering around the back roads is a joy in itself.

Springbok is 560km from Cape Town, 375km from Upington and 1275km from Jo'burg, so just getting there is a reasonable undertaking. It's a solid six or seven hour drive from Cape Town, obviously considerably more to Jo'burg. To do justice to the area when the flowers are out, you need to budget on spending a minimum of two or three days in the district. Most varieties of wildflowers are protected by law and heavy fines can be imposed if you pick them.

During flower season there are plenty of sightseeing tours of the area run from Cape Town. More personal is the tour run by a Kamieskroon local Lita Cole (☎ (0257) 762 after 7 pm; fax 675). She organises one to three-day hikes or drives (in your car) through the best flower areas. She charges about R200 per group for a day trip and R65 per night on overnight hikes. ■

NORTHERN CAPE PROVINCE

is characterised by a phenomenal variety of daisies, but there are also mesembryanthemums, gladioli, aloes, euphorbias, violets, pelargoniums and many other species.

The area is sparsely populated, mainly by Afrikaans-speaking sheep farmers and, in the north-west, by the Namaqua, a Khoikhoi tribe. The Namaqua were famous for their metal-working skills, particularly in copper which occurs in the region. Not surprisingly, this attracted the attention of Dutch explorers, who first came into contact with the tribe in 1661. Because of the isolation of the region, however, the copper rush in Namaqualand did not begin in earnest until the 1850s.

The first commercial copper mine (now a national monument) was started just outside Springbok in 1852, and there are still a number of large operations, including one at Nababeep.

Namaqualand is also an important source for alluvial diamonds. In 1925 a young soldier, Jack Carstens, found a glittering stone near Port Nolloth. Prospectors converged on the area, and it soon became clear (notably to Ernest Oppenheimer of De Beers) that an enormously rich resource of diamonds had been discovered.

In order to prevent an oversupply of diamonds and the collapse of prices, the government took control of the diggings. Eventually all major mines were brought into the De Beers fold and all production was brought under the control of a global cartel, the Central Selling Organisation (CSO). All of the major west coast alluvial diamond fields are classified as prohibited areas – they are closed to the general public. Diamonds can only be bought and sold by licensed traders.

The diamonds are harvested from gravel beds on the sea floor and from beneath the sandveld. The sandveld is the narrow, sandy plain, between mountains and sea, which was itself once under the sea. Enormous amounts of sand are moved to expose the bedrock (up to 15m below the surface), where the diamond-bearing gravel is found. Underwater diamonds are dredged, or mined

## Merinos

In 1789 Charles V of Spain gave William IV of Holland six Escorial merinos. These were prized for their fine wool, and the Spanish carefully protected their monopoly. Six of these merinos were sent to the Cape and placed in the care of an RJ Gordon. They thrived and multiplied.

The Spanish got wind of this and demanded that their sheep be returned. Gordon obeyed the request to the letter, returning the original six sheep, but keeping their progeny. Most of the flock was later shipped to Australia. ∎

by specially licensed divers using boats equipped with suction pumps.

The bleak and beautiful landscape, and the diamond miners, contribute to a definite frontier atmosphere. Namaqualand can get very cold in winter (average minimums around 5°C with a high wind-chill factor) and hot in summer (average maximums around 30°C).

Aside from buses on the N7 and R27 (between Vanrhynsdorp and Upington), public transport is sparse. The major operators offer tours of Namaqualand leaving from Jo'burg and Cape Town, but if you want to comb the region you'll need your own car.

## CALVINIA

Calvinia is an attractive rural centre surrounded by 'Wild West' country with a great sense of scale and space – the air has an exhilarating clarity. This is no illusion, as the town's 'starlight factor' is an extremely high 80%. A ridge of the Hantamsberg range dominates the town, which is itself over 1000m above sea level. As the Calvinia church clock quietly tolls away the hours it's easy to imagine that decades, if not centuries, have slipped away.

The surrounding countryside can have magnificent spring wildflowers on a Namaqualand scale, even though it is more properly considered the Hantam region. It is in a transitional zone with floral elements from the Namaqualand, Karoo and Cape.

Calvinia's economy is dependent on the surrounding merino sheep farms, and like similar communities in Australia it has been hard hit by the collapse of wool prices. Amazingly, 80% of sheep in the region are still shorn with hand clippers (not electric). Cheap labour has a tremendous distorting effect on the economy.

## Information

The information office (☎ (0273) 41 1712), PO Box 28, Calvinia 8190, adjoining the museum is one of the best you'll come across in South Africa. It has a range of suggestions for interesting accommodation and things to do, and a walking-tour map of the town. Farm stays and B&Bs are thriving in the region, and the information office will help you to arrange accommodation; bookings are advisable in flower season. The office is open Monday to Friday from 8 am to 1 pm and 2 to 5 pm, and Saturday until noon.

## Calvinia Museum

For a small country town, this museum is of a surprisingly high standard and is definitely worth visiting. The main building was a synagogue – it's incongruous but not unusual to find disused Jewish buildings in tiny, remote towns. The museum concentrates on the white settlement of the region, sheep and farming activities, and there are some wonderful oddities like a four legged ostrich chick (a fake used by a travelling shyster) and a room devoted to a local set of quadruplets. It has the same opening hours as the information office; admission is R1 for adults, 0.50c for children.

## Places to Stay & Eat

The undistinguished *Calvinia Caravan Park* (☎ (0273) 41 1011), close to the centre of town, is flat and ordinary. The facilities are fine, and the town's public pool is next door. Sites are R25 – they may be all you get during the August Meat Festival.

The best place to stay is any one of the trio of restored historic buildings now run as guesthouses. *Die Tiushuis*, *Die Dorphuis* and *Bothasdal* are wonderful old places fur-

### Traut Ties

The barman at Holden's Commercial Hotel is an engaging old character by the name of Cecil Traut. His claim to fame (and he has a modicum) is his collection of ties from around the country and the world. He has more than 500, which cover a wall of the bar, and he will be only too happy to show them to you. He has worked behind bars for a long time, and pours a good beer. ■

JON MURRAY

nished with antiques. Depending on where you stay, rooms start at R70 per person or R110 with breakfast. Bookings (☎ (0273) 41 1606) can be made at Die Hantamhuis on Hoop St, the oldest building in town and now a café. This is where you'll have breakfast if you stay at one of the guesthouses. Breakfast (from 7.30 to 9 am) is available to nonresidents (daily, except on Sunday), and it's recommended. If you order a day in advance you can try *skilpadjie*, or 'tortoise' (lambs fry wrapped in caul).

The *Hantam Hotel* (☎ (0273) 41 1512) on Kerk St is plain but comfortable, and it's as clean as a whistle. Rooms are a reasonable R90 per person, plus R25 for breakfast. The hotel has an à la carte steakhouse, the *Busibee*, where braaied lamb is a perennial feature of the menu.

*Holden's Commercial Hotel* (☎ (0273) 41 1020) on Water St is also of a pretty high standard, but is hideously ugly, which is a shame considering it was a beautiful old

NORTHERN CAPE PROVINCE

building before 'modernisation'. There is talk of replacing its old verandah. The rooms are good (although they may smell of that dreadful air-freshener that's the bane of South African hotels) and cost R80 per person; breakfast is another R25. Carefully select your bait and try and catch Cecil Traut behind the bar.

The information office can suggest B&B possibilities; you will be forgiven for thinking that the list reads like a local Afrikaner social register. There are also a number of farmhouse B&Bs; most charge around R65 per person. Try the *Vinknes Guesthouse* (☎ (0273) 41 2214), on a farm about 30km from Calvinia on the road to Nieuwoudtville. A number of the farms have San paintings and excellent hiking possibilities.

### Getting There & Away

**Bus** Intercape goes through Calvinia on its Cape Town to Upington service, departing from Calvinia at 12.45 am on Monday, Tuesday, Thursday and Saturday heading north; at 12.15 am on Monday, Wednesday, Friday and Saturday heading south. Fares and running times from Calvinia include Cape Town, R120, 5¾ hours; Clanwilliam, R80, 2½ hours; and Upington, R110, 3¾ hours. This service involves a lot of inconvenient times! Book at the travel agency (☎ (0273) 44 1373) incongruously sited in the *slaghuis* (butcher shop); buses stop at the *trokkie* (truck) stop on the west side of town.

City to City/Transtate has slightly cheaper and slightly slower buses to/from Cape Town and Upington, although the departure times are still late at night. On Monday, Friday and Saturday, it departs from the Calvinia post office at 12.55 am heading for Upington; on Sunday, Monday and Friday it departs at 10.30 pm heading for Cape Town. Fares are perhaps 20% less than Intercape.

**Minibus Taxi** Go to the trokkie stop for minibus taxis. It's R75 to either Cape Town or Upington, but taxis don't run every day. If you have no luck here, try the Total station on the east (Upington) side of town.

## AROUND CALVINIA
### Akkerendam Nature Reserve

This reserve is about 2km north of town and is managed by the Calvinia municipality. It covers around 2500 hectares of country at the foot of the Hantamsberg, including part of the southern slopes. There are two hiking trails – the 2km walk takes one hour (easy), and the other, which heads up the mountain, takes around seven hours (strenuous, but great views). Apart from the wealth of plants (and flowers in season), there are a number of small antelope species.

### Calvinia to Clanwilliam

The R364 between Clanwilliam and Calvinia is a superb road through unspoilt, empty countryside and several magnificent passes. There are excellent displays of flowers if you happen to be here at the right time. There's a great view from the top of **Botterkloof**, and a couple of nice flat rocks overlooking the gorge that are perfect for a picnic. Sit and dream what this country must have been like 300 years ago, before the San and the game were shot out ...

You hit irrigation country around Doringbos and start to get dramatic views of the Cederberg range. The **Pakhuis Pass** takes you through an amazing jumble of multicoloured rocks. There's an excellent *camping ground* on the Clanwilliam side of the pass. Allow at least two hours for the road – more if you have a picnic or are tempted to take the side road to **Wuppertal**, which is an old Rhenish mission station, little changed since its establishment in 1830. It features whitewashed, thatched cottages, as well as cypresses and donkeys.

### Calvinia to Vanrhynsdorp

There is a stunning road between Vanrhynsdorp and Calvinia, with magnificent views over the Knersvlakte from **Vanrhyns Pass**. In spring there can be a dramatic contrast between green and fertile wheat fields and flowers at the top and the desert far below.

Just beyond the pass on the Calvinia side, but off the main road, is the small town of **Nieuwoudtville**, which has a handsome church, and a couple of nearby nature reserves. There's a small hotel, some guesthouses (contact through the Calvinia information office) and the shady municipal caravan park.

The small **Nieuwoudtville Wildflower Reserve**, just to the north of the R27 (which is clearly signposted), has a fantastic range of flowers, including gladioli and other bulb plants. Accommodation is possible here in a small flat at *Theresa Rabe's* (☎ (02726) 81139) from R60 per person.

The 5000 hectare **Oorlogskloof Nature Reserve** runs along the eastern bank of the Oorlogskloof River and overlooks the plains. The terrain is rugged, and there's rich bird and floral life and a superb waterfall. There are hiking trails ranging from day hikes to three-night hikes. All access must be arranged in advance (☎ (02726) 81010), since there's no public access road.

## GARIES

Just off the main road, Garies (after a species of local grass 'th'aries') does not have the same appeal as Kamieskroon, although there are some nice old homes and buildings lining the main street. The municipal office (☎ (027) 652 1014) has an information desk, but despite the sign, it's not very helpful about flower information. There are a couple of banks, a post office and a couple of petrol stations.

The inexpensive *Garies Caravan Park* (☎ (027) 652 1014), near the sports ground, would be OK, although there isn't much in the way of shade. The old-style *Garies Hotel* (☎ (027) 652 1042) is not particularly welcoming. Rooms with shared bath cost R60/90 a single/double, and rooms with bath are R75/110.

## KAMIESKROON

Kamieskroon (the Nama name means 'jumble') is an ordinary little town, but it is perched high in the mountains and is surrounded by boulder-strewn hills. There are some beautiful drives and walks in the area. The dirt roads west to Hondeklip Bay and east to Witwater are truly spectacular, partic-

ularly in spring. For information contact the municipality (☎ (027) 672 1627).

Kamieskroon is a great spot to get away from it all and is an ideal base for exploring the area. The climate can be extreme – very hot in summer (commonly 40°C) and very cold in winter. Snow is not unusual and with strong winds there is a very high chill factor.

About 18km north-west of Kamieskroon is the **Skilpad Wildflower Reserve**, established by the World Wide Fund for Nature to increase world awareness of the floral heritage of Namaqualand. It's on the first ridge in from the coast, so it receives good rain.

### Mountain Biking

There are a number of mountain-biking routes in the mountainous Kamiesberg area, east of Kamieskroon. These include the 29km Nourivier circular route (easy); the short 8.2km Leliefontein route (easy); the 49km Leliefontein route (difficult); and the 7.5km Vissersplaat circular route (easy). You need your own bike, plenty of water and R10 for a permit. The best time to bike here is from August to October when the wildflowers are out.

### Places to Stay

*Kamieskroon Hotel* (☎ (027) 672 1614 or 706; fax 6721675) is a very civilised hideaway and it is deservedly popular, especially from July to September (when bookings are essential and prices rise). Singles/doubles are R80/125 without breakfast, R100/160 with breakfast and R135/235 for dinner, bed and breakfast. The hotel also manages a small number of shaded camp sites (R25).

There is also *Verbe Caravan Park* (☎ (027) 672 1605) and a few farmstays in the region – *Pedroskloof* (☎ (027) 672 1666) and *Arkoep* (☎ (027) 672 1759), for example.

### Getting There & Away

Namaqualand Busdiens (☎ (0251) 22061) and Intercape run buses along the N7. Kamieskroon is an hour south of Springbok – see its entry for details.

## HONDEKLIP BAY

In most ways, Hondeklip Bay is just a smaller, less interesting version of Port Nolloth. It's a small, dusty little town on a bleak stretch of the coastal plain. There's a shop, petrol and a depressing little *caravan park* – there are no showers, and you would be wise to bring your own water.

The local dirt roads are spectacular, however. After climbing through rocky hills, you drop onto the desert-like coastal plain which is dotted with enormous diamond mines. The flora is fascinating – make sure you take time to walk around, even if it's just off the side of the road.

## SPRINGBOK

Springbok considers itself the capital of Namaqualand, and it lies in a valley among harsh rocky hills that explode with colour in the flower season. The first European-run copper mine was established on the town's outskirts in 1852, and from a rough-and-tumble frontier town it has been transformed into a busy service centre for the copper and diamond mines in the region.

In the 1920s, Springbok had a large Jewish population who traded in the region. Most have moved away, and their synagogue (built in 1929) has been converted into a small but interesting local **museum**. There are some interesting historical photos and relics. It's open Monday, Wednesday and Friday from 9 am to noon.

### Orientation & Information

The town is quite spread-out, but most places are within walking distance of the small *koppie* (hill) in the elbow of the main street's right-angled bend. The koppie is covered with Namaqualand's strange flora.

On the main street, the Springbok Lodge & Restaurant (☎ (0251) 21321), is a unique phenomenon run by the ebullient Jopie Kotze. This is the best spot in town to get a meal and to collect information on the surrounding region. There is an extensive rock and gem collection, with some pieces for sale, as well as books, postcards, maps – pretty much anything you can think of.

There's also the Regional Tourism Information Office (☎ (0251) 22071 or 22011) in the old church next to the post office. It's open from 7.30 am to 4.15 pm on weekdays, and from 8 am to 1 pm on weekends during the flower season.

### Places to Stay

During the flower season accommodation in Springbok can fill up. The information office can tell you about private overflow accommodation. There is a big difference between low and flower season prices.

*Springbok Caravan Park* (☎ (0251) 81584) is 2km from town on Goegap Rd, the road to the nature reserve and the airport. Occasional buses run past, otherwise it's a very long walk. Tent sites are R15 (more during the flower season).

The *Namastat* (☎ (0251) 22435 for bookings) is an interesting place, with accommodation in traditional woven Nama 'mat' huts, similar in shape to Zulu 'beehive' huts. In Afrikaans they're called *matjieshuis*. Each hut has two beds and costs R45 per person (R10 more during the flower season) if you need a bed, considerably less if you have your own bedding. There's a common ablutions block, but no electricity. It serves traditional Nama foods and it has a non-traditional bar. It's about 3km west of the centre of town, on the Cape Town road (not the highway). It's at the head of a valley and there are good views.

*Springbok Lodge* (☎ (0251) 21321) has rooms in a street full of workers' cottages behind the restaurant. The yellow and white cottages have been steadily upgraded over the years and all exude character. Rates start at R60 per person, or self-catering flats are available for R75.

On Van Riebeeck St, under the lee of a huge basalt outcrop, *The Old Mill Lodge* (☎ (0251) 81705) is an upmarket B&B; rates are R150/230 for a single/double, and breakfast is an extra R25. The upmarket *Naries Guesthouse* is 25km west of town. It costs R250 per person, including four course meal.

One family runs three of Springbok's places to stay: the Springbok and Masonic

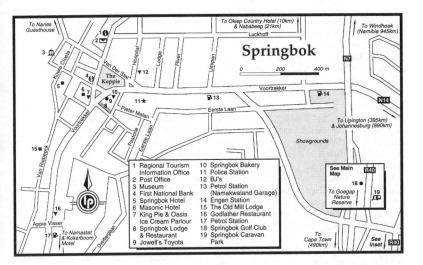

Springbok

| | |
|---|---|
| 1 Regional Tourism Information Office | 10 Springbok Bakery |
| 2 Post Office | 11 Police Station |
| 3 Museum | 12 BJ's |
| 4 First National Bank | 13 Petrol Station (Namakwaland Garage) |
| 5 Springbok Hotel | 14 Engen Station |
| 6 Masonic Hotel | 15 The Old Mill Lodge |
| 7 King Pie & Oasis Ice Cream Parlour | 16 Godfather Restaurant |
| 8 Springbok Lodge & Restaurant | 17 Petrol Station |
| 9 Jowell's Toyota | 18 Springbok Golf Club |
| | 19 Springbok Caravan Park |

hotels and the Kokerboom Motel. The *Springbok Hotel* (☎ (0251) 21161) is a plain, old-style hotel, a bit dowdy, but reasonable value nonetheless. Rooms are R118/183, with breakfast an additional R20. The nearby *Masonic Hotel* (☎ (0251) 22008) has been upgraded recently. Rooms without bath cost R124/188, breakfast is R25 and dinner R35.

The *Kokerboom Motel* (☎ (0251) 22685) is more like an army barracks and it is inconveniently located on the outskirts of town. The rates are as for the Springbok Hotel.

About 10km north-east of Springbok is the *Okiep Country Hotel* – the owner takes local historical tours. It costs R192 for a double in well-presented rooms.

**Places to Eat**

For takeaways, there is the ubiquitous *King Pie*, next to the *Oasis Ice Cream Parlour* and opposite the Koppie, and *Springbok Bakery*, close by.

The *Springbok Hotel* has a certain faded country-town grandeur. Its dining room has à la carte meals: entrees cost between R10 and R20; fish or steak starts around R25; and good-value stews are R20 or less. *BJ's*, a

fully licensed steakhouse, has a quite extensive menu – a burger with chips and salad is R13; a number of readers have recommended it.

For something more informal and fun, the *Springbok Restaurant* at the Springbok Lodge can't be beaten. It's rare to find such a pleasant place in a small South African town, where you usually have to resort to something Wimpyesque for a snack or a coffee. The menu is extensive and includes grills (from R30), breakfast, pizzas, snacks and salads. Avoid the pizzas – they are covered with a thick slime of orange cheese which renders them indigestible – the only negative in a sea of positives. The Springbok stays open until 10 pm.

Just down the hill from the Koppie, the *Godfather Restaurant* is a pizza place which is also open 24 hours for takeaways.

**Getting There & Away**

**Air** There are weekday flights from Springbok to Cape Town with National Airlines (☎ (021) 934 0350 in Cape Town, (0251) 22061 in Springbok) for R730. Flights continue on to Alexander Bay.

NORTHERN CAPE PROVINCE

**Bus** Intercape's service from Windhoek to Cape Town runs through Springbok. Buses leave Cape Town at 2 pm on Sunday, Tuesday, Wednesday, Thursday and Friday, and arrive at Windhoek at 6.30 am the next day; they come through Springbok (Springbok Lodge) at 8.15 pm. Buses leave from Windhoek at 7 pm on Monday, Wednesday, Thursday, Friday and Sunday, and arrive at Cape Town at 11 am the next day; they pass through Springbok at 4.45 am. From Springbok to Cape Town is R170; Springbok to Windhoek is R240.

Van Wyk's Busdiens (☎ (0251) 38559) has a bus to Cape Town for between R60 and R90. You could also try Titus Taxis & Bus (☎ (0251) 21524), Carstens (☎ (0251) 21847) and Bezuidenhout (☎ (0251) 21271).

**Minibus Taxi** Van Wyk's Busdiens (☎ (0251) 38559) runs a daily door-to-door taxi to Cape Town for R80. You'll find ordinary leave-when-full taxis to Cape Town for about R60. Ask at the taxi rank at the rear of the First National Bank.

VIP Taxis (☎ (0251) 22006) operates a weekday taxi service from Port Nolloth to Upington costing R60 to R70. It picks up at the Masonic Hotel in Springbok at 3 pm, returning from Upington the following morning at 7 am; it reaches Springbok at about 11 am.

**Car** Ask at the Springbok Lodge or at the Regional Tourism Information Office about car hire from local garages such as Jowell's Toyota.

## AROUND SPRINGBOK
### Nababeep
Nababeep is the site of a large copper mine, and the surrounding hills often have spectacular flowers. For those who are interested in mining, a visit to the **O'Kiep Copper Company Museum** is worthwhile. Phone ☎ (0251) 38121 for opening times.

### Goegap Nature Reserve
This semi-desert reserve, which is famous for its extraordinary display of spring

flowers and its nursery of 200 amazing Karoo and Namaqualand succulents (the Hester Malan Wildflower Garden), shouldn't be missed.

There are a couple of driving routes, but you'll see more on one of the circular walks of 4km, 5.5km and 7km. There are two incredible mountain biking routes of 14km and 20km, particularly memorable during flower season; bring your own bikes. There's a permit fee of R10 per person. The **horse trails** are for riders with their own horses.

In addition to the flora, there are springbok, ostrich, zebra and birds. The reserve (☎ (0251) 21880) is open from 8 am to 4 pm daily. Admission is R4 per person, and R5 for the vehicle.

## PORT NOLLOTH
Port Nolloth is a sandy and exposed little place, but it has a certain fascination. It was originally developed as the shipping point for the region's copper, but it is now dependent on the small fishing boats that catch diamonds and crayfish. The boats are fitted with pumps, and divers vacuum up the diamond-bearing gravel found on the ocean floor. The town has attracted a multicultural group of fortune-seekers, who give the town frontier vitality.

This area is one of South Africa's driest, and until recently the town received its drinking water by boat. Despite this, Port Nolloth is notorious for mists, known to the Nama people as *malmokkie*.

Unlike most other towns in South Africa, there's a feeling of 'just getting by' among the white population (and the all-too-familiar feeling of not quite getting by among the coloured population), and most houses are modest wooden buildings. For the visitor this is a nice change – presumably the inhabitants wouldn't agree.

### Information
The information centre is in the town hall, just off the main road into town. There's a branch of the First National Bank, a petrol station, a pharmacy and a few shops. For

## Illegal Diamond Buying

It is illegal in South Africa to sell diamonds except to De Beers. The diamond mines are hives of security, but the independent divers who work Port Nolloth and other submarine diamond fields on the west coast have more opportunity to get away with extracting diamonds from their catch and selling them on the black market. Diamond diving is hard work and it isn't lucrative; the divers can only work about 10 days a month because of the weather. Illegal diamond buying (IDB) is a sub-current of life in this area, and chances are that a few of your fellow patrons in a diamond town bar are undercover members of the police IDB branch. You may meet locals who offer to sell you cheap diamonds – not only is this highly illegal, you are also likely to end up with what is known as a *slenter*, or fake diamond. These are cut from lead crystal and only an expert can pick them. ■

information, contact the Port Nolloth municipality (☎ (0255) 8229) on Hoof Rd.

Should you want to swim in this cold water, the best beach is to the north of town – unless diamond miners have taken up their option and begun digging up the dunes there.

### Places to Stay

There's *Bedrock* (☎ (0255) 8865), a guesthouse in one of the old wooden cottages lining the seafront. As well as being a friendly and comfortable place to stay, with big rooms and sea views, it's a social must, as it's owned by Grazia de Beer ('Mama'), a local identity. To get to Bedrock, turn right onto the beachfront road as you come into town and it's the second building along. In the guesthouse you'll pay R100 per person for dinner, bed and breakfast. There are two-bedroom self-catering cottages for R150, a house which sleeps seven for R210 and another cottage where backpackers can stay for R35 (when space is available). Mama also owns a couple of nearby houses, so there is a range of accommodation options.

Comfortable *Scotia Inn* (☎ (0255) 8353) has pleasant rooms, a peg or two above what you might expect in this rough-and-tumble

town, and the prices reflect this. Singles with/without bath are R165/125 or doubles are R275/200.

*McDougall's Bay Caravan Park* (☎ 0255) 8657) is acceptable, but don't expect five-star comforts (bring your own towels and dish cloths). Basic huts are R45, chalets sleeping six are R100 in winter, rising to R125 at peak times, and camping sites (on gravel) are R25. The park is 4km south of Port Nolloth by road, less on foot if you can find a path through the shantytown (and if it's safe to take it). A taxi runs half-hourly for R5.

### Places to Eat

*Crow's Nest*, attached to the Bedrock, has seafood, meat and pasta dishes (from R13 to R20); it is the place in town to get a pizza. For fresh-baked bread go to the *Welcome Bakery*.

*Captain Pete's Tavern*, across from the hotel, has meals for between R28 and R35. It's owned by a diamond diver who struck it rich. *Scotia Inn* has a dining room and there are meals at the *Country Club*, a few kilometres out of town.

### Getting There & Away

There is little public transport, and hitching from the N7 turn-off at Steinkopf would be slow. Port Nolloth Busdiens (☎ (0255) 8408) operates a service on weekdays. It departs from behind the First National Bank for Springbok at 7 am, returning at 4 pm, and costs R30 to R50 return.

It's a great drive from Springbok (145km), with bare mountains looming to the north and the exhilarating drop down to the coastal plain through the Aninaus Pass. There was once a Port Nolloth to Springbok train service, but mules had to pull the train up the pass! As you drive along the coastal flats you'll notice that the land is all fenced. This isn't to keep stock in, but to keep poachers out of diamond leases. It's illegal to enter.

### ALEXANDER BAY & VIOOLSDRIF

Alexander Bay is a government-controlled diamond mine on the south bank of the

Orange River mouth – Namibia is across the river. The road from Port Nolloth is open to the public, but the Namibian border is closed. Restrictions on access are beginning to lift and the town is looking at its tourism potential. There are mine tours (☎ (0256) 831 1330, one day in advance) on Thursday at 8 am and a museum.

*Brandkaros* (☎ (0265) 831 1856 or 831 1464) is a farm by the river about 30km from Alexander Bay, with self-catering rondavels (R140 a double) as well as tent sites. It also has a great swimming pool. It's en route to Richtersveld National Park and is a good base.

Vioolsdrif is the border crossing on the N7, 677km north of Cape Town. The drive from Steinkopf is spectacular and there are views of the Orange River carving its way through desolate mountains. The border is open 24 hours.

## RICHTERSVELD NATIONAL PARK

The Richtersveld National Park is an enormous (162,000 hectares) park in the northern loop of the Orange River, west of Vioolsdrif and the N7. The park is the property of the local Nama people, who continue to lead a semi-traditional, semi-nomadic pastoral existence; hopefully they will benefit from increased job opportunities and the rent paid by the park authorities.

The area is a mountainous desert, a spectacular wilderness, with jagged rocky peaks, deep ravines and gorges; the hiking possibilities, though demanding, are excellent. Despite its apparent barrenness, the region has a prolific variety of succulents.

At present, most of the park is virtually inaccessible without a properly equipped expedition and local guides. Apparently the southern section is accessible by 2WD vehicles, but it would pay to check before going in. Only a small number of people are allowed into the park at any time, so ring (☎ (0256) 831 1506) or write (Richtersveld National Park, PO Box 406, Alexander Bay 8290) and see if you can get in. A good companion is *Tracks and Trails of the*

*Richtersveld* by Heinz Reck. Admission to the park is R28/14 for adults/children.

There is guesthouse accommodation at Sendelingsdrift on the western edge of the park. *Arieb House* and *Kokerboom* cost R280 for one to four persons (R70/35 for extra adults/children), and *Fish Eagle* is R140 for two persons (R70/35); camping at the five designated camp sites is R12 per person.

Fill up your tank at Alexander Bay before entering the park; fuel emergencies only are dealt with at Selingsdrift. Visitors should be in the park by 4 pm, allowing time to get to their night camps.

Rey van Rensburg (☎ (0251) 21905; fax 81460) is a Springbok photographer who also runs tours (the 'Richtersveld Challenge'), between April and October, into the national park. Rey is enthusiastic, experienced and very knowledgeable about the area. A five day vehicle tour costs R1750 per person, and a five day tour that includes some hiking costs R1200 per person. You'll need at least eight people and your own bedding. Book two or so months in advance.

### Hiking Trails

Three hiking trails have been established in the park. The 42km four day **Ventersvalle Trail** takes in the mountainous south-west wilderness; the 23km three day **Lelieshoek-Oemsberg Trail** takes in a waterfall and a huge amphitheatre; and the 15km two day **Kodaspiek Trail** allows the average walker to view stunning mountain desert scenery. Accommodation is in matjieshuise (traditional huts) and there are field toilets. The costs of the trails are R145, R110 and R80 respectively, including the services of a field guide.

### NAMAKWA 4WD ROUTE

The Namakwa 4WD route is over 610km long and traverses some of South Africa's most remote and rugged territory. The route has been divided into two parts – Pella Mission Station to Vioolsdrif (328km, R40 per vehicle) and Vioolsdrif to Alexander Bay (284km, R30). At the end of the journey

4WDers have the option of visiting the Richtersveld National Park; the cost is R30, excluding entry to the park. Permits to visit the park are obtained from the Regional Tourism Information Office (☎ (0251) 22011) in Springbok.

An incredible diversity of succulent plants will be seen along the way, many of which are unique to the region. The terrain varies as much as the plant types – it can be mountainous, green along the riverbeds or just miles of sandy dunes.

Four wheel drive vehicles can be hired in Upington; the cost is about R450 with unlimited kilometres. Try Avis (☎ (054) 25746) or Upington 4WD Hire (☎ (054) 25441).

# KwaZulu-Natal

KwaZulu-Natal manages to cram in most of the things that visitors come to South Africa to see, plus a few that they don't expect.

There's the spectacular Drakensberg range in the south-east, a long coast of sub-tropical surf beaches with water warmed by the Agulhas current, remote lowveld savanna in the far north, and historic Anglo-Boer War and Anglo-Zulu War battlefields. In the middle of it all is Zululand, the Zulu heartland. The Natal Parks Board has many excellent parks which offer good opportunities to see the best-known Southern African animals. A final plus is Durban, a city with a great holiday atmosphere and, in parts, an Indian flavour.

If you're planning to spend much time in Natal Parks Board parks and reserves (and if you have a car you could tour most of the province from bases in the good-value accommodation at the various parks) your first stop should be the Natal Parks Board headquarters in Pietermaritzburg to make bookings. You can make credit-card bookings over the phone, but there's such an array of accommodation in most parks that it's better to do it in person. Alternatively, there's a Natal Parks Board agent at the Tourist Junction centre in Durban. Camp sites are booked directly with individual parks.

The latest South African census revealed that KwaZulu-Natal has the biggest official population of any province, with 7,670,000 people – this doesn't include illegal immigrants, however.

## HISTORY

Just before the 1994 elections Natal Province was renamed KwaZulu-Natal, a belated recognition that the Zulu heartland of KwaZulu comprised a large part of the province – and an acknowledgment that the mainly Zulu Inkatha Freedom Party (IFP) was about to take the province by a landslide in the elections.

Natal was named by the Portuguese explorer Vasco da Gama, who sighted the coast

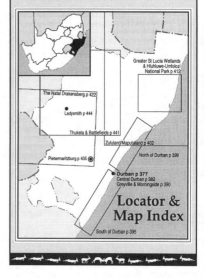

**HIGHLIGHTS**

- Durban – a big, fun city with surf on its doorstep and a sub-tropical climate
- Outstanding national parks
- Traditional Zulu culture, plus many Boer War battlefields
- Long, unspoilt coastline with excellent remote beaches and good diving
- The Natal Drakensberg – great hiking and walking, spectacular views, and San rock-paintings

Greater St Lucia Wetlands & Hluhluwe-Umfolozi National Park p 412

The Natal Drakensberg p 422

Ladysmith p 444

Thukela & Battlefields p 441

Zululand/Maputaland p 402

Pietermaritzburg p 435

North of Durban p 399

Durban p 377
Central Durban p 382
Greyville & Morningside p 390

Locator & Map Index

South of Durban p 395

on Christmas Day 1497 and named it for the natal day of Jesus. It was not until 1843 that Natal was proclaimed a British colony, and in 1845 it was made part of Cape Colony. In 1856, with a European population of less than 5000, Natal was again made a separate colony.

The introduction of Indian indentured labour in the 1860s and the consequent development of commercial agriculture (mainly sugar) boosted development, and from

KwaZulu-Natal

0      100      200 km

1895 when railways linked Durban's port (dredged to accommodate big ships) with the booming Witwatersrand, the colony thrived.

The recorded history of the province until the Union of South Africa is full of conflict: the difaqane, the Boer-Zulu and the Anglo-Zulu wars which saw the Zulu kingdom subjugated, and the two wars between the British and the Boers. All these are covered in the Facts about the Region chapter.

More recent troubles, which could almost be called a civil war, occurred during and after the negotiations for majority rule. Although the indigenous population is almost entirely Zulu, the people were split between the African National Congress (ANC) and Chief Buthelezi's IFP. Evidence is emerging that the apartheid government supplied the KwaZulu 'Homeland' government (and thus Inkatha) with arms and 'advisers' to carry out attacks on ANC-supporting villages. There were some horrific massacres. Less violent problems continue today, as anti-ANC sentiment still runs high among Inkatha politicians. There are still occasional attacks on villages but these are always highly targeted and occur in remote regions. Individual visitors have nothing to fear from random political violence.

To get a feel of the early days of European settlement in Natal, read *Travels in Southern Africa Vol I* by Adulphe Delegorgue, who was part amateur scientist and part amateur historian but above all a traveller and a hunter. His engaging book was first published in 1847 and the Killie Campbell Africana Library (Durban) has issued a reprint (paperback, R65).

Delegorgue arrived in Natal the year after the Battle of Blood River and witnessed battles between the Voortrekkers and the Zulu. He was also the guest of both sides. As a Frenchman, Delegorgue is able to give a relatively impartial – and refreshingly quirky – assessment of Boer, British and Zulu culture. Luckily for modern sensibilities he doesn't dwell overmuch on hunting, although you might want to avoid the gory bits about hippo killing.

While travelling with a Boer raiding party Delegorgue was told to stop writing his journal as the Boers had a historian and they didn't want non-official views to be recorded – a very early example of the repression of free speech which was to become an important weapon for the apartheid regime.

**Jon Murray**

# Durban

Durban is a big subtropical city on a long surf beach. It is a major port, but it is better known as a mecca for holiday-makers. It is the largest city in the province and the third largest in South Africa, but it isn't the capital of KwaZulu-Natal; Pietermaritzburg is.

Every summer, thousands of Transvaalers ('Vaalies') used to trek down to Durban ('Durbs') for sun, sand and a hint of sin. Now that Transvaal no longer exists, the Vaalies don't know what to call themselves (Gauties?) but whatever their name, their numbers are again increasing after a fall-off due to a post-election increase in crime. The city seems to have regained control of the major tourist areas, but it still pays to be alert. However, the situation is nowhere near as bad as in Jo'burg.

The city centre is no longer a white enclave but the ghetto-like situation which is developing in downtown Jo'burg seems unlikely to be repeated here. West and Smith streets, once the city's main shopping centres, are losing customers to suburban malls, which are still white enclaves.

The weather (and the water, thanks to the Agulhas current) stays warm year-round and there are about 230 sunny days a year. Over summer the weather is quite hot and very humid, with spectacular thunderstorms.

Durban is home to the largest concentration of Indian-descended people in the country – about 800,000. Muslims number about 200,000, so it not surprising to find the biggest mosque in South Africa here.

## HISTORY

It took quite some time for Durban to be established. Natal Bay, around which Durban is centred, provided refuge for seafarers at least as early as 1685, and it's thought that Vasco da Gama anchored here in 1497. The Dutch bought a large area of land around the bay from a local chief in 1690, but their ships didn't make it across the sandbar at the entrance to the bay until 1705, by which time the chief had died, and his son refused to acknowledge the deal.

With a good port established at Delagoa Bay (now Maputo, Mozambique), Natal Bay attracted little attention from Europeans until 1824, when Henry Fynn and Francis Farewell set up a base here to trade for ivory with the Zulu. Shaka granted the trading company land around the bay and it was accepted in the name of King George IV.

The settlement was slow to prosper, partly because of the chaos Shaka was causing in the area. By 1835 there was a small town with a mission station, and that year it took the name D'Urban, after the Cape Colony governor.

In 1837 the Voortrekkers crossed the Drakensberg and founded Pietermaritzburg, 80km north-west of Durban. The next year, after Durban was evacuated during a raid by the Zulu chief Dingaan's impis (regiments), the Boers claimed control. It was reoccupied by a force of British infantry later that year, but the Boers stuck by their claim. The Boers had crushed the Zulu by 1840 and seemed ready to claim most of Natal. The British sent a contingent of troops to Durban to secure their claim, but they were soundly defeated by the Boers, under Andries Pretorius, at the Battle of Congella in 1842.

The Boers retained control for a month until a British frigate arrived (fetched by teenager Dick King who rode the 1000km of wild country between Durban and Grahamstown in Eastern Cape in 10 days) and dislodged them. Durban was again under British control, and the next year the whole of Natal was annexed by the British. A year later the Natal Turf Club had been formed and Durban began its growth into an important colonial port city, although there were still elephants roaming the Berea Ridge into the 1850s.

In 1860 the first indentured Indian labourers arrived to work the canefields. Despite the iniquitous system – slave labour by another name – many more Indians arrived, including, in 1893, Mohandas Gandhi.

## ORIENTATION

A good way to get an idea of the layout of the city is to take one of the Mynah buses, which run several circular routes. See the Getting Around section.

Marine Pde, fronting long surf beaches, is Durban's focal point. Many places to stay and eat are on the parade or in the streets behind it, and much of the entertainment is here as well. The hub of all this activity is around the intersection of West St and Marine Pde. West St is a mall here, but further west it becomes one of downtown Durban's main streets.

Marine Pde continues south, leading to Erskine Pde which runs along the Point, the arm of land enclosing the north side of the harbour, Natal Bay. The Point is an old docklands area, with some colonial-era buildings and residential areas – low-key after the glitter of Marine Pde, but potentially dangerous at night.

The city hall, an imposing monument to colonial confidence, is about 1.5km west of the beach, straddling West and Smith Sts. This is the centre of the downtown area, which continues west another kilometre or so.

On the western side of the city centre, around Grey and Victoria Sts, is the Indian

Andries Pretorius, victor of the Battle of Congella in 1842.

## Gandhi in South Africa

Mohandas Karamchand Gandhi was born 2 October 1869 in Porbandar, by the sea on the Kathiawar Peninsula in western India. In 1888 he sailed for England to study law; he was called to the bar in June 1891 and immediately returned to India. He practised law in India for two years and, unimpressed with the petty politics of Porbandar, he left for South Africa in 1893.

Gandhi was soon embroiled in the politics of South Africa and became a victim of the widespread prejudice against his people. He was ejected from a train in Pietermaritzburg, and when he returned to South Africa after fetching his family he was beaten up at the docks by an angry mob. He founded the Natal Indian Congress in 1894 to fight for Indian emancipation.

During the Anglo-Boer War Gandhi raised a volunteer corps of stretcher bearers to assist the British. Gandhi and his bearers distinguished themselves on the battlefield, even at the bloody battle of Spioenkop, braving enemy fire to bring wounded to the base hospital.

Inspired by the writings of British essayist John Ruskin, he purchased a farm, Phoenix, just outside Durban in 1903. He transferred the printing presses and office of the magazine *Indian Opinion* here. He and his followers, known as Satyagrahis, lived a self-sufficient lifestyle and practised self-denial, truth and love.

In 1907 the Asiatic Registration Act was passed to prevent Indians from entering the Transvaal. Gandhi saw it as an affront and his law offices in Jo'burg became the HQ for opposition to the repressive law. Opposition slowly evolved into mass resistance. Thousands of indentured labourers went on strike and Gandhi's followers where thrown into already overflowing prisons (Gandhi himself joined them on occasion), as negotiations between General Jan Smuts and Gandhi dragged on.

In June 1914 Smuts and Gandhi agreed on the terms of the Indian Relief Bill and a victory of sorts (with many conditions) was won for the Indian community. Gandhi was happy that this struggle was over and he sailed for England in July 1914, never to return. Ironically, Gandhi's Phoenix, part of what the Zulu called Bhambayi (Bombay), was destroyed by squatters from the surrounding Inanda township in violent clashes in 1985. Hopefully it will rise from the ashes. ∎

area. There's a bustle and vibrancy missing from most commercial districts in South Africa and (as a tourist brochure puts it) 'the acrid smell of curry'. Grey St has been described as 'the real soul of the city'. Unfortunately, the apartheid government didn't like the idea of Indians living in the city centre, so their residential area was bulldozed and the people were forced out to distant nonwhite areas. This means that the Indian area in the city shuts down when the shops close and people make the long trek home. The old Indian residential area is now a wasteland of open space and government buildings north-east of the city centre.

Near the Indian area, especially around Berea station, thousands of Zulu squatters have set up camp to make an extraordinarily jumbled 'township' right on the city's doorstep. Most of these people are near-destitute and live in appalling conditions, so conspicuously wealthy tourists are an obvious target for 'informal wealth redistribution', but it's

an interesting place, with muti shops and a vibrant street life.

The suburb of Berea (pronounced b-*ree*-a) is further inland, on a ridge overlooking the city centre. The ridge marks the beginning of the white suburbs, with real estate prices climbing with altitude: the higher you get, the more breezes there are, and thus relief from the summer humidity.

The increasingly popular areas of Greyville and Morningside have many restaurants and clubs, around Florida and Windermere Rds.

The Umgeni River, which flows past some impressive cliffs and enters the sea near Blue Lagoon Beach, marks the north boundary of the city, although the suburbs have sprawled over the river all the way up the coast to Umhlanga Rocks, a big resort and retirement town. Inland from Umhlanga Rocks is Phoenix, an Indian residential area named after the Gandhi commune.

South of the city the sprawl merges into

To North Coast
To Stanger
To Umhlanga Rocks, Stanger & North Coast Beaches
N2
Sea Cow Lake
Greenwood Park
R102
Northway
M4
Briardene

**Durban**

0    0.5    1 km

Riverside
North Coast Road
Inanda Road
Umgeni Canal
Umgeni River Bird Park
Riverside Road
Beachwood Mangroves Nature Reserve

Springfield Park
Athlone Drive
Blue Lagoon Beach

Umgeni Road
Laguna Beach
Tekweni Beach

Springfield
Puntans Hill
See Greyville/Morningside Map (Page 390)
Country Club Beach

Alpine
Morningside
Goble
Sydenham
Mitchell Park
Innes
NMR Avenue

M10
Eastwood
Musgrave
Florida
Argyle
Windermere Road
Stamford Hill Road
Greyville
Waterworld
INDIAN
Overport
Oasis Beach

M15
Overport City
Cowey
M17
Dunes Beach

OCEAN

YWCA
M8
Arcadia
Epsom
Blue Waters
Battery Beach

To Pinetown & 1000 Hills
Ridge
St Thomas
Umgeni
Durban Train Station
Stanger
Shell Pde
Somtseu
Bay of Plenty Beach

N3
Musgrave Centre
Greyville Racecourse
Marine Parade
North Beach

Berea
Botanic Gardens
Municipal Sportsground
M15
Fort
Dairy Beach

Berea Rd North
M8
Old Dutch
Moore Rd
Clark
Davenport
New Berea Centre
Grey
Old
Pine
Point Rd
Esplanade
South Beach

South Ridge
West
Smith
Addington Beach

Umbilo
Gale
Victoria Embankment
See Central Durban Map (Page 382)
Bells Beach

Sydney Rd
Albert Park
Fishing Boat Jetty
Shipping Terminal
330
Seafarer's Club & Hostel
The Point Market & Restaurants
North Pier

Nicholson
Sugar Terminal
Natal Bay
Cave Rocks

M4
Maydon Road
Pier No 1
The Bluff

Congella
Maydon Wharf
Pier No 2
Salisbury Island

Southern Freeway
Graving Dock
To Airport & South Coast Beaches
To Brighton Beach

the resort towns of the south coast. On the city's western fringe is Pinetown, a vast collection of dormitory suburbs. A fair proportion of Durban's population, mainly black, lives in townships surrounding the city. These include Richmond Farm, Kwa-Mashu, Lindelani, Ntuzuma and the Greater Inanda area.

There are two good viewpoints where you can look down over the city. The best is at the University of Natal on Ridge Rd; entry is free, but check with security at the gate first. The view from the Cube (a cubical sculpture) near the reservoir on Innes Rd is especially good at night.

## INFORMATION
### Tourist Information

The main tourist information centre (☎ (031) 304 4934) is in the old railway station on the corner of Pine and Gardiner Sts; the complex is known as Tourist Junction. It's open weekdays from 8 am to 5 pm and Saturday from 9 am to 2 pm. There's also a branch at the beach (☎ (031) 32 2608, 32 2595) open every day, although this might close soon.

There are various booking agencies in the complex, including one which takes reservations for both the Natal Parks Board and the National Parks Board (☎ (031) 304 4934). You can also book train tickets at the complex, which saves a dispiriting visit to the huge new train station.

Tourist information is also available at the airport.

**Publications** Pick up a copy of the *What's On in Durban* pamphlet at the Tourist Junction. The monthly *Durban for all Seasons* is available from most hotels. There is also information in the *KwaZulu-Natal Experience* magazine. The Durban municipal library (☎ (031) 37 6246) produces a full *Clubs & Societies* listing.

The best introduction to Durban is the superb *ADA (Art, Design, Architecture): Durban and Surrounds* (R29) by Jennifer Sorrell. If ever a book gets into the heart of a city, this one does. An illustrated A-Z of

cultural activities and artistic personalities, it covers all races and religions.

Also useful is *A Guide to the History & Architecture of Durban* (R4) by Bennett, Brusse & Adams, available from the Local History Museum, among other places. It gives an interesting history, describes four walks and has good maps. The AA has a good map of Durban, and their *Natal Holiday Coast & Hinterland* is also handy.

### Other Services

One of several central laundromats is on Prince Alfred St near the corner of West St. A bag wash (you drop it off and they wash, dry and fold it) costs R12.25.

Adam's Books, on Smith St west of Gardiner St, is excellent and on the 1st floor they stock textbooks, which include some dictionaries and phrasebooks in the many South African languages.

The shops in the city centre and the small shopping centres in the nearby suburbs will cater to most of your needs, but if you want to see one of the potential futures for South Africa, where the wealthy minority hides from the poor majority in a glitzy local version of the American dream, drop into the enormous Pavilion complex. It's on the city's outskirts but is a quick drive from the centre, on the N3 towards Pietermaritzburg.

### Money

The foreign exchange counter at the First National Bank on the corner of West and Gillespie Sts is open from 3 to 7 pm on weekdays, 11 am to 6 pm on Saturday and 10 am to 3 pm on Sunday. However, because of its extended hours it gives a slightly poorer rate than other foreign exchange outlets.

Rennies Travel (the Thomas Cook agent) (☎ (031) 305 3800) has several forex offices, including one in the 320 Arcade off Smith St just west of Gardiner St. American Express (☎ (031) 301 5551) is in Denor House on Smith St, next to the AA office.

The French Bank of SA is in the Durdoc Centre, on Smith St, just north of Broad St. Other banks include Nedbank, in Durban Club Place; United Bank, on the corner of

Smith and Gardiner Sts; and Standard Bank, also on the corner of Smith and Gardiner Sts. Most banks open on Saturday morning.

### Post & Communications
Poste restante is at the GPO. Go through the doors on the right in the entrance foyer and ask at the desk immediately inside. They keep letters for a month.

You can make international phone calls at Cash Call Telkom, on the 1st floor of 320 West St, from 8 am to 9.50 pm Monday to Saturday (but closed for lunch) and 6 to 9 pm on Sunday.

Java@Java is an Internet café on Marriott St, just west of Greyville Racecourse.

### Foreign Consulates
Consulates in Durban include:

Austria
    3 Bellvue Rd (☎ (031) 304 9522)
Belgium
    37B Jonsson Lane (☎ (031) 303 2840)
Denmark
    Saambou Building, 399 Smith St (☎ (031) 305 1888)
France
    7011 Overport City, Ridge Rd (☎ (031) 29 9330)
Germany
    320 West St (☎ (031) 305 5677)
India
    Durban Unlimited Building (the Tourist Junction) cnr Pine & Gardiner Sts (☎ (031) 304 7020)
Italy
    Sanlam Building, West St (☎ (031) 301 4107)
Netherlands
    65 Victoria Embankment (☎ (031) 304 1770)
Sweden
    115 Musgrave Rd, Berea (☎ (031) 202 6911)
UK
    10th Floor, Fedlife House, 320 Smith St (☎ (031) 305 2929)
USA
    Durban Bay House, 333 Smith St (☎ (031) 304 4737)

### Emergency
For an ambulance phone 10177, or 261 6887 for a private service. For police it's 10111 (flying squad) or 306 4422.

### Dangers & Annoyances
Many areas are potentially dangerous at night, notably the Indian area and parts of Point Rd. At night central Durban takes on the feel of a ghetto as people head to the restaurants in places like Morningside or to the big hotels and clubs along the beachfront.

The crowded beachfront promenade is a happy hunting ground for pickpockets, and there are occasional violent robberies in the less well-lit areas between the beach and the promenade. If you are confronted by armed muggers, hand over your valuables!

### BEACHFRONT AREA
Durban's prime attraction is its long string of surf beaches. The Golden Mile is 6km long, with shark nets protecting warm-water beaches all the way from Blue Lagoon (at the mouth of the Umgeni River) south to Addington on The Point. In between, from north to south, the main beaches are Laguna, Tekweni, Country Club, Oasis, Dunes, Battery, Bay of Plenty, North, Dairy, South, Addington and Bells. Lifesavers patrol the beaches between 8 am and 5 pm – always swim in a patrolled area, indicated by flags.

The brilliantly revamped promenade fronts the surf. It's a good place to watch the crowds and there are a number of things to do. Across the road is a screen of high-rise buildings with many hotels and restaurants. Marine Pde, especially around the West St Mall, is the centre of the action.

It's worth walking out on one of the long piers which jut into the surf for a good view of the city. Another good view can be had from the chairlift in the small **amusement park** on the promenade near West St. It's definitely worth R5 for the view (and the fear – it's a long way down).

Nearby is **Seaworld**, open from 9 am to 9 pm daily. The fish are hand-fed daily by divers (sharks are fed on Monday, Wednesday and Friday). There are dolphin and seal shows each day; call ☎ (031) 37 4079 for times. Admission is R22 (R14 children).

A Sunday **flea market** is held near the amphitheatre, Bay of Plenty, weekly in summer and every second week at other times. Phone ☎ (031) 301 3200 for times.

Nowadays, there are only about a dozen

KWAZULU-NATAL

**rickshaws** in Durban, usually to be found on the beachfront near Seaworld. In 1904 there were about 2000 registered rickshaw pullers and they were a means of transport rather than a tourist novelty. A five minute ride costs R10 plus R2 for the mandatory photo.

Nearby is **Mini Town**, a tacky model city which has replicas of Durban's best-known buildings. The **Snake Park** (☎ (031) 37 6456) on Snell Pde, North Beach, has about five venom-milking demonstrations daily; admission is R10 (R5 children).

Back from the beach on Gillespie St is **The Wheel** complex, with shops, restaurants, bars and a dozen cinemas, as well as that incongruous Ferris wheel spinning above the street. Take a walk through the huge complex, which is well designed. Some travellers report that the centre is not so safe at night.

On the Umgeni River, near Blue Lagoon Beach, is the **Model Yacht Pond** where enthusiasts sail their craft on the weekend. Nearby, also on the river but on the north side, is **Umgeni River Bird Park** where the birds live in cliff-face aviaries. At the mouth of the Umgeni you will see many species of waterbird coming and going as they please.

**Waterworld**, between the beach and the King's Park stadium, is a large complex with waterslides and other amusements. Not far away, and south of Argyle Rd, is a **drive-in cinema**.

## NATAL BAY & VICTORIA EMBANKMENT

Durban's harbour is the busiest in Africa (and the ninth busiest in the world), and much of the activity centres on the **Shipping Terminal** near Stanger St, where there are public viewing areas. You can also see the activity on the water from the ferry that runs across the harbour mouth from North Pier on The Point to South Pier on the Bluff.

The small **Natal Maritime Museum** on Victoria Embankment has two tugboats and the minesweeper SAS *Durban*. It's open from 8.30 am to 4 pm Monday to Saturday, and 11 am to 4 pm Sunday; admission is R3.

The **Vasco Da Gama Clock**, a florid Victorian monument on the Embankment

---

### 'Durbs' 4 Kids

Well supervised, kids will have a ball at the beach and when they get out of the water they can go to Mini Town, the Children's Farm, Seaworld, Funworld and Water Wonderland or even have a rickshaw ride – all along the waterfront. Funworld has carousel and bumper rides and Water Wonderland has waterslides and a pulsating river ride. The Children's Ed-U-Fun Farm, Battery Beach Rd, is open from 9 am to 4 pm. It has pigs, goats, lambs, and tractor and pony rides (entry is R6 for 'big' kids and R5 for little kids).

Other distractions: the Fitzsimmons Model railway exhibition adjacent to the Snake Park (there are rides for the under-fives on the Orient Express); mini golf on the banks of the Umgeni River at Blue Lagoon and indoor mini golf at 100 Brickhill Rd; the Entertainment Centre in The Wheel; *T rex*, a dodo skeleton, a discovery room and other attractions in the Natural History Museum; and The Little Top on the water's edge at South Beach. The latter has competitions for the kids and provides deck chairs for adults (to collapse in after chasing the little fiends around). ■

---

east of Aliwal St, was presented by the Portuguese government in 1897, the 400th anniversary of Vasco da Gama's sighting of Natal. Continue west and you come to the **Dick King Statue**, near Gardiner St, which commemorates his ride in 1842.

West of Gardiner St is the **Durban Club**, a solid jumble of Victorian and Edwardian architectural elements.

**Maydon Wharf**, running along the south-western side of the harbour, contains the **Sugar Terminal** at 57 Maydon Rd (☎ (031) 301 0331 if you are interested in going on one of eight daily tours), the **Graving Dock** and the **Fishing Jetty**, where deep-sea fishing boats leave. Phone the Charter Boat Association (☎ (031) 261 6010) for prices. Make sure you take Maydon Rd to get there, not the Southern Freeway (the M4).

There are also boat tours of the harbour running from the Gardiner St jetty. Sarie Marais Pleasure Cruises (☎ (031) 305 4022) has timetables.

Down at the south end of the beachfront,

**The Point** is an old area on a spit of land between the harbour and the ocean. At the very end of The Point you can watch ships coming through the quite narrow heads into the harbour. There's a weekend market, and a bar and restaurant or two, which are popular on weekends.

## CITY CENTRE

The impressive **city hall**, built in 1910 in modern renaissance style, is worth a look inside and out. It is similar in design to the city hall of another colonial city – Belfast. In front of the hall is **Francis Farewell Square**, where Fynn and Farewell made their camp in 1824. Here there are several statues and memorials to historical figures.

In the city hall building is the **Natural Science Museum** (enter from Smith St), open daily from 8.30 am to 5 pm (from 11 am Sunday). Check out the cockroach display, the reconstructed dodo and the life-size dinosaur model. There are sometimes free films here – some dull, some very good.

Upstairs is the **Art Gallery**, which houses a good collection of contemporary South African works, especially arts and crafts of Zululand. In particular, see the collection of baskets from Hlabisa, finely woven from a variety of grasses and incorporating striking natural colours. Admission is free. The **municipal library** is also in this complex.

The **Local History Museum** is in the 1863 courthouse behind the city hall (enter from Aliwal St). It has interesting displays on colonial life as well as a useful bookshop; admission is free.

Across West St, on the corner of Gardiner St, is the **GPO**, which predates the city hall. On the east side of the GPO is **Church Square**, with its old vicarage and the 1909 **St Paul's Church** at the rear on Pine St. Next to Church Square is a swimming pool, open from 7 am to 4.30 pm. **Medwood Gardens**, with an outdoor café, is next to the pool.

The **old railway station**, on the corner of Soldiers Way (Gardiner St) and Pine St, was built in 1894 and gives an idea of Durban's size and importance at the end of last century. The building now houses the Tourist Junc-

tion information centre. **The Workshop**, a shopping centre on Commercial Rd, was another railway building (a train shed, hence the huge doors) which became redundant when the new station opened. It is open daily.

From The Workshop, walk north across some vacant land to Ordnance Rd, where you'll find the excellent **KwaMuhle Museum** in the former Bantu Administration building. The museum has a permanent display (with good oral history tapes) on the 'Durban System' by which whites subjugated blacks, and temporary exhibitions relating to Zulu culture and contemporary issues.

Nearby, across Aliwal St from The Workshop, is the Durban Exhibition Centre (DEC), which hosts the **Durban Military Tattoo** each year in July. On Sundays a **flea market** is held in the DEC's South Plaza.

The **African Art Centre** is in the Guildhall Arcade, running off Gardiner St near Leslie St, a block west of the Victoria Embankment. It is not a curio shop but a nonprofit gallery with exciting work by rural artists.

The **Old House Museum** is at 31 St Andrews St, the restored home of Natal's first prime minister. It's open daily.

The **Old Fort**, north of the centre on Old Fort Rd, is where the British were besieged by the Boers in 1842. Just east is **Warriors Gate**, the general headquarters of the MOTHs (Memorable Order of Tin Hats), an ex-servicepersons' club. There's a small collection of militaria here; it's open daily except Saturday.

## INDIAN AREA

The **Victoria Street Market** at the west end of Victoria St replaces the old Indian Market which burned down in 1973. It is the main tourist attraction of the area and is worth wandering around, but a walk through the nearby bustling streets is equally interesting. Just be on the lookout for pickpockets.

Grey St ('not black, not white ...' is how a taxi driver described both the street and the predicament of Indians in South Africa), between Victoria and West Sts, is the main shopping area. Prices are low and you can

Central Durban

0   200   400 m

INDIAN

OCEAN

KWAZULU-NATAL

Bay of Plenty Pier
North Beach Pier
Dairy Beach Pier
New Pier
Wedge Pier

Snell Parade
Sol Harris Crescent
Somtseu
Playfair
Pavilion Terrace
Brickhill
Prince Alfred
Stanger
Promenade
Marine Parade
Boscombe
Victoria Park
Brickhill
Morrison
Hunter
Milne
Farewell
Pine
Palmer
John Milne Rd.
Prince Alfred
West
Stanger
Kitchener
Mills
Cato Square
Aliwal
Walnut
Aliwal
Commercial
Gardiner
Smith
Pine
Field
Soldiers Way
Ordnance
Old Fort
Kingsmead Cricket Ground
NMR Avenue
Taylor Crescent
Umgeni
Umgeni
Albert
Albert
Beatrice Lane
Fountain Lane
Lorne
Prince Edward
Queen
Commercial
Broad
Grey
Grey
Cross
Cross
Victoria
Russell
Russell
Efilat Viaduct
Theatre
West
St Georges
St Andrews
Russell
Brook
Market
Warwick
Warwick
Winterton
Berea
Centenary
Carlisle
Darnell Crescent
Alice
Leopold
Sydenham Road
DLI Avenue
Greyville Racecourse
Municipal Sportsground
Botanic Gardens
May
Mitchell
North
First
Newmarket
Fynn
Ascot
Epsom
Natal Bay
Victoria Embankment
Alexandra
Gull
Fisher
Pickering
Mazeppa
Roy
Creek
Cato
Winder
Bay Terrace
Point
Prince
Sea View
Gillespie
West
Tyzack
Smith
Brighton
Beatty
Grenville
Shamrock
Thistle
Rochester
Trafalgar
Rutherford

Sol Harris Crescent
Playfair

M4
M2
M5
R102

To Umhlanga Rocks & North Coast
To Morningside & Mitchell Park
To Africana Museum
To YWCA
To Pietermaritzburg (N3)
To South Coast & Durban (Louis Botha) Airport

Old Dutch
Canongate

| PLACES TO STAY | | |
|---|---|---|
| 7 | Holiday Inn Garden Court North Beach | |
| 11 | City Lodge | |
| 45 | Tudor House Hostel | |
| 52 | Royal Hotel | |
| 64 | PL Maharaj Lodge | |
| 65 | Banana Backpackers | |
| 70 | The Palace Protea Hotel | |
| 72 | Holiday Inn Garden Court South Beach | |
| 74 | Balmoral Hotel | |
| 77 | Palmerston Hotel | |
| 79 | Marine Parade | |
| 82 | Tropicana | |
| 84 | Palm Beach | |
| 85 | Durban Beach Youth Hostel | |
| 86 | Four Seasons | |
| 88 | Impala Holiday Flats | |
| 90 | Hawaii Resort | |

| PLACES TO EAT | | |
|---|---|---|
| 22 | Victory Lounge | |
| 34 | Taj Mahal | |
| 44 | Medwood Gardens Cafe; Swimming Pool | |
| 55 | Aliwal Lighthouse | |
| 67 | Gringo's Cantina | |
| 71 | Joe Kool's | |
| 75 | Coimbra Portuguese Restaurant | |
| 76 | Thatcher's | |
| 81 | Lord Prawn | |
| 83 | The Haven | |
| 89 | Aldo's Italian | |
| 91 | Finnegan's Pub | |

| OTHER | | |
|---|---|---|
| 1 | Long-Distance Minibus Taxis | |
| 2 | Durban Train Station | |
| 3 | Hindu Temple | |
| 4 | Ocean City (Theatre & Ice Rink) | |
| 5 | Snake Park | |
| 6 | Mini Town | |
| 8 | Parking | |
| 9 | Military Museum; Sunday Flea Market | |
| 10 | Parking | |
| 12 | Old Fort; Warriors Gate | |
| 13 | KwaMuhle Museum | |
| 14 | Bus Depot | |
| 15 | Victoria Bus Terminus | |
| 16 | Fruit & Vegetable Market | |
| 17 | Berea Train Station; Minibus Taxis | |
| 18 | Minibus Taxi to Lusikisiki (Transkei) | |
| 19 | Cemetery | |
| 20 | Emmanuel Cathedral | |
| 21 | Victoria Street Indian Market | |
| 23 | Juma Mosque | |
| 24 | Madrassa Arcade | |
| 25 | West St Mosque | |
| 26 | Bank of France (SA) | |
| 27 | AA Office | |
| 28 | Old House Museum | |
| 29 | Yacht Mole | |
| 30 | First National Bank | |
| 31 | Rennies Travel; US Consulate | |
| 32 | American Express | |
| 33 | AA Office | |
| 35 | 320 Towers; Arcade | |
| 36 | GPO | |
| 37 | Tourist Junction | |
| 38 | Local Buses to Umhlanga Rocks | |
| 39 | The Workshop | |
| 40 | Parking | |
| 41 | Durban Exhibition Centre | |
| 42 | Local Bus Terminus | |
| 43 | St Paul's Church | |
| 46 | Local History Museum | |
| 47 | Natural Science Museum; Library; Art Gallery | |
| 48 | City Hall | |
| 49 | Francis Farewell Square | |
| 50 | Standard Bank | |
| 51 | Dick King Statue | |
| 53 | The Natal Playhouse | |
| 54 | Albany Hotel | |
| 56 | SAA Office; Airport Bus | |
| 57 | Outdoor Inn | |
| 58 | Hilmark Car Rental | |
| 59 | Natal Maritime Museum; Boat Cruises | |
| 60 | BAT Centre | |
| 61 | Vasco Da Gama Clock | |
| 62 | Laundrette | |
| 63 | Bavarian Deli | |
| 66 | Fairport Market | |
| 68 | Mike Lamont Surf Shop | |
| 69 | Cool Runnings | |
| 73 | U-Tours; Rennies Travel; Rickshaws | |
| 78 | First National Bank | |
| 80 | Seaworld | |
| 87 | The Wheel Shopping Centre | |
| 92 | Al's Bike Hire | |

bargain. Most Muslim shops close between noon and 2 pm on Friday.

The big **Juma Mosque**, the largest in the southern hemisphere, on the corner of Queen and Grey Sts, is open to visitors on weekdays and Saturday morning; phone ☎ (031) 304 0326 for a guided tour. The **Madrassa Arcade** runs between the mosque and the Catholic **Emmanuel Cathedral**, exemplifying a commercial ecumenicism.

On West St, near the corner of Grey St, is the less flamboyant **West St Mosque**. Further up West St, opposite the cemetery, is **The Mansions**, a big Edwardian building,

all verandahs and wrought iron. West of Berea train station is a big, bustling **fruit & vegetable market**, now the centre of the maelstrom of a squatter settlement – it's still interesting but don't take valuables if you visit.

The **Alayam Hindu Temple** is the oldest and biggest in South Africa. It's away from the main Indian area, on Somtseu Rd, which runs between Stanger St and NMR Ave. It is open from 7 am to 6 pm daily.

## AFRICANA MUSEUM

The Africana Museum at 220 Marriot Rd, near the corner of Musgrave Rd, is an old

KWAZULU-NATAL

## Hindu & Muslim Festivals

The annual **Kavadi Festival**, held twice annually (January to February and April to May), is the major Hindu festival. It honours the god **Muruga** who heals and dispels misfortune, and much self-inflicted pain, as a sign of devotion, accompanies the ceremony. In April or May an 18-day festival is held to honour the goddess **Draupadi** and it culminates with firewalking. For 10 days during July and August the **Mariamman**, or Porridge Festival, is celebrated; Mariamman is both the cause and cure of infectious diseases.

Two other festivals are the three-day **Deepvali** (Diwali), the Festival of Lights, celebrated in November; and the colourful five-day Hare Krishna Festival **Ratha Yatra** (Festival of Chariots) celebrated in December.

Each year there's the Muslim observance of the death of the Prophet's grandson, which culminates in a parade down Centenary Rd. ■

home preserving Dr Killie Campbell's important collection of Zulu craftworks, art, furniture and paintings. It's open on Tuesday and Thursday from 8 am to 1 pm.

### MITCHELL PARK

Further north, Musgrave St becomes Innes St and, on the corner of Nimmo St, passes Mitchell Park. There is a small zoo here with birds and a few animals, and an outdoor restaurant. King's House, on the edge of the park, was the Natal governor's residence and is now the Durban home of the president.

### BOTANIC GARDENS

The 20 hectare Botanic Gardens (☎ (031) 21 3022), on Sydenham Rd west of Greyville Racecourse, are open daily from 7.30 am to 5.15 pm in winter, and until 5.45 pm in summer. The Orchid House is open from 9.30 am to 12.30 pm and 2 to 5 pm daily. One of the rarest cycads, *Encephalartos woodii*, can be seen here, as well as many species of bromeliad. There is a picturesque tea garden.

### THE TEMPLE OF UNDERSTANDING

The biggest Hari Krishna temple in the southern hemisphere is just outside Durban.

The building is unusual and there's a vegetarian restaurant inside. Follow the N3 towards Pietermaritzburg and then branch off to the N2 south. Take the Chatsworth turn-off and turn right towards the Chatsworth centre; phone ☎ (031) 43 3328 for opening times and tour details.

### ORGANISED TOURS

Perhaps the best way to experience Durban is in the company of someone who knows what they are looking at. Durban Unlimited (☎ (031) 304 4934) conducts three walking tours of the city, each with a different flavour; the R25 charge is well spent. Tours leave from the Tourist Junction at 9.45 am (but get there 15 minutes early).

The U-Tour Coach Company office (☎ (031) 368 2848), on the beachfront just south of West St, has some interesting bus tours of the city and the surrounding area. A half-day city tour costs R90.

Tekweni Ecotours (☎ (031) 303 1199; fax 303 4369; email tekeco@javajava.co.za) – that's 'eco' as in economical as well as in ecological – has some good day tours, such as the Valley of 1000 Hills (R120) and the Cato Manor Experience (R95), which takes you from KwaMuhle Museum to a *shebeen* (drinking establishment) in an informal settlement. There are also longer tours: the Zululand Grassroots Experience (three days, R735) which includes Lake St Lucia and Hluhluwe-Umfolozi, and Drakensberg Hikes (three days, R535).

African Routes (☎ (031) 562 8724; fax (031) 562 8673) trips are about a week in duration. You would see a fair slice of Mpumalanga, KwaZulu-Natal and the Cape if you took their combined two week trip from Jo'burg to Cape Town via Durban. There's a booking office in the Tourist Rendezvous Junction.

Africa South Tours operates out of the Amazulu hostel in KwaMbonambi and has a three day tour (picking up and dropping off in Durban) which includes Hluhluwe-Umfolozi and St Lucia for R580.

A reader highly recommends Masakhane Zulu Tours (☎ (083) 675 4034 or (031) 29

0743), run by Tim Shobalembuzi. His tour to the Valley of 1000 Hills avoids the tourist traps and takes you into traditional villages, where you stay overnight. The cost is around R200. Let us know what you think of it. See Club Tropicana in the Hibiscus Coast section later in this chapter for more overnight stays in villages, and the chance to do voluntary work in a lovely rural area.

## ACTIVITIES
### Hiking
Outdoor Inn, on Aliwal St near Victoria Embankment, has hiking supplies.

There are a couple of hiking clubs, the Durban Ramblers and the Mountain Backpackers. Their contact numbers depend on the office-holders, so try the phone book or ask at the Outdoor Inn.

The Ramblers take things more easily and concentrate on the social and aesthetic pleasures of hiking. The Mountain Backpackers are more likely to be seen sweating it out on

a high traverse of the Drakensberg. The club welcomes visitors, even novices. The Mountain Club of SA (Natal Section) members are the spider-like forms you will see scaling the sides of the Monk's Cowl in the central Drakensberg.

The Durban Parks & Recreation Department (☎ (031) 21 1303) holds weekend walks through reserves and parks in the area.

### Diving
If you're a qualified diver you can hire equipment from the Undersea Club (☎ (031) 32 0654) and go diving through it. Simply Scuba (☎ /fax (031) 23 9442), 200D Florida Rd, Morningside (down a small lane off the main street), offers PADI or NAUI courses, equipment hire and sales. Another school for specialised NAUI courses is Eco Diving (☎ (031) 96 4239).

### Surfing
If you're a surfer and you're in Durban then

### The KwaZulu-Natal Surf Scene
Durban and the KwaZulu-Natal coast has a surf culture, quality and history to match anywhere in the world. It is the home of true legends like Shaun Tomson and up-and-comers like (hotdogger deluxe) Frankie Oberholzer.

'Town' itself is a smorgasbord of quality breaks, all best when the sou'wester blows. South Beach and Addington are normally the best beginner spots, but with the right swell they can throw some gaping barrels. Wedge Reef, next to Old West Street Pier can be testy, while Dairy Pier has the best left-hander of the lot. New Pier, North Beach, Bay of Plenty and Snake Park can be long and hollow, often with picture perfect right-handers breaking off the piers.

In July, North Beach is the home of the Gunston 500, the feature event of the Ocean Africa Festival. Ocean Africa is a unique extravaganza encompassing every beach activity possible, including night surfing, beauty contests, fashion shows, beer tents, bands and stands selling everything imaginable. The turnout is usually huge and the action on the beach rivals that in the water. Joe Kool's and the Cattleman, right on North Beach, are the most popular after-surfing 'jols'.

The northern town beaches, Battery and Tekweni, can also have quality waves with less crowds. Further north are breaks too numerous to mention. The pick of these are Westbrook (arguably the hollowest wave around), Ballito Bay and Zinkwasi.

The Bluff, just south of Durban, has some good spots with the infamous Cave Rock being its showpiece. Often compared with Hawaii's Backdoor, The Rock is for experienced surfers only.

The KwaZulu-Natal Coast really comes into its own south from the Bluff. The best time is winter, from April to August, before 10 or 11 am, when you're basically guaranteed a north-west land breeze. The solid groundswells roll in from the south, hitting Greenpoint, Scottsburgh, Happy Wanderers and The Spot (all right-handers) at a perfect angle. Each produces incredibly rideable four to eight-foot-plus grinders over rock and sand bottom, with the occasional couple-of-hundred-metre rides. Plenty of barrels are to be had, but check with locals to be safe. Further south are more right-hand points right along the Transkei coast with plenty of quality waves in between.

**Patrick Moroney**

you've cruised to the right place. There are a multitude of good beaches with any number of breaks. (See the boxed text on the KwaZulu-Natal surf scene.) *Zigzag* magazine has surfing information crammed in between glossy ads; it comes out every two months.

### Sailing

Durban is an excellent place to learn to sail. Travellers have recommended the Ocean Sailing Academy (☎ (031) 301 5726; fax 307 1257), 38 Fenton Rd. It offers five-day courses for yacht hands/skippers (R1500 for either, R2700 for both); the student rate is R850.

### Horse-Racing

Horse-racing, very popular in Durban, is held throughout the year at Greyville Racecourse near the Botanic Gardens, and at Clairwood Park Turf Club near the freeway south of the city. South Africa's main racing event is the Rothman's July, held on the first Saturday of that month at Greyville. It's worth driving along DLI Avenue, which cuts across Greyville, for its banks of carefully tended tropical flowers.

### Canoeing

Durban is the canoeing centre of South Africa, and the Natal Canoe Union (☎ (031) 46 0984; fax 65225) looks after clubs throughout the province. All types of canoeing are catered for – marathon, slalom, white-water, canoe polo and sea kayaking.

Each year the popular Dusi Marathon starts 80km inland at Pietermaritzburg and ends at the mouth of the Umgeni River.

### White-Water Rafting

The mighty Tugela River (in Zulu it is *uThukela*, 'the startling one') is the scene of most of the rafting in KwaZulu-Natal. When the water level is high, usually from November to April, you can ride through Horrible Horace, the Rollercoaster, Four-Man Hole and the Tugela Ravine. Rafting operators include Tugela River Adventures (☎ (0331)

65018) and The River Rafters (☎ (011) 884 1652).

### Golf

KwaZulu-Natal is a great place to vent your frustration on the small white ball. The area to the south of Durban is known as the Golf Coast (pick up the free *Golf: Southern Natal* for contact numbers from the Tourist Junction). A bit of trivia: the 3rd at the Durban Country Club is touted in the video *Fairways to Heaven* as the best 3rd hole in the world.

### Spectator Sports

Several different codes of football are played in KwaZulu-Natal, but the most popular is soccer, or plain football. Professional teams such as AmaZulu and Manning Rangers play in town and international teams visit.

Rugby is usually associated with the white population. Natal has always been a strong rugby province and won the interprovincial Currie Cup in 1990 and 1992. The 60,000 seat King's Park Rugby stadium staged some of the games of the 1995 Rugby World Cup.

Durban's large Indian population is a contributing factor to the popularity of cricket. Kingsmead hosts international sides, and recent Natal stars include the fine opener Andrew Hudson and the mercurial master fieldsman Jonty Rhodes.

---

#### The Comrades Marathon

This is the most famous athletics event in South Africa. The race was conceived to honour the comrades who fought in WW I, and every year since May 1921, runners from throughout the country and all over the world have come to run between Durban and Pietermaritzburg (PMB). The race is reversed on alternate years – up from Durban to PMB one year and down from PMB to Durban the next.

In 1921 the distance (89km) was completed by the winner, Bill Rowan, in 8 hours 59 minutes. Today the times are much faster. Women could only officially compete from 1975 but many had completed the distance long before that. The undisputed king of the event was Bruce Fordyce who won nine times between 1980 and 1990. ■

## PLACES TO STAY – BOTTOM END
### Caravan Parks

*Queensburgh Caravan Park* (☎ (031) 44 5800) is in Northdene, about 12km west of the city centre. It's in a nice spot, by a creek with a nature reserve on the other side. There are only a few tent sites as yet but the new owners are investing a lot of money to add more. Sites cost around R25 and you can rent vans. To get there take the M7 west and exit at Bellville Rd/Old Main Rd/M5. Travel west on the M5 for some way and just after the civic centre turn right onto St Augustine Rd then right onto Haslam Rd. The caravan park is at the end of Haslam Rd.

*Durban Caravan Park* (☎ (031) 47 3929) is a long way from town at 55 Greys Inn Rd. There are camp sites for R22 per person plus R2 per vehicle and on-site vans (usually full) for R120 for four people. To get there, take the Brighton Beach exit from the N2 and head south-east on Edwin Swales VC Drive which meets Bluff Rd, near the intersection of Greys Inn Rd.

### Hostels

Durban doesn't have the range of hostels you'll find in Cape Town or even Jo'burg, but there are some good ones here.

*Durban Beach Youth Hostel* (☎ (031) 32 4945; fax 32 4551) is superbly located near the beach at 19 Smith St; dorm beds are R22. It has been poorly maintained and not particularly pleasant for the past few years, but the owners say they are cleaning up their act.

Not too far from the beach is *Banana Backpackers* (☎ (031) 368 4062), on the 1st floor (that's 2nd floor to Americans) at 61 Pine St (corner of Prince Alfred). It's a big, relaxed place that gets good feedback. Its location is excellent for both the beach and the city centre, although there's a fair bit of traffic noise. Dorms are R30, singles are R70, twins are R80 and small doubles are R110. The hostel is owned by the African Routes adventure travel people.

Down in The Point area is a new place, *Seafarer's Club* (☎ (031) 32 0511), 154 Point Rd (it's also called Backpackers International). It's in a very big, old building and

has potential, with a big bar and venues for local bands. The area isn't great, although it isn't far from Marine Pde. Dorms are R25 and there are small singles/doubles for not much more. They do airport pick-ups.

Out in Morningside, *Tekweni Backpackers* (☎ (031) 303 1433; fax 303 4369), 167 9th Ave, is a manageable distance north of the centre, and it is popular. Dorm beds are R30, double rooms are R40 per person. Not far away at 743 Currie Rd is another good place, *Traveller's Rest* (☎ (031) 303 1064). To get to either place take a Mitchell Park, Musgrave Rd, Kensington or St Mathias Rd Mynah bus.

Up in the suburb of Umgeni Park (Riverside), near Blue Lagoon, *Riverside Lodge* (☎ (031) 83 6570; email riversidelodge@ mail.saix.net), 31 Ridgeside Rd, is in a private house and offers camping (R20), dorms (R25) and doubles (R90). A taxi from town costs about R15.

### Hotels & Apartments

Gillespie St (a block back from the beach) and the nearby area is crammed with holiday apartments and hotels, many of which are good value in the off-season. Some places stay affordable year-round, although getting a room might be a problem during the Christmas holidays. However, along with low prices you're likely to find cockroaches, poor maintenance and possible security problems. Some of the better places are listed in the following section.

## PLACES TO STAY – MIDDLE

Most of the middle to top-range places are listed in the *Natal Accommodation Guide*, available for R3 at the Tourist Junction. There's an accommodation booking desk in the complex, and they should be able to find you a B&B from around R120/170 a single/ double.

The streets near the beach, especially Gillespie St, are the places to look for cheaper hotels and apartments. Be warned that as more and more expensive accommodation opens in this area, standards at the cheaper

KWAZULU-NATAL

places are slipping, so check the room before handing over your cash.

Try the *Palmerston Hotel* (☎ (031) 37 6363), 42 Palmer St, which charges R60/120 a single/double; *Palm Beach* (☎ (031) 37 3451), on Gillespie St at the corner of Tyzack St, which charges from R95/130 (R160 a double at Christmas); *Impala Holiday Flats* (☎ (031) 32 3232), 40 Gillespie St, with singles/doubles from R95/130 (doubles R160 at Christmas); and the big *Four Seasons* (☎ (031) 37 3381), 81 Gillespie St, where singles/doubles start at R90/180 (much more at Christmas).

Away from the beach but a bargain is the small *Tudor House Hotel* (☎ (031) 37 7328), on West St, east of Aliwal St. Rooms with air-con, phone and TV are R110/160, with breakfast. It's one of the few cheaper city hotels to maintain standards and it's popular – book ahead. Across the road a little closer to the beach is the high-rise *PL Maharaj Lodge* (☎ (031) 368 3304) at 158 West St; slightly odd self-contained apartments sleeping up to four people cost from R150.

## PLACES TO STAY – TOP END
Many top-end places line the beachfront. The classic *Blue Waters* (☎ 0800 31 2044 toll-free; fax (031) 37 5817) is a bargain with singles/doubles for R195/290 with break-fast. *Tropicana* (☎ (031) 368 1511; fax 368 2322), on Marine Pde south of West St, charges R329/458 for singles/doubles. *Marine Parade* (☎ (031) 37 3341; fax 32 9885), at 167 Marine Pde, is a four star member of the Holiday Inn Garden Court chain and has singles/doubles from R289/318. There are two other members of the chain at the beachfront, *South Beach* (☎ (031) 37 2231), from R220 per room, and *North Beach* (☎ (031) 32 7361), from R289 per room.

*City Lodge* (☎ (031) 32 1447; fax 32 1483), a big, motel-like place on the corner of Brickhill and Old Fort Rds, has singles/doubles from R230/260.

You have to leave the beach area to find Durban's best hotel, the *Royal* (☎ (031) 304 0331; fax 304 5055), which is near the city hall at 267 Smith St. Single/double rooms cost R700/880 and suites are R1110, with weekend specials.

## PLACES TO EAT
Most of Durban's many hotels have restau-rants or dining rooms, ranging from one-star pubs where you can get bar meals to classy à la carte places.

### Beach Area
Many of the hotels around the beachfront have cheap meals, especially at lunch. There are also several restaurants in The Wheel complex but don't expect cheap tucker.

*Aldo's Italian*, on the corner of Gillespie and Rochester Sts, has good food (lunch is about R40), and *Villa d'Este* across the street is another Italian place, with daily specials. Next door, at 37 Gillespie St, is *Ahmed's*, a basic Indian place with seafood specials. *Taiwan*, 124 Gillespie St, near the mall, has main courses for about R22 and daily spe-cials. *Coimbra Portuguese*, 130 Gillespie St, has genuine Portuguese food. *Thatcher's*, in a block of apartments on the corner of Gil-lespie and Sea View Sts, is a sedate place with surprisingly inexpensive dishes – steaks cost from R20.

*The Haven* restaurant and bar is a small place on Tyzack between Gillespie and Erskine, with steaks and seafood – try the seafood curry (R35). It doesn't look espe-cially upmarket but the service is good. *Lord Prawn*, in the Coastlands Building (2nd floor) on the corner of West St and Marine Pde, is open daily for seafood feasts.

If you head north along North Beach Promenade you get to an enclave of eating places which overlook the sea. *Joe Kool's* is a legendary nightspot that serves reasonable food at fair prices. Next door is *Cattleman* where a steak meal is about R40. Above this is *The Deck*, a hangout for surfies and the spot for breakfast after catching those morning waves.

### City Area
*Tudor House* in the Tudor House Hotel, on West St, has inexpensive bar meals and a

slightly more expensive bistro. *Aliwal Lighthouse*, on Aliwal St next to the SAA office on the corner of Smith St, opens at 8 pm and stays open very late, sometimes until breakfast.

While you're waiting for your washing at the nearby laundrette, you can have a cheap pub lunch (from R6.50) at the *Bavarian Deli*, a pleasant bar on Prince Alfred St between West and Smith Sts.

At 267 Smith St is a Durban institution, the Royal Hotel – it has the *Royal Steakhouse* (with relatively cheap pub lunches), the *Royal Grill*, the *Ulundi* (see Indian Food in this section) and the popular (and cheapish) *Coffee Shoppe*. Most of the restaurants have a Sunday lunch deal where a buffet or set menu costs about R50 (plus drinks). On the Old Well Arcade, just off Smith St, is *Africafé*, decked out Ndebele style, and *the* place for African food.

The inexpensive outdoor *café* in Medwood Gardens on West St, near the GPO, is a good place to read your mail. Breakfast is served all day and the curry is worth trying. It's open daily except Sunday from 8.30 am to 4 pm. In the next block west, on West St, is the huge complex at No 320 with several places to eat including *At Lindis*, a casual café which serves a good breakfast for about R20.

*Roma Revolving Restaurant* (☎ (031) 37 6707) is on the 32nd floor of John Ross House at the east end of Victoria Embankment. The view is amazing and the Italian food isn't horrifyingly expensive – for two people, three courses with coffee and wine will cost around R120 or closer to R200 if you order lobster. It's open daily except Sunday for lunch and dinner; there is parking in adjacent Mills Lane.

In the Musgrave Centre, a shopping centre on Musgrave Rd in Berea, west of the city centre, *Bellissima* and *Legends* are recommended by locals. Legends stays open most of the night.

**Indian Food** Takeaway places around the city have good Indian snacks, including bunny chow (half a loaf of bread hollowed out and filled with a curry stew). It's cheap and filling.

Indian taxi drivers are a good source of information about which restaurants are currently popular. *Victory Lounge*, upstairs from a good pastry shop on the corner of Grey and Victoria Sts, is an excellent and lively café, open during the day; biryanis are R15. Other places on Grey St are the Gujarati-style *Patel's Vegetarian* (closes 3 pm), *Khyber* and *New Delhi*. Down on Gardiner St, across from the town hall, the more expensive *Taj Mahal* is reportedly very good.

*Ulundi* in the Royal Hotel is the place to sample a Bombay fish curry or lamb tharkaree. You'll spend around R50 for several courses.

### Greyville & Morningside

On Florida Rd in Morningside are several places to eat and drink. *Christina's Kitchen* near the corner of 8th St has pre-made gourmet dishes, and next door is *Christina's Restaurant*, with main courses such as roast duck for R32. Nearby is the *Keg & Thistle* pub. Upstairs there's a *Thai restaurant* with main courses at around R25. Some way further up is the *Continental Deli*, a must for Aussies hanging out for a decent salad roll. *Florida Café* is nothing special but it is around the corner from the Travellers Rest hostel and serves breakfast.

At 16 Stamford Hill Rd, in an historic building, is the atmospheric *Queen's Tavern*. Unfortunately the food is now fairly ordinary, but it's a nice place for a beer.

For some excellent food in the light, healthy and spicy Australian/Californian style, go to *Bean Bag Bohemia* (the sign says 'BBB'), on Windermere Rd at the corner of Campbell Ave (near the Florida Rd junction). The downstairs café and bar is open from 11 am and the upstairs restaurant from noon, daily. Café meals start at around R16, with larger main courses at around R40; it's recommended.

Head down Lambert Rd into Windermere Rd for some more places, including *El Turko*, corner of Innes Rd, with dolmades, dips and fresh pitta. Keep heading north on

## Greyville & Morningside

0    250    500 m

**PLACES TO STAY**

| | |
|---|---|
| 6 | Lily Shell Manor |
| 8 | Squire's Loft |
| 12 | Florida Guesthouse |
| 14 | Travellers' Rest |
| 20 | Tekweni Backpackers' |
| 21 | Hotel California (Bonkers Nightclub underneath) |

**PLACES TO EAT**

| | |
|---|---|
| 1 | RJ's Steakhouse |
| 2 | Billy the Bum's |
| 3 | El Turko |
| 5 | Mitchell Park Restaurant |

| | |
|---|---|
| 9 | Continental Deli |
| 13 | Carry Out Curry; Spar Supermarket |
| 17 | Tea Room & The Deli |
| 19 | Debonair's |
| 25 | Joop's Place |
| 26 | Sandanado's on Seventh Avenue |
| 27 | Mr Mozzie's Butchery |
| 28 | Bean Bag Bohemia |
| 31 | Queen's Tavern |

**OTHER**

| | |
|---|---|
| 4 | King's House |
| 7 | The Cube |
| 10 | Telephone Service |

| | |
|---|---|
| 11 | Post Office |
| 15 | First National Bank |
| 16 | Simply Scuba Diving Shop |
| 18 | Standard Bank |
| 22 | Windermere Shopping Centre (laundromat) |
| 23 | Keg & Thistle Pub |
| 24 | Africana Museum |
| 29 | Post Office |
| 30 | Game City Shopping Centre |
| 32 | Royal Durban Turf Club |
| 33 | Java@Java |

Windermere Rd and after a couple of blocks you'll come to *Billy the Bum's*, a trendy bar and restaurant, and next door the much more down-to-earth *RJ's Steakhouse*.

## ENTERTAINMENT
Durban is a fun city with a vibrant cultural scene and heaps of nightlife. Many events can be booked with Computicket (☎ (031) 304 2753).

The *BAT Centre*, on the Victoria Embankment and overlooking the Small Craft Harbour, is a new arts centre which is worth checking out for a range of entertainment, exhibitions, theatre and dance.

### Cinemas
*The Wheel* houses the biggest cinema complex and there are more in *The Workshop*, the *Sanlam Centre* in Pinetown, *The Pavilion* in Westville and the *Musgrave Centre*. *The Movies* (☎ (031) 37 5270) in the old Oscar Cinema on Aliwal St has arthouse fare.

The University of Natal hosts the International Film Festival in September; the *Elizabeth Sneddon Theatre* is the main venue.

### Pubs & Clubs
*The Wheel* on Gillespie St has several bars, and not far away the *Bagdad Café* on Winder St features live bands. The *London Town Pub*, complete with double-decker bus, is in the Palm Beach Hotel. *Magoo's Bar* in the Parade Hotel, Marine Pde, has a band each night. A block or so back from the beach on Hunter St, *Cool Runnings* is the place for reggae.

The Florida Rd precinct of Morningside also attracts the late-night crowd, with several pubs.

In the little enclave of Albany Grove in central Durban there are few late-night places. *The Keg & Fiddle* is at No 58, *The Grove* is in the Albany Hotel at the Smith St corner, and *Murphy's Pub* – 'open 25 hours a day eight days a week' – is at No 14.

*Le Plaza Hotel*, on the corner of Broad and St Andrews Sts, has various styles of music, from folk to jazz to pop on different nights.

Monday night is folk night; there is a small cover charge, waived if you play.

On Point Rd, *No 330* is a glossy dance club on Saturday night and an 'alternative' club on Friday night. This place plays all types of dance music – techno, hip-hop, acid house, garage – and stays open late (the steep entry fee is designed to keep out undesirables). At No 154, *Mariners* (which is also Seafarers Hostel) has bands.

In the New Berea Centre, Berea Rd, the *Rockadilly* (formerly the Hard Rock Café) plays rock music and serves pub lunches (about R6). It is closed on Sunday.

### Jazz & Jazz Fusion
The jazz scene in Durban deserves a special mention. There is a real blend of styles utilising American jazz rhythms as a base. Imagine what effect the sprinkling of Indian classical, indigenous South African and township jazz influences has on the sound.

There are plenty of venues. Rockadilly and the Queen's Tavern have been mentioned. The *Octagon Jazz Forum* is a popular jazz club on the corner of Field and Queen Sts. Other well-known jazz venues are *Bassline* on Rutherford St, *Club Zoom* at 19 Dick King St and *The Moon Hotel* at 522 South Coast Rd, Rossborough.

*The Rainbow*, 23 Stanfield Lane, Pinetown, is a monthly Sunday jazz venue attracting top musicians, black and white (R15 entry). One reader reports seeing the African Jazz Pioneers, Ladysmith Black Mambazo, and Sakhile (with jazz-fusion king Sipho Gumede) here.

### Classical Music & Theatre
The *Natal Playhouse*, opposite the city hall on Smith St, has dance, drama and music most nights. It's built in two old movie theatres, and there are restaurants. The Natal Philharmonic Orchestra has an interesting spring concert programme with weekly performances in the *Opera House*; phone ☎ (031) 304 3631 for information.

The University of Natal's Music Department has free lunchtime concerts on Monday in *Howard College*, with concerts on many evenings. On Wednesday at 1 pm, go to the city hall steps and listen to a variety of musicians and exceptional gospel choirs.

### Gay & Lesbian

There's a small gay scene in Durban. *The Riviera Hotel* in The Esplanade is probably the best place to meet people. The Bar is Durban's oldest gay club and it is open every night with a DJ on Wednesday, Friday and Saturday. The other club on the premises is *Images* (which has a mix of men and women); it's open every night except Monday. There's a small cover charge at both places. *Grumpy's Complex* in the Alexander Hotel on Point Road is another option.

On the first Sunday of each month, *Cheers*, a wine bar at 65 Pine City Centre, Imperial Lane, Pinetown, hosts a predominantly lesbian clientele.

## GETTING THERE & AWAY
### Air

Durban international airport (which used to be called Louis Botha) is off the N2, about 15km south of the city. The SAA office building is on the corner of Smith and Aliwal Sts (☎ (031) 361 1111 for bookings).

SAA flies to Cape Town (R787), East London (R490), George (R775), Jo'burg (R445), Kimberley (R536), Port Elizabeth (R536) and Richards Bay (R148). Sun Air (☎ (031) 469 3444) flies to Cape Town and Jo'burg at cheaper fares than SAA, and Comair/British Airways (☎ toll-free 0800 131 4155) might also be a cheaper way of getting to Cape Town, Jo'burg and Port Elizabeth. SA Airlink (☎ (031) 42 2676) flies to destinations including Bloemfontein (R581), Nelspruit (R581), Port Elizabeth (R536) and Umtata (R410).

A new airport is planned, to be built north of the city and to be called King Shaka.

### Bus

Most long-distance buses leave from the rear of Durban train station. If you're coming here by car, enter from NMR Ave, not Umgeni Rd. Translux (☎ (031) 361 8333) is here and Greyhound's office (☎ (031) 309

7830) is nearby. You can also book Translux and Greyhound on the beachfront at U-Tours (☎ (031) 368 2848; fax 32 8945).

The Margate Mini Coach (☎ (03931) 21600) also leaves from the rear of the station.

Don't forget the Baz Bus (☎ (021) 439 2323 or book through hostels), with its services to Cape Town and Jo'burg.

**Bloemfontein & Kimberley** Several Translux and Greyhound services stop in Bloemfontein (R160).

**Cape Town** Translux has a daily service to Cape Town (R340) via Bloemfontein. There's a daily service to Port Elizabeth which connects with a service to Cape Town. Greyhound runs to Cape Town for R350, via either Bloemfontein or the Garden Route, both daily.

**Drakensberg & Sani Pass** Sani Pass Couriers (☎ (033) 701 1017) picks up at hostels and runs via Pietermaritzburg to Underberg, Himeville and Sani Lodge three times a week.

**Illovo & Amanzimtoti** Enbee runs commuter buses to Illovo and Amanzimtoti from the Dick King Statue (on Victoria Embankment) on weekday afternoons and at 1.30 pm on Saturday.

**Margate** The Margate Mini Coach runs between Margate and Durban daily for R40 (same-day return R60). You should book seats (☎ (03931) 21406). Some services run all the way south to the Wild Coast Sun (just over the border in Eastern Cape).

**Jo'burg/Pretoria** The Translux express to Jo'burg/Pretoria (R145) via the N3 runs at least daily, taking eight hours. There's another daily service stopping at more places and taking an hour longer. Greyhound runs four times each day via the N3 to Jo'burg/Pretoria (R155). Only the 10 am bus stops at most places en route. Greyhound also has a daily service running via Richards Bay (R70), Melmoth (R80) and Vryheid (R110). The fare to Jo'burg/Pretoria is the same as on the N3 services but the trip is several hours longer.

**Pietermaritzburg** Cheetah Coaches runs to Pietermaritzburg (R23) on weekdays at 10.30 am and 4.45 pm, Friday 4.15 & 6.30 pm, Saturday 10.45 am and 2.45 pm and Sunday at 4.45 pm only. The bus leaves from Aliwal St outside the Natural Science Museum.

KWAZULU-NATAL

**Richards Bay** Interport (☎ (0351) 91791) runs north to Mandini, Gingindlovu, Mtunzini, Empangeni and Richards Bay daily at 7 am and 4.30 pm. The three hour trip to Richards Bay costs R50. The bus departs outside St Paul's on Pine St. One of Greyhound's Jo'burg buses also runs this route.

**Umhlanga Rocks** The Umhlanga Express bus (☎ (031) 561 2860) leaves from a number of points in Durban, including Pine St, Commercial Rd and the corner of Brickhill and Somtseu Rds. The fare is R9.

**Umtata & Port Elizabeth** Translux has a daily service to Port Elizabeth from Durban; stops include Kokstad (R95), Umtata (R135), East London (R165), Grahamstown (R200) and Port Elizabeth (R210). One of Greyhound's daily Cape Town services also runs this route. The fares are slightly higher but the trip is in daylight.

## Train
The huge Durban train station (☎ (031) 361 7621) is on Umgeni Rd. There's a booking desk (☎ (031) 361 8270) at the Tourist Junction, but it isn't open on weekends.

The daily *Trans Natal* (Durban-Jo'burg via Kimberley and Bloemfontein) and the weekly *Trans Oranje* (Durban-Cape Town via Newcastle) run from Durban. Some 1st/2nd/3rd class fares are:

| | |
|---|---|
| Bethlehem | R111/76/46 |
| Bloemfontein | R178/121/75 |
| Cape Town | R425/286/179 |
| Estcourt | R57/39/23 |
| Jo'burg | R164/108/67 |
| Kimberley | R213/145/90 |
| Ladysmith | R71/48/29 |
| Newcastle | R97/65/39 |
| Pietermaritzburg | R33/23/13 |

There are also commuter trains running down the coast as far as Kelso and north to Stanger. The service once ran south as far as Port Shepstone, and might do so again (☎ (031) 361 7609 for information). You can catch southbound commuter trains at the Berea train station as well as at Durban station.

## Minibus Taxi
Some long-distance minibus taxis leave from ranks in the streets opposite the Umgeni Rd entrance to the train station. To Jo'burg it's R70 and to the Swaziland border, about R65. Other taxis, running mainly to the south coast and Transkei, are around the Berea Rd station. From a rank on Theatre Lane, near the cemetery at the west end of West St, several minibuses a day run to Lusikisiki in Transkei for about R40.

## Car Rental
All the major car rental companies have offices here: Avis (☎ toll-free 08000 21111), Budget (☎ toll-free 0800 016 622) and Imperial (☎ toll-free 0800 131 000).

There are smaller companies with lower rates, including Tempest (☎ toll-free 0800 031 666) and Alisa (☎ (031) 368 1013).

## Hitching
Heading south, hitch from the N2 interchange near Albert Park. The N2 north starts at the top end of Stanger St.

## GETTING AROUND
### The Airport
A bus (☎ (031) 465 5573, after hours 21 1434) runs to the airport from the SAA office on the corner of Aliwal and Smith Sts for R20. Some hostels can get discounts and pickups for backpackers on the return trip. By taxi, the same trip costs nearly R200!

### Bus
The main DTMB (Durban Transport Management Board) terminus and information centre is on Commercial Rd across from The Workshop.

The Mynah service of small, fairly frequent buses covers most of the central and beachfront areas. The disadvantage is that the service stops early in the evening on most routes. All trips cost R2.50 and you get a slight discount if you pre-buy 10 tickets. Routes are as follows:

KWAZULU-NATAL

North Beach
> From Sandown Rd, which meets Snell Pde near Battery Beach, down Playfair Rd, Boscombe Terrace and Sea View St, to join Smith St. It then runs up Smith to Russell St and St Andrews St and returns down West St.

South Beach
> From Bell St north up Gillespie/Prince St, up Smith St to Russell St and St Andrews St, and back along West St.

Musgrave Rd Circle
> From the terminus near The Workshop north along Smith St, up Berea Rd past the Berea Centre, east along Musgrave Rd to Mitchell Park, and returns down Florida Rd, Kent Rd, Umgeni Rd (passing the train station) and Soldiers Way. Some buses (Musgrave Rd Circle via Market) take a loop past Berea train station and through the Indian area on Russell and Leopold Sts and Market Rd.

Mitchell Park Circle
> This route is the same as the Musgrave Rd route but runs anticlockwise, using West St rather than Smith St, and Field St rather than Soldiers Way.

The Ridge/Vause
> This service runs up Smith St to Berea Rd, north along Ridge Rd to Earl Haig Rd and Valley Rd, and then back along Vause Rd, Berea Rd and West St. Some buses (the Ridge via Market) make a detour along Russell St, Leopold St and Market Rd.

Tollgate
> The same as The Ridge route but runs only as far as Entabeni Hospital on Ridge Rd.

Botanic Gardens
> This route goes up Smith St and Berea Rd, then past the Botanic Gardens on Botanic Gardens Rd and Cowey Rd, down Clarence Rd and back to the city on 1st Ave and Soldiers Way. It runs clockwise and anticlockwise (using West St rather than Smith St).

Kensington/Mathias Rd
> North along Soldiers Way, 1st Ave and Windermere Rd. From Kensington it heads west into Trematon Drive and runs to North Ridge Rd and returns from there (this is the service to take to get to the Morningside restaurants). The St Mathias route keeps going north on Goodwin Drive and returns from Salisbury Rd. Both routes run past the train station.

As well as the Mynah services there are slower and less frequent full-size buses, also departing from the terminus near The Workshop. They run more routes and travel further from the city centre than Mynah. At off-peak times (8.30 am to 3.30 pm and after 5.30 pm daily), the most you will pay is R3.

### Taxi
A taxi between the beach and the train station costs about R15. Bunny Cabs (☎ (031) 32 2914) runs 24 hours – the drivers we met were honest and friendly. Other taxi companies include Eagles (☎ (031) 37 8333) and Aussies (☎ (031) 37 2345).

### Tuk-Tuk
Tuk-tuks (Asian-style three-wheelers) congregate on the beachfront near Palmer St. Over short distances their fares are lower than taxis, but for anything more than a kilometre or so the fares are comparable.

## AROUND DURBAN
### Pinetown
Pinetown, a centre of light industry, is the third biggest population centre in KwaZulu-Natal and the second largest industrial area. There are areas of this city that possess a certain charm – Paradise Valley and Marian-hill nature reserves, and the Japanese Gardens in Sarnia, for example. A visit to Pinetown gives a taste of modern South African suburbia, and shows the massive task of integration yet to be undertaken.

### Valley of 1000 Hills
The Umgeni Valley runs from the ocean at Durban to Nagle Dam, east of Pietermaritzburg. The rolling hills and traditional Zulu villages are the main reason visitors drive through here, usually on the R103 which begins in Hillcrest, off the M13 freeway. You can also get to Hillcrest from the N3 between Durban and Pietermaritzburg. If you want to see more of the valley you'll have to head north from this road, which just skirts the southern edge.

PheZulu (meaning 'high up') and the adjacent Assegay Safari Park, which features reptiles, are on the R103. These places are open daily and have touristy cultural displays.

See Organised Tours in the Durban section

for a chance to stay with a Zulu family in a traditional village.

**Places to Stay & Eat** *Chantecler* (☎ (031) 75 2613; fax 765 6101) on Clement Stott Rd, Botha's Hill, is an old-style place with singles/doubles for R105/165, with breakfast. Also in Botha's Hill, *Rob Roy* (☎ (031) 777 1305; fax 777 1364) is reminiscent of the Lookover Hotel in Stanley Kubrick's *The Shining*; single/double rooms cost from R250/330, with breakfast.

Many Durbanites visit the hills for the food. The Chantecler and Rob Roy have restaurants, and the Chantecler has music on Sunday afternoon. Other places are *Falcon Crest Estate*, 18 Old Main Rd, Botha's Hill, for pub lunches every day except Monday and a carvery meal with music on Sunday; and the *Swan & Rail* in the old Hillcrest station, Inanda Rd, for pub lunches. Several other old railway stations in the area, such as Botha's Hill and Kloof, have been renovated into English-style pubs and tea gardens.

# South of Durban

There are some good beaches on the south coast, the strip between Durban and Transkei. There are also shoulder-to-shoulder resorts for much of the 150km, and in summer there isn't a lot of room to move.

The south coast begins at Amanzimtoti, a huge resort and residential area not far from Durban international airport. South of here the major centres are Umkomaas, Scottburgh, Park Rynie and Hibberdene. This area is called the **Sunshine Coast**. From just after Hibberdene a large built-up area begins, centring on Port Shepstone and Margate. This region, the **Hibiscus Coast**, continues almost unbroken to Marina Beach near the Trafalgar Marine Reserve (see the Hibiscus Coast section). Port Edward is the last centre before Transkei and the Umtamvuna River.

**Getting There & Around**
**Air** SA Airlink (☎ (03931) 73267) flies

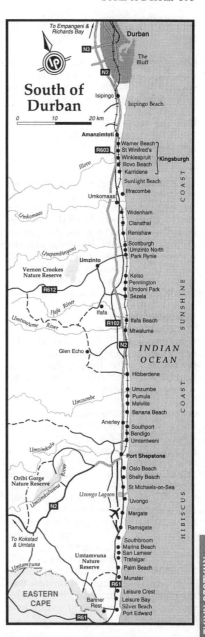

between Margate and Jo'burg daily for R440.

**Train** Commuter trains run from Durban down the coast as far as Kelso, on the northern edge of Pennington. The line further on to Port Shepstone may be reopened.

**Bus** The Margate Mini Coach runs from Durban down to Margate (R40), with some services running down to the Wild Coast Sun casino, just over the border in Eastern Cape.

**Car & Motorbike** The freeway system down the coast should reach all the way to Port Edward soon, but there's no reason not to use the old coast road – on which you don't pay tolls. Now that most traffic uses the freeway, the coast road is quite a good run, although summer weekends are very busy. The N2 (which is currently signposted as both the freeway and the coast road) runs down to Port Shepstone, where it heads west.

## SUNSHINE COAST

The Sunshine Coast stretches about 60km from Amanzimtoti to Mtwalume. All of the beaches are easily accessible from the N2, but the area suffers from its proximity to Durban – Amanzimtoti is almost in the shadow of the southern industrial areas.

### Amanzimtoti & Kingsburgh

Called 'Toti' for short, Amanzimtoti ('sweet waters') is a high-rise jungle of apartment blocks which sees over 300,000 visitors a year. It merges into Kingsburgh to the south. Winklespruit, Illovo and Karridene are beaches nearby.

The helpful Amanzimtoti Publicity Association visitors' bureau (☎ (031) 903 7493; fax 903 7382) is on Beach Rd, not far from the Inyoni Rocks. It is open from 7.45 am to 12.45 pm and 1.45 to 4.30 pm daily.

The tiny **Ilanda Wilds Nature Reserve** is on the Manzimtoti River and many birds live in its forest. Even smaller is **Umdoni Bird Sanctuary**, off Umdoni Rd. There are hides for bird-watching (over 150 species have been spotted), and feeding times are 7 am

and 3 pm; entry is free. The **Umbogovango Nature Reserve**, near the corner of Umdoni Rd and Blaze Way, has been established in an industrial area to conserve bird and tree species.

**Places to Stay** There are many caravan parks in the area. *Ocean Call Caravan Park* (☎ (031) 96 2644) is 1.5km from the train station in Winklespruit; sites are R22/40 per adult in the low/high season. *Winklespruit Resort* (☎ (031) 96 2318) is not far away. *Illovo Beach Caravan Park* (☎ (031) 96 3472) and *Villa Spa* (☎ (031) 96 4939) are at Illovo Beach. A site for two at the Villa is R45/65 (even more around Christmas), chalets are R120/150 in the low/high season.

*Angle Rock Backpackers* (☎ (031) 96 2996; email rayjan@iafrica.com) has opened at 5 Ellcock Rd in Warner Beach. It's close to the beach and they will do free pickups from Durban. Warner Beach is at the south end of Amanzimtoti and while it's still a built-up area the atmosphere is more relaxed.

*Karridene Protea* (☎ (031) 903 3355) has singles/doubles for R260/285.

There are B&Bs, flats and holiday homes; see the Amanzimtoti visitors' bureau.

### Umkomaas to Mtwalume

The main towns in this strip are Umkomaas, Scottburgh, Park Rynie, Kelso and Pennington. Umkomaas and Scottburgh have a publicity association (☎ (0323) 21364).

Off the coast road between Umkomaas and Scottburgh is **Croc World** (☎ (0323) 21103), with many crocs and other reptiles; feeding time is 3 pm on Sunday. The **Umnini Craft Stalls** are at the Shell Ultra City on the N2 between Umgababa and Widenham.

**Places to Stay** *Clansthal Caravan Park* (☎ (0323) 30211) is opposite the train station in Umkomaas. Four-person chalets cost R60 plus R10 per person; there are camp sites for R15 per person. The Scottburgh municipal *caravan park* (☎ (0323) 20291) is opposite the station. *Happy Wanderers* (☎ (0323) 51104) in Kelso is a resort on the beach about

2km from the Kelso station; it has chalets and sites.

*Blue Marlin* (☎ (0323) 21214; fax 22197), 180 Scott St, Scottburgh, costs about R125/200 for dinner, bed and breakfast. At *Cutty Sark Protea* (☎ (0323) 21230; fax 22197) in Scottburgh, singles/doubles are R250/290 with breakfast. At peak times the minimum rate is R480 a double.

There are plenty of B&Bs and out of season you might get away with R50 per person – ask at the various information centres.

### Vernon Crookes Nature Reserve

Inland from Park Rynie, off the R612 past Umzinto, this reserve has a few game animals and some indigenous forest. If you walk through the reserve beware of ticks. There are four-bed huts for R45 per person (minimum R90); entry is R6 per person. Unlike most Natal Parks Board reserves, you can book locally (☎ (0323) 42222 between 8 am and 7 pm).

### HIBISCUS COAST

This section of the south coast includes the seaside towns of Hibberdene, Port Shepstone, Shelly Beach, St Michaels-on-Sea, Uvongo, Margate, Ramsgate and Marina Beach. Port Shepstone is an unattractive industrial centre and Margate is a large, tizzy resort town which compares itself with the English Margate. Enough said. Near Port Edward the rugged coastal bush grows almost to the water's edge. Port Edward adjoins the Transkei region of Eastern Cape and the Wild Coast is to the south. Just south of town, opposite the entrance to the Wild Coast Sun hotel and casino, is the interesting **Mzamba Village market** where a range of Xhosa crafts are sold.

You can get information on these places from the South Coast Publicity Association (☎ (03931) 22322) at Main Beach, Margate.

### The Banana Express

This steam train (☎ (0391) 82 4821 for bookings) departs from Port Shepstone at 10 am on Wednesday and Saturday for day trips to

Paddock Station (R50). There are 1½-hour excursions to Izotsha at 10 am on Tuesday and Thursday and 11 am on Sunday (R24).

### Oribi Gorge Nature Reserve

Oribi Gorge is inland from Port Shepstone, off the N2. The spectacular gorge on the Umzimkulwana River is one of the highlights of the south coast. Apart from the scenery there are many animals and birds. Entry costs R6 per person.

The *Oribi Gorge Hotel* (☎ (03967) 91753), near a viewing site overlooking the gorge, has B&B for R110 per person. The Natal Parks Board has huts (R65/130 a single/double) and a cottage (R125 per person, minimum R500). You can't camp.

### Trafalgar Marine Reserve

This reserve protects ancient fossil beds, but for most visitors it is the surfing and especially sailboarding here which are the attractions. When there's a westerly wind, **Trafalgar Point** is the best place for sailboarding on the south coast.

### Umtamvuna Nature Reserve

On a gorge on the Umtamvuna River, which forms part of the border with Eastern Cape, this reserve is densely forested and in spring there are wildflowers. There are also quite a number of animals and birds, including peregrine falcons. Beware of bilharzia in the river. There is no accommodation here. To get to the reserve, head to Banner Rest, a small town south-west of Port Edward, and drive north towards Izingolweni for a few kilometres.

### Places to Stay

**Caravan Parks** There are many caravan parks, including *Villa Siesta* (☎ (039681) 3343), in Anerley, with four-person chalets from R90/180 and sites for R35/45. There are three caravan parks in Margate, all expensive. On the beach at St Andrews Ave, *De Wet* (☎ (03931) 21022) has only a few tent sites. The *Margate* (☎ (03931) 20852) is opposite the police station and sandwiched between the R620 and Valley Rd, and 1km from the beach on the corner of Varley and Hanau Sts is *Constantia* (☎ (03931) 20482). There is a good family resort in Port Edward, *Old Pont* (☎ (03930) 32211; fax 32033), with caravan and camp sites.

**Hostel** *Club Tropicana Youth Sanctuary* (☎ (039) 681 3547) is a hostel overlooking the sea near Anerley, north of Port Shepstone between Melville (Banana Beach) and Bendigo. The Margate Mini Coach stops nearby, as do the main intercity buses running the N2. It's on an old tropical fruit farm which is the headquarters for a nonprofit project teaching craft and hospitality skills to people living in traditional villages in the beautiful hinterland. You can treat this place as an ordinary hostel (dorms R20, camping R10, big meals R9), but it would be much better to stay a while and take advantage of the hikes and activities in participating villages. Better yet, volunteer your time to live in the villages and help with building trail huts, schools, clinics or whatever. This costs R30 per night, including meals, and while conditions can be basic it is probably the best bargain to be had in South Africa.

**Hotels, Apartments & B&Bs** A cheap hotel in Margate is *Sunlawns* (☎ (03931) 21078), on Uplands Rd, which charges R95 per person for dinner, bed and breakfast. There are many other hotels, resorts and self-catering apartments in Margate. Rather than trekking around, you're better off booking something through an agency such as Beach Holidays (☎ (03931) 22543; fax 73753) or the Information Centre for Holiday Accommodation (☎ (03931) 50265).

One of the nicer resorts is the *Pumula Hotel* (☎ (039) 684 6717), a little place on the beach at 67 Steve Pitts Rd in Umzumbe, south of Hibberdene. The single/double tariff, which includes meals, is R195/250, rising to R440 a double in the highest season. Less expensive hotels include the *Alexander* (☎ (039) 699 2309), on Barracuda Blvd, Hibberdene (R75/100).

In Port Shepstone the *Bedford Inn* (☎ (0391) 20419), 64 Colley St, and the *Marine Hotel*

(☎ (0391) 20281), Bisset St, are fair midrange hotels.

Nature lovers may choose to stay in the self-catering accommodation at *Clearwater Camp* (☎ (03930) 32684), overlooking the Umtamvuna River near Port Edward. Rates are just R20 per person (minimum R60).

## TRAVELLING ON

The R61, which runs north-west from Port Edward to meet the N2 12km west of Kokstad, runs through the Xhosa villages of eastern Transkei, beginning in pleasant, rolling country then, after Bizana, rising into the foothills. Coming from Port Edward, when you come to a T-intersection in a bustling little trading town turn left. Further on, the R61 splits, with the left-hand road going to Lusikisiki (and on to Port St Johns) and the right to the N2 and Kokstad.

The road is in good condition but it is narrow and the usual warnings about watching out for pedestrians and animals on the roads of ex-Homelands apply.

There are local buses and minibus taxis running between villages along this route but few run long distances, so there's a chance that the trip (about 120km between Port Edward and the N2) would take more than a day. There is no formal accommodation. However, it's worth asking around at the craft stalls near the Wild Coast Sun (across the provincial border from Port Edward) as people there might know of something.

# North of Durban

The stretch of coast from Umhlanga Rocks north to Tugela Mouth is less developed than the coast south of Durban, and the beaches are better. With lots of time-shares and retirement villages, things aren't very lively.

Before swimming at the beaches on the north coast you might want to check on the current status of the shark netting. There's no problem at Umhlanga Rocks, but further north some of the nets protecting the area have been removed.

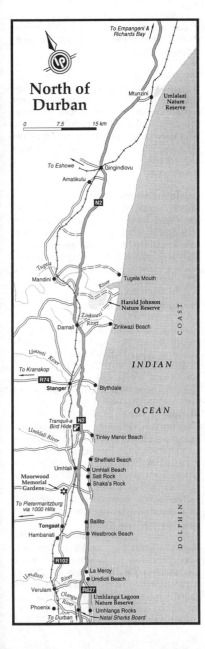

Other than some commuter services between Durban and Umhlanga there is very little public transport along the coast. There are, however, commuter trains and plenty of buses and minibus taxis between Durban and Stanger and other inland towns.

## UMHLANGA ROCKS
This resort town is only about 15km north of Durban. Umhlanga means 'place of reeds'; the 'h' is pronounced something like a 'sh', so it's beautifully onomatopoeic.

On the mall, near the intersection of Lagoon Drive and Lighthouse St (the continuation of the road in from the main Durban road), there's an information kiosk (☎ (031) 561 4257), open from 8.30 am to 4.30 pm on weekdays (closing for lunch) and Saturday morning. If you can't find out what you need to know here, try the Shaka Tours & Safaris bus kiosk nearby.

### Natal Sharks Board
The Natal Sharks Board (☎ (031) 561 1001) is a research institute dedicated to studying sharks, specifically in relation to their danger to humans. With the great white shark, a big shark with a fearsome (but perhaps undeserved) reputation for attacks on humans, frequenting the KwaZulu-Natal coast, this has more than academic interest. You can visit at 9 am Tuesday, Wednesday and Thursday; 11 am and 2 pm on Wednesday; and 2 pm on the first Sunday of the month for R10. The squeamish should note that the tour includes watching a dissection of a shark.

The Board is about 2km out of town, up the steep Umhlanga Rocks Drive (the M12 leading to the N3) – a tuk-tuk costs from R15.

### Umhlanga Lagoon Nature Reserve
This reserve is on a river mouth just north of the town. Despite its small size (26 hectares) there are many bird species. The trails lead through dune forest, across the lagoon and onto the beach. There is no entry fee. The adjacent **Hawaan Nature Reserve**, with a forest that includes rare tree species, is privately run.

KWAZULU-NATAL

## Places to Stay & Eat

**Self-Catering** Umhlanga is crowded with holiday apartments, mostly close to the beach. They fill up in the high season, when you'd be lucky to rent one for less than a week, but away from peak times it's possible to take one for as few as two days.

A two bedroom apartment costs from about R190/380 per night in the low/high seasons, and three-bedroom apartments are from R210/400. Contact Umhlanga Flat Service (☎ (031) 561 1511) or Umhlanga Accommodation (☎ (031) 561 2012).

**Hotels** Most hotels charge around R400/600 a single/double. Along Lagoon Drive you'll find *Umhlanga Rocks* (☎/fax (031) 561 1321), *Umhlanga Sands* (☎ (031) 561 2323; fax 561 4408), *Cabana Beach* (☎ (031) 561 2371; fax 561 3522), *Oyster Box* (☎ (031) 561 2223; fax 561 4072) and *Breakers* (☎ (031) 561 2271; fax 561 2722).

Most of the hotels have restaurants. A reader recommends splashing out at the *Beverley Hills Hotel*. Vegetarians are catered for at *Health Nut* in the Village Centre, on Chartwell Drive.

## Getting There & Away

A commuter bus (☎ (031) 561 2860) runs from the publicity kiosk in Umhlanga to Durban seven times a day for R9.

## Getting Around

Umhlanga has tuk-tuks and they're a cheap way to get around. There's a rank near the publicity kiosk or phone ☎ (031) 561 2860. You have to have pre-paid tickets; several shops in town sell books of tickets.

## DOLPHIN COAST

The Dolphin Coast starts at Umdloti Beach and stretches north to the Tugela River. It includes the areas of Tongaat, Ballito, Shaka's Rock, Umhlali (Salt Rock), Blythdale, Stanger, Zwinkazi and Tugela Mouth. The coast gets its name from the pods of bottlenose dolphins that frolic offshore.

The Dolphin Coast Publicity Association (☎ (0322) 61997) is near the BP service station, just where you leave the N2 to enter Ballito. They book B&Bs and list other accommodation.

## Tongaat

A big, sedate sugar town with some fine old buildings, Tongaat is on the railway running north from Durban. Many Indians live here, and there's a Jaggernath temple. There are 90-minute tours of the Maidstone **sugar mill** (☎ (0322) 24551) on Tuesday, Wednesday and Thursday at 9 and 11 am and 2 pm. Bookings are required.

## Ballito to Sheffield Beach

Ballito, Shaka's Rock, Umhlali (Salt Rock) and Sheffield Beach form a continuous settled strip, although the density of settlement is nothing like that on the south coast. They are connected by the old coast road, so you don't have to jump back and forth on the N2 to travel between them.

**Places to Stay & Eat** There are *caravan parks* in Ballito and Umhlali (Salt Rock). Most other accommodation is in apartments, and in season most are let by the week. Rental agencies in Ballito include Coastal Holiday Letting (☎ (0322) 62155). To give you an idea, a three room flat costs as little as R100 a night (from R330 in peak season).

## Stanger

This town is definitely not a resort-and-retirement enclave – it's an industrial town and altogether on the wrong side of the tracks. Most people on the street are black or Indian, and the town has a gritty, run-down feel. As the biggest service centre on this section of coast, however, it has a lively feel after all those pristine coastal villages basking in their exclusivity.

On Couper St are the **Shaka Memorial Gardens** where you can see the memorial stone erected in 1932 over Shaka's burial chamber, originally a grain pit. Shaka founded the original settlement as his capital, called KwaDukuza. He was murdered here in 1828 by his half-brother Dingaan.

The **Tranquil-a Bird Hide** (☎ (0324) 90

## Shaka Sites

Shaka established a royal settlement called *Dukuza* ('maze') on the site of present-day Stanger in July 1825. The settlement of 2000 beehive huts was intended as a halfway station between Zululand and the settlers of Port Natal (Durban). Shaka's royal residence was near the site of the old police station, in the centre of modern Stanger.

In front of the municipal offices in Roodt St is an old *mkuhla* tree (Natal mahogany), referred to as Shaka's *indaba*, where Shaka is reputed to have conducted meetings. A large fig tree stood in the Nyakambi kraal at the opposite end of Dukuza. Shaka was murdered here, by his half brothers Dingaan and Umhlanga, in September 1828.

Dukuza was abandoned and choked by weeds until the site was surveyed for the town of Stanger in 1872. Other sites in town associated with Shaka are the Mavivane execution cliff, north of the R74 at the end of Lindley St, and the Mbozambo Valley (now the site of Shakaville township). Known as his 'playground', it's where Shaka reputedly bathed and relaxed. ∎

2222) is south of Stanger at the Sappi Paper mill. Newman (of the bird-book fame) saw 48 species here in less than two hours. There's no entry fee but you have to collect a key from the mill security; visits are restricted to two hours.

**Places to Stay** The friendly *Victoria Hotel* (☎ (0324) 21803; fax 24896) is on the corner of Couper and Reynolds Sts. Single/doubles cost R90/130, or R70/100 with shared bathroom, both including breakfast. The *Luthando Hotel* (☎ (0324) 22208; fax 23237) on King George Rd costs about the same.

### Blythdale

Blythdale is a quiet town with a sandy beach and decidedly noisy surf. *La Mouette Caravan Park* (☎ (0324) 22547) has sites from R44 for two people in the low season rising to R135 for four (minimum) in the December holidays. *Mini Villas* (☎ (0324) 21277) has bungalows which sleep six, costing from R90/250 in the low/highest seasons; during

school holidays there's a minimum stay of up to a week. North of Blythdale, *Zinkwazi Resort* (☎ (0324) 3344; fax 3340) has chalets and sites at similar prices.

Occasional minibus taxis or buses run between Blythdale and Stanger, 7km away.

### Tugela Mouth

The Tugela River, once an important tribal boundary, enters the sea here to end its journey from Mont-aux-Sources in the Drakensberg. Several major battles took place near the river mouth, notably the Battle of Ndondasuka in which Cetshwayo defeated his brother, Mbuyasi, and many thousands were killed.

The **Harold Johnson Nature Reserve** is on the south bank of the Tugela, east of the highway. Entry is R6 per person and tent sites cost R17 per person. There's a crocodile dam where feeding time is 2 pm Saturday (summer only). Nearby are the ruins of Fort Pearson, a small British fort from the Anglo-Zulu War of 1879, and the **Ultimatum Tree**, where the British presented their demands to Cetshwayo's representatives in 1878.

# Zululand

For many travellers in South Africa this is the first and often the only taste they get of the real Africa. It is a region dominated by one tribal group, the Zulu, and a place replete with their customs, historical traditions and culture. The name Zulu ('heaven') comes from an early chief. His descendants were *abakwaZulu*, or people of Zulu.

Zululand covers a large part of central KwaZulu-Natal and extends in a rough triangle from the Tugela River mouth to Kosi Bay on the border of Mozambique, across to Vryheid, and back to Tugela Mouth. The area east of the N2 and north of the Mtubatuba-St Lucia road is known as Maputaland and is covered separately later in this chapter. North of the Tugela you'll find the Zulu capital, Ulundi, the large port of Richards Bay, the big adjacent Hluhluwe-Umfolozi

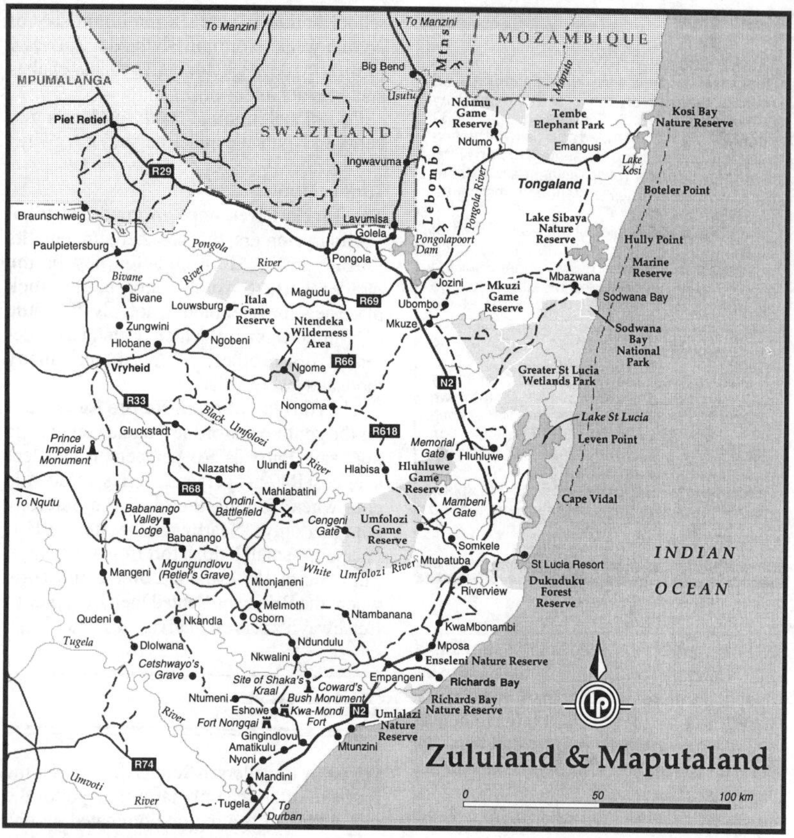

Zululand & Maputaland

0    50    100 km

Park (see the Maputaland section), and many traditional Zulu villages.

Much of Zululand is a mass of attractive rolling hills. The climate becomes steadily hotter as you go north and summers are steamy and almost tropical, thanks to the warm Indian Ocean. Although few white South Africans live here, there are several major holiday centres, especially in the St Lucia area.

The humid coastal air causes frequent dense mists on the inland hills, with visibility cut to a few metres. Be careful of pedestrians and animals suddenly appearing around a

corner. In the sugar areas slow-moving vehicles are common.

### Warning

There is malaria in Zululand and other places in the north of KwaZulu-Natal, and bilharzia in some waterways and dams.

### GINGINDLOVU

After crossing the Tugela River, the first town of any size is Gingindlovu ('the swallower of the elephant'), at the junction of the R68 to Eshowe and the N2 north. It was once one of Cetshwayo's strongholds. Two battles of the Anglo-Zulu War of 1879 were fought in the vicinity – the town itself was razed.

In town there's the mid-range *Imperial Hotel* (☎ (0353) 30 1202) on Main Rd, but it's tempting to splurge on *Mine Own Guest House* (☎ (0353) 30 1262; fax 30 1025), a very fine old homestead on a sugar plantation, with B&B from R400 a double.

Perhaps the best and certainly the cheapest souvenir of South Africa is the booklet-style brochure for *Inyezane* (☎ (083) 255 7345; email inyezane@dbn.lia.net), a great new hostel on an old plantation near Gingindlovu. Maybe the next best souvenir will be the one you make for yourself while you stay there – there are regular craft workshops, as well as plenty of other events from Zulu music to battlefield walks to learning about medicinal plants. Accommodation is in huts, either dorms (R30), tiny singles (R50) or doubles, one with an en suite (R180). It's quirky, a little rough around the edges and great fun.

The Interport bus between Durban and Richards Bay stops in Gingindlovu, from where it's 3km to Inyezane. Phone and they'll pick you up.

## MTUNZINI

If you want to stay on the coast while exploring this part of KwaZulu-Natal, Mtunzini makes a good base. You can get information from the Trade Winds (☎ (0353) 40 1411).

This quiet coastal town had a colourful beginning. John Dunn, the first European to settle in the area, was granted land by Cetshwayo. He became something of a chief himself, took 49 wives and fathered 117 children. He held court here under a tree, hence the town's name – *mtunzi* is Zulu for shade.

Near the mouth of the Mlalazi River there is lush tropical forest where you'll find the **Raffia Palm Monument**. The raffia palm is monocarpic, meaning that it only seeds once in its 25 year cycle, and its presence this far south is a mystery. Its closest relatives are found in the far north of Tongaland, near Kosi Bay, and it is believed that this unusual grove was planted around 1910 from seeds

## Zulu Leaders

See Facts about the Region for the early history of the Zulu people. Briefly, the small Zulu clan had become a huge and disruptive force in Southern Africa under the fanatical leader Shaka Zulu. Dingaan, Shaka's successor, continued the reign of terror and murdered the party of trekboers lead by Piet Retief. That massacre was avenged at the Battle of Blood River, when 3000 Zulu were slaughtered.

After the disaster of Blood River, facing internal dissent and further attacks by the Boers and the British colonists, Dingaan lost support and fled to Swaziland, where he was killed in 1840. His successor, Mpane, has been seen as a puppet ruler installed by the Europeans, but there is evidence that he played off the British and Boers against each other. Nevertheless, during his reign much Zulu land was signed over to European interests, especially to the British who had by this stage established the colony of Natal. He was succeeded by his son Cetshwayo in 1873.

Cetshwayo inherited a reasonably stable kingdom but pressures from the land-grabbing Boers in Transvaal was growing. While the British colonial government in Natal agreed that Boer encroachment was illegal it gave little assistance to the Zulu, largely because the British had plans of their own – a grand imperial scheme of a British wedge into Africa heading north from Durban. The Zulu kingdom was directly in the way. Diplomatic chicanery ended with a British ultimatum with which Cetshwayo could not comply, and in January 1879, the British invaded the kingdom, beginning the Anglo-Zulu War.

The Zulu decisively defeated the British at the Battle of Isandlwana but failed to capture the small station at Rorke's Drift, despite overwhelming superiority in numbers. After that things went downhill and on 4 July at Ulundi, Cetshwayo was defeated.

Cetshwayo was jailed and his power was divided between 13 British-appointed chiefs, many of whom opposed him. In 1882 Cetshwayo travelled to England to plead for his restoration, but the British response was to partition the kingdom according to the pro and anti-Cetshwayo factions. This lead to chaos and bloodshed, and in 1887, the British annexed Zululand. Dinizulu, Cetshwayo's son and the last independent Zulu king, was exiled to St Helena in the Cape Province. In 1897 the British handed over Zululand to the colony of Natal.

The current Zulu king is King Goodwill Zwelithini but tussling for power is Chief Mangosuthu Buthelezi, leader of the IFP, great-grandson of Cetshwayo, and a cabinet member in the new South African government. ■

obtained near Maputo. There is a wooden boardwalk through the grove and you might spot the rare palmnut vulture *(Gypohierax angolensis)*, which favours raffia palms.

### Umlalazi Nature Reserve

The entrance to Umlalazi ('place of the whetstone') Nature Reserve is 1.5km east of the town, on the coast. There are some crocodiles here, as well as plentiful bird life in the dense vegetation of the sand-dune forest and mangrove swamp. There are three walking trails.

Entry is R6 per person. This is a Natal Parks Board reserve, so book accommodation other than camp sites in Pietermaritzburg or Durban. Camp sites (book on ☎ (0353) 40 1836) are R22 per person, five-bed log cabins are R100 per person.

### Places to Stay

There are two caravan parks in town, *Xaxaza* (☎ (0353) 40 1843) and nearby *Casa Benri* with sites from around R15 per person (R35 in season) and cabins. However, it's a 4km walk to the beach from here, so if you want to be on the coast you'd be better off staying at the Umlalazi Nature Reserve.

*Trade Winds Hotel* (☎ (0353) 40 1411; fax 40 1629), on the main street, is a friendly place and has singles/doubles from R130/220 with breakfast (less on weekends). *Forest Inn* (☎ (0353) 40 1431; fax 40 1363) on the highway is similar.

*Mtunzini Chalets* (☎ (0353) 40 1953) are in dune forest near the coast and cost from R78 per person (minimum R216), rising to R86 (minimum R258) during school holidays.

### RICHARDS BAY

The port at Richards Bay is second to Durban's in size, but it handles more cargo than any other in the province. The town feels as though it was meticulously planned for a boom which hasn't quite happened yet. It's spread out, with tourist-oriented facilities a long way from what passes for the centre.

The Richards Bay Publicity Association (☎ (0351) 31111; fax 31897), at 48 Anglers

Rd, has information on things to do in the region.

### Places to Stay

The municipal *caravan park* (☎ (0351) 31971; fax 31897) has camp sites. It's near the harbour and the beach at the end of the road in from Empangeni.

The town's hotels are pricey. Cheapest, at R230 for a room with two double beds, is *Quay West* (☎ (0351) 53 3065).

### Getting There & Away

Interport (☎ (0351) 91791) runs to Durban daily at 6 am. The three hour trip costs R50. Greyhound also stops here on one of its runs between Durban and Jo'burg.

### EMPANGENI

Empangeni (pronounced m'pan-*gay*-nee) started out as a sugar town, but the huge eucalypt plantations nearby are rivalling the cane in importance to the town's economy. It's a jumping-off point for the coast and the inland areas of Zululand.

### Places to Stay & Eat

The *Imperial Hotel* (☎ (0351) 92 1522), at 52 Maxwell St, has singles/doubles for R160/240, or R130/180 with shared bathroom. There's also the more expensive *Royal Hotel* (☎ (0351) 21601) on Turnbull St.

The restaurant in the Royal is called *Palms* and next door is a *Portuguese restaurant* known for its prawn piri-piri. There are also a *Spur* and a *Mike's Kitchen* in town.

*Harbour Lights* (☎ (0351) 96 6239) is a caravan park (not a brand of cigarettes) off the N3 between Empangeni and Richards Bay, with dorms and private rooms.

### Getting There & Away

The daily Interport (☎ (0351) 91791) bus between Durban and Richards Bay runs past Empangeni.

### ENSELENI NATURE RESERVE

This small reserve, 13km north-east of Empangeni on the N2, is on a bend in the Nseleni River. As well as game species and zebra there are hippo and crocodile in the river. There are several walks (the longest is a 5km swamp trail) but no accommodation. The reserve is open daily between 8 am and 5 pm.

## WINDY RIDGE GAME PARK

About 20km north-west of Empangeni, 10km beyond Heatonville, Windy Ridge (☎ (0351) 23465; fax 27206) has a large variety of animals in its 1300 hectares, including white rhino and crocodile. This area was once the hunting ground of Zulu kings. You can drive through the park or go on a guided walk. There are inexpensive huts but you can't camp.

## ESHOWE

This town, on the R68, is inland in the misty Zululand hills. The name Eshowe is said to be the sound the wind made when passing through the trees. Eshowe was Cetshwayo's stronghold before he moved to Ondini, and like Ondini, Eshowe was destroyed during the Anglo-Zulu War. The British occupied the site and built Fort Nongqai in 1883, establishing Eshowe as the administrative centre of their newly captured territory.

For information, the Eshowe Publicity Association (☎ (0354) 41141) is worth a visit.

### Things to See & Do

If you arrive on a day of thick mist, seeing *anything* might be a problem. In the mud-and-brick three turreted **Fort Nongqai** is the Zululand Historical Museum, open daily from 10 am to 5 pm; entry is by donation. The fort has only three towers because, according to rumour, it collapsed while it was being built and they couldn't salvage enough bricks to complete the fourth tower. In the museum is a copy of *The Sausage Wrapper*, an early news sheet. It contains a quite funny parody of Henry Rider-Haggard.

The shop here sells souvenirs, crafts and some interesting books. Perhaps coincidentally, the white staff member persuaded me to buy *Fearful Hard Times*, a fairly gung-ho account of the 1879 siege and relief of British

forces in Eshowe (hardback, R179), while the black staff member sold me *The Destruction of the Zulu Kingdom*, the story of the aftermath of the Anglo-Zulu War (paperback, R63).

From the museum you can walk to **Mpushini Falls**, but don't swim or drink the water as there is bilharzia.

The **Dlinza Forest Reserve** is a 200 hectare strand of forest – on a misty day this is an eerie place. There are a few animals, rich bird life and walking trails, some of them believed to have been made by British soldiers stationed here after the Anglo-Zulu War.

Bird-watchers should look for crowned eagles *(Stephanoaetus coronatus)*, green coucals *(Ceuthmochares aereus)*, Narina trogons *(Apaloderma narina)* and Delegorgue's pigeon *(Columba delegorguei)*.

### Places to Stay & Eat

The *Eshowe Caravan Park* (☎ (0354) 41141), run by the municipality, costs around R25 for a site. It's some way from the town centre but close to Dlinza Forest. Follow Osborn Rd west, continue along Main Rd as it doglegs, and turn right onto Saunders St. The park is on your left after a couple of blocks.

It was still under construction when we called, but the new *hostel* behind the George Hotel seems as though it will be a good one, with two or three-bed rooms, a good outside area and trips available. Check other hostels for brochures or call the hotel.

The *George Hotel* (☎ (0354) 74919) is fair and charges R148/168 a single/double (more for air-con) and R125 for a single with shared bath.

### Getting There & Away

The minibus taxi and bus park is at the old railway station, off Main Rd near Osborn Rd. The fare to Empangeni is R15 and to Melmoth (the best place to catch taxis deeper into Zululand) it's R8.

Washesha Buses (☎ (0354) 74504) runs several services in the area, including a scenic but rough run on dirt roads through forest areas to Nkandla for R14. There's no

KWAZULU-NATAL

accommodation at Nkandla but you can get a taxi from there to Melmoth, where there's a hotel. A bus from Eshowe to Empangeni costs R10 and this is also a dirt-road run through rural areas. Washesha (the name means 'hurry' in Zulu) is pretty reliable, but on dirt roads rain can strand the buses. For more information ask at the office, behind KFC on the main street. Washesha also has a very cheap service to Durban – R16.

## AROUND ESHOWE

**Entumeni Nature Reserve**, larger than Dlinza, preserves indigenous mist-belt forest and has some animals and many birds. It's 16km west of town, off the road to Ntumeni and Nkandla; entry is free. On the south-east side of Eshowe, off the R68, the **Ocean View Game Park** has some animals and many birds; it is open from 7 am to 5 pm daily.

Head east from Eshowe on the Gezinsela road (the continuation of Kangella) for a few kilometres and you'll come to Imbomboty-ana (Signal Hill to the British in the Anglo-Zulu War). From here there are good views, sometimes all the way to the coast.

## NKWALINI VALLEY

Shaka's kraal, KwaBulawayo, once loomed over this beautiful valley but today the valley is regimented into citrus orchards and can-efields rather than impis. A marker shows where the kraal was. From Eshowe head north for 6km on the R68 and turn off to the right onto the P230 (a dirt road which will eventually get you to the R34 and Empangeni) and keep going for about 20km.

Across the road from the KwaBulawayo marker is **Coward's Bush**, now just another marker, where warriors who returned from battle without their spears or who had received wounds in the back were executed.

Further west, a few kilometres before the P230 meets the R68, the **Mandwe Cross** was erected in the 30s against the wishes of the Zulu. There are good views from the hill.

### Stewart's Farm

The old Stewart's Farm tourist trap has been taken over by a local Zulu family and is

operated as a craft and cultural centre (☎ (03546) 644), with the proceeds supporting a health clinic. The craft shop is open daily (closed for lunch) and a tour of the kraal, with dancing and traditional meals, is by appointment only.

Take the R34, which runs east to Empangeni from the R68 near Nkwalini village, which is about 20km north of Eshowe on the R68. Turn off the R34 onto a dirt road about 6km east of the intersection with the R68. From here it's 5km on a dirt road, the last section of which is very difficult when wet.

### Mfuli Game Ranch

This ranch is off the R34, 13km east of the R68. Although there isn't yet a lot of game on this new ranch (☎ (0354600) 620) it is a friendly place in nice country and is a good base for the region. Accommodation is in self-contained cabins and costs R150/230 for singles/doubles; in the high season add about 20%. There's a good restaurant here.

### Shakaland

Created as a set for the telemovie *Shaka Zulu* and managed by the Protea chain (complete with have-a-nice-day reception staff), this isn't exactly a genuine Zulu village. The Nandi Experience, a display of Zulu culture and customs, is held daily at 11 am and 12.30 pm and costs R50. (Nandi was Shaka's mother.) The 'experience' plus accommodation costs R340/560 for dinner, bed and breakfast.

Shakaland (☎ (0354600) 912; fax 824) is at Norman Hurst Farm, Nkwalini, a few kilometres off the R68 and 14km north of Eshowe.

### KwaBhekithunga Zulu kraal

This craft centre on the road into Nkwalini (Shakaland) is a genuine Zulu village, although it doesn't look much like a traditional one. A live-in 'Zulu Experience' is offered here too, but only for large groups. Phone ☎ (0354600) 644 to book if you can muster 15 or more people. Even if you can't, it's worth visiting for the handicraft centre.

## MELMOTH

Named after the first Resident Commissioner of Zululand, Melmoth is a small town dozing in the hills, on the point of going to seed. Until recently the major local industry was the harvesting of wattle bark.

### Place to Stay

*Melmoth Inn* (☎ (03545) 2074; fax 2075), on Victoria St, has singles/doubles without bath for R110/160, including breakfast (a double with bath is R170). The rooms are ordinary but it's a friendly place with a nice bar and a fair restaurant with somnambulistic service.

## ULUNDI

Ulundi was the capital of the KwaZulu Homeland, and there is a possibility that it will replace Pietermaritzburg as the capital of KwaZulu-Natal. The town is new but this area has been the stronghold of many Zulu kings, and several are buried in the area. Although Ulundi is a small town it is spread out, with residential areas dotted around the neighbouring countryside. The town itself offers little to see, but there are important historical sites in the area.

For information go to the KwaZulu Monuments Council (☎ (0358) 79 1854) at Ondini. Their interesting booklet *Ulundi: Yesterday, Today, Tomorrow* (R10) seems to be a plug for Ulundi to be the provincial capital.

The former **KwaZulu Legislative Assembly** is just north of the railway line, and has some interesting tapestries and a statue of Shaka. The building isn't always open to visitors.

Opposite the Legislative Assembly is the site of King Mpande's *iKhanda* (palace), **kwaNodwengu**. Mpande won control from Dingaan after the disaster at Blood River. He seized power with assistance from the Boers, but Zululand declined during his reign. The king's grave is here, and a small museum.

Close to Ulundi is **Fort Nolela**, near the drift on the White Umfolozi River where the British camped before attacking Ondini in 1879, and **KwaGqokli**, where Shaka celebrated victory over the Ndwandwe in 1818.

Another place of great significance to the Zulu is **eMakhosini**, Valley of the Kings. The great *makhosi* (chiefs) Nkhosinkulu (Zulu), Senzangakhona (father of Shaka, Dingaan and Mpande) and Dinizulu are buried here.

### Ondini

Ondini ('the high place') was established as Cetshwayo's capital in 1873, but it was razed by British troops after the Battle of Ulundi (4 July 1879), the final engagement of the 1879 Anglo-Zulu War.

It took the British nearly six months to defeat the Zulu army but the Battle of Ulundi went the way of most of the campaign, with the number of Zulu deaths 10 to 15 times higher than British deaths. Part of the reason for the British victory at Ulundi was that they adopted the Boer laager tactic, with troops forming a hollow square to protect the cavalry, which attacked only after the Zulu army had spent itself trying to penetrate the walls.

The **royal kraal** section of the Ondini site is still being rebuilt, but you can see where archaeological digs have uncovered the floors of identifiable buildings. The floors, of mud and cow dung, were preserved by the heat of the fires which destroyed the huts above them. The huge area is enclosed in a defensive perimeter of gnarled branches, some of which act as fencing for a herd of white Nguni cattle, prized by Zulu kings.

Also at Ondini is the **KwaZulu Cultural-Historical Museum** (entry R4), with good exhibits on Zulu history and culture and an excellent audiovisual show. You can buy souvenirs, including some interesting books.

To get to Ondini, take the airport turn-off from the highway just south of Ulundi and keep going for about 5km on a dirt road. This road continues on to Hluhluwe-Umfolozi Park. Minibus taxis occasionally pass Ondini.

### Mgungundlovu

This was Dingaan's capital from 1829 to 1839, and it's here that Piet Retief and the other Voortrekkers were killed by their host

## A Zulu Dwelling

At Ondini, in the main museum, there is a reconstruction of a Zulu dwelling *(indlu)* with all the goods and chattels of a traditional home. A collection of indlu, often surrounded by a palisade, was known as an *imuzi*, or homestead.

The indlu was circular and the archetypal 'beehive' shape. A number of pliable branches would be bound together to form a dome. These would then be covered with a woven grass mat before thatching was added. The binding string was made from the umbrella thorn tree *(Acacia tortillis)*. The floor is ant bed (crushed termite soil) mixed with clay and fresh cow dung. There was no chimney as the smoke was used to kill insects in the thatch.

The **entrance** was kept clear as the ancestral spirits gathered there. It was also small, forcing people entering to stoop low in respect. In front of the entrance was the **hearth**, also important to ancestors *(amadlozi)* as a place to get warmth and food.

JEFF WILLIAMS

On one side of the indlu, women would prepare food, sleep, grind meal, eat, and weave. The men kept to the other side where they would eat, sleep, socialise, drink sorghum beer and do woodwork.

At the back of the indlu, directly opposite the entrance, is the **unsamo**. It was used to store utensils and prepared food, especially meat, sour milk and sorghum beer. Precious objects were also kept here. The unsamo was sacred to the amadlozi as it was here that prayers and offerings to them would be made. ■

Zulu huts are a major feature of the landscape throughout KwaZulu-Natal

---

in 1838, the event which precipitated the Boer-Zulu War. The site of the *iKhanda* is being restored and there's a small museum and a monument to the Voortrekkers nearby. In 1990 excavations revealed the site of Dingaan's *ndlunkulu* (great hut). The museum is open daily from 8 am to 5 pm and guides take visitors around the current archaeological excavations.

The site is 5km off the R34, running between Melmoth and Vryheid. Turn off to the left (west) about 5km north-east of the intersection with the R66 to Ulundi. There are several variations of the spelling of Mgungundlovu, such as Ungungundhlovu.

### Places to Stay

*Ulundi Holiday Inn Garden Court* (☎ (0358) 21121) has singles/doubles from R274/318. Out at Ondini (☎ (0358) 79 1223) there's accommodation in traditional *umuzi* ('bee-

hive' huts) for R65 per person, with dinner and breakfast. Unless you've made other arrangements you must be there by 6 pm.

### Getting There & Away

The minibus taxi park is opposite the Holiday Inn. To Eshowe the fare is R18, to Vryheid R14 and to Jo'burg about R60.

### BABANANGO

This village is on the R68 between Melmoth and Dundee. Babanango (literally, 'father, there it is') is near interesting battlefields. An essential stop is Stan's pub. His *Babanango Hotel* (☎ (0358) 35 0029), near the police station and the town's main crossroads, is rough around the edges but exudes atmosphere. Dinner, bed and breakfast costs R150 per person. *Hall's Habitat* (☎ (0358) 350 035), Lot 6 Wilson St, is a good B&B charging R340 a double.

Another excellent place is *Babanango Valley Lodge* (☎ /fax (0358) 35 0062) on historic Goudhoek Farm in the beautiful Nsubeni Valley. A double with dinner and breakfast costs from R550. It is run by John and Meryn Turner, extremely friendly hosts. John organises tours of nearby battlefields for R100 per person. He's an outstandingly good guide who has a knack of communicating his enthusiasm. This sylvan valley is quite isolated, off the R68 about halfway between Melmoth and Dundee. Turn north off the R68 about 4km west of Babanango and continue on (stay left at the fork) for about 12km – you are on the right track if you head down a very steep hill.

# Maputaland

Maputaland is one of the wildest and most fascinating regions of South Africa and an absolute must for nature lovers. It takes its name from the Maputo River which splits, on the border of Mozambique and South Africa, into the Usutu and Pongola rivers.

This section includes Hluhluwe-Umfolozi Park, the Pongola area, and all of the region north of the Mtubatuba-St Lucia road and to the north-east of the N2. Maputaland is sparsely settled and much of it is protected in parks and reserves. It contains three huge lakes, including the significant St Lucia Wetlands; the last wild elephants in the country in Tembe reserve; coral reefs; and many game reserves with all of the Big Five represented.

Sea-fishing is a major attraction and the coral reefs are popular with divers – and also with sharks. You'd be unwise to dive without consulting locals.

### Getting There & Away

With the collapse of Transtate's services in KwaZulu-Natal, getting around this area by public transport isn't simple, but it is possible. There is a good network of minibus taxis, and local bus companies are filling the void left by Transtate. However, timetables and routes are still vague, so be prepared for delays and hassles. But then, this is Africa.

One of Greyhound's daily Durban/Jo'burg services runs through the area, stopping in Gingindlovu (R65 from Durban, R155 from Jo'burg), Richards Bay (R70, R155), Empangeni (R70, R155), Melmoth (R80, R155) and Vryheid (R110, R125).

The Baz Bus also runs up the coast on the run between Durban and Johannesburg via Swaziland.

### KWAMBONAMBI

KwaMbonambi (often called just 'Kwambo') is a tiny but lush and beautiful town off the N2 about 30km north of Empangeni and the same distance south of Mtubatuba. There would be no reason to stop here, except that it has two hostels, making it an ideal base for backpackers exploring St Lucia, Hluhluwe/Umfolozi and other attractions in northern Zululand and Maputaland.

One of the hostels says that KwaMbonambi means 'place of the gathering of kings', the other that it means 'place of the blacksmith', as Shaka's spears were made here.

### Places to Stay

*Cuckoos Nest* (☎ (035) 580 1001/2), 28 Albizia St, is a pleasant, relaxed hostel with few rules and lots of activities. Breakfast and dinner are available. Dorms are R25, doubles are R75 and you can put up your tent for R18. They offer trips to Umfolozi Game Reserve and Sodwana Bay, and excursions (sometimes free) to a secluded stretch of beach where they have beach camping. There's a boat and they can arrange dive courses.

The other hostel, *Amazulu* (☎ (035) 580 1009; email amazulu@cdrive.co.za), 5 Killarney Place, is a pretty fabulous place with a variety of accommodation including doubles with air-con (R80), small dorms (R20), some tiny singles by the pool (which is a decent size), a huge dorm for groups and camping (R15). Africa South tours operate from here, so there are plenty of well-organised trips. They do pickups from Richards Bay and also from Durban a couple of times a week.

How to choose between the hostels? Both are very friendly. Amazulu's facilities are excellent but that doesn't mean that Cuckoos Nest's aren't good. Cuckoos Nest would be the place to hang out for a while, but then Amazulu is good for a bit of a comfortable breather between grottier hostels ... sorry, I can't recommend one over the other.

### Getting There & Away

Greyhound and Interport run to Richards Bay from Durban (R65), and Greyhound runs there from Jo'burg (R145).

### MTUBATUBA

This is a trading town, busy on weekends, but the main reason to visit is that buses and minibus taxis run through here on the way south to Durban, north to Pongola (via Mkuze and Hluhluwe) and west into Zululand. Coming from those destinations, Mtubatuba is the stop for St Lucia. St Lucia Resort is about 25km east (R4 by minibus

taxi). The name comes from a local chief, Mthubuthubu, meaning 'he who was pummelled out', referring to a difficult birth.

On the southern side of Mtubatuba is **Riverview**, a poor but neat town with a sugar mill.

**Dukuduku Forest Reserve** (including Mihobi Nature Reserve), on the R620 between Mtubatuba and St Lucia, is one of the largest remaining coastal forests in KwaZulu-Natal. It is home to many varieties of butterfly as well as other insects, birds and animals. There are walking trails and a nice picnic spot. Camping is not permitted.

### Places to Stay

The *Sundowner Hotel* (☎ (035) 550 0153) is an older place and a bit run-down but it has a good atmosphere and friendly Portuguese managers. Singles/doubles are R80/150, or R70/130 with shared bath; breakfast is included. They say that they intend to offer backpacker beds for about R40. Heading into Mtubatuba from the N2, turn right at the T-intersection at the edge of town (ie towards Riverview) and the hotel is nearby on the right.

*Mtubatuba* (☎ (035) 550 0538), 243 Celcis Drive, is a good B&B which charges R145/250. It also has a self-catering unit.

### DUMAZULU

Probably the best of the 'Zulu experience' villages, Dumazulu (☎ (035) 562 0144 for bookings) is east of the N2, north of Mtubatuba. Four shows are held daily for about R50 and lunch and dinner are available. There's accommodation for about R240 per person, with breakfast.

### HLUHLUWE

Hluhluwe village (roughly pronounced 'shloo-shloo-wee') is equidistant from the Memorial Gate of Hluhluwe-Umfolozi Park and the north of the Greater St Lucia Wetlands.

You can get information on accommodation and activities in the region from Zululand Information Services (☎ (035) 562 0353) at 15 Main St. There is as good a selection of Zulu baskets, beadwork and other handicrafts as you will see anywhere (and at much lower prices than most shops) at Ilala Weavers (☎ (035) 562 0630); make an appointment to visit.

## Places to Stay

The *Sisalana Hotel* (☎ (035) 562 0177) has chalets, for R150 per person, and rooms. Also in town is the *Hluhluwe Hotel* (☎ /fax (035) 562 0251) with dinner, bed and breakfast for around R300.

*Bonamanzi* (☎ (035) 562 0181), south of Hluhluwe village, is a private reserve with a range of accommodation including self-catering tree houses for about R220 a double.

## HLUHLUWE-UMFOLOZI PARK

The two reserves were first proclaimed in 1897 and today they are among the best in South Africa. They don't adjoin, but a 'corridor' between them allows animals to move freely from one park to the other. The reserves, now combined into one park, and the corridor have a combined area of nearly 100,000 hectares.

Both reserves have lion, elephant, many rhino (black and white), giraffe and other animals and birds. The land is quite hilly except on the river flats: the White Umfolozi River flows through Umfolozi, and the Black Umfolozi forms the northern border of the park; the Hluhluwe River bisects Hluhluwe, and the dam on it attracts game.

The park is best visited in winter as the animals can range widely without congregating at water sources, although the lush vegetation sometimes makes viewing difficult. However, summer visits can also be very rewarding, especially at Umfolozi where there is more open savanna country.

Entry to each reserve is R6 per person, R25 per vehicle.

The reserves are in a malarial area and there are plenty of mosquitos, so come prepared.

Maybe I was lucky, but in a couple of days in Umfolozi (in mid-November) I saw so many white rhinos at close quarters that I became almost blasé about them.

**Jon Murray**

## Wilderness Trails

One of Umfolozi's main attractions is its trail system, open from March to the end of November, in a special 24,000 hectare wilderness area. Accompanied by an armed ranger and donkeys to carry supplies, hikers spend three days walking in the reserve; the average distance covered each day is from 12 to 15km. The first and last nights are spent at a base camp, with two nights out in the wilderness area. Bookings are accepted up to six months in advance and it's advisable to book early, with alternative dates if possible. The cost is R880 per person, including all meals and equipment, and a 50% deposit is required. On weekends there is a two night trail which costs R495 per person. A variation on this is the 'primitive trail', on which you provide everything except food and carry it all yourself. Taking a primitive trail might be more fun as you get to participate more – hikers must sit up in 90-minute watches during the night, for example.

There is a hitch, though: both types of hikes require parties of eight and these must be pre-arranged: the Natal Parks Board doesn't make up groups. Trail bookings can be made on ☎ (035) 550 1261.

Hluhluwe offers guided day walks of two to three hours for R25 per person (no children under 12).

## Tours

Several tours include Hluhluwe-Umfolozi. One inexpensive option is the three day trip with Tekweni Ecotours (☎ (031) 303 1199; fax 303 4369), which also takes in the Greater St Lucia Wetlands. However, unless you are watching every rand you're better off hiring a car and travelling at your own pace through the park.

## Places to Stay & Eat

Book accommodation through the Natal Parks Board in Pietermaritzburg or the agent in Durban's Tourist Junction.

In Hluhluwe, *Hilltop Camp* (☎ (035) 562 0255; fax 562 0113), at the top of a forested ridge, has absolutely stupendous views over the Hluhluwe section of the park and Zulu-

1 Dugandlovu Camp
2 Hilltop Lodge;
   Mtwazi Lodge
3 Muntulu
4 Munyawaneni
5 Thiyeni Waterhole
6 Sontuli
7 Gqoyeni
8 Mpila Camp
9 Nselwesi
10 Masinda Camp
11 Mndindini
12 Mphafa Waterhole

**Greater St Lucia Wetlands & Hluhluwe-Umfolozi Park**

land. It is a great place to stay; self-catering two and four-bed chalets cost from R165 per person (minimum R248); rondavels without bath are R80 per person (minimum R206); and two-bed non-catering chalets are R206/330 a single/double. *Mpunyane Restaurant* serves game dishes at reasonable prices.

There are drawbacks to the good views and facilities at Hilltop: it's the most popular destination for tour buses and is generally quite busy. If you want peace and quiet and can't afford a bush lodge, try one of the accommodation centres in Umfolozi, which are smaller.

There are bush lodges at *Muntulu*, perched high above the Hluhluwe River, and at *Munyawaneni*, which is secluded and self-contained. These sleep eight and cost a minimum of R1080.

There are two main accommodation centres in Umfolozi: *Mpila* in the centre of the reserve and *Masinda* closer to Mambeni Gate. Both have four-bed huts for R80 per

person (minimum R160). There are also eight-bed bush camps *(Sontuli* and *Nselweni)* for R120 per person, minimum R1080 (including your own ranger and cook), a bush lodge at *Gqoyeni* (minimum R1080) and a tented camp at *Mndindini* operating from December to February (minimum R720).

### Getting There & Away

The main entrance to Hluhluwe, Memorial Gate, is about 15km west of the N2, about 50km north of Mtubatuba. Alternatively, just after Mtubatuba, turn left off the N2 onto the R618 to Nongoma and take the right turn to the reserve after 17km. This road is more interesting, but it isn't in very good condition and you'll have to slow down for animals on the road – you enter the reserve through Gunjaneni Gate. Petrol is available at Hilltop Camp.

Umfolozi also has two gates. On the west side is the Cengeni Gate, accessible by rough roads from Ulundi. The Mambeni Gate on the east side sees more traffic and you can get there from the R618. Turn off to the west a few kilometres north of the turn-off to Hluhluwe, itself 17km north of the R618 junction with the N2. Petrol is available at Mpila Camp.

## GREATER ST LUCIA WETLANDS
One of the world's great ecotourism destinations stretches for 80km from Sodwana Bay, in the north of Maputaland, to Mapelane at the south end of Lake St Lucia. The area is gradually being consolidated as the Greater St Lucia Wetlands. The Convention on Wetlands of International Importance has listed St Lucia as having international conservation value. The region also satisfies the criteria for listing as a UNESCO World Heritage area.

The park protects five interconnected ecosystems – marine (coral reefs, beaches); shore (barrier between lake and sea); Mkuze reed and sedge swamps; the lake (the largest estuary in Africa); and western shores (fossil corals, sand forest, bushveld, grasslands).

At present, Lake St Lucia, its surrounds and the nearby ocean beaches are popular holiday destinations, and the area is made up of a number of parks and reserves: St Lucia Park, St Lucia Game Reserve, False Bay Park, Tewati Wilderness Area, Mfabeni Section, Ozabeni Section, Sodwana Bay National Park, Mapelane Nature Reserve and the St Lucia and Maputaland marine reserves. To the south is Mhlatuze State Forest. The main population centres in the area are Mtubatuba and St Lucia Resort.

All the parks and reserves are administered by the Natal Parks Board, but there is also private accommodation in the town of St Lucia (here called St Lucia Resort to avoid confusion), which is a sizeable holiday village – evidenced by the fact that you can buy bait here 24 hours a day. There aren't too many places in South Africa where you can buy food for *yourself* late at night, much less food for fish.

Remember that all non-camping accommodation run by the Natal Parks Board must be booked in Pietermaritzburg or at the agency in Durban's Tourist Junction.

### Warning
This is a malarial area, and there are plenty of mosquitos. Ticks and leeches can also be a problem. You should also be aware of crocs and hippos – both potentially deadly. Be careful at night, as hippos roam. In more remote areas hippos might be encountered on shore during the day – treat them with respect and retreat quietly. Sharks sometimes venture up the estuary near St Lucia Resort.

### Hiking Trails
The main walks are the four-night, guided Wilderness Trail and the three-day Mziki Trail, both in the Cape Vidal area, and the Dugandlovu Trail in False Bay Park – see that section for details. There are also day walks, detailed in Natal Parks Board literature available at the office at St Lucia Resort.

### Boat Tours
One of the highlights of a trip to the St Lucia Wetlands is the boat trip on the *Santa Lucia*. It leaves from St Lucia Resort, from the wharf on the west side of the bridge on the Mtubatuba road, at 8 and 10.30 am and 2.30 pm daily (R35). The number of trips each day might increase or decrease seasonally.

The slow-moving launch is a great platform from which to photograph and observe. The sparse commentary allows you to get on with watching – hippos, a lone crocodile, white and black mangroves, a hovering pied kingfisher, breeding fish eagles, a stalking goliath heron or nesting hadeda ibis. At least that's what we saw. Other travellers had less luck:

The boat trip was rather disappointing, although it was amusing to look at 80 people fighting each other to shoot the best pictures of two hippo's eyes.
**Henk Lodeweges**

### St Lucia Resort
This is the main centre for the area, with Natal Parks Board's offices, shops, boat hire and other services, as well as a lot of private

accommodation. In season it's a very busy place.

As well as the Natal Parks Board office there's a local information centre (☎ (035) 590 1075) on the main street. It's open weekdays and Saturday morning. You can book tours and accommodation here.

There is only one ATM in town, in the Dolphin supermarket. The First National and Standard banks are open on Monday, Wednesday and Friday from 9 am to noon.

About 2km north of St Lucia on the road to Cape Vidal is the **Crocodile Centre** where there are displays on the ecosystems in the region and other information; entry is R7. At 13 McKenzie St is the excellent Vukani Association shop selling arts and crafts, especially basketware.

**Tours** Lanie Toere (☎ (035) 590 1259, book at the office next to the Dolphin supermarket) offers two good trips. The Mziki Trail includes a 2km walk through dune forest to the Mfansana pans, and visits to hides and a beach cave (R25, 8 am to 3 pm). The Cape Vidal trip includes snorkelling, swimming and fishing (R60, also 8 am to 3 pm). Anglers can head out on the *San Jan* (☎ (035) 590 1257) for R200 per person per day.

**Places to Stay** There are three Natal Parks Board camping grounds (☎ (0352) 590 1340): *Sugarloaf*, *Eden Park* and *Iphiva*. Costs are R25 per person except in Sugarloaf, which has power points and costs R30 per person.

There is also a huge range of private accommodation, mainly in self-contained holiday apartments. You can make bookings at the information centre (☎ (035) 590 1075; AH 590 1328). B&Bs start at around R40 per person, although you're unlikely to find something this cheap (or even a vacancy) at peak times.

One of the cheaper places to stay is *St Lucia Wilds* (☎ (035) 590 1033), where apartments sleeping six cost from R45 per person. To get there, head all the way down the main street but instead of following the road around to the left to the Natal Parks

Board office, keep going straight on down the small road. St Lucia Wilds is at the end of this road.

**Places to Eat** Places to eat include a *Wimpy*, the small *North Coast Restaurant* next to the Spar, *St Pizza*, with a shaded outdoor area, the upmarket *Lake View* (for seafood) and the *Quarterdeck*, with fresh fish from R30.

### St Lucia Park & Game Reserve

St Lucia Game Reserve, which takes in the water body of the lake, the islands and Mapelane Nature Reserve, is the oldest reserve in South Africa, having been declared in 1897. The park also takes in a ribbon of land around the lake. Entry is R6.

Lake St Lucia is in fact a large and meandering estuary (Africa's largest) with a narrow sea entrance, and its depth and salinity alter as a result of seasonal and ecological factors. It is mainly shallow and the warm water is crowded with fish, which in turn attract huge numbers of waterbirds. There are lots of pelican and flamingo, and fish eagle breed in the area. Frogs produce a din during the summer mating season. However, the area is best known as a crocodile and hippo reserve.

**Places to Stay** As well as the accommodation at St Lucia Resort, the Natal Parks Board has camping and huts at *Fanies Island* and a cottage and huts at *Charters Creek*. Book these on (☎ (035) 550 1631). Charters Creek is on the western shore of the lake's southern arm, and is accessible from a turn-off from the N2 20km north of Mtubatuba. Fanies Island is by the lake 11km north of Charters Creek.

### False Bay Park

False Bay Park runs along the western shore of Lake St Lucia; entry is R6 per person. As well as the lake's hippos and crocs, the park has several antelope species and other animals, including zebra and warthog. The park boasts prolific bird life and a great variety of vegetation. There are several hiking trails, including the easy two day, 17km

**Dugandlovu Hiking Trail**, which hugs the lake and passes through *Acacia* and *Terminalia* woodlands. There are huts at the turnaround point (Dugandlovu Camp). Book this trail through the Natal Parks Board in Pietermaritzburg or Durban.

In the northern part of False Bay is the **Mpophomeni Trail**, divided into two routes suitable for families – the longer 10km section takes about four to five hours, the shorter 7km section, three hours.

**Places to Stay** There are camp sites for R17 per person and rustic four-bed huts for R46 per person (minimum R92) on the Dugandlovu trail, about 9km from the entrance gate; you can drive there. Book these direct on ☎ (035) 562 0425.

**Getting There & Away** The main road into the park runs from Hluhluwe village (the Zulu village, not the park), off the N2. Hluhluwe village is also the nearest place to buy fuel and other supplies.

### Tewati Wilderness Area (Cape Vidal)

This wilderness area takes in the land between the lake and the ocean, north from Cape Vidal. Some of the forested sand dunes are 150m high. Entry costs R6 per person plus R10 per vehicle.

The Cape Vidal office is the starting place for the four night **St Lucia Wilderness Trail**, a guided hike costing R880 per person, including all equipment and meals (book with the Natal Parks Board in Pietermaritzburg or Durban). Walks are available only from April to September. The minimum number of people is four. There is a lot of wading involved, so bring spare shoes.

The 38km, three day **Mziki Trail** is in the Mfabeni section of St Lucia (formerly the Eastern Shores State Forest). Entry to Mfabeni costs R6 per person and R10 per vehicle; the trail costs R30 per person, which includes accommodation in a trail hut. The base camp for this trail is Mt Tabor, inland just north of Mission Rocks and accessible from the road running between St Lucia and Cape Vidal. Mt Tabor was a base for subma-

rine-spotting Catalina flying-boats during WWII, and the wreckage of one of the planes can be seen in the lake south-west of the camp.

The Mziki is actually three easy trails. Day 1 (10km) is a walk south through dune forest and along the coastline; Day 2 (10km) is west through indigenous forest to the freshwater Mfazana pan, along the shore of Lake St Lucia, then east over Mt Tabor; and Day 3 (18km) descends into Bokkie Valley (named after the reedbuck or *mziki* there) and returns through dune forest and along some pristine coastline. The trail is part of a system which will eventually link St Lucia with Cape Vidal.

**Places to Stay** In the *Bhangazi* complex there are camp sites for R25 per person (book on (035) 590 1404), log cabins from R105 per person (minimum R315), dormitory cabins for R55 (minimum R440) and an eight bed bush lodge for R150 (minimum R900).

**Getting There & Away** From St Lucia head north past the Crocodile Centre and through the entrance gates. Cape Vidal is about 30km further on.

### St Lucia & Maputaland Marine Reserves

Combined, these reserves cover the coastal strip and three nautical miles out to sea, running from Cape Vidal right up to Mozambique. The reserves include the world's most southerly coral reefs, especially around Sodwana Bay (itself a national park and covered later in this chapter), and nesting sites of leatherback and loggerhead turtles.

### Mapelane Nature Reserve

South across the estuary from St Lucia, this popular fishing spot will probably become the major visitors' centre for Mhlatuze State Forest when that area is developed for recreational use. The dense bush around the camp is flanked by a giant dune, the Mjakaja.

Entry costs R6. Camp sites are R25 per person (book on ☎ (035) 590 1407), five-bed cabins cost R100 per person (minimum R300).

## Marine Turtles

Five species of turtle occur off the South African coast but only two actually nest on the coast – leatherback (*Dermochelys coriacea*) and loggerhead (*Caretta caretta*) turtles. The nesting areas of the leatherback extend from the St Lucia mouth north into Mozambique but the loggerhead only nests in the Maputaland reserve.

Both species nest at night in summer. The female moves above the high-tide mark, finds a suitable site and lays her eggs. The loggerheads' breeding area is much greater as they clamber over rocks in the intertidal zone whereas the leatherbacks will only nest on sandy beaches. The hatchlings scramble out of the nest about 70 days later (at night) and make a dash for the sea. Only one or two of each thousand hatchlings survive to maturity. The females return from 12 to 15 years later to the same beach to nest.

The Natal Parks Board has night turtle tours in December and January. The cost is R45 per person (children R12) in park vehicles, R25 per person (R15 children) in your own vehicle. ■

Although it's across the estuary from St Lucia, travel between the two centres is circuitous unless you have a boat. Mapelane is reached by 40km of sandy and sometimes tricky road from KwaMbonambi, off the N2 south of Mtubatuba. Follow the KwaMbonambi Lighthouse sign.

## SODWANA BAY

When travellers debate the best spots in South Africa, Sodwana Bay is invariably mentioned. Its appeal is in its isolation, the accessibility of the world's most southerly coral reef, walking trails, fishing and magic coastal scenery.

The small **Sodwana Bay National Park** is on the coast east of Mkuze. Entry costs R6 per person. There are some animals and the dunes and swamps are worth visiting, as well as the offshore coral reefs, but the area packs out during holidays and things get noisy and crowded. Over Christmas there are turtle-viewing tours.

For a more peaceful look at a similar eco-

system, head south to the adjoining Sodwana State Forest, now called **Ozabeni**, which runs all the way down to Lake St Lucia. Entry to Ozabeni is R6 per person and R25 per vehicle. North of the lake is a prohibited area. Bird-watchers will go wild, as over 330 species have been recorded.

### Places to Stay

There is Natal Parks Board accommodation at Sodwana Bay, with cabins from R105 per person (minimum R315) and camp sites for R35. Book early on ☎ (035) 571 0051/2. There is a shop in the resort and fuel is available. *Sodwana Bay Lodge* (☎ (035) 571 0095; fax 571 0144) is a private resort with dinner, bed and breakfast singles/doubles for R295/510 (see the note on Snorkelling & Diving in this section).

In Ozabeni (☎ 03562, ask for 2302), part of the Greater St Lucia Wetlands Park, open camp sites are R12.

### TONGALAND

The area of Maputaland on the Mozambique

## Snorkelling & Diving

The coastline near Sodwana Bay, which includes the southernmost coral reefs in Africa, is a diver's paradise. Schools of fish glide through the beautiful coral, turtles swim by, and moray eels peer inquisitively from rock crevices. Predominantly soft coral over hard, the reef has one of the world's highest recorded numbers of tropical fish species. All of these wonders can be seen using scuba or snorkelling equipment, and excellent visibility and warm winter waters allow for diving year round.

Popular snorkelling spots are Cape Vidal, Two-Mile Reef off Sodwana Bay, Mabibi and the Kosi Mouth with its famous 'aquarium', so named because of the diversity of fish. Scuba users should head for Tenedos Shoal, between the Mlalazi River and Port Durnford, and Five, Seven and Nine-Mile reefs. Courses are conducted at Two-Mile Reef.

The Sodwana Bay Lodge specialises in diving packages (it has NAUI instructors). A four-night, six-dive package costs R1185/2200 a single/double. A five-night, seven-dive package is R1407/2624. ■

border was once known as Tongaland, as it was settled by the Tonga people of Mozambique. It's a distinct ecological region and the only part of South Africa to lie east of the Lebombo range, the southern tail of which, known as the Ubombo, peters out near Mkuze. The soil of this flat, hot region is sandy and the sluggish rivers harbour crocodile and hippo. Inland there are forests of huge figs, especially along the Pongola River, and nearer the coast, palms grow among the salt pans and thornveld.

There has been little development and there are some good game reserves. One of the most common creatures is the mosquito, so take precautions against malaria.

### Mkuze

Mkuze, a small town on the N2 and the Mkuze River, is west of a pass over the Lebombo range. The road through the pass is one route to Sodwana Bay. **Ghost Mountain**, south of the town, was an important burial place for the Ndwandwe tribe and has a reputation for eerie occurrences, usually confined to strange lights and noises. The human bones which are sometimes found near Ghost Mountain date from a big battle between rival Zulu factions in 1884.

*Ghost Mountain Inn* (☎ (035) 573 1025) is a nice place with small rooms for R95 per person and larger rooms from R145/230 a single/double.

### Mkuzi Game Reserve

Established in 1912, this 36,000 hectare Natal Parks Board reserve lacks lion and elephant but just about every other sought-after animal is represented, as well as over 400 species of bird (including the rare Pel's fishing owl, *Scotopelia peli*).

Better still, the reserve has hides at pans and water holes which offer some of the best wildlife viewing in the country. The walk to Nsumu pan features two bird-watching hides, and there are six game-viewing hides, the most notable being Bube and Masinga. Morning is the best time.

Nestled below the Ubombo range, the country is partly dense thornveld, partly open savanna and gets very hot in summer although winters are generally mild.

There's an entry fee of R6 per person and R25 per vehicle. There are guided walks (R25) and night drives (R40). Between April and October there are twice-monthly three-day hikes through the reserve, similar to the wilderness trails run through Umfolozi (R740 per person).

From the north you can get here from Mkuze town; from the south, turn off the N2 35km north of Hluhluwe village. Fuel is sold at the main gate.

**Places to Stay**  Self-contained bungalows cost from R115 per person (minimum R230) and the safari camp costs from R95 (minimum R143). Camp sites (☎ (035) 573 0003 for bookings) cost R20 per person. There is also a bush lodge (minimum R930) and tented bush camps in summer (minimum R540). Book accommodation other than camp sites through the Natal Parks Board in Pietermaritzburg or the agency in Durban's Tourist Junction.

### Phinda Resource Reserve

This 17,000 hectare reserve, very much an 'ecotourism' showpiece, is to the north-west of Lake St Lucia. It was set up by The Conservation Corporation, a private reserves chain.

There are nine different ecosystems in the park. They include hilly terrain, sand forest, riverine woodland, natural pans and savanna grasslands. This diversity attracts a great variety of bird life (over 360 species) as well as promoting a diverse range of plant life. There are about 10,000 head of game, many reintroduced, including nyala and the rare suni antelope *(Neotragus moschatus)*. Lion and cheetah kills can occasionally be seen and leopard are now seen during game drives. In addition to the game drives there are accompanied walks, canoeing and riverboat cruises.

The only problem with Phinda is that all the 'eco'-pluses don't come cheap: from R2085/2780 a single/double for full board, activities included. For bookings phone ☎ (011) 784 7077; fax 784 7667.

Just south of Phinda, *Zulu Nyala Lodge* (☎ (011) 484 1560; fax 484 2893) also has a reserve and offers several of the Big Five (but not lion), walks, horse-riding, game drives and a cruise. The all-inclusive rates are much cheaper than those at Phinda: from R950/1390 a single/double.

To get to either place, take the Southern Maputaland turn-off from the N2 and follow the signs.

### Pongola

Pongola is a tiny town in a sugar-growing district near the Mpumalanga border and not far from Swaziland.

The inexpensive municipal *caravan park* (☎ (03841) 31233) is in the centre of town; it's basic but green and shaded. Across the street the *Pongola Hotel* (☎ (03841) 31352) has rooms from about R100/125 with a good breakfast – make sure you know which standard of room you're paying for. The public bar is a lively place where you can meet local farm workers.

### Ndumu Game Reserve

Right on the Mozambique border and close to the Swaziland border, about 100km north of Mkuze, this reserve of 10,000 hectares is looked after by the KwaZulu Department of Nature Conservation (KDNC) (☎ (0331) 94 6696; fax 42 1948) in Pietermaritzburg. The KDNC also administers the Coastal Forest Reserve. Ndumu has black and white rhino, hippo, crocs and antelope species, but it is the bird life on the Pongola and Usutu rivers and their flood plains and pans which attracts visitors.

Guided walks (one for game viewing, two for bird-watching, one for trees) and vehicle tours are available. This is the southernmost limit of the range of many bird species and the reserve is a favourite of bird-watchers, with over 400 species having been recorded – watch for the southern banded snake eagle (*Circaetus fasciolatus*), yellow-spotted nicator (*Nicator gularis*) and the green-capped eremomela (*Eremomela scotops*).

Fuel and limited supplies are usually available 2km outside the park gate. You can't camp at the reserve; accommodation is in three-bed cottages near the Pongola River and there are cooking facilities.

### Tembe Elephant Park

South Africa's last free-ranging elephants are protected in the sandveld forests of this park on the Mozambique border. There are now about 100 elephants in the area, many of them the last remnants of the elephants from the Maputo Elephant Reserve saved from Mozambique's civil war. There are also white rhino and leopard.

Accommodation costs just R85 per person (minimum R255) and a maximum of eight people is allowed into the park at a time. This is a good start, but the downside is that you need a 4WD to get into the park, and once there you must take a tour pre-booked with the KDNC (☎ (0331) 94 6696; fax 42 1948) in Pietermaritzburg.

## COASTAL FOREST RESERVE

This reserve stretches from Mozambique in the north to Sodwana Bay in the south, and includes Lake Sibaya, Kosi Bay, Bhanga Nek, Black Rock, Rocktail Bay, Manzengwenya, Mabibi and Nine-Mile Beach. The reserve is administered by the KDNC.

### Lake Sibaya Nature Reserve

This reserve protects the largest freshwater lake in South Africa, covering between 60 and 70 sq km depending on the water level. It lies very close to the coast, and between the eastern shore and the sea there is a range of sand dunes up to 165m high. There are hippos, some crocs and a large range of birds (over 280 species have been recorded). The lake is popular for fishing – you can hire boats (complete with skipper) for fishing trips.

There is accommodation in cabins at *Baya Camp*, on the south side of the lake. You must bring your own food but there are cooks to prepare it if you want. Book accommodation through the KDNC (☎ (0331) 94 6696; fax 42 1948) in Pietermaritzburg.

The main route here is via the village of Mbazwana, south of the lake, either from Mkuze or from Mhlosinga, off the N2 north of Hluhluwe village.

## Kosi Bay Nature Reserve

Kosi Bay, like Sodwana, is another place listed by travellers as among the 10 best South African destinations. On the coast near the Mozambique border, this remote reserve encompasses fig and raffia palm forests, mangrove swamps, sand dunes and freshwater lakes (the 'bay' is in fact a string of four lakes – Nhlange, Mpungwini, Sifungwe and Amanzimnyama). There are pristine beaches that are usually deserted, and a coral reef with great snorkelling.

There are antelope species in the drier country and hippos, Zambezi sharks and some crocs in the lake system. There are over 250 bird species, including the rare palmnut vulture. The research station here studies the local population of leatherback turtles; during the nesting season there are turtle-viewing tours.

Canoes are available for hire. The **Kosi Bay Trail** is a four night/five day guided hike around the Kosi estuarine system (R165), stopping each night in remote camps which focus on different aspects of the reserve. This trail includes a walk to the Kosi Mouth.

Entry costs R5 per person and R12 per car. Because the ecosystems here are in such delicate balance the number of visitors is limited; to enter the reserve you need a permit from the KDNC in Pietermaritzburg (☎ (0331) 94 6696; fax 42 1948). Only five permits a day are issued for visits to Kosi Mouth and a 4WD vehicle is needed. Beach driving is only permitted from Sodwana Bay to Nine-Mile Beach and 20 permits are issued each day to allow drivers to continue past Nine-Mile to the boom gate before Mabibi.

You can camp at KDNC sites (R15 per person, minimum R60) or stay at the privately-run *Rocktail Bay Lodge* (☎ (011) 884 1458 for bookings), a coastal camp. The lodge was built so that it blends into the coastal forest canopy – large trees provide shade, and beds are at canopy level.

On the road to the reserve is a small settlement where you can buy supplies and fuel.

**Getting There & Away** To get there, take the Jozini turn-off from the N2 and head towards Ndumu Game Reserve, but turn hard right (east) just before Ndumo village. Most of the road is sealed but you might still encounter deep sand – you might need a 4WD.

# Northern Zululand

This section covers the region north of Ulundi and west of the N2. Although it is a large area, it is not as diverse as the coastal region of Zululand. It does, however, contain two spectacular natural areas, Itala Game Reserve and the Ntendeka Wilderness Area. The main towns are Louwsburg, Nongoma, Vryheid and Paulpietersburg.

## NTENDEKA WILDERNESS AREA

This is a truly beautiful and tranquil area of grassland and indigenous coastal and inland tropical forest, with some dramatic dolerite and sandstone cliffs (*Ntendeka* means 'place of precipitous heights'). More than 180 tree, 60 fern and 190 bird species have been recorded. The rare Ngoye red squirrel is found in the forest. Rare birds such as the blue swallow (*Hirundo atrocaerulea*) and cuckoo hawk (*Aviceda cuculoides*) can also be spotted. The wilderness area is bordered by **Ngome State Forest**, a good example of inland tropical forest.

This is an important region in Zulu history, and Cetshwayo was once holed up here – his rock-shelter refuge is in the north-eastern corner of the park. Another famous figure to hide out here was Mzilikazi, one of Shaka's disloyal generals. Mzilikazi was eventually chased north, where his descendants established the Ndebele tribe in the Pretoria area and the Matabele in modern-day Zimbabwe.

There are walking trails, but you can't drive through the wilderness area. There's a camp site with ablution facilities on the north-eastern edge of the park, the only place in the wilderness where you can camp. Phone ☎ (0386) 71883 or call at the Ngome Forest Station, south off the R618 just past the south-eastern corner of the wilderness area, to see if permits are still necessary.

The nearest town is Nongoma (which is an important trading town but has no facilities for visitors), about 60km north-east of Ulundi, with 50km of unsealed road. Alternatively, get to Ntendeka by travelling south from Vryheid on the R618 for about 70km, or south from Pongola on the R66, then north-west on the R618.

## VRYHEID

Vryheid ('liberty') is the largest town in north-eastern KwaZulu-Natal. Today Vryheid is an agricultural and coal-mining centre but in 1884 it was the capital of the Nieuwe Republiek, which was absorbed into the ZAR four years later. After the Anglo-Boer War, the area was transferred to Natal. There are Anglo-Boer War sites and several people offer guided tours of the battlefields – contact the information centre.

The information centre (☎ (0381) 81 2133) is on the corner of Market and High Sts. There are three **museums** in town. One, devoted to the short-lived Nieuwe Republiek, is in the Old Raadsaal building on Landdrost St. South of Kerk St, the main street, is a small museum of local history in the old Lucas Meijer House (Meijer was the only president of the Nieuwe Republiek). The other museum is in the old Carnegie library.

Just north of town, the **Vryheid Nature Reserve** has zebra and antelope species and there's a bird hide next to a salt pan.

### Places to Stay

The municipal *caravan park* (☎ (0381) 81 2133) is not far from both the town's centre and the train station. *Klipfontein Resort* (☎ (0381) 4383) is a centre for fishing and water sports. Entry is R6 per person and there are basic camp sites for about R20 per

person. Take the Melmoth road, the R33, south from Vryheid for about 5km.

In town there's the inexpensive *Vryheid Lodge* (☎ (0381) 5201) and 6km out on the Dundee road is the *Stilwater Protea Hotel* (☎ (0381) 6181) which charges R199/245, with breakfast.

*Villa Prince Imperial* (☎ (0381) 80 2610), 201 Deputasie St, is a quality B&B charging from R170/280, plus R18 for a continental breakfast or R25 for a full breakfast.

If you want to stay with a family of German descent in Vryheid or the nearby area (there are many), contact Building Bridges – German Guest Homes (☎ (0381) 80 8644), 106 Deputasie St.

### Getting There & Away

The well-organised minibus taxi park is near the train station. Drop into the taxi association office for information. Vryheid is the centre for minibus taxis in this part of KwaZulu-Natal. From Vryheid, some destinations and fares are Dundee R15, Pongola R18, Nongoma R14, Ulundi R14, Eshowe R22, Durban (via Melmoth) R40 and Jo'burg R50.

## ITALA GAME RESERVE

The Natal Parks Board's Itala now has all the trappings of a private game reserve but much lower prices. Entry costs R6 per person plus R25 per vehicle.

Most of the 30,000 hectares is taken up by the steep valleys of six rivers (tributaries of the Pongola), with some open grassland on the heights, rugged outcrops and about 25% bushveld.

Animals, mostly reintroduced, include black and white rhino, elephant, tsessebe (the only herd in KwaZulu-Natal), nyala, hyena, buffalo, baboon, leopard and cheetah. There are over 75 mammal species in the park, plus crocodile and 100 or so other species of amphibians and reptiles, and 20 species of indigenous fish. The diverse habitats support over 320 species of bird, including the endangered southern bald ibis (*Geronticus calvus*).

## Places to Stay

*Ntshondwe* is the main centre, with superb views of the reserve below. There's a restaurant and a shop here, as well as a swimming pool. Accommodation starts at R120 for a unit with communal kitchen and R135 (minimum R203) for a chalet. There are a few basic camp sites for R12 per person. Book these on ☎ (0388) 75239.

There are three bush camps, offering privacy and proximity to wildlife but without the luxuries of the main camp. They are geared to single groups so unless you have a few people you'll find the minimum charges high.

## Getting There & Away

Itala is entered from Louwsburg, about 55km east of Vryheid on the R69, and about the same distance south-west of Pongola via the R66 and the R69. Louwsburg is much smaller than many maps indicate.

## PAULPIETERSBURG

This town is a centre for timber and agricultural production. It gets its name from Paul Kruger and Pieter Joubert. The information bureau (☎ (038) 995 1729) has information on the town and surrounds. Outside town is the Natal Spa (☎ (038) 995 1630), where you can lie back in the warm or cold mineral pools.

This region has many descendants of the original German settlers from the Hermannsburg Missionary Society established in 1848. The main German towns are Gluckstadt, Braunschweig and Luneberg.

# The Natal Drakensberg

The awesome Drakensberg is a mountainous basalt escarpment forming the border between KwaZulu-Natal and Lesotho, and continuing a little way into the Free State. The escarpment continues to the north, less spectacularly, before rearing up again in Mpumalanga's Klein Drakensberg.

'Drakensberg' means dragon mountains;

the Zulu named it *Quathlamba* (Battlement of Spears). The Zulu word is a more accurate description of the sheer and jagged escarpment, but the Afrikaans name captures something of the Drakensberg's otherworldly atmosphere. Although people have lived here for thousands of years – there are many San rock painting sites – some of the peaks and rocks were first climbed by Europeans less than 50 years ago.

The San, already under pressure from the tribes who had moved into the Drakensberg foothills, were finally destroyed with the coming of white settlers. Some moved into Lesotho where they were absorbed into the Basotho population, but many were killed or simply starved when their hunting grounds were occupied by others. Khoisan cattle raids annoyed the white settlers to the extent that the settlers forced several black tribes to relocate into the Drakensberg foothills to act as a buffer between the whites and the Khoisan. These early 'bantu locations' meant that there was little development in the area, which later allowed the creation of a chain of parks and reserves. (It also meant, of course, that the 'bantus' were again forced out.)

## Orientation

The Drakensberg is usually divided into three sections, although the distinctions aren't strict. The northern Drakensberg runs from the Golden Gate Highlands National Park in the Free State (covered in that chapter) to the Royal Natal National Park. Harrismith and Bergville are sizeable towns in this area.

The central Drakensberg's main feature is Giant's Castle, the largest reserve in the area. North of Giant's Castle is Cathedral Peak and wilderness areas. Bergville, Estcourt and Winterton are towns adjacent to the central Drakensberg.

The southern Drakensberg runs down to the Transkei area of Eastern Cape. This area, where the Drakensberg bends around to the south-west, is less developed than the others but is no less spectacular. Here there's a huge wilderness area and the Sani Pass route into

KWAZULU-NATAL

The Natal Drakensberg

To Bethlehem
N5
R720
R712
Harrismith
Phuthaditjhaba
Sterkfontein Dam
Swinburne
N3
To Johannesburg
FREE STATE
Van Reenens Pass
N11
To Newcastle
Ventetspruit
Olivieshoek Pass
Little Switzerland
Cavern Berg Resort
Rugged Glen Nature Reserve
Hlalanathi Berg Resort
Hotel
Royal Natal National Park
R74
R616
Spioenkop Nature Reserve
Spioenkop Dam
Ladysmith
N11
Roosboom
Bergville
Tugela River
Mont-aux-Sources (3282m)
Woodstock Dam
M'Weni
Winterton
R103
Colenso
Bloukrans
Cathedral Peak (3004m)
Mlambonja
R600
Little Tugela
Loskop
R74
Frere
Weenen
Cleft Peak (3280m)
Cathedral Peak Hotel
Nkenka
Cathkin Peak (3181m)
Drakensberg Sun
Champagne Castle Hotel
Draycott
R103
Weenen Game Reserve
R74
Mlambonja Wilderness Area
Mdedelelo Wilderness Area
Champagne Castle (3377m)
Injasuti (3409m)
White Mountain Lodge
Estcourt
To Greytown
Motsitseng
Mafadi (3450m)
Popple Peak (3330m)
Hillside Camp
Giant's Castle Game Reserve
Bushmans
Wagendrif Nature Reserve
N3
Mokhotlong
LESOTHO
Main Camp
Little Mooi
Mooi River
Mooi River
Craigie Burn Dam Nature Reserve
Rietvlei
R622
Giant's Castle (3314m)
Redi (3298m)
Highmoor State Forest
Loteni Nature Reserve
Redcliffe
Kamberg Nature Reserve
Mooi
Rosetta
Karkloof
Thabana-Ntlenyana (3482m)
Mkhomazi Wilderness Area
Umkomaas
Vergelegen Nature Reserve
Cobham State Forest
Lower Loteni
Nottingham Road
Lions
R103
Howick
Sani Pass
Sani Pass Hotel
Loteni
Mzimkulwana Nature Reserve
Umkomazana
Umgeni River
Midmar Public Resort Nature Reserve
Hilton
R33
Garden Castle State Forest
Mzimkulu Wilderness Area
Sani Lodge
Himeville Nature Reserve
Bushman's Nek & Border Post
Drakensberg Garden Hotel
Himeville
Underberg
R617
Pietermaritzburg
Bushman's Nek Hotel
Mzimkulwana Nature Reserve
Coleford Nature Reserve
R626
Sehlabathebe National Park (Lesotho)
To Kokstad
R612
Bulwer
Deepdale
Ncwadi
Umlazi
Edendale
R56
To Durban
To Ixopo
To Richmond

0    15    30 km

southern Lesotho. Pietermaritzburg to the east and Kokstad to the south are the main access points to the southern Drakensberg, but up in the hills are some pleasant little towns, notably Underberg and Himeville.

## Information
As well as the various KwaZulu-Natal Parks Board offices in the reserves, the Drakensberg Publicity Association (☎ /fax (036) 448 1557), which covers only the north and central Drakensberg, is based in Bergville. The Southern Drakensberg Publicity Association (☎ (033) 701 1096) is on Main St, Underberg.

## Climate
If you want to avoid most of the sharp frosts and, on the heights, snowfalls, you should visit in summer, although this is when most of the rain falls and views can be obscured by low cloud. However, what you lose in vistas you'll gain in atmosphere, as the stark and eerie peaks are at their best looming out of the mist. Much of the rain falls in sudden thunderstorms so you should always carry wet-weather gear. Cold snaps are possible even in the middle of summer.

## Places to Stay
The best way to see the Drakensberg is to stay at one of the Natal Parks Board's excellent reserves. The biggest and most popular are Royal Natal and Giant's Castle, but accommodation and camp sites can also be found in the state forests and other reserves. Free camping is allowed in most designated wilderness areas, but check in at the Parks Board or Forestry offices; there's a small fee.

Usually more expensive than the Parks Board's accommodation are the private resorts which dot the foothills near Royal Natal and Giant's Castle. Places to stay in the southern Drakensberg are covered under the towns following the parks entries.

## Getting There & Away
There is little public transport in the northern and central Drakensberg, although there is a lot of tourist traffic; and with so many resorts

### Hiking in the Drakensberg
The Drakensberg has some superb walks and hikes, ranging from gentle day walks to strenuous treks of two or more days. There's an ambitious plan to create a trail from the top of Sani Pass all the way to the coast.

The trails in the Mkhomazi and Mzimkulu wilderness areas and the Mzimkulwana Nature Reserve in the southern Drakensberg offer some of the most remote and rugged hiking in South Africa. For the less experienced there's also the five-day Giant's Cup Trail, part of the National Hiking Way, running from near Sani Pass Hotel in the north down to Bushman's Nek. (See the Southern Drakensberg Wilderness Areas section for more information.)

Summer hiking on the less frequented trails can be made frustrating and even dangerous by rivers flooded by sudden torrential storms; in winter, frosts and snow are the main hazards. April and May are the best months for hiking.

Make sure you get the relevant 1:50,000-scale Forestry Department maps, which show trails and have essential information for hikers. They are available at most trailheads.

Permits are needed on most of the hikes, especially in the wilderness areas; get them from Natal Parks Board offices at the various trailheads. Trail accommodation, especially in Royal Natal and Giant's Castle, is often in huts and caves (meaning that you don't need a tent).

Accommodation in the northern Drakensberg must be booked well in advance, but in the wilderness areas of the southern Drakensberg, this isn't a problem. ■

all needing staff there are some minibus taxis. The main jumping-off points are on or near the N3. See the sections on Estcourt, Mooi River, Winterton and Bergville later in this chapter. The Baz Bus drops off and picks up at a hostel in the area. To get to the southern Drakensberg you can arrange a lift to the hostels near Sani Pass and Himeville through hostels in Durban.

Sani Pass is the best-known Drakensberg route into Lesotho. There are other passes over the escarpment, but most don't connect with anything in Lesotho larger than a walking track (if that) a long way from anywhere.

Many roads in the Drakensberg area are unsealed and after rain some are impassable, but it's usually possible to find an alternative route. Tourist routes in the northern and central Drakensberg are indicated by brown signs with a lammergeyer (bearded vulture) symbol.

## ROYAL NATAL NATIONAL PARK

Although it is only a little over 8000 hectares in extent, Royal Natal has some of the Drakensberg's most dramatic and accessible scenery. The southern boundary of the national park is formed by the Amphitheatre, an 8km stretch of cliff which is spectacular from below and even more so from the top. Here the Tugela Falls drop 850m in five stages (the top one often freezes in winter). Looming up behind is Mont-aux-Sources, so called because the Tugela, Elands and Western Khubedu rivers rise here – the latter eventually becomes the Orange and flows all the way to the Atlantic.

Other notable peaks in the area are Devil's Tooth, the Eastern Buttress and the Sentinel. Rugged Glen Nature Reserve adjoins the park on the north-eastern side.

The park's big visitor centre is a kilometre or so in from the main gate. There's a bookshop here where you can pick up a copy of the Natal Parks Board's excellent booklet *Royal Natal National Park* for more detailed information, including descriptions of walks and a handy sketch map. The Board also produces a good 1:20,000 topographical map, *Mont-aux-Sources*. Entry to the park is R6 per person, which is astoundingly good value. Fuel is available in the park.

### Flora & Fauna

With plentiful water, a range of more than 1500m in altitude and distinct areas such as plateaux, cliffs and valleys, it isn't surprising that the park's flora is extremely varied. Broadly speaking, though, much of the park is covered in grassland, with protea savanna at lower altitudes. This grassland depends on fire for reproduction and to discourage other vegetation. In areas which escape the park's periodic fires, scrub takes over. At lower levels, but confined to valleys, are small yellowwood forests. At higher altitudes grass yields to heath and scrub.

Royal Natal is not as rich in wildlife as Giant's Castle and other sections of the Drakensberg, but there is still quite a lot to be seen. Of the half-dozen species of antelope, the most common is the mountain reedbuck. Hyraxes are everywhere, as are hares, and you'll probably meet some baboons. Most other species in the reserve are shy and not often seen. They include otter, jackal and mongoose. More than 200 species of bird have been recorded.

### Rock Paintings

There are several San rock painting sites, although Royal Natal's are fewer and not as well preserved as Giant's Castle, because the latter has many more rock shelters and caves – and has suffered less from vandalism. The notable sites are Sigubudu Shelter, north of the road just past the main gate; and Cannibal Caves, on Surprise Ridge, outside the park's northern boundary.

### Hiking Trails

Except for the walk to Mont-aux-Sources, all of the 30-odd walks are day walks. Only 50 day visitors and 50 overnighters are allowed on **Mont-aux-Sources** each day. There are two ways to approach the summit. The easiest way is to drive to the Sentinel car park on the road from Phuthaditjhaba in QwaQwa (see the QwaQwa section in the Free State chapter). By doing this it's possible to get to the summit and back in a day. Otherwise, having completed the mountain register at the visitor centre, you walk up to Basotho Gate then take the road to Sentinel car park.

If you plan to camp on the mountain you should book with Free State Agriculture Department (☎ (058) 713 4444; fax 713 4342) in Phuthaditjhaba. Otherwise there's a basic mountain hut on the escarpment near Tugela Falls. Unlike other Natal Parks Board accommodation you don't need to book (except for registering before walking here) and there's no fee for the hut.

Walking is very popular here, particularly up the Tugela River to its gorge. We did another walk 'that no-one should miss', but most people must as the trail was so overgrown in places that we had to concentrate on our feet, not the mountains and the sandstone cliffs and bluffs, forested ravines, wildflowers and butterflies. There was no signpost at the midpoint to show where the objective of the walk (a cave) was. If the long trails are anything like the short ones, tackling them would be foolhardy, and with any we've inspected closely, the routes are silly.

**Noel Gross**

## Climbing

As some of the peaks and faces were first climbed by mountaineers only about 50 years ago, the park is a mecca for climbers. You must apply for a permit from the office before you attempt a climb: unless you are experienced, it might not be granted. Take

---

### Taming the Dragons

The mountains of South Africa don't stand as a single, solid range like the European Alps. They are a series of ranges, each imbued with its own particular character. The most majestic of the ranges is the Drakensberg, stretching from Eastern Cape to Northern Province. The Natal Drakensberg were the last of the 'dragons' to be tamed, as most activity had concentrated on peaks near Cape Town – the Mountain Club was formed there in 1891.

In 1888, the Reverend A Stocker, a member of the Alpine Club, was the first to climb Champagne Castle (3375m) and Sterkhorn Peak. He attempted Cathkin Peak (3167m) but it was not climbed until 1912 when a group which included a black guide, Melatu, scaled it. Cathedral Peak (3004m) was conquered in 1917 by two climbers, R Kingdon and D Bassett-Smith.

The next intensive period of climbing was in the 1940s. Dick Barry had attempted the Monk's Cowl (3234m) in 1938, but was killed doing so. In 1942 a group led by Hans Wongtschowski scaled its basalt faces. Two years later, Hans and his wife Elsa clawed up the seemingly impregnable Bell (2991m).

The region's great challenge was the Devil's Tooth (3022m) and, after several attempts, this was climbed in 1950. Shortly after it was surveyed, in 1954, Thabana-Ntlenyana ('little black mountain') in Lesotho, at 3482m Southern Africa's highest peak, was climbed as a relatively simple excursion. ∎

---

your passport if you plan to venture into Lesotho.

### Places to Stay

The main camp is *Tendele*, where there are bungalows for R125/188 a single/double and a variety of more expensive chalets. At *Mahai* there's a camp site costing R17 (R25 with power) per person, and at Rugged Glen Nature Reserve, on the north-eastern edge of the park, there's a camp site for the same price. Book either site on ☎ (036) 438 6303. An overnight hiking permit costs R7.

Also in the reserve, near the visitor centre, is the privately-run *Royal Natal National Park Hotel* (☎ (036) 438 6200; fax 438 6101) with rooms for about R390, including all meals.

**Outside the Park** Just off the R74, near Oliviershoek Pass, *Little Switzerland* (☎ /fax (0364) 438 6220) is a large place with self-catering chalets sleeping four for about R400 in the high season, much less in the low season. Single/double hotel-style rooms cost from R270/370. The rugged scenery around here is impressive, but the escarpment is some way off. Little Switzerland will collect you from Swinburne, on the N3 near Harrismith (in the Free State), where Translux buses stop.

Off the road into Royal Natal from the R74, *Hlalanathi Berg Resort* (☎ (036) 438 6308) has camp sites for R30/45 in the low/high season, and chalets from R125 a double in the low season. There is a small shop at the resort entrance. Nearby, the upmarket *Mont-aux-Sources Hotel* (☎ /fax (036) 438 6230) charges R240/390 (more on weekends) for dinner, bed and breakfast.

About 10km north of Hlalanathi, the family-oriented *Cavern Berg Resort* (☎ (036) 438 6270; fax 438 6334) offers horse-riding and walks. Single/double rooms with all meals cost from R195/360.

Secluded *Isibongno Lodge & Backpackers* (☎ (036) 438 6707) is about 15km from the park and has dorms (R35), singles (R70) and doubles (R100), or you can camp for

R15. Meals are available. They can pick you up from Harrismith or Bergville.

### Getting There & Away
The only road into Royal Natal runs off the R74, about 30km north of Bergville and about 5km from Oliviershoek Pass, but see the previous Hiking Trails section for information on a route to Mont-aux-Sources.

## BERGVILLE
This small town is a handy jumping-off point for both the northern Drakensberg and the Midlands – if you have a car.

The Drakensberg Publicity Association has an office here, open from 9 am to 4 pm on weekdays only.

On the third Friday of each month there are local cattle sales and the sleepy town takes on an altogether different atmosphere.

In the courthouse grounds is the **Upper Tugela Blockhouse**, built by the British during the Anglo-Boer War.

### Places to Stay & Eat
In town, *Hotel Walter* (☎ (036) 448 1022) has reasonable single/double rooms for R119/195, with breakfast. A few kilometres out of Bergville off the R616 to Ladysmith, *Sanford Park Lodge* (☎ (036) 448 1001; fax 448 1047) has good rooms in thatched rondavels or in a big 150-year-old farmhouse from about R250 per person, including all meals. It's a little too large to feel personal, but it's a nice place.

Off the Bergville to Harrismith road, at Jagersrust, *Drakensville Resort* (☎ (036) 438 6287; fax 438 6524) is a big place, with 70 three-bedroom homes. It seems to be a recycled workers' village (the houses are not old) and it's a little bleak, but it isn't bad value. A house sleeping six people can cost as little as R140. You must provide your own linen. You can camp here for R40/50 a double in the low/high season.

### Getting There & Away
None of the long-distance bus lines run very close to Bergville. You'll probably have to get to Ladysmith and take a minibus taxi

from there. The Translux service from Durban to Bloemfontein stops at both Montrose (at the Shell Ultra on the N3 near Swinburne) and Ladysmith. Translux's Jo'burg/Pretoria-Umtata and Jo'burg/Pretoria-Durban services also stop at Montrose. A daily Greyhound bus stops at Estcourt, Swinburne in the Montrose bus service area and Ladysmith.

The minibus taxi park is behind the Score supermarket. Taxis run into Royal Natal National Park area for about R8 but few run all the way to the park entrance. The number of hitchhikers in this area is a sign that taxis are infrequent.

## CENTRAL BERG
In some ways the Central Berg is the most attractive part of the range. Some of the most challenging climbs of the Drakensberg – Cathkin Peak (3181m), the Monk's Cowl (3234m) and Champagne Castle (3377m) – are found here. The central region also includes the grand Giant's Castle Peak. Midway between Cathedral and Cathkin peaks is Ndedema Gorge, where there are some fine San rock paintings.

The area between Cathedral Peak and Giant's Castle, in the Central Berg, comprises two wilderness areas, Mlambonja and Mdedelelo (together some 35,000 hectares). Both are administered by the Natal Parks Board.

Grey rhebok, klipspringer and mountain reedbuck occur naturally in the area. And so do boys with extremely high voices. Just off the Dragon Peaks road is the Drakensberg Boys' Choir School (☎ (036) 468 1012). There are public performances on Wednesday and Saturday at 4 pm.

### Cathedral Peak State Forest
Cathedral Peak (3004m) lies between Royal Natal and Giant's Castle, west of Winterton. It's part of a small chain of peaks which jut out east of the main escarpment. The others, challenging for climbers, include the Bell, the Horns, the Pyramid and Needles. Cathedral Peak is a long day's climb (a trail begins

near the hotel), but other than being fit no special ability or equipment is required.

The forest office, where you can book camp sites and overnight hiking (R12), is off the road running west from Winterton, near the Cathedral Peak Hotel; entry to the state forest is R6 per person.

There's a fee of R25 to drive up Mike's Pass, where there are good views.

**Places to Stay** The Natal Parks Board has camp sites (☎ (036) 488 1880) for R17 per person. *Cathedral Peak Hotel* (☎ /fax (036) 488 1888), 40km from Winterton, is close to the escarpment, near Cathedral Peak. Single/ double rooms cost from R220/360 including meals. The hotel will collect you from Estcourt.

### Monk's Cowl State Forest (Champagne Castle)

The forest office (☎ (036) 468 1103) is 3km beyond the Champagne Castle Hotel, which is at the end of the R600 running south-west from Winterton. Entry, camping and hiking fees are the same as for Cathedral Peak State Forest.

If you're driving into this area don't get carried away by the good road; there are a couple of very steep sections and a nightmarish hairpin with reverse camber and a long drop.

**Places to Stay & Eat** As well as camping in the state forest there are some other options.

*Dragon Peaks Park* (☎ (036) 468 1031; fax 468 1104) is a Club Caravelle resort with the usual maze of prices and minimum stays depending on seasons and school holidays. Sites cost R22 per person (high season R48, minimum R96) and the cheapest cottages are R80 per person, minimum R120 (high season R110, minimum R165).

*Cayley Lodge* (☎ /fax (036) 468 1222) charges R310/500 a single/double, including meals. *Champagne Castle* (☎ /fax (036) 468 1063) is one of the best-known resorts and it's well located, right in the mountains at the end of the road to Champagne Castle peak. There are cottages, rondavels and units,

costing from R180 per person in the low season, with meals – good value. The hotel will collect you from Estcourt (a Greyhound stop) for R50. The *Drakensberg Sun* (☎ (036) 468 1000) has singles/doubles for R470/760, with packages available.

### WINTERTON

This pretty little town is the gateway to the central Drakensberg and is not too far from the northern end. There is a great little museum on Kerk St which concentrates on the geology, flora and fauna of the Drakensberg – a good place to read up before venturing further. It is open Wednesday and Friday from 1 to 4 pm, and on Saturday from 9 am to noon.

The *Bridge Hotel* (☎ (036) 488 1554) is a friendly local pub with singles/doubles for R120/185 and self-catering units for R100/ 165 per person.

*Ntabeni Backpackers* (☎ (036) 488 1773/1372) is on a farm 5km from Winterton and charges R25. *Vilamoura Country Estate* (☎ (036) 488 1128) charges about the same. The Baz Bus will stop at either place.

A minibus taxi to Cathedral Peak costs R7. To Bergville it's R5 and to Estcourt R7.

### GIANT'S CASTLE GAME RESERVE

This reserve of 34,500 hectares was established in 1903, mainly to protect the eland. It's in high country: the lowest point is 1300m and the highest tooth of the Drakensberg in the reserve is the 3409m Injasuti Dome, also the highest peak in South Africa. With huge forest reserves to the north and south and Lesotho's barren plateau over the escarpment to the west, it's a rugged and remote place, despite the number of visitors it attracts.

There's an entry fee of R6 per person. Limited supplies (including fuel) are available at Main Camp and there's a basic store near the White Mountain Lodge, but the nearest shops are in Estcourt, 50km away.

### Flora & Fauna

The reserve is mainly grassland, wooded gorges, high basaltic cliffs with small forests

in the valleys, and some protea savanna surviving the grass-fires caused by lightning
strikes and, recently, controlled burning.
During spring there are many wildflowers.

Because of the harsh conditions many of
the reserve's animals lead a precarious existence, and the balance of numbers and
available food is delicate – an event such as
a hard winter can disturb the equation and
threaten a species' existence.

The reserve is home to 12 species of antelope, with relatively large numbers of eland,
mountain reedbuck, black wildebeest, red
hartebeest, grey rhebok and oribi. The rarest
antelope is the klipspringer, sometimes
sighted on the higher slopes. The rarest
species is a small short-tailed rodent called
the ice rat, which lives in the boulders near
the mountain summits. Altogether there are
thought to be about 60 mammal species, but
some, such as the leopard and aardwolf, have
not been positively sighted.

The rare lammergeyer, or bearded vulture
(Gypaetus barbatus), which is found only in
the Drakensberg, nests in the reserve.
Because there's a danger that the birds will
feed on poisoned carcasses, which some
farmers in the area use to kill jackals, the
reserve puts out meat on weekend mornings
between May and September to encourage
the birds to feed in the reserve. **Lammergeyer Hide** has been built nearby, and it's
the best place to see the vultures. The fee for
using the hide is R30 (minimum R180), and
you must book.

The number of other bird species to have
been sighted in the reserve is around 200.
There are also about 30 reptile species,
including the puff adder.

## Rock Paintings

The reserve is rich in San rock paintings,
with at least 50 sites. It is thought that the last
San lived here at the turn of the century.

The two main sites of paintings are Main
Cave (about 550 paintings) and Battle Cave
(750 paintings), both of which have an entry
fee of R6. Main Cave is 2km south of Main
Camp (30 minutes walk) and there's also a
display on San life here. The cave is open on

weekends and holidays from 9 am to 3 pm;
on weekdays you have to go with a tour
which departs from the camp office at 9 am
and 3 pm. Battle Cave is near Injasuti and
must be visited on a tour which leaves the
camp daily at 9 am. It's an 8km walk each
way, and there's a good chance of seeing
wildlife en route. Battle Cave is so called
because some of the paintings here record a
fight between San groups.

Other painting sites near Main Camp are
Bamboo Hollow, where there are two rich
sites – Steel's Shelter and Willcox's Shelter,
where you can see a figure known as the
Moon Goddess. Near Injasuti are Grindstone
Cave and Fergie's Cave (fires are not allowed). Ask the Environmental Officer at
Main Camp for maps and information about
more remote sites.

## Hiking Trails

There are three mountain huts (R30 per
person plus R12 trail fee) for which you'll
need sleeping bags and cooking utensils – a
gas stove is provided. Meander Hut is a 2½
hour walk from Main Camp and is on a cliff
above the Meander Valley. Giant's Hut is a
four hour walk from Main Camp and is hard
against the escarpment, under Giant's Castle
itself. Bannerman's Hut is also a four hour
walk from Main Camp and is close to the
escarpment near Bannerman's Pass. If
you're planning to walk between huts rather
than returning to Main Camp you have to
arrange to collect keys. Unless you've booked
out the whole hut you must share it with other
hikers.

The reserve's booklet *Giant's Castle
Game Reserve* gives details and has a basic
map of the trails. There's also a two night
guided trail for R300.

Before setting out on a long walk you must
fill in the rescue register; those planning to
go higher than 2300m must report to the
warden.

Don't confuse trails described here with
the Giant's Cup Trail, further south in the
Drakensberg and covered in the Southern
Drakensberg Wilderness Areas section later
in this chapter.

## Horse-Riding

From the centre at Hillside there is a variety of horse rides. There are short guided rides costing R28 per hour, and R200 overnight rides for experienced riders only. On the overnight rides everything is provided except food, and accommodation is in huts and caves. Horse trails must be booked through the Natal Parks Board in Pieter-maritzburg or the agency in Durban's Tourist Junction. They are not available during July and August and at other times routes are liable to change because of bad weather. Book day rides directly at Hillside on ☎ (0363) 24435 between 9 am and noon daily.

Some of the places to stay in the area, notably Champagne Castle, also offer riding.

## Places to Stay

**Giant's Castle Game Reserve** There are three main areas, as well as trail huts and caves for hikers. Note that nowhere in the park are you allowed to cut or even collect firewood; hikers are not allowed to light fires, so bring a stove. Litter must be brought back, not burned or buried. There's a small supermarket near Main Camp, and a restaurant is planned to open soon.

*Main Camp* has a range of accommodation from R105/158 a single/double in bungalows. You can't camp here.

There's a camp site at *Hillside* in the reserve's north-east corner. It's a long way from Main Camp, let alone the escarpment, but there are good day and overnight walks offering great views of the Drakensberg. Entry costs R6 and sites are R17 per person. There's an eight bed hut for R45 per person (minimum R180) but it's often taken by groups doing horse rides. Book accommodation at Hillside direct (☎ (0363) 24435).

*Injasuti Hutted Camp* (☎ (036) 488 1050 for bookings) is on the north side of the reserve. There's a camp site (R17 per person), and cabins from R75 per person (minimum R150); entry is R6 per person. It's a secluded and pleasant spot.

**Around Giant's Castle Reserve** There are several places on and near the R600 which

runs south-west from Winterton towards Cathkin Peak and Champagne Castle, some of which have been listed earlier in the Central Berg section. *Inkosana Lodge* (☎ (036) 468 1202) is a base for treks and has rooms for R155/260 with breakfast and dinner. Their policy on backpackers has changed a few times over the years, so it's best to ring and check. Currently they do have a dorm (R55) and doubles (R100), with breakfast. But you can't cook, so if you stay for more than a night you have to pay the full-board rates.

Off the road running from Estcourt to Giant's Castle, *White Mountain Lodge* (☎ /fax (0363) 24437) has powered camp sites from R40 (R80 in the high season) and self-catering cottages from R130 a double, depending on the season. In the high season there's a minimum stay of a week, and two days at other times. There's a small shop. The lodge will collect you from Estcourt (free) if you arrange it beforehand.

## Getting There & Away

**Main Camp** The best way into Main Camp is via the dirt road from Mooi River although the last section can be impassable when wet. It's also possible to get here by following the route for Hillside, taking the Hillside turn-off. However, until the road is sealed don't attempt it in wet weather.

Infrequent minibus taxis run from Estcourt to villages near the main entrance (KwaDlamini, Mahlutshini and KwaMankonjane), but these are still several kilometres from Main Camp.

**Hillside** Take the Giant's Castle road from Estcourt, signposted at the Anglican church. Turn left at the White Mountain Lodge junction and after 4km turn right onto the Hillside road. Take the right turn at the two minor intersections which follow.

Minibus taxis, running between Estcourt and the large village of Malutshini on the Bushmans River where you turn off for Main Camp, pass near here. Ask to be let off at Hillside (about 10km before Malutshini) and from here it's about a 5km walk.

KWAZULU-NATAL

**Injasuti** Injasuti is accessible from the township of Loskop, north-west of Estcourt. Turn south 4km west of Loskop or 6km east of the R600; the road is signposted.

## SOUTHERN DRAKENSBERG WILDERNESS AREAS

Four state forests, Highmoor, Mkhomazi, Cobham and Garden Castle, run from Giant's Castle south beyond Bushman's Nek, to meet Lesotho's Sehlabathebe National Park. The big Mkhomazi Wilderness Area and the Mzimkulu Wilderness Area are in the state forests.

The wilderness areas are close to the escarpment, with the Kamberg, Loteni, Vergelegen and Mzimkulwana nature reserves to the east of them, except for a spur of Mzimkulwana which follows the Mkhomazana River (and the road) down from Sani Pass, separating the two wilderness areas.

The wilderness areas are administered by the Natal Parks Board. Entry to each is R4 per person and overnight hiking costs R6.

### Kamberg Nature Reserve

South-east of Giant's Castle and a little away from the main escarpment area, this small (2232 hectares) Natal Parks Board reserve has a number of antelope species. The country in the Drakensberg foothills is pretty, but it's trout fishing which attracts most visitors. The reserve's office sells fishing permits (R15 per rod per day).

Entry to the reserve costs R6 per person and overnight hiking costs R12. The cheapest accommodation is in rest huts, at R65/130 a single/double.

You can get here from Rosetta, off the N3 south of Mooi River, travelling via either Nottingham Road or Redcliffe.

### Highmoor State Forest

Part of the Mkhomazi Wilderness Area is in Highmoor. The forest station (☎ (0333) 37240) is off the road from Rosetta to Giant's Castle and Kamberg. Turn off to the south just past the sign to Kamberg, 31km from Rosetta. Camp sites with limited facilities cost R12, as does overnight hiking.

### Loteni Nature Reserve

There is a **Settlers' Museum** in this reserve and some very good day walks.

There are camp sites (R17) and a variety of accommodation (from R55/83). Phone (☎ (033) 702 0540) to book camp sites. Entry is R6 and the fee for overnight hiking is R12.

The access road runs from the hamlet of Lower Loteni, about 30km north-east of Himeville or 65km south-west of Nottingham Road (off Mooi River). The roads aren't great and heavy rain can close them. They are, however, some of the most scenic in South Africa, with the Drakensberg as a backdrop and many picturesque Zulu villages in the area.

### Mkhomazi State Forest

This is the southern part of Mkhomazi Wilderness Area. The 1200 hectare **Vergelegen Nature Reserve** is along this road; the entry fee is R4 and there are no established camp sites here. The turn-off to the state forest is 44km from Nottingham Road, off the Lower Loteni/Sani Pass road, at the Mzinga River. From here it's another 2km.

### Cobham State Forest

The Mzimkulu Wilderness Area and the Mzimkulwana Nature Reserve are in Cobham state forest. The forest office (☎ (033) 702 0831) is about 15km from Himeville on the D7 and this is a good place to get information on the many hiking trails in the area (some with trail huts). Entry costs R6 and basic camp sites cost R12, as does overnight hiking.

### Garden Castle State Forest

The forest office (☎ (033) 712 1722) is 3km on from the Drakensberg Gardens Hotel, 30km west of Underberg.

You can walk to the top of the escarpment and back in about eight hours if you're fit (and prepared with cold-weather gear) and early risers might make it to the top of spectacular Rhino Peak and back in a day.

You can't camp near the office but there's a nearby hut (part of the Giant's Cup trail) which you can use if it isn't fully booked – it often is. You can camp at the Drakensberg Gardens Hotel or walk at least 3km into the state forest and go wilderness camping, which is allowed and costs R6.

### Sani Pass
This steep route into Lesotho, the highest pass in South Africa (2865m) and the only road between KwaZulu-Natal and Lesotho, is one of the most scenic parts of the Drakensberg (see Sani Pass in the Lesotho chapter). The drive up the pass is magic, with stunning views out across the Umkhomaz-ana River to the north and looming cliffs, almost directly above, on the south side. There are hikes in almost every direction and inexpensive horse rides are available (from R20 for a half day).

Travel Underberg (☎ (033) 701 1466) runs a 4WD up to the Sani Top lodge in Lesotho (R100 return), and at least one of the hostels offers cheaper trips. You need a passport to cross into Lesotho.

See the following Underberg section for some transport options.

**Places to Stay** There are two budget places at the bottom of the pass. *Sani Lodge* (☎ (033) 722 1330) is behind Mokhotlong Transport (also known as Giant's Cup Motors), just before the Sani Pass Hotel and 19km from Underberg. The lodge is run by Russell Suchet, author of *A Backpackers' Guide to Lesotho*. Russell can tell you about the many excellent walks in the area. The hostel is a simple place but pleasant, and you're more likely to meet travellers than party animals here. Dorms are R24, doubles are R56 and camping is R16 per person. You can buy drinks and cakes here but bring other supplies.

Another 5km along the road, *Wild West Sani Youth Hostel* (☎ (033) 702 0340) has dorms, doubles and rondavels, all for R25 per person. The owner is a keen conservationist and offers free accommodation to travellers who help him with conservation projects.

The *Sani Pass Hotel* (☎ (033) 722 1320),

complete with guards and razor-wire fences, is also at the bottom of the pass, 14km from Himeville. It has pricey dinner, bed and breakfast packages.

### Bushman's Nek
This is a South Africa/Lesotho border post. From here there are hiking trails up into the escarpment, including to Lesotho's Sehla-bathebe National Park. You can walk in or hire a horse for R40. How often do you get to enter a country on horseback?

A few kilometres east of the border post is *Bushman's Nek Hotel* (☎ (033) 701 1460), which has rooms for R175 per person (cheaper out of season) and four-person self-catering chalets from R170. Closer to the border post is *Silver Streams Caravan Park* (☎ (033) 701 1249) with sites and huts.

### GIANT'S CUP HIKING TRAIL
The five day, 60km Giant's Cup Trail, which runs from Sani Pass to Bushman's Nek, is one of the great walks of South Africa. It's designed so that any reasonably fit person can walk it, so it's very popular. Early booking (up to nine months ahead, through the Natal Parks Board in Pietermaritzburg or the agency at Durban's Tourist Junction) is advisable. Although the walking is relatively easy, the usual precautions necessary for the Drakensberg apply – expect severe cold snaps at any time of the year.

The stages are as follows: Day 1 – 14km, Day 2 – 9km, Day 3 – 12km, Day 4 – 13km and Day 5 – 12km. The highlights include the Bathplug Cave with San rock paintings, beautiful Crane Tarn, and the breathtaking mountain scenery on Day 4.

Tents are not permitted on this trail; accommodation in shared huts costs R30 per person. No firewood is available so you'll need a stove and fuel. The Sani Lodge (☎ (033) 722 1330) is almost at the trailhead; arrange for the lodge to pick you up from Himeville or Underberg.

### UNDERBERG
This quiet little town in the foothills of the southern Drakensberg is the centre of a

farming community. There's a First National
Bank here. The southern Drakensberg offers
excellent wilderness hiking, and the Underberg Hiking Club is a very good source of
information. The Natal Parks Board has an
office in the main street.

South of Underberg, off the R626 to
Kokstad, the Natal Parks Board's **Coleford
Nature Reserve** (1272 hectares) has some
game, but it's more of a recreation than a
nature reserve. Trout fishing is popular here
and you can get a permit and hire equipment
in the reserve. You can't camp here, but there
are inexpensive rustic cabins and chalets.

**Places to Stay & Eat**
The archaic *Underberg Hotel* (☎ (033) 701
1412) has rooms for R95 per person, including breakfast. For B&Bs (from R85) and
cottages to rent in the area contact Travel
Underberg (☎ (033) 701 1466; email
travel.underberg@pixie.com.za), just off the
main street, on the Himeville road. Jonathan
Aldous, who runs Travel Underberg and also
the lodge at the top of Sani Pass in Lesotho,
is a good source of information on the area
and travel into Lesotho.

In the new shopping centre is the frilly
*White Cottage Café* and on the southern edge
of town is the *Bull & Tankard* restaurant.

West of Underberg, on the Garden Castle
Forest Station road and in a magnificent
valley, is the *Drakensberg Gardens Hotel*
(☎ (033) 701 1355), a fairly impersonal
resort-style place with rooms from R169/
278, for full board. You can camp here. The
unsealed 29km road from the R617 to
Drakensberg Gardens is in good condition
but slippery after rain, especially the last
6km. There are quite a number of other
places to stay along this road.

Also out of town and set on 10 hectares is
*Eagle's Rock* (☎ (0033) 701 1757), with self-
catering thatched cottages for R65, or R85
with breakfast.

**Getting There & Away**
Transtate/City to City runs between Matat-
iele (west of Kokstad) and Jo'burg via
Underberg, from Sunday to Friday. The

buses stop diagonally opposite the Mobil
station on the main street.

Sani Pass Carriers (☎ (033) 701 1017) runs
here from Durban three times a week (R70) and
from Pietermaritzburg every weekday (R50).
Minibus taxis run to Pietermaritzburg (R17)
and Himeville (R2) and you might find one
running to the Sani Pass Hotel.

The main routes to Underberg and nearby
Himeville are from Pietermaritzburg on the
R617 and from Kokstad on the R626, but it's
possible to drive here from the north-east via
Nottingham Road, south of Mooi River, and
Lower Loteni. These roads are mainly
unsealed and can be closed after rain.

**HIMEVILLE**
Not far from Underberg, this smaller but
nicer town is above 1500m so winters are
coolish. A good place for a spot of tennis and
a pink gin! There's a **museum** on the main
street, in a building which was originally a
small fort and nowadays has displays on
local history. It's open from 10 am to noon
on Wednesday, Friday and weekends.

The **Himeville Nature Reserve**, on the
north-east side of town, is popular for trout
fishing (you can hire rowing boats) and there
are a few antelopes around. On the Pevensey
Rd, 14km east of Himeville, is the **Swamp
Nature Reserve**, which has the Polela River
as 3km of its southern boundary. This is a
small wetlands reserve, home to many
species of waterbird, including the rare
wattled crane.

**Places to Stay & Eat**
There is a Natal Parks Board *camp site* in the
Himeville Nature Reserve not far from town,
where open camp sites are R17 per person;
the entry fee is R6 per person. The *Himeville
Arms* (☎ /fax (033) 702 1305) has good
rooms from R130/240, including breakfast.
At the 'black bar', a little further down the
road to Underberg, you'll be made much
more welcome.

**Getting There & Away**
About the only regular transport from Himeville are minibus taxis to Underberg (R2) and

twice-daily KZT buses to Pietermaritzburg. The road to Underberg is lined with oak trees, the result of a reconciliation between the two towns after a feud.

## GRIQUALAND EAST

Historically the Voortrekkers had been moving into the Griqua territory between the Vaal and the Orange rivers, around Philippolis, since the 1820s. The Griqua chief, Adam Kok III, realising that there would soon be no land left, encouraged his people to sell off their remaining titles and move elsewhere.

In 1861, Kok's entire community of 2000 with about 20,000 head of cattle began their epic, two year journey over the rugged mountains of Lesotho to Nomansland, a region on the far side of the Drakensberg. When they reached the southern slopes of Mt Currie they set up camp. Later, in 1869, they moved to the present site of Kokstad. Nomansland was called Griqualand East after annexation by the Cape in 1874. Kok died the following year when he was thrown from his cart.

Today the main towns in the area are Kokstad, Matatiele and Cedarville. It is a pleasant place to visit and the residents are extremely friendly.

### Kokstad

Kokstad is named in honour of Adam Kok III. It lies 1280m above sea level in the Umzimhlava River valley, between Mt Currie and the Ngele mountains. Today it's a pleasant little place with some solid buildings and, despite its backwater air, excellent transport connections.

The library (☎ (037) 727 3133) in the impressive town hall has information on the area. There's a telephone service off the entrance to the Royal Hotel where you can make calls without coins.

**Places to Stay & Eat** The shady municipal *caravan park* (☎ (037) 727 3133) is next to the sports ground, near the town centre.

*The Balmoral* (☎ (037) 727 2070) is OK, sort of, and charges R152/280 with break-

fast. It's on Hope St, the main road, so rooms at the front might be noisy. The *Royal Hotel* (☎ (037) 727 2060), 85 Main St, is cheaper.

Apart from the hotels there's a *Spur* steakhouse at the Balmoral, a *Wimpy* next to the Mount Currie Motel, and *Norah's Pie Place* on Barkley St.

**Getting There & Away** Various Transtate/City to City services depart from the train station for Pietermaritzburg, Umtata, Jo'burg and Underberg. There's also a slow but scenic service to Welkom via Transkei and Maclear. The City to City (book through Translux) Jo'burg-Umtata service runs via Kokstad. Greyhound and Translux run to Umtata, Durban and Port Elizabeth. Greyhound and City to City stop at the Wimpy Bar, a little way from the town centre on the Durban to Umtata road.

The train station is a few blocks west (downhill) from the main street. You can book buses here or through Keval Travel (☎ (037) 727 3124), which is on Main St in the same building as the Kokstad Pharmacy. The minibus taxi park is between Hope and Main Sts and regular taxis go to Pietermaritzburg, Durban, Mt Frere and Matatiele.

### Around Kokstad

A few kilometres north of Kokstad, off the R626 to Franklin, is the **Mt Currie Nature Reserve** (☎ (037) 727 3844). There are walking trails and several antelope species in this grassy 1800 hectare reserve. A memorial marks the site of Adam Kok's first laager. Open camp sites in the reserve cost R17 per person.

Out of Kokstad, on the R56 and just before the N2, is the *Mount Currie Motel* (☎ /fax (037) 727 2178). It's slightly more upmarket than the Kokstad hotels and has a restaurant.

There is an isolated chunk of Eastern Cape Province north-east of Kokstad called Umzimkulu; the boundaries are subject to a referendum in the future.

### Ngele Hiking Trail

In the **Weza State Forest**, off the N2 east of Kokstad near Staffords Post, is the Ngele

KWAZULU-NATAL

Trail system (*ngele* means 'precipitous place'). There are a variety of hiking possibilities and the main trail is either a four day (64km) or five day (95km) excursion. The additional day is extremely tough as it takes in the 28km Fairview Loop and an ascent of 2268m Ngele mountain.

The forest is in hilly country and is partly a huge pine plantation and partly indigenous forest. The trail also leads through mountain grassland, highland sourveld ('sour' because it loses its palatability in winter). The orange-yellow flowers of the Christmas bell (*Sandersonia aurantiaca*), endemic to South Africa, appear here in December. There is a population of well over 1000 bushbuck, as well as common duiker and mountain reedbuck. Predators include the African wild cat, caracal, large-spotted genet and serval. Well over 70 bird species have been recorded.

During August and September the trail is usually closed because of fire danger – be very careful at other times too. Accommodation in old farm buildings costs R18 per person and is booked, along with the trails, through the Natal Parks Board in Pietermaritzburg or the agency in Durban's Tourist Junction.

# The Midlands

The Midlands run north-east from Durban to Estcourt, skirting Zululand to the north-east. This is mainly farming country with not a lot to interest visitors. The main town is Pietermaritzburg – the capital of KwaZulu-Natal.

West of Pietermaritzburg there is pretty, hilly country, with horse studs and plenty of European trees. This area was settled mainly by English farmers and looks a little like England's West Country. The various artists' and potters' galleries in this area are included in the *Midlands Meander*; pick up a brochure from one of the larger tourist offices.

## PIETERMARITZBURG
After defeating the Zulu at the decisive Battle of Blood River, the Voortrekkers began to establish their republic of Natal. Pietermaritzburg (usually known as PMB) was named in honour of leader Pieter Mauritz Retief, and was founded in 1838 as the capital (later the 'u' was dropped and, in 1938, it was decreed that Voortrekker leader Gert Maritz be remembered in the title). Here in 1841 the Boers built their Church of the Vow to honour the Blood River promise. The British annexed Natal in 1843 but they retained Pietermaritzburg – well positioned, less humid than Durban and already a neat little town – as the capital.

As well as the Afrikaner and British presence there's a big Indian population. Streets around Retief St, such as Church and Longmarket Sts, echo the Subcontinent.

PMB rightly bills itself as the heritage city, as it has numerous historic buildings and a British colonial air. Get a copy of the *Mini-Guide* from the Publicity Association – it details the interesting buildings in the centre of town.

### Orientation
The central grid of Pietermaritzburg contains most places of interest to travellers, although as is becoming depressingly common in South Africa, white businesses are beginning to flee the city centre. South-east of the centre is the University of Natal.

The north end of the city, beyond Retief St, is a largely Indian commercial district. It shuts down at night and is the least safe part of the city centre. North of here is the Indian residential area of Northdale (with suburbs such as Bombay Heights and Mysore Ridge). To the south-west of the city is Edendale, the black dormitory suburb. West, on the Old Howick Rd beyond Queen Elizabeth Park, is the village of Hilton, a leafy and slightly twee residential area. Hilton is only about 10km from PMB but it's a long way up. If it's rainy in PMB then Hilton will probably be in the clouds.

### Information
The helpful Publicity Association (☎ (0331) 45 1348; fax 94 3535) is in Publicity House at 177 Commercial Rd, on the corner of

**PLACES TO STAY**
5 'Sunduzi Backpackers
6 Summer Place
18 Karos Capital Towers
22 Tudor Inn
28 Imperial Hotel
29 Crown Hotel
36 Cumberland Hotel
40 Kismet Hotel
42 City Royal Hotel
45 YMCA

**PLACES TO EAT**
8 Cheap Cafés
19 Golden Dragon Restaurant
23 Drifter's Pub & Grub
37 Indian Cafe

**OTHER**
1 Polo Tavern
2 Keg & Elephant
3 Rennies Travel
4 KwaZulu Department of
  Nature Conservation
7 Bus Station; KZT Buses
9 Minibus Taxis to Underberg
10 Train Station;
11 Minibus Taxis to Ladysmith
12 Minibus Taxis to Johannesburg
13 Black Stag
14 Macrorie House Museum
15 First National Bank
16 Standard Bank
17 Old Colonial Buildings
20 City Hall
21 Statue of Gandhi
24 American Express
25 Old Supreme Court
  (Tatham Art Gallery)
26 GPO
27 Natal Museum
30 Post Office
31 Publicity Association
32 Long-Distance Buses;
  City Buses
33 Modern Memorial Church
34 Voortrekker Museum
35 Islamia Mosque
38 Hindu Temple
39 Hindu Temple
41 Spotted Dog
43 Voortrekker Cemetery
44 Flea Market

Pietermaritzburg

## From Pietermaritzburg Station to Mahatma?

Anyone who has seen Richard Attenborough's film *Gandhi* will recall the scene when Gandhi is ejected from the train and his suitcases are unceremoniously dumped onto the station platform.

The station was Pietermaritzburg. The 24-year-old Gandhi was on his way to Pretoria in the Transvaal for legal business. He had boarded the train with a 1st-class ticket and duly went to his allocated compartment. A white passenger complained to railway officials who ordered Gandhi to the baggage car.

When he protested, displaying his 1st-class ticket, they called a policeman who threw him out. He could have gone to 3rd class but he refused. Instead, he meditated in the station's cold waiting room. Some years later, in India, when asked about the most influential experiences in his life, he cited this incident. There is now a plaque at the station where the incident occurred. ■

Longmarket St. Rennies Travel (☎ (0331) 94 1571) is at 207 Pietermaritz St, near the corner of Levy St. The AA (☎ (0331) 42 0571) is in Brasfort House at 191 Commercial Rd.

**Natal Parks Board Headquarters** This office, where you book most of the accommodation and walks in KwaZulu-Natal parks, is a long way from the city centre, in Queen Elizabeth Park, a small nature reserve. You can make phone bookings with a credit card but it's better to visit to collect the useful literature. For general inquiries phone (☎ (0331) 47 1986); for bookings call (☎ (0331) 47 1981).

Head out to the Old Howick Rd (Commercial Rd) and turn right onto Link Rd about 1km past the big roundabout. The office is about 2km further on. A Wembley bus from stand 10 at the city bus rank behind the Publicity Association will get you to the roundabout.

**KwaZulu Department of Nature Conservation** The KDNC's office (☎ (0331) 94 6696; fax 42 1948) is in the old YWCA building at 108 Chapel St, between Pietermaritz and Berg. It's open on weekdays from 8 am to 4.15 pm.

**Forestry Branch Library** In the Southern Life Building on Church St, this library (☎ (0331) 42 8101), is worth visiting for information on the area's state forests.

### Things to See & Do

Two of PMB's best features are its avenues of huge old **jacaranda trees** (some under threat because they are taking up parking spaces) and the maze of narrow pedestrian **lanes** running off the mall between Church and Longmarket Sts.

There are a number of colonial-era buildings. The massive red brick **city hall**, on the corner of Church and Commercial Sts, is a good example, as is the old **Supreme Court** across the road (now the Tatham Art Gallery). The **Publicity Association office**, itself housed in the old borough police and fire complex (1884), has a walking-tour map.

**Macrorie House Museum**, on the corner of Loop and Pine Sts, displays items related to early British settlement. It's open from 9 am to 1 pm Tuesday to Thursday, from 11 am to 4 pm on Sunday. For another view, visit the **Voortrekker Museum** on Church St near the city hall. It's open on weekdays from 9 am to 4 pm and on Saturday morning. The museum is in the **Church of the Vow**, built in 1841 to fulfil the Voortrekkers' part of the Blood River bargain. Afrikaner icons on display include Retief's prayerbook and waterbottle, and a replica of a trek wagon. The words of the Vow are in the **Modern Memorial Church** next door.

The **Natal Museum** has a range of displays, including African ethnography. It's on Loop St, south-west of Commercial Rd and is open from 9 am to 4.30 pm Monday to Saturday, and on Sunday from 2 to 5 pm.

The **Tatham Art Gallery**, housed in the old Supreme Court, is open every day except Monday, from 10 am to 6 pm. It has a good collection of French and English 19th and early 20th-century works. Perhaps the best collection of artworks in PMB is the least known: the **Natal Provincial Administration Collection** at 330 Longmarket St. Included are some of the finest examples of indigenous art, including beadwork, pottery and weaving; it is open by appointment only (☎ (0331) 45 3201).

Architect Phillip Dudgeon modelled the **Standard Bank** in the Church St mall on the Bank of Ireland in Belfast. It has an unusual set of stained-glass windows depicting the four seasons as one would experience them in the northern hemisphere (someone messed up!).

There are two **Hindu temples** at the north end of Longmarket St. The main **mosque** is nearby, on Church St. Recently a **statue of Gandhi** was erected opposite the old colonial buildings on Church St.

The **Natal Botanic Gardens**, 2km west of the train station on the continuation of Berg St, has exotic species and a garden of indigenous mist-belt flora.

The **Natal Steam Railway Museum** (☎ (0331) 43 1857) is in Hilton on the corner of Hilton Ave and Quarry Rd. There are occasional steam train excursions.

There's a good view of the city from **World's View**, a lookout on a hill reached from the Old Howick Rd.

### Places to Stay – bottom end

The municipal *caravan park* (☎ (0331) 65342) is on Cleland Rd, nearly 5km from the train station. Head south-east on Commercial Rd, which becomes Durban Rd after you cross the creek. Go left onto Blackburrow Rd across the freeway then take the first road to the right.

There's a reasonable hostel, *'Sunduzi Backpackers* (☎ (0331) 94 0072), 140 Berg St. The owner is a licensed game hunter, so there are a lot of animal skins about the place and photos of hunters gloating over the bodies of big cats. There are dorms and doubles, and you can arrange to stay at the owner's game farm.

Other cheap accommodation can be found at the *Jan Richter Centre* (☎ (0331) 69252),

on the corner of New Scotland Rd and Stalkers Alley (walk south-east on West St, cross the creek, and New Scotland Rd is 1km further on the right).

There are a few cheap hotels, such as *Kismet* (☎ (0331) 45 1141), corner of Longmarket and Retief Sts (R80/100), and the nearby *Cumberland* (☎ (0331) 45 0793), which is very run-down. You're much better off at the hostel.

### Places to Stay – middle & top end

The *Crown Hotel* (☎ (0331) 94 1601), at 186 Commercial St, is handy to the long-distance bus stop and the town centre. It's a small place, with singles/doubles from R150/190. The excellent *Tudor Inn* (☎ (0331) 42 1778), at 18 Theatre Lane, has doubles only for R230. Some of the rooms are very large and it's in a good location.

The *City Royal Hotel* (☎ (0331) 94 7072; fax 94 7080), 301 Burger St, doesn't look all that impressive from the outside but the rooms are very good and it's off the main streets so there's no traffic noise. There's a restaurant and bar, secure parking and courteous and helpful staff. Rooms are good value at R250/280 a single/double, slightly less on weekends.

*Karos Capital Towers* (☎ (0331) 43 3267), 121 Commercial St, charges R215/225, plus R30 for breakfast. The *Imperial* (☎ (0331) 42 2857), 224 Loop St, charges from R265/295, with breakfast.

*Rehoboth* (☎ (0331) 96 2312), 276 Murray Rd in the suburb of Lincoln Meade, has Victorian-style self-catering cottages in a large garden, which cost between R120 and R300.

There are many B&Bs and the Publicity Association provides a full list.

**Hilton** In nearby Hilton you'll find the Tudor-style *Hilton Hotel* (☎ (0331) 33311; fax 33722), which isn't a member of the chain. Singles/doubles cost R250/300, with breakfast. Another good place is *Crossways Country Inn* (☎ /fax (0331) 43 3267), which charges R130/200 for singles/doubles, breakfast included. There are some good

B&Bs and guesthouses in Hilton, including *The Stables at Highcroft* (☎ (0331) 43 4009), 21 Hilton Ave, with bedrooms in old stables costing R130/250, and *Whytten House* (☎ (0331) 43 4421), 50 Groenkloof Rd, from R140/200.

## Places to Eat

Across from the train station and up Church St are a couple of basic cafés selling take-away-style food. More upmarket snacks are sold near the long-distance bus stop on Longmarket St at *Upper Crust Patisserie*. Up in the Indian area there is a good place for Indian food opposite the Cumberland Hotel.

The meals at *Café Bavaria*, in the NBS Building, are good value. *Ristorante da Vinci*, at 117 Commercial Rd, is a good Italian place with cheap lunches.

*Golden Dragon*, on the corner of Commercial Rd in the Karos Capital Towers, has been recommended by locals. *Tuskers* at 60 Boshoff St was once a good member of the Mike's Kitchen chain, and is worth trying. Most of the hotels have restaurants and we recommend the City Royal Hotel.

The best Indian food in town is found at *Pakeesa's*, on the corner of Naidoo and Greytown Sts, in the Indian suburb of Raisethorpe.

## Entertainment

PMB is not the most exciting place in the province – catch a bus to Durban if you want full-on entertainment. *Ristorante da Vinci* at 117 Commercial Rd is a popular nightspot. Not far away, at 80 Commercial Rd, is the *Keg & Elephant*, an atmospheric watering hole. The *Spotted Dog* at 363 Burger St, the *Black Stag* at 24 Longmarket St and *Drifters Pub & Grub* on Theatre Lane are good for imbibing beer.

For something completely different try the *Polo Tavern*, on West St at the corner of Greyling St. This grungy neighbourhood pub always has music and is good fun.

## Getting There & Away

**Air** SA Airlink (☎ (0331) 69286) flies to Durban (R114), Jo'burg (R445) and Ulundi (R114).

**Bus** Greyhound and Translux stop near the Publicity Association on a little road between Church and Longmarket Sts. Translux goes to Bloemfontein (R135) via Bethlehem (R95), and Jo'burg/Pretoria (R110) via Harrismith (R55). Greyhound has several services each day between Durban and Jo'burg/Pretoria via Ladysmith and Newcastle. The Durban-Kimberley run also stops in PMB. Book Translux and Greyhound at the Publicity Association.

Cheetah Coaches (☎ (0331) 42 0266; 42 2673) runs daily between Durban, PMB and Durban international airport; its offices are in the Main City Building at 206 Longmarket St. The fare to Durban is R23.

KZT (☎ (0331) 42 8133) runs local services around the former KwaZulu Homeland, departing from the local bus depot on Havelock Rd, near the train station. The fare to Newcastle is R35 and to Estcourt R35.

Sani Pass Carriers (☎ (033) 701 1017) runs up into the southern Drakensberg on weekdays. The fare to Underberg is R50.

**Train** The train station has had its Victorian charms partially restored. Here, you can catch the weekly *Trans Oranje* (Durban-Cape Town) and the daily *Trans Natal* (Durban-Jo'burg).

**Minibus Taxi** Most minibus taxi ranks are near the train station. Fares include: Jo'burg R55, Newcastle R35, Estcourt R17 and Ladysmith R23. Other taxis depart from Market Square (behind Publicity House), and you might find taxis running to Umtata and Maseru here.

**Car & Motorbike** If you're heading north, a nicer route than the N3 is the R103 which runs through pretty country between Howick and Mooi River. For a long but scenic drive to Durban, head north on the R33 (the continuation of Church St) to Sevenoaks, then cut back to the coast on the R614. Watch out for pedestrians and slow-moving cane trucks on this road.

Avis (☎ toll-free 08000 21111), Budget (☎ toll-free 0800 16622) and Imperial (☎ toll-free 0800 131 000) have agents here.

**Hitching** If you're hitching in on the N3, get off at Exit 81 (Church St) for the city centre, Exit 76 (northbound) or Exit 74 (southbound) for the municipal caravan park.

### Getting Around
The main rank for city-area buses is on the road running behind the Publicity Association on the corner of Longmarket St and Commercial Rd.

For a taxi, phone Springbok (☎ (0331) 42 4444), Junior (☎ (0331) 94 5454) or Unique (☎ (0331) 91 1238).

## AROUND PIETERMARITZBURG
### Howick
In the town of Howick, about 25km northwest of Pietermaritzburg on the N3, are the popular Howick Falls. Just before the falls there is the small **Howick Museum**, an unabashedly parochial celebration of the town; it is open from 9 am to noon and 2 to 3.30 pm Tuesday to Friday, and from 10 am to 1 pm on Sunday.

The small (656 hectare) **Umgeni Valley Nature Reserve**, with walks and some more falls, is nearby. This is one of the best conservation education centres in South Africa. Over 200 bird species have been recorded in the confines of the reserve.

The municipal *caravan park* (☎ (0332) 30 6124) is near the falls on Morling St and *Orient Park* (☎ (0332) 30 2067) is near the Midmar Dam wall. The *Howick Falls Hotel* (☎ (0332) 30 2809), 2 Main St, charges just R75 per person with breakfast. *Harrow Hill Guest Farm* (☎ (0332) 30 5033), 8 Karkloof Rd (4km from Howick), charges R240 a double.

### Midmar Public Resort
This resort is a few kilometres from Howick. Although there are some animals in the reserve it is mainly a recreation area, with water sports on the dam. There's an entry fee of R6 per person. There's accommodation at *Munro Bay*, cheapest in chalets, and camping at *Dukududku*, *Morgenzon* and *Munro Bay* (phone ☎ (0331) 47 1981 to book sites).

### Midmar Historical Village
This village (☎ (0332) 30 5351), which is open daily from 9 am to 4 pm, adjoins the resort. The project aims to recreate a typical Natal village of the 1900-10 era. There are already a number of interesting exhibits including Durban's last steam-driven tugboat, a Shiva temple and Zulu huts. The entrance fee is R8 and train rides are R6 per person.

### Albert Falls Public Resort
This resort is also run by the Natal Parks Board and is 25km from PMB, off the road north to Greytown. Tent sites at *Notuli* are R17 per person (book on ☎ (03393) 202), and there are inexpensive rondavels and chalets. Note that there have been outbreaks of bilharzia in the dam.

## MOOI RIVER
Mooi River is a nondescript town, but the early Voortrekkers probably had high hopes for it, as *mooi* means beautiful. The Zulu were more matter of fact, calling it *mpofana*, 'place of the eland'. The surrounding countryside, especially to the west, is worth exploring. It's horse-stud country on rolling land dotted with old European trees.

Mooi River is closer to Giant's Castle than Estcourt and, while there are fewer minibus taxis from here, the town is right on the N3 so hitching to and from here may be easier.

### Places to Stay & Eat
In town there's a caravan park, *Riverbank* (☎ (0333) 32144) and the *Argyle Hotel* (☎ (0333) 31106), charging R85/140.

If you continue past the caravan park for about 15km you will come to *Sierra Ranch* (☎ (0333) 31073) where chalets and rondavels start at R145 per person, including dinner and breakfast. Rates are a little lower on weekends.

See the following Nottingham Road & Around section for some excellent country guesthouses in this area.

There's a restaurant and bar, the *Station Masters Arms*, in the refurbished old railway station. The *golf club*, reached from town by taking the underpass on the north side of the river, serves solid lunches for about R25 – ask a member to sign you in.

### Getting There & Away

Transtate/City to City buses on the Jo'burg/Pretoria to Umtata route stop here, but not often. Greyhound buses running between Durban and Jo'burg/Pretoria stop at the Wimpy, at the big truck stop on the Rosetta road near the N3, 1km from the centre.

The *Trans Oranje* and *Trans Natal* trains stop here. Book tickets at the goods office, across the tracks from the old station.

Minibus taxis aren't frequent and run mainly to nearby villages.

### NOTTINGHAM ROAD & AROUND

The quaint little town of Nottingham Road was named to honour the Nottinghamshire Regiment of the British Army, which was garrisoned here. This is probably the most gentrified corner of the country and there are some expensive but excellent guesthouses in the area. Most have extensive gardens.

One place that isn't so expensive but is still good is *The Outpost* (☎ (0333) 36836), 2km from Nottingham Road on Old Main Rd. Rooms cost from around R200 a double. *Thatchings* (☎ (0333) 36275) is 3km from town and is well equipped. Doubles, with breakfast, cost R360.

One of the better-known places is *Granny Mouse Country House* (☎ /fax (0333) 234 4071), near the village of Balgowan, south of Mooi River. It's off the R103, a pretty road running parallel to the N3 between Howick and Mooi River. B&B costs from around R300 per person. Not far away but north of the N3, *Old Halliwell* (☎ (0332) 30 2602) charges around R400 per person. *Rawdon's* (☎ /fax (0333) 36044) has doubles from R400. *Hartford House* (☎ (0333) 32713) was the home of Natal's last prime minister.

You pay from R400/550 (and way up) to experience the luxury.

# Thukela

Bird-watchers may be attracted to the St Lucia Wetlands, walkers and climbers to the Drakensberg and wildlife lovers to Kruger, but the historian will be happy in Thukela. The Thukela region, at the headwaters of the Tugela ('the startling one') officially also includes the northern and central Drakensberg, but these are covered in a separate section of this chapter.

Some of the more important conflicts in South Africa's history took place in the area, including the Siege of Ladysmith, the Battle of Spioenkop, the bloody defeat of the British by the Zulu at Isandlwana, the heroic Defence of Rorke's Drift and the battles of Majuba Hill and Blood River – the region is often described as the Battlefields Route. Get free copies of *Natal Battlefields Route*, *Dundee* and *Natal Battlefields Chronicle* from local publicity associations and the Tourist Junction in Durban.

### ESTCOURT

Estcourt, named after an early sponsor of an immigration scheme to the area, is at the southern edge of Thukela. The town is close to the central Drakensberg resorts and the Giant's Castle, and it's on the Jo'burg/Pretoria-Durban bus route. It also has good train and minibus taxi connections. About 8km west of Estcourt is the black township of Wembesi.

### Things to See & Do

Now a museum, **Fort Durnford** was built in 1874 to protect Estcourt from Zulu attack; the museum is open from 9 am to noon and 1 to 4 pm on weekdays. There are interesting displays and a reconstructed Zulu village in the grounds.

There's not much to do or see at **Wagendrift Public Resort** (☎ (0363) 22550) but you can swim and fish in the dam, camp for

## Thukela & Battlefields

R20 per person or stay in the one four-bed chalet for R50 per person (minimum R100). Entry is R3 during the week, R6 on weekends. The resort is 7km south-west of Estcourt on the road to Ntabamhlope. A little further on from the resort, at the head of the dam, is the **Moor Park Nature Reserve**, which overlooks Wagendrift Dam and Bushmens River. There are zebra, wildebeest and antelope.

About 25km north-east of Estcourt is the 5000 hectare **Weenen Game Reserve**, which has black and white rhino, buffalo, giraffe and several antelope species, including the rare roan. There are two good walking trails – Amanzimyama and Reclamation. Entry costs R5 per person and R10 per vehicle. Camp sites (☎ (0363) 41809) are R15 per person.

Almost at the point where the R103 meets the R74, 16km north of Estcourt, is the site where the young Winston Churchill was captured by the Boers in 1899 when they derailed the armoured train he was travelling in; there is a plaque just off the road.

### Places to Stay

The inexpensive municipal *caravan park*

KWAZULU-NATAL

(☎ (0363) 23000) isn't far from the town centre on Lorne St. *Lucey's Plough Hotel* (☎ (0363) 23040), 86 Harding St, has singles/doubles for R115/196 with bath and rooms for R88 without, including breakfast.

### Getting There & Away

**Bus** Transtate/City to City services between Welkom and Port Shepstone, via Pieter-maritzburg, sometimes stop in Estcourt. Greyhound buses on the Durban-Kimberley and Durban-Jo'burg/Pretoria route leave from the municipal library on Victoria St.

Wembezi Tours has local buses departing from the minibus taxi rank to Durban (R30), Ladysmith (R14) and Bergville (R6).

**Train** The weekly *Trans Oranje* (Cape Town-Durban) and the daily *Trans Natal* (Jo'burg/Pretoria-Durban) stop here. Book tickets at the goods (freight) depot, not at the train station. The depot is a few blocks south-west of the station, past the Nestlé factory and under the railway overpass.

**Minibus Taxi** The main minibus taxi rank is at the bottom of Phillips St in the town centre, downhill from the post office. Taxis beside the post office are for the local area only. Examples of fares are Durban R25, Winterton R7, Ladysmith R12, Pietermaritz-burg R18 and Jo'burg R55.

### COLENSO

As well as Spioenkop, there are several other Anglo-Boer War battlefields near Colenso, a small town about 20km south of Ladysmith. Colenso was the British base during the Relief of Ladysmith, and there is a museum and several memorial sites relating to the Battle of Colenso on 15 December 1899, another disaster for the hapless General Buller at the hands of Louis Botha. The **museum** is in the toll house adjacent to the bridge. You can get the keys from the police station between 8 am and 6 pm.

Lord Roberts' only son, Freddy, was among those slaughtered here (with about 1100 other British) – he is buried in the

**Chieveley military cemetery**, south of the town.

There is a *caravan park* (☎ (03622) 2737) run by the municipality in town and the *Old Jail Lodge* (☎ (03622) 2594), which has a restaurant.

### SPIOENKOP NATURE RESERVE

This 6000 hectare Natal Parks Board reserve is based on the Spioenkop Dam on the Tugela River. The reserve is handy to most of the area's battlefield sites and not too far from the Drakensberg for day trips. Animals in the small game reserves (there are two reserves in the resort) include white rhino, giraffe, zebra and various antelope species. There's a swimming pool, and horse-riding and tours of the Spioenkop battlefield are available. Entry costs R6.

Accommodation at the eight bed bush camp at *Ntenjwa* costs R75 per person (minimum R150) and the four bed tented camp at *iPika* costs R60 (minimum R120). Camp sites at iPika cost R22 per person. Book accommodation direct (☎ (036) 488 1578).

The resort is just north of Bergville but the entrance is on the eastern side, off the R600, which runs between the N3 and Winterton. If you are coming from the south on the N3 take the turn off to the R74 to get to Winterton.

### LADYSMITH

Ladysmith (not to be confused with the town of Ladismith in Western Cape) was named after the wife of Cape Colony governor Sir Harry Smith, but it could well have had a much more colourful name. She wasn't just plain Lady Smith, she was Lady Juana Maria de los Dolores ... Smith.

The 'smith' in Ladysmith is sometimes pronounced 'smit'.

The town achieved fame during the 1899-1902 Anglo-Boer War, when it was besieged by Boer forces for 118 days. Apart from the historical aspect – several buildings in the city centre were here during the siege – Ladysmith is a pleasant place to walk around.

## The Battle of Spioenkop

On 23 January 1900 the British, led by General Buller, made a second attempt to relieve Ladysmith, which had been under siege by the Boers since late October 1899. After 15,000 of his men had been prevented from crossing the Tugela River by 500 Boers at Trichardt's Drift, Buller decided that he needed to take Spioenkop. This flat-topped hill would make a good gun emplacement from which to clear the annoying Boers from their trenches.

During the night 1700 British troops climbed the hill and chased off the few Boers guarding it. They dug a trench and waited for morning. Meanwhile the Boer commander, Louis Botha, heard of the raid. He ordered his field guns to be trained onto Spioenkop and positioned some of his men on nearby hills. A further 400 soldiers began to climb Spioenkop as the misty dawn broke.

The British might have beaten off the 400, but the mist finally lifted, and was immediately replaced by a hail of bullets and shells. The British retreated to their trench and by mid-afternoon, continuous shellfire combined with the summer heat caused many to surrender. By now, reinforcements were on hand (summoned, according to some, by the young Winston Churchill) and the Boers could not overrun the trench. A bloody stalemate was developing.

After sunset the British evacuated the hill; so did the Boers. Both retreats were accomplished so smoothly that neither side was aware that the other had left. That night Spioenkop was held by the dead.

It was not until the next morning that the Boers again climbed up Spioenkop and found that it was theirs. The Boers had killed or wounded 1340 British and taken 1000 prisoners, at a loss of 230 casualties, unusually high for their small army. Gandhi's stretcher-bearer unit performed with distinction at this battle. Buller relieved Ladysmith a month later on 28 February. ■

Sadly, Ladysmith is a microcosm of modern South Africa. The whites live in relative comfort in the best parts of town; most of Ladysmith's large Indian population lives south and west of the river in Leonardsville and Rose Park; the coloured population lives in Limit Hill; and the blacks live in townships around eZakheni (once in the KwaZulu Homeland), 20km away.

The information office (☎ (0361) 22992) is in the town hall on Murchison St and is open on weekdays during office hours. Ask here about guided tours of the battlefields.

## Things to See

The very good **Siege Museum** is next to the town hall in the Market House (built in 1884) which was used to store rations during the siege. You can pick up a walking-tour map of Ladysmith here. The museum is open between 8 am and 4.20 pm on weekdays and until noon on Saturday. If you phone ☎ (0361) 22231 (ask for the museum) you can arrange for someone to open the museum for you between 2 and 4 pm on Saturday or from 10 to 11.30 am on Sunday.

Outside the town hall are two guns, **Castor** and **Pollux**, used by the British in defence of Ladysmith. Nearby is a replica of **Long Tom**, a Boer gun capable of heaving a shell 10km. Long Tom was put out of action by a British raiding party during the siege, but not before it had caused a great deal of damage.

On the corner of King St and Settlers Drive is the police station, which includes the wall with loopholes from the original **Zulu Fort**, built as a refuge from Zulu attack.

Across the river on the west side of town (there's a footbridge) is a **Sufi mosque**, built by the Muslim community which has been in Ladysmith almost since the town's inception. The mosque is worth seeing. There's also a Hindu **Vishnu temple**, and while the building is undistinguished you'll meet some friendly people there. As well as religious statues inside the temple, in the garden is a **statue of Gandhi**. The statue was imported from Bombay and depicts Gandhi as the Mahatma and not as a stretcher bearer with Buller's forces at Spioenkop, which might have been more appropriate.

South of town, near the junction of the N11 and R103, is an area generally known as **Platrand** (or Wagon Hill). There is an unusual monument to the Boers who died attempting to wrest Wagon Hill from the British on 6 January 1900.

Ladysmith

0        150        300 m

1  Travel Agency
2  Siege Museum
3  Town Hall (Information)
4  Railway Station
5  Zulu Fort
6  NG Kerk
7  Royal Hotel
8  Minibus Taxi Park
9  Vishnu Temple &
    Gandhi Statue
10 Crown Hotel
11 Greyhound Bus Stop
12 Anglican Church
13 Natalasia Hotel
14 Settlers Park
15 Sufi Mosque

## Places to Stay & Eat

The municipal *caravan park* (☎ (0361) 26050) is on the north side of town; follow Poort Rd over the hill, where it becomes the Harrismith road.

Near the town hall, on Murchison St, the main street, there are two staid old hotels. The *Crown* (☎ (0361) 22266) has B&B for R185/260 a single/double and the *Royal* (☎ /fax (0361) 22176) charges R180/235. Out on the Durban road, 3km from the town, the *Andrew Motel* (☎ /fax (0361) 26908) is cheaper.

The Indian-owned modern *Natalasia Hotel* (☎ (0361) 26821), on the corner of Leonards and Kandahar Sts, has unfortunately gone downhill, and a reader reports not being able to buy an Indian meal in the restaurant. Still, it's OK. Rooms go for R120/200, slightly cheaper on weekends.

The information office has details of farmstays and B&Bs. Prices range between R75 and R180 per person.

*Swainson's Restaurant* in the Royal Hotel, has the usual steaks (R25) and salads, plus some game and seafood (around R35). Also in the Royal is a grill for pub meals and *Mario's*, an Italian restaurant with lunch specials such as tagliatelle for R12. They do play Italian pop music, but they also have a menu full of the 'rich and creamy', rather than the 'light and zesty' more usually associated with Mediterranean cuisine. For cheap eats, try the stalls and shops around the large minibus taxi park.

## Getting There & Away

**Bus** Transtate/City to City buses originating in Welkom and travelling via Bethlehem sometimes stop at Ladysmith train station en route to Pietermaritzburg and Port Shepstone.

Translux buses leave from the train station and run to Durban (R80) and Bloemfontein (R140). Greyhound has daily services to Johannesburg/Pretoria (R115) and Durban (R100). Book at the Shell service station on the corner of Murchison and King Sts, or at Destinations Travel (☎ (0361) 31 0831).

There are local companies serving the former QwaQwa Homeland in Free State and the immediate area, some of which will get you fairly close to the Drakensberg.

**Train** The *Trans Oranje* (Durban-Cape Town) and the daily *Trans Natal* (Durban-Jo'burg/Pretoria) both stop here, but at inconvenient times.

**Minibus Taxi** The main (and surprisingly large) taxi rank is east of the centre of town near the corner of Queen and Lyell Sts. Taxis bound for Harrismith and Jo'burg are nearby on Alexandra St. Some destinations are Jo'burg (R50), Durban (R28) and Harrismith (R10).

## NEWCASTLE

Not surprisingly, Newcastle is a coal-mining and steel-producing town. The white population is 25,000, and there are 16,000 Indians in Lennoxton and Lenville, and 250,000 blacks in the nearby townships of Madadeni and Osizweni.

There's an Anglo-Boer War museum in **Fort Amiel**, open Tuesday to Thursday 9 am to 1 pm, Friday 11 am to 4 pm and Saturday 9 am to 1 pm. Fort Amiel was established in 1876 when the British anticipated conflict with the Zulu. The colonial-era **town hall** (☎ (03431) 53318), Scott St, is worth a look, and you can get information, including details of local accommodation, from the enthusiastic staff.

Tours of the two large black **townships**, Madadeni and Osizweni, are being arranged; inquire at the town hall. There is a **handicraft centre** in Osizweni which is worth a visit.

The turn-off to **Chelmsford Dam Nature Reserve** is on the R23 about 25km south of Newcastle. As well as water sports on the dam there is a small game reserve with white rhino, and there is Natal Parks Board accommodation. Entry is R3 (R6 on weekends). Chalets sleeping three cost R150 and camp

sites (☎ (03431) 77205) at Leokop, Richgate and Sandford cost R20 per person.

### Holkrans Walking Trail

This trail is 25km south-west of Newcastle just off the Normandien road and in the Drakensberg foothills. The trail is 25km long and divided into two stages – an 11.5km walk to the night stop, a *holkrans* (overhang) in the sandstone cliffs, and a 6km walk via a ravine and grassveld back to the start point. For information, telephone ☎ (03435) 600.

### Places to Stay & Eat

The municipal *caravan park* (☎ (03431) 81273) is out of town at Amcor Dam; a powered site is R30 plus R5 per person.

Cheaper hotels include *Kings* (☎ (03431) 26101), on the corner of Harding and Hardwick Sts, and the upgraded *Royal* (☎ (03431) 25895), 20 Voortrekker St. On the corner of Victoria and Hunter Sts, there's a *Holiday Inn Garden Court* (☎ (03431) 28151; fax 24142) with single/double rooms for R110/219.

Ask travelling salespeople what is the best accommodation in Newcastle and they will shout '*Majuba Lodge*'. The lodge (☎ (03431) 55011; fax 55023) is opposite the Holiday Inn at 27 Victoria Rd; the cost is R219 a single or double. The restaurant here is the best place to eat in town.

The *House Next Door* in Harding St is a good restaurant with ladies' bar attached, and not far away is *Beagles* on the corner of Allen and Harding Sts. There is an unnamed Chinese restaurant opposite the information office, a *Spur* steakhouse on Voortrekker St and *Longhorn*, also for steak, on Allen St. The meals at the *Newcastle Golf Club* have been recommended.

### Getting There & Away

Greyhound runs to Jo'burg (R85) and Durban (R120) daily, from the Shell station on Allen St. *Eagle Liner* (KwaZulu Transport) operates to Osizweni. Minibus taxis to Jo'burg cost about R35.

The daily *Trans Natal* train runs to Jo'burg and Durban.

Car rental companies with agents in Newcastle are Imperial (☎ (03431) 22806), based at Newcastle airport, and Avis (☎ (03431) 21274) at Leon Motors, Allen St.

## MAJUBA HILL

The first Anglo-Boer War ended abruptly 40km north of Newcastle, with the British defeat at **Majuba Hill** in early 1881. The site has been restored and a map is available; there is a small entry fee. The Laings Nek and Schuinshoogte battlefields are also signposted.

Peace negotiations took place at **O'Neill's**

---

### Battle of Majuba Hill – 1881

The British annexed the first South African Republic (ZAR) of Transvaal on 12 April 1877. After peaceful protest failed, over 8000 armed Boers met at Paardekraal and pledged to reinstate the ZAR government as from 13 December, using force if necessary. The first shots were fired at Potchefstroom on 16 December and several British garrisons were besieged. The obvious route for British reinforcements sent to relieve the garrisons would be from Durban to Transvaal via Newcastle. Piet Joubert moved 2000 mounted troops to the strategic position of Laings Nek, north of Newcastle, in anticipation of this move.

The British under Sir George Colley attacked the Boers on 28 January 1881 at Laings Nek but had to retreat after an hour. On 8 February a British wagon column was encircled by Boers at Schuinshoogte (Ingogo) and suffered heavy casualties.

On the night of 26 February, Colley and nearly 600 troops climbed Majuba Hill to overlook the Boer positions. The British in their bright uniforms, cumbersome helmets and armed with Martini Henry rifles (with their sights incorrectly adjusted) were no match for the highly mobile Boers. The British panicked and began to flee. About 1 pm on the 27th, Colley was fatally wounded; in all, 285 British soldiers were killed, wounded or taken prisoner.

When news was received of Colley's death, General Sir Evelyn Wood was sworn in as acting governor of Natal. On 6 March he met the Boer commanders at O'Neill's Cottage, at the base of Majuba, to negotiate peace. The battle and events before and after are described in GA Chadwick's *The First War of Independence in Natal: 1880-1881* (R4). ∎

---

**Cottage** in the foothills near Majuba. The cottage, used as a hospital during the battle, has been restored and has a photographic display; it is open daily.

## UTRECHT

Today a quiet little town in prime cattle country, Utrecht was once the capital of one of the original Voortrekker republics, this one measuring just 30 by 65km! The town was the British headquarters during the Anglo-Zulu War, and a number of fine 19th century buildings still remain. There's a museum in the old parsonage, which is open weekdays from 8 am to 6 pm but closed for lunch; pick up a brochure there on the town's attractions.

*Balele Resort* (☎ (03433) 3041) is 5km north of town on the Wakkerstroom road. Rondavels are R51 per person, sites are R13.70 plus R4.60 per person. You book here to do the two day, 25km **Balele Hiking Trail** which passes through the Enhlanzeni Valley in the Langalibalele Range. Accommodation costs R19 per person; the first night is in an old farmhouse, and the overnight camp has beehive huts.

## DUNDEE

Dundee is a large coal-mining town, not especially attractive but perhaps useful as a base for the area's historical sites. It was named by an early settler who came from a village near Dundee in Scotland.

On the Vryheid road, 1.5km out of town, is the **Talana Museum**, dedicated to 'small men who had to take root or die, not to the captains and kings who departed'. It's still being developed but it's already a large place with several old buildings and displays on coal mining and local history, which includes both the Anglo-Zulu and the Anglo-Boer Wars. Some good pamphlets on the area's history are available. The museum is open on weekdays and on weekend afternoons. Entry is R2.

You can get information from the Talana Museum or the town hall. Both can put you in touch with battlefield guides, who charge between R100 and R200 for a one-day tour.

To the east of Dundee, 52km away via the R33 and R68, is the fascinating regional centre of **Nqutu**. This is an important trading centre for the surrounding Zulu community and about as close to a buzzing urban black town as you will see. A minibus to Nqutu is about R40 from Jo'burg. About 30km north of Nqutu near Nondweni is the memorial to the **Prince Imperial Louis Napoleon**, the last of the Bonaparte dynasty, who was killed here on 1 June 1879.

### Places to Stay & Eat
The municipal *caravan park* (☎ (0341) 22121) has sites for about R25. To get there take the Ladysmith road out of the town centre and turn right at the traffic lights.

There are several B&Bs in Dundee and nearby; check at the Talana Museum (☎ (0341) 22654) or the town hall. *Penny Farthing* (☎ /fax (03425) 925), 30km south of Dundee, is typical of the B&Bs and charges R130 per person, with dinner and breakfast.

The *Royal Hotel* (☎ (0341) 22147) on Victoria St opposite the town hall has single/double rooms for R165/260, with breakfast. The nearby *El Mpati Hotel* (☎ (0341) 21155), 59 Victoria St, charges R165/240, also with breakfast. The *Etna Hotel* (☎ (0341) 24191), Wilson St, is cheaper.

At the licensed *Buffalo Steakhouse*, near the corner of Gladstone and Victoria Sts, a steak meal starts at R30. *Miner's Rest* at Talana serves lunch and the golf, cricket and rugby clubs offer pub lunches from R15.

### Getting There & Away
Transtate/City to City's Jo'burg/Pretoria-Empangeni and Welkom-Nongoma buses stop at Dundee.

Minibus taxi destinations from Dundee include Vryheid (R12), Ladysmith (R12), Durban (R35) and Jo'burg (R40).

### ISANDLWANA & RORKE'S DRIFT
You have probably heard of the Defence of Rorke's Drift but not the Battle of Isandlwana – the former was a British imperial

---

### The Battle of Isandlwana
The Battle of Isandlwana was the first major engagement of the 1879 Anglo-Zulu War, precipitated by an ultimatum to Cetshwayo which the British knew he would not and could not meet. The demands included the complete re-organisation of the Zulu political structure and the abolition of the Zulu army.

On 22 January 1879 a soldier from one of the five British forces sent to invade Zululand happened to look over a ridge near Isandlwana Hill. He was surprised to discover 25,000 Zulu warriors sitting in the gully below, silently awaiting the time to attack. This was to have been the following day, the day after the full moon, but on being discovered the impis adopted their battle formation – two enclosing 'horns' on the flanks and the main force in the centre – and attacked the utterly unprepared British camp. By the end of the day almost all of the British were dead, along with many Zulus.

Meanwhile, the small British contingent which had remained at Rorke's Drift (where the army had crossed into Zululand) to guard supplies, heard of the disaster and fortified their camp. They were attacked by about 4000 Zulus but the defenders, numbering fewer than 100 fit soldiers, held on through the night until a relief column arrived. Victoria Crosses were lavished on the defenders – 11 in all – and another couple went to the two officers at Fugitive's Drift.

Many people will know of these battles by the movies made of them: *Zulu Dawn* for Isandlwana and *Zulu* for Rorke's Drift. Perhaps the best account of the Anglo-Zulu War is *The Washing of the Spears* by D Morris. ■

---

victory of the misty-eyed variety, the latter was a bloody disaster.

Isandlwana should not be missed. At the base of this sphinx-like rock there are many graves and memorials to those who fell in battle on 22 January 1879. The Isandlwana museum, with artefacts taken from the battlefield, is in St Vincent's (the bluestone buildings in the nearby village) just outside the site. You pay the R5 entry here.

At Rorke's Drift, 42km from Dundee, there is a splendid museum, a self-guided trail around the battlefield, several memorials and the ELC Zulu craft centre, open from Monday to Saturday. The rugs and tapestries woven and sold here are world-renowned and therefore not cheap; a small wall-hanging costs over R1000.

The Zulu know this site as *Shiyane*, their name for the hill at the back of the village. The *Rorke's Drift-Shiyane Self-Guided Trail* brochure is helpful for understanding the close nature of the fighting in this battle.

About 10km south of Rorke's Drift is **Fugitive's Drift**. Two British officers were killed at Fugitive's Drift attempting to prevent the Queen's Colours from falling into Zulu hands (losing colours was a definite no-no in the British Army). *Elmpati Drift Lodge* (☎ (0341) 21155) has rooms for R155 per person.

While you are in this area it is worthwhile taking a side trip to the spectacular **Mangeni Falls**, at the head of a tributary of the Buffalo River. About 35km east of Babanango, at Silutshana, turn south and follow the road to Mangeni. At Mangeni you will probably have to ask the way to the falls as the track is not obvious.

### Getting There & Away
The battle sites are south-east of Dundee. Isandlwana is about 70km from Dundee, off the R68; Rorke's Drift is 42km from Dundee, also accessible from the R68 or R33 (the R33 turn-off is 13km south of Dundee). The road to Isandlwana is sealed but the roads to Rorke's Drift and Fugitive's Drift can be dusty and rough.

### BLOOD RIVER MONUMENT
The Blood River battle site is marked by a full-scale recreation of the 64-wagon laager in bronze. The cairn of stones was built by the Boers after the battle to mark the centre of their laager. The monument is 20km

**The Battle of Blood River**

The Battle of Blood River occurred on 16 December 1838 when a small party of Voortrekkers avenged the massacre of Piet Retief's party by the Zulus. The Voortrekkers defeated 12,000 Zulu warriors, killing 3000 while sustaining only a few casualties. This battle is a seminal event in Afrikaner history. The victory came to be seen as the fulfilment of God's side of the bargain and seemed to prove that the Boers had a divine mandate to conquer and 'civilise' Southern Africa; that they were in fact a chosen people.

However, Afrikaner nationalism and the significance attached to Blood River grew in strength simultaneously and it has been argued (by Leach in *The Afrikaners – Their Last Great Trek* and others) that the importance of Blood River was deliberately heightened and manipulated for political ends. The standard interpretation of the victory meshed with the former apartheid regime's world view: hordes of untrustworthy black savages were beaten by Boers who were on an Old Testament-style mission from God. ■

Relief of carving on the Blood River Monument.

JON MURRAY

DAVID ELSE

DEANNA SWANEY

Top: The Namastat 'hotel' in Springbok provides two beds in each traditional woven
  Nama hut, Northern Cape.
Left: South African rural towns are usually religious, in this case Calvinia, Northern Cape.
Right: Springtime in Namaqualand is a spectacular sight, Northern Cape.

Top: A multitude of beach activities close to Durban's harbour entrance, KwaZulu-Natal.
Middle: Fifty Mile Beach, KwaZulu-Natal; Victoria Bay, south of George, Western Cape.
Bottom: Scaling Table Mountain high above the resort of Camps Bay, Western Cape.

south-east of the R33; the turn-off is 27km from Dundee and 45km from Vryheid. Admission is R2.50 and there's a small café.

The rationale behind this place is so utterly politically incorrect that it's almost worth a visit for that reason alone. And the village kids, kept out by a high fence, certainly want you to visit so they can sell you handicrafts.

# Mpumalanga

There's a lot to do in this province. There are many hiking, horse-riding and mountain-bike trails in the vicinity of the Klein Drakensberg escarpment; picturesque and historic towns like Pilgrim's Rest, Sabie, Graskop and Barberton; great fishing valleys; and the world-famous Kruger National Park, bordered by private game reserves.

Mpumalanga (meaning 'place of the rising sun', formerly Eastern Transvaal) was once part of the larger Transvaal Province. See the Gauteng and Northern Province chapters for the white history of the region.

## Klein Drakensberg

The highveld ends suddenly at this dramatic escarpment which tumbles down to the eastern lowveld. The Klein ('small') Drakensberg (as opposed to the more impressive Drakensberg in KwaZulu-Natal and still often known by its old name of Transvaal Drakensberg) is not so much peaks as cliffs, and there are some stunning views. As it is prime vacation territory there's a lot of accommodation available, much of it expensive, but it fills up at peak times. The population density is low, so there's little public transport.

Winters are cold, with occasional snow-falls. Summers are warm, but after the sweltering lowveld it's a relief to get up here. The difference in temperature between Hazyview and Graskop is well worth the 40km drive up Kowyns Pass. Mists can be a driving and hiking hazard year-round.

Get a copy of the excellent and free publication *The Lowveld* from information centres. *Transvaal Weekender* (R30) and the free *Mpumalanga Tourist Map* are also good.

### BLYDE RIVER CANYON

The 26,000 hectare Blyde River Canyon

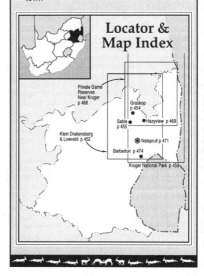

Locator & Map Index

Private Game Reserves Near Kruger p 468

Graskop p 454

Sabie p 455 • Hazyview p 469

Klein Drakensberg & Lowveld p 452

Nelspruit p 471

Barberton p 474

Kruger National Park p 459

Nature Reserve snakes north almost 60km from Graskop, following the escarpment and meeting the Blyde River as it carves its way down to the lowveld. The Blyde's spectacular canyon, nearly 30km long, is one of South Africa's scenic highlights.

This description, from north to south, begins near the Manoutsa Cliffs (see the aside on bird-watching in this section) at the junction of the Tzaneen road (R36) and the R527 (marked on some maps as a continuation of the R531).

Following the R36 as it turns south and

climbs up from the lowveld through the JG Strijdom Tunnel and scenic Abel Erasmus Pass, you pass the turn-off to the R532 and come to the village of Mogaba and the road to the **Museum of Man**, an archaeological site with rock paintings and other finds on show daily between 8 am and 5 pm. Also in the area are the **Echo Caves** where Stone Age relics have been found. The caves get their name from dripstone formations which echo when tapped. There are guided tours at R15 for half an hour. The guide might demand a huge tip.

If you return to the R532 junction and proceed east along the R532 you come to the Aventura Blydepoort resort. There is a good view of the **Three Rondavels** from a viewpoint a few kilometres past the resort. The Rondavels are huge cylinders of rock with hut-like pointy 'roofs', rising out of the far wall of the canyon. There are a number of short walks in the area to points where you can look down to the Blydepoort Dam.

**Bourke's Luck Potholes**, at the confluence of the Blyde and Treur rivers, are weird cylindrical holes carved into the rock by whirlpools in the river. They are interesting, although perhaps not as great an attraction as

MPUMALANGA

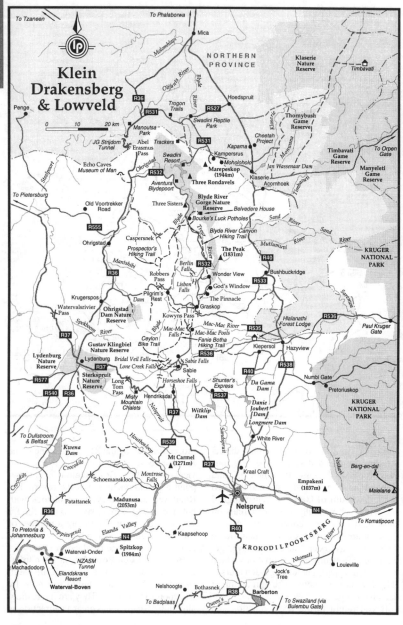

# Klein Drakensberg & Lowveld

they are touted to be. Still, it's worth stopping off as there is a good visitors' centre with information on the geology, flora and fauna of the canyon. There's a fee of R4.50 to see the potholes.

The R532 follows the Treur south to its source, and further on is a turn-off to the R534 loop road. This road leads to the spectacular viewpoints of **Wonder View** and **God's Window**, now tightly controlled by the Mpumalanga Parks Board. (You can also take the R532 north from Graskop to get here; it is well signposted.) The atmosphere here has changed considerably – once you could park quietly and enjoy the view at the lookouts, now there are entry gates and a battery of souvenir sellers. At God's Window there's a short trail to views of the lowveld 1000m below.

A few kilometres further on you pass the **Pinnacle**, an impressive rock formation, which juts out from the escarpment; lock up your car here as there have been thefts. The R534 joins the R532 3km north of Graskop.

### Hiking Trails

There are several great hiking trails in the area but some have been closed for redevelopment, notably the 38.5km **Protea** and the 25km **Yellowwood** trails. The **Op-de-Berg Trail** (four days) begins at the potholes and takes you into the canyon. This trail costs R20 per person per night (students R10) and should be booked in advance (☎ (013) 758 1216, from 9 am to 12.30 pm weekdays) as there are limits on the number of people. No camping is permitted in the reserve. A good map of the trail is available from the visitors' centre at the potholes.

The 65km **Blyderivierspoort Hiking Trail** begins at God's Window and ends on the lowveld near the Swadini resort. This is done as a five day hike and lets you explore the spectacular Blyde River Canyon. There is a maximum of 30 and a minimum of two persons on this trail; the cost is R15/7.50 per person per night. For bookings (well in advance as this area is very popular) and more information contact the Blyde River

Canyon Nature Reserve (☎ (013) 759 4000), PO Box 1990, Nelspruit 1200.

The 77km **Fanie Botha Hiking Trail** is a five day walk (less if you do only a section), mainly through plantations, but with some good views; it begins at the Ceylon Forest Station near Sabie and ends at God's Window north of Graskop. The 69km, five day **Prospector's Trail** meanders through the Sabie and Pilgrim's Rest area and it isn't too strenuous. You can book these two trails through SAFCOL (South African Forest Commission Ltd) (☎ (013) 764 1058), Private Bag X503, Sabie 1260.

The interesting **Elandskrans Trail** takes in part of the highveld and lowveld of southern Mpumalanga. Combining a 24km walk with a 12km rail journey, the trail begins and ends at the Elandskrans holiday resort near Waterval-Boven. Book at Elandskrans Resort (☎ (013262), ask for 176; fax 321), Private Bag X05, Waterval-Boven 1195.

### Places to Stay

As well as accommodation in the towns on top of the escarpment, there are a number of places to stay close to the canyon. *Aventura Blydepoort* (☎ (013) 769 8055) is a large resort and has all the usual facilities. Tent sites cost R20/35 in the low/high season plus R15 per person, two-bed units cost from R170/230 and standard four-bed units are R190/305; luxury units are considerably more. At the bottom of the escarpment, on the eastern side but still on the Blyde River, is Aventura's *Swadini Resort* (☎ (01528) 35141); camping (R15 per site) and four-bed units are the same as at Blydepoort.

Mpumalanga Parks Board (reservations ☎ (013) 759 4000) operates the self-catering *Belvedere House*, which sleeps nine people and costs R730 per night, and *Paradise Camp*, near Wonder View (R160 per chalet for two persons).

One of the area's best places to stay is also at the bottom of the escarpment, to the north of Swadini. The Rushworths' *Trackers* (☎ (015) 795 5033) is a beautifully situated private reserve taking in the strikingly different ecosystems of the highveld and the

**MPUMALANGA**

lowveld. The reserve caters mainly to educational groups, but individuals are welcome. Basic camping costs R15, a cottage R60 per person or R130 for dinner, breakfast and bed (the meals are excellent). Trips to study the natural vegetation of the region are conducted from Trackers by Tamboti Botanical Trails; the cost is R15/30 per person for a morning/day. They also have two day whitewater rafting trips on the Blyde River for R550.

To get to Trackers take the R527 west from Hoedspruit and after about 20km turn south onto the small Driehoek road, just after you cross the Blyde River. After 6.5km you will see their signpost; it's a steep climb to Trackers up towards the escarpment.

*Trogon Trails* (☎ /fax (015) 795 5581) has self-catering accommodation for R100 per person (R80 if there are three or more people). It's a great spot for an 'alternative big five' – cheap digs, peace, quiet, views and beautiful birds like the narina trogon. Trogon Trails is 4.5km west of the Blyde River bridge on the R531; it is signposted. The camp is 3km from the main gate down a dirt road.

## GRASKOP

Graskop is on the edge of the Drakensberg escarpment, at the top of Kowyns Pass. Nearby are some spectacular views of the lowveld, almost 1000m below. A walking trail, including places described in *Jock of the Bushveld*, starts at the municipal resort; the resort will provide a map.

There are good **mountain biking** trails in the region. Maps are available from the Graskop information office (☎ (013) 767 1126), opposite the entrance to the municipal tourist park; permits cost R5.

### Places to Stay

*Panorama Rest Camp* (☎ (013) 767 1090) is about 2km east of town on the road to Kowyns Pass. It's stunningly situated at the top of a deep gorge: the small pool is right on the edge and has astounding views down to the lowveld. Camp sites are about R30 plus R15 per person. Chalets with cooking

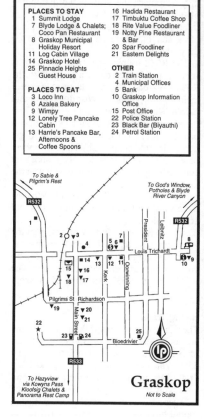

Graskop
Not to Scale

facilities cost R95 for two people or R150 for up to five.

The *Graskop Municipal Holiday Resort* (☎ (013) 767 1126) is in town; tent sites are R17 plus R7 per person, and four-bed bungalows are R125.

*Summit Lodge* (☎ (013) 767 1058), some 500m down the road to Pilgrim's Rest, charges R105 per person for B&B. The revamped *Graskop Hotel* (☎ (013) 767 1244) on the main street charges R210/370 for good single/double B&B (R180/240 in low season).

*Blyde Lodge & Chalets* (☎ (013) 767 1316;

fax 767 1798) has fully equipped chalets from R175 per person with breakfast, depending on the season. In the lodge, B&B is from R110 to R130 per person.

Other places include *Log Cabin Village* (☎ (013) 767 1974), at the east end of Louis Trichardt St; *Pinnacle Heights Guesthouse* (☎ (013) 767 1847) on Bloedrivier St; and *Kloofsig Chalets* (☎ (01315) 71488) on the Kowyns Pass Rd.

### Places to Eat

This town is a gourmet's delight. On Louis Trichardt St are *Azalea Bakery* for '*die beste mosbolletjies in die laeveld*', and the famous *Harrie's Pancake Bar*, recommended to me by Jo'burg's Chosen Few motorcycle gang (pancakes are from R18). Nearby are *Lonely Tree Pancake Cabin* for black forest cake, *Afternoons & Coffee Spoons* for light meals, and *Leonardo's Trattoria* for pizzas.

In Main St, try *Eastern Delights* for Indian food such as bunny chow (R6.50), samosas and biryani. A good three course meal costs about R35 at the *Hadida Restaurant*, next to the Graskop Hotel. Around the corner in Richardson St is *Notty Pine*, known for its excellent trout dishes.

Last but not least, *Loco Inn*, across from the library and well signposted, is 'your passport to pleasure' (their words, not mine) – as well as pub lunches, there is a pool table and a lively bar.

### SABIE

Sabie is the largest town in this region, but it's still a manageable size. The town is quite prosperous, being a tourist centre and a timber town. Tourists come for the cool climate, trout fishing and the extensive pine and eucalypt plantations in the area, but if you prefer your forests wild this might not be such an attraction. The plantations were established last century to replace indigenous forest cut down for the mining industry.

To see how the area looked before most of the indigenous forest was destroyed, visit the **Mt Sheba Nature Reserve**, about 10km west of Pilgrim's Rest.

### Orientation & Information

Sabie is a good base for visiting the area, but Graskop is closer to both the Blyde River Canyon and Kruger. Sondela Central Reservations (☎ /fax (013) 764 3492), on Main St on the Lydenburg and Long Tom Pass side of town, happily provides information on accommodation and activities. For further details contact the new information office at the end of 8th Lane.

### Things to See & Do

The **Forestry Museum**, next to the information centre, has displays on local forests, as

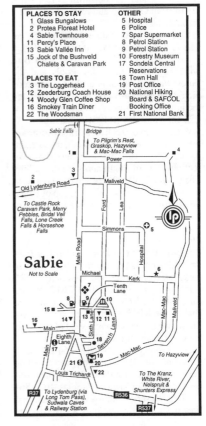

well as exhibits like match paintings, which 'will take your breath away'. It's open on weekdays and Saturday morning; entry is R4/2 for adults/children.

There are a number of **waterfalls** in the area. Closest are the Sabie Falls, just beyond town on the R532 (Graskop road). Southwest of Sabie, off the Old Lydenburg road, are the 70m Bridal Veil Falls. Also off the Old Lydenburg road are the 68m Lone Creek Falls; there is wheelchair access to the falls on the right-hand path. Nearby are Horse Shoe Falls. Off the R532 to Graskop are the Mac-Mac Falls, named because of the many Scottish names on the area's mining register (R3 entry), and the beautiful Forest Falls, 10km from Graskop and reached by a walk through the forest.

There are several nature **walks** near Sabie. The Jantjiesbos and Waterfall walks start at Lone Creek Waterfall. The Secretary Bird walk begins at Mac-Mac Pools and the Forest Falls walk starts at the Groenerferis picnic site. **Horse-riding** is also popular and the information offices can arrange rides for R25 for a half day (R40 with lunch).

There are two excellent marked **mountain bike** trails. The Long Tom Trail, in the vicinity of Long Tom pass, consists of two sections, one of 36km and the other 20km. The Ceylon Trail is 21km and there is a steep section, which takes you to the top of Bridal Veil Falls. There is an entrance fee of R4 for both trails.

### Places to Stay
**Bottom End** At *Castle Rock Caravan Park* (☎ (013) 764 1242), the municipal caravan park, sites cost R25 and electricity is R7 extra. *Merry Pebbles* (☎ (013) 764 2266) has camp sites for R65 as well as self-contained chalets for R175; both prices are for two. These two places are north-west of town, off the Old Lydenburg road.

*Glass Bungalows* (☎ (013) 764 2227), on the corner of Old Lydenburg and Graskop roads, has chalets for R290. *Jock of the Bushveld Chalets & Caravan Park* (☎ (013) 764 2178) is closer to the town centre and has sites from R28 for two plus R5 per person.

This place is also a *youth hostel* charging R35 per person.

*Percy's Place* (☎ (013) 764 3302) on 6th Lane, behind the Forestry Museum, is a B&B costing from R140 for two.

Some 25km from Sabie on the Long Tom road is *Misty Mountain Chalets* (☎ (013) 764 3377), ideally located for mountain-bikers; self-catering cottages are from R150 for two in low season.

SAFCOL operate the *Hlalanathi Forest Lodge* (☎ (013) 764 1058), a tranquil place in the Frankfort plantation/avocado farm, 17km from Sabie; chalets are R275/220 in/out of season.

**Middle & Top End** *Sabie Vallée Inn* (☎ (013) 764 2182), on 10th Lane, charges R155 per person, with all meals. *Protea Floreat* (☎ (013) 764 2160) on the Old Lydenburg road has singles/doubles from R225/250, including breakfast. *Sabi Star Chalets* (☎ (013) 764 3328) has two-bed chalets from R130 in low season, R150 in high season. These are 3km out of town on the R536.

South-east of Sabie, on the R537 to White River, is *Shunter's Express* (☎ /fax (013) 751 1777), which has accommodation in 1930s railway coaches; B&B is R150 per person, dinner is R25 extra. Their horse-riding packages cost R450 for the weekend.

There are many B&B places in the area; inquire at the information offices for details. *Sabie Townhouse* (☎ (013) 764 2292), on Power St, is a popular place with rooms from R160 to R240 per person; it's often fully booked.

### Places to Eat
*Loggerhead* near Sabie Falls is a good steak and fish place where you'll pay about R35 for a meal. *Zeederburg Coach House* specialises in trout braais but also serves filling pastas for R30. The *Woodsman*, at the corner of Main Rd and Mac Mac St, has a great Greek menu.

There are vegetarian choices at *Woody Glen Coffee Shop* on Main Rd and the dedicated Afrikaner diner can get potjiekos (stew cooked in a three legged pot) from the easily recognised *Smokey Train Diner*, at the western end of Main Rd. There are fabulous Italian provincial dishes at the *Artists Café*, out at Hendriksdal, on the R37.

### Getting There & Away
There are daily regular buses from Jo'burg to Lydenburg and Nelspruit, from where you can take minibus taxis to Sabie. To return to Jo'burg catch a minibus taxi to either Nelspruit or Lydenburg, then catch another minibus taxi or regular bus to Jo'burg.

Sabie's minibus taxi park is behind the Spar supermarket on Main St. Most taxis run only in the local area. The fare to Hazyview is R15 and to Lydenburg it's R17.50.

## PILGRIM'S REST
In 1873 gold was discovered here and for 10 years the area buzzed with diggers working small-scale alluvial claims. When the big operators arrived in the 1880s, Pilgrim's Rest became a company town, and when the gold finally fizzled out in 1972 the town was sold to the government as a ready-made historical village. It's a nice little place, where people once worked hard and lived simply – an ethos which doesn't come across in many other old towns in South Africa, burdened by grandiose town halls and churches. Avoid it on weekends, however.

The information centre is on the main street, and is open daily from 9 am to 12.45 pm and 1.15 to 4.30 pm.

### Things to See & Do
There are three **museums**: the Pilgrim's Rest & Sabie News, a printing shop; the House Museum, a restored home; and the Drezden Shop & House Museum, a general store. Admission to all three is R1.50; buy tickets at the information centre. Also worth a visit is historic **Alanglade**, a former mine manager's residence furnished with period objects from the 1920s. There are guided tours daily (except Sunday) at 10.30 am and 4 pm; entry is R2/1 for adults/children.

The nearby **nature reserve** doesn't have many animals and the vegetation isn't all indigenous, but it's a nice place for walks.

There is a **tractor cart**, which shuttles between Uptown and Downtown; it is R5/3 for adults/children.

### Places to Stay & Eat
The *Royal Hotel* (☎ (013) 768 1100) is an atmospheric, historic place with over 40 suites furnished in Victorian-era style; singles/doubles are from R220/280 but prices rise sharply on weekends and holidays. More economic are the *District Six Miners' Cottages* (☎ (013) 768 1277); these cost from R135 a double. Cheapest of all is the *caravan park* (☎ (013) 768 1376) on the banks of the Blyde River in Downtown. Resorts abound. The luxurious *Mt Sheba Hotel* (☎ (013) 768 1241), in the Mt Sheba Nature Reserve, has half-board singles/doubles from R300/360 (considerably more in high season). The self-catering lodges at the superbly situated *Crystal Springs Mountain Lodge* (☎ (013) 768 1153), near Pilgrim's Rest, cost R140/70 for adults/children in high season, R90/45 out of season. The *Inn on Robbers Pass* (☎ (013) 768 1491), on the Lydenburg road, costs from R190 per person for dinner, bed and breakfast.

For light meals during the day try *Scott's Restaurant* in Uptown; a lunch is around R30. *The Vine* in Downtown is a pub, which also serves light meals described as 'South African' (R25). The best place for a relaxing ale is the *Church Bar* next to the Royal Hotel.

### Getting There & Away
There is little public transport: the roads are narrow and steep so buses are disinclined to make the trip, and because there are few blacks living in the area minibus taxis are infrequent.

## LYDENBURG
Lydenburg is at the bottom of Long Tom Pass, which is named after the big gun used by the Boer forces in the Anglo-Boer War. Lydenburg ('town of suffering') was established by Voortrekkers in 1849 and was once the capital of the Republic of Lydenburg. Today it's a quiet service centre for the farming district. The **museum** is on the Long

Tom Pass road, a few kilometres from town. The information office (☎ (013) 235 2096) is at 50 Kantoor St.

The **Gustav Klingbiel Nature Reserve** is east of Lydenburg, on the R37. As well as antelope species there are Iron Age sites and Anglo-Boer War trenches. There's also a hiking trail. Phone the town clerk at Lydenburg (☎ (013) 235 2121) for information.

### Places to Stay

On Viljoen St, the road to Jo'burg, just before the intersection with Lydenburg's main street, is *Uitspan Caravan Park* (☎ (013) 235 2914). Camp sites are about R30, and rondavels sleeping three people are R130 or R95 with common bathroom.

*Morgan's Hotel* (☎ (01323) 2165), 14

---

### Middleveld Fishing Valleys

The Middleveld region to the south of Lydenburg is noted for its fine trout fishing, and visitors come from all over the world in the search for that elusive bite during the evening rise. The area sandwiched between the R540, R36 and the N4 is where anglers will achieve most success. The main fishing towns are **Dullstroom**, **Machadodorp** and **Waterval-Boven**. A trout-fishing licence from the local authority is required. The Mpumalanga Tourist Association's *Trout Fishing* brochure is useful for contact addresses and accommodation. The Federation of Southern African Flyfishers (☎ (011) 887 8787), PO Box 37035, Birnham Park 2015, will also provide information.

There are a number of exclusive trout lodges in the region. The most famous is *Walkerson's* (☎ (01325) 40246) in Dullstroom, a fly-fisher's haven; it's very expensive with singles/doubles in the lakeside suites for R550/780, equipment included. Another option, *Critchley Hackle* (☎ (01325) 40145) is also expensive. The cheapest option is the *Dullstroom Inn* (☎ (01325) 40071), which costs about R145 per person, breakfast included. Travellers have recommended the *Tonteldoos Café* in Dullstroom for a meal. Near Waterval-Boven there are a number of places. The cheapest of these is the *Wayside Inn* (☎ (013262), ask for 425) with B&B for about R150 per person. The *Bambi Hotel* (☎ (013252) ask for 101) in Machadodorp costs about the same as the Wayside. ∎

Voortrekker St, has singles/doubles from R135/210, including breakfast.

### Getting There & Away

City to City/Transtate (☎ (011) 774 3333) passes through Lydenburg on its Sunday, Tuesday and Thursday service from Jo'burg to Phalaborwa (it travels in the other direction on Monday, Wednesday and Friday).

The minibus taxi park is in a yard off the main shopping street. Taxis to Sabie are R17.50 and to Jo'burg R40. The fare to Nelspruit is R18 but few taxis run there. Your own transport is the best bet for touring.

# The Eastern Lowveld

To the north the lowveld is dry and hot – extremely so in summer, when there are storms and high humidity. Further south the temperatures moderate and the scrubby terrain gives way to lush subtropical vegetation around Nelspruit and the Crocodile River. South, near Barberton, the dry country resumes with a vengeance – gold prospectors last century dubbed it the Valley of Death.

Much of the eastern lowveld is taken up by Kruger National Park and the private game reserves which border it.

### Warning

The lowveld is a malarial area and bilharzia occurs in waterways and dams.

### KRUGER NATIONAL PARK

Kruger National Park is, justifiably, one of the most famous wildlife parks in the world (with over 900,000 visitors each year). It's also one of the biggest and oldest. Sabie Game Reserve was established by the ZAR president Paul Kruger in 1898. The reserve, since renamed and much expanded, is now nearly two million hectares in extent (about the size of Wales).

The park authorities claim Kruger has the greatest variety of animals of any park in Africa, with lion, leopard, elephant, buffalo and black and white rhino (the 'big five') as well as cheetah, giraffe, hippo, and many species of antelope and smaller animals. Altogether, these include 147 mammals, 507 birds, 114 reptile and 34 amphibian species. There are also 336 tree and 49 fish species.

Unlike some of the parks in East Africa, Kruger does not offer a true wilderness experience (although some would argue that the walking trails do approach this ideal). The infrastructure, including a network of sealed roads and comfortable camps, is too highly developed and organised. The park is too accessible and popular, and many animals are acclimatised to the presence of cars.

None of this should deter you, however, because Kruger will undoubtedly be a highlight of your South African trip. The positive side of the park's excellent organisation and facilities is that you can explore the park at leisure, without having to depend on organised tours or guides. The accommodation ranges from cheap camp sites to self-catering huts and a range of more luxurious and expensive alternatives.

The landscape is both beautiful and fascinating, and although you have to be lucky to

**Suggested Itinerary**

If you have a car and want to start and finish in Jo'burg and drive the length of the park, say from Crocodile Bridge to Punda Maria, you'll need at least four days. Given speed limits and the fact that you will, at times, want to travel much more slowly, and/or get off the bitumen, you may be driving virtually all day, every day. This might sound easy, but it's actually quite demanding, especially when it's hot and you are concentrating on spotting animals (and staying on the road).

The ideal minimum would be five days (from Monday to Friday). Allow the first day to get to the park and perhaps stay at Pretoriuskop, Berg-en-dal or Crocodile Bridge; spend the second day in the south with a night at Lower Sabie or Skukuza; the third day in the middle with a night at Olifants, Balule or Letaba; the fourth day in the north, perhaps staying at Shingwedzi or Punda Maria; and allow most of the fifth day to get back to Jo'burg.

This schedule allows you the opportunity to see the park's main ecological zones. ∎

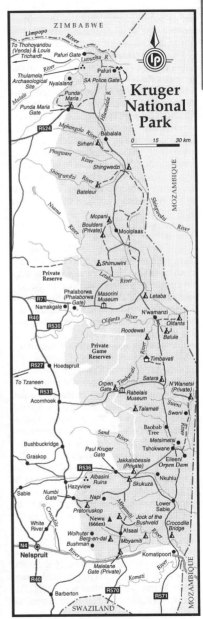

see all the large predators you will almost certainly see some of the 'big five' and an extraordinary variety of smaller mammals and birds. That many of the animals are used to the presence of cars means that you can get really close to them.

Speedy visits aren't recommended – you should spend at least one night in the park. Although the park is popular, the crowds are by no means intrusive if you avoid weekends and school holidays. Numbers are even lower north of the Phalaborwa Gate and on gravel roads. It's not unusual to travel for an hour or so without seeing another vehicle, and there's nothing to stop you finding a spot near a water hole, and just waiting to see what comes by.

## Orientation

Kruger stretches almost 350km along the Mozambique border and has an average width of 60km. There are also several large private game reserves adjoining the western boundaries (see Private Game Reserves in Northern Province and in this chapter), and there are hopes that when the political situation in Mozambique stabilises, Kruger will merge with a proposed park in that country.

Most of the park consists of flat grass and bush-covered plains (savanna bushveld), sometimes broken by rocky outcrops. The unspectacular Lebombo mountains mark both the eastern border of the park and South Africa's border with Mozambique. A number of rivers flow across the park from east to west – from the north they are the Limpopo, Luvuvhu, Shingwedzi, Letaba, Olifants, Timbavati, Sabie and Crocodile.

There are seven entrance gates (heks in Afrikaans): Malelane and Crocodile Bridge on the southern edge, and accessible from the N4 (the quickest direct route from Jo'burg); the Numbi and Paul Kruger gates, accessible from Hazyview (turn off the N4 before Nelspruit); Orpen, which is convenient if you have been exploring Blyde River; Phalaborwa, accessible from Pietersburg/Polokwane; Punda Maria, accessible from Louis Trichardt; and Pafuri, in the far north, accessible from Thohoyandou, Venda.

There are a number of sealed roads within the park, one of which runs the entire spine of the park, and a number of gravel side roads, which are recommended if you want to get away from the crowds. Altogether, the road network extends for nearly 2000km.

## Information

**Bookings** Accommodation can be booked through the National Parks Board. Its head office (☎ (012) 343 1991; fax 343 0905) is in Pretoria; the postal address is PO Box 787, Pretoria 0001, and the telex is 3-21324SA. There is also an office in Cape Town (☎ (021) 22 2810; fax 24 6211); PO Box 7400, Rogge Bay 8012.

Written applications for rest camps and wilderness trails can be made 13 months in advance. Except at peak times (school holidays, Christmas and Easter) and weekends, booking is advisable but not essential.

Day excursion drives or night game drives

---

### Thulamela – the Great Crocodile

The ancient stone ruins of Thulamela, in the northern part of Kruger National Park near Pafuri, remain an enigma – an enigma which archaeologists are desperately trying to solve.

The stone walls of Thulamela Palace were rediscovered in 1983 and intense archaeological activity was only commenced in 1993. Slowly the pieces were linked and a royal enclosure was reconstructed from the scattered stones. It was determined that the site was inhabited as early as 1500 AD, in the late Iron Age. There were a few surprises – white and blue Chinese porcelain suggesting contact across the Indian Ocean; a holy gong similar to those found in Ghana, West Africa; and the remains of an ancient ruler, the 'Great Crocodile of Thulamela', with gold beads in his jaw and gold wire and bracelets entangled with the rest of his bones.

It is a mystical place, a complete contrast to present-day Kruger with its tour vehicles and legions of tourists. Marvel at the V-shaped cornerstones of the royal enclosure, which symbolise the crocodile's tail, and the *muzinda*, the pool or place of the Great Crocodile, and then ponder the fact that this chiefdom was established 400 years ago, after the abandonment of Great Zimbabwe. ■

are available for R105/60 per person (R50/30 for children under 12); bookings are advisable. The knowledgeable rangers who conduct them know where to find the game.

**Entry** It costs R15 per person for a day visit and R10 for an overnight visit (children two to 15 are R7.50) to enter the park plus R20 for a car (bicycles, motorbikes and open vehicles are not admitted). A minibus with less than 15 seats is R25. Maps and publications are sold in the larger rest camps.

During school holidays you can stay for a maximum of 10 days in the park and five days at any one rest camp (10 days if you're camping). The park authorities restrict the total number of visitors within the park, so at peak times it pays to arrive early if you don't have a booking.

The entrance gates open at 5.30 am except in April (6 am), from May to August (6.30 am) and September (6 am). The camps, which are fenced, open at 4.30 am in November and December; 5 am in January; 5.30 am in February and March; 6 am in April and September; and 6.30 am from May to August.

Entrance gates and camps close at 6.30 pm from November to February, 6 pm in March, September and October, and 5.30 pm from April to August. It's an offence to arrive late at a camp and you can be fined. With speed limits of 50km/h on tar and 40km/h on dirt it can take a while to travel from camp to camp, especially if you meet a traffic jam near an interesting animal.

**Facilities** Skukuza, near the Kruger and Numbi gates, is the biggest rest camp and has a large information centre with interesting displays and the exceptional Stevenson-Hamilton library. There's an AA workshop for vehicle repairs, a bank, post office and photo-developing service. A doctor is available. Letaba and Satara rest camps also have workshops, and there are also staffed information centres at Letaba, Berg-en-dal and Mopani. Many of the rest camps show films on Kruger's wildlife in the evenings on

weekends and during school holidays. All camps have telephones and first-aid centres.

The larger camps all have reasonable-value restaurants (a sandwich is R2.60, coffee is R2 and a large hamburger is R6) and decent shops that stock a range of essentials (including cold beer and wine), but if you are planning to do your own cooking it is worth stocking up outside the park.

## Climate

Summers are very hot (averaging around 30°C), with violent thunderstorms; this means that the game viewing is most pleasant early and late in the day. The whole park is in a summer rainfall area, with the rainfall generally decreasing as you go north. In the winter, the days are pleasant, but the temperature at night can sometimes fall below 0°C).

## Plant & Animal Distribution

Kruger takes in a variety of landscapes and ecosystems, in part related to the rainfall, with each ecosystem favouring a particular group of species. Most mammals are distributed throughout the park, but some show a distinct preference for particular regions. The excellent *Find It* booklet and accompanying maps, available at all rest camp stores and entrance gates, point out the most likely places to see a particular species.

Impala, buffalo, Burchell's zebra, blue wildebeest, kudu, waterbuck, baboon, vervet monkey, cheetah, leopard and other smaller predators are all widely distributed. Bird life is prolific along the rivers, and north of the Luvuvhu River.

The south-west corner between the Olifants and Crocodile rivers, where the rainfall is highest (700mm a year), is thickly wooded, with a variety of trees, including acacias and bushwillows, but also bigger trees like sycamore figs and flowering species like the red and orange coral tree. This terrain is particularly favoured by white rhino and buffalo, but is less favoured by antelope and, therefore, by predators.

In the eastern section to the south of the Olifants River, on the plains around Satara and south to the Crocodile River, there's

## Wildlife Viewing

Viewing is best in the winter dry season, because trees lose their leaves and plant growth is sparser, making visibility easier. The animals also tend to be concentrated around the dwindling water sources. On the other hand, the park is more attractive in summer, with lots of fresh green growth, and this is when most animals have their young.

It can be quite difficult to spot animals at any time of the year. It is amazing how often you first notice one animal, stop the car, and suddenly realise that there are many more individuals and species in the immediate area. Even elephant, which you imagine would be fairly conspicuous, can be very well camouflaged, especially if they are still.

Patience and perseverance are vital prerequisites. Drive slowly. If you find any decent vantage point, stop the car and scan the surrounding countryside. It is always rewarding to sit still and stake out a water hole. Sunglasses and binoculars are essential; ideally there should be one set of binoculars per person.

Different animals display different behaviours at different times of the day, but there is always something to be seen. Despite the following observations, animals do not follow rules. A hungry or thirsty animal will be much more concerned about eating or drinking than taking midday siestas.

An early morning drive should begin around 6 am. Many animals (including lion, leopard and rhino) and birds are at their most active from first light to around 10 am.

Conventional wisdom says you are much less likely to see animals at midday (particularly if it is very hot), but given that most people have a very limited time in the park it is still definitely worthwhile going for a drive in the middle of the day. Knowing that many animals will look for shade can actually help you locate them.

The middle of the day is when cheetah are often seen hunting. It's also a good time to see giraffe, zebra and hippo, which continue to be active. Antelopes often move close to water holes, and may attract hungry lions.

A third drive is worthwhile in the late afternoon, from about 3.30 pm, when animals and birds become more active once again. Look for the big cats enjoying the views and breezes from rocky knolls. Leopard, particularly, will often rest high off the ground in the branches of trees. The later you return to camp the better, but don't forget you can be fined for arriving after the official camp closing times.

The more you know about the animals (especially their distribution and behaviour) the better your chance of finding them, so it is worth buying more detailed books. Many are available in the rest camp shops. Two obvious signals to look for in the field are circling vultures, or a number of parked cars.

Warthog, baboon, zebra, giraffe and many antelope species will happily graze together, so if you see one species, there will often be more close by. The presence of feeding herbivores does not preclude the possibility of a predator in the vicinity. For a start, of course, most predators are expert stalkers, and may not be obvious. In addition, most animals seem to know whether a predator is actually hunting; if it isn't they will be quite relaxed in its presence.

Antelopes will be unusually nervous and alert if they are aware of a predator on the hunt, but they will not immediately flee. They know they can nearly always out-run a predator if they have a sufficient head start, so they maintain a 'flight distance' between themselves and the threat. If the hunter encroaches, the antelope will move, but will try to keep the hunter in sight. If the hunter charges, the antelope will obviously flee, but will probably not leave the immediate area.

It is not necessarily best to drive as close as possible to an animal. The closer you are, the more likely you are to disturb its natural behaviour. Sudden movements will disturb most animals, so if you do approach make it slow and steady. Avoid frequent stopping and starting of the car engine, but bear in mind that engine vibrations might create a problem with camera shake. There are only a few designated spots where you are allowed to get out of your car. ■

reasonable rainfall (600mm) and fertile soils. There are large expanses of good grazing, with buffalo and red grass interspersed with acacia thorn trees (especially knobthorn), leadwood and marula trees. This favours large populations of impala, zebra, wildebeest, giraffe and black rhino. Predators, particularly lion, prey on the impala, zebra and blue wildebeest.

North of the Olifants River the rainfall drops below 500mm and the veld's dominant tree is mopane. This grows strongly in the west, where it is interspersed with red bush-willow, but has a tougher time on the basalt plains of the north-east, where it tends to be more stunted. The mopane is the favoured diet of elephants, which are most common north of the Olifants, and mopanes are also eaten by tsessebi, eland, roan and sable.

Perhaps the most interesting area is in the far north around Punda Maria and Pafuri. This has a higher rainfall (around 700mm at Punda Maria) than the mopane country and therefore supports a wider variety of plants (baobabs are particularly noticeable) and a higher density and variety of animals. There's woodland, bushveld, grass plains and, between the Luvuvhu and Limpopo rivers, a tropical riverine forest.

All the rivers have forest along their banks, often with enormous fig trees, which support populations of bushbuck and nyala. Needless to say, the rivers are where you will find hippo and crocodile.

## Wilderness Trails

There are seven guided 'trails', offering a chance to walk through the park. Small groups are guided by highly knowledgeable armed guides. Usually you don't walk *to* anywhere, nor are the walks terribly strenuous – you explore the area around your base camp and the itinerary is determined by the interests of the group, the time of year and the disposition of the wildlife.

Most trails last two days and three nights, over a weekend. Accommodation is in basic, though comfortable, huts and you don't need to provide food or equipment (bring your own beer and wine).

Wilderness Trails are popular and must be booked well in advance, through the National Parks Board in Pretoria or Cape Town. The maximum number of people on any trail is eight, at R985 per person. Trails, and (in parenthesis) the camps to report to, are: Bushman and Wolhuter (Berg-en-dal), Metsimetsi (Skukuza), Napi (Pretoriuskop), Nyalaland (Punda Maria), Olifants (Letaba) and Sweni (Satara).

On the **Bushman** trail, in the south-west corner of the park near Berg-en-dal, you can trek to rock paintings as well as see the large herds of antelope, lion and rhino. **Wolhuter**, based near the Bushman Trail camp, is also in an area inhabited by lion and rhino. The name commemorates legendary father and son rangers, Harry and Henry.

**Metsimetsi** is midway between Lower Sabie and Satara, in an area of plentiful and diverse animals. The terrain consists of undulating savanna, ravines and rocky gorges.

**Sweni** is a new trail, east of Satara, in an area with many lion attracted here by the herds of wildebeest, zebra and buffalo.

With a base on the Olifants River, the **Olifants** trail offers the chance to get close to elephant, hippo and crocodile as well as other animals.

The **Nyalaland** trail is in the far north of the park, a region of strikingly diverse ecosystems. This trail is famous for its birdlife, and there are many mammals.

The **Napi** trail runs through mixed bushveld midway between Skukuza and Pretoriuskop. There are black and white rhino, lion, leopard, cheetah, wild dog, buffalo and elephant – good for the 'big five'.

## Places to Stay

There are several styles of accommodation in Kruger, all of a high standard. Book through the National Parks Board.

Most visitors stay in rest camps. These have a wide range of facilities. Their restaurants are good and prices reasonable. They usually have a fairly standard menu, and steak and fish dishes cost around R35.

The accommodation varies, but usually includes huts (some of which have communal kitchens and bathrooms) and self-contained cottages. Booking is advisable, especially during holidays. In addition to huts and cottages, some rest camps also have 'sponsored accommodation' (privately owned and often better equipped and more comfortable), which should also be booked through the National Parks Board. Camping facilities are available at most camps; booking is not really necessary.

Bushveld camps are smaller, more remote camps without shops and restaurants, and private camps cater for small groups, which must take the entire camp. Bookings are essential for both types of camp.

All huts and cottages are supplied with bedding and towels. Most have air-conditioning or fans, and fridges. Visitors in accommodation without a kitchen who want to prepare their own meals must provide their own utensils. Camping sites are not equipped with power points. Large plastic groundsheets for tents are not allowed where lawn has been planted.

**Rest Camps** Unless otherwise stated in the following descriptions, the camps all have electricity, a shop, a restaurant, public telephones, communal cooking facilities (sinks, hotplates and braais) and fuel supplies (petrol and diesel).

All camps are fenced, attractively laid out and immaculately maintained. There are swimming pools at Pretoriuskop, Mopani, Shingwedzi and Berg-en-dal.

Most of the accommodation has a minimum charge for two or four people, with an additional charge of R60/30 for each additional adult/child.

*Berg-en-dal* is a modern, medium-sized camp near Malelane Gate. It's laid out in natural bush on the banks of Matjulu Spruit, about 5km from a water hole popular with rhino. There's a visitors' centre and, during school holidays, nature trails.

Camping in tents is R45 for one to two people plus R14 per extra person. Huts cost from R275 for one or two people, and six-bed cottages are R545 for up to six. All of

these include kitchens and bathrooms. There are two sponsored cottages.

*Crocodile Bridge*, near the gate of the same name, is a small camp in a great position by the Crocodile River. There are crocodile and hippo pools a few kilometres away and large numbers of zebra, impala, buffalo and wildebeest in the surrounding acacia.

There is no restaurant and diesel fuel is not available. Camping in tents costs R45 for one to two people plus R14 for each extra person. Huts with kitchens and bathrooms cost R275 for one or two people.

*Pretoriuskop*, Kruger's oldest camp, is near Numbi Gate and in higher country than other places in the park, so it's a little cooler in summer. The surrounding country is attractive, with granite outcrops, and is frequented by white rhino. The large camp has a certain old-style charm and includes a natural-rock swimming pool.

Camping in tents costs R45 for one to two people plus R14 for each extra person. Huts without air-conditioning or bathrooms cost from R90 for one or two people, or R100 with air-conditioning and a fridge. Huts with bathrooms cost R265, and huts with bathrooms and kitchens cost R315; both costs are for one or two people. There are also cottages from R485 for up to four people (R610 for up to six people, two bathrooms), and two sponsored cottages.

*Lower Sabie*, a medium-sized camp about an hour (35km) from Crocodile Bridge Gate, is in a prime game-viewing region. It overlooks a dam on the Sabie River, which attracts many animals. Elephant, buffalo, cheetah and rhino are often seen in the surrounding country. There's an excellent road along the Sabie River to Skukuza.

Camping in tents costs R45 for one to two people plus R14 for each extra person. Huts with common bathrooms are R60/105 a single/double, self-contained huts cost from R275 for two and cottages sleeping up to four persons are R640. There is one sponsored cottage.

*Skukuza* (☎ (013) 735 5611), on the Sabie River, is the main camp in Kruger and has facilities approaching those in a small town. There's a bank (Volkskas), an AA workshop, a doctor, a library, police, a post office and an excellent information centre. Comair flies to the nearby airfield from Jo'burg, and it is possible to hire cars.

There are a number of interesting historical sites in Skukuza, including the **Campbell Hut Museum**, one of the first huts to be restored, which houses a collection of furniture and photographs.

There is a huge variety of different accommodation and, although the camp is large, it's well laid out and doesn't overwhelm. Camping in tents costs R45 for one to two persons plus R14 for each extra person; the camp sites are distinctly average (furnished tents are R110 for one to two persons, R30/12 for extra adults/children). There is a variety of huts (from R275 for one or two people) and cottages (from R530 for up to four people and from R610 for up to six people), plus four sponsored cottages.

*Orpen*, near Orpen Gate, is a small, attractive camp. A nearby water hole attracts wildlife. There is no restaurant; cooking facilities are communal and no utensils are provided. Some accommodation doesn't have electricity (bring a torch).

There are basic camp sites available at Maroela, 4km away; you can camp in tents for R45 for one to two people plus R14 for each extra person. Huts at Orpen, with communal facilities, cost from R140 for one or two people, and a cottage sleeping up to six people is R640.

*Satara* (☎ (013) 735 6306), east of Orpen Gate, is a camp in an area of flat and fertile plains, which attract large numbers of grazing animals and have the highest lion population in the park. There are several water holes – you can watch one of them from the terrace of the pleasant self-serve restaurant. It's the second largest camp, and although it is not the most appealing (it's a bit flat for a start), there's a range of facilities.

Camping in tents costs R45 for one to two people plus R14 for each extra person. Huts with shower, toilet and fridge cost from R275 for one or two people (no cooking

utensils provided) and there are cottages from R730 for up to five people. There are three sponsored cottages.

*Olifants* (☎ (013) 735 6606) has a fantastic position on the bluff high above the Olifants River – there are spectacular views. You can see elephant, hippo and many other animals from the camp, as they come down to the river 100m below. Much of the camp is terraced and some of the huts are literally on the edge of the cliffs. There's an interesting information centre, concentrating on elephants.

There are no camp sites at Olifants, but it is possible to camp at nearby Balule. Huts with shower, toilet and fridge cost from R275 for one or two people or with a kitchen from R305 for one or two people. Fully equipped cottages cost from R535 for up to four people (with two bathrooms, R610). There are also two sponsored cottages.

*Balule* is a small rest camp 11km from Olifants. There are no services except hot water and wood stoves. It's quiet and atmospheric, however, and you'll almost certainly hear hippo grunting in the nearby river. Camping in tents costs R45 for one to two people plus R14 for each extra person. Basic huts with communal facilities and no electricity cost R85 for one or two people. Definitely bring a torch.

*Letaba* (☎ (013) 735 6636) is a camp with excellent views over a wide bend of the Letaba River. It's an attractive camp with lots of shade, trees and grassy camping sites. There are plenty of animals, especially in winter. The restaurant overlooks the river.

The **museum** here focuses on the elephant and includes mounted tusks of the big bulls (Mafunyane, Dzombo, Shingwedzi and Shawu), which have died in the park. There is also a section on poaching, the illegal ivory trade, geomorphology, biology and descriptions of elephant habits.

Tent camping costs R45 for one to two people plus R14 for each extra person. There is a variety of other accommodation in this camp, including furnished tents with lighting, fan and fridge but no kitchen (R110 for one or two people); huts with common bathroom (from R120 for one or two people); fully equipped huts (from R275 for one or two people) and cottages (R750 for up to six people); and two sponsored cottages.

*Mopani* (☎ (013) 735 6536) is a superb modern rest camp on the edge of the Pioneer Dam, 45km north of Letaba. Natural materials have been extensively used and all the buildings are thatched. There are some great spots overlooking the dam. The huts are from R315 for one or two persons, cottages for up to six persons are R750. There's a sponsored cottage but no camp sites.

*Shingwedzi* (☎ (013) 735 6806/7) is the largest camp in the northern section of the park. It's an old-style place, with many huts and cottages arranged in circles and shaded by tall mopane trees and palms. A restaurant overlooks the Shingwedzi River, and there's a swimming pool. There are excellent drives in the vicinity.

Camping in tents costs R45 for one to two people plus R14 for each extra person. Huts with fans and fridges cost R115 for two people, from R255 with kitchen and bathroom. A cottage with fans costs R340 for up to four people.

*Punda Maria* (☎ (013) 735 6873) is the northernmost rest camp in sandveld country by Dimbo Mountain. It's a long-established camp with an attractive setting and a wilderness atmosphere. Plans to modernise and expand it are in train; hopefully the atmosphere won't be spoilt. The area's ecology is fascinating and there is a wide range of animals, including lion and elephant. It's the perfect place for a night-time braai – come prepared.

Camping is R45 for one to two people plus R14 for each extra person, huts with bath but communal kitchens are R255 for two people (with kitchen it's R265) and cottages are R510 for up to four people.

**Bushveld Camps** These small clusters of self-catering cottages don't have the facilities of the rest camps, nor do they have the numbers of people passing through. Most are reasonably close to a rest camp where you can buy supplies. Except for Jakkalsbessie,

which is a more upmarket camp and almost a suburb of Skukuza, all bushveld camps have solar power – you can't use electrical appliances other than lights, fans and fridges. (Prices quoted are the minimum charges. For additional adults/children add R60/30.)

*Biyamiti*, on the south border of Kruger, between Malelane and Crocodile Bridge gates, has one and two-bedroom cottages (R325 for one or two people, R630 for up to five people, respectively).

*Jakkalsbessie* is 7km from Skukuza. There is electricity and air-conditioning, and an airfield nearby. There are eight two-bedroom cottages (from R705 to R840 for up to four people).

*Talamati*, on the western border of Kruger about 30km south of Orpen Gate, has one-bedroom cottages at R325 for one or two people and two-bedroom cottages at R630 for up to four people.

*Shimuwini* is on the Letaba River, 50km north of the Phalaborwa Gate. There are one-bedroom cottages for R325 for one or two people, two-bedroom cottages for R630 for up to five people and one three-bedroom cottage (R705 for up to four).

*Bateleur*, about 40km south of Shing-wedzi, has two and three-bedroom cottages which cost, respectively, R575 and R660 for up to four people.

*Sirheni*, about 55km south-east of Punda Maria, has one and two-bedroom cottages for R325 for one or two people and R630 for up to four people.

**Private Camps** Not to be confused with the private reserves which border Kruger, the following five camps are privately owned. They are all secluded and you have to book the whole camp, so there's plenty of privacy. Unless you're in a largish group they are pretty expensive, at R2280 (for up to 12 people plus R60/30 for each additional adult/child). Take all your own supplies except bedding, and book through the National Parks Board (☎ (012) 343 1991; fax 343 0905).

*Malelane*, 3km from Malelane Gate on the Berg-en-dal road, has rondavels with air-conditioning and electricity which sleep 19 people; the nearest shop is at Berg-en-dal.

At *Jock of the Bushveld*, about 40km from Berg-en-dal on the Skukuza road, huts sleep 12 people in total and have solar power for lighting but no other electricity.

*Nwanetsi*, 27km from Satara on the Nwanetsi road, has huts which sleep 16 people in total but there is no electricity.

At *Roodewal*, 40km from Olifants on the road to Timbavati, there is a cottage and three huts which sleep a total of 19 people; a viewing platform overlooks a water hole.

*Boulders*, 50km north of Letaba on the Mooiplaas-Phalaborwa road, sleeps 12 people and is built on stilts; there is no fencing, so animals can wander below.

### Getting There & Away
**Air** Comair flies between Jo'burg and Skukuza twice daily for R422. InterAir has services from Nelspruit, Durban and Jo'burg to Phalaborwa (see Phalaborwa in the Northern Province chapter). Airlink flies from Jo'burg to Nelspruit and Phalaborwa.

**Bus & Minibus Taxi** For most visitors, Nelspruit is the most convenient large town near Kruger, and it's well served by buses and minibus taxis to/from Jo'burg. However, once in Nelspruit you still have a fair way to go to get into the park. Near Nelspruit and closer to Kruger (15km from Numbi Gate) is the small village of Hazyview, where there are a couple of backpacker hostels.

City to City/Transtate buses to/from Jo'burg run through Hazyview, and there are minibus taxis to Nelspruit. A minibus taxi from Hazyview to Skukuza is R7. Phalaborwa, in the north, is right on the edge of Kruger and is served by regular bus services, both City to City/Transtate and North Link Tours. In the Venda area, minibus taxis run to near the Punda Maria Gate. See the relevant towns for details.

**Train** The *Komati* runs from Jo'burg to Komatipoort (via Nelspruit), about 12km from Kruger's Crocodile Bridge Gate.

**Car** Skukuza is 500km (six hours) from Jo'burg. Punda Maria is about 620km from Jo'burg and can be reached in eight hours. Hire cars are available at Skukuza, Nelspruit and Phalaborwa.

**Hitching** Hitching is definitely not a good way to see Kruger – forget it. If you're low on funds, you're better off joining a group of people and hiring a car.

**Tours** There are many tour operators. For those with limited funds one of the best ways to get a glimpse of the park is with African Routes (☎ (031) 562 8724; fax 562 8673). The safari includes pick-up from Jo'burg, visits to the Klein (Mpumalanga) Drakensberg, Kruger (two days), Swaziland, and the KwaZulu-Natal Drakensberg (two days) and drop off in Durban. The cost is from R1350 to R1650 for seven days, all-inclusive. Smaller tour operators include Bundu Bus (☎ (011) 693 1808), with four-day tours (departing on Monday and Friday) of Mpumalanga and Kruger Park for about R685; Sebata Safaris (☎ (082) 855 9669), which has three-day tours of the park from Jo'burg/Nelspruit for R675/545; and the reliable Jo'bu Tours & Safaris (☎ (011) 964 2329), which has four-day camping trips for R750, all inclusive.

Other operators include: Max Maximum Tours (☎ (011) 933 4177, (082) 553 1587); Safari Tours Hazyview (☎ (013) 737 7113); Livingstone Trails (☎ (011) 867 2586); Wagon Trails (☎ (011) 643 3762); Wildlife Safaris (☎ (011) 888 6896); Wilderness Wheels (☎ (011) 648 5737); and Mopani Tours (☎ (011) 640 6431).

## PRIVATE GAME RESERVES – MPUMALANGA
The area just west of Kruger contains a large number of private reserves, usually sharing a border with Kruger and thus most of the 'big five' are seen. They are often extremely expensive – R650 per person is only mid-range – but with an economic stake in their guests getting close to animals they have good viewing facilities. It is possible to find

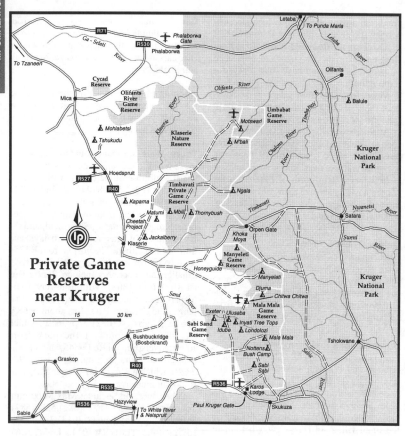

## Private Game Reserves near Kruger

cheaper places, and these may be more enjoyable because accommodation is in bush camps. For Klaserie & Manyeleti reserves, see the Northern Province chapter.

Listed below are some of the reserves and accommodation options. Before deciding which private reserve to visit, it's worth contacting a travel agent to find out if there are any special deals going. Sondela Central Reservations (☎ (013) 764 3492) in Sabie, Enter Africa (☎ (011) 487 1557) in Jo'burg, the Publicity Association (☎ (013) 752 4547) and Bushveld Breakaways (☎ (013) 750 1998; fax 750 0383) in White River, as well

as the Phalaborwa Association for Tourism (☎ (01524) 85860), all handle bookings.

**Sabi Sand Game Reserve** is a very large private conservation area on the south-west edge of Kruger Park. Within Sabi Sand are a number of prestigious private reserves, all sharing the same lowveld country and its wealth of birds and animals. There are no fences between this area and Kruger. Following are some reserves and lodges within Sabi Sand; for fuller listings, ask a travel agent.

**Sabi Sabi** ( ☎ (011) 483 3939) consists of two parts: Sabi Sabi in the south on the Sabie River, and Inyati Tree Tops (☎ (011) 493

0755) in the north, on the Sand River. While the 'big five' are found in both, you have a better chance of seeing lion at Sabi Sabi. For hippo and crocodile, Inyati is better. Accommodation is in luxury chalets, with Inyati's considerably cheaper. The tariff will include meals, drives and guided walks.

The luxurious *Idube* (☎ (011) 888 3713; fax 888 2181) is north-west of Sabi Sabi (from R1500 per person). Other accommodation nearby includes *Djuma Game Reserve* (☎ (011) 789 2722) and *Chitwa Chitwa* (☎ (011) 883 1354). The latter has specials from R840 per person sharing, which includes three meals, bush walks and game drives; that's cheap for this part of the world. The rock lodge at *ulu Saba* (☎ (013) 735 5460), set in bush west of Inyati, has winter specials from R1000 per person sharing.

There is a variety of accommodation at **Londolozi Game Reserve**, from a main camp with luxury chalets to bush camps. Prices include meals and game drives; book on ☎ (011) 803 8421. Take the R536 from Hazyview west towards Kruger Gate and Skukuza, and turn to the left after 36km. The reserve is 28km further on.

The world-famous **Mala Mala** reserve is geared towards safari-suited foreigners who want to see the 'big five' while remaining in a small five-star cocoon (Yeoville in Jo'burg won't feature in post-trip slide shows, I bet). *Mala Mala* (☎ (011) 789 2677) costs over US$500 per person per night. Take the roads to Londolozi then follow the signposts.

## HAZYVIEW

Hazyview is a small village with a large shopping centre serving the black community. Kruger Park's Numbi and Kruger gates are nearby (15km and 43km, respectively). Hazyview is near the junction of the R535 (which runs down the escarpment from Graskop), the R536 from Sabie and the R538 from White River.

The Hazyview Tourist Association (☎ (013) 737 7414) in the Numbi Hotel is open weekdays from 8.30 am to 4.30 pm, Saturday from

8 am to 1 pm. There are banks and supermarkets near the four-way stop.

### Places to Stay

Three km up the hill from the junction of the R40 and R538 is the new *Big 5 Backpackers* (☎ (011) 622 3663). The adequate dorms are R35 and private rooms R50 per person. The owner has cleverly converted water reservoirs into bomas where you can cook or rest; above these is a 'contemplation' area from where you can see distant Kruger, write postcards or enjoy a 'sundowner'.

*Kruger Park Backpackers'* (☎ /fax (013) 737 7224) has camping for R15, dorm beds for R35 and Zulu-style huts for R50; all costs are per person. The hostel is about 2km south of Hazyview, just past the White River turnoff. They pick up from Nelspruit for R50 per person. In the bar, local whites horrifically reveal their true thoughts about the 'new' South Africa.

Not far from the main junction is *Hotel*

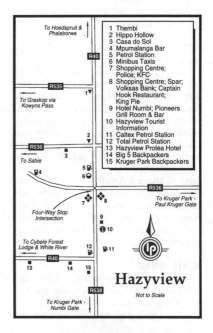

| 1 | Thembi |
| 2 | Hippo Hollow |
| 3 | Casa do Sol |
| 4 | Mpumalanga Bar |
| 5 | Petrol Station |
| 6 | Minibus Taxis |
| 7 | Shopping Centre; Police; KFC |
| 8 | Shopping Centre; Spar; Volksas Bank; Captain Hook Restaurant; King Pie |
| 9 | Hotel Numbi; Pioneers Grill Room & Bar |
| 10 | Hazyview Tourist Information |
| 11 | Caltex Petrol Station |
| 12 | Total Petrol Station |
| 13 | Hazyview Protea Hotel |
| 14 | Big 5 Backpackers |
| 15 | Kruger Park Backpackers |

Hazyview

Not to Scale

*Numbi* (☎ (013) 737 7301), which has single/double bungalows for R190/260, and rooms for R250/350. There is camping here; a tent site is about R60 a double.

*Hazyview Protea Hotel* (☎ (013) 737 7332) is near Hazyview at Burgershall; it charges R294/398. On the R536 to Sabie, *Casa do Sol* (☎ (013) 737 8111) has cottages and villa units from R350. Off the R40, *Cybele Forest Lodge* (☎ (01311) 50511) is about R400 in a studio, R520 in a cottage.

On the north side of the R536, just 200m before the Kruger Gate (and not part of a reserve), is the flash *Karos Lodge* (☎ (013) 735 5671), which has singles/doubles for R520/750 for dinner, bed and breakfast.

### Places to Eat

There are *takeaways* near the four-way stop. The Hotel Numbi's *Pioneer Grill* has jacket potatoes for R8.50, black mushrooms for R12.50, salads for R12 and a huge meal of roquefort rump for R35. Other recommended places are *Thembi*, near the junction of the R535 and R40, and *Hippo Hollow* to the south, which sometimes has an African game menu. There are places in the mall (where the R536 and R538 meet) including the *Captain Hook Restaurant*.

The brave (foolhardy) can try out the *Mpumalanga Bar*, where the serving area is surrounded by a metal grill, to hear the many shouts of 'Amstel' and to enjoy rowdy conversation; ask a local black for directions. *Hunter's Nightclub* is *the* place to party. It has a large bar and a pizza restaurant; turn north off the R40 to Kiepersol.

### Getting There & Away

City to City/Transtate's Friday night only Jo'burg to Acornhoek buses stop at Hazyview, as do many minibuses and buses serving the local area. A minibus to Nelspruit or Sabie is R15.

### WHITE RIVER

White River (Witrivier) is a little higher and less humid than nearby Nelspruit, but it is still warm enough to be a green, pleasant little town with a colonial feel. There are also numerous artists in the area; get their addresses from the town hall or the Artists' Trading Post. The town is the self-styled 'nut capital of South Africa', and in **Nutcracker Valley** just south of the town off the R40 you can visit some plantations.

On the R40 near the hamlet of Rocky Drift, about halfway to Nelspruit, **Kraal Kraft** claims to have the largest collection of African artefacts in the country.

### Places to Stay & Eat

The inexpensive municipal *caravan park* (☎ (01311) 31176) is in the park in the centre of town. In nearby Rocky Drift, on the Nelspruit road, *Flamboyant Rondavels* (☎ (01311) 58 1133) are R70/95 for singles/doubles. *Karula Hotel* (☎ (01311) 32277) is on the Old Plaston road, the R538, which is more reminiscent of an English country lane than a South African road. The hotel is also pleasant and charges R145/240 for dinner, bed and breakfast.

South of White River is the upmarket *Jatinga Country Lodge* (☎ (01311) 31932), in 30 acres of gardens. Full board is over R400 per person.

*Timbuctoo Restaurant*, open for lunch and dinner, serves game dishes, steaks and prawns, and there is also a great wine list; it is closed on Sunday.

### Getting There & Away

Minibus taxis run to Nelspruit for R4. Prestige Travel (☎ (01311) 31228) has daily buses running to Jo'burg for R75.

### NELSPRUIT

Nelspruit, in the Crocodile River valley, is the largest town in Mpumalanga's steamy subtropical lowveld; it is also the provincial capital.

Nelspruit's growth began only in the 1890s, when the South African Republic decided that it must put a railway through to Delagoa Bay (Maputo) so it would have access to a non-British port. The Anglo-Boer War upset these plans and it wasn't until 1905 that Nelspruit was proclaimed a town.

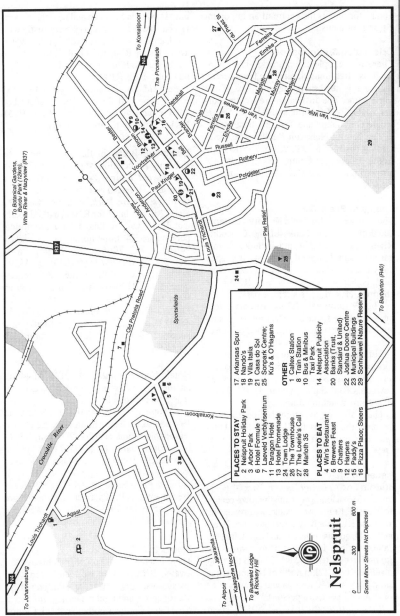

# Nelspruit

0   300   600 m

Some Minor Streets Not Depicted

**PLACES TO STAY**
2   Nelspruit Holiday Park
3   Arbor Park
6   Hotel Formule 1
7   Laeveld Verblyfsentrum
11  Paragon Hotel
13  Hotel Promenade
24  Town Lodge
26  The Townhouse
27  The Loerie's Call
28  Marloth 35

**PLACES TO EAT**
4   Win's Restaurant
5   Brewers Feast
9   Chatters
12  Harpers
15  Paddy's
16  Pizza Place; Steers

17  Arkansas Spur
18  Nando's
19  Villa Italia
21  Casa do Sol
25  Sonpark Centre;
    Ku's & O'Hagans

**OTHER**
1   Caltex Station
8   Train Station
10  Bus & Minibus
    Taxi Park
14  Nelspruit Publicity
    Association
20  Banks (Trust,
    Standard & United)
22  Joshua Doore Centre
23  Municipal Buildings
29  Sonhuewel Nature Reserve

Today, the area is the centre of an important citrus-fruit industry.

## Orientation & Information
There are a couple of landmarks. The Promenade is a tree-lined street in the town centre, with a big new shopping complex of the same name. The Joshua Doore Centre, corner of Louis Trichardt and Kruger Sts, is where Greyhound and Translux buses stop.

The helpful Nelspruit Publicity Association (☎ (013) 755 1988/9; fax 755 1350) is in the Promenade Centre. It's open from 8 am to 5 pm on weekdays, 9 am to 4 pm on weekends.

## Things to See & Do
The 150 hectare **Lowveld National Botanic Garden** is on the banks of the Crocodile River (take the R37) and includes formal gardens and indigenous forest. It's open daily between 7 am and 4.30 pm and admission is R2.50 for adults and R0.50 for children. Next door is a reptile park.

The **Sonheuwel Nature Reserve** features antelope species, vervet monkeys and leguan lizards; there are some rock paintings here. There is no entrance fee.

This area of Mpumalanga is home to many species of birds, some of which do not occur further west in South Africa. The renowned Lawson's Bird Safaris (☎ (013) 755 2147) offers bird-watching tours.

There are two overnight **hiking trails** in the area, the Kaapsche Hoop and the Uitsoek. For trail and hut bookings, contact SAFCOL (☎ (013) 764 1058) in Sabie.

## Places to Stay
**Bottom End** *Nelspruit Holiday Park* (☎ (013) 759 2113) is a long way from the town centre. Sites cost R40 for two people, and rondavels cost from R150 for two. To get there head west on the N4, go past Agaat St and turn left at the Caltex station. It's about 1km further on. *Bundu Park* (☎ (013) 758 1221), off the road to White River, 12km north of Nelspruit, has camp sites for R40 for two and caravan sites for R50 (R5 per extra person).

*Rockery Hill* (☎ (013) 741 5011), 11km

out of town via Mataffin and near the airport, is a backpackers' place. It is very rustic with no electricity although there is gas hot water. Tent sites are R30, dorm beds R30, A-frame double cabins R70 for two, and there's a four bed cottage for R100.

*Laeveld Verblyfsentrum* (☎ (013) 753 3380) is on Old Pretoria Rd. A dorm bed costs about R40 (with full board it is R65). It's used mainly by youth groups.

**B&Bs** For B&Bs in the area contact the Publicity Association (☎ (013) 755 1988/9).

*Bushveld Lodge* (☎ (013) 43219) on Kaapsche Hoop Rd is R150 for two, sharing facilities; *Arbor Park*, also on Kaapsche Hoop Rd, has units for R105 (without bath) and R115 with a shared bath (additional persons are R40); the upmarket *Townhouse* (☎ (013) 752 7006) is at 5 Ferreira St (R195/295); *Marloth 35* (☎ (013) 752 4529), at the reverse of the name, has singles/doubles for R120/160 and will pick you up from the bus depot or airport; and *The Loerie's Call* at 2 du Preez St (☎ (013) 752 4844) is a well-presented guesthouse in a peaceful suburb – single/double rooms are R190/300.

**Hotels** *Hotel Formule 1* (☎ (013) 741 4490), on the N4, has rooms for R119; a rather sparse breakfast is R7.

*Paragon Hotel* (☎ /fax (013) 753 3205) at 19 Anderson St has an impressive façade and reasonable rooms at R206/268 with breakfast. *Town Lodge* (☎ (013) 741 1444) in General Dan Pienaar Rd has singles/doubles for R178/200, excluding breakfast (R24).

*Hotel Promenade* (☎ (013) 753 3000) is the old town hall. It's a very pleasant place and charges from R320/380, with weekend specials (R120 per person B&B).

## Places to Eat
There is a fair sprinkling of franchised takeaways. Brown St is well endowed with restaurants. For pizza, there's *Pappa's* at No 56; for coffee and light meals, try *Harpers* at No 31 and *Chatters* in the Nedbank Centre;

and *Nando's*, for spicy Portuguese food, is at No 47.

In the Promenade, *Mike's Kitchen* has hearty meals for about R30 (and lunch specials for R17 with help-yourself salad platter). Nearby is a local favourite *Café Mozart* with quality meals.

*Villa Italia*, on the corner of Louis Trichardt and Kruger Sts, is popular with the young set; a delectable pasta meal costs from R25. In the same complex is *Casa do Sol*, a quaint little Portuguese restaurant. Not far away, on Louis Trichardt St, is *Arkansas Spur* for burgers and chips.

On the opposite side of the road from the Town Lodge is *O'Hagan's*, which tries hard to be a 'real' Irish pub, and the ever-reliable Chinese place *Ku's*. Close to the Formule 1 is *Brewers Feast*, a convenient late-night stop for travellers.

### Getting There & Away

**Air** The airport is 8km south of town on the Kaapsche Hoop road. There are daily SA Airlink (☎ (013) 752 5257) flights to Jo'burg (Apex one way is R251) and Durban (R296). Metavia (☎ (011) 453 3352, (013) 741 3141) has flights to Maputo in Mozambique (R456 one way).

**Bus** There is a daily Jo'burg to Maputo (Mozambique) service with Tropical Express (☎ (011) 337 9169, (013) 755 1988/9), returning daily (from Nelspruit it costs R80 one way to Maputo and R80 to Jo'burg). Jo'burg to Maputo is R150.

Greyhound (☎ (013) 752 5134) has a daily service to Jo'burg for R125, departing from the Joshua Doore Centre at 7.30 am, except on Sunday when it leaves at 3.30 pm.

**Train** The *Komati* (☎ (011) 773 2944) runs to/from Jo'burg and Maputo via Nelspruit on Sunday, Tuesday and Thursday (returning on Monday, Wednesday and Friday), from Jo'burg via Nelspruit to Komatipoort daily; the Maputo train crosses the border and it is necessary to carry out immigration formalities at Lebombo and Ressano Garcia (Mozambique). Fares from Jo'burg to Ko-

matipoort in 1st/2nd class are R121/85, Komatipoort to Maputo is R30/23.

**Minibus Taxi** The large local bus and minibus taxi park is near the corner of Brown and Henshall Sts, about 80m from The Promenade. Minibus taxi destinations and fares include: Jo'burg R55, Sabie R10, Barberton R6.50, Hazyview R15, White River R4, Graskop R35 and Komatipoort R40.

The City Bug (☎ (013) 755 3792) operates in town; the cost door to door is R8.

**Car Rental** Avis (☎ (013) 741 1087), Budget (☎ (013) 741 3871), Europcar (☎ (013) 741 3062) and Imperial (☎ (013) 741 3210) have offices at the airport.

## SUDWALA CAVES

In the Mankelekele mountains west of Nelspruit and south of Sabie, the Sudwala caves have the usual stalactite and stalagmite formations with fanciful names and mood lighting. They are worth a visit; there are one-hour tours (☎ (01311) 64152) for R20.

Near the caves is the **Dinosaur Park**, which is more interesting for its indigenous forest than the model saurians. It's open daily between 8.30 am and 4.30 pm. The caves are about 2km up a steep hill; at the bottom of the hill is *Sudwala Lodge* (☎ (01311) 63073) with singles/doubles for R200/320, and chalets from R210 for up to three people.

## MALELANE

Malelane, on the banks of the Crocodile River, is right on the border of the Kruger National Park. It's a modern town with a distinctive wagon-wheel layout, and it is surrounded by sugar-cane fields. There are two **game reserves** in the vicinity. The 700 hectare **Mahushe Shongwe**, on the Lebombo Flats, has the Mzinti River flowing through it. The 9000 hectare **Mthethomusha**, adjoining Kruger, has a variety of wildlife, and over 200 bird species have been recorded here.

The self-catering *Mthomeni Tented Camp* (☎ (013) 759 4000), administered by the Mpumalanga Parks Board, in Mahushe Shongwe, costs a very reasonable R80 per

MPUMALANGA

person and the rate includes two game drives and bush walks. *Malelane Hotel* (☎ /fax (01313) 30274) at 21 Impala St has B&B for about R110 per person.

About 20km away near Kaapmuiden is *Kudu Lodge* (☎ (01313) 98 0080). A tent site is R10.50 plus R7.50 per person, and single/double B&B is R100/180 (children are charged R30 for B&B).

## KOMATIPOORT

This border town is at the foot of the Lebombo mountains near the confluence of the Komati and Crocodile rivers. It is only 10km to the Crocodile Bridge into Kruger.

Just outside town there is a *caravan park* (☎ (01313) 50213). *Border Country Inn* (☎ (01313) 50328) is on the N4 close to both the Mozambique border post and Kruger; B&B is R145 per person.

### Border Formalities

To cross into Mozambique you need a visa paper (not in your passport) stamped. It is worth paying R30 to one of the Portuguese-speakers, who hang around for this purpose, to help with this. The exit formalities are carried out at Komatipoort and the entry into Mozambique takes place at Ressano Garcia. If you have a car you will need a breakdown-warning triangle, seat belts in the car and the relevant vehicle papers, especially for hire cars. The black market rate for conversion of rand to meticais is 20% better than at a bank. As in any such currency exchange, beware.

## BARBERTON

Barberton, 50km south of Nelspruit, was something of a boom town during gold rushes last century and had South Africa's first stock exchange. However, most miners soon moved onto the newly discovered Rand fields near Jo'burg. Today, all working gold mines in the region are over 100 years old.

Barberton is a quiet but alluring town in harsh but interesting lowveld country. The

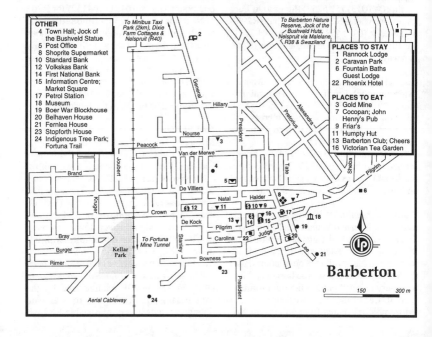

**OTHER**
4 Town Hall; Jock of the Bushveld Statue
5 Post Office
8 Shoprite Supermarket
10 Standard Bank
12 Volkskas Bank
14 First National Bank
15 Information Centre; Market Square
17 Petrol Station
18 Museum
19 Boer War Blockhouse
20 Belhaven House
21 Fernlea House
23 Stopforth House
24 Indigenous Tree Park; Fortuna Trail

**PLACES TO STAY**
1 Rannock Lodge
2 Caravan Park
6 Fountain Baths Guest Lodge
22 Phoenix Hotel

**PLACES TO EAT**
3 Gold Mine
7 Cocopan; John Henry's Pub
9 Friar's
11 Humpty Hut
13 Barberton Club; Cheers
16 Victorian Tea Garden

To Minibus Taxi Park (2km); Dixie Farm Cottages & Nelspruit (R40)

To Barberton Nature Reserve, Jock of the Bushveld Huts, Nelspruit via Malelane, R38 & Swaziland

General
Hillary
President
Nourse
Peacock
Van der Merwe
De Villiers
Natal
Halder
Crown
De Kock
Pilgrim
Carolina
Bowness
Judge
Stanley
Joubert
Brand
Kruger
Bray
Burger
Rimer
Kellar Park
To Fortuna Mine Tunnel
Aerial Cableway

Alexandra
Pretorius
Tate
Sheba
Pilgrim
Lee

**Barberton**

0    150    300 m

large township outside Barberton is **Emjin-dini**. Readers of *The Power of One* may be interested to know that its author, Bryce Courtenay, was born in Barberton.

The information centre (☎ (013) 712 2121) in Market Square on Crown St is extremely well organised. It is open from 8 am to 4.30 pm Monday to Friday (lunch is from 1 to 2 pm), 8.30 am to noon Saturday.

### Things to See & Do

There are several restored houses in town. **Belhaven House** on Lee Rd, a middle-class home built at the turn of the century, is open for inspection (entry is R1/0.50 for adults/children). It is open on weekdays for a guided tour at 10 and 11 am, noon, 2 and 3 pm. **Stopforth House** in Bowness St, a typical middle-class home dating from the diggers' period (1890s), is open the same hours as Belhaven; entry is free. **Fernlea** in Lee Rd, open weekdays from 9 am to 4 pm, has temporary exhibits.

Barberton has a modern **museum** in Pilgrim St, open daily from 9 am to 4 pm; admission is free. In between Lee and Judge Sts is an iron and wood **blockhouse** from the Anglo-Boer War, part of the chain built by the British when the war entered its guerrilla phase. There's a statue of **Jock of the Bushveld** outside the town hall. Not far from town is an umbrella thorn tree, **Jock's Tree**; it was his favourite territorial marker.

The 20.3km aerial cableway, purported to be the longest industrial cableway in the world, brings asbestos down from a mine in Swaziland. Coal is carried in the other direction to provide counterweight.

**Barberton Nature Reserve** is just northeast of the town, on the R38 to Kaapmuiden. The country is lowveld, with some high hills, especially towards the Swaziland border. As mining still takes place in the reserve, there aren't all that many animals to be seen other than birdlife, which is plentiful, and a few species of monkey and ungulates.

**Lone Tree Hill**, about 7km from town, is a prime paragliding launch site, just being discovered by people who are doing such things. Find out about keys and access from the information centre.

**Hiking Trails** There is the interesting 2km **Fortuna Mine** walk close to town. About 600m of it is through an old tunnel, so you need to bring a torch. The rocks excavated from the tunnel are 4200 million years old, the oldest sedimentary rocks yet found.

Several overnight hiking trails begin in Barberton, including the two-day **Pioneer** and **Umvoti** trails. The countryside combines beautiful scenery and old mine workings. The **Gold Nugget Trail** follows old prospectors' trails on the northern slopes of the Makhonjwa range. Contact the information centre for details.

### Places to Stay

At the *caravan park* (☎ (013) 712 3323) tent sites are R35 (up to three people, extra persons R7), van sites are R45, and chalets with kitchens are from R140 for two people or R220 for six.

A good place to stay is *Fountain Baths Guest Lodge* (☎ (013) 712 2707) (also called *FB Holiday Cottages)* at the southern end of Pilgrim St, where it resumes after merging into Sheba Rd (Crown St). Self-contained rooms cost R85 per person. This place, built in 1885, used to be Barberton's public pool, and has pleasant gardens.

On Pilgrim St on the corner of President St, the newly renovated *Phoenix Hotel* (☎ (013) 712 4211), is a clean, old-style country pub. With B&B for R165 per person, it is the most expensive place in Barberton. There's a ladies bar, mens pub, tea garden and intimate dining room.

Fourteen km out on the R38 to Kaapmuiden, *Diggers' Retreat* (☎ (013) 719 9681) has B&B for R125 per person; it also has a pool, and organises gold-panning trips and day visits to Eureka City.

Small, intimate B&B places seem the way to go around here and there is no shortage. *Rannoch Lodge* (☎ (013) 26417) is in town and upmarket (R135 per person); *Dixie Farm Cottages* (☎ (013) 9625) are 10km north of Barberton (R125); and the thatched

MPUMALANGA

*Jock of the Bushveld Huts* (☎ 712 4002) have self-contained rooms, a pool, horse-riding and microlighting (R75) – the backpackers' rooms for R45 include the use of a communal kitchen.

### Places to Eat

*Humpy Hut* and *Friar's*, in Crown St, are the places for takeaways; a hamburger with the lot is R5. *Gold Mine* next to Checkers supermarket covers most tastes; for a bar lunch it is R18 and a dinner is R35. *Cocopan*, on Crown St opposite the museum, is a casual place with *John Henry's Pub* attached. They specialise in casual food with a limited á la carte menu. The licensed *Victorian Tea Garden* is the place to relax and watch the passing parade; light meals cost R15.

*Cheers* in President St at the Barberton Club (☎ (013) 712 3226) has a full menu and lots of drunks; in the attached pub, you may meet some local characters.

### Getting There & Away

The scenic R40 road from here to Swaziland (via the Josefdal/Bulembu border posts) is unsealed and *very* rough but is all-weather. There's a checkpoint at the Bulembu mine.

There is a small minibus taxi rank by Emjindini, about 3km from town on the Nelspruit road, or you can find taxis in town. To Nelspruit it is R6, to Badplaas R10.

### BADPLAAS

This town certainly doesn't equate with its English-sounding name 'bad place'. It's a nice spot with pleasant sulphur springs and the dramatic Hlumuhlumu mountains as a backdrop.

*Aventura Badplaas* (☎ (017) 844 1020) releases mineral water twice daily in the doubles and suites; the cost, we guess, for this dunking is about R130/210 in the doubles. At *Badplaas Valley Inn* (☎ (017) 844 1040) it is R110 per person (you can sneak into the resort to take the waters).

### SONGIMVELO NATURE RESERVE

This spectacular 56,000 hectare reserve is in harsh lowveld country south of Barberton,

with some highveld on the eastern side which runs along the mountainous Swaziland border. The lack of dangerous predators in the reserve means that walking and horse-riding are popular activities.

There are big plans for this wilderness region – 1930s period costumes and 'gangster' cars for game drives included. We can only hope it is done sympathetically without the total ruination of one of South Africa's most pristine regions.

The *Komati River Lodge* (☎ (013) 759 4000), looked after by Mpumalanga Parks Board, has tented singles/doubles for R450/700 per night, all-inclusive, with two game drives and transfers to/from the gate.

# Centre & South

### VAAL DAM NATURE RESERVE

This area is a watersports recreation area for Gauteng, and it gets crowded. It's open daily between 7 am and 6 pm. There's a camp site. To get there take the N3 south from Jo'burg and turn off at Villiers, or just north of Villiers, to reach the northern side of the dam.

### MIDDELBURG

Middelburg, so called because it is midway between Pretoria and Lydenburg, is a large and stock-standard town on the N4.

Accommodation is geared towards businesspeople and is expensive. The cheapest option is *Oliphants River Lodge* (☎ (0132) 22 9114) on President Rd, with single/double rooms in the R100/130 range.

### NDEBELE VILLAGES

There are a number of places relating to the fascinating Ndebele culture, a link between the Zulu of KwaZulu-Natal and the Matabele people of Zimbabwe, which tourists can visit; the Vuka-Tsoga ('Wake up – Arise') region is an hour's drive from Pretoria. The main town in the region is KwaMhlanga.

The **Ndebele Traditional Village & Museum** is just across the road from the

Loopspruit Wine Estate (on the R568 north); there are fine examples of beadwork, decorative house design and woodcarving. You can also visit the **Royal Kraal, Emthambothini** (Weltevrede) by prior arrangement (☎ (013) 937 1841).

## LOSKOP DAM NATURE RESERVE
This reserve around the Loskop Dam has a fair range of animals inhabiting the dry, rolling hills of the Waterberg range, including white rhino, buffalo, zebra and leopard. It's off the R35 (turnoff from the R555), about 45km from Middelburg.

*Aventura Eco Loskop Dam* resort (☎ (01202) 3075) has camp sites for R25 plus R15 per person, and standard four-bed units for R195 (R270 in high season).

## PIET RETIEF
This solid, medium-sized town has few attractions, but it is the largest in the south of Mpumalanga and might be a good stopover on the way to Swaziland or KwaZulu-Natal.

There's a small **museum** off Church St, on one side of the minibus taxi park. It's open from 2 to 4 pm on weekdays, 10 am until noon on Saturday.

### Places to Stay & Eat
The pleasant, shady municipal *caravan park* (☎ (01343) 2619) is about 500m from the town centre, off the Pongola road. Van sites are R35, tent sites R30.

The *Imperial Hotel* (☎ (01343) 4251) on Church St, the main street, has B&B singles/doubles for R100/130. A few blocks along Church St, on the corner of du Toit St, the *Central Hotel* (☎ (01343) 4344) is smaller and cheaper.

There are several restaurants on Church St. *Green Door* is a friendly place with a comfortable bar and a big menu; takeaway pizzas are R18. It's open daily from 10 am until late.

### Getting There & Away
City to City/Transtate buses on the 10 hour Jo'burg to Swaziland route stop in Piet Retief (R65 to Hlathikulu).

They cross the border at Mahamba and run via Nhlangano to Hlathikulu. Buses from Jo'burg depart weekdays at 7.30 pm and return daily, except Saturday. There is also a service departing Jo'burg at 10 pm on Friday.

The minibus taxi park is in the large open space on Church St opposite the Old Mutual building. From here to the Swaziland border post at Mahamba costs R8.

# Gauteng

Gauteng Province (seSotho for Place of Gold and pronounced 'how-teng') takes in the mineral-rich area once known as PWV – Pretoria, Witwatersrand and Vereeniging. After 1994 it was briefly called PWV, but, as Krijan Lemmer noted in the *Weekly Mail & Guardian*, who wants to live in a place that sounds like a livestock disease?

Gauteng is by far the smallest province of South Africa (about 19,000 sq km), but with around 7 million people (including more than 40% of the country's whites) it has the second largest population. There is also an unknown number of illegal immigrants from other African countries. It has been claimed that Gauteng accounts for 65% of South Africa's gross domestic product and some 25% of the gross product of all Africa!

The area is rich in history (see the Johannesburg and Pretoria sections), but for most visitors a quick visit to Johannesburg and perhaps Pretoria will be more than enough. The province's countryside is crowded, surrounded by fields of *mielies* (maize) and polluted by power stations.

### Orientation

Johannesburg lies at the centre of an enormous conurbation, rapidly developing into a megalopolis. Diminishing green belts separate it from Pretoria to the north, but in all other directions the sprawl rolls on apace.

The Witwatersrand, which is often shortened to 'the Rand', literally means Ridge of White Waters. The ridge runs from Randfontein through Johannesburg and east beyond Brakpan and Springs. The term is now used to describe most of southern Gauteng, heavily developed and urbanised.

Although the ridge is over 1700m above sea level at its highest point, it is not particularly impressive. It's more famous for its underground geology than its above-ground form. At Carletonville, the Western Deep mine gets ore 3.5km below the surface.

The Vaal Triangle lies to the south of the

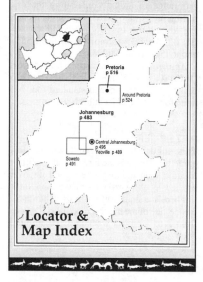

## HIGHLIGHTS

- Johannesburg – a huge, scary, exhilarating city embodying the best and worst of the new South Africa
- Guided tour of Soweto – essential and safe!
- Sedate Pretoria – history and nightlife

Pretoria
p 516

Around Pretoria
p 524

Johannesburg
p 483

Central Johannesburg
p 496
Yeoville p 489

Soweto
p 491

**Locator & Map Index**

Rand and is another heavily developed area, occupying the triangle formed by Vanderbijlpark, Vereeniging and Sasolburg (the latter is across the border in the Free State).

# Johannesburg

It can be quite a shock arriving in Johannesburg (also called Jo'burg, Jozi or eGoli – the City of Gold). A mere 100 years old, it's by far the largest city in South Africa and the largest city in Africa south of Lagos. It's a brash, fast-growing, ugly infant with the

478

redeeming features of wealth, energy and climate.

For the poor and the ambitious, Jo'burg is an irresistible lure. In the 1985 census, the population of greater Jo'burg was three million. In 1991, some estimates placed the population of Soweto, the largest black township, at over two million, which would mean that greater Jo'burg was probably approaching six million. Since the repeal of the Group Areas Act in 1991, the population has increased significantly, and with illegal immigrants no-one is sure of the exact figure.

On first appearances, Jo'burg is just an-other anonymous, big, western-style city that could just as easily be in the USA. You can expect fortified middle-class suburbs, a city centre dominated by modern skyscrapers, air-conditioned shopping malls, some pretty scary crime, black ghettos (townships) and lots of weapons.

Jo'burg's sole reason for existence is the reef of gold that lies under the highveld. Greed plays a role in building every city, but it is as naked and unashamed in Jo'burg as it is in Manhattan. Inhabitants – black, coloured and white – single-mindedly pursue the rand.

Cities also seem to answer a deep human need for interaction. This need is usually met by restaurants, cafés, pubs, bars, clubs, markets, churches and theatres. In most cities these cultural assets are an integral and prized part of urban life, but not in Jo'burg. In Jo'burg the main idea seems to have been to keep people apart. For a city at the centre of a huge conurbation, cultural assets are thin on the ground.

You can count the number of pleasant pubs and bars on one hand. There is no world-class gallery, museum or concert theatre. Not counting the township shebeens, the few inner-city bars seem often to be pick-up joints. The restaurants are generally scattered in suburbs, accessible only by car, and isolated in shopping centres.

When this book went to press the townships were still off-limits to lone wanderers, but not to those accompanied by black friends or with a reputable tour company.

### Why Visit Jo'burg?

If your time and finances are limited, it is best to go through Jo'burg as quickly as possible, or miss it altogether. However, you may not have a choice in the matter as Jo'burg has the major South African international airport and is a major hub for all forms of domestic transport. Most tourists only stay a day or two and few have a kind word to say about the city.

However, if you really do want to try to understand South Africa, Jo'burg has to be on your itinerary. Not even the old regime succeeded in completely crushing the life from the city. Beginning with the reforms of 1990 and accelerating since the elections there have been some radical and positive changes. Hillbrow, Berea and Yeoville remain the only multiracial suburbs of note in South Africa.

It's still difficult to cross the racial divide in South Africa, but you stand a better chance of meeting blacks on relatively equal terms in Jo'burg than almost anywhere else. Unlike many South African cities where there are so few black faces you could forget that you are in Africa, the centre of Jo'burg has been reclaimed and the sidewalks are jammed with black hawkers and stalls of every description. There's also a growing multiracial music and theatre scene. ∎

Although large-scale outbreaks of violence are things of the past, violent crime is still rampant, especially in the centre and the Hillbrow area.

If your time isn't limited and you can get some night transport (private car or taxi) you'll find Jo'burg a stimulating and interesting place that *is* definitely worth a few days of your time. This is the heart of the new South Africa, and this is where change – good and bad – is happening first. Remember, life goes on for its inhabitants – you are here only for a brief moment.

## HISTORY

At the beginning of 1886 the undistinguished stretch of the Transvaal highveld that was to become Johannesburg consisted of four sleepy farms: Braamfontein, Doornfontein, Turffontein and Langlaagte. In March of that year, however, an Australian prospector, George Harrison, found traces of gold on Langlaagte. Poor George didn't realise that he had stumbled on the only surface outcrop of the richest gold-bearing reef ever discovered. He sold his claim for £10.

Within a matter of months thousands of diggers descended on this site and by December, vacant land between the original farms had been surveyed, subdivided and auctioned. Initially, diggers lived in tents and covered ox-wagons, but permanent buildings soon appeared – and kept on appearing.

Because the gold was deep – in reef form, not the more easily accessible alluvial form – mining was quickly concentrated in the hands of men who had the capital to finance large underground mines. Mining magnates who had made their money at the Kimberley diamond field bought up the small claims and soon came to be known as the Randlords – Cecil Rhodes and Barney Barnato were among them.

By 1889 Jo'burg was the largest town in Southern Africa, full of the inevitable bars and brothels. The multicultural fortune seekers – blacks and whites – were regarded with deep distrust by the Boers, by the Transvaal government, and especially by the president, Paul Kruger. Although mining

JON MURRAY

LUBA VANGELOVA

Top: The Sufi mosque in Ladysmith, built by the local muslim community which has been in the town almost since its inception, KwaZulu-Natal.
Bottom: Zulu Shaka dancers perform with cowhide shields and traditional weapons, KwaZulu-Natal.

MIKE REED

RICHARD EVERIST

RICHARD EVERIST

LUBA VANGELOVA

Top: Council workers taking a break in Johannesburg, Gauteng.
Middle: Tribal dances are performed at Gold Reef City outside Johannesburg, Gauteng.
Bottom: The extravagant entrance to the Palace Hotel, Sun City, North-West Province.

boosted the government coffers the Boers feared their hard-won independence would be swamped by the huge influx of English-speaking *uitlanders* (outsiders, mainly from the USA and the British colonies) and blacks. Kruger introduced electoral laws that effectively restricted voting rights to Boers, and laws aimed at controlling the movement of blacks were passed.

The tensions between the Randlords and uitlanders on one side and the Transvaal government on the other were crucial factors in the lead-up to the Anglo-Boer War of 1899-1902. Jo'burg, which had a population in excess of 100,000, became a ghost town during the war, but it recovered quickly when the British took control and massive new mines were developed to the east and west. The British entrenched the privileged position of white workers.

By 1921 the 21,000 white miners earned almost twice as much as the 180,000 black miners, which suggested an obvious possibility to the mining companies. In 1922 the Chamber of Mines attempted to lower costs by employing blacks in skilled jobs that had previously been reserved for whites. The strike called by the white unionists soon became an open revolt – the Imperial Light Horse was ambushed at Ellis Park and artillery and aircraft were used against the strikers. By the time peace was restored, over 200 people, including 129 soldiers and policemen, had died in the Rand Revolt.

Although gold mining remained the backbone of the city's economy, manufacturing industries soon began to spring up, gaining fresh impetus during WWII. Under increasing pressure in the countryside, thousands of blacks moved to the city in search of jobs. Racial segregation had become entrenched during the interwar years, and from the 1930s onwards, vast squatter camps had sprung up around Jo'burg, particularly around Orlando to the south-west.

Under black leadership – most notably of James Mpanza, who is regarded as the founder of Soweto – the camps became well-organised cities, despite their gross overcrowding and negligible services. In the late

James Mpanza, the founder of Soweto.

1940s, many of the camps were destroyed by the authorities and the people were moved to new suburbs known as the South-Western Townships, shortened to Soweto.

The development of apartheid during the 1960s did nothing to slow the expansion of the city or the arrival of black squatters. Large-scale violence finally broke out in 1976 when the Soweto Students' Representative Council organised protests against the use of Afrikaans (regarded as the language of the oppressor) in black schools.

On 12 June, police opened fire on a student march, beginning a round of demonstrations, strikes, mass arrests and riots that took over 1000 lives over the next 12 months. Jo'burg and South Africa were never to be the same again – a generation of young blacks committed themselves to a revolutionary struggle against apartheid, and the black communities were politicised.

The regulations of apartheid were finally abandoned in February 1990, and since the 1994 elections the city has in theory been free of discriminatory laws. The black townships are being integrated into the municipal government system; the city centre is vibrant with black hawkers and street stalls; and a

GAUTENG

number of inner suburbs are quickly becoming multiracial.

Unfortunately, serious problems remain. Crime is rampant and middle class whites are retreating to the northern suburbs where new shopping malls and satellite business centres are mushrooming. It's another world out there in the northern suburbs, practically a *Volkstaat* by default.

Gold mining is no longer undertaken in the city area, and the old, pale-yellow mine dumps that created such a surreal landscape on the edge of the city are being carted away and reprocessed. Modern recovery methods allow metallurgists to recover gold from tailings that were regarded as valueless waste. The classic view of Jo'burg with a mine dump in the foreground and skyscrapers in the background will be retained, however, as some dumps are being preserved as historical monuments.

## ORIENTATION

Despite its size, it's not difficult to find your way around Jo'burg. Johannesburg International (formerly Jan Smuts) airport is 25km north-east of the city centre, accessible by freeway. Regular buses connect the airport with the Rotunda bus terminal, which is beside Jo'burg train station on the northern edge of the city centre.

Two major communication towers on the ridges to the north of the city centre make good landmarks. The Berea Tower, just behind Hillbrow, is 269m high and used by the post office. North-west of the city, the South African Broadcasting Commission runs the 239m Brixton Tower.

The city centre, which is laid out in a straightforward grid, is dominated by office blocks, in particular the 50 storey Carlton Centre on Commissioner St. The observation deck is ideal for orienting yourself.

There's no particular advantage in staying in the city centre. It becomes a virtual ghost town after the shops close – and it becomes extremely unsafe unless you're in a car, and maybe even then.

North of the city centre, a steep ridge runs east-west from the dangerous suburbs of Hillbrow and Berea across to Braamfontein. To the north-east is Yeoville, with the best budget accommodation and entertainment for those wishing to stay near the city centre.

The northern suburbs are white middle-class ghettos stretching away to the north within an arc formed by the N1 and N3 freeways. This is where to go if you want to pretend you're not in Africa. White people driving Mercs and BMWs whisk to busy, antiseptic shopping centres and the only blacks are neatly uniformed maids and gardeners waiting for minibus taxis. There is little communal life, although scattered about you'll find many of the city's best restaurants and shops. Serious shoppers are lured to the malls at Rosebank, or even further out to Randburg and Sandton. Those after a meal also hit the shopping centres, or a smattering of inner-city restaurant 'strips' such as Melville, Illovo and Norwood.

If you've noted the lack of trees in the city centre, you'll find the northern suburbs compensate. The enormous houses and private gardens are dominated by beautiful purple-flowering jacarandas in spring, and the lawns are always green and manicured. Most properties have high walls and large dogs – which go into a frenzy at the sound of pedestrians' footsteps. New offices are springing up in areas like Parktown (often in old mansions) as the whites' lemming-like rush to abandon the city centre accelerates.

The so-called black townships ring the city and are a grotesque contrast to the northern suburbs. Conditions within them range from basic to appalling. Accessibility and convenience were never factors in their planning, so they are a considerable distance from the city centre and the white suburbs (out of sight and out of mind). Black workers are forced to live away from their families, or to commute, which is both time-consuming and expensive. The main township is Soweto, but there are also big townships at Tokoza (south of Alberton), Kwa-Thema and Tsakane (south of Brakpan), Daveyton (east of Benoni), Tembisa (to the north-east) and Alexandra (inside the N3 freeway to the north).

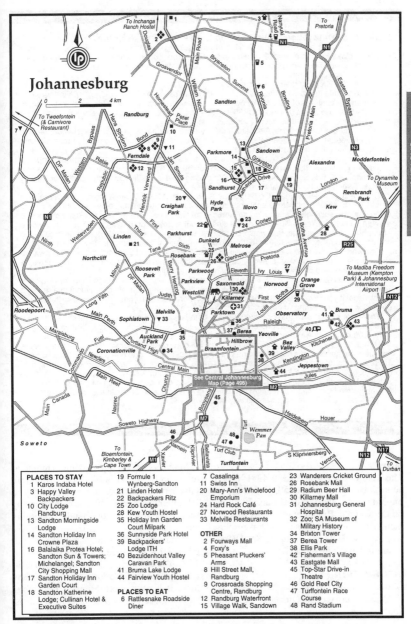

GAUTENG

**PLACES TO STAY**
1 Karos Indaba Hotel
3 Happy Valley Backpackers
10 City Lodge Randburg
13 Sandton Morningside Lodge
14 Sandton Holiday Inn Crowne Plaza
16 Balalaika Protea Hotel; Sandton Sun & Towers; Michelangel; Sandton City Shopping Mall
17 Sandton Holiday Inn Garden Court
18 Sandton Katherine Lodge; Cullinan Hotel & Executive Suites
19 Formule 1 Wynberg-Sandton
21 Linden Hotel
22 Backpackers Ritz
25 Zoo Lodge
28 Kew Youth Hostel
35 Holiday Inn Garden Court Milpark
36 Sunnyside Park Hotel
39 Backpackers' Lodge ITH
40 Bezuidenhout Valley Caravan Park
41 Bruma Lake Lodge
44 Fairview Youth Hostel

**PLACES TO EAT**
6 Rattlesnake Roadside Diner
7 Casalinga
11 Swiss Inn
20 Mary-Ann's Wholefood Emporium
24 Hard Rock Café
27 Norwood Restaurants
33 Melville Restaurants

**OTHER**
2 Fourways Mall
4 Foxy's
5 Pheasant Pluckers' Arms
8 Hill Street Mall, Randburg
9 Crossroads Shopping Centre, Randburg
12 Randburg Waterfront
15 Village Walk, Sandton
23 Wanderers Cricket Ground
26 Rosebank Mall
29 Radium Beer Hall
30 Killarney Mall
31 Johannesburg General Hospital
32 Zoo; SA Museum of Military History
34 Brixton Tower
37 Berea Tower
38 Ellis Park
42 Fisherman's Village
43 Eastgate Mall
45 Top-Star Drive-in Theatre
46 Gold Reef City
47 Turffontein Race Course
48 Rand Stadium

**Dangers & Annoyances: Surviving Jo'burg – the First 48 Hours**

Many people don't have problems walking around Jo'burg, but there are enough true-life horror stories to make caution essential. South Africa has an appalling tradition of violence and there's a huge gulf between rich and poor. It's a rough city, hence these survival tips (A Lonely Planet guide is worth this advice alone!).

If your hostel/hotel lift does not arrive at the airport, bus station or railway station when expected, catch a legitimate taxi to your intended destination (even pay up to R100, US$20), as it will be worth more than the contents of your pack and money belt. Don't become one of the many independent travellers who lose the lot (R25,000, US$5000-plus) in their first moments in the city – ie, those trying to walk or catch a bus to their accommodation to save money.

When you get to your hostel/hotel immediately store your passport, travellers' cheques, airline tickets and spare cash in their safe. It is usually safer here than in the dorms and rooms where interlopers, including fellow travellers, prey.

When you head off for your first meal or pub experience, carry as much money as you are prepared to lose (in your pocket), and more in your socks for the taxi home – maybe they won't find it – and forget cameras, videos, watches, jewellery (including gold studs in your ears) and good quality clothes. T-shirt, shorts and sandals are reasonably inconspicuous.

Don't head into Central (near the Carlton Centre or Smal St Mall), Braamfontein, Hillbrow or Berea to discover the real South Africa until you have well and truly sussed these places out. The places where you are staying will advise 'no go' areas – definitely heed their advice. Avoid the city centre at night and on weekends when the shops close and the crowds drop. With the exception of some of the busy Yeoville streets, you would be crazy to walk around at night. Daylight muggings in the city centre and other inner suburbs, notably Hillbrow (at gun and knife point), are not uncommon.

Be aware of what's going on around you. Walk on the road side of the footpath and don't hesitate to cross the street to avoid an alleyway or a threatening individual or group. In general, you're safe so long as there are plenty of people around, or you're in a group.

If you have a car, make sure your doors are locked, and when you're at stop lights leave a car's length between you and the vehicle in front so you can drive away if necessary. Running a red light is not illegal if you're in reasonable fear of assault. When you leave your car, immobilise it, attach a gear stick lock or steering wheel lock ('Gorilla') – or do all three.

There are plenty of beggars on the streets – both black and white. Some of them can be very insistent. Consider carrying a rand or two in change in an accessible pocket, so that you can give without flashing your wallet or purse around.

Have a healthy respect for your circumstances, but don't be overly paranoid – most of the people you meet are genuine and not trying to rip you off. But don't succumb to offers that you 'can't' refuse. There are a lot of scumbags out there ready to make you a victim. If the situation looks bleak, run! If the muggers produce a knife or gun, give them all they want. A smile often goes a long way to ameliorate the situation – if you have been mugged, sort of accept it. When all else fails, head to Soweto with a black friend, to reaffirm that there are a heap of nice South African people out there.

(This advice has been comprehensively roadtested.) ∎

## Maps

The Map Office (☎ (011) 339 4951; postal address Box 207, Wits 2050, Gauteng), on the 3rd floor of the Standard Bank Building on De Korte St, Braamfontein, sells government maps for R11.50 a sheet. (Drakensberg maps are available only from the Natal Parks Board in KwaZulu-Natal.)

## INFORMATION
### Climate & When to Go

Jo'burg has an excellent climate; uncomfortable extremes are rare.

Summers are hot, but maximum temperatures rarely exceed 30°C. Most of the rain falls between October and April, usually in late afternoon storms, often accompanied by spectacular displays of thunder, lightning and hail.

Winter days are sunny and warm with crisp nights; temperatures range from 6°C to 17°C. There's no right or wrong time to visit, although accommodation can be tight at any time. It is even more acute in December, when a great many whites head for the coast on holidays.

## Tourist Offices

Greater Johannesburg Tourism has offices at the airport (☎ (011) 970 1220), open from 5 am, at the Rotunda bus terminal (☎ (011) 337 6650) and in the city centre (☎ (011) 336 4961) on the corner of Market and Kruis Sts. They have the excellent (if inconveniently large) *Johannesburg Gateway*, the smaller *Gauteng: Quick Reference Guide*, the very detailed *Jo'burg Tourist Map* and good information on restaurants and places to stay. To get a feel for the cultural side of the city you definitely want ADA's *Johannesburg: A to Z Cultural Update*.

Some provinces and neighbouring countries have information offices in Jo'burg. They include:

Captour (Western Cape Province)
    123 Rosebank Mall, Rosebank (☎ (011) 442 4707)
Mozambique
    3 Siemens St, Braamfontein (☎ (011) 339 7275/81; fax 339 7295)
Namibia
    209 Redroute, Carlton Centre, Commissioner St (☎ (011) 331 7055; fax 331 2037)
North-West Province Tourism
    Suite 4702, Carlton Towers, Commissioner St (☎ (011) 331 9336)
Zimbabwe
    PO Box 9398, Johannesburg 2000 (☎ (011) 331 3137, 331 3155)

## National Parks Board

Unfortunately, the National Parks Board doesn't have an office in Jo'burg. To make bookings you either have to phone the Pretoria office (☎ (012) 343 1991), which is sometimes difficult because the lines are often engaged, or visit their desk at Pretoria's Tourist Rendezvous centre. The head office is inconveniently located on the southern outskirts of Pretoria at 643 Leyds St, Muckleneuk. If desperate, ring the Cape Town office (☎ (021) 22 2810).

## Hiking Federation

For details about hiking, contact the Hiking Federation of South Africa in Johannesburg at (☎ (011) 886 6524).

## Foreign Consulates & Trade Missions

Most countries have their main embassy in Pretoria, with an office or consulate in Cape Town, which becomes the official embassy during Cape Town's parliamentary sessions. However, many countries also have consulates (which can arrange visas and passports) in Jo'burg. An office of Rennies Travel, or the Visa Service (☎ (011) 403 3538; fax 403 1492), 10th Floor, Traduna Centre, 188 Jorissen St, Braamfontein, will arrange visas; charges are reasonable. For South African visa extensions, contact the Department of Home Affairs (☎ (011) 836 3228), 77 Harrison St (near the corner of Plein St). The British consular service no longer has a presence in Jo'burg (see Pretoria).

Australia
    Rennies Travel, 7th Floor, Safren House, 19 Ameshoff St, Braamfontein (☎ (011) 407 3211); open weekdays from 9 am to 3 pm
Belgium
    1st Floor, 158 Jan Smuts Building, Rosebank (☎ (011) 447 5495); weekdays 9 am to noon
Botswana
    2nd Floor, Futura Bank House, 123 De Korte St, Braamfontein (☎ (011) 403 3748); open weekdays from 8 am to 1 pm
France
    35th Floor, Carlton Centre, Commissioner St (☎ (011) 331 3478); open weekdays from 8.30 am to 1 pm
Germany
    4th Floor, Community Centre of the German Lutheran Church, 16 Kapteijn St, Hillbrow (☎ (011) 725 1573); open Monday to Thursday from 7.30 to 11 am, Friday 7.30 to 10.30 am (visa collections 11.45 am to 12.30 pm)
Malawi
    1st Floor, Sable House, 41 De Korte St, Braamfontein (☎ (011) 339 1569); open weekdays from 8.30 am to noon, 1.30 to 4.30 pm
Mozambique
    7th Floor, Cape York House, 252 Jeppe St (☎ (011) 336 1819; fax 336 9921)
Namibia
    209 Redroute, Carlton Centre, Commissioner St (☎ (011) 331 7055); open weekdays from 8.30 am to 4.30 pm
Swaziland
    6th Floor, Braamfontein Centre, PO Box 8030, Johannesburg 2000 (☎ (011) 403 3026); open weekdays from 9.30 am to 12.30 pm

GAUTENG

Switzerland
  2nd Floor, Cradock Heights, 21 Cradock Ave,
  Rosebank (☎ (011) 442 7500; fax 442 7891);
  open weekdays from 9 am to noon
USA
  11th Floor, Kine Centre, on the corner of Commissioner and Kruis Sts (☎ (011) 331 1681; fax
  331 1327); open weekdays from 8 am to noon
Zimbabwe
  6th Floor, Bank of Lisbon Building, 37 Sauer St
  (☎ (011) 838 2156; fax 838 5620); open weekdays from 8.30 am to noon (except Wednesday)

**GAUTENG**

## Money

Banks are open Monday to Friday from 9 am to 3.30 pm, Saturday from 8.30 to 11 am. The foreign-exchange counters at the airport open two hours before all international departures and stay open two hours after arrivals.

The main Amex office (☎ (011) 339 5494) is in the lobby of the Carlton Hotel; it is open 8 am to 8 pm weekdays, 8 am to 6 pm Saturday and 10 am to 4 pm Sunday. There are offices in the northern suburbs: in Sandton, the office (☎ (011) 884 6161) is in Shop U20 A, Upper Level 6, Sandton City Mall; in Randburg (☎ (011) 789 3204), at Shop 176, Randburg Waterfront; and the efficient Rosebank Mall office (☎ (011) 880 8859) organises most replacements for lost/stolen cheques within an hour.

Rennies Travel is the Thomas Cook agent. They have many foreign exchange outlets: 36A Rissik St (☎ (011) 29 6341); Shop 14A, Sandton Mall (☎ (011) 783 1110); and Shop L20A, Eastgate Mall, Bradford Rd, Bedfordview (☎ (011) 616 1241).

## Post & Communications

Telephone 1023 for local directory inquiries and 0903 for international inquiries. The GPO is on Jeppe St, between Von Brandis St and the Smal St Mall. It's open from 8 am to 4.30 pm weekdays, 8 am to noon Saturday. There's a poste restante service (in theory you need some sort of identification but they're not very strict about this) and an international telephone exchange. For normal business use the charming Rissik St post office, opposite the city hall – it's less hectic than the GPO.

There are many commercial phone services in the city; a handy one is in the Bridge shopping centre. Always check rates before calling. Phonecards, purchased at Telkom branches, are the best way to make calls.

## Travel Agencies

The SA Students' Travel Service (SASTS) is a national organisation with offices around the country. They offer all the regular facilities plus student and youth cards, special fares and flights. The Student Union Building branch, Wits University (☎ (011) 716 3045) is open weekdays from 9 am to 4 pm.

Rennies Travel has a comprehensive network of agencies throughout SA, including Jo'burg. They handle international and domestic bookings, are the Thomas Cook agents, and also arrange visas for a fee. Their main office is on the 11th Floor, ISM Building, 124 Main St (☎ (011) 331 5898).

Backpacker hostels should have info on cheap packages to Kruger, as well as the best (and cheapest) travel links to Cape Town, Durban, Swaziland, Lesotho, Namibia, Botswana and Zimbabwe. If they don't (and they should, as they're well commissioned for such advice), stay elsewhere.

## Bookshops

Rockey St, Yeoville, has a smattering of secondhand bookshops that can be a bibliophile's delight, with interesting old histories and travel guides, and the odd first edition. Books Galore, at No 15B, has a good old books section; and Yeoville Books, No 28, has new titles.

There are CNA bookstores throughout Jo'burg including one in Rockey St. They have great South African sections, road atlases, locally published guidebooks and tonnes of glossy picture books. Exclusive Books, one of the best bookshops in town, has outlets in the northern suburbs. There are a couple of good bookshops in the Rosebank Mall (including CNA and Exclusive Books).

## Walking Tour

Jo'burg has shown scant regard for its architectural and historical legacy, and even less regard for pedestrians and quality of life. You get the distinct feeling that buildings more than 30 years old have survived through some oversight – and that the mistake will soon be rectified. The more recent office blocks are insensitive, alienating and ugly – the Carlton Centre, the Johannesburg Holiday Inn (on the corner of Jeppe and Von Weilligh), and No 11 Diagonal St are all memorable examples.

In spite of this, the centre of Jo'burg is an interesting and vibrant place. At street level, it's very much an African city and the pavements are crowded with shoppers and hawkers. It's not really vital to have a set walking tour, but the suggested route gives a pretty comprehensive introduction. It's a circuit so you could start at any point.

**Warning** Before you set out on this walk, check the newspapers to see if there are any ongoing disturbances in the city centre and divest yourself of all valuables. Wear discreet clothes.

The **Johannesburg Railway Station**, slowly being revamped, serves more than 200,000 short and long-distance commuters daily – it's the terminal for all country trains. Train buffs should check out the first train to serve the Witwatersrand, which is at the north end of the concourse outside the train information office, and the **Spoornet Museum** – note that this may all change with the current redevelopment of the station. Walk towards the city and the old southern entry on De Villiers St.

Turn left into De Villiers and proceed until you reach Hoek Mall and **St Mary's Anglican Cathedral**, built of dressed sandstone in 1926 and designed by Sir Herbert Baker. Walk down the mall and take the second left into Bree St. Jo'burg's rowdy past lives on in the blatant 'massage parlours' around the intersection of Bree, Klein and Von Weilligh.

Turn right into Von Weilligh and first right into Jeppe past the extraordinary **Johannesburg Holiday Inn Hotel**. Immediately after the hotel and before the GPO, turn left into the **Smal St Mall**, which is full of trendy shops, including a number of art and craft galleries – show heaps of caution here as this is a favourite mugging spot.

Continue down the mall and through the Nedbank Mall (a continuation) to Commissioner St and the **Carlton Centre** with its huge shopping complex and tower (which houses an observation floor, **The Panorama**). From the Carlton Centre head down to Fox St; the **Rand Club** is on the right between Loveday and Harrison Sts. It was built in 1904, modelled on the Reform Club in London, and was the favourite haunt of the Randlords.

Commissioner St takes you west to one of the only surviving sections of old Jo'burg – a couple of blocks of interesting Indian shops with shady verandahs and a comfortable lived-in atmosphere. There's a **Hindu Temple** on the corner of Commissioner and Becker. Turn right into Becker and right again into Market. Backtrack until you get to Diagonal St, the only exception to the the city's grid plan. There's a muti shop, **Kwa Dabulamanzi** on the corner (No 14) which sells African herbal remedies that are prescribed by a sangoma.

Diagonal St is home to an extraordinary skyscraper (No 11), designed by Chicago architect Helmut John, that towers incongruously over a section of old Indian shops that have been tarted up and trendified. The **Stock Exchange**, on the corner of Diagonal and Pritchard, has guided tours on weekdays at 11 am and 2.30 pm. From here it's a relatively short walk to the Market Theatre and Oriental Plaza, which are both good places for lunch.

If you choose to continue the circuit, however, from Pritchard turn right into Sauer, which takes you past the offices of the Jo'burg *Star* newspaper. Then turn left into President which takes you past the Library. President will also take you past the **Johannesburg City Hall**, and the impressive **Rissik St Post Office**, which hasn't changed significantly (inside or out) since 1897. The city hall has public toilets – a rare luxury – on the corner of President and Harrison.

To finish the circuit, turn left into the tree-lined and pleasant Eloff, which will take you back to the railway station past several of the major department stores. ∎

## Laundry

There's a generous smattering of laundrettes. A service wash (drop your clothes in the morning, pick them up in the afternoon) is only marginally more expensive than doing it yourself. International Laundromat is reliable. They have branches at 296 Bree St, City, and at High-Rise Flats, Primrose Terrace, Berea. An average wash costs R20.

Most Jo'burg hostels will get staff to wash gear very cheaply; pay the person doing the washing.

**GAUTENG**

## Medical Services

Medical services are of a high standard, but expensive (make sure you're insured). Doctors are listed under Medical in the phone book. They generally arrange for hospitalisation, although in an emergency you can go direct to the casualty department of Jo'burg General Hospital (☎ (011) 488 4911), less than 1km north of Hillbrow. Ring the Flying Squad (a ready reaction force of armed police in fast cars; ☎ 10111) to get directions to the nearest hospital. The Yeoville Medical Centre on Rockey St stays open until 9 pm every night. A Daelite Pharmacy in Sandton (☎ (011) 883 7520) is open until 10.30 pm daily.

## Emergency

For ambulances call ☎ 999 (St Johns, ☎ (011) 403 4227); for the police Flying Squad call ☎ 10111; for the fire brigade call ☎ (011) 624 2800.

There is a Crisis Centre (☎ (011) 787 9555), on the corner of Tudhope and Honey Sts, Berea, which is open from 5 to 11 pm. The radio station 702 has a help line (☎ (011) 884 8448).

The phones at POWA – Battered Women and Rape Crisis Centre (☎ (011) 642 4345) are staffed from 6 am to 10 pm. There's a Lifeline service (☎ (011) 728 1347) and an AIDS line (☎ (011) 725 6710). For information on the Sandton Crisis Centre call (☎ (011) 883 2800).

## HILLBROW & BEREA

On the ridge to the north-east of the train station (a 20 minute walk, if you are silly), Hillbrow and adjoining Berea were once the most lively and interesting suburbs in Jo'burg, South Africa's answer to Soho (London), Greenwich Village (New York) and King's Cross (Sydney).

This is now one of the most densely populated and dangerous areas in Africa, dominated by towering apartment buildings and cheap residential hotels. Over the last few years it has become increasingly dominated by black arrivals (many of whom are destitute), giving the area a 'half-way house'

feel. The Ponte Centre, with its flashing neon 'Coca Cola' sign, is rightly nicknamed 'little Kinshasa'. This said, the 'Brow' is one of the very few places in SA where mixed-race couples don't create a sensation. Venture here only after you have got your bearings, and stringently observe the Dangers & Annoyances rules (see the earlier boxed text).

## YEOVILLE

Raleigh and Rockey Sts (they change name midway), Yeoville, once formed the counterculture 'capital' of South Africa. Black clothes (perhaps with an embroidered T-shirt from Kathmandu), long hair and earnest conversations over cappuccinos were the rule. That has changed somewhat, and some of the old Hillbrow seediness is creeping in, but despite (or because of) this the atmosphere is relaxed, congenial and nonracial. These are practically the only streets in Jo'burg (and among a few in South Africa) where walking around at night is relatively safe and stimulating.

There are plenty of good-value restaurants and bars, some of which have live music. There are also some interesting craft and secondhand shops. The 'far east' end of Rockey St has acquired a reputation as a distribution centre for heavy drugs; be careful if you head this way to go to a live-music venue.

Raleigh/Rockey St is a short taxi ride north of the centre (R25 maximum). It would not be wise to walk here, especially with your valuables. Buses (R3) run to Rockey St, via Cavendish St, from Pritchard St (a fair walk down Harrison St from the Rotunda). Look for bus Nos 22, 23 and 24 – all intersect Rockey St at some point. Bus Nos 19a and 20 reach Rockey St via Hillbrow; you get these from Vanderbijl Square. Buses are frequent from 6.45 to 8.40 am, from 4 to 7 pm, hourly during the middle of the day, and nonexistent after 7 pm.

When you first arrive in Jo'burg, most Yeoville/Bez Valley hostels will pick you up from the airport, train station or Rotunda. If not, take a taxi!

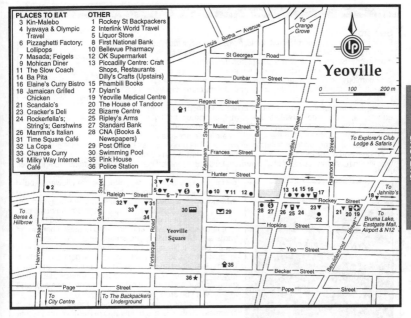

PLACES TO EAT
3 Kin-Malebo
4 Iyavaya & Olympic Travel
6 Pizzaghetti Factory; Lollipops
7 Masada; Feigels
9 Mohican Diner
11 The Slow Coach
14 Ba Pita
16 Elaine's Curry Bistro
18 Jamaican Grilled Chicken
21 Scandalo's
23 Cracker's Deli
24 Rockerfella's; String's; Gershwins
26 Mamma's Italian
31 Time Square Café
32 La Copa
33 Charros Curry
34 Milky Way Internet Café

OTHER
1 Rockey St Backpackers
2 Interlink World Travel
5 Liquor Store
8 First National Bank
10 Bellevue Pharmacy
12 OK Supermarket
13 Piccadilly Centre: Craft Shops, Restaurants Dilly's Crafts (Upstairs)
15 Phambili Books
17 Dylan's
19 Yeoville Medical Centre
20 The House of Tandoor
22 Bizarre Centre
25 Ripley's Arms
27 Standard Bank
28 CNA (Books & Newspapers)
29 Post Office
30 Swimming Pool
35 Pink House
36 Police Station

## MUSEUMS

There are several museums in the centre of Jo'burg, a number within the Newtown cultural precinct; get a free copy of *Museums Map: Gauteng*, which lists over 40. Not covered here, but worth a look, are the **Dynamite Museum** (☎ (011) 606 3206), 2 Main St, Modderfontein; the **SA Transnet Railway Museum** (☎ (011) 773 9118) in the Jo'burg train station complex, Pim St; and also the several collections at **Wits University** (☎ (011) 716 3472).

### Museum Africa

Founded in the 1930s, this important museum (☎ (011) 833 5624) is now housed in the impressive old Bree St fruit market, next to the Market Theatre complex.

Part of the museum concentrates on the evolution of Jo'burg ('Transformations') and even includes a simulated descent into one of the gold mines. The Sophiatown

display (with jazz music seemingly appearing from nowhere) and a re-creation of the township is outstanding. There's also a large collection of rock art, a geological museum and the Bensusan Museum of Photography. At the time of writing, there was a superb exhibit on the Treason Trials, 1956-61 (which featured most of the important figures in the 'new' South Africa).

The museum is open daily except Monday from 9 am to 5 pm. Entry is R2/1 for adults/children, free on Sunday. If you walk from the city centre, it's reputedly safer to walk along Jeppe St than Bree St. Sadly, the museum often seems deserted and its souvenir store has closed – it needs visitors to keep afloat, so go.

### SA Breweries Museum

This very popular museum (☎ (011) 836 4900), in the Newtown cultural precinct, is at the opposite end of the spectrum from

## Soweto

For the majority of Jo'burg's inhabitants, home is in one of the black townships surrounding the city – probably Soweto. Despite this, most white South Africans are completely ignorant of life in the townships and very few have ever been inside one. Their picture is of unmitigated hostility, and a nightmare environment of drugs, superstition, tribal warfare, depravity and violent crime of every kind.

JEFF WILLIAMS

The first impression as one approaches a township is of an enormous, grim, undifferentiated sprawl, punctuated by light towers that would seem more appropriate in a concentration camp. In fact, some suburbs within the townships are quite acceptable, not all that far removed from suburbs anywhere, while others are as bad as any Third World slum.

In descending order there's a tiny wealthy elite that live in comfortable bungalows; the privileged who live in monotonous rows of government-built three-roomed houses with an outside tap and toilet;

JEFF WILLIAMS

'Faces of the departed' – those killed in the 1976 riots in Soweto. The pictures are only representations of those killed, a common practice when no photos were available.

the lucky who have been provided with a block of land, a prefabricated toilet and a tap, and who are allowed to build whatever they can; the fortunate who live in shacks erected in backyards; the squatters who build wherever they can and have virtually no facilities at all; and at the bottom of the pile, the men who live in dormitories in vast dilapidated hostels.

It is striking how neat and clean the houses, shacks and yards are. Unfortunately the streets and open places are buried under a blizzard of plastic bags and rubbish. This is at least partly because each house only gets one rubbish bin that is emptied once a week. This may be adequate when one family lives in a house; it is hopelessly inadequate when three or four additional families live in the backyard, and irrelevant if you are a squatter.

The townships played a crucial role in the struggle against apartheid. This was a struggle against a government that routinely used bullets, tear gas, imprisonment without trial, torture and summary execution of men, women and children. Soweto was in a virtual state of war from 1976, when the first protesting school students were killed, until the 1994 elections. During that time many thousands died. No one is quite sure exactly how many. The struggle is graphically depicted in a photographic exhibition, temporarily housed in old shipping containers, which surround the Hector Peterson monument – many award-winning photos taken by Peter Magubane, the Pulitzer Prize winner, are displayed.

Given the townships' recent history, the courtesy and friendliness that is generally shown to white visitors is almost shocking. If you visit on a Sunday, the most militant sight you will see is thousands of Christians dressed in immaculate uniforms (based on those worn by European medieval religious orders) on their way to and from church. The majority of people in Soweto still seem to have entirely middle-class aspirations – they want a job, decent housing, affordable education and a reasonable opportunity for their children to better themselves.

Although outsiders, including whites, are *not* automatically targeted, the townships are still in a state of acute social trauma, and violent crime is commonplace. Try to get objective advice on the current situation. This isn't easy, however, since most whites would not dream of visiting and have no first-hand experience of doing so. Certainly, unless things change markedly for the better, visiting without a companion who has local knowledge is likely to be disastrous. If a trustworthy black friend is happy to escort you, however, you should have no problems, and tours have operated safely for over seven years.

JEFF WILLIAMS

Detail from the Hector Peterson monument. Despite an intensive search, the man carrying Peterson was never found.

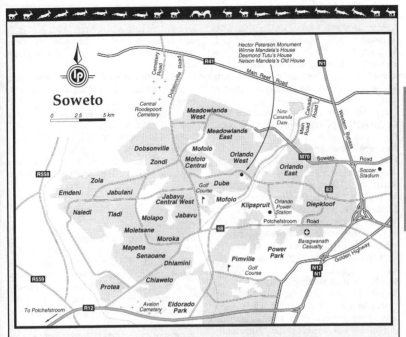

Soweto

GAUTENG

Visiting a large township is an unforgettable experience. It may seem grotesque treating these places as just another tourist attraction, but to get any kind of appreciation for South African reality you have to visit them. If the only way you can do it safely is with a tour, then a tour it must be.

A number of operators take tourists into Soweto. Most tours are designed to be serious educational experiences, so they can be earnest, and a little dry. But you should see the poignant Peterson monument (and current photographic display), a squatter camp, Winnie Mandela's house, Nelson Mandela's old house, Desmond Tutu's house, Soweto 'architecture' (shacks to brick palaces), Avalon cemetery (with Helen Joseph's and Joe Slovo's graves) and the Freedom Charter (on the side of a container) in Kliptown.

Max Maximum Tours (☎ (011) 933 4177, ☎ 938 8703 or ☎ (082) 533 1587) is recommended. Max is a long-time Soweto resident, a nice bloke and a good guide. He charges about R85/40 for adults/ children (Rosebank or Sandton pick-ups are R100/ 50). Max might also be available to take you further afield – have a beer and discuss it with him. Abantu Tours (☎ (011) 648 7066; fax 487 1557) is another good operator; its three-day tour for R690 has a great itinerary including a visit to Sophiatown ('Kofifi'), the start of the Group Areas Act fiasco, and two nights in Soweto with a local family.

The biggest operator is Jimmy's Face to Face Tours (☎ (011) 331 6109, 331 6209). Its popular morning and afternoon tours leave from Rosebank and Sandton (R100), and city hotels (R90). ■

JON MURRAY

Squatter housing is a major feature of most suburbs in the Soweto township.

Museum Africa. It unlocks the secrets of brewing in South Africa from the time when sorghum beer first passed the lips of early Africans. In the Ales Pavilion, the European tradition of brewing ales and lagers is described; sorghum brewing is covered in the 'Ukhamba' exhibit and there is a re-creation of a 1965 Soweto shebeen.

It's open from 11 am to 6 pm, Tuesday to Saturday; the R10 entry includes free beer.

### Workers' Museum
This museum (☎ (011) 834 2181), in the restored Electricity Department compound (built in 1910 for 300-plus municipal workers) at 52 Jeppe St, Newtown, has been declared a national monument. There is a workers' library/resource centre and a display of the living conditions of migrant workers. It is open from 8.30 am to 5 pm weekdays, 9.30 am to 5 pm Saturday.

### SA Museum of Military History
One might have hoped that this would only appeal to a few Rambos and warmongers, with its collection of guns, swords, grenades and other war memorabilia. Apparently, however, it's the most popular museum in Jo'burg. You can see artefacts and implements of destruction from the Anglo-Boer War through to the Namibian wars. The museum (☎ (011) 646 5513), at the east end of the zoo grounds, is open daily from 9 am to 4.30 pm.

### Madiba Freedom Museum
It's early days, but no doubt this will become a shrine to Madiba (Mandela's affectionate title), the main player in the evolution of the new South Africa. It covers the political history of the man, concentrating on the long struggle for equality and featuring many photographs from the time.

It's in the Erikson Diamond Centre, Monument Rd, Kempton Park; ring ☎ (011) 970 1355 to find out opening times.

### MARKETS
A market is held in **Market Square**, on Saturdays between 9 am and 1 pm, in the car park opposite the Market Theatre. There's a lively, cheerful atmosphere (with buskers), and although most of the stalls sell fleamarket rubbish, there's also some reasonable craftwork among the dross.

The **Windybrow People's Market** is a small-scale market in Hillbrow on Claim St, between Kapteijn and Pietersen Sts. Browse here for shoes, clothing and electrical goods at any time of the day.

**Flea Market World** is big and fairly commercial, open daily except Monday. It's on Marcia St, not far from Bruma Lake and Eastgate Mall. On the opposite footpath are many craft stalls. There is a very wide range, although you'll look hard for high quality.

### GALLERIES
### Johannesburg Art Gallery
This gallery (☎ (011) 725 3130), on the Klein St side of Joubert Park, was once disappointing, despite being housed in a lovely little building. The exhibits were mostly uninspiring European and white South African landscape and figurative paintings. These are still here, along with an increasing number of exhibitions featuring more adventurous contemporary work and long-overdue retrospectives of black artists.

As well as the art, the gallery (and its pleasant coffee shop) makes a quiet escape from the real world. Entry is free. It's open daily except Monday from 10 am to 5 pm.

### Standard Bank Centre Gallery
On the corner of Simmonds and Frederick, this gallery (☎ (011) 636 4231) has changing exhibitions, often of a high standard (some from the Grahamstown Festival). It's open weekdays from 8 am to 4.30 pm, Saturday from 9 am to 1 pm; there is secure parking by arrangement.

### Gertrude Posel Gallery
This gallery (☎ (011) 716 3632), in the University Art Galleries, Senate House, Wits University, houses the Standard Bank Foundation Collection of African tribal art, which includes masks, beadwork and Ndebele fer-

tility dolls. It's open Monday to Saturday from 10 am to 4 pm.

## CARLTON CENTRE & PANORAMA

The **Carlton Centre** – all 50 floors of it – is an unmistakable landmark on Commissioner St. It has a three-tier shopping centre built around the Rondehof, a central display area used for exhibitions and promotions.

The **Carlton Panorama** ($\pi$ (011) 331 6608) is on the 50th floor and is accessible by lifts from level 100 of the Rondehof (fare R10). The view is spectacular and it's a good way to orient yourself. You can still see how the city grew up alongside its mines, although the evidence is fast disappearing as the old mine tailings are reprocessed. It was described by a traveller as being '50 floors above the mayhem'.

On top of one artificial mountain, in the distance, is the spectacularly sited Top-Star Drive-in Theatre, just to the south of the M2 freeway. The freeway divides the city from the area that was mined – the extensive tunnelling (and resulting instability) means that high-rises cannot be built to the south.

The luxury **Carlton Hotel**, the starting point for many local tours, is in the centre's south-west corner (Main and Kruis Sts).

## MARKET THEATRE

The Market Theatre complex ($\pi$ (011) 832 1641) on Bree St, at the north-west corner of the city centre, is one of the highlights of Jo'burg. There are galleries, live-theatre venues, a coffee shop and the recently reopened Kippie's Bar ($\pi$ (011) 823 1645), which is an excellent jazz venue (named after Kippie 'Morolong' Moeketsi, a legendary black saxophonist).

There is always some interesting theatre, ranging from sharply critical contemporary plays to musicals and stand-up comedy; check in the *Weekly Mail & Guardian* entertainment section.

Housed in old, recycled market buildings, the complex is an attractive and enjoyable place to hang around. With the Museum Africa nearby, this corner of Jo'burg could easily absorb most of a day and a fair part of the night – especially on Saturday when the market sets up nearby.

## ORIENTAL PLAZA

A short walk from the Market Theatre complex, further west along Bree St (between Bree St and Main Rd, Fordsburg), the Oriental Plaza has over 300 Indian-owned shops. If you have a rough idea of prices and don't mind bargaining, you'll make some good purchases. At the least, you'll find cheap, delicious samosas.

## JOHANNESBURG FORT

The old fort at the end of Kotze St in Hillbrow was built in the 1890s to defend and garrison the military forces who were responsible for keeping the miners under control. It has never seen action and after the Anglo-Boer War it was converted into a prison. Number Four, as it was known, was where pass-law violators (in apartheid days) were imprisoned – it's recalled with dread.

## JOHANNESBURG ZOO

It seems rather bizarre going to a zoo in Africa, but you can combine a visit to Johannesburg Zoo with the SA Museum of Military History. The zoo ($\pi$ (011) 646 2000) is open daily from 8.30 am to 5.30 pm and admission is R10. There are also thrice-weekly night tours for R30 (no children); book through Computicket.

Take bus No 78, 80 or 80B from Eloff St or No 79 from Rissik St.

## WITS UNIVERSITY

The University of Witwatersrand, Jan Smuts Ave, Braamfontein, is the largest English-language university in the country with over 20,000 students. It's an attractive campus; visitors might choose to visit the Gertrude Posel Gallery (see the previous Galleries section) or Jan Smuts' House to see the great man's study. There's also the Student Union Building for a cheap café meal, and the Student Travel (SASTS) office.

Also found on campus is the **Planetarium** ($\pi$ (011) 716 3199), on Yale Rd. It has various programmes that have been recommended by travellers. They last an hour and cost R15/8 for adults/children and seniors.

## GOLD REEF CITY

Gold Reef City (☎ (011) 496 1600) is a tourist trap that can't quite make up its mind whether it's a Disneyland clone or a serious historical reconstruction of old Jo'burg. It helps fill a Jo'burg weekend.

It features scary rides, a Victorian fun fair and various historical reconstructions (including a bank, brewery, pub and newspaper office). You can go down a shaft to see a gold mine (220m below), watch a gold pour and see a programme of tribal or 'Gumboot' dancing. Tribal dancers perform twice daily on weekdays, thrice daily on weekends – it is a lot of fun; ring for performance times.

There are numerous places to eat and drink, and a particularly good craft/souvenir shop (Gold Reef City Arts & Crafts Centre – it's along the street from the more obvious eGoli Village craft shop). There are often special programmes on weekends, sometimes with live music in an amphitheatre, and fireworks. Check the entertainment section in the *Star*.

The complex is open from 9 am to 5 pm and admission is R18 (R20 on weekends). All rides and exhibits are free except for the mine tour, which costs R14. Many of the eating and drinking places stay open until 11 pm; entry after 5 pm is free. The complex is closed Monday (except public holidays).

Gold Reef City is 6km south of the city, just off the M1 freeway. Unfortunately, it's a bit tricky to reach by public transport, and a taxi would be expensive. By bus, catch the No 55 (R3) from Vanderbijl Square, the main local bus terminus in the city. From Tuesday to Saturday buses leave every 20 minutes or so; on Sunday the frequency drops to one every two hours, so check the timetable. Get off at stop 14, Althan Rd, Robertsham; walk west along Alamein Rd, go under the freeway and you'll see Gold Reef City on your right. Most day tours include Gold Reef City on their itineraries.

There are luxurious rooms in *Gold Reef City Hotel* (☎ (011) 496 1626); single/double B&B starts at R350/425.

## GOLD MINES

The Chamber of Mines (☎ (011) 498 7100) runs excellent tours of working gold mines. However, their tours are dependent on the hospitality of the mining companies, which, apparently, aren't very enthusiastic. There is rarely more than one tour per week (on Tuesday, Wednesday or Thursday) and in December there are none at all. Contact the chamber as far in advance as possible. You have to be committed because the all-day tours cost at least R160 (R200 if you go all the way down to the Free State goldfields), and depart as early as 5.45 am.

## RANDBURG WATERFRONT

Poor ol' inland Jo'burg didn't have a real waterfront like Cape Town's Victoria & Alfred. The solution was to toss lots of rand at a small pond on the Jukskei River, and then to surround it with shops, 50-plus restaurants and pubs and a Harbour Flea Market with over 360 stalls. The result isn't that bad – a day at the Randburg Waterfront can be a pleasure, especially if you have kids in tow.

The Waterfront (☎ (011) 789 5052), on Republic Rd, Ferndale, is open daily (the flea market is not open on Monday).

## ORGANISED TOURS

Springbok Atlas (☎ (011) 493 3780), the largest tour operator in the country, has half-day city tours for R140, longer tours that include Gold Reef City for R200, evening cultural tours for R330 and a full-day tour to Pretoria for R390 per person (children are half-price in all cases). Dumela Africa (☎ (011) 837 9928) is a little cheaper. Historical Walks of Johannesburg (☎ (011) 837 9928) offers two-hour walking tours in the city for a minimum of four people; you will meet a *sangoma* and drink in the city's oldest pub.

See the earlier boxed text on Soweto for Soweto tours. The *Gateway* booklets lists many other options.

## FESTIVALS

The big **Arts Alive Festival** is held in September and October. Since South Africa's liberation the arts have been going through an exciting time, with an explosion of optimism and the mainstream acceptance of long-suppressed talents. A strong element in the festival is workshops exposing South Africans to their continent's rich cultures, so long denigrated by the Eurocentrism of the apartheid years. The festival is a particularly good time to hear excellent music, on and off the official programme.

Other festivals include **Chinese New Year** at Wemmer Pan; the **Guinness Jo'burg Jazz Festival** in late September; and the annual **Gay Pride March**, held in spring.

## PLACES TO STAY – BOTTOM END
### Caravan Parks

*Safari Caravan Park* (☎ (011) 942 1404) is on the M27, the old Jo'burg-Vereeniging highway (sometimes shown on maps as the R82), 12km south of the city. There are caravan stands, tents are allowed and there are nearby shops. A stand costs R25, more or less, depending on whether or not you have an electricity hook-up. Not far south of Safari, on the R554, are the *Protea*, *Lion Rampant*, *Riverside* and *Blossom Valley* parks, all on the Klip River. The best-placed park is the *Bezuidenhout Valley Caravan Park* (☎ (011) 648 6302), 180 Third Ave, off Observatory Avenue, Bezuidenhout Valley, near Bruma Lake and 4km east of Hillbrow. A van site is R25 and foreigners are allowed to pitch tents.

### Hostels

**Central Jo'burg** Campers don't need to go to a caravan park as Jo'burg has many hostels which allow you to pitch a tent. Most hostels will also pick you up from the airport, train station or the bus Rotunda for free.

There are a few good choices in Yeoville, arguably the best area to stay in central Jo'burg. *Rockey St Backpackers* (☎ (011) 648 8786; fax 648 8423) isn't on Rockey St, but it is just a short (and safe) walk away at 34 Regent St. The staff are friendly, the atmo-sphere good, the facilities reasonable – with a plunge pool and a well-patronised shebeen (bar) – and they are in the process of tidying up the bathrooms. Dorms go for R30, and singles/doubles are R65/75. They arrange trips around Jo'burg, to Kruger and further afield, and organise rentals.

The clean *Explorer's Club Lodge* (☎ (011) 648 7138; fax 648 4673) at 9 Innes St, Observatory, is also recommended. In an old 1900s mansion, it has spacious gardens and a pool. There's a travel agency on the premises. Dorms are R35, singles/doubles (some with en suites) are R80/105.

The *Pink House* (☎ (011) 487 1991), 73 Becker St, receives good press from backpackers. It doesn't do airport pick-ups. Dorms are R30, singles/doubles are R50/80. You can camp if the hostel is full. *Backpackers Underground* (☎ (011) 648 6132) at 20 Harley St is a small place, a 10 minute walk from Rockey St. It has a pool, bar, cable TV and personal safes; dorms are R27, twins are R70 and camping is R20.

One km or so south-east of Yeoville, in the Bez (Bezuidenhout) Valley, *Backpackers Lodge ITH* (☎ (011) 614 4640), 55 First St, is bigger than it looks from the street. We were denied entry to the 'castle', even after producing a business card, so tell us if it has improved or not. Are there still triple-decker bunks? Dorms are R30, and singles/doubles are R65/85. It's a long walk from Rockey St. The overflow for the ITH, *Egoli*, at 109 Third Ave, looked spartan from the outside, a partially dismantled car the only thing in the front yard.

*Fairview Youth Hostel* (☎ (011) 618 2048), 4 College St, is 3km east of the city centre in unlovely Troyeville. It's run down, has a pokey kitchen and a backyard full of litter and rubbish. Dorm beds are R28. There are better choices in Yeoville.

The *YMCA* (☎ (011) 403 3426), 104 Rissik St, Braamfontein, is a depressing place; and the *YWCA* (☎ (011) 403 3830), 128 De Korte St, Braamfontein, is just fractionally better. Both are in a grotty part of town (necessitating curfews) and both should be 'last resorts'.

GAUTENG

GAUTENG

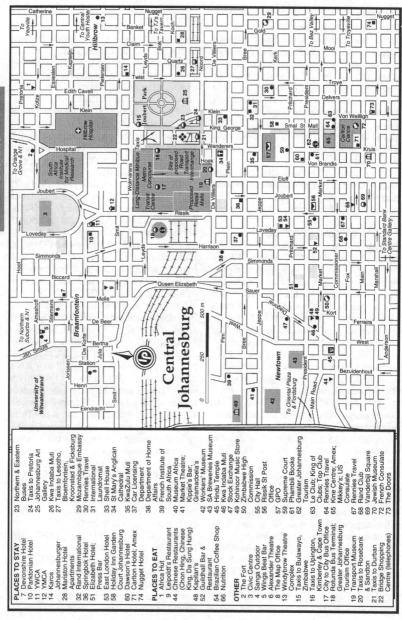

**PLACES TO STAY**
7 Devonshire Hotel
10 Parktonian Hotel
11 YWCA
12 YWCA
14 Karos Johannesburger
28 Mariston Hotel
Johannesburger Apartments
32 Rand International
36 Sunnbrook Hotel
51 Elizabeth Hotel; Press Bar
53 East London Hotel
58 Holiday Inn Garden Court Johannesburg
60 Dawson's Hotel
71 Carlton Hotel; Amex
74 Nugget Hotel

**PLACES TO EAT**
1 Africa Hut
9 Leipoldt's Restaurant
44 Chinese Restaurants (Chon Hing, Chinese King, Da Sung Hung)
48 Kapitan's
52 Guildhall Bar & Restaurant
54 Brazilian Coffee Shop
66 Nutrition

**OTHER**
2 The Fort
3 Civic Centre
4 Sanga Outdoor
5 Wings Beat Bar
6 Alexander Theatre
8 The Map Office
13 Windybrow Theatre Complex
15 Taxis to Bulawayo, Zimbabwe
16 Taxis to Upington, Kimberley & Cape Town
17 City to City Bus Office
18 Rotunda Bus Terminal; Greater Johannesburg Tourism Office
19 Transport Museum
20 Taxis to Rosebank & Sandton
21 Taxis to Durban
22 Bridge Shopping Centre (telephones)

23 Northern & Eastern Buses
24 Taxis to Pretoria
25 Johannesburg Art Gallery
26 Kwa Indaba Muti
27 Taxis to Lesotho, Bloemfontein, Kroonstad & Ficksburg
29 Mozambique Embassy
30 Rennies Travel
31 International Laundromat
33 Shell House
34 St Mary's Anglican Cathedral
35 KwaZulu Muti
37 Car Licensing Department
38 Department of Home Affairs
39 French Institute of South Africa
40 Museum Africa
41 Market Theatre; Kippie's Bar; Gramadoela's
42 Workers' Museum
43 SA Breweries Museum
45 Hindu Temple
46 Kwa Indaba Muti
47 Stock Exchange
49 Kohinoor Music Store
50 Zimbabwe High Commission
55 City Hall
56 Rissik St Post Office
57 GPO
59 Supreme Court
61 Phambili Books
62 Greater Johannesburg Tourism
63 Le Club; King of Clubs; Top Club
64 Rennies Travel
65 Kine Centre; Amex; Mikkey's; US Consulate
67 Rennies Travel
68 Rand Club
69 Vanderbijl Square
70 Jewish Museum
72 French Consulate
73 The Doors

*Central Youth Hostel* (☎ (011) 643 1213), 4 Fife Ave, Berea, should *not* be your first stop in town. It is on the edge of Hillbrow and, therefore, close to a lot of crime. If you wish to be in this part of the city, stay here for a while only after you have sussed things out – many seasoned travellers are happy with the location. The hostel café sells food but the bar is open to all and sundry. The place is rough, from its 'electric-fenced' walls to smelly cubicles. Dorms are R28, doubles are R70.

**Suburbs** *Bruma Lake Lodge* (☎ (011) 615 1092) at 41 Hans Pirow Ave, just walking distance from the lake and flea market, is a very impressive, clean two-storey mansion with a pool. Dorms are a reasonable R25, and singles/doubles are R70/80. Unfortunately, when we visited, it was unattended for at least half an hour, no staff at all – an absolute 'no-no' in Jo'burg.

*Zoo Lodge* (☎ (011) 788 3292), 233A Jan Smuts Ave in Parktown North, is no longer close to the zoo. It has moved to a pleasant house with a large back garden, a shaded braai/bar area at the side of the main building and a pool. It was still being improved when we visited, with work under way to improve the dorms. Dorms are R25, singles/doubles are R50/70 and breakfasts/dinners are from R8/15.

Even further out, but within an easy walk of the Hyde Park (Dunkeld) shopping centre, is the *Backpackers' Ritz* (☎ (011) 327 0229; fax 792 1376). The Ritz has recently moved to a magnificent mansion at the far end of North St, but is still close to bars and restaurants. It's a huge place with some of the best dorm rooms you will ever hope to see. It also has plenty of recreation areas, including a crypt-like bar. As victim of probably the greatest backpacker heist in SA's history, it is now more security conscious than the Jo'burg Fort, with individual safes and strict means of entry and exit. The dorms are R30, and singles/doubles are R60/70. Camping in the grounds (a pleasant option) costs R20. Bus Nos 73 and 80B from Eloff St and No 80 from the Rotunda run to the Dunkeld shops, a short walk from the Ritz.

*Kew Youth Hostel* (☎ (011) 887 9072) is at 5 Johannesburg Rd (the M20), Kew, 10km from the city centre. It is worth considering if you have a car and want some distance between you and the city. The hostel is a nice suburban home with a pool, and they allow camping. Dorms are R28, doubles R70. Bus Nos 13 and 13B run nearby.

One of the most pleasant alternatives in Jo'burg is the 55 acre *Inchanga Ranch Hostel* (☎ (011) 708 1304), Inchanga Rd, Witkoppen. It has a floodlit tennis court, jacuzzi and pool, and there is horse-riding nearby. Dorms are R28 (the beds are in the relaxed hostel, which seems like a beach house), doubles ('wendy houses') are R70 and camping is R15 per person. To get there, head for the Fourways Mall shopping centre north of the city (a Putco bus from the Carlton Centre) then call the hostel from Entrance 5; they will pick up.

Similar is *The Woodpecker Inn* (☎ /fax (011) 964 2593), on a huge parcel of land in Bapsfontein, north-east of Jo'burg. The main house, thatched roof and all, is huge and used mainly for B&B (R200 for a double). Backpackers can stay in one of 10 'wendy houses' arranged around a central *lapa* area/bar (R50 per person), or in a dorm (R40). There is free pick-up from the airport.

Last but not least is *Happy Valley Backpackers* (☎ /fax (011) 807 0972), 86 Nanyuki Rd, Sunninghill Park. It is a well-set place with a great patio near the bar, and plenty of grounds for pitching a tent or parking a campervan (R20 per person). Clean dorms/doubles are R30/60. It is close to Foxy's for the big Sunday arvo blast (see Music & Dancing in the Entertainment section).

### Hotels

**Hillbrow & Berea** Hillbrow and Berea were once the cheapest, most interesting and convenient suburbs in which to stay – not any more. We have given a couple of choices if you have the urge to stay here. When you realise all transactions between guests and management usually take place through a thick metal grille, you'll get the picture.

The staff of *Hillbrow Inn*, Van der Merwe St, thought it was a great joke when I turned up to look at their rooms – 'You want to send foreign travellers to stay here?'. In spite of their protestations and the becoming smiles from the legion of prostitutes in the foyer, the rooms were clean and good value at R90/119 for doubles/twins. From the rooms on the higher levels it seemed you could reach out and touch the Berea Tower.

The *Crest Hotel* (☎ (011) 642 7641), 7 Abel Rd, is comfortable, convenient and well run. Rooms are large and well maintained, with radios and telephones, and there's security parking. Singles/doubles cost about R80/110 – a bargain. There are only a limited number of rooms.

The *Mark Hotel* (☎ (011) 643 6731), 24 O'Reilly Rd, Berea, is also recommended. It's a modern, comfortable, multistorey hotel, a five minute walk from Hillbrow's centre. There's parking, and singles/doubles (with telephones) are both R110.

*Formule 1* (☎ (011) 484 5551), 1 Mitchell St, Berea (just off Louis Botha Ave), is part of the very successful chain. One to three people can share a small room for R119 (breakfast is R7 per person extra).

**City Centre** Most of the bottom-enders in the city centre are run down and depressing. The problem with staying in the city is that you can't really go out at night on foot.

*Dawson's Hotel* (☎ (011) 337 5010), 117 President (corner of Von Brandis St), is good and recommended. It's a clean and comfortable old-style hotel with a restaurant (breakfast R15), a couple of bars and live music. It's listed in the bottom end section because of its low prices, not its standards. Rooms (single or double) go for just R95 from Sunday to Thursday and R125 on weekends. Larger luxury rooms are R105, or R130 on weekends.

The *Nugget Hotel* (☎ (011) 334 0059), corner of Nugget and Marshall Sts, is fairly run down but not a complete dive. It's spartan but clean and the beds are good. Singles

with shared bath are R75 and singles/doubles with bath are R90/105.

With all the backpacker places close by (and many of them pick up for free), there is no reason for you to descend any lower. There are also *Formule 1* hotels at 130 Boeing Rd East, Edenvale (☎ (011) 453 5945); corner of Herman and Kruin Sts, Isando, close to Jo'burg International Airport (☎ (011) 392 1453); and at 1 Maree St, Bramley Park, near Wynberg/Sandton (☎ (011) 887 5555). All cost R119 for one to three people.

## PLACES TO STAY – MIDDLE
### B&Bs

There are surprisingly few independent bed & breakfast operations. One exception is *Joel House* (☎ (011) 642 4426), 61 Joel Rd, Berea, which is an extremely comfortable old house that has been specially restored. There are five bedrooms with en suites which cost R185/275 a single/double.

Fortunately the excellent Bed & Breakfast organisation (☎ (011) 482 2206/7; fax (011) 726 6915) has a number of members in and around the northern suburbs of Jo'burg. The accommodation is exceptionally good value. Most rooms are in large, luxurious suburban houses (often with pools) and all have private baths. The only problem is that Bed & Breakfast prefers advance bookings (usually at least a week) and most houses are difficult to get to without private transport. Prices range from R110/175 to R225/300 for singles/doubles.

### Hotels & Apartments

**Hillbrow & Berea** Some of the better hotels in this area are good value as escalating crime has chased away custom.

*The Ridge* (☎ (011) 643 4911), 8 Abel Rd, Berea, has an excellent situation on the edge of Hillbrow/Berea. It's nothing spectacular – a typical large soulless hotel, but it is comfortable and very convenient. There's off-street parking and singles/doubles are R110/175 with breakfast.

The nearby *Park Lane* (☎ (011) 642 7425), 54 Van der Merwe St, is similar.

Singles/doubles are R140/175 with breakfast. Rooms are a little small but they do have balconies. It's in good condition but you get the impression that it could go to seed fairly quickly. The *Protea Gardens Hotel* (☎ (011) 643 6610), 35 O'Reilly Rd, Berea, is a comfortable place to stay. It should be, with singles or doubles, room only, for R250.

**City Centre** One of the few old-style places to maintain standards is the *Springbok Hotel* (☎ (011) 337 8336), on the corner of Joubert and Bree Sts. It offers frilly singles/doubles from R130/155.

*Mariston Hotel Apartments* (☎ (011) 725 4130), on the corner of Claim and Koch Sts, is an enormous multistorey hotel halfway between the city centre and Hillbrow. You get most facilities, including security parking, and prices have dropped in the past few years because of the rough neighbourhood. Singles or doubles can go as low as R110 (R700 per week).

Nearer Joubert Park, *Karos Johannesburger* (☎ (011) 725 3753), 60 Twist St, is another large international-style hotel with covered parking. It too has dropped its prices recently (R179/220). *Rand International* (☎ (011) 336 2724), 290 Bree St, is in the heart of downtown; single/double rooms are R159/189.

*Holiday Inn Garden Court Johannesburg* (☎ (011) 336 7011), 84 Smal St, is a striking modern tower, bang in the middle of the city. While it's a luxury hotel, the crime rate in the city centre has lowered its appeal; room rates can drop to R220 a double.

**Northern & Eastern Suburbs** *Linden Hotel* (☎ (011) 782 4905) on the corner of 7th St and 4th Ave, Linden, is an attractive, comfortable personalised hotel. Unfortunately, it's a long way from the city. Single/double B&B starts at R180/230.

*Duneden Hotel* (☎ (011) 453 2002), 46 Van Riebeeck Ave, Edenvale, is close to shops and the airport, but a long way from Jo'burg; it is good value, with singles from a little more than R110.

The City Lodge group offers good-value, mid-range accommodation at a few locations; singles/doubles are about R220/240. *Jo'burg Airport Lodge* (☎ (011) 392 1750) is at the Isando exit on the R24 freeway to the airport; they will arrange airport transfers. *Randburg City Lodge* (☎ (011) 706 7800) is a couple of kilometres north of the Randburg centre, close to restaurants and shops. *Sandton Katherine Lodge* (☎ (011) 444 5300), corner of Katherine and Grayston Drive, and *Sandton Morningside Lodge* (☎ (011) 884 9500), corner of Rivonia and Hill Rds, are both within jogging distance of the Sandton shops. Also run by the City Lodge group is *Town Lodge Airport* (☎ (011) 974 5202), on Herman Rd, Germiston (take the R24/Barbara Rd exit).

## PLACES TO STAY – TOP END
### Hotels
**City Centre** The five-star *Carlton Hotel* (☎ (011) 331 8911; fax 331 3555), adjoining the Carlton Centre, has a great position if you are doing business in the city and, although the area is a bit barren at night, there are plenty of restaurants and bars to keep you busy within the building. There are special offers, but expect to pay from around R460/570 a single/double.

The *Parktonian Hotel* (☎ (011) 403 5740), 120 De Korte St, charges R375/470, with weekend specials at R200/250 if you stay two nights. Technically, it is in Braamfontein but it isn't too far from the city centre. Further west, also in Braamfontein, the *Devonshire Hotel* (☎ (011) 339 5611), corner of Melle and Jorissen Sts, is a comfortable medium-sized hotel. It has all the mod-cons, including undercover parking. Single/double B&B is from R315/340.

**Northern Suburbs** The four-star *Sunnyside Park Court Hotel* (☎ (011) 643 7226), 2 York Rd (the entrance is actually off Carse O'Gowrie Rd), Parktown, is recommended. An old-style hotel set in attractive gardens, it's a 20 minute walk north of Hillbrow. Singles/doubles go for R430/480, with weekend specials about half that. It's not far from the city or Yeoville, so basing yourself here and taxiing wouldn't be too expensive.

There are a few *Holiday Inn Garden Courts* scattered around – the city option has been mentioned. They're all of a dependable high standard. The one at the airport (☎ (011) 975 1121) is R279/308 a single/double on weekends; the one at Milpark (☎ (011) 726 5100) on the corner of Owl and Empire Rds, 5km from the centre and set in a pleasant garden, is R254/268 for singles/doubles; and the one at Sandton (☎ (011) 884 5660), corner of Katherine and Rivonia Rds, is R279/318. *Sandton Holiday Inn Crowne Plaza* (☎ (011) 783 5262), corner of Grayston and Rivonia Rds, is more upmarket; rooms are R549/700. The last two places are close to great shopping and restaurants.

The Sandton district definitely has many ritzy places. *Karos Indaba* (☎ (011) 465 1400) is on Hartbeespoort Dam Rd, Witkoppen, and singles/doubles are R490/580. Although you might assume the *Balalaika Protea Hotel* (☎ (011) 884 1400), 20 Maud St, Sandown, is a Greek-style hotel, you'd be wrong. The theme is English, with thatched roofs, a re-created English pub, an outdoor Village Green and so on. It's a short walk from the Sandton shops. Singles/doubles are R482/588. *Cullinan Hotel & Executive Suites* (☎ (011) 884 8544) in Katherine St is a really nice place to stay and, considering the level of luxury, prices are good; standard singles/doubles are R425/495, and luxury rooms are R485/555.

The superb *Sandton Sun & Towers* (☎ (011) 780 5000), just across the road from the Sandton City shopping Centre, hoists the flag for the Southern Sun Group; singles/doubles are R835/1035 in the Sun and about R100 more in the Towers. Top of the 'sleep heap' is the luxurious *Michelangelo* (☎ (011) 784 7022) at Deodar St (off West St), close to Sandton Square; single/double rooms are R875/1000.

## PLACES TO EAT

Jo'burg is stacked with places to eat. There are cuisines of every type catering for almost every budget. Unfortunately for visitors, especially those without cars, most of the safe places are scattered around the northern suburbs and can be difficult to find. The *Greater Jo'burg*, *Hello Jo'burg* and *Hello Gauteng* brochures list restaurants.

The major hotels all have high-quality restaurants. In shopping centres, you'll find franchised steakhouses like *Spur* or family places like *Mike's*.

### City Centre

**Snacks** There's a marked shortage of cafés and cheap eating places in the city. There's no shortage of takeaways, but they are uninspiring (eg roasted mielies in their husks). You'll find a few alternatives in the Holiday Inn and the Carlton Centre – *El Gaucho*, a fully licensed Mexican place in the Carlton Hotel, is recommended.

The best selection of cheap eateries is in Chinatown, a colourful district at the west end of Commissioner St near John Vorster Square. Our favourites are the ever-reliable *Chon Hing Cantonese*, for dim sums to Peking duck, patronised by office workers; *Chinese King Takeaways*, at 8A Commissioner St, for a huge variety of fast meals; and *Da Sung Hung*, another takeaway for much of the same.

Just finding somewhere to sit down is a major problem. The *Guildhall Bar & Restaurant*, corner of Harrison and Market Sts, has tables on a 1st floor balcony, offering a rare chance to take a leisurely look at the bustling streets without having to worry about being mugged. The coffee shop in the *Jo'burg Art Gallery* is another possibility.

On New St North, opposite the Vanderbijl Square bus information office, the *Nutrition* snack bar promises 'health food'. Compared with most downtown Jo'burg snackeries the fare is healthy, but there's a lot of meat on the menu. Sandwiches/rolls cost from R6, salads from R5.

For a cheap meal of pap and stew and braaied meat (just follow the enticing smells), try the *stalls* by the long-distance taxi ranks on Wanderers St, or nearby.

**Meals** Upstairs at 11A Kort St, one of the few

remaining Indian streets (just behind Diagonal St), *Kapitan's* (☎ (011) 834 8048) is a cheerful, old-fashioned restaurant with authentic Indian food. Vegetable curry is R18, meat curries are R25, and chicken vindaloo or biryani is R30. On the wall is a photocopied letter of appreciation from one of its famous diners, Nelson Mandela.

A mixed Pakistani/Indian place worth a visit is *The Taj Palace* (☎ (011) 836 4925), 21 Bree St, Fordsburg (corner of Mint St). The tandoori king prawns, chicken tikka masala and nurgusi kofta come with tandoori naan; superb value at R40.

In Braamfontein, at 94 Juta St, *Leipoldt's Restaurant* (☎ (011) 339 2765) is the place for authentic South African food, buffet-style. It is open weekdays for lunch and dinner, Saturday just for dinner; a huge plate costs about R45. Plan on spending several hours and don't schedule any strenuous activities after your meal! Another place for 'trad' South African food is *Anton van Wouw*, in the house of the renowned sculptor, at 111 Sivewright Ave, Doornfontein; it is worth visiting for the Strandloper potjie, a concoction rivalling the best of paellas. They have secure parking.

In the bedraggled Market Theatre complex, hopefully soon to undergo rebirth (with added security), you will be able to get basic pub-style meals and sit outside. The magnificent *Gramadoela's* (☎ (011) 838 6960), in the complex, is arguably the city's best restaurant. It has a bright and interesting decor, matched by an interesting nouveau-style menu; the specialities are based on Cape Dutch/Malay (eg bean soup and venison) and African cuisine. It's open Monday to Saturday for lunch and dinner. A full meal will cost around R50. Famed diners include Hillary Clinton, Denzel Washington and Madiba. If you can, get a copy of their *Egoli Recipe Book*.

Troyeville was once a run-down, lower middle class white suburb on the eastern edge of the city, but gentrification has proceeded apace.

The good *Quasimodo Bistro*, a pleasant coffee shop/restaurant on Commissioner St

(just before it becomes College St), has snacks for R12, mains under R25 and vegetarian dishes for R18. Troyeville's gem is *Kitchenboy*, on Op de Bergen St, an eclectic jumble of eye-openers (you have to see to believe) concocted by artist/nut/foodie Braam Kruger. The food, prepared in an open-plan kitchen, is always '3S' – surprising, sensational and succulent. The menu is in the form of graffiti on the restaurant's outer wall; food is tossed about in Brueghelian mayhem; and five hours' dining, at least, is needed to tame your bewilderment.

Sadly, Hillbrow, once a great haunt for travellers on a budget looking for street life and informal atmosphere, is now almost 'no go'. Cafés *Gattopardo* and *Kranzler*, and the fine *Porterhouse Carvery*, for instance, have retreated to the northern suburbs. For 24 hour African fast food such as stew and rice for R8, try *Africa Hut* on the corner of Edith Cavell and Kotze Sts.

### Yeoville
In general, Yeoville restaurants are unpretentious, informal places. Most are strung along Rockey St between Cavendish and Bezuidenhout Sts, although the strip is expanding and there are now places further east and west. Time Square, on Raleigh St at the corner of Fortesque Rd, is the best place to start an exploration of the street's delights. The following places run from west to east.

*La Copa* is the pick of the cafés, where you are bound to meet some black Africans; the food is good and R35-plus will see two people (black or white) well fed. Close by is *Time Square Café* and the *Milky Way Internet Café* (☎ (011) 487 1340; ndilo@milkyway.co.za), a few flights upstairs. When it adjusts, it will be the place to communicate with friends in the outside world.

At the back of the courtyard is *Charros Curry*, a good place for authentic Indian food. Curries are around R18 (vegetarian R13), plus papadams, dhal, raita, etc. Try their excellent homemade pickles (R4.50). There is secure parking behind the Square; tip the guards to ensure it stays so.

In the next block east, opposite Yeoville

Square, is *Pizzaghetti Factory* for wood-fired pizzas; *Masada* and *Feigel's* for good Jewish fare (to satisfy the suburb's Jewish populace); and *Mohican Diner*, on the corner of Rockey and Kenmere Sts, for huge breakfasts, freshly squeezed orange juice, burgers for under R8 and a collection of hideous Hollywood memorabilia.

*The Slow Coach*, at 65 Raleigh St, midway between Kenmere St and Bedford Rd, is a great place for light meals and a respite from the street stalls below. When you cross over Cavendish St, you enter 'buzzing' Jo'burg – enjoy it.

On the corner is *Mamma's Italian*, with the best and cheapest Italian fare around – real minestrone, choked with vegies, for a minuscule R10 and several other delights. Across the road, in the Piccadilly Centre, are places for coffee and snacks.

At No 5 Rockey St, *Ba Pita* was once the place to agonise over existentialist dilemmas to the accompaniment of coffee and Pink Floyd. Not much has changed, except the tapes are now more likely to be local bands. The atmosphere is pleasant and the food is simple, cheap and tasty. Nearby at No 9A, *Elaine's Curry Bistro* is a curry restaurant with a large menu and good reputation. Vegetarian mains are under R20, others are around R25.

If consciousness allows, and you don't feel threatened by the flood of yuppies, recently reopened *Rockerfella's*, a combination café, bar and restaurant, serves meals (a little behind the action). To its direct west is *Ripley's Arms*, a great place to order a meal at the bar and retreat to the 'outdoor' meals area (R12 pub lunches).

*Scandalo's*, 24A Rockey St, is a pleasant, casual Greek restaurant with reasonable prices. The usual dips/dolmades are well under R12 and main courses, both Greek dishes and steaks, cost from R25. Further east along Rockey, *The House of Tandoor* (☎ (011) 487 1569) is both a venue and a café. With a combination of good food and live music it has everything going for it. As well as the restaurant there's a barn-like space for bands and a roof-top bar. Curries

cost from R16 and most other dishes are around R20. There's a cover charge for the music, usually R10. Further east are *Jamaican Grilled Chicken* – takeaway chook heaven – and an ever-reliable *KFC*.

For African food, head to *Iyavaya*, at 42 Hunter St near the corner of Fortesque Rd. It's pleasant, but the service is very slow and indifferent (our mate from Soweto was appalled). Two meals will cost around R70. Better still is *Kin-Malebo* (☎ (011) 648 5303), nearby at the corner of Hunter and Fortesque; it's the place for hot Congolese (Zaïrese) dishes sweltering in piment (hot chillies), and best washed down with tangawuisi (home-made ginger beer).

*Jahnito's* at 43 Rockey St, Bellevue East, is better known as a live-music venue; the menu is West African influenced, with the curries simply delicious.

### The Waterfronts

It's worth considering an expedition to the kitsch Fisherman's Village, beside Bruma Lake, or to the Randburg Waterfront in the northern suburbs. There are a number of popular restaurants at Bruma, including *Mar-e-Sol* (☎ (011) 622 6162), which is an interesting Portuguese/Mozambique restaurant. Chinese food lovers will appreciate the 100-plus item menu (jellyfish, sea cucumber and trotters included) at *The Great Wall*, in Finance House, Ernest Oppenheimer Drive. These are 4km east of Yeoville; continue along Rockey St, which becomes Observatory, then along Marcia St.

The popular Randburg Waterfront has something for everyone, pulsating fountain included. Places which stand out are *Laughing Buddha* (Shop 212) for delicious eastern food, *Mezzaluna* (Shop 171/2) for Portuguese and *Kiri Pani* (Shop 202B) for Sri Lankan cuisine. There is also a *MacRib* (for families), a *McGinty's* pub and the trendy *Waterfront Arms*.

### Northern Suburbs

In general, the restaurants in the northern suburbs are high quality and, relatively speaking, highly priced. There are restaurant/coffee shop enclaves in Melville, Brixton, Norwood and Illovo, and many restaurants scattered throughout the shopping malls in Rosebank and Sandton.

**Melville** Trendy Melville, just north-west of Braamfontein, is becoming popular for its restaurants and coffee shops. You'll find a selection on 7th St. Between 2nd and 3rd Aves, *Bass Line*, a fine jazz venue, has meals for around R20 (R30 for steaks). When there's music (six nights a week) there's an admission charge of R15. Other nearby cafés are *Hard Times* at 63A 4th Ave, open daily until late; *Sam's* at 11B 7th St; and *The Mixer*, corner of 4th Ave and 7th St.

Seafood lovers will revel in the catch at licensed *Horatio's* (☎ (011) 726 2890), at the corner of 3rd Ave and 7th St; a full meal will cost around R50. It is open weekdays for lunch and dinner, weekends for dinner only. Those expecting Australian fare at *Koala Blu*, near the corner of 4th Ave and 7th St, will be rather surprised – the meals are Thai (no kangaroo), but the entrées for R20 and mains for R35-plus are well worth it.

**Illovo** *La Margaux*, 3 Rivonia Rd, is an institution in Jo'burg. Much of the food is prepared at the table, but the menu varies from assorted pasta to seafood and steaks. It is a classy place, French with an Italian influence, and much loved by the local elite. They like pseudo-French ambience in the north.

Many foreign visitors gravitate to the *Hard Rock Café* in the New Thrupps Centre, Oxford Rd, to buy a T-shirt (some people actually collect these!) The food is good and reasonably priced; it is open daily until late and there is a happy hour from 5 to 7 pm.

**Norwood** This enclave, reached by taking Louis Botha Ave north-east, is coming of age. In a close group on Grant Ave, you can choose from the excellent *Fishmonger* – great sushi and sashimi for about R35 a plate; the cosy Italian *Trattoria da Renato & Carla*; and the very popular open-plan *Jabberwock*. For reasonable pizzas, try *Pasquino* in the Grant Centre, at the corner of Iris Rd.

**The Far North** The choice is enormous but the myriad slick places in the Rosebank and Sandton malls are much of a muchness – if you discover a really special place, tell us. *Le Chablis* (☎ (011) 884 1000), in the Sandown Centre, on the corner of Maud St and Rivonia Rd, Sandown, is a relaxed bistro with exceptional, imaginative food.

Two Rivonia favourites are *Rattlesnake Roadside Diner*, a Tex-Mex place in the Mutual Village; and the English pub *Pheasant Pluckers' Arms*, corner of 11th Ave and Rivonia Rd. After several beers at the latter, practise: 'I'm not a pheasant plucker, I'm a pheasant pluckers son, And I'll be pheasant plucking, until the pheasant plucking's done'. Good luck.

In this 'meat-mad' country it's a pleasant change to find a great vegetarian restaurant. *Mary-Ann's Wholefood Emporium*, The Colony, 345 Jan Smuts Ave, Craighall Park, will satisfy every fastidious eater; excellent additive-free mains range from R15 to R30. There are further branches of this chain in the Heathway Centre, off DF Malan Drive, Blackheath; and corner of 7th Ave and Rivonia Rd, Rivonia.

**Other Options** If you are inclined to eat some of the animals you have seen in SA's game parks, *Carnivore*, Plot 69, Drift Boulevard, Muldersdrift, is the place to go. There is a good selection of salads and desserts, potjie soups, and 'all-the-meat-you-can-eat', carved from Maasai tribal sword skewers at your table. For something a little less 'meaty', the Italian *Casalinga*, at the Rocky Ridge Driving Range, Muldersdrift Rd, Honeydew, is open Wednesday to Sunday (lunch only Sunday).

*Swiss Inn* (☎ (011) 787 9903) at 170 Hendrik Verwoerd Drive, Bordeaux Gardens, Randburg, is worth the long drive. Our local friends rave about the ambience and food; it is open Tuesday to Sunday (dinner only Saturday, lunch only Sunday).

### ENTERTAINMENT

The best entertainment guide for Jo'burg is in the *Weekly Mail & Guardian* (R3.50); you can't do without a copy. 'Tonight' in the *Star*

**GAUTENG**

(http://www.inc.co.za/online/tonight) is also good. For entertainment bookings by credit card contact Computicket (☎ (011) 445 8000) – it has *every* seat for *every* theatre, cinema and sports venue on its system.

## Theatres

The Market Theatre complex (☎ (011) 832 1641) is the most important venue for live theatre. The quality varies, of course, but a visit is highly recommended. Other venues worth keeping your eye on include the Windybrow Theatre Complex (☎ (011) 720 7009) on Nugget St, north of Smit between Joubert Park and Hillbrow; the Alexander Theatre (☎ (011) 339 3461), on Stiemens St between Melle and De Beer Sts, Braamfontein; and the Alhambra Theatre complex (☎ (011) 402 7726), at 109 Sivewright Ave, Doornfontein.

## Music & Dancing

*Kippie's* (☎ (011) 832 1641) at the Market Theatre complex is one of the best places to see South African jazz talent, which happens to be exceptional; it's closed on Monday. Another good place to see jazz and township music on weekends is the *Get Ahead Shebeen* (☎ (011) 442 5964) in the Rosebank Mall, an unlikely venture which has successfully transported a shebeen (township bar) to a rich white suburb.

The *Radium Beer Hall* (see the previous Bars section) also sometimes has jazz. There's more music (of the rhythm 'n' blues ilk) at *Mojo's Jazz Blues & Beyond*, 206 Louis Botha Ave, Orange Grove.

*Bass Line* (☎ (011) 482 6915), on 7th St in Melville, has jazz nightly except Sunday. On Friday and Saturday the emphasis is on blues. The cover charge is R15. A few blocks west on Main Rd, Melville, are some clean-cut clubs and bars catering mainly to a clean, young 'half-cut' crowd. *Roxy Rhythm Bar* in the Melville Hotel is the best known. A usurper is the *Bohemian Club* in Park Rd, which attracts an eclectic mix of punters.

Downtown there is a constantly changing batch of dance clubs. Weekends are the busiest times. Check the *Weekly Mail &*

*Guardian* for current favourites. A club that has been around for a while is *The Doors*, 161 Marshall St, which has a young crowd, loud rock (also ska, goth and reggae) and pool tables. You get the choice of three clubs at 154 Market St – *Le Club* is the place for alternative sounds, or try *King of Clubs* or *Top Club*.

Braamfontein has a good scene. For a student crowd check out *Wings Beat Bar* (☎ (011) 339 4492), 8 Ameshoff St. Entry is just R7.50 and there is live music Tuesday to Sunday. *La Rumba* in the Orchidea Hotel, 90 De Korte St, is one of the 'vibe-iest' places around, attracting a mainly black clientele from all parts of Africa. If neither of these suits your pretensions, then you will revel in *Caesar's Palace* at 61 Jorissen St.

In Yeoville, one of the best venues for interesting music and a mixed crowd is the *House of Tandoor* (☎ (011) 487 1569) at the east end of Rockey St. There's usually something on Wednesday and Saturday nights, with a cover charge of around R10 to R20, depending on who is playing. Be warned that the venue is just a smoky barn with a concrete floor – pretty depressing unless there's a good crowd. If not, go upstairs to the rooftop bar. Elsewhere on Rockey St there are venues such as *Dylan's* and *Rockerfella's* where the emphasis is more on drinking (and drinking) and dancing. At *Kartouche*, 13A Raymond St, Yeoville, and *Jahnito's*, Bellevue East, music is the important factor. At the latter you'll see acts ranging from the Springbok Nude Girls to Mahlathini & the Queens.

In nearby Hillbrow, the buzzing place is *La Frontiere* in the Squash Court Centre, 19-25 Pretoria St – it attracts a crowd that is fully representational of the continent and the beat is swing and Congolese (Zaïrean) soukous.

In the northern 'white ghetto' of Rosebank, the timid ('I've never been into the city, it's too violent'), almost all-white crowd exact their own rhythmical demise, à la *Cabaret* and Berlin pre-WWII, at a succession of venues. On Oxford Rd, there is *Pearl Harbour*, the herpetological *Viper Room*, *Picasso's* and *Storyville*. In nearby Illovo there is the *Hard Rock Café* (see the earlier Places to Eat section), with occasional live music, and the *Illovo Blues Room* (☎ (011) 442 4093), in the New Thrupps Centre.

Put the 'north' in perspective at *Foxy's* (☎ (011) 803 2202), 79 Kikuyu Rd, Sunninghill Park. On a Sunday afternoon or evening, if you are black (among 1500 well-heeled whites), you are well and truly on your own. *Synergy's*, described as 'triffic', is a weekend techno/dance music venue at Fourways Mall, 194 Witkoppen Rd. The cover charge is R10 on weekends. And for other rave venues, get a copy of *The Vibe* street paper or just turn up for the Essential Session at *Insomnia*, New Thrupps Centre, Illovo. Bring water – the taps are off.

### Bars & Other Hang-outs

If your best outfit consists of a clean pair of jeans, the best place to stroll is **Yeoville**, where there are some late-night bars and music venues, most on Rockey St between Cavendish and Bezuidenhout or at the west (Berea) end on Raleigh St. It all tends towards the grungy, but it's also the only area of town where you're likely to meet interesting people and hear non-mainstream music in a safe environment. Try *Ripley's Arms* and *Rockerfella's*, the more standard of watering troughs, and the nearby *String's* and *Gershwin's*. *Dylan's* and *The House of Tandoor* (go upstairs to the roof garden or through to the rear disco) are where those in the know hang out. Other places come and go. On a hot evening, the Time Square courtyard of cafés and surrounding restaurants (corner of Fortesque Rd and Raleigh St) are good places for a drink.

Hillbrow & Berea are a bit too exciting for late-night wandering these days, although with a knowledgeable local and a car or a taxi you should be OK. Just don't take anything you can't afford to lose. *Brazil Bar* in Johnston St, Berea, is not for the faint-hearted – if you go, get a cab to wait for an hour or so – it is not a place to walk home from. *Summit Club* at the corner of Pretoria and Claim Sts, and *The Red Lion*, Kotze St, Hillbrow, are

### The World's Meanest Guard Dogs

'Did you hear about the guy who crossed a rottweiler with a hyena? It bit blacks and laughed.'

This 'joke' was printed in a conservative white newspaper a few years ago. Times have changed a little – the newspaper would no longer print it, but many readers would probably still find it funny. And there are still a lot of big dogs, especially in Jo'burg's white suburbs, which go ballistic at the sight of a non-white person.

The scariest is the boerebul, reputedly a cross between a bloodhound, a doberman and a rottweiler. Weighing as much as a large man and originally bred by racist white farmers to kill black trespassers, boerebuls are ferocious and almost unstoppable.

The apartheid army's covert scientific unit also tried to breed killer dogs. Its triumph was a cross between an alsatian and a wolf, a monster with huge fangs, unbelievable strength and a very bad temper. ∎

definite walks on the wild side – go with big, streetwise friends, or stay home.

There's a surprising lack of civilised bars in the city centre, although there are suitably flashy saloons in the big hotels. Some would dispute that 'civilised' was the appropriate word, but the *Press Bar* in the Elizabeth Hotel, on the corner of Pritchard and Sauer Sts opposite the *Star* newspaper offices, is a good spot to stop for refreshment in the city. Other possibilities are *Dawson's Hotel*; *TJ's* (also called *The Koppie*), at the east end of Bok St, Doornfontein, a real Afrikaner haunt where your liberal views must take a temporary back seat (talk about cricket, rugby, *boevewors*); and *Duke's*, 12 Henri St, Braamfontein, for food and music.

Fortunately, *Kippie's* in the Market Theatre complex has reopened. What a tragic corner of earth this was whilst Kippie's was closed. A small but very popular jazz venue named after the great Kippie 'Morolong' Moeketsi, it's a 'must do' when in Jo'burg. Perhaps the classic *Yard of Ale*, nearby, may reopen.

The *Radium Beer Hall*, 282 Louis Botha Ave in Orange Grove, is one of the few neighbourhood pubs left in Jo'burg. It's the sort of pub that you might imagine would be ubiquitous in South Africa – masculine but civilised and dedicated to the thirst of workers. That isn't the case, though; the Radium is almost unique. The bar counter dates from 1895, although the Radium is much younger than that, and the ceiling is of pressed metal. Bar meals cost less than R12 and there's plenty of choice.

There are a couple of possibilities in Gold Reef City (☎ (011) 496 1600) – *Barney's* and the *Consolidated Saloon*. After 5 pm it's free to enter the complex. There are often special events on weekends – they are promoted in the *Star*.

Both Bruma Lake and the Randburg Waterfront have plenty of *bars* in settings with water and fountains will allow you temporary respite from the big city and its slag heaps.

### Gay & Lesbian Jo'burg

Apart from the annual Gay Pride March, most of the gay scene in Jo'burg is rather surreptitious. The pages of the country's longest-running gay mag, *Exit*, and the gay/lesbian lifestyle mag *Outright* are the best places to start your search. It's also worthwhile getting in touch with the Gay & Lesbian Organisation of Witwatersrand (GLOW) – the number is in the phone book.

There is not the scene of Cape Town but there are a healthy smattering of clubs. *Krypton* (☎ (011) 788 4708), in the Constantia Centre, Trywhitt Ave, Rosebank, is a popular gay/bi venue for the outrageous (and admiring 'out-ragers'). The cover charge is R10 Wednesday, R20 weekends. Another gay spot is *Pandora's Piano Lounge*, across the road. The infamous Dungeon has gone but gay venturers will find solace in *Skyline Bar*, near the entrance to the Harrison Reef Hotel in Hillbrow; *Gotham City* (also called *58*), a block away; *Champions* in Braamfontein; or *Champs Elysees* in Yeoville.

### SPECTATOR SPORT

Jo'burg boasts some excellent spectator venues. Sport (or rather the restrictions upon it) probably contributed more than any other

single factor to opening SA to the world. **Ellis Park** in Doornfontein, east of the city centre, is the headquarters of Rugby Union, and the main stadium hosts everything from rugby to rock concerts. Rugby supporters are fanatics, and Ellis Park can hold 100,000 of them – a Saturday afternoon at the football can be quite an experience. Ellis Park is also home to the SA Open tennis tournament.

The most important cricket venue is **Wanderers**, on Corlett Drive, Melrose North, just off the M1 freeway to Pretoria. It's one of the most beautiful cricket grounds in the world. The uninitiated will find the game fairly obscure, but if you go to a one day game with someone who can explain the rules you'll get plenty of entertainment. Believe it or not, Test matches go for five days. A new first class cricket ground has opened in Soweto, called Elkah Oval. (Australia's Test team played here in 1997.)

**Kyalami**, off the M1 between Jo'burg and Pretoria, is the venue for motor sports and home of the November SA Formula One Grand Prix. It also hosts saloon car and motorcycle events.

Of the many horse-racing tracks, the best known is **Turffontein** (☎ (011) 683 9330), 3km south of the city. There are almost weekly race meetings.

The **Rand Stadium** on Turf Rd near Turffontein, and **Soccer City**, further west on Soweto Rd, are the major venues for soccer, which is the sport that most black South Africans follow passionately. The enormous new Soccer City holds 130,000 spectators. The popular teams are the Orlando Pirates (known as the Bucs) and the 'mighty, all conquering' Kaiser Chiefs.

### THINGS TO BUY

Jo'burg prides itself on its shops. The big shopping malls are jammed with western consumer goods of every description.

Shopaholics would do well to start in the Carlton Centre and Smal St Mall, but if you're a serious buyer make an expedition to Rosebank, which has an interlocking series of malls. (There's central parking on the corner of Cradock Ave and Baker St.)

Sandton and Randburg also have large malls; both are a 30 minute drive north of the city. Another handy mall is Eastgate, off the N12 just east of Bruma Lake.

One of the best sources of ethnic/African music is Kohinoor, which has a number of branches including 11 Kort St, downtown (off Market St). You can get most of the titles you seek in all of the big malls.

If you wish to remind yourself that you're still in Africa, visit a *muti* shop. Kwa Indaba is at 14 Diagonal St, City, and on the corner of Koch and Twist Sts opposite the Art Gallery. Muti shops sell herbs and potions prescribed by a sangoma. Many problems, from broken hearts to headaches, are treated. Despite being dim, pungent caves of animal parts, muti shops are definitely businesses – the KwaZulu Muti on Kruis St offers a wholesale discount to *inyangas* (medicine men). The muti tradition, which has religious overtones, is regarded with great seriousness by most black South Africans. Don't demean the sangomas or yourself by treating it as a joke. Cynicism is fine, but have the decency to show respect. Some who would argue that there are equally strange western beliefs – like blind faith in science.

### Crafts

A number of good shops sell traditional carvings, beadwork, jewellery and fertility dolls, although prices in Jo'burg are high. Unfortunately, you may not get a better chance to see and buy such a wide range of items.

Street vendors set up on the footpaths around town and sell crafts. Bargaining is expected. There are a couple of good stalls along Pretoria St in Hillbrow. In Yeoville, Rockey St has a fascinating collection. Across from Flea Market World, near Bruma Lake, there are craft sellers with a wide range but lots of kitsch.

### Camping Equipment

A number of specialist camping stores sell all kinds of up-to-date equipment. The biggest group is the combined ME Stores and Camp & Climb. ME Stores have branches at the Kine Centre, 146 Market St, City (☎ (011)

331 6811), and at the Crossroads Shopping Centre, Hill St, Randburg (☎ (011) 789 1604). Camp & Climb (☎ (011) 403 1354) has a shop on the corner of Juta and De Beer, Braamfontein, and in the same area is Sanga Outdoor on Ameshoff St (next to the Wings Beat Bar). Another good shop is Camping in Africa (☎ (011) 787 3524) in the Hill St Mall, Oak Ave, Randburg.

### GETTING THERE & AWAY
### Air

Jo'burg International (☎ (011) 356 1111; 975 9963 for flight inquiries) is SA's major international and domestic airport.

Distances in SA are large, so if you're in a hurry some domestic flights are definitely worth considering. There are flights to Cape Town, Port Elizabeth, East London, Durban, Kimberley and Upington, with smaller airlines reaching most places in the country. See the South Africa Getting Around chapter for fares.

Comair (☎ (011) 921 0111) charges R595 to Cape Town and R365 to Durban, with significant advance-purchase discounts. Sun Air (☎ (011) 397 2244) has daily flights to Sun City for R230. There are also flights to/from Cape Town (R787) and Durban (R433), VAT included.

Lesotho Airways flies at least daily between Moshoeshoe airport, 18km from Maseru, and Jo'burg; a one-way ticket costs R330; note, it is R390 Jo'burg to Maseru. Royal Swazi Airlines flies between Manzini and Jo'burg daily; a one-way fare is R400 – there are good deals on Apex return fares.

Most airlines have city offices:

Air Afrique
   1st Floor, Sanlam Arena, Cradock Ave, Rosebank
   (☎ (011) 880 9888; fax 880 8669)
Air France
   1st Floor, Oxford Manor, 196 Oxford Rd, Illovo
   (☎ (011) 880 8055; fax 880 7772)
Air Mauritius
   701 Carlton Towers, Commissioner St (☎ (011)
   331 1918; fax 331 1954)
Air Namibia
   1st Floor, Dunkeld Place, 12 North Rd, Dunkeld
   West (☎ (011) 442 4461; fax 442 4111)

GAUTENG

Air Zimbabwe
    Carlton Centre, Commissioner St (☎ (011) 331 1541; fax 331 6970)
Alitalia
    1st Floor, Oxford Manor, corner of Oxford and Chaplin Rds, Illovo (☎ (011) 880 9254)
British Airways
    158 Jan Smuts Ave, Rosebank (☎ (011) 441 8600; fax 880 5784)
Comair
    Corner of Atlas and Marignane Rds, Bonaero Park (☎ (011) 921 0222; fax 973 3913)
Eastern Air
    Office No 43, International Departure Lounge, Jo'burg airport (☎ (011) 970 2057)
KLM
    (☎ (011) 881 9696; fax 881 9691)
Metavia
    Terminal 5, Jo'burg airport (☎ (011) 394 3780; fax 394 3726)
Qantas Airways
    3rd Floor, Village Walk, Sandton (☎ (011) 884 5300; fax 884 5312)
Royal Swazi Airlines
    2nd Floor, Finance House, Ernest Oppenheimer Drive, Bruma (☎ (011) 616 7323; fax 616 7757)
SAA
    ☎ (011) 356 1111; airport (international) ☎ 978 3370; airport (domestic) ☎ 978 3119
SA Airlink
    ☎ (011) 394 2430; fax 394 2649
SA Express
    ☎ (011) 978 5577; fax 978 5578
Sun Air
    302 Administration Building, international airport (☎ (011) 397 2244; fax 397 1008)
Varig
    134 Fox St (☎ (011) 331 2231; fax 331 7447)

## Bus

Many international bus services depart from Jo'burg for Lesotho, Botswana, Mozambique, Namibia, Swaziland and Zimbabwe. Panthera Azul (☎ (011) 337 7409) runs to Maputo, and Silverbird (☎ (011) 337 7215) runs to Harare. See the introductory South Africa Getting There & Away chapter for details.

The main long-distance bus lines (national and international) currently depart and arrive from the Rotunda, a short walk west of the Jo'burg train station. There are booking counters and a Jo'burg information desk (☎ (011) 337 6650) in the Rotunda. City to City/Transtate, the inexpensive government

bus service, leaves from the train station, not far from the Rotunda – walk through the underpass across the road from the Rotunda and turn right. (These arrangements will change – see the boxed text 'The New Park Station' further on.)

The most comprehensive range of services are offered by the government-owned lines, Translux (☎ (011) 774 3313) and City to City/Transtate (☎ (011) 773 6002 from 7 to 10 am and 5 to 9 pm; otherwise try the head office, ☎ 774 7741). In general, Translux has slightly cheaper fares than Greyhound (☎ (011) 830 1400), while City to City/Transtate is the cheapest of the lot. Another company with a wide coverage is Intercape (☎ (011) 333 5231).

Backpackers can travel to the most popular destinations (Swaziland, Durban, Garden Route, Cape Town) by the excellent Baz Bus (☎ (021) 439 2323), ☎ (031) 23 6585). The beauty is that they pick up at hostels, saving you the hassle of going into the city to arrange transport.

**Mpumalanga & Kruger National Park** The nearest large town to Kruger is Nelspruit, and Greyhound runs there daily for R120 (five hours). City to City/Transtate has slow, cheap services from Jo'burg to Nelspruit (R55, seven hours) that continue on to Acornhoek, via Hazyview (R65, eight hours). Hazyview is closer to Kruger than Nelspruit and has backpacker hostels which arrange trips into the park. See Routes North later this section for buses to the Phalaborwa Gate.

**Durban** Translux has at least one daily bus to Durban for R140. Greyhound has four buses a day between Jo'burg and Durban for R155 (seven hours); their rapid direct service takes six hours (R160).
    Several small companies, such as Golden Wheels (☎ (011) 852 1423) and Roadshow Intercity (☎ (082) 449 9037), run to Durban (R95). The Baz Bus costs R120 and departs on Tuesday, Friday and Sunday.

**Cape Town** Translux has at least one daily bus running from Pretoria/Jo'burg to Cape Town via Bloemfontein (16 hours to Cape Town). Also, five services (daily, except Tuesday and Thursday) run via Kimberley (18 hours to Cape Town). From Jo'burg the fare on either service is R320.

From Jo'burg to Bloemfontein costs R160, to Kimberley it's R165.

Greyhound has daily buses to Cape Town via Bloemfontein for R340. Note that Greyhound has a daily express bus to Kimberley for just R90.

Intercape has five services a week to Upington (R175). From Upington there are four services weekly to Cape Town (R150). You might have to wait to change buses in Upington but total road travel time Jo'burg to Cape Town is 19 hours. From Upington you can also get an Intercape bus to Windhoek in Namibia (R200), but there isn't a direct connection.

The hop-on hop-off return price with Baz Bus is R850, but this means you can go via Durban and the Garden Route to Cape Town, and then return up the centre via Kimberley (or return the way you came). Given the flexibility, this is really good value.

**South Coast** Translux runs a daily service from Jo'burg to East London, via Bloemfontein. The fare is R220 and the trip takes 12 hours. Translux also has five services weekly (Sunday and Tuesday excepted) from Jo'burg to Port Elizabeth via Bloemfontein and Graaff-Reinet. The fare is R240 and the trip takes 11 hours. Greyhound has daily (overnight) buses from Jo'burg to Port Elizabeth for R275.

Translux runs to Knysna (R230) via Kimberley (Sunday and Thursday) or Bloemfontein (daily, except Thursday and Sunday) then Oudtshoorn, Mossel Bay and George (all R230); the trip takes 17 hours.

City to City/Transtate runs to Umtata, the closest large town to Port St Johns and Coffee Bay, daily at 6 pm (on Tuesday and Friday at 7 pm); the fare is R95.

The Baz Bus departs from Durban on Wednesday and Saturday, from East London on Thursday and Sunday, and from Knysna on Friday and Monday, in the direction of Cape Town (and the Garden Route); ask your hostel/hotel for details and prices.

**Routes North** Several services run north up the N1. Translux has a daily bus to Beitbridge and on to Harare (R210) and Lusaka (R320) via Pietersburg/Polokwane (R80), Louis Trichardt (R90) and Messina (R105).

A budget service leaves Jo'burg daily at 8.30 am for Beitbridge (R70) – that is all the info we have. There is also a daily City to City/Transtate service to Sibasa in Venda for R60. This and various City to City/Transtate services winding north through townships and ex-Homelands also stop in the major towns on the N1.

North Link Tours (☎ (0152) 291 1867) also runs buses between Jo'burg and Phalaborwa (R140). Fares (from Jo'burg/ Phalaborwa) are Pretoria (R15/125), Naboomspruit (R55/85), Potgietersrus (R70/75), Pietersburg/Polokwane (R80/55) and Tzaneen (R115/30). There is a separate service to Louis Trichardt (R115). Kruger's Phalaborwa Gate is further from Jo'burg than some of the others, but you might want to enter the park in the north and work your way down. You can hire cars in Phalaborwa.

Two recommended companies going to Zimbabwe are Mini-Zim Travel (☎ (012) 543 1236) – twice weekly to Bulawayo, R210/420 one way/ return; and Zimi-Bus (☎ (011) 678 2308) – three times weekly to Harare, R350/685.

**Routes West** City Link (☎ (011) 333 4412) runs twice daily to Mafikeng from the Rotunda (R60). City to City/Transtate has a variety of useful services, including a daily run to Mafikeng (R50) via Krugersdorp and Zeerust. Greyhound passes through Rustenburg (R50) and Zeerust (R85) on its daily Johannesburg to Gaborone (Botswana) service.

Intercape runs to Cape Town and Windhoek (Namibia) via Upington – see Upington in the Northern Cape chapter.

### Train

Overseas visitors are no longer eligible for a 25% discount, but there has been a long-running special whereby *everyone* is entitled to a 25% discount on train fares, so ask if this is still available. If it is, 1st class fares are very competitive with Translux and Greyhound buses. If not, 2nd class fares are less than bus fares. For more information contact Mainline (☎ (011) 773 2944).

At the Mainline ticket office on the main concourse at Jo'burg station, you can make bookings between 7.30 am and 5 pm on weekdays and until 1 pm on Saturday. The station's left-luggage department is open daily from 6 am to 7 pm (7 am to 6 pm on Sunday). There's a R2 per day charge for each piece of luggage.

**Blue Train to Cape Town** The *Blue Train* (☎ (011) 774 4469) is an extremely luxurious train between Cape Town and Jo'burg. It has individual suites and compartments of varying degrees of comfort and expense. There are departures on Monday, Wednesday and Friday, but it is essential to book in advance. The train leaves Pretoria at 9 am and arrives in Cape Town at noon the next

GAUTENG

## The New Park Station

A huge and much-needed redevelopment of the train station is underway, so transport arrangements will change during the life of this guide. The area being developed is 22 city blocks, bounded by Wolmarans, Rissik, De Villiers, Hoek, Noord and Wanderers Sts.

A new Transit Centre will connect luxury buses to mainline trains from Platforms 11 to 19. A Metro Concourse will be built for Metro trains from Platforms 1 to 10. Later, a Road Transport Interchange will be built over the web of railway tracks between the Metro Concourse and Wanderers St. Eventually it will deal with about 150 long-distance taxis and some 1200 minibus taxis.

The 700 or so homeless who currently occupy the station are being moved elsewhere. Security cameras are being installed, and there are hopes for the development of pedestrian malls, retail malls, a museum, a budget hotel and covered car parking. Good news for all, except the homeless. ■

day. Northbound, it leaves Cape Town at 11 am. Luxury suites are well over 100 times the cost of this guidebook; compartments over 25 times the cost. Enough said.

**Trans Karoo to Cape Town** The *Trans Karoo* runs daily to Cape Town via Kimberley, De Aar and Worcester. The southbound train leaves Jo'burg at 12.30 pm and arrives in Cape Town 26 hours later at 2.15 pm. The northbound train leaves Cape Town at 9.20 am and arrives in Jo'burg at 10.15 am. First/2nd class tickets are R345/235. Although it takes an extra eight hours, it is worth considering taking the train rather than the bus.

**Durban** The *Trans Natal* runs every night between Jo'burg and Durban. The train leaves Jo'burg at 6.30 pm and arrives in Durban at 8 am. First/2nd class tickets are R165/110. The train fares are competitive, but buses run during the day and only take about seven hours.

**East London** The *Amatola* runs daily between Jo'burg and East London via Bloemfontein. The train leaves Jo'burg at 12.45 pm and gets to East London at 8.30 am the next morning. First/2nd class tickets are R215/150 (to Bloemfontein it is R95/65).

**Port Elizabeth** The *Algoa* operates daily between Jo'burg and Port Elizabeth via Bloemfontein.

The southbound train departs from Jo'burg at 2.30 pm and arrives in PE at 9.25 am the next day. First/2nd class tickets are R245/165.

**Diamond Express** A special service runs from Jo'burg to Bloemfontein, via Kimberley, daily except Saturday; it departs Jo'burg about 7 pm. First/2nd class tickets, Jo'burg to Bloemfontein, are R115/80.

**Komati** The *Komati* runs east to Komatipoort, on the border with Mozambique, via Nelspruit. It's a daily service (on Monday, Wednesday and Friday it continues on to Maputo, capital of Mozambique). The train leaves Jo'burg at 5.45 pm, arrives in Nelspruit at 3.30 am the next day and in Komatipoort at 6 am. First/2nd class tickets, Jo'burg to Komatipoort, are R121/85. To continue on to Maputo, the additional cost is R32/25.

### Minibus Taxi

The main long-distance taxi ranks are currently sandwiched between the train station and Joubert Park, mainly on Wanderers and King George Sts (with luck they will soon be in the New Park Station – see the boxed text). There are set areas for taxis to particular destinations (shown on the Central Johannesburg map).

Despite the apparent chaos, the ranks are well organised; ask for the queue marshal. You'll find taxis for Kimberley, Cape Town and Upington on Wanderers St near Leyds St; Bulawayo taxis at the north end of King George St; Pretoria taxis on Noord St; Lesotho, Bloemfontein (and other Free State destinations) on Noord St, east of Joubert Park; and Durban taxis near the corner of Wanderers and Noord Sts. Because of the risk of mugging, it isn't a good idea to go searching for a taxi while carrying your luggage.

Some examples of destinations and fares from Jo'burg are: Cape Town, R170; Durban, R70; Harrismith, R45; Kimberley, R60; Pietersburg/Polokwane, R50; Nelspruit, R65; Tzaneen, R60; Thohoyandou (Venda), R60; Pretoria, R10; Gaborone (Botswana), R60; Komatipoort, R80; Maputo (Mozambique), R100; Manzini (Swaziland), R55; and Bulawayo (Zimbabwe), R155.

As well as these taxis (which leave when

they are full), there are a few door-to-door services which you can book. Durban is well served by these; the cost is about R80 (many can be booked through hostels).

## Car

**Rental** All the major rental operators have counters at Jo'burg airport and at various locations around the city. Operators include Avis (☎ (0800) 021 111 toll free); Budget (☎ (0800) 016 622 toll free); Imperial (☎ (0800) 13 1000 toll free); Dolphin (☎ (011) 394 6605); Levitt's (☎ (011) 394 3580) and Tempest (☎ (011) 397 5402).

There aren't many budget alternatives, and the few that do exist are not very conveniently located (although many will deliver). Try Alisa (☎ (0800) 21515) or ask around the hostels/hotels. We thrashed a Delta car through the Kalahari and returned satisfied; they're worth consideration.

**Purchase** Jo'burg is the best place in SA to buy a car, although since this process is inevitably time-consuming it might be preferable to buy/sell in Cape Town, which is a more congenial place to waste a week or two.

Jules St, a 30 minute walk east of the city centre, is the main drag for used-car dealers. It's a jungle out there! The yards are open weekdays from 9 am to 5 pm and to noon on Saturday. There can be no guarantees with cheap, old cars, but Mike Ephron Motors (☎ (011) 614 6865), at No 167, could be the place to start. ZZ Cars, No 200, is another place to look.

A couple of Jo'burg dealers offer buy-back deals; the better Jo'burg hostels can advise on how best to draw up a contract that should make the deal stick when the time comes to sell back. One example: a 1983 Datsun 1400 pick-up was purchased for R11,000 with roadworthy certificate. The buy-back deal included R1000 per month depreciation while the vehicle was away – after six months the buyer could hope to get R5000 returned (much cheaper than a rental). You need time – the buyer in this case waited two weeks for delivery.

Dealers have to make a profit; you'll pay much less if you buy privately. The *Star* has ads every day and a motoring supplement on Thursday; look for the 'Bargains' section (usually under R8000). A vehicle trading-post magazine, known locally as 'Junk Mail', is used by prospective sellers and buyers.

The Sunday Car Market (☎ (011) 643 1183), at the Top Star Drive-in, Simmonds Southway, Park Central, Jo'burg, operates every Sunday from 9 am to 1 pm. It's best to arrive here early. There are usually around 200 cars to choose from. Buyers pay no commission or entrance fees, and change of ownership forms and advice about roadworthies and registering are available. Sellers pay a once-only fee of R50.

Unfortunately, there seem to be very few decent-quality used cars at low prices. You will be lucky to find a decent vehicle for much less than R13,000 (anything under R8000 is a definite gamble). You might be able to find something like a 1983 Passat wagon for about R10,000 (not considered good value), a 1986 1.6L Ford Sierra for R13,500, a 10-year-old Toyota Corolla (with 180,000km on the clock) for R12,000-plus and VW Golfs for about R1000 less than a Corolla. Of course, if nothing serious goes wrong, you may get your money back when you sell. There are few guarantees.

Whoever you buy from, make sure that the car's details correspond accurately with the ownership papers. Check the owner's name against their identity document and the engine and chassis numbers. Consider getting the car tested by the AA (Automobile Association); see the address at the end of this section. A full test can cost up to R300; less detailed tests are around R100.

Cheap cars are often sold without a roadworthy certificate. A roadworthy is required when you register the change of ownership and pay tax. The testers are fussy, so the certificates can be both difficult and expensive to get. There are various roadworthy centres; check the phone book. A test costs about R110. Once you have your roadworthy, take it, the ownership papers signed by the seller, your passport, and

GAUTENG

around R100 (for the 12 month Gauteng road tax) to the Licensing Department (☎ (011) 836 1951), 79 Loveday St, City. In an amazingly short time (well, a couple of hours) you'll receive new ownership papers and a tax disk to fix inside your windscreen.

Insurance, for third-party damages and damage to or loss of your vehicle, is a very good idea. It's easy enough to take out a year's insurance but most travellers don't want that much. Unfortunately, if you want to buy insurance by the month it is surprisingly difficult to find an insurance company to take your money if you don't have a permanent address and/or a local bank account. If this concerns you, start shopping around early so you can figure out a way to meet their conditions – before you purchase the car.

It might be possible to take out a year's insurance on the understanding that you'll get a rebate for the unused months when you sell the car, but you'd be wise to get this in writing. We would be interested to hear of any companies that are helpful to travellers. The AA has Limited Fire & Theft insurance for R145 per month, but full insurance is closer to R420.

Membership of the SA Automobile Association (the AA) is highly recommended. It has an efficient breakdown service and a good supply of maps and information. (The important things to get are the window stickers they give you for breakdown service.) Joining costs R50 (waived for members of many foreign motoring associations – bring your membership details) plus R235 per year. The main office (☎ (011) 407 1000) is in Braamfontein, on De Korte St, between De Beer St and Louis Botha Ave. There's a useful office in the Eastgate Mall shopping centre.

Repairs are horrendously expensive. One story described to us involved, shortly after purchase, a new clutch kit, two CV joints, an engine mounting and seals – R2200 for parts, R1000 for labour and R500 VAT. It may be worth taking out a major parts insurance (engine, gearbox, etc) with the AA for R2000 per year.

## Hitching

We do not recommend hitching, especially in Jo'burg. If you are picked up by black drivers they usually expect you to contribute to the cost of the trip. Whites usually speed past with looks of disbelief on their faces. Many hitchers load their packs into a car only to see the vehicle drive off before they get in. But if you must, then heading north, a popular place to begin hitching is on the N1 near the Killarney Mall, a couple of kilometres north-west of Yeoville. The N12 running east towards Kruger begins just east of Eastgate Mall. Heading south on the N1 (eg, to Cape Town) many hitchers try to pick up lifts on the freeway on-ramps; this is illegal and highly dangerous.

The hostels always have noticeboards with details of free or shared-cost lifts. Don't expect hostels to take any responsibility, and they shouldn't – it is up to you to check out the lift giver and to decide whether or not you wish to travel with them.

## GETTING AROUND
### To/From the Airport

Between 5 am and 10 pm, buses run every half-hour (a quarter to and a quarter past the hour) between Jo'burg International and the Rotunda, Leyds St, just to the east of Jo'burg train station. Journey time is about 25 minutes and the fare is R35; call ☎ (011) 394 6902 for details. There's also the Magic bus, which costs R50 and drops off at the more expensive hotels. For hotels in Sandton, take the Sandton Shuttle (☎ (011) 884 3957); it is also R50. Taxis are expensive (R95).

Some hostels will collect you from the airport, and several hostels 'tout' there. For hostels, only go to Yeoville or the northern suburbs. Avoid the city on your first day.

### Bus

For inquiries about bus services phone ☎ (011) 838 2125, or visit the information counter on Vanderbijl Square (the main city bus station, two blocks west of the Carlton).

The current fare scheme (these things change) is that any ticket costs R3 (or R4 during the evening rush, from 4 until 5.30 pm or so). Not many buses run later than this.

Routes 19 (Berea), 19A and 20 (Yeoville) are useful. Starting at Vanderbijl Square, they run north up Eloff St (stopping on the corner of Pritchard St) and Edith Cavell to Hillbrow, east along Pretoria, north along Harrow, then east along Raleigh St to Kenmere St. At Kenmere, the bus turns north then east following Hunter St to its end. It returns along Raleigh to Rockey (which is one way). They're frequent from 6.45 to 8.40 am, hourly in the middle of the day, then frequent from 4 to 7 pm, when they stop.

The buses that run out to Sandton are not part of the municipal fleet; they're operated by Padco (☎ (011) 474 2634). They leave the city centre from the corner of Kruis and Commissioner Sts. The buses run hourly from 6.30 am to 5.15 pm, more frequently at peak times; the fare to Sandton is R5.

### Minibus Taxi

Fares differ with routes, but R2 will get you around the inner suburbs and the city centre. It's easy enough to get a minibus taxi into the city – if you're waiting at a bus stop, chances are that a taxi will arrive before the bus does. Getting a minibus taxi home from the city is a more difficult proposition. Even locals often give up and take the bus. Heading for Yeoville, try Eloff St.

There's a complex system of hand/finger signals to tell a passing taxi where you want to go (the driver will stop if he/she is going the same way). Just raising your index finger in the air will stop most taxis – but it means 'town'. A down-turned index finger means 'Sandton'. The last three fingers held up is 'Dobsonville, Soweto' – you'll win the lottery before you see this indicated by a white hand.

### Taxi

There are taxi ranks in the city centre outside the Carlton Hotel and the Jo'burg Holiday Inn Garden Court, and at the airport. All taxis operate meters which, unfortunately, seem to vary markedly in their assessment. Some taxi companies seem to be cheaper than others; taxis from the Yeoville rank seem more expensive. From the Rotunda to Yeoville should cost between R15 and R20. Once you ascertain the cost of a trip, agree on a price rather than use the meter. Two reputable firms are Rose's Taxis (☎ (011) 725 3333) and Flash Taxis (☎ (011) 886 6816).

### Train

For inquiries about trains phone ☎ (011) 773 5878, or visit the helpful info office at the northern end of the train station concourse. There was a very serious problem with violent crime on the metro system, mostly on lines connecting with black townships, so ask the safety question before jumping on. Most whites use buses, and most blacks use buses and minibus taxis. A rail ticket costs about R3.50.

# Pretoria

Pretoria (known as Tshwane by the Sotho population) is South Africa's administrative capital. It is a bland city, superficially a bit like a northern Jo'burg suburb. After all, it's only 60km away and suburban sprawl is shrinking the green belt that separates the two. In some ways this is Paul Kruger's worst nightmare come true. Despite all the bitter struggles, all the wars and all the statutes, the uitlanders are now engulfing the old capital of the first Zuid-Afrikaansche Republiek (ZAR).

Nonetheless, Pretoria's history bears no relation to Jo'burg's – although their destinies have naturally been linked – and this has created cities with very different atmospheres. Pretoria is uncompromisingly 'Boer', owing its existence and growth to the Boer dreams of independence from the British as well as domination of black South Africans.

As the administrative capital of South Africa, Pretoria is home to embassies, military and civilian bureaucracies, military bases and educational institutions. Although Greater Pretoria has a population of 1.6 million it seems more like a large country

GAUTENG

town, increasingly irrelevant to the new South Africa, which centres on tumultuous Jo'burg. Most blacks living here are Sotho people; about 60% of the whites are Afrikaners. There are several sites that are central to the Afrikaners' semi-mystical folk history – some are virtual 'holy ground'.

Pretoria is quite an attractive city, especially during October and November when it is dominated by tens of thousands of flowering jacarandas. There are still a few old houses, incongruous not just for their size when compared with the neighbouring ranks of apartment blocks, but for their lack of high walls and razor wire. This is a *much* more relaxed place than Jo'burg.

Jo'burg is only 60km of freeway away, so if you *want* to stay there it's quite possible to cover most of Pretoria's sights in a day trip, especially if you have a car.

## HISTORY

The well-watered and fertile area around the Apies River supported a large population of cattle farmers for hundreds of years. These were Nguni-speaking people (from the same offshoot as the Zulus and Swazis), who came to be known as the Ndebele by the Sotho people of the Transvaal, and as the Matabele by the Europeans. The disruption caused by the difaqane, however, resulted in massive dislocation and the Boers trekked into a temporary vacuum.

The Great Trek reached its logical conclusion in the early 1850s when the British granted independence to the ZAR, north of the Vaal River, and to the Orange Free State, between the Orange and Vaal rivers.

At this stage there were an estimated 15,000 whites and 100,000 blacks between the Vaal and Limpopo rivers. As the whites were widely scattered, a central capital was needed. In 1853, two farms on the Apies River were bought as the site for the republic's capital. It became the capital of the ZAR in 1860.

The ZAR was a shaky institution. There were ongoing wars with the black tribes, and violent disputes among the Boers themselves. Pretoria, which was named after Andries Pretorius, hero of Blood River, was the scene of fighting during the 1863-69 Boer Civil War.

With scarcely any money in the government's coffers, there was very little material development. Pretoria was nothing more than a tiny frontier village with a grandiose title. Despite this, the servants of the British Empire watched it with growing misgivings. They acted in 1877, annexing the republic. The Boers went to war – Pretoria came under siege at the beginning of 1881 – and won back their independence. Paul Kruger was elected president in 1883.

The discovery of gold on the Witwatersrand in the late 1880s revolutionised the situation. A small community of farmers suddenly controlled some of the richest real estate land in the world. For hardliners like Kruger, however, the advantage of an overflowing treasury was almost outweighed by the flood of English-speaking uitlanders who threatened to undermine the Boers' hard-won independence.

Kruger's misgivings were soundly based – in 1899 the Boer Republics were once again at war with the British. Pretoria was abandoned by Kruger and the Boer forces in June 1900, but the war ground on until 31 May 1902 when the Peace of Vereeniging was signed at Melrose House.

After the war, a fabulous new source of wealth was found on Pretoria's doorstep. One of the biggest and most productive diamond-bearing kimberlite pipes in the world was discovered 40km east at Cullinan. It has produced three of the largest diamonds ever found. The largest, the Cullinan, as it was called, was 11cm by 6cm in rough form and was presented to King Edward VII.

After the war, the British made efforts towards reconciliation. Self-government was again granted to the Transvaal in 1906 and moves towards the union of the separate South African provinces were instituted.

The thorny issue of which city should be the capital was solved by the unwieldy compromise of making Pretoria the administrative capital, Cape Town the seat of the legislature and Bloemfontein the seat of the Appellate

Division of the Supreme Court. The Union of South Africa came into being in 1910, but Pretoria was not to regain its republican status again until 1961, when the Republic of South Africa came into existence under the leadership of Dr Verwoerd.

Ironically, the city now has a black mayor, Slo Ramokhoase, and a black-dominated council. Kruger's worst dream has finally materialised.

## ORIENTATION

If you arrive by car you'll encounter the usual nightmare of one-way streets and poor signage but on foot the city centre is easy to get around.

The main east-west through-road is Church (Kerk) St, which, at 26km, is claimed to be one of the longest straight streets in the world. Fortunately, the city centre, most of the sights, decent hotels and restaurants are not so far apart. Church St runs through Church Square, the historic centre of the city, and east to Arcadia, home of hotels, embassies and the Union Buildings (the seat of government). The nightlife zones (pale imitations of Yeoville) are Sunnyside and Hatfield.

## INFORMATION

The well-organised Tourist Rendezvous Centre is on Prinsloo St between Church and Vermeulen Sts, in the big Sammy Marks Centre. Open from 7 am to 7 pm daily, it's an excellent source of information. Here you'll find the Pretoria information centre (☎ (012) 323 1222, 313 7694), a National Parks Board desk (☎ (012) 323 0930), travel agents, transport (airport shuttle bus), foreign exchange, a bar and a coffee lounge. The staff at the information centre are helpful and have a wide range of brochures. If only Jo'burg had a centre like this!

The *Be My Guest* monthly magazine is widely available, as is the informative *Pretoria: Window on Africa*.

The head office of the National Parks Board (☎ (012) 343 0930) at 643 Leyds St, Muckleneuk, is not far from the university, south-east of the city centre.

## Money

Most banks are open from 9 am to 3.30 pm weekdays and from 8.30 to 11 am on Saturday; all exchange foreign currency.

Amex (☎ (012) 322 2620) is in the Tramshed, a shopping complex in a renovated building on the corner of Van der Walt and Schoeman Sts. Rennies Travel (☎ (012) 325 3800) has a couple of branches, including one in the Sanlam Centre, Andries St.

## Post & Communications

The GPO, on the corner of Pretorius and Van der Walt Sts, is open weekdays from 8 am to 4.30 pm, Saturday from 8 am to noon. There is a branch post office in Sunnyside.

## Visa Extensions

Apply for visa extensions at the Department of Home Affairs (☎ (012) 324 1860), Sentrakor Building, Pretorius St.

## Foreign Embassies

Many countries have diplomatic representation in both Jo'burg and Cape Town, but some only have trade missions in Jo'burg. Check the Foreign Consulates sections of this book for both those cities before you make a special trek to Pretoria.

The Lesotho embassy (☎ (012) 322 6090; fax 322 0376), the only place in South Africa where you can get visas to Lesotho, is on the 6th floor, West Tower, Momentum Centre, 343 Pretorius St. It is open from 9 am to noon on weekdays for visa applications. You'll need a passport photo and R30 for a one month visa; they take 24 hours to issue.

The addresses for embassies not listed here are available from the tourist information bureau (☎ (012) 313 7694). Ring ahead to check opening hours.

Australia
    292 Orient St, Arcadia (☎ (012) 342 3740; fax 342 4222)
Botswana
    Infotech Building, 1090 Arcadia St, Arcadia (☎ (012) 342 4760; fax 342 1845)
Canada
    1103 Arcadia St, Hatfield (☎ (012) 342 6923; fax 342 3837)

GAUTENG

GAUTENG

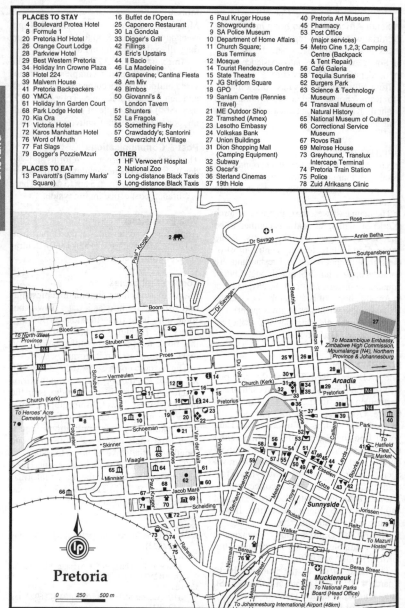

**PLACES TO STAY**
4 Boulevard Protea Hotel
8 Formule 1
20 Pretoria Hof Hotel
26 Orange Court Lodge
28 Parkview Hotel
29 Best Western Pretoria
34 Holiday Inn Crowne Plaza
38 Hotel 224
39 Malvern House
41 Pretoria Backpackers
60 YMCA
61 Holiday Inn Garden Court
68 Park Lodge Hotel
71 Kia Ora
71 Victoria Hotel
72 Karos Manhattan Hotel
76 Word of Mouth
77 Fat Slags
79 Bogger's Pozzie/Mzuri

**PLACES TO EAT**
13 Pavarotti's (Sammy Marks' Square)
16 Buffet de l'Opera
25 Caponero Restaurant
30 La Gondola
33 Digger's Grill
42 Fillings
43 Eric's Upstairs
44 Il Bacio
46 La Madeleine
47 Grapevine; Cantina Fiesta
48 Am Miv
49 Bimbos
50 Giovanni's & London Tavern
51 Shunters
52 La Fragola
55 Something Fishy
57 Crawdaddy's; Santorini
59 Oeverzicht Art Village

**OTHER**
1 HF Verwoerd Hospital
2 National Zoo
3 Long-distance Black Taxis
5 Long-distance Black Taxis
6 Paul Kruger House
7 Showgrounds
9 SA Police Museum
10 Department of Home Affairs
11 Church Square; Bus Terminus
12 Mosque
14 Tourist Rendezvous Centre
15 State Theatre
17 JG Strijdom Square
18 GPO
19 Sanlam Centre (Rennies Travel)
21 ME Outdoor Shop
22 Tramshed (Amex)
23 Lesotho Embassy
24 Volkskas Bank
27 Union Buildings
31 Dion Shopping Mall (Camping Equipment)
32 Subway
35 Oscar's
36 Sterland Cinemas
37 19th Hole
40 Pretoria Art Museum
45 Pharmacy
53 Post Office (major services)
54 Metro Cine 1,2,3; Camping Centre (Backpack & Tent Repair)
56 Café Galeria
58 Tequila Sunrise
62 Burgers Park
63 Science & Technology Museum
64 Transvaal Museum of Natural History
65 National Museum of Culture
66 Correctional Service Museum
67 Rovos Rail
69 Melrose House
73 Greyhound, Translux Intercape Terminal
74 Pretoria Train Station
75 Police
78 Zuid Afrikaans Clinic

Pretoria

France
807 George Ave, Arcadia (☎ (012) 43 5564; fax 43 3481)
Germany
180 Blackwood St, Arcadia (☎ (012) 344 3854; fax 343 9401)
Mozambique
199 Beckett St, Arcadia (☎ (012) 343 7840; fax 343 6714)
Netherlands
825 Arcadia St, Arcadia (☎ (012) 344 3910; fax 343 9950)
Swaziland
Infotech Building, 1090 Arcadia St, Hatfield (☎ (012) 342 5782; fax 342 5682)
Sweden
9th Floor, Old Mutual Building, 167 Andries St (☎ (012) 21 1050; fax 323 2776)
Switzerland
818 George St, Arcadia (☎ (012) 43 6707; fax 43 6771)
UK
Greystoke, 225 Hill St, Arcadia (☎ (012) 43 3121)
USA
7877 Pretorius St, Arcadia (☎ (012) 342 1048; fax 342 2244)
Zimbabwe
798 Merton St, Arcadia (☎ (012) 342 5125; fax 342 5126)

**Travel Agencies**
There are travel agencies in the Tourist Rendezvous Centre. See also Rennies Travel in the earlier Money section. There is a list in the free *Pretoria: Window on Africa*.

**Medical Services**
The HF Verwoerd Hospital (☎ (012) 329 1111) is north-west of the Union Buildings on Dr Savage Rd. (It's highly likely that the hospital's name will change.) There are numerous other medical centres and many pharmacies – the Zuid Afrikaans Clinic, on Berea St, is handy to Sunnyside. The pharmacy on the north-west corner of Esselen and Celliers Sts is open until 10 pm.

**Emergency**
For police call ☎ 10111, fire brigade ☎ (012) 323 2781 and ambulance ☎ (012) 326 0111. For Life Line ring ☎ (012) 343 8888.

**Dangers & Annoyances**
Pretoria is much safer and more relaxed than Jo'burg, but it's a big city so reasonable precautions should be observed. The square roughly formed by Pretorius, Andries, Boom, and Du Toit Sts has a bad reputation.

**Other Information**
A member of ME Stores (☎ (012) 322 7464), an outdoor chain, is in the Sanlam Plaza West on Schoeman St; and a Big Five outdoor shop is in the Hatfield Plaza.
The Gay & Lesbian Counselling number is ☎ (012) 46 9888.

**CHURCH SQUARE**
Church Square, the heart of Pretoria, is surrounded by imposing public buildings, including the Reserve Bank and Palace of Justice (on the north side). In the centre, the Old Lion, Paul Kruger, looks disapprovingly at office workers lounging on the grass. In the early days, Boers from the surrounding countryside would gather in the square every three months for *Nagmaal* (communion). They would come in their ox-wagons which would outspan (unyoke) in the square.

**HEROES' ACRE**
This cemetery, 1.5km west of Church Square on Church St, is the burial place for a number of historical figures, including Andries Pretorius, the hero of Blood River; Paul Kruger, president of the first ZAR; and Hendrik Verwoerd, the prime minister from 1958 to 1966 (when he was assassinated). An Australian, 'Breaker' Morant, a Boer War anti-hero who was executed by the British for war crimes, is also buried here. Take a West Park No 2 or Danville bus from Church Square.

**JG STRIJDOM SQUARE**
A striking example of neo-fascist architecture, the square is dominated by the huge head of JG Strijdom and a group of charging horses (apparently an archetypal heroic and martial image). Ironically, Strijdom, the prime minister from 1954 to 1958 and an architect of apartheid, now looks over the black street

GAUTENG

### Embarrassing Statues

The statue of JG Strijdom may have been demolished by the time you get to Pretoria, but it's a sign of the amazing restraint shown by the black majority that it was not blown up within hours of the ANC winning the 1994 elections.

There are many other statues of apartheid figures around the country. A perfect resting place for them would be a particularly remote, bleak and arid corner of the Karoo. They could sit and look at each other in the drab and silent isolation they so craved. ■

vendors who have set up by the square. They must get right up his nose.

## UNION BUILDINGS

The Union Buildings are an impressive red sandstone construction – with a self-conscious imperial grandeur – surrounded by expansive gardens. They are the headquarters of government, and the South African equivalent of the Kremlin. The architect was Sir Herbert Baker, who is responsible for many of the best public buildings built in the years immediately after the Union of South Africa was formed in 1910. They are best viewed at night – take a picnic and sit in the gardens.

The buildings are quite a long walk from the city centre. Catch just about any bus heading east on Church St and walk up through the gardens from Church St.

## MUSEUMS

In addition to museums covered here there are a few others, such as the **Correctional Services Museum** (☎ (012) 314 1766) and the hands-on **Science & Technology Museum**. See the Around Pretoria section later in this chapter for some museums a short way out of town, including the 'must-see' Voortrekker Monument.

The **National Museum of Culture**, on the corner of Visagie and Bosman Sts, focusses on the archaeological and anthropological records of Southern Africa. Special emphasis is given to the African tribes of Gauteng.

The Tourist Rendezvous has details of all these and other places.

### Kruger House

A short walk west from Church Square, at 60 Church St, the residence of Kruger has been turned into a museum. It's interesting but, partly because of its setting right on a busy street, it's curiously difficult to get a feeling for the man (unlike at Doornkloof, Smuts' house), despite the fact that he was undoubtedly an extraordinary human being.

There are clues. The house is unpretentious, although there would have been few grander homes in 1883 when it was built. Among all sorts of bric-a-brac there's the knife that Kruger used to amputate his thumb after a shooting accident (the thumb isn't on display!). Legend has it that he would sit on the front porch and chat with passers-by. The Dutch Reformed Church where he worshipped and preached is across the road.

The house is open from 8.30 am to 4 pm Monday to Saturday and from 11 am to 4 pm on Sunday; admission is R5.

### Melrose House

Melrose House, 275 Jacob Maré St, opposite Burgers Park, is a mansion that was built in 1886 for George Heys in a somewhat fanciful cross between English Victorian and Cape Dutch styles.

During the 1899-1902 Anglo-Boer War (sometimes known as the Second War of Independence) both Lords Roberts and Kitchener (British commanders) lived here. On 31 May 1902 the Peace of Vereeniging that ended the war was signed in the dining room. The house has been restored and has an excellent collection of period furniture, including the furniture that was used when the treaty was signed.

It's open from 10 am to 5 pm Tuesday to Saturday and from 2 to 5 pm on Sunday; entry is R4. Take the station bus outside the Standard Bank, Church Square. It goes down Kruger St, so get off at Jacob Maré St.

### Transvaal Museum of Natural History

This museum has traditional static displays

of animals and birds in glass exhibition cases. The most dramatic exhibit is the enormous skeleton of a whale found outside the building. The museum is on Kruger St between Visagie and Minnaar Sts (not all that far from Melrose House). It's open from 9 am to 5 pm Monday to Saturday and from 11 am to 5 pm on Sunday; entry is R4.

### Pretoria Art Museum
In the grounds of Arcadia Park, between Schoeman and Park Sts a kilometre or so east of the city, this museum (☎ (012) 344 1807) displays South African art from all periods of the country's history. It's open Tuesday to Saturday from 10 am and 5 pm (till 8 pm on Wednesday) and Sunday from 10 am to 6 pm; admission is R4.

### Police Museum
This museum has changed a little now that South Africa is no longer a 'police' state. In a way, it would have been a useful historical artefact if it remained as it was – a somewhat amateurish propaganda vehicle for the old SAP. It has dioramas of various crimes, murder weapons and blood-stained clothing – perhaps not the best place to bring children. The entrance is on Pretorius St, near Volkstem St, two minutes from Church Square. It's open from 8 am to 3.30 pm weekdays, 8.30 am to 12.30 pm Saturday and 1.30 to 4.30 pm Sunday; entry is free.

### NATIONAL ZOO
This zoological garden is impressive and a pleasant enough spot to while away an afternoon. There's a decent cafeteria and some lawn areas. The highlight is a cable car that runs up to the top of a *koppie* (rocky hill) overlooking the city. Entry is R12, plus the cable-car fare. It's open daily from 8 am to 5.30 pm (to 5 pm in winter).

### MARKETS
On Sunday a flea market is held in the Sunnypark shopping centre on Esselen St. There is also a Sunday flea market in Hatfield; stalls are open from 9 am to 4.30 pm. East out of town, on the N4 opposite the CSIR

complex, a *boeremark* (farmers' market) is the place to find fresh produce and old-style Boers, with traditional food and music. It's held on Saturday from 6 to 9 am.

There are interesting **craft stalls** along Boom St to the west of the zoo, with particularly good beadwork. You can bargain.

### ORGANISED TOURS
Many companies offer tours of Pretoria and the surrounding area, some running from Jo'burg. The Tourist Rendezvous Centre has information on most of the operators. Sakabula Safaris & Tours (☎ /fax (012) 98 1585) has informative half-day city tours for R110. The Expeditionary Force (☎ (012) 667 2833) conducts specialist history tours.

### FESTIVALS
The **Jacaranda Festival** is held annually during the third week of October, when the blooms are at their peak. There are flea markets, shows, concerts and food stalls. The immensely popular **Pretoria Show** is held during the third week of August at the showgrounds.

### PLACES TO STAY – BOTTOM END
### Caravan Parks & Hostels
*Fountains Valley Caravan Park* (☎ (012) 44 7131; fax 341 3960) is a good facility with plenty of sites, a pool, a restaurant and tennis courts; tent sites are R32 for two.

*Pretoria Backpackers* (☎ (012) 343 9754), 34 Bourke St, Sunnyside, is a short walk from Esselen St. It's a great travellers' place run by Françoise, a registered tour guide and Pretoria enthusiast. Dorm beds are R30 and doubles are R80; there is limited camping. Transfers to/from the airport (Jo'burg) are R42 with the hourly Pretoria Airport Shuttle (this is available to all Pretoria hostels and accommodation).

*Word of Mouth* (☎ (012) 341 9661), 145 Berea St, Muckleneuk, does everything within its power to lure backpackers away from evil Jo'burg. It advertises its 'safe' position (as opposed to 'jungle' Jo'burg) but doesn't add 'dull' re its location (Pretoria). No Jo'burg, no real glimpse of South Africa, in our view. Anyway, the WOM is OK and trying hard to make your stay in Pretoria as comfortable as possible; dorms (including one for snorers) are R30, singles/doubles are R60/90. They have an overflow, *WOM Too*, at 246 Preller St.

There are a few other places. *Bogger's Pozzie/Mzuri* (☎ (012) 343 7782), 503 Reitz St, also plugs the 'no go Jo'burg' ethic (poor misguided 'boggers'); it charges R30 in dorms. *Kia Ora* (☎ (012) 322 4803) at 257 Jacob Maré St ('on the way to the rest of Africa') must survive on its New Zealand greeting alone; dorms are R25, singles and doubles R75. *Fat Slags* (☎ (012) 341 1259) at 243 Mears St, Muckleneuk, offers free condoms. This is good value/insurance for a dorm price of R30.

### Hotels & Guesthouses

*Parkview Hotel* (☎ (012) 325 6787), on Leyds St opposite the Union Buildings' gardens, is spartan but friendly and very clean, with small rooms for R70/90. Each room has a shower but toilets are shared. If you're wearing sneakers the squeaking on the highly polished lino floors will drive you insane!

*Malvern House* (☎ (012) 341 7212), 575 Schoeman St, Arcadia, is a large guesthouse in a good position, within walking distance of the city and Sunnyside. It's spotlessly clean and comfortable but bathrooms are shared. Singles/doubles/triples are R80/110/120, including a good breakfast.

### PLACES TO STAY – MIDDLE

*That's It* (☎ (012) 344 3404), 5 Brecher St, near the corner of Farenden St, is a guesthouse in a leafy corner of Sunnyside, not too far from Esselen St. It's a pleasant suburban house with good-sized rooms and a big garden with a pool. Prices range from R85 to R105 for a single and R135 to R165 for a double, with breakfast. Farenden St runs into Park St, a main road out of Pretoria.

*La Maison* (☎ (012) 43 4003), 235 Hilda St, Hatfield, has three beautiful rooms upstairs in an old Pretoria house that is surrounded by a leafy garden (including a pool).

The owner is a cordon bleu chef and offers superb buffet breakfasts; dinner is R50. Singles/doubles are R185/230, with some smaller singles at R160.

*Lady Godiva Guest House* (☎ (012) 71 5729) at 16 Godiva St, Valhalla, gets in because of its name – but there's no 'Certificate X' (singles are from R100).

*Jane-Anne's Junction* (☎ (012) 83 3535), 175 Rubida St, Murrayfield, has singles/doubles from R120/200; and *Clydesdale Cottage* (☎ (012) 344 2988), 417 Kirkness St, Sunnyside, provides rates on application.

The Tourist Rendezvous Centre has a list of B&Bs and guesthouses. You can also contact the Bed 'n' Breakfast organisation (☎ (011) 482 2206/7; fax (011) 726 6915) based in Jo'burg; prices start around R100/170 a single/double. The Jacana accommodation agency (☎ (012) 346 3550; fax 346 2499) also has several places, from R150/240 for singles/doubles.

*Park Lodge Hotel* (☎ (012) 320 8230), on Jacob Maré St near the corner of Andries St, isn't great but the price is low; B&B costs R100/115. Rooms are small, uninspiring and some have shared toilets.

*Orange Court Lodge* (☎ (012) 326 6346), 7 Orange Court, 540 Vermeulen St, on the corner of Hamilton St, is an excellent option – comfortable, homely and well placed. It offers serviced apartments (with one, two or three bedrooms) in a historic building, with phone, TV, equipped kitchens and linen. There's a welter of rates, starting at R240 for doubles in a one-bedroom apartment, up to R350 for six people in a three-bedroom apartment.

The large *Hotel 224* (☎ (012) 44 2581; fax 44 3063), on the corner of Schoeman and Leyds Sts, Arcadia, is starting to fray at the edges and the rooms are small but it's still reasonable, and fair value with rooms starting around R140 a double.

There's a member of the basic but inexpensive *Formule 1* chain (☎ (012) 323 8331) at 81 Pretorius St. Rooms sleeping up to three people (in cramped circumstances) cost around R119; a paltry breakfast is R7 extra.

## PLACES TO STAY – TOP END

*Meintjieskop Guesthouse* (☎ (012) 43 3711), 145 Eastwood St, Arcadia, has guest rooms for R240/330 (less if you stay longer than three days) and also self-catering units.

*Victoria Hotel* (☎ (012) 323 6052), on the corner of Kruger and Scheiding Sts, is the oldest hotel building in Pretoria still used for its original purpose. It was built in 1896 and has a gracious Victorian atmosphere. It's associated with Rovos Rail (a company that operates a luxurious restored steam train). Suites range from R250 to R700, with breakfast included (it should be!).

The remaining top-end hotels are all large international-style places with all mod-cons. There's not much to separate them apart from position, and in this department *Holiday Inn Garden Court Pretoria* wins.

Other places, in alphabetical order, are: *Best Western Pretoria* (☎ (012) 341 3473) at 230 Hamilton St with rooms for R314/348, breakfast included; *Boulevard Protea Hotel* (☎ (012) 326 4806), 186 Struben St, with rooms from R300; *Holiday Inn Crowne Plaza* (☎ (012) 341 1571), Beatrix St, handy to the city and nightlife, from R510/630; *Holiday Inn Garden Court* (☎ (012) 322 7500), Van der Walt St, from R280/310; *Karos Manhattan Hotel* (☎ (012) 322 7635), on the corner of Van der Andries and Scheiding Sts, R260/325 midweek; and *Pretoria Hof Hotel* (☎ (012) 322 7570), corner of Pretorius and Van der Walt Sts, a solid old place, well located in the centre of town, with B&B from R280 a double.

## PLACES TO EAT

There are places in the centre but most people head to Arcadia/Sunnyside and Hatfield for meals. Below is just a selection; for more see the *Be My Guest* guide.

*Sammy's Coffee Bar*, in the Tourist Rendezvous Centre is licensed and sells snacks such as omelettes and burgers from R12 to R17. Also in the city centre, *Roberto's Italian* is on Schoeman St next to the Tramshed complex. Despite the upmarket decor and service, prices aren't bad and the food is good, although much richer than genuine

Italian dishes. Soup is R8, pasta around R18 and meat dishes around R27. They also have pizzas. *Buffet de l'Opera*, in Church St near the State Theatre, has a buffet for R40 or à la carte dishes for about R15.

*Pavarotti's* in Sammy Marks Square tries its hardest to feed clients as vast as its namesake. A huge, but relatively inexpensive dinner, best enjoyed before or after the theatre, is from R35; there is often live music, but not of the large tenor variety.

One of the most atmospheric possibilities is the old dining room at the *Victoria Hotel* (☎ (012) 323 6052), on the corner of Scheiding and Kruger Sts. Breakfast is R20 and an impressive set-lunch is R50.

### Arcadia & Sunnyside

Esselen St, Sunnyside, has numerous restaurants/takeaways – the following description is east to west. Near the corner of Bourke and Esselen Sts is *Fillings*, a trendy café selling snacks such as pancakes (from R3.50) and pap, 'wors and sous (sauce or gravy) for R12. They have a happy hour every night when local beers are R2.50 and use of the Cybercafé is R20 per hour. Across the road, *Il Bacio*, at No 286, is popular for its large pizzas (R16) and steaks (there's another *Il Bacio* in Burnett St, Hatfield).

Close to the corner of Celliers is *Am Miv*, a tiny Israeli takeaway where you get great felafels (R8), shawarma (R12) and roast chicken (R14). *La Madeleine* at No 258 is an expensive French place but the meals (R45) are well worth it; there is an extensive wine list. *Grapevine* offers an outdoor area with goof coffee and excellent cakes. On the corner of Troye there's a 24 hour *Bimbos* hamburger joint and on the other side of the street is *Shunters*, a 24 hour bar and grill. *Giovanni's*, upstairs at No 151, is fairly expensive. There's a large menu, with pasta for R20 and good salads for R12 (there's another branch in Hatfield).

At the western end of Esselen St, two places get the nod. *Santorini* at No 67 is for those craving traditional Greek food – a shared meal of dips, calamari, gyros and spicy sausages will cost about R22 a head.

Nearby is *Crawdaddy's*, a steakhouse with half-kilo rumps for R27, a kilo of lamb chops for R33 and salads; meals come with salad, chips or a baked potato. Its only drawback is the slow service.

On Jeppe St just south of Schoeman St, *La Fragola* is a lively place with music, where pizzas start from R15 and steaks from R22. The *Oeverzicht Art Village*, on Gerhard Moerdyk St, has a number of good restaurants, including the excellent *Le Temps des Fondues*; the complex is open daily from 9 am until late.

Arcadia, north of Sunnyside, also has plenty of eateries. The traditional South African *Gerhard Moerdyk* at 752 Park St has waterblommetjie (waterlily), bobotie (curried hash) and oxtails; a meal is around R35.

### Hatfield

There are many places to eat in Hatfield and it is safe to walk along Burnett St, the main drag, at night. A number of places are covered in the following entertainment section. *Bugatti's*, a bar/coffee shop, is great for breakfast (R10). *O'Hagan's*, on the corner of Duncan and South Sts, is open daily until late; Sunday lunch is R25. *Villa di' Amici*, 1065 Arcadia St, serves traditional Italian food and has a great wine list. There are a few places in The Yard complex, Duncan St – the *Boere Bar* has Moroccan food.

### ENTERTAINMENT

Upstairs in the Tramshed complex on the corner of Van der Walt and Schoeman Sts, *Crossroads Blues Bar*, a live-music venue, stays open late nightly and is usually crowded. *Steamers*, near the train station, is a gay-friendly club, as is *Incognito* in the Belgrave Hotel, 22 Railway St.

Several bars and nightspots in trendy Hatfield cater for all types. *Ed's Easy Diner* in the Hatfield Galleries has been recommended for drinking and dancing. *Sports Frog*, 1048 Burnett St, is the place to listen to the appreciative shouts of Afrikaners as they watch their cricket and rugby heroes on the big screen. Similar is *McGinty's*, an Irish pub; it is open daily from 11 am until late.

*Things & Themes* (known as T'n'T) is a laid-back place where reggae rules. Nearby, *Upstairs at Morgan's* is usually pumping out rock.

Sunnyside and Arcadia have their share of places. *Oscar's*, at 501 Beatrix St in Arcadia, is a late-night American diner which features live music; the nearby *Subway* is a rave club. On Esselen St, Sunnyside, *Café Galeria* is a buzzing live-music venue, open nightly. Opposite is the *Viper Room* (the entrance is through the Hollywood Café), a huge venue. Next to it is *Tequila Sunrise*, a laid-back venue which features reggae and impromptu jamming sessions.

The surrounding townships, especially Mamelodi and Atteridgeville, have plenty of shebeens, best visited with a black friend – *Maggie's Jazz Club*, *Mum's Sports Tavern* and *Sunny's* are recommended.

Quite a range of high culture (opera, music, ballet and theatre) is offered at the State Theatre complex (☎ (012) 322 1665) on the corner of Prinsloo and Church Sts. There are five theatres: the Arena, Studio, Opera, Drama and Momentum. Check local newspapers for listings. The Computicket office is in the Tramshed.

There are several enormous cinema complexes. The largest is Sterland, on the corner of Pretoria and Jeppe Sts, which has no fewer than 13 cinemas, an ice rink and possibly the most horrible fluorescent decor in Africa. There are a few cinemas around Esselen St, including Metro Cine 1, 2 & 3 on the corner of Esselen and Jeppe Sts.

### GETTING THERE & AWAY
#### Bus

Many interprovincial and international bus services commence in Pretoria before picking up in Jo'burg – see the introductory South Africa Getting There & Away chapter for details. Most buses leave from the Pretoria train station forecourt.

The best method of transport between Pretoria and Jo'burg is the train because almost all buses between the two cities are en route to other destinations and charge high prices for this short sector.

GAUTENG

Most Translux (☎ (012) 315 2111) and Greyhound (☎ (012) 328 4040) services running from Jo'burg to Durban, the south coast and Cape Town originate in Pretoria. See the Jo'burg Getting There & Away section earlier in this chapter for more information – add an hour to travel times. Translux and City to City/Transtate services running north up the N1 also stop here – see the earlier Jo'burg Getting There & Away section and deduct an hour from travel times.

Examples of Translux fares from Pretoria are: Beitbridge, R115; Bloemfontein, R155; Cape Town, R315; Durban, R140; East London, R225; Kimberley, R160; Knysna, R235; Louis Trichardt, R90; Pietersburg/Polokwane, R80; and Port Elizabeth, R245. Greyhound's fares are a little higher.

Intercape (☎ (012) 328 4599) leaves from the train station and has services to Upington (R175), connecting with a service to Cape Town (R150 from Upington). From Upington you can get to Windhoek, Namibia (R200), but there is no direct connection.

The Baz Bus (☎ (021) 439 2323) will pick up and drop off at Pretoria hostels (R30 to Jo'burg). Elwierda Buses (☎ (012) 664 5880) has a weekday service to Jo'burg, departing from the State Theatre, Prinsloo St, at 6.25 am; it returns from the Carlton Hotel, Jo'burg, at 4.45 pm (R45 return). North Link Tours (☎ (012) 323 0379) runs north to Pietersburg/Polokwane (R70).

### Train
The train station is about a 20 minute walk south of the city centre. Buses run along Kruger St to Church Square, the main local bus terminus.

A 1st class train ticket to Jo'burg on the Metro system is R12 (there's no 2nd class). The journey takes over one hour. From Monday to Friday trains run every half-hour early in the morning, then hourly until 10 pm. On weekends trains run about every 1½ hours. For exact times call Jo'burg (☎ (011) 773 5878) or Pretoria (☎ (012) 315 2007).

Taking a mainline (long-distance) train (☎ (012) 315 2401) on the Pretoria to Jo'burg section costs R32/23, 1st/2nd class.

Mainline trains running through Pretoria are the *Diamond Express* (Pretoria to Kimberley and Bloemfontein, daily except on Saturday); the *Komati* (Johannesburg to Komatipoort via Nelspruit, daily) and the three trains that run north via Pietersburg/Polokwane and Messina to Beitbridge at the Zimbabwe border – the *Limpopo* on Friday, the *Bulawayo* on Tuesday and the *Bosvelder* daily. First/2nd class fares from Pretoria are R14/10 less or more than from Jo'burg, depending on your direction of travel.

### Car
The larger local and international car rental companies are represented. You can make bookings at the Tourist Rendezvous. Local firms include Alisa (☎ (012) 324 4782), Pender (☎ (012) 46 8016) and, for the impecunious, Rent a Jalopy (☎ (012) 333 4374).

## GETTING AROUND
### To/From Jo'burg International Airport
Pretoria Airport Shuttle (☎ (012) 323 1222) operates between the airport and the Tourist Rendezvous. The journey takes a bit under an hour and costs R45.

### Bus
There is an extensive network of local buses. The main terminus and the inquiry office (☎ (012) 313 0839) are on the south-east corner of Church Square. A booklet of timetables and route maps is available from the inquiry office. Fares range from R2.50 to R5 depending on distance. Quite a few services, including the one to Sunnyside, run until about 10.30 pm – unusually late for South Africa. The standard fare for a minibus taxi around town is R2.50 to R3.

### Taxi
Taxis are relatively inexpensive – about R2 per kilometre. There are stands on the corner of Church and Van der Walt Sts and at Vermeulen and Andries Sts, or telephone Rixi Taxis (☎ (012) 325 8072/3).

GAUTENG

# Around Pretoria

## SMUTS' HOUSE MUSEUM

General JC Smuts was a brilliant scholar, Boer general, politician and international statesman. He was an architect of the Union of South Africa, and the prime minister from 1919 to 1924 and from 1939 to 1948.

His home, Doornkloof, has been turned into an excellent museum that is well worth visiting if you have private transport and are travelling to or from Pretoria. The building was originally a British officers' mess at Middelburg, but Smuts bought it and re-erected it on his 4000 acre property at Irene, 16km south of Pretoria. Surrounded by a wide veranda and shaded by trees, it still has a warm family atmosphere, and it gives a vivid insight into Smuts' amazing life. Some of his furniture is at Wits University, but much is original.

There's a small cafeteria with an outdoor tea garden, and an adjacent caravan park. The house (☎ (012) 667 1176) is open daily from 9.30 am to 1 pm and from 1.30 to 4.30 pm (until 5 pm on weekends); entry is R4,

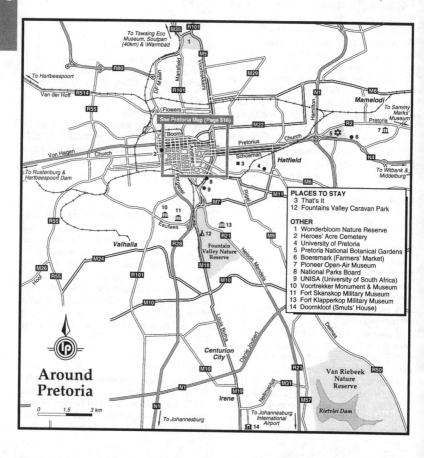

Around Pretoria

0    1.5    3 km

PLACES TO STAY
3  That's It
12  Fountains Valley Caravan Park

OTHER
1  Wonderbloom Nature Reserve
2  Heroes' Acre Cemetery
4  University of Pretoria
5  Pretoria National Botanical Gardens
6  Boeremark (Farmers' Market)
7  Pioneer Open-Air Museum
8  National Parks Board
9  UNISA (University of South Africa)
10  Voortrekker Monument & Museum
11  Fort Skanskop Military Museum
13  Fort Klapperkop Military Museum
14  Doornkloof (Smuts' House)

free to the garden. The pleasant, small caravan park on the property (☎ (012) 667 1176) has sites for R30. This would make a peaceful and economic alternative to staying in either Jo'burg or Pretoria.

Unfortunately, there is no access by public transport. The house is signposted from both the N1 freeway (R28) and the R21. The most direct route from Pretoria is along Louis Botha Ave to Irene, the nearest town.

## FORT KLAPPERKOP MUSEUM
One of four forts built after the Jameson Raid, Fort Klapperkop, on Johann Rissik Drive 6km south of the city, never fired a shot in anger, but it now illustrates South Africa's military history from 1852 to the end of the Anglo-Boer War. The museum is open every day from 10 am to 3.30 pm; entry is free.

## PIONEER OPEN-AIR MUSEUM
The open-air museum (☎ (012) 803 6086) is a reconstructed pioneer farmyard and restored thatched cottage. It gives a brief insight into the past. Unfortunately it's very difficult to get to without a car, as it's about 12km east of the city centre at Silverton, off Pretoria Rd (the R104). You could take the Silverton bus from Church St. It is open daily from 8.30 am to 4 pm and entry is R5.

## NATIONAL BOTANICAL GARDENS
The botanical gardens cover 77 hectares and are planted with indigenous flora from around the country. The 20,000 or so plant species are labelled and grouped according to their region of origin, so a visit is a must for keen botanists. The gardens are 11km east of the city centre and are open daily from 8 am to 5.30 pm; entrance is free weekdays, R2 on weekends.

By car, head east along Church St (the R104) for about 9km, then turn right into Cussonia Rd; the gardens are on the left-hand side. Or catch the Meyerspark or Murrayfield bus from Church Square.

## SAMMY MARKS' MUSEUM
This museum (☎ (012) 803 6158) is housed in one of the country's most splendid Victor-

ian mansions (which dates from 1884). Sammy was an English magnate, with his fingers in a lot of pies – industry, mining and agriculture. It is a good example of the sort of house you can build for yourself if you strike it rich (and of the expensive goodies you can fill it with). After visiting here, go north to historic **Cullinan**, where the huge 3106-carat diamond was found in 1905 and where there are some fine sandstone houses. The diamond was presented to King Edward VII by the Transvaal government, and cut into 105 gems weighing 1063 carats in total.

The poorer of us can see the mansion on weekdays from 9 am to 4 pm, weekends from 10 am to 4 pm (it is closed on Monday); entry is R5. To get there, take Church St (the R104) towards Bronkhorstspruit.

## TSWAING ECO MUSEUM
This museum (☎ (01214) 98 7302), in Soutpan, 40km north-west of Pretoria, is in a huge meteorite crater. A cross between a nature reserve and a museum, it's open daily from 9 am to 4 pm.

## VOORTREKKER MONUMENT
The enormous Voortrekker Monument was built in 1938 to commemorate the extraordinary achievements of the Boers who trekked north over the coastal mountains of the Cape into the heart of the African veld. In particular, it commemorates the Battle of Blood River, when, on 16 December 1838, 470 Boers under the command of Andries Pretorius defeated approximately 12,000 Zulus. Supposedly, three trekkers were wounded and 3000 Zulus were killed.

The trekkers went on to found independent republics that in many ways form the genesis of the modern South African state. In terms of drama, determination, courage, vision and tragedy their story surpasses the history of European colonists (or invaders if you like) anywhere else in the world. Some Afrikaners go one step further: the trek parallels the biblical Exodus and the Battle at Blood River was a miracle that can only be explained by divine intervention, proof that the trekkers were a chosen people.

GAUTENG

The Voortrekker Monument commemorates the achievements of the Boers in the Great Trek.

The monument was built at the time of a great resurgence of Afrikaner nationalism. The scars of their defeat in the Second War of Independence (the 1889-1902 Anglo-Boer War) were still fresh and the monument provided an emotional focal point for the Afrikaners' ongoing struggle. The inauguration of the building in 1949 was attended by 250,000 people. It remains a powerful symbol of the 'white tribe of Africa', and their historical relationship to South Africa.

The edifice is surrounded by a stone wall carved with 64 ox-wagons in a traditional defensive *laager* (circle). The building itself is a huge stone cube inspired by the ruins of Great Zimbabwe. Above the entrance is the head of a buffalo, which many believe to be the most unpredictable and dangerous of all African animals, especially when wounded. Inside, a detailed bas-relief tells the story of the trek and of the Battle of Blood River. On 16 December a shaft of light falls on the words *Ons vir jou, Suid Africa* (We for thee, South Africa). A staircase leads to the roof and a panoramic view of Pretoria and the highveld.

Below the car park is an excellent small museum that re-creates the lives of the trekkers. There is a reconstruction of a homestead, two wagons, photographs, clothing and, of course, weapons. The monument and the museum are open daily from 9 am to 4.45 pm. Entrance to the monument is R5/3 for adults/children and to the museum it's R5/2.50. There's also a restaurant that sells reasonable meals, and an open-air café.

### Getting There & Away

The monument, 6km south of the city, just to the west of the N1 freeway, is clearly signposted. It is possible to catch the Voortrekkerhoogte or Valhalla bus from Kruger St near the corner of Church Square. Ask the driver to let you off at the entrance road to the monument, from where it is a 10 minute walk uphill.

# Free State

The landlocked Free State consists largely of the plains of the Southern African plateau. To the east is highland with weirdly eroded sandstone hills.

The Free State's borders reflect the prominent role it has played in South African history. To the south is the Orange River, which the Voortrekkers crossed to escape from Cape Colony. The northern border is defined by the Vaal River, which was the next frontier of Boer expansion – see the Facts about the Region chapter. To the east, across the Caledon River, is Lesotho, where mountains and King Moshoeshoe I halted the tide of Boer expansion. To the south-east, however, the Free State spills across the Caledon as the mountains dwindle to grazing land, harder for Moshoeshoe to defend.

There are important gold mines in and around Welkom and diamonds are also mined in the Free State. The western half of the province is bare, rolling grazing country, while the hillier east is a major grain-growing region. It is a wealthy province and while there are fewer attractions in the Free State than in other provinces, many of the quiet *dorps* (towns) and prosperous burgs have a Rip van Winkle air, where dreams of an Afrikaner Arcadia linger.

## HIGHLIGHTS

- Golden Gate Highlands National Park – best place to view the region's colourful sandstone formations
- Dignified Bloemfontein – capital of an early Boer republic
- Small, conservative towns – a taste of pre-democratic South Africa
- QwaQwa Conservation Area – excellent hiking opportunities

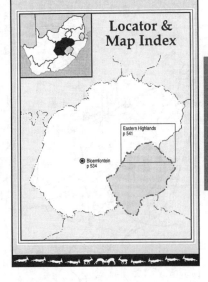

## Northern Free State & Goldfields

Gold was discovered in the Free State in April 1938 and a rush started immediately. Now the Free State goldfields produce more than a third of the country's output. The extraction of gold is centred on three towns – Welkom, Virginia and Odendaalsrus.

Much of the region is given over to intensive farming, mainly maize. The largest town between Jo'burg and Bloemfontein is Kroonstad. The other towns are sleepy, pleasant places and if a farm holiday is your bag you have come to the right place. If the quiet of this part of the Free State gets to you, it's only two hours north to Johannesburg!

### WINBURG

It's difficult to imagine that this sleepy little town, founded in 1842, was the first capital of a Boer republic in today's Free State. It's a forceful reminder of just how the Boer republics really began at a grass roots level. It was in the dining room of Ford's Hotel that

527

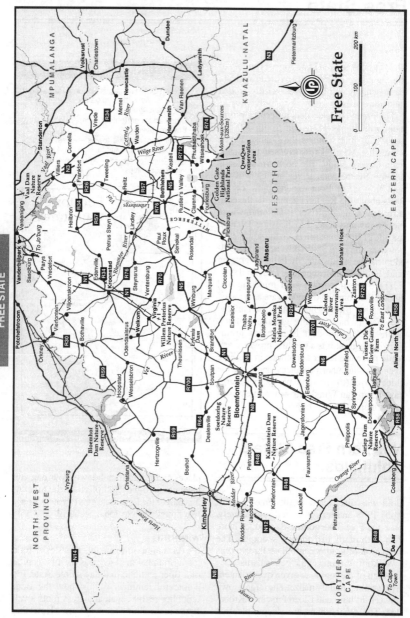

# Free State

the leaders of five Voortrekker groups finally agreed to form a government under the leadership of Piet Retief.

Information is available at the library, in the town square.

The **church** on the town square was used as a hospital and school during the Anglo-Boer War. There are some old photos of the town here. The **Voortrekker Monument**, about 3km from town, is composed of five columns symbolising the five trek parties (those of Louis Trichardt, Hendrik Potgieter, Gert Maritz, Piet Retief and Pieter Uys) who created the republic. You may well have been wondering why just about every town in the Free State has variations of these as street names! Nearby there's a small **museum** and the small dwelling in which a later president, MT Steyn, was born.

### Places to Stay & Eat

The basic and cheap *municipal caravan park* is near the creek at the end of Edward St, not far from the post office. The historic Ford's Hotel, with its wrought-iron sign on the roof, has closed, but the old-style *Winburg Hotel* (☎ (051) 881 0160) is still operating and is good value at R75 per person. It's a simple place with some character. The dining room here is the only place to eat, apart from crummy takeaways.

### Getting There & Away

City to City/Transtate buses between Welkom and Thaba 'Nchu, Welkom and Maseru (Lesotho), and Welkom and Ficksburg stop here.

There are minibus taxis running to the goldfields area and some heading towards Bloemfontein, but not many. Ask at the petrol station on the north edge of town.

If you want to hitch, walk down Victoria St (it begins at the square with the post office on the corner) to the T-junction. Turn left for the 5km walk to the N1, which takes you past the Voortrekker Monument, or right if you want to cut through the small black township and save yourself a few kilometres.

## AROUND WINBURG
### Willem Pretorius Game Reserve

This game reserve is on the Allemanskraal Dam, off the N1 about 20km north of Winburg and 70km south of Kroonstad. The Aventura resort has a conference centre, golf course and bowling greens, but there are also animals including giraffes, white rhinos, buffaloes and various antelopes. Fishing is popular (get a Free State angling licence from the resort) and there are hiking trails. Entry costs R15 per car.

Aventura's *Aldam Resort* (☎ (05777) 4077; fax 4078) has a range of accommodation, including camping (from R71 for a site), two-bed chalets (from R65) and four-bed units (from R160). Prices rise steeply in high season.

### KROONSTAD

Kroonstad, on the N1, is a typical large rural town in the Free State. It dates back to 1855 and the Voortrekker Sarel Celliers was one of the first settlers. The town may have been named after his horse, Kroon.

The best place to get information is from the efficiently run Central Free State Publicity Association (☎ /fax (0562) 22601) in the old town hall on Cross St.

If you want a taxi, phone ☎ (0562) 22704 or (0562) 33424 after hours.

### Things to See & Do

The **Old Market Building**, opposite the pretty **Magistrate's Building** on the corner of Mark and Murray Sts, is a national monument. Upstairs in the library there's the small **Sarel Celliers Museum**, open weekdays (closing for lunch) and on the second and fourth Saturday morning of each month.

You can see the **Celliers statue** in the grounds of the impressive NG Moederkerk (Mother Church) on Cross St. Celliers is standing on a gun carriage making the Blood River vow. His farm, **Doornkloof**, is 45km out of town and can be visited by appointment – ask at the Publicity Association.

**Kroon Park** offers swimming and other water activities. Day visitors are charged R10.

FREE STATE

The national tournament of **Jukskei** (an Afrikaner game in which clubs are tossed at a peg) is held annually in Kroonstad.

The 4000 hectare **Koppies Dam Nature Reserve**, north-east of Kroonstad, is on the Rhenoster River. There's wildlife and waterbirds, but fishing is the main pursuit; the reserve is open from 7 am to 9 pm daily.

### Places to Stay & Eat

*Kroon Park* (☎ (0562) 31942) is more like a resort than a municipal park, with a couple of swimming pools and good facilities. It's across the river and further south down Cross St (which becomes Louw St). There are sites from R15 plus R12 per person, apartments from R160 for two people and chalets from R135. This is the best accommodation in town and it can be booked out.

There are a couple of cheap hotels, *Hotel Emillo* (☎ (0562) 23271) on Louw St and *Hotel Zeederberg* (☎ (0562) 51674) on Market St, and the more expensive but very run-down *Toristo Protea* (☎ (0562) 25111) on the corner of Du Toit and Rautenbach Sts. None are appealing – you're better off staying at Kroon Park or asking the Publicity Association for its list of holiday farms and B&Bs in the area.

*Angelo's Trattoria* on Reitz St is good for Italian food, *Sleepers* is a steakhouse with quite a few beers on tap, and there's a *Spur* on Buitekant St.

### Getting There & Away

**Bus** The City to City/Transtate service between Welkom and Jo'burg stops at the train station.

Three Translux services (between Jo'burg/ Pretoria and East London, Port Elizabeth and Knysna) stop out on the highway at the Shell Ultra City, as does Greyhound's Jo'burg/Pretoria-Port Elizabeth service.

**Train** The *Amatola* (Jo'burg-East London) and *Algoa* (Jo'burg-Port Elizabeth) trains stop here.

**Minibus Taxi** Across from the train station is the minibus taxi park. Most taxis go only to relatively nearby towns, although there are occasional services to Jo'burg – get there early in the morning.

## WELKOM

About 30% of South Africa's gold is mined in the Free State and this modern town is at the centre of the goldfields. It's something of a showpiece, as it was completely planned – there are no *robots* (traffic lights), a fact which is touted as proof of a masterpiece of town planning. However, this just means that it's sprawling, soulless and hell to get around if you don't have transport. The whites number 65,000 but there are over 300,000 blacks living in town or working on the mines. There's some black wealth here and some of the suburbs are a little more integrated than usual. There's white wealth, too, with the highest per capita income in the country.

### Orientation & Information

The 'publicity tower' (☎ (057) 352 9244, 352 9501) is in the clocktower at the civic centre on Stateway, the main street. Rennies Travel (☎ (057) 353 3041), the Thomas Cook agent, is at Shop 11, Sanlam Plaza (also known as Checkers, after the plaza's supermarket), also on Stateway.

Not far away from Stateway is Mooi St, which encloses most of the central shopping area in its horseshoe curve. The First National Bank is on Elizabeth St, the Standard Bank is on Tulbagh St and the main post office is on Bok St.

There's a taxi rank on Mooi St, near the south-west corner of Central Park, or phone ☎ (057) 55945 or 396 1429.

### Things to See & Do

Approximately once a month you can tour one of the dozen or so mines and see gold being poured (free). Contact the tourist office for more information. If no tours are on offer here, you could try phoning ☎ (057) 212 3111 to see if there are any in nearby Virginia.

The area's huge mine evaporation pans are home to a wide variety of **bird life**, including the greater flamingo *(Phoenicopterus ruber)* and the lesser flamingo *(Phoenicopterus minor)* and the greyheaded gull *(Larus cirrocephalus)*. More than 200 species of birds have been seen around the city – 90% of all waterfowl species found in South Africa. Try Flamingo Pan off the R30 just west of the town, or Witpan at Oppenheimer Park, about 4km south-east of the town centre on the continuation of Stateway. Two other bird-watching spots are Theronia and Flamingo lakes.

### Places to Stay

The pleasant and central *municipal caravan park*, between the Welkom Inn and the swimming pool, may have reopened. About 2km from the town centre is *Sirkel Caravan Park* (☎ (057) 53987) at 281 Koppie Alleen Rd in the Reitz Park area, north of the centre, with sites for R25.

*Hotel 147* (☎ (057) 352 5381), on Stateway, is reasonable and has singles/doubles for about R90/150. The three-star *Welkom Hotel* (☎ (057) 51411), 283 Koppie Alleen Rd, charges R195/228. The more modern *Welkom Inn* (☎ (057) 357 3361; fax 352 1458) is also three-star rated and is on Stateway at the corner of Tempest Rd, a few blocks east of the centre, and has rooms from R196/228.

### Places to Eat

*Giovanni's Pizzaghetti* at 15 Mooi St has pasta and pizza from R20 and also steak and seafood. There are plenty of steakhouses, such as *Al's Grill* and *The Blues Grill* on Van Bruggen St, *Indiana Spur* in the Volksblad Building and *JJ's* at the Liberty Centre. A solid meal will cost from R35 at these places. For a bit more variety try *Mike's Kitchen* in Sanlam Plaza.

### Getting There & Away

**Train** Passenger trains don't stop here; Virginia is the nearest town with a passenger service.

**Bus** Being a mining town, Welkom is a major depot for City to City/Transtate, with

a few services to Jo'burg/Pretoria and more south to QwaQwa, Lesotho and Transkei.

Several Translux services stop on Buiten St on the way to destinations including Bloemfontein (R95), Cape Town (R300), Jo'burg (R145) and Knysna (R230). Greyhound buses stop at the Orange Hotel on Stateway. Book either line at Rennies Travel in Sanlam Plaza.

**Minibus Taxi** The taxis in the supermarket car park in town are mainly for the local area, but you might find long-distance taxis here in the early morning. You can usually get a ride out to the main minibus taxi park on the outskirts of town.

## VIRGINIA

This well planned mining town, about 20km south-east of Welkom, is on the banks of the Sand River. The library (☎ (057) 212 3111), in the picturesque Virginia Gardens, has tourist information.

There are **mine tours** to the Harmony Gold Mining Company and Western Holdings. A **hiking trail** runs along the banks of the Sand River and there is a **bird sanctuary** at Virginia Park. Bird-watching is fruitful in this town, as there is a variety of habitats attracting different species.

### Places to Stay

*Virginia Park Resort* (☎ (057) 212 3306), west of town on the banks of the Sand River, has a comfortable hotel and a fenced-off area for caravans. Three hotels in town charge about R130 per person for bed and breakfast.

## CANNA CIRCLE

This region takes its name from the annual cultivation of masses of colourful cannas. These are in bloom from the end of December to April, and each of the towns within the circle cultivates a different colour.

If you are travelling between Jo'burg and the Free State's Eastern Highlands it is easy to deviate to several of these pleasant towns. Reitz is at the junction of the R57 and R26, Frankfort is on the R26 and R34, Heilbron is

FREE STATE

## Free State Battlefields

The most significant of the Voortrekker battle-fields is **Vegkop**, south of Heilbron, the scene of a bloody battle between Hendrik Potgieter and the Ndebele army of Mzilikazi in 1836. When confronted by the Ndebele, who employed Zulu-style fighting meth-ods, about 50 Voortrekkers formed their wagons into a laager and held off the attackers.

There are at least 20 major battlefields and sites from the Anglo-Boer War in and around Free State. **Kimberley**, actually in the Northern Cape but just across the Free State border, was besieged for 126 days from 14 October 1899 until 15 February 1900. Not far across the border, at **Paardeberg** in Free State, General Cronj's Boers surrendered in February 1900 after being besieged by Lord Roberts' force.

There were a number of battles around Bloemfontein and the most significant site is **Sannapos**, east towards Thaba 'Nchu, where Free Staters inflicted heavy losses on the Brit-ish on 31 March 1900. Bloemfontein had been captured by the British on 13 March 1900 and the Boers were withdrawing eastwards; two other significant battles took place at this time – Mostertshoek on 4 April, and Jamm-erberg Drift, five days later.

In May 1900 the battles raged near the Sand River, which flows through the Goldfields region. During a battle at **Biddulphsberg**, between Winburg and Bethlehem, the veld caught fire and many British soldiers died in the flames. At **Surrender Hill**, near Fouriesburg, on 31 July 1900 a major Boer force led by General Prinsloo surrendered to the British.

Conventional warfare ended in mid 1900 and the Boers resorted to guerrilla tactics for the next two years. Commandos operated all over the country and, in many places, barbed-wire fences were erected to prevent the free movement of the Boers. Concentration camps were set up. Many Boer memorials remain from this 'dirty' phase of the war. The war ended with the Peace of Vereeniging in May 1902. ∎

on the R57 and R34, and Vrede is on the R34 about 20km east of the N3.

Frankfort, Heilbron, Lindley, Villiers, Reitz and Vrede all have *caravan parks*. There are hotels in most of the towns. The *Frankfort Hotel* (☎ (0588) 31080), at 55A Brand St, charges about R140/170 per person, bed and breakfast.

# Bloemfontein

Bloemfontein is the provincial capital and South Africa's judicial capital. It occupies an important place in the country's history. Bloemfontein means 'Fountain of Flowers'; the Tswana name for the area is Mangaung, 'Place of Cheetahs'.

At first sight it seems to be just another sprawling, modernised town, but there are a few places worth seeing and pockets of impressive buildings. As well as the legal community there's a university and a large military camp, so you can meet a wide range of people. Most of the blacks are still forced by economic realities to live in the enclaves they were shunted into during the apartheid days. Botshabelo, on the Thaba 'Nchu road, is one of the largest 'locations' in the country.

The city straddles the Bloem stream, which now resembles a drain rather than a stream as it was lined with stone after the disastrous 1904 flood. It is spanned by a series of pretty little sandstone bridges.

JRR Tolkien, author of *Lord of the Rings*, was born here in 1892. He moved to England when he was four but his memory of the Bloemfontein district as '...hot, dry and barren' might well have influenced his creation of Mordor. We saw some graffiti in a Cape Town pub claiming that JRR was 'just another Bloemfontein boy on acid'.

## HISTORY

Bloemfontein wasn't the first Boer capital in the lands across the Orange River. The Voortrekkers established their first settlement near modern-day Thaba 'Nchu, and various embryonic republics, as well as a period of British sovereignty after the Anglo-Boer War, came and went. In 1854 the Orange Free State was created, with Bloemfontein as the capital. Bloemfontein was named after a farm built in 1840 by Johannes Brits. By 1854 it was only a small village, but it had its own parliament, presiding over the republic's 12,000 scattered white citizens.

In 1863 Johannes Brand began his 25 year

term as president, and it was during this time that Bloemfontein grew from a struggling frontier town, in constant danger of being wiped out by Moshoeshoe's warriors, to a wealthy little capital city with railway links to the coast and many public buildings.

## ORIENTATION & INFORMATION

As usual there are endless sprawling suburbs, but the central area is laid out on a grid and it is easy to find your way around. Hoffman Square is the centre of the downtown area. Not far to the north-east is Naval Hill, where there are good views of the town and surrounding plains.

The friendly information centre (☎ (051) 405 8489) is on Park Ave, not far from the stadium. The Free State Tourism Board (☎ (051) 447 1363) is at Shop 9, Sanlam Parkade, Charles St. The local bus information office (☎ (051) 405 8135) is in the town centre on Hoffman Square. The GPO is on Groenendal St across from Hoffman Square and there's a coin laundry on 1st Ave (Eerstelaan) just north of Zastron Rd.

La Scala Internet Café is at 4A Ella St, not far from the information centre.

## MUSEUMS
### National Museum

The National Museum, on the corner of Charles and Aliwal Sts, is open daily from 8 am to 5 pm (1 to 6 pm on Sunday); entry is R3. The most interesting display is a great re-creation of a 19th century street.

### Queens Fort

Now restored as a military museum, Queens Fort was built in 1848 during the Orange Free State-Basutho Wars. The fort, on Church St south of the stream near the corner of Goddard St, is open on weekends and Monday from 8 am to 4 pm; entrance is free.

### Military Museum of the Boer Republics

This museum, devoted to the Anglo-Boer Wars, has some interesting displays and a great deal of trivia, a sign of how deeply the war still affects the national psyche.

It is open from 9 am to 4.30 pm on week-

> ## Concentration Camps
> During the 1899-1902 Anglo-Boer War the British invented the concentration camp in response to harassment by guerrilla bands which were helped by – and included – Afrikaner farmers. The British response was to burn the farms of suspected combatants and ship the women and children to concentration camps. In the first years of the 20th century, before the invention of most medicines and vaccines and without modern engineering, any large-scale incarceration of people was bound to be disastrous.
>
> By the end of the war 200,000 Afrikaner women and children were prisoners. More than 26,000 of them, mostly children, had died, accounting for about 70% of Afrikaner deaths in the war. There were also concentration camps for blacks and of the 80,000 people interned it is estimated that 14,000 died.
>
> For Afrikaners, the image of a man returning from his defeated kommando to find his farm destroyed and his children dead remains a powerful one. The loss of political independence and the destruction of family, home and farm left little but the Bible, deep bitterness and a determination to survive against any odds. ∎

days, 9 am to 5 pm on Saturday and 2 to 5 pm on Sunday; admission is R2. The museum is south of the centre, on Monument Rd. From Hoffman Square, bus Nos 14 and 16 run to near the museum.

### National Women's Monument

The monument, which is outside the military museum, commemorates the 26,000 Afrikaner women and children who died in British concentration camps during the 1899-1902 Anglo-Boer War. Emily Hobhouse, the British 'turncoat' hero who alerted the world to this infamy, is buried here.

### Freshford House Museum

To get an idea of how Bloemfontein burghers lived at the turn of the century, visit this house at 31 Kellner St. It's open from 10 am to 1 pm on weekdays, 2 to 5 pm on weekends; entry is R3.

FREE STATE

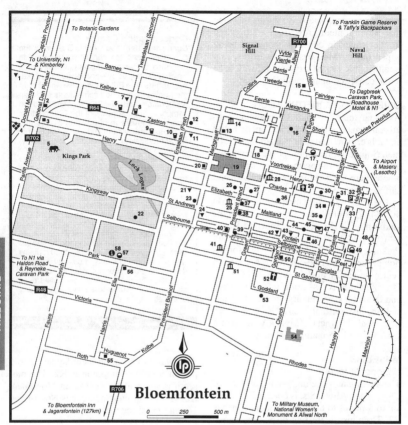

Bloemfontein

FREE STATE

## National Afrikaans Literature Museum
This museum is in the Old Government Building on President Brand St across from Maitland St. It houses an Afrikaans research centre and has displays on Afrikaans literature. It is open from 8 am to 12.15 pm and 1 pm to 4 pm on weekdays, 9 am to noon Saturday; entry is free.

## Old Presidency
On President Brand St, just north of the corner of St Georges St, is this grand Victorian-style building. Orange Free State presidents once lived in these spacious chambers, in what must have seemed extraordinary opulence to the rural citizens. The museum is open from 10 am to noon and 1 to 4 pm Tuesday to Friday, and from 1 to 5 pm on weekends; admission is free. Behind the Old Presidency is a collection of old agricultural machinery.

## Hertzog House
This humble house on Goddard St was the home of JBM Hertzog, prime minister of South Africa 1924-1939 and a prominent figure in the Anglo-Boer War. It's open Tuesday to Friday from 9 am to 4 pm and entry is free.

**PLACES TO STAY**
2   Holiday Inn Garden
    Court; Hard Rock
    Café
3   City Lodge
13  Christopher's Hotel
15  Hotel President
18  Stanville the Inn
20  Hotel Halevy House
34  Bloemfontein Hotel
46  Cecil Hotel
50  Boulevard Hotel
55  Roberta Guesthouse
56  Stadium Inn

**PLACES TO EAT**
1   Mimosa Mall &
    Barba's Café
7   Characters & Braai
    Burger
11  Schillaci's Trattoria
21  Revolving Restaurant
24  John Malcolms
33  Mary's Kitchen
42  The Mexican
    Restaurant

43  Silvano's

**OTHER**
4   Cottage Square
5   Zoo
6   O'Hagan's
8   McGinty's
9   Sportsmans Pub
10  Kegg & Goose
12  Coin Laundry
14  Freshford House
    Museum
16  Rambler's Cricket
    Ground
17  Translux Bus
    Stop
19  City Hall
22  Stadium
23  Sand du Plessis
    Theatre
25  Old Government
    Building & National
    Afrikaans
    Literature Museum
26  Appeal Court
27  Fourth Raadsal

28  National Museum
29  Twin-Towered
    Church
30  Satour Office
31  Old Market
32  Car Parking
35  Sanlam Parkade
36  Rennies Travel
37  Waldorf Building
38  Jubileum Building &
    Hall
39  Supreme Court
40  Fire Station
41  Old Presidency
44  Hoffman Square
45  Bus Information
47  Post Office
48  Train Station
49  Minibus Taxis
51  First Raadsal
52  Anglican Cathedral
53  Hertzog House
54  Queens Fort
57  Bus Stop
58  Information
    Centre

FREE STATE

## INTERESTING BUILDINGS
### President Brand St

The best selection of interesting buildings is along President Brand St, where aromatic cypress trees improve the air. These solid buildings demonstrate how comfortable and self-assured burgher life once was – as well as emphasising the hideousness of modern South African architecture.

If you head south down President Brand St from Voortrekker St, the **City Hall** (1934), with its reflecting pool, is on the right. On the next block, on the same side of the road, is the **Appellate Court** (1929) in understated neoclassical style. The carvings and panelling inside are worth a look. On the left, opposite the court, is the **Fourth Raadsaal** (1893), which was the parliament house of the Free State republic, where almost light-hearted Renaissance-style architecture blends well with down-to-earth red brick.

On the corner of Elizabeth St is the **Waldorf Building** (1928), not all that impressive until you remember how few buildings of this vintage survive in South African cities. Opposite is the **Old Government Building** (1908), which now houses the National Afri-

kaans Literary Museum. Diagonally opposite, on the block between Maitland and St Andrew, are the **Jubileum Building & Hall**. The building, despite its authoritarian façade, was designed as a coffee house and meeting place for young people. The pompous and menacing hall was once the headquarters for the Free State's Dutch Reformed Church.

Further down, on the corner of Fontein St, are the **Fire Station** (1933) and the imposing **Supreme Court** (1906).

### First Raadsaal

On St Georges St, just east of President Brand St, is the oldest building in town and the original parliament house, still with its thatched roof and dung floors. Visiting hours are from 10.15 am to 3 pm on weekdays, 2 to 5 pm on weekends; entry is R1.

### Old Market

The old market, on the corner of Charles and East Burger Sts, is a fanciful building now housing a shopping complex.

**FREE STATE**

### Sand du Plessis Theatre
A modern building of interest is the Sand du Plessis Theatre (1985). There are artworks on display and there are tours of the complex on Thursday at 2.30 pm; entry is R3. The theatre is on the corner of Markgraaff and Andrews Sts. The local paper lists music, ballet, drama and opera performances.

### NAVAL HILL
This hill, dominating the town to the northeast, was the site of the British naval gun emplacements during the Anglo-Boer War. On the east side of the hill is a large white horse, a landmark for the returning British cavalry during the Anglo-Boer War; it was laid out by a regiment homesick for its similar but prehistoric horse in Wiltshire.

There are good views from the hill, and on the hilltop is the **Franklin Game Reserve**, where you may see antelopes. You can walk in the reserve, although one traveller reports being chased by a wildebeest! Naval Hill and the reserve are open from 8 am to 5 pm; entrance is free.

On Union Ave, north of where the road up the hill turns off, is the **Orchid House** with a large collection of flowers. It's open from 10 am to 4 pm on weekdays, 10 am to 5 pm on weekends; entry is free.

### BLOEMFONTEIN ZOO
There is an extensive collection of primates, among many other animals. And yes there is a 'liger', a cross between a lion and a tiger, here. The entrance to the zoo (☎ (051) 405 8911) is on Henry St. In summer it is open from 8 am to 6 pm, and in winter 8 am to 5 pm; admission is R10 for adults, R4 for children.

### BOTANICAL GARDENS
The 45 hectare Free State National Botanical Gardens are on Rayton Rd, about 10km north of the city centre. The gardens protect some natural vegetation – open woodland, Karoo species and grassland. They are open daily from 8 am to 6 pm; entry costs R5.

### PLACES TO STAY
The information centre can give you an excellent accommodation list. Bloemfontein hosts important cricket and rugby games, and accommodation can be scarce on match weekends.

### Caravan Parks
More than walking distance from the centre on Andries Pretorius St, *Dagbreek Caravan Park* (☎ (051) 33 2490) has tent sites for R30 and rooms in old railway coaches at R35/65 for singles/doubles. Two km out on the Petrusburg Rd is the new *Reyneke Park* (☎ (051) 23888) with caravan sites (for up to five people) for R50 and chalets for R200. Neither place is convenient if you don't have a vehicle.

### Hostels
*Taffy's Backpackers* (☎ (051) 31 4533), 18 Louis Botha St, Waverley, is in a private home (it describes itself as 'a B&B for overseas travellers') and has dorms for R30, singles/doubles for R55/80, and you can camp in the well-maintained garden for R15. Breakfast costs from R7. It's pleasant, clean and friendly but not for party animals.

### B&Bs/Guesthouses
B&Bs and guesthouses are the best option. The information centre has an up-to-date list and makes bookings.

*The Lions' Den* (☎ (082) 416 0571, or (051) 436 6561 after hours), 6 Captain Dawson St, is a fully equipped two bedroom flat costing just R75/140 for a single/double. Phone for directions. For something a little different, *The Deanery* (☎ (051) 447 3649; fax 448 3078), 1A Saltzmann St, *is* the Deanery of the Anglican Cathedral next door, and you are the B&B guest of the Dean of Bloemfontein. Single/double rooms cost around R115/140.

*Roberta Guesthouse* (☎ (051) 448 4601), 14 Roth Ave, Willows, has singles/doubles for R110/130. One of the nicest guesthouses is the excellent *Hobbit House* (☎ (051) 447 0663), 19 President Steyn Ave, Westdene. The rates are around R150 per person.

## Hotels

*Stadium Inn* (☎ (051) 47 4747) on Park Ave, Willows, opposite the Stadium swimming pool, is good value. There are 30 or so flats at R95/120 for singles/doubles, plus R20 for each additional person. The run-down *Boulevard Hotel* (☎ (051) 447 7236; fax 30 6217) on the corner of Gordon and Douglas Sts charges R125 for a room. On Zastron Rd, near the corner of Aliwal St, *Stanville the Inn* (☎ (051) 447 7471) is reasonable at R100/110; rooms facing the street are noisy.

There are a number of mid-range hotels close to the city centre, although some are becoming run down. Try the *Cecil Hotel* (☎ (051) 48 1155; fax 30 8323), on St Andrew's St opposite Hoffman Square. It's a big old-style hotel charging R150 for a room and is still in reasonable shape.

More expensive places include the pleasant *Hotel President* (☎ (051) 430 1111), at 1 Union Ave, with rooms from R250; the older *Bloemfontein Hotel* (☎ (051) 430 1911), in Sanlam Plaza on East Burger St, with singles/doubles from R310/340; *City Lodge* (☎ (051) 447 9888), on the corner of Henry St and General Dan Pienaar Ave, with singles/doubles for R199/220; and the new *Holiday Inn Garden Court Bloemfontein* (☎ (051) 447 0310), on the corner of Melville and Zastron Rds, with rooms from R244.

## PLACES TO EAT

Steak lovers have the usual wide choice for their R35, including *Camelot Carvery*, 149 Voortrekker St; *Steers*, 200 Zastron Rd; and the *Beef Baron* (perhaps the best of them all), 2nd Ave, Westdene.

*Schillaci's Trattoria* on Zastron Rd is a good and very popular Italian restaurant with some shady outdoor tables. Main courses start at R25 and there are mid-week specials, such as all the pizza you can eat for R20. On the corner of Kellner St and Tweedelaan is *Characters*, a fairly lively but expensive Italian restaurant with a pleasant bar. Not far away in the Mimosa Mall on Kellner St is *Barba's Café*, recommended by locals.

*Distrik Six Café*, upstairs at the western end of the arcade that runs off West Burger St into Sanlam Plaza, is a slightly surprising place to find in Bloem. It's run by a genial Cape Towner (who remains very much a Cape man, despite years in the Free State) who serves interesting, Asian-influenced dishes. You can eat and drink well for about R50.

On top of the tall CR Swart Building on Elizabeth St is the *Revolving Restaurant*, which revolves (it used to be called the Carousel – maybe the name wasn't sufficiently obvious) and has meals from around R50. Behind the Old Presidency on President Brand St is *Die Stalle* café, pleasant enough if you find it open.

## ENTERTAINMENT

Downstairs from Characters (but you have to go upstairs to the restaurant level to get in) is *Braai Burger*, a bar and restaurant popular with all types; it's a fairly clean-cut, middle-of-the-road place. If you're looking for something a bit grungier, try *Hotel Christophers*, which has music in the bar some nights.

'Haven't I seen your face before?' – this line gets worn out at *Deja Vu* in Voortrekker St, a club near the *Kegg & Goose*, another favoured watering hole. On the same side of Voortrekker St but a little further west is *Sportsman's Pub*.

To meet students, go to the *Tavern* at Brandwag or to *Barry's Bar* at the university; usually live entertainment is provided at the latter. Another place the scholarly set 'existentialise' in is the *Hard Rock Café*, just off Donald Murray St, and part of the Holiday Inn.

## GETTING THERE & AWAY

### Air

Bloemfontein airport (it used to be called the JBM Hertzog airport) is 10km from the city centre and there is no airport transport (except taxis).

SAA connects Bloemfontein with Cape Town, Durban, George, Kimberley, Port Elizabeth, Upington and Jo'burg. SA Airlink flies to Jo'burg and Port Elizabeth.

**Minibus Taxi**

Most minibus taxis leave from opposite the train station. A taxi to Kimberley costs R25, to Maseru (Lesotho) it's R20.

**Bus**

The City to City/Transtate bus from Welkom to Thaba 'Nchu passes through Bloemfontein. There is also a Welkom-Umtata service.

Translux (☎ (051) 408 2262) runs to Cape Town (R265), Durban (R150), East London (R180), Knysna (R210), Jo'burg/Pretoria (R150) and Port Elizabeth (R180). Buses leave from 164 Zastron St.

Greyhound (☎ (051) 430 2361) has services to Durban, Pretoria, Cape Town, Port Elizabeth, Kimberley and Upington. Buses leave from the information centre on Park Ave.

Intercape Mainliner (☎ (021) 386 4400, 24 hours, or book at a travel agent) stops at the Shell Ultra City out on the freeway and runs to Cape Town (R220) and Jo'burg (R140).

Local buses to Thaba 'Nchu town leave a long way from the centre, on the main road to Thaba 'Nchu just before the corner of Mimosa St.

**Train**

For information phone ☎ (051) 408 2946; for bookings, ☎ (051) 408 2941. The *Trans Oranje* (Durban-Cape Town), the *Amatola* (Jo'burg-East London) and the *Algoa* (Jo'burg-Port Elizabeth) stop here. There is also the *Diamond Express* (Bloemfontein-Pretoria via Kimberley).

**Car Rental**

Companies include Avis (☎ (051) 33 2331) and Budget (☎ (051) 33 1178).

**Hitching**

Coming from the N1, get dropped off at the Zastron Rd exit, although it's quite a walk into the centre (there are infrequent buses once you get to the university); or at the Haldon Rd exit, which is further from the centre but better served by public transport (but not at night). Bus No 9 runs near here from Hoffman Square.

**GETTING AROUND**

There's a public bus system although services stop early in the evening. At off-peak times (8.30 am to 12.55 pm and 2.10 to 3.45 pm) there's a flat fare of R0.90; at other times the fare varies with distance, up to R2.10. All buses run through Hoffman Square, and the bus information office (☎ (051) 405 8135) has timetables. To get to Franklin Game Reserve on Naval Hill take bus No 2 to Union Ave and walk from there.

For taxis, try Vrystaat Taxis (☎ (051) 30 6354) or Bloem Taxis (☎ (051) 33 3776).

**AROUND BLOEMFONTEIN**
**Soetdoring Nature Reserve**

On the Modder River, Soetdoring (☎ (051) 33 1011) is about 35km north-west of Bloemfontein on the R700. The dam is home to waterbirds and martial eagles, and secretary birds breed in the reserve. Power boats are banned here so it's quieter than some of the other Free State dams, but there's no accommodation and you can't camp.

**Thaba 'Nchu**

Thaba 'Nchu (pronounced ta-*baan*-chu) is a small Tswana town east of Bloemfontein. The surrounding area was once a small piece of the scattered Bophuthatswana Homeland, and this too was known as Thaba 'Nchu. As with most Homeland territories, a Sun casino was built here.

There's an information office on the main street, at the other end of town from the supermarkets. There are a few historical buildings in town and a church designed by the priest-cum-artist Father Claerhout. Look out for the Aran jerseys handcrafted in town.

**Maria Moroka National Park** This beautiful park centres on a natural amphitheatre formed by Thaba 'Nchu (Black Mountain) and includes the Groothoek Dam. It has a large variety of wildlife such as zebras, elands, blesboks, springboks and red hartebeests.

There are two relatively short hiking trails. The **Volstruis Hiking Trail** takes about one to two hours to walk; it passes through a wooded ravine and winds by an old kraal and the Groothoek Dam. The **Eland Hiking Trail** takes about four to five hours. It too passes through the ravine and by the kraal, but the stiff climb up to a viewpoint adds to its difficulty.

**Places to Stay & Eat** In town, the *Thaba 'Nchu Hotel* (☎ (051871) 51514) is basic but clean with singles/doubles at R65/120 with attached bathroom, R50/90 with shared bathroom. Coming from the main turn-off to Bloemfontein, continue up the main street, turn left onto Market Square and follow the road around to the right. For food, try the *Morocco Restaurant*.

The *Naledi Sun* (☎ (051) 33 1505) is quite pricey at R278/380. It's a friendly place with a good restaurant, bar and 'slots'. You are likely to meet talkative blacks and whites in the bar, eagerly discussing the merits of the 'new' South Africa.

The five-star *Thaba 'Nchu Sun* (☎ (051) 33 1505), about 10km from Thaba 'Nchu, costs R347/440 during the week, R401/515 on weekends. The casino is here.

**Getting There & Away** City to City/Transtate has a service to Thaba 'Nchu which leaves Welkom at 7 am, arriving in town at noon; it passes through Bloemfontein at about 9.30 am. There are minibuses between Bloemfontein and Thaba 'Nchu (about R6) and to Ladybrand (R14). A minibus from Thaba 'Nchu town to the casino costs R5 but it's simpler to take the free shuttle which operates between the Naledi and Thaba 'Nchu Sun hotels. Tours to the casino run from Bloemfontein.

# Southern Free State

The southern Free State typifies much of the province – it is dusty, harsh and dry and the many windmills make it reminiscent of the Australian Outback. Much of the marginal land is cultivated and grazed, but there are a few fairly interesting reserves.

## FAURESMITH

Fauresmith is famous for the railway line which runs along the main street. North of town on the Petrusburg road is the 4500 hectare **Kalkfontein Dam Nature Reserve**, a great place to see the local black population harvesting yellowfish.

## TUSSEN DIE RIVIERE GAME FARM

This 23,000 hectare reserve (☎ (051762) 2803) has more animals than any other in the Free State, mostly various antelope species and small mammals but also white rhinos and hippos. The country is varied, with plains and ridges and a long frontage on the Orange River. Between May and the end of August the reserve is closed for the annual cull. For keen hikers there are the 7km Middelpunt, the 12km Klipstapel and the 16km Orange River hiking trails; water must be carried on all of them.

There are tent sites and inexpensive chalets but no food is available. The entrance gate is on the road between Bethulie and Smithfield (R701), about 15km from Bethulie or 65km east of the N1

## STOKSTERT HIKING TRAIL

This 22km overnight trail is in the Caledon River Conservancy Area, around Smithfield. This huge area (300,000 hectares) is on the land of over 60 farmers who have adopted conservation-minded techniques. The area has a wide range of flora and fauna and is of historic interest – the occupation of land west of the Caledon River by Boer farmers lead to the Basutho Wars in the 19th century, which resulted in the present-day borders of Lesotho. French missionaries established missions in the area and you can see the remains of some of the buildings.

To book hikes contact The Secretary, Caledon River Conservancy Area (☎ (05562) 2014), PO Box 71, Smithfield 9966.

FREE STATE

## GARIEP DAM NATURE RESERVE

West of Tussen Die Riviere, on the Orange River, this reserve surrounds one of the largest dams in South Africa (which used to be called the Hendrik Verwoerd Dam). Be warned, the dam is described in brochures as 'a mecca for motorboats'. In the flat, arid Karoo grassland, several animal species, including Cape mountain zebra, can be seen.

On the west side of the reserve, off the N1 south of the town of Donkerpoort, Aventura's *Midwaters Resort* (☎ (052172), ask for 45; fax (052172), ask for 135) is expensive. Camping costs R78 (R90 in high season), two-bed chalets cost R220 (R350), four-bed chalets are R210/340 and six-bed units are R230 (R390).

## PHILIPPOLIS

On the R717, Philippolis is a beautiful little place; it's the oldest town in the Free State, founded in 1823 as a mission station. The Griquas who settled here in 1826 sold the town and then trekked overland, through Lesotho, to settle in Griqualand East (see Kokstad in the KwaZulu-Natal chapter). There are a number of interesting buildings, including the NG Kerk, the library, an old jail and many places built in the Karoo style.

# Eastern Highlands

This is the most beautiful part of the Free State, stretching from Zastron in the south to Harrismith in the north. Roughly, it is the area which fringes the R26 and the R49 east of Bethlehem to Harrismith. In addition to being a tremendously scenic area, it is also archaeologically and historically important. It includes the quaint towns of Clarens, Ficksburg and Bethlehem, the 'alternative' enclave of Rustler's Valley and the walker's paradise of QwaQwa. The drives alone, past sandstone monoliths which tower above rolling fields, are reason enough to visit.

## ZASTRON

Zastron, on the R726, is a quiet little town under the foothills of the Aasvoëlberg and Maluti mountains. It's the centre of a rural community and, with Lesotho forming an arc around this section of the Free State, Zastron has long-established trading links with the kingdom. The nearest town in Lesotho is Mohale's Hoek, 55km away on a dirt road.

There are some **San paintings** in the area; the best are in the Seekoei and Hoffman caves. There are also various walks and climbs. The **Eye of Zastron**, a mildly interesting rock formation with a 9m hole, is best seen from the road to Aliwal North.

### Places to Stay

The *caravan park* (☎ (051) 673 1397) is a few kilometres out of town; tent sites are R28. It's a nice walk down a wooded gorge. In town, the three-star *Maluti Hotel* (☎ (051) 673 1657) is a rather pleasant place with singles/doubles for R145/210.

### Getting There & Away

The City to City/Transtate Jo'burg to Lady Grey service passes through. There are also the daily Queenstown to Jo'burg and Welkom to Sterkspruit services. Minibus taxis are few and most run only to small nearby towns.

## WEPENER & HOBHOUSE

Both these small towns are on the R26. Wepener, a 'nice' little town at the base of the Jammerberg, has some good examples of sandstone architecture. South of town is the Welbedacht Dam on the Caledon River. There is a small game reserve here and hiking trails are being set up. Wepener is near the Van Rooyen's Gate border post into Lesotho.

Hobhouse is popular with anglers; you will see them on the banks of the Leeu, at Armenia Dam and at DonDon on the Caledon. For information call *Koos Taljaard Caravan Park* (☎ (05662), ask for 13). There are tent and caravan sites.

## LADYBRAND

Ladybrand, on the R26, is the closest South African town to the main border crossing

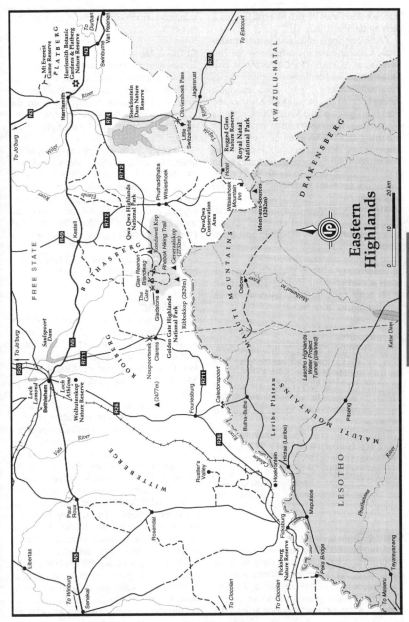

FREE STATE

Eastern Highlands

into Lesotho. From here to Maseru, the Lesotho capital, it is 16km.

There are some nice **sandstone buildings**, including the town hall and the Old Magistrate's Court. The **Catharina Brand Museum** has archaeological displays, including rock paintings, instruments and tools dating back to the Stone Age. Also housed here is a replica of the fossil *Diathrognatus protozoan* which was found in a quarry near the town; this is important as it provides a glimmer of a link between reptile and mammal in the evolutionary process. Ashes taken from an ancient hearth in the **Rose Cottage Cave**, not far from Ladybrand, are 50,000 years old.

About 12km from Ladybrand you can visit one of the quaintest churches you are ever likely to see. The **Modderpoort Cave Church**, built in 1869, is nestled under a huge boulder in scenic surroundings.

The overnight **Steve Visser Hiking Trail** starts at the Leliehoek Holiday Resort; book at the town hall (☎ (05191) 40654), which also has tourist information.

### Places to Stay

*Leliehoek Holiday Resort* (☎ (05191) 40260), 2km south of the town hall, has camping sites for R35 and chalets from R70. Ladybrand's one hotel is *Country Lodge* (☎ (05191) 3209), 23 Joubert St, which charges R135/169 a for single/double rooms for bed and breakfast.

There are several B&Bs, including the good *My Housy* (☎ (05191) 2777), 17A Prinsloo St (from R135/250), and *Cranberry Cottage* (☎ (05191) 2290), 37 Beeton St (from R158/280). Cranberry Cottage also has rooms in the nearby recycled train station.

### Getting There & Away

The minibus taxi fare to Bloemfontein is about R22. A basic bus runs daily between Bethlehem (R25) and Bloemfontein (R20) via Maseru (R4) – it comes through Ladybrand mid-morning but needs to be flagged down. Ask for more information around the minibus taxi ranks near the church on Piet Retief St.

## CLOCOLAN

Established in 1906, this is a small but important junction town on the R26, as the R708 goes north from here to Winburg and Senekal. The name is derived from the seSotho word *hlohlolane*, which means 'ridge of the battle', after the heights above town.

There are a number of places to stay in and around Clocolan. *Ikebana Mountain Resort* (☎ (05652) 1702), about 10km south-west on the Tandjiesberg road, has chalets scattered on the slopes of Klein-Suikerkop. Horses, ponies and guides are available for the many trails. *Clocolan Caravan Park* (☎ (051) 943 0516) has tent sites for about R20.

The City to City/Transtate Welkom-Ficksburg service (Monday to Saturday) stops in Clocolan.

## FICKSBURG

This town is in sandstone country and there are some fine buildings built from the stone, including the town hall, the NG Kerk and the post office. Tourist information is available from the Highlands Tourism office (☎ (05192) 5447/8), across the square from the town hall.

The **museum** has displays on local history, including that of the Basotho people.

The mild summers and cold winters of this area (the Maluti mountains across the river in Lesotho often have snow) are good for growing stone fruits, and Ficksburg is the centre of the Free State's cherry industry. There's a Cherry Festival in November. September and October are the best time to see the trees in bloom. The **Cherry Trail** is a tourist route around the district. There are several orchards to visit, various art and craft shops, some guest farms and hiking trails.

There are quite a few **hiking trails** in the area, mostly on private property, so you need to book and usually pay a small fee. Highlands Tourism has details. Another outfit has put together a variety of day walks and overnight hikes of easy and moderate difficulty in conservation areas on private property in the area. Most have accommodation (from barns to caves) and you can camp. For details phone ☎ (012) 346 3550; fax 346 2499.

### Places to Stay & Eat
*Thom Park* (☎ (05192) 2122), the municipal caravan park, is on Voortrekker St. You can camp at *Meulspruit Dam*, 5km from town on the R26 to Clocolan; contact the town hall (☎ (05192) 2122).

The *Hoogland Hotel* (☎ (05192) 2214), on Market Square near Voortrekker St, has singles/doubles for R130/194 on weekends, a little more during the week. The dining room in the hotel has a reasonable à la carte menu (from R25). *Bella Rosa Guest House* (☎ (05192) 2623), 21 Bloem St, charges R135/230 for rooms, including breakfast; the meals are superb. There is a *Pizza Parlour* on Piet Retief St.

## RUSTLER'S VALLEY
This remote valley, in the heart of the conservative Free State, is in the vanguard of the 'dare to be different' in the new South Africa. Rustler's attracts a diverse crowd – yuppies from Jo'burg, remnant hippies from all parts of the continent and 'ideas' people from all over the globe.

At the end of the valley is a hidden canyon where stolen cattle were concealed until they could be smuggled away for sale, hence the name.

You can swim in the pool, wander into the valley, swim or fish in the many dams, walk up onto sandstone escarpments, climb imposing Nyakalesoba (Witchdoctor's Eye), ride into the labyrinthine *dongas* (gullies) on a placid horse or discuss existential philosophy in the bar with the semi-permanent residents of Rustler's.

The Easter music festival here is a highlight of the year for alternative South Africans – although lately there has been a cultural split between the ravers and the rest, and the 'peace and love' has been somewhat disturbed.

Rustler's (☎ /fax (05192) 3939) has a variety of accommodation, including rooms for R100/140 a single/double and a cottage for R150. There is backpackers' space for R30 per person and camping is encouraged (R10 per person). There's also a restaurant, predominantly vegetarian.

### Getting There & Away
The main turn-off is about 25km south of Fouriesburg on the R26 to Ficksburg. Head west on a dirt road which crosses a railway line. From the turn-off it is about 12km to Rustler's. When you reach a prominent crossroads where there are numerous signposts, take the sharp turn to the right (the road to Nebo is behind). A few kilometres on there is another junction; Rustler's is to the right. You can also reach Rustler's from the south.

You can get to Ficksburg by taking a minibus taxi from Jo'burg to Bethlehem. At Bethlehem change buses for Ficksburg and call Rustler's to see if they can pick you up (there will be a small fee).

## FOURIESBURG
This is another town on the scenic R26, only 10km from the Caledonspoort border post into Lesotho and 50km from the Golden Gate Highlands National Park. It is surrounded by mountains, the Witteberge to the west and the Malutis to the east. Two nearby peaks, Snijmanshoek and Visierskerf, are the highest in the Free State.

During the Anglo-Boer War, the town was proclaimed capital of the Free State when the Boer government moved from Bloemfontein and the British occupied Bethlehem.

There are a number of fine old sandstone buildings in the town, including President Steyn's house. The oldest dwelling, Tuishuis, is still occupied.

### Brandwater Hiking Trail
The Brandwater offers a 72km, five day circular walk from the Meiringskloof Caravan Park, some 3km from Fouriesburg, through varied sandstone country with good views of the Rooiberg, Maluti and Witteberge ranges. Three of the overnight stops

are in caves and a fourth night is spent in an old sandstone farm building. Most of the walk, the longest in the Free State, is over private land and there's a fee of R50 per person. Book on ☎ (058) 223 0050. If the Brandwater is too long for you, ask about overnight hikes in the same area, such as the Dikitla and the Ventersberg.

### Places to Stay

*Meiringskloof Caravan Park* (☎ (058) 233 0067), 3km from town, has tent sites for R15 plus R5 per person. There are also chalets from R110 for two. The *Fouriesburg Hotel* (☎ (058) 223 0207), part of the original Fourie farm, has singles/doubles for R115/ 180, with breakfast.

There are a number of B&B places, including *Carolina Lodge* (☎ (058) 223 0552), off the Butha-Buthe road, from R165 per person for full board, or R144 with shared bathroom, and *Wynford Holiday Farm* (☎ (058) 223 0274), a cosy little place with comfortable rooms from R124 to R195 per person for full board.

### CLARENS

This pretty little town on the R711, a back road between Bethlehem and Fouriesburg, is well worth a detour from the main drag (the R711 is prettiest between Fouriesburg and Clarens). The town is surrounded by large limestone rocks, including **Titanic Rock**, and the magnificent Malutis are in the background.

Artists have set up studios in and around Clarens. Perhaps the only detraction from this otherwise picturesque town is Cinderella's Castle, constructed from more than 50,000 beer bottles. Kids will love it, however. (Of course, there's also the usual detraction of the compact but desperately poor 'location' on the edge of town.)

### Places to Stay & Eat

There is plenty of accommodation in and around Clarens. *Bokpoort Holiday Farm & Game Ranch* (☎ (058) 256 1181) is back-packer-friendly and is in a great location between Clarens and Golden Gate. You can

camp for R10, there is a dorm (R25) and B&B costs R75/150 a single/double. There is horse-riding and you can hire mountain bikes. To get here, travel 5km from Clarens on the Golden Gate road, then turn off at the big Bokpoort Holiday Farm sign and travel another 3km along the dirt road.

*Maluti Mountain Lodge* (☎ (058) 256 1422), on Steil St in Clarens, is a proper 'pub'; rooms start at R186.50/299 per person, with breakfast. There is a great little restaurant in this hotel serving home-style meals. *Berg Cottage* (☎ (058) 256 1112; fax 256 1406) is north on the road which runs on the east side of President Square. Ask the owners about another B&B place, *Strawberry Fayre*.

*The Street Café*, on the main street, is a good place for a snack or a meal, and the pub next door has live music on weekends.

### GOLDEN GATE HIGHLANDS NATIONAL PARK

Golden Gate preserves the unique and spectacular scenery of the foothills of the Maluti mountains, specifically the beautifully coloured sandstone cliffs and outcrops. The western approach to the park is guarded by immense sandstone cliffs which turn a glowing golden colour in the late afternoon, hence the name. There are also quite a few animal species, including the grey rhebok, blesbok, eland, oribi, Burchell's zebra, jackal and baboon.

Winters can be very cold here, with frost and snow; summers are mild but most rain falls at this time and cold snaps are possible – if you're out walking take warm clothing.

### Rhebok Hiking Trail

The circular 33km Rhebok Hiking Trail is a great way to see the park, although we've had reports that it is no longer reliably marked and could use some maintenance. The trail takes its name from the grey rhebok, a species of antelope which prefers exposed mountain plateaus, and you will probably see them when walking. The trail starts at the Glen Reenen Rest Camp, and on the second day the track climbs up to a viewpoint on the

## Bird-watching in Golden Gate

The bird-watching opportunities in Golden Gate Highlands National Park are particularly good; more than 140 species have been identified. You may see species such as the rare bearded vulture (lammergeyer), black eagle, jackal buzzard, southern bald ibis, the endemic orange-throated longclaw *(Macronyx capensis)*, the grass-bird *(Sphenoaceus afer)* and the ground woodpecker *(Geocolaptus olivaceus)*. Langtoon Dam is a good place to see waterbirds. Look out for the African black duck *(Anas sparsa)*, grey heron *(Ardea cineria)*, Egyptian goose *(Alopochen aegyptiacus)* and the very odd-looking hamerkop *(Scopus umbretta)*. ■

Boasting a wingspan of up to 2.8m, the lammergeyer is a ferocious sight.

side of Generaalskop (2732m), the highest point in the park, from where Mont-aux-Sources and the Malutis can be seen. The return trail to Glen Reenen passes Langtoon Dam.

There are some steep sections so hikers should be reasonably fit. The trail is limited to 18 people and must be booked through the National Parks Board or by phoning ☎ (058) 256 1471; fax 256 1471. There's a fee of R30 per person.

### Places to Stay

At *Brandwag Camp*, where there's a restaurant, rooms cost from R135/190 for a single/double, and a four bed self-catering chalet with TV is R220 for two people. You can't camp at Brandwag.

At *Glen Reenen* three-bed rondavels start at R120 for two people, and there's a house (from R220). A camp site costs R40 for two people. Book accommodation through the National Parks Board.

### Getting There & Away

The R711 is a sealed road into the park from Clarens, between Bethlehem and Fouriesburg. Alternatively, midway between Bethlehem and Harrismith on the N5, head

south on the R712 and after a few kilometres turn west on a dirt road, or continue south on the R712 and head west about 7km before Phuthaditjhaba.

## QWAQWA AREA

QwaQwa (master the 'click' pronunciation and you'll win friends and influence people) was once a small and extremely poor Homeland east of the Golden Gate Highlands National Park. The name QwaQwa means 'Whiter than White', after the sandstone hill which dominates the area.

QwaQwa was created in the early 80s as a Homeland for southern Sotho (Sotho ba Borwa) people. The dumping of 200,000 people on a tiny patch of agriculturally unviable land, remote from employment centres, was one of the more obscene acts of apartheid. Today, this area is one of the best spots to visit in the Free State, now that the 'free' part of that appellation has been realised.

### Orientation & Information

Phuthaditjhaba, adjacent to the town of Witsieshoek and about 50km south of Harrismith, was the 'capital' of QwaQwa. Here there's a tourist information centre (☎ (058) 713 4444; fax 713 4342) and some

FREE STATE

craft shops. Pick up the free QwaQwa tourist pamphlet, which details hiking trails.

## Places to Stay & Eat

There is a mid-sized modern hotel, the *QwaQwa* (☎ (058) 713 0903), in Phuthaditjhaba. The clean rooms are carpeted and have phones, TVs and radios; bed and breakfast is about R95/115 a single/double. More basic rooms are available.

About 25km south of Phuthaditjhaba is *Witsieshoek Mountain Inn* (☎ (058) 713 6361), reputedly South Africa's highest hotel. It charges from R185/300 for dinner, bed and breakfast, less out of season. *Fika Patso Mountain Resort* (☎ (058) 713 3656), near the dam of the same name, has chalets for R105 per person self-catering or R195 per person with dinner, bed and breakfast.

In Phuthaditjhaba, the *Golden Restaurant* on Kestell Rd has takeaways as well as a fully licensed section and *Matshidiso* is recommended for 'African-style' meals.

## QwaQwa Highlands National Park

This newly proclaimed park adjoins the eastern side of Golden Gate and shares the scenery. Here you'll find the small but interesting **Basutho Cultural Village**, open daily. A tour (the only way to see it) costs R15. There's a curio shop and tearoom which is pleasant and cheap – boerewors, pap and spinach costs R12. Try the home-made ginger beer.

## QwaQwa Conservation Area

The conservation area covers 30,000 hectares in the foothills of both the Maluti mountains and the Drakensberg. The usual warnings about sudden changes of temperature in the mountains apply, with storms and mists in summer and snow in winter.

There are some animals and rare birds, such as the Cape vulture, but the main reason to visit is for the great hiking trails. Even if you don't want to hike, it's well worth making the drive up to the Sentinel car park along an amazing road following the twisting ridge-tops. There's an R3 toll.

## Hiking Trails

There are three good hiking trails in QwaQwa. The most famous is the 10km **Sentinel Hiking Trail**, which commences in the Free State and ends in KwaZulu-Natal. The trail starts at the Sentinel car park at an altitude of 2540m and runs for 4km to the top of the Drakensberg Plateau, where the average height is 3000m; it's about a two hour ascent for those of medium fitness. At one point you have to use a chain ladder. Those who find the ladder frightening can take the route up The Gully, which emerges at Beacon Buttress. The reward for the steep ascent is majestic mountain scenery and the opportunity to climb Mont-aux-Sources. See also the Royal Natal National Park section in the KwaZulu-Natal chapter.

The two day **Metsi Matsho Hiking Trail** begins at the Witsieshoek Mountain Inn at 2200m above sea level. From the hotel it follows the provincial border to Cold Ridge. It then drops, almost in a due northerly direction, to Metsi Matsho (Swartwater) Dam, where there is an overnight hut. Beginning with beautiful views of the mountains, the walk also passes sandstone formations, caves, slopes of protea and, finally, the dam, where fishing is possible.

Book both hiking trails at least two weeks in advance through the tourist office in Phuthaditjhaba.

The **Fika Patso Hiking Trail** begins at the resort on the Fika Patso Dam. It is intended that this trail connect with the Metsi Matsho trail. It will leave the Fika Patso Dam at its far eastern side and join the Metsi Matsho trail near the Witsieshoek Mountain Inn. Book this hike through the Fika Patso Mountain Resort (☎ (058) 713 3656; fax (058) 713 2253), which might insist that you stay there before allowing you to use the trail.

## Getting There & Away

City to City/Transtate has a Welkom-Phuthaditjhaba via Bethlehem service.

If you're driving into Phuthaditjhaba from the north you'll eventually get through the urban sprawl to the tourist information centre, a cluster of roofs on the left shaped like Mt Paul. If you're heading for the Witsieshoek Mountain Inn or the Sentinel, turn left at the robots at the information centre and keep going. If you don't turn left and keep going into the commercial centre, you'll need to turn left at the last set of robots – trouble is, you won't know that they're the last until you've gone past. If you get to a Stop sign not at an intersection but outside a paramilitary establishment then you've gone too far.

## BETHLEHEM

This is one of the more pleasant towns in the Free State. Voortrekkers came to this area in the 1840s and Bethlehem was established on the farm Pretoriuskloof in 1864. Devout Voortrekkers gave the name Jordaan to the river which flows through town. It's now a large town and the main centre of the eastern Free State.

The tourist office (☎ (058) 303 5732; fax 303 5076) is in the civic centre on Muller St, near the corner of Roux St. A good art market is held on the Moederkerkplein on the last Saturday of the month. There are no taxis in Bethlehem, which means some long walks. It can *rain* here, too.

### Things to See & Do

As usual for this area there are some impressive sandstone buildings, including the **Old Magistrate's Office** on the corner of Louw and Van der Merwe Sts and the **NG Moederkerk** in the centre of town. Right in town is the tiny **Pretoriuskloof Nature Reserve**, on the banks of the Jordaan near the corner of Kerk and Kort Sts.

The easy, two day **Wolhuterskop Hiking Trail** covers a 23km loop through the Wolhuterskop Nature Reserve, beginning at the Loch Athlone Holiday Village. There is a hut on the trail, 18km out, where you can stay overnight, and there is also a camp site; a fee of R23.50 per person is charged. From the hut it is only a 5km return to the resort. There is also a horse trail here; the 1½ hour ride costs R30. The overnight 36km **Houtkop Hiking Trail** also begins at Loch Athlone.

Book either walk at the Loch Athlone resort or phone ☎ (012) 346 3550; fax 346 2499.

### Places to Stay

*Loch Athlone Holiday Resort* (☎ (058) 303 5732) is about 3km from the town centre and charges R40 for a site plus R6 per person. There are chalets from R130/160 per person, more on weekends.

The *Park Hotel* (☎ (058) 303 5191), 23 Muller St, on the corner of High St, has singles/doubles in the old section for R125/175, with breakfast; rooms in the newer three-star part cost R192/242. The *Royal Hotel* (☎ (058) 303 5448), at 9 Boshoff St, is reasonable value at R135/175 for singles/doubles, including breakfast.

There are also some good B&Bs in the area. *Fisant Guest House* (☎ (058) 303 7144), 10 Thoi Oosthuyse St (R135/210) and *Hoogland Guest House* (☎ (058) 303 3633), 47 De Leeuw St (from R135/200). The information centre has a full list, including some cheaper places.

### Places to Eat

The *Long Kong* Chinese restaurant on Louw St is open until 11.30 pm; set menus cost from R20. At *Mike's Kitchen* in the Park Hotel a meal costs from R30. *Nix Pub* on Kerk St, across from the church, is a cosy place for a drink and next door is the *Wooden Shoe* restaurant. *Athlone Castle*, at the Loch Athlone resort, is shaped like the mail ship of the same name and is full of memorabilia.

### Getting There & Away

Several City to City/Transtate services pass through Bethlehem, including Welkom to Lusikisiki in Eastern Cape via Kokstad, and Welkom to Phuthaditjhaba. Translux runs to Durban (R120) and Cape town (R310), as does Greyhound at similar fares. Both lines stop at the Wimpy on Church/Kerk St.

From the bus station (on the corner of Cambridge and Gholf Sts, north of the centre on the way to the train station) there's a slow local bus running daily to Bloemfontein via Maseru.

The weekly *Trans Oranje* (Cape Town to

FREE STATE

Durban) train stops here. The station is north of the centre; head up Commissioner St.

## HARRISMITH

Harrismith is a quiet rural centre, well sited as a base for exploring the northern Drakensberg and QwaQwa.

The friendly little information centre (☎ (05861) 23525) is at the back of the old brick town hall. It's open on weekdays and Saturday morning.

The extensive **botanic gardens**, about 5km south of town at the foot of the Platberg, has many species from the Drakensberg. There's an information centre and a British blockhouse from the Anglo-Boer War. The garden is open daily from 7 am (7.30 in winter) to 4.45 pm and admission is R5 if there's anyone there to collect it. Next door, the **Platberg Nature Reserve** has quite a lot of game animals, including wildebeest and ostrich.

### Mt Everest Game Reserve

This 1000 hectare private reserve (☎ (05861) 30235) is 21km north-east of Harrismith, off the Verkykerskop road. The variety of animals (22 species at last count) includes rhinos. With horse-riding (R15 per hour) and hiking available, you might get close to the animals.

Camping costs from R20 per person (R30 in the high season), budget beds in an old stone farmhouse cost R28 (R48), rondavels for two cost R195 (R250 in high season) and there are more expensive chalets.

### Sterkfontein Dam Nature Reserve

This is a small reserve in the Drakensberg foothills, 23km south of Harrismith on the Olivershoek Pass road into KwaZulu-Natal. It is a very beautiful area and looking out

over this expansive dam with rugged peaks as a backdrop is like gazing across an inland sea. There's a **vulture restaurant** at one of the viewpoints, but there's no set day or time for feeding. There is a *caravan park* (☎ (05861) 23520) with rondavels.

### Places to Stay

*President Brand Caravan Park* (☎ (05861) 21061) is on Cloete St along the banks of the Wilge River. Tent sites cost R22. Facing the train station, turn left, and after about 300m turn right under the railway overpass and keep going for about 1km.

The old-style *Grand National Hotel* (☎ (05861) 21060), on the corner of Warden and Boshoff Sts, has rooms for R79/143, and doubles with a shared bathroom for R118. It's a family-run, backpacker-friendly place. There's also the *Harrismith Inn* (☎ (05861) 21011) and the *Sir Harry Motel* (☎ (05861) 22151), both on McKechnie St.

### Getting There & Away

Harrismith is on some useful City to City/ Transtate routes running between Jo'burg/ Pretoria or Welkom and Nongoma, Umtata and Maseru (Lesotho).

Translux runs to Durban (R90), Bloemfontein (R135) and Cape Town (R310), stopping to pick-up at the Sir Harry Motel on McKechnie St.

Maluti Bus Service (☎ (058) 71 30045/9) runs many routes in this area, but the ticket office at the modern bus and minibus taxi station (further along from the train station) sells only five-day passes. Perhaps you can come to a private arrangement with a driver.

The Trans Oranje (Durban-Cape Town) train stops here.

# North-West Province

The North-West is a region of wide, hot plains. It was once covered entirely in bushveld and thorn trees, but is now an important agricultural region. The dominant crop is maize (better known as *mielies*), but sunflowers, tobacco, cotton and groundnuts (peanuts) are also grown, and cattle are important. Diamonds were discovered in the 1870s and there was an enormous rush to the fields around Lichtenburg. Mining is still important, and the world's largest platinum mines are in the Rustenburg region.

San paintings attest to the original inhabitants of the region, but when the first white missionaries arrived in the 1830s, the region had been settled by the Batswana – the stone walls that surrounded their huts and towns can still be seen. The Batswana, however, were dispersed by the Ndebele, themselves swept up in the wave of disruption unleashed during the *difaqane* (forced migration).

As part of the apartheid regime's Homeland policy, the Batswana were relocated to Bophuthatswana; the North-West Province takes in most of the area once covered by this fragmented creation. The provincial capital, Mmabatho (now renamed Mafikeng), was capital of Bophuthatswana.

The Voortrekkers who carved out their farms in the 1840s had a hard battle to survive the vicissitudes of nature and also the political turmoil of the region. Their descendants are a tough and uncompromising lot – many towns today remain strongholds of the AWB, an extremist white right-wing group. Ventersdorp is perhaps the most conservative 'dorp' in modern South Africa, and is mentioned here as 'the town to avoid'.

Although the region's towns sometimes have interesting histories, today they're generally uninspiring places with little to see and do. Nonetheless, many people will travel through the region en route to more interesting places.

The provincial population is 3.3 million, and about two-thirds live in rural areas.

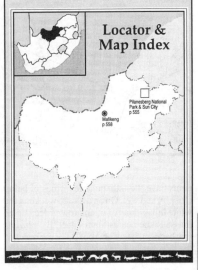

## HIGHLIGHTS

- Sun City – one of the great icons of glittery kitsch
- Pilanesberg National Park – attractive park set around a complex of extinct volcanoes
- Lotlamoreng Dam & Cultural Village – an all too rare insight into fast-disappearing traditional cultures

Locator & Map Index

Pilanesberg National Park & Sun City p 555

Mafikeng p 558

### Warning

Precautions should be taken against malaria during the summer months. Many of the dams and rivers carry bilharzia, so don't swim in them or drink from them.

### HARTBEESPOORT DAM & THE MAGALIESBERG

Visitors to South Africa will soon realise what an important role dams (reservoirs) play in the recreational life of the Afrikaners. Those who visit South Africa's magnificent coastline may well find the popularity of inland dams bizarre, but for the locals the

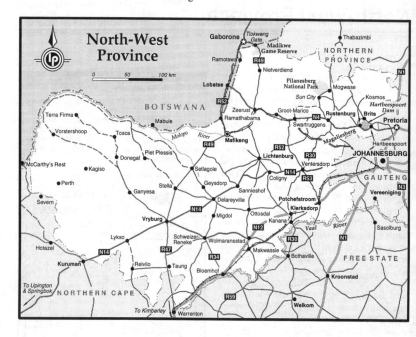

dams have the indisputable virtues of being close by and wet. On an average weekend the white inhabitants of inland towns decamp en masse to the nearest dam – the 3Bs – *braais* (barbecues), beers and boats are the order of the day.

Hartbeespoort Dam is on the edge of Gauteng Province and is the water sports resort for Pretoria and, to a lesser extent, Jo'burg. There are several fully fledged holiday towns perched on the north-eastern side of the dam on the slopes of the Magaliesberg – including Hartbeespoort and the trendy and expensive Kosmos. They're pleasant enough places – particularly Kosmos – and both towns would, no doubt, look even better if you were resident in one of the nearby cities over summer. If you are a short-term overseas visitor, however, they needn't be given any priority.

The Magaliesberg has attractive mountain scenery and there are some good walks but, once again, the range will really be of interest

only if you are based in the region. Private transport is essential. The tourist information office (01211) 30037) on Marais St, Schoemanville, is just south of Hartbeespoort.

## RUSTENBURG

Rustenburg is a large and prosperous town lying at the western edge of the Magaliesberg. It was founded in 1841.

Rustenburg is about 120km north-west of Jo'burg at the centre of a thriving agricultural region and close to two huge platinum mines. Sun City is 40km north.

The information centre (☎ (0142) 94 3194) is in the museum, on the corner of Plein and Burger Sts, behind the Civic Centre and across from the old church. It is open daily except for weekends.

### Things to See & Do

The **museum** is in an old building. It's small but interesting, with some Iron Age archaeological finds, but it mainly concentrates on

## The Batswana

Controversy surrounds much of South Africa's history, and the history of the Batswana people is no exception. Bantu-speaking peoples had extensive settlements on the highveld by 500 AD. These were Iron Age communities, and their inhabitants grew crops and kept domestic animals. In a process that can only be guessed at, linguistic and cultural distinctions developed between the Nguni people, who lived along the coast, and the Sotho-Tswana, who lived on the highveld.

The peoples of the highveld often built their houses and animal pens from stone and, in places, lived in large communities that can only be described as towns. In parts of the former Transvaal some communities specialised in mining and metal production.

The Tswana, in common with the rest of the Bantu-speaking peoples, formed clans within a larger tribal grouping. This was a dynamic situation, with people entering or leaving clans and tribal groups, and the groups themselves consolidating or fragmenting. The Tswana oral tradition describes a number of dynastic struggles, often with competing sons splitting clans on the death of the old chief. This segmentation often occurred peacefully, partly because there was sufficient land available for groups of people to move on to fresh pastures.

By the 19th century, Batswana tribes dominated much of present-day Northern Province, North-West Province, Northern Cape Province and large parts of Botswana. Fresh pastures were starting to look few and far between, however, and all hell broke loose in the terrible years of the difaqane. Although the Batswana did not come up directly against Shaka and his Zulus, they were ravaged by Mzilikazi and the Ndebele. (There is some confusion in the use of the terms Tswana and Batswana. For a start, both terms were first used by Europeans to describe a group of independent tribes who happened to be culturally and linguistically similar; they were not used by the tribes themselves. The terms are now often used interchangeably.)

Such was the devastation when the first whites crossed the Vaal River in the 1830s that they believed the land was largely uninhabited. However, as the Boers moved further north, the Batswana rallied and fought back, sometimes with the help of white mercenaries. They also petitioned the British for protection. Eventually, in 1885, the British responded to the Boer expansion, which they saw as a threat to their own interests, by establishing the British Protectorate of Bechuanaland, which has become Botswana.

Mafeking (now Mafikeng) was set up as the capital of Bechuanaland, even though it was in South Africa – giving unintended recognition to the fact that the protectorate by no means included all Batswana land.

The Transvaal Batswana were left to the tender mercies of the new Union of South Africa when it was created after the Boer War. Many were forced to seek work in the new mines and industries that sprang up around Johannesburg. From the time the National Party came to power in 1948, however, the idea of creating black Homelands (based on existing black reserves) was pursued enthusiastically. Although the move was resisted by many black activists and leaders, Bophuthatswana finally accepted 'independence' in 1977.

Bophuthatswana was one of the most depressing and least coherent of the Homelands created by the apartheid regime to serve as dumping grounds for unwanted blacks. Its territory was made up of seven enclaves. Six of the chunks were scattered in an arc running from north of Pretoria to the west, with one of the main chunks bordering Botswana. The most isolated chunk lay on the highveld within the Free State just west of Bloemfontein.

Lucas Mangope was the first and only president of Bophuthatswana. Although in some ways he jealously guarded Bophuthatswana's 'independence', he only survived a 1988 coup attempt thanks to the violent intervention of South African troops. His regime had a dismal human rights record.

Economically, Bophuthatswana was the most independent of the Homelands and provided over 80% of its own revenue – largely through the wages of around 400,000 workers employed in South Africa. The next main source of income was mining; Bophuthatswana supplied around 60% of the platinum produced in Southern Africa and nearly 30% of total world production. Tourism, especially the Sun City complex, remains important to the new North-West Province. ∎

the early Boer settlers. The original flag of the Zuid-Afrikaansche Republiek (ZAR – the first Republic of South Africa) is on display. It's open on weekdays from 8.30 am to 4.30 pm, Saturday from 9 am to 1 pm and Sunday from 3 to 5 pm.

Paul Kruger's farm **Boekenhoutfontein**, just north of town, is worth visiting. A small

NORTH-WEST PROVINCE

section of the farm and several buildings have been preserved. These include a pioneer cottage built in 1841, the house that Paul built for himself in 1863 (which now serves as a coffee shop) and the main family homestead built in 1875 (a fine example of the Colesberg Cape Dutch style). It's open from 8 am to 5 pm Tuesday to Saturday and 3 to 5 pm on Sunday.

The **Rustenburg Nature Reserve**, at the western end of the Magaliesberg range, is dominated by rocky ridges and well-wooded ravines. It lies to the south of the town and is well signposted. It's open daily from 8 am to 1 pm. There is an enormous number of plant species, including quite a few that are both rare and protected. Smaller antelope are well represented, and there are shy predators like the leopard, hyena and black-backed jackal.

### Places to Stay & Eat

The information centre has a list of guesthouses and B&Bs in town, and there are a few hotels. These hotels are mainly pricey places, such as the *Cashane Hotel* (☎ (0142) 28541) on Van Staden St, with singles/doubles for R175/215, including breakfast, and *Karos Safari Hotel* (☎ (0142) 97 1220) on the outskirts of town, with singles/doubles from R305/435.

Some 12km from Rustenburg off the R24 is *Bill McGill's B&B* (☎ (0142) 92333), which costs R90 per person.

*Hunter's Rest Hotel* (☎ (0142) 92140) is an attractive resort 14km south of Rustenburg on the R30, in the Magaliesberg. Full board costs from R240 per person. There's a big swimming pool and extensive sports facilities, including horse-riding.

*Rustenburg Kloof Holiday Resort* (☎ (0142) 97 1351) is another large and popular resort near a magnificent rocky gorge. It's 7km south-west of Rustenburg on the Donkerhoek road and is well signposted from the town. There are pools, excellent facilities and the usual range of bungalows from R75 for three people. Unfortunately, it no longer allows tents.

*Mike's Kitchen*, part of the popular chain, is on Van Staden St, Rustenburg's main

street. There are also a number of fast-food places catering to through traffic – they probably won't kill you. For desserts, frozen yoghurt and ice creams, hunt out *Purple Cow* in the Biblio Plaza.

### Getting There & Away

Greyhound has a service from Jo'burg to Gaborone (Botswana) via Rustenburg and Zeerust. See Getting There & Away in the following Zeerust section for details. City to City/Transtate runs daily from the train station to Jo'burg at 1.30 pm for about R25.

The taxi park is west of the corner of Van Staden and Malan Sts, on the Sun City side of the town centre.

## ZEERUST

The countryside around Zeerust is rather attractive hilly bushveld, but it soon gets flat as you head south-west to Mafikeng. Zeerust's main claim to fame is as a jumping-off point for Gaborone, and there are always a lot of people moving through. It can get very hot in Zeerust, with temperatures in January averaging a fierce 40°C. Even in June, the average is 30°C.

The town is quite large; there are plenty of shops strung along Church St, including a couple of 24 hour petrol stations and banks.

The **Zeerust Museum** opens occasionally, or you could inquire at the town hall (☎ (01428) 21081) for information on the local Mampoer Route, which refers to a fiery distilled liquor brewed in the region.

### Places to Stay

*Transvaal Hotel* (☎ (01428) 22003), Church St, is an old-style country hotel – pretty much unchanged since the 1920s. It must get warmish in summer. The prices might reflect its historical interest but otherwise aren't great value, starting at R80 per person or R90 with bath.

The most comfortable option is *Abjaterskop Hotel* (☎ (01428) 22008), 2km from the town centre. There's a swimming pool, and rooms are air-conditioned. Singles/doubles are R160/220, including breakfast.

## Getting There & Away

Greyhound passes through Rustenburg and Zeerust daily on its Jo'burg to Gaborone service. From Rustenburg to Gaborone is R85, Zeerust to Gaborone is R50. To Jo'burg, it's R50 and R85 respectively. Lehurutshe Transport (☎ (0140) 63 3606) runs buses around the local area.

The minibus taxi park is on Church St (the main street), on the Mafikeng side of the town centre. The fare to Mafikeng is R12 and to Rustenburg it's R25.

## SUN CITY

Sun City is the extraordinary creation of Mr Sol Kerzner. It's a large entertainment complex focusing on a couple of big spaces full of slot (poker) machines. In addition to the pokies, there are the usual casino games of chance, two excellent golf courses (thanks to Gary Player and an army of ground staff), swimming pools, sports facilities (including the spectacular Valley of the Waves), dancing girls, a concert venue, cinemas, restaurants and high-quality accommodation.

Sol took advantage of the 'independent' status of Bophuthatswana to bypass the apartheid regime's Calvinist views on gambling and bare flesh. Combining the densely populated Pretoria-Witwatersrand-Vereeniging region nearby, the dry and sunny climate and the Homeland's cheap labour, he was on a winner. Of course, to really meet the classic tourist fantasy you also need a sandy beach, waves and palm trees – hence the Valley of the Waves. Since April 1994 there have been no Homelands and Sun City is now in South Africa. Luckily for Sol, the new South Africa is much more relaxed about the human body – even more luckily, he seems set to retain his monopoly on large-scale casino gambling.

All this extravagance in the middle of one of the poorest corners of the country is, at best, incongruous. Sun City has, nonetheless, been fantastically successful and South Africans flock here to walk on a (very tame) wild side, and to fling their money around. Losers can console themselves with the thought that they are helping to pay over 3500 salaries.

Some might argue that entertainment and feeding money into slot machines are mutually exclusive concepts, but if you do get a kick out of gambling and like the idea of being pampered in luxurious hotels, this is the place for you. There are occasionally concerts, which attract big crowds.

## Orientation & Information

The Sun City complex has a Welcome Centre (☎ (01465) 71544), where you can get maps and information. It's at the entrance to the Entertainment Centre, right by the bus station. Admission to Sun City is R10, with one or two of the attractions having separate admission charges, notably the Valley of the Waves, which costs another R35.

The complex is really not all that big, but it is a bit confusing. The car park for day visitors is at the entrance, about 2km from the Entertainment Centre. An elevated train shuttles from the car park to the Cabanas, Sun City Hotel, The Cascades and the Entertainment Centre. You walk through the garish entertainment centre to reach The Lost City.

## Things to See & Do

The **Entertainment Centre** is a gambling venue apparently aimed primarily at daytrippers and slot-machine addicts. It's mega tacky. The **Sun City Hotel** also has ranks of slot machines, a sophisticated casino area, shops, bars, restaurants and nightclubs.

The spectacular centrepiece of Sun City is **The Lost City**, an extraordinary piece of kitsch that would be fun if the publicity didn't talk about it symbolising African heritage and so on. It has less to do with African heritage than Euro-Disneyland has to do with French heritage. As well as some Disneyesque attractions there's the **Valley of the Waves**, where there is, not surprisingly, a large-scale wave machine. This is the best reason for non-gamblers to come to Sun City.

At the heart of The Lost City is **The Palace**, a hotel which could inspire hallucinations – unfortunately, you can't wander around much unless you're a guest, and you can't be a guest unless you are wealthy.

Golf at the superb **Gary Player Country Club** is R75 for 18 holes if you're a resident, or R95 for day visitors. A caddie is compulsory and will cost R40; club hire is R60. Even more expensive is the new **Lost City Golf Course**, at R95 for residents and R120 for day visitors; golf carts are mandatory. We know of backpackers who have played the 'Player' course – they love the course, but moan about the big tips expected by caddies inured to well-heeled visitors.

**Waterworld**, on the shores of a large artificial lake, has facilities for parasailing, water skiing and windsurfing.

There are tours into the adjoining **Pilanesberg National Park**, departing at 7.30 am and 2.30 pm daily – a 2½ hour tour in an open vehicle costs R75/48 per adult/child.

Near the main entrance is the **Kwena Gardens Crocodile Sanctuary**; entry is R12.

### Places to Stay & Eat

*The Palace* is the top place to stay at Sun City. Standard rooms start around R940, and R1095 on Friday and Saturday. A night in a suite will set you back as much as R10,000!

The Palace has displaced *The Cascades* as the most luxurious hotel in the complex, although it too is surrounded by elaborate landscaped grounds with a swimming pool, waterfalls and so on. Standard rooms (easily described as palatial) start at R670, or nearly R840 on weekends.

*Sun City Hotel* is the oldest of the five-star hotels, and it's the cheapest. It's by no means shabby, however, and cheap is hardly the right word. It's the most lively of the hotels, with gambling facilities on the premises, as well as a number of restaurants, an enormous pool and bar, a disco and nightclubs. According to the promotional hype, it 'pulsates' at night. Standard rooms start at R555, or R675 on weekends.

The cheapest alternative is the more laid-back *Sun City Cabanas*, which seems to be aimed at family groups. Guests can make use of all the facilities in the Sun City Hotel, but it also has its own adventure playground and

pool. The pleasant rooms are fully equipped; standard rooms start at R380, or R475 on weekends.

All these hotels can be contacted or booked through Sun City (☎ (01465) 21000; fax 74277) or booked through Sun International central reservations (☎ (011) 780 7800; fax 780 7449). If they are too expensive (and you have your own transport), consider staying at Pilanesberg National Park (see the following section). The other alternative is just to make a day trip.

All the hotels have a selection of restaurants. The cheapest alternative is *Palm Terrace* in the Cabanas, which is open for breakfast, lunch and dinner. There are a number of reasonably priced restaurants representing a variety of cuisines in the Entertainment Centre. The best of the bars here is *Crazy Monkey*, with its giant video screen. Expect to pay from R35 to R45 for a pretty straightforward meal.

### Getting There & Away

**Air** Tiny Pilanesberg airport (☎ (01465) 21261) once gloried in the name 'Pilanesberg International Airport'. It's about 7km north-west of the entrance to Sun City. Sun Air (☎ (011) 397 2244; fax 397 2284) has flights from Jo'burg daily for R228. There are also Sun Air flights to/from Jo'burg to Cape Town (R690) and Durban (R380). Sun Air was once the 'national' airline of Bophuthatswana (then called Bop Air).

**Bus** Sun City Buses (bookings through Computicket ☎ (011) 331 9991) has daily buses from the Rotunda in Jo'burg at 9 am, 11.45 am and 3 pm Monday to Thursday; 9 am, 11 am and 5 pm on Friday; 9 am, 11.45 am and 2 pm on Saturday; and 9 and 11.45 am on Sunday. The return fare is R60, which includes a few freebies, or R80 with entry to the Valley of the Waves. If you are at a hostel, you could get a group together, hire a car and tour both Pilanesberg and Sun City in the same day.

There are weekend buses from Pretoria (departing from the Tourist Rendezvous) to Sun City. Prices are the same as for Jo'burg.

**Car** Sun City is surprisingly poorly sign-posted, so navigators will need to pay attention. From Jo'burg it's a two hour drive. The most straightforward route is via Rustenburg, although the Sun City people recommend you travel via Brits.

## PILANESBERG NATIONAL PARK

The superb Pilanesberg National Park surrounds Sun City, so it is easy to combine a visit to both places. It protects over 500 sq km of an unusual complex of extinct volcanoes and is the fifth largest national park in South Africa. The countryside is attractive, with rocky outcrops, ridges and craters, mostly covered in sparse woodland. There are two vegetation zones – Kalahari thornveld and sour bushveld – and the atmosphere is quintessentially African.

Until the 1970s, the Pilanesberg was farmed, but it was recognised as an ideal site for a national park, partly because the hills provide a natural barrier to the more densely populated surrounding plains. As a result, the land was acquired by the Bop government, and an ambitious and imaginative rehabilitation and game-stocking programme was instituted. This has been successful and it is now impossible to imagine that the area was ever anything other than wilderness.

The park is once again home to extensive populations of many of Africa's most impressive animals. There are white and black rhinos, elephants, giraffes, hippos, buffaloes, a wide variety of bucks (including sables, elands, kudus, gemsboks), zebras, leopards, jackals, hyenas and even a small number of cheetahs. The region also has a diverse population of birds – over 300 species have been recorded. (Psst! This park has been described by some, including us, as a better wildlife viewing experience than faraway Kruger.)

There is an excellent 100km network of gravel roads, hides, picnic spots and some good-value accommodation options. Since it is no more than 25km from one end of the

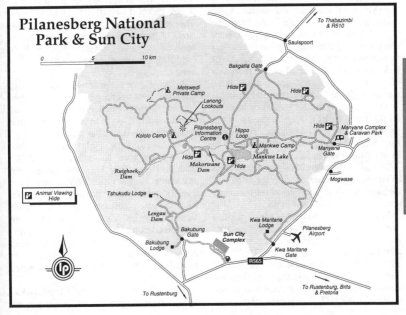

park to the other, it is easy to cover the range of different environments in the park and see a wide variety of animals. To do any real justice to it, however, you need at least one full day (and on no account miss the viewpoints over the crater from Lenong). Bear in mind that the best game-viewing times are in the morning and evening, and that you'll average around 10 to 15km/h while driving.

### Orientation & Information

Signposting in this area, even around Sun City and the Pilanesberg, is less than terrific – you can't really go wrong once you get to Sun City, however, because the Pilanesberg are the only significant hills in the region.

The Manyane and Kwa Maritane gates are on the Sun City-Thabazimbi road. From Sun City follow the R565 for 4km to the Mogwase turn-off. Kwa Maritane gate is 2km along. The best entrance is Manyane gate – proceed past Mogwase village and turn left after the Caltex station.

The Pilanesberg range forms four concentric mountain rings, with Mankwe Lake at the centre. Information and useful sketch maps are available at the main Manyane Gate, where overnight visitors must enter and report to the reception office (excluding those staying at Kwa Maritane, Tshukudu or Bakubung lodges). The Manyane reception office is open from 7.30 am to 8 pm daily, although it's closed between 1 and 2 pm.

The entrance fee for adults/children is R13/7. From April to August gates into the park proper (beyond Manyane) are closed from 6 pm to 6 am, and from September to March from 7 pm to 5.30 am.

There is an interpretative display and shop in an old magistrates court in the centre of the park; the shop sells curios, refreshments and a range of basic food items.

Pilanesberg Safaris (☎ (01466) 55588) runs several activities from Sun City. There are 2½-hour game drives in the morning, afternoon and at night for R75/48 for adults/children (minimum of six); guided three hour hikes for R80 (minimum six); and four-hour balloon rides (a great way to see wildlife) for R1150 (minimum eight).

### Places to Stay

The park (☎ (01465) 56135) was administered by the now-defunct Bophuthatswana National Parks Service. Currently accommodation bookings are taken on ☎ (011) 465 5423, but that might change. You could try the new North-West Province tourist office (☎ (0140) 84 3040) in Mafikeng.

The *Manyane Complex & Caravan Park* (☎ (011) 465 5423), near the Manyane Gate, is excellent – thoughtfully designed and laid out, with high-quality facilities. There's a small pool, a shop with basic food items and a decent restaurant. Sites are R50 (R60 in high season) for up to four people, so it isn't cheap; however, it's only about 20km from Sun City and it's a lot cheaper than any accommodation there. There are also chalets from R175 a double.

*Mankwe Camp* is a smaller place, overlooking Mankwe Lake. This camp provides self-catering bungalows and safari tents scattered among natural trees, with communal washing and kitchen facilities (including fridges). The bungalows sleep up to four people and cost R80 (R105 in high season). The tents sleep three people and cost R60 (R80 in high season). They're pitched on concrete floors and have comfortable beds (bedding provided), chairs and paraffin lamps.

*Kololo Camp* is the smallest camp, with only four tents sleeping 12 people and basic cooking facilities (including a fridge). It has a great location on a hilltop and has fine panoramas. It's booked as a single unit.

There are a couple of upmarket time-share resorts with hotel accommodation in the park, such as *Kwa Maritane Lodge* and *Bakubung Lodge* (☎ (01465) 21861; fax 21621); book both at Bakubung. The Kwa Maritane gate is about 5km north-east of the Sun City turn-off, on the road to Manyane Gate; Bakubung Gate is about 5km southwest of the Sun City turn-off. Both lodges charge from R565/850 a single/double on weekdays or R650/910 on weekends. Rates include all meals.

*Tshukudu Lodge*, accessible from Bakubung Gate, is an upmarket resort with just six cottages. Rates, which include a welcome drink, all meals, game drives and walks, are a whopping R1150/1900. Book at Bakubung Lodge.

## MAFIKENG (MMABATHO)

Mafikeng and Mmabatho are twin towns about 3km apart. Mafeking, as it was known, was the original capital of the British Protectorate of Bechuanaland (now Botswana). It is most famous for its role in the 1899-1902 Anglo-Boer War, when British forces under Colonel Baden-Powell were besieged by the Boers. Nearby Mmabatho is a modern town built as the capital of the 'independent' homeland of Bophuthatswana; it's now the capital of North-West Province. In 1997 the towns were renamed as simply Mafikeng.

Mafikeng has some vitality – the streets are busy. There is a reasonable selection of shops and a few interesting historical sites. Mmabatho was developed as Bop's showcase. As a result it has a number of suitably grandiose and ugly buildings; they're quite widely scattered as the planners obviously presumed cars would be the primary form of transport in this city of the future. Among other things, there's a sports stadium and a huge US-style shopping mall, Megacity.

The history of Mafikeng is interesting, but you don't have to visit it to discover this. The present reality is mundane and hot.

### History

In the 1870s, various European mercenaries who had fought on the northern frontier against Tswana tribes were rewarded with farms in the Mafikeng region; they created the Republic of Goshen. The British, who had been petitioned by the Tswana tribes further north and who saw the new republic as a threat, sent a force under Sir Charles Warren to annexe the territory. In 1885 Mafeking (as the Europeans called it) was established as the administrative capital of the British Protectorate of Bechuanaland.

The small frontier town was besieged by Boer forces from 14 October 1899 to 17 May 1900. The lifting of the siege was such an event in the British Empire that Australian Rules football matches in Melbourne were postponed for the civic celebrations. The dispatches written by Baden-Powell led to the siege becoming a symbol of British courage and steadfastness. In reality, the Boers made only one determined attempt to capture the town and were for the most part content to maintain a civilised siege – there was seldom fighting on Sundays.

Perhaps its most lasting significance was the role it played in the development of Baden-Powell's ideas. During the siege he created a cadet corps for the town's boys – the forerunner of the Boy Scout movement. The boys carried messages, ran errands and, no doubt, did good deeds.

I said to one of these boys on one occasion, when he came through a rather heavy fire:

'You will get hit one of these days, riding about like that when shells are flying.'

'I pedal so quick, sir, they'll never catch me!' he replied.

These boys didn't seem to mind the bullets one bit. They were ready to carry out orders, though it meant risking their lives every time.

**Scouting for Boys**, Robert Baden-Powell

### Orientation & Information

It's easy to get around Mafikeng on foot. Most shops and banks are grouped around the central bus park. It's 5km from the Mafikeng centre to Megacity in Mmabatho; catch one of the numerous local buses.

Megacity is a useful starting point if you are heading further north or west. There are banks, an adjoining post office, a number of large, well-stocked department stores (good for food and camping equipment) and numerous smaller shops, as well as several restaurants of the fast-food chain ilk.

Look for the free *What's New in Mmabatho* and the glossy *North-West Province*, available in most of the hotels.

**Tourist Office** The North-West Province tourist office (☎ (0140) 84 3040), on the ground floor of Borekelong House, Lucas Mangope Highway, Mmabatho, is struggling to come to terms with its new responsibilities – but it is all there is, as the Mafikeng office

NORTH-WEST PROVINCE

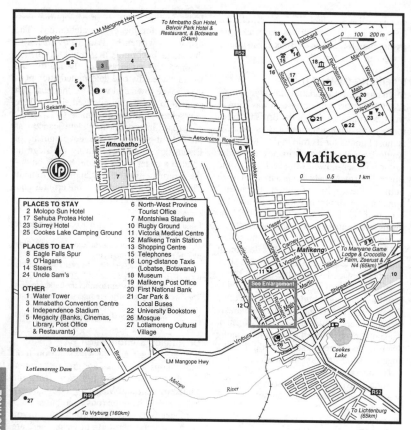

PLACES TO STAY
2   Molopo Sun Hotel
17  Sehuba Protea Hotel
23  Surrey Hotel
25  Cookes Lake Camping Ground

PLACES TO EAT
8   Eagle Falls Spur
9   O'Hagans
14  Steers
24  Uncle Sam's

OTHER
1   Water Tower
3   Mmabatho Convention Centre
4   Independence Stadium
5   Megacity (Banks, Cinemas,
    Library, Post Office
    & Restaurants)
6   North-West Province
    Tourist Office
7   Montshiwa Stadium
10  Rugby Ground
11  Victoria Medical Centre
12  Mafikeng Train Station
13  Shopping Centre
15  Telephones
16  Long-distance Taxis
    (Lobatse, Botswana)
18  Museum
19  Mafikeng Post Office
20  First National Bank
21  Car Park &
    Local Buses
22  University Bookstore
26  Mosque
27  Lotlamoreng Cultural
    Village

has closed. This office is open Monday to Friday from 8 am to 4.30 pm but is closed on weekends (when it is needed by tourists!).

**Money** There are no Amex or Rennies travel agencies in Mafikeng or Mmabatho, so for changing money, banks in Mafikeng and Megacity are your only option. First National has a branch in Mafikeng, on Robinson St between Main and Shippard Sts.

**Post & Communications** The main post office is next to Megacity. The Mafikeng

post office is on Carrington St between Main and Martin Sts.

**Travel Agencies** Tswana Travel (☎ (0140) 23555) and North-West Travel, both in Megacity, handle travel bookings.

**Bookshops** The University Bookstore (☎ (0140) 81 0272) on the corner of Carrington and Shippard Sts, Mafikeng, has a reasonable collection of books and stationery. There is a branch of the CNA bookshop chain in Megacity.

**Medical Services** Andre Pharmacy, 19 Voortrekker St, is open Monday to Friday from 8 am to 9 pm, Saturday until 1 pm and 5 to 9 pm, and Sunday from 11 am to 1 pm and 7 to 9 pm. For dentists and doctors, go to the Victoria Medical Centre (☎ (0140) 81 2043), Victoria Rd, Mafikeng.

**Emergency** You can contact police on ☎ 10111 and ambulance on ☎ (0140) 23333.

## Mafikeng Museum
The museum is not large, but it does have some interesting relics, mainly relating to the famous siege. Among the relics is a menu for a dinner for senior officers given to celebrate the Queen's Birthday on 24 May 1900 – life may have been tough for some, but the senior officers managed to maintain standards. Admission is free, and it's open Monday to Friday from 8 am to 4 pm, and Saturday from 10 am to 12.30 pm.

## Lotlamoreng Dam & Cultural Village
The Lotlamoreng Cultural Village is an unabashed tourist attraction, but it has been well handled and gives an all-too-rare insight into fast-disappearing traditional cultures. In the western half of South Africa it is almost impossible to find any surviving traditional housing, so Lotlamoreng is playing a vital role. It is the brainchild of Vusamazulu Credo Mutwa, a Tswana priest, historian, artist and author.

A number of small traditional villages and *kraals* (cattle stockades) have been developed on the banks of the Lotlamoreng Dam. Among the ten groups represented are the Tswana, including the Barolong (blacksmith people) and Batlhaping (boat people), Xhosa, Zulu, Pedi, Ndebele and San. These are not just static displays, but are in full use by people practising traditional crafts – from dancing and singing to pottery and beadwork. As you explore the village you are likely to stumble on people doing any number of things, basically without regard to visitors (and there aren't many).

The complex is open daily from 8 am to 5 pm; entry is R5/2 for adults/children. It can easily absorb a full afternoon. Right beside the dam there's an aviary, refreshment kiosk, lawns and braais.

## Places to Stay
*Cookes Lake Camping Ground* is dusty and unattractive, with few facilities; it would do in a pinch and a camp site costs only R10. Apparently you can stay at *St Joseph's Centre* at St Mary's Mission (☎ (0140) 83 2646) in Lomanyaneng, about 2km south of the train station, for R50.

There are a few B&Bs, starting around R100 per person. Ask at the North-West Province tourist office for a complete list. For example, *Royal Palm* (☎ (0140) 81 2218) at 70 Shippard St, Mafikeng, has singles/doubles for R90/120; 'dishes of the day' are R20.

The *Surrey Hotel* (☎ (0140) 81 0420), 32 Shippard St, is not cheap but it's the cheapest alternative. It is pretty rowdy and not very inspiring. Singles/doubles cost R100/125 or R115/140 with bath. *Sehuba Protea Inn* (☎ (0140) 81 0117) on the corner of Station Rd and Martin St, Mafikeng, charges R165/ 220 for half-board, or R270/320 for three/ four people.

If you have the money, it's definitely worth considering one of the ubiquitous Sun hotels. As in virtually all the Sun hotels, gambling is encouraged! The *Molopo Sun* (☎ (0140) 24184), Dr Mokgobo Ave (University Dr), Mmabatho, is close to Megacity for shopping, and a courtesy bus runs people to/from the Mmabatho Sun for gambling and other nightlife. It has a couple of decent-value places to eat, and there's a pool. Rooms are all fully equipped and pleasant, with prices from R225/280 and occasional specials in the off season. A continental/full breakfast is R27/41.

Prices are considerably more at the luxurious *Mmabatho Sun* (☎ (0140) 89 1111) on Lobatse Rd. There's a pool, fountains, tennis courts, a casino and a cinema.

There's a hotel school, *Belvoir Park Hotel & Restaurant* (☎ (0140) 86 2200), next to the Mmabatho Sun, which offers rooms for R230/340.

*Manyane Game Lodge & Crocodile Farm* (☎ (0140) 81 6020), about 6km out of town on the Zeerust road, has fully equipped chalets for R180/220, or R300/350 for three/four people. It has a restaurant, shop and laundry.

## Places to Eat

For budget eaters, *Uncle Sam's Restaurant & Takeaway*, 38 Shippard St, Mafikeng, has standard takeaway fare, such as stew and pap (R7) and curry and rice (R9). Inexpensive takeaways are available from *Botsalano Chinese Restaurant* at 54 Station Rd, Mafikeng, including spring rolls (R4 each), beef chop suey (R11) and chicken chow mein (R12). *Wimpy* is just one of Megacity's many takeaway places.

For chain-store food, there's a *Steers* in Mafikeng's Station Towers centre, on Hatchard St not far from the train station; and *Eagle Falls Spur*, a steak place at the corner of Voortrekker and Aerodrome Rds. The latter has specials such as steak and calamari (surf 'n' turf) for R30 and kids burgers (with free drinks) for R14. In Mafikeng's Golf View is *O'Hagan's*, on the corner of Tillard and Gemsbok Sts, with entrees from R7.50 and mains approaching R30.

There are surprisingly good options at the Molopo Sun hotel, Mmabatho. *Letsatsi* has inexpensive snacks and the *Ditha Restaurant* has buffet lunches for about R30.

## Getting There & Away

Many people come through Mafikeng on their way to/from Botswana. Ramatlabama, 26km north, is the busiest border crossing and lies on the main route to/from Lobatse (Botswana) and Gaborone.

**Air** SA Airlink (☎ (0140) 85 1119) has flights to Jo'burg (R456) daily, except Saturday, with connections to other cities.

**Bus** City Link (☎ (0140) 81 2680, (0110) 333 4412 in Jo'burg) runs daily from Megacity to Jo'burg for R50. A City to City/Transtate service from Jo'burg to Mafikeng (R50) departs Jo'burg daily at 7 am, except

Sunday, and returns daily, except Saturday. Buses depart from Mafikeng train station at 12.30 pm and arrive in Jo'burg at 5.45 pm.

**Train** Occasionally there is a Botswana Railways passenger train from Mafikeng, via Gaborone, to Bulawayo; ring the station (☎ (0140) 28259) for information. From Mafikeng to Gaborone and Bulawayo in 1st/2nd class is R50/35 and R160/135 respectively.

**Minibus Taxi** Minibus taxis leave from the forecourt of the Mafikeng train station. As usual, most leave early in the morning. Examples of destinations and fares are: Botswana border, R4 (running all day); Gaborone, R30; Jo'burg, R40; Lobatse, R15; Pretoria, R40; Rustenburg, R30; Vryburg, R25 (very few taxis); and Zeerust, R12.

## Getting Around

Numerous city buses travel between Mafikeng (corner of Main St and Station Rd) and Mmabatho (Megacity) for a few rand. Buses also run out to Lotlamoreng.

## POTCHEFSTROOM

Potchefstroom, known locally as Potch, is off the N12 about 115km south-west of Jo'burg. It's a large town, verging on a city, that looks rather unappetising from the main road. There are some pleasant leafy suburbs, however, including an oak avenue which claims the title of the longest in the southern hemisphere. There's also a large lakeside resort about 4km west of the town centre.

It might not appear so, but Potchefstroom was the first European town to be established in the former Transvaal. It was founded by the Voortrekker leader Andries Potgieter in 1838, and was the original capital of the ZAR. It remains a staunchly conservative town.

The information office (☎ (0148) 293 1611) is in the town hall on Church (Kerk) St and can give you a map of Potch. There's also a North-West Province office (☎ (0148) 293 1611) on the 1st floor of the Royal Building, 44 Lombard St.

The **Potchefstroom Museum** is worth

visiting, particularly to see the only remaining ox-wagon dating from the Battle of Blood River. It's open from 10 am to 1 pm and 2 to 5 pm weekdays, 9 am to 12.45 pm Saturday and 2.30 to 5 pm Sunday.

**Places to Stay & Eat**
The *Lake Recreation Resort* (☎ (0148) 299 5470) is a dam classic – the whole of Potch can be found here on a sunny weekend. Signposting is a bit erratic, but anyone should be able to direct you – it's about 4km from the N12, on the north side of town. There are swimming pools, fairground attractions, boats, a café and plenty of braais. There is a range of bungalows (from R60) and camp sites (R35) for two.

There are a number of hotels in town, including the decent *Kings Hotel* (☎ (0148) 297 5505), 25 Potgieter St (on the corner of Church St), with rooms from R95/155 per person, and the more luxurious *Elgro Hotel* (☎ (0148) 297 5411), 60 Wolmarans St, which has rooms starting from R100 per person (and a disco).

On Church St, *Espressivo* is a good place for coffee and cake. There are other restaurants, including a *Mike's Kitchen*.

**VRYBURG**
The country around Vryburg is flat, dry and scrubby, so you don't get any unpleasant surprises when you arrive. The only unexpected factor is the size of the town – it's a large place, and a major shopping and service centre for the surrounding farms. Other than the well-maintained gardens on the main street and one or two pubs with accommodation, there's absolutely nothing else to interest visitors.

Hope springs eternal – advertising for Stellaland (as the Vryburg region was proclaimed in 1882) describes the place 'as the tourist destination of the nineties'. To delve deeper, contact Vryburg Publicity (☎ (05391) 78 2200). Please write to us and tell us what you found! The **Armoedsvlatke Bull Testing Station** is definitely not an acceptable answer.

Carlsberg | De Beers | CASTLE LAGER | SOUTHERN SUN GROUP | De Beers | SAA

# Northern Province

Northern Province (once the north and west of the old Transvaal Province, later briefly known as Northern Transvaal) is a combination of highveld and lowveld, but most of it is savanna and it is very hot in summer, with high humidity and electrical storms on the lowveld. The lush Letaba Valley – with its tropical fruit farms and nearby cycad forests surrounding the Rain Queen's home – and the forested Soutpansberg range provide some contrast to the bushveld plains.

To the west of the N1 is the fascinating Waterberg region; north of the Soutpansberg you're well into tropical, baobab-studded plains; and to the east is the mystical Venda area. As well as Kruger National Park and its bordering private game reserves, there are many other reserves and good hiking trails in the area.

Mining in this region is important both as an employer of a fair percentage of the local black population and as an earner of foreign currency. Fourteen of the 20 main (strategic) minerals are mined here and nine of the deposits are the biggest of their type in the world. The biggest coalfields in SA are near Ellisras; gold, beryllium, asbestos and antimony are mined near Gravelotte; platinum and iron near Thabazimbi; and the biggest copper mine, with a hole seven times larger than Kimberley's, is in Phalaborwa.

A large part of Kruger National Park is in Northern Province, but the park is covered in the Mpumalanga chapter.

## HISTORY

The region was not densely populated prior to white settlement, but it was nonetheless home to a considerable number of indigenous peoples. Among others, there were the Ndebele (north of Pretoria), Venda (in the north-east), Langa (in the Waterberg) and the Batswana of the Sotho group (in the southwest).

The Voortrekkers first crossed the Vaal River in 1836. A number of bloody conflicts

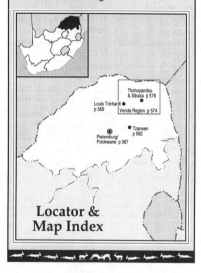

**HIGHLIGHTS**

- Strong traditional cultures, especially in the Venda region
- Excellent private reserves bordering Kruger
- Horse-riding and hiking in the game reserves of the wild Waterberg

Thohoyandou & Sibasa p 576
Louis Trichardt p 569
Venda Region p 574
Tzaneen p 582
Pietersburg/ Polokwane p 567

**Locator & Map Index**

between the blacks and whites followed. In 1852 at Sand River, Andries Pretorius successfully negotiated with the British for the independence of the trekkers north of the Vaal River – and created the first of the Boer republics. In 1853 the name Zuid-Afrikaansche Republiek (ZAR) was adopted. Pretoria was founded as the capital in 1855.

Boer independence did not last long. The republic was annexed by the British in 1877 and became the province of Transvaal. The Boers fought for and won their independence and the Transvaal was once again a republic by 1884.

Gold was discovered on the Witwatersrand in 1886, with consequences that no-one

# Northern Province

could have foreseen. One of these was a new British interest in the region and, in 1899, the Boers were once again locked in a war of independence with the British. The British won, but the Transvaal regained representative government before the end of 1906 and was finally incorporated in the new Union of South Africa. Pretoria was not to be a republican capital again until 1961.

## WARNING
Take precautions against both malaria and bilharzia while in Northern Province.

# The N1 North

The N1 highway from Jo'burg and Pretoria to the Zimbabwe border neatly divides Northern Province. Along this artery are the main towns of the province.

### Getting There & Away
The Jo'burg to Pietersburg route (N1) is well served by transport. North Link Tours (☎ (0152) 307 2950) buses pass through most N1 towns on the Jo'burg-Phalaborwa or Jo'burg-Louis Trichardt runs; see Getting There & Away in the Gauteng chapter. City to City/Transtate and Translux buses also serve most of the N1 towns.

The minibus taxi system is easy to work out, as it costs about R10 to travel between the main towns. Fares from Warmbad to Nylstroom, Nylstroom to Naboomspruit, Naboomspruit to Potgietersrus and Potgietersrus to Pietersburg are all more or less R10.

The *Bosvelder* train stops at most N1 towns, but not at Nylstroom.

### WARMBAD (WARMBATHS)
This sleepy little town, 90km north of Pretoria off the N1, has become a popular holiday spot because of its **mineral springs**. Day visits to the baths cost R20 (children R12); this gets you access to all facilities.

The information centre (☎ (014) 736 3694) is at the corner of Voortrekker and

Pretoria Sts. Most of the town's inhabitants are black and live in the township of Bela.

### Places to Stay & Eat
The baths are part of an *Aventura Eco Resort* (☎ (014) 736 2200), which offers powered camp sites for R20, plus R15 per person (R28 in high season). Two-bed/four-bed units are R170/190 (R230/305 in high season).

The *New White House Hotel* (☎ (014) 736 2876) is in the town centre opposite the post office on the corner of Pretoria and Voortrekker Sts. It's a country pub with rooms from R80 per person, with breakfast.

There are numerous holiday flats, many of which are along Moffat St. Included are *Casa Blanca Holiday Flats* (☎ (014) 736 2480) at No 42 and *Dula Monate Holiday Flats* (☎ (014) 736 3341) at No 17.

There are plenty of places to get a meal within walking distance of the baths. A steak at the *Spur* is about R30, *Pizza Bela Bela* has pizzas from R18 to R27.50 and *Paul's Pub & Grill* has pub lunches from R10.

### NYLSTROOM
Nylstroom, a small town in cattle country, was named by Voortrekkers who thought they'd found the source of the Nile. After all, the river here seemed to fit the biblical description of the Nile: it was a river, it was in Africa and it had papyrus reeds growing along the banks. The library (☎ (014) 717 2211) provides limited information.

### Places to Stay
About 3km from Nylstroom on the old Naboomspruit road, the *Stokkiesdraai Motel & Caravan Park* (☎ (014) 717 4005) has sites from about R40 for two and large holiday chalets for R250. It has all that is needed for the weary Voortrekker wishing to rest, water the horses and oil the wagon wheels.

About 10km from the Kranskop toll gate on the Eersbewoond Rd is *Shangri-La Lodge* (☎ (014) 717 5381). A studio room with bath is R250 per person for half board, while a thatched rondavel is R285.

## No Moses, but Plenty of Birds

When the Nylsvley (Nyls Valley) floods in summer, a cacophony of sound emanates from the reeds, but it is no baby crying. This flood plain is rich in waterbirds – both in numbers and diversity of species.

More than 100 different species of waterbird have been recorded here and in the adjoining private **Mosdene Nature Reserve**. This number includes 85 of the 94 species known to have bred in South Africa, which is more than any other wetland in the Republic.

After the rains, the food supply in the *vlei* (valley) is plentiful and the flocks of birds begin to arrive. Some 17 species of ducks are to be found, including the white-faced whistling duck *(Dendrocygna viduata)* and the southern pochard *(Netta erythrophthalma)*. Up to 17 species of heron, such as the great white egret *(Egretta alba)*, squacco *(Ardeola ralloides)* and black egret *(Egretta ardesiaca)* – more than 12,000 birds – begin hunting in the shallow water. Bird-watchers get the opportunity to see rare species such as the bittern *(Botaurus stellaris)*, dwarf bittern *(Ixobrychus sturmii)* and rufous-bellied heron *(Ardeola rufiventris)*. Apart from waterbirds, more than 300 other species have been recorded in the valley, making it one of the premier places to see birds in Africa. ■

The black-headed heron is one of the most widespread waterbird species found in Southern Africa.

## NABOOMSPRUIT

This town (called 'Naboom' by all) is in the centre of a rich agricultural and mining district. There are many mineral springs in the area. It's a conservative place, but after a few glasses of *mampoer* (local schnapps) the clothes may well come off as there is a huge nudist camp nearby.

The 3000 hectare **Nylsvley Nature Reserve** is 20km south of Naboomspruit. It's one of the best places in the country to see birds (see the boxed text 'No Moses, but Plenty of Birds'). The reserve is open daily between 6 am and 6 pm. There's a basic *camp site* (☎ (014) 743 1074). To get to the reserve, head south on the N1 for 13km and turn off to the east on the road to Boekenhout. (The N1 may well have been rerouted – there should be new signposts.)

### Places to Stay & Eat

The municipal *caravan park* (☎ (014) 743 1111) is a central and cheap option for campers. There are nine caravan parks in the vicinity! *Naboom Hotel* (☎ /fax (014) 743 0321) has single/double rooms from R65/90 and an à la carte restaurant. *Kings & Queens Restaurant*, on Louis Trichardt St, has reasonable meals from about R30.

## POTGIETERSRUS

This conservative town (they all seem to be up this way), 227km north of Pretoria, was settled early by Voortrekkers, but not without resistance from the people already living there. The **Arend Dieperink Museum** on the N1, open weekdays until 4.30 pm, tells the story of local resistance. The Bosveld Publicity Association (☎ (0154) 2244) is based here.

**Makapan's Caves**, 23km north-east of town, are of world significance to palaeontology, yielding bones of *Australopithecus africanus* carbon-dated to be three million years old. You must book at the Dieperink museum to visit.

NORTHERN PROVINCE

### Reserves near Potgietersrus

The **Game Breeding Centre** (☎ (0154) 4314), a few kilometres north of Potgietersrus on the N1, is a breeding centre for the National Zoological Gardens (Pretoria) and has a wide variety of native and exotic animals. One of the breeding aviaries covers over a hectare. You can drive through the reserve, which is open weekdays from 8 am to 4 pm and weekends until 6 pm. Entry is R5. There is a *camp site* opposite the entrance to the breeding centre.

The **Percy Fyfe Nature Reserve**, 26km from town (☎ (0154) 5678), is a breeding centre for species of rare antelopes, and has other species of mammals as well. It's open from 8 am to 5 pm.

### Places to Stay & Eat

*Potgietersrus Caravan Park* (☎ (0154) 3101) and *Kiepersol Resort* (☎ (0154) 5609) both have camp sites and rondavels. *Lonely Oak* on Hooge St (☎ (0154) 4560) has singles/doubles from R95/115. *Protea Park Hotel* (☎ (0154) 3101) has singles/doubles from R235/285.

*Jaagbaan* (☎ (0154) 7833), a B&B 8km south of town, is recommended by readers; it costs R80 per person.

There are a number of places on the N1 (Voortrekker St) where you can get a half-decent meal, including *Casanova*, *Pizza Den* and *Spur Steak Ranch*.

### PIETERSBURG/POLOKWANE

Pietersburg, the provincial capital, was founded in 1886 by a group of Voortrekkers who had been forced to abandon a settlement further north because of malaria and 'hostile natives'. Today, Pietersburg (now renamed Pietersburg/Polokwane, after the large black township in the vicinity) is a big, sedate place serving agricultural and mining communities. It is pleasant enough, with coral trees and jacarandas lining the broad streets and, reputedly, the lowest crime rate of any South African provincial capital.

The Pietersburg/Polokwane Marketing Company office (☎ (0152) 295 2011) is in the Civic Square on Landdros Mare St; it will provide basic information. The best source of information is Vis Streicher at SA Tours & Bookings (☎ (0152) 297 2177) at 89A Schoeman St. Vis knows all there is to know about the region and attractions and goes out of his way to put you on the right track (and even to serve you a welcome cup of tea and biscuits).

### Things to See & Do

The **donkey statue** on the corner of Vorster and Landdros Mare Sts commemorates the part donkeys played in the white development of the Transvaal. Horses were susceptible to equine fever so the donkey replaced them in transport, agriculture and mining roles. Apparently they often committed suicide by jumping off cliffs rather than face another day's toil!

The **Pietersburg Nature Reserve** is in Union Park, south of the town centre on the road to Silicon. It's very big for a reserve adjacent to a city – the largest such reserve in the country. You can see zebras, giraffes and white rhinos from the Rhinoceros walking trail. All of the South African antelopes are represented. It is open daily from 7 am to 6 pm.

The **Bakoni Malapa Northern Sotho Open-Air Museum**, 9km south-east of Pietersburg on the R37 to Chuniespoort, is devoted to northern Sotho culture and includes an authentic 'living' village. There are archaeological remains and paintings dating back to 1000 AD and evidence of Ndebele iron and copper smelting. It is open on weekdays except Monday afternoon, when it closes at 12.30 pm; admission is R5.

Australian visitors might want to visit the house where anti-hero Harry Harbord Morant ('the Breaker') was tried for crimes committed during the Anglo-Boer War. SA Tours & Bookings will direct you to the house at 4 Hans van Rensburg St.

### Places to Stay

Accommodation is generally pricey and can fill up with travelling salespeople.

*Union Caravan Park* (☎ (0152) 295 2011) is in Union Park, about 5km from the town

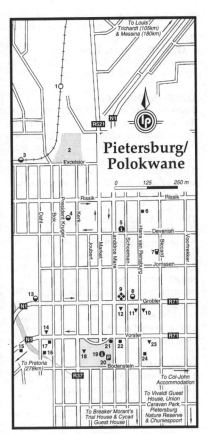

**PLACES TO STAY**
6  Kiepersol Overnight Accommodation
15  Pietersburg Lodge
16  Travellers' Lodge
17  Holiday Inn Garden Court
22  Great Northern Hotel
24  Arnotha's

**PLACES TO EAT**
10  Die Klause; San Antonio Spur;
    Checkers Supermarket
11  Villa Italia; Publo's Bar & Restaurant
12  Nando's
14  Golden Egg
18  Mike's Kitchen
23  Porterhouse Restaurant

**OTHER**
1  Train Station
2  Oriental Plaza
3  Minibus Taxi Rank
4  Minibus Taxi Rank
5  SA Tours & Bookings
7  O'Hagans
8  North Link Tours Office;
    Library Gardens
9  OK Bazaar
13  City to City Buses
19  Pietersburg/Polokwane Marketing
    Company
20  Car Parking
21  Donkey Statue; Public Toilets

centre, past the stadium. Sites cost R25 for a tent and R30 for a caravan, or there are chalets for R110 for up to six people. If you're walking the trail in the adjacent nature reserve, sites are R10.

*Arnotha's* (☎ (0152) 291 3390) at 42 Hans van Rensburg St is a comfortable salespersons' refuge with rooms for R120/200, including breakfast. Of a similar standard are *Travellers' Lodge* (☎ (0152) 291 5511) at R150/125 on weekdays/weekends, and *Pietersburg Lodge* (☎ (0152) 292 1214) at R155/195.

The *Holiday Inn Garden Court* (☎ (0152) 291 2030) on Vorster St has rooms from R239/258, with breakfast. The *Ranch Hotel* (☎ (0152) 7293 7180), 25km south of town, is expensive at R240/340.

The best place to stay is *Vivaldi Guest House* (☎ (0152) 297 0816) at the corner of Voortrekker and South Sts; shared rooms cost from R150 to R160 per person. Also recommended are the new *Cycad Guest House* (☎ (0152) 291 2181) on the corner of Schoeman and South Sts (R280/340 on weekdays, R150/250 on weekends); *Col-John Accommodation* (☎ (0152) 295 9340) at 35 Burger St (R228/285 with breakfast); and *Kiepersol Overnight Accommodation* (☎ (0152) 297 0943) at 102 Hans van Rensburg St (R110/180).

**Places to Eat**
There is no shortage of eateries in town and along the N1. *Nando's* at 59 Schoeman St has

NORTHERN PROVINCE

spicy whole chicken packs for R33 and jumbo burgers for R19. *Mike's Kitchen* in the Glass House, by the Civic Centre, has steak (R30) and seafood. *San Antonio Spur*, for huge burgers (R16), and the once-renowned *Die Klause*, for continental food, are both in the Checkers Centre. *Villa Italia*, on Hans van Rensburg St, has pasta from R15.

Last time we were in Pietersburg there were very few night venues. Now there is *O'Hagan's* on Biccard St for Irish-style boozing, plus the friendly *Publo's Bar & Restaurant*, on Hans van Rensburg St, for a most pleasant night out with friendly staff (they sell healthy salads at the bar for R7.50).

### Getting There & Away
**Air** SA Airlink flies daily to and from Jo'burg; the Apex fare is R215 one way.

**Bus** City to City/Transtate runs between Jo'burg and Sibasa daily, and stops at the garage on the corner of Grobler and Dahl Sts. The Greyhound and Translux services between Jo'burg and Harare stop at the Shell Ultra on the highway about 10km south of town (at 2.30 and 2.45 am respectively); a taxi from here to town is R30 (try City Taxis ☎ (0152) 297 4493). North Link Tours services between Phalaborwa and Jo'burg stop at the Library Gardens bus stop on Hans van Rensburg St. Buy tickets at the North Link Tours head office (☎ (0152) 291 1867) nearby in the mall; the cost is R55 to Phalaborwa, R80 to Jo'burg, R30 to Tzaneen and R30 to Louis Trichardt.

**Train** The *Bosvelder* (Jo'burg-Beitbridge) stops here, as does the *Limpopo* (Jo'burg-Harare). Jo'burg to Louis Trichardt on the *Bosvelder* is R112/78 in 1st/2nd class; the *Limpopo* is R321/220.

**Minibus Taxi** The main minibus taxi rank is opposite the OK supermarket on Kerk St. There's another on Excelsior St near the train station – most Jo'burg taxis leave from here. To get to Phalaborwa take a minibus taxi (R6) to Boyne east of Pietersburg, and from Boyne take another one to Tzaneen (R9.50),

where you'll get another to Phalaborwa for R16.

Other fares from Pietersburg include: Louis Trichardt, R20; Thohoyandou, R28; Pretoria, R40; and Jo'burg, R45.

## LOUIS TRICHARDT
Louis Trichardt nestles into the south side of the Soutpansberg range and is cooler and wetter than the harsh thornbush country which suddenly appears north of the range.

The Soutpansberg tourist office (☎ (015) 516 0040) is on the N1 at the northern entrance to town; the staff here are knowledgeable and helpful. Get a copy of the free, fact-packed *Soutpansberg & Limpopo*. There's a Standard Bank on Krogh St and a First National Bank on Trichardt St.

The **Church of the Covenant**, on the corner of Erasmus and Krogh Sts, was built to fulfil the vow made by General Piet Joubert on the eve of his successful attack against the VhaVenda on Hangklip, in 1898. Behind the municipal buildings on Erasmus St is **Fort Hendrina**, an armour-plated structure once used as a base for attacks against local tribes.

### Places to Stay
There's a municipal *caravan park* (☎ (015) 516 0212) near the town centre off Grobler St; tent sites cost about R22.

*Ezriel Lodge* (☎ (015) 516 2222) is on the N1; take the turn-off at the Caltex petrol station at the northernmost four-way stop. Ezriel has rooms for R85/115; book in advance if you want a TV. In town, on Rissik St, the *Bergwater Hotel* (☎ (015) 516 0262) charges R163/234, including breakfast.

There are a couple of excellent guesthouses in town charging R80 to R100 per person. *Carousel Lodge* (☎ (015) 516 4482), down a side street off Rissik St, has singles/doubles with kitchen and bath for R100/140; breakfast is R15. *Lutombo Guesthouse* (☎ (015) 516 0850) at 141 Anderson St and *Die Grasdak* (☎ (015) 516 1773) at 45 Erasmus St are also recommended.

On the N1 north of Louis Trichardt are three more places. The best is the *Punch*

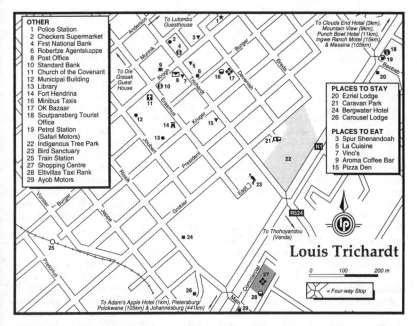

OTHER
1 Police Station
2 Checkers Supermarket
4 First National Bank
6 Robertze Agentskappe
8 Post Office
10 Standard Bank
11 Church of the Covenant
12 Municipal Building
13 Library
14 Fort Hendrina
16 Minibus Taxis
17 OK Bazaar
18 Soutpansberg Tourist Office
19 Petrol Station (Safari Motors)
22 Indigenous Tree Park
23 Bird Sanctuary
25 Train Station
27 Shopping Centre
28 Eltivillas Taxi Rank
29 Ayob Motors

PLACES TO STAY
20 Ezriel Lodge
21 Caravan Park
24 Bergwater Hotel
26 Carousel Lodge

PLACES TO EAT
3 Spur Shenandoah
5 La Cuisine
7 Vino's
9 Aroma Coffee Bar
15 Pizza Den

**Louis Trichardt**

*Bowl Hotel* (☎ (015) 517 7088) about 11km north of town. It's a small place on the dry side of the Soutpansberg, with some nice scenery. Rooms cost R85 per person and breakfast is R20 – this is where locals go to escape the ennui of their town. *Mountain View* (☎ (015) 517 7031) is 9km north of Louis Trichardt and has rooms from R130/210 for singles/doubles with breakfast; dinner is R35. *Clouds End Hotel* (☎ (015) 517 7021), 3km north of town, offers 'booze & snooze', but it isn't as tacky as that. It's a solid old place charging R130/230, including breakfast (dinner is R44). Watch out for the voracious vervet monkeys!

*Adam's Apple Hotel* (☎ (015) 516 4817), 16km south of Louis Trichardt on the N1, has singles/doubles from R135/210; including breakfast, and there is a variety of more expensive rooms. *Ingwe Ranch Motel* (☎ (015) 517 7087), 15km north of Louis Trichardt on the N1 (just before the tunnels), offers B&B for about the same price.

In the area around the scenic Levubu River, about 48km east of Louis Trichardt, *Lalani Lodge* (☎ (015) 583 0405) has single/double rooms for R150/240. Close to Albasini Dam is *Shiluvari Lakeside Lodge* (☎ (015) 583 3406) with thatched chalets and an excellent restaurant. It has singles/doubles for R135/225, including breakfast. Dinner is R30.

**Places to Eat**

*La Cuisine*, on the corner of Trichardt and Krogh Sts, is reasonable. It opens early for breakfast (steak and eggs are R25) and there's a good *bakery* in an adjoining café. At *Pizza Den*, on Trichardt St (between Kruger and President Sts) a large vegetarian pizza is R19 and those with meat toppings are R26. There's a *Spur Shenandoah* on Krogh St.

*Aroma Coffee Bar*, on Krogh St opposite the post office, is a hub for home industry enthusiasts. On the opposite side of the road

NORTHERN PROVINCE

from La Cuisine is *Vino's*, a restaurant/pub with continental food. *Tamboekie*, at Ingwe Ranch Motel (see Places to Stay), is a pleasant coffee shop.

### Getting There & Away

**Bus** City to City/Transtate buses running between Jo'burg and Sibasa stop at the train station, while the Translux service between Jo'burg and Harare stops outside the tourist office on the N1. You can book Translux tickets at the Robbertze Agentskappe (☎ (015) 516 5042) on Trichardt St. North Link Tours buses running to Jo'burg leave from the Bergwater Hotel. To Jo'burg it is R115, to Pietersburg is R30.

**Train** The train station is at the south-west end of Kruger St. The *Bosvelder* (Jo'burg-Beitbridge) and the *Limpopo* (Jo'burg-Harare) stop here.

**Minibus Taxi** The taxi park is in the OK Bazaar supermarket car park, off Burger St, a block north-east of Trichardt St. There is another taxi rank in Eltivillas. Fares from Louis Trichardt are: Zimbabwe border, R20; Messina, R17; Tzaneen, R20; Pietersburg, R20; Thohoyandou, R20; and Jo'burg, R60.

### AROUND LOUIS TRICHARDT
### Soutpansberg Hiking Trails

The original trail between Hangklip and Entabeni forest stations has closed, but there are still two good walks in the Soutpansberg. The two day, 20.5km **Hangklip Trail** includes a climb up a 1719m peak; it begins at the Hangklip Forest Station. The 52km **Entabeni Circular Route**, about 40km east of Louis Trichardt, has a number of options, including a less strenuous four day route and an arduous two day route, which should only be undertaken by fit hikers.

Watch out for malaria, bilharzia and ticks.

Overnight accommodation is in huts and there is a trail fee of R25 per person per day (this includes a good-quality walking map). To book these walks contact SAFCOL (☎ (013) 764 1058) in Sabie.

Keen hikers can stay in the western end of

the Soutpansberg at *Medike* (☎ (015) 516 0481) surrounded by the Sand River gorge. There are a number of trails where you can see rock paintings. Self-contained cottages are R85 per person and rustic camp sites are R25 per person. To get there from Louis Trichardt, follow Rissik St, which becomes the R522, and turn right onto a gravel road after 35km, just after you cross the Sand River. Continue on steeply for 8km, then turn right to the signposted entrance.

*George's Place* (☎ (01554) 641) is in the Sand River gorge in northern Soutpansberg; the comfortable accommodation in rustic wood cabins costs from R80 per person. To get there take the R523 to Waterpoor, cross the Sand River and take the signposted turn-off to the south.

### Lesheba Wilderness

Up on the top of the western Soutpansberg range, Lesheba Wilderness is a long, narrow reserve which is home to a range of animals. This is dramatic, varied country, with grassland, forests, plains and the cliffs of the Sand River gorge. Accommodation at *Duluni* and *Hamasha* is in cottages with cooking facilities, which cost about R80 per person; there are 4WD tours available. You must book (☎ (015) 593 0076) and the minimum stay is two nights.

To get there from Louis Trichardt, follow Rissik St, which becomes the R522, and turn right onto a gravel road after 35km, just after you cross the Sand River. Continue on for a steep drive of 10km to the entrance.

### Ben Lavin Nature Reserve

This 2500 hectare reserve (☎ (015) 516 4534) is worth visiting. There are four marked trails, all rewarding. The 8km Tabajwane Trail is good for wildlife viewing, while the Fountain Trail follows the Doring River; there are hides at water holes. There is quite a range of birds (about 240 species have been recorded) and animals, including giraffes, zebras and jackals. The African rock python, the only python species in this part of Africa, may be spotted in the reserve.

The park is open daily from 6 am to 7 pm.

Tent sites are R25, or you can stay in tents for R45, huts for R70 or the lodge for R88. You have to bring your own food.

To get there, travel south from Louis Trichardt on the N1 for about 3km and take the Elim turn-off to the left. After about 1km, turn off to the right to Fort Edward.

## TSHIPISE

This small settlement, east of the N1, is centred on the *Aventura Eco Tshipise* resort (☎ (015539) 608/9). Even if you've previously rejected such resorts for their holiday-camp atmosphere, Tshipise's bars, pools, shady tent sites and air-conditioned rooms will seem attractive in this hot, harsh area.

A powered camp site is R35, plus R15 per extra person, while standard two-bed units are R170 and four-bed units are R222 in the low season (in the high season they are R230/400). Rooms in the old hotel are R50 per person.

### Greater Kuduland Safaris

This upmarket private game reserve company (☎ (015539) 720; fax 808) has reserves at three locations – Tshipise, Alldays and Makuya. The 10,000 hectare Tshipise Reserve, consisting of mopane trees and mixed bush, includes many species of game. In addition to shy leopards and cheetahs, there are gemsboks, klipspringers, nyalas and other antelope species. The three to five-day hiking trails might be worth trying.

Accommodation in the main camp is in luxury huts and costs around R350 per person, with all meals included (minimum two day stay). There is the self-catering *Sunset Bushcamp* deep in the reserve. The R100 per person charge includes the 23km transfer to the camp, plus linen and crockery.

## MESSINA

The closest town to the Zimbabwe border, Messina is a hot, dusty little town with a frontier feel to it. The town grew around the copper mines which began operating in 1905 and are still functioning today. Road maps show Messina as being the same size as Pietersburg – it isn't. Away from the mines,

the town centre is a sleepy place. Groups of Zimbabweans wait patiently under the coral trees with mounds of luggage. A dog wanders down the street. The arrival of the train stirs the populace out of lethargy.

The Zimbabwean border is 12km away at Beitbridge (on the Limpopo River) and is open from 5.30 am to 10.30 pm. There is a R20 vehicle toll at the new bridge. Few hire vehicles are permitted to cross the border. South Africans need a visa to get into Zimbabwe, but can obtain it at the border.

You can change money at the First National Bank, which is open from 9 am to 12.45 pm and 2 to 3.30 pm on weekdays, and 8.30 am to 1 pm on Saturday.

You'll see some big baobab trees on the road south of here and, 5km south of the town just off the N1, is the **Messina Nature Reserve** (☎ (01553) 3235), established to protect the trees. There are some animals such as the nyala, kudu, Sharpe's grysbok and over 50 species of reptile. You can camp here now in permanent tents (all with reed-enclosed lapa areas) or stay in the three bedroom guesthouse. There is an 8km hiking trail and picnic facilities; entry to the reserve is free.

### Places to Stay & Eat

*Baobab Caravan Park* (☎ (01553) 40221) is on the southern outskirts of town, about 1.5km from the town centre. Sites cost around R15. Next door, *Impala Lielie Hotel* (☎ (01553) 40127) has a pool and restaurant; single/double rondavels are R100/130. *Limpopo River Lodge* (☎ /fax (01553) 40204) has single/double rooms for R105/140. *Ilala Lodge* (☎ (01553) 3220) is 8km out of Messina on the Venetia Mine road and is signposted from the Beitbridge road. It costs R90 per person here for grass-roofed rondavels.

*Matombo Lodge* (☎ (01553) 40115) is just north of Messina; the chalets here are R120 per person including breakfast. Not far away, *Mudzwiri Lodge* (☎ (01553) 41131/2) has singles/doubles for R171/274, including breakfast.

The best place in town for a meal is the

restaurant-cum-frontier bar *Meet 2 Eat* on the N1. There are also several fried chicken places and *Limpopo* in the lodge of the same name. There is also a *Buffalo Ridge Spur* on the N1 – Spur comes to Messina!

### Getting There & Away
**Bus** Translux buses on the Jo'burg to Harare route stop at the Limpopo River Lodge (R100 to Jo'burg and R125 to Harare via Bulawayo). Greyhound stops at Beitbridge on the other side of the border.

**Train** The *Bosvelder* terminates at Beitbridge, north of Messina. First/2nd class fares to Jo'burg are R143/96. The *Limpopo* stops here on the Friday run between Jo'burg and Harare at 8.30 pm (9 am on Sunday in the other direction). Those lucky enough to be travelling on the *Limpopo* can carry out border-crossing formalities on the train.

**Minibus Taxi** If you're coming from Zimbabwe and want to take a taxi further south than Messina, catch one at the border – there are many more there than in Messina. To Jo'burg it's R70, to Louis Trichardt it's R17 and to Pietersburg it's R33. Taxis between the border and Messina cost as little as R4.50, but you might have to pay more.

# The Waterberg

The Waterberg, west of the N1, gets its name from the many swamps, springs and streams in the range. The 150km-long range stretches from Thabazimbi in the south to the Lapalala River in the north-east and is usually divided into southern and northern regions. It is a wild and inspirational place, with sourveld and bushveld etched by rivers.

The poet and naturalist Eugene Marais wrote his famous works on termites and baboons *(The Soul of the White Ant* and *The Soul of the Ape)* here. He also discovered a rare cycad, but forgot to record its location. Rediscovered years later, it was named *Encephalartos eugenemaraisii* after him.

One unpleasant feature of the Waterberg is the hunting lodges. Their advertising depicts hunters with high-powered rifles posing with dead zebra, kudu and leopard. Avoid!

### Horse-riding
The Waterberg is a great location for horse-riding and there are a number of places where you can ride in an area rich in wildlife. Equus Trails, within the Touch Stone Game Ranch (☎ (014) 765 0230), is south-east of Marken off the R518. It can be reached from Potgietersrus or Vaalwater. The trails pass through Waterberg bushveld and near to the Lapalala River. It's not unusual to encounter rhino and many other wildlife species. Accommodation is in overnight bush camps.

### BONWA PHALA & MABULA
In the Waterberg area there are several private game reserves and lodges, including *Bonwa Phala* (☎ (014) 736 4101), 30km west of Warmbad, which charges more than R400 per person, including meals and game drives.

*Mabula Game Lodge* (☎ (014734) 771) is luxurious; singles/doubles are R460/750, including breakfast, and R40 extra per person on weekends. Mabula is near the Waterberg and 'big five' animals can be found here. To get to Mabula from Warmbad, take the R516; turn off to Rooiberg after 34km, and 4km on turn right to Rhenosterhoekspruit. Mabula is 7km further on.

### THABAZIMBI
Thabazimbi (Mountain of Iron) is 126km west of Warmbad on the R516 and 129km north of Rustenburg on the R510. Nearby is the imposing Kransberg, highest peak of the Waterberg. The **Ben Alberts Nature Reserve**, 7km south of town, has an abundance of wildlife and good game-viewing vantage points; there is a *caravan park* (☎ (014773) 21509) here. *Hotel Kransberg* (☎ (014773) 71586) charges R125 per person for bed and breakfast.

## VAALWATER & MELKRIVIER

Vaalwater, the centre of the Waterberg, is 60km north-west of Nylstroom on the R517. There are a number of attractions in the region, including the Lapalala Wilderness to the north. The moderately priced *Vaalwater Hotel* (☎ (014775) 3600) is the only source of nightlife in the region.

From Vaalwater there's a circular drive on an extremely scenic dirt road through the Waterberg. Head north-west of town on the R517 for 10km, then turn south for 37km. At the prominent junction turn right for 20km to **Palace of the Vultures**, a breeding colony of the Cape vulture *(Gyps coprotheres)*. Return to the junction, but then continue straight ahead over Rankin's Pass. Here, take the Tweestroom road back to the R517 and turn left to Vaalwater or right to Nylstroom.

North-east of Vaalwater is the pleasant little town of Melkrivier (Milk River) on the banks of the Lapalala. *Emaweni Game Lodge* (☎ (014775) 2714) is an upmarket place with a magnificent aspect on the banks of the Lapalala. Note that some of our readers have questioned the level of service here.

To get to Melkrivier take the Vaalwater road from Nylstroom. In Vaalwater, turn north and drive for 45km to Melkrivier.

## LAPALALA WILDERNESS

This big, private reserve (25,600 hectares) is an area of high ecological value. It has a number of animals – including black and white rhinos, zebras, blue wildebeests and several antelope species, plus hippos and crocodiles in bilharzia-free rivers – but it's best known as a conservation area. More than 270 species of birds have been recorded. In 1990, Lapalala was the first private reserve to obtain black rhinos. The pamphlet *Lapalala Wilderness: A Natural Heritage*, provided at the reserve, contains a comprehensive species checklist.

The reserve is divided into three areas. In the wilderness area you don't have to take a guide when canoeing or hiking. Once you have driven in you are alone. The second area is an environmental school comprising Molope and Moletse, and the third contains Kolobe Lodge and Rhino Camp.

Ask the rangers to point out the unusual **termite mounds** built under layers in the sandstone. It almost appears that the ants have lifted the sandstone slabs and built beneath them, earning the builders the name 'Arnold Schwarzenegger ants'.

There are many **San paintings** in the reserve, especially along the Kgogong and Lapalala rivers. There are also a number of prehistoric **Iron Age sites**.

### Places to Stay

Six small camps are scattered through the wilderness, with accommodation from R50 to R100 per person, depending on numbers. The camps are *Tambuti*, *Mukwa*, *Umdoni*, *Lepotedi*, *Munadu* and *Marula* – all named after trees indigenous to the area. There are cooking facilities, but you must bring all your own supplies. The minimum stay is two nights; book on (☎ (011) 453 7645), as Lapalala is popular.

*Kolobe Lodge*, also (☎ (011) 453 7645), has a 16 bed lodge, four luxury rondavels, a pool, a restaurant and guided walks. For R300 per person you get all meals and game drives. Visitors usually have their own car, but the lodge will pick you up from the train station in Vaalwater. Clive Walker Safari's *Rhino Camp* (with the same ☎ number) accommodates eight in luxury-style tents for R250, all inclusive.

### Getting There & Away

From Nylstroom take the R517 to Vaalwater and from there head to Melkrivier. After 40km take the turn-off to Melkrivier school and continue for 25km. The gates close at 7 pm.

## MARAKELE NATIONAL PARK

We don't have much information on this newest of the national parks; it protects a section of the Waterberg on the Sterkstroom River. West of Vaalwater, it is reached by a dirt road to the west of Hermanusdorings. There is limited, four-bed tent accommodation; it costs R120 for two and R40/20 for each extra adult/child.

# Venda

The Venda area, the Homeland of the Vha-
Venda people under the apartheid regime, is
a fascinating place to visit for its culture and
scenery. More than any other region in South
Africa, you might feel that you are 'in Africa'
here, with perhaps the exception of parts of
the former Transkei.

The Soutpansberg harbours rainforest and
is strikingly lush compared with the hot, dry
lowveld to the north. Several forests and
lakes in the region are of great religious
significance to the VhaVenda people.

Endear yourself to the locals with traditional VhaVenda greetings. When a man
enters a house he says *Ndaa!* (Hello) and a
woman says *Aa!* The response is *Ndaa!* or
*Aa!* depending on the sex. When you leave
the simple farewell is *Salani.* You might also
want to try local delicacies, *nziya* (locusts)

or *mopane worms* (caterpillars living on the
mopane tree) – a crunchy snack, often dried
on an open fire and added to a thick, spicy
sauce.

### WARNING
Venda is in a malarial area and bilharzia is
present in many of the dams and streams.
Marauding crocodiles are also a reality.

### THOHOYANDOU & SIBASA
Created as the capital of the former Venda
Homeland, Thohoyandou has a casino, a
large shopping mall, some impressive public
buildings and not much else. The huge mall
buzzes, however, and is about the closest you
will come to a true 'African' city in South
Africa – disorganisation, ghetto blasters,
rows of 'takkies' for sale, street stalls and all.
The adjacent town (more a suburb, really) of
**Sibasa** is a few kilometres north. Most public transport leaves from Sibasa.

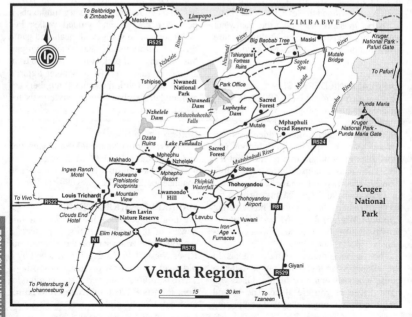

Venda Region

## History of the VhaVenda People

Just when the VhaVenda people arrived in the Soutpansberg range, and where they came from, are matters of dispute among historians. There are elements of Zimbabwean culture, including stone structures similar in style (if not scale) to Great Zimbabwe, and mining and metalworking have long been important elements in the VhaVenda economy and culture. The Lemba people, another group living in Venda, appear to have had contact with Islam.

What is known is that in the early 18th century a group of VhaSenzi and VhaLemba, led by Chief Dimbanyika, crossed the Limpopo and located a tributary which they called the Nzhelele (Enterer). They moved up the Nzhelele and into the Soutpansberg, calling their new land Venda, believed to mean 'Pleasant Land'.

At Lwandali they set up a chief's kraal and called it Dzata. When Dimbanyika died some of his people moved south down the Nzhelele, where they established another Dzata. Under the new chief, Thohoyandou, the VhaVenda flourished and their influence was felt widely. When Thohoyandou disappeared mysteriously, this Dzata was abandoned and there was a period of unrest as his offspring fought for succession.

Several invaders then tried to take over the VhaVenda lands. First came the Boers under Paul Kruger, then the Swazis, the BaPedi and the Tsonga. The VhaVenda, however, managed to avoid being overrun throughout the 19th century and did not even admit missionaries into their territory. This was partly due to the geography of the Soutpansberg, which made attack difficult, and partly to the tsetse fly, which made this area unattractive to graziers.

It was not until 1898 that a Boer army of 4000 men conquered Venda. Perhaps if the VhaVenda had been able to hold out for a year, the defeat of the Boer republics in the 1899-1902 Anglo-Boer War would have given them time to negotiate a place in the Union of South Africa. That was not to be, and Venda was absorbed into the Transvaal, to be granted 'independent Homeland' status in 1979.

Today the region is part of Northern Province, but retains its unique culture. ■

The Venda tourist office (☎ (0159) 41577; fax 41048) is at the Ditike Craft Centre, on the Louis Trichardt road. You can book accommodation for Acacia Park (Thohoyandou), Nwanedi National Park, Mphephu Resort and Sagole Spa there.

To find out what is happening in Venda get a copy of the Friday *Mirror* (R1).

### Organised Tours

Several interesting tours run from the Ditike Craft Centre. Not far from Thohoyandou, the **Phiphidi Waterfall** on the Mutshindudi River is often included in the tours; entry to the falls is R2.

The highlight of the day tour through Southern Venda is meeting Noria Mabasa, a woman who sculpts traditional VhaVenda characters in clay and wood (the latter medium was traditionally an occupation for men only).

A half-day tour costs R80 per person and a full-day tour is R120 (both with a minimum of three people). Longer tours and guided walks are also available. There is an extra charge of R180 when the guide is away overnight.

### Places to Stay & Eat

Thohoyandou/Sibasa does not have much in the way of accommodation; it remains as it was two years ago. *Acacia Park* (☎ (0159) 22506) has 16 self-contained chalets for R120 a double, serviced caravan sites for R30 and camp sites for R20.

The motel-style *Bougainvillea Lodge* (☎ (0159) 82 4064) is about a kilometre from Thohoyandou, up the hill towards Sibasa. It is friendly, clean and comfortable, but singles/doubles are not cheap at R160/200, breakfast included.

*Venda Sun Hotel* (☎ (0159) 21011), in the centre of Thohoyandou, has rooms from R280/380, with breakfast. There's a casino, restaurant and pool.

Things change! Once there was only the Sun for half-decent food. Now, at the bus park you have *Nando's*, *Zapa's Eating Land*

NORTHERN PROVINCE

PLACES TO STAY
7  Venda Sun Hotel
10  Bougainvillea Lodge
19  Acacia Park

PLACES TO EAT
5  Nando's; Zapa's Eating Land; Pie City
18  Fish & Chix; Super Munch

OTHER
1  24-hour Petrol Station
2  Tourist Office; Ditike Craft Centre
3  Total Petrol Station
4  Shell Petrol Station
6  Police
8  Automatic Tellers
9  Venda University
11  Minibus Taxis
12  Shopping Centre
13  Buses
14  Radio Thohoyandou
15  Government Buildings
16  Shopping Centre; Minibus Taxis
17  Venda Open Market Mall

Thohoyandou & Sibasa

0      0.5      1 km
Approximate Scale

and *Pie City*. In the Venda open market there is *Fish & Chix* and *Super Munch*. All are not up to much, but at least there is some choice these days.

### Getting There & Away

**Air** It's possible to fly from Lanseria airport in Randburg (41km from Jo'burg) to Thohoyandou with Theron Airways (☎ (011) 659 2738) on weekdays. The fare is about R460 and the flight takes two hours.

**Bus** City to City/Transtate runs between Pretoria and Thohoyandou/Sibasa (R60); there is a second service via Nzhelele. Magweba company has a daily bus, Sibasa to Sagole (R8), departing at 1 pm from Sibasa bus park.

**Minibus Taxi** In Thohoyandou taxis congregate in the car park of the shopping centre across the road from the Venda Sun Hotel. The fare to Sibasa is R2.30. The main taxi park is in Sibasa, on the corner of the road from Thohoyandou. Fares include: Mutale, R4.50; Punda Maria (frequent taxis), R15; Sagole Spa, R7; Messina (three daily), R15;

Louis Trichardt, R16; Mphephu Resort, R4.50; and Jo'burg, R65.

### NWANEDI NATIONAL PARK

The dry, northern side of the Soutpansberg provides an extremely scenic backdrop to the park, although it's a contrast to Venda's other lush landscapes. The vegetation is mainly mopane and mixed woodland. It can be very hot here in summer. The main attraction for most visitors is fishing on the Nwanedi and Luphephe dams (on tributaries of the Nwanedi which feed into the Limpopo River). The major walk in the park is to the very scenic **Tshihovhohovho Falls**.

There is limited wildlife viewing, including white rhinos, warthogs, kudus, blue wildebeests, impalas, elands, klipspringers and the common duiker. There are lions and cheetahs, but they are in enclosures. The park gates are open from 6 am to 6 pm.

### Places to Stay & Eat

*Tent sites* cost R16 and there are four-person *chalets* for R120. Four-bed luxury *rooms* (two beds on the ground floor and two on a mezzanine level are R230/380 for singles/

## VhaVenda Arts & Crafts

VhaVenda culture is extremely rich and diverse, and a visit to the many arts and crafts outlets in this region is always rewarding. About 4000 people are actively engaged in local arts and crafts industries.

Perhaps most interesting are the many traditional potteries. Here you can see Venda pots, famous throughout South Africa, thrown and fired. As the potteries are a cottage industry it is necessary to have a guide so you can enter the village workplaces.

The 'master' potters in Venda tradition are all women. The pots are fashioned from mud by hand, smoothed with a piece of leather, dried in the sun for about three days (depending on the weather), glazed and fired. Originally the glaze was graphite, but now many different types of paint are added.

Firing is done in a wide, shallow hole. Thin saplings of carefully selected local trees are added to control the rate of firing. If there is too much heat the pots will crack. Usually the firing takes about four hours.

Traditional pots come in 10 different sizes and designs. Each has a different function – cooking, serving food or liquids, or storage. The pots, which feature brightly coloured geometric designs, are more ornamental than functional.

Traditional clay figures *(zwifanyiso)* are fashioned from clay like the pots, but are sun-dried rather than fired. These figures may depict a group scene or individuals, such as important tribal personalities.

Woodcarvings are also popular. Traditionally woodcarving was a men-only occupation, but a modern master is the talented Noria Mabasa (see Organised Tours). A number of local woods are used such as *mudzwin, mutango* and *musimbiri*. Carved items include chains attached to calabashes and bowls, salad bowls, spoons, trays, pots, walking sticks and knobkerries (a stick with a round knob at one end, used as a club or missile). ∎

doubles, breakfast included. Similar rooms, without air-conditioning, are R220/340. Basic supplies are available and there's a fully licensed *restaurant*. You can hire canoes for R40.

### Getting There & Away

You can reach the park from Thohoyandou, entering at the Nwanedi Gate, but while the road is scenic there's a good chance of getting lost, and there are several kilometres of bad dirt road. It's simpler to come via Tshipise and enter from the west. Tshipise is the nearest place to buy fuel.

By public transport you could take a minibus taxi from Sibasa to Gomela, a tiny village 3km from the Nwanedi Gate. From the gate it's another 6km to the office and accommodation along a quiet road.

### MPHEPHU RESORT

This resort, known for its hot springs, is 34km west of Thohoyandou. (Mphephu was one of the great chiefs of the VhaVenda and ruled from the late 19th century until his death in 1924. He was the son of Makhado, the 'Lion of the North'.)

Day visits cost R3. Accommodation is in 20 chalets which cost from R120. Book at the Ditike Craft Centre in Thohoyandou. There is a licensed self-service *restaurant* in the complex.

### LAKE FUNDUDZI

This lake is a sacred site, as its water is believed to have come from the great sea which covered the earth before land was created. The python god, which holds an important place in the rites of Venda's matriarchal culture and once required human sacrifice, lives here. The lake is 35km west of Thohoyandou, but unfortunately it's impossible to visit it without permission – unlikely to be granted – from the lake's priestess. (Another home of the python god is the hot spring at Sagole.) You do get a glimpse of the lake if you take a tour from Thohoyandou.

Near the lake is **Thathe-Vondo**, the Sacred Forest. A spirit lion guards the burial grounds of VhaVenda chiefs in the forest.

### Mabudashango Hiking Trail

The four day (50km) Mabudashango Hiking

Trail starts at Mabudashango Hut near the Thathe-Vondo forest station and heads for 15.3km through the Sacred Forest to Fundudzi Rest Camp. Day 2 is through the forest for 16km to Mukumbani Dam; Day 3 is a return loop of 12.2km via the Mahovhohovho Waterfall to Mukumbani Dam; and the last day is a 10km walk to the Thathe-Vondo forest station.

Take precautions against ticks, mosquitoes and malaria. Accommodation is in basic trail shelters and in the forester's cottage at the Thathe-Vondo forest station. Book with the Department of Water Affairs & Forestry (☎ (0159) 31001, ext 2235), Private Bag X2247, Sibasa, Northern Province.

## SAGOLE

This VhaVenda town is near Sagole village and the hot springs spa of the same name. To the north-west of Sagole are the **Tshiungane stone fortifications** and nearby, in caves, are the remains of dwellings with clay grain bins built into the rocky walls. What is believed to be the biggest **baobab** in Africa is close to the ruins.

Sagole Spa has two six-bed cottages with plunge pools fed by the nearby hot spring; these are a bargain at R180. The three-bed rondavels are R45 per person or R60 with showers and toilets. Dorm beds (usually booked for groups of children) are R10 and camp sites/caravan sites are R10/12. Book at the Ditike Craft Centre in Thohoyandou.

## MUTALE, VUWANI & MASHAMBA

Near **Mutale**, north of Thohoyandou, there is a wood-carving workshop where you can see the ceremonial *domba* drums being made. The drums are beaten during the python dance, an integral part of the female puberty ceremony.

South of **Vuwani**, you can see the remains of Iron Age furnaces where the VhaVenda smelted high-grade iron for centuries. Many of their metal-working skills have been lost, but the craft of making attractive pottery continues. **Mashamba** also has several metal-working foundries.

### Land of Legend

The lakes, rivers, mountains, caves and forests of Venda form a rich spirit world. Stories of natural and ancestral beings abound. Almost every body of water, whether it be a stream, waterfall or lake, is inhabited by 'water elves' or spirits.

Most famous of these is sacred Lake Fundudzi, which can only be visited with the permission of the priestess of the lake (which is not likely to be given). Around the lake there are a number of spirit gardens where spirits tend their crops, large rocks in the shape of drums where spirits meet in celebration and other sacred rocks where the VhaVenda make offerings to allow the spirits to sample recent crops.

In the Thathe-Vondo forest, west of Thohoyandou, is the Sacred Forest, which no strangers are permitted to enter. At Lwamondo Hill, south-west of Thohoyandou, the baboons (which once warned the VhaVenda of approaching enemies) are venerated. The nearby forest manifests a plague of snakes if anyone tries to steal firewood without the permission of the priest Tshifhe. If you are observant, you may see the furtive Ditutwane when you visit Phiphidi Waterfall. These water spirits resemble half people and have only one eye and a single leg and arm.

The most important of the initiation ceremonies is the fertility rite *(domba)*. Drums made in Mutale resound night after night as VhaVenda maidens are prepared for adulthood. The ceremony culminates in the famous python dance when many VhaVenda girls join in a writhing 'conga' formation.

Herbalists and traditional doctors are very much part of daily life. By using an intricately carved divining bowl *(ndilo)*, a diviner is able to communicate with spirits and share their wisdom. ■

# The North-East

The north-east, often overlooked because of the more popular Blyde River and Klein Drakensberg areas to the south, is well worth a visit.

It is very culturally rich, being the traditional home of the Tsonga-Shangaan and Lobedu people. It is also popular for a north-south traverse through Kruger National Park or a visit to one of the many private game reserves in the Hoedspruit area. The main town of Tzaneen is pleasant and a good base for trips into the nearby scenic Modjadji and Magoebaskloof regions.

## VENDA TO TZANEEN

A popular route goes all the way through Kruger National Park from the Punda Maria Gate to one of the numerous exits in the south (see Kruger National Park in the Mpumalanga chapter). If you are coming from Venda, the Tzaneen/Letaba region can also be reached via the R529 and there are a number of interesting places close to this route.

The former Homeland of the Tsonga-Shangaan people, Gazankulu, is extremely poor. Yet the population carries on in spite of dust, flies and poor sanitation. Kids laugh as they kick a football around on the barren plains. Hopefully, these stoic people will be afforded more of a chance in future.

The main centre, **Giyani**, is north of Phalaborwa and has a frontier atmosphere. It is best reached on the road running north from the R36 at Mooketsi or the R529 road running south from the R524, 45km east of Thohoyandou. Few visitors come here and there is almost no tourist development. In fact, we could only find one place to stay, *Giyani Hotel* (☎ (0158) 23230). For traditional food such as chicken offal, pap and vleis try the *Bush Spaza Shop*.

City to City/Transtate buses run between Jo'burg and Giyani, via Louis Trichardt.

### Hans Merensky Nature Reserve

This 5000 hectare reserve (☎ (015) 386 8632) is bordered by the Letaba River, but you risk bilharzia if you swim in the river, not to mention the risk from larger denizens – crocs and hippos. You'd have to be lucky to see a lion or a leopard, but there is plenty of other game.

The **Tsonga Kraal** (☎ (015) 386 8727), an open-air museum of Tsonga traditional life, is in the reserve. It comprises sleeping huts, a chief's hut, grain stores, cooking shelters, a sacrificial place and domestic animal enclosures. The village people wear tradi-tional dress and play their own musical instruments. There are guided tours at 10 am and 3 pm Monday to Friday and 10 am on Saturday; it is closed on Sunday.

*Aventura Eiland Eco* (☎ (015) 386 8667) in the reserve has rondavels for R180 (R240 in high season) and unpowered sites for R20 plus R15 per person.

To get to the reserve, take the R71 east from Tzaneen towards Phalaborwa, and turn off to the left onto the R529 after 27km. The reserve is 40km further on. Occasional minibus taxis run along the R71, but the rest of the journey will require hitching.

### Modjadji Nature Reserve

This small reserve (☎ (015) 632 6144) of 305 hectares protects forests of the ancient Modjadji cycad. In the summer mists this place takes on an ethereal atmosphere.

Take the Duiwelskloof/Ga-Kgapane turn-off from the R36 about 10km north of Duiwelskloof; the turn-off to the reserve is a few kilometres further on.

### Duiwelskloof/Ga-Kgapane

This small village is in the wooded hills north of Tzaneen. The name refers to the devilishly hard time the early European settlers had getting their wagons up and down the hills. In 1916 it was to be called Modjadji, after the Rain Queen, but the white population objected because of 'heathen connotations'

### The Modjadji Cycad

The Modjadji cycad *(Encephalartos transvenosus)*, a living fossil, is one of the largest cycads in the world. It averages a height of 5 to 8m and can grow to 13m. It dates back to the Mesozoic era, approximately 50 to 60 million years ago, when dinosaurs roamed the landscape.

Some claim that cycads have survived here because they grow on land protected by the Rain Queen (see boxed text 'Modjadji - the Rain Queen'). It is more likely that they have survived because local inhabitants have found no use for them. ■

## Modjadji – the Rain Queen

In Africa it is unusual for a woman to be sovereign of a tribe, but the Rain Queen is an exception. The Queen resides in the town of Ga-Modjadji in the Bolebodu district near Duiwelskloof. Every year, around November, a festival is held to celebrate the coming of the rains, which is presided over by the Queen. The *indunas* (tribal headmen) select people to dance naked and call for rain, to perform traditional rituals and to undergo male and female initiation ceremonies. After the ceremony, the rain falls. The absence of rain is usually attributed to some event such as the destruction of a sacred place – a situation only resolved by further ritual.

During the rest of the year the Queen has a number of other functions. She never marries, yet still bears children. When she dies, succession normally falls to the eldest of her daughters (the fathers have very insignificant roles). The Queen is buried in the evening and only close relatives and indunas are permitted to go to the burial place. ■

– they named it after the devil instead! It now combines the name of the large nearby black community, Ga-Kgapane. Tourist information is available from the town hall (☎ (015) 309 9246).

There are a number of **hiking trails** in the vicinity. The Panorama and Piesangkop trails are accessible to most people. The library provides free walking notes.

**Places to Stay** *Duiwelskloof Municipal Chalets & Caravan Park* (☎ (015) 309 9246) has sites for R35, two-bed rondavels for R60 and four-person rondavels (with attached kitchen and bathroom) for R110. There are guest farms and holiday cottages in the area; ask at the tourist office.

*Imp Inn* (☎ (015) 309 9253), a nice country pub (but with a disillusioned, grumpy and often uniformed Afrikaner clientele), has singles/doubles for R110/160, including breakfast (R90/120 on weekends).

## LETABA DISTRICT

The Letaba Valley, to the south-east of Tzaneen and east of Pietersburg/Polokwane, is

between two chunks of the former Lebowa Homeland. Tzaneen is the main town in the area and most places of interest are easily reached from here. The valley is subtropical and lush, with tea plantations and crops of tropical fruits, while on the hills are forests, mainly of the plantation variety. Tours of the **Sapekoe Tea Plantation** (☎ (0152) 307 3120) are held from Tuesday to Friday.

The 100km drive along the R71 from Pietersburg to Tzaneen is scenic. Some 24km east of Pietersburg at Turfloop is the **University of the North**, the largest black university in the country. A further 6km on, at Boyne, is **Zion City Moria**, the headquarters of the Zion Christian Church. At Easter, millions of followers (identifiable by their badge with a silver star on a green background) congregate here.

At Haenertsburg the road splits, with the R71 reaching Tzaneen via the steep Magoebaskloof Pass, while the R528 runs along the more gentle George's Valley.

### Haenertsburg & the Magoebaskloof

Haenertsburg, a village established during the 1887 gold rush, is on the escarpment above the Letaba Valley and is the centre of a forestry and cherry-growing region. The Cherry Blossom Festival is held at Cheerio Halt Farm in late September/early October.

The Magoebaskloof is the escarpment on the edge of the highveld, and the road here drops quickly down to Tzaneen and the lowveld, passing through plantations and large tracts of thick, indigenous forest. The high summer rainfall means that there are a number of waterfalls in the area, including **Debengeni Falls** in the De Hoek State Forest. You can swim in the pool at the bottom, but be careful as there have been many deaths here. To get there turn west off the R71 at Bruphy Sawmills.

Author John Buchan once lived here, near the present Magoebaskloof Hotel, and his book *Prester John* (a good read, if incredibly racist and imperialist) is set in the area.

**Woodbush Indigenous Forest** This is the largest indigenous forest in Northern Province and there are some very tall trees. Leopards are found here.

**Magoebaskloof Hiking Trails** There are several trails in the area. Walks take up to three days and pass through some beautiful country. The walking can be challenging and you should be fit before setting out.

Two recommended walks are the two day, 21km **Debengeni** trail and the three day, 37km **Dokolewa Waterfall** trail; both are rated moderately difficult. Overnight stays during the Dokolewa Waterfall trail are in huts placed near waterfalls and streams.

There is also a three day Dokolewa House trail in which overnight stops are in old forestry houses. Book these with SAFCOL (☎ (013) 764 1058) in Sabie.

**Places to Stay** About 8km north of Haenertsburg, *Troutwaters Inn* (☎ (0152) 276 4245) has fairly pricey camp sites and chalets, and hotel rooms for R150/210 with breakfast (R65 for each extra adult). Some 2.5km from Haenertsburg on the R71 to the Magoebaskloof is the comfortable *Glenshiel Country Lodge* (☎ (0152) 276 4335); rooms start at R325 per person, all inclusive.

*Magoebaskloof Hotel* (☎ /fax (015) 276 4276) has singles/doubles from R160/250, including breakfast.

*The Coach House* (☎ /fax (0152) 307 3641), about 15km south of Tzaneen near the New Agatha Forest, is a refurbished old hotel with views and good food. Rooms start at R275/500 for a single/double (or R300 per person for shared luxury rooms); breakfast is not included.

**Tzaneen**

Tzaneen, the largest town in the Letaba district, is a good place to base yourself. Tourist information is available from the town hall (☎ (0152) 307 1411; fax 307 1507) or from Letaba Tourism (☎ (015) 276 4307; fax 276 4386). The small **Tzaneen Museum** has an interesting collection of Tsonga cultural artefacts, including a Rain Queen ceremonial drum, and is well worth a visit; entry is free.

You can change money at the ABSA Trust Bank or the First National Bank in the town centre. Opposite the Trust Bank, near the Karos Tzaneen Hotel, is a telephone bureau where you can make hassle-free international calls. Nu Metro cinemas, open every day for two showings, are in the Oasis Mall on Aqua St.

Clarke's Backpackers Bus and Tours (☎ (0152) 307 2000) offers tours throughout Letaba. They have day/overnight trips to Kruger National Park for R175/280 (minimum of four people). Letaba Active Tours (☎ (0152) 307 3538) also offers trips in the Letaba region.

**Places to Stay** *Fairview Lodge & Caravan Park* (☎ (0152) 307 4809) is 1km from the town centre, just off the R71. In the Arbor Park shopping centre, on the corner of Soetdoring and Geelhout Sts, *Arborpark Travel Lodge* (☎ (0152) 307 1831) has singles/doubles for about R150/210, with breakfast an extra R10.

*Karos Tzaneen Hotel* (☎ /fax (0152) 307 3140) charges from R250/330, including breakfast.

Five km out of town on the R71 is *Steffi's Sun Lodge* (☎ (0152) 307 1475), a very pleasant B&B with friendly owners; singles/doubles are R120/170. The balcony of this Cape Dutch-style house is a great place to relax. There are a number of other B&Bs in the area, at around R100 to R120 per person; inquire at the information office on the corner of Pienaar and Peace Sts. As examples, *La Borie* (☎ (0152) 307 5282) at 23B Circle Rd and *Tamboti Lodge* (☎ (0152) 307 4526) on Tamboti St are both good.

**Places to Eat** *Nando's*, on the corner of Lannie Ave and Danie Joubert St, has half/full chicken packs for R30/49. *Tino's Pizzeria* on Agatha St and *The Villa Italiana*, on Danie Joubert St next to Nando's, have smallish pizzas from R22. *Atelier Koffiehuis* at 46 Boundary St has great pancakes.

There are two steakhouses – *Porterhouse*, near the Oasis Mall on Aqua St, and *Emerald Creek Spur*, at 16 Morgan St. *Addison's* at Arborpark Travel Lodge, open daily (except

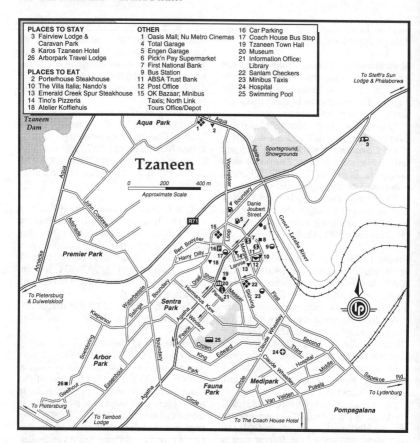

PLACES TO STAY
3  Fairview Lodge &
   Caravan Park
8  Karos Tzaneen Hotel
26 Arborpark Travel Lodge

PLACES TO EAT
2  Porterhouse Steakhouse
10 The Villa Italia; Nando's
13 Emerald Creek Spur Steakhouse
14 Tino's Pizzeria
18 Atelier Koffiehuis

OTHER
1  Oasis Mall; Nu Metro Cinemas
4  Total Garage
5  Engen Garage
7  Pick'n Pay Supermarket
7  First National Bank
9  Bus Station
11 ABSA Trust Bank
12 Post Office
15 OK Bazaar; Minibus
   Taxis; North Link
   Tours Office/Depot

16 Car Parking
17 Coach House Bus Stop
19 Tzaneen Town Hall
20 Museum
21 Information Office;
   Library
22 Sanlam Checkers
23 Minibus Taxis
24 Hospital
25 Swimming Pool

---

Sunday) for meals, gets favourable reviews from locals.

**Getting There & Away** The minibus taxi park is behind the OK Bazaar, off the main street in the centre of town. Destinations and fares include Jo'burg, R60; Phalaborwa, R20; Pietersburg (change at Boyne), R18; Haenertsburg, R10; Duiwelskloof, R5; and Lydenburg, R25.

North Link Tours (☎ (0152) 307 2950) buses stop at the rear of the OK Bazaar. These buses run from Phalaborwa (R30) to Jo'burg (R115), via Pietersburg (R30).

**Lekgalameetse Nature Reserve**

A reserve of 20,000 hectares in mountainous country intersected by the Ga-Selati River, Lekgalameetse also includes some remaining indigenous forest. As a transition region between the lowveld and the Drakensberg, it is particularly rich in plants, with over 1200 species, including the rare *Aloe monotropa*. The huge yellowwoods and sneezewoods found here are some of the biggest in the country.

Occasionally antelopes can be seen, plus there are leopards and some rare butterflies. Cabins are available (about R75), as well as tents on the hiking trails. The area is still sometimes known as 'the Downs' as, in parts, it resembles England's Surrey Downs.

The park office (☎ (0152302), ext 1514) is near Trichardtsdal, west off the R36 about 55km south of Tzaneen.

## Wolkberg Wilderness Area

South of Tzaneen in the northern tail of the Drakensberg, this 22,000 hectare wilderness area (☎ (0152) 295 9713) has hiking trails and, in the valleys to the south and east, stands of indigenous forest. Some animals are returning – including a few shy leopards and hyenas – after the area was shot-out by hunters and the *dagga* growers who flourished here until the 1950s; it's rumoured that their crop still grows in some of the ravines. Hikers should be aware of snakes – particularly the black mamba, puff adder and berg adder. More than 150 bird species have been recorded. It rains a lot here in summer, while in winter it can get cold.

There is a *camp site* at the Serala Forest Station on the western side (the nearest town is Haenertsburg), although from Tzaneen the main access point is via the New Agatha Forest Station to the north. You can't drive in the wilderness area, so plan your trip well. Fires aren't permitted so you'll need a gas or fuel stove. Book the hiking trails (a permit is essential) through SAFCOL (☎ (013) 764 1058) in Sabie.

## PHALABORWA

Phalaborwa is new, clean and planned. The town has an interesting mix of cultures – Tsonga, Shangaan, Pedi, Sotho, VhaVenda and Afrikaners. The majority of the black population lives in the nearby townships of Nawakgale, Lulekani, Majeje and Namakushan. The BaPhalaborwa (which means 'better than the south') Festival is celebrated in late August and well worth seeing; entry is a ridiculously cheap R2.50 per person.

Phalaborwa is a copper-mining town and the metal has been mined here for at least 1200 years. You can tour the current mine, a big open-cut operation, at 9 am on Friday. Phone first on ☎ (01524) 80 2337.

Just near the airport turn-off there is a **mystery tree** – part mopane with a marula growing out of its side!

The Phalaborwa Gate into Kruger National Park is 3km from the town itself. The sluggish Phalaborwa Association for Tourism (☎ (01524) 85860) is close by. It's open 7.30 am to 5 pm on weekdays and 8 am to noon on Saturday.

Jumbo River Safaris (☎ (01524) 86168) has game-viewing raft trips down the Olifants River at sunset; the cost is R40 per person. There are Microflight Flips over private game parks adjacent to the Kruger National Park with great game viewing; the cost is R50 for 10 minutes or R150 for 30 minutes. There are also night drives into the park from the town for R60. For these trips, contact the Phalaborwa Association for Tourism.

## Touring Kruger National Park

For people with limited time in South Africa, it is possible to visit Kruger by flying from Jo'burg to Phalaborwa, hiring a car for touring the park and then returning the car at Phalaborwa airport before returning by air to Jo'burg. SA Airlink and InterAir's Fly-Drive packages are good. Best of all is the package which includes the superb Khoka Moya Wildlife Encounters (☎ (01524) 87107).

Hire cars are available from Avis (☎ (01524) 5169), Imperial (☎ (01524) 2376) and Budget (☎ (01524) 85404). Bell's Bushveld Safaris (☎ (01524) 4805) provides good guided tours of the park for R500 per day per vehicle (maximum of seven people), mileage included.

## Places to Stay & Eat

*Elephant Walk* (☎ /fax (01524) 4758, mobile phone (082) 495 0575) is a new and much-needed backpackers' place at 30 Anna Scheepers St. A tent site is R15 per person and a dorm bed is R40/50 without/with breakfast. The friendly owner, Christa, can pick you up from the tourist office. She can also organise trips to Kruger, to the white lions of Timbavati and to the Valley of the

Elephants (R250 for one or two people, extra people R50).

*Lantana Hotel* (☎ (01524) 85855), on the corner of Kiaat and Hall Sts, has caravan sites for R30, plus R5 per person and R5 for electricity. Flatlets are R125/185 for rooms. *Impala Protea Inn* (☎ (01524) 5681/2) is at 52 Essenhout St; rooms cost from R195/240.

*Selati Lodge* (☎ (01524) 89 2122), on Rooibos St, costs from R130/230. *Sefapane* (☎ (01524) 87041) – the name means 'Southern Cross' – on the corner of Koper and Essenhout Sts has a range of rooms from R95 per person.

There are also a number of B&Bs. Two good ones are *Daan & Zena's* (☎ (01524) 86049) at 15 Birkenhead St (R90/140) and *Steyn's Cottage* (☎ (01524) 2836) at 67 Bosvlier St (R95/140).

*Bushveld Tavern* (☎ /fax (01524) 2381), 13km south-west of town on the R530 to Mica, has shared chalets from R90 per person, including breakfast.

*Campico Spur* is in the Sanlam Centre. *Monroes*, near Selati Lodge, specialises in South African food.

### Getting There & Away

**Air** SA Airlink (☎ (01524) 85823) flies to Jo'burg (R479/250 for full/Apex fare).

**Bus** There is a City to City/Transtate (book with Translux) Jo'burg/Phalaborwa via Lydenburg service on Tuesday, Thursday and Sunday (R95).

North Link Tours has buses daily, except Saturday, between Phalaborwa and Jo'burg and other towns on the N1. In Phalaborwa purchase tickets from Turn Key Travel (☎ (01524) 4492) in the Rentmeester Building; buses leave from the Impala Protea Inn.

North Link destinations and fares include: Pretoria, R125; Potgietersrus, R75; Pietersburg, R55; and Tzaneen, R30. The total fare from Jo'burg to Phalaborwa is R140.

**Minibus Taxi** There aren't many minibus taxis in this area and even fewer run south to the lowveld between Kruger National Park and the Drakensberg escarpment. Most run

to Tzaneen (R20) and south as far as Hoedspruit (R15). There's a taxi park near the corner of Sealene Rd and Mellor Ave, 300m south-west of the town centre.

## HOEDSPRUIT

Hoedspruit, at the junction of the R527 and R40, is a good jumping-off point for trips to the northern private reserves which border Kruger. The town has big army and air force bases (and 'revved up' service-people).

Information can be obtained from Central Lowveld Tourism (☎ (01528) 31678). There are three banks in town – the First National, Standard and United.

South of Hoedspruit on the R40, the **Cheetah Breeding Project** (☎ (01528) 31633) is both a breeding station and study centre (but is somewhat disappointing as the graceful cheetah are captive). It is open from 8 am and 4 pm daily; entry is R20.

*Fort Copieba Hotel* (☎ (01528) 31175) has B&B for R110 per person. 'The fort' was the place to eat and party, but recent incidents of violence make it less desirable.

Comair flies to and from Jo'burg daily (R422 one way). There is a minibus taxi rank near the train station; minibuses go to Jo'burg, Phalaborwa and Pietersburg. The thrice-weekly City to City/Transtate Jo'burg service stops here; book through Translux.

### Organised Tours

Off Beat Safaris (☎ (082) 494 1735) in Hoedspruit operates trips (from seven to 21 days) into Mozambique. The cost is R260 per person, per day which includes the use of an inflatable dinghy, spear guns and cooking items, but not drinks or visas).

## PRIVATE GAME RESERVES – NORTHERN PROVINCE

The area just west of Kruger contains a large number of private reserves, usually sharing a border with Kruger, and thus they have most of the 'big five' (buffalo, lion, leopard, elephant and black rhino). These reserves are often extremely pricey, but with an economic stake in their guests getting close to animals, they have good viewing facilities.

The famous and expensive reserves are just north of the Kruger Gate in Mpumalanga (see that chapter). Around Hoedspruit, and Kruger's Orpen and Phalaborwa gates, there is another group of much cheaper reserves.

## Lodges Near Phalaborwa

To the east of the R527, on the road between Mica and Hoedspruit, are two reputable reserves. *Mohlabetsi* (☎ (01528) 32166) has singles/doubles for R360/530 and *Tshukudu* (☎ (015) 793 2476; fax 793 2078) charges from R700/1180.

There are a number of private lodges near the Kruger's Phalaborwa Gate, including: *Mfubu* (☎ (01524) 4071), with self-catering from R110 per person, the beautifully presented *Tintshaba* (☎ (01528) 33234) and *Tulani Safari Lodge* (☎ /fax (01524) 85414). All of these places arrange game drives.

South of Phalaborwa and east of Hoedspruit, the **Klaserie Reserve** covers 60,000 hectares and contains a similar range of birds and animals (including lions and elephants) to Kruger; to visit you must book on ☎ (01528) 32461. South of Hoedspruit off the R40, the 11,000 hectare *Kapama Game Reserve* (☎ (012) 804 1711) has guesthouse and camp accommodation ranging from R400 to R480 per person, all inclusive.

## Manyeleti Game Reserve

This 23,000 hectare reserve is between Sabi Sand Game Reserve and Kruger National Park's Orpen Gate. It shares a border, and thus animals (all the 'big five' included), with Kruger and offers some of the area's least expensive accommodation in the public camp (☎ (013) 735 5733). There are a few private operations within Manyeleti, including *Khoka Moya* (see following), *Honeyguide* (☎ (011) 483 2734) and *Pungwe* (☎ (011) 823 2623).

## Khoka Moya

Khoka Moya (☎ (01528) 31729; (012) 543 2134) means 'Capture the Spirit', and this is a great place to experience the South African bush. You can go 'rhino monitoring' with very professional guides. Full board in the

main camp is R850 per person per day, all inclusive. *Molwareng Sky Beds,* at R350 per person, are huts on stilts with a kitchen, built well off the ground above a water hole.

In the future, rhino monitoring units may be established in Manyeleti, Andover, Letaba Ranch and Atherston reserves – these will be administered from Khoka Moya.

## Nyani Cultural Village

For an opportunity to see how a traditional Tsonga family lives, visit this non-touristy village, home of the descendants of former local chief Kapama. Within the village all of the idiosyncrasies of daily life, customs and architecture are explained. It is like taking a journey back 150 years. This village recreates all aspects of tribal culture and there are also explanations of traditional foods and medicines.

The village (☎ (01528) 33816) is on the Guernsey Rd (the road into Thornybush Game Reserve), 4km up the road from the R531 and near Klaserie (formerly Jan Wassenaar) Dam; entry is R15.

## Timbavati Private Nature Reserve

Timbavati, known for its white lion population, has a good reputation. The reserve is jointly owned by a large number of people dedicated to conservation.

On the road into Timbavati is *Thornybush* (☎ (01528) 31976), a luxurious place in its own reserve which costs R1080 per person sharing, all inclusive. Other places to stay in the Timbavati area include *Tanda Tula* (book on ☎ (021) 794 6500), *Motswari* and *M'Bali* (book both on ☎ (011) 463 1990). Both Motswari and M'Bali start from R725 per person sharing, while Tanda Tula is R870 per person in winter and about R300 more in summer, all inclusive.

## The 'Last Frontier'

For a unique experience in the real African wilderness contact Expeditions Africa (☎ (01528) 33816, (083) 700 7987). The journey starts at Phalaborwa and continues north through the **Marietta Corridor**, a buffer of land set up for the protection of animals moving between tribal Homelands and Kruger National Park. You then zigzag through traditional Tsonga villages, occasionally overnighting, before entering an under-utilised region of Kruger near Punda Maria Gate. After a brief excursion into Kruger, the tour exits via the Pafuri Gate into traditional VhaVenda lands, where there is another buffer zone, **Makuya Park**. Here there are large groups of elephants and lions.

The **Levuvhu River** (River of Hippo) is the focus of the trip. It is best known as the southern limit of a number of bird species, including the black eagle, Pel's fishing owl, crested guinea fowl and giant kingfisher. There also are many species of trees unique to the area, including the baobab.

It is rugged terrain with many 4WD trails, 72km of river frontage and rapids for canoeing. The 4WD trail eventually reaches the flood plains and pans of the Limpopo, notable for its fever trees and lala palms.

# Lesotho

## Around the Country

# Lesotho

Lesotho offers the rare opportunity to meet and stay with people living traditional lifestyles, whether you hike or take one of the well-organised pony treks. After spending time in South Africa it's a real relief to visit a country which isn't suffering the after-effects of apartheid. Although Lesotho is a poor Third World country you don't have to rough it – unless you want to, of course. There are good accommodation options in Maseru and with an ordinary hire car you can see some spectacular scenery and reach at least one of the pony trekking centres. Public transport is quite good (if uncomfortable) in much of the country, or you can just head off into the mountains and valleys and walk.

## Facts about the Country

Lesotho (pronounced le-*soo*-too) is a mountainous kingdom about the size of Belgium which is surrounded by South Africa. Its forbidding terrain and the defensive walls of the Drakensberg and Maluti (sometimes spelt Maloti) ranges gave both sanctuary and strategic advantage to the Basotho (the people of Lesotho), who forged a nation while playing a key role in the manoeuvrings of the white invaders on the plains below.

### HISTORY

Archaeological and linguistic evidence suggests that the group of peoples described as Sotho lived in Southern Africa as early as the 10th century AD, and possibly much earlier. By the beginning of the 19th century they had become a dominant group on the highveld of what is now South Africa. Because of the different terrains into which they moved, various groups began to differ in culture and custom, but the unifying seSotho language and persisting marriage customs have encouraged anthropologists to retain the broad label of Sotho. The major groups

### Highlights

- Pony-trekking on sure-footed Basotho ponies through the rugged and beautiful interior (pages 608, 612)
- A night in a hut in one of the remote highland's traditional villages
- Challenging wilderness hiking along the top of the Drakensberg escarpment (page 598)

today are the Tswana (western Sotho), the northern Sotho and the people who today live in Lesotho, the southern Sotho. Strangely, the Lesotho royal family's symbol is the crocodile – a creature that does not occur in Lesotho.

## Lesotho

Lesotho was settled by Sotho peoples comparatively recently, possibly as late as the 16th century. Already here were the Khoisan, with whom there was some inter-marriage and mingling of language. There might also have been some Nguni people.

The early society was made up of small chiefdoms, which fragmented as groups broke away in search of new land. Cattle and cultivation were the mainstays of the economy, and extensive trade links were forged. Grain and hides were exported in exchange for iron from the Transvaal area.

By the early 19th century white traders were on the scene, exchanging beads for cattle. They were soon followed by the Voortrekkers (Boer pioneers) and pressure on Sotho grazing lands grew. Even without white encroachment Sotho society was due to face the fact that it had expanded as far as it could and would have to adapt to living in a finite territory. On top of this came the disaster of the difaqane (forced migration).

The rapid consolidation and expansion of the Zulu state under the leadership of Shaka, and later Dingaan, resulted in a chain reaction of turmoil throughout the whole of Southern Africa. Huge numbers of people were displaced, their tribes shattered and their lands lost, and they, in turn, attacked other tribes. Old alliances were upset and agriculture and herding became impossible in many areas. Some bands of refugees didn't stop moving until they came to the area now known as Tanzania.

That the loosely organised southern Sotho society survived this period was largely due to the abilities of King Moshoeshoe.

## Moshoeshoe the Great

Moshoeshoe began as a leader of a small village and, in about 1820, he led his villagers to Butha-Buthe. From this mountain stronghold his people survived the first battles of the difaqane and, in 1824, Moshoeshoe began his policy of assisting refugees on the condition that they help in his defence. Later in the same year he moved his people further, to Thaba-Bosiu, a mountain top which was even easier to defend.

From Thaba-Bosiu, Moshoeshoe played a patient game of placating the stronger local rulers and granting protection – as well as land and cattle – to groups of refugees. By 1840 his people numbered about 40,000 and

King Moshoeshoe the Great played a major role in the emergence and survival of Basutholand.

his power base was protected by groups who had settled on his outlying lands and were partially under his authority. These people and others like them were to form Basutholand, which, by the time of Moshoeshoe's death in 1870, had a population exceeding 150,000.

Another factor in Basutholand's emergence and survival was Moshoeshoe's welcoming of Catholic missionaries, and his ability to take their advice without being dominated by them. The first missionaries to arrive in the area, in 1833, were from the Paris Evangelical Missionary Society. Moshoeshoe made one of them his adviser, and the sophisticated diplomacy which had marked his dealings with local chiefs now extended to his dealings with Europeans. The missions, often situated in remote parts of the kingdom, served as tangible symbols of his authority, and in return for some Christianisation of Sotho customs, the missionaries were disposed to defend the rights of 'their' Basotho against the new threat – British and Boer expansion.

The Boers had crossed the Orange River in the 1830s, and by 1843 Moshoeshoe was sufficiently concerned by their numbers to ally himself with the British Cape Colony government. The resulting treaties defined his borders but did little to stop squabbles with the Boers, who regarded the grazing rights they had been granted as title to the land they occupied – the fertile lowlands west of the Mohokare (Caledon) River.

The British Resident, installed in Basutholand as a condition of the treaties, decided that Moshoeshoe was too powerful and engineered an unsuccessful attack on his kingdom. In 1854, the British withdrew from the area having fixed the boundaries of Basutholand. The Boers pressed their claims on the land and increasing tension led to the 1858 Free State-Basotho War. Moshoeshoe won yet another major battle, and the situation simmered along until 1865 when another Free State-Basotho War erupted. This time Moshoeshoe suffered setbacks and, as a consequence, was forced to sign away much of the western lowlands.

The Boers' land hunger showed no sign of diminishing and, in 1868, Moshoeshoe again called on British assistance, this time on the imperial government in London. A High Commission was formed to adjudicate the dispute and the result was the loss of more Basotho land. It was obvious that no treaty between Boers and Basotho would hold for long, and continual war between the Free State and Basutholand was not good for British interests. The British solution was to simply annex Basutholand.

## After Moshoeshoe
The British, their imperial policy changing yet again, gave control of Basutholand to the Cape Colony in 1871. Moshoeshoe had died the year before and squabbles over succession were dividing the country. The Cape government exploited this and reduced the powers of chiefs and limited them to their individual areas.

The Gun War of 1880 began as a protest against the Cape government's refusal to allow the Basotho to own firearms, but it quickly became a battle between rebel chiefs on one side and the Cape government and collaborating chiefs on the other. The war ended in a stalemate (making it one of the few wars in Southern Africa which didn't result in Africans being crushed by Europeans) with the Cape government discredited.

A shaky peace followed until another war appeared imminent, and the British government again took over direct control of Basutholand in 1884. The imperial government decided to back strong local leaders rather than rule through its own officers, and this helped to stabilise the country. One unexpected benefit of direct British rule was that, when the Union of South Africa was created, Basutholand was a British protectorate and was not included in the Union. If the Cape government had retained control, Lesotho would have been part of South Africa and have become a Homeland under the apartheid regime.

Ruling through chiefs might have defused power struggles between rival chiefs but it did nothing to develop democracy in the country. If anything it created a feudal state more open to abuse than Moshoeshoe's loose confederation of subordinate chiefs.

## Home Rule & Independence
In 1910 the Basutholand National Council was formed. This official advisory body was composed of members nominated by the chiefs, but after decades of allegations of corruption and favouritism, reforms were made in the 1940s which introduced some democracy into appointments to the council.

In the mid-1950s the council requested internal self-government from the British and, in 1960, a new constitution was in place and elections were held for a Legislative Council. Half its members were elected by the (male) people and the other half was made up of chiefs and the appointed representatives of the king.

Meanwhile, political parties had formed. The main contenders were the Basutholand Congress Party (BCP), similar to South Africa's ANC, and the Basutholand National Party (BNP), a conservative party headed by Chief Leabua Jonathan.

The BCP won the 1960 elections and demanded full independence from Britain. This was eventually agreed to and a new constitution was drawn up, with independence to come into effect in 1966. However, at the elections in 1965 the BCP lost power to the BNP and Chief Jonathan became the first prime minister of the new Kingdom of Lesotho. Just why the BCP lost is debatable, but the fact that the BNP promised cooperation with the South African apartheid regime and in turn received massive support from it must be significant.

However, as most of the civil service was still loyal to the BCP, Jonathan did not have an easy time. Stripping King Moshoeshoe II of the few powers that the new constitution had left him did not endear Jonathan's government to the people and, in the 1970 election, the BCP won government.

Jonathan responded by suspending the constitution, arresting then expelling the king and banning opposition parties. The king, after an exile in Holland, was allowed to return, and Jonathan attempted to form a government of national reconciliation. This ploy was partly successful, with several BCP members joining the sham government, but some, including the leader Ntsu Mokhehle, resisted and attempted to stage a coup in 1974. The coup failed miserably and resulted in the death of many BCP supporters and the jailing or forced exile of the BCP leadership. Lesotho was effectively a one-party state.

Trouble continued and repressive measures were applied. It's possible that Jonathan would have continued to cling to power had he not changed his attitude towards South Africa, although this change was partly caused by a need to placate popular opposition to South Africa. He called for the return of land in the Orange Free State that had been stolen from the original Basutholand, and, more seriously from the South African point of view, began criticising apartheid, allegedly offering refuge to ANC guerrillas and flirting with Cuba. Relations soured to the point where South Africa closed Lesotho's borders, strangling the country.

The Lesotho military took action and Jonathan was deposed in 1986. The military council, headed by Major General Lekhanya, restored the king as head of state. This was a popular move, but eventually agitation for democratic reform again rose to the point where there were disturbances in the country. In 1990 King Moshoeshoe II was deposed by the army in favour of his son, Prince Mohato Bereng Seeisa (Letsie III). Elections in 1993 resulted in the return of the BCP and Mokhehle became prime minister.

In early 1994 two rival army factions, each supporting a different political party, began fighting near Maseru. After a short battle an uneasy peace was established, although South Africa mounted major military exercises along the border shortly after the fighting. With the Highlands Water Project nearing completion, South Africa was probably warning Lesotho not to threaten its interests.

In January 1995 Letsie III abdicated in favour of his father, and five years after being deposed, Moshoeshoe II was reinstated, restoring some calm to Lesotho after a year of

unrest. Tragically, a year later in January 1996 he was killed when his 4WD plunged over a cliff in the Maluti mountains. Letsie III is again the king, and while there have been some rumblings in the army and police, most visitors will not notice anything amiss.

## GEOGRAPHY

Lesotho's borders are mainly natural and it is completely surrounded by South Africa. From Lesotho's northern tip to its western side where it juts out almost to the town of Wepener in South Africa, the border is formed by the Mohokare (Caledon) River. The eastern border is defined by the rugged escarpment of the Drakensberg, and high country forms much of the southern border.

All of Lesotho exceeds 1000m in altitude, with peaks in the Central Ranges and near the escarpment over 3000m. The tourist slogan, 'kingdom in the sky', is not far wrong, as Lesotho has the highest lowest point of any country on earth.

The highest mountain in Southern Africa (the highest point south of Kilimanjaro) is the 3841m Thabana-Ntlenyana, near Sani Pass in eastern Lesotho.

## CLIMATE

Winters are cold and clear. Frosts are common and there are snowfalls in the high country and sometimes at lower altitudes. At other times of the year, snow has been known to fall (especially on the high peaks where the weather is dangerously changeable), but rain and mist are more common bugbears for drivers and hikers. Nearly all of Lesotho's rain falls between October and April, with

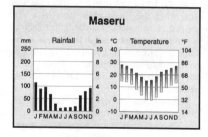

spectacular thunderstorms in summer – quite a few people are killed by lightning every year. Down in the valleys, summer days can be hot, with temperatures over 30°C.

Never go out into the mountains, even for an afternoon, without a sleeping bag, tent and sufficient food for a couple of days in case you get fogged in. Even in summer it can be freezing.

## GOVERNMENT

The country is in the process of writing a new constitution. Its draft constitution allowed free elections in 1993 after some years of military rule. The head of state is King Letsie III, and the prime minister is Ntsu Mokhehle of the BCP. Under traditional law, the king can be deposed by a majority vote of the College of Chiefs.

## ECONOMY

Lesotho is one of the world's poorest countries. Erosion is a major problem and the already scarce arable land is becoming degraded. Much of Lesotho's food is imported, although in the 19th century Lesotho exported grain. The main export is now labour; perhaps 60% of male Basotho wage earners work in South Africa.

The huge Highlands Water Project is creating a series of dams on the Orange River in Lesotho, and sales of water and hydroelectricity to South Africa might make Lesotho more economically independent. Very little manufacturing takes place in the kingdom and most goods are imported from South Africa.

## POPULATION & PEOPLE

The two million citizens of Lesotho are known as the Basotho people. Culturally, most are southern Sotho and most speak seSotho. The melding of the Basotho nation was largely the result of Moshoeshoe I's 19th century military and diplomatic triumphs and many diverse subgroups and peoples have somehow merged into a homogeneous society. Maseru, with about 300,000 people, is the only large city.

### Highlands Water Project

This project is being implemented in stages to provide water and electricity for a large tract of southern Africa. When construction is finished (circa 2020) there will be four major dams, many smaller dams and many km of tunnels.

Phase 1 includes the recently completed 180m-high Katse Dam on the Malibamat'so River, to the north of Thaba-Tseka. A transfer tunnel 4m in diameter and 45km long will carry water to a hydroelectric plant at Muela near Butha-Buthe. After generating electricity, the water will flow through a 37km tunnel across the border to Clarens and into the Axle River, a tributary of the Vaal. Eventually this water will reach the Vaal Dam, an essential reservoir for Jo'burg. The other three major dams will be on the Senqu (Orange) River.

The immediate effect of the development has been improved roads into Lesotho's interior. Farmers who have lost land are promised compensation. There are, however, several environmental questions to consider and critics of the scheme feel that satisfactory answers still have to be provided. ■

## CULTURE

The first people to occupy Lesotho were the Khoisan. They have left many examples of their rock art in the valleys.

Although traditional Basotho culture is breaking down through contact with the rest of the world and changes in the society, much of the culture remains because it relates so strongly to the way people live. Also, rich and vibrant cultures have a way of surviving through change: a belief might live on in a proverb or a ritual may have transformed into a game.

Traditional culture in Lesotho consists largely of the customs, rites and superstitions with which ordinary people explain and flavour their lives. As in all cultures, the milestones of birth, puberty, marriage and death are associated with ceremonies. Cattle, both as sacrificial animals and as a symbol of wealth and worth, play a large part in the culture, as do the cultivation of crops and the vagaries of the weather – Basotho farmers have to worry about drought, flood, hailstorms, snow and lightning.

Much of the folklore puts common sense into practice: toasting fresh rather than stale bread is bad (it causes rheumatism); when working at straining beer take an occasional drink (or your hands will swell); a spider in a hut should not be molested (it's the strength of the family); a howling dog must be silenced immediately (or it will bring evil).

Music and dance play their part in traditional culture, both in ceremonial occasions and in everyday life. There are various kinds of musical instruments, from the *lekolulo* (a flute-like instrument) played by herd-boys, to the *thomo* (a stringed instrument played by women) and the *setolo-tolo* (a stringed instrument played with the mouth, by men).

Traditional medicine mixes rites and customs, with healers (sangomas) developing their own charms and rituals. The Basotho are traditionally buried in a sitting position, ready to leap up when called, and facing the rising sun.

Much of the traditional culture is associated with avoiding misfortune, and reflects the grim realities of life in a marginal agricultural region. For example, a feeble old man, unwilling to die and relieve his relatives of the burden of supporting him, is liable to be placed at the entrance to a cattle kraal, to be trampled in the evening by the homecoming beasts. But there are also many other lighthearted customs, such as the last-resort ceremony for rainmaking which is detailed in the pamphlet *Customs & Superstitions in Basutholand* by Justinus Sechefo (see the boxed text 'Rainmaking').

## RELIGION

Thanks to the important role that French and Canadian missionaries played in the creation of Moshoeshoe the Great's Lesotho, most people are at least nominally Christian and a high percentage of Christians follow Catholicism. However, traditional beliefs are still strong in rural areas and seem to coexist with Christianity, probably because the beliefs are tied so closely to the important and trivial details of everyday life.

Broadly, traditional religion among the Basotho is similar to that of the other Sotho people in Southern Africa. They believe in a masculine supreme being but place a great deal of emphasis on ancestors *(balimo)*, who act as intermediaries between the people and the capricious forces of nature and the spirit world.

Evil is a constant danger, caused by *boloi* (witchcraft; witches can be either male or female) and *thkolosi*, maliciously playful beings having much in common with leprechauns, imps and pixies in their sinister, pre-Disney form. A *ngaka* is a learned man, a combination of sorcerer and doctor, who can combat these forces.

### Rainmaking

A first attempt at bringing rain is made by the men of the village, who climb to the top of a nearby mountain and kill everything they can find. The entrails of the animals are thrown into streams and the men return home, drenched from the heavy rain. If the rain *isn't* falling, the village calls in a *moroka-pula* (rainmaker). If he fails, it's the turn of the village's young women.

They go to a neighbouring village and the quickest of them enters a hut and steals the *lesokoana*, which can be any wooden cooking utensil. She flees from the village with the lesokoana, raising the alarm herself if she hasn't already been spotted. When the village women run out to reclaim the lesokoana, the young women toss it back and forth, sometimes losing it and sometimes regaining it. This game of long-distance 'keepings-off' attracts spectators from both villages and ends when one group makes it back to their village with the lesokoana.

The winners 'enter the village with merriment, wearing green leaves about the head and waist, and singing with great joy an anthem.'

Sechefo doesn't say what happens if this still fails to bring rain – but at least everyone stops worrying about the drought for a while. ∎

## The Basotho Hat

A distinctive feature of Basotho dress is the conical hat with its curious top adornment; it is known to the Basotho as *mokorotlo* or *molianyeoe*.

The style of this hat is taken directly from the shape of a hill near Moshoeshoe I's Thaba-Bosiu fortress. The hill is called Qiloane and it stands proudly alone with a few villages at its base.

These hats can be purchased in Maseru at the appropriately named Basotho Hat, from the vendors in front of the tourist office and at the border posts. A large adult-sized hat costs about M30. You'll pay M15 for one which could hang from your rear-vision mirror next to those cute FIFA soccer boots. The large hats are highly prized in South Africa; I lost mine to a local angler in an eel-fishing competition in western Transkei.

**Jeff Williams**

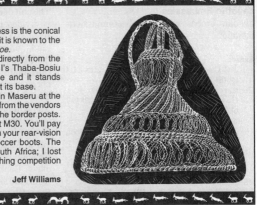

## LANGUAGE

The official languages are seSotho and English. For more about seSotho see the main language section in the Facts about the Region chapter.

# Facts for the Visitor

## VISAS & DOCUMENTS

The visa situation has changed a couple of times lately and it might have changed again by the time you get here. It's hard to imagine a change that wouldn't be for the better.

Most people need a visa, unless they are citizens of Denmark, Finland, Greece, Iceland, Ireland, Israel, Japan, Norway, Sweden or South Africa. Citizens of Commonwealth countries do not need a visa, with the significant exceptions of visitors from Australia, Canada, Ghana, India, New Zealand, Nigeria, Pakistan and Namibia.

The nearest Lesotho high commission is in Pretoria (South Africa), so getting a visa is a hassle if, for example, you want to travel from Cape Town to Lesotho. If you arrive at the Maseru Bridge border without a visa you might be given a temporary entry permit, which allows you to go into Maseru and

apply for a visa at the Ministry of Immigration office on Kingsway. Don't count on this, as it depends on the whim of the border officials who are heartily sick of foreigners arriving without visas and demanding to be let in.

A single-entry visa costs M20 and a multiple-entry visa is M40. At most border posts you get two weeks stay (although a traveller reports asking for two days and being given two months), renewable by either leaving the country and re-entering or by application at the Ministry of Immigration in Maseru.

For a longer stay in Lesotho, apply in advance to the Director of Immigration & Passport Services, PO Box 363, Maseru 100, Lesotho.

Remember that when you leave South Africa your visa/entry permit expires. This isn't a hassle if you qualify for an entry permit (most people do) or if you have a multiple-entry visa, but if you only had a single-entry visa you'll have to apply for a new South African visa in Maseru and that could be time-consuming. There's no other way out of Lesotho except through South Africa.

No vaccination certificates are necessary to enter Lesotho unless you have recently been in a yellow fever area.

## EMBASSIES
### Lesotho Embassies
Lesotho embassies and high commissions include:

Canada
202 Clemow Ave, Ottawa, Ontario H1S 2B4 (☎ (613) 236-9449)
Germany
Godersberger Alle 50 5300, Bonn 2 (☎ (228) 37 6868/9)
South Africa
343 Pretorius St, Momentum Centre, 6th Floor, West Tower, Pretoria 001 (☎ (012) 322 6090)
UK
7 Chesam Place, Belgravia, London SW1 8AN (☎ (0171) 373 8581/2; fax 235 5686)
USA
2511 Massachusetts Ave NW, Washington, DC 20008 (☎ (202) 797-5533/4)

### Foreign Embassies in Lesotho
A number of embassies closed after South Africa rejoined the international community. The remaining include:

Canada
☎ 31 4187
France
37 Qoaling Rd, Maseru (☎ 32 6050)
Ireland
Christie House, 2nd Floor, Orpen Rd, Maseru (☎ 31 4068)
Netherlands
c/o Lancer's Inn, Maseru (☎ 31 2144)
South Africa
10th Floor, Lesotho Bank Centre, Kingsway, Maseru (☎ 31 5758)
Sweden
1st Floor, Lesotho Bank Centre, Kingsway, Maseru (☎ 31 1555)
UK
Linare Rd, Maseru (☎ 31 3961)
USA
Kingsway, Maseru (towards Maseru Bridge border post) (☎ 31 2666; fax 31 0116)

## CUSTOMS
Customs regulations are broadly the same as those for South Africa, but you can't bring in alcohol unless you're arriving from a country other than Botswana, Swaziland or South Africa – and that isn't likely. If you're entering through Sani Pass there's a chance that alcohol will be confiscated.

## MONEY
The unit of currency is the maloti (M), which is divided into 100 liesente. The maloti is fixed at a value equal to the South African rand, and rands are accepted everywhere – there is no real need to convert your money into maloti. When changing travellers cheques you can usually get rand notes and this saves having to convert unused maloti. You will invariably get maloti in change.

The only banks where you can change foreign currency, including travellers cheques, are in Maseru. The banks are the Lesotho Development Bank, Standard Bank and Barclays. Banks are open Monday to Friday from 8.30 am to 3 pm (to 1 pm on Thursday), Saturday from 8.30 am to 11 am.

### Costs
Lesotho is a cheaper country to travel in than South Africa if you take advantage of the opportunities to stay with local people and to camp in remote areas. Otherwise hotel prices are the same as in South Africa and there aren't many cheaper options. Transport is a bit cheaper but only compared with South Africa's upmarket buses.

Examples of costs are: hostel in Maseru, M25; hotel in Maseru, from M120/150 for a single/double room; street food, M5 a plate; steak, M30; bus ride from Maseru to Thaba-Tseka, M24.

### Currency Exchange
The rate is fixed at the same value as the South African rand (see the currency exchange table in the Money section of the South Africa Facts for the Visitor chapter).

### Taxes
A GST tax of 10% is added to most transactions. Note that hotels don't usually include the GST when quoting rates.

## POST & COMMUNICATIONS
The telephone system works reasonably well in Maseru but is less reliable outside the capital. There are no area codes within Lesotho; to call from South Africa dial the

prefix 09-266. See the Maseru section for information on international calls.

Post offices are open Monday to Friday from 8 am to 4.30 pm, Saturday from 8 am to noon. Delivery is slow and unreliable.

## BOOKS & MAPS

Russell Suchet, owner of the Sani Lodge hostel at the bottom of Sani Pass in South Africa, has put together a handy little guide, *A Backpackers' Guide to Lesotho*, R15. For a little more background than we have room for here, look for Marco Turco's *Visitors' Guide to Lesotho* (paperback, R55.95), widely available in South Africa. Marco has a real enthusiasm for the country.

Some interesting books about Basotho culture and history are produced in Lesotho, and you'll find a selection at the Basotho Hat craft shop in Maseru. Look for *I am a Mosotho* (paperback) by Patrick Mohlalefi Bereng. It's a collection of stories, poetry and other writings celebrating the culture and making it accessible to outsiders. *History of the Basotho* (hardback) is a facsimile reprint of a 1912 work by DF Ellenberger, a missionary. It's a detailed look at the Basotho and their society, researched at a time when the old ways were beginning to fade.

The Land, Surveys & Physical Planning Department in Maseru sells good 1:50,000 topographic maps of the country (about M10 per sheet). They also sell a high quality 1:250,000 map of the country (M30). A lot of the new roads built for the Highlands Water Project are not shown. The office is open between 8 am and 12.45 pm, and 2 and 4.30 pm on weekdays. It's on Lerotholi Rd, near the corner of Constitution Rd in Maseru.

## MEDIA

Several thin newspapers, such as *Lesotho Today*, are available in the morning in Maseru and later elsewhere. Day-old South African newspapers are available in Maseru.

If you're a fan of the BBC World Service, Lesotho is a mecca as there's a transmitter here and you can pick up the Beeb on short wave, medium wave (1197kHz) and FM.

## TIME

Lesotho time is the same as in South Africa – GMT/UTC plus two hours year-round.

## HEALTH

There is neither malaria nor bilharzia in Lesotho, but avoid drinking untreated water. The weather is the greatest threat to your health, and it could be a lot more serious than catching a cold if you're trapped on a mountain without proper clothing.

Several lives are lost each year from lightning strikes; remember to keep off the high ground during an electrical storm and avoid camping in the open. The sheer ferocity of an electrical storm in Lesotho has to be seen to be believed. With the thunder and torrential rain comes a strong wind and if you don't have waterproof gear you'll be soaked (and cold) in seconds. The storms don't last long but they can be frequent.

See the Health section in the Regional Facts for the Visitor chapter for more details.

## BUSINESS HOURS & HOLIDAYS

Most businesses are open from 8 am to 5 pm weekdays, until noon on Saturday. The civil service works between 8 am and 4.30 pm on weekdays and lunch is from 12.45 to 2 pm.

Public holidays include the usual Christmas, Boxing and New Year's days, Good Friday and Easter Monday, plus Independence Day, 4 October, and Moshoeshoe Day, in early March.

## ACTIVITIES
### Pony Trekking

Lesotho's tough little Basotho ponies can take you to some remote and beautiful places. Just keep reminding yourself, as your pony nonchalantly negotiates an apparently sheer cliff, that next to 'tough', the most popular cliché describing these beasts is 'sure-footed'.

The main trekking centres are the Basotho Pony Trekking Centre on God Help Me Pass, and Malealea Lodge near the Gates of Paradise (see the relevant entries for further details) and isolated Semonkong Lodge. You might be able to join a day ride without

## The Basotho Pony

The Basotho pony is strong and sure-footed and generally docile. Its size and physique is the result of cross-breeding between short Javanese horses and European full mounts.

A few horses were captured from invading Griqua forces by Basotho warriors in the early 1800s and Moshoeshoe I is recorded as having ridden a horse in 1830. Since that date the pony has become an integral part of life in the highlands and the preferred mode of transport for many villagers. In 1983 the Basotho Pony Trekking Centre was set up near God Help Me (Molimo-Nthuse) Pass in an attempt to prevent dilution of the ponies' gene pool.

Visitors do not need prior riding experience to go pony trekking into the interior. There are several places which conduct pony treks: see the Basotho Pony Trekking Centre, Semonkong and Malealea sections later in this chapter. ■

booking at these places but it's a long way to go to be turned away.

Whichever you choose, you have to take all your own food. There are basic stores near all these centres but it's better to bring food from Maseru. On an overnight trek you'll need to take food, a sleeping bag and warm and waterproof clothing, plus the usual trekking extras, such as sunscreen, a torch (flashlight), a water bottle and water-purification tablets. Check whether you'll need cooking utensils.

### Hiking

Lesotho offers great remote-area trekking in a landscape reminiscent of the Tibetan plateau. David Ambrose's *Guide to Lesotho* (Winchester Press) is a good guide.

In all areas, but especially the remote eastern highlands, walking is dangerous if you aren't prepared. Temperatures can plummet to near zero even in summer, and thunderstorms are common. Waterproof gear and plenty of warm clothes are absolutely essential. In summer many of the rivers flood, and fords can become dangerous. Be prepared to change your route or wait until the river

subsides. Thick fogs can also delay you. By the end of the dry season good water can be scarce, especially in the higher areas.

There are stores in the towns but these stock only very basic foodstuffs. Bring all you need from Maseru, or from South Africa if you want specialist hiking supplies. There are trout streams in the east – if you don't catch your own, buy some from locals.

Hikers should respect the mounds of stones which mark graves. On the other hand, a mound of stones near a trail, especially between two hills, should be added to by passing travellers, who can ensure their good luck by spitting on a stone and throwing it onto the pile. Also keep in mind that a white flag waving from a village means that local sorghum beer (*joala*) has just been brewed; a yellow flag indicates maize beer, red is for meat and green for vegetables.

The whole country is good for trekking, but the eastern highlands and the Drakensberg's crown attract serious hikers, with the walks between Qacha's Nek and Butha-Buthe offering the best challenge.

One three-day walk in this area which you could try before attempting something more ambitious is from the Sani Top chalet (at the top of Sani Pass), south along the edge of the escarpment, to the Sehlabathebe National Park. From here there's a track leading down to Bushman's Nek in South Africa. As the crow flies the distance from Sani Top to Nkonkoana Gate is about 45km but the walk is longer than that. Much of this area is over 3000m and it's remote even by Lesotho's standards: there isn't a horse trail, much less a road or a settlement. Don't try this unless you are well prepared, experienced and in a party of at least three people.

A number of other walks are outlined in Russell Suchet's *A Backpackers' Guide to Lesotho*. In addition to the Sani Top to Sehlabathebe walk he also outlines walks from Semonkong to Malealea (three days); Sehonghong to Sehlabathebe (two to three days); Mokhotlong to Sani Top via Thabana-Ntlenyana (three to four days); and Ha Lejone to Oxbow (three to four days). He also suggests the ultimate Lesotho challenge

– from Mahlesela Pass in the north near Oxbow Lodge, all the way to Sehlabathebe via Mont-aux-Sources (14 to 20 days).

The beauty is that you can walk just about anywhere in Lesotho as there are no organised hiking trails, just footpaths and bridles. There are few fences, so you can head in almost any direction.

A word of warning: make sure you know how to use a map and compass and get the relevant 1:50,000 maps from the map office at the Department of Land, Surveys & Physical Planning on Lerotholi Rd, Maseru.

Malealea Lodge also offers hiking, with a pony to carry your gear if you want.

### Bird-watching

About 280 species of birds have been recorded in Lesotho – surprising for a landlocked country. The mountainous terrain provides suitable habitats for many species of raptor (birds of prey). If lucky, you will see the Cape vulture *(Gyps coprotheres)*, the rare bearded vulture or lammergeyer *(Gypaetus barbatus)* – not found below 2000m, the steppe buzzard *(Buteo buteo)*, the black eagle *(Aquila verreauxii)* and the rare gymnogene *(Polyboroides typus)*.

Another bird to look out for is the southern bald ibis *(Geronticus calvus)*, found in Lesotho as it breeds in crevices in cliffs. You can distinguish it from other ibises as it has a bald red head and a white face. The name Mokhotlong means 'Place of the Bald Ibis'.

Good bird-watching places include eyries in the Malutis, along Mountain Rd and near the eastern Drakensberg escarpment.

### Fishing

Trout fishing is very popular in Lesotho and these fish are caught in many of the dams and river systems. The trout season commences in September and continues until the end of May; from 1 June to 31 August it is closed. For more information contact the Ministry of Agriculture Livestock Division (☎ (266) 32 3986), Private Bag A82, Maseru 100; there is a minimal licence fee, a bag limit of 12 fish, a size limit, and only rod and line and artificial non-spinning flies may be used.

The nearest fishing area to Maseru is the Makhaleng River, 2km downstream from the Molimo-Nthuse Hotel (a two hour drive from Maseru). Other places to fish are in the Malibamat'so near Butha-Buthe, 2km below the Oxbow Lodge; in the De Beers' Dam and Khubelu and Mokhotlong rivers near Mokhotlong; the Tsoelikana River, Park Ponds and Leqooa River near Qacha's Nek; and the Thaba-Tseka main dam.

Indigenous fish include the barbel in lowland rivers, the yellowfish in the mountains and the rare Maloti minnow in the upper Tsoelikana.

## ACCOMMODATION
### Camping & Hostels

Camping isn't really feasible close to towns, but away from population centres, you can camp anywhere as long as you have local permission. As well as being an essential courtesy, you might be offered a hut for the night; pay about M15 for this.

There are a couple of hostels in Maseru and one near Butha-Buthe.

There are missions scattered around the country (the 1:250,000 Lesotho map shows them) and you can often get a bed. There are also Agricultural (or Farmer) Training Centres in several places which provide a bed for about M20.

### Hotels

Maseru has a good range of hotel accommodation. In a few larger towns there are reasonable mid-range hotels. Most towns have small hotels which have survived from Protectorate days. These are usually now just run-down bars and liquor stores but with some persuasion you might get a room. Just remember that you don't come to Lesotho for high-class accommodation.

## THINGS TO BUY

Unfortunately, Lesotho's all-purpose garment, the blanket, is usually made elsewhere. There are plenty of other handicrafts to buy, including mohair tapestry, and woven grass products such as mats, baskets and, of course, the Basotho hat. If you're trekking you might want a sturdy stick. They come plain or decorated and can be found everywhere from craft shops to bus parks, where prices start at about M40 but bargaining is essential.

In and around the town of Teyateyaneng there are many craft shops and cottage industries.

# Getting There & Away

## AIR
Lesotho Airways flies daily between Moshoeshoe airport, 18km north-east of Maseru, and Jo'burg in South Africa for M313, one way (advance-booked return tickets are cheaper). There is an airport departure tax of M20.

## LAND
### Bus & Minibus Taxi
Minibus taxis run between Jo'burg and Maseru for about R65. Buses from Maseru for South African destinations leave from the bridge on the South African side of the border. The simplest way to get to a fair-sized South African town and link up with other transport is to take a minibus taxi from the bridge to Ladybrand (Free State).

South Africa's inexpensive Transtate system used to have several slow services running to or near Lesotho but Transtate routes are contracting. The thrice-weekly bus from Johannesburg to Maseru Bridge (six hours, R60) seems to be the only remaining service.

Vrystaat Tours has a daily bus running between Bethlehem and Bloemfontein, via Maseru Bridge. This is a slow local service and the timetable is hazy. Mid-morning seems to be the time to expect the bus to Bloemfontein (about M30) and early afternoon for the Bethlehem bus (about M25).

## Car & Motorcycle
You can't enter via Sani Pass unless your vehicle is 4WD, but you can leave that way in a conventional vehicle (if you dare). Most of the other entry points in the south and the east of the country also involve very rough roads. If you're driving in via Sani Pass make sure that you fill up with fuel in Himeville, as it's a long way to the nearest fuel.

Hertz ($\pi$ 31 4460) and Avis ($\pi$ 31 4325) have agents in Maseru, but it's cheaper to hire in South Africa. Don't forget to take a letter from the hirer giving you permission to take the car into Lesotho. With the major companies the letter is just a formality to prevent you being accused by the police (the Royal Lesotho Mounted Police!) of having stolen the car, and it's rarely asked for. However if you're with a smaller company there might be insurance complications if you take

### Lesotho Border Posts
All the land borders are with South Africa. Most people enter via Maseru Bridge. The major border posts are:

| Border Post | Hours | Nearest South African Town |
| --- | --- | --- |
| Caledonspoort | 24 hours | Fouriesburg (near Butha-Buthe) |
| Ficksburg Bridge | 24 hours | Ficksburg (Maputsoe) |
| Makhaleng | 8 am - 4 pm | Zastron (near Mohale's Hoek) |
| Maseru Bridge | 6 am - 10 pm | Ladybrand |
| Ngoangoana Gate | 8 am - 4 pm | Bushman's Nek (near Sehlabathebe) |
| Qacha's Nek | 8 am - 10 pm | north of Matatiele |
| Ramatseliso's Gate | 8 am - 6 pm | north-east of Matatiele |
| Sani Pass | 8 am - 4 pm | Himeville |
| Sephapho's Gate | 8 am - 4 pm | Boesmanskop (south of Mafeteng) |
| Van Rooyen's Gate | 6 am - 10 pm | Wepener (north of Mafeteng) |

the car out of South Africa, so it pays to get the letter.

There is a road tax of M2, payable on departure.

# Getting Around

## AIR

Lesotho Airways used to fly to several internal destinations and fares were low – this is no longer the case. Currently the only flight from Maseru is to Qacha's Nek (about M100). Note that the free-luggage allowance is only 15 kg.

The airline's timetable changes frequently, partly because of weather conditions and partly because of economic problems, so check whether other routes are again operating. The main booking office (☎ 32 4500, 32 4507) is on Kingsway, Maseru.

## BUS & MINIBUS TAXI

There is a good network of slow buses running to many towns. Minibus taxis are quicker but tend not to run long distances. In more remote areas you might have to arrange a ride with a truck, for which you'll have to negotiate a fare. Be prepared for long delays once you're off the main routes.

You'll be quoted long-distance fares on the buses but it's better to just buy a ticket to the next major town, as most of the passengers will get off there and you'll be stuck waiting for the bus to fill up again, and other buses might leave before yours. Buying tickets in stages is only slightly more expensive than buying a direct ticket.

Heading north-east from Maseru you almost always have to change at Maputsoe, although this sometimes happens on the road into town if your bus meets another coming the other way.

Unlike many buses in South Africa, buses in Lesotho are strictly nonsmoking.

Some examples of bus fares are: Maseru to Teyateyaneng, M4; Maseru to Maputsoe, M12; and Maseru to Thaba-Tseka, M24.

## TRAIN

No passenger trains run to or in Lesotho.

## CAR & MOTORCYCLE

Driving in Lesotho is getting easier as new roads are built in conjunction with the massive Highlands Water Project, but once you get off the tar there are still plenty of places where even a 4WD vehicle will get into trouble. Apart from rough roads, rivers flooding after summer storms present the biggest problems, and you can be stuck for days. People and animals on the roads are another hazard. There are sometimes army roadblocks (usually searching for stolen cars), although 'respectable' cars are often waved through.

Before attempting a difficult drive try to get some local knowledge of current conditions; ask at a police station. The bar at the Maseru Club contains a good cross section of people working all over Lesotho.

You can use any driving licence as long as it's in English or you have a 'certified translation'. There's a fine for not wearing a seat belt.

## ORGANISED TOURS

The tourist office in Maseru sporadically organises tours to places of scenic and cultural interest for locals. Day tours cost around M75 and there are sometimes weekend trips as well. Foreigners might be able to tag along but don't force the issue if it seems that you aren't wanted. The minimum number of people on a tour is three.

Malealea Lodge (see the Malealea entry later in this chapter) organises vehicle safaris and pony trekking. African Routes (☎ South Africa (031) 562 8724; fax 562 8673) has trips to Lesotho from Durban and Jo'burg which include pony trekking.

# Maseru

Maseru has been a quiet backwater for much of its history. Kingsway was paved for the 1947 visit by British royals and remained the capital's only tarred road for some time.

Most of Maseru's 300,000 people have arrived since the 1970s, but for a rapidly expanding Third World city Maseru remains an easy-going place. Despite this, it's very much a capital city and a recreation centre for the many foreign aid workers.

Maseru is fairly safe but be on your guard at night, especially off the main street. Kids begging for money can be a bit of a hassle.

### Orientation & Information

Maseru's main street, Kingsway, runs from the border post at the bridge right through the centre of town to the Circle, a traffic round-about and landmark. At the Circle it splits to become two important highways: Main North Rd and Main South Rd.

**Tourist Office** The tourist office (☎ 31 2896; fax 32 3638) is on Kingsway, next to the Hotel Victoria. The staff are friendly and helpful. They have a good but not very detailed map of Maseru; if they're out of stock try the Basotho Hat craft shop across the road.

The Land, Surveys & Physical Planning Department has a more detailed map but it's harder to read and more out of date. You can also buy good topographic maps of the country here. The office is open between 8 am and 12.45 pm, and 2 and 4.30 pm on weekdays. It's on Lerotholi Rd, near the corner of Constitution Rd.

The Maseru Club is a meeting place for expats and aid workers, good sources of information on out-of-the-way places.

**Sehlabathebe National Park** For bookings at the park contact the Conservation Division (☎ 32 3600, ext 30), in the Ministry of Agriculture building (the sign says Bosiu Rural Development Project) on Raboshabane Rd, which is off Moshoeshoe Rd, near the train station.

**Money** With so many foreigners in town the banks are used to changing money and there's no hassle except for the short banking hours: 8.30 am to 3 pm weekdays (except Thursday when they are only open until 1

pm) and 8.30 to 11 am Saturday. The last Friday of the month is pay day and huge slow-moving queues wind down the street.

Three bank branches – Lesotho, Barclays and Standard – are all on Kingsway. These are the only places in the country where you can change money.

**Post & Communications** If you can help it don't use Maseru as a poste restante address, or you'll join the permanent group of people waiting to complain about missing mail.

To make international phone calls go to the public call office, down the lane on the west side of the post office. It's open from Monday to Friday between 8 am and 5 pm, Saturday between 8 am and noon. Calls are very expensive, so if you can, wait until you are back in South Africa.

**Medical Services** If you need a doctor or a dentist contact an embassy; they have lists of recommended practitioners. In an emergency go to the Queen Elizabeth II Hospital on Kingsway, near the Lesotho Sun Hotel.

**Cultural Centres** There's a British Council, an Alliance Française and an American Cultural Center.

### Things to See & Do

There are several good walks on the mountain ridges which protrude into the city, such as the walk beginning at the gate of the Lesotho Sun Hotel which takes you up to a plateau where there are great views of Maseru. *Hill Walks In & Around Maseru* (M3.75), available at the Basotho Hat and nearby craft shops, describes other walks. Note that some walks in the book have been overwhelmed by urban sprawl and are no longer possible.

Take some time to go into the 'urban villages' which surround Maseru. You will be welcomed and, if you are lucky, you may be invited to spend the night there. It makes a pleasant change from the western-style hotels in Maseru.

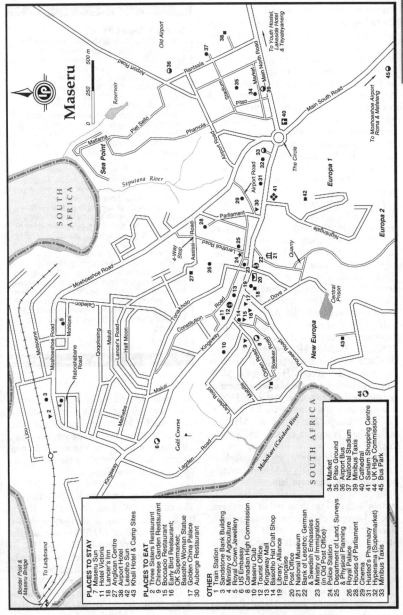

Maseru

0   250   500 m

**PLACES TO STAY**
1   Maseru Sun
11  Hotel Victoria
18  Lancer's Inn
27  Anglican Centre
38  Airport Hotel
42  Lesotho Sun
43  Khali Hotel & Camp Sites

**PLACES TO EAT**
2   Three Sisters Restaurant
9   Chinese Garden Restaurant
15  Boccacio Restaurant
16  Early Bird Restaurant;
    Basotho Woman Statue
    OK Supermarket;
17  Golden China Palace
30  Auberge Restaurant

**OTHER**
1   Train Station
3   Sandstone Bank Building
4   Ministry of Agriculture
5   Royal Crown Jewellery
6   US Embassy
8   Canadian High Commission
10  Maseru Club
12  Tourist Office
13  Kingsway Mall
14  Basotho Hat Craft Shop
19  Library; Alliance
    Française
20  Post Office
21  National Museum
22  Bank of Lesotho; German
    & Swedish Embassies
23  Ministry of Immigration
    (in Old Post Office)
24  Police Station
25  Department of Land, Surveys
    & Physical Planning
26  Royal Palace
28  Houses of Parliament
29  Cathedral
31  Lesotho Pharmacy
32  Cinema
33  Hyperama (Supermarket)
33  Minibus Taxis
34  Market
35  Pitso Ground
36  Airport Bus
37  National Stadium
39  Minibus Taxis
40  Cathedral
41  Sanlam Shopping Centre
44  UK High Commission
45  Bus Park

## Places to Stay – bottom end

**Camping & Hostels** There is no camp-ground in Maseru and free-camping would be risky, but you can camp at the *Khali Hotel/Motel* (see below) for M40.

Still, with a couple of hostels it's possible to find inexpensive accommodation. The *Anglican Centre* (☎ 32 2046) charges M25 per person in austere dorms or twin rooms. Meals are available if you give notice. The centre is only about 500m north of Kingsway on the bend where Assisi Rd becomes Lancer's Rd, but getting there isn't simple – see the map. If you get lost ask for St James Church, which is next door, or Machabeng High School, which is at least in the area.

*Phomolong Youth Hostel* (☎ 33 2900) is a long way from town; it charges M25 per person per night. Head out on Main North Rd, go over the bridge and turn right down the Lancers Gap road. This turn-off is not signposted but near the turn-off is a sign, 'Gold Medal Enterprises'. The hostel is about 2km further on. Minibuses to Lancers Gap run past it. This place is quite relaxed and doesn't keep strict hours.

If you're desperate, you could stay at the *Lesotho Workcamps Association* (☎ 31 4862), 917 Cathedral Rd, behind the Catholic Cathedral near the large traffic circle at the end of Kingsway. Head down Main North Rd until you come to a garage; nearby is a dirt road where taxis accumulate. Follow this road until you come to the buildings of the work camp. The dorms are M15 per night. There is a place to wash and a small kitchen.

You used to be able to stay at a couple of the aid workers' hostels in Maseru but they no longer welcome travellers.

**Hotels** Add 10% tax to the prices given here. About 5km east of the centre is the *Lakeside Hotel* (☎ 31 3646), off Main North Rd. Singles/doubles are M110/150 and it's good for the price. Out on the Lancer's Gap road is the *Palace Hotel* (☎ 50 0700, 50 0617), a small place which has rooms from M100.

The *Khali Hotel/Motel* (☎ 31 0501) is a large and friendly local place south of

---

### Urban Village Life

Urban village life sounds like an impossibility, but in the townships surrounding Maseru you have an opportunity to experience Basotho village life on the edge of a city.

Phomolong, just outside Maseru and at the foot of Lancer's Gap, is a good example. The moment you leave the sealed Lancer's Gap road the adventure begins. The reality of these places is an absence of street signs, complex mazes of dirt roads and a seemingly never-ending expanse of rudimentary houses. You may cross a dam wall, pass a small shop and zigzag through a corridor of wire and brick fences.

Village life here is like anywhere where trading and bartering are common. Negotiate a price for a dozen 'free-range' eggs before you enter your hosts' house, or observe the locals tending their small vegetable plots and milking cows. As evening descends look upwards to the masses of stars, a view undisturbed by street lighting, and listen to the dogs barking, the locals chattering as they fetch water and the children singing folk songs.

In the morning the staccato crowing of an undetermined sum of roosters awakes you and you soon head to the village tap to fetch water for washing, drinking and cooking. The sun pops up from behind the surrounding limestone cliffs as the locals emerge from the ramshackle labyrinth to catch buses to their jobs in Maseru.

**Jeff Williams**

---

Kingsway, beyond the prison. It has rooms from M80/120 and there's a restaurant. You can camp for M40 (two people). The hotel runs an hourly shuttle-bus or you can take a Thetsane minibus on Pioneer Rd, near Lancer's Inn, and get off at the turn-off for the suburb of New Europa.

## Places to Stay – middle & top end

The tall *Hotel Victoria* (☎ 31 2922; fax 31 0318), on Kingsway, is deteriorating and is not good value at M170/240 for singles/doubles. *Lancer's Inn* (☎ 31 2114; fax 31 0223), on Kingsway, is a comfortable colonial-era hotel with rooms from M135/167, and self-contained chalets for M192/224.

There are two Sun hotels: the *Maseru Sun* (☎ 31 2434; fax 31 0158), near the river south-west of Kingsway, which has singles/ doubles from M225/315, and the *Lesotho Sun* (☎ 31 3111; fax 31 0104), on a hillside further east. It's more of a luxury resort hotel, charging from M358/484.

### Places to Eat

On Kingsway there are street stalls, mainly open during the day, selling good grilled meat for about M5. Serves of curry and rice cost M4.

Opposite the Kingsway Mall construction site (which in the future will be a happy hunting ground for food) there is a small plaza with a statue of a Basotho woman. Head left of the statue to the *Early Bird*, a friendly local café serving a reasonable range of inexpensive food.

At the Lancer's Inn there's a bakery and deli. All the hotels have restaurants. The *Rendezvous*, at Lancer's Inn, is gloomy and often empty but it's OK. The 1st floor (that's 2nd floor to you North Americans) restaurant at the *Hotel Victoria* is much livelier and the food is good. Also on Kingsway, on the corner of Airport Rd, is the popular *Auberge*; it has a bar which is frequented by expats and locals.

The food at *Boccacio*, an Italian-run Italian restaurant off Kingsway on Bowker Rd, is reliable. Pasta dishes are about M20. Boccacio is closed on Monday.

*Chinese Garden* is a big place on Orpen Rd, off Kingsway. The food is reasonable. There is also the *Golden China Palace* in the Lesotho National Development Corporation Centre on Kingsway. On Moshoeshoe Rd, near the railway station, is *Three Sisters*, a big local eatery.

### Entertainment

Maseru is the headquarters of the many aid organisations working in Lesotho, so there are a lot of volunteers passing through. Currently most of them are Irish, the Canadians having moved on to Rwanda. Aid volunteers receive tiny wages, so buy them beers (Lion Maluti is good) in return for some interesting stories.

The *Maseru Club* is on Lagden Rd. It's a fine old colonial club and a meeting place for expats and aid workers. There's a bar and restaurant and various sports, including squash, tennis and cricket. Temporary membership costs M30 a month but it's easy enough to be signed in as a guest.

On top of the Hotel Victoria there's *The Penthouse*, which has good jazz on weekends, with an entry charge of about M10. The hotel's disco, *Cross Roads*, is in the building to the west of the tower. It is really worth a visit as many locals come here to dance into the wee small hours of the night.

A trip to the *Seapoint Hotel*, 1km or so north-east from the centre, might be fun, but be warned that it's a basic neighbourhood bar and there's the risk of mugging in the area.

You can take in a movie at the *cinema*. Coming from the border end of town, turn left just before the Auberge. Take the first street to the right; the cinema is on the left, just a little way down the road.

Both of the Sun hotels have bars and slot machines and the Lesotho Sun has tenpin bowling.

### Things to Buy

The Basotho Hat, on Kingsway opposite the Hotel Victoria, is a government-run craft shop. It's well worth a look but the prices are generally higher than you'll find in rural areas. If you plan on pony trekking or walking it's a good idea to buy a horsehair fly-whisk. Caboodles is another craft shop nearby on Kingsway which has unusual gifts and some books. Further down Kingsway, towards the Circle, is a large bookshop stocking mainly school texts, but also with some interesting locally published books and pamphlets.

### Getting There & Away

**Bus** The main bus park has been relocated quite a way from the centre on Main South Rd. There have been complaints about this and it might move again. Meanwhile, it's common to see men pushing wheelbarrows full of luggage. There have been complaints about them, too – unless the passenger hurries along beside him, the wheelbarrow-man has been known to vanish with the load.

Examples of fares from Maseru are: Mafeteng, M9; Mafeteng to Quthing, M12; Mohale's Hoek, M15; Pony Trekking Centre (God Help Me Pass), M10.

**Minibus Taxi** Taxis congregate in the streets between the Circle and the market, and there are others near the new Hyperama supermarket off Kingsway near the Circle. The destination is displayed on the left side of the taxi's front window.

### Getting Around
**To/From the Airport** Moshoeshoe airport is 18km from town, off Main South Rd. A Lesotho Airways staff bus runs out there from the old airport (now used by the military and the flying doctor) in town half a dozen times a day. The times often vary and the staff at the ticket office on Kingsway might not have the latest ones. You'll be told the trip takes 15 minutes but by the time the driver has meandered around giving lifts to friends it can be closer to 45 minutes. The plane doesn't wait for the bus. The Khali Hotel's shuttle bus runs to the airport.

**Local Transport** The standard minibus taxi fare around town is M1.40. There are a few conventional taxi services – try Moonlite Telephone Taxis (☎ 31 2695).

# Around Lesotho

Most towns have risen around trading posts or Protectorate-era administration centres and none approach Maseru in size or facilities.

## THABA-BOSIU
Moshoeshoe I's mountain stronghold, first occupied in July 1824, is east of Maseru. Thaba-Bosiu (Mountain at Night), the most important historical site in Lesotho, played a pivotal role in the consolidation of the Basotho nation in the 19th century. The name may have been bestowed because the site

was first occupied at night, but another legend suggests that Thaba-Bosiu, a hill in daylight, grows into a mountain at night.

There's a visitor information centre at the base of Thaba-Bosiu where you pay the M4 entry fee; they provide a map and a pamphlet. An official guide will accompany you to the top of the mountain. The guides are generally friendly and knowledgeable, although some of their knowledge is dubious. For example, it's highly unlikely that Moshoeshoe held court under the big eucalypt on top of the hill, as the trees hadn't been introduced when he was there.

There are good views from the summit of Thaba-Bosiu, including the Qiloane pinnacle, inspiration for the Basotho hat. On the summit are the remains of fortifications, Moshoeshoe's grave and parts of the original settlement.

### The Battles for Thaba-Bosiu
The Basotho atop Thaba-Bosiu repulsed invaders for nearly 40 years. First, the amaNgwane led by one Matiwane attacked the fortress in 1828. After a fierce battle the attacking regiments were driven off and ceased to be a threat. Early in 1831 the heavily armed Kornnas (raiders) were driven away. Next, in 1831, from north of the Vaal came the Ndebele of Mzilikazi. They attacked Thaba-Bosiu at Rafutho's Pass but were repulsed by defenders hurling spears and rocks from above.

It was then the turn of the British. In 1852 Sir George Cathcart, governor of the Cape colony, made a punitive attack on Moshoeshoe's people. On the way to the fortress, about 5km west of Thaba-Bosiu, Cathcart's troops were forced to withdraw by 5000 heavily armed and mounted Basotho warriors.

The Boer republic of the Orange Free State was established in 1854 and Basotho land between the Orange and Caledon rivers began to be taken. There were a number of clashes with the Free State. The most serious started in 1865, when a determined Free State commando (an army unit) led by Commandant Louw Wepener attempted to storm Thaba-Bosiu. The commando was repulsed in what was to be the last attack on Thaba-Bosiu in Moshoeshoe's lifetime. Wepener was killed at Khubelu Pass and today this pass is sometimes referred to as Wepener's Pass. ■

## Places to Stay & Eat

About 2km before the Thaba-Bosiu visitor centre is *'Melesi Lodge* (☎ 35 7215) with single/double rooms for M90/115 and a great restaurant.

## Getting There & Away

To get to Thaba-Bosiu look for a minibus taxi near the Hyperama supermarket (off Kingsway near the Circle); these go as far as the visitor centre at the base of the mountain. If you're driving, head out on Main South Rd, take the turn-off to Roma and after about 6km (near Mazenod) turn off to the left. Thaba-Bosiu is about 10km further along.

## TEYATEYANENG

Teyateyaneng ('Place of Quicksand') is usually known as TY. The town has been developed as the craft centre of Lesotho and there are several places worth visiting.

Some of the best tapestries come from Helang Basali Crafts in the St Agnes Mission, a couple of kilometres before TY on the Maseru road. More tapestries are available from Hatooa-Mose-Mosali and wool products from Setsoto Design, Tebetebeng, and Letlotlo Handcrafts.

The *Blue Mountain Inn* (☎ 50 0362) has single/double rooms for M90/105 and a family room for M140 or you can camp (make sure you get permission from the local chief).

## MAPUTSOE

This border town, 86km north of Maseru, is across the Mohokare (Caledon) River from Ficksburg in South Africa. It has a new shopping centre and a few other civic amenities, but its status as a black dormitory suburb of Ficksburg is still apparent – it is very run-down and impoverished. When it rains the streets turn to slippery mud. Still, it is handy to a border crossing with good transport connections, especially now that it is a gateway to the Highlands Water Project.

## Places to Stay

The run-down *Express Sekekete Hotel* (☎ 43 0621) is inexpensive but you're better off

staying across the border in Ficksburg; see the Free State chapter.

## LERIBE (HLOTSE)

A large town by Lesotho's standards, Leribe (the old name, Hlotse, is still sometimes used) is a quiet village serving as a regional shopping and market centre. It was an administrative centre under the British and there are some old buildings slowly decaying in the leafy streets. **Major Bell's Tower**, on the main street near the market, was built in 1879. A very humble symbol of the might of the British Empire, it spent most of its career as a storehouse for government records.

The **Leribe Craft Centre**, off the highway between the turn-off to Leribe and the turn-off to Katse Dam, sells woollen goods at reasonable prices.

There is a set of **dinosaur footprints** a few kilometres south of Leribe at Tsikoane village. Coming north towards Leribe, take the small dirt road going off to the right towards some rocky outcrops. Follow it up to the church and ask someone to direct you to the *minwane*. It's a 15 to 20 minute slog up the mountainside to a series of caves. The prints are clearly visible on the ceiling of the rock.

About 10km north of Leribe are the **Subeng River dinosaur footprints**. There is a signpost indicating the river but not the footprints. Walk down to the river from the road to a concrete causeway (about 250m). The footprints, of at least three species of dinosaur, are about 15m downstream on the right bank. They are fairly worn.

## Places to Stay & Eat

The *Agricultural Training Centre* is just outside town, or try the *Catholic Mission* about 10km past Leribe. The old-style *Leribe Hotel* (☎ 40 0362), on Main St, has singles/doubles for about M100/160. There is also a tea garden surrounded by well-established trees.

## KATSE & HIGHLANDS WATER PROJECT

One of the effects of the Lesotho Highlands Water Project has been the improvement of roads into the interior of the country. As Phase 1A (construction of the Katse Dam to the north of Thaba-Tseka) proceeds it gets easier for travellers to get into this remote part of Lesotho.

From Leribe (Hlotse) you can now take a sealed road all the way to the project headquarters at Katse. This road passes the lowland village of Pitseng and climbs over the Maluti mountains to drop to Ha Lejone (which one day will be at the edge of the dam's lake). It continues south past Mamohau Mission, crosses the impressive Malibamat'so Bridge, climbs over another series of hills to the Matsoku Valley, recrosses the Malibamat'so and ends in Katse. From Katse you can continue on an improved dirt road to Thaba-Tseka, 45km to the south.

Information about the project is available from the Lesotho Highlands Development Authority in Katse (look for the modern yellow building with a blue roof). A visit can be organised in advance; phone ☎ 31 4324. The dam is now completed, and at 185m high (the highest in Africa) the wall is an impressive sight.

### Place to Stay & Eat

*Katse Lodge* (☎ 91 0202) is reportedly reasonable although it fills up with sightseers on weekends. On Friday nights they have a steak special (M20). For a beer with good views and satellite TV head for Bruno's Pub, on the hillside above the turn-off for Katse Village. Things can get out of hand on Friday nights.

### Getting There & Away

There are taxis from Leribe (Hlotse) to Katse for about M30. There's plenty of traffic if you want to hitch.

### BUTHA-BUTHE

Moshoeshoe named this town Butha-Buthe (Place of Lying Down) because it was here that his people first retreated during the chaos of the difaqane. The small town is built alongside the Hlotse River and has the beautiful Maluti mountains as a backdrop.

### Places to Stay & Eat

There are signs on the road pointing to the *Ha Thabo Ramakatane Youth Hostel*, though you may have to ask directions (say *hasechele*). It's about 4km from the village. There are no supplies so buy food in the village before arriving. There is no electricity; you cook using gas and you fetch your own water just as the villagers do. Basic accommodation costs around M20 per night.

The *Crocodile Inn* (☎ 46 0223), Reserve Rd, has single/double rooms from M88/110 and the *Butha-Buthe Hotel* (☎ 46 0233) is similar.

Apart from the usual crop of liquor restaurants, there is the *Venice Italian*, the *Sekekete Café* and the *Roadside Café* for a choice of ordinary fare.

### OXBOW

South African skiers used to come to Oxbow in winter but the place has slowly died as a ski resort. The *New Oxbow Lodge* (book on ☎ (05192) 2247), on the banks of the Malibamat'so River, charges M105/175 for singles/doubles. A few kilometres further north is a private chalet belonging jointly to the Maluti and Witwatersrand University ski clubs. It's possible to sleep here for M25 although winter weekends are crowded. See the caretaker or write to Club Maluti, PO Box 783308, Sandton 2146, South Africa.

### BASOTHO PONY TREKKING CENTRE

The pony trekking centre is on the road between Maseru and Thaba-Tseka on the top of God Help Me Pass. By bus it's M10 from Maseru and takes about two hours. There *should* be four daily buses each way, but there have been problems with the road lately.

Treks range from a two hour ride (about M30) to a week-long ride (about M350). There are minimum numbers on some of the longer rides, but they are only two or four, so it's easy to get a group together. There are discounts for larger groups. Contact the tourist office in Maseru for details and bookings.

Accommodation on overnight treks is in villages along the way, and they charge about

M10 per person a night or M5 if you have a tent. This is not included in the trekking fees, so bring enough money to cover costs. You can't stay at the centre (although travellers have wangled floor space), so if your trek departs early in the morning you'll have to camp out or stay at the *Molimo-Nthuse Lodge* (☎ 31 2922 for booking), 3km back down the pass. This means a steep walk the next morning. The lodge still charges from M100/130 for singles/doubles (good value).

Pony treks are also available from Malealea Lodge; see Malealea in this chapter.

### THABA-TSEKA
This remote town is on the western edge of the Central Ranges, over the sometimes tricky Mokhoabong Pass. It was established in 1980 as a centre for the mountain district.

You can usually get a bed at the *Farmer Training Centre* for about M12 per person.

About four buses a day run from Maseru to Thaba-Tseka (M25), but continuing on is not so easy. There's reportedly a minibus taxi heading north at about 6 am daily, which will get you to a settlement from where there is plenty of transport to Leribe. Heading south from Thaba-Tseka to Sehonghong and Qacha's Nek is more difficult – you'll probably have to negotiate with a truck driver. As the Highlands Water Project progresses there should be more traffic and better roads.

### MOKHOTLONG
The first major town north of Sani Pass and Sehlabathebe National Park, Mokhotlong (Place of the Bald Ibis) has basic shops and transport to Oxbow and Butha-Buthe. The town, some 270km from Maseru and 200km from Butha-Buthe, has the reputation as being the coldest, driest and most remote place in Lesotho. The nearby Senqu (Orange) River, the biggest in Lesotho, has its source near Mokhotlong. The town is a good base for walks to the Drakensberg escarpment.

At the *Farmer Training Centre* you can get a bed for M12 per night; there are cold-water washing facilities and a kitchen. The *(Lefu) Senqu Hotel* (☎ 92 0330), 5km from the airport, has rooms for M100/120.

Some 15km south-west of Mokhotlong in Upper Rafalotsane village is *Molumong Lodge*; it costs from M25 per person but you need to bring your own sleeping bag. There are three buses a day to the lodge from Mokhotlong. The owner, Mike Campbell, might be able to take you to/from Himeville (South Africa) but there's no fixed schedule.

One of the few places in Mokhotlong where you can get a half-decent meal is the *Hunter's Restaurant*.

### SANI PASS
This steep pass is the only dependable road into Lesotho from the KwaZulu-Natal Drakensberg. On the South African side the nearest towns are Underberg and Himeville.

From the chalet at the top of the pass there are several day walks, including a long and arduous one to **Thabana-Ntlenyana** (3482m), the highest peak in Africa south of Mt Kilimanjaro. There is a path but a guide would come in handy. Horses can do the trip so consider hiring one. The height of the mountain was only calculated in 1951, and it took another 30 years for this calculation to be confirmed by satellite technology.

Another walk leads to **Hodgson's Peaks**, 6km south, from where you get the benefit of views to Sehlabathebe National Park and to KwaZulu-Natal.

### Places to Stay
*Sani Top*, at the top of the pass, has dorms (R24) and doubles (R56) or you can camp for R16. There are also non-backpacker rooms for R50 per person. There is a bar and cooking facilities but you must bring all your own food. In winter the snow is often deep enough to ski (there are a few pieces of antique equipment) and horse trekking is available with prior arrangement. Book through Travel Underberg (☎ (033) 701 1466) in South Africa.

The other obvious places to stay are *Sani Lodge* and *The Wild West Youth Hostel*, on the South African side of the pass. See the KwaZulu-Natal chapter.

## Getting There & Away

The South African border guards won't let
you up the pass unless you have a 4WD,
although you can come down from Lesotho
without one. The South African border is
open between 8 am and 4 pm; the Lesotho
border stays open an hour later to let the last
vehicles through. Hitching up or down the
pass is best on weekends when there is a fair
amount of traffic to and from the lodge.

The hostels in South Africa at the bottom
of the pass arrange transport up the pass and
Travel Underberg (☎ (033) 701 1466) in
Underberg will also take you up. They have
a 'standby' backpacker rate of R45.

There's no public transport from the pass
to other places in Lesotho, although there are
several trucks each day heading for Mokhotlong (52km north-west) and you might be
able to hitch, but expect to pay.

## SEHLABATHEBE NATIONAL PARK

Lesotho's first (and only) national park, proclaimed in 1970, is remote and rugged, and
it is always an adventure to get to. The park's
main attraction is its sense of separation from
the rest of the world. Other than a rare Maloti
minnow, thought to be extinct but rediscovered in the Tsoelikana River, rare birds such
as the bearded vulture, and the odd rhebok
or baboon, there are relatively few animals.
As well as hikes and climbs, the park has
horse-riding and guided horseback tours cost
M50.

This is a summer-rain area, and thick mist,
potentially hazardous to hikers, is common.
Winters are clear but cold at night and there
are sometimes light falls of snow.

Near the village of Sehonghong is **Soai's
Cave**. Soai, the last chief of the Maloti San
people, was attacked and defeated here by
Cape and Basotho forces in 1871.

## Places to Stay & Eat

You can camp in the park but except at the
lodge, where camping costs M10, there are
no facilities besides plenty of water. The
lodge has hotel beds for M20, single/double
rooms for M30/50 and four-bed family
rooms for M90. The whole lodge costs M240

per night. You can buy firewood and coal
here, but for food (very limited) and petrol
or diesel you'll have to rely on a small store
about 5km west of the park entrance and
quite a way from the lodge and hostel. You
have to book the lodge in Maseru at the
Conservation Division of the Ministry of
Agriculture (☎ 32 3600, ext 30).

In Sehlabathebe village is the new, clean
*Range Management Education Centre*. It is
1.5km down the road to Sehonghong and it
costs M20 per person in dorms. At the café
next to the Sehonghong airstrip there is occasionally accommodation for M20 per night;
this is a handy option if you fly in.

## Getting There & Away

Sometimes there are charter flights from
Maseru to Ha Paulus, a village near the park
entrance, and you can arrange to be picked
up from there for M40.

Driving into the park can be a problem, as
the roads are 4WD tracks which become
impassable after heavy rain, which falls in
spring and summer. Bear in mind that having
got to the park you could be stuck here
waiting for a river to go down. Still, people
usually do make it in and out without too
many problems and most agree that the
journey has been worth it. The road-building
accompanying the hydroelectric scheme
should improve at least some of the routes.
Check with the Conservation office in Maseru when you book accommodation.

There are several routes into the park, all
of which currently require 4WD. The longest
is the southern route via Quthing and
Qacha's Nek. There's also a route via Thaba-
Tseka, then down the Senqu River valley
past the hamlet of Sehonghong and over the
difficult Matebeng Pass. The park can also
be reached from Matatiele in the extreme
west of KwaZulu-Natal. This route doesn't
have as many difficult sections as the other
routes but it is less well maintained so it is
sometimes closed; check in Matatiele before
trying it.

There is a daily bus between Qacha's Nek
and Sehlabathebe village. The relatively
short distance takes 5½ hours and costs

M19; the bus departs from Sehlabathebe at 5.30 am and returns from Qacha's Nek at noon.

Probably the simplest way in is to hike the 10km up the escarpment from Bushman's Nek in South Africa. From Bushman's Nek to Nkonkoana Gate, the Lesotho border post, takes about six hours. You can also take a horse up or down for M40.

## QACHA'S NEK
This pleasant town, with a number of sandstone buildings, was founded in 1888 near the pass (1980m) of the same name. There are Californian redwood trees nearby, some over 25m high. The *Nthatuoa Hotel* (☎ 95 0260) offers adequate accommodation starting at M93/126.50. It is within walking distance from the airstrip.

There are cafés in town including the *Vuka Afrika* and you can get meals at the hotel.

### Getting There & Away
Weather permitting (this area can get snowed-in during winter) a bus to Sehlabathebe leaves daily at around noon (M19). There is more transport between here and Quthing (Moyeni). A bus leaves from both towns at 9 am, takes about six hours and costs M30. It is a spectacular drive.

## ROMA
Roma, only 35km from Maseru, is a university town and a good place to meet students. There are some attractive sandstone buildings dotted around the town and the entry to town by the southern gorge is spectacular.

North from Roma is the important **Ha Baroana rock-painting** site. Although the site suffers from neglect and vandalism (including damage done by tourists who spray water on the paintings to produce brighter photos) this site is worth seeing.

To get there from Roma head back to the Maseru road and turn right onto the road heading west to Thaba-Tseka and the pony trekking centre. After about 12km turn off to the left, just after the Ha Ntsi settlement on the Mohlsks-oa-Tuka River. To get to the site by minibus taxi from Maseru head for Naza-reth and get off about 1.5km before Nazareth. A signpost indicates the way to the paintings off to the left. Follow this gravel track 3km to the village of Ha Khotso, then turn right at a football field. Follow this track a further 2.5km to a hilltop overlooking a gorge. A footpath zigzags down the hillside to the rock shelter where the paintings can be found.

### Places to Stay & Eat
Outside Roma, off the Maseru road, is the *Trading Post Guest House* (☎ 34 0202 or 34 0267). The trading post has been here since 1903, as has the Thorn family which owns the store and the guesthouse. There are walks and horse-riding in the area, including a 20 minute walk to dinosaur footprints. The accommodation is good value at M35 per person in rondavels, M40 in the main house (a nice old stone building), and camping costs M7 per person. There is no restaurant but you can use the kitchen. Everything is provided except towels. In Roma, try the *Roberto Restaurant*.

## SEMONKONG
The **Maletsunyane Falls**, also known as Lebihan Falls after the French missionary who reported them in 1881, are about a 1½ hour walk from Semonkong (Place of Smoke). The 192m falls are at their most spectacular in summer and best appreciated from the bottom of the gorge (where there are camp sites).

The remote 122m **Ketane Falls** are also worth seeing. These are a solid day's ride (30km) from Semonkong or a four day return horse-ride from Malealea Lodge.

### Places to Stay
You can usually find a bed at the *Roman Catholic Mission* for a small contribution. Fraser's *Semonkong Lodge* charges M18 for a camp site, M30 per night for a dorm bed and M156 for a double. The Lodge offers hiking and pony trekking, with rates and options similar to those at Malealea Lodge. Book the lodge and trekking through Peacock Sports (☎ South Africa (05192) 2730

LESOTHO

or 3106) in Fontein St, Ficksburg, South Africa.

### Getting There & Away
Buses between Maseru and Semonkong (M15) leave from either end in the morning and arrive late afternoon.

### MORIJA
This small village, about 40km south of Maseru on the Main South Rd, is where you will find the **Morija Museum & Archives** (☎ 36 0308). The collection includes archives from the first mission to Basutholand, and as the missionary was associated with King Moshoeshoe the collection is of great importance. Part of the tea set given to the king by the mission society is on display at the museum, together with displays of Basotho culture, some Stone and Iron Age finds and dinosaur relics. The museum is open Monday to Saturday from 8.30 am to 4.30 pm, Sunday from 2 to 4.30 pm; admission is M2.

Near the museum is the *Mophato Oa Morija* (☎ 36 0219), an ecumenical centre with beds for M40 and camping for M20 per person. There's also *Ha Matel* (call the museum at ☎ 36 0308, ask for Stephen Gill – he works there), a pleasant self-catering cottage which costs M60 per person (no minimum – it's a good deal).

### MAFETENG
The name Mafeteng derives from 'Place of Lefeta's People'. An early magistrate, Emile Rolland, was called Lefeta (One who Passes By) by local Basotho. Nearby is the 2908m Thaba-Putsoa (Blue Mountain), the highest feature in this part of Lesotho.

There is not much of interest in town, although it is important as a bus and minibus taxi interchange. There's a memorial to soldiers of the Cape Mounted Rifles who fell in the 1880 Gun War.

The *Mafeteng Hotel* (☎ 70 0236) has singles/doubles for M105/120.

### MOHALE'S HOEK
This comfortable town is 125km from Ma-

seru on a sealed road. The younger brother of Moshoeshoe I, Mohale, gave this land to the British for administrative purposes in 1884. It is a much nicer little place than nearby Mafeteng.

Mohale's Hoek has the *Hotel Mount Maluti* (☎ 78 5224) with singles/doubles from M96/146. For desperados there is a possibility of a bed at the *Farmer Training Centre* at M20 per night. There are a number of places where you can buy an uninspiring meal – try *Koena's Corner* on Hospital Rd or the *Majantja General Café* on Kou St.

### MALEALEA
Malealea is a small village, a store and a large lodge. This is one of the gems of Lesotho and is appropriately advertised as 'Lesotho in a nutshell'. The owners, Mick and Di Jones, work tirelessly to promote Lesotho throughout Southern Africa. You can go on a well-organised pony trek from here or wander freely through the hills and villages.

The valleys around Malealea have been occupied for many hundreds of years, as shown by the many San paintings in rock shelters. The original Malealea Trading Store was established in 1905 by Mervyn Smith, a teacher, diamond miner and soldier. The owners of the lodge may show you the protected spiral aloe *(Aloe polyphylla)*, a plant unique to Lesotho.

A reader reports that the Mafiteng Children's Choir practices in the village and that just hearing them is worth the trip from Maseru.

### Pony Trekking
Malealea Lodge is the best place in Lesotho to go pony trekking. These treks offer a good chance to come face to face with Basotho villagers as well as experience the awesome scenery of the mountains and deep valleys. These treks are conducted by the villagers in conjunction with the lodge, so if you undertake a trek you are contributing to the local village economy.

The two most popular treks are those to the Ribaneng Waterfall (two days, one night) and to the Ribaneng/Ketane waterfalls (four days, three nights). The lodge will organise a trek to any destination that takes your fancy, however. You need to bring food, sleeping bag, rainwear, sunscreen, warm clothing, torch and water purification tablets.

Day rides cost M70 per person or M60 each for four or more people. Overnight treks cost M100 per person per day. There is an additional cost of M20 for each night spent in one of the Basotho village huts.

### Walks

You may elect to go walking if 'ye are of tender buttocks' and cannot face seven-hour stints on the ponies. Mick and Di have put together a number of walking options and provide a map. They can arrange for your packs to be carried on ponies. Day walks include a two hour return walk to the Botso'ela Waterfall; a six hour return walk to the Pitseng Gorge (don't forget your swimwear); an easy one hour walk along the Pitseng Plateau; a walk along the Makhaleng River; and a hike from the Gates of Paradise Pass back to Malealea. The scenery along any of these walks is nothing less than stunning and all include the local villages which dot the landscape. Overnight and longer walks can easily be planned.

### Drives

Although it is slow-going on the dirt roads in this region there are some very scenic drives. Perhaps the best is the road which forms part of the Roof of Africa Rally. Take a right turn at the first junction you come to when leaving Malealea. The road passes through some picturesque villages before crossing the top of the Botso'ela Waterfall. A few kilometres on it reaches an impressive lookout over the Makhaleng and Ribaneng valleys. In a conventional car it takes an hour to reach the viewpoint from Malealea; rally drivers take 20 minutes to cover this same distance!

If you continue north from the lookout to Sebelekoane you can return to Maseru via Roma. This scenic road leads to Basotho villages and missions tucked away in the valleys. Be warned, it is rough in places and

the going can be slow; allow three hours from Sebelekoane to Maseru.

### Places to Stay & Eat

*Malealea Lodge* is part of Smith's old colonial trading post. There is a variety of accommodation including backpackers' rooms (there's a good chance that you'll have a room to yourself) where beds are M35 per person or M30 if you don't need linen, huts with communal facilities for M50 per person and rooms with private facilities (some with a private kitchen for M70 per person). You need to bring your own towel. Camping costs M15 per person.

There are communal kitchens or you can arrange to have meals (the food is good), at M18 for breakfast, M25 for lunch and from M30 for dinner.

There's a bar at the lodge and the village shop sells basic supplies.

There's usually room if you just turn up but sometimes there are groups which take up the whole place so you should book. There's no phone at the lodge (there is a radio) so allow a few days for your booking to go through. To book, call South Africa (☎ (51) 447 3200; fax 448 3001), or Lesotho (☎ 78 5727; fax 78 5336; email malealea@ pixie.co.za).

About 6km from the Malealea Lodge turn-off is *Qaba Lodge* (☎ (05192) 2370), which has accommodation in run-down surroundings for M50 per person; it does have a fully equipped kitchen, bar and store where you can buy supplies.

### Getting There & Away

Maseru to Malealea is 84km. From Maseru, head south on the well-signposted Mafeteng road for 52km to the town of Motsekuoa (the first town after Morija). Look out for the Golden Rose restaurant, the proliferation of taxis and the huddles of potential passengers. Opposite the restaurant turn left (east) onto the dirt road and follow it for 24km. When you reach the signposted turn-off to Malealea, it is a further 7km to the lodge. You know that you are on the right track when you pass through the Gates of Paradise and are rewarded with a stunning view of your destination. The plaque here announces 'Wayfarer – Pause and look upon a gateway of Paradise'. Romantic stuff. Look east from here and you can just make out the Ribaneng Waterfall.

The road to Malealea from the south, via Mpharane and Masemouse, is much rougher. Most drivers take the Motsekuoa road.

It's sometimes possible to arrange transport between Bloemfontein (Free State) and Malealea. Inquire when booking or ask at Taffy's Backpackers in Bloemfontein.

Abantu Tours (☎ South Africa (011) 648 7066; fax 648 2186) arranges packages from Jo'burg or Bloemfontein, including transport to/from Malealea, pony trekking and two nights accommodation. The minimum group size is four. From Jo'burg this costs R850 per person and from Bloemfontein it's R790. Abantu is run by Lancelot Ntsepileng Sello, otherwise known as Porky. We haven't had any feedback on them but the people at Malealea say that they are good.

## QUTHING (MOYENI)

Quthing, the southernmost major town in Lesotho, is often known as Moyeni (a Sephuthi word meaning 'Place of the Wind'). The town was established in 1877, abandoned three years later during the 1880 Gun War and then rebuilt at the present site.

Most of the town is in Lower Quthing; up on the hill overlooking the dramatic Orange River Gorge is Upper Quthing, where there is a good hotel, a mission and sundry colonial-era structures. A minibus taxi between the two costs M1.50 – you can hitch but you should still pay.

Pony trekking is sometimes available; see the Royal Lesotho Mounted Police in Upper Quthing or book through the Orange River Hotel.

Off the highway, about 5km west of Quthing, is the five-room **Masitise Cave**

**House**. This mission building was built into a San rock shelter in 1866 by one Rev Ellenberger. His son Edmund, a latter-day troglodyte, was born in the cave in 1867. Edmund later became the mayor of Bethlehem in the Free State. Inquire at the school about access to the cave house and someone will unlock it for you. There are San paintings nearby.

Probably the most easily located of the **dinosaur footprints** in Lesotho are close to Quthing. To get to these, go up the Mt Moorosi road from Quthing until you reach a thatched-roofed orange building. There is a short walk to the footprints, which are believed to be 180 million years old.

Between Quthing and Masitise there is a striking twin-spired **sandstone church**, part of the Villa Maria Mission.

Near Qomoqomong, 10km from Quthing, there is a good gallery of **San paintings**; inquire at the General Dealers store about acquiring a guide for the 20 minute walk to the paintings.

### Places to Stay & Eat

The cheapest place is the *Merino Stud Farm*, which has clean double rooms with bath for M35 per person; breakfast and dinner are about M10 each.

The *Orange River Hotel* (☎ 75 0252) in Upper Quthing is a pleasant place with stunning views across the gorge to the bleak hills behind. Single/double rooms cost M85/120. There's a restaurant and a bar, but for a better place to drink, head up the driveway to the old thatched pub and sit with the locals on the lawn under an oak tree.

In Lower Quthing, the *Mountain Side Hotel* (☎ 75 0257) is a basic pub with a restaurant which might have rooms, depending on who's behind the bar when you ask. If you do get in, expect to pay M70 for either a single or double.

# Swaziland

# Swaziland

Swaziland comes as a breath of fresh air after travelling through South Africa. Very few of the animosities so evident in post-apartheid era South Africa will be experienced in Swaziland, and it is comforting being in a country where everyone seems to get along with each other.

Outside of Mbabane, the capital, and Manzini, the commercial centre, the country is rural and dotted with small villages. It is easy to get from place to place – Swaziland is compact and the distances between points of interest are relatively small. But with a blood alcohol limit of 0.15, some of the most notorious stretches of road in the world, very few fences, stock wandering freely, pea-soup fogs and jam-packed minibus taxis, driving is a real experience – you just have to be careful.

As one of Africa's monarchies – almost an absolute monarchy at that – there is much evidence of royalty and right royal relationships. Chances are that the man or woman you are talking to in a shop or at the bar is a prince or princess, without the obvious trappings normally associated with such titles. The monarchy fortunately clings to tradition, and there are several chances each year to see cultural spectaculars such as the Incwala and Umhlanga (Reed) dances at the Royal Kraal in Lobamba.

The Swaziland national parks are special. After a hard and often bloody fight the threat to the black and white rhino populations is not as critical as it once was, and these majestic animals can now be seen in Mkhaya Game Reserve. The lion, symbol of the king, has been returned to the kingdom at Hlane Royal National Park; and the Mlilwane Wildlife Sanctuary, in the Ezulwini Valley, is one of the few places where you can see wildlife on foot, from a bicycle or on horseback. There is good hiking in Malolotja, plenty of horse-riding centres in the old British 'expat' hill towns, and adventurous white-water rafting on the Great Usutu River.

## SWAZILAND AT A GLANCE

**Area:** 17,363 sq km
**Population:** 1,031,000
**Population Growth Rate:** 3.2%
**Capital:** Mbabane
**Head of State:** King Mswati III
**Official Languages:** English, siSwati
**Currency:** Emalangeni (E) (plural), Lilangeni (singular)
**Exchange Rate:** E4.3 = US$1
**Per Capita GNP:** US$1060 (Purchasing power parity: US$3700)
**Literacy:** 77%
**Infant Mortality:** around 9%

### Highlights

- Game-viewing and safari camps in the splendid Mkhaya Game Reserve (page 636)
- Hiking, night drives and white-water rafting (pages 631, 632, 635)
- Ezulwini Valley – the Royal heartland (page 630)
- Swazi handicrafts (page 624)

Most visitors enjoy Swaziland – it is still a comparatively poor country so just be careful in the larger towns, where theft is rife. Above all, the friendliness and openness of the people of Swaziland will leave a lasting impression.

SWAZILAND

Swaziland

0          15          30 km

# Facts about the Country

## HISTORY

The area which is now Swaziland has been inhabited by various groups for a very long time – in eastern Swaziland archaeologists have discovered human remains dating back 110,000 years – but the Swazi people themselves arrived relatively recently.

In the great Bantu migration into Southern Africa, one group, the Nguni, moved down the east coast. One clan settled in the coastal area around modern Maputo in Mozambique, and eventually a dynasty was founded by the Dlamini family. By the middle of the 18th century increasing pressure from other clans in the area forced a Dlamini king, Ngwane III, to lead his people south to lands around the Pongola River, in what is today southern Swaziland. The Swazi consider Ngwane III to have been the first king of Swaziland.

This move didn't stop the problem of tribal encroachment and the next king, Sobhuza I, came under pressure from the Zulu. He withdrew to the Ezulwini Valley, which remains the centre of Swazi royalty and ritual. Trouble with the Zulu continued and there was a further retreat by the next king, Mswazi (or Mswati) – this time as far as the Hhohho area in northern Swaziland.

However, King Mswazi, with a combination of martial skill and diplomacy, managed to unify the whole kingdom and by the time he died in 1868, the Swazi nation was secure. Mswazi's subjects called themselves people of Mswazi or Swazis.

## European Interference

Meanwhile, the Zulu were coming under increasing pressure from both the British and the Boers, which created frequent respites for the Swazis. The European presence might have indirectly helped the Swazis with their Zulu problem but it caused a number of others. From the mid-19th century onwards Swaziland attracted increasing numbers of European hunters, traders and missionaries, and farmers in search of land for their cattle. Mswazi's successor, Mbandzeni, inherited a kingdom rife with European carpetbaggers, and more and more of the kingdom's land was being alienated by leases granted to Europeans. Bribes for the king featured heavily in some of the deals.

Furthermore, the Boers' fledgling South African Republic (ZAR) decided to extend its control east to Delagoa Bay (Maputo). Swaziland was in the way and the republic decided to annex the kingdom, but before this could take place, the republic itself was annexed by the British in 1877.

The Pretoria Convention of 1881 guaranteed Swaziland's independence, but also defined its borders and Swaziland lost large chunks of territory. 'Independence' in fact meant that both the British and the Boers had responsibility for administering their various interests in Swaziland, and the result was chaos. The Boer administration collapsed with the 1899-1902 Anglo-Boer War and afterwards the British took control of Swaziland as a protectorate.

During this troubled time, when Swazis were coming to grips with their loss of sovereignty, King Sobhuza II was only a young child but Labotsibeni, his mother, ably acted as regent until her son took over in 1921. Throughout the regency and for most of Sobhuza's long reign, the Swazis fought to again become an independent nation and to regain their lands. After the petitions and delegations to England failed, Labotsibeni encouraged Swazis to buy the land back, and many sought work in the Witwatersrand (near Jo'burg) mines to raise money. Gradually land was returned to the kingdom, by both direct purchase and British government action, and by the time of independence (in 1968), about two-thirds of the kingdom was again in Swazi control.

Land ownership was not just a political and economic issue. Swazi kings are considered to hold the kingdom in trust for their subjects, and having a large proportion of the country owned by foreigners threatened the credibility of the monarchy and thus the viability of Swazi culture.

## Independence

In 1960, King Sobhuza II proposed the creation of a Legislative Council, to be composed of Europeans elected along European lines and a National Council formed in accordance with Swazi culture. One of the Swazi political parties formed at this time was the Mbokodvo (Grindstone) National Movement, which pledged to maintain traditional Swazi culture but also to eschew racial discrimination. When the British finally agreed to elections in 1964, Mbokodvo won a majority and, at the next elections in 1967, won all the seats. Independence, now certain, was achieved on 6 September 1968.

The country's constitution was largely the work of the British and, in 1973, the king suspended it on the grounds that it did not accord with Swazi culture. Four years later the parliament reconvened under a new constitution which vested all power in the king. Sobhuza II, then the world's longest reigning monarch, died in 1982, having ensured the continued existence of his country and culture, under threat since his father's reign. He is still referred to as 'the late king'.

The surprising feature of Britain's 66 year rule of Swaziland was the lack of violence with which it was resisted and overthrown. That many of the streets in the capital city, Mbabane, retain their colonial-era names is surely indicative of the goodwill which was maintained. In fact, the capital city's main street is named after the first European to be born there.

## Today

Mswati III ascended the throne in 1986 and continues to represent and maintain the traditional way of life. Although most Swazis seem happy with their political system there is some dissent. The main concern of most Swazis, however, is to ensure that Swazi culture survives modernisation. Currently, King Mswati and a small core of advisers (Council of Ministers) run the country.

Opposition parties remain illegal, but the main players, Pudemo (People's United Democratic Movement) and Swayoco (Swaziland Youth Congress), have only minimal support. In October 1993 the electoral system was changed slightly in response to pressure from the United Nations and World Bank. In 1995 student riots led to the torching of the National Assembly and the homes of the deputy prime minister and the vice chancellor of the University of Swaziland. The Swaziland Youth Congress claimed responsibility, and following a general strike in that year there was a gradual easing of the almost total autocratic control of the king. In 1997, the heads of South Africa and Mozambique held talks with the king, discussing further democratisation of the country.

## GEOGRAPHY

Swaziland, one of the smallest countries in the southern hemisphere, has a wide range of ecological zones, from rainforest in the north-west to savanna scrub in the east.

The western edge of the country is highveld, consisting mainly of short, sharp mountains. It is known as *nkhangala* (treeless) in Swazi but now there are large plantations of exotic pine and eucalyptus, especially around Piggs Peak in the north. The mountains dwindle to middleveld in the centre of the country, where most of the people live. The eastern half is scrubby lowveld, once lightly populated because of malaria (still a risk), but now home to sugar estates. The eastern border with Mozambique is the harsh Lebombo range.

## CLIMATE

Most rain falls in summer, usually in torrential thunderstorms and mostly in the western mountains. Summers on the lowveld are

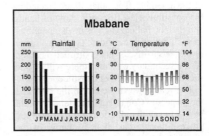

very hot, with temperatures often over 40°C; in the high country the temperatures are lower and in winter it can get cool. Winter nights on the lowveld are sometimes very cold.

October can be the hottest month. The rains usually begin around early December and last until April. May to August are the coolest months, with frosts common in June and July.

## NATIONAL PARKS & RESERVES

The five main reserves in Swaziland have all been created comparatively recently, but they are all worth visiting and reflect the country's geographical diversity. Easiest to get to is Mlilwane Wildlife Sanctuary in the Ezulwini Valley. Mkhaya Game Reserve and Hlane Royal National Park are also well worth visiting. These three reserves are privately run as part of the Big Game Parks organisation (☎ 44541; fax 40957).

The National Trust Commission (☎ 61151, 61178/9) has an office in the National Museum near Lobamba. It runs Malolotja and Mlawula nature reserves. Malolotja is a western highlands reserve with some good hiking trails. Mlawula is in harsh lowveld country near the Mozambique border.

## GOVERNMENT

Swaziland is governed by a parliament but final authority (and ownership of much of the country's resources) is vested in the king. The king can dissolve parliament at any time.

There is a Senate as well as a House of Assembly. Half of the 30 senators are elected by the assembly, the other are appointed by the king. The king also appoints 20 members of the assembly. The other 40 are elected in the constituencies, first by a show of hands and then by ballot. There is no campaigning as such but each candidate is given a range of subjects to discuss at a controlled meeting. At the secondary elections there will be one successful candidate per constituency.

The real power is vested in the king and the 16 person Council of Ministers. It would be fair to say that dilution of the democratic process means that about a quarter of the

council actually represent the interests of the average Swazi. Not that the average Swazi is demanding rapid change.

## ECONOMY

Swaziland is a poor country but it is by no means in crisis and the economy is modestly healthy. The major export is sugar, and forest products are also important. Although most foreign investment in the country is still British, South African investment is extremely important and fluctuations in that country's economy affect Swaziland.

Nearly 75% of the population works in agriculture, mostly at a subsistence level, but the country is not self-sufficient in food.

## POPULATION & PEOPLE

Almost all of the one million people are Swazi. The rest are Zulu, Tsonga-Shangaan and European. There are also Mozambican refugees, of both African and Portuguese descent. About 5% of Swazis still live and work in South Africa.

The dominant clan is the Dlamini and you'll meet people with that surname all over the country. It's sometimes felt that ordinary Dlaminis put on unwarranted royal airs and there's a little resentment towards them, usually expressed as friendly jibes. There are a lot of princes and they come from all walks of life. They might be dripping with supercilious world-weariness or be a struggling local farmer like the others at the bar.

## LANGUAGE

The official languages are siSwati and English, and English is the official written language. For information on siSwati see the Language section in the Facts about the Region chapter.

# Facts for the Visitor

Many Swazis have a sophistication which is totally unexpected in such a small, rural country. Maybe it's because of their strong culture or because there are so few Swazis

### Swazi Ceremonies

**Incwala** The Incwala (sometimes Ncwala) is the most sacred ceremony of the Swazi people. It is a 'first fruits' ceremony, as the king gives permission for his people to eat the first crops of the new year.

Preparation for the Incwala begins some weeks beforehand, according to the moon. *Bemanti* (learned men) journey to the Lebombo Mountains to gather plants, other groups collect water from Swaziland's rivers and some travel across the mountains to the Indian Ocean (where the Dlamini clan lived long before the Swazi nation came into being), to skim foam from the waves. Meanwhile, the king goes into retreat.

On the night of the full moon, young men all over the kingdom harvest branches of *lusekwane*, a small tree, and trek to the Royal Kraal at Lobamba. They arrive at dawn and their branches are used to build a kraal. If a branch has wilted it is a sign that the young man bearing it has had illicit sex. Songs prohibited during the rest of the year are sung and the bemanti arrive with their plants, water and foam.

On the third day of the ceremony a bull is sacrificed. On the fourth day, to the pleadings of all the regiments of Swaziland, the king breaks his retreat and dances before his people. He eats a pumpkin, the sign that Swazis can eat the new year's crops. Two days later there's a ritual burning of all items in the ceremony, after which the rains are expected to fall.

**Umhlanga** Not as sacred as the Incwala, the Umhlanga Dance serves a similar function in drawing the nation together and reminding the people of their relationship to the king. It is something like a week-long debutante ball for marriageable young Swazi women, who journey from all over the kingdom to help repair the queen mother's home at Lobamba.

After arriving at Lobamba they spend a day resting, then set off in search of reeds, some not returning until the fourth night. On the sixth day the reed dance is performed as they carry their reeds to the queen mother. The dance is repeated the next day. Those carrying torches (flashlights) have searched for reeds by night. Those with red feathers in their hair are princesses.

As the Swazi queen mother must not be of the royal clan, the reed dance is also a showcase of potential wives for the king. As with the Incwala, there are signs which identify the unchaste, a powerful incentive to avoid premarital sex.

**Umcwasho** This dance has not been performed for some time. Young women wear a necklace of beads from which a long wooden tassel (the *umcwasho*) is suspended. The necklace is worn for two years, and during this time the girls are not allowed to be courted. After two years they go to the Royal Kraal for dancing and feasting. At the end of the dance the umcwasho, now a bad omen, was traditionally thrown at a female elder who could no longer bear children. ■

and they are like a huge extended family. In Swaziland there are rarely unwarranted hassles with officialdom.

With Swazi men encountering new ideas while working in South Africa and with Mozambican refugees, Swazi culture is having to deal with foreign values and it's feeling the strain. For the visitor, the Mozambicans add a cosmopolitan touch and there are some good bars and restaurants.

## VISAS & DOCUMENTS

Most people don't require a visa to visit Swaziland, but there are some significant exceptions, including Austrian, French, Swiss and German citizens. However, citizens of these and other EU countries can get visas free at the border or the airport.

Anyone staying for more than 60 days must apply for a temporary residence permit from the Chief Immigration Officer (☎ 42941), PO Box 372, Mbabane.

No vaccination certificates are required to enter Swaziland unless you have recently been in a yellow-fever area.

## EMBASSIES
### Swazi Embassies

Addresses of Swazi representation in other countries include:

Canada
    130 Albert St, Ottawa, Ontario KIP 5G4 (☎ (613) 567 1480)
Kenya
    PO Box 41887, Nairobi (☎ (00254) 2-33 9231)

Mozambique
608 Av do Zimbabwe, PO Box 4711, Maputo (☎ 49 2451)
UK
20 Buckingham Gate, London SW1E 6LB (☎ (0171) 630 6611)
USA
3400 International Dr NW, Suite #3M, Washington DC 20008 (☎ (202) 362 6683/4)

In South Africa, visas can be obtained from the Swaziland High Commission (☎ (012) 342 5782/4; fax 342 5682), Suite 105 Infotech Building, 1090 Arcadia St, Arcadia, Pretoria 0083, open from Monday to Friday from 8 am to 3 pm; and the Swaziland Trade Attache (☎ (011) 29 9776/7; fax 29 9763) at 165 Jeppe St, PO Box 8030, Jo'burg 2000, open Monday to Friday from 7.45 am to 3 pm. There are honorary consulates in a number of other countries, including Greece, Spain, Switzerland, Japan and Germany.

### Foreign Embassies in Swaziland

The Mozambique High Commission in Mbabane (☎ 43700) issues one-month visas for E80 with two photos. They usually take a week to issue but the friendly staff might do it faster in an emergency. The fee is considerably less than you'd pay in Jo'burg. The embassy is open between 9 am and 1 pm on weekdays. To get there head out onto the Manzini road, turn left down the road to the Mountain Inn, turn left onto the dirt road just past the hotel entrance and then left again at the next corner. The embassy is 100m or so further on.

Other diplomatic representation in Swaziland includes:

Belgian Consulate
PO Box 124, Malkerns (☎ 83180)
Danish Consulate
Ground Floor, Sokhamlilo Building, Johnson St, Mbabane (☎ 43547)
Dutch Consulate
Business Machine House, Mbabane (☎ 45178)
German Embassy
3rd Floor, Dhlan'ubeka House, Mbabane (☎ 43174)
Israeli Embassy
PO Box 146, Mbabane (☎ 42626)
Mozambique High Commission
Princess Drive, Mbabane (☎ 43700)

UK High Commission
Allister Miller St, Mbabane (☎ 42581/3)
US Embassy
Central Bank Building, Warner St, Mbabane (☎ 46441/2)

## CUSTOMS

Customs regulations are similar to those for South Africa (Swaziland is in the Customs Union of Southern Africa). If you are arriving from South Africa there are no restrictions.

## MONEY

The unit of currency is the lilangeni (the plural is emalangeni – E) which is fixed at a value equal to the South African rand. Rands are accepted everywhere and there's no need to change them, although many places will not accept South African coins. Emalangeni are difficult to change for other currencies outside Swaziland.

Several banks change travellers' cheques. Barclays Bank has the most branches: Mbabane (☎ 42691), Manzini (☎ 52411), Nhlangano (☎ 78377), Piggs Peak (☎ 71100) and Big Bend (☎ 74100). There are now a number of automatic teller machines (ATMs) which accept various (but not all) credit cards.

Barclays is open between 8.30 am and 2.30 pm on weekdays, and until 11 am on Saturday. Other banks keep similar hours. There's a Swaziland Development Bank branch at Matsapha airport, open for flights.

### Exchange Rates

The rate is the same as for the South African rand (see Exchange Rates in the South Africa Facts for the Visitor chapter).

### Costs

Costs are similar to those in South Africa, with food a little cheaper. The game reserves here are particularly good value.

## TOURIST OFFICES

The main tourist office is in the Swazi Plaza, Mbabane (☎ 46721), but Royal Swazi Big Game Parks (☎ 44541), in the new Mall, Mbabane, is also a mine of information.

## PUBLIC HOLIDAYS & SPECIAL EVENTS

In addition to Christmas, Boxing and New Year's days holidays, and Good Friday and Easter Monday, other holidays observed in Swaziland are:

| | |
|---|---|
| *King Mswati III's Birthday* | 19 April |
| *National Flag Day* | 25 April |
| *King Sobhuza II's Birthday* | 22 July |
| *Umhlanga (Reed) Dance Day* | variable; in August or September |
| *Somhlolo Day (Independence)* | 6 September |
| *Incwala Day* | variable; December or January |

*Sibhaca* dancing developed fairly recently, but it is very popular and there are national competitions at the Manzini Trade Fair – it's practically a team sport. This martial dance is vigorous, with teams lined up, bedecked in warrior costumes and wielding long wooden staffs. There is much shouting and choreographed stomping as the teams attempt to outdo each other. Local competitions are held frequently, and the Mbabane tourist office in the Swazi Plaza has details. The Sun hotels in the Ezulwini Valley sometimes have performances.

The most important cultural events in Swaziland are the *Incwala* ceremony, held sometime between late December and early January, and the *Umhlanga* (Reed) Dance held in August or September. The venue for both is near Lobamba in the Ezulwini Valley. Ask at the tourist office in Mbabane for exact dates. Photography is not permitted at the Incwala but it is at the Umhlanga Dance.

## POST & COMMUNICATIONS

Post offices are open from 8 am to 4 pm on weekdays, and until 11 am on Saturday.

There are no telephone area codes within Swaziland; if you're calling from South Africa use the code ☎ 09 268. You can make international calls (but not reverse charges) at the post office in Mbabane.

## NEWSPAPERS

There are two English-language daily newspapers – *The Times of Swaziland* (founded in 1887 by Allister Miller senior) and the *Swazi Observer*.

## HEALTH

Beware of both bilharzia and malaria. See the Health section in the Regional Facts for the Visitor chapter for information on avoiding these potentially deadly diseases.

If you need medical assistance there is the Mbabane Clinic Service (☎ 42423), the Mbabane Government Hospital (☎ 42111), the Raleigh Fitkin Hospital in Manzini (☎ 52211) and the Piggs Peak Government Hospital (☎ 71111).

## ACCOMMODATION

There are few designated camp sites in Swaziland except in some of the national parks and nature reserves. There's a good caravan park in the Ezulwini Valley, 10km from Mbabane.

Away from the few population centres it's usually possible (and safe) to find your own place to pitch a tent, but *always* ask permission from local people, who will probably have to seek permission in turn from their local leader. Be patient. Swazis' hospitality is genuine but so is their dislike of people imposing on them or disregarding their social structures.

If you're stuck for a room in rural areas you could try the local school, where you'll probably be welcomed. Many of the country's hotels are geared towards South African tourists and are expensive. Some towns have smaller, pub-like places left over from the Protectorate days which are cheaper, and some are good value.

## ACTIVITIES

Although Swaziland is a small country, there are enough activities to keep you interested for some days. White-water rafting and abseiling (rap jumping) at Mkhaya Game Reserve are becoming popular.

There are plenty of opportunities to go horse-riding and a number of stables offer lessons, rides and children's riding camps in areas only accessible by foot or on horseback. In Mlilwane Wildlife Sanctuary, not far from Mbabane, it is possible to view wildlife on horseback. Guests at several hotels have access to stables: Meikles Mount (☎ 74110) and the Foresters Arms Hotel (☎ 74117) in the Mhlambanyatsi region, the Ezulwini Valley Sun hotels (☎ 61001) and the Protea Piggs Peak Hotel (☎ 71104). There are also stables at Hawana Park (☎ 24109, 42619) near Malolotja and at Nyanza (☎ 83090) near Malkerns.

As well as walking trails in several parks, especially Malolotja Nature Reserve, you can set out on foot to explore the country, following countless tracks which are generations old. If you have time, this would be the best way to see Swaziland.

### THINGS TO BUY

Swaziland's handicrafts are worth looking out for. Because of the strength of traditional culture many items are made for the local market as much as for tourists.

Woven grassware, such as *liqhaga* (grassware 'bottles', so well made that they are used for carrying water) and mats are popular, as are wooden items, ranging from bowls to knobkerries. The best place to see dyed and woven items is at Gone Rural in Malkerns. Other Swazi crafts to look for include jewellery, pottery, weapons and implements.

If you come in through the Oshoek border post there are small stalls nearby. There are also outlets in Mbabane's SEDCO estate, including a pottery shop and Swaziland Arts & Crafts. Mbabane's Swazi Market is worth visiting to ascertain prices.

In the Ezulwini Valley, there are several crafts shops, the biggest being the Mantenga Craft Centre, off the highway between Smokey Mountain Village and the Mantenga Hotel. Tishweshwe Cottage Crafts, 2km down the Malkerns road and next to Gone Rural, is a large showroom and workshop.

High-quality hand-woven mohair is produced at Rosecraft in Mankayane. Coral Stephen's weaving workshop near Piggs Peak has an international reputation; phone ☎ 71140 for an appointment to visit. Also in Piggs Peak is Tintsaba Crafts, at the High-

lands Inn. At the casino, 10km north, is Tekwane Crafts.

The trade fair held in Manzini each year from the end of August is a showcase for handicrafts as well as industrial products.

# Getting There & Away

If you're arriving from South Africa, remember that you won't be allowed to return unless you have a multiple-entry visa.

### AIR

Royal Swazi Airlines operates out of Matsapha international airport, north of Manzini. Schedules and tickets often refer to the airport as Manzini. Royal Swazi Airways flies to:

Jo'burg – daily; E430, return E540
Maputo (Mozambique) – Tuesday, Wednesday, Saturday and Sunday; E320
Harare (Zimbabwe) – Monday and Friday; E1310
Lusaka (Zambia) – Monday and Friday; E1580
Dar es Salaam (Tanzania) – Tuesday and Saturday; E1970
Nairobi (Kenya) – Tuesday and Saturday; E2150

Lesotho Airways flies twice a week to Maseru for E530 one way. Comair flies to/from Jo'burg on Monday, Tuesday, Wednesday, Friday and Saturday, for E360. The airport departure tax is E20.

### LAND
#### Border Crossings

Swaziland's 12 border posts are all with South Africa, with the exception of the Namaacha/Lomahasha border post in the extreme north-east, which is the entry point to Mozambique. The small posts close at 4 or 6 pm; the main border posts with South Africa are:

*Oshoek/Ngwenya* This post is open from 7 am to 10 pm and takes most of the traffic, so it can be clogged with South Africans arriving on Friday and leaving on Sunday. It's a good place to pick up lifts.

Top: Sani Pass, the remote border trail between Lesotho and KwaZulu-Natal.
Middle: Tough Basotho ponies take visitors through highlands near Malealea, Lesotho.
Bottom: The snowclad Maluti Mountains in Lesotho seen from neighbouring Free State.

JEFF WILLIAMS

JEFF WILLIAMS

Top: A sangoma or herbalist/witchdoctor, Malealea, Lesotho.
Bottom: Basotho men wearing 'morokotlo' hats, Maseru, Lesotho.

Top: 'The Regiment': white rhino at Mkhaya Game Reserve, Swaziland.
Middle Left: Traditional Swazi singing & dancing at Hlane Royal National Park, Swaziland.
Middle Right: Entrance to a family compound, National Museum, Lobamba, Swaziland.
Bottom: Rafting on the Great Usutu River is not for the fainthearted.

MIKE REED

MIKE REED

Top: Women in national dress dance at a festival, Swaziland.
Bottom: Women dancing at the coronation of King Mswat III, Swaziland.

*Mahamba* Open from 7 am to 10 pm, this is the best post to use from Piet Retief, South Africa. It's close to Nhlangano and Hlathikulu.

*Golela/Lavumisa* Open from 7 am to 10 pm, this post is in the south-east, opposite Golela in South Africa. From here it's a quick run to Big Bend.

*Josefsdal/Bulembu* Open from 8 am to 4 pm, it is on the rough dirt road from Piggs Peak to Barberton, South Africa. It is tricky in wet weather.

*Mozambique (Namaacha/Lomahasha)* This post is open from 7 am to 4.45 pm daily. Purchasing visas at the border is an on/off affair so it's best to get them in advance. If you get your visa in South Africa it will cost R120 but the Mozambique High Commission in Mbabane arranges them for around E80.

## Bus

There is a twice-weekly service from Mbabane to Maputo (Mozambique); inquire at the tourist office.

The Baz Bus (☎ (021) 439 2323, (031) 23 6585) now has a route from Jo'burg to Durban via Mlilwane in Swaziland's Ezulwini Valley. It departs Jo'burg on Monday, Tuesday, Thursday and Saturday; the cost is R115 (to continue further on to Cape Town costs R495).

City to City/Transtate, the old South African 'third class' bus line runs to and near Swaziland. A minibus taxi costs a little less and is much faster. However, the buses are safe, relatively comfortable and rarely crowded. Two useful City to City/Transtate bus routes are:

**Jo'burg to Hlathikulu** This route takes 10 hours, via Piet Retief and Nhlangano, departing from Jo'burg at 7.30 am daily (also 10 pm Friday), and returning daily except Saturday (R65). This overnight trip leaves you short of Mbabane; you will need to take a minibus taxi.

**Jo'burg to Mbabane & Manzini** This service takes 10½ hours, via Ermelo, the Ezulwini Valley and Manzini. It departs from Jo'burg weekdays at 7.30 am (also Friday at 10 pm), returning daily except Saturday. It's the best way into Swaziland from Jo'burg. (Jo'burg to Mbabane is R65.)

## Train

There is no ordinary passenger train, but five times a year there are four-day tours from

Jo'burg on the *Royal Swazi Express* (☎ (011) 822 1295) for information).

### Minibus Taxi

There are some minibus taxis running direct between Jo'burg and Mbabane for E55, but to most other destinations in Swaziland you'll have to take a minibus taxi to the border and another from there to the nearest town, where you'll probably have to change again. This can be slow.

### Car & Motorcycle

There's an E12 tax on vehicles entering Swaziland. If you're entering Mozambique, your car must have a vehicle-breakdown warning triangle, seat belts and official papers (for your hire car to cross from Swaziland or South Africa into Mozambique).

### Hitching

Most South Africans enter through the Oshoek/Ngwenya border post, with the casinos in the north (near the Matsamo/Jeppe's Reef border post) and south (near the Mahamba border post) attracting traffic, especially on weekends.

# Getting Around

## BUS & MINIBUS TAXI

There's a good system of buses running regular routes (some express), but not very frequently. Minibus taxis usually run shorter routes at prices a little higher than the buses.

Some examples of bus routes and fares are Manzini to Siteki, E8; Manzini to Big Bend, E10; Manzini to Mbabane, E4.50; Big Bend to Lavumisa (border post), E6; and Mbabane to Piggs Peak, E7.

A minibus from the Mahamba border post to Nhlangano is E1.50; to Hlathikulu it's E10. There are also 'normal' nonshare taxis in some of the larger towns.

## CAR & MOTORCYCLE

Most roads are quite good and there are also some satisfyingly rough backroads through the bush. Driving down the Ezulwini Valley in heavy traffic can be slow and dangerous – Malagwane Hill, from Mbabane into the Ezulwini Valley, was once listed in the *Guinness Book of Records* as the most dangerous stretch of road in the world! It is currently being improved but with all the earthmoving equipment in the region it is as dangerous as ever.

Away from the few population centres the main dangers are people and animals on the road. On narrow gravel roads beware of speeding buses and wandering cattle. There are very few fences in this country, a fact attributable to a royal decree defending the rights of cattle to roam freely. The other danger is drunk drivers – the permitted blood-alcohol limit is 0.15%!

Wearing seat belts is compulsory. If an official motorcade approaches, you must pull over and stop. The speed limit is 80km/h on the open road, 60km/h in built-up areas.

Many petrol stations are open 24 hours, and there are AA agents in Manzini, Mbabane and Piggs Peak.

### Car Rental

Swaziland is so small that hiring a car for a couple of days will give you a good idea of the whole country. Rates are similar to those in South Africa.

Both Avis (☎ 86226) and Hertz/Imperial (☎ 84862) are at Matsapha airport, near Manzini. Hertz/Imperial also has an agent in Mbabane (☎ 41384). The minimum age for hiring a car with these companies is 23.

### HITCHING & WALKING

Hitching is easier here than in South Africa, as the colour of the driver and the colour of the hitchhiker aren't factors in the decision to offer a lift. You might wait a long time for a car on backroads, and everywhere you'll have lots of competition from locals.

Transport for most people in rural Swaziland is on foot, which has left trails all over the country.

### TOURS & PACKAGES

Royal Swazi Airways has various packages

from Jo'burg, mostly with accommodation in the more expensive hotels in Ezulwini Valley, but there's an option with accommodation at the small Foresters Arms Hotel which includes car hire. Phone ☎ 74117 for more information.

Swazi Trails (☎ 62180; fax 40957) is based at the Royal Swazi Sun and at Mlilwane Wildlife Sanctuary in the Ezulwini Valley. It offers a variety of tours, with some of the day tours being good value if you're short of time or don't have transport.

The tours include an in-depth look at Swazi culture, visits to top craft outlets, a historical trip through Swazi's colourful past and wildlife excursions to the Big Game Parks. Adventurous options include whitewater rafting, horse-riding, mountain biking, and abseiling (rap jumping) at Mlilwane's 'rock of execution'. For example, a half day tour of your choice is E80. Rafting is about E250, and includes lunch and transport.

# Mbabane

With about 50,000 people, Mbabane (if you say 'mba-*baa*-nay' you'll be close enough) is the second largest town in Swaziland and it's growing fast. There isn't much to see or do here – the adjacent Ezulwini Valley has the attractions – but Mbabane is a relaxing place in a nice setting in the Dlangeni Hills. The altitude makes Mbabane cooler than Manzini. That's why the British, in 1902, moved their administrative centre here from Manzini.

### Orientation

Despite recent development, Mbabane is still a pleasant town (but not without the odd danger – crime is an issue). The main street is Allister Miller St. Off Western Distributor Rd is Swazi Plaza, a large, modern shopping mall with most services and a good range of shops; it's also a good landmark. Across OK Rd are the Mall and adjoining New Mall, a showpiece.

## Information

**Tourist Office** The government tourist office (☎ 42531) is in Swazi Plaza. The *Swaziland Jumbo Tourist Guide* (E20) has information tucked away between platitudinous rambling and advertising, and the *Swaziland Tour Sales Manual*, intended for people in the tourist industry, is a helpful guide (if you can get a copy).

For trustworthy information on the Royal Swazi Big Game Parks (☎ 44541; fax 40957) inquire at their office in the Mall.

**Money** There's a Barclays branch in Swazi Plaza and on Allister Miller St. The Standard Chartered, 21 Allister Miller St, has a 24 hour ATM, and the Stanbic (Standard) Bank in the Swazi Plaza accepts most foreign credit cards, including MasterCard.

**Post & Communications** There are no area codes within Swaziland. Some places in Swaziland are not on automatic exchanges and to call them you have to book a trunk call (☎ 90) and the operator will call you back.

You can make international calls (but not reverse charges) at the post office between 8 am and 4 pm on weekdays, and until noon

SWAZILAND

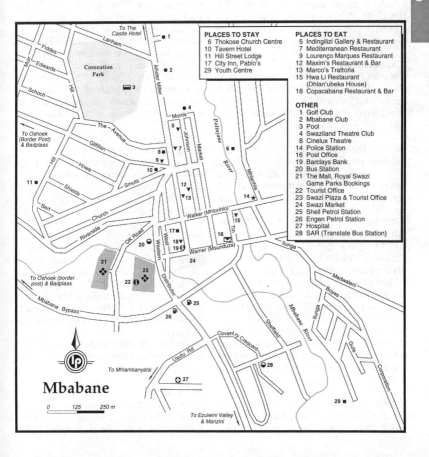

**PLACES TO STAY**
6 Thokose Church Centre
10 Tavern Hotel
11 Hill Street Lodge
17 City Inn, Pablo's
29 Youth Centre

**PLACES TO EAT**
5 Indingilizi Gallery & Restaurant
7 Mediterranean Restaurant
9 Lourenço Marques Restaurant
12 Maxim's Restaurant & Bar
13 Marco's Trattoria
15 Hwa Li Restaurant
  (Dhlan'ubeka House)
18 Copacabana Restaurant & Bar

**OTHER**
1 Golf Club
2 Mbabane Club
3 Pool
4 Swaziland Theatre Club
8 Cinelux Theatre
14 Police Station
16 Post Office
19 Barclays Bank
20 Bus Station
21 The Mall, Royal Swazi
  Game Parks Bookings
22 Tourist Office
23 Swazi Plaza & Tourist Office
24 Swazi Market
25 Shell Petrol Station
26 Engen Petrol Station
27 Hospital
28 SAR (Transtate Bus Station)

Mbabane

0      125      250 m

on Saturday. There are often long queues. (You will need gold E1 coins from the post office for the phone.)

**Bookshops** There are several branches of Webster's, a good book chain, throughout the country.

**Emergency** In case of fire, call ☎ 43333. For medical assistance, call ☎ 42423 or 42111. For police, call ☎ 42221 in Mbabane, 52221 in Manzini.

**Dangers & Annoyances** Mbabane is a little unsafe at night, especially on the back streets. The Malagwane Hill route into the Ezulwini Valley is extremely dangerous to drive, especially when fog descends.

### Places to Stay

**Caravan Parks** The nearest caravan park is about 10km away in the Ezulwini Valley. See the Around Swaziland section for details. It is definitely not advisable to camp in city parks.

**Hostels** There are no youth hostels as such but there is accommodation in a couple of church missions. The drawback with these places is that they are some way from the centre of town and walking back at night isn't safe (take a taxi).

*Thokose Church Centre* (☎ 46682) is on Mhlanhla Rd; single/double rooms are E35/40, but it's often full, especially around Christmas. From Allister Miller St turn onto Walker St, cross the bridge at the bottom of the hill, turn left at the police station and head along a dirt road up the hill for about 10 minutes. A taxi there is E7 from Swazi Plaza.

Further out, south-east of the city centre on Isomi St, the *Youth Centre* (☎ 42176) charges E30 per person, including breakfast, in two-bed rooms – you might have to share. The gates are locked at 10 pm. A taxi there is E10, or E15 at night.

**Hotels** A longtime travellers' favourite is *City Inn* (☎ 42406), in the centre on Allister Miller St. Singles/doubles cost from E150/

190 or E77/110 with shared bathroom. There are more expensive rooms with air-conditioning. Check out the rooms with shared bathrooms as you might decide they're better than the cheaper rooms with a bathroom. The noisy disco behind the hotel has recently closed – so sweet dreams.

Quieter, but a fair walk from the centre on Hill St, is *Hill Street Lodge* (☎ 46342). Singles or doubles with shared bathroom cost E60. For the price it's good value.

The *Tavern Hotel* (☎ 42361), off Gilfillan St, charges E118/202 (poolside rooms are E163/218), with breakfast. Some of the rooms are tiny. There's a dirty swimming pool and a couple of bars.

*Mountain Inn* (☎ 42781) is 1km or so south of the centre, overlooking the Ezulwini Valley. Rooms in the south wing cost E270/320, north-wing rooms are E230/280 and poolside rooms are E250/290; all prices include breakfast. *Swazi Inn* (☎ 42235), 3km out on the Ezulwini Valley road, is similar; single/double rooms with breakfast are E193/238.

The most bizarre place near town, *The Castle* (☎ 44506), is perched on a rocky outcrop north of Mbabane. It is a place where, seemingly, Henry VIII meets *Psycho*'s Bates Motel, but it is not as bad as that. The self-catering apartments, decorated with medieval implements such as crossbows, are far from dungeon-like with singles/ doubles/ triples good value at E176/220/270; breakfast is E25, lunch E28 and a three course dinner E48. Getting there is difficult: follow the Golf Course Rd north until you see The Castle signpost. Turn onto Mantshok Rd and follow it until you reach another Castle signpost near the US Ambassador's residence. This is Valhalla Rd; follow it for 1km to The Castle gates.

See Ezulwini Valley in the Around Swaziland section for other accommodation near Mbabane.

### Places to Eat

The restaurant by the entrance to the City Inn is called *Pablo's* – the decor and food are Wimpyesque, with some steak dishes added to the menu. It's a good place for a coffee and breakfast. Further south on Allister Miller St, on the corner of Warner (Msunduza) St, *Copacabana* is a Portuguese-run place serving simple food. Stew with rice costs E12, a big salad is E7.

*Maxim's* on Johnson St has a fine bar and its food is pretty good as well. There's a pavement eating area with good service and a relaxed atmosphere. The restaurant is open daily from 9 am to 1 am. Breakfast costs E12, steaks are from E25 and good salads E8. Best value are their outstandingly good pizzas, which only cost E12.

Further down Johnson St, at No 112, the *Indingilizi Gallery* has a relaxed outdoor café with African food and other relatively inexpensive, healthy meals (a quiche costs E11). It's open from 8 am to 5 pm on weekdays and until 2 pm on Saturday.

The *Mediterranean* on Allister Miller St is in fact Indian, although the menu also has steaks, seafood and vegetarian dishes; curries cost E15. It's open for lunch and until 11 pm for dinner. *Marco's Trattoria*, also on Allister Miller St, is upstairs and there's a small balcony. The owner is Italian, the food is good, pizzas are from E12 and there's a good range of other Italian dishes. More pizzas are to be found at the *Continental Pizzeria* in Swazi Plaza; it is open daily except Sunday from 9 am to 11 pm.

For Portuguese-style food try *LM (Lourenço Marques)*, on the corner of Gilfillan and Allister Miller Sts; the chicken peri peri and the king and queen prawns are excellent. More spicy fare is available at *Nando's* in the New Mall.

In Dhlan'ubeka House on Walker (also known as Mhlonhlo) St is *Hwa Li*, a Chinese place specialising in spring rolls, chow mein and spicy soups. For Chinese takeaway, try *Kowloon* in the New Mall.

In Swazi Plaza the popular *Longhorn Steakhouse* has salads from E8, and large steaks from E25 to E30, depending on the sauces added. Across the road in the Mall is the new *Phoenix Spur* – Swazi's first of the ubiquitous chain. It puts on a good Mexican 'fiesta' meal on Tuesday nights.

### Entertainment

The *Cinelux Theatre* at the north end of Allister Miller St shows mainstream movies each night at 8 pm, with 3 pm matinees on Wednesday, Saturday and Sunday.

At the river side of Swazi Plaza is the very crowded and popular *Plaza Bar*, where you will meet a blend of locals and travellers. Beware – shifty types lurk in the shadowy walkways outside.

*Maxim's*, the watering hole of a wide range of people – locals, visitors and expats – is a good meeting place. There's a popular *bar*, complete with pool tables, in the cellar beneath the Tavern Hotel. There's a rough, yet popular, *bar* on the Tavern's eastern side (for the adventurous only).

### Things to Buy

The Swazi Market at the end of Allister Miller St has a good range of handicrafts. If you have some time in the country check here first to get an idea of standards and prices. You'll usually do better in rural areas if you know what you're looking for.

The Indingilizi Gallery at 112 Johnson St has an idiosyncratic collection, pricey but well worth a look. There is traditional craft, including some interesting old pieces, and some excellent art and craft works by contemporary Swazi artists. Living in Africa at Sunny Bananas, in Swazi Plaza, sells practical household goods but there are plenty of interesting smaller items as well. In the Mall, opposite Swazi Plaza, African Fantasy has locally made T-shirts.

### Getting There & Away

City to City/Transtate buses leave from the train station on Coventry Crescent. Minibus taxis to South Africa leave from the taxi park near Swazi Plaza, where you'll also find buses and minibus taxis to destinations in Swaziland.

### Getting Around

**The Airport** A nonshare taxi from Mbabane to Matsapha international airport costs E70. It is about E50 to Manzini and E60 to the far end of Ezulwini Valley. Buses and minibuses from Mbabane to Manzini go past the turn-off to the airport, from where it's a walk of several kilometres to the terminal.

**Bus & Minibus Taxi** The main bus/minibus park is near Swazi Plaza. Vehicles heading towards Manzini or Matsapha pass through the Ezulwini Valley.

**Taxi** Non-share taxis congregate near the bus rank by Swazi Plaza, and at night you can usually find one near the City Inn, or try phoning ☎ 42014/42530. Non-share taxis to the Ezulwini Valley cost at least E25, more to the far end of the valley, and still more at night.

# Around Swaziland

## EZULWINI VALLEY

The royal valley begins just outside Mba-bane and extends down past Lobamba village, 18km away. Most of the area's attractions are near Lobamba. It's a pretty valley but fast turning into a hotel strip, the one exception being Mlilwane Wildlife Sanctuary.

### Lobamba

This is the heart of Swaziland's royal valley, and has been almost since the beginning of the Swazi people. The royal palace, the Embo State Palace, isn't open to visitors, and you are not allowed to take photos of it. This palace was built by the British; Swazi kings now live in the Lozitha State House about 10km from Lobamba. Given the size of the royal family (Sobhuza II had 600 children), this is a large complex.

You can see the monarchy in action at the Royal Kraal in Lobamba during the Incwala ceremony and the Umhlanga dance. The nearby **Somhlolo Stadium** hosts big sports events (mainly soccer) and important state occasions, such as coronations.

The **National Museum** has some interesting displays on Swazi culture and there's a traditional beehive village beside it. The museum is open weekdays from 9 am to 3.45

pm, on weekends from 10 am to 3.45 pm. The National Trust Commission offices, where you can make bookings for Mlawula and Malolotja nature reserves, are here.

Next to the museum is the **Parliament**, which is sometimes open to visitors; wear neat clothes and use the side entrance. Across the road from the museum is the **King Sobhuza II memorial**, to the most revered of the Swazi kings. The memorial is open on weekdays from 8.30 am to 4.30 pm, on weekends from 9.30 am to 4 pm.

**Mantenga Falls** are worth a look, but ask for advice at the nearby Mantenga Lodge (directions to the lodge are in the Places to Stay section) before you go. The road is steep and sometimes dangerous, and there have been muggings and worse at the falls. About 3km from Mantenga Lodge is the **Swazi Cultural Village**, with authentic beehive huts and cultural displays.

### Mlilwane Wildlife Sanctuary

This sanctuary near Lobamba was the first in Swaziland. It's a private reserve and was created by Ted Reilly on his family farm in the 50s. Reilly has gone on to open Mkhaya Game Reserve and has supervised the setting up of Hlane Royal National Park. Read about conservation efforts at the reserve (and throughout the kingdom) in the excellent *The Mlilwane Story*, available from the sanctuary (E20).

The reserve is dominated by the precipitous Nyonyane ('little bird') peak, and there are several nice walks around it.

Among the animals to be seen are zebra, giraffe and many antelope species, as well as crocodile and hippo and a variety of birds. In summer, black eagles *(Aquila verreauxii)* are seen near Nyonyane. There is a pair of resident, exhibitionist blue cranes *(Anthropoides paradisea)* at Main Camp.

You can walk, cycle or ride a horse through the reserve and there are night drives. Bikes can be rented for E25 per hour, less for longer rides. Horse-riding is E35 per hour.

Watching the hippos from the *Hippo Haunt* restaurant is great entertainment, especially at feeding time (3 pm daily). At 'human'

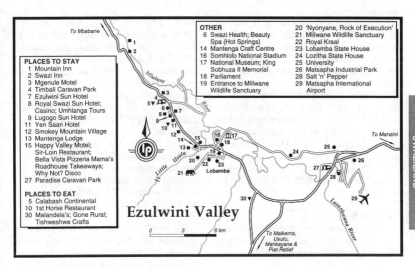

**OTHER**
6 Swazi Health; Beauty Spa (Hot Springs)
14 Mantenga Craft Centre
16 Somhlolo National Stadium
17 National Museum; King Sobhuza II Memorial
18 Parliament
19 Entrance to Mlilwane Wildlife Sanctuary
20 'Nyonyane, Rock of Execution'
21 Mlilwane Wildlife Sanctuary
22 Royal Kraal
23 Lobamba State House
24 Lozitha State House
25 University
26 Matsapha Industrial Park
28 Salt 'n' Pepper
29 Matsapha International Airport

**PLACES TO STAY**
1 Mountain Inn
2 Swazi Inn
3 Mgenule Motel
4 Timbali Caravan Park
7 Ezulwini Sun Hotel
8 Royal Swazi Sun Hotel; Casino; Umhlanga Tours
9 Lugogo Sun Hotel
11 Yen Saan Hotel
12 Smokey Mountain Village
13 Mantenga Lodge
15 Happy Valley Motel; Sir-Loin Restaurant; Bella Vista Pizzeria Mama's Roadhouse Takeaways; Why Not? Disco
27 Paradise Caravan Park

**PLACES TO EAT**
5 Calabash Continental
10 1st Horse Restaurant
30 Malandela's; Gone Rural; Tishweshwe Crafts

**Ezulwini Valley**

SWAZILAND

feeding time, a full breakfast is E18.50 (E12.50 for kids), lunch or supper is E20 for a full meal (E12.50), a campfire braai of hog on the spit is E25 (E15) and puddings (desserts) are about E6.50.

Entry to the reserve (☎ 44541; fax 40957) is E7 on weekdays, E10 on weekends and E13 during peak season. The reserve is on the route of a number of backpackers' buses. The new entrance is 2km south of the Happy Valley Motel on the Manzini road; it is signposted from the turn-off. At the entry point you can get hold of a sanctuary map and ask about night access via an alternative gate.

**Places to Stay** Camping and caravanning are E20 per person. Beehive huts in the *Main Camp* cost from E95 per person sharing, E111 on the weekend (single rates are E156/196). In the timber dorm in the *Beehive Village*, the cost (with bedding) is E45 per person sharing, or E55 on the weekend (single rates are E75/85); without bedding it is slightly less. There's a store and restaurant here. During South African school holidays Mlilwane is very busy. (Phone ☎ 44541 to book accommodation.)

Also in the sanctuary, further north from the camp, is the well-equipped *Sondzela Backpackers' (IYHF) Lodge* (☎ 44541), which has dorm beds for E31. This is a spacious building with a large verandah and central living area. The road through the reserve is signposted or it is a 1\$1/2 hour walk on a signed trail from the Main Camp.

Swazi Trails operates a daily shuttle from the Royal Swazi Sun, to the Lobamba bus rank (from where you can catch local taxis), into Mlilwane Rest Camp and on to Sondzela. It departs Sondzela at 7.30 am and Royal Swazi Sun at 5 pm (be there at 4.30 pm). The Baz Bus overnights at Sondzela on Monday, Tuesday, Thursday and Saturday.

There are self-catering cottages with all facilities – hot water, toilets etc – at *Nyonyane Camp* on the eastern border of the park; the cost is E86 per person on weekdays and E99 on weekends and public holidays.

**White-Water Rafting**
One of the attractions of Swaziland is white-water rafting on the Great Usutu River. The river is usually sluggish and quite tame but near the reserve it passes through the narrow Bulungu Gorge between the Mabukabuka and

Bulunga mountains, generating rapids. At one stage a 10m waterfall has to be portaged. The second half of the day is a sedate trip through scenic country with glimpses of the 'flat dogs' (crocodiles) sunning on the river bank.

The trips, operated by Swazi Trails in two-person 'crocodile rafts', take a full day and cost E250 per person (minimum of four people or E1000), all equipment and lunch included. Phone ☎ 44541 (62366 after hours) for more information. The water is Grade IV and not for the faint-hearted, although brave beginners should handle the day easily.

### Places to Stay

As well as the camp sites and beehive huts at Mlilwane (the best budget accommodation in the valley) there is a range of other places.

**Caravan Parks** *Timbali Caravan Park* (☎ 61156) has sites and accommodation in rondavels and caravans. It's a well-run place and has a swimming pool and a restaurant which is open daily. Services offered include tent cleaning! There's a supermarket nearby.

Camp sites are E33/44 in the low/high season plus E9/12 per person, two-berth on-site caravans are E82/94, rondavels are E94/110 and four-bed rooms are E110/132; all are plus E14/19 per extra person and electricity is E5 per day. During the high season (December, January and holidays) you pay for a minimum of three nights.

See Mlilwane Wildlife Sanctuary for more budget options.

**Hotels** Off the main valley road, on a wooded hillside near Mlilwane, is *Mantenga Lodge* (☎ 61049). It's an old place with only 10 rooms and its atmosphere is nothing like that of the glitzy valley strip. At E95/120 for singles/doubles it's good value. To get there, take the turn-off from the highway at Lobamba for Mlilwane Wildlife Sanctuary but turn right rather than left at the T-intersection. The hotel is 400m along.

The *Mgenule Motel* (☎ 61041) is the closest of the valley's hotels to Mbabane and one of the cheapest. Doubles cost from E110/145 on weekdays/weekends, rising to E165 during the high season, and a cottage for four is E175/185, rising to E275 in the high season. There's a pool and an halal tandoori restaurant.

*Smokey Mountain Village* (☎ 61291; fax 46465) is a small place, with self-contained chalets costing E210/260/350 for three/four/six people.

Near here is the *Happy Valley Motel* (☎ 61061; fax 61050), which has comfortable weekend singles and doubles at E190 and weekday singles/doubles for E140/190; all rooms have cable TV and the cost includes breakfast and free entry to the Why Not? Disco.

The *Yen Saan Hotel* (☎ 61051) has only 34 rooms and a restaurant. It's designed in Chinese style, which is rather incongruous for the royal valley of the Kingdom of Swaziland; singles/doubles are E110/165.

**Expensive** At the top of the scale are three of the Sun group's hotels: the *Royal Swazi Sun & Casino* (☎ 61001), the *Lugogo Sun* (☎ 61101) – which is in the grounds of the Royal Swazi – and the *Ezulwini Sun* (☎ 61201), across the road from the other two. In this complex there are the usual international-hotel features such as pools, tennis courts and, at the Royal Swazi, a golf course and casino. Rooms at the Royal Swazi start at E375, singles/doubles at the Lugogo are E365/445 (weekends E490/590) and the revamped Ezulwini has midweek singles/doubles for E385/515, B&B.

### Places to Eat

All three Sun hotels have restaurants – a buffet lunch which includes a selection from the carvery, salads and desserts is E45. At the top of Malagwane Hill, the Mountain Inn and Swazi Inn also have restaurants.

Next to Timbali Caravan Park is *Calabash Continental*, open seven days, which specialises in German and Swiss cuisine. On the south side of the road into the Yen Saan is *1st Horse Restaurant*, so called because it is next to Swaziland Tattersalls. Mantenga Lodge and Smokey Mountain Village serve pub meals for E25.

At the Happy Valley Motel there is *Bella Vista Pizzeria* (☎ 61061 for takeaways) with large vegetarian pizzas for E17 and hearty seafood pizzas for E22.50. There is also *Sir-Loin* steakhouse, *Mama's* coffee bar and an outside takeaway, the *Roadhouse*.

### Entertainment

The best-known nightspot in the area is the *Why Not?* Disco at the Happy Valley Motel which charges E20 admission and E30 on weekends when there are shows. This place would have to rate as one of the great incongruities of Africa. It looks innocent enough from the outside but inside it is a veritable den of iniquity, a complete enigma in conservative Swaziland. The Why Not? is a huge auditorium reserved for crowds ogling visiting European strippers, and the dimly lit If Not has strippers dancing along the bar. Questions continue to be asked in parliament about all this immorality and it might be stopped.

An interesting crowd gathers at the *Lugogo Sun* on Wednesday at about 8 pm, and the venue is now the most popular for the country's many expats – get there early to reserve a spot where you can listen to local musician Dieter Uken. On Friday and Saturday nights there's a live band at *Gigi's* in the Royal Swazi Sun.

### Getting There & Away

Taxis from Mbabane cost at least E35, and from E60 if you want to go to the far end of the valley. At night you'll have to negotiate. During the day you could get on a Manzini-bound bus, but make sure the driver knows you want to alight in the valley. Even some nonexpress buses aren't keen on stopping.

### MALKERNS

About 7km south of Lobamba there is a turn-off to the fertile Malkerns Valley, known for its arts and crafts outlets. At Gone Rural (☎ 83439), 1km from the turn-off, lutindzi grass is dyed and woven into baskets and mats. Swazi Candles and Tishweshwe

Crafts are also based near Malkerns, and Baobab Batik is near Nyanza Stables on the Manzini road.

The best restaurant in the region is *Malandela's*, next to Tishweshwe Crafts. Good old-fashioned meals such as pork pie (individually E8), fresh carrots, boiled potatoes and broccoli, and pecan pie cost about E35. The prawn nights are very popular and it is not unusual for 100 dozen to be consumed in an evening. Several English beers are available. Pete Thorne, the owner, is a dab hand at shove-halfpenny (an English pub game) and a noted pumpkin connoisseur.

### MANZINI

Manzini is now the country's industrial centre, but between 1890 and 1902 it was the combined administrative centre for the squabbling British and Boers, and during the Anglo-Boer War a renegade unit of Boer kommandos burnt it down. Downtown Manzini isn't large but it feels like a different country from easy-going rural Swaziland. There are reckless drivers (confused by the city's perplexing one-way system), city slickers and a hint of menace. Be careful walking at night.

The market on Thursday and Friday mornings is highly recommended. Get there at dawn if possible, as the rural people bring in their handicrafts to sell to retailers.

### Places to Stay

About 7km north of Manzini on the Mbabane road, just past Matsapha, *Paradise Caravan Park* (☎ 84935) is a reasonable place. Tent sites cost E8, van sites are E25, and rondavels are E55 a double.

There's nothing very cheap in the way of hotels in Manzini, but 7km out on the highway, opposite the Paradise, is a turn-off for a *rest camp* with 'cottages' for E50. It's pleasant enough but pretty basic.

The *Mozambique Hotel* (☎ 52489) is on Mahleka St. It has a good dingy bar and a popular restaurant. The distinctly average double rooms with common bath are E95, and with own bath they are E145. It's not great value, but the place has a lively buzz.

SWAZILAND

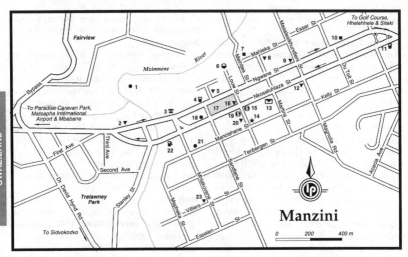

Manzini

**PLACES TO STAY**
7  Mozambique Hotel
10  New George Hotel

**PLACES TO EAT**
2  R & H Restaurant;
   Total Garage
5  OK Restaurant
8  Gil Vincente
   Restaurant
9  KFC
12  Smuggler's Inn

16  Chicken Licken'
20  Cheap Restaurants
23  The Hub (Fontana di
    Trevi Pizzeria;
    Nando's; Sailor
    Sam Restaurant)

**OTHER**
1  Showgrounds
3  Manzini Telephone
   Exchange
4  Checkers

6  Bus & Minibus Park
11  Manzini Club
13  Post Office
14  Police Station
15  Nedbank
17  Bhunu Mall (Steers;
    OK Bazaar;
    Parking)
18  Library
19  Barclays Bank
21  Market
22  Total Petrol Station

The most expensive hotel is the *New George* (☎ 52061) on Ngwane St, once a colonial hotel but now almost totally rebuilt. There is a pool, restaurants and all of the mod cons except efficient staff. Economy singles/doubles/triples cost from E145/195/250 with breakfast; luxury rooms are E170/230/295, and family rooms, E360.

### Places to Eat

The *café* at the bus station has cheap local food. In town, on Louw St, there are a few basic food outlets, open during the day. The most notable is the *OK Restaurant*.

In The Hub, on the corner of Villiers and

Mhlakuvane Sts, are *Fontana di Trevi Pizzeria*, *Nando's* and *Sailor Sam*. The latter, an inexpensive, tackily furnished place, has traditional Pakistani and tandoori food as well as seafood takeaways – and great caramel-dip ice creams.

There's a Portuguese restaurant at the Mozambique Hotel, and a block away is another, *Gil Vincente* on Martins St. *Smuggler's Inn*, corner of Nkoseluhlaza and Masalesikhundleni Sts, almost didn't make it into the book because of the spelling of its location.

About 8km east of Manzini, at Hhelehhele, is the rustic *Gobble & Gossip*, where there is usually a great Sunday braai. For a wilder night out, venture into *Salt 'N 'Pepper Club* (the replacement for the notorious *Jimmy's*) to swill beer in an oft-successful try at self-imposed oblivion.

### Getting There & Away
A non-share taxi to Matsapha international airport costs around E50. The main bus and minibus taxi park is at the north end of Louw St. Buses run up the Ezulwini Valley to Mbabane for E1.50.

City to City/Transtate runs from here to South Africa via either Mbabane or Hlathikulu and Nhlangano. See the Getting There & Away section at the beginning of this chapter.

### NGWENYA
This town (the name means 'The Crocodile') is 5km east of the Oshoek border post on the road to Mbabane. The **Ngwenya Glass factory** is located here. Recycled glass is used to create African animals and birds as well as vases and tableware. The showroom is open daily from 8 am to 5 pm. Another 1km up the road is **Endlotane Studios/Phumulanga Tapestries** (☎ 45447/9). Tapestries from here are featured in galleries throughout the world; the studio is open daily from 8 am to 5 pm.

There is accommodation at *Hawana Park* (☎ 24335), near the Hawana Dam, to the east of the Piggs Peak road and not far from the Ngwenya-Mbabane road junction. A tent site is E25, a two bed honey hut is E75 (or E10 extra in peak season) and a self-contained, three bed chalet is E175 (E225 peak).

### MALOLOTJA NATURE RESERVE
This highveld/middleveld reserve, in the hilly north-west, has mainly antelope species (and recently two bull elephants in the Nkomati Valley). Over 280 species of bird have been recorded in the reserve, a number of them rare. Southern bald ibis nest on the cliffs near the Malolotja Falls and there are also nesting blue swallows *(Hirundo atrocaerulea)* in the reserve. Wildflowers and rare plants are also main attractions. Several

of the plants are found only in this part of Africa, including the woolly Barberton and Kaapschehoop cycads. The Nkomati River cuts a gorge through the park and flows east in a series of falls and rapids until it meets the lowveld.

Ngwenya has one of the world's oldest known mines, dating from 41,000 BC. The mine can be visited by vehicle but a ranger must accompany you; arrange one day in advance. You can also visit the Forbes Reef Goldmine in Forbes Reef Forest.

Entry to the reserve is E10 per person and E5 per vehicle. Camping costs E16.50 at the established sites and E10 on the trails. There are fully equipped cabins sleeping six for E130, or E180 on weekends. Book through the National Trust Commission (☎ 61178/9), National Museum, Lobamba.

The park entrance is about 35km from Mbabane, on the Piggs Peak road; the gates are open from 6 am to 6 pm in summer, and from 6.30 am in winter.

### Hiking Trails
The reserve is a true wilderness area, rugged and in the most part unspoilt. There are a number of hiking trails, ranging from short day walks to a week-long trail which extends from Ngwenya in the south to the Mgwayiza range in the north.

For the extended trails a free permit and map must be obtained from the reserve office. You need to bring all your own food and a camp stove as fires are not permitted outside the base camp. Shorter walks include the Nkomati viewpoint, the Upper Majolomba River, and Malolotja Falls and Vlei (swamp).

### MANKAYANE
This small town south-west of Manzini is surrounded by hills and pine plantations. *Inyatsi Inn* (☎ 88244) has single/double rooms without bath for about E50/70, and doubles with bathroom for E85.

### NHLANGANO
'Nhlangano' means 'meeting place', and it's here that King Sobhuza II met England's

King George VI in 1947. In 1961, British prime minister Harold Macmillan met Swazi leaders here on the fact-finding visit to South Africa which eventually led to Swaziland's independence.

Nhlangano is the closest town to the border crossing at Mahamba, but unless you want to visit the *Nhlangano Sun Casino* (☎ 78211), 4km out of town (with single/double rooms for E225/378 plus 10%), there's no reason to come here. The run-down *Phoenix Hotel* (☎ 78488), 5th St, is poor value – the Sun is the town's best choice.

## HLATHIKULU
The basic *Assegi Inn* (☎ 76126), Prince Arthur St, is good value at about E90 a double (no breakfast). Hlathikulu is the terminus for City to City/Transtate's bus running from Jo'burg via Ermelo, Piet Retief and Nhlangano (weekdays only).

## MKHAYA GAME RESERVE
Mkhaya (☎ 44541; fax 40957) is a private reserve off the Manzini-Big Bend road, near the hamlet of Phuzumoya. It is run by the people who administer Mlilwane near Mba-bane, and the same hands-on commitment to conservation is evident.

The reserve is on rehabilitated cattle farms, although the area had always been popular with hunters for its game. Mkhaya takes its name from the mkhaya tree (or knobthorn, *Acacia nigrescens)*, which abounds on the reserve. Mkhayas grow only on good land, and are valued not only for their fruit, from which Swazis brew beer, but for the insect and bird life they support.

Although small, Mkhaya has a wide range of animals, including white and black rhino (including six black rhino donated by the Taiwanese government in a gesture of good-will), roan and sable antelope, and elephant. The reserve's boast is that you're more likely to meet a black rhino in the wild here than anywhere else in Africa. There are also herds of the indigenous and rare Nguni cattle which make the reserve economically self-supporting.

---

### Rhino Wars
In 1965 white rhino were re-established in the kingdom after an absence of 70 years and since then there has been an ongoing battle to protect them from poachers. At the forefront of this battle has been Ted Reilly and a band of dedicated, hand-picked rangers.

This defence has not been easy as the poachers have received hefty financial backing from Taiwanese interests. Poaching escalated in the late 80s and there were determined efforts to change the laws in Swaziland relating to rhino poaching. Rhinos were dehorned and confined to enclosures for their own protection. After Hlane was attacked in January 1992 by poachers with AK47s, the rangers armed themselves. With the rhinos dehorned at Hlane, the poachers shifted to Mkhaya. The battle commenced.

In April 1992 there was a shoot-out between rangers and poachers at Mkhaya, and some poachers were captured. Not long after there was a big shoot-out at Big Bend and two poachers were killed.

The last rhino (the majestic bull Mthondvo) was killed for horn in December 1992 while the Swazi courts still agonised over action relating to the Big Bend incident. The young king, Mswati III, intervened on behalf of Reilly's rangers and poaching declined dramatically. The rangers still wait with their rifles at the ready. You can help – your presence at any one of the big game parks assists in rhino conservation.

A happy postscript was the donation by the Taiwanese government in 1996 of enough money to purchase six black rhino – a gesture of good faith which was welcomed with open arms. ∎

---

Day tours are available (E145/124 per adult on weekends/weekdays, including lunch and a game drive), plus guided walking safaris for E68/56. Mkhaya is worth staying at for at least a night. At E364 per person sharing in safari tents (with shared facilities), and including three meals and three game-viewing drives and walks, it's better value than many of the private reserves near Kruger in South Africa. Self-contained safari tents are E406 per person; the single rate is E550. There is also *Nkonjane* (the 'Swallow's Nest'), a luxurious stone cottage, at E720/860 per person for singles/doubles on weekdays, more on weekends – an experience in itself.

If accommodation described as 'luxury' puts you off, don't worry, it's better than that – *Stone Camp*, the safari-tent option, is like a comfortable 19th century hunting camp rather than a hotel sitting incongruously in the wilderness. The floors of the tents are on sand, allowing you to see ant trails and the tracks of the small animals which come in at night. The food is simple and good, with traditional methods and ingredients (such as wild mushrooms) used.

Note that you can't visit without having booked, and even then you can't drive in alone; you'll be met at Phuzumoya at a specified pickup time, usually 10 am or 4 pm.

## MHLAMBANYATSI

This town, its name meaning 'watering place of the buffaloes', is 27km from Mbabane. The popular *Foresters Arms* (☎ 74177; fax 74051) has single/double rooms for E195/ 220 plus 10% tax. It is likely to be full of locals on the weekend as they drift up here from Mbabane for home-made bread and Sunday lunch. You can sail, windsurf or canoe on the nearby **Luphohlo Dam**, or relax in the Foresters' library.

Some 6km from Mhlambanyatsi, on the road to Mbabane, is *Meikles Mount* (☎ 74110), a great B&B hideaway; singles/ doubles are E100/140 (more in the high season). There's horse-riding here and at Foresters.

## BIG BEND

Big Bend is a neat sugar town on, not surprisingly, a big bend in the Lusutfu River. It's quite a picturesque spot.

The *New Bend Inn* (☎ 36111), on a hill just south of town and with good views across the river, is good value at E118/147 for singles/doubles, without breakfast. There's a restaurant and a pleasant outdoor bar overlooking Big Bend. There's also a friendly workers' bar, *Vibes*, with a lively disco on Friday and Saturday. The *Riverside Motel* (☎ 36012; fax 36032) is a 10 minute drive south of Big Bend on the road to KwaZulu-Natal; rooms with breakfast are E126/160.

*Lubombo Lobster*, a few kilometres south of Big Bend, serves 'Highway hen' (spatchcock cooked with peri-peri) for E25 and tasty steak rolls for E8 each. There is also a restaurant in the Riverside Motel, which also specialises in Portuguese food.

There is a *hotel* on the Swazi/South Africa border at Lavumisa/Golela – it has a bar but no restaurant, but is close to fast-food places; a double with bathroom (cold water) is E50.

### Getting There & Away

About four buses a day run south to the South African border at Lavumisa for E6. The other way, they go on to Manzini for E10.

## SITEKI

This trading town isn't really on the way to anywhere anymore, but it's a nice enough little place and a bit cooler up here in the Lebombo Mountains than down on the plains. There are good views on the steep road up. The town is sometimes still known by its colonial-era name of Stegi.

The town was originally named when Mbandzeni (great-grandfather of the present king) gave his frontier troops permission to

---

**Nguni Cattle**

Mkhaya started out in 1979 as a stud-breeding programme for the indigenous Nguni cattle. The Nguni is an old breed, and centuries of natural selection have made it heat tolerant, disease immune, self-sufficient and, importantly, tick resistant. It was and still is highly prized by the Nguni tribes who led these cattle south during the Great Migration (difaqane). The Zulu king has a herd of Royal White Nguni (*Inyonikayiphumuli*) near Ulundi in KwaZulu-Natal.

Nguni are small and were interbred with larger foreign breeds to increase beef production. This led to a degeneration of their gene pool, hence the attempts at Mkhaya to preserve their purity. When supplemental feeding of other breeds became expensive the Nguni came into its own as an effective beef producer and they are now highly valued. Conservation activities at Mkhaya are funded entirely by the sale of these cattle. ■

SWAZILAND

marry – Siteki means 'marrying place'. Later, the area was the haunt of highwaymen such as Robert MacNab and Charles Dupont.

The *Siteki Hotel* (☎ 34126) has dinner, bed and breakfast for E90 per person – host, Graham Duke, knows lots about the area.

Several express buses run between Manzini and Siteki daily for E8. The local bus company is Tit For Tat Bus (☎ 34304).

## NORTH-EAST SWAZILAND

The north-eastern corner of Swaziland is a major sugar-producing area. It's hot, and in the arid foothills of the Lebombo range the scenery approaches what most people think of when you say 'Africa'.

The company towns of Tshaneni, Mhlume, Tambankulu and Simunye are the main population centres. Simunye is a show-piece and is worth a look. It describes itself as a village, but that's being coy. It's a neat, lush town with excellent facilities, a bit like Australia's Darwin on a manageable scale.

The **Sand River Reservoir**, west of Tshaneni, has no facilities, but you can camp there. Don't swim in the water or drink it untreated, as it's teeming with bilharzia.

### Places to Stay

Unfortunately, the only hotel accommodation in the area is at Tshaneni (pronounced Jan-*ay*-ni), probably the least attractive of the towns. The run-down *Impala Arms* (☎ 31244) has singles/doubles for E80/90, with breakfast, but many Swazis would rather push on than stay in this town.

At Simunye there is the *Tambankulu Recreational Club* (☎ 38111; fax 38213), off the Tshaneni road about 8km west of the junction with the Manzini-Lomahasha highway. It has rooms for E45 per person and a restaurant. Inquire here about accommodation in the Mlawula Nature Reserve. The *Simunye Country Club* (☎ 52646) also has accommodation and a great restaurant.

### Getting There & Away

Regular buses run to this region from Manzini. There are fewer on the run across to Piggs Peak, mainly on dirt roads.

## HLANE ROYAL NATIONAL PARK

This park (its name means 'wilderness'), Swazi's largest protected area, is in the north-east near the former royal hunting grounds. There are white rhino and many antelope species. Elephant, lion, cheetah and leopard have been successfully reintroduced. There are guided walking trails at E15 per person, with the opportunity to see elephant and rhino on foot. The park entrance is about 4km from Simunye. For more information get a copy of *The History & Significance of Hlane Royal National Park*, published in 1994 to celebrate the return of lions to Swaziland.

Entry to the reserve is E7 on weekdays, E10 on weekends, and E13 in peak season. Camping and caravanning cost from E20 per person. There are thatched huts at *Ndlovu Camp* from E75 per person sharing midweek or E87 on weekends or in peak season (single rates are E140/170), and self-contained huts at *Bhubesi Rest Camp* from E95 per person sharing midweek and E110 on weekends and in peak season (single rates are E160/195); ☎ 44541 or fax 40957 to make bookings.

## MLAWULA NATURE RESERVE

In the east, taking in both plains and the Lebombo Mountains, this 18,000 hectare reserve is in harsh but beautiful country. Walking trails are being established. The reserve has antelope species and there are shy hyena in remote areas. Aquatic dangers include both bilharzia and crocodiles. Watch out for ticks, too. A deadly trio of snakes – black mamba, puff adder and spitting cobra – are found here.

Entry to the reserve is E10 per person (E5 for kids) and a car is E5. Camping is E15 (E8 for children), or E10 on the hiking trails.

There is also tent accommodation at Mbuluzi, from E60 on weekdays and E80 on the weekend, and at *Mapelepele House* which is E180 per person. Phone ☎ 38885 for bookings, or contact the National Trust Commission, National Museum, Lobamba (☎ 61151 or 61178/9). The reserve's entrance is about 10km north of Simunye. It is open in summer from 6.30 am to 6.30 pm (winter from 7 am to 6 pm) but day visitors must leave the park by 6 pm. (The Ndzindza Trails cottage is only for the use of day hikers.)

## PIGGS PEAK

In hilly country in the north-western corner of the country, this small town is the centre of the logging industry and there are huge pine plantations in the area.

The town was named after a prospector who found gold here in 1884. There was a rush, but only one deep mine ever made much money and it has been closed for 35 years. West of Piggs Peak is **Bulembu** and the Havelock asbestos mine. The aerial cableway carries the asbestos to Barberton, 20km away in South Africa. The cableway would be the easiest way to travel – the 60km of dirt to Barberton includes some of the roughest tracks in Africa – expect the descent to take two hours on this shocking road.

As well as its scenery, including the **Phophonyane Falls** about 8km north of town, this area is known for the quality of its handicrafts. At the Highlands Inn in Piggs Peak, **Tintsaba Crafts** (☎ 71260) displays a good range; there are several other craft places.

### Places to Stay & Eat

The only place to stay in town is the *Highlands Inn* (☎ 71144), about 1km south of the town centre on the main road. Singles/doubles cost from E111/202 plus tax, including breakfast. The rooms are clean and nice enough, but it isn't great value. There's a pleasant garden area with views.

In the area is one of the nicest places to stay in Swaziland. *Phophonyane Lodge* (☎ /fax 71319) is in its own nature reserve of lush indigenous forest on the Phophonyane River, where you can swim in rock pools. There is a system of walking trails. With a maximum of just over 20 guests in three separate locations, this is a quiet and friendly place. This isn't a malarial area but there are mosquitoes in summer, so bring repellent.

Accommodation is in cottages from E183 or tents from E118; both rates are per person. On weekends there's a minimum stay of two nights and prices rise in holidays. There are cooking facilities or you can eat in the tiny restaurant, the *Dining Hut* – breakfast is E23, main courses are E25 and desserts E9. Day visitors are charged E9.

To get there head north-east from Piggs Peak towards the casino, 10km away, and take the signposted turn-off about 1km before the casino (minibus taxis will drop you off here). Continue down this road until you cross a bridge over a waterfall and the turn-off to the lodge is about 500m further on, to the right. You can usually arrange to be collected from Piggs Peak.

About 10km north-east of Piggs Peak, on the road to the Jeppe's Reef border with South Africa, is the *Protea Piggs Peak Hotel* (☎ 71104). The midweek specials (singles/doubles with B&B are E385/410) are affordable if gambling is what you seek.

### Getting There & Away

Heading across to the north-east of the country the roads are mainly dirt, but they're in reasonable condition. If you're driving, beware of buses coming the other way (running between Piggs Peak and Tshaneni) – they speed and hog the gravel road.

There are nonshare taxis; to the casino the fare is about E20, to Mbabane it's E100. The bus and minibus taxi rank is next to the market at the top end of the main street. There's an express bus to Mbabane for E7.

# Glossary

**ablutions block** – a building containing a toilet, bath, shower and washing facilities (found mainly in caravan parks and game reserves)

**af** – derogatory reference to a black person, as bad as 'nigger' or 'abo'

**ANC** – African National Congress

**animism** – various definitions, but most useful seems to be: 'beliefs based on an existence of the human soul, and on spirits that inhabit or are represented by natural objects and phenomena, which have the power to influence human life for good or ill'

**apartheid** – literally 'the state of being apart'; a political system in which peoples are segregated according to ethnic background

**AWB** –Afrikaner Weerstandsbeweging (Afrikaner Resistance Movement). Extremist right-wing group active in pre-election South Africa, led by the recently jailed Eugene Terre-Blanche.

**bakkie** – utility, pick-up

**bantustans** – see Homelands

**bazaar** – market

**bhundu** – bush, wilderness

**bilharzia** – disease caused by blood flukes which are passed on by freshwater snails

**biltong** – dried and salted meat that can be made from just about anything from eland or ostrich to mutton or beef

**black taxi** – minibus taxi

**blikkiesdorp** – the quintessential small town

**bobotie** – dish consisting of curried mincemeat with a topping of beaten egg baked to a crust, probably of Cape Malay origin

**boerewors** – spicy sausages, often sold by street vendors, and consumed at a braai, literally 'farmers sausage'

**Bokkies** – affectionate name for a national sports team, usually a rugby team

**bottle store** – shop selling alcohol

**braai** – a barbecue featuring tons of grilled meat and beer ('and a small salad for the ladies'), a South African institution, particularly among whites

**Broederbond** – secret society only open to Protestant Afrikaner men, highly influential under National Party rule

**buck** – antelope

**buppies** – black yuppies

**buy a donkey** – 'thank you very much', 'many thanks', actually, it's *baie dankie*

**café** smalltown shops selling odds and ends, plus unappetising fried food

**campground** – area where tents can be pitched and caravans parked

**camp site** – an individual pitch on a campground

**cassper** – armoured vehicle

**coloureds** – South Africans of mixed race

**comma** – point, as in decimal point

**dagga** or **zol** – marijuana

**dam** – reservoir

**donga** – steep-sided gully created by soil erosion

**dorp** – rural settlement where a road crosses a river

**drankwinkel** – literally 'drink shop'; South African off-licence

**drift** – river ford

**dumpy** – smallest size of beer bottle

**eh** – (pronounced to rhyme with hay) all purpose ending to sentences, even very short ones such as 'Thanks, eh.'

**Fanagalo** – a language spoken mainly by migrant mine workers, a mixture of English, Afrikaans and various Bantu languages

**farm stall** – small shop or shelter by a road, selling farm produce

**Flying Squad** – ready reaction force of armed police, originally established to stem interracial violence, now augmented in response to the burgeoning crime rate

**forest** – in this mainly unforested region, any large collection of trees, usually a pine or eucalypt plantation

**fynbos** – term for the vegetation of the area

around Cape Town, literally means fine or delicate bush

**Homelands** – reserves for the black peoples of South Africa established under apartheid, reabsorbed into South Africa after 1994; also called bantustans
**hoofweg** – main road
**howzit?** – all purpose greeting

**IFP** – Inkatha Freedom Party; KwaZulu-Natal based political party, a longtime rival of the ANC
**indaba** – originally an assembly of Zulu chiefs; now applied to political meetings
**inyanga** – medicine man, herbalist
**Izzit?** – rhetorical question which most closely translates as 'Really?' and is used without regard to gender, person, or number of the subject. Therefore, it could mean 'Is it?', 'Is that so?', 'Did you?', 'Are you?', 'Is he?', 'Are they?', 'Is she?', 'Are we?', 'Amazing!', etc. Also 'How izzit?', for 'How are things?', 'How's it going?', etc.

**jol** – party, both verb and noun
**just now** – indeterminate future, but reasonably imminent

**kaffir** – black person (derogatory – do not use)
**kloof** – ravine
**knobkerrie** – traditional African weapon, a stick with a round knob at the end, used as a club or missile
**koeksesters** – small doughnuts dripping in honey – very gooey and figure-enhancing
**kopje or koppie** – little hill, usually flat-topped
**kraal** – Afrikaans version of the Portuguese curral, an enclosure for livestock or fortified village

**laager** – a defensive circular formation of ox-carts, used by the voortrekkers for protection against attack
**lapa** – a circular building with low walls and a thatched roof, used for cooking, partying, etc
**larney** – posh, smart, high quality

**lekker** – (pronounced lakker), very good, enjoyable or tasty
**location** – another word for township, more usually in rural areas

**Madiba** – a name by which Nelson Mandela is sometimes known
**mampoer** – home-distilled brandy made from peaches, prickly pear, etc, often stronger than schnapps
**mfecane** – forced migration by several Southern African tribes in the face of Zulu aggression
**mielie pap** or **mealie meal** – maize porridge – black African staple
**muti** – traditional medicine

**now** – soon (eg 'I'll serve you now' means in a little while. 'Just now' means 'I understand that you're impatient, and I'll be with you soon', or 'When I can get around to it'.)
**now-now** – immediately

**oke** – bloke, guy

**plus-minus** – meaning 'about', this is scientific/mathematical term has entered common parlance, particularly among people who don't speak English as their first language: eg 'the bus will come in plus-minus 10 minutes', 'I have been working here for plus-minus four years'
**pronking** – strange bouncing leaping by antelope, apparently just for fun

**robot** – traffic light
**rondavel** – a round hut with a conical roof, frequently seen in holiday resorts
**rooibos** – literally 'red bush' in Afrikaans; herbal tea which reputedly has therapeutic qualities
**Russian** – large, red sausage, fried but often served cold (and revolting)

**SAB** – South African Breweries, brewers of Black Label, Castle, etc; loved and hated
**samp** – crushed maize used for porridge
**sangoma** – a witchdoctor or herbalist
**shame!** – what a pity!

**shebeen** – drinking establishment in black townships, often illegal

**sjambok** – short whip, traditionally made from rhino hide

**Spar** – supermarket chain; becoming generic for any large supermarket

**spruit** – shallow river

**squaredavel** – see rondavel and work out the rest

**stad** – used on road signs to indicate the city centre

**strand** – beach

**takkie** – gym shoe

**tickie box** – public phone on private premises

**township** – black residential district, usually hidden on the outskirts of a white town

**toyi toyi** – jubilant dance often associated with political demonstrations

**tsotsi** – township hoodlum, gangster

**uitlanders** – 'foreigners'; name given by Afrikaners to the immigrants who poured into the Transvaal after the discovery of gold

**Vaalies** – slang name for whites from the former Transvaal Province

**Van der Merwe** – archetypal Boer country bumpkin and butt of English jokes

**veld** – open grassland (pronounced 'felt'); variations: lowveld, highveld, bushveld, sandveld

**veldskoens** – comfortable shoes made of soft leather (also called 'vellies')

**Vienna** – smaller version of Russian (see that entry)

**vlei** – any low open landscape, sometimes marshy (pronounced 'flay')

**volkstaat** – Homeland for whites, or rather Afrikaners. Conservative Afrikaner groups still agitate for their own volkstaat.

**Voortrekkers** – original Afrikaner settlers of the Orange Free State and Transvaal who migrated from the Cape Colony in the 1830s

**...weg** – literally 'way', but translated as 'street' or 'road' (eg Abelweg means Abel Rd)

**yah well no fine** – yes-no-maybe-perhaps

In African English, repetition for emphasis is common: something that burnt you would be 'hot hot'; fields after the rains are 'green green'; a crowded minibus with no more room is 'full full', and so on.

For Food terms, see the Food section in the South Africa Facts for the Visitor chapter.

# Index

644 Index

## BOXED TEXT

## TEXT

## NATIONAL PARKS & WILDLIFE RESERVES

658 Thanks

## Thanks

Thanks to the many travellers who wrote in with comments about our last edition, and with tips and comments about South Africa, Lesotho and Swaziland (apologies if we've misspelt your name). If you wish to contact us by e-mail with responses to this edition, you can reach us on talk2us@lonelyplanet. com.au.

T & M Andreassen, Hettie Anema, NC Appleyard, Eric & Mary Baber, Paul Bailey, TS Bailey, Gianni Baldassini, Grant Balfour, Trevor Ball, Antje Barabasch, David Barnes, Ward Barnes, Dagmar Barth, Richard Batt, Julia Beamish, Marcel Bechers, Joanne Bennett, Gerald N Berstell, Kathrin Beuermann, Pia Boelum, Agnes Gonxha Bojaxhiu, S & J Braiden, Leanne Brandis, M & D Brewster, Robert Brockman, Katherine Brown, Aidan Browne, Marjolein Bruning, Sandy Brutschin, Lynda Bywaters, Christopher Case, C Cavasco, Agnes Chague, Ann Charles, Yannick Chevalier, Kathy Church, X Ci Escarra, Alan Clark, Al & Meg Clark, J & M Clifton, Richard Crocker, R Curis, P DeGraaf, Ben Dipple, Tina Donath, Cameron Douglas, M Drayer, Tina Drayton, Lars Eckhardt, Jon Edgall, Chris Edwards, Beatrice Elar, Jean Ettridge, Peter Everett, Ione Feifer, Chris Fenner, Solveig Fetz, Sabine Fischer, Naomi Fisher, Kristen Flogstad, John Frederick, Celina Freitas, Takashi Fuwa, O & L Gaubert, Tom Gehrels, Bryan Geon, Emma Golding, A Golebiowska, Anne Marie & James Gormley, Jenny Gough, Romano Grandis, Alexa Grant, Ian Greasby, Frances Green, Paula Hailstone, Ken Haley, Armando Hamel, Helen Harper, Ann Harris, Donna Hattern, D Haye, Hjalmer Heiner, Thomas Henchel, Lucian Hernick, Thomas Herrington, Tom Hetley, NG Hetterley, Tim Hill, Sally Hodges, Geraldine Hodgkins, P & M Hoedemakers, HC Holman, Ron Hoogsteen, Sarah Hotter, Martin Huckerby, Reiner Huhn, Mr & Mrs GJ Hunt, Daniel Hunter, Malcolm Hunter Jnr, A Ililunk, Hamish Imrie, Victor Isaac, Benjamin Isgur, Jon Isherwood, H Jahn, Alex Jannic, A Jannis, Sylvio Jansen, Ian Jeffreys, Matthew Johnson, Margaret Johnson, Rachel Johnson, Peter Johnson, Brian Jones, Hugh & Maire Jones, Nigel Jones, Tanya Joseph, Sabine Joyce, Erwin Karl, Irma & Kai Keller, Danielle Kent, Philip Kestelman, Claire Keysell, Michael Kilpatrick, SE Kinghorn, Jessica Kirsten, DT & MR Knight, Britta Kowalski, Saskia Krawczynski, Elke Kretrschann, Jerome Kruemcke, Eoin Langan, Jeff Layman, Margaret Le Rick, D Leus, Lawrie Little, Henk Lodeweges, Phil Lord, Matteo Lorenzi, Mike Lourens, Nicola Lugaresi, Jon MacCallum, Jane Maltais, Dr Marcus Markus, Gabrielle Marley, L & J Matilainen, Bernhard Matzinger, Roger McEvilly, Pat McGee, D McMillan, Julian Mellor, Brenda Melum, Jo Mercuri, Lucy Metcalfe, Louise Meyer, Alexander Mitchell, A Moller, Carol Monaghan, Angel Montoro, Elwyn Morris, Jeremy Morris, Marti Morthorst, Anna Mulsarczyk, Chanouk Nap, Vered Ne'eman, Ben Niblett, Jennilyn Noack, Kala Nobbs, E & C Norman, R Oestermeicher, Darryl Page, A & L Pansaru, Stuart Park, Joanne Passaro, Henri Paul, Carolyn Payne, C Phoenix, Nancy Pickering, Judith Pickett, Dominic Pinto, Perry Pohlmann, David Pratten, Kate Prevedello, K Rammeloo, Maxim & Nancy Rice, Phil Richardson, Anna Rickards, Andy Ring, Alexandra Robak, David Rowlandson, Jenni Scarrott, Benjamin Schmidt, Stephen Seit, Pam Shaffer, Greesh Sharma, Nicholas Shear, Julie Sheard, Nathan Shearing, Tom Sheppard, Michael Siassi, Kay Simonson, U & P Skerritt, Christine Sleight, Peter Small, Jackie Smit, Dan Smith, Suzanne Smith, A & B Soltysiak, Charles Spencer, K Spuijbroek, Keith Sread, Hilda Srnoy, Tom & Arek Stafiej, Jane Stewart, Malin Strand, B & O Strandholdt, B & T Summers, Jonathan Sykes, Phillipa Taylor, DP Taylor, Robert Theile, Deborah Tobis, Renmans Toon, Gordon Travis, PH Treuanion, Christa Troger, Charles Twigger, Thom Tyson, Stephan Ulbrich, R Van, P van der Waaij, Manfred van Eyk, Ruud Vantrijp, Luc Vermeire, Hannu Visti, Brandon Vogt, Sharon Waddington, Deborah Walee, Jill Walker, Lynn Watkins, Penny Weal, Kirstin Wells, Thomas Welschof, Joe West, Seb White, NE & BK Whitehead, Dr J D Wigdahl, Tim Williams, Pia Willumsen, Joan Wilson, Alexander Winter, E Wolf, B Wolfer, Sandra Wolton, Peter Wood, Denis Woodward, Claus Wunschmann, Dianne Young and Rodger Young.

# LONELY PLANET PHRASEBOOKS

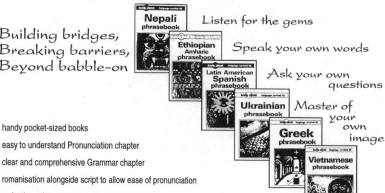

Building bridges,
Breaking barriers,
Beyond babble-on

Listen for the gems

Speak your own words

Ask your own questions

Master of your own image

- handy pocket-sized books
- easy to understand Pronunciation chapter
- clear and comprehensive Grammar chapter
- romanisation alongside script to allow ease of pronunciation
- script throughout so users can point to phrases
- extensive vocabulary sections, words and phrases for every situations
- full of cultural information and tips for the traveller

*'...vital for a real DIY spirit and attitude in language learning'* – Backpacker

*'the phrasebooks have good cultural backgrounders and offer solid advice for challenging situations in remote locations'* – San Francisco Examiner

*'...they are unbeatable for their coverage of the world's more obscure languages'* – The Geographical Magazine

---

Arabic (Egyptian)
Arabic (Moroccan)
Australia
  *Australian English, Aboriginal and Torres Strait languages*
Baltic States
  *Estonian, Latvian, Lithuanian*
Bengali
Burmese
Brazilian
Cantonese
Central Europe
  *Czech, French, German, Hungarian, Italian and Slovak*
Eastern Europe
  *Bulgarian, Czech, Hungarian, Polish, Romanian and Slovak*
Egyptian Arabic
Ethiopian (Amharic)
Fijian
French
German
Greek
Hindi/Urdu
Indonesian

Italian
Japanese
Korean
Lao
Malay
Mandarin
Mediterranean Europe
  *Albanian, Croatian, Greek, Italian, Macedonian, Maltese, Serbian, Slovene*
Mongolian
Moroccan Arabic
Nepali
Papua New Guinea
Pilipino (Tagalog)
Quechua
Russian
Scandinavian Europe
  *Danish, Finnish, Icelandic, Norwegian and Swedish*
South-East Asia
  *Burmese, Indonesian, Khmer, Lao, Malay, Tagalog (Pilipino), Thai and Vietnamese*

Spanish (Castilian)
  *Also includes Catalan, Galician and Basque*
Spanish (Latin American)
Sri Lanka
Swahili
Thai
Thai Hill Tribes
Tibetan
Turkish
Ukrainian
USA
  *US English, Vernacular Talk, Native American languages and Hawaiian*
Vietnamese
Western Europe
  *Basque, Catalan, Dutch, French, German, Greek, Irish, Italian, Portuguese, Scottish Gaelic, Spanish (Castilian) and Welsh*

# LONELY PLANET JOURNEYS

JOURNEYS is a unique collection of travel writing – published by the company that understands travel better than anyone else. It is a series for anyone who has ever experienced – or dreamed of – the magical moment when they encountered a strange culture or saw a place for the first time. They are tales to read while you're planning a trip, while you're on the road or while you're in an armchair, in front of a fire.

JOURNEYS books catch the spirit of a place, illuminate a culture, recount a crazy adventure, or introduce a fascinating way of life. They always entertain, and always enrich the experience of travel.

---

## THE RAINBIRD
### A Central African Journey
### *Jan Brokken*
#### *translated by Sam Garrett*

*The Rainbird* is a classic travel story. Following in the footsteps of famous Europeans such as Albert Schweitzer and H.M. Stanley, Jan Brokken journeyed to Gabon in central Africa. A kaleidoscope of adventures and anecdotes, *The Rainbird* brilliantly chronicles the encounter between Africa and Europe as it was acted out on a side-street of history. It is also the compelling, immensely readable account of the author's own travels in one of the most remote and mysterious regions of Africa.

*Jan Brokken* is one of Holland's best known writers. In addition to travel narratives and literary journalism, he has published several novels and short stories. Many of his works are set in Africa, where he has travelled widely.

---

## SONGS TO AN AFRICAN SUNSET
### A Zimbabwean Story
### *Sekai Nzenza-Shand*

*Songs to an African Sunset* braids vividly personal stories into an intimate picture of contemporary Zimbabwe. Returning to her family's village after many years in the West, Sekai Nzenza-Shand discovers a world where ancestor worship, polygamy and witchcraft still govern the rhythms of daily life – and where drought, deforestation and AIDS have wrought devastating changes. With insight and affection, she explores a culture torn between respect for the old ways and the irresistible pull of the new.

*Sekai Nzenza-Shand* was born in Zimbabwe and has lived in England and Australia. Her first novel, *Zimbabwean Woman: My Own Story*, was published in London in 1988 and her fiction has been included in the short story collections *Daughters of Africa* and *Images of the West*. Sekai currently lives in Zimbabwe.

*This project has been assisted by the Commonwealth Government through the Australia Council, its arts funding and advisory body.*

# LONELY PLANET TRAVEL ATLASES

Lonely Planet has long been famous for the number and quality of its guidebook maps. Now we've gone one step further and produced a handy companion series: Lonely Planet travel atlases – maps of a country produced in book form.

Unlike other maps, which look good but lead travellers astray, our travel atlases have been researched on the road by Lonely Planet's experienced team of writers. All details are carefully checked to ensure the atlas corresponds with the equivalent Lonely Planet guidebook.

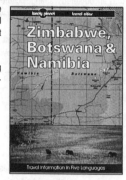

The handy atlas format means no holes, wrinkles, torn sections or constant folding and unfolding. These atlases can survive long periods on the road, unlike cumbersome fold-out maps. The comprehensive index ensures easy reference.

- full-colour throughout
- maps researched and checked by Lonely Planet authors
- place names correspond with Lonely Planet guidebooks
  – no confusing spelling differences
- legend and travelling information in English, French, German, Japanese and Spanish
- size: 230 x 160 mm

*Available now:*
Chile & Easter Island • Egypt • India & Bangladesh • Israel & the Palestinian Territories •Jordan, Syria & Lebanon • Kenya • Laos • Portugal • South Africa, Lesotho & Swaziland • Thailand • Turkey • Vietnam • Zimbabwe, Botswana & Namibia

---

# LONELY PLANET TV SERIES & VIDEOS

Lonely Planet travel guides have been brought to life on television screens around the world. Like our guides, the programmes are based on the joy of independent travel, and look honestly at some of the most exciting, picturesque and frustrating places in the world. Each show is presented by one of three travellers from Australia, England or the USA and combines an innovative mixture of video, Super-8 film, atmospheric soundscapes and original music.

Videos of each episode – containing additional footage not shown on television – are available from good book and video shops, but the availability of individual videos varies with regional screening schedules.

*Video destinations include:* Alaska • American Rockies • Australia – The South-East • Baja California & the Copper Canyon • Brazil • Central Asia • Chile & Easter Island • Corsica, Sicily & Sardinia – The Mediterranean Islands • East Africa (Tanzania & Zanzibar) • Ecuador & the Galapagos Islands • Greenland & Iceland • Indonesia • Israel & the Sinai Desert • Jamaica • Japan • La Ruta Maya • Morocco • New York • North India • Pacific Islands (Fiji, Solomon Islands & Vanuatu) • South India • South West China • Turkey • Vietnam • West Africa • Zimbabwe, Botswana & Namibia

*The Lonely Planet TV series is produced by:*
**Pilot Productions**
The Old Studio
18 Middle Row
London W10 5AT UK

**For video availability and ordering information contact your nearest Lonely Planet office.**

*Music from the TV series is available on CD & cassette.*

# PLANET TALK

## Lonely Planet's FREE quarterly newsletter

We love hearing from you and think you'd like to hear from us.

**When...**is the right time to see reindeer in Finland?
**Where...**can you hear the best palm-wine music in Ghana?
**How...**do you get from Asunción to Areguá by steam train?
**What...**is the best way to see India?

*For the answer to these and many other questions read PLANET TALK.*

Every issue is packed with up-to-date travel news and advice including:

* a letter from Lonely Planet co-founders Tony and Maureen Wheeler
* go behind the scenes on the road with a Lonely Planet author
* feature article on an important and topical travel issue
* a selection of recent letters from travellers
* details on forthcoming Lonely Planet promotions
* complete list of Lonely Planet products

*To join our mailing list contact any Lonely Planet office.*

*Also available: Lonely Planet T-shirts. 100% heavyweight cotton.*

---

# LONELY PLANET ONLINE

## Get the latest travel information before you leave or while you're on the road

Whether you've just begun planning your next trip, or you're chasing down specific info on currency regulations or visa requirements, check out Lonely Planet Online for up-to-the minute travel information.

As well as travel profiles of your favourite destinations (including maps and photos), you'll find current reports from our researchers and other travellers, updates on health and visas, travel advisories, and discussion of the ecological and political issues you need to be aware of as you travel.

There's also an online travellers' forum where you can share your experience of life on the road, meet travel companions and ask other travellers for their recommendations and advice. We also have plenty of links to other online sites useful to independent travellers.

And of course we have a complete and up-to-date list of all Lonely Planet travel products including guides, phrasebooks, atlases, Journeys and videos and a simple online ordering facility if you can't find the book you want elsewhere.

***www.lonelyplanet.com***
***or***
***AOL keyword: lp***

# LONELY PLANET PRODUCTS

Lonely Planet is known worldwide for publishing practical, reliable and no-nonsense travel information in our guides and on our web site. The Lonely Planet list covers just about every accessible part of the world. Currently there are eight series: *travel guides, shoestring guides, walking guides, city guides, phrasebooks, audio packs, travel atlases* and *Journeys* – a unique collection of travel writing.

## EUROPE

Amsterdam • Austria • Baltic States phrasebook • Britain • Central Europe on a shoestring • Central Europe phrasebook • Czech & Slovak Republics • Denmark • Dublin • Eastern Europe on a shoestring • Eastern Europe phrasebook • Estonia, Latvia & Lithuania • Finland • France • French phrasebook • German phrasebook • Greece • Greek phrasebook • Hungary • Iceland, Greenland & the Faroe Islands • Ireland • Italian phrasebook • Italy • Mediterranean Europe on a shoestring • Mediterranean Europe phrasebook • Paris • Poland • Portugal • Portugal travel atlas • Prague • Russia, Ukraine & Belarus • Russian phrasebook • Scandinavian & Baltic Europe on a shoestring • Scandinavian Europe phrasebook • Slovenia • Spain • Spanish phrasebook • St Petersburg • Switzerland • Trekking in Greece • Trekking in Spain • Ukrainian phrasebook • Vienna • Walking in Britain • Walking in Switzerland • Western Europe on a shoestring • Western Europe phrasebook

*Travel Literature:* The Olive Grove: Travels in Greece

## NORTH AMERICA

Alaska • Backpacking in Alaska • Baja California • California & Nevada • Canada • Florida • Hawaii • Honolulu • Los Angeles • Mexico • Miami • New England • New Orleans • New York City • New York, New Jersey & Pennsylvania • Pacific Northwest USA • Rocky Mountain States • San Francisco • Southwest USA • USA phrasebook • Washington, DC & the Capital Region

## CENTRAL AMERICA & THE CARIBBEAN

Bermuda • Central America on a shoestring • Costa Rica • Cuba • Eastern Caribbean • Guatemala, Belize & Yucatán: La Ruta Maya • Jamaica

## SOUTH AMERICA

Argentina, Uruguay & Paraguay • Bolivia • Brazil • Brazilian phrasebook • Buenos Aires • Chile & Easter Island • Chile & Easter Island travel atlas • Colombia • Ecuador & the Galápagos Islands • Latin American Spanish phrasebook • Peru • Quechua phrasebook • Rio de Janeiro • South America on a shoestring • Trekking in the Patagonian Andes • Venezuela

*Travel Literature:* Full Circle: A South American Journey

## ANTARCTICA

Antarctica

## ISLANDS OF THE INDIAN OCEAN

Madagascar & Comoros • Maldives• Mauritius, Réunion & Seychelles

## AFRICA

Africa - the South • Africa on a shoestring • Arabic (Moroccan) phrasebook • Cape Town • Central Africa • East Africa • Egypt • Egypt travel atlas• Ethiopian (Amharic) phrasebook • Kenya • Kenya travel atlas • Malawi, Mozambique & Zambia • Morocco • North Africa • South Africa, Lesotho & Swaziland • South Africa, Lesotho & Swaziland travel atlas • Swahili phrasebook • Trekking in East Africa • West Africa • Zimbabwe, Botswana & Namibia • Zimbabwe, Botswana & Namibia travel atlas

*Travel Literature:* The Rainbird: A Central African Journey • Songs to an African Sunset: A Zimbabwean Story

# MAIL ORDER

Lonely Planet products are distributed worldwide. They are also available by mail order from Lonely Planet, so if you have difficulty finding a title please write to us. North American and South American residents should write to Embarcadero West, 155 Filbert St, Suite 251, Oakland CA 94607, USA; European and African residents should write to 10 Barley Mow Passage, Chiswick, London W4 4PH; and residents of other countries to PO Box 617, Hawthorn, Victoria 3122, Australia.

## NORTH-EAST ASIA

Beijing • Cantonese phrasebook • China • Hong Kong • Hong Kong, Macau & Guangzhou • Japan • Japanese phrasebook • Japanese audio pack • Korea • Korean phrasebook • Mandarin phrasebook • Mongolia • Mongolian phrasebook • North-East Asia on a shoestring • Seoul • Taiwan • Tibet • Tibet phrasebook • Tokyo

*Travel Literature*: Lost Japan

## MIDDLE EAST & CENTRAL ASIA

Arab Gulf States • Arabic (Egyptian) phrasebook • Central Asia • Iran • Israel & the Palestinian Territories • Israel & the Palestinian Territories travel atlas • Istanbul • Jerusalem • Jordan & Syria • Jordan, Syria & Lebanon travel atlas • Middle East • Turkey • Turkish phrasebook • Turkey travel atlas • Yemen

*Travel Literature:* The Gates of Damascus • Kingdom of the Film Stars: Journey into Jordan

## ALSO AVAILABLE:

Travel with Children • Traveller's Tales

## INDIAN SUBCONTINENT

Bangladesh • Bengali phrasebook • Delhi • Hindi/Urdu phrasebook • India • India & Bangladesh travel atlas • Indian Himalaya • Karakoram Highway • Nepal • Nepali phrasebook • Pakistan • Rajasthan • Sri Lanka • Sri Lanka phrasebook • Trekking in the Indian Himalaya • Trekking in the Karakoram & Hindukush • Trekking in the Nepal Himalaya

*Travel Literature:* In Rajasthan • Shopping for Buddhas

## SOUTH-EAST ASIA

Bali & Lombok • Bangkok • Burmese phrasebook • Cambodia • Ho Chi Minh City • Indonesia • Indonesian phrasebook • Indonesian audio pack • Jakarta • Java • Laos • Lao phrasebook • Laos travel atlas • Malay phrasebook • Malaysia, Singapore & Brunei • Myanmar (Burma) • Philippines • Pilipino phrasebook • Singapore • South-East Asia on a shoestring • South-East Asia phrasebook • Thailand • Thailand's Islands & Beaches • Thailand travel atlas • Thai phrasebook • Thai audio pack • Thai Hill Tribes phrasebook • Vietnam • Vietnamese phrasebook • Vietnam travel atlas

## AUSTRALIA & THE PACIFIC

Australia • Australian phrasebook • Bushwalking in Australia • Bushwalking in Papua New Guinea • Fiji • Fijian phrasebook • Islands of Australia's Great Barrier Reef • Melbourne • Micronesia • New Caledonia • New South Wales & the ACT • New Zealand • Northern Territory • Outback Australia • Papua New Guinea • Papua New Guinea phrasebook • Queensland • Rarotonga & the Cook Islands • Samoa • Solomon Islands • South Australia • Sydney • Tahiti & French Polynesia • Tasmania • Tonga • Tramping in New Zealand • Vanuatu • Victoria • Western Australia

*Travel Literature:* Islands in the Clouds • Sean & David's Long Drive

# THE LONELY PLANET STORY

Lonely Planet published its first book in 1973 in response to the numerous 'How did you do it?' questions Maureen and Tony Wheeler were asked after driving, bussing, hitching, sailing and railing their way from England to Australia.

Written at a kitchen table and hand collated, trimmed and stapled, *Across Asia on the Cheap* became an instant local bestseller, inspiring thoughts of another book.

Eighteen months in South-East Asia resulted in their second guide, *South-East Asia on a shoestring*, which they put together in a backstreet Chinese hotel in Singapore in 1975. The 'yellow bible', as it quickly became known to backpackers around the world, soon became *the* guide to the region. It has sold well over half a million copies and is now in its 9th edition, still retaining its familiar yellow cover.

Today there are over 240 titles, including travel guides, walking guides, language kits & phrasebooks, travel atlases and travel literature. The company is the largest independent travel publisher in the world. Although Lonely Planet initially specialised in guides to Asia, today there are few corners of the globe that have not been covered.

The emphasis continues to be on travel for independent travellers. Tony and Maureen still travel for several months of each year and play an active part in the writing, updating and quality control of Lonely Planet's guides.

They have been joined by over 70 authors and 170 staff at our offices in Melbourne (Australia), Oakland (USA), London (UK) and Paris (France). Travellers themselves also make a valuable contribution to the guides through the feedback we receive in thousands of letters each year and on our web site.

The people at Lonely Planet strongly believe that travellers can make a positive contribution to the countries they visit, both through their appreciation of the countries' culture, wildlife and natural features, and through the money they spend. In addition, the company makes a direct contribution to the countries and regions it covers. Since 1986 a percentage of the income from each book has been donated to ventures such as famine relief in Africa; aid projects in India; agricultural projects in Central America; Greenpeace's efforts to halt French nuclear testing in the Pacific; and Amnesty International.

*'I hope we send people out with the right attitude about travel. You realise when you travel that there are so many different perspectives about the world, so we hope these books will make people more interested in what they see. Guidebooks can't really guide people. All you can do is point them in the right direction.'*

– Tony Wheeler

# LONELY PLANET PUBLICATIONS

**Australia**
PO Box 617, Hawthorn 3122, Victoria
tel: (03) 9819 1877  fax: (03) 9819 6459
e-mail: talk2us@lonelyplanet.com.au

**USA**
Embarcadero West, 155 Filbert St, Suite 251,
Oakland, CA 94607
tel: (510) 893 8555  TOLL FREE: 800 275-8555
fax: (510) 893 8563
e-mail: info@lonelyplanet.com

**UK**
10 Barley Mow Passage, Chiswick,
London W4 4PH
tel: (0181) 742 3161  fax: (0181) 742 2772
e-mail: lonelyplanetuk@compuserve.com

**France:**
71 bis rue du Cardinal Lemoine, 75005 Paris
tel: 1 44 32 06 20  fax: 1 46 34 72 55
e-mail: 100560.415@compuserve.com

**World Wide Web: http://www.lonelyplanet.com**
**or *AOL keyword: lp***